ADVISORY BOARD

THE WESLEYAN EDITION OF THE
WORKS OF HENRY FIELDING

———

THE HISTORY OF TOM JONES

A FOUNDLING

HENRY FIELDING

The History of
TOM JONES
A FOUNDLING

WITH AN INTRODUCTION AND
COMMENTARY BY
MARTIN C. BATTESTIN

THE TEXT EDITED BY
FREDSON BOWERS

WESLEYAN UNIVERSITY PRESS

WESLEYAN UNIVERSITY PRESS
Published by University Press of New England,
Hanover, NH 03755

Copyright © 1975 by Martin C. Battestin & Fredson Bowers
All Rights Reserved

Printed in the United States of America 10 9 8 7 6
First American Paperback Edition, 1975

LIBRARY OF CONGRESS CATALOGING IN PUBLICATION DATA

Fielding, Henry, 1707–1754.
    The history of Tom Jones, a foundling.

    (The Wesleyan edition of the works of Henry Fielding)
    Bibliography: p.
    Includes index.
    I. Bowers, Fredson Thayer. II. Title. III. Series:
Fielding, Henry, 1707–1754. Works. 1983.
[PR3454.H5 1983]   823'.5   83–10633
ISBN 0–8195–6048–0 (pbk.)

TO RUTHE

What you do
Still betters what is done.

PREFACE

During Fielding's lifetime *Tom Jones* went through four editions, all in 1749, although the fourth was dated 1750. The second and third editions are simple reprints, but Fielding revised the fourth edition by annotating a copy of the third. The present text is based on the first 1749 edition as copy-text but incorporates the identifiable revisions that Fielding made in the fourth of 1750 while rejecting the corruptions of the third edition passed on to the fourth and some of the printer's errors in the fourth itself. The text is printed by offset from the two-volume Wesleyan–Clarendon Press edition of 1975 but with the omission of its extensive general and textual introductions and of the six appendices of apparatus. Occasion has been taken to correct some misprints and oversights noted by the kindness of Eric Rothstein, Clive T. Probyn, Colin Mayrhofer, and Pat Rogers, and particularly of Dr. Hugh Amory. Dr. Amory's recent discovery that sheet O in the first edition, taking in text from Book VIII, chapters xiii–xv, is a cancel substituted for an original the text of which has been preserved, reprinted by an extraordinary accident in the third edition, only (*Harvard Library Bulletin*, 25 [1977], 101–13), has led in the present edition to some revisions in the text of these chapters. A list of page-line references for all changes made from the 1975 Wesleyan–Clarendon text will be found on page 991 of this volume.

M. C. B.

F. B.

Charlottesville, Virginia
1 November 1976

LIST OF CONTENTS

INTRODUCTION

HENRY FIELDING's masterpiece, *The History of Tom Jones, a Foundling*, was published in February, 1749. Seven years earlier, in reaction to *Pamela*, Fielding had founded, as he put it, "a new Province of Writing," introducing into English letters the "Comic Epic-Poem in Prose." In *Joseph Andrews* (February, 1742), he had turned away from the brooding, claustrophobic world of Richardson's beleaguered virgins to follow Cervantes along the open road—a way cheerful and panoramic, leading not merely through Georgian England, but, because his eye was steadily fixed on "Nature," which is ever the same, through a timeless country. In this sense, as he remarked of the author of *Don Quixote*, Fielding's subject was "the History of the World in general"; for he described "not Men, but Manners; not an Individual, but a Species" (III. i). *Tom Jones* fulfilled the promise of that ambitious, splendid beginning. It is, as few books have managed to be, the realization of a particular form and conception of literary art.

To be sure, in our century as in his own, Fielding has suffered from the criticisms of those who either have misunderstood his fiction or have found it not very much to their taste. The grounds of Dr. Johnson's preference for Richardson, "who knew how a watch was made," over Fielding, who could merely "tell the hour by looking on the dial-plate," are not very far from those of Ian Watt's, who distinguishes, to Fielding's disadvantage, between Richardson's technique of "formal realism" and Fielding's "realism of assessment."[1] Between them these two great novelists, in conscious rivalry, marked out the divergent directions that modern fiction was to take—Richardson in *Pamela* (1740) and *Clarissa* (1747–48) turning inward to explore the dark corners of the personality, Fielding in *Joseph Andrews* (1742) and *Tom Jones* ranging outward to encompass the variegated panorama of society. In their best and most representative works, *Clarissa* and *Tom Jones*, the differences that separate these authors are absolute, as diametrical as the difference between tragedy and

[1] *The Rise of the Novel: Studies in Defoe, Richardson, and Fielding* (Berkeley and Los Angeles: University of California Press, 1957).

comedy, between the novel of character and the novel of manners and action, between the "realistic" mode and the paradigmatic.

Inevitably, therefore, the claims of Richardson and of Fielding for pre-eminence have been debated by readers for more than two centuries. In his own day, the most damaging charge against Fielding was the "lowness" of his themes—his preoccupation with the adventures (chiefly sexual) of footmen and foundlings, of country wenches and Mayfair demi-reps. Dr. Johnson was appalled that Hannah More had read so "vicious," so "corrupt" a book as *Tom Jones*, and a writer in *Old England* fancied that the earthquakes that shook London in 1750 were signs of God's wrath at the enthusiastic reception accorded Fielding's novel. But the very qualities that offended the prudish and the proper among Fielding's first readers have recommended *Tom Jones* to a twentieth-century audience; Fielding's wit and hearty good humor and, above all, his tolerant humanity have seemed more congenial to us than has the sober—one might almost say pathological—prudentialism of Richardson, however compelling the force of his art in a book like *Clarissa*.

We are, in fact, still very much in the midst of the "Fielding revival" that Kingsley Amis remarked some time ago, one sign of which has been the brilliant success of Tony Richardson's film *Tom Jones* (1963) and the same director's more recent adaptation of *Joseph Andrews* (1977). In *The New York Times Book Review* of July 7, 1957, Amis observed that Fielding's humor was "closer to our own than that of any writer before the present century," and he further found that in rejecting "the novel of consistent tone," contemporary authors have followed Fielding in attempting "to combine the violent and the absurd, the grotesque and the romantic, the farcical and the horrific within a single novel." One thinks, for example, of Saul Bellow's *Adventures of Augie March*, of John Barth's *The Sot-Weed Factor*, and of Amis's own *Lucky Jim* as books in which Fielding would have recognized a form and an impulse similar to his own. The fact of Fielding's relevance to the novelists of our new Age of Satire is perhaps most eloquently stated by Bowen, the young writer of Amis's *I Like It Here*, who, standing before the white stone sarcophagus in which the author of *Tom Jones* rests near Lisbon, reflects upon the significance of the master:

Bowen thought about Fielding. Perhaps it was worth dying in your forties if two hundred years later you were the only noncontemporary novelist who could be read with unaffected and wholehearted interest, the only one who never had to be apologized for or excused on the grounds of changing taste. And how enviable to live in the world of his novels, where duty was plain, evil arose out of malevolence and a starving wayfarer could be invited indoors without hesitation and without fear. Did that make it a simplified world? Perhaps, but that hardly mattered beside the existence of a moral seriousness that could be made apparent without the aid of evangelical puffing and blowing.[1]

II

As Wayne Booth has observed,[2] the most important "character" in *Tom Jones* is the narrator himself, whose voice, as he relates the story to his "good-natured" and (he hopes) "sagacious" reader, or as he digresses in his comments and prefaces, sounds very like Fielding's own. More than any other major novelist of the period, Henry Fielding—or rather that heightened and idealized projection of him which has been called his "second-self"—is immanent in his book. From the first sentence to the last, he is, to use his own analogy (XVIII. i), the reader's close companion on this stagecoach journey through the imaginary world of the novel. It is useful, therefore, to know something about the man whose wit entertains us and whose genial wisdom instructs.

The circumstances of Fielding's life and, what is more important, the force of his convictions—political, religious, and critical —in large part determined the particular shape and character of *Tom Jones*. Though this is neither an autobiographical novel nor a *roman à clef*, Fielding's constant method as a writer of fiction was to translate the particular facts of his experience into symbols of universal relevance. Consider, for instance, the setting of the book. Paradise Hall, where Fielding's foundling hero was born and raised, is, like Eden itself, an imaginary estate. Yet it is composed of elements associated in the novelist's mind with his own heritage, his own ideal identity: the distinctive features of Allworthy's seat are drawn both from the estates of Fielding's benefactors, George Lyttelton and Ralph Allen, and more

[1] From Kingsley Amis, *I Like It Here* (New York: Harcourt, Brace and World, Inc., 1958), p. 185.
[2] *The Rhetoric of Fiction* (Chicago: University of Chicago Press, 1961), pp. 215–18.

especially from the prospect westward from atop Tor Hill in Glastonbury, Somerset, which, though Fielding does not mention it by name, may be taken as the specific locale of the novel's first six books. From the threshold at Sharpham Park, the home of Fielding's maternal grandfather and the place of the novelist's birth in 1707, Glastonbury Tor rises in full view only a short distance across the moors. The roads Tom Jones follows from Glastonbury to Wells, Gloucester, Upton-upon-Severn, and Meriden and at last from Coventry to London are those Fielding often had traveled, and the time of Tom's journey is that critical moment in the late autumn of 1745 when the Jacobite rebels under the Young Pretender, Charles Edward Stuart, had crossed the Tweed and were advancing deep into the heart of England.

Certain of the principal characters in the novel, furthermore, were broadly modeled on Fielding's friends and acquaintances. Lyttelton and Allen are reflected in Squire Allworthy, and Sophia Western, the girl whom Tom Jones loves and marries, is in part an idealization of Fielding's first wife, Charlotte Cradock—"one," he declared before her death in 1744, "from whom I draw all the solid comfort of my life." To notice these correspondences is by no means to imply that *Tom Jones* is not a work of fiction after all, but a mere transcription of actuality. Fielding's true subject, announced in the first chapter, is "HUMAN NATURE"; the world he presents is an imaginative creation, more symbol than fact, and his hero's progress is ultimately the journey, at least as arduous as amusing, we all must take from innocence to wisdom. Yet, although *Tom Jones* is finally concerned with universals— with presenting, as Fielding said of *Don Quixote*, "the History of the World in general"—it is also a book, like Joyce's *Ulysses*, firmly rooted in the soil of contemporary life.

More important than the actual people and events reflected in the novel are the factors in Fielding's experience that helped to condition his attitudes and thought. Both by birth and by education, Fielding was a gentleman, proud of his family's connection with the aristocracy and intellectually at home in the great philosophical tradition of Christian humanism. His father, though too improvident to leave him any money, was a military man who rose to the rank of general; his mother, Sarah Gould, was the daughter of a distinguished judge. After a childhood spent in the country village of East Stour, Dorset—a fact perhaps reflected in the novels, in which the naturalness and simplicity of the country provide the antithesis to the affectation and vice of the town—Fielding received an excellent formal education, first at Eton College (1719–24) and then at the University of Leyden (1728–29), across the Channel in Holland. From this period stems the intimate knowledge of the classics and of their ancient and modern commentators that informs nearly everything he wrote and that lies behind his conception of the novel itself.

In need of money, as he seems always to have been, Fielding returned from Holland determined to make his mark as a dramatist in London. From 1730 to 1737, he produced more than a score of plays—all of them comedies, farces, or satires. Most popular were *Tom Thumb* (1730), an hilarious burlesque of heroic tragedy, and *Pasquin* (1736) and *The Historical Register* (1737), political satires aimed chiefly, and to Fielding's cost, at the Prime Minister, Sir Robert Walpole. As Colley Cibber remarked in a passage in his autobiography typical of the wit for which he is celebrated in Pope's *Dunciad*, Fielding, "like another Erostratus, set fire to his stage, by writing up to an Act of Parliament to demolish it": Fielding's satires so incensed the Minister that he forced the passage of the Licensing Act of 1737, which closed the doors of Fielding's Little Theatre in the Haymarket and ended his career as a playwright. If Fielding was the most successful dramatist of his time, whose plays may still be read with enjoyment, it is surely too much to say, with Bernard Shaw, that he was "the greatest dramatist, with the single exception of Shakespeare, produced by England between the Middle Ages and the nineteenth century."[1] His years as a playwright were important primarily for what they meant to the novels: the theatre sharpened Fielding's ear for comic dialogue and perfected that sense of form, of significant design, which is one of his chief contributions to the art of fiction.

Although the period between the end of Fielding's theatrical career and the publication of *Tom Jones* was too eventful to be traced here in detail, yet it is too important to an understanding of that novel to be ignored. Having married in 1734, Fielding found himself three years later with no apparent means of supporting his family. In November, 1737, he entered the Middle

[1] Shaw's *Plays: Pleasant and Unpleasant* (New York: Brentano's, 1909), I, xiii.

Temple, determined to prepare himself for the law. Less than three years later, he was called to the Bar, but despite his diligence in term time and on the Western Circuit, he could not make a living at his new profession. To supplement his meager income, he was obliged to turn hackney author; it was preferable, he once facetiously remarked, to becoming a hackney coachman. During 1739–41, he renewed his attacks against the man who had driven him from the stage, editing *The Champion* and publishing a number of pamphlets and poems calculated to serve the Opposition's cause against Walpole. But the great event of this period was literary rather than political—the appearance in November, 1740, of Richardson's first novel, *Pamela: or, Virtue Rewarded*. At once exasperated and amused at the enthusiastic reception accorded the epistolary adventures of Richardson's shrewdly chaste young servant maid, Fielding responded first by parodying the book in *Shamela* (1741) and then by offering in *Joseph Andrews* (1742) his own alternative conception of the art of the novel. Though less ambitious, and perhaps less profound, than *Tom Jones*, *Joseph Andrews* is none the less the first masterly comic novel in English. In the theory set forth in his preface and introductory chapters, and in the deft execution of the narrative, Fielding had invented a new genre, which he called the "comic Romance" or "comic Epic-Poem in Prose"—a new literary form whose promise and potential he fully realized in *Tom Jones*. For our present purpose, only one other production of this period need be mentioned, the collection in three volumes of Fielding's *Miscellanies* (1743). Except for *Jonathan Wild*, the pieces here assembled are undistinguished in themselves, but valuable for the light they shed on the novels. In verse epistles such as "Of Good-Nature" and "Of True Greatness," or in essays such as "On Conversation" and "On the Knowledge of the Characters of Men," Fielding sets forth discursively the values and ethical beliefs that are enacted dramatically in the characters of Parson Adams and Tom Jones, of Allworthy and Dr. Harrison, of Jonathan Wild and Blifil.

In July, 1744, Fielding contributed to a second edition of his sister's novel *The Adventures of David Simple* a preface in which he affected to despise the insubstantial favors of the Muse, protesting that he had neither leisure nor inclination to write another work of fiction. This resolution happily was short-lived, for to judge from internal evidence, he was soon—perhaps even before the year was out—to begin work on his masterpiece. From the fact that the first six books of *Tom Jones* contain not a single definite allusion to the Jacobite uprising (and from certain other evidence too complex to be presented here), it seems clear that Fielding had finished about a third of the novel before the late summer of 1745, when news of the rebellion interrupted him. By October of that year and for several months thereafter, there were matters more urgent than novel-writing to occupy him. In earnest support of the Hanoverian Establishment, he published in rapid succession three hortatory pamphlets designed to acquaint the public with the pernicious consequences of a Jacobite victory and to arouse them in defense of their Constitution and religion. These works, issued within a fortnight in October, 1745, were *A Serious Address to the People of Great Britain*, *The History of the Present Rebellion*, and *A Dialogue between the Devil, the Pope, and the Pretender*. The same motives prompted him to undertake *The True Patriot*, a weekly journal that he conducted from November 5, 1745, to June 17, 1746. The winter of 1745 was indeed bleak and ominous—a critical moment in England's history, when the political and religious institutions Fielding cherished were threatened by a successful rebellion at home and when the war with France was going badly on the Continent. These dark and perilous months chilled his spirits and continued to trouble his thoughts long after the immediate danger had passed. It was a time, he recalled, when the nation was faltering at "the very Brink of Ruin" (*The True Patriot*, April 22–29, 1746), a time "far more terrible to all the Lovers of Liberty and the Protestant Religion, than this Age had ever seen before, or is, I hope, in any Danger of seeing again" (*The Jacobite's Journal*, August 13, 1748). No wonder, then, that when he returned to *Tom Jones* after the Jacobites had been defeated at Culloden (April 16, 1746), Fielding set the action of his central narrative in November, 1745, "the very Time when the late Rebellion was at the highest" (VII. xi), or that he made his hero—"a hearty Well-wisher to the glorious Cause of Liberty, and of the Protestant Religion"— volunteer to join the King's forces marching north against the rebels.

Since the fall of Walpole in 1742 and the formation of the so-called "Broad-Bottom" Administration in 1744, the government now included many of the men whom Fielding most

admired—among them Lyttelton and the Duke of Bedford, to
name the two he compliments in the dedication to *Tom Jones.* The
"Forty-five" having drawn him back into politics, this time on
the side of the ministry, Fielding continued to support his friends
in print, most notably in *The Jacobite's Journal* (December 5,
1747–November 5, 1748), the irony of whose title points at the
Tory Opposition, that ardent and vociferous faction whose principles Fielding was at the same time writing into the memorable
character of Squire Western. For his services to the government,
Fielding was rewarded, shortly before the publication of *Tom
Jones*, by being appointed justice of the peace, first for the City
of Westminster and then also for the County of Middlesex.
Though the Opposition journalists sneered, Fielding brought
to his new office an energetic concern for the cause of justice and
the public welfare that few of his predecessors could boast of.
As satirist and now as magistrate, he constantly addressed himself to the betterment of society, to the detection of vice and the
correction of folly. In the few remaining years of his life, he
worked to reform the bench and to control the spreading evils
of crime and poverty, devoting himself so assiduously to these
tasks that he injured his health. By refusing the lucrative per-
quisites by which his predecessors had made a "job" of the
administration of justice, he also suffered financially. These years,
moreover, appear to have exacted their price spiritually. In his
last novel, *Amelia* (1751), as in his other writings of the fifties
(*The Covent-Garden Journal* and the pamphlets on crime and the
poor), the genial, easy voice of the narrator of *Tom Jones* has
changed to tones graver and more constrained. Fielding's wit
and eloquence remain, but the feast of life he celebrated in *Tom
Jones* has staled for him. Whatever the cause, whether the
sobering effects of his magistracy or the pain he suffered from the
hideous disease that killed him, no one who reads that last sad
testament of his life, *The Journal of a Voyage to Lisbon* (1755), can
fail to be moved by Fielding's weariness and disenchantment. He
died in Lisbon on October 8, 1754.

III

Although, as we have said, Fielding is immanent in *Tom Jones*,
it is the work itself, his "great Creation" (x. i), that chiefly

concerns us. Despite the petulant protests by Richardson and by
Dr. Johnson, *Tom Jones* was a splendid and instantaneous success.
Tirelessly "puffed" by Fielding's friends Lyttelton and William
Pitt, who had read the work in manuscript, the entire first edition
of 2,000 copies was sold before the announced date of publication,
February 10, 1749. It was, as Joseph Spence observed with
admiration, "perhaps an unheard-of case." By the end of that
month, a second edition, of 1,500 copies, was issued, and before
the year was out, two further editions had been called for, together
amounting to 6,500 copies. Richardson persisted in his haughty
refusal to read the book, but clearly he set no very influential
example. *Tom Jones*, as even Fielding's antagonists had to admit,
was "in every Hand, from the beardless Youth, up to the hoary
Hairs of Age." The fact of its popularity did not, to be sure,
discourage Fielding's critics from roundly damning a book "so
truly profligate, of such evil Tendency, and offensive to every
chaste Reader, so discouraging to Virtue and detrimental to
Religion!" Such was the opinion expressed by "Aretine" in *Old
England* (May 27, 1749) and echoed at length by "Orbilius,"
his colleague in pseudonymous invective, in the *Examen* of the
novel published in December. Yet there were other, juster voices
to praise it. Fresh from reading Fielding's "Amazing entertainment," Captain Lewis Thomas exclaimed in a letter to a friend on
April 3, 1749: "Character, Painting, Reflexions, Humour,
excellent each in its Kind. . . . If my design had been to propagate
virtue by appearing publickly in its defense, I should rather have
been ye Author of Tom Jones than of five Folio Volumes of
sermons."

    Indeed, as Fielding declared in dedicating his book to Lyttel-
ton, to recommend "the Cause of Religion and Virtue" had been
his "sincere Endeavour" in writing *Tom Jones*. To understand
how he achieved that purpose in a work of art is to know what
Fielding understood by "religion" and "virtue," and what he
conceived to be the art of the novel. Though Fielding, like Tom
Jones, was a hearty well-wisher to the Protestant religion, his
membership in the Church of England was of a very different
sort from that of Thwackum, the ferocious and pharisaical
upholder of orthodoxy who demonstrates the doctrines of natural
depravity and grace by frequent applications of birch to the
posteriors of his pupils. "When I mention Religion," Thwackum

declares, "I mean the Christian Religion; and not only the Christian Religion, but the Protestant Religion; and not only the Protestant Religion, but the Church of *England*" (III. iii). Unlike Thwackum, his author was a Christian of the Low-Church, Latitudinarian tradition, whose chief spokesman in the eighteenth century, the controversial Bishop Benjamin Hoadly, Fielding compliments early in the novel (II. vii). As set forth by Hoadly—and earlier by Isaac Barrow and John Tillotson, whom Fielding also admired and drew upon in his works—the Latitudinarian position was essentially rationalist and mystery-dispelling. In striving for greater comprehension within the Church, and in attempting to accommodate Christianity to an Age of Reason, Hoadly preached that the Church of Christ was nothing less than the whole community of believers. He argued that the Sacrament of the Lord's Supper had no special efficacy, but was instituted merely as a memorial of Christ's sacrifice and as an occasion for renewing Christian feelings of brotherhood. Stressing the importance of works over faith, the Latitudinarians in effect revived the old quarrel between Pelagius and Augustine: man, they maintained against Hobbes and Calvin, was by nature capable of much goodness, and he was free to choose between virtue and vice. As George Whitefield plainly saw (he was the fiery evangelist who, together with Wesley, had begun the Methodist movement in the 1730's), the tendency of such principles was to de-emphasize the role of Christ in salvation and to transform Christianity into a moral system hardly distinguishable from the Stoicism of Cicero or the Deism of Shaftesbury. To Fielding, the religion of Whitefield and his followers, as Parson Adams declares in *Joseph Andrews* (I. xvii), was at best mere "Nonsense and Enthusiasm," at worst a "pernicious" and "detestable" doctrine; for a persuasion that salvation was a matter of belief rather than virtuous practice, of the passive receiving of grace rather than an active charity, could lead only to the subversion of society. For Fielding, Whitefield, more than any other Englishman of his time, was the Enemy, his doctrine a convenient rationale for the selfish and hypocritical. In *Tom Jones*, the despicable Captain Blifil is "not a little suspected of an Inclination to *Methodism*" (I. x), and his son, the villain of the piece, is last heard of as a member of "that Sect" (XVIII. xiii). When Tom Jones pauses to refresh himself at an inn owned by Whitefield's brother (VIII. viii), the evangelist himself, together with his "pernicious Principles," becomes the subject of a sardonic digression.

Fielding's morality and his religion are founded upon the benevolist theories inculcated by the Latitudinarians and given additional currency by Shaftesbury. "Good nature," that innate sympathetic disposition which causes us to feel the happiness and misfortunes of others and prompts us to do whatever we can to promote the one and relieve the other, is the chief virtue in his system. The "glorious Lust of doing Good," he called it in his verse essay on the subject. In order to be meaningful, however, the generous impulses of the good-natured man must be expressed in practice. So it is that Allworthy, like his author, represents an active charity as "an indispensable Duty, enjoined both by the Christian Law, and by the Law of Nature itself" (II. v). All the good men of Fielding's fiction share this conviction. He did not believe, of course, that everyone was capable of that high pitch of benevolence evident in a Parson Adams or a Tom Jones. With Pope, Fielding subscribed to the theory of a predominant passion that in part accounted for the individual characters of different men; self-love was as powerful as social, and more generally to be met with. For every Tom Jones, he implies, there is a Blifil. Nevertheless, assisted by the compelling incentives of religion, men could, through the proper exercise of reason and the will, live virtuously and charitably, thereby contributing to the health of society and of the private soul. In all this, Fielding preferred the practical Christianity of the Latitudinarians to the insubstantial theories of deists such as his own philosopher Square, whose abstract speculations on "*the natural Beauty of Virtue*" and "the *eternal Fitness of Things*" prove inadequate to the business of life. Square's deism, a mixture of vague notions drawn from Shaftesbury and from the intellectualist school of Tindal, flatters the philosopher's opinion of himself but provides no effective moral imperative. His exposure in Molly Seagrim's bedroom (v. v)—a scene which, as the hilarious revelation of the naked truth behind the drapery of pretension, may be taken as the quintessential dramatization of Fielding's theory of "the true Ridiculous"—demonstrates the irrelevancy of Square's metaphysics to the moral life. At the end of the novel (XVIII. iv) his conversion makes the point explicit.

The ideals of good nature and charity, and the tenets of Latitudinarian Christianity, may be said to define, in a general way, the
ethos of all Fielding's fiction. Yet Fielding gave to each of his
novels a distinctive character and theme of its own: the mock
heroics of *Joseph Andrews* define the nature of Chastity and
Charity; the irony of *Jonathan Wild* explores the meaning of
Greatness; *Amelia* is the rather sentimental story of a marriage.
Tom Jones is more ambitious in conception; for it may be seen
as the summarizing expression of an entire world view, as the
formal embodiment of a system of values characteristic of that
period in English literary history (roughly 1660 to 1750) which
most scholars call the "Augustan Age." There are many ways of
defining Augustanism, all of them perhaps equally true and all
equally in need of qualification. For the present, mine centers
upon the correlative ideas of Art and Order that distinguish
much of the thought of the age of Newton and Pope—an age
whose cast of mind saw the moral drama of the individual life
enacted within a frame of cosmic and social order conceived in
the then still compatible terms of Christian humanism and New-
tonian science, and whose view of art, conditioned by the principles of neo-Aristotelian aesthetics, saw the poem as fundamentally mimetic of this universal design. The philosophic and
aesthetic assumptions of the Augustan Age are perhaps most
memorably and explicitly expressed in Pope's complementary
poems, the *Essay on Criticism* (1711) and the *Essay on Man*
(1733–34), in which the neoclassical concept of Nature and of
the poetic imitation of her are set forth in couplets as finely
wrought and balanced as the poet's universe itself. The point is
most succinctly made in these familiar lines from the poem that,
Fielding once remarked, "*taught me a System of Philosophy in
English Numbers*":

> All Nature is but Art, unknown to thee;
> All Chance, Direction, which thou canst not see;
> All Discord, Harmony, not understood;
> All partial Evil, universal Good. . . .

Pope's universe is Fielding's; Art and Order are its distinguishing
characteristics, as they should be of the poem or novel that seeks
to imitate "what really exists" (to cite Fielding's translation of

Aristotle in *Tom Jones*, vii. i), and as they will be of the micro-cosm, man, as long as he realizes his true identity. More than any other production of the age—more even than the *Essay on Man*, which presents a similar doctrine in discursive form—*Tom Jones* embodies this philosophy in a work of the creative imagination.

Art, in this peculiarly Augustan sense, is both the subject and the characteristic of *Tom Jones*. To promote "the Cause of Religion and Virtue," as Fielding promised in his dedication, the major themes of the novel are the assertion of the doctrine of Providence, or "the Art of God," and the recommendation of Prudence, or "the Art of Life." Together these two concepts define Fielding's world of Order. As Providence is to the macro-cosm, the universe at large, so is Prudence to the microcosm, man—the latter being that rational, pragmatic virtue that, in the moral sphere, is analogous to the Deity's wise and omniscient government of the creation. To a remarkable degree, the art of *Tom Jones* itself is the formal expression of these themes.

In Book X, Chapter i, Fielding applies to his novel a metaphor made familiar by Pope, Ralph Cudworth, and countless other philosophers or divines who saw the world as the work of a divine Artificer, a wise and benevolent Deity whose Word brought Order out of Chaos and whose careful providence con-ducts all men toward that final denouement in which the virtuous will be rewarded and the vicious punished. "This Work," Fielding declares, "may, indeed, be considered as a great Creation of our own; and for a little Reptile of a Critic to presume to find Fault with any of its Parts, without knowing the Manner in which the Whole is connected, and before he comes to the final Catastrophe, is a most presumptuous Absurdity." *Tom Jones* is a paradigm of the Augustan world view. Consider, for example, what may be called the "Palladian" architecture of the novel—that nice symmetry of structure by which the eighteen books of the novel are divided into three equal parts treating, respectively, the country, the journey, and the city, with the adventures at Upton forming the keystone of the arch at the mathematical center of the narrative and being balanced on either side by the digressions of the Man of the Hill and Mrs. Fitzpatrick. The design of *Tom Jones* mirrors a similar Order, a similar harmony and symmetry of parts, in Fielding's universe. Another, equally celebrated feature of the book, the omniscient narrator himself, functions, as both Thackeray and Wayne Booth have observed, as a kind of surrogate Providence in the world of the novel, whose wit and wisdom we rely on and whose intrusions into the story keep us constantly aware of the shaping intelligence that arranges and governs all contingencies and will bring the characters at last to their just rewards. Though Professor Crane has brilliantly analyzed the "intricate scheme of probabilities" by which Fielding's plot develops organically,[1] and though Fielding himself insists at length that the Probable is preferable to the Marvelous in fiction (viii. i), it is no less true that many of the events in *Tom Jones* are the highly improbable contrivances of "Fortune." Tom's lucky encounter at the crossroads with the illiterate beggar who has found Sophia's lost pocketbook (xii. iv) is but one among many instances of the important role coincidence plays in the novel. As the divines whom Fielding read and admired were at pains to make clear, however, and as Tom Jones himself frequently acknowledges, it is Providence, not Fortune, that contrives the extraordinary casualties of life. The happy accidents and surprising reversals in Fielding's novel remind us of the manipulating intelligence of the author who conducts the story, as those in real life are signs of the Deity's providential care.

Chance, then, *is* Direction in the world of *Tom Jones*, as in the world celebrated in the *Essay on Man*. And the events in the novel ultimately lead toward a comic apocalypse—that last, improbable, joyous catastrophe in which true identities are discovered, the innocent redeemed, and unerring justice meted out to one and all. How is it, then, that one of the absurdities of *Pamela* that Fielding ridiculed was Richardson's insistence that virtue was rewarded in this world? "A very wholesome and comfortable Doctrine," Fielding remarked in *Tom Jones* (xv. i), "and to which we have but one Objection, namely, That it is not true." Why, one may well ask, should the happy conclusion of Fielding's own fiction be considered any less intellectually reprehensible than that of *Pamela*? The answer is implicit in what we have been saying so far about the relation of form to meaning in *Tom Jones*. Whereas Richardson offers *Pamela* to us as a literal transcription

---

1 "The Plot of *Tom Jones*," reprinted in Battestin, ed., *Twentieth Century Interpretations of "Tom Jones"* (Englewood Cliffs, N. J.: Prentice-Hall, 1968), pp. 68–93.

of reality, Fielding's intention is ultimately symbolic. In the preface to *Joseph Andrews*, Fielding saw the business of the comic novelist, as he saw that of his friend Hogarth, the "Comic History-Painter," as "the exactest copying of Nature"; but he meant this in an Aristotelian, not a Baconian, sense. He would have agreed with Imlac in Johnson's *Rasselas* that the poet was not concerned to number the streaks of the tulip; his subject was "not Men, but Manners; not an Individual, but a Species." Richardson's eye is on the fact, Fielding's on the abstraction that the fact implies. The happy ending of *Pamela* is unacceptable because the novel asks to be taken as a faithful (even in a pious sense) representation of actuality. Fielding's fiction makes no such claim. Ultimately he asks us to consider not Tom Jones, but "HUMAN NATURE," not so much the particular story of one man's fall and redemption as that rational and benign scheme of things which the story and its witty, genial author imply. *Tom Jones* asks to be taken as a work of Art, as paradigm and emblem of that wise Design which Pope celebrated and in terms of which "partial Evil"—however real, however terrible—may be seen as "universal Good." The form of *Tom Jones*—its omniscient narrator and symmetrical design, its progression through probabilities and improbabilities to a fortunate conclusion—is the embodiment of its author's Christian vision: the vision of a world ordered and benign, and therefore "comic" in the profoundest sense.

The form of Fielding's masterpiece has, then, an ontological significance, the art of the novel implying the art of God. This, the assertion of Providence, is the book's implicit meaning; the recommendation of Prudence, "the Art of Life"—as Fielding, echoing Cicero, calls this virtue in *Amelia* (I. i)—is the explicit ethical purpose of the novel.[1] The word *prudence* (or the synonymous term *discretion*) recurs and reverberates throughout *Tom Jones*, acquiring something of the quality and function of a musical motif. But its meanings are curiously ambiguous: on the one hand, prudence is the summarizing vice of Blifil or Lady Bellaston, and on the other hand, prudence is that virtue Tom Jones must acquire before he reaches maturity as a moral agent. The

---

[1] For a full discussion of the themes of Providence and prudence in *Tom Jones*, see Battestin, *The Providence of Wit: Aspects of Form in Augustan Literature and the Arts* (Oxford: The Clarendon Press, 1974), chs. 5–6.

problem for Tom, as for the reader, is to distinguish true prudence from false. It is a problem no less difficult than the definition of Wisdom itself.

In his dedication to Lyttelton, Fielding provides a clue to both the substance and the form of his major theme: invoking the Platonic metaphor comparing Virtue to a beautiful woman whose irresistible charms demand our love, he states that he intends not only to display "that Beauty of Virtue which may attract the Admiration of Mankind," but also to convince men "that their true Interest directs them to a Pursuit of her." The passage epitomizes the distinction familiar in the Christian humanist tradition between the two kinds of virtue or moral wisdom, *sophia* and *prudentia*. The apprehension of *sophia*, or speculative wisdom, was the goal of Plato's philosopher; the acquisition of *prudentia*, or practical wisdom, was the quest of Cicero's *vir honestus*. Prudence in this sense was the chief of the four cardinal virtues in antiquity. It is the ability, through the proper exercise of the rational faculties of memory, intelligence, and foresight, to distinguish truth from appearances and to estimate the future consequences of our present actions. It implies, furthermore, the power to choose between good and evil and to determine the right and effective means of achieving the one and of avoiding the other. This, as Allworthy observes, "is indeed the Duty which we owe to ourselves" (xviii. x). On the other hand, as it describes the less admirable characters in the novel—Blifil, Lady Bellaston, Deborah Wilkins, Jenny Jones, Mrs. Western, and Partridge, among a crowded gallery of the worldly and hypocritical —prudence reflects the modern definition of the term that had gained currency during the seventeenth century. Cicero had warned that cunning (*malitia*) was the counterfeit of wisdom (*prudentia*), and by Fielding's time, the popularity among middle-class readers of such works as Gracian's *The Art of Prudence* and William de Britaine's *Humane Prudence* had, in effect, transformed the supreme rational virtue of the ancients into that selfish and mean-spirited sense of expediency which the term now signifies. Robinson Crusoe and Pamela, the archetypal hero and heroine of the new bourgeois mythology, are "prudent" in this latter sense, the sagacity of the *vir honestus* having become, in Defoe and Richardson, the worldly wisdom of the *vir œconomicus*. Fielding's ambiguous use of prudence is calculated to test the reader's own ability to distinguish true from false, to involve us, as it were, in his hero's progress toward the acquisition of *prudentia*.

In this context the story of Tom Jones's disgrace and redemption, of his arduous journey toward reconciliation with his foster father and marriage with the woman he loves, takes on a broadly allegorical dimension; it is the story of our own deep need to live our lives with Wisdom. *Tom Jones* is not, of course, an allegory in the same sense or in the same way that *The Faerie Queene*, let us say, is an allegory. Fielding's novel differs from the conventional allegory in that its story is primary and autonomous. Characters, events, and setting have an integrity of their own and compel our interest in and for themselves; they do not require, at every point in the narrative, to be read off as signs and symbols in some controlling ideational system. Whereas Spenser's Una is "the One," Sophia Western is the girl Tom Jones loves and her family bullies. At the same time, however, within the world of the novel, Sophia is both cynosure and avatar—as her name implies, the center of the theme of Virtue and its incarnation. In her, to refer again to Fielding's use of the Platonic metaphor in his dedication, Virtue becomes "an Object of Sight." Similarly, though he is not of the same symbolic company as the Red Cross Knight or Bunyan's pilgrim, Tom Jones appears in the novel as a kind of Everyman striving toward maturity against his own weaknesses and the pressures of a hostile world. Tom's "Pursuit" of Sophia shadows the quest of us all to find wisdom and our own true identities; like his, ours is also a journey we must make essentially alone, assisted though we may be by the occasional kindness of strangers and assured (as Fielding, at least, believed) of the friendly guidance of Providence. Tom's status as a foundling, prominently underscored in the title Fielding gave to his book, supplies the chief clue to this theme: the circumstances of his hero's birth are Fielding's metaphor of the human condition, for, as children of erring parents in Eden, we are all foundlings in this world. Such would seem to be the import of that curious passage (ii. ii) in which Captain Blifil and Squire Allworthy debate the consequences of Tom's bastardy in language echoing the arguments for and against the theological doctrine of absolute reprobation. We will be judged, Allworthy and his author imply, not for any taint in the blood beyond our control, but according to our own success or failure in the pursuit of Virtue.

Fielding's hero is possessed of every private and social virtue but one: he is honest, brave, and generous, but he is imprudent, and therefore imperfect as a moral agent. For want of prudence, Tom Jones is cast out of Paradise Hall, commits one good-natured indiscretion after another, and finds himself at last clapped into prison, rejected by Sophia and his foster father, and guilty (for all he knows) of incest and murder. After his expulsion from Paradise Hall, Tom's journey is at first aimless and uncertain: "*The World*, as *Milton* phrases it, *lay all before him*; and *Jones*, no more than *Adam*, had any Man to whom he might resort for Comfort or Assistance" (VII. ii). After the crisis at Upton, however, when his mistress discovers his infidelity with Mrs. Waters, Tom's pursuit of Sophia will signify his gradual and painful attainment of *prudentia*. This, we recall, had been Fielding's purpose in writing the novel—to convince men "that their true Interest directs them to a Pursuit" of Virtue. In prison, at the nadir of his misfortunes, Tom Jones arrives at the crucial moment of self-awareness toward which the novel has been moving: " 'Sure . . . Fortune will never have done with me, till she hath driven me to Distraction. But why do I blame Fortune? I am myself the Cause of all my Misery. All the dreadful Mischiefs which have befallen me, are the Consequences only of my own Folly and Vice' " (XVIII. ii). At the moment when Fielding's hero confesses his folly and learns the lesson of prudence, the prison doors miraculously open, his "crimes" are undone, his enemies exposed, his true identity discovered. His marriage with Sophia follows inevitably. Within the frame of Fielding's comic vision of a just and ordered world, of a world in which wisdom *is* attainable, it is the only possible conclusion.

Ideally, Fielding saw life as he saw art, not merely as energy, but as order. What he admired in men and in the natural world was a sort of benign exuberance rationally controlled and directed toward the attainment of a desirable end. The world of *Tom Jones* is dynamic, charged with the energy of sunshine and laughter and love. And it is at the same time a celebration of that rational design which gives meaning to vitality, and which alone, perhaps, makes it a source of joy and of wonder.

THE

HISTORY

OF

TOM JONES,

A

FOUNDLING.

In SIX VOLUMES.

By HENRY FIELDING, Esq;

——*Mores hominum multorum vidit.*——

LONDON:

Printed for A. MILLAR, over-against
Catharine-street in the *Strand.*
MDCCXLIX.

To the HONOURABLE

George Lyttleton, *Esq* ;[1]

One of the Lords Commissioners of
the TREASURY

SIR,

NOTWITHSTANDING your constant Refusal, when I
have asked Leave to prefix your Name to this Dedication,
I must still insist on my Right to desire your Protection of this
Work.

To you, Sir, it is owing that this History[2] was ever begun.
It was by your Desire that I first thought of such a Composition.

---

[1] *Note to title-page.* Horace, *Ars Poetica*, 141–2: 'Sing, Muse, for me the man who on Troy's fall / Saw the wide world, its ways and cities all'—trans. H. R. Fairclough, Loeb Classical Library (1929). Advising the poet to begin his work simply and modestly, Horace here cites the example of Homer, paraphrasing the exordium of the *Odyssey*. Fielding used the same motto in *The Champion* (20 March 1739/40).

[1] George Lyttelton (1709–73) of Hagley Park, Worcestershire; later first Baron Lyttelton (1757). When the Pelham administration was formed in 1744, Lyttelton was appointed to the Treasury. An appropriate model for Squire Allworthy, he was widely esteemed for his piety, benevolence, and taste. Though Lyttelton was himself an author of modest abilities—e.g., *Letters from a Persian in England* (1735), *Observations on the Conversion and Apostleship of St. Paul* (1747), *Dialogues of the Dead* (1760)—in letters he is perhaps best remembered as the friend of Pope and the patron of Thomson and Fielding. His close and lasting association with Fielding probably began at Eton in the early 1720s; certainly, they were on the friendliest terms in 1733, the year of Fielding's unpublished poem, 'An Epistle to Mr. Lyttelton', censuring Pope for his satire of Lady Mary Wortley Montagu (see Isobel Grundy, 'New Verse by Henry Fielding', *PMLA*, lxxxvii (1972), 213–45). Together with Pitt, Chesterfield, and Dodington—to name only the most prominent of those who befriended Fielding—Lyttelton was a member of the Opposition during Walpole's last years as prime minister, when Fielding was supporting the 'Patriot' cause in his plays and in *The Champion* (1739–41). Throughout this period, if one may judge from Fielding's compliments to Lyttelton in the poems 'Of True Greatness' (1741) and 'Liberty' (1743, in *Miscellanies*, i), relations between the two men remained cordial.

In the months preceding the publication of *Tom Jones*, Fielding's obligations to Lyttelton, whom he praised in *The Jacobite's Journal* (16 July 1748) as 'almost the only Patron which the Muses at present can boast of among the Great', were widely known and jeeringly remarked by their enemies. The writers of *Old England* (5 March, 12 November 1748) asserted that Lyttelton had hired his friend to edit *The Jacobite's Journal* as an administration organ and had arranged to distribute the paper gratis throughout the kingdom. According to Horace Walpole, it was owing to Lyttelton's influence that Fielding was

Notes 1 and 2 continued overleaf.

So many Years have since past, that you may have, perhaps, forgotten this Circumstance: But your Desires are to me in the Nature of Commands; and the Impression of them is never to be erased from my Memory.

Again, Sir, without your Assistance this History had never been completed. Be not startled at the Assertion. I do not intend to draw on you the Suspicion of being a Romance Writer. I mean no more than that I partly owe to you my Existence during great Part of the Time which I have employed in composing it: another Matter which it may be necessary to remind you of; since there are certain Actions of which you are apt to be extremely forgetful; but of these I hope I shall always have a better Memory than yourself.

Lastly, it is owing to you that the History appears what it now is. If there be in this Work, as some have been pleased to say, a stronger Picture of a truly benevolent Mind than is to be found in any other, who that knows you, and a particular Acquaintance of yours,[1] will doubt whence that Benevolence hath been copied? The World will not, I believe, make me the Compliment of thinking I took it from myself. I care not: This they shall own,

appointed Justice of the Peace for Middlesex (see the General Introduction, p. xxix, n. 3). And it was Lyttelton's enthusiastic commendation of *Tom Jones* that stimulated public interest in the novel before it was published (see the General Introduction, p. xlvi).

For further discussion of Lyttelton and his relations with Fielding, see Rose Mary Davis, *The Good Lord Lyttelton* (Bethlehem, Pa., 1939). For other allusions to Lyttelton in *Tom Jones*, see below, pp. 405, n. 2; 687; 925, n. 2.

[2] On Fielding's association of his new species of fiction with the genre of history, see below, p. 489, n. 2.

[1] Ralph Allen (1693–1764) of Bath, philanthropist and patron of letters. Though of humble birth, Allen made a fortune by improving the system of cross-country posts in England and Wales, and then purchased the valuable stone quarries at Combe Down. With this stone Allen and the architect John Wood transformed Bath into a new Roman city and built Allen's own magnificent Palladian mansion at Prior Park, Widcombe (see p. 42, n. 1; 613, n. 1). For his various charities—especially his donations to hospitals, such as the General Hospital at Bath and the Foundling Hospital and St. Bartholomew's in London— Allen was celebrated as the very type of 'the Benevolent Man'. (See, for example, the anonymous poem 'Of the Characters of Men. An Epistle to Ralph Allen, Esq.' [1750].) Among men of letters, Pope and Richardson were his good friends; but from the time of their first meeting in 1741, Allen took a particular beneficent interest in Fielding and his family. Fielding, in turn, warmly acknowledged these favours, praising Allen in *Joseph Andrews* (1742; III. i, vi), *A Journey from This World to the Next* (1743; I. v), and *The Covent-Garden Journal* (11 April 1752), and to Allen he dedicated his last novel, *Amelia* (1751). For an authoritative biography, see Benjamin Boyce, *The Benevolent Man: A Life of Ralph Allen of Bath* (Cambridge, Mass., 1967). For other allusions to Allen in *Tom Jones*, see below, pp. 38, n. 1; 42, n. 1; 403–4; 613, n. 1; 687.

that the two Persons from whom I have taken it, that is to say, two of the best and worthiest Men in the World, are strongly and zealously my Friends. I might be contented with this, and yet my Vanity will add a third to the Number; and him one of the greatest and noblest, not only in his Rank, but in every public and private Virtue. But here whilst my Gratitude for the princely Benefactions of the Duke of *Bedford*[1] bursts from my Heart, you must forgive my reminding you, that it was you who first recommended me to the Notice of my Benefactor.

And what are your Objections to the Allowance of the Honour which I have sollicited? Why, you have commended the Book so warmly, that you should be ashamed of reading your Name before the Dedication. Indeed, Sir, if the Book itself doth not make you ashamed of your Commendations, nothing that I can here write will, or ought. I am not to give up my Right to your Protection and Patronage, because you have commended my Book: For though I acknowledge so many Obligations to you, I do not add this to the Number; in which Friendship, I am convinced, hath so little Share: Since that can neither biass your Judgment, nor pervert your Integrity. An Enemy may at any Time obtain your Commendation by only deserving it; and the utmost which the

---

[1] John Russell (1710–71), fourth Duke of Bedford, succeeded to the dukedom in 1732. He had been associated with Lyttelton in Opposition, working at first against Walpole and then, after the Minister's resignation in 1742, against the Hanoverian policies of Carteret. When the Broad-Bottom coalition was formed in December 1744, Bedford was appointed First Lord of the Admiralty; on 12 February 1748 he replaced Chesterfield as Secretary of State for the Southern Department, an office which he held until 1751. He was Lord Justice in 1745, 1748, 1750, and in 1746 was appointed Warden of the New Forest (see below, p. 259, n. 4). Among his public benefactions, Bedford was Head of the Corporation of the Foundling Hospital, receiving the royal charter from Captain Coram in 1739 (see below, p. 761, n. 3).

The personal favours he bestowed upon Fielding began at least as early as 1743, when Bedford's name appeared among the subscribers to the *Miscellanies*. The 'princely Benefactions' to which the novelist refers in the present passage were doubtless more substantial and of more recent date. Since, however, the first two volumes of *Tom Jones* had been issued as early as November 1748, the reference here—contrary to what most scholars have assumed—could not be to the best-known instance of Bedford's generosity to Fielding: not until 13 December did Fielding write to his patron requesting the lease of certain properties having a rental value of £100, the gift of which made it possible for him to qualify as Justice of the Peace for Middlesex (see Cross, ii. 96–8). Some years later, in the Introduction to the *Journal of a Voyage to Lisbon* (1755), Fielding acknowledged further obligations to his 'great Patron', who granted him a yearly pension out of the public service-money. For complimentary references to Bedford, see also *The Jacobite's Journal* (30 January and 20 February 1748).

Faults of your Friends can hope for is your Silence; or, perhaps, if too severely accused, your gentle Palliation.

In short, Sir, I suspect, that your Dislike of public Praise is your true Objection to granting my Request. I have observed, that you have, in common with my two other Friends, an Unwillingness to hear the least Mention of your own Virtues; that, as a great Poet says of one of you, (he might justly have said it of all three) you

Do Good by stealth, and blush to find it Fame.[1]

If Men of this Disposition are as careful to shun Applause, as others are to escape Censure, how just must be your Apprehension of your Character falling into my Hands; since what would not a Man have Reason to dread, if attacked by an Author who had received from him Injuries equal to my Obligations to you!

And will not this Dread of Censure increase in Proportion to the Matter which a Man is conscious of having afforded for it? If his whole Life, for Instance, should have been one continued Subject of Satire, he may well tremble when an incensed Satyrist takes him in Hand. Now, Sir, if we apply this to your modest Aversion to Panegyric, how reasonable will your Fears of me appear!

Yet surely you might have gratified my Ambition, from this single Confidence, that I shall always prefer the Indulgence of your Inclinations to the Satisfaction of my own. A very strong Instance of which I shall give you in this Address; in which I am determined to follow the Example of all other Dedicators, and will consider not what my Patron really deserves to have written, but what he will be best pleased to read.

Without further Preface then, I here present you with the Labours of some Years of my Life. What Merit these Labours have is already known to yourself. If, from your favourable Judgment, I have conceived some Esteem for them, it cannot be imputed to Vanity; since I should have agreed as implicitly to your Opinion, had it been given in Favour of any other Man's Production. Negatively, at least, I may be allowed to say, that

[1] Pope's famous, if somewhat condescending, compliment to Ralph Allen in *Epilogue to the Satires. Dialogue I* (1738), 135–6: 'Let humble ALLEN, with an aukward Shame, / Do good by stealth, and blush to find it Fame.' Later in *Tom Jones* (p. 404, n. 4). Fielding seems again to allude to these lines, this time betraying his irritation at the inadequacy of Pope's praise.

had I been sensible of any great Demerit in the Work, you are the last Person to whose Protection I would have ventured to recommend it.

From the Name of my Patron, indeed, I hope my Reader will be convinced, at his very Entrance on this Work, that he will find in the whole Course of it nothing prejudicial to the Cause of Religion and Virtue; nothing inconsistent with the strictest Rules of Decency, nor which can offend even the chastest Eye in the Perusal. On the contrary, I declare, that to recommend Goodness and Innocence hath been my sincere Endeavour in this History. This honest Purpose you have been pleased to think I have attained: And to say the Truth, it is likeliest to be attained in Books of this Kind; for an Example is a Kind of Picture, in which Virtue becomes as it were an Object of Sight, and strikes us with an Idea of that Loveliness, which *Plato* asserts[1] there is in her naked Charms.

Besides displaying that Beauty of Virtue which may attract the Admiration of Mankind, I have attempted to engage a stronger Motive to Human Action in her Favour, by convincing Men, that their true Interest directs them to a Pursuit of her. For this Purpose I have shewn, that no Acquisitions of Guilt can compensate the Loss of that solid inward Comfort of Mind, which is the sure Companion of Innocence and Virtue; nor can in the least balance the Evil of that Horror and Anxiety which, in their Room, Guilt introduces into our Bosoms. And again, that as these Acquisitions are in themselves generally worthless, so are the Means to attain them not only base and infamous, but at best incertain, and always full of Danger. Lastly, I have endeavoured strongly to inculcate, that Virtue and Innocence can scarce ever be injured but by Indiscretion; and that it is this alone which often betrays them into the Snares that Deceit and Villainy spread for them. A Moral which I have the more industriously laboured, as the teaching it is, of all others, the likeliest to be attended with

---

[1] Cf. *Phaedrus,* 250d: 'wisdom would arouse terrible love, if such a clear image of it were granted as would come through sight' (trans. H. N. Fowler, Loeb Classical Library, 1914). See also Cicero, *De Finibus,* II. xvi, and *De Officiis,* I. v; and Seneca, *Epistulae Morales,* cxv. 6. The specific notion of the naked charms of Virtue, imaged as a beautiful woman, is only implicit in Plato. Fielding was especially fond of this commonplace: see, for example, *The Champion* (24, 26 January 1739/40) and the essays 'On Conversation' and 'On the Knowledge of the Characters of Men'—both in the *Miscellanies* (1743). For a later allusion in *Tom Jones,* see below, p. 537, n. 1.

Success; since, I believe, it is much easier to make good Men wise, than to make bad Men good.

For these Purposes I have employed all the Wit and Humour of which I am Master in the following History; wherein I have endeavoured to laugh Mankind out of their favourite Follies and Vices. How far I have succeeded in this good Attempt, I shall submit to the candid Reader, with only two Requests: First, That he will not expect to find Perfection in this Work; and Secondly, That he will excuse some Parts of it, if they fall short of that little Merit which I hope may appear in others.

I will detain you, Sir, no longer. Indeed I have run into a Preface, while I professed to write a Dedication. But how can it be otherwise? I dare not praise you; and the only Means I know of to avoid it, when you are in my Thoughts, are either to be entirely silent, or to turn my Thoughts to some other Subject.

Pardon, therefore, what I have said in this Epistle, not only without your Consent, but absolutely against it; and give me at least Leave, in this public Manner, to declare, that I am, with the highest Respect and Gratitude,

SIR,

Your most Obliged,

Obedient Humble Servant,

Henry Fielding

CONTENTS OF THE
FIRST VOLUME

BOOK I

Containing as much of the Birth of the Foundling as is necessary or proper to acquaint the Reader with in the Beginning of this History.

BOOK II

Containing Scenes of matrimonial Felicity in different Degrees of Life; and various other Transactions during the first two Years after the Marriage between Captain Blifil, *and Miss* Bridget Allworthy.

Contents

BOOK III

Containing the most memorable Transactions which passed in the Family of Mr. Allworthy, *from the Time when* Tommy Jones *arrived at the Age of Fourteen, till he attained the Age of Nineteen. In this Book the Reader may pick up some Hints concerning the Education of Children.*

CONTENTS OF THE SECOND VOLUME

BOOK IV

Containing the Time of a Year.

BOOK V

Containing a Portion of Time, somewhat longer than Half a Year.

Contents

BOOK VI
Containing about three Weeks.

CONTENTS OF THE THIRD VOLUME

BOOK VII
Containing three Days.

BOOK VIII

Containing above two Days.

Contents

BOOK IX

Containing twelve Hours.

CONTENTS OF THE
FOURTH VOLUME

BOOK XII

Containing the same individual Time with the former.

CONTENTS OF THE
FIFTH VOLUME

BOOK XIII
Containing the Space of Twelve Days.

BOOK XIV

Containing two Days.

BOOK XV

In which the History advances about two Days.

CONTENTS OF THE
SIXTH VOLUME

BOOK XVI

Containing the Space of Five Days.

BOOK XVII

Containing three Days.

BOOK XVIII
Containing about Six Days.

Contents

THE HISTORY OF
A FOUNDLING

BOOK I

Containing as much of the Birth of the Foundling as is necessary or proper to acquaint the Reader with in the Beginning of this History.

CHAPTER I

The Introduction to the Work, or Bill of Fare to the Feast.

AN Author ought to consider himself, not as a Gentleman who gives a private or eleemosynary Treat, but rather as one who keeps a public Ordinary, at which all Persons are welcome for their Money. In the former Case, it is well known, that the Entertainer provides what Fare he pleases; and tho' this should be very indifferent, and utterly disagreeable to the Taste of his Company, they must not find any Fault; nay, on the contrary, Good-Breeding forces them outwardly to approve and to commend whatever is set before them. Now the contrary of this happens to the Master of an Ordinary. Men who pay for what they eat, will insist on gratifying their Palates, however nice and whimsical these may prove; and if every Thing is not agreeable to their Taste, will challenge a Right to censure, to abuse, and to d—n their Dinner without Controul.

To prevent therefore giving Offence to their Customers by any such Disappointment, it hath been usual, with the honest and well-meaning Host, to provide a Bill of Fare, which all Persons may peruse at their first Entrance into the House; and, having thence acquainted themselves with the Entertainment which they may expect, may either stay and regale with what is provided for them, or may depart to some other Ordinary better accommodated to their Taste.

As we do not disdain to borrow Wit or Wisdom from any Man who is capable of lending us either, we have condescended to take a Hint from these honest Victuallers, and shall prefix not only a general Bill of Fare to our whole Entertainment, but shall likewise give the Reader particular Bills to every Course which is to be served up in this and the ensuing Volumes.

The Provision then which we have here made is no other than HUMAN NATURE. Nor do I fear that my sensible Reader, though most luxurious in his Taste, will start, cavil, or be offended, because I have named but one Article. The Tortoise, as the Alderman of *Bristol*,[1] well learned in eating, knows by much Experience, besides the delicious *Calibash* and *Calipee*, contains many different Kinds of Food;[2] nor can the learned Reader be ignorant, that in *Human Nature*, tho' here collected under one general Name, is such prodigious Variety, that a Cook will have sooner gone through all the several Species of animal and vegetable Food in the World, than an Author will be able to exhaust so extensive a Subject.

An Objection may perhaps be apprehended from the more delicate, that this Dish is too common and vulgar; for what else is the Subject of all the Romances, Novels, Plays and Poems, with which the Stalls abound. Many exquisite Viands might be rejected by the Epicure, if it was a sufficient Cause for his contemning of them as common and vulgar, that something was to be found in the most paultry Alleys under the same Name. In reality, true Nature is as difficult to be met with in Authors, as the *Bayonne* Ham or *Bologna* Sausage is to be found in the Shops.

1 Owing to the extravagant feasts consumed on such civic occasions as the Lord Mayor's Day, the gluttony of aldermen was proverbial (see, for example, the anonymous poem, *Bath* [1748], p. 18). By mid-century, turtle, imported to Bristol and London from the West Indies, was considered a great delicacy. Perhaps the best gloss on the passage occurs in Lyttelton's *Dialogues of the Dead* (1760), xix, in which Apicius remarks: 'I am credibly informed, that they [turtles] are now as plentiful in England as sturgeons. There are turtle-boats that go regularly to London and Bristol from the West Indies. I have just received this information from a fat alderman, who died in London last week, of a surfeit he got at a turtle-feast in that city.' (Lyttelton's *Works*, ed. G. E. Ayscough, 3rd ed. [1776], ii. 263–4.)

2 Calipash and calipee are the edible substances found, respectively, under the upper shell and inside the lower shell of a turtle. According to William Verral, who learned to cook under the Duke of Newcastle's celebrated French chef, M. de St. Clouet (see p. 33, n. 2), a turtle made 'a pretty first-course' of seven dishes—'the calliopash and calliopee at top and bottom, soup in the middle, and the other four [i.e., fins, head, tripe, and innards] the corners'. (See Verral's *Complete System of Cookery* [1759], p. 240.)

But the whole, to continue the same Metaphor, consists in the Cookery of the Author; for, as Mr. *Pope* tells us,

> True Wit is Nature to Advantage drest,
> What oft' was thought, but ne'er so well exprest.[1]

The same Animal which hath the Honour to have some Part of his Flesh eaten at the Table of a Duke, may perhaps be degraded in another Part, and some of his Limbs gibbeted, as it were, in the vilest Stall in Town. Where then lies the Difference between the Food of the Nobleman and the Porter, if both are at Dinner on the same Ox or Calf, but in the seasoning, the dressing, the garnishing, and the setting forth. Hence the one provokes and incites the most languid Appetite, and the other turns and palls that which is the sharpest and keenest.

In like manner, the Excellence of the mental Entertainment consists less in the Subject, than in the Author's Skill in well dressing it up. How pleased therefore will the Reader be to find, that we have, in the following Work, adhered closely to one of the highest Principles of the best Cook[2] which the present Age, or perhaps that of *Heliogabalus*,[3] hath produced. This great Man,

[1] *Essay on Criticism* (1711), 297–8.

[2] Not, as Cross surmised (ii. 105), a reference to Lebeck, proprietor of a tavern in the Strand, who flourished much earlier (*c.* 1690–1710). In the preceding paragraph Fielding's mention of 'the Table of a Duke' provides the clue to what is doubtless a facetious compliment to Thomas Pelham-Holles (1693–1768), Duke of Newcastle and since 1744 Secretary of State in the government headed by his brother, Henry Pelham (see below, p. 612, n. 1). During the 1740s the most famous cook in England was Newcastle's French chef, M. de St. Clouet, known as 'Cloe'. For several contemporary references to him, see Walpole's letters to Horace Mann (7 July 1742), to Sir Charles Hanbury Williams (6 August 1745), and to Lady Hervey (17 October 1758); see also Print No. 3378 ('A Scene in Hell, or the Infernal Jubilee'), *Catalogue of Prints and Drawings in the British Museum*, Division I (Political and Personal Satires), Vol. iii, Pt. ii (1877). A satiric print of 1745 (No. 2684, 'The Duke of N—tle, and his Cook') depicts Newcastle and 'Cloe' and suggests how closely they were associated in the public mind. For a character of 'Cloe' and an admiring description—with recipes—of his culinary arts, see William Verral, *A Complete System of Cookery* (1759).

[3] Elagabalus, emperor of Rome (A.D. 218–22), was notorious for his licentiousness and gluttony. His lavish banquets, which sometimes lasted for days, are reported in detail by Lampridius, *Scriptores Historiae Augustae*, xviii. 4–xxxiii. In *The True Patriot* (3 December 1745) Fielding anticipated the present analogy between the two feasts, gastronomic and literary. Posing as the epicure 'Heliogabalus', he addressed a letter to himself, observing 'that you had cooked up the Entertainment you *serve* to the Public with much Propriety: You give us first a Dish of substantial Food, when our Appetites are brisk and keen; you then *serve up* several *petit Plats* from the News Papers; and lastly, send us away with a *Bon Bouche* of your own.' Among Fielding's contemporaries Horace Walpole, at least, would not have been puzzled by the juxtaposition of allusions to Elagabalus and the Duke of Newcastle (see above, n. 2): writing in 1756, Walpole described the Duke as having 'the

as is well known to all Lovers of polite eating, begins at first by setting plain Things before his hungry Guests, rising afterwards by Degrees, as their Stomachs may be supposed to decrease, to the very Quintessence of Sauce and Spices. In like manner, we shall represent Human Nature at first to the keen Appetite of our Reader, in that more plain and simple Manner in which it is found in the Country, and shall hereafter hash and ragoo it with all the high *French* and *Italian* Seasoning of Affectation and Vice which Courts and Cities afford. By these Means, we doubt not but our Reader may be rendered desirous to read on for ever, as the great Person, just above-mentioned, is supposed to have made some Persons eat.

Having premised thus much, we will now detain those, who like our Bill of Fare, no longer from their Diet, and shall proceed directly to serve up the first Course of our History, for their Entertainment.

CHAPTER II

A short Description of Squire Allworthy, *and a fuller Account of Miss* Bridget Allworthy *his Sister.*

IN that Part of the western Division of this Kingdom, which is commonly called *Somersetshire*, there lately lived (and perhaps lives still) a Gentleman whose Name was *Allworthy*, and who might well be called the Favourite of both Nature and Fortune;[1] for both of these seem to have contended which should bless and enrich him most. In this Contention, Nature may seem to some to have come off victorious, as she bestowed on him many Gifts; while Fortune had only one Gift in her Power; but in pouring forth this, she was so very profuse, that others perhaps may think this single Endowment to have been more than equivalent to all the various Blessings which he enjoyed from Nature. From the former of these, he derived an agreeable Person, a sound Constitution, a solid Understanding, and a benevolent Heart; by the latter, he was decreed to the Inheritance of one of the largest Estates in the County.

monkey disposition of Heliogabalus' (see *Memoirs of the Reign of King George the Second*, ed. Lord Holland, 2nd ed. [1847], i. 373).

1 Cf. 'Liberty. To George Lyttleton, Esq.;' (1743), in which Fielding paid a similar compliment to his friend and patron—one 'Whom Nature vy'd with Fortune to adorn!'

This Gentleman had, in his Youth, married a very worthy and beautiful Woman, of whom he had been extremely fond: By her he had three Children, all of whom died in their Infancy. He had likewise had the Misfortune of burying this beloved Wife herself, about five Years before the Time in which this History chuses to set out. This Loss, however great, he bore like a Man of Sense and Constancy; tho' it must be confest, he would often talk a little whimsically on this Head: For he sometimes said, he looked on himself as still married, and considered his Wife as only gone a little before him, a Journey which he should most certainly, sooner or later, take after her; and that he had not the least Doubt of meeting her again, in a Place where he should never part with her more.[1] Sentiments for which his Sense was arraigned by one Part of his Neighbours, his Religion by a second, and his Sincerity by a third.

He now lived, for the most Part, retired in the Country, with one Sister, for whom he had a very tender Affection. This Lady was now somewhat past the Age of 30,[2] an Æra, at which, in the Opinion of the malicious, the Title of Old Maid may, with no Impropriety, be assumed. She was of that Species of Women, whom you commend rather for good Qualities than Beauty, and who are generally called by their own Sex, very good Sort of

---

[1] The sentiments which comfort Allworthy were commonplaces of the Christian *consolatio*: thus in his 'Consolatory Discourse' (1660) Simon Patrick observed that 'my friend is not gone, but gone before. . . . He hath taken a journey into a far Country, and there I may go to see him' (quoted in H. K. Miller, *Essays on Fielding's 'Miscellanies'* [Princeton, N.J., 1961], p. 246, n. 137). But the present passage may glance specifically at Lyttelton, whose wife died on 19 January 1747. Lyttelton's monody on her death (published 30 October 1747) closes with an expectation similar to Allworthy's that his wife awaits him in heaven. Still closer to the squire's sentiments are those Lyttelton expressed to Doddridge shortly after the death of Thomson: 'It often occurs to my mind that the death of our friends is one of the most powerfull ordinary means made use of by Providence to detach our affections and hopes from this world, and convince us that we have here *no enduring city, but are to look for a better*. By that time we have run half our course, those who set out with us, and of whose company we are most fond, are parted from us, and got to the end of their journey. If we were never to meet again, to what purpose has nature implanted in us such strong, such bitter, such lasting regrets at this separation; these affections are not in vain, they are not fixed upon what is no more; they are intimations and notices of a life to come, and are designed to carry our views, our wishes, I could almost say our passions, on to that life.' (Letter from Hagley, 30 September 1748; R. Phillimore, ed. *Memoirs and Correspondence of George Lord Lyttelton, from 1734 to 1773* [1845], i. 407.) Cf. also, *Tom Jones*, p. 117.

[2] Later in this Book (ch. viii) Bridget Allworthy is said to be approaching forty years of age.

Women—as good a Sort of Woman, Madam, as you would wish
to know. Indeed she was so far from regretting Want of Beauty,
that she never mention'd that Perfection (if it can be called one)
without Contempt; and would often thank God she was not as
handsome as Miss such a one, whom perhaps Beauty had led
into Errors, which she might have otherwise avoided. Miss
Bridget Allworthy (for that was the Name of this Lady) very
rightly conceived the Charms of Person in a Woman to be no
better than Snares for herself, as well as for others, and yet so
discreet was she in her Conduct, that her Prudence[1] was as much

---

[1] The first occurrence in *Tom Jones* of the idea of *prudence* (and of the more or less
synonymous term, *discretion*), the dominant ethical theme of the novel. Prudence in *Tom
Jones* is an ambiguous concept, shifting in connotation from pejorative to positive according to the context, which Fielding carefully controls. In the present instance Bridget
Allworthy's prudence suggests the usual modern understanding of the term, a certain self-
protective caution and mean-spirited sense of expediency. (In this sense the word is also
used to describe a host of other characters: e.g. Deborah Wilkins [I. v, vi], Jenny Jones [I.
ix], Mrs. Seagrim [IV. viii], Mrs. Western [VI. xiv], Partridge [VIII. ix], Mrs. Honour [X.
ix], Lady Bellaston [XIII. iii, xv. ix].) Yet in the penultimate paragraph of the novel, Tom
Jones is said to be a fit partner for Sophia only because he has 'by Reflexion on his past
Follies, acquired a Discretion and Prudence very uncommon in one of his lively Parts';
prudence in this sense is the indispensable requisite of the moral man—'the Duty', as
Allworthy puts it, 'which we owe to ourselves' (XVIII. x). In still another sense, prudence is
the summarizing attribute of Blifil, the villain of the piece.

In *Tom Jones* this single term thus carries with it at least three distinct meanings. (1) In
the Christian humanist tradition, two kinds of wisdom were distinguished: *sophia*, or
speculative wisdom, and *prudentia*, or practical wisdom. (See Cicero, *De Officiis*, I. xliii.)
Prudentia, the chief of the cardinal virtues, is the rational ability to distinguish between
goods real and only apparent and, by the proper use of the intellectual faculties of memory,
judgement, and foresight, to estimate the future consequences of present actions and events.
(See Cicero, *De Inventione*, II. liii. 160; *De Natura Deorum*, III. xv. 38; *De Finibus*, v. vi.
16.) This is the *ars vivendi*, or, as Fielding has it in *Amelia* (I. i), 'the Art of Life'—the
virtue which Tom Jones, like the *vir honestus*, must acquire. (2) On the other hand, in *Tom
Jones*, 'prudence' may signify the false wisdom of this world, the self-interested cunning of
a Blifil: it is 'wisdom [*prudentia*]', Cicero writes, 'which cunning [*malitia*] seeks to counterfeit' (*De Officiis*, III. xxv, trans. W. Miller, Loeb Classical Library, 1913; see also
ibid., II. iii, III. xvii). (3) By the eighteenth century, however, the concept of *prudentia* had
suffered from reinterpretation by writers of bromidic conduct books addressed chiefly to a
middle-class audience of shopkeepers and schoolboys. In the process, ironically, its counterfeit and shadow came to be taken for the thing itself: self-discipline, discretion, foresight,
expediency came to be valued for mercenary reasons—not as the way to self-knowledge and
virtuous conduct, but as the surest means of prospering in the world. (See, for example,
William de Britaine, *Humane Prudence* [1680]; Balthazar Gracian, *The Art of Prudence*
[English trans. 1685]; Thomas Fuller, *Introductio ad Prudentiam*, 3rd ed. [1731]; Nathaniel
Lardner, *Counsels of Prudence for the Use of Young People* [1735].) Thus the hard-earned
wisdom of the *vir honestus* had become—if in name only—the property of the *vir œconomicus*, of a Robinson Crusoe or a Pamela, or in *Tom Jones* of Bridget Allworthy and a
crowded gallery of meretricious and self-interested characters from every rank of society.

on the Guard, as if she had all the Snares to apprehend which
were ever laid for her whole Sex. Indeed, I have observed (tho'
it may seem unaccountable to the Reader) that this Guard of
Prudence, like the Trained Bands,[1] is always readiest to go on
Duty where there is the least Danger. It often basely and cowardly
deserts those Paragons for whom the Men are all wishing, sighing, dying, and spreading every Net in their Power; and constantly attends at the Heels of that higher Order of Women, for
whom the other Sex have a more distant and awful Respect, and
whom (from Despair, I suppose, of Success) they never venture
to attack.

Reader, I think proper, before we proceed any farther together,
to acquaint thee, that I intend to digress, through this whole
History, as often as I see Occasion: Of which I am myself a
better Judge than any pitiful Critic whatever; and here I must
desire all those Critics to mind their own Business, and not to
intermeddle with Affairs, or Works, which no ways concern
them: For, till they produce the Authority by which they are
constituted Judges,[2] I shall plead to their Jurisdiction.

CHAPTER III

An odd Accident which befel Mr. Allworthy, *at his Return home.
The decent Behaviour of Mrs.* Deborah Wilkins *, with some proper
Animadversions on Bastards.*

I HAVE told my Reader, in the preceding Chapter, that Mr.
Allworthy inherited a large Fortune; that he had a good Heart,
and no Family. Hence, doubtless, it will be concluded by many,

By using the same term to convey these antithetical meanings, Fielding's rhetorical
strategy in *Tom Jones* requires the reader to exercise his own prudential faculties, to distinguish between true wisdom and false. The reader, too, is implicated, as it were, in Tom
Jones's awkward progress toward the acquisition of prudence. For a full discussion of this
theme, see Battestin, 'Fielding's Definition of Wisdom: Some Functions of Ambiguity
and Emblem in *Tom Jones*', ELH, xxxv (1968), 188–217. (See also below, pp. 141, n. 1;
770, n. 3).

[1] Companies of citizen soldiers. For an earlier ironic allusion to their courage, see *Joseph
Andrews* (1742), II. vii.

[2] Sarcasm at the expense of critics recurs throughout *Tom Jones*. Implicit in the present
passage is an etymological joke later developed at length in XI. i: the derivation of *critic*
from the Greek word signifying a judge (see below, p. 566, n. 2). For a discussion of
Fielding's estimate of critics, see R. C. Beatty, *PMLA*, xlix (1934), 1095–1100.

that he lived like an honest Man, owed no one a Shilling, took nothing but what was his own, kept a good House, entertained his Neighbours with a hearty Welcome at his Table, and was charitable to the Poor, *i.e.* to those who had rather beg than work, by giving them the Offals from it; that he dy'd immensely rich, and built an Hospital.

And true it is, that he did many of these Things; but, had he done nothing more, I should have left him to have recorded his own Merit on some fair Free-Stone over the Door of that Hospital.[1] Matters of a much more extraordinary Kind are to be the Subject of this History, or I should grossly mispend my Time in writing so voluminous a Work; and you, my sagacious Friend, might, with equal Profit and Pleasure, travel through some Pages, which certain droll Authors have been facetiously pleased to call *The History of England*.[2]

Mr. *Allworthy* had been absent a full Quarter of a Year in *London*, on some very particular Business, tho' I know not what it was; but judge of its Importance, by its having detained him so long from home, whence he had not been absent a Month at a Time during the Space of many Years. He came to his House very late in the Evening, and after a short Supper with his Sister, retired much fatigued to his Chamber. Here, having spent some

[1] Doubtless a compliment to Ralph Allen (see above, p. 4, n. 1), for whom hospitals were a favourite public charity. In a very particular sense Allen 'built' the General Hospital at Bath, completed in 1742: the building was constructed entirely of the 'fair Free-Stone' from Allen's quarries, which he donated free of charge. Allen similarly contributed to the building of St. Bartholomew's Hospital in London.

[2] Fielding was both exasperated and amused at the inaccuracies of contemporary historians, who distorted the facts according to personal or political bias. In *Joseph Andrews* (1742; III. i) he distinguished between the true 'history' or 'biography' he was writing and the 'romances' of such English historians as Clarendon, Echard, Whitelocke, and Rapin, who, he insisted, were not historians at all, but rather mere 'Topographers or Chorographers'. The present passage, however, may point specifically at Thomas Carte's *General History of England*, the first volume of which (published 1 January 1747/8) revealed the author's Jacobital sympathies. Fielding ridiculed Carte in several numbers of *The Jacobite's Journal* (20, 27 February, 12 March 1748), calling him a 'learned and facetious Novelist', and urging him to issue the remaining volumes of his 'great Romance . . . in the same manner with those true and delectable Histories of *Argalus* and *Parthenia*, *Guy* Earl of *Warwick*, the *Seven Champions*, &c. in which Form, at the Price of 1*d.* each, when embellished by our Frontispiece, I make no doubt of assuring him as universal a Sale, as the inimitable Adventures of *Robinson Crusoe* formerly had throughout this Kingdom'. Other works hostile to Carte's *History* were published in 1748, among them the anonymous *Remarks upon Mr. Carte's Specimen of His General History of England* and the pseudonymous *Letter to John Trot-Plaid, Esq; Author of the Jacobite's Journal, concerning Mr. Carte's General History of England* by 'Duncan MacCarte a Highlander'.

Minutes on his Knees, a Custom which he never broke through
on any Account, he was preparing to step into Bed, when, upon
opening the Cloaths, to his great Surprize, he beheld an Infant,
wrapt up in some coarse Linnen, in a sweet and profound Sleep,
between his Sheets. He stood some Time lost in Astonishment
at this Sight; but, as Good-nature[1] had always the Ascendant in
his Mind, he soon began to be touched with Sentiments of Compassion for the little Wretch before him. He then rung his Bell,
and ordered an elderly Woman Servant to rise immediately and
come to him, and in the mean Time was so eager in contemplating
the Beauty of Innocence, appearing in those lively Colours with
which Infancy and Sleep always display it, that his Thoughts
were too much engaged to reflect that he was in his Shirt, when
the Matron came in. She had indeed given her Master sufficient
Time to dress himself; for out of Respect to him, and Regard to
Decency, she had spent many Minutes in adjusting her Hair at
the Looking-glass, notwithstanding all the Hurry in which she
had been summoned by the Servant, and tho' her Master, for
ought she knew, lay expiring in an Apoplexy, or in some other Fit.

It will not be wondered at, that a Creature, who had so strict a
Regard to Decency in her own Person, should be shocked at the
least Deviation from it in another. She therefore no sooner opened
the Door, and saw her Master standing by the Bedside in his
Shirt, with a Candle in his Hand, than she started back in a most
terrible Fright, and might perhaps have swooned away, had he
not now recollected his being undrest, and put an End to her
Terrors, by desiring her to stay without the Door till he had
thrown some Cloaths over his Back, and was become incapable
of shocking the pure Eyes of Mrs. *Deborah Wilkins*, who, tho'

---

[1] 'Good-nature' is the distinguishing characteristic of all Fielding's moral men—of
Parson Adams, Heartfree, Allworthy, Jones, Captain Booth, Dr. Harrison. It signifies
those benevolent, social affections which lead us to empathic involvement in the concerns of
others and which prompt us to charitable actions. In his poem, 'Of Good-Nature' (1743),
Fielding calls this virtue 'the glorious Lust of doing Good'. In 'An Essay on the Knowledge of the Characters of Men' (1743) he is more specific: Good-Nature is that benevolent and amiable Temper of Mind which disposes us to feel the Misfortunes, and enjoy the
Happiness of others; and consequently pushes us on to promote the latter, and prevent the
former; and that without any abstract Contemplation on the Beauty of Virtue, and without
the Allurements or Terrors of Religion.' For discussion of this concept in Fielding, and of
its genesis in the theories of the latitudinarian divines, see Battestin, *The Moral Basis of
Fielding's Art* (Middletown, Conn., 1959), pp. 14–19, 54–63, 65–81, and Miller, *Essays on
Fielding's 'Miscellanies'*, pp. 54–88.

in the 52d Year of her Age, vowed she had never beheld a Man without his Coat. Sneerers and prophane Wits may perhaps laugh at her first Fright, yet my graver Reader, when he considers the Time of Night, the Summons from her Bed, and the Situation in which she found her Master, will highly justify and applaud her Conduct; unless the Prudence, which must be supposed to attend Maidens at that Period of Life at which Mrs. *Deborah* had arrived, should a little lessen his Admiration.

When Mrs. *Deborah* returned into the Room, and was acquainted by her Master with the finding the little Infant, her Consternation was rather greater than his had been; nor could she refrain from crying out with great Horror of Accent as well as Look, 'My good Sir! what's to be done?' Mr. *Allworthy* answered, she must take care of the Child that Evening, and in the Morning he would give Orders to provide it a Nurse. 'Yes, Sir,' says she, 'and I hope your Worship will send out your Warrant to take up the Hussy its Mother (for she must be one of the Neighbourhood) and I should be glad to see her committed to *Bridewel*, and whipt at the Cart's Tail.[1] Indeed such wicked Sluts cannot be too severely punished. I'll warrant 'tis not her first, by her Impudence in laying it to your Worship.' 'In laying it to me, *Deborah*,' answered *Allworthy*, 'I can't think she hath any such Design. I suppose she hath only taken this Method to provide for her Child; and truly I am glad she hath not done worse.' 'I don't know what is worse,' cries *Deborah*, 'than for such wicked Strumpets to lay their Sins at honest Men's Doors; and though your Worship knows your own Innocence, yet the World is censorious; and it hath been many an honest Man's Hap to pass for the Father of Children he never begot; and if your Worship should provide for the Child, it may make the People the apter to believe: Besides, why should your Worship provide for what the Parish is obliged to maintain?[2] For my own Part, if it was an honest Man's Child indeed; but for my own part, it goes against me to touch these misbegotten Wretches, whom I don't look

[1] According to 7 James I, cap. 4, the mother of a bastard child chargeable to the parish (see below, n. 2) could be committed by order of two justices to the house of correction, there to be corporally punished and set to work for the term of one year. (See Theodore Barlow, *The Justice of the Peace* [1745], s.v. 'Bastards', p. 55.)

[2] According to the provisions of the Elizabethan Poor Law (43 Elizabeth, cap. 2), each parish was taxed in order to provide shelter and sustenance for its impotent poor, such as foundling infants.

upon as my Fellow Creatures. Faugh, how it stinks! It doth not smell like a Christian. If I might be so bold to give my Advice, I would have it put in a Basket, and sent out and laid at the Church-Warden's Door.[1] It is a good Night, only a little rainy and windy; and if it was well wrapt up, and put in a warm Basket, it is two to one but it lives till it is found in the Morning. But if it should not, we have discharged our Duty in taking proper care of it; and it is, perhaps, better for such Creatures to die in a state of Innocence, than to grow up and imitate their Mothers; for nothing better can be expected of them.'

There were some Strokes in this Speech which, perhaps, would have offended Mr. *Allworthy*, had he strictly attended to it; but he had now got one of his Fingers into the Infant's Hand, which by its gentle Pressure, seeming to implore his Assistance, had certainly out-pleaded the Eloquence of Mrs. *Deborah*, had it been ten times greater than it was. He now gave Mrs. *Deborah* positive Orders to take the Child to her own Bed, and to call up a Maid-servant to provide it Pap and other things against it waked. He likewise ordered that proper Clothes should be procured for it early in the Morning, and that it should be brought to himself as soon as he was stirring.

Such was the Discernment of Mrs. *Wilkins*, and such the Respect she bore her Master, under whom she enjoyed a most excellent Place, that her Scruples gave way to his peremptory Commands; and she took the Child under her Arms, without any apparent Disgust at the Illegality of its Birth; and declaring it was a sweet little Infant, walked off with it to her own Chamber.

Allworthy here betook himself to those pleasing Slumbers, which a Heart that hungers after Goodness, is apt to enjoy, when thoroughly satisfied. As these are possibly sweeter than what are occasioned by any other hearty Meal, I should take more Pains to display them to the Reader, if I knew any Air to recommend him to for the procuring such an Appetite.

---

[1] Churchwardens were among those overseers of the poor whose duty it was to levy a 'poor's rate' and to care for the impotent poor of the parish.

CHAPTER IV

*The Reader's Neck brought into Danger by a Description, his Escape,
and the great Condescension of Miss Bridget Allworthy.*

THE *Gothick* Stile of Building could produce nothing nobler
than Mr. *Allworthy*'s House.[1] There was an Air of Grandeur in it, that struck you with Awe, and rival'd the Beauties of
the best *Grecian* Architecture; and it was as commodious within,
as venerable without.

It stood on the South-east Side of a Hill, but nearer the Bottom
than the Top of it, so as to be sheltered from the North-east by
a Grove of old Oaks, which rose above it in a gradual Ascent of
near half a Mile, and yet high enough to enjoy a most charming
Prospect of the Valley beneath.

In the midst of the Grove was a fine Lawn sloping down towards the House, near the Summit of which rose a plentiful
Spring, gushing out of a Rock covered with Firs, and forming a
constant Cascade of about thirty Foot, not carried down a regular
Flight of Steps, but tumbling in a natural Fall over the broken
and mossy Stones, till it came to the bottom of the Rock; then

---

[1] Appropriately enough, the description of Allworthy's seat—the place of Tom Jones's
birth and the home of his spiritual father—is an imaginative synthesis of details associated
primarily with Sharpham Park, Fielding's own birthplace and the home of his maternal
grandfather, Sir Henry Gould, and secondarily with Hagley Park and Prior Park, the
estates, respectively, of Fielding's patrons, George Lyttelton and Ralph Allen (see above,
pp. 3, n. 1; 4, n. 1). From the threshold at Sharpham Park, Fielding would have looked
across the moors at Glastonbury and Tor Hill. The prospect from Allworthy's Paradise
Hall corresponds in general to the view westward from atop Tor Hill (see Cross, ii. 165).
The 'Stile' of Paradise Hall itself doubtless compliments a mutual friend of Fielding's and
Lyttelton's, Sanderson Miller (1717–80), amateur architect and pioneer of the Gothic
revival. In 1747–8 and 1749–50 Lyttelton erected a ruined castle and a rotunda of Miller's
design at Hagley Park; indeed, until his second wife disapproved, he had wanted Miller to
build him a Gothic house. Like Allworthy's mansion, furthermore, Hagley Hall is situated
on the south side of a hill, nearer the bottom than the top, yet high enough to command a
pleasant view of the valley. And, what is especially noteworthy, many of the details in
Fielding's description echo Thomson's celebration of Hagley Park in 'Spring', ll. 900–58
(*Seasons*, 1744 ed.); with Fielding's introduction of Allworthy later in this chapter, compare, too, Thomson's description of Lyttelton, strolling through Hagley and delighting
both in the natural scene and in the thoughts of benevolence which the season inspires. At
the same time, in the third paragraph of the chapter, Fielding does not forget Ralph Allen,
whose house, an example of 'the best *Grecian* Architecture', he had praised earlier in *Joseph
Andrews* (III. i, vi) and *A Journey from This World to the Next* (I. v): Allen's Palladian
mansion stands on the summit of a hill down which a stream falls into a lake which is
visible 'from every Room in the Front'.

running off in a pebly Channel, that with many lesser Falls winded along, till it fell into a Lake at the Foot of the Hill, about a quarter of a Mile below the House on the South Side, and which was seen from every Room in the Front. Out of this Lake, which filled the Center of a beautiful Plain, embellished with Groupes of Beeches and Elms, and fed with Sheep, issued a River, that for several Miles was seen to meander through an amazing Variety of Meadows and Woods, till it emptied itself into the Sea, with a large Arm of which, and an Island beyond it, the Prospect was closed.

On the right of this Valley opened another of less Extent, adorned with several Villages, and terminated by one of the Towers of an old ruined Abbey, grown over with Ivy, and Part of the Front which remained still entire.

The left Hand Scene presented the View of a fine Park, composed of very unequal Ground, and agreeably varied with all the Diversity that Hills, Lawns, Wood and Water, laid out with admirable Taste, but owing less to Art than to Nature,[1] could give. Beyond this the Country gradually rose into a Ridge of wild Mountains, the Tops of which were above the Clouds.

It was now the Middle of *May*, and the Morning was remarkably serene, when Mr. *Allworthy* walked forth on the Terrace, where the Dawn opened every Minute that lovely Prospect we have before described to his Eye. And now having sent forth Streams of Light, which ascended the blue Firmament before him as Harbingers preceding his Pomp, in the full Blaze of his Majesty, up rose the Sun; than which one Object alone in this lower Creation could be more glorious, and that Mr. *Allworthy* himself presented; a human Being replete with Benevolence, meditating in what manner he might render himself most acceptable to his Creator, by doing most good to his Creatures.

Reader, take care, I have unadvisedly led thee to the Top of as

---

[1] The observation would apply equally to the estates of both Fielding's patrons. Influenced principally by the example of William Kent, who broke with continental theories of the classic, formal garden, Lyttelton developed Hagley Park—his '*British Tempe*', as Thomson called it—into one of the monuments of the natural school of English landscape gardening. (See R. M. Davis, *Good Lord Lyttelton*, Pt. III, ch. iii.) At Prior Park, too, nature, as Fielding remarks later in *Tom Jones* (XI. ix), seemed 'to triumph' over art. In September 1746, on his first visit to Allen's estate, Charles Yorke was similarly impressed: 'The natural beauties of wood, water, prospect, hill and vale, wildness and cultivation, make it one of the most delightful spots I ever saw, without adding any thing from art.' (Quoted in B. Boyce, *Benevolent Man*, p. 169.)

high a Hill as Mr. *Allworthy's*, and how to get thee down without breaking thy Neck, I do not well know. However, let us e'en venture to slide down together, for Miss *Bridget* rings her Bell, and Mr. *Allworthy* is summoned to Breakfast, where I must attend, and, if you please, shall be glad of your Company.

The usual Compliments having past between Mr. *Allworthy* and Miss *Bridget*, and the Tea being poured out, he summoned Mrs. *Wilkins*, and told his Sister he had a Present for her; for which she thanked him, imagining, I suppose, it had been a Gown or some Ornament for her Person. Indeed, he very often made her such Presents, and she in Complacence to him spent much time in adorning herself. I say, in Complacence to him, because she always exprest the greatest Contempt for Dress, and for those Ladies who made it their Study.

But if such was her Expectation, how was she disappointed, when Mrs. *Wilkins*, according to the Order she had receiv'd from her Master, produced the little Infant. Great Surprises, as hath been observed,[1] are apt to be silent, and so was Miss *Bridget*, till her Brother began and told her the whole Story, which as the Reader knows it already, we shall not repeat.

Miss *Bridget* had always exprest so great a regard for what the Ladies are pleased to call Virtue, and had herself maintained such a Severity of Character, that it was expected, especially by *Wilkins*, that she would have vented much Bitterness on this Occasion, and would have voted for sending the Child, as a kind of noxious Animal, immediately out of the House; but on the contrary, she rather took the good-natur'd side of the question, intimated some Compassion for the helpless little Creature, and commended her Brother's Charity in what he had done.

Perhaps the Reader may account for this Behaviour from her Condescension to Mr. *Allworthy*, when we have informed him, that the good Man had ended his Narrative with owning a Resolution to take care of the Child, and to breed him up as his own; for, to acknowledge the Truth, she was always ready to oblige her Brother, and very seldom, if ever, contradicted his

---

[1] Cf. the proverbial observation that great joys, like great griefs, are silent—to which Fielding alludes below, pp. 228.3–4, 978.10–12. (For examples from Seneca, Shakespeare, and Shackerley Marmion, see Stevenson's *Book of Quotations Classical and Modern* [n.d.], pp. 842, 1018; and the *Oxford Dictionary of Quotations*, 2nd ed. [Oxford, 1953], pp. 331, 468.)

Sentiments; she would indeed sometimes make a few Observations, as, that Men were headstrong and must have their own way, and would wish she had been blest with an independent Fortune; but these were always vented in a low Voice, and at the most amounted only to what is called Muttering.

However, what she withheld from the Infant, she bestowed with the utmost Profuseness on the poor unknown Mother, whom she called an impudent Slut, a wanton Hussy, an audacious Harlot, a wicked Jade, a vile Strumpet, with every other Appellation with which the Tongue of Virtue never fails to lash those who bring a Disgrace on the Sex.

A Consultation was now entered into, how to proceed in order to discover the Mother. A Scrutiny was first made into the Characters of the female Servants of the House, who were all acquitted by Mrs. *Wilkins*, and with apparent Merit; for she had collected them herself, and perhaps it would be difficult to find such another Set of Scarecrows.

The next Step was to examine among the Inhabitants of the Parish; and this was referred to Mrs. *Wilkins*, who was to enquire with all imaginable Diligence, and to make her Report in the Afternoon.

Matters being thus settled, Mr. *Allworthy* withdrew to his Study, as was his Custom, and left the Child to his Sister, who, at his Desire, had undertaken the Care of it.

CHAPTER V

Containing a few common Matters, with a very uncommon Observation upon them.

WHEN her Master was departed, Mrs. *Deborah* stood silent, expecting her Cue from Miss *Bridget*; for as to what had past before her Master, the prudent Housekeeper by no means relied upon it, as she had often known the Sentiments of the Lady in her Brother's Absence to differ greatly from those which she had expressed in his Presence. Miss *Bridget* did not, however, suffer her to continue long in this doubtful Situation; for having looked some time earnestly at the Child, as it lay asleep in the Lap of Mrs. *Deborah*, the good Lady could not forbear giving it a hearty Kiss, at the same time declaring herself wonderfully pleased with its Beauty and Innocence. Mrs. *Deborah* no sooner observed this, than she fell to squeezing and kissing with as great Raptures as sometimes inspire the sage Dame of forty and five towards a youthful and vigorous Bridegroom, crying out in a shrill Voice, 'O the dear little Creature, the dear, sweet, pretty Creature! well, I vow, it is as fine a Boy as ever was seen!'

These Exclamations continued till they were interrupted by the Lady, who now proceeded to execute the Commission given her by her Brother, and gave Orders for providing all Necessaries for the Child, appointing a very good Room in the House for his Nursery. Her Orders were indeed so liberal, that had it been a Child of her own, she could not have exceeded them; but lest the virtuous Reader may condemn her for shewing too great Regard to a base-born Infant, to which all Charity is condemned by Law as irreligious,[1] we think proper to observe, that she concluded the whole with saying, 'Since it was her Brother's Whim to adopt the little Brat, she supposed little Master must be treated with great Tenderness; for her part, she could not help thinking it was an Encouragement to Vice; but that she knew too much of the Obstinacy of Mankind to oppose any of their ridiculous Humours.'

With Reflections of this nature, she usually, as hath been hinted, accompany'd every Act of Compliance with her Brother's Inclinations; and surely nothing could more contribute to heighten the Merit of this Compliance, than a Declaration that she knew at the same time the Folly and Unreasonableness of those Inclinations to which she submitted. Tacit Obedience implies no Force upon the Will, and consequently may be easily, and without any Pains, preserved; but when a Wife, a Child, a Relation, or a Friend, performs what we desire, with Grumbling, and Reluctance, with Expressions of Dislike and Dissatisfaction, the manifest Difficulty which they undergo, must greatly enhance the Obligation.

[1] Fielding's remark appears to be ironical. The Poor Law (43 Elizabeth, cap. 4) specifically provided for the efficient management of all 'Lands, Goods, and Stocks of Money' donated to the uses of the poor, including foundling infants. In 1739, furthermore, the Foundling Hospital 'for the Maintenance and Education of Exposed and Deserted Young Children' was granted the royal charter (see below, p. 761, n. 3). Perhaps, however, Fielding alludes to the legal *status* of bastards, who were prevented by law from inheriting property by descent (see below, p. 79, n. 3).

As this is one of those deep Observations which very few Readers can be supposed capable of making themselves, I have thought proper to lend them my Assistance; but this is a Favour rarely to be expected in the Course of my Work. Indeed I shall seldom or never so indulge him, unless in such Instances as this, where nothing but the Inspiration with which we Writers are gifted, can possibly enable any one to make the Discovery.

CHAPTER VI

Mrs. Deborah *is introduced into the Parish, with a Simile. A short Account of* Jenny Jones*, with the Difficulties and Discouragements which may attend young Women in the Pursuit of Learning.*

MRS. *Deborah*, having disposed of the Child according to the Will of her Master, now prepared to visit those Habitations which were supposed to conceal its Mother.

Not otherwise than when a Kite, tremendous Bird, is beheld by the feathered Generation soaring aloft, and hovering over their Heads, the amorous Dove, and every innocent little Bird spread wide the Alarm, and fly trembling to their Hiding-places: He proudly beats the Air, conscious of his Dignity, and meditates intended Mischief.

So when the Approach of Mrs. *Deborah* was proclaimed through the Street, all the Inhabitants ran trembling into their Houses, each Matron dreading lest the Visit should fall to her Lot. She with stately Steps proudly advances over the Field, aloft she bears her tow'ring Head, filled with Conceit of her own Pre-eminence, and Schemes to effect her intended Discovery.

The sagacious Reader will not, from this Simile, imagine these poor People had any Apprehension of the Design with which Mrs. *Wilkins* was now coming towards them; but as the great Beauty of the Simile may possibly sleep these hundred Years, till some future Commentator shall take this Work in hand, I think proper to lend the Reader a little Assistance in this Place.

It is my Intention therefore to signify, that as it is the Nature of a Kite to devour little Birds, so is it the Nature of such Persons as Mrs. *Wilkins*, to insult and tyrannize over little People. This being indeed the Means which they use to recompense to themselves their extreme Servility and Condescension to their

Superiors; for nothing can be more reasonable, than that Slaves and Flatterers should exact the same Taxes on all below them, which they themselves pay to all above them.

Whenever Mrs. *Deborah* had Occasion to exert any extraordinary Condescension to Miss *Bridget*, and by that means had a little sowered her natural Disposition, it was usual with her to walk forth among these People, in order to refine her Temper, by venting, and, as it were, purging off all ill Humours; on which Account, she was by no means a welcome Visitant; to say the Truth, she was universally dreaded and hated by them all.

On her Arrival in this Place, she went immediately to the Habitation of an elderly Matron; to whom, as this Matron had the good Fortune to resemble herself in the Comeliness of her Person, as well as in her Age, she had generally been more favourable than to any of the rest. To this Woman she imparted what had happened, and the Design upon which she was come thither that Morning. These two began presently to scrutinize the Characters of the several young Girls, who lived in any of those Houses, and at last fixed their strongest Suspicion on one *Jenny Jones*, who they both agreed was the likeliest Person to have committed this Fact.

This *Jenny Jones* was no very comely Girl, either in her Face or Person; but Nature had somewhat compensated the Want of Beauty with what is generally more esteemed by those Ladies, whose Judgment is arrived at Years of perfect Maturity; for she had given her a very uncommon Share of Understanding. This Gift *Jenny* had a good deal improved by Erudition. She had lived several Years a Servant with a Schoolmaster, who discovering a great Quickness of Parts in the Girl, and an extraordinary Desire of learning, (for every leisure Hour she was always found reading in the Books of the Scholars) had the Good-nature, or Folly (just as the Reader pleases to call it,) to instruct her so far, that she obtained a competent Skill in the Latin Language, and was perhaps as good a Scholar as most of the young Men of Quality of the Age. This Advantage, however, like most others of an extraordinary Kind, was attended with some small Inconveniencies: For as it is not to be wondered at, that a young Woman so well accomplished should have little Relish for the Society of those whom Fortune had made her Equals, but whom Education had rendered so much her Inferiors; so is it Matter of no greater

Astonishment, that this Superiority in *Jenny*, together with that Behaviour which is its certain Consequence, should produce among the rest some little Envy and Ill-will towards her; and these had perhaps secretly burnt in the Bosoms of her Neighbours, ever since her Return from her Service.

Their Envy did not however display itself openly, till poor *Jenny*, to the Surprize of every Body, and to the Vexation of all the young Women in these Parts, had publickly shone forth on a *Sunday* in a new Silk Gown, with a laced Cap, and other proper Appendages to these.

The Flame, which had before lain in Embrio, now burst forth. *Jenny* had, by her Learning, encreased her own Pride, which none of her Neighbours were kind enough to feed with the Honour she seemed to demand; and now, instead of Respect and Adoration, she gained nothing but Hatred and Abuse, by her Finery. The whole Parish declared she could not come honestly by such Things; and Parents, instead of wishing their Daughters the same, felicitated themselves that their Children had them not.

Hence perhaps it was, that the good Woman first mentioned the Name of this poor Girl to Mrs. *Wilkins*; but there was another Circumstance that confirmed the latter in her Suspicion: For *Jenny* had lately been often at Mr. *Allworthy's* House. She had officiated as Nurse to Miss *Bridget*, in a violent Fit of Illness, and had sat up many Nights with that Lady; besides which, she had been seen there the very Day before Mr. *Allworthy's* Return, by Mrs. *Wilkins* herself, tho' that sagacious Person had not at first conceived any Suspicion of her on that Account: For, as she herself said, 'She had always esteemed *Jenny* as a very sober Girl, (tho' indeed she knew very little of her) and had rather suspected some of those wanton Trollops, who gave themselves Airs because, forsooth, they thought themselves handsome.'

Jenny was now summoned to appear in Person before Mrs. *Deborah*, which she immediately did: When Mrs. *Deborah*, putting on the Gravity of a Judge, with somewhat more than his Austerity, began an Oration with the Words 'You audacious Strumpet,' in which she proceeded rather to pass Sentence on the Prisoner, than to accuse her.

Tho' Mrs. *Deborah* was fully satisfied of the Guilt of *Jenny*, from the Reasons above shewn, it is possible Mr. *Allworthy* might have required some stronger Evidence to have convicted her; but she saved her Accusers any such Trouble, by freely confessing the whole Fact with which she was charged.

This Confession, tho' delivered rather in Terms of Contrition, as it appeared, did not at all mollify Mrs. *Deborah*, who now pronounced a second Judgment against her, in more opprobrious Language than before; nor had it any better Success with the Bye-standers, who were now grown very numerous. Many of them cried out, 'They thought what Madam's Silk Gown would end in;' others spoke sarcastically of her Learning. Not a single Female was present, but found some Means of expressing her Abhorrence of poor *Jenny*; who bore all very patiently, except the Malice of one Woman, who reflected upon her Person, and, tossing up her Nose, said, 'The Man must have a good Stomach, who would give Silk Gowns for such Sort of Trumpery.' *Jenny* replied to this, with a Bitterness which might have surprized a judicious Person, who had observed the Tranquility with which she bore all the Affronts to her Chastity; but her Patience was perhaps tired out: For this is a Virtue which is very apt to be fatigued by Exercise.

Mrs. *Deborah*, having succeeded beyond her Hopes in her Enquiry, returned with much Triumph, and at the appointed Hour made a faithful Report to Mr. *Allworthy*, who was much surprized at the Relation; for he had heard of the extraordinary Parts and Improvements of this Girl, whom he intended to have given in Marriage, together with a small Living, to a neighbouring Curate. His Concern therefore on this Occasion, was at least equal to the Satisfaction which appeared in Mrs. *Deborah*, and to many Readers may seem much more reasonable.

Miss *Bridget* blessed herself, and said, 'For her Part, she should never hereafter entertain a good Opinion of any Woman:' For *Jenny* before this had the Happiness of being much in her good Graces also.

The prudent Housekeeper was again dispatched to bring the unhappy Culprit before Mr. *Allworthy*, in order, not, as it was hoped by some and expected by all, to be sent to the House of Correction; but to receive wholesome Admonition and Reproof, which those who relish that kind of instructive Writing, may peruse in the next Chapter.

CHAPTER VII

Containing such grave Matter, that the Reader cannot laugh once through the whole Chapter, unless peradventure he should laugh at the Author.

WHEN *Jenny* appeared, Mr. *Allworthy* took her into his Study, and spoke to her as follows:

'You know, Child, it is in my Power, as a Magistrate, to punish you very rigorously for what you have done;[1] and you will perhaps be the more apt to fear I should execute that Power, because you have, in a manner, laid your Sins at my Door.

'But perhaps this is one Reason which hath determined me to act in a milder Manner with you: For, as no private Resentment should ever influence a Magistrate, I will be so far from considering your having deposited the Infant in my House, as an Aggravation of your Offence, that I will suppose, in your Favour, this to have proceeded from a natural Affection to your Child; since you might have some Hopes to see it thus better provided for, than was in the Power of yourself, or its wicked Father, to provide for it. I should indeed have been highly offended with you, had you exposed the little Wretch in the Manner of some inhuman Mothers, who seem no less to have abandoned their Humanity, than to have parted with their Chastity. It is the other Part of your Offence therefore upon which I intend to admonish you, I mean the Violation of your Chastity. A Crime, however lightly it may be treated by debauched Persons, very heinous in itself, and very dreadful in its Consequences.

'The heinous Nature of this Offence must be sufficiently apparent to every Christian, inasmuch as it is committed in Defiance of the Laws of our Religion, and of the express Commands of him who founded that Religion.

'And here its Consequences may well be argued to be dreadful; for what can be more so, than to incur the divine Displeasure, by the Breach of the divine Commands; and that in an Instance, against which the highest Vengeance is specifically denounced.

'But these Things, tho' too little, I am afraid, regarded, are so plain, that Mankind, however they may want to be reminded,

---

[1] See above, p. 40, n. 1.

can never need Information on this Head. A Hint therefore to awaken your Sense of this Matter shall suffice; for I would inspire you with Repentance, and not drive you to Desperation.

'There are other Consequences, not indeed so dreadful or replete with Horror as this; and yet such, as if attentively considered, must, one would think, deter all, of your Sex at least, from the Commission of this Crime.

'For by it you are rendered infamous, and driven, like Lepers of old, out of Society; at least from the Society of all but wicked and reprobate Persons; for no others will associate with you.

'If you have Fortunes, you are hereby rendered incapable of enjoying them; if you have none, you are disabled from acquiring any, nay almost of procuring your Sustenance; for no Persons of Character will receive you into their Houses. Thus you are often driven by Necessity itself into a State of Shame and Misery, which unavoidably ends in the Destruction of both Body and Soul.

'Can any Pleasure compensate these Evils? Can any Temptation have Sophistry and Delusion strong enough to persuade you to so simple a Bargain? Or can any carnal Appetite so overpower your Reason, or so totally lay it asleep, as to prevent your flying with Affright and Terror from a Crime which carries such Punishment always with it?

'How base and mean must that Woman be, how void of that Dignity of Mind, and decent Pride, without which we are not worthy the Name of human Creatures, who can bear to level herself with the lowest Animal, and to sacrifice all that is great and noble in her, all her Heavenly Part, to an Appetite which she hath in common with the vilest Branch of the Creation! For no Woman sure, will plead the Passion of Love for an Excuse. This would be to own herself the meer Tool and Bubble of the Man. Love, however barbarously we may corrupt and pervert its Meaning, as it is a laudable, is a rational Passion, and can never be violent, but when reciprocal; for though the Scripture bids us love our Enemies,[1] it means not with that fervent Love,

---

1 Cf. Matthew 5: 44, Luke 6: 27, 35. 'FORGIVE THE ACTS OF YOUR ENEMIES', Fielding remarked in 'An Essay on the Knowledge of the Characters of Men' (1743), 'hath been thought the highest Maxim of Morality'. In *The Champion* (27 March 1740) he insisted that 'this excellent Doctrine' was distinctively Christian, teaching 'us something beyond what the Religion of Nature and Philosophy could arrive at' (see also *The Champion*, 5 April 1740).

which we naturally bear towards our Friends; much less that we should sacrifice to them our Lives, and what ought to be dearer to us, our Innocence. Now in what Light, but in that of an Enemy, can a reasonable Woman regard the Man, who solicits her to entail on herself, all the Misery I have described to you, and who would purchase to himself a short, trivial, contemptible Pleasure, so greatly at her Expence! For by the Laws of Custom the whole Shame, with all its dreadful Consequences, falls entirely upon her. Can Love, which always seeks the Good of its Object, attempt to betray a Woman into a Bargain, where she is so greatly to be the Loser? If such Corrupter, therefore, should have the Impudence to pretend a real Affection for her, ought not the Woman to regard him, not only as an Enemy, but as the worst of all Enemies; a false, designing, treacherous, pretended Friend, who intends not only to debauch her Body, but her Understanding at the same Time?'

Here *Jenny* expressing great Concern, *Allworthy* paused a Moment, and then proceeded: 'I have talked thus to you, Child, not to insult you for what is past, and irrevocable, but to caution and strengthen you for the future. Nor should I have taken this Trouble, but from some Opinion of your good Sense, notwithstanding the dreadful Slip you have made; and from some Hopes of your hearty Repentance, which are founded on the Openness and Sincerity of your Confession. If these do not deceive me, I will take care to convey you from this Scene of your Shame, where you shall, by being unknown, avoid the Punishment which, as I have said, is allotted to your Crime in this World; and I hope by Repentance, you will avoid the much heavier Sentence denounced against it in the other. Be a good Girl the rest of your Days, and Want shall be no Motive to your going astray: And believe me, there is more Pleasure, even in this World, in an innocent and virtuous Life,[1] than in one debauched and vicious.

'As to your Child, let no Thoughts concerning it, molest you;

---

[1] Hobbes and the Calvinists having asserted the essential selfishness and depravity of human nature, the latitudinarian divines answered this cynical view by accommodating what Professor Crane called 'a strain of egoistic hedonism' within the system of benevolism —the notion that virtuous behaviour was attended with a 'Self-approving Joy'. For Tillotson, 'There is no sensual Pleasure in the World comparable to the Delight and Satisfaction that a good Man takes in doing good.' (See Crane, 'Suggestions toward a Genealogy of the "Man of Feeling" ', *ELH*, i (1934), esp. 227–9.) For other instances of this concept in *Tom Jones*, see pp. 96, n. 1; 659.

I will provide for it in a better manner than you can ever hope. And now nothing remains, but that you inform me who was the wicked Man that seduced you; for my Anger against him will be much greater than you have experienced on this Occasion.'

Jenny now first lifted her Eyes from the Ground, and with a modest Look, and decent Voice, thus began:

'To know you, Sir, and not love your Goodness, would be an Argument of total want of Sense or Goodness in any one. In me it would amount to the highest Ingratitude, not to feel, in the most sensible manner, the great Degree of Goodness you have been pleased to exert on this Occasion. As to my Concern for what is past, I know you will spare my Blushes the Repetition. My future Conduct will much better declare my Sentiments, than any Professions I can now make. I beg leave to assure you, Sir, that I take your Advice much kinder, than your generous Offer with which you concluded it. For as you are pleased to say, Sir, it is an Instance of your Opinion of my Understanding—' Here her Tears flowing apace, she stopped a few Moments, and then proceeded thus, 'Indeed, Sir, your Kindness overcomes me; but I will endeavour to deserve this good Opinion; for if I have the Understanding you are so kindly pleased to allow me, such Advice cannot be thrown away upon me. I thank you, Sir, heartily, for your intended Kindness to my poor helpless Child; he is innocent, and I hope will live to be grateful for all the Favours you shall shew him. But now, Sir, I must on my Knees intreat you, not to persist in asking me to declare the Father of my Infant. I promise you faithfully, you shall one Day know; but I am under the most solemn Ties and Engagements of Honour, as well as the most religious Vows and Protestations, to conceal his Name at this Time. And I know you too well to think you would desire I should sacrifice either my Honour, or my Religion.'

Mr. *Allworthy*, whom the least Mention of those sacred Words was sufficient to stagger, hesitated a Moment before he replied, and then told her she had done wrong to enter into such Engagements to a Villain; but since she had, he could not insist on her breaking them. He said, it was not from a Motive of vain Curiosity he had enquired, but in order to punish the Fellow; at least, that he might not ignorantly confer Favours on the Undeserving.

As to these Points, *Jenny* satisfied him by the most solemn Assurances, that the Man was entirely out of his Reach, and was neither subject to his Power, nor in any probability of becoming an Object of his Goodness.

The Ingenuity of this Behaviour, had gained *Jenny* so much Credit with this worthy Man, that he easily believed what she told him: For as she had disdained to excuse herself by a Lie, and had hazarded his farther Displeasure in her present Situation, rather than she would forfeit her Honour, or Integrity, by betraying another, he had but little Apprehension that she would be guilty of Falshood towards himself.

He therefore dismissed her with Assurances, that he would very soon remove her out of the Reach of that Obloquy she had incurred, concluding with some additional Documents, in which he recommended Repentance, saying, 'Consider, Child, there is one still to reconcile yourself to, whose Favour is of much greater Importance to you than mine.'

CHAPTER VIII

A Dialogue between Mesdames Bridget, *and* Deborah; *containing more Amusement, but less Instruction than the former.*

WHEN Mr. *Allworthy* had retired to his Study with *Jenny Jones*, as hath been seen, Miss *Bridget*, with the good Housekeeper, had betaken themselves to a Post next adjoining to the said Study; whence, through the Conveyance of a Key-hole, they sucked in at their Ears the instructive Lecture delivered by Mr. *Allworthy*, together with the Answers of *Jenny*, and indeed every other Particular which passed in the last Chapter.

This Hole in her Brother's Study Door, was indeed as well known to Miss *Bridget*, and had been as frequently applied to by her, as the famous Hole in the Wall was by *Thisbe*[1] of old. This served to many good Purposes. For by such Means Miss *Bridget* became often acquainted with her Brother's Inclinations, without giving him the Trouble of repeating them to her. It is true, some Inconveniencies attended this Intercourse, and she had sometimes Reason to cry out with *Thisbe*, in *Shakespear*,[2] 'O wicked, wicked Wall!' For as Mr. *Allworthy* was a Justice of Peace, certain

---

[1] See Ovid, *Metamorphoses*, iv. 55–166.
[2] In fact, it is Pyramus who cries out—*A Midsummer Night's Dream*, v. i.

Things occurred in Examinations concerning Bastards, and such like, which are apt to give great Offence to the chaste Ears of Virgins, especially when they approach the Age of forty,[1] as was the Case of Miss *Bridget*. However, she had, on such Occasions, the Advantage of concealing her Blushes from the Eyes of Men, and *De non apparentibus, et non existentibus eadem est ratio.*[2] In *English*: 'When a Woman is not seen to blush, she doth not blush at all.'

Both the good Women kept strict Silence during the whole Scene between Mr. *Allworthy* and the Girl; but as soon as it was ended, and that Gentleman was out of hearing, Mrs. *Deborah* could not help exclaiming against the Clemency of her Master, and especially against his suffering her to conceal the Father of the Child, which she swore she would have out of her before the Sun set.

At these Words Miss *Bridget* discomposed her Features with a Smile (a Thing very unusual to her.) Not that I would have my Reader imagine, that this was one of those wanton Smiles, which *Homer* would have you conceive came from *Venus*, when he calls her the laughter-loving Goddess;[3] nor was it one of those Smiles, which Lady *Seraphina* shoots from the Stage-Box, and which *Venus* would quit her Immortality to be able to equal. No, this was rather one of those Smiles, which might be supposed to have come from the dimpled Cheeks of the august *Tysiphone*,[4] or from one of the Misses her Sisters.

With such a Smile then, and with a Voice, sweet as the Evening Breeze of *Boreas*[5] in the pleasant Month of *November*, Miss *Bridget* gently reproved the Curiosity of Mrs. *Deborah*, a Vice with which it seems the latter was too much tainted, and which the former inveighed against with great Bitterness, adding, 'that among all her Faults, she thanked Heaven, her Enemies could not accuse her of prying into the Affairs of other People.'

She then proceeded to commend the Honour and Spirit with which *Jenny* had acted. She said, she could not help agreeing with her Brother, that there was some Merit in the Sincerity of her

---

[1] Earlier Bridget was said to be 'somewhat past the Age of 30' (see above, p. 35).

[2] 'That which is not seen must be treated as if it did not exist'—a legal maxim found in Sir Edward Coke's *Reports* (1658), v. 343. Fielding quotes it again in *The Covent-Garden Journal* (7 January 1752).   [3] *Iliad*, iii. 424.

[4] One of the Erinyes or Furies of classical mythology.

[5] The north wind.

Confession, and in her Integrity to her Lover. That she had always thought her a very good Girl, and doubted not but she had been seduced by some Rascal, who had been infinitely more to blame than herself, and very probably had prevailed with her by a Promise of Marriage, or some other treacherous Proceeding.

This Behaviour of Miss *Bridget* greatly surprized Mrs. *Deborah*; for this well-bred Woman seldom opened her Lips either to her Master or his Sister, till she had first sounded their Inclinations, with which her Sentiments were always strictly consonant. Here, however, she thought she might have launched forth with Safety; and the sagacious Reader will not perhaps accuse her of want of sufficient Forecast in so doing, but will rather admire with what wonderful Celerity she tacked about, when she found herself steering a wrong Course.

'Nay, Madam,' said this able Woman, and truly great Politician, 'I must own I cannot help admiring the Girl's Spirit, as well as your Ladyship. And, as your Ladyship says, if she was deceived by some wicked Man, the poor Wretch is to be pitied. And to be sure, as your Ladyship says, the Girl hath always appeared like a good, honest, plain Girl, and not vain of her Face, forsooth, as some wanton Husseys in the Neighbourhood are.'

'You say true, *Deborah*,' said Miss *Bridget*, 'if the Girl had been one of those vain Trollops, of which we have too many in the Parish, I should have condemned my Brother for his Lenity towards her. I saw two Farmers Daughters at Church, the other Day, with bare Necks. I protest they shock'd me. If Wenches will hang out Lures for Fellows, it is no matter what they suffer. I detest such Creatures; and it would be much better for them, that their Faces had been seamed with the Small-Pox; but I must confess, I never saw any of this wanton Behaviour in poor *Jenny*; some artful Villain, I am convinced, hath betrayed, nay perhaps forc'd her; and I pity the poor Wretch with all my Heart.'

Mrs. *Deborah* approved all these Sentiments, and the Dialogue concluded with a general and bitter Invective against Beauty, and with many compassionate Considerations for all honest, plain Girls, who are deluded by the wicked Arts of deceitful Men.

CHAPTER IX

Containing Matters which will surprize the Reader.

JENNY returned home well pleased with the Reception she had met with from Mr. *Allworthy*, whose Indulgence to her she industriously made public; partly perhaps as a Sacrifice to her own Pride, and partly from the more prudent Motive of reconciling her Neighbours to her, and silencing their Clamours.

But though this latter View, if she indeed had it, may appear reasonable enough, yet the Event did not answer her Expectation; for when she was convened before the Justice, and it was universally apprehended, that the House of Correction would have been her Fate; tho' some of the young Women cry'd out, 'it was good enough for her,' and diverted themselves with the Thoughts of her beating Hemp in a Silk Gown;[1] yet there were many others who began to pity her Condition: But when it was known in what manner Mr. *Allworthy* had behaved, the Tide turned against her. One said, 'I'll assure you, Madam hath had good Luck.' A second cry'd, 'See what it is to be a Favourite.' A third, 'Ay, this comes of her Learning.' Every Person made some malicious Comment or other, on the Occasion; and reflected on the Partiality of the Justice.

The Behaviour of these People, may appear impolitic, and ungrateful to the Reader, who considers the Power, and the Benevolence of Mr. *Allworthy*: But as to his Power, he never used it; and as to his Benevolence, he exerted so much, that he had thereby disobliged all his Neighbours: For it is a Secret well known to great Men, that by conferring an Obligation, they do not always procure a Friend, but are certain of creating many Enemies.

Jenny was, however, by the Care and Goodness of Mr. *Allworthy*, soon removed out of the Reach of Reproach; when Malice, being no longer able to vent its Rage on her, began to seek another Object of its Bitterness, and this was no less than Mr. *Allworthy* himself; for a Whisper soon went abroad, that he himself was the Father of the foundling Child.

---

[1] The activity and attire of Kate Hackabout in Plate 4 of Hogarth's *Harlot's Progress* 1732). For references to Hogarth in *Tom Jones*, see below, p. 66, n. 1.

This Supposition so well reconciled his Conduct to the general Opinion, that it met with universal Assent; and the Outcry against his Lenity soon began to take another Turn, and was changed into an Invective against his Cruelty to the poor Girl. Very grave and good Women exclaimed against Men who begot Children and then disowned them. Nor were there wanting some, who, after the Departure of *Jenny*, insinuated, that she was spirited away with a Design too black to be mentioned, and who gave frequent Hints, that a legal Inquiry ought to be made into the whole Matter, and that some People should be forced to produce the Girl.

These Calumnies might have probably produced ill Consequences (at the least might have occasioned some Trouble) to a Person of a more doubtful and suspicious Character than Mr. *Allworthy* was blessed with; but in his Case they had no such Effect; and, being heartily despised by him, they served only to afford an innocent Amusement to the good Gossips of the Neighbourhood.

But as we cannot possibly divine what Complexion our Reader may be of, and as it will be some Time before he will hear any more of *Jenny*, we think proper to give him a very early Intimation, that Mr. *Allworthy* was, and will hereafter appear to be, absolutely innocent of any criminal Intention whatever. He had indeed committed no other than an Error in Politics, by tempering Justice with Mercy, and by refusing to gratify the good-natured Disposition of the Mob,* with an Object for their Compassion to work on in the Person of poor *Jenny*, whom, in order to pity, they desired to have seen sacrificed to Ruin and Infamy by a shameful Correction in a *Bridewel*.[1]

So far from complying with this their Inclination, by which all Hopes of Reformation would have been abolished, and even the

---

* Whenever this Word occurs in our Writings, it intends Persons without Virtue, or Sense, in all Stations, and many of the highest Rank are often meant by it.

---

1 '*Bridewel*'—after Bridewell Hospital in London, rebuilt in 1720, the name given to any house of correction, wherein minor offenders, such as whores and vagabonds, were set to work beating hemp and supported on a penny-loaf of bread a day. In Fielding's opinion, commitment to these prisons was a severe punishment which, instead of reforming prisoners, generally confirmed them in the practice of vice. During his own tenure as magistrate he, like Squire Allworthy, refused to commit any but the most hardened offenders to Bridewell. (See *An Enquiry into the Causes of the Late Increase of Robbers* [1751], section iv, and *The Covent-Garden Journal* [1 August 1752].)

Gate shut against her, if her own Inclinations should ever hereafter lead her to chuse the Road of Virtue, Mr. *Allworthy* rather
chose to encourage the Girl to return thither by the only possible
Means; for too true I am afraid it is, that many Women have
become abandoned, and have sunk to the last Degree of Vice
by being unable to retrieve the first Slip. This will be, I am afraid,
always the Case while they remain among their former Acquaintance; it was therefore wisely done by Mr. *Allworthy*, to remove
Jenny to a Place where she might enjoy the Pleasure of Reputation, after having tasted the ill Consequences of losing it.

   To this Place therefore, wherever it was, we will wish her a
good Journey, and for the present take leave of her, and of the
little Foundling her Child, having Matters of much higher Importance to communicate to the Reader.

CHAPTER X

The Hospitality of Allworthy; with a short Sketch of the Characters of
two Brothers, a Doctor, and a Captain, who were entertained by that
Gentleman.

NEITHER Mr. *Allworthy's* House, nor his Heart, were shut
against any Part of Mankind, but they were both more particularly open to Men of Merit. To say the Truth, this was the only
House in the Kingdom where you was sure to gain a Dinner by
deserving it.

   Above all others, Men of Genius and Learning shared the
principal Place in his Favour; and in these he had much Discernment: For though he had missed the Advantage of a learned
Education, yet being blest with vast natural Abilities, he had so
well profited by a vigorous, though late Application to Letters,
and by much Conversation with Men of Eminence in this Way,
that he was himself a very competent Judge in most Kinds of
Literature.

   It is no Wonder that in an Age when this Kind of Merit is so
little in Fashion, and so slenderly provided for, Persons possessed
of it should very eagerly flock to a Place where they were sure
of being received with great Complaisance; indeed where they
might enjoy almost the same Advantages of a liberal Fortune as if

they were entitled to it in their own Right; for Mr. *Allworthy* was not one of those generous Persons, who are ready most bountifully to bestow Meat, Drink, and Lodging on Men of Wit and Learning, for which they expect no other Return but Entertainment, Instruction, Flattery, and Subserviency; in a Word, that such Persons should be enrolled in the Number of Domestics, without wearing their Master's Cloaths, or receiving Wages.

On the contrary, every Person in this House was perfect Master of his own Time: and as he might at his Pleasure satisfy all his Appetites within the Restrictions only of Law, Virtue and Religion; so he might, if his Health required, or his Inclination prompted him to Temperance, or even to Abstinence, absent himself from any Meals, or retire from them whenever he was so disposed, without even a Solicitation to the contrary: For indeed, such Solicitations from Superiors always savour very strongly of Commands. But all here were free from such Impertinence, not only those whose Company is in all other Places esteemed a Favour from their Equality of Fortune, but even those whose indigent Circumstances make such an eleemosynary Abode convenient to them, and who are therefore less welcome to a great Man's Table because they stand in need of it.

Among others of this Kind was Dr. *Blifil*, a Gentleman who had the Misfortune of losing the Advantage of great Talents by the Obstinacy of a Father, who would breed him to a Profession he disliked. In Obedience to this Obstinacy the Doctor had in his Youth been obliged to study Physick, or rather to say he studied it; for in reality Books of this Kind were almost the only ones with which he was unacquainted; and unfortunately for him, the Doctor was Master of almost every other Science but that by which he was to get his Bread; the Consequence of which was, that the Doctor at the Age of Forty had no Bread to eat.

Such a Person as this was certain to find a Welcome at Mr. *Allworthy's* Table, to whom Misfortunes were ever a Recommendation when they were derived from the Folly or Villany of others, and not of the unfortunate Person himself. Besides this negative Merit, the Doctor had one positive Recommendation. This was a great Appearance of Religion. Whether his Religion was real, or consisted only in Appearance, I shall not presume to say, as I am not possessed of any Touch-stone, which can distinguish the true from the false.

If this Part of his Character pleased Mr. *Allworthy*, it delighted Miss *Bridget*. She engaged him in many religious Controversies; on which Occasions she constantly expressed great Satisfaction in the Doctor's Knowledge, and not much less in the Compliments which he frequently bestowed on her own. To say the Truth, she had read much *English* Divinity, and had puzzled more than one of the neighbouring Curates. Indeed her Conversation was so pure, her Looks so sage, and her whole Deportment so grave and solemn, that she seemed to deserve the Name of Saint equally with her Name-sake,[1] or with any other Female in the *Roman* Kalendar.

As Sympathies of all Kinds are apt to beget Love, so Experience teaches us that none have a more direct Tendency this Way than those of a religious Kind between Persons of different Sexes. The Doctor found himself so agreeable to Miss *Bridget*, that he now began to lament an unfortunate Accident which had happened to him about ten Years before; namely, his Marriage with another Woman, who was not only still alive, but what was worse, known to be so by Mr. *Allworthy*. This was a fatal Bar to that Happiness which he otherwise saw sufficient Probability of obtaining with this young Lady; for as to criminal Indulgencies, he certainly never thought of them. This was owing either to his Religion, as is most probable, or to the Purity of his Passion, which was fixed on those Things, which Matrimony only, and not criminal Correspondence, could put him in Possession of, or could give him any Title to.

He had not long ruminated on these Matters before it occurred to his Memory that he had a Brother who was under no such unhappy Incapacity. This Brother he made no doubt would succeed; for he discerned, as he thought, an Inclination to Marriage in the Lady; and the Reader perhaps, when he hears the Brother's Qualifications, will not blame the Confidence which he entertained of his Success.

This Gentleman was about 35 Years of Age. He was of a middle Size, and what is called well built. He had a Scar on his Forehead, which did not so much injure his Beauty, as it denoted his Valour (for he was a half-pay Officer.) He had good Teeth,

---

[1] St. Brigid (*c.* 451–525), patroness of Ireland, whose feast day in the Roman calendar is 1 February. Not only Bridget Allworthy, but Bridewell Hospital, the house of correction for loose women, was named after St. Brigid (or St. Bride).

and something affable, when he pleased, in his Smile; though naturally his Countenance, as well as his Air and Voice, had much of Roughness in it, yet he could at any Time deposite this, and appear all Gentleness and good Humour. He was not ungenteel, nor entirely void of Wit, and in his Youth had abounded in Spriteliness, which, though he had lately put on a more serious Character, he could, when he pleased, resume.

He had, as well as the Doctor, an Academic Education; for his Father had, with the same Paternal Authority we have mentioned before, decreed him for holy Orders; but as the old Gentleman died before he was ordained, he chose the Church Military, and preferred the King's Commission to the Bishop's.

He had purchased the Post of Lieutenant of Dragoons, and afterwards came to be a Captain; but having quarrelled with his Colonel, was by his Interest obliged to sell; from which Time he had entirely rusticated himself, had betaken himself to studying the Scriptures, and was not a little suspected of an Inclination to *Methodism*.[1]

[1] The Methodist movement had begun in the late 1730s under the leadership of the great evangelists, John Wesley (1703–91) and George Whitefield (1714–70). Its purpose was to reform the Church of England, both the worldliness of the clergy and the rationalistic, Pelagian tendencies of the latitudinarian divines. From the first, however, Fielding distrusted the movement and repeatedly attacked the fiery, calvinistic bias of Whitefield in particular, who, as Parson Adams declares in *Joseph Andrews* (I. xvii), was calling 'Nonsense and Enthusiasm to his Aid' and preaching the 'pernicious' doctrine of justification by faith and grace alone, without regard to good works. The latitudinarian divines whom Fielding admired—Barrow, Tillotson, and Hoadly, for example—stressed an opposite doctrine, denouncing emotionalism and mystery in religion and making salvation conditional upon an active charity. Whereas Whitefield condemned Tillotson and his followers for disregarding the calvinistic tenor of the Articles of the Church and for transforming Christianity into a mere moral system, little preferable to deism or to the stoicism of Cicero or Seneca, Fielding in turn decried the Antinomian implications of Whitefield's theology. Virtually repeated by Parson Adams, the popular rendering of Whitefield's position was, 'So you say you believe in the Lord Jesus Christ, you may live the life of devils.' After incidental allusions to Whitefield in *The Champion* (5 April, 24 May 1740), Fielding vigorously began his campaign against the new 'sect' in *Shamela* (1741), where, with the aid of Whitefield's works, Fielding's heroine rationalizes her frequent fornication and the hypocritical Parson Williams is made to parrot Whitefield's sermons. In *The Female Husband* (1746) Mary Hamilton is said to have been first corrupted by a recent convert to Methodism, and in *Amelia* (I. iv), the Methodist Cooper preaches the 'cant' doctrine of grace versus works and ends by picking Booth's pocket. As may be seen from his representation of Shamela and Mary Hamilton, Fielding suspected that the enthusiastical behaviour of the Methodists was often a convenient cover for sexual licence. For other derogatory allusions to Whitefield and his 'Sect' in *Tom Jones*, see below, pp. 430, 726, 980; also pp. 79, n. 4; 93, n. 1; 96, n. 2. A discussion of the subject may be found in Battestin, *The Moral Basis of Fielding's Art*, pp. 22–5, 81–4.

It seemed therefore not unlikely that such a Person should succeed with a Lady of so Saint-like a Disposition, and whose Inclinations were no otherwise engaged than to the married State in general; but why the Doctor, who certainly had no great Friendship for his Brother, should for his Sake think of making so ill a Return to the Hospitality of *Allworthy*, is a Matter not so easy to be accounted for.

Is it that some Natures delight in Evil, as others are thought to delight in Virtue? Or is there a Pleasure in being accessary to a Theft when we cannot commit it ourselves? Or Lastly, (which Experience seems to make probable) have we a Satisfaction in aggrandizing our Families, even tho' we have not the least Love or Respect for them?

Whether any of these Motives operated on the Doctor we will not determine; but so the Fact was. He sent for his Brother, and easily found Means to introduce him at *Allworthy's* as a Person who intended only a short Visit to himself.

The Captain had not been in the House a Week before the Doctor had Reason to felicitate himself on his Discernment. The Captain was indeed as great a Master of the Art of Love as *Ovid*[1] was formerly. He had besides received proper Hints from his Brother, which he failed not to improve to the best Advantage.

CHAPTER XI

Containing many Rules, and some Examples, concerning falling in love: Descriptions of Beauty, and other more prudential Inducements to Matrimony.

IT hath been observed by wise Men or Women, I forget which, that all Persons are doomed to be in Love once in their Lives. No particular Season is, as I remember, assigned for this; but the Age at which Miss *Bridget* was arrived seems to me as proper a Period as any to be fixed on for this Purpose: It often indeed

---

[1] In late February 1747, Fielding published his own version of Ovid's *Ars Amatoria*, Book I, entitled *Ovid's Art of Love Paraphras'd and Adapted to the Present Times*. See *The Jacobite's Journal* (12 March 1748), where Fielding recommends this work to the 'unlearn'd Reader'.

happens much earlier; but when it doth not, I have observed, it seldom or never fails about this Time. Moreover, we may remark that at this Season Love is of a more serious and steady Nature than what sometimes shews itself in the younger Parts of Life. The Love of Girls is uncertain, capricious, and so foolish that we cannot always discover what the young Lady would be at; nay, it may almost be doubted, whether she always knows this herself.

Now we are never at a Loss to discern this in Women about Forty; for as such grave, serious and experienced Ladies well know their own Meaning, so it is always very easy for a Man of the least Sagacity to discover it with the utmost Certainty.

Miss *Bridget* is an Example of all these Observations. She had not been many Times in the Captain's Company before she was seized with this Passion. Nor did she go pining and moping about the House, like a puny foolish Girl, ignorant of her Distemper: She felt, she knew, and she enjoyed, the pleasing Sensation, of which, as she was certain it was not only innocent but laudable, she was neither afraid nor ashamed.

And to say the Truth, there is in all Points, great Difference between the reasonable Passion which Women at this Age conceive towards Men, and the idle and childish Liking of a Girl to a Boy, which is often fixed on the Outside only, and on Things of little Value and no Duration; as on Cherry Cheeks, small Lily-white Hands, slow-black Eyes, flowing Locks, downy Chins, dapper Shapes, nay sometimes on Charms more worthless than these, and less the Party's own; such are the outward Ornaments of the Person, for which Men are beholden to the Taylor, the Laceman, the Perriwigmaker, the Hatter, and the Milliner, and not to Nature. Such a Passion Girls may well be ashamed, as they generally are, to own either to themselves or to others.

The Love of Miss *Bridget* was of another Kind. The Captain owed nothing to any of these Fop-makers in his Dress, nor was his Person much more beholden to Nature. Both his Dress and Person were such as, had they appeared in an Assembly, or a Drawing-room, would have been the Contempt and Ridicule of all the fine Ladies there. The former of these was indeed neat, but plain, coarse, ill-fancied, and out of Fashion. As for the latter, we have expressly described it above. So far was the Skin on his Cheeks from being Cherry-coloured, that you could not discern what the natural Colour of his Cheeks was, they being totally overgrown by a black Beard, which ascended to his Eyes. His Shape and Limbs were indeed exactly proportioned, but so large, that they denoted the Strength rather of a Ploughman than any other. His Shoulders were broad, beyond all Size, and the Calves of his Legs larger than those of a common Chairman. In short, his whole Person wanted all that Elegance and Beauty, which is the very reverse of clumsy Strength, and which so agreeably sets off most of our fine Gentlemen; being partly owing to the high Blood of their Ancestors, *viz.* Blood made of rich Sauces and generous Wines, and partly to an early Town Education.

Tho' Miss *Bridget* was a Woman of the greatest Delicacy of Taste; yet such were the Charms of the Captain's Conversation, that she totally overlooked the Defects of his Person. She imagined, and perhaps very wisely, that she should enjoy more agreeable Minutes with the Captain, than with a much prettier Fellow; and forewent the Consideration of pleasing her Eyes, in order to procure herself much more solid Satisfaction.

The Captain no sooner perceived the Passion of Miss *Bridget*, in which Discovery he was very quick-sighted, than he faithfully returned it. The Lady, no more than her Lover, was remarkable for Beauty. I would attempt to draw her Picture; but that is done already by a more able Master, Mr. *Hogarth* himself, to whom she sat many Years ago, and hath been lately exhibited by that Gentleman in his Print of a Winter's Morning,[1] of which she was no improper Emblem, and may be seen walking (for walk she doth in the Print) to *Covent-Garden* Church, with a starved Foot-boy behind carrying her Prayer-book.

The Captain likewise very wisely preferred the more solid

---

[1] See 'Morning' from Hogarth's *The Four Times of the Day* (1738); the print is reproduced as Plate I of this edition. Fielding's great admiration for the works of his good friend William Hogarth (1697–1764) is amply attested. In a famous passage in *The Champion* (10 June 1740) he pronounced 'the ingenious Mr. *Hogarth*' to be 'one of the most useful Satyrists any Age hath produced'. In the Preface to *Joseph Andrews* Fielding refers to his friend's works in order to illustrate the distinction between comic art and caricature; and in *Tom Jones*, besides the allusion to 'Morning' in the present passage, Fielding directs his readers to other specific paintings by Hogarth in order to clarify the description of Mrs. Partridge (II. iii) and Thwackum (III. vi). Compliments to Hogarth also appear in *The Vernon-iad* (1741), 'An Essay on Conversation' (1743), the Preface to Sarah Fielding's *Familiar Letters* (1747), *Amelia* (1751; I. vi, III. iii, xii), *The Covent-Garden Journal* (21 January, 30 June 1752), and *The Journal of a Voyage to Lisbon* (1755). For other references in *Tom Jones*, see below, pp. 82, 138, 282, 555, 742.

Enjoyments he expected with this Lady, to the fleeting Charms of
Person. He was one of those wise Men, who regard Beauty in
the other Sex as a very worthless and superficial Qualification;
or, to speak more truly, who rather chuse to possess every Convenience of Life with an ugly Woman, than a handsome one
without any of those Conveniencies. And having a very good
Appetite, and but little Nicety, he fancied he should play his
Part very well at the matrimonial Banquet, without the Sauce of
Beauty.

To deal plainly with the Reader, the Captain, ever since his
Arrival, at least from the Moment his Brother had proposed the
Match to him, long before he had discovered any flattering
Symptoms in Miss *Bridget*, had been greatly enamoured; that is
to say, of Mr. *Allworthy's* House and Gardens, and of his Lands,
Tenements and Hereditaments; of all which the Captain was so
passionately fond, that he would most probably have contracted
Marriage with them, had he been obliged to have taken the
Witch of *Endor*[1] into the Bargain.

As Mr. *Allworthy* therefore had declared to the Doctor, that
he never intended to take a second Wife, as his Sister was his
nearest Relation, and as the Doctor had fished out that his Intentions were to make any Child of hers his Heir, which indeed
the Law, without his Interposition, would have done for him;[2] the
Doctor and his Brother thought it an Act of Benevolence to give
Being to a human Creature, who would be so plentifully provided
with the most essential Means of Happiness. The whole Thoughts
therefore of both the Brothers, were how to engage the Affections
of this amiable Lady.

But Fortune, who is a tender Parent, and often doth more for
her favourite Offspring than either they deserve or wish, had
been so industrious for the Captain, that whilst he was laying
Schemes to execute his Purpose, the Lady conceived the same
Desires with himself, and was on her Side contriving how to give
the Captain proper Encouragement, without appearing too forward; for she was a strict Observer of all Rules of Decorum. In

[1] See 1 Samuel 28: 7–25.

[2] Since Allworthy has no children of his own to survive him, upon his death his estate
would pass by law to the person who is '*next of Kin* in the *Collateral* Line of the whole Blood
(tho' never so Remote)'—in this case, to his sister and her children. (See Thomas Wood, *An
Institute of the Laws of England,* 7th ed. [1745], p. 228.)

this, however, she easily succeeded; for as the Captain was always on the Look-out, no Glance, Gesture, or Word, escaped him.

The Satisfaction which the Captain received from the kind Behaviour of Miss *Bridget,* was not a little abated by his Apprehensions of Mr. *Allworthy;* for, notwithstanding his disinterested Professions, the Captain imagined he would, when he came to act, follow the Example of the rest of the World, and refuse his Consent to a Match, so disadvantageous in point of Interest, to his Sister. From what Oracle he received this Opinion, I shall leave the Reader to determine; but, however he came by it, it strangely perplexed him how to regulate his Conduct so, as at once to convey his Affection to the Lady, and to conceal it from her Brother. He, at length, resolved to take all private Opportunities of making his Addresses; but in the Presence of Mr. *Allworthy* to be as reserved, and as much upon his Guard as was possible; and this Conduct was highly approved by the Brother.

He soon found Means to make his Addresses, in express Terms, to his Mistress, from whom he receiv'd an Answer in the proper Form; *viz.* The Answer which was first made some thousands of Years ago, and which hath been handed down by Tradition from Mother to Daughter ever since. If I was to translate this into Latin, I should render it by these two Words, *Nolo Episcopari;*[1] a Phrase likewise of immemorial Use on another Occasion.

The Captain, however he came by his Knowledge, perfectly well understood the Lady; and very soon after repeated his Application with more Warmth and Earnestness than before, and was again, according to due Form, rejected; but as he had encreased in the Eagerness of his Desires, so the Lady, with the same Propriety, decreased in the Violence of her Refusal.

Not to tire the Reader, by leading him through every Scene of this Courtship, (which, tho' in the Opinion of a certain great Author,[2] it is the pleasantest Scene of Life to the Actor, is perhaps as dull and tiresome as any whatever to the Audience) the

---

[1] 'I do not wish to be made a bishop'—the formal (and entirely perfunctory) reply traditionally made upon the royal offer of a bishopric. Cf. *A Journey from This World to the Next* (I. ix.).

[2] Joseph Addison in *The Spectator,* No. 261 (29 December 1711): 'The pleasantest Part of a Man's Life is generally that which passes in Courtship, provided his Passion be sincere, and the Party beloved kind with Discretion. Love, Desire, Hope, all the pleasing Motions of the Soul rise in the Pursuit.'

Captain made his Advances in Form, the Citadel was defended in Form, and at length, in proper Form, surrendered at Discretion.

During this whole Time, which filled the Space of near a Month, the Captain preserved great Distance of Behaviour to his Lady, in the Presence of the Brother, and the more he succeeded with her in private, the more reserved was he in public. And as for the Lady, she had no sooner secured her Lover, than she behaved to him before Company with the highest Degree of Indifference; so that Mr. *Allworthy* must have had the Insight of the Devil (or perhaps some of his worse Qualities) to have entertained the least Suspicion of what was going forward.

CHAPTER XII

Containing what the Reader may perhaps expect to find in it.

IN all Bargains, whether to fight, or to marry, or concerning any other such Business, little previous Ceremony is required, to bring the Matter to an Issue, when both Parties are really in earnest. This was the Case at present, and in less than a Month the Captain and his Lady were Man and Wife.

The great Concern now was to break the Matter to Mr. *Allworthy*; and this was undertaken by the Doctor.

One Day then as *Allworthy* was walking in his Garden, the Doctor came to him, and with great Gravity of Aspect, and all the Concern which he could possibly affect in his Countenance, said, 'I am come, Sir, to impart an Affair to you of the utmost Consequence; but how shall I mention to you, what it almost distracts me to think of!' He then launched forth into the most bitter Invectives both against Men and Women; accusing the former of having no Attachment but to their Interest, and the latter of being so addicted to vicious Inclinations, that they could never be safely trusted with one of the other Sex. 'Could I,' said he, 'Sir, have suspected, that a Lady of such Prudence, such Judgment, such Learning, should indulge so indiscreet a Passion; or could I have imagined that my Brother—why do I call him so? He is no longer a Brother of mine.——'

'Indeed but he is,' said *Allworthy*, 'and a Brother of mine too.'
——'Bless me, Sir,' said the Doctor, 'do you know the shocking

Affair ?'—— 'Look'ee, Mr. *Blifil*,' answered the good Man, 'it hath been my constant Maxim in Life, to make the best of all Matters which happen. My Sister, tho' many Years younger than I, is at least old enough to be at the Age of Discretion. Had he imposed on a Child, I should have been more averse to have forgiven him; but a Woman upwards of thirty must certainly be supposed to know what will make her most happy. She hath married a Gentleman, tho' perhaps not quite her Equal in Fortune; and if he hath any Perfections in her Eye, which can make up that Deficiency, I see no Reason why I should object to her Choice of her own Happiness; which I, no more than herself, imagine to consist only in immense Wealth. I might, perhaps, from the many Declarations I have made, of complying with almost any Proposal, have expected to have been consulted on this Occasion; but these Matters are of a very delicate Nature, and the Scruples of Modesty perhaps are not to be overcome. As to your Brother, I have really no Anger against him at all. He hath no Obligations to me, nor do I think he was under any Necessity of asking my Consent, since the Woman is, as I have said, *Sui Juris*,[1] and of a proper Age to be entirely answerable only to herself for her Conduct.'

The Doctor accused Mr. *Allworthy* of too great Lenity, repeated his Accusations against his Brother, and declared that he should never more be brought either to see, or to own him for his Relation. He then launched forth into a Panegyric on *Allworthy's* Goodness, into the highest Encomiums on his Friendship; and concluded, by saying, He should never forgive his Brother for having put the Place which he bore in that Friendship, to a Hazard.

Allworthy thus answer'd: 'Had I conceived any Displeasure against your Brother, I should never have carried that Resentment to the Innocent: But, I assure you, I have no such Displeasure. Your Brother appears to me to be a Man of Sense and Honour. I do not disapprove the Taste of my Sister; nor will I doubt but that she is equally the Object of his Inclinations. I have always thought Love the only Foundation of Happiness in a married State; as it can only produce that high and tender Friendship, which should always be the Cement of this Union; and, in my Opinion, all those Marriages which are contracted

---

[1] 'Of one's own right'—the state of being able to exercise one's legal rights.

from other Motives, are greatly criminal; they are a Profanation of a most holy Ceremony, and generally end in Disquiet and Misery: For surely we may call it a Profanation, to convert this most sacred Institution into a wicked Sacrifice to Lust, or Avarice: And what better can be said of those Matches to which Men are induced merely by the Consideration of a beautiful Person, or a great Fortune!

'To deny that Beauty is an agreeable Object to the Eye, and even worthy some Admiration, would be false and foolish. Beautiful is an Epithet often used in Scripture, and always mentioned with Honour. It was my own Fortune to marry a Woman, whom the World thought handsome, and I can truly say, I liked her the better on that Account. But, to make this the sole Consideration of Marriage, to lust after it so violently, as to overlook all Imperfections for its Sake, or to require it so absolutely as to reject and disdain Religion, Virtue, and Sense, which are Qualities, in their Nature of much higher Perfection, only because an Elegance of Person is wanting; this is surely inconsistent either with a wise Man, or a good Christian. And it is, perhaps, being too charitable to conclude that such Persons mean any thing more by their Marriage, than to please their carnal Appetites, for the Satisfaction of which we are taught it was not ordained.

'In the next Place, with respect to Fortune. Worldly Prudence perhaps exacts some Consideration on this Head; nor will I absolutely and altogether condemn it. As the World is constituted, the Demands of a married State, and the Care of Posterity, require some little Regard to what we call Circumstances. Yet this Provision is greatly encreased beyond what is really necessary, by Folly and Vanity, which create abundantly more Wants than Nature. Equipage for the Wife, and large Fortunes for the Children, are by Custom enrolled in the List of Necessaries; and, to procure these, every thing truly solid and sweet, and virtuous, and religious, are neglected and overlooked.

'And this in many Degrees; the last and greatest of which seems scarce distinguishable from Madness. I mean, where Persons of immense Fortunes contract themselves to those who are, and must be, disagreeable to them; to Fools and Knaves, in order to encrease an Estate, already larger even than the Demands of their Pleasures. Surely such Persons, if they will not be thought mad, must own, either that they are incapable of tasting the

Sweets of the tenderest Friendship, or that they sacrifice the greatest Happiness of which they are capable, to the vain, uncertain, and senseless Laws of vulgar Opinion, which owe as well their Force, as their Foundation, to Folly.'

Here *Allworthy* concluded his Sermon, to which *Blifil* had listened with the profoundest Attention, tho' it cost him some Pains to prevent now and then a small Discomposure of his Muscles. He now praised every Period of what he had heard, with the Warmth of a young Divine who hath the Honour to dine with a Bishop the same Day in which his Lordship hath mounted the Pulpit.

CHAPTER XIII

Which concludes the first Book, with an Instance of Ingratitude,
which we hope will appear unnatural.

THE Reader, from what hath been said, may imagine that the Reconciliation (if indeed it could be so called) was only Matter of Form; we shall therefore pass it over, and hasten to what must surely be thought Matter of Substance.

The Doctor had acquainted his Brother with what had past between Mr. *Allworthy* and him; and added with a Smile. 'I promise you, I paid you off; nay, I absolutely desired the good Gentleman not to forgive you: For you know, after he had made a Declaration in your Favour, I might, with Safety, venture on such a Request with a Person of his Temper; and I was willing, as well for your Sake as for my own, to prevent the least Possibility of a Suspicion.'

Captain *Blifil* took not the least Notice of this, at that Time; but he afterwards made a very notable Use of it.

One of the Maxims which the Devil, in a late Visit upon Earth, left to his Disciples, is, when once you are got up, to kick the Stool from under you. In plain *English*, when you have made your Fortune by the good Offices of a Friend, you are advised to discard him as soon as you can.

Whether the Captain acted by this Maxim, I will not positively determine; so far we may confidently say, that his Actions may be fairly derived from this diabolical Principle; and indeed it is difficult to assign any other Motive to them: For no sooner was he possessed of Miss *Bridget*, and reconciled to *Allworthy*, than he began to shew a Coldness to his Brother, which encreased daily; till at length it grew into Rudeness, and became very visible to every one.

The Doctor remonstrated to him privately concerning this Behaviour, but could obtain no other Satisfaction than the following plain Declaration: 'If you dislike any thing in my Brother's House, Sir, you know you are at Liberty to quit it.' This strange, cruel, and almost unaccountable Ingratitude in the Captain, absolutely broke the poor Doctor's Heart: For Ingratitude never so thoroughly pierces the human Breast, as when it proceeds from those in whose Behalf we have been guilty of Transgressions. Reflections on great and good Actions, however they are received or returned by those in whose Favour they are performed, always administer some Comfort to us; but what Consolation shall we receive under so biting a Calamity as the ungrateful Behaviour of our Friend, when our wounded Conscience at the same Time flies in our Face, and upbraids us with having spotted it in the Service of one so worthless?

Mr. *Allworthy* himself spoke to the Captain in his Brother's Behalf, and desired to know what Offence the Doctor had committed; when the hard-hearted Villain had the Baseness to say, that he should never forgive him for the Injury which he had endeavoured to do him in his Favour; which, he said, he had pumped out of him, and was such a Cruelty, that it ought not to be forgiven.

Allworthy spoke in very high Terms upon this Declaration, which, he said, became not a human Creature. He expressed, indeed, so much Resentment against an unforgiving Temper, that the Captain at last pretended to be convinced by his Arguments, and outwardly professed to be reconciled.

As for the Bride, she was now in her Honey-moon, and so passionately fond of her new Husband, that he never appeared, to her, to be in the wrong; and his Displeasure against any Person, was a sufficient Reason for her Dislike to the same.

The Captain, at Mr. *Allworthy's* Instance, was outwardly, as we have said, reconciled to his Brother, yet the same Rancour remained in his Heart; and he found so many Opportunities of giving him private Hints of this, that the House at last grew insupportable to the poor Doctor; and he chose rather to submit to any Inconveniencies which he might encounter in the World, than longer to bear these cruel and ungrateful Insults, from a Brother for whom he had done so much.

He once intended to acquaint *Allworthy* with the whole; but he could not bring himself to submit to the Confession, by which he must take to his Share so great a Portion of Guilt. Besides, by how much the worse Man he represented his Brother to be, so much the greater would his own Offence appear to *Allworthy*, and so much the greater, he had Reason to imagine, would be his Resentment.

He feigned, therefore, some Excuse of Business for his Departure, and promised to return soon again; and took leave of his Brother with so well-dissembled Content, that, as the Captain played his Part to the same Perfection, *Allworthy* remained well satisfied with the Truth of the Reconciliation.

The Doctor went directly to *London*, where he died soon after of a broken Heart; a Distemper which kills many more than is generally imagined, and would have a fair Title to a Place in the Bill of Mortality,[1] did it not differ in one Instance from all other Diseases, *viz.* That no Physician can cure it.

Now, upon the most diligent Enquiry into the former Lives of these two Brothers, I find, besides the cursed and hellish Maxim of Policy above-mentioned, another Reason for the Captain's Conduct: The Captain, besides what we have before said of him, was a Man of great Pride and Fierceness, and had always treated his Brother, who was of a different Complexion, and greatly deficient in both those Qualities, with the utmost Air of Superiority. The Doctor, however, had much the larger Share of Learning, and was by many reputed to have the better Understanding. This the Captain knew, and could not bear. For, tho' Envy is at best a very malignant Passion, yet is its Bitterness greatly heightened by mixing with Contempt towards the same Object; and very much afraid I am, that whenever an Obligation is joined to these two, Indignation, and not Gratitude, will be the Product of all three.

---

[1] Since 1592, when plague broke out, the Company of Parish Clerks had published weekly records of deaths (and later of births and baptisms) occurring in 109 parishes in and around London.

BOOK II

Containing Scenes of matrimonial Felicity in different Degrees of Life; and various other Transactions during the first two Years after the Marriage between Captain Blifil, *and Miss* Bridget Allworthy.

CHAPTER I

Shewing what Kind of a History this is; what it is like, and what it is not like.

THO' we have properly enough entitled this our Work, a History, and not a Life; nor an Apology for a Life, as is more in Fashion;[1] yet we intend in it rather to pursue the Method of those Writers who profess to disclose the Revolutions of Countries, than to imitate the painful and voluminous Historian, who to preserve the Regularity of his Series thinks himself obliged to fill up as much Paper with the Detail of Months and Years in which nothing remarkable happened, as he employs upon those notable Æras when the greatest Scenes have been transacted on the human Stage.

Such Histories as these do, in reality, very much resemble a News-Paper, which consists of just the same Number of Words,

---

[1] Doubtless another hit at Colley Cibber (1671–1757), actor, playwright, and poet laureate. Cibber's autobiography, *An Apology for the Life of Mr. Colley Cibber, Comedian* (1740), was a favourite target of Fielding's satire: see, especially, *The Champion* (1, 15, 22, 29 April, 3, 6, 17 May 1740), *Shamela* (1741)—the full title of which parodies Cibber's own—*Joseph Andrews* (1742; I. i), and *Jonathan Wild* (1743; I. xiii). For a full sketch of Fielding's relations with Cibber, see the notes to the Wesleyan Edition of *Joseph Andrews*.

While *Tom Jones* was nearing completion, moreover, other writers followed Cibber's example by publishing autobiographical 'apologies'. On 30 November 1747 appeared *An Apology for the Conduct of a late celebrated Second-rate Minister*, a spurious work purporting to disclose the unscrupulous politics of Thomas Winnington, recently deceased, and incidentally accusing Fielding's Whig friends in the government of being Jacobites in disguise; Fielding's *Proper Answer to a Late Scurrilous Libel* (24 December 1747) was written to refute this pamphlet. In April 1748 the scandalous 'Con' Phillips began to issue her own *Apology*, to which Fielding alludes in *Amelia* (1751; IV. i). This Cibberian device continued to be 'fashionable' after the publication of *Tom Jones*: late in 1749 there appeared the popular *Apology for the Life of Mr. Bampfylde-Moore Carew, Commonly call'd The King of the Beggars.*

whether there be any News in it or not. They may likewise be compared to a Stage-Coach, which performs constantly the same Course, empty as well as full. The Writer, indeed, seems to think himself obliged to keep even Pace with Time, whose Amanuensis he is; and, like his Master, travels as slowly through Centuries of monkish Dulness, when the World seems to have been asleep, as through that bright and busy Age so nobly distinguished by the excellent *Latin* Poet.[1]

> *Ad confligendum venientibus undique pœnis;*
> *Omnia cum belli trepido concussa tumultu*
> *Horrida contremuere sub altis ætheris auris:*
> *In dubioque fuit sub utrorum regna cadendum*
> *Omnibus humanis esset, terraque marique.*

Of which, we wish we could give our Reader a more adequate Translation than that by Mr. *Creech*.[2]

> When dreadful *Carthage* frighted *Rome* with Arms,
> And all the World was shook with fierce Alarms;
> Whilst undecided yet, which Part should fall,
> Which Nation rise the glorious Lord of all.

Now it is our Purpose in the ensuing Pages, to pursue a contrary Method. When any extraordinary Scene presents itself (as we trust will often be the Case) we shall spare no Pains nor Paper to open it at large to our Reader; but if whole Years should pass without producing any thing worthy his Notice, we shall not be afraid of a Chasm in our History; but shall hasten on to Matters of Consequence, and leave such Periods of Time totally unobserved.

These are indeed to be considered as Blanks in the grand Lottery of Time. We therefore who are the Registers of that Lottery, shall imitate those sagacious Persons who deal in that which is drawn at *Guild-Hall*,[3] and who never trouble the Public with

---

[1] Lucretius, *De Rerum Natura*, iii. 833–7. Fielding apparently followed the Creech text of 1717 (in his library), which differs in several readings from the text of the Loeb Classical Library edition (trans. W. H. D. Rouse, 1924), here cited.

[2] Thomas Creech (1659–1700), whose popular translation of Lucretius was first published in 1682.

[3] From 1694 to 1826 state lotteries were held at intervals to raise money for such purposes as the construction of Westminster Bridge and the establishment of the British Museum. Draws were held in November–December at the Guildhall, the Hall of the Corporation of the City of London. The lottery system, which encouraged gambling even among the poor and which led to profiteering by unscrupulous ticket-mongers, was often satirized by

the many Blanks they dispose of; but when a great Prize happens to be drawn, the News-Papers are presently filled with it, and the World is sure to be informed at whose Office it was sold: Indeed, commonly two or three different Offices lay claim to the Honour of having disposed of it; by which I suppose the Adventurers are given to understand that certain Brokers are in the Secrets of Fortune, and indeed of her Cabinet-Council.

My Reader then is not to be surprised, if in the Course of this Work, he shall find some Chapters very short, and others altogether as long; some that contain only the Time of a single Day, and others that comprise Years; in a word, if my History sometimes seems to stand still, and sometimes to fly. For all which I shall not look on myself as accountable to any Court of Critical Jurisdiction whatever: For as I am, in reality, the Founder of a new Province of Writing, so I am at liberty to make what Laws I please therein.¹ And these Laws, my Readers, whom I consider as my Subjects, are bound to believe in and to obey; with which that they may readily and chearfully comply, I do hereby assure them that I shall principally regard their Ease and Advantage in all such Institutions: For I do not, like a *jure divino* Tyrant,²

Fielding, most notably in his ballad-opera, *The Lottery* (1732), and in *The Champion* (29 December 1739, 3 January 1739/40). Incidental jibes at the lottery and at the 'Puffs' of 'Lottery-Mongers' occur in *The True Patriot* (12, 19, 26 November 1745). In the present passage, however, Fielding may allude specifically to the advertisements of two well-known brokers, Francis Wilson and J. Hazard: on 24 December 1746 and 4 December 1747 both these men claimed in the newspapers to have sold identical tickets, prizes of £5,000 and £500, respectively. (See *The General Advertiser*, 24 December 1746, and *The Penny London Post*, 24–6 December 1746; and *The Daily Advertiser*, 4 December 1747.)

¹ An echo of the famous critical axiom enunciated by Le Bossu in the opening chapter of his *Traité du poëme épique* (Paris, 1675). Dryden paraphrases as follows: 'That all excellent arts, and particularly that of poetry, have been invented and brought to perfection by men of a transcendent genius; and that, therefore, they, who practise afterwards the same arts, are obliged to tread in their footsteps, and to search in their writings the foundation of them; for it is not just that new rules should destroy the authority of the old' ('Preface to *Troilus and Cressida* [1679], containing The Grounds of Criticism in Tragedy'; in W. P. Ker, ed. *Essays of John Dryden* [New York, 1961], i. 211).

² The political metaphor developed in this passage is the first of many anti-Jacobitical strokes in *Tom Jones*. Specifically, Fielding's argument recalls Locke's *Two Treatises of Government* (1690), which maintained the principles of a limited, constitutional monarchy against the doctrine of absolutism propounded by Sir Robert Filmer in *Patriarcha* (1680). Filmer's view that the king ruled *jure divino*, by divine right, provided the ideological basis of Jacobitism. Locke, on the other hand, was the great apologist for the Revolution Settlement of 1689, insisting that the supreme power resided in the legislature, which governs only by consent of the governed. Fielding always subscribed to this view (cf. 'Liberty' [1743], l. 79, where he ironically reflects on 'the strange Divinity of Kings'); but from

imagine that they are my Slaves or my Commodity. I am, indeed, set over them for their own Good only, and was created for their Use, and not they for mine. Nor do I doubt, while I make their Interest the great Rule of my Writings, they will unanimously concur in supporting my Dignity, and in rendering me all the Honour I shall deserve or desire.

CHAPTER II

Religious Cautions against shewing too much Favour to Bastards; and a great Discovery made by Mrs. Deborah Wilkins.

EIGHT Months after the Celebration of the Nuptials between Captain *Blifil* and Miss *Bridget Allworthy*, a young Lady of great Beauty, Merit, and Fortune,[1] was Miss *Bridget*, by reason of a Fright, delivered of a fine Boy. The Child, was indeed, to all Appearance, perfect; but the Midwife discovered, it was born a Month before its full Time.

Tho' the Birth of an Heir by his beloved Sister was a Circumstance of great Joy to Mr. *Allworthy*, yet it did not alienate his Affections from the little Foundling, to whom he had been Godfather, had given his own Name of *Thomas*, and whom he had hitherto seldom failed of visiting at least once a Day, in his Nursery.

He told his Sister, if she pleased, the new-born Infant should be bred up together with little *Tommy*, to which she consented, tho' with some little Reluctance: For she had truly a great Complacence for her Brother; and hence she had always behaved towards the Foundling with rather more Kindness than Ladies of

the time of the Jacobite uprising in 1745 he was especially outspoken in applying Lockean principles to defend the Hanoverian Establishment. In *A Serious Address to the People of Great Britain* (1745) he represents James II as a king whose 'Mind was strongly tainted with all the Notions of absolute Power. Passive Obedience, and Non-resistance on the Part of the Subject, and a *dispensing Power* in the Crown, with an indefeasible Hereditary Right, *Jure Divino*, were as much Articles of his political Creed, as the Supremacy of the Pope, or Transubstantiation, were of his religious one . . .' (p. 5). Later, in the third number of *The Jacobite's Journal* (19 December 1747), Fielding cited the doctrine of the king's rule *jure divino* as the fundamental 'Mystery' of Jacobitism.

1 The phrasing parodies the fulsome and pretentious language of wedding-notices in the newspapers, a subject which Fielding frequently ridiculed in his journals. See below, p. 705, n. 1, where the hyperbole here applied to Bridget Allworthy reappears verbatim in a similar satire from *The Jacobite's Journal* (13 February 1748).

rigid Virtue can sometimes bring themselves to shew to these Children, who, however innocent, may be truly called the living Monuments of Incontinence.

The Captain could not so easily bring himself to bear what he condemned as a Fault in Mr. *Allworthy*. He gave him frequent Hints, that to adopt the Fruits of Sin was to give countenance to it. He quoted several Texts (for he was well read in Scripture) such as, *He visits the Sins of the Fathers upon the Children;*[1] and, *the Fathers have eaten sour Grapes, and the Children's Teeth are set on edge,*[2] &c. Whence he argued the Legality of punishing the Crime of the Parent on the Bastard. He said, 'Tho' the Law did not positively allow the destroying such base-born Children, yet it held them to be the Children of no body; that the Church considered them as the Children of no body;[3] and that at the best, they ought to be brought up to the lowest and vilest Offices of the Commonwealth.'

Mr. *Allworthy* answered[4] to all this and much more which the

---

[1] The second commandment (Exodus 20: 5, Deuteronomy 5: 9): 'Thou shalt not bow down thyself to them [graven images], nor serve them: for I the LORD thy God *am* a jealous God, visiting the iniquity of the fathers upon the children unto the third and fourth *generation* of them that hate me.'

[2] Ezekiel 18: 2–3: 'What mean ye, that ye use this proverb concerning the land of Israel, saying, The fathers have eaten sour grapes, and the children's teeth are set on edge?/ *As* I live, saith the Lord GOD, ye shall not have *occasion* any more to use this proverb in Israel.' (Cf. Jeremiah 31: 29–30 and Numbers 14: 18.)

[3] 'A *Bastard* is he that is born out of Marriage. He shall never inherit or be Heir to any one. He cannot be of kin to one. For in Law he is *Quasi nullius Filius*, and no Man's Issue.' (Wood, *Institutes*, 7th ed. [1745], p. 67.) Since 1160 the position of the Church had been that children born out of wedlock should be considered legitimate; but in 1235 (20 Henry III, cap. 9) the secular courts denied the bishops' plea to this effect. (Edmund Gibson, *Codex Juris Ecclesiastici Anglicani* [1713], ii. 1129–30.)

[4] Though ostensibly a question of the guilt or innocence of bastards, the dispute between Captain Blifil and Allworthy is actually a rehearsal of contemporary arguments for and against the theological doctrine of absolute reprobation. Blifil, 'not a little suspected of an Inclination to *Methodism*' (p. 63, n. 1), echoes the harsh Calvinistic views of George Whitefield, who cited the same scriptural texts as the captain in asserting the doctrines of original sin and justification by grace and faith alone. Thus in his sermon, 'The Potter and the Clay', Whitefield promised that those who attended to his message 'will then no longer have any thing to say against the doctrine of *Original Sin*; or charge the Almighty foolishly, for suffering our first parents to be prevailed on to eat such sour grapes, and permitting thereby their children's teeth to be set on edge'. (Sermon xiii, *Works* [1771–2], v. 214.) It was Whitefield's belief in absolute reprobation that caused him to break with Wesley, whose Methodism was milder and more Arminian in character. (See Whitefield's 'Letter to the Reverend Mr. John Wesley: In Answer to his Sermon, Entituled, Free-Grace' [24 December 1740]; ibid., **iv.** 67 and *passim*.)

On the other hand, Allworthy's refutation of Blifil closely follows the arguments of John

Captain had urged on this Subject, 'That however guilty the Parents might be, the Children were certainly innocent. That as to the Texts he had quoted, the former of them was a particular Denunciation against the *Jews* for the Sin of Idolatry, of relinquishing and hating their heavenly King; and the latter was parabolically spoken,[1] and rather intended to denote the certain and necessary Consequences of Sin, than any express Judgment against it. But to represent the Almighty as avenging the Sins of the Guilty on the Innocent, was indecent, if not blasphemous, as it was to represent him acting against the first Principles of natural Justice, and against the original Notions of Right and Wrong, which he himself had implanted in our Minds; by which we were to judge not only in all Matters which were not revealed, but even of the Truth of Revelation itself. He said, he knew many held the same Principles with the Captain on this Head; but he was himself firmly convinced to the contrary, and would provide in the same Manner for this poor Infant, as if a legitimate Child had had the Fortune to have been found in the same Place.'

While the Captain was taking all Opportunities to press these and such like Arguments to remove the little Foundling from Mr. *Allworthy's*, of whose Fondness for him he began to be jealous,

Tillotson (see below, p. 145), Archbishop of Canterbury and leader of the latitudinarians. In his sermon, 'The goodness of God', for example, Tillotson vehemently denounced 'the doctrine of absolute reprobation: by which I mean the decreeing the greatest part of mankind to eternal misery and torment, without any consideration or respect to their sin and fault. . . . God is infinitely better than the best of men, and yet none can possibly think that man a good man, who should absolutely resolve to disinherit and destroy his children, without the foresight and consideration of any fault to be committed by them. We may talk of the goodness of God; but it is not an easy matter to devise to say any thing worse than this of the devil.' (Sermon cxlv, *Works* [1757], viii. 277–9.) To assert this view of the Deity, Tillotson elsewhere declared, is 'little less than a horrid and dreadful blasphemy'. (Sermon cxxxvi, 'The wisdom, glory, and sovereignty of God', ibid., viii. 124.) The text Allworthy applies to Blifil's position, furthermore, had been recommended by Tillotson in rejecting the doctrine of reprobation. In Sermon cxv, 'The sins of men not chargeable upon God; but upon themselves', Tillotson insisted that 'one of the surest ways of reasoning in religion' is 'from the natural notions which men have of God. . . . And if any thing be, upon good grounds in reason, received for a divine revelation, (as the holy scriptures are amongst christians) no man ought to be regarded, who from thence pretends to maintain any doctrine contrary to the natural notions, which men have of God; such as clearly contradict his holiness, or goodness, or justice, or do by plain and undeniable consequence make God the author of sin, or the like; because the very attempt to prove any such thing out of the scripture, does strike at the divine authority of those books' (ibid., vii. 93–5).

[1] According to William Warburton, Origen was the first to offer a parabolical interpretation of the texts cited by Captain Blifil. (See *The Divine Legation of Moses Demonstrated*, ii [1741], 460–1.)

Mrs. *Deborah* had made a Discovery, which in its Event threatned at least to prove more fatal to poor *Tommy*, than all the Reasonings of the Captain.

Whether the insatiable Curiosity of this good Woman had carried her on to that Business, or whether she did it to confirm herself in the good Graces of Mrs. *Blifil*, who, notwithstanding her outward Behaviour to the Foundling, frequently abused the Infant in private, and her Brother too for his Fondness to it, I will not determine; but she had now, as she conceived, fully detected the Father of the Foundling.

Now as this was a Discovery of great Consequence, it may be necessary to trace it from the Fountain-head. We shall therefore very minutely lay open those previous Matters by which it was produced; and for that Purpose, we shall be obliged to reveal all the Secrets of a little Family, with which my Reader is at present entirely unacquainted; and of which the Oeconomy was so rare and extraordinary, that I fear it will shock the utmost Credulity of many married Persons.

CHAPTER III

The Description of a domestic Government founded upon Rules directly contrary to those of Aristotle.[1]

MY Reader may please to remember he hath been informed that *Jenny Jones* had lived some Years with a certain Schoolmaster, who had, at her earnest Desire, instructed her in *Latin*, in which, to do justice to her Genius, she had so improved herself, that she was become a better Scholar than her Master.

Indeed, tho' this poor Man had undertaken a Profession to which Learning must be allowed necessary, this was the least of his Commendations. He was one of the best-natured Fellows in the World, and was at the same time Master of so much Pleasantry and Humour that he was reputed the Wit of the Country; and all the neighbouring Gentlemen were so desirous of his Company, that as denying was not his Talent, he spent much

[1] Cf. *Politics*, I. v. 1–2, where Aristotle states that the husband is by nature meant to govern his wife and family.

Time at their Houses, which he might with more Emolument have spent in his School.

It may be imagined, that a Gentleman so qualified, and so disposed, was in no danger of becoming formidable to the learned Seminaries of *Eton* or *Westminster*. To speak plainly, his Scholars were divided into two Classes. In the upper of which was a young Gentleman, the Son of a neighbouring Squire, who at the Age of Seventeen was just entered into his Syntaxis;[1] and in the lower was a second Son of the same Gentleman, who, together with seven Parish-boys, was learning to read and write.

The Stipend arising hence would hardly have indulged the Schoolmaster in the Luxuries of Life, had he not added to this Office those of Clerk and Barber, and had not Mr. *Allworthy* added to the whole an Annuity of Ten Pound, which the poor Man received every Christmas, and with which he was enabled to chear his Heart during that sacred Festival.

Among his other Treasures, the Pedagogue had a Wife whom he had married out of Mr. *Allworthy's* Kitchen, for her Fortune, *viz.* Twenty Pound, which she had there amassed.

This Woman was not very amiable in her Person. Whether she sat to my Friend *Hogarth*,[2] or no, I will not determine; but she exactly resembled the young Woman who is pouring out her Mistress's Tea in the third Picture of the Harlot's Progress. She was besides a profest Follower of that notable Sect founded by *Xantippe*[3] of old; by means of which, she became more formidable in the School than her Husband: for to confess the Truth, he was never Master there, or any where else, in her Presence.

Tho' her Countenance did not denote much natural Sweetness of Temper, yet this was perhaps somewhat soured by a Circumstance which generally poisons matrimonial Felicity. For Children are rightly called the Pledges of Love; and her Husband, tho' they had been married nine Years, had given her no such Pledges; a Default for which he had no Excuse, either from Age or Health,

---

[1] The construction of grammar—usually the second stage in the teaching of Latin.

[2] See above, p. 66, n. 1. Plate 3 of Hogarth's *A Harlot's Progress* (1732) is reproduced as Plate 2. For this satiric series and for the later *Rake's Progress* (1735) Fielding had the highest praise: 'I almost dare affirm', he remarked in *The Champion* (10 June 1740), that these two works 'are calculated more to serve the Cause of Virtue, and for the Preservation of Mankind, than all the *Folio's* of Morality which have been ever written'.

[3] The shrewish wife of Socrates.

being not yet thirty Years old, and, what they call a jolly, brisk, young Man.

Hence arose another Evil which produced no little Uneasiness to the poor Pedagogue, of whom she maintained so constant a Jealousy, that he durst hardly speak to one Woman in the Parish; for the least Degree of Civility, or even Correspondence with any Female, was sure to bring his Wife upon her Back, and his own.

In order to guard herself against matrimonial Injuries in her own House, as she kept one Maid Servant, she always took Care to chuse her out of that Order of Females, whose Faces are taken as a Kind of Security for their Virtue; of which Number *Jenny Jones*, as the Reader hath been before informed, was one.

As the Face of this young Woman might be called pretty good Security of the before-mentioned Kind, and as her Behaviour had been always extremely modest; which is the certain Consequence of Understanding in Women; she had passed above four Years at Mr. *Partridge's*, (for that was the Schoolmaster's Name) without creating the least Suspicion in her Mistress. Nay, she had been treated with uncommon Kindness, and her Mistress had permitted Mr. *Partridge* to give her those Instructions, which have been before commemorated.

But it is with Jealousy, as with the Gout. When such Distempers are in the Blood, there is never any Security against their breaking out; and that often on the slightest Occasions, and when least suspected.

Thus it happened to Mrs. *Partridge*, who had submitted four Years to her Husband's teaching this young Woman, and had suffered her often to neglect her Work, in order to pursue her Learning. For passing by one Day, as the Girl was reading, and her Master leaning over her, the Girl, I know not for what Reason, suddenly started up from her Chair; and this was the first Time that Suspicion ever entered into the Head of her Mistress.

This did not, however, at that Time, discover itself, but lay lurking in her Mind, like a concealed Enemy, who waits for a Reinforcement of additional Strength, before he openly declares himself, and proceeds upon hostile Operations; and such additional Strength soon arrived to corroborate her Suspicion: For not long after, the Husband and Wife being at Dinner, the Master said to his Maid, *Da mihi aliquid Potum*;[1] upon which the

---

[1] Partridge tries to say, 'Give me something to drink.'

poor Girl smiled, perhaps at the Badness of the Latin, and when her Mistress cast her Eyes on her, blushed, possibly with a Consciousness of having laughed at her Master. Mrs. *Partridge*, upon this, immediately fell into a Fury, and discharged the Trencher on which she was eating, at the Head of poor *Jenny*, crying out, 'You impudent Whore, do you play Tricks with my Husband before my Face?' and, at the same Instant, rose from her Chair, with a Knife in her Hand, with which, most probably, she would have executed very tragical Vengeance, had not the Girl taken the Advantage of being nearer the Door than her Mistress, and avoided her Fury, by running away; for, as to the poor Husband, whether Surprize had rendered him motionless, or Fear (which is full as probable) had restrained him from venturing at any Opposition, he sat staring and trembling in his Chair; nor did he once offer to move or speak, till his Wife returning from the Pursuit of *Jenny*, made some defensive Measures necessary for his own Preservation; and he likewise was obliged to retreat, after the Example of the Maid.

This good Woman was, no more than *Othello*,[1] of a Disposition,

> ——To make a Life of Jealousy,
> And follow still the Changes of the Moon
> With fresh Suspicions——

with her, as well as him;

> ——To be once in doubt
> Was once to be resolved——

she therefore ordered *Jenny* immediately to pack up her Alls, and be gone; for that she was determined she should not sleep that Night within her Walls.

Mr. *Partridge* had profited too much, by Experience, to interpose in a Matter of this Nature. He therefore had Recourse to his usual Recipe of Patience; for, tho' he was not a great Adept in Latin, he remembered and well understood the Advice contained in these Words:

> ——*Leve fit, quod bene fertur Onus.*[2]

In English: 'A Burden becomes lightest, when it is well borne.'

---

[1] *Othello*, III. iii.
[2] Ovid, *Amores*, I. ii. 10. Cf. *Amelia* (1751), III. x.

Which he had always in his Mouth, and of which, to say the Truth, he had often Occasion to experience the Truth.

Jenny offered to make Protestations of her Innocence; but the Tempest was too high for her to be heard. She then betook herself to the Business of Packing, for which a small Quantity of brown Paper sufficed; and, having received her small Pittance of Wages, she returned home.

The Schoolmaster and his Consort pass'd their Time unpleasantly enough that Evening; but something or other happened before the next Morning, which a little abated the Fury of Mrs. *Partridge*; and she at length admitted her Husband to make his Excuses. To which she gave the readier Belief, as he had, instead of desiring her to recall *Jenny*, professed a Satisfaction in her being dismissed, saying, She was grown of little Use as a Servant, spending all her Time in reading, and was become, moreover, very pert and obstinate: For indeed she and her Master had lately had frequent Disputes in Literature; in which, as hath been said, she was become greatly his Superior. This, however, he would by no means allow; and, as he called her persisting in the Right, Obstinacy, he began to hate her with no small Inveteracy.

CHAPTER IV

Containing one of the most bloody Battles, or rather Duels, that were ever recorded in Domestic History.

FOR the Reasons mentioned in the preceding Chapter, and from some other matrimonial Concessions, well known to most Husbands; and which, like the Secrets of Free Masonry,[1]

[1] Incidental satire directed against the esotericism of Freemasonry occurs in several of Fielding's publications during 1747: e.g. in *Ovid's Art of Love Paraphrased*, in the Preface to Sarah Fielding's *Familiar Letters*, and in the three first numbers of *The Jacobite's Journal* (5, 12, 19 December 1747), where a facetious comparison is drawn between the 'mysterious' doctrines of Freemasonry and Jacobitism. This, indeed, may be the connection that prompted Fielding's sarcasm. As may be seen in James Anderson's *Constitutions of the Free-Masons* (1723; 2nd ed., 1738) the brothers took a special pride in claiming the Stuart kings for their fraternity; in particular, Anderson praised James I as 'a *Mason* King' who, by patronizing 'our *great Master-Mason* INIGO JONES', became 'the *First* Prince in the World that recover'd the *Roman* Architecture from the Ruins of *Gothick* Ignorance' (see L. Vibert, ed. [1923], pp. 38–41). According to the constitution of

should be divulged to none who are not Members of that honourable Fraternity; Mrs. *Partridge* was pretty well satisfied, that she had condemned her Husband without Cause, and endeavoured, by Acts of Kindness, to make him Amends for her false Suspicion. Her Passions were, indeed, equally violent, which ever Way they inclined: for, as she could be extremely angry, so could she be altogether as fond.

But tho' these Passions ordinarily succeeded each other, and scarce twenty-four Hours ever passed in which the Pedagogue was not, in some Degree, the Object of both; yet, on extraordinary Occasions, when the Passion of Anger had raged very high, the Remission was usually longer, and so was the Case at present; for she continued longer in a State of Affability, after this Fit of Jealousy was ended, than her Husband had ever known before: And, had it not been for some little Exercises, which all the Followers of *Xantippe* are obliged to perform daily, Mr. *Partridge* would have enjoyed a perfect Serenity of several Months.

Perfect Calms at Sea are always suspected by the experienced Mariner to be the Forerunners of a Storm: And I know some Persons, who, without being generally the Devotees of Superstition, are apt to apprehend, that great and unusual Peace or Tranquility, will be attended with its opposite: For which Reason the Antients used, on such Occasions, to sacrifice to the Goddess *Nemesis*; a Deity who was thought by them to look with an invidious Eye on human Felicity, and to have a peculiar Delight in overturning it.

As we are very far from believing in any such Heathen Goddess, or from encouraging any Superstition, so we wish Mr. *John Fr*———,[1] or some other such Philosopher, would bestir

the Order, furthermore, no brother could be expelled from a lodge merely for being a rebel, a stipulation designed to accommodate powerful Jacobite elements in the fraternity (ibid., pp. xxix, 50). For a later reference to Freemasonry in *Tom Jones*, see below, p. 236, n. 1.

1 John Freke (1688–1756), F.R.S. and Surgeon at St. Bartholomew's Hospital, London. In 1746 the publication of William Watson's *Experiments and Observations* generated considerable popular and scientific interest in electricity and electrical phenomena. Freke entered the controversy in mid October, publishing an absurdly theoretical and pretentious work entitled, *An Essay to Shew the Cause of Electricity; and Why Some Things are Non-Electricable . . . In a Letter to Mr. William Watson, F.R.S.* (The first edition was announced in *The Daily Advertiser*, 11 October 1746; the second edition appeared on 3 November 1746—see *The Daily Advertiser* and *The London Courant* for that date.) Freke's claims for his pamphlet were extravagant, to say the least. His subject, he declared, '*can, with more Nobleness and Dignity employ the Mind of Man, than any I can think of relating to the sub-*

himself a little, in order to find out the real Cause of this sudden Transition, from good to bad Fortune, which hath been so often remarked, and of which we shall proceed to give an Instance; for it is our Province to relate Facts, and we shall leave Causes to Persons of much higher Genius.

Mankind have always taken great Delight in knowing and descanting on the Actions of others. Hence there have been, in all Ages, and Nations, certain Places set apart for public Rendezvous, where the Curious might meet, and satisfy their mutual Curiosity. Among these, the Barbers Shops have justly borne the Pre-eminence. Among the *Greeks*, Barbers News was a proverbial Expression,[1] and *Horace*, in one of his Epistles,[2] makes honourable Mention of the *Roman* Barbers in the same Light.

Those of *England* are known to be no wise inferior to their *Greek* or *Roman* Predecessors. You there see foreign Affairs discussed in a Manner little inferior to that with which they are handled in the Coffee-houses; and domestick Occurrences are much more largely and freely treated in the former, than in the latter. But this serves only for the Men. Now, whereas the Females of this Country, especially those of the lower Order, do associate themselves much more than those of other Nations, our Polity would be highly deficient, if they had not some Place set apart·likewise for the Indulgence of their Curiosity, seeing they are in this no way inferior to the other half of the Species.

In enjoying, therefore, such Place of Rendezvous, the *British* Fair ought to esteem themselves more happy than any of their foreign Sisters; as I do not remember either to have read in

lunary Part of the World. For by it you may be acquainted with the immediate Officer of God Almighty, *which he seems to send to all Things living. Nay, this Power, according to my Conception, seems to be the Cause, under* HIM, *both of Life and Death*' (pp. v–vi). Having discovered the '*Flamma Vitalis*' (p. 4) of the ancient philosophers, he saw himself enshrined among the Harveys and Newtons of modern science (pp. vii–viii). Others besides Fielding were amused by Freke's hobby-horsical performance. In *Remarks on a Rhapsody of Adventures of a Modern Knight-Errant in Philosophy* (Bath, 1746), Benjamin Martin likened Freke to a scientific Don Quixote performing 'Feats of *Electrical Chivalry*' (p. 25). For a later allusion to Freke's essay in *Tom Jones*, see below, p. 187, n. 1.

[1] Cf. Plutarch, 'De Garrulitate', *Moralia*, 509; also Lucian, *How to Write History*, 24. But Fielding may be allowed his own gloss on the passage: in a note to his and William Young's translation of Aristophanes' *Plutus, the God of Riches* (1742; II. iii), he describes barber shops as 'the Coffee-Houses of the Antients. . . . They were Assemblies of all idle gossipping Fellows, who there assembled to vent their Malignity against their Betters. The Barbers themselves were likewise the most talkative and impertinent of all People.'

[2] Fielding probably means Horace's *Satires*, I. vii. 2–3.

History, or to have seen in my Travels, any thing of the like Kind.

This Place then is no other than the Chandler's Shop; the known Seat of all the News; or, as it is vulgarly called, Gossiping, in every Parish in *England*.

Mrs. *Partridge* being one Day at this Assembly of Females, was asked by one of her Neighbours, if she had heard no News lately of *Jenny Jones*. To which she answered in the negative. Upon this, the other replied, with a Smile, That the Parish was very much obliged to her for having turned *Jenny* away as she did.

Mrs. *Partridge*, whose Jealousy, as the Reader well knows, was long since cured, and who had no other Quarrel to her Maid, answered boldly, She did not know any Obligation the Parish had to her on that Account, for she believed *Jenny* had scarce left her Equal behind her.

'No, truly,' said the Gossip, 'I hope not, tho' I fancy we have Sluts enow too. Then you have not heard, it seems, that she hath been brought to bed of two Bastards; but as they are not born here, my Husband, and the other Overseer, says we shall not be obliged to keep them.'[1]

'Two Bastards!' answered Mrs. *Partridge* hastily, 'you surprize me. I don't know whether we must keep them; but I am sure they must have been begotten here, for the Wench hath not been nine Months gone away.'

Nothing can be so quick and sudden as the Operations of the Mind, especially when Hope, or Fear, or Jealousy to which the two others are but Journeymen, set it to work. It occurred instantly to her, that *Jenny* had scarce ever been out of her own House, while she lived with her. The leaning over the Chair, the sudden starting up, the Latin, the Smile, and many other Things rushed upon her all at once. The Satisfaction her Husband expressed in the Departure of *Jenny*, appeared now to be only dissembled; again, in the same Instant, to be real; but yet to confirm her Jealousy, proceeding from Satiety, and a hundred other bad Causes. In a Word, she was convinced of her Husband's Guilt, and immediately left the Assembly in Confusion.

[1] A bastard child was considered to be settled in, and therefore chargeable to, the parish in which it was born, even though it was conceived elsewhere. (See Michael Dalton, *The Country Justice* [1746], p. 172.)

As fair *Grimalkin*, who, though the youngest of the Feline
Family, degenerates not in Ferosity from the elder Branches of
her House, and, though inferior in Strength, is equal in Fierceness to the noble Tyger himself, when a little Mouse, whom it
hath long tormented in Sport, escapes from her Clutches for a
while, frets, scolds, growls, swears; but if the Trunk, or Box,
behind which the Mouse lay hid, be again removed, she flies like
Lightning on her Prey, and, with envenomed Wrath, bites,
scratches, mumbles, and tears the little Animal.

Not with less Fury did Mrs. *Partridge* fly on the poor Pedagogue. Her Tongue, Teeth, and Hands, fell all upon him at once.
His Wig was in an Instant torn from his Head, his Shirt from
his Back, and from his Face descended five Streams of Blood,
denoting the Number of Claws with which Nature had unhappily
armed the Enemy.

Mr. *Partridge* acted for some Time on the defensive only;
indeed he attempted only to guard his Face with his Hands; but
as he found that his Antagonist abated nothing of her Rage, he
thought he might, at least, endeavour to disarm her, or rather to
confine her Arms; in doing which, her Cap fell off in the Struggle,
and her Hair being too short to reach her Shoulders, erected
itself on her Head; her Stays likewise, which were laced through
one single Hole at the Bottom, burst open, and her Breasts,
which were much more redundant than her Hair, hung down
below her Middle; her Face was likewise marked with the Blood
of her Husband; her Teeth gnashed with Rage; and Fire, such
as sparkles from a Smith's Forge, darted from her Eyes. So that,
altogether, this Amazonian Heroine might have been an Object
of Terror to a much bolder Man than Mr. *Partridge*.

He had, at length, the good Fortune, by getting Possession of
her Arms, to render those Weapons, which she wore at the Ends
of her Fingers, useless; which she no sooner perceived, than the
Softness of her Sex prevailed over her Rage, and she presently
dissolved in Tears, which soon after concluded in a Fit.

That small Share of Sense which Mr. *Partridge* had hitherto
preserved through this Scene of Fury, of the Cause of which he
was hitherto ignorant, now utterly abandoned him. He ran
instantly into the Street, hollowing out, that his Wife was in the
Agonies of Death, and beseeching the Neighbours to fly with the
utmost Haste to her Assistance. Several good Women obeyed his

Summons, who entering his House, and applying the usual Remedies on such Occasions, Mrs. *Partridge* was, at length, to the great Joy of her Husband, brought to herself.

As soon as she had a little recollected her Spirits, and somewhat composed herself with a Cordial, she began to inform the Company of the manifold Injuries she had received from her Husband; who, she said, was not contented to injure her in her Bed; but, upon her upbraiding him with it, had treated her in the cruelest Manner imaginable; had torn her Cap and Hair from her Head, and her Stays from her Body, giving her, at the same Time, several Blows, the Marks of which she should carry to the Grave.

The poor Man, who bore on his Face many and more visible Marks of the Indignation of his Wife, stood in silent Astonishment at this Accusation; which the Reader will, I believe, bear Witness for him, had greatly exceeded the Truth; for indeed he had not struck her once; and this Silence being interpreted to be a Confession of the Charge, by the whole Court, they all began at once, *una voce*, to rebuke and revile him, repeating often, that none but a Coward ever struck a Woman.

Mr. *Partridge* bore all this patiently; but when his Wife appealed to the Blood on her Face, as an Evidence of his Barbarity, he could not help laying Claim to his own Blood, for so it really was; as he thought it very unnatural, that this should rise up (as we are taught[1] that of a murdered Person often doth) in Vengeance against him.

To this the Women made no other Answer, than that it was Pity it had not come from his Heart, instead of his Face; all declaring, that if their Husbands should lift their Hands against them, they would have their Heart's Bloods out of their Bodies.

After much Admonition for what was past, and much good Advice to Mr. *Partridge* for his future Behaviour, the Company, at length, departed, and left the Husband and Wife to a personal Conference together, in which Mr. *Partridge* soon learned the Cause of all his Sufferings.

---

[1] Cf. Genesis 4: 10. Fielding alludes to this text in the introduction to *Examples of the Interposition of Providence in the Detection and Punishment of Murder* (1752).

CHAPTER V

Containing much Matter to exercise the Judgment and Reflection of the Reader.

I BELIEVE it is a true Observation, that few Secrets are divulged to one Person only; but certainly, it would be next to a Miracle, that a Fact of this Kind should be known to a whole Parish, and not transpire any farther.

And, indeed, a very few Days had past, before the Country, to use a common Phrase, rung of the Schoolmaster of *Little Baddington*; who was said to have beaten his Wife in the most cruel Manner. Nay, in some Places, it was reported he had murdered her; in others, that he had broke her Arms; in others, her Legs; in short, there was scarce an Injury which can be done to a human Creature, but what Mrs. *Partridge* was somewhere or other affirmed to have received from her Husband.

The Cause of this Quarrel was likewise variously reported; for, as some People said that Mrs. *Partridge* had caught her Husband in Bed with his Maid, so many other Reasons, of a very different Kind, went abroad. Nay, some transferred the Guilt to the Wife, and the Jealousy to the Husband.

Mrs. *Wilkins* had long ago heard of this Quarrel; but, as a different Cause from the true one had reached her Ears, she thought proper to conceal it; and the rather, perhaps, as the Blame was universally laid on Mr. *Partridge*; and his Wife, when she was Servant to Mr. *Allworthy*, had in something offended Mrs. *Wilkins*, who was not of a very forgiving Temper.

But Mrs. *Wilkins*, whose Eyes could see Objects at a Distance, and who could very well look forward a few Years into Futurity, had perceived a strong Likelihood of Captain *Blifil's* being hereafter her Master; and, as she plainly discerned, that the Captain bore no great Good-will to the little Foundling, she fancied it would be rendering him an agreeable Service, if she could make any Discoveries that might lessen the Affection which Mr. *Allworthy* seemed to have contracted for this Child, and which gave visible Uneasiness to the Captain; who could not entirely conceal it even before *Allworthy* himself; though his Wife, who acted her Part much better in public, frequently recommended to him her own Example, of conniving at the Folly of her Brother,

which, she said, she at least as well perceived, and as much resented as any other possibly could.

Mrs. *Wilkins* having therefore, by Accident, gotten a true
Scent of the above Story, though long after it had happened, failed
not to satisfy herself thoroughly of all the Particulars, and then
acquainted the Captain, that she had at last discovered the true
Father of the little Bastard, which she was sorry, she said, to see
her Master lose his Reputation in the Country, by taking so much
Notice of.

The Captain chid her for the Conclusion of her Speech, as an
improper Assurance in judging of her Master's Actions: For if his
Honour, or his Understanding, would have suffered the Captain
to make an Alliance with Mrs. *Wilkins*, his Pride would by no
means have admitted it. And, to say the Truth, there is no Conduct less politic, than to enter into any Confederacy with your
Friend's Servants, against their Master. For, by these Means,
you afterwards become the Slave of these very Servants; by
whom you are constantly liable to be betrayed. And this Consideration, perhaps, it was which prevented Captain *Blifil* from
being more explicit with Mrs. *Wilkins*; or from encouraging the
Abuse which she had bestowed on *Allworthy*.

But though he declared no Satisfaction to Mrs. *Wilkins* at this
Discovery, he enjoyed not a little from it in his own Mind, and
resolved to make the best Use of it he was able.

He kept this Matter a long Time concealed within his own
Breast, in Hopes that Mr. *Allworthy* might hear it from some
other Person; but Mrs. *Wilkins*, whether she resented the Captain's Behaviour, or whether his Cunning was beyond her, and
she feared the Discovery might displease him, never afterwards
opened her Lips about the Matter.

I have thought it somewhat strange, upon Reflection, that the
House-keeper never acquainted Mrs. *Blifil* with this News, as
Women are more inclined to communicate all Pieces of Intelligence to their own Sex, than to ours. The only Way, as it
appears to me, of solving this Difficulty, is, by imputing it to
that Distance which was now grown between the Lady and the
House-keeper: Whether this arose from a Jealousy in Mrs.
Blifil, that *Wilkins* shewed too great a Respect to the Foundling;
for while she was endeavouring to ruin the little Infant, in order
to ingratiate herself with the Captain, she was every Day more

and more commending it before *Allworthy*, as his Fondness for
it every Day encreased. This, notwithstanding all the Care she
took at other Times to express the direct contrary to Mrs. *Blifil*,
perhaps offended that delicate Lady, who certainly now hated
Mrs. *Wilkins*; and though she did not, or possibly could not,
absolutely remove her, from her Place, she found, however, the
Means of making her Life very uneasy. This Mrs. *Wilkins*, at
length, so resented, that she very openly shewed all Manner of
Respect and Fondness to little *Tommy*, in Opposition to Mrs.
Blifil.

The Captain, therefore, finding the Story in Danger of perishing, at last took an Opportunity to reveal it himself.

He was one Day engaged with Mr. *Allworthy* in a Discourse
on Charity:[1] In which the Captain, with great Learning, proved

---

[1] In their 'Discourse on Charity' which Fielding develops over the next several paragraphs, Captain Blifil again reveals his Methodistical inclinations while Allworthy, in
answering him, draws upon one of Fielding's favourite latitudinarian divines, Isaac Barrow.
Blifil begins by echoing Whitefield (see pp. 63, n. 1; 79, n. 4; 96, n. 2; 430, n. 1; 929,
n. 1). In his sermon on 1 Corinthians 13, 'The great Duty of Charity recommended'
(1740), Whitefield replied to those critics who, he said, had falsely accused him of denying
the efficacy of moral actions. Nevertheless, the definition of charity he proposed makes it a
much less practical virtue than that recommended by the latitudinarians. Most commentators agree that the Greek word *agape*, translated as 'charity' in the King James version, is
more accurately rendered as 'spiritual love'; thus Whitefield, referring to St. Paul, informs
his congregation 'what the apostle means by charity; and that is, LOVE' (Sermon xlvii,
Works [1771–2], vi. 228). Though he does not quite disparage almsgiving, he denies that
St. Paul intended us 'to hurt ourselves or our families' by an imprudent generosity (ibid.,
vi. 227) and he further declares that charity is 'much more valuable . . . when it extends to
the souls of men' (ibid., vi. 233) than when it ministers to their bodies only. For Whitefield,
true charity is the 'grace of love' (ibid., vi. 237), not the mere performance of good works:

'It is not the leading of a moral life, being honest, and paying every man his just due;
this is not a proof of your being in a state of grace, or of being born again, and renewed
in the spirit of your minds: No, you may die honest, just, charitable, and yet not be in
a state of salvation.

'It is not the preaching of that morality, which most of our pulpits now bring forth,
that is sufficient to bring you from sin unto GOD. . . .

'Therefore, let me advise you to be charitable to the souls of one another; that is, by
advising them with all love and tenderness, to follow after CHRIST, and the things which
belong to their immortal peace, before they be for ever hid from their eyes.' (Ibid., vi.
234–5.)

For Whitefield as for Captain Blifil, the latitudinarians, in preaching the doctrine of works,
were feeding their flocks 'only with the dry husks of dead morality' (Sermon xxxviii, 'The
Indwelling of the Spirit, the Common Privilege of All Believers', ibid., vi. 95): 'My dear
brethren,' he admonished, '*Seneca, Cicero, Plato*, or any of the heathen philosophers, would
have given as good a definition as this' (Sermon ix, 'The Folly and Danger of Being Not
Righteous Enough', ibid., v. 126).

to Mr. *Allworthy*, that the Word *Charity*, in Scripture, no where means Beneficence, or Generosity.

'The Christian Religion,' he said, 'was instituted for much nobler Purposes, than to enforce a Lesson which many Heathen Philosophers had taught us long before, and which, though it might, perhaps, be called a moral Virtue, savoured but little of that sublime Christian-like Disposition, that vast Elevation of Thought, in Purity approaching to angelic Perfection, to be attained, expressed, and felt only by Grace. Those (he said) came nearer to the Scripture Meaning, who understood by it Candour, or the forming of a benevolent Opinion of our Brethren, and passing a favourable Judgment on their Actions; a Virtue much higher, and more extensive in its Nature, than a pitiful Distribution of Alms, which, though we would never so much prejudice, or even ruin our Families, could never reach many; whereas Charity, in the other and truer Sense, might be extended to all Mankind.'

He said, 'Considering who the Disciples were, it would be absurd to conceive the Doctrine of Generosity, or giving Alms, to have been preached to them. And, as we could not well imagine this Doctrine should be preached by its divine Author to Men who could not practise it, much less shall we think it understood so by those who can practise it, and do not.

'But though,' continued he, 'there is, I am afraid, little Merit in these Benefactions; there would, I must confess, be much Pleasure in them to a good Mind, if it was not abated by one Consideration. I mean, that we are liable to be imposed upon, and to confer our choicest Favours often on the Undeserving, as you must own was your Case in your Bounty to that worthless Fellow *Partridge*: For two or three such Examples must greatly lessen the inward Satisfaction, which a good Man would otherwise find in Generosity; nay, may even make him timorous in bestowing, lest he should be guilty of supporting Vice, and encouraging the Wicked; a Crime of a very black Dye, and for which it will by no means be a sufficient Excuse, that we have not actually intended such an Encouragement; unless we have used the utmost Caution in chusing the Objects of our Beneficence. A Consideration which, I make no Doubt, hath greatly checked the Liberality of many a worthy and pious Man.'

Mr. *Allworthy* answered,[1] 'He could not dispute with the Captain in the *Greek* Language, and therefore could say nothing as to the true Sense of the Word, which is translated *Charity*; but that he had always thought it was interpreted to consist in Action, and that giving Alms constituted at least one Branch of that Virtue.

'As to the meritorious Part,' he said, 'he readily agreed with the Captain; for where could be the Merit of barely discharging a Duty; which (he said) let the Word Charity have what Construction it would, it sufficiently appeared to be from the whole Tenor of the New Testament. And as he thought it an indispensable Duty, enjoined both by the Christian Law, and by the Law of Nature itself; so was it withal so pleasant, that if any Duty could be said to be its own Reward, or to pay us while we are discharging it, it was this.

[1] If Allworthy is unsure about the true signification of *agape*, his author had no such doubts. In *The Champion* (5 April 1740) Fielding offered his own interpretation of 1 Corinthians 13, declaring that the word *agape*, 'which some Versions, render Charity, is better rendered by others Love'. Like Allworthy, however, he further insists that this is above all an active virtue, 'not confined to our Wishes merely, but our Actions, under which Head I shall introduce Liberality. . . . By this Virtue, which is generally called Charity itself, (and perhaps it is the chief Part of it) is not meant the ostentatious giving a penny to a Beggar in the Street . . . as if Charity was Change for Sixpence, but the relieving the Wants and Sufferings of one another to the utmost of our Abilities. It is to be limited by our Power, I say, only.'

The arguments Allworthy adduces in defence of an active charity may be found in countless homilies by the latitudinarian divines. (See, for example, R. S. Crane, *ELH*, i [1934], esp. 208–13; and Battestin, *Moral Basis of Fielding's Art*, pp. 17–22.) But in the succeeding paragraphs his particular emphasis on the 'Duty' and 'Reward' of Beneficence, and his notion of the 'epicurean' pleasures which the charitable man enjoys, point to a specific source for the passage in Isaac Barrow's 'The Duty and Reward of Bounty to the Poor', a classic charity sermon of the period. Fielding's admiration for 'our favourite Dr. Barrow' (1630–77) is well attested by complimentary references in *Amelia* (1751; VI. vii; XII. v), where Booth is saved from infidelity by perusing Barrow's works, and in *The Covent-Garden Journal* (14 January, 24 March, 11 April, 16 May, 2 June, 4 November 1752), in which Barrow's sermon is frequently quoted. With Allworthy's view that charity consists principally in action, not, as Captain Blifil asserts, merely in 'Candour', compare Barrow: 'And of charity, works of bounty and mercy are both the chief instances, and the plainest signs: for whereas all charity doth consist either in mental desire, or in verbal signification, or in effectual performance of good to our neighbour; this last is the end, the completion, and the assurance of the rest. Good-will is indeed the root of charity; but that lies under ground, and out of sight; nor can we conclude its being or life without visible fruits of beneficence. Good words are at best but fair leaves thereof, such as may (and too often do) proceed from a weak and barren disposition of mind. . . . It is to decline spending their goods, or their pains, that men forge and feign; pretending to make up in wishing well, the defect of doing so, and paying words instead of things' (Sermon xxxi, *Works*, 5th ed. [1741], i. 308–9).

'To confess the Truth,' said he, 'there is one Degree of Generosity, (of Charity I would have called it) which seems to have some Shew of Merit, and that is, where from a Principle of Benevolence, and Christian Love, we bestow on another what we really want ourselves; where, in order to lessen the Distresses of another, we condescend to share some Part of them by giving what even our own Necessities cannot well spare. This is, I think, meritorious; but to relieve our Brethren only with our Superfluities; to be charitable (I must use the Word) rather at the Expence of our Coffers than ourselves; to save several Families from Misery rather than hang up an extraordinary Picture in our Houses, or gratify any other idle, ridiculous Vanity, this seems to be only being Christians, nay indeed, only being human Creatures. Nay, I will venture to go farther, it is being in some degree Epicures:[1] For what could the greatest Epicure wish rather than to eat with many Mouths instead of one; which I think may be predicated of any one who knows that the Bread of many is owing to his own Largesses.

'As to the Apprehension of bestowing Bounty on such as may hereafter prove unworthy Objects, because many have proved such; surely it can never deter a good Man from Generosity: I do not think a few or many Examples of Ingratitude can justify a Man's hardening his Heart against the Distresses of his Fellow-Creatures; nor do I believe it can ever have such Effect on a truly benevolent Mind. Nothing less than a Persuasion of universal Depravity can lock up the Charity of a good Man; and this Persuasion must lead him, I think, either into Atheism, or Enthusiasm;[2] but surely it is unfair to argue such universal

---

[1] Cf. Barrow, 'The Duty and Reward of Bounty to the Poor': Nature has 'made the communication of benefits to others to be accompanied with a very delicious relish upon the mind of him that practices it; nothing indeed carrying with it a more pure and savoury delight than beneficence. A man may be virtuously voluptuous, and a laudable epicure by doing much good; for to receive good, even in the judgment of *Epicurus* himself, (the great patron of pleasure) is no wise so pleasant as to do it' (Sermon xxxi, op. cit., i. 322). In *The Covent-Garden Journal* (11 April 1752) Fielding quotes this passage from 'my beloved Author Dr. Barrow'.

[2] The cynical view of human nature that Allworthy here rejects, Fielding attributed chiefly to the 'atheistical' philosophies of Hobbes and Mandeville, on the one hand (see below, p. 268, n. 2), and to Whitefield and the Calvinists, on the other. In his sermon, 'The Folly and Danger of being not righteous enough', Whitefield thus assured his congregation that 'There is no difference between you, by nature, and the greatest malefactor that ever was executed at *Tyburn*: the difference made, is all owing to the free, the rich, the undeserved grace of GOD'(Sermon ix, op. cit., v. 137). His insistence that 'we must feel that

Depravity from a few vicious Individuals; nor was this, I believe, ever done by a Man, who upon searching his own Mind found one certain Exception to the general Rule.' He then concluded by asking who that *Partridge* was whom he had called a worthless Fellow.

'I mean,' said the Captain, '*Partridge*, the Barber, the Schoolmaster, what do you call him? *Partridge*, the Father of the little Child which you found in your Bed.'

Mr. *Allworthy* exprest great Surprise at this Account, and the Captain as great at his Ignorance of it: For he said, he had known it above a Month, and at length recollected with much Difficulty that he was told it by Mrs. *Wilkins*.

Upon this, *Wilkins* was immediately summoned, who having confirmed what the Captain had said, was by Mr. *Allworthy*, by and with the Captain's Advice, dispatched to *Little Baddington* to inform herself of the Truth of the Fact: For the Captain exprest great Dislike at all hasty Proceedings in criminal Matters, and said he would by no means have Mr. *Allworthy* take any Resolution either to the Prejudice of the Child or its Father, before he was satisfied that the latter was guilty: For tho' he had privately satisfied himself of this from one of *Partridge's* Neighbours, yet he was too generous to give any such Evidence to Mr. *Allworthy*.

CHAPTER VI

The Trial of Partridge, *the Schoolmaster, for Incontinency; The Evidence of his Wife; A short Reflection on the Wisdom of our Law; with other grave Matters, which those will like best who understand them most.*

IT may be wondered that a Story so well known, and which had furnished so much Matter of Conversation, should never have been mentioned to Mr. *Allworthy* himself, who was perhaps the only Person in that Country who had never heard of it.

To account in some measure for this to the Reader, I think proper to inform him that there was no one in the Kingdom less

Spirit upon our hearts' encouraged displays of religious fervour amongst Whitefield's followers which his critics condemned as 'enthusiasm and madness' (ibid., v. 125).

interested in opposing that Doctrine concerning the Meaning of the Word Charity, which hath been seen in the preceding Chapter, than our good Man. Indeed, he was equally intitled to this Virtue in either Sense: For as no Man was ever more sensible of the Wants, or more ready to relieve the Distresses of others, so none could be more tender of their Characters, or slower to believe any thing to their Disadvantage.

Scandal, therefore, never found any Access to his Table: For as it hath been long since observed that you may know a Man by his Companions;[1] so I will venture to say, that by attending to the Conversation at a great Man's Table, you may satisfy yourself of his Religion, his Politics, his Taste, and indeed of his entire Disposition: For tho' a few odd Fellows will utter their own Sentiments in all Places, yet much the greater Part of Mankind have enough of the Courtier to accommodate their Conversation to the Taste and Inclination of their Superiors.

But to return to Mrs. *Wilkins*, who having executed her Commission with great Dispatch, tho' at fifteen Miles Distance, brought back such a Confirmation of the Schoolmaster's Guilt, that Mr. *Allworthy* determined to send for the Criminal, and examine him *viva voce*. Mr. *Partridge*, therefore, was summoned to attend, in order to his Defence (if he could make any) against this Accusation.

At the Time appointed, before Mr. *Allworthy* himself, at *Paradise-Hall*, came as well the said *Partridge*, with *Anne* his Wife, as Mrs. *Wilkins*, his Accuser.

And now Mr. *Allworthy* being seated in the Chair of Justice, Mr. *Partridge* was brought before him. Having heard his Accusation from the Mouth of Mrs. *Wilkins*, he pleaded, Not guilty, making many vehement Protestations of his Innocence.

Mrs. *Partridge* was then examined, who, after a modest Apology for being obliged to speak the Truth against her Husband, related all the Circumstances with which the Reader hath already been acquainted; and at last concluded with her Husband's Confession of his Guilt.

Whether she had forgiven him or no, I will not venture to determine: But it is certain, she was an unwilling Witness in this Cause, and it is probable, from certain other Reasons would never have been brought to depose as she did, had not Mrs. *Wilkins*,

[1] Cf. the proverb, 'Noscitur a socio', cited pp. 119, 542.

with great Art, fished all out of her, at her own House, and had she not indeed made Promises in Mr. *Allworthy's* Name, that the Punishment of her Husband should not be such as might any wise affect his Family.

Partridge still persisted in asserting his Innocence, tho' he admitted he had made the above-mentioned Confession; which he however endeavoured to account for, by protesting that he was forced into it by the continued Importunity she used, who vowed, that as she was sure of his Guilt, she would never leave tormenting him till he had owned it, and faithfully promised, that in such Case, she would never mention it to him more. Hence, he said, he had been induced falsely to confess himself guilty, tho' he was innocent; and that he believed he should have confest a Murder from the same Motive.

Mrs. *Partridge* could not bear this Imputation with Patience; and having no other Remedy, in the present Place but Tears, she called forth a plentiful Assistance from them, and then addressing herself to Mr. *Allworthy*, she said, (or rather cried) 'May it please your Worship, there never was any poor Woman so injured as I am by that base Man: For this is not the only Instance of his Falshood to me. No, may it please your Worship, he hath injured my Bed many's the good time and often. I could have put up with his Drunkenness and Neglect of his Business, if he had not broke one of the sacred *Commandiments*. Besides, if it had been out of Doors I had not mattered it so much; but with my own Servant, in my own House, under my own Roof; to defile my own chaste Bed, which to be sure he hath with his beastly stinking Whores. Yes, you Villain, you have defiled my own Bed, you have; and then you have charged me with *bullocking* you into owning the Truth. It is very likely, an't please your Worship, that I should *bullock* him.—I have Marks enow about my Body to shew of his Cruelty to me. If you had been a Man, you Villain, you would have scorned to injure a Woman in that Manner. But you an't half a Man, you know it.—Nor have you been half a Husband to me. You need run after Whores, you need, when I'm sure——And since he provokes me, I am ready, an't please your Worship, to take my bodily Oath, that I found them a-bed together. What, you have forgot, I suppose, when you beat me into a Fit, and made the Blood run down my Forehead, because I only civilly taxed you with your Adultery! but I can prove it by all my Neighbours. You have almost broke my Heart, you have, you have.'

Here Mr. *Allworthy* interrupted, and begged her to be pacified, promising her that she should have Justice; then turning to *Partridge*, who stood aghast, one half of his Wits being hurried away by Surprise and the other half by Fear, he said, he was sorry to see there was so wicked a Man in the World. He assured him, that his prevaricating and lying backward and forward was a great Aggravation of his Guilt: For which, the only Attonement he could make was by Confession and Repentance. He exhorted him, therefore, to begin by immediately confessing the Fact, and not to persist in denying what was so plainly proved against him, even by his own Wife.

Here, Reader, I beg your Patience a Moment, while I make a just Compliment to the great Wisdom and Sagacity of our Law, which refuses to admit the Evidence of a Wife for or against her Husband. This, says a certain learned Author,[1] who, I believe, was never quoted before in any but a Law-book, would be the Means of creating an eternal Dissention between them. It would, indeed, be the Means of much Perjury, and of much Whipping, Fining, Imprisoning, Transporting, and Hanging.

Partridge stood a while silent, till being bid to speak, he said, he had already spoken the Truth, and appealed to Heaven for his Innocence, and lastly, to the Girl herself, whom he desired his Worship immediately to send for; for he was ignorant, or at least pretended to be so, that she had left that Part of the Country.

Mr. *Allworthy*, whose natural Love of Justice, joined to his Coolness of Temper, made him always a most patient Magistrate in hearing all the Witnesses which an accused Person could produce in his Defence, agreed to defer his final Determination of this Matter, till the Arrival of *Jenny*, for whom he immediately dispatched a Messenger; and then having recommended Peace between *Partridge* and his Wife (tho' he addressed himself chiefly to the wrong Person) he appointed them to attend again the third Day: For he had sent *Jenny* a whole Day's Journey from his own House.

[1] Sir Edward Coke (1552–1634) in his *Commentary upon Littleton*, I. i: 'It hath been resolved by the Justices, That a Wife cannot be produced either against or for her Husband, *quia sunt duae animae in una carne*; and it might be a Cause of implacable Discord and Dissension between the Husband and the Wife, and a Means of great Inconvenience' (11th ed. [1719], p. 6).

At the appointed Time the Parties all assembled, when the Messenger returning brought word, that *Jenny* was not to be found: For that she had left her Habitation a few Days before, in company with a recruiting Officer.

Mr. *Allworthy* then declared, that the Evidence of such a Slut as she appeared to be, would have deserved no Credit; but he said he could not help thinking that had she been present, and would have declared the Truth, she must have confirmed what so many Circumstances, together with his own Confession, and the Declaration of his Wife, that she had caught her Husband in the Fact, did sufficiently prove. He therefore once more exhorted *Partridge* to confess; but he still avowing his Innocence, Mr. *Allworthy* declared himself satisfied of his Guilt, and that he was too bad a Man to receive any Encouragement from him. He therefore deprived him of his Annuity, and recommended Repentance to him, on account of another World, and Industry to maintain himself and his Wife in this.

There were not, perhaps, many more unhappy Persons, than poor *Partridge*. He had lost the best Part of his Income by the Evidence of his Wife, and yet was daily upbraided by her for having, among other Things, been the Occasion of depriving her of that Benefit; but such was his Fortune, and he was obliged to submit to it.

Tho' I called him, poor *Partridge*, in the last Paragraph, I would have the Reader rather impute that Epithet to the Compassion in my Temper, than conceive it to be any Declaration of his Innocence. Whether he was innocent or not, will perhaps appear hereafter; but if the Historic-Muse[1] hath entrusted me with any Secrets, I will by no means be guilty of discovering them till she shall give me leave.

Here therefore, the Reader must suspend his Curiosity. Certain it is, that whatever was the Truth of the Case, there was Evidence more than sufficient to convict him before *Allworthy*; indeed much less would have satisfied a Bench of Justices on an Order of Bastardy;[2] and yet, notwithstanding the Positiveness of Mrs. *Partridge*, who would have taken the Sacrament upon the Matter,

---

[1] Clio.

[2] By order of two justices of the parish (one being of the quorum), the mother and father of a bastard child could be punished and compelled to provide for the care of the child, which would otherwise become chargeable to the parish. (See Dalton, *The Country Justice* [1746], p. 33.)

there is a Possibility that the Schoolmaster was entirely innocent: For tho' it appeared clear, on comparing the Time when *Jenny* departed from *Little Baddington*, with that of her Delivery, that she had there conceived this Infant, yet it by no means followed, of Necessity, that *Partridge* must have been its Father: For, to omit other Particulars, there was in the same House a Lad near Eighteen, between whom, and *Jenny*, there had subsisted sufficient Intimacy to found a reasonable Suspicion; and yet, so blind is Jealousy, this Circumstance never once entered into the Head of the enraged Wife.

Whether *Partridge* repented or not, according to Mr. *Allworthy's* Advice, is not so apparent. Certain it is, that his Wife repented heartily of the Evidence she had given against him; especially when she found Mrs. *Deborah* had deceived her, and refused to make any Application to Mr. *Allworthy* on her Behalf. She had, however, somewhat better Success with Mrs. *Blifil*, who was, as the Reader must have perceived, a much better-tempered Woman; and very kindly undertook to solicit her Brother to restore the Annuity. In which, tho' Good-nature might have some Share, yet a stronger and more natural Motive will appear in the next Chapter.

These Solicitations were nevertheless unsuccessful: For tho' Mr. *Allworthy* did not think, with some late Writers,[1] that Mercy consists only in punishing Offenders; yet he was as far from thinking that it is proper to this excellent Quality to pardon great Criminals wantonly, without any Reason whatever.[2] Any Doubtfulness of the Fact, or any Circumstance of Mitigation, was never disregarded; but the Petitions of an Offender, or the Inter-

---

[1] In the summer of 1746, the question of whether or not mercy should be shown to the defeated rebels occasioned a heated controversy in the newspapers which may be followed in the pages of *The Gentleman's Magazine*, xvi (June–October). A certain Andrew Horne was most vehement in urging the severest punishment (see *The General Evening-Post*, 22 July and 21 August 1746). Others, however, advocated clemency and applauded the king's decision to pardon the Earl of Cromarty, one of three Jacobite lords sentenced to be executed on 18 August.

[2] Cf. Fielding in *An Enquiry into the Causes of the Late Increase of Robbers* (1751), section x: 'To speak out fairly and honestly, tho' Mercy may appear more amiable in a Magistrate, Severity is a more wholesome Virtue; nay Severity to an Individual may, perhaps, be in the End the greatest Mercy, not only to the Public in general . . . but to many Individuals.' When confronted with villainy, Fielding continues, 'the Passions of the Man are to give Way to the Principles of the Magistrate. Those may lament the Criminal, but these must condemn him.' Contrast, in different circumstances, Jones's leniency towards the highwayman (XII. xiv) with Allworthy's sternness towards Black George (XVIII. xi).

cessions of others, did not in the least affect him. In a word, he never pardoned, because the Offender himself, or his Friends, were unwilling that he should be punished.

Partridge and his Wife were therefore both obliged to submit to their Fate; which was indeed severe enough: For so far was he from doubling his Industry on the account of his lessened Income, that he did in a manner abandon himself to despair; and as he was by Nature indolent, that Vice now increased upon him, by which means he lost the little School he had; so that neither his Wife nor himself would have had any Bread to eat, had not the Charity of some good Christian interposed, and provided them with what was just sufficient for their Sustenance.

As this Support was conveyed to them by an unknown Hand, they imagined, and so, I doubt not, will the Reader, that Mr. *Allworthy* himself was their secret Benefactor; who, though he would not openly encourage Vice, could yet privately relieve the Distresses of the Vicious themselves, when these became too exquisite and disproportionate to their Demerit. In which Light, their Wretchedness appeared now to Fortune herself; for she at length took pity on this miserable Couple, and considerably lessened the wretched State of *Partridge*, by putting a final end to that of his Wife, who soon after caught the Small-Pox, and died.

The Justice which Mr. *Allworthy* had executed on *Partridge*, at first met with universal Approbation; but no sooner had he felt its Consequences, than his Neighbours began to relent, and to compassionate his Case; and presently after, to blame that as Rigour and Severity, which they before called Justice. They now exclaimed against punishing in cold Blood, and sang forth the Praises of Mercy and Forgiveness.

These Cries were considerably increased by the Death of Mrs. *Partridge*, which, tho' owing to the Distemper above mentioned which is no Consequence of Poverty or Distress, many were not ashamed to impute to Mr. *Allworthy's* Severity, or, as they now termed it, Cruelty.

Partridge, having now lost his Wife, his School, and his Annuity, and the unknown Person having now discontinued the last-mentioned Charity, resolved to change the Scene, and left the Country, where he was in Danger of starving with the universal Compassion of all his Neighbours.

CHAPTER VII

A short Sketch of that Felicity which prudent Couples may extract from Hatred; with a short Apology for those People who overlook Imperfections in their Friends.

THO' the Captain had effectually demolished poor *Partridge*, yet had he not reaped the Harvest he hoped for, which was to turn the Foundling out of Mr. *Allworthy's* House.

On the contrary, that Gentleman grew every Day fonder of little *Tommy*, as if he intended to counterbalance his Severity to the Father with extraordinary Fondness and Affection towards the Son.

This a good deal soured the Captain's Temper, as did all the other daily Instances of Mr. *Allworthy's* Generosity: For he looked on all such Largesses to be Diminutions of his own Wealth.

In this, we have said, he did not agree with his Wife; nor indeed, in any thing else: For tho' an Affection placed on the Understanding is by many wise Persons thought much more durable than that which is founded on Beauty, yet it happened otherwise in the present Case. Nay, the Understandings of this Couple were their principal Bone of Contention, and one great Cause of many Quarrels which from time to time arose between them; and which at last ended, on the Side of the Lady, in a sovereign Contempt for her Husband, and on the Husband's, in an utter Abhorrence of his Wife.

As these had both exercised their Talents chiefly in the Study of Divinity, this was, from their first Acquaintance, the most common Topic of Conversation between them. The Captain, like a well-bred Man, had, before Marriage, always given up his Opinion to that of the Lady; and this, not in the clumsy, aukward Manner of a conceited Blockhead, who, while he civilly yields to a Superiour in an Argument, is desirous of being still known to think himself in the Right. The Captain, on the contrary, tho' one of the proudest Fellows in the World, so absolutely yielded the Victory to his Antagonist, that she, who had not the least Doubt of his Sincerity, retired always from the Dispute with an Admiration of her own Understanding, and a Love for his.

But tho' this Complaisance to one whom the Captain thoroughly despised, was not so uneasy to him, as it would have been, had any Hopes of Preferment made it necessary to shew the same Submission to a *Hoadley*,[1] or to some other of great Reputation in the Science, yet even this cost him too much to be endured without some Motive. Matrimony, therefore, having removed all such Motives, he grew weary of this Condescention, and began to treat the Opinions of his Wife with that Haughtiness and Insolence, which none but those who deserve some Contempt themselves can bestow, and those only who deserve no Contempt can bear.

When the first Torrent of Tenderness was over, and when in the calm and long Interval between the Fits, Reason began to open the Eyes of the Lady, and she saw this Alteration of Behaviour in the Captain, who at length answered all her Arguments only with Pish and Pshaw, she was far from enduring the Indignity with a tame Submission. Indeed, it at first so highly provoked her, that it might have produced some tragical Event, had it not taken a more harmless Turn, by filling her with the utmost Contempt for her Husband's Understanding, which somewhat qualified her Hatred towards him; tho' of this likewise, she had a pretty moderate Share.

The Captain's Hatred to her was of a purer Kind: For as to any Imperfections in her Knowledge or Understanding, he no more despised her for them than for her not being six Feet high. In his Opinion of the female Sex, he exceeded the Moroseness of *Aristotle* himself.[2] He looked on a Woman as on an Animal of domestic Use, of somewhat higher Consideration than a Cat, since her Offices were of rather more Importance; but the Difference between these two, was in his Estimation so small, that in his Marriage contracted with Mr. *Allworthy's* Lands and

---

[1] Benjamin Hoadly (1676–1761), Bishop of Winchester and the chief contemporary spokesman for the latitudinarians. Hoadly's famous sermon, 'The Nature of the Kingdom, or the Church, of Christ' (1717), began the Bangorian controversy by asserting that, since religion was a matter of sincerity and not of external forms of worship, the true Church was the whole community of Christians. In 1735 Hoadly's *Plain Account of the Nature and End of the Sacrament of the Lord's Supper*—a rational, mystery-dispelling analysis of the eucharist —involved him in another dispute with a host of more strictly orthodox clergymen. In *Joseph Andrews* (1742; I. xvii) Parson Adams praises this work, whose author Fielding himself had commended in *Of True Greatness* (1741) as the exemplary divine. For Fielding's use of Hoadly's sermon against the Jacobites, see below, p. 671, n. 1.

[2] Several passages in the *Politics* attest to Aristotle's belief that, with respect to virtue, women were by nature inferior to men (e.g., I. v and II. vi).

Tenements, it would have been pretty equal which of them he had taken into the Bargain. And yet so tender was his Pride, that it felt the Contempt which his Wife now began to express towards him; and this, added to the Surfeit he had before taken of her Love, created in him a Degree of Disgust and Abhorrence, perhaps hardly to be exceeded.

One Situation only of the married State is excluded from Pleasure; and that is, a State of Indifference; but as many of my Readers, I hope, know what an exquisite Delight there is in conveying Pleasure to a beloved Object, so some few, I am afraid, may have experienced the Satisfaction of tormenting one we hate. It is, I apprehend, to come at this latter Pleasure, that we see both Sexes often give up that Ease in Marriage, which they might otherwise possess, tho' their Mate was never so disagreeable to them. Hence the Wife often puts on Fits of Love and Jealousy, nay, even denies herself any Pleasure, to disturb and prevent those of her Husband; and he again, in return, puts frequent Restraints on himself, and stays at home in Company which he dislikes, in order to confine his Wife to what she equally detests. Hence too must flow those Tears[1] which a Widow sometimes so plentifully sheds over the Ashes of a Husband with whom she led a Life of constant Disquiet and Turbulency, and whom now she can never hope to torment any more.

But if ever any Couple enjoyed this Pleasure, it was at present experienced by the Captain and his Lady. It was always a sufficient Reason to either of them to be obstinate in any Opinion, that the other had previously asserted the contrary. If the one proposed any Amusement, the other constantly objected to it. They never loved or hated, commended or abused the same Person. And for this Reason, as the Captain looked with an evil Eye on the little Foundling, his Wife began now to caress it almost equally with her own Child.

The Reader will be apt to conceive, that this Behaviour between the Husband and Wife did not greatly contribute to Mr. *Allworthy's* Repose, as it tended so little to that serene Happiness which he had designed for all three, from this Alliance; but the Truth is, though he might be a little disappointed in his sanguine Expectations, yet he was far from being acquainted with the whole Matter: For, as the Captain was, from certain obvious

[1] See below, p. 415, n. 3.

Reasons, much on his Guard before him, the Lady was obliged, for fear of her Brother's Displeasure, to pursue the same Conduct. In fact, it is possible for a third Person to be very intimate, nay even to live long in the same House, with a married Couple, who have any tolerable Discretion, and not even guess at the sour Sentiments which they bear to each other: For though the whole Day may be sometimes too short for Hatred, as well as for Love; yet the many Hours which they naturally spend together, apart from all Observers, furnish People of tolerable Moderation with such ample Opportunity for the Enjoyment of either Passion, that, if they love, they can support being a few Hours in Company, without toying, or if they hate, without spitting in each other's Faces.

It is possible, however, that Mr. *Allworthy* saw enough to render him a little uneasy; for we are not always to conclude, that a wise Man is not hurt, because he doth not cry out and lament himself, like those of a childish or effeminate Temper. But indeed it is possible he might see some Faults in the Captain, without any Uneasiness at all: For Men of true Wisdom and Goodness are contented to take Persons and Things as they are, without complaining of their Imperfections, or attempting to amend them. They can see a Fault in a Friend, a Relation, or an Acquaintance, without ever mentioning it to the Parties themselves, or to any others; and this often without lessening their Affection. Indeed unless great Discernment be tempered with this overlooking Disposition, we ought never to contract Friendship but with a Degree of Folly which we can deceive: For I hope my Friends will pardon me, when I declare I know none of them without a Fault; and I should be sorry if I could imagine I had any Friend who could not see mine. Forgiveness, of this Kind, we give and demand in Turn. It is an Exercise of Friendship, and, perhaps, none of the least pleasant. And this Forgiveness we must bestow, without Desire of Amendment. There is, perhaps, no surer Mark of Folly, than an Attempt to correct the natural Infirmities of those we love. The finest Composition of human Nature, as well as the finest China, may have a Flaw in it; and this, I am afraid, in either Case, is equally incurable; though, nevertheless, the Pattern may remain of the highest Value.

Upon the whole then, Mr. *Allworthy* certainly saw some Imperfections in the Captain; but, as this was a very artful Man,

and eternally upon his Guard before him, these appeared to him
no more than Blemishes in a good Character; which his Goodness
made him overlook, and his Wisdom prevented him from discovering to the Captain himself. Very different would have been
his Sentiments, had he discovered the whole; which, perhaps,
would, in Time, have been the Case, had the Husband and Wife
long continued this Kind of Behaviour to each other; but this
kind Fortune took effectual Means to prevent, by forcing the
Captain to do that which rendered him again dear to his Wife,
and restored all her Tenderness and Affection towards him.

CHAPTER VIII

*A Receipt to regain the lost Affections of a Wife, which hath never
been known to fail in the most desperate Cases.*

THE Captain was made large Amends for the unpleasant
Minutes which he passed in the Conversation of his Wife
(and which were as few as he could contrive to make them) by
the pleasant Meditations he enjoyed when alone.

These Meditations were entirely employed on Mr. *Allworthy's*
Fortune; for first, he exercised much Thought in calculating, as
well as he could, the exact Value of the whole; which Calculations he often saw Occasion to alter in his own Favour: And
secondly, and chiefly, he pleased himself with intended Alterations in the House and Gardens, and in projecting many other
Schemes, as well for Improvement of the Estate, as of the Grandeur of the Place. For this Purpose he applied himself to the
Studies of Architecture and Gardening, and read over many
Books on both these Subjects; for these Sciences, indeed, employed his whole Time, and formed his only Amusement. He
at last completed a most excellent Plan; and very sorry we are,
that it is not in our Power to present it to our Reader, since even
the Luxury of the present Age, I believe, would hardly match
it. It had, indeed, in a superlative Degree, the two principal
Ingredients which serve to recommend all great and noble
Designs of this Nature: For it required an immoderate Expence
to execute, and a vast Length of Time to bring it to any Sort of
Perfection. The former of these, the immense Wealth of which the

Captain supposed Mr. *Allworthy* possessed, and which he thought himself sure of inheriting, promised very effectually to supply; and the latter, the Soundness of his own Constitution, and his Time of Life, which was only what is called Middle Age, removed all Apprehension of his not living to accomplish.

Nothing was wanting to enable him to enter upon the immediate Execution of this Plan, but the Death of Mr. *Allworthy*; in calculating which he had employed much of his own Algebra; besides purchasing every Book extant that treats of the Value of Lives, Reversions,[1] &c. From all which, he satisfied himself, that as he had every Day a Chance of this happening, so had he more than an even Chance of its happening within a few Years.

But while the Captain was one Day busied in deep Contemplations of this Kind, one of the most unlucky, as well as unseasonable Accidents, happened to him. The utmost Malice of Fortune could indeed have contrived nothing so cruel, so mal-a-propos, so absolutely destructive to all his Schemes. In short, not to keep the Reader in long Suspence, just at the very Instant when his Heart was exulting in Meditations on the Happiness which would accrue to him by Mr. *Allworthy's* Death, he himself—died of an Apoplexy.

This unfortunately befel the Captain as he was taking his Evening Walk by himself, so that no Body was present to lend him any Assistance, if indeed any Assistance could have preserved him. He took, therefore, Measure of that Proportion of Soil, which was now become adequate to all his future Purposes, and he lay dead on the Ground, a great (though not a living) Example of the Truth of that Observation of *Horace*:[2]

> Tu secanda marmora
> Locas sub ipsum funus: et sepulchri
> Immemor, struis domos.

Which Sentiment, I shall thus give to the *English* Reader: 'You provide the noblest Materials for Building, when a Pick-ax and a Spade are only necessary; and build Houses of five hundred by a hundred Feet, forgetting that of six by two.'

[1] See below, p. 748, n. 1; also p. 278. 6.

[2] *Odes*, II. xviii. 17–19: 'yet thou on the grave's verge dost contract for the cutting of marble slabs, and, forgetful of the tomb, dost rear a palace' (trans. C. E. Bennett, Loeb Classical Library, 1914).

CHAPTER IX

A Proof of the Infallibility of the foregoing Receipt, in the Lamenta-
tions of the Widow; with other suitable Decorations of Death, such as
Physicians, &c. and an Epitaph in the true Stile.

MR. *Allworthy*, his Sister, and another Lady, were assembled
at the accustomed Hour in the Supper Room, where having
waited a considerable Time longer than usual, Mr. *Allworthy*
first declared he began to grow uneasy at the Captain's Stay (for
he was always most punctual at his Meals,) and gave Orders that
the Bell should be rung without the Doors, and especially towards
those Walks which the Captain was wont to use.

All these Summons proving ineffectual, (for the Captain had,
by perverse Accident, betaken himself to a new Walk that Evening) Mrs. *Blifil* declared she was seriously frightned. Upon which
the other Lady, who was one of her most intimate Acquaintance,
and who well knew the true State of her Affections, endeavoured
all she could to pacify her; telling her—To be sure she could not
help being uneasy; but that she should hope the best. That,
perhaps, the Sweetness of the Evening had enticed the Captain
to go farther than his usual Walk, or he might be detained at some
Neighbour's. Mrs. *Blifil* answered, No; she was sure some Accident had befallen him; for that he would never stay out without
sending her Word, as he must know how uneasy it would make
her. The other Lady, having no other Arguments to use, betook
herself to the Entreaties usual on such Occasions, and begged
her not to frighten herself, for it might be of very ill Consequence
to her own Health; and, filling out a very large Glass of Wine,
advised, and at last prevailed with, her to drink it.

Mr. *Allworthy* now returned into the Parlour; for he had been
himself in Search after the Captain. His Countenance sufficiently
shewed the Consternation he was under, which indeed had a good
deal deprived him of Speech; but as Grief operates variously on
different Minds, so the same Apprehension which depressed his
Voice, elevated that of Mrs. *Blifil*. She now began to bewail
herself in very bitter Terms, and Floods of Tears accompanied
her Lamentations, which the Lady, her Companion, declared
she could not blame; but at the same Time dissuaded her from
indulging; attempting to moderate the Grief of her Friend, by

philosophical Observations on the many Disappointments to which human Life is daily subject, which, she said, was a sufficient Consideration to fortify our Minds against any Accidents, how sudden or terrible soever. She said, her Brother's Example ought to teach her Patience, who, though indeed he could not be supposed as much concerned as herself, yet was doubtless very uneasy, though his Resignation to the Divine Will had restrained his Grief within due Bounds.

'Mention not my Brother,' said Mrs. *Blifil,* 'I alone am the Object of your Pity. What are the Terrors of Friendship to what a Wife feels on these Occasions? O he is lost! Somebody hath murdered him—I shall never see him more.'——Here a Torrent of Tears had the same Consequence with what the Suppression had occasioned to Mr. *Allworthy,* and she remained silent.

At this Interval, a Servant came running in, out of Breath, and cried out, the Captain was found; and, before he could proceed farther, he was followed by two more, bearing the dead Body between them.

Here the curious Reader may observe another Diversity in the Operations of Grief: For as Mr. *Allworthy* had been before silent, from the same Cause which had made his Sister vociferous; so did the present Sight, which drew Tears from the Gentleman, put an entire Stop to those of the Lady; who first gave a violent Scream, and presently after fell into a Fit.

The Room was soon full of Servants, some of whom, with the Lady visitant, were employed in Care of the Wife, and others, with Mr. *Allworthy,* assisted in carrying off the Captain to a warm Bed, where every Method was tried, in order to restore him to Life.

And glad should we be, could we inform the Reader that both these Bodies had been attended with equal Success; for those who undertook the Care of the Lady, succeeded so well, that after the Fit had continued a decent Time, she again revived, to their great Satisfaction; but as to the Captain, all Experiments of bleeding, chafing, dropping, *&c.* proved ineffectual. Death, that inexorable Judge, had passed Sentence on him, and refused to grant him a Reprieve, though two Doctors who arrived, and were fee'd at one and the same Instant, were his Counsel.

These two Doctors, whom, to avoid any malicious Applications, we shall distinguish by the Names of Dr. *Y*. and Dr. *Z*., having felt his Pulse; to wit, Dr. *Y*. his right Arm, and Dr. *Z*. his left, both agreed that he was absolutely dead; but as to the Distemper, or Cause of his Death, they differed, Dr. *Y*. holding that he had died of an Apoplexy, and Dr. *Z*. of an Epilepsy.

Hence arose a Dispute between the learned Men, in which each delivered the Reasons of their several Opinions. These were of such equal Force, that they served both to confirm either Doctor in his own Sentiments, and made not the least Impression on his Adversary.

To say the Truth, every Physician, almost, hath his favourite Disease, to which he ascribes all the Victories obtained over human Nature. The Gout, the Rheumatism, the Stone, the Gravel, and the Consumption, have all their several Patrons in the Faculty; and none more than the nervous Fever, or the Fever on the Spirits.[1] And here we may account for those Disagreements in Opinion, concerning the Cause of a Patient's Death; which sometimes occur between the most learned of the College;[2] and which have greatly surprized that Part of the World who have been ignorant of the Fact we have above asserted.

The Reader may, perhaps, be surprized, that instead of en-

[1] Otherwise known as the vapours, hypo, or the spleen, this was a hysteric disorder to which 'weak and tender Women' were most susceptible. One prominent 'Patron', as Fielding says, of this disease was Sir Richard Manningham, who in November 1745 published a popular treatise on the subject, entitled *The Symptoms, Nature, Causes, and Cure of the Febricula, or Little Fever: Commonly Called the Nervous or Hysteric Fever; the Fever on the Spirits; Vapours, Hypo, or Spleen*. The narrator of *A Journey from This World to the Next* (1743) believes he has died from this malady, but he searches in vain for it in the City of Diseases (I. iii). In *Amelia* (1751; III. vii), however, Fielding seems to have considered the distemper very real indeed, for his heroine suffers from it. See also *Tom Jones*, p. 579.

[2] The Royal College of Physicians, founded in 1518 and situated during the eighteenth century in Warwick Lane. Until 1858 no one except graduates of Oxford or Cambridge could legally practise medicine without a licence from the College.

Throughout this passage Fielding's amusement at learned doctors who dispute the cause of a patient's death recalls his earlier satire, *The Charge to the Jury: or, The Sum of the Evidence, on the Trial of A. B. C. D. and E. F. All M. D. for the Death of one Robert at Orfud, at a Special Commission of Oyer and Terminer held at Justice-College, in W[arwi]ck-Lane* (2 July 1745). After Walpole's death on 18 March 1745 the physicians who had attended him became embroiled in an unseemly public debate, defending their methods of treating the disease that killed him. On 10 April 1745 Fielding's friend John Ranby began the controversy by publishing his *Narrative* of Walpole's last illness. Ranby, who had correctly diagnosed the case, criticized his colleagues Drs. Jurin, Hulse, and Crowe for their incompetency and their reliance upon such questionable nostrums as the 'Lithontriptic Lixivium' prescribed by Jurin. For complimentary allusions to Ranby in *Tom Jones*, see below, pp. 468, 911.

deavouring to revive the Patient, the learned Gentlemen should fall immediately into a Dispute on the Occasion of his Death; but in reality, all such Experiments had been made before their Arrival: For the Captain was put into a warm Bed, had his Veins scarified, his Forehead chafed, and all Sorts of strong Drops applied to his Lips and his Nostrils.

The Physicians, therefore, finding themselves anticipated in every thing they ordered, were at a Loss how to employ that Portion of Time which it is usual and decent to remain for their Fee, and were therefore necessitated to find some Subject or other for Discourse; and what could more naturally present itself than that before-mentioned?

Our Doctors were about to take their Leave, when Mr. *Allworthy*, having given over the Captain, and acquiesced in the divine Will, began to enquire after his Sister, whom he desired them to visit before their Departure.

This Lady was now recovered of her Fit, and, to use the common Phrase, as well as could be expected for one in her Condition. The Doctors, therefore, all previous Ceremonies being complied with, as this was a new Patient, attended, according to Desire, and laid hold on each of her Hands, as they had before done on those of the Corpse.

The Case of the Lady was in the other Extreme from that of her Husband; for, as he was past all the Assistance of Physic, so, in reality, she required none.

There is nothing more unjust, than the vulgar Opinion by which Physicians are misrepresented, as Friends to Death. On the contrary, I believe, if the Number of those who recover by Physic could be opposed to that of the Martyrs to it, the former would rather exceed the latter. Nay, some are so cautious on this Head, that, to avoid a Possibility of killing the Patient, they abstain from all Methods of curing, and prescribe nothing but what can neither do good nor harm. I have heard some of these, with great Gravity, deliver it as a Maxim, That Nature should be left to do her own Work, while the Physician stands by, as it were to clap her on the Back, and encourage her when she doth well.

So little then did our Doctors delight in Death, that they discharged the Corpse after a single Fee; but they were not so disgusted with their living Patient; concerning whose Case they immediately agreed, and fell to prescribing with great Diligence.

Whether, as the Lady had at first persuaded her Physicians to believe her ill, they had now, in return, persuaded her to believe herself so, I will not determine; but she continued a whole Month with all the Decorations of Sickness. During this Time she was visited by Physicians, attended by Nurses, and received constant Messages from her Acquaintance, to enquire after her Health.

At length, the decent Time for Sickness and immoderate Grief being expired, the Doctors were discharged, and the Lady began to see Company; being altered only from what she was before by that Colour of Sadness in which she had dressed her Person and Countenance.

The Captain was now interred, and might, perhaps, have already made a large Progress towards Oblivion, had not the Friendship of Mr. *Allworthy* taken Care to preserve his Memory, by the following Epitaph, which was written by a Man of as great Genius as Integrity, and one who perfectly well knew the Captain.[1]

Here lies,
In Expectation of a joyful Rising,
The Body of
Captain JOHN BLIFIL.
LONDON
had the Honour of his Birth,
OXFORD
of his Education.
His Parts
were an Honour to his Profession
and to his Country.
His Life to his Religion
and human Nature.
He was a dutiful Son,
a tender Husband,

[1] With Fielding's opinion of '*the true Stile*' of epitaphs (as he ironically remarks in the heading to this chapter), compare Pope's definition in *The Dunciad* (1729), I. 41: 'Sepulchral lyes our holy walls to grace.' Epitaphs, Pope later observed in a letter to Ralph Allen (30 April 1736), were synonymous with 'flatteries and false history'. The true nature of this abused genre was the subject of an essay by Samuel Johnson in *The Gentleman's Magazine*, x (December 1740), 593–6. In the notes to a satiric elegy published not long after *Tom Jones*, a pseudonymous Oxonian expressed his delight in Fielding's mock-epitaph for Captain Blifil, wherein 'this prevailing Folly' is ridiculed 'with great Humour' (see 'Jo: Freinshemius', *Threnodia: or, An Elegy on the unexpected and unlamented Death of the M[aster] of B[alliol]* [Oxford, 1753], pp. 13–14).

an affectionate Father,
a most kind Brother,
a sincere Friend,
a devout Christian,
and a good Man.
His inconsolable Widow
hath erected this Stone,
The Monument of
His Virtues,
and Her Affection.

BOOK III

Containing the most memorable Transactions which passed in the Family of Mr. Allworthy, *from the Time when* Tommy Jones *arrived at the Age of Fourteen, till he attained the Age of Nineteen. In this Book the Reader may pick up some Hints concerning the Education of Children.*

CHAPTER I

Containing little or nothing.

THE Reader will be pleased to remember, that at the Beginning of the Second Book of this History, we gave him a Hint of our Intention to pass over several large Periods of Time, in which nothing happened worthy of being recorded in a Chronicle of this Kind.

In so doing, we do not only consult our own Dignity and Ease; but the Good and Advantage of the Reader: For besides, that by these Means we prevent him from throwing away his Time in reading either without Pleasure or Emolument, we give him at all such Seasons an Opportunity of employing that wonderful Sagacity, of which he is Master, by filling up these vacant Spaces of Time with his own Conjectures; for which Purpose, we have taken care to qualify him in the preceding Pages.

For Instance, what Reader but knows that Mr. *Allworthy* felt at first for the Loss of his Friend,[1] those Emotions of Grief, which on such Occasions enter into all Men whose Hearts are not composed of Flint, or their Heads of as solid Materials? Again, what Reader doth not know that Philosophy and Religion, in time, moderated, and at last extinguished this Grief? The former of these, teaching the Folly and Vanity of it, and the latter, correcting it, as unlawful, and at the same time

---

[1] Allworthy's grief on this occasion and his eventual triumph over it by attending to the precepts of philosophy and religion recall Fielding's consolatory essay, 'Of the Remedy of Affliction for the Loss of our Friends' (1743), written upon the death of his daughter Charlotte in March 1742. For a comprehensive discussion of this work and of its place in the Christian humanist tradition of the *consolatio*, see Miller, *Essays on Fielding's 'Miscellanies'*, pp. 228–71.

assuaging it by raising future Hopes and Assurances which enable a strong and religious Mind to take leave of a Friend on his Death-bed with little less Indifference than if he was preparing for a long Journey;[1] and indeed with little less Hope of seeing him again.

Nor can the judicious Reader be at a greater Loss on Account of Mrs. *Bridget Blifil*, who, he may be assured, conducted her-self through the whole Season in which Grief is to make its Appearance on the Outside of the Body, with the strictest Regard to all the Rules of Custom and Decency, suiting the Alterations of her Countenance to the several Alterations of her Habit: For as this changed from Weeds to Black, from Black to Grey, from Grey to White, so did her Countenance change from Dismal to Sorrowful, from Sorrowful to Sad, and from Sad to Serious, till the Day came in which she was allowed to return to her former Serenity.

We have mentioned these two as Examples only of the Task which may be imposed on Readers of the lowest Class. Much higher and harder Exercises of Judgment and Penetration may reasonably be expected from the upper Graduates in Criticism. Many notable Discoveries will, I doubt not, be made by such, of the Transactions which happened in the Family of our worthy Man, during all the Years which we have thought proper to pass over: For tho' nothing worthy of a Place in this History occurred within that Period; yet did several Incidents happen, of equal Importance with those reported by the daily and weekly Historians of the Age, in reading which, great Numbers of Persons consume a considerable Part of their Time, very little, I am afraid, to their Emolument. Now, in the Conjectures here proposed, some of the most excellent Faculties of the Mind may be employed to much Advantage, since it is a more useful Capacity to be able to foretel the Actions of Men in any Circumstance from their Characters; than to judge of their Characters from their Actions.[2] The former, I own, requires the greater Penetration; but may be accomplished by true Sagacity, with no less Certainty than the latter.

[1] See above, p. 35, n. 1.

[2] Cf. Fielding's 'Essay on the Knowledge of the Characters of Men' (1743) where, however, he warns that a man's actions are 'a more infallible Guide' to his character than his appearance or reputation.

As we are sensible that much the greatest Part of our Readers are very eminently possessed of this Quality, we have left them a Space of twelve Years to exert it in; and shall now bring forth our Heroe, at about fourteen Years of Age, not questioning that many have been long impatient to be introduced to his Acquaintance.

CHAPTER II

The Heroe of this great History appears with very bad Omens. A little Tale, of so LOW *a Kind, that some may think it not worth their Notice. A Word or two concerning a Squire, and more relating to a Game-keeper, and a Schoolmaster.*

AS we determined when we first sat down to write this History, to flatter no Man; but to guide our Pen throughout by the Directions of Truth, we are obliged to bring our Heroe on the Stage in a much more disadvantageous Manner than we could wish; and to declare honestly, even at his first Appearance, that it was the universal Opinion of all Mr. *Allworthy's* Family, that he was certainly born to be hanged.

Indeed, I am sorry to say, there was too much Reason for this Conjecture. The Lad having, from his earliest Years, discovered a Propensity to many Vices, and especially to one, which hath as direct a Tendency as any other to that Fate, which we have just now observed to have been prophetically denounced against him. He had been already convicted of three Robberies, *viz.* of robbing an Orchard, of stealing a Duck out of a Farmer's Yard, and of picking Master *Blifil's* Pocket of a Ball.

The Vices of this young Man were moreover heightened by the disadvantageous Light in which they appeared, when opposed to the Virtues of Master *Blifil*, his Companion: A Youth of so different a Cast from little *Jones*, that not only the Family, but all the Neighbourhood resounded his Praises. He was indeed a Lad of a remarkable Disposition; sober, discreet, and pious beyond his Age. Qualities, which gained him the Love of every one who knew him, while *Tom Jones* was universally disliked, and many expressed their Wonder that Mr. *Allworthy* would suffer such a Lad to be educated with his Nephew, lest the Morals of the latter should be corrupted by his Example.

An Incident which happened about this Time, will set the Characters of these two Lads, more fairly before the discerning Reader, than is in the Power of the longest Dissertation.

Tom Jones, who, bad as he is, must serve for the Heroe of this History, had only one Friend among all the Servants of the Family; for, as to Mrs. *Wilkins*, she had long since given him up, and was perfectly reconciled to her Mistress. This Friend was the Game-keeper, a Fellow of a loose kind of Disposition, and who was thought not to entertain much stricter Notions concerning the Difference of *meum* and *tuum*, than the young Gentleman himself. And hence, this Friendship gave Occasion to many sarcastical Remarks among the Domestics, most of which were either Proverbs before, or at least are become so now; and indeed, the Wit of them all may be comprised in that short *Latin* Proverb, '*Noscitur a socio*,' which, I think, is thus expressed in *English*, 'You may know him by the Company he keeps.'

To say the Truth, some of that atrocious Wickedness in *Jones*, of which we have just mentioned three Examples, might perhaps be derived from the Encouragement he had received from this Fellow, who, in two or three Instances, had been what the Law calls an Accessary after the Fact. For the whole Duck, and great Part of the Apples, were converted to the Use of the Game-keeper and his Family. Tho' as *Jones* alone was discovered, the poor Lad bore not only the whole Smart, but the whole Blame; both which fell again to his Lot, on the following Occasion. Contiguous to Mr. *Allworthy's* Estate, was the Manor of one of those Gentlemen, who are called *Preservers of the Game*. This Species of Men, from the great Severity with which they revenge the Death of a Hare or a Partridge, might be thought to cultivate the same Superstition with the Bannians in *India*;[1] many of whom, we are told, dedicate their whole Lives to the Preservation and Protection of certain Animals; was it not that our *English* Bannians, while they preserve them from other Enemies, will most unmercifully slaughter whole Horse-loads themselves, so that they stand clearly acquitted of any such heathenish Superstition.

I have, indeed, a much better Opinion of this Kind of Men than is entertained by some, as I take them to answer the Order of Nature, and the good Purposes for which they were ordained

[1] A Hindu caste of merchants who, because they believe that all animal life is sacred, observe a strict vegetarian diet. See *The Champion* (22 March 1739/40).

in a more ample Manner than many others. Now, as *Horace* tells us,[1] that there are a Set of human Beings,

Fruges consumere nati.

'Born to consume the Fruits of the Earth.' So, I make no manner of Doubt but that there are others

Feras consumere nati.

'Born to consume the Beasts of the Field,' or, as it is commonly called, the Game; and none, I believe, will deny, but that those Squires fulfil this End of their Creation.

Little *Jones* went one Day a shooting with the Game-keeper; when, happening to spring a Covey of Partridges, near the Border of that Manor, over which Fortune, to fulfil the wise Purposes of Nature, had planted one of the Game-Consumers, the Birds flew into it, and were *marked* (as it is called) by the two Sportsmen, in some Furze Bushes, about two or three hundred Paces beyond Mr. *Allworthy's* Dominions.

Mr. *Allworthy* had given the Fellow strict Orders, on Pain of forfeiting his Place, never to trespass on any of his Neighbours, no more on those who were less rigid in this Matter, than on the Lord of this Manor. With regard to others, indeed, these Orders had not been always very scrupulously kept; but as the Disposition of the Gentleman with whom the Partridges had taken sanctuary, was well known, the Game-keeper had never yet attempted to invade his Territories. Nor had he done it now, had not the younger Sportsman, who was excessively eager to pursue the flying Game, over-persuaded him; but *Jones* being very importunate, the other, who was himself keen enough after the Sport, yielded to his Persuasions, entered the Manor, and shot one of the Partridges.

The Gentleman himself was at that time on horseback, at a little Distance from them; and hearing the Gun go off, he immediately made towards the Place, and discovered poor *Tom*: For the Game-keeper had leapt into the thickest Part of the Furze-brake, where he had happily concealed himself.

The Gentleman having searched the Lad, and found the Partridge upon him, denounced great Vengeance, swearing he would

---

[1] *Epistles,* I. ii. 27. The phrase describes Penelope's suitors and the idle youths at King Alcinous' court in the *Odyssey.* Cf. *Jonathan Wild* (1743), I. viii, and *An Enquiry into the Causes of the late Increase of Robbers* (1751), sec. i.

acquaint Mr. *Allworthy*. He was as good as his Word, for he rode immediately to his House, and complained of the Trespass on his Manor, in as high Terms, and as bitter Language, as if his House had been broken open, and the most valuable Furniture stole out of it. He added, that some other Person was in his Company, tho' he could not discover him: for that two Guns had been discharged almost in the same Instant. And, says he, 'we have found only this Partridge, but the Lord knows what Mischief they have done.'

At his Return home, *Tom* was presently convened before Mr. *Allworthy*. He owned the Fact, and alledged no other Excuse but what was really true, *viz.* that the Covey was originally sprung in Mr. *Allworthy's* own Manor.[1]

Tom was then interrogated who was with him, which Mr. *Allworthy* declared he was resolved to know, acquainting the Culprit with the Circumstance of the two Guns, which had been deposed by the Squire and both his Servants; but *Tom* stoutly persisted in asserting that he was alone; yet, to say the Truth, he hesitated a little at first, which would have confirmed Mr. *Allworthy's* Belief, had what the Squire and his Servants said, wanted any further Confirmation.

The Game-keeper being a suspected Person, was now sent for, and the Question put to him; but he, relying on the Promise which *Tom* had made him, to take all upon himself, very resolutely denied being in Company with the young Gentleman, or indeed having seen him the whole Afternoon.

Mr. *Allworthy* then turned towards *Tom*, with more than usual

---

[1] Legally, Tom and the gamekeeper would have been judged guilty of an offence only if they had trespassed on a game warren (i.e. a place especially privileged by the King's licence for the preservation of game). Earlier in this chapter the squire of this manor (identified as Western in III. ix) is ironically referred to as 'one of those Gentlemen, who are called *Preservers of the Game*'; but it seems unlikely that Fielding, who knew the law and therefore the significance of this point to the determination of Tom's guilt, would have neglected specifically to designate Western's estate a warren if he had meant the reader to think of it as such. The law is summarized as follows in Giles Jacob, *A New Law-Dictionary*, 4th ed. (1739), s.v. 'Game': 'An Action was brought against a Person for entering another Man's Warren; the Defendant pleaded that there was a Pheasant on his Land, and his Hawk pursued it into the Plaintiff's Ground; it was resolved that this doth not amount to a sufficient Justification, for in this Case he can only follow his Hawk and not take the *Game*. *Poph.* 162. though it is said to be otherwise where the Soil of the Plaintiff is not a Warren. 2 *Roll. Abr.* 567. If a Man in Hunting starts a Hare upon his own Ground, and follows and kills it on the Ground of another, yet still the Hare is his own, because of the fresh Suit.... *Cro. Car.* 553.' (Cf. Barlow, *The Justice of the Peace* [1745], s.v. 'Game'.)

Anger in his Countenance, and advised him to confess who was with him; repeating, that he was resolved to know. The Lad, however, still maintained his Resolution, and was dismissed with much Wrath by Mr. *Allworthy*, who told him, he should have to the next Morning to consider of it, when he should be questioned by another Person, and in another Manner.

Poor *Jones* spent a very melancholy Night, and the more so, as he was without his usual Companion: for Master *Blifil* was gone abroad on a Visit with his Mother. Fear of the Punishment he was to suffer was on this Occasion his least Evil; his chief Anxiety being, lest his Constancy should fail him, and he should be brought to betray the Game-keeper, whose Ruin he knew must now be the Consequence.

Nor did the Game-keeper pass his Time much better. He had the same Apprehensions with the Youth; for whose Honour he had likewise a much tenderer Regard than for his Skin.

In the Morning, when *Tom* attended the Reverend Mr. *Thwackum*, the Person to whom Mr. *Allworthy* had committed the Instruction of the two Boys, he had the same Questions put to him by that Gentleman, which he had been asked the Evening before, to which he returned the same Answers. The Consequence of this was, so severe a Whipping, that it possibly fell little short of the Torture with which Confessions are in some Countries extorted from Criminals.

Tom bore his Punishment with great Resolution; and tho' his Master asked him between every Stroke, whether he would not confess, he was contented to be flead rather than betray his Friend, or break the Promise he had made.

The Game-keeper was now relieved from his Anxiety, and Mr. *Allworthy* himself began to be concerned at *Tom's* Sufferings: For, besides that Mr. *Thwackum*, being highly enraged that he was not able to make the Boy say what he himself pleased, had carried his Severity much beyond the good Man's Intention, this latter began now to suspect that the Squire had been mistaken; which his extreme Eagerness and Anger seemed to make probable; and as for what the Servants had said in Confirmation of their Master's Account, he laid no great Stress upon that. Now, as Cruelty and Injustice were two Ideas, of which Mr. *Allworthy* could by no Means support the Consciousness a single Moment, he sent for *Tom*, and after many kind and friendly Exhortations, said, 'I am convinced, my dear Child, that my Suspicions have wronged you; I am sorry that you have been so severely punished on this Account.'—And at last gave him a little Horse to make him amends; again repeating his Sorrow for what had past.

Tom's Guilt now flew in his Face more than any Severity could make it. He could more easily bear the Lashes of *Thwackum*, than the Generosity of *Allworthy*. The Tears burst from his Eyes, and he fell upon his Knees, crying, 'Oh! Sir, you are too good to me. Indeed, you are. Indeed, I don't deserve it.' And at that very Instant, from the Fullness of his Heart, had almost betrayed the Secret; but the good Genius of the Game-keeper suggested to him what might be the Consequence to the poor Fellow, and this Consideration sealed his Lips.

Thwackum did all he could to dissuade *Allworthy* from shewing any Compassion or Kindness to the Boy, saying, 'He had persisted in an Untruth;' and gave some Hints, that a second Whipping might probably bring the Matter to Light.

But Mr. *Allworthy* absolutely refused to consent to the Experiment. He said, the Boy had suffered enough already, for concealing the Truth, even if he was guilty, seeing that he could have no Motive but a mistaken Point of Honour for so doing.

'Honour!' cry'd *Thwackum*, with some Warmth, 'mere Stubbornness and Obstinacy! Can Honour teach any one to tell a Lie, or can any Honour exist independent of Religion?'

This Discourse happened at Table when Dinner was just ended; and there were present Mr. *Allworthy*, Mr. *Thwackum*, and a third Gentleman who now entered into the Debate, and whom, before we proceed any farther, we shall briefly introduce to our Reader's Acquaintance.

CHAPTER III

The Character of Mr. Square *the Philosopher, and of Mr.* Thwackum *the Divine; with a Dispute concerning————*

THE Name of this Gentleman who had then resided some time at Mr. *Allworthy's* House, was Mr. *Square*.[1] His

[1] Fielding's biographers have rather too categorically identified Square with Thomas Chubb (1679–8 February 1747), tallow-chandler of Salisbury and the prolific author of deistical tracts. (See Cross, ii. 169–70, and Dudden, ii. 647–9.) Though Square's views

natural Parts were not of the first Rate, but he had greatly improved them by a learned Education. He was deeply read in the
Antients, and a profest Master of all the Works of *Plato* and

correspond with Chubb's at several points (see below), in every other respect the two are
diametrically different. Chubb, for example, was recognized even by his enemies as 'a Man of
uncommon Genius, and *natural* Capacities', but who had not had the advantage of a learned
education. Unlike Square, who 'was a comely Man' (III. vi) and attractive to the ladies,
Chubb was short and portly, his appearance '*despicable* and *mean*'; and far from being a
philanderer, as is the case with Square (v. v), he had a reputation for perfect chastity with
respect to women, though his effeminate manner led his detractors to suspect him of being
homosexual. Finally, whereas Square is converted to Christianity on his deathbed (XVIII.
iv), Chubb died suddenly and without renouncing his heterodox views. (See the accounts of
Chubb published shortly after his death: *A Short and Faithful Account of the Life and
Character of the Celebrated Mr. Thomas Chubb* [1747] and the reply, *Memoirs of Mr.
Thomas Chubb, Late of Salisbury* [1747].) Personally, indeed, Square and Chubb are so
completely antithetical that one may suspect Fielding's character of being a sort of negative
image of the man.

However that may be, Fielding clearly intended Square as a satire not on any one
philosopher, but on the whole tribe of deists and free-thinkers who sought to base religion
solely on the grounds of reason and natural law, neglecting the authority of divine revelation. In sum, Square epitomizes the two principal schools of contemporary deism: the
school of 'moral sentiment', whose chief spokesman was Shaftesbury (see below, p. 217),
and the 'intellectualist' school descended from the Cambridge Platonists through Samuel
Clarke, Matthew Tindal, Chubb, and many others. (See A. R. Humphreys, ' "The
Eternal Fitness of Things": An Aspect of Eighteenth-Century Thought', *MLR*, xlii
[1947], 188–98—which, however, errs in identifying Square exclusively with the 'intellectualists'.) The distinction between these schools was widely recognized. In *Deism
Revealed* (2nd ed., 1751) Dechaine thus defines 'the light of nature' as consisting of both
natural sentiment and *reason*: the former is 'that perception of beauty in a good, and of
deformity in a bad, action, which every man feels in himself'; the latter is 'that divine
faculty of the mind, by which all men are enabled to judge and direct themselves in the
choice of such means, as are necessary to bring about the ends suggested to them by their
natural sentiments, to decide between them according to the fitness of things' (i. 40).

Square's 'favourite Phrase . . . *the natural Beauty of Virtue*' and his belief that 'Vice was a
Deviation from our Nature in the same Manner as Deformity of Body is' may be traced
ultimately to Shaftesbury, who maintained that the moral sense consisted 'in a real Anti-
pathy or Aversion to *Injustice* or *Wrong*, and in a real Affection or Love towards *Equity* and
Right, for its own sake, and on the account of its own natural Beauty and Worth' ('An
Inquiry concerning Virtue or Merit', I. iii. 1; *Characteristicks*, 5th ed. [1732], ii. 42). In
'The Moralists' (III. ii) Shaftesbury had asked: 'Is there then . . . a natural Beauty of
Figures? and is there not as natural a one of ACTIONS ? No sooner the Eye opens upon
Figures, the Ear to *Sounds*, than straight *the Beautiful* results, and *Grace* and *Harmony* are
known and acknowledg'd. No sooner are ACTIONS view'd, no sooner the *human Affections*
and *Passions* discern'd . . . than straight *an inward* EYE distinguishes, and sees *the Fair* and
Shapely, *the Amiable* and *Admirable*, apart from *the Deform'd*, *the Foul*, *the Odious*, or *the
Despicable*. How is it possible therefore not to own, "That as these *Distinctions* have their
Foundation *in Nature*, the Discernment it-self is *natural*, and from NATURE *alone?*" ' (ibid.,
ii. 414–15).

On the other hand, Square's method of measuring 'all Actions by the *unalterable Rule of
Right* and the *eternal Fitness of Things*' derives from the 'intellectualists', who believed that

Aristotle. Upon which great Models he had principally form'd himself, sometimes according with the Opinion of the one, and sometimes with that of the other. In Morals he was a profest *Platonist*, and in Religion he inclined to be an *Aristotelian.*[1]

But tho' he had, as we have said, formed his Morals on the *Platonic* Model, yet he perfectly agreed with the Opinion of *Aristotle*, in considering that great Man rather in the Quality of a Philosopher or a Speculatist, than as a Legislator.[2] This Sentiment he carried a great way; indeed, so far, as to regard all Virtue as Matter of Theory only. This, it is true, he never affirmed, as I have heard, to any one; and yet upon the least Attention to his Conduct, I cannot help thinking, it was his real Opinion, as it will perfectly reconcile some Contradictions which might otherwise appear in his Character.

morality could be made into a rational science as systematic and as infallible as Euclidian geometry. Chubb, to choose only one among many possible exemplars of this school, insisted that natural religion was 'grounded upon the unalterable nature, and the eternal reason of things' and, as such, did not depend on the sanctions of 'any *divine revelation*, or any *promulged law*'; Christ, he maintained, taught nothing contradictory 'to the eternal rule of right and wrong' ('The Author's Farewel to his Readers', in *The Ground and Foundation of Morality Considered* [1745], pp. 40–1, 42). Indeed, Square's favourite phrases recur throughout Chubb's works: 'By moral duties', he explained, 'I understand the performance of such actions as are in themselves right and fit to be performed by every intelligent being, or moral agent, in equal circumstances; which fitness results solely from the nature and reason of things, when considered abstractedly from, and antecedent to any promulgated law, whether human or divine. And . . . there is such a fitness and unfitness arising from, and founded in the natural and essential differences in things' ('Some Reflections upon the comparative Excellency and Usefulness of moral and positive Duties', in *A Discourse concerning Reason, with regard to Religion and Divine Revelation* [1731], pp. 33–4; see also *The True Gospel of Jesus Christ Asserted* [1738], pp. 18, 38). But by mid century such formulas had become part of the common vocabulary of deism; they cannot with certainty be traced to any one author.

Perhaps the most useful gloss on Fielding's intentions with regard to Square is the first volume (1738) of Warburton's *Divine Legation of Moses.* Here, after addressing his work 'to the Free-Thinkers', Warburton proceeds in some detail to refute those authors who had recently flooded the bookstalls with 'a Deluge of Moral Systems, in which either the *Moral Sense*, or the *Essential Difference* makes the sole Foundation' (i. 41). His chief argument, to which Fielding would have subscribed, is that only the supreme authority of the divine will could render such abstract notions efficacious as a moral imperative. (On Warburton, see below, p. 687, n. 3.)

[1] Cf. Warburton on the ultimate sources of deism: 'And indeed, the following the antient Philosophers too servilely, has occasioned the Errors of modern Moralists, in unnaturally separating the Grounds of Obligation: *Plato* being the Patron of the *Moral Sense*; *Aristotle* of the *Essential Differences*; and the *Stoics* of *Arbitrary Will*' (*Divine Legation*, i [1738], 41, n. *e*).

[2] Cf. the general tenor of Aristotle's criticism of Plato's *Republic* and *Laws* (*Politics*, II. i–iii).

This Gentleman and Mr. *Thwackum* scarce ever met without a Disputation; for their Tenets were, indeed, diametrically opposite to each other. *Square* held human Nature to be the Perfection of all Virtue, and that Vice was a Deviation from our Nature in the same Manner as Deformity of Body is. *Thwackum,* on the contrary, maintained that the human Mind, since the Fall, was nothing but a Sink of Iniquity, till purified and redeemed by Grace. In one Point only they agreed, which was, in all their Discourses on Morality never to mention the Word *Goodness.* The favourite Phrase of the former, was *the natural Beauty of Virtue*; that of the latter, was the *divine Power of Grace.* The former measured all Actions by the *unalterable Rule of Right,* and the *eternal Fitness of Things*; the latter decided all Matters by Authority; but, in doing this, he always used the Scriptures and their Commentators, as the Lawyer doth his *Coke upon Lyttleton,*[1] where the Comment is of equal Authority with the Text.

After this short Introduction, the Reader will be pleased to remember, that the Parson had concluded his Speech with a triumphant Question, to which he had apprehended no Answer; *viz.* Can any Honour exist independent of Religion?

To this *Square* answered, that it was impossible to discourse philosophically concerning Words, till their Meaning was first established;[2] that there were scarce any two Words of a more

---

[1] Sir Edward Coke's commentary (1628) on the *Tenures* of Sir Thomas Littleton (*c.* 1422–81), a standard authority on real property law. (See above, p. 100, n. 1.)

[2] Rigid in his orthodoxy and morose in his Augustinian view of human nature, Thwackum throughout this chapter interprets 'Honour' as a 'Mode of divine Grace' strictly dependent on the Church of England. In attempting to refute this position, Square's method and argument, though in accord with the strategies of deism in general, correspond quite closely to those of Chubb in 'The Author's Farewel to His Readers' (1745). In this work Chubb methodically attacks 'the doctrine of *grace,* or *special grace,* as it is sometimes called' (ibid., p. 57), advocating instead a 'doctrine' of moral '*self-sufficiency*' (p. 62), our ability to perform moral actions being entirely natural to us and '*antecedent*' (p. 60) to any alleged (and in his view illusory) dispensation of divine grace. He further disposes of the narrow assumptions of religious sects that their beliefs alone are divinely authorized. Like Square, Chubb typically begins each division of his argument by 'fixing' his subject, defining his terms (e.g., pp. 47, 57). Keeping in mind Square's objections to Thwackum's orthodoxy, consider Chubb on '*religious parties*': 'I am sensible, that the doctrine of divine impressions has been adhered to, and maintained by *most,* if not *all, religious parties* in the world; but then they all seem inclined to *confine* the favour to their *own party,* or, at least, to think it is *chiefly,* and *more certainly* with them; and therefore, they are apt to *draw back,* and are unwilling to submit to what is dictated to them as a *divine oracle,* when it comes from any *other quarter*; and thus, a christian would scarce think himself *concerned,* much less *obliged* to attend to what may be delivered to him as the *produce* of *divine impression* by

vague and uncertain Signification, than the two he had mentioned: For that there were almost as many different Opinions
concerning Honour, as concerning Religion. 'But,' says he, 'if by
Honour you mean the true natural Beauty of Virtue, I will maintain it may exist independent of any Religion whatever. Nay
(added he) you yourself will allow it may exist independent of
all but one; so will a *Mahometan*, a *Jew*, and all the Maintainers of
all the different Sects in the World.'

Thwackum replied, This was arguing with the usual Malice
of all the Enemies to the true Church. He said, he doubted not
but that all the Infidels and Hereticks in the World would, if
they could, confine Honour to their own absurd Errors, and
damnable Deceptions; 'But Honour,' says he, 'is not therefore
manifold, because there are many absurd Opinions about it;
nor is Religion manifold, because there are various Sects and
Heresies in the World. When I mention Religion, I mean the
Christian Religion; and not only the Christian Religion, but the
Protestant Religion; and not only the Protestant Religion, but
the Church of *England*.[1] And, when I mention Honour, I mean
that Mode of divine Grace which is not only consistent with,
but dependent upon, this Religion; and is consistent with, and
dependent upon, no other. Now to say that the Honour I here
mean, and which was, I thought, all the Honour I could be supposed to mean, will uphold, much less dictate, an Untruth, is to
assert an Absurdity too shocking to be conceived.'

'I purposely avoided,' says *Square*, 'drawing a Conclusion which
I thought evident from what I have said; but if you perceived it,
I am sure you have not attempted to answer it. However, to
drop the Article of Religion, I think it is plain, from what you
have said, that we have different Ideas of Honour; or why do

---

a *Mahometan*; and the like of a *Mahometan*, by a christian' (pp. 55–6). Similarly, with
Square's rejection of Thwackum's Augustinianism, compare Chubb, who derisively
notices 'what is sometimes urged in *favour* of the doctrine of *special grace*, or rather of
what is urged *against* the doctrine of *self-sufficiency*, which seems to stand in *competition* with
it; namely, *first*, That it must be *great pride* and *arrogance* in man to consider himself as an
independent, *self-sufficient* creature, as one who can, *of himself*, do *many good* actions; whereas
man, especially *since* the *fall*, is most *corrupt*, *impotent*, and *weak*, who cannot, *of himself*, so
much as *think* a *good thought*, much less bring forth any thing that is good, without the
special aid of his Maker' (pp. 64–5).

[1] Thwackum's narrow and rigid orthodoxy should be contrasted with the latitudinarian-
ism of, for example, Bishop Hoadly (see above, p. 105).

we not agree in the same Terms of its Explanation? I have asserted, that true Honour and true Virtue are almost synonimous Terms, and they are both founded on the unalterable Rule of Right, and the eternal Fitness of Things; to which an Untruth being absolutely repugnant and contrary,[1] it is certain that true Honour cannot support an Untruth. In this, therefore, I think we are agreed; but that this Honour can be said to be founded on Religion, to which it is antecedent, if by Religion be meant any positive Law——'

'I agree,' answered *Thwackum*, with great Warmth, 'with a Man who asserts Honour to be antecedent to Religion!—Mr. *Allworthy*, did I agree——?'

He was proceeding, when Mr. *Allworthy* interposed, telling them very coldly, they had both mistaken his Meaning; for that he had said nothing of true Honour.—It is possible, however, he would not have easily quieted the Disputants, who were growing equally warm, had not another Matter now fallen out, which put a final End to the Conversation at present.

CHAPTER IV

Containing a necessary Apology for the Author; and a childish Incident, which perhaps requires an Apology likewise.

BEFORE I proceed farther, I shall beg leave to obviate some Misconstructions, into which the Zeal of some few Readers may lead them; for I would not willingly give Offence to any, especially to Men who are warm in the Cause of Virtue or Religion.

I hope, therefore, no Man will, by the grossest Misunderstanding, or Perversion, of my Meaning, misrepresent me, as endeavouring to cast any Ridicule on the greatest Perfections of Human Nature; and which do, indeed, alone purify and enoble the Heart of Man, and raise him above the Brute Creation. This, Reader, I will venture to say, (and by how much the better Man you are yourself, by so much the more will you be inclined to

---

[1] Again Square recalls Chubb, who argued that 'lying and deceiving' were invariably wrong because contrary to the 'essential *difference* in things' and because 'one thing or action is *preferable* to another in nature', as truth is preferable to a lie, or as a promise, once made, must be kept, not broken (*The True Gospel of Jesus Christ Asserted* [1738], p. 189).

believe me) that I would rather have buried the Sentiments of these two Persons in eternal Oblivion, than have done any Injury to either of these glorious Causes.

On the contrary, it is with a View to their Service that I have taken upon me to record the Lives and Actions of two of their false and pretended Champions. A treacherous Friend is the most dangerous Enemy; and I will say boldly, that both Religion and Virtue have received more real Discredit from Hypocrites, than the wittiest Profligates or Infidels could ever cast upon them: Nay farther, as these two, in their Purity, are rightly called the Bands of civil Society, and are indeed the greatest of Blessings; so when poisoned and corrupted with Fraud, Pretence and Affectation, they have become the worst of civil Curses, and have enabled Men to perpetrate the most cruel Mischiefs to their own Species.

Indeed, I doubt not but this Ridicule will in general be allowed; my chief Apprehension is, as many true and just Sentiments often came from the Mouths of these Persons, lest the whole should be taken together, and I should be conceived to ridicule all alike. Now the Reader will be pleased to consider, that as neither of these Men were Fools, they could not be supposed to have holden none but wrong Principles, and to have uttered nothing but Absurdities; what Injustice, therefore, must I have done to their Characters, had I selected only what was bad, and how horridly wretched and maimed must their Arguments have appeared!

Upon the whole, it is not Religion or Virtue, but the Want of them which is here exposed. Had not *Thwackum* too much neglected Virtue, and *Square* Religion, in the Composition of their several Systems; and had not both utterly discarded all natural Goodness of Heart, they had never been represented as the Objects of Derision in this History; in which we will now proceed.

This Matter, then, which put an end to the Debate mentioned in the last Chapter, was no other than a Quarrel between Master *Blifil* and *Tom Jones*, the Consequence of which had been a bloody Nose to the former; for though Master *Blifil*, notwithstanding he was the younger, was in Size above the other's Match, yet *Tom* was much his Superior at the noble Art of Boxing.

Tom, however, cautiously avoided all Engagements with that

Youth: For besides that *Tommy Jones* was an inoffensive Lad amidst all his Roguery, and really loved *Blifil*; Mr. *Thwackum* being always the Second of the latter, would have been sufficient to deter him.

But well says a certain Author,[1] No Man is wise at all Hours; it is therefore no Wonder that a Boy is not so. A Difference arising at Play between the two Lads, Master *Blifil* called *Tom* a *Beggarly Bastard*. Upon which the latter, who was somewhat passionate in his Disposition, immediately caused that Phænomenon in the Face of the former, which we have above remembred.

Master *Blifil* now, with his Blood running from his Nose, and the Tears galloping after from his Eyes, appeared before his Uncle, and the tremendous *Thwackum*. In which Court an Indictment of Assault, Battery, and Wounding, was instantly preferred against *Tom*; who in his Excuse only pleaded the Provocation, which was indeed all the Matter that Master *Blifil* had omitted.

It is indeed possible, that this Circumstance might have escaped his Memory; for, in his Reply, he positively insisted, that he had made Use of no such Appellation; adding, 'Heaven forbid such naughty Words should ever come out of his Mouth.'

Tom, though against all Form of Law,[2] rejoined in Affirmance of the Words. Upon which Master *Blifil* said, 'It is no Wonder. Those who will tell one Fib, will hardly stick at another. If I had told my Master such a wicked Fib as you have done, I should be ashamed to shew my Face.'

'What Fib, Child?' cries *Thwackum* pretty eagerly.

'Why, he told you that Nobody was with him a shooting when he killed the Partridge; but he knows, (here he burst into a Flood of Tears) yes, he knows; for he confessed it to me, that *Black George* the Game-keeper was there. Nay, he said,—Yes you did,—deny it if you can, That you would not have confest the Truth, though Master had cut you to Pieces.'

At this the Fire flashed from *Thwackum's* Eyes; and he cried out in Triumph: 'Oh ho! This is your mistaken Notion of

---

[1] See below, pp. 677, n. 3; 856.

[2] In this mock trial, the plaintiff, Blifil, has made his accusation and has been answered by the defendant, Tom, who 'pleaded the Provocation'. Blifil then makes his reply or *replication* and is answered by Tom's *rejoinder*, which, however, because merely a rehearsal of his original plea, would be disallowed in a court of law. (See Wood's *Institutes*, 7th ed. [1745], pp. 609–11.)

Honour! This is the Boy who was not to be whipped again!'
But Mr. *Allworthy*, with a more gentle Aspect, turned towards the
Lad, and said, 'Is this true, Child? How came you to persist so
obstinately in a Falshood?'

Tom said, 'He scorned a Lie as much as any one; but he thought
his Honour engaged him to act as he did; for he had promised
the poor Fellow to conceal him; which,' he said, 'he thought
himself farther obliged to, as the Game-keeper had begged him
not to go into the Gentleman's Manor, and had at last gone himself in Compliance with his Persuasions.' He said, 'this was the
whole Truth of the Matter, and he would take his Oath of it;'
and concluded with very passionately begging Mr. *Allworthy*,
'to have Compassion on the poor Fellow's Family, especially as
he himself only had been guilty, and the other had been very
difficultly prevailed on to do what he did.' 'Indeed Sir,' said he,
'it could hardly be called a Lie that I told; for the poor Fellow
was entirely innocent of the whole Matter. I should have gone
alone after the Birds; nay, I did go at first, and he only followed
me to prevent more Mischief. Do, pray, Sir, let me be punished,
take my little Horse away again; but pray, Sir, forgive poor
George.'

Mr. *Allworthy* hesitated a few Moments, and then dismissed
the Boys, advising them to live more friendly and peaceably
together.

CHAPTER V

*The Opinions of the Divine and the Philosopher concerning the two
Boys; with some Reasons for their Opinions, and other Matters.*

IT is probable, that by disclosing this Secret, which had been
communicated in the utmost Confidence to him, young *Blifil*
preserved his Companion from a good Lashing: For the Offence
of the bloody Nose would have been of itself sufficient Cause for
Thwackum to have proceeded to Correction; but now this was
totally absorbed, in the Consideration of the other Matter; and
with Regard to this, Mr. *Allworthy* declared privately, he thought
the Boy deserved Reward rather than Punishment; so that
Thwackum's Hand was withheld by a general Pardon.

Thwackum, whose Meditations were full of Birch, exclaimed against this weak, and, as he said he would venture to call it, wicked Lenity. To remit the Punishment of such Crimes was, he said, to encourage them. He enlarged much on the Correction of Children, and quoted many Texts from *Solomon*,[1] and others; which being to be found in so many other Books, shall not be found here. He then applied himself to the Vice of Lying, on which Head he was altogether as learned as he had been on the other.

Square said, he had been endeavouring to reconcile the Behaviour of *Tom* with his Idea of perfect Virtue; but could not. He owned there was something which at first Sight appeared like Fortitude in the Action; but as Fortitude was a Virtue, and Falshood a Vice, they could by no Means agree or unite together. He added, that as this was in some measure to confound Virtue and Vice, it might be worth Mr. *Thwackum's* Consideration, whether a larger Castigation might not be laid on, upon that Account.

As both these learned Men concurred in censuring *Jones*, so were they no less unanimous in applauding Master *Blifil*. To bring Truth to light, was by the Parson asserted to be the Duty of every religious Man; and by the Philosopher this was declared to be highly conformable with the Rule of Right, and the eternal and unalterable Fitness of Things.

All this, however, weighed very little with Mr. *Allworthy*. He could not be prevailed on to sign the Warrant for the Execution of *Jones*. There was something within his own Breast with which the invincible Fidelity which that Youth had preserved, corresponded much better than it had done with the Religion of *Thwackum*, or with the Virtue of *Square*. He therefore strictly ordered the former of these Gentlemen to abstain from laying violent Hands on *Tom* for what had past. The Pedagogue was obliged to obey those Orders; but not without great Reluctance, and frequent Mutterings, that the Boy would be certainly spoiled.

Towards the Game-keeper the good Man behaved with more Severity. He presently summoned that poor Fellow before him, and after many bitter Remonstrances, paid him his Wages, and dismist him from his Service; for Mr. *Allworthy* rightly observed that there was a great Difference between being guilty of a

---

[1] c.g. Proverbs 13: 24, 19: 18, 22: 15, 23: 13–14, 29: 15.

Falsehood to excuse yourself, and to excuse another. He likewise urged, as the principal Motive to his inflexible Severity
against this Man, that he had basely suffered *Tom Jones* to
undergo so heavy a Punishment for his Sake, whereas he ought
to have prevented it by making the Discovery himself.

When this Story became public, many People differed from
Square and *Thwackum*, in judging the Conduct of the two Lads on
the Occasion. Master *Blifil* was generally called a sneaking Rascal,
a poor-spirited Wretch; with other Epithets of the like Kind;
whilst *Tom* was honoured with the Appellations of a brave Lad,
a jolly Dog, and an honest Fellow. Indeed his Behaviour to
Black George much ingratiated him with all the Servants; for
though that Fellow was before universally disliked, yet he was no
sooner turned away than he was as universally pitied; and the
Friendship and Gallantry of *Tom Jones* was celebrated by them
all with the highest Applause; and they condemned Master
Blifil, as openly as they durst, without incurring the Danger of
offending his Mother. For all this, however, poor *Tom* smarted in
the Flesh; for though *Thwackum* had been inhibited to exercise
his Arm on the foregoing Account; yet, as the Proverb says,[1] *It is
easy to find a Stick*, &c. So was it easy to find a Rod; and, indeed,
the not being able to find one was the only thing which could
have kept *Thwackum* any long Time from chastising poor Jones.

Had the bare Delight in the Sport been the only Inducement
to the Pedagogue, it is probable, Master *Blifil* would likewise
have had his Share; but though Mr. *Allworthy* had given him
frequent Orders to make no Difference between the Lads, yet
was *Thwackum* altogether as kind and gentle to this Youth, as
he was harsh, nay even barbarous, to the other. To say the Truth,
Blifil had greatly gained his Master's Affections; partly by the
profound Respect he always shewed his Person, but much more
by the decent Reverence with which he received his Doctrine;
for he had got by Heart, and frequently repeated his Phrases,
and maintained all his Master's religious Principles with a
Zeal which was surprising in one so young, and which greatly
endeared him to the worthy Preceptor.

Tom Jones, on the other hand, was not only deficient in outward
Tokens of Respect, often forgetting to pull off his Hat, or to

---

[1] 'It is easy to find a stick to beat a dog.' (See W. G. Smith and P. Harvey (edd.), *Oxford Dictionary of English Proverbs*, 2nd ed. [Oxford, 1948], p. 617.)

bow at his Master's Approach; but was altogether as unmindful both of his Master's Precepts and Example. He was indeed a thoughtless, giddy Youth, with little Sobriety in his Manners, and less in his Countenance; and would often very impudently and indecently laugh at his Companion for his serious Behaviour.

Mr. *Square* had the same Reason for his Preference of the former Lad; for *Tom Jones* shewed no more Regard to the learned Discourses which this Gentleman would sometimes throw away upon him, than to those of *Thwackum*. He once ventured to make a Jest of the Rule of Right; and at another Time said, He believed there was no Rule in the World capable of making such a Man as his Father (for so Mr. *Allworthy* suffered himself to be called.)

Master *Blifil*, on the contrary, had Address enough at sixteen to recommend himself at one and the same Time to both these Opposites. With one he was all Religion, with the other he was all Virtue. And when both were present, he was profoundly silent, which both interpreted in his Favour and in their own.

Nor was *Blifil* contented with flattering both these Gentlemen to their Faces; he took frequent Occasions of praising them behind their Backs to *Allworthy*; before whom, when they two were alone, and his Uncle commended any religious or virtuous Sentiment, (for many such came constantly from him) he seldom fail'd to ascribe it to the good Instructions he had received from either *Thwackum* or *Square*: For he knew his Uncle repeated all such Compliments to the Persons for whose Use they were meant; and he found by Experience the great Impressions which they made on the Philosopher, as well as on the Divine: For, to say the Truth, there is no kind of Flattery so irresistible as this, at second Hand.

The young Gentleman, moreover, soon perceived how extremely grateful all those Panegyricks on his Instructors were to Mr. *Allworthy* himself, as they so loudly resounded the Praise of that singular Plan of Education which he had laid down:[1] For

---

[1] Like Parson Adams in *Joseph Andrews* (1742; III. v), Allworthy naïvely trusts in the superior moral efficacy of a private education over a public one. The 'Fault in the Plan', as Fielding remarks later in this chapter, had been stated by Joseph Andrews in his reply to Adams: 'I remember when I was in the Stable, if a young Horse was vicious in his Nature, no Correction would make him otherwise; I take it to be equally the same among Men: if a Boy be of a mischievous wicked Inclination, no School, tho' ever so private, will ever make him good; on the contrary, if he be of a righteous Temper, you may trust him to *London*,

this worthy Man having observed the imperfect Institution of our public Schools, and the many Vices which Boys were there liable to learn, had resolved to educate his Nephew, as well as the other Lad, whom he had in a Manner adopted, in his own House; where he thought their Morals would escape all that Danger of being corrupted, to which they would be unavoidably exposed in any public School or University.

Having therefore determined to commit these Boys to the Tuition of a private Tutor, Mr. *Thwackum* was recommended to him for that Office, by a very particular Friend, of whose Understanding Mr. *Allworthy* had a great Opinion, and in whose Integrity he placed much Confidence. This *Thwackum* was Fellow of a College, where he almost entirely resided; and had a great Reputation for Learning, Religion and Sobriety of Manners. And these were doubtless the Qualifications by which Mr. *Allworthy's* Friend had been induced to recommend him; tho' indeed this Friend had some Obligations to *Thwackum's* Family, who were the most considerable Persons in a Borough which that Gentleman represented in Parliament.

Thwackum, at his first Arrival, was extremely agreeable to *Allworthy*; and indeed he perfectly answered the Character which had been given of him. Upon longer Acquaintance, however, and more intimate Conversation, this worthy Man saw Infirmities in the Tutor, which he could have wished him to have been without; tho' as those seemed greatly over-ballanced by his good Qualities, they did not incline Mr. *Allworthy* to part with him; nor would they indeed have justified such a Proceeding: For the Reader is greatly mistaken, if he conceives that *Thwackum* appeared to Mr. *Allworthy* in the same Light as he doth to him in this History; and he is as much deceived, if he imagines, that the most intimate Acquaintance which he himself could have had with that Divine, would have informed him of those Things which we, from our Inspiration, are enabled to open and discover. Of Readers who from such Conceits as these, condemn the Wisdom or Penetration of Mr. *Allworthy*, I shall not scruple to say, that they make a very bad and ungrateful Use of that Knowledge which we have communicated to them.

or where-ever else you please, he will be in no danger of being corrupted.' This view, to which Fielding doubtless subscribed, is merely a paraphrase of Quintilian, *Institutio Oratoria*, I. ii. 4–5.

These apparent Errors in the Doctrine of *Thwackum*, served greatly to palliate the contrary Errors in that of *Square*, which our good Man no less saw and condemned. He thought indeed that the different Exuberancies of these Gentlemen, would correct their different Imperfections; and that from both, especially with his Assistance, the two Lads would derive sufficient Precepts of true Religion and Virtue. If the Event happened contrary to his Expectations, this possibly proceeded from some Fault in the Plan itself; which the Reader hath my Leave to discover, if he can: For we do not pretend to introduce any infallible Characters into this History; where we hope nothing will be found which hath never yet been seen in human Nature.

To return therefore; the Reader will not, I think, wonder that the different Behaviour of the two Lads above commemorated, produced the different Effects, of which he hath already seen some Instance; and besides this, there was another Reason for the Conduct of the Philosopher and the Pedagogue; but this being Matter of great Importance, we shall reveal it in the next Chapter.

CHAPTER VI

Containing a better Reason still for the before-mentioned Opinions.

IT is to be known then, that those two learned Personages, who have lately made a considerable Figure on the Theatre of this History, had from their first Arrival at Mr. *Allworthy's* House, taken so great an Affection, the one to his Virtue, the other to his Religion, that they had meditated the closest Alliance with him.

For this Purpose they had cast their Eyes on that fair Widow, whom, tho' we have not for some Time made any Mention of her, the Reader, we trust, hath not forgot. Mrs. *Blifil* was indeed the Object to which they both aspired.

It may seem remarkable that of four Persons whom we have commemorated at Mr. *Allworthy's* House, three of them should fix their Inclinations on a Lady who was never greatly celebrated for her Beauty, and who was, moreover, now a little descended into the Vale of Years; but in reality Bosom Friends, and intimate Acquaintance, have a kind of natural Propensity to particular Females at the House of a Friend; *viz.* to his Grand-mother,

Mother, Sister, Daughter, Aunt, Niece or Cousin, when they are rich, and to his Wife, Sister, Daughter, Niece, Cousin, Mistress or Servant Maid, if they should be handsome.

We would not, however, have our Reader imagine, that Persons of such Characters as were supported by *Thwackum* and *Square*, would undertake a Matter of this Kind, which hath been a little censured by some rigid Moralists, before they had thoroughly examined it, and considered whether it was (as *Shakespear* phrases it)[1] 'Stuff o' th' Conscience' or no. *Thwackum* was encouraged to the Undertaking, by reflecting, that to covet your Neighbour's Sister is no where forbidden, and he knew it was a Rule in the Construction of all Laws, that '*Expressum facit cessare Tacitum,*'[2] the Sense of which is, 'When a Law-giver sets down plainly his whole Meaning, we are prevented from making him mean what we please ourselves.' As some Instances of Women, therefore, are mentioned in the divine Law, which forbids us to covet our Neighbours Goods, and that of a Sister omitted, he concluded it to be lawful. And as to *Square*, who was in his Person what is called a jolly Fellow, or a Widow's Man, he easily reconciled his Choice to the eternal Fitness of Things.

Now, as both these Gentlemen were industrious in taking every Opportunity of recommending themselves to the Widow, they apprehended one certain Method was, by giving her Son the constant Preference to the other Lad; and as they conceived the Kindness and Affection which Mr. *Allworthy* shewed the latter, must be highly disagreeable to her, they doubted not but the laying hold on all Occasions to degrade and villify him, would be highly pleasing to her; who, as she hated the Boy, must love all those who did him any Hurt. In this *Thwackum* had the Advantage; for while *Square* could only scarify the poor Lad's Reputation, he could flea his Skin; and indeed he considered every Lash he gave him as a Compliment paid to his Mistress; so that he could with the utmost Propriety repeat this old flogging Line, '*Castigo te non quod odio habeam, sed quod* AMEM;[3] I chastize thee

---

[1] Iago's speech in *Othello*, I. ii: 'Though in the trade of Warre I have slaine men,/ Yet do I hold it very stuffe o' th' conscience/ To do no contriv'd Murder.'

[2] A legal maxim meaning literally: 'That which is expressed nullifies [i.e., causes to cease] that which is tacitly assumed.'

[3] Cf. Proverbs 13: 24: 'He that spareth his rod hateth his son: but he that loveth him chasteneth him betimes.' Not only Thwackum apparently (see above, p. 132, n. 1), but also the Church fathers cited this text in defending the practice of corporal discipline (see

not out of Hatred, but out of Love.' And this indeed he often had in his Mouth, or rather, according to the old Phrase, never more properly applied, at his Fingers Ends.

For this Reason principally, the two Gentlemen concurred, as we have seen above, in their Opinion concerning the two Lads; this being indeed almost the only Instance of their concurring on any Point: For beside the Difference of their Principles, they had both long ago strongly suspected each other's Design, and hated one another with no little Degree of Inveteracy.

This mutual Animosity was a good deal increased by their alternate Successes: For Mrs. *Blifil* knew what they would be at long before they imagined it; or indeed intended she should: For they proceeded with great Caution lest she should be offended, and acquaint Mr. *Allworthy*; but they had no Reason for any such Fear. She was well enough pleased with a Passion of which she intended none should have any Fruits but herself. And the only Fruits she designed for herself were Flattery and Court-ship; for which Purpose, she soothed them by Turns, and a long Time equally. She was indeed rather inclined to favour the Parson's Principles; but *Square's* Person was more agreeable to her Eye; for he was a comely Man; whereas the Pedagogue did in Countenance very nearly resemble that Gentleman, who in the Harlot's Progress is seen correcting the Ladies in *Bridewel*.[1]

Whether Mrs. *Blifil* had been surfeited with the Sweets of Marriage, or disgusted by its Bitters, or from what other Cause it proceeded, I will not determine; but she could never be brought to listen to any second Proposals. However, she at last conversed with *Square*, with such a Degree of Intimacy, that malicious Tongues began to whisper Things of her, to which, as well for the Sake of the Lady, as that they were highly disagreeable to the Rule of Right, and the Fitness of Things, we will give no Credit; and therefore shall not blot our Paper with them. The Pedagogue, 'tis certain, whipt on without getting a Step nearer to his Journey's End.

Indeed he had committed a great Error, and that *Square* dis-covered much sooner than himself. Mrs. *Blifil* (as perhaps the

the Abbé Boileau, *Histoire des flagellans* [Amsterdam, 1701], pp. 162–3). Cf. the sadistic priest in *A Journey from This World to the Next* (1743; I. xv).

1 Plate 4 of Hogarth's *A Harlot's Progress* (1732) is reproduced as Plate 3. See also above, pp. 58, 66, 82.

Reader may have formerly guess'd) was not over and above pleased with the Behaviour of her Husband; nay, to be honest, she absolutely hated him, till his Death at last a little reconciled him to her Affections. It will not be therefore greatly wondered at, if she had not the most violent Regard to the Offspring she had by him. And, in fact, she had so little of this Regard, that in his Infancy she seldom saw her Son, or took any Notice of him; and hence she acquiesced, after a little Reluctance, in all the Favours which Mr. *Allworthy* showered on the Foundling; whom the good Man called his own Boy, and in all Things put on an intire Equality with Master *Blifil*. This Acquiescence in Mrs. *Blifil* was considered by the Neighbours, and by the Family, as a Mark of her Condescension to her Brother's Humour, and she was imagined by all others, as well as *Thwackum* and *Square*, to hate the Foundling in her Heart; nay, the more Civility she shewed him, the more they conceived she detested him, and the surer Schemes she was laying for his Ruin: For as they thought it her Interest to hate him, it was very difficult for her to perswade them she did not.

Thwackum was the more confirmed in his Opinion, as she had more than once slily caused him to whip *Tom Jones*, when Mr. *Allworthy*, who was an Enemy to this Exercise, was abroad; whereas she had never given any such Orders concerning young *Blifil*. And this had likewise imposed upon *Square*. In reality, though she certainly hated her own Son; of which, however monstrous it appears, I am assured she is not a singular Instance, she appeared, notwithstanding all her outward Compliance, to be in her Heart sufficiently displeased with all the Favour shewn by Mr. *Allworthy* to the Foundling. She frequently complained of this behind her Brother's Back, and very sharply censured him for it, both to *Thwackum* and *Square*; nay, she would throw it in the Teeth of *Allworthy* himself, when a little Quarrel or Miff, as it is vulgarly called, arose between them.

However, when *Tom* grew up, and gave Tokens of that Gallantry of Temper which greatly recommends Men to Women, this Disinclination which she had discovered to him when a Child, by Degrees abated, and at last she so evidently demonstrated her Affection to him to be much stronger than what she bore her own Son, that it was impossible to mistake her any longer. She was so desirous of often seeing him, and discovered such Satisfaction and Delight in his Company, that before he was eighteen Years old, he was become a Rival to both *Square* and *Thwackum*; and what is worse, the whole Country began to talk as loudly of her Inclination to *Tom*, as they had before done of that which she had shewn to *Square*; on which Account the Philosopher conceived the most implacable Hatred for our poor Heroe.

CHAPTER VII

In which the Author himself makes his Appearance on the Stage.

THO' Mr. *Allworthy* was not of himself hasty to see Things in a disadvantageous Light, and was a Stranger to the public Voice, which seldom reaches to a Brother or a Husband, tho' it rings in the Ears of all the Neighbourhood; yet was this Affection of Mrs. *Blifil* to *Tom*, and the Preference which she too visibly gave him to her own Son, of the utmost Disadvantage to that Youth.

For such was the Compassion which inhabited Mr. *Allworthy's* Mind, that nothing but the Steel of Justice could ever subdue it. To be unfortunate in any Respect was sufficient, if there was no Demerit to counterpoise it, to turn the Scale of that good Man's Pity, and to engage his Friendship, and his Benefaction.

When therefore he plainly saw Master *Blifil* was absolutely detested (for that he was) by his own Mother, he began, on that Account only, to look with an Eye of Compassion upon him; and what the Effects of Compassion are in good and benevolent Minds, I need not here explain to most of my Readers.

Henceforward, he saw every Appearance of Virtue in the Youth thro' the magnifying End, and viewed all his Faults with the Glass inverted, so that they became scarce perceptible. And this perhaps the amiable Temper of Pity may make commendable; but the next Step the Weakness of human Nature alone must excuse: For he no sooner perceived that Preference which Mrs. *Blifil* gave to *Tom*, than that poor Youth, (however innocent) began to sink in his Affections as he rose in hers. This, it is true, would of itself alone never have been able to eradicate *Jones* from his Bosom; but it was greatly injurious to him, and prepared Mr. *Allworthy's* Mind for those Impressions, which afterwards

produced the mighty Events, that will be contained hereafter in
this History; and to which, it must be confest, the unfortunate
Lad, by his own Wantonness, Wildness, and Want of Caution,
too much contributed.

In recording some Instances of these, we shall, if rightly
understood, afford a very useful Lesson to those well-disposed
Youths, who shall hereafter be our Readers: For they may here
find that Goodness of Heart, and Openness of Temper, tho' these
may give them great Comfort within, and administer to an honest
Pride in their own Minds, will by no Means, alas! do their
Business in the World. Prudence[1] and Circumspection are necessary even to the best of Men. They are indeed as it were a Guard
to Virtue, without which she can never be safe. It is not enough
that your Designs, nay that your Actions are intrinsically good,
you must take Care they shall appear so. If your Inside be never
so beautiful, you must preserve a fair Outside also. This must
be constantly looked to, or Malice and Envy will take Care to
blacken it so, that the Sagacity and Goodness of an *Allworthy* will
not be able to see through it, and to discern the Beauties within.
Let this, my young Readers, be your constant Maxim, That no
Man can be good enough to enable him to neglect the Rules of
Prudence; nor will Virtue herself look beautiful, unless she be
bedecked with the outward Ornaments of Decency and Decorum.
And this Precept, my worthy Disciples, if you read with due
Attention, you will, I hope, find sufficiently enforced by Examples
in the following Pages.

I ask Pardon for this short Appearance, by Way of Chorus on

---

[1] See above, p. 36, n. 1. Most contemporary discussions of prudence stressed the importance of one's preserving the appearance, at least, of virtue. In *The Art of Prudence*
(1702) Gracián had warned that 'THINGS are not taken for what they really are, but for
what they appear to be. . . . It is not enough to have a good Intention, if the Action look
ill' (maxim xcix; see also cxxx), and Fuller's apothegms similarly emphasize that 'a fair
Reputation' is necessary to all men (*Introductio ad Prudentiam*, 3rd ed. [1731], Nos. 1425,
1590). As may be seen from *The Champion* (22 November 1739), Fielding agreed with this
much at least of the worldly wisdom inculcated by the writers of conduct books, though,
unlike them, he took care to distinguish a proper sense of discretion from a hypocritical
dissimulation: 'I would . . . by no Means recommend to Mankind to cultivate Deceit, or
endeavour to appear what they are not; on the contrary, I wish it were possible to induce the
World to make a diligent Enquiry into Things themselves, to withold them from giving
too hasty a Credit to the outward Shew and first Impression; I would only convince my
Readers, *That it is not enough to have Virtue, without we also take Care to preserve, by a
certain Decency and Dignity of Behaviour, the outward Appearance of it also.*' Cf. also Mrs.
Raffler in *The Universal Gallant* (1735), II. i.

the Stage. It is in Reality for my own Sake, that while I am discovering the Rocks on which Innocence and Goodness often
split, I may not be misunderstood to recommend the very Means
to my worthy Readers, by which I intend to shew them they will
be undone. And this, as I could not prevail on any of my Actors
to speak, I myself was obliged to declare.

CHAPTER VIII

*A childish Incident, in which, however, is seen a good-natur'd Dis-
position in* Tom Jones.

THE Reader may remember, that Mr. *Allworthy* gave *Tom
Jones* a little Horse, as a kind of smart Money for the Punishment, which he imagined he had suffered innocently.

This Horse *Tom* kept above half a Year, and then rode him to a
neighbouring Fair, and sold him.

At his Return, being questioned by *Thwackum*, what he had
done with the Money for which the Horse was sold, he frankly
declared he would not tell him.

'Oho!' says *Thwackum*, 'you will not! then I will have it out of
your Br—h;' that being the Place to which he always applied
for Information, on every doubtful Occasion.

Tom was now mounted on the Back of a Footman, and every
Thing prepared for Execution, when Mr. *Allworthy* entering the
Room, gave the Criminal a Reprieve, and took him with him
into another Apartment; where being alone with *Tom*, he put the
same Question to him which *Thwackum* had before asked him.

Tom answered, He could in Duty refuse him nothing; but as
for that tyrannical Rascal, he would never make him any other
Answer than with a Cudgel, with which he hoped soon to be
able to pay him for all his Barbarities.

Mr. *Allworthy* very severely reprimanded the Lad, for his
indecent and disrespectful Expressions concerning his Master;
but much more for his avowing an Intention of Revenge. He
threatened him with the entire Loss of his Favour, if he ever heard
such another Word from his Mouth; for he said, he would never
support or befriend a Reprobate. By these and the like Declarations, he extorted some Compunction from *Tom*, in which that

Youth was not over sincere: For he really meditated some Return for all the smarting Favours he had received at the Hands of the Pedagogue. He was, however, brought by Mr. *Allworthy* to express a Concern for his Resentment against *Thwackum*; and then the good Man, after some wholesome Admonition, permitted him to proceed, which he did, as follows.

'Indeed, my dear Sir, I love and honour you more than all the World; I know the great Obligations I have to you, and should detest myself, if I thought my Heart was capable of Ingratitude. Could the little Horse you gave me speak, I am sure he could tell you how fond I was of your Present: For I had more Pleasure in feeding him, than in riding him. Indeed, Sir, it went to my Heart to part with him; nor would I have sold him upon any other Account in the World than what I did. You yourself, Sir, I am convinced, in my Case, would have done the same: For none ever so sensibly felt the Misfortunes of others. What would you feel, dear Sir, if you thought yourself the Occasion of them?—Indeed, Sir, there never was any Misery like theirs.'—'Like whose, Child,' says *Allworthy*, 'what do you mean?' 'Oh, Sir,' answered *Tom*, 'your poor Game-keeper, with all, his large Family, ever since your discarding him, have been perishing with all the Miseries of Cold and Hunger. I could not bear to see these poor Wretches naked and starving, and at the same Time know myself to have been the Occasion of all their Sufferings.—I could not bear it, Sir, upon my Soul, I could not.' (Here the Tears run down his Cheeks, and he thus proceeded) 'It was to save them from absolute Destruction, I parted with your dear Present, notwithstanding all the Value I had for it.—I sold the Horse for them, and they have every Farthing of the Money.'

Mr. *Allworthy* now stood silent for some Moments, and before he spoke, the Tears started from his Eyes. He at length dismissed *Tom* with a gentle Rebuke, advising him for the future to apply to him in Cases of Distress, rather than to use extraordinary Means of relieving them himself.

This Affair was afterwards the Subject of much Debate between *Thwackum* and *Square*. *Thwackum* held, that this was flying in Mr. *Allworthy's* Face, who had intended to punish the Fellow for his Disobedience. He said, in some Instances, what the World called Charity appeared to him to be opposing the Will of the Almighty, which had marked some particular Persons for

Destruction; and that this was in like manner acting in Opposition to Mr. *Allworthy*; concluding, as usual, with a hearty Recommendation of Birch.

Square argued strongly, on the other Side, in Opposition perhaps to *Thwackum*, or in Compliance with Mr. *Allworthy*, who seemed very much to approve what *Jones* had done. As to what he urged on this Occasion, as I am convinced most of my Readers will be much abler Advocates for poor *Jones*, it would be impertinent to relate it. Indeed it was not difficult to reconcile to the *Rule of Right*, an Action which it would have been impossible to deduce from the *Rule of Wrong*.

CHAPTER IX

Containing an Incident of a more heinous Kind, with the Comments of
Thwackum *and* Square.

IT hath been observed by some Man of much greater Reputation for Wisdom than myself, that Misfortunes seldom come single. An Instance of this may, I believe, be seen in those Gentlemen who have the Misfortune to have any of their Rogueries detected: For here Discovery seldom stops till the whole is come out. Thus it happened to poor *Tom*; who was no sooner pardoned for selling the Horse, than he was discovered to have some time before sold a fine Bible which Mr. *Allworthy* gave him, the Money arising from which Sale he had disposed of in the same Manner. This Bible Master *Blifil* had purchased, though he had already such another of his own, partly out of Respect for the Book, and partly out of Friendship to *Tom*, being unwilling that the Bible should be sold out of the Family at half Price. He therefore disbursed the said half Price himself; for he was a very prudent Lad, and so careful of his Money, that he had laid up almost every Penny which he had received from Mr. *Allworthy*.

Some People have been noted to be able to read in no Book but their own.[1] On the contrary, from the Time when Master *Blifil* was first possessed of this Bible, he never used any other. Nay, he was seen reading in it much oftner than he had before been

[1] Said proverbially of the Parson of Saddleworth. (See John Ray's *Collection of English Proverbs* [1670].)

in his own. Now, as he frequently asked *Thwackum* to explain difficult Passages to him, that Gentleman unfortunately took Notice of *Tom's* Name, which was written in many Parts of the Book. This brought on an Enquiry, which obliged Master *Blifil* to discover the whole Matter.

Thwackum was resolved, a Crime of this Kind, which he called Sacrilege, should not go unpunished. He therefore proceeded immediately to Castigation; and not contented with that, he acquainted Mr. *Allworthy*, at their next Meeting, with this monstrous Crime, as it appeared to him; inveighing against *Tom* in the most bitter Terms, and likening him to the Buyers and Sellers who were driven out of the Temple.[1]

Square saw this Matter in a very different Light. He said, He could not perceive any higher Crime in selling one Book, than in selling another. That to sell Bibles was strictly lawful by all Laws both divine and human, and consequently there was no Unfitness in it. He told *Thwackum* that his great Concern on this Occasion brought to his Mind the Story of a very devout Woman, who out of pure Regard to Religion, stole *Tillotson's* Sermons[2] from a Lady of her Acquaintance.

This Story caused a vast Quantity of Blood to rush into the Parson's Face, which of itself was none of the palest; and he was going to reply with great Warmth and Anger, had not Mrs. *Blifil*, who was present at this Debate, interposed. That Lady declared herself absolutely of Mr. *Square's* Side. She argued, indeed, very learnedly in Support of his Opinion; and concluded with saying, If *Tom* had been guilty of any Fault, she must confess her own Son appeared to be equally culpable; for that she could see no Difference between the Buyer and the Seller; both of whom were alike to be driven out of the Temple.

Mrs. *Blifil* having declared her Opinion, put an End to the Debate. *Square's* Triumph would almost have stopt his Words,

[1] Cf. Matthew 21: 12–13, Mark 11: 15–17, John 2: 14–16.

[2] John Tillotson (1630–94), Archbishop of Canterbury and a leader of the latitudinarians. Because of his 'natural and easy' style, Tillotson's sermons were much admired. (See, for example, Henry Felton, *A Dissertation on Reading the Classics, and Forming a Just Style*, 5th ed. [1753], pp. 178–9.) In *Tom Jones* Allworthy apparently draws upon Tillotson's works in disputing a theological point with Captain Blifil (see above, p. 79, n. 4). Indeed, complimentary allusions to this distinguished divine occur frequently in Fielding's writings: see, for example, *The Champion* (22 January, 15 March 1739/40), *Joseph Andrews* (1742; I. xvi), *The Covent-Garden Journal* (14 January 1752), and *A Proposal for Making an Effectual Provision for the Poor* (1753).

had he needed them; and *Thwackum*, who, for Reasons before-mentioned, durst not venture at disobliging the Lady, was almost choaked with Indignation. As to Mr. *Allworthy*, he said, Since the Boy had been already punished, he would not deliver his Sentiments on the Occasion; and whether he was, or was not angry with the Lad, I must leave to the Reader's own Conjecture.

Soon after this, an Action was brought against the Game-keeper by Squire *Western* (the Gentleman in whose Manor the *Partridge* was killed) for Depredations of the like Kind. This was a most unfortunate Circumstance for the Fellow, as it not only of itself threatened his Ruin, but actually prevented Mr. *All-worthy* from restoring him to his Favour: For as that Gentleman was walking out one Evening with Master *Blifil* and young *Jones*, the latter slily drew him to the Habitation of *Black George*; where the Family of that poor Wretch, namely, his Wife and Children, were found in all the Misery with which Cold, Hunger, and Nakedness, can affect human Creatures: For as to the Money they had received from *Jones*, former Debts had consumed almost the whole.

Such a Scene as this could not fail of affecting the Heart of Mr. *Allworthy*. He immediately gave the Mother a couple of Guineas, with which he bid her cloath her Children. The poor Woman burst into Tears at this Goodness, and while she was thanking him, could not refrain from expressing her Gratitude to *Tom*; who had, she said, long preserved both her and hers from starving. We have not, says she, had a Morsel to eat, nor have these poor Children had a Rag to put on, but what his Good-ness hath bestowed on us: For indeed, besides the Horse and the Bible, *Tom* had sacrificed a Night-gown and other Things to the Use of this distressed Family.

On their Return home, *Tom* made use of all his Eloquence to display the Wretchedness of these People, and the Penitence of *Black George* himself; and in this he succeeded so well, that Mr. *Allworthy* said, He thought the Man had suffered enough for what was past; that he would forgive him, and think of some Means of providing for him and his Family.

Jones was so delighted with this News, that though it was dark when they returned home, he could not help going back a Mile in a Shower of Rain to acquaint the poor Woman with the glad Tidings; but, like other hasty Divulgers of News, he only brought on himself the Trouble of contradicting it: For the Ill-fortune of *Black George* made use of the very Opportunity of his Friend's Absence to overturn all again.

CHAPTER X

In which Master Blifil *and* Jones *appear in different Lights.*

MASTER *Blifil* fell very short of his Companion in the amiable Quality of Mercy; but he as greatly exceeded him in one of a much higher Kind, namely, in Justice: In which he followed both the Precepts and Example of *Thwackum* and *Square*; for though they would both make frequent Use of the Word *Mercy*, yet it was plain, that in reality *Square* held it to be inconsistent with the Rule of Right; and *Thwackum* was for doing Justice, and leaving Mercy to Heaven. The two Gentlemen did indeed somewhat differ in Opinion concerning the Objects of this sublime Virtue; by which *Thwackum* would probably have destroyed one half of Mankind, and *Square* the other half.

Master *Blifil* then, though he had kept Silence in the Presence of *Jones*, yet when he had better considered the Matter, could by no Means endure the Thoughts of suffering his Uncle to confer Favours on the Undeserving. He therefore resolved immediately to acquaint him with the Fact which we have above slightly hinted to the Readers. The Truth of which was as follows:

The Game-keeper, about a Year after he was dismissed from Mr. *Allworthy's* Service, and before *Tom's* selling the Horse, being in Want of Bread, either to fill his own Mouth, or those of his Family, as he passed through a Field belonging to Mr. *Western*, espied a Hare sitting in her Form. This Hare he had basely and barbarously knocked on the Head, against the Laws of the Land, and no less against the Laws of Sportsmen.

The Higler to whom the Hare was sold, being unfortunately taken many Months after with a Quantity of Game upon him, was obliged to make his Peace with the Squire by becoming Evidence against some Poacher.[1] And now *Black George* was

---

[1] According to the Game Laws (viz. 5 Anne [Session 2], cap. 14), any higgler or other unauthorized person found to have game in his possession could be prosecuted. If convicted within three months of the offence, he was liable to a fine of £5 for each bird, etc.,

pitched upon by him as being a Person already obnoxious to Mr. *Western*, and one of no good Fame in the Country. He was, besides, the best Sacrifice the Higler could make, as he had supplied him with no Game since; and by this Means the Witness had an Opportunity of screening his better Customers: For the Squire, being charmed with the Power of punishing *Black George*, whom a single Transgression was sufficient to ruin, made no further Enquiry.

Had this Fact been truly laid before Mr. *Allworthy*, it might probably have done the Game-keeper very little Mischief. But there is no Zeal blinder than that which is inspired with the Love of Justice against Offenders. Master *Blifil* had forgot the Distance of the Time. He varied likewise in the Manner of the Fact; and, by the hasty Addition of the single Letter S, he considerably altered the Story; for he said that *George* had wired Hares. These Alterations might probably have been set right, had not Master *Blifil* unluckily insisted on a Promise of Secrecy from Mr. *Allworthy*, before he revealed the Matter to him; but by that Means, the poor Game-keeper was condemned, without having any Opportunity to defend himself: For as the Fact of killing the Hare, and of the Action brought, were certainly true, Mr. *Allworthy* had no Doubt concerning the rest.

Short-lived then was the Joy of these poor People; for Mr. *Allworthy* the next Morning declared he had fresh Reason, without assigning it, for his Anger, and strictly forbad *Tom* to mention *George* any more; though as for his Family, he said, he would endeavour to keep them from starving; but as to the Fellow himself, he would leave him to the Laws, which nothing could keep him from breaking.

Tom could by no Means divine what had incensed Mr. *Allworthy*: For of Master *Blifil* he had not the least Suspicion. However, as his Friendship was to be tired out by no Disappointments, he now determined to try another Method of preserving the poor Game-keeper from Ruin.

Jones was lately grown very intimate with Mr. *Western*. He

or, if unable to pay the money, he could be imprisoned. By supplying evidence leading to the conviction of some other offender within three months of the offence, he would, however, not only escape punishment himself, but be rewarded with half the amount of all fines paid. (See Wood's *Institutes*, 7th ed. [1745], pp. 462–3.) As Hugh Amory has noticed, however, in 1728 and 1738 the King's Bench had held that the higgler's interest in the conviction disqualified him as a witness.

had so greatly recommended himself to that Gentleman, by leaping over five-barred Gates, and by other Acts of Sportsmanship, that the Squire had declared *Tom* would certainly make a great Man, if he had but sufficient Encouragement. He often wished he had himself a Son with such Parts; and one Day very solemnly asserted at a drinking Bout, that *Tom* should hunt a Pack of Hounds for a thousand Pound of his Money with any Huntsman in the whole Country.

By such kind of Talents he had so ingratiated himself with the Squire, that he was a most welcome Guest at his Table, and a favourite Companion in his Sport: Every Thing which the Squire held most dear; to wit, his Guns, Dogs, and Horses, were now as much at the Command of *Jones*, as if they had been his own. He resolved therefore to make use of this Favour on Behalf of his Friend *Black George*, whom he hoped to introduce into Mr. *Western's* Family in the same Capacity in which he had before served Mr. *Allworthy*.

The Reader, if he considers that this Fellow was already obnoxious to Mr. *Western*, and if he considers farther the weighty Business by which that Gentleman's Displeasure had been incurred, will perhaps condemn this as a foolish and desperate Undertaking; but if he should not totally condemn young *Jones* on that Account, he will greatly applaud him for strengthening himself with all imaginable Interest on so arduous an Occasion.

For this Purpose then *Tom* applied to Mr. *Western's* Daughter, a young Lady of about seventeen Years of Age, whom her Father, next after those necessary Implements of Sport just beforementioned, loved and esteemed above all the World. Now as she had some Influence on the Squire, so *Tom* had some little Influence on her. But this being the intended Heroine of this Work, a Lady with whom we ourselves are greatly in Love, and with whom many of our Readers will probably be in Love too before we part, it is by no Means proper she should make her Appearance in the End of a Book.

The End of the First Volume.

BOOK IV

Containing the Time of a Year.

CHAPTER I

Containing five Pages of Paper.

AS Truth distinguishes our Writings, from those idle Romances which are filled with Monsters, the Productions, not of Nature, but of distempered Brains;[1] and which have been therefore recommended by an eminent Critic[2] to the sole Use of the Pastry-cook: So, on the other hand, we would avoid any Resemblance to that Kind of History which a celebrated Poet seems to think is no less calculated for the Emolument of the Brewer, as the reading it should be always attended with a Tankard of good Ale.

> *While—History with her Comrade Ale,*
> *Sooths the sad Series of her serious Tale.*[3]

For as this is the Liquor of modern Historians, nay, perhaps

---

[1] See also *Tom Jones* (IX. i) and *Joseph Andrews* (1742; III. i), where Fielding similarly distinguishes between the confused and unnatural productions of romance-writers and the 'true histories' of authors such as Cervantes and LeSage, 'who are contented to copy Nature'.

[2] Cf. the Preface to *The Journal of a Voyage to Lisbon* (1755), where Fielding tentatively identifies this critic as Joseph Addison (1672–1719). Fielding's memory, however, seems to have failed him in this instance, for, though both Addison and Steele facetiously allude to the pastry-cooks, who used the sheets of ephemeral books and pamphlets to line pie plates, they do not specifically recommend that romances be dismembered for this purpose. (See *The Spectator*, No. 85 [7 June 1711] and No. 304 [18 February 1712].) Closer to the present context are two passages from Shaftesbury which Fielding may have confused: in 'Advice to an Author' (III. iii), Shaftesbury deplores the contemporary taste for novels and romances, 'Things the most *unnatural* and *monstrous*'; in his 'Miscellaneous Reflections' (chap. ii), he takes comfort in the fact that another kind of fugitive literature, the works of polemical pamphleteers, 'have been long since paying their attendance to the *Pastry-cooks*'. (See *Characteristicks*, 5th ed. [1732], i. 347, iii. 14.) Cf. *The Covent-Garden Journal* (21 January 1752), where Fielding offers the following translation of the epigraph from Martial: '*How many fear the Moth's and Bookworm's Rage,/ And Pastry-Cooks, sole Buyers in this Age?*'

[3] Fielding imperfectly recalls a couplet from the original version of Pope's *Dunciad* (1728), III. 171–2: 'While happier *Hist'ry* with her comrade *Ale*,/ Sooths the sad series of her tedious tale.' The lines are part of the passage beginning, 'each *Science* by its modern type/ Stands known' (III. 167–8). See also below, p. 684. 10–11.

their Muse, if we may believe the Opinion of *Butler*,[1] who attributes Inspiration to Ale, it ought likewise to be the Potation of their Readers; since every Book ought to be read with the same Spirit, and in the same Manner, as it is writ.[2] Thus the famous Author of *Hurlothrumbo*[3] told a learned Bishop, that the Reason his Lordship could not taste the Excellence of his Piece, was, that he did not read it with a Fiddle in his Hand; which Instrument he himself had always had in his own, when he composed it.

That our Work, therefore, might be in no Danger of being likened to the Labours of these Historians, we have taken every Occasion of interspersing through the whole sundry Similes, Descriptions, and other kind of poetical Embellishments. These are, indeed, designed to supply the Place of the said Ale, and to refresh the Mind, whenever those Slumbers which in a long Work are apt to invade the Reader as well as the Writer, shall begin to creep upon him. Without Interruptions of this Kind, the best Narrative of plain Matter of Fact must overpower every Reader; for nothing but the everlasting Watchfulness, which *Homer* hath ascribed[4] only to *Jove* himself, can be Proof against a News-Paper of many Volumes.

---

[1] In Part i of *Hudibras* (1663), Samuel Butler (1613–80) invokes the nameless Muse who
> . . . with Ale, or viler Liquors,
> Didst inspire *Withers, Pryn*, and *Vickars*,
> And force them, though it were in spight
> Of nature and their stars, to write. . . .
(i. i. 639–42; ed. J. Wilders [Oxford, 1967].)
For other allusions to Butler and *Hudibras* in *Tom Jones*, see below, pp. 178, 399, 561.

[2] Cf. Pope's *Essay on Criticism* (1711), 233–4: 'A perfect Judge will *read* each Work of Wit/ With the same Spirit that its Author *writ*. . . .' Cf. also the Preface to Swift's *Tale of a Tub* (1704), where the author lays down the following 'general Maxim' for the benefit of those readers with 'the Taste of Wit' who would fully sound the depths of that sublime work: 'Whatever Reader desires to have a thorow Comprehension of an Author's Thoughts, cannot take a better Method, than by putting himself into the Circumstances and Postures of Life, that the Writer was in, upon every important Passage as it flow'd from his Pen; For this will introduce a Parity and strict Correspondence of Idea's between the Reader and the Author.'

[3] *Hurlothrumbo: or, The Super-Natural*, a heroic extravaganza by Samuel Johnson (1691–1773), dancing-master of Cheshire, had a spectacular run when it was first produced at the Haymarket in 1729. Johnson, who took the part of Lord Flame, fiddled and danced and ranted his way through the role. Fielding alludes facetiously to Johnson and his nonsensical drama in *The Author's Farce* (1730; i. v and iii), in the Preface to *Tom Thumb* (1730), in *Pasquin* (1736; v. i), and in *The Champion* (19 February 1739/40, 15 April 1740).

[4] *Iliad*, ii. 1–2. For an earlier reference, see Fielding's note to *A Journey from This World to the Next* (1743), i. ii.

We shall leave to the Reader to determine with what Judgment we have chosen the several Occasions for inserting those ornamental Parts of our Work. Surely it will be allowed that none could be more proper than the present; where we are about to introduce a considerable Character on the Scene; no less, indeed, than the Heroine of this Heroic, Historical, Prosaic Poem. Here, therefore, we have thought proper to prepare the Mind of the Reader for her Reception, by filling it with every pleasing Image, which we can draw from the Face of Nature. And for this Method we plead many Precedents. First, this is an Art well known to, and much practised by, our Tragic Poets; who seldom fail to prepare their Audience for the Reception of their principal Characters.

Thus the Heroe is always introduced with a Flourish of Drums and Trumpets,[1] in order to rouse a martial Spirit in the Audience, and to accommodate their Ears to Bombast and Fustian, which Mr. *Lock's* blind Man[2] would not have grossly erred in likening to the Sound of a Trumpet. Again, when Lovers are coming forth, soft Music often conducts them on the Stage, either to sooth the Audience with the Softness of the tender Passion, or to lull and prepare them for that gentle Slumber in which they will most probably be composed by the ensuing Scene.

And not only the Poets, but the Masters of these Poets, the Managers of Playhouses, seem to be in this Secret; for, besides the aforesaid Kettle Drums, &c. which denote the Heroe's Approach, he is generally ushered on the Stage by a large Troop of half a dozen Scene-shifters; and how necessary these are imagined to his Appearance, may be concluded from the following Theatrical Story.

King *Pyrrhus*[3] was at Dinner at an Alehouse bordering on the

[1] Facetious allusions to this dramatic convention occur earlier in *The Tragedy of Tragedies* (1731), I. i and note k, and in *Jonathan Wild* (1743), I. iii.

[2] John Locke (1632–1704) in *An Essay concerning Human Understanding* (1690), III. iv 11: 'A studious blind Man, who had mightily beat his Head about visible Objects, and made use of the Explication of his Books and Friends, to understand those Names of Light and Colours, which often came in his way; bragged one Day, That he now understood what *Scarlet* signified. Upon which his Friend demanding, what *Scarlet* was? The blind Man answered, it was like the Sound of a Trumpet' (12th ed. [1741], ii. 29). See also *Tom Jones*, p. 271.

[3] Barton Booth (1681–1733), the celebrated tragedian, who first acted the part of Pyrrhus in Ambrose Philips's *The Distrest Mother* (1712). From 1711 Booth was associated with Cibber and Robert Wilks (1665–1732) in the management of Drury Lane.

Theatre, when he was summoned to go on the Stage. The Heroe, being unwilling to quit his Shoulder of Mutton, and as unwilling to draw on himself the Indignation of Mr. *Wilks*, (his Brother Manager) for making the Audience wait, had bribed these his Harbingers to be out of the Way. While Mr. *Wilks*, therefore, was thundering out, 'Where are the Carpenters to walk on before King *Pyrrhus*,' that Monarch very quietly eat his Mutton, and the Audience, however impatient, were obliged to entertain themselves with Music in his Absence.

To be plain, I much question whether the Politician, who hath generally a good Nose, hath not scented out somewhat of the Utility of this Practice. I am convinced that awful Magistrate my Lord Mayor contracts a good deal of that Reverence which attends him through the Year, by the several Pageants which precede his Pomp.[1] Nay, I must confess, that even I myself, who am not remarkably liable to be captivated with Show, have yielded not a little to the Impressions of much preceding State. When I have seen a Man strutting in a Procession, after others whose Business was only to walk before him, I have conceived a higher Notion of his Dignity, than I have felt on seeing him in a common Situation. But there is one Instance which comes exactly up to my Purpose. This is the Custom of sending on a Basket-woman,[2] who is to precede the Pomp at a Coronation, and to strew the Stage with Flowers, before the great Personages begin their Procession. The Antients would certainly have invoked the Goddess *Flora* for this Purpose, and it would have been no Difficulty for their Priests or Politicians to have persuaded the People of the real Presence of the Deity, though a plain Mortal had personated her, and performed her Office. But we have no such

[1] Occurring annually in late October, the day on which the new Lord Mayor of London took the oaths of office was an occasion of much pomp and pageantry. The following account is from *The General Advertiser* (29 October 1748): 'This Day the new Lord-Mayor, accompanied by the late Lord-Mayor, Aldermen, Recorder, and Sheriffs in their Scarlet Gowns, will go in their Coaches to the Water-Side, the Sword and Mace carried before them, and the City Officers attending, and from thence proceed in the City Barge, attended by the several Companies in their respective Barges, adorned with Streamers and Pendants to Westminster; and after having walked round the Hall and solemnly Saluted all the Courts, they will go to the Exchequer-Bar, and the Lord-Mayor will there take the Oaths appointed, and having recorded Warrants of Attorney in the proper Courts, they will return by Water to Black-Fryars, and from thence in Coaches with the usual Solemnity to Guildhall; where a magnificent Entertainment will be provided for them. . . .'
[2] This convention is alluded to in *Pasquin* (1736), III. i.

Design of imposing on our Reader, and therefore those who object to the Heathen Theology, may, if they please, change our Goddess into the above-mentioned Basket-woman. Our Intention, in short, is to introduce our Heroine with the utmost Solemnity in our Power, with an Elevation of Stile, and all other Circumstances proper to raise the Veneration of our Reader. Indeed we would, for certain Causes, advise those of our Male Readers who have any Hearts, to read no farther, were we not well assured, that how amiable soever the Picture of our Heroine will appear, as it is really a Copy from Nature,[1] many of our fair Country-women will be found worthy to satisfy any Passion, and to answer any Idea of Female Perfection, which our Pencil will be able to raise.

And now, without any further Preface, we proceed to our next Chapter.

CHAPTER II

A short Hint of what we can do in the Sublime, and a Description of Miss Sophia Western.

HUSHED be every ruder Breath. May the Heathen Ruler of the Winds[2] confine in iron Chains the boisterous Limbs of noisy *Boreas*, and the sharp-pointed Nose of bitter-biting *Eurus*. Do thou, sweet *Zephyrus*, rising from thy fragrant Bed, mount the western Sky, and lead on those delicious Gales, the Charms of which call forth the lovely *Flora* from her Chamber, perfumed with pearly Dews, when on the first of *June*, her Birth-day, the blooming Maid, in loose Attire, gently trips it over the verdant Mead, where every Flower rises to do her Homage, till the whole Field becomes enamelled, and Colours contend with Sweets which shall ravish her most.

So charming may she now appear; and you the feather'd Choristers of Nature, whose sweetest Notes not even *Handel*[3] can

[1] See below, p. 156, n. 3.

[2] Aeolus. The names that follow are those, respectively, of the north, east, and west winds.

[3] George Frideric Handel (1685–1759), the celebrated composer, had been residing in England since 1712. Fielding, who delighted in 'the enchanting Harmony' of his music (see *The Champion*, 10 June 1740), paid frequent compliments to Handel: see, for example,

excel, tune your melodious Throats, to celebrate her Appearance. From Love proceeds your Music, and to Love it returns. Awaken therefore that gentle Passion in every Swain: for lo! adorned with all the Charms in which Nature can array her; bedecked with Beauty, Youth, Sprightliness, Innocence, Modesty, and Tenderness, breathing Sweetness from her rosy Lips, and darting Brightness from her sparkling Eyes, the lovely *Sophia* comes.

Reader, perhaps thou hast seen the Statue of the *Venus de Medicis*.[1] Perhaps too, thou hast seen the Gallery of Beauties at *Hampton-Court*.[2] Thou may'st remember *each bright* Churchill *of the Gallaxy*,[3] and all the Toasts of the *Kit-Cat*.[4] Or if their Reign was before thy Times, at least thou hast seen their Daughters, the no less dazling Beauties of the present Age; whose Names, should we here insert, we apprehend they would fill the whole Volume.

Now if thou hast seen all these, be not afraid of the rude Answer which Lord *Rochester* once gave[5] to a Man, who had seen

---

Of True Greatness (1741), The True Patriot (5 November 1745, 28 January–4 February 1746), Letter xl of Sarah Fielding's *Familiar Letters* (1747), The Jacobite's Journal (19 March 1748), *Amelia* (1751; IV. ix), and The Covent-Garden Journal (16 September 1752). See also below, p. 169.

[1] Done by a follower of Praxiteles, this famous statue now stands in the Uffizi Gallery, Florence. According to Joseph Spence, the body of the Venus de Medici 'will ever be the standard of all female beauty and softness' (*Polymetis* [1747], p. 66). Burlington placed a copy of the statue in the Rotunda at Chiswick, and prints of it were very popular in England (see, for example, the advertisements in *The General Advertiser*, 4–6 February 1746/7).

[2] The 'Hampton Court Beauties' were the series of eight portraits by Godfrey Kneller (1649?–1723) representing the principal ladies who attended upon Queen Mary. Completed in 1691, the series hung first in the Water Gallery and then in the Eating Room at Hampton Court. Engravings were made by John Faber.

[3] Cf. The Dispensary (1706), p. 68, by Samuel Garth (1661–1719): 'And each bright Churchill of the Galaxy.' The four daughters of John and Sarah Churchill, Duke and Duchess of Marlborough, were celebrated for their beauty. In his Apology (1740), Cibber complimented the Duchess on having 'given the World four of the loveliest Daughters, that ever were gaz'd on', who were 'the reigning Toasts of every Party of Pleasure' (2nd ed., pp. 59–60). Fielding alludes to these 'fair' ladies again in his poem, 'To a Friend on the Choice of a Wife' (1743). See also Pope's Epistle to Mr. Jervas (1716), ll. 46, 59, on the beauty of 'Churchill's race'.

[4] The Kit-Cat Club (*fl.* 1700–20) was composed of the most eminent Whig statesmen and wits of the day—Garth (see n. 3 above), Robert Walpole, Vanbrugh, Congreve, Addison, and Steele. The name presumably derives from one Christopher Cat, a pastrycook at whose house the members originally met. It was the club's custom to toast the fair ladies of their acquaintance—the Churchill 'galaxy' among them—in glasses inscribed with appropriate verses. See 'Verses Written for the Toasting-Glasses of the Kit-kat Club, in the Year 1703' in Tonson's *Miscellany Poems*, v (1716), [60–70].

[5] John Wilmot (1647–80), second Earl of Rochester. Fielding refers to the poem 'To all

many Things. No. If thou hast seen all these without knowing what Beauty is, thou hast no Eyes; if without feeling its Power, thou hast no Heart.

Yet is it possible, my Friend, that thou mayest have seen all these without being able to form an exact Idea of *Sophia*: for she did not exactly resemble any of them. She was most like the Picture of Lady *Ranelagh*;[1] and I have heard more still to the famous Dutchess of *Mazarine*;[2] but most of all, she resembled one whose Image never can depart from my Breast,[3] and whom, if thou dost remember, thou hast then, my Friend, an adequate Idea of *Sophia*.

But lest this should not have been thy Fortune, we will endeavour with our utmost Skill to describe this Paragon, though we are sensible that our highest Abilities are very inadequate to the Task.

Sophia then, the only Daughter of Mr. *Western*, was a middle-sized Woman; but rather inclining to tall. Her Shape was not only exact, but extremely delicate; and the nice Proportion of her Arms promised the truest Symmetry in her Limbs. Her Hair, which was black, was so luxuriant, that it reached her Middle, before she cut it, to comply with the modern Fashion; and it was now curled so gracefully in her Neck, that few could believe it to be her own. If Envy could find any Part of the Face which demanded less Commendation than the rest, it might possibly think her Forehead might have been higher without Prejudice to her. Her Eye-brows were full, even, and arched beyond the Power of Art to imitate. Her black Eyes had a Lustre in them, which all her Softness could not extinguish. Her Nose was exactly regular, and her Mouth, in which were two Rows of Ivory, exactly answered Sir *John Suckling's* Description[4] in those Lines,

Curious Criticks and Admirers of Metre', which, though probably not in fact by Roches-ter, originally appeared in his *Poems* (1680) and continued to be attributed to him. Organ-ized in a manner similar to Fielding's preceding paragraph, the poem proceeds through a series of questions—'Have you seen' a ship tossed by a storm, a jealous bull, fairies dancing, etc. ?—to a rude conclusion: 'If you have seen all this, then kiss mine A[rs]e.'

1 Margaret Cecil (1673–1727), Countess of Ranelagh, was one of the 'Hampton Court Beauties' painted by Kneller (see above, p. 155, n. 2, and Plate 4).

2 Hortense Mancini (1646–99), Duchess of Mazarin, was a famous beauty who, after emigrating to England from France in 1676, was taken into the court of Charles II. Sir Peter Lely (1618–80) painted her portrait several times, from which engravings were made. One of these prints is reproduced as Plate 5.

3 Charlotte Cradock, Fielding's first wife, who died in November 1744.

4 'A Ballad upon a Wedding', ll. 61–3, by Sir John Suckling (1609–42).

Her Lips were red, and one was thin,
Compar'd to that was next her Chin.
Some Bee had stung it newly.

Her Cheeks, were of the oval Kind; and in her right she had a Dimple which the least Smile discovered. Her Chin had certainly its Share in forming the Beauty of her Face; but it was difficult to say it was either large or small, tho' perhaps it was rather of the former Kind. Her Complexion had rather more of the Lilly than of the Rose; but when Exercise, or Modesty, encreased her natural Colour, no Vermilion could equal it. Then one might indeed cry out with the celebrated Dr. *Donne*,[1]

——*Her pure and eloquent Blood*
Spoke in her Cheeks, and so distinctly wrought,
That one might almost say her Body thought.

Her Neck was long and finely turned; and here, if I was not afraid of offending her Delicacy, I might justly say, the highest Beauties of the famous *Venus de Medicis* were outdone. Here was Whiteness which no Lillies, Ivory, nor Alabaster could match. The finest Cambric might indeed be supposed from Envy to cover that Bosom, which was much whiter than itself,—It was indeed,

Nitor splendens Pario marmore purius.[2]

'A Gloss shining beyond the purest Brightness of *Parian* Marble.'

Such was the Outside of *Sophia*; nor was this beautiful Frame disgraced by an Inhabitant unworthy of it. Her Mind was every way equal to her Person; nay, the latter borrowed some Charms from the former: For when she smiled, the Sweetness of her Temper diffused that Glory over her Countenance, which no Regularity of Features can give. But as there are no Perfections of the Mind which do not discover themselves, in that perfect Intimacy, to which we intend to introduce our Reader, with this charming young Creature; so it is needless to mention them here: Nay, it is a Kind of tacit Affront to our Reader's Understanding, and may also rob him of that Pleasure which he will receive in forming his own Judgment of her Character.

[1] John Donne (*c.* 1572–1631), Dean of St. Paul's from 1621. The passage describing Elizabeth Drury from Donne's *Second Anniversarie*, ll. 244–6, had been quoted by Steele in *Spectator*, No. 41 (17 April 1711), who used the lines to praise the charms of 'Statira'.

[2] Horace, *Odes*, I. xix. 5–6: 'urit me Glycerae nitor,/ splendentis Pario marmore purius' ('I am enamoured of Glycera's beauty, more dazzling than Parian marble'—trans. C. E. Bennett, Loeb Classical Library, 1914).

It may however, be proper to say, that whatever mental Accomplishments she had derived from Nature, they were somewhat improved and cultivated by Art: for she had been educated under the Care of an Aunt, who was a Lady of great Discretion, and was thoroughly acquainted with the World, having lived in her Youth about the Court, whence she had retired some Years since into the Country. By her Conversation and Instructions, *Sophia* was perfectly well-bred, though perhaps she wanted a little of that Ease in her Behaviour, which is to be acquired only by Habit, and living within what is called the polite Circle. But this, to say the Truth, is often too dearly purchased; and though it hath Charms so inexpressible, that the *French*, perhaps, among other Qualities, mean to express this, when they declare they know not what it is,¹ yet its Absence is well compensated by Innocence; nor can good Sense, and a natural Gentility ever stand in need of it.

CHAPTER III

Wherein the History goes back to commemorate a trifling Incident that happened some Years since; but which, trifling as it was, had some future Consequences.

THE amiable *Sophia* was now in her eighteenth Year, when she is introduced into this History. Her Father, as hath been said, was fonder of her than of any other human Creature. To her, therefore, *Tom Jones* applied, in order to engage her Interest on the Behalf of his Friend the Game-keeper.

But before we proceed to this Business, a short Recapitulation of some previous Matters may be necessary.

Though the different Tempers of Mr. *Allworthy*, and of Mr. *Western* did not admit of a very intimate Correspondence, yet they

---

¹ The French phrase, *je ne sais quoi,* was commonly used by aestheticians to denote that indefinable quality of grace which lies, as Pope put it, 'beyond the Reach of Art' (*An Essay on Criticism* [1711], l. 155). Thus Shaftesbury advised his author to 'fix his Eye upon that consummate *Grace*, that Beauty of *Nature*, and that *Perfection* of Numbers, which the rest of Mankind, feeling only the Effect, whilst ignorant of the Cause, term the *Je-ne-sçay-quoy*, the unintelligible, or the I know not what; and suppose to be a kind of *Charm*, or *Inchantment*, of which the Artist himself can give no account' ('Soliloquy: or, Advice to an Author', in *Characteristicks*, 5th ed. [1732], i. 332).

lived upon what is called a decent Footing together; by which Means the young People of both Families had been acquainted from their Infancy; and as they were all near of the same Age, had been frequent Play-mates together.

The Gaiety of *Tom's* Temper suited better with *Sophia*, than the grave and sober Disposition of Master *Blifil*. And the Preference which she gave the former of these, would often appear so plainly, that a Lad of a more passionate Turn than Master *Blifil* was, might have shewn some Displeasure at it.

As he did not, however, outwardly express any such Disgust, it would be an ill Office in us to pay a Visit to the inmost Recesses of his Mind, as some scandalous People search into the most secret Affairs of their Friends, and often pry into their Closets and Cupboards, only to discover their Poverty and Meanness to the World.

However, as Persons who suspect they have given others Cause of Offence, are apt to conclude they are offended; so *Sophia* imputed an Action of Master *Blifil*, to his Anger, which the superior Sagacity of *Thwackum* and *Square* discerned to have arisen from a much better Principle.

Tom Jones, when very young, had presented *Sophia* with a little Bird, which he had taken from the Nest, had nursed up, and taught to sing.

Of this Bird, *Sophia*, then about thirteen Years old, was so extremely fond, that her chief Business was to feed and tend it, and her chief Pleasure to play with it. By these Means little *Tommy*, for so the Bird was called, was become so tame, that it would feed out of the Hand of its Mistress, would perch upon her Finger, and lie contented in her Bosom, where it seemed almost sensible of its own Happiness; tho' she always kept a small String about its Leg, nor would ever trust it with the Liberty of flying away.

One Day, when Mr. *Allworthy* and his whole Family, dined at Mr. *Western's*, Master *Blifil*, being in the Garden with little *Sophia*, and observing the extreme Fondness that she shewed for her little Bird, desired her to trust it for a Moment in his Hands. *Sophia* presently complied with the young Gentleman's Request, and after some previous Caution, delivered him her Bird; of which he was no sooner in Possession, than he slipt the String from its Leg, and tossed it into the Air.

The foolish Animal no sooner perceived itself at Liberty, than forgetting all the Favours it had received from *Sophia*, it flew directly from her, and perched on a Bough at some Distance.

Sophia, seeing her Bird gone, screamed out so loud, that *Tom Jones*, who was at a little Distance, immediately ran to her Assistance.

He was no sooner informed of what had happened, than he cursed *Blifil* for a pitiful, malicious Rascal, and then immediately stripping off his Coat, he applied himself to climbing the Tree to which the Bird escaped.

Tom had almost recovered his little Name-sake, when the Branch, on which it was perched, and that hung over a Canal, broke, and the poor Lad plumped over Head and Ears into the Water.

Sophia's Concern now changed its Object. And as she apprehended the Boy's Life was in Danger, she screamed ten times louder than before; and indeed Master *Blifil* himself now seconded her with all the Vociferation in his Power.

The Company, who were sitting in a Room next the Garden, were instantly alarmed, and came all forth; but just as they reached the Canal, *Tom*, (for the Water was luckily pretty shallow in that Part) arrived safely on shore.

Thwackum fell violently on poor *Tom*, who stood dropping and shivering before him, when Mr. *Allworthy* desired him to have Patience, and turning to Master *Blifil*, said, Pray, Child, what is the Reason of all this Disturbance?

Master *Blifil* answered, 'Indeed, Uncle, I am very sorry for what I have done; I have been unhappily the Occasion of it all. I had Miss *Sophia's* Bird in my Hand, and thinking the poor Creature languished for Liberty, I own, I could not forbear giving it what it desired: for I always thought there was something very cruel in confining any Thing. It seemed to me against the Law of Nature, by which every Thing hath a Right to Liberty; nay, it is even unchristian; for it is not doing what we would be done by: But if I had imagined Miss *Sophia* would have been so much concerned at it, I am sure I would never have done it; nay, if I had known what would have happened to the Bird itself: for when Master *Jones*, who climbed up that Tree after it, fell into the Water, the Bird took a second Flight, and presently a nasty Hawk carried it away.'

Poor *Sophia*, who now first heard of her little *Tommy's* Fate; (for her Concern for *Jones* had prevented her perceiving it when it happened) shed a Shower of Tears. These Mr. *Allworthy* endeavoured to assuage, promising her a much finer Bird; but she declared she would never have another. Her Father chid her for crying so for a foolish Bird; but could not help telling young *Blifil*, if he was a Son of his, his Backside should be well flea'd.

Sophia now returned to her Chamber, the two young Gentlemen were sent home, and the rest of the Company returned to their Bottle; where a Conversation ensued on the Subject of the Bird, so curious, that we think it deserves a Chapter by itself.

CHAPTER IV

Containing such very deep and grave Matters, that some Readers, perhaps, may not relish it.

*S*QUARE had no sooner lighted his Pipe, than addressing himself to *Allworthy*, he thus began: 'Sir, I cannot help congratulating you on your Nephew; who, at an Age when few Lads have any Ideas but of sensible Objects, is arrived at a Capacity of distinguishing Right from Wrong. To confine any thing, seems to me against the Law of Nature, by which every thing hath a Right to Liberty.[1] These were his Words; and the Impression they have made on me is never to be eradicated. Can any Man have a higher Notion of the Rule of Right, and the Eternal Fitness of Things? I cannot help promising myself from such a

---

[1] The hypocritical intent of Blifil's words is clear enough. What may be obscure is that his statement of the 'law of nature' would have been regarded by most authorities on the subject—Grotius (1583–1645) and Pufendorf (1632–94), for example—as excessively libertarian, blurring the distinction between the conditions of life in a 'state of nature' and in society. To Grotius, the possession of wild creatures was 'certainly *Natural . . .* now *Property* is Establish'd'; for, he continued, 'Nature gives all these to him who *finds*, and lays hold on 'em *first*' (*Of the Rights of War and Peace* [1715], ii. 196, 199). Since the formation of societies, when the 'law of nations' superseded the 'law of nature' in certain crucial respects, not even human beings could consider that they were exempt from being the subjects or property of others: men, he remarked, are '*by Nature* in a State of *Freedom* [;] *by Nature* is to be understood the *Right of Nature*, as 'tis antecedent to all Human Acts to the contrary; and the *Freedom* there meant is a *Freedom* in a *private*, and not a *Contradictory* Sense, that is, tho' a Man be not *by Nature* a *Slave* or *subject* to any, yet from thence he cannot derive a Right of being always exempted from *Slavery* and *Subjection*, for in this Sense no body living is *Free*' (ibid., ii. 580).

Dawn, that the Meridian of this Youth will be equal to that of either the elder or the younger *Brutus*.'[1]

Here *Thwackum* hastily interrupted, and spilling some of his Wine, and swallowing the rest with great Eagerness, answered, 'From another Expression he made use of, I hope he will resemble much better Men. The Law of Nature is a Jargon of Words, which means nothing. I know not of any such Law, nor of any Right which can be derived from it. To do as we would be done by, is indeed a Christian Motive, as the Boy well expressed himself, and I am glad to find my Instructions have born such good Fruit.'

'If Vanity was a thing fit (says *Square*) I might indulge some on the same Occasion; for whence only he can have learnt his Notions of Right or Wrong, I think is pretty apparent. If there be no Law of Nature, there is no Right nor Wrong.'

'How! (says the Parson) do you then banish Revelation? Am I talking with a Deist or an Atheist?'

'Drink about, (says *Western*) Pox of your Laws of Nature. I don't know what you mean either of you, by Right and Wrong. To take away my Girl's Bird was wrong in my Opinion; and my Neighbour *Allworthy* may do as he pleases; but to encourage Boys in such Practices, is to breed them up to the Gallows.'

Allworthy answered, 'that he was sorry for what his Nephew had done; but could not consent to punish him, as he acted rather from a generous than unworthy Motive.' He said, 'if the Boy had stolen the Bird, none would have been more ready to vote for a severe Chastisement than himself; but it was plain that was not his Design:' And, indeed, it was as apparent to him, that he could have no other View but what he had himself avowed. (For as to

---

[1] See also p. 163. According to tradition, Lucius Junius Brutus was one of the first two Roman consuls (*c.* 509 B.C.). After having liberated Rome from the Tarquins, he put to death his own two sons for conspiring to restore that tyrannical regime. In *An Enquiry into the Causes of the late Increase of Robbers* (1751), section x, Fielding calls him 'a worthy Pattern' of the maxim that, for the good of society, the tenderness of the man must give way to the rigour of the magistrate. (See also *The Jacobite's Journal*, 26 March 1748.) From selfless motives of patriotism Marcus Junius Brutus (78 ?–42 B.C.) led the conspiracy to assassinate Caesar (44 B.C.), even though he was under the strongest personal obligations to the dictator. In the Preface to the *Miscellanies* (1743), Fielding cites Brutus, together with Socrates, as a rare example of the great and good man, the '*true Sublime* in Human Nature'. In *The Jacobite's Journal* (11 June 1748) the two Brutuses are again linked to illustrate the observation that the motives even of those 'deserving our highest Commendation' may be misconstrued.

that malicious Purpose which *Sophia* suspected, it never once entered into the Head of Mr. *Allworthy*.) He, at length, concluded with again blaming the Action as inconsiderate, and which, he said, was pardonable only in a Child.

Square had delivered his Opinion so openly, that if he was now silent, he must submit to have his Judgment censured. He said, therefore, with some Warmth, 'that Mr. *Allworthy* had too much Respect to the dirty Consideration of Property. That in passing our Judgments on great and mighty Actions, all private Regards should be laid aside; for by adhering to those narrow Rules, the younger *Brutus* had been condemned of Ingratitude, and the elder of Parricide.'

'And if they had been hanged too for those Crimes,' cried *Thwackum*, 'they would have had no more than their Deserts. A couple of heathenish Villains! Heaven be praised, we have no *Brutus's* now-a-days. I wish, Mr. *Square*, you would desist from filling the Minds of my Pupils with such Antichristian Stuff: For the Consequence must be, while they are under my Care, its being well scourged out of them again. There is your Disciple *Tom* almost spoiled already. I overheard him the other Day disputing with Master *Blifil*, that there was no Merit in Faith without Works. I know that is one of your Tenets, and I suppose he had it from you.'

'Don't accuse me of spoiling him,' says *Square*. 'Who taught him to laugh at whatever is virtuous and decent, and fit and right in the Nature of Things? He is your own Scholar, and I disclaim him. No, no, Master *Blifil* is my Boy. Young as he is, that Lad's Notions of moral Rectitude I defy you ever to eradicate.'

Thwackum put on a contemptuous Sneer at this, and replied, 'Ay, ay, I will venture him with you. He is too well grounded for all your philosophical Cant to hurt. No, no, I have taken Care to instil such Principles into him——'

'And I have instilled Principles into him too,' cries *Square*. 'What but the sublime Idea of Virtue could inspire a human Mind with the generous Thought of giving Liberty? And I repeat to you again, if it was a fit thing to be proud, I might claim the Honour of having infused that Idea——'

'And if Pride was not forbidden,' said *Thwackum*, 'I might boast of having taught him that Duty which he himself assigned as his Motive.'

'So between you both,' says the Squire, 'the young Gentleman hath been taught to rob my Daughter of her Bird. I find I must take Care of my Partridge Mew. I shall have some virtuous, religious Man or other set all my Partridges at Liberty.' Then slapping a Gentleman of the Law, who was present, on the Back, he cried out, 'What say you to this, Mr. Counsellor? Is not this against Law?'

The Lawyer, with great Gravity, delivered himself as follows:

'If the Case be put of a Partridge, there can be no Doubt but an Action would lie: For though this be *feræ Naturæ*, yet being reclaimed, Property vests;[1] but being the Case of a Singing Bird, though reclaimed, as it is a Thing of base Nature, it must be considered as *nullius in Bonis*.[2] In this Case, therefore, I conceive the Plaintiff must be nonsuited; and I should disadvise the bringing any such Action.'

'Well, (says the Squire) if it be *nullus Bonus*, let us drink about, and talk a little of the State of the Nation, or some such Discourse that we all understand; for I am sure I don't understand a Word of this. It may be Learning and Sense for aught I know; but you shall never persuade me into it. Pox! you have neither of you mentioned a Word of that poor Lad who deserves to be commended. To venture breaking his Neck to oblige my Girl, was a generous spirited Action; I have Learning enough to see that. D—n me, here's *Tom's* Health, I shall love the Boy for it the longest Day I have to live.'

Thus was this Debate interrupted; but it would probably have been soon resumed, had not Mr. *Allworthy* presently called for his Coach, and carried off the two Combatants.

Such was the Conclusion of this Adventure of the Bird, and of

---

[1] In law, *feræ naturæ* signified wild beasts and birds (as opposed to domestic), which no one could claim as his 'absolute real *Property*'; if, however, such beasts were reclaimed—i.e. 'inclosed and made Tame'—then 'there may be a qualified and possessory *Property* in them.' (See Giles Jacob, *New Law Dictionary*, 4th ed. [1739], s.v. 'Feræ Naturæ' and 'Property'.)

[2] *Nullius in bonis*: literally, 'among the goods of nobody'—i.e. nobody's natural property. In this case the law does not admit the possibility of larceny where there can be no motive of personal gain. Cf. Wood's *Institutes*, 7th ed. (1745): 'Besides, The Law does not presume, that any one would Steal such Things that are of no Value or Use to any one but the Owner. The Personal Goods also must not be of a *Base Nature*, as Dogs or Cats, if They may be said to be One's Personal Goods. Some Things that are *Wild* by Nature, and made Tame, cannot be Taken away feloniously as Personal Goods; as (for Example) . . . Singing Birds, &c.' (p. 386).

the Dialogue occasioned by it, which we could not help recounting to our Reader, though it happened some Years before
that Stage, or Period of Time, at which our History is now
arrived.

CHAPTER V

Containing Matter accommodated to every Taste.

PARVA leves capiunt Animos,[1] 'Small Things affect light
Minds,' was the Sentiment of a great Master of the Passion
of Love. And certain it is, that from this Day *Sophia* began to
have some little Kindness for *Tom Jones*, and no little Aversion
for his Companion.

Many Accidents from time to time improved both these
Passions in her Breast; which, without our recounting, the Reader
may well conclude, from what we have before hinted of the
different Tempers of these Lads, and how much the one suited
with her own Inclinations more than the other. To say the Truth,
Sophia, when very young, discerned that *Tom*, though an idle,
thoughtless, rattling Rascal, was no-body's Enemy but his own;
and that Master *Blifil*, though a prudent, discreet, sober young
Gentleman, was at the same Time strongly attached to the Interest only of one single Person; and who that single Person was,
the Reader will be able to divine without any Assistance of ours.

These two Characters are not always received in the World
with the different Regard which seems severally due to either;
and which one would imagine Mankind, from Self-interest,
should shew towards them. But perhaps there may be a political
Reason for it: In finding one of a truly benevolent Disposition,
Men may very reasonably suppose, they have found a Treasure,
and be desirous of keeping it, like all other good Things, to
themselves. Hence they may imagine, that to trumpet forth the
Praises of such a Person, would, in the vulgar Phrase, be crying
Roast-meat;[2] and calling in Partakers of what they intend to apply
solely to their own Use. If this Reason doth not satisfy the Reader,
I know no other Means of accounting for the little Respect which

[1] Ovid, *Ars Amatoria*, i. 159.
[2] Foolishly proclaiming a piece of private good fortune. (See W. G. Smith and P.
Harvey (eds.), *Oxford Dictionary of English Proverbs*, 2nd ed. [Oxford, 1948], p. 121.)

I have commonly seen paid to a Character which really doth great Honour to Human Nature, and is productive of the highest Good to Society. But it was otherwise with *Sophia*. She honoured *Tom Jones*, and scorned Master *Blifil*, almost as soon as she knew the Meaning of those two Words.

Sophia had been absent upwards of three Years with her Aunt; during all which Time she had seldom seen either of these young Gentlemen. She dined, however, once together with her Aunt, at Mr. *Allworthy's*. This was a few Days after the Adventure of the Partridge, before commemorated. *Sophia* heard the whole Story at Table, where she said nothing; nor indeed could her Aunt get many Words from her, as she returned home; but her Maid, when undressing her, happening to say, 'Well, Miss, I suppose you have seen young Master *Blifil* to Day.' She answered with much Passion, 'I hate the Name of Master *Blifil*, as I do whatever is base and treacherous; and I wonder Mr. *Allworthy* would suffer that old barbarous Schoolmaster to punish a poor Boy so cruelly for what was only the Effect of his Good-nature.' She then recounted the Story to her Maid, and concluded with Saying— 'Don't you think he is a Boy of a noble Spirit?'

This young Lady was now returned to her Father; who gave her the Command of his House, and placed her at the upper End of his Table, where *Tom* (who for his great Love of Hunting was become a great Favourite of the Squire) often dined. Young Men of open, generous Dispositions are naturally inclined to Gallantry, which, if they have good Understandings, as was in reality *Tom's* Case, exerts itself in an obliging, complaisant Behaviour to all Women in general. This greatly distinguished *Tom* from the boisterous Brutality of mere Country Squires on the one hand; and from the solemn, and somewhat sullen, Deportment of Master *Blifil* on the other: And he began now, at Twenty, to have the Name of a pretty Fellow among all the Women in the Neighbourhood.

Tom behaved to *Sophia* with no Particularity, unless, perhaps, by shewing her a higher Respect than he paid to any other. This Distinction her Beauty, Fortune, Sense, and amiable Carriage, seemed to demand; but as to Design upon her Person he had none; for which we shall at present suffer the Reader to condemn him of Stupidity; but perhaps we shall be able indifferently well to account for it hereafter.

Sophia, with the highest Degree of Innocence and Modesty, had a remarkable Sprightliness in her Temper. This was so greatly encreased whenever she was in Company with *Tom*, that, had he not been very young and thoughtless, he must have observed it; or had not Mr. *Western's* Thoughts been generally either in the Field, the Stable, or the Dog-kennel, it might have, perhaps, created some Jealousy in him; but so far was the good Gentleman from entertaining any such Suspicions, that he gave *Tom* every Opportunity with his Daughter which any Lover could have wished. And this *Tom* innocently improved to better Advantage, by following only the Dictates of his natural Gallantry and Good-nature, than he might, perhaps, have done, had he had the deepest Designs on the young Lady.

But, indeed, it can occasion little Wonder, that this Matter escaped the Observation of others, since poor *Sophia* herself never remarked it, and her Heart was irretrievably lost before she suspected it was in Danger.

Matters were in this Situation, when *Tom* one Afternoon finding *Sophia* alone, began, after a short Apology, with a very serious Face, to acquaint her, that he had a Favour to ask of her, which he hoped her Goodness would comply with.

Though neither the young Man's Behaviour, nor indeed his Manner of opening this Business, were such as could give her any just Cause of suspecting he intended to make Love to her; yet, whether Nature whispered something into her Ear, or from what Cause it arose I will not determine, certain it is, some Idea of that Kind must have intruded itself; for her Colour forsook her Cheeks, her Limbs trembled, and her Tongue would have faultered, had *Tom* stopped for an Answer: But he soon relieved her from her Perplexity, by proceeding to inform her of his Request, which was to sollicit her Interest on Behalf of the Gamekeeper, whose own Ruin, and that of a large Family, must be, he said, the Consequence of Mr. *Western's* pursuing his Action against him.

Sophia presently recovered her Confusion, and with a Smile full of Sweetness, said, 'Is this the mighty Favour you asked with so much Gravity. I will do it with all my Heart. I really pity the poor Fellow, and no longer ago than Yesterday sent a small Matter to his Wife.' This small Matter was one of her Gowns, some Linnen, and ten Shillings in Money, of which *Tom* had heard, and it had, in reality, put this Solicitation into his Head.

Our Youth, now emboldened with his Success, resolved to push the Matter farther; and ventured even to beg her Recommendation of him to her Father's Service; protesting that he thought him one of the honestest Fellows in the Country, and extremely well qualified for the Place of a Game-keeper, which luckily then happened to be vacant.

Sophia answered, 'Well, I will undertake this too; but I cannot promise you as much Success as in the former Part, which I assure you I will not quit my Father without obtaining. However, I will do what I can for the poor Fellow, for I sincerely look upon him and his Family as Objects of great Compassion.—And now, Mr. *Jones*, I must ask you a Favour——'

'A Favour, Madam, (cries *Tom*) if you knew the Pleasure you have given me in the Hopes of receiving a Command from you, you would think by mentioning it you did confer the greatest Favour on me; for by this dear Hand I would sacrifice my Life to oblige you.'

He then snatched her Hand, and eagerly kissed it, which was the first Time his Lips had ever touched her. The Blood, which before had forsaken her Cheeks, now made her sufficient Amends, by rushing all over her Face and Neck with such Violence, that they became all of a scarlet Colour. She now first felt a Sensation to which she had been before a Stranger, and which, when she had Leisure to reflect on it, began to acquaint her with some Secrets, which the Reader, if he doth not already guess them, will know in due Time.

Sophia, as soon as she could speak, (which was not instantly) informed him, that the Favour she had to desire of him, was not to lead her Father through so many Dangers in Hunting; for that, from what she had heard, she was terribly frightened every Time they went out together, and expected some Day or other to see her Father brought Home with broken Limbs. She therefore begged him, for her Sake, to be more cautious; and, as he well knew Mr. *Western* would follow him, not to ride so madly, nor to take those dangerous Leaps for the future.

Tom promised faithfully to obey her Commands; and after thanking her for her kind Compliance with his Request, took his Leave, and departed highly charmed with his Success.

Poor *Sophia* was charmed too; but in a very different Way. Her Sensations, however, the Reader's Heart (if he or she have any) will better represent than I can, if I had as many Mouths as ever Poet wished for,[1] to eat, I suppose, those many Dainties with which he was so plentifully provided.

It was Mr. *Western's* Custom every Afternoon, as soon as he was drunk, to hear his Daughter play on the Harpsichord: for he was a great Lover of Music, and perhaps, had he lived in Town, might have passed for a Connoisseur: for he always excepted against the finest Compositions of Mr. *Handel.*[2] He never relished any Music but what was light and airy; and indeed his most favourite Tunes, were *Old Sir* Simon *the King, St.* George *he was for* England, *Bobbing* Joan,[3] and some others.

His Daughter, though she was a perfect Mistress of Music, and would never willingly have played any but *Handel's,* was so devoted to her Father's Pleasure, that she learnt all those Tunes to oblige him. However, she would now and then endeavour to lead him into her own Taste, and when he required the Repetition of his Ballads, would answer with a 'Nay, dear Sir,' and would often beg him to suffer her to play something else.

This Evening, however, when the Gentleman was retired from his Bottle, she played all his Favourites three Times over, without any Solicitation. This so pleased the good Squire, that he started from his Couch, gave his Daughter a Kiss, and swore her Hand was greatly improved. She took this Opportunity to execute her Promise to *Tom,* in which she succeeded so well, that the Squire

---

[1] Cf. *Iliad*, ii. 489, where Homer wishes for ten tongues and ten mouths.

[2] See above, p. 154, n. 3. Early in 1745 Handel's popularity, always precarious at best, sank to a new low, chiefly owing to the opposition of the opera party led by the Earl of Middlesex. A certain fashionable lady (probably Lady Brown) carried her hostility to the composer so far as to give a 'drum' or 'rout' whenever Handel was to perform. Subscribers to his oratorio concerts were so few that Handel publicly lamented 'the loss of the publick Favour' and sadly predicted his 'Ruin' (see *The Daily Advertiser*, 17 January 1745). His friends rallied to his aid, complaining that the neglect of so great a genius was a 'National Disgrace' (see the poem 'To Mr. Handel' in *The Daily Advertiser*, 21 January 1745), but their efforts were ineffectual. On 2 April 1745 Mrs. Elizabeth Carter summarized the situation in a letter to Catherine Talbot: 'Handel, once so crowded, plays to empty walls in that opera house [i.e. the King's Theatre in the Haymarket], where there used to be a constant *audience* as long as there were any dancers to be *seen*. Unfashionable that I am, I was I own highly delighted the other night at his last oratorio.' (See O. E. Deutsch, *Handel: A Documentary Biography* [1955], pp. 602–10.)

[3] These old tunes, especially popular during the Restoration period, are discussed in W. Chappell, *Old English Popular Music*, ed. H. Ellis Wooldridge (1893), i. 280–2, 312; ii. 102–4.

declared, if she would give him t'other Bout of old Sir *Simon*, he would give the Game-keeper his Deputation[1] the next Morning. Sir *Simon* was played again and again, till the Charms of the Music soothed Mr. *Western* to sleep. In the Morning *Sophia* did not fail to remind him of his Engagement, and his Attorney was immediately sent for, and ordered to stop any further Proceedings in the Action, and to make out the Deputation.

Tom's Success in this Affair soon began to ring over the Country, and various were the Censures past upon it. Some greatly applauding it as an Act of good Nature, others sneering, and saying, 'No Wonder that one idle Fellow should love another.' Young *Blifil* was greatly enraged at it. He had long hated *Black George* in the same Proportion as *Jones* delighted in him; not from any Offence which he had ever received, but from his great Love to Religion and Virtue: For *Black George* had the Reputation of a loose kind of a Fellow. *Blifil* therefore represented this as flying in Mr. *Allworthy's* Face; and declared with great Concern, that it was impossible to find any other Motive for doing Good to such a Wretch.

Thwackum and *Square* likewise sung to the same Tune: They were now (especially the latter) become greatly jealous of young *Jones* with the Widow: For he now approached the Age of Twenty-one,[2] was really a fine young Fellow; and that Lady, by her Encouragements to him, seemed daily more and more to think him so.

Allworthy was not, however, moved with their Malice. He declared himself very well satisfied with what *Jones* had done. He said, the Perseverance and Integrity of his Friendship was highly commendable, and he wished he could see more frequent Instances of that Virtue.

But Fortune, who seldom greatly relishes such Sparks as my Friend *Tom*, perhaps because they do not pay more ardent Addresses to her, gave now a very different Turn to all his Actions, and shewed them to Mr. *Allworthy* in a Light far less agreeable than that Gentleman's Goodness had hitherto seen them in.

---

[1] According to 9 Anne, cap. 25, the appointment of a game-keeper by the Lord of the Manor had to be formally recorded and certified by the clerk of the parish. (See Dalton, *The Country Justice* [1746], p. 108.)

[2] Emended from 'Twenty'. In all editions Fielding here overlooked the fact that in the errata to the first edition he had earlier in this chapter changed Jones's age from nineteen to twenty (see above, p. 166.32).

CHAPTER VI

An Apology for the Insensibility of Mr. Jones, *to all the Charms of the lovely* Sophia; *in which possibly we may, in a considerable Degree, lower his Character in the Estimation of those Men of Wit and Gallantry, who approve the Heroes in most of our modern Comedies.*

THERE are two Sorts of People, who I am afraid, have already conceived some Contempt for my Heroe, on Account of his Behaviour to *Sophia*. The former of these will blame his Prudence in neglecting an Opportunity to possess himself of Mr. *Western's* Fortune; and the latter will no less despise him for his Backwardness to so fine a Girl, who seemed ready to fly into his Arms, if he would open them to receive her.

Now, though I shall not perhaps be able absolutely to acquit him of either of these Charges; (for Want of Prudence admits of no Excuse; and what I shall produce against the latter Charge, will, I apprehend, be scarce satisfactory;) yet as Evidence may sometimes be offered in Mitigation, I shall set forth the plain Matter of Fact, and leave the whole to the Reader's Determination.

Mr. *Jones* had Somewhat about him, which, though I think Writers are not thoroughly agreed in its Name,[1] doth certainly

---

[1] The usual name for the moral faculty to which Fielding here refers is, of course, the 'conscience'—an important corollary of his concept of 'good-nature' (see above, p. 39, n. 1). As he defines the functions of this 'active Principle' in the ensuing paragraphs, Fielding may be seen to side with those Christian philosophers and divines who opposed Locke's attempt to discredit the doctrine of innate knowledge. Traditionally, the conscience was regarded not as an acquired, but as a natural, faculty which enabled men to recognize God's laws and which prompted them to do good and to eschew evil. In theological terms, it comprised two distinct, yet complementary, departments: *synteresis*, which functions as a guide for conduct, directing one's actions towards virtuous ends; and *syneidesis*, which passes judgement on actions already performed, signalling approval or disapproval. This theory, therefore, placed the foundation of morality in the very nature of man.

A useful gloss on Fielding's account of the conscience is supplied by Richard Carpenter, who describes synteresis as the 'treasury of morall principles, and of sacred rules wherewith the practicall understanding is furnished, for the saving direction of us in all actions'; it is 'a nobel and diuine power and faculty, planted of God in the substance of mans soule, working vpon itself by reflection, and taking exact notice, as a Scribe or Register, and determining as Gods Viceroy and deputy, Judge of all that is in the mind, will, affections, actions, and whole life of man' (*The Conscionable Christian* [1623], pp. [2], 41). Similarly, in Thomas Nabbes's moral masque, *Microcosmus* (1637), v, Conscience is represented in ways that suggest Fielding's general agreement with this pre-Lockean tradition:

inhabit some human Breasts; whose Use is not so properly to distinguish Right from Wrong, as to prompt and incite them to the former, and to restrain and with-hold them from the latter.

This Somewhat may be indeed resembled to the famous Trunk-maker in the Playhouse:[1] for whenever the Person who is possessed of it doth what is right, no ravished or friendly Spectator is so eager, or so loud in his Applause; on the contrary, when he doth wrong, no Critic is so apt to hiss and explode him.

To give a higher Idea of the Principle I mean, as well as one more familiar to the present Age; it may be considered as sitting on its Throne in the Mind, like the LORD HIGH CHANCELLOR[2] of this Kingdom in his Court; where it presides, governs, directs, judges, acquits and condemns according to Merit and Justice; with a Knowledge which nothing escapes, a Penetration which nothing can deceive, and an Integrity which nothing can corrupt.

> Conscience the judge of actions
> Is neither power, nor habit, but an act;
> To wit an application of that knowledge
> That shewes the difference. Its Synteresis,
> Or purer part, is th'instigation
> Of will to good and honest things, and seates
> The mind in a rich throne of endlesse quiet.

For a discussion of this theory and of Locke's opposition to it, see J. W. Yolton, *John Locke and the Way of Ideas* (Oxford, 1956), pp. 30–5, 55–7. For 'An Account of the Nature and Measures of Conscience' with which Fielding was certainly familiar, see Robert South's two sermons by that title (1691–2). In the latter, South to a degree anticipates Fielding's metaphor of 'the Lord High Chancellor' by characterizing the conscience as 'the viceregent of God', remarking 'the extraordinary quickness and sagacity of its sight' and 'its great and rigorous impartiality' which no 'power, rhetoric, or riches' can corrupt (see *Sermons Preached upon Several Occasions* [1865], i. 195–6, 200–1).

¹ See *The Spectator*, No. 235 (29 November 1711). The '*Trunk-maker*', who stationed himself in the upper-gallery and expressed his approbation of the play by loud knocks upon the benches and wainscot, is represented by Addison as the type of the true critic: 'his Stroaks are always just, and his Admonitions seasonable; he does not deal about his Blows at Random, but always hits the right Nail upon the Head.' In his essay on trunks in *The Champion* (31 May 1740), Fielding refers again to this 'great Judge of Dramatic Poetry'.

² Philip Yorke (1690–1764), Baron Hardwicke, was Lord Chancellor from 1737 to 1756; in the summer of 1746 he presided over the trials of the Jacobite lords. Fielding frequently expressed his admiration for 'this Great Man', whose 'Ability, Clemency and Justice' in the administration of his office had 'made the inferior Branches to regard him in the Light of a Father' (*The True Patriot*, 11–18 February 1746). In 1751 Fielding dedicated *An Enquiry into the Causes of the late Increase of Robbers* to Hardwicke. Other compliments to him may be found in *The Jacobite's Journal* (23 January, 12 March 1748) and in *A True State of the Case of Bosavern Penlez* (1749). With the present passage, compare Fielding's characterization of the conscience in the Preface to the *Miscellanies* (1743): 'there is still a Judge in every Man's Breast, which none can cheat nor corrupt. . . .'

This active Principle may perhaps be said to constitute the most essential Barrier between us, and our Neighbours the Brutes; for if there be some in the human Shape, who are not under any such Dominion, I chuse rather to consider them as Deserters from us to our Neighbours; among whom they will have the Fate of Deserters, and not be placed in the first Rank.

Our Heroe, whether he derived it from *Thwackum* or *Square* I will not determine, was very strongly under the Guidance of this Principle: for though he did not always act rightly, yet he never did otherwise without feeling and suffering for it. It was this which taught him, that to repay the Civilities and little Friendships of Hospitality by robbing the House where you have received them, is to be the basest and meanest of Thieves. He did not think the Baseness of this Offence lessened by the Height of the Injury committed; on the contrary, if to steal another's Plate deserved Death and Infamy,[1] it seemed to him difficult to assign a Punishment adequate to the robbing a Man of his whole Fortune, and of his Child into the Bargain.

This Principle therefore prevented him from any Thought of making his Fortune by such Means (for this, as I have said, is an active Principle, and doth not content itself with Knowledge or Belief only.) Had he been greatly enamoured of *Sophia*, he possibly might have thought otherwise; but give me Leave to say, there is great Difference between running away with a Man's Daughter from the Motive of Love,[2] and doing the same Thing from the Motive of Theft.

Now though this young Gentleman was not insensible of the Charms of *Sophia*; tho' he greatly liked her Beauty, and esteemed all her other Qualifications, she had made, however, no deep Impression on his Heart: For which, as it renders him liable to the Charge of Stupidity, or at least of Want of Taste, we shall now proceed to account.

The Truth then is, his Heart was in the Possession of another Woman. Here I question not, but the Reader will be surprized at our long Taciturnity as to this Matter; and quite at a Loss to

---

[1] Grand larceny was defined as the theft of personal goods 'above the Value of Twelve Pence' and was punishable by death. (See Wood's *Institutes,* 7th ed. [1745], p. 383.)

[2] On two occasions in his youth Fielding seems to have done just this: in 1725 he attempted to 'abduct' Sarah Andrew, an attractive girl of fifteen with whom he was in love; and in 1734 he married Charlotte Cradock, apparently after eloping with her. (See Cross, i. 51, 169.)

divine who this Woman was; since we have hitherto not dropt a
Hint of any one likely to be a Rival to *Sophia*: For as to Mrs.
Blifil, though we have been obliged to mention some Suspicions
of her Affection for *Tom*, we have not hitherto given the least
Latitude for imagining that he had any for her; and, indeed, I
am sorry to say it, but the Youth of both Sexes are too apt to
be deficient in their Gratitude, for that Regard with which
Persons more advanced in Years are sometimes so kind to honour
them.

That the Reader may be no longer in Suspence, he will be
pleased to remember, that we have often mentioned the Family
of *George Seagrim*, commonly called *Black George*, the Game-
keeper, which consisted at present of a Wife and five Children.

The second of these Children was a Daughter, whose Name
was *Molly*, and who was esteemed one of the handsomest Girls
in the whole Country.

Congreve well says,[1] *There is in true Beauty something which
vulgar Souls cannot admire*; so can no Dirt or Rags hide this
Something from those Souls which are not of the vulgar Stamp.

The Beauty of this Girl made, however, no Impression on
Tom, till she grew towards the Age of Sixteen, when *Tom*, who
was near three Years older, began first to cast the Eyes of Affection upon her. And this Affection he had fixed on the Girl long
before he could bring himself to attempt the Possession of her
Person: for tho' his Constitution urged him greatly to this, his
Principles no less forcibly restrained him. To debauch a young
Woman, however low her Condition was, appeared to him a very
heinous Crime; and the Good-will he bore the Father, with the
Compassion he had for his Family, very strongly corroborated
all such sober Reflections; so that he once resolved to get the
better of his Inclinations, and he actually abstained three whole
Months without ever going to *Seagrim's* House, or seeing his
Daughter.

Now though *Molly* was, as we have said, generally thought a
very fine Girl, and in reality she was so, yet her Beauty was not of
the most amiable Kind. It had indeed very little of Feminine
in it, and would have become a Man at least as well as a Woman;

---

[1] In *The Old Batchelour* (1693), IV. iii. When Belinda and Araminta unmask, Sharper
declares: 'There is in true Beauty, as in Courage, somewhat, which narrow Souls cannot
dare to admire.'

for, to say the Truth, Youth and florid Health had a very considerable Share in the Composition.

Nor was her Mind more effeminate than her Person. As this
was tall and robust, so was that bold and forward. So little had
she of Modesty, that *Jones* had more Regard for her Virtue than
she herself. And as most probably she liked *Tom* as well as he
liked her, so when she perceived his Backwardness, she herself
grew proportionably forward; and when she saw he had entirely
deserted the House, she found Means of throwing herself in his
Way, and behaved in such a Manner, that the Youth must have
had very much, or very little of the Heroe, if her Endeavours had
proved unsuccessful. In a Word, she soon triumphed over all
the virtuous Resolutions of *Jones*: For though she behaved at
last with all decent Reluctance, yet I rather chuse to attribute
the Triumph to her: Since, in Fact, it was her Design which
succeeded.

In the Conduct of this Matter, I say, *Molly* so well played her
Part, that *Jones* attributed the Conquest entirely to himself, and
considered the young Woman as one who had yielded to the
violent Attacks of his Passion. He likewise imputed her yielding,
to the ungovernable Force of her Love towards him; and this the
Reader will allow to have been a very natural and probable Supposition, as we have more than once mentioned the uncommon
Comeliness of his Person: And indeed he was one of the handsomest young Fellows in the World.

As there are some Minds whose Affections, like Master
Blifil's, are solely placed on one single Person, whose Interest
and Indulgence alone they consider on every Occasion; regarding
the Good and Ill of all others as merely indifferent, any farther
than as they contribute to the Pleasure or Advantage of that
Person: So there is a different Temper of Mind which borrows a
Degree of Virtue even from Self-love; such can never receive any
kind of Satisfaction from another, without loving the Creature to
whom that Satisfaction is owing, and without making its Well-
being in some sort necessary to their own Ease.

Of this latter Species was our Heroe. He considered this poor
Girl as one whose Happiness or Misery he had caused to be dependent on himself. Her Beauty was still the Object of Desire,
though greater Beauty, or a fresher Object, might have been
more so; but the little Abatement which Fruition had occasioned

to this, was highly over-ballanced by the Considerations of the Affection which she visibly bore him, and of the Situation into which he had brought her. The former of these created Gratitude, the latter Compassion; and both together with his Desire for her Person, raised in him a Passion, which might, without any great Violence to the Word, be called *Love*; though, perhaps, it was at first not very judiciously placed.

This then was the true Reason of that Insensibility which he had shewn to the Charms of *Sophia*, and that Behaviour in her, which might have been reasonably enough interpreted as an Encouragement to his Addresses: For as he could not think of abandoning his *Molly*, poor and destitute as she was, so no more could he entertain a Notion of betraying such a Creature as *Sophia*. And surely, had he given the least Encouragement to any Passion for that young Lady, he must have been absolutely guilty of one or other of those Crimes; either of which would, in my Opinion, have very justly subjected him to that Fate, which at his first Introduction into this History, I mentioned to have been generally predicted as his certain Destiny.

CHAPTER VII

Being the shortest Chapter in this Book.

HER Mother first perceived the Alteration in the Shape of *Molly*, and in order to hide it from her Neighbours, she foolishly clothed her in that Sack which *Sophia* had sent her. Though indeed that young Lady had little Apprehension, that the poor Woman would have been weak enough to let any of her Daughters wear it in that Form.

Molly was charmed with the first Opportunity she ever had of shewing her Beauty to Advantage; for though she could very well bear to contemplate herself in the Glass, even when drest in Rags; and though she had in that Dress conquered the Heart of *Jones*, and perhaps of some others; yet she thought the Addition of Finery would much improve her Charms, and extend her Conquests.

Molly, therefore, having dressed herself out in this Sack, with a new laced Cap, and some other Ornaments which *Tom* had given her, repairs to Church with her Fan in her Hand the very next *Sunday*. The Great are deceived, if they imagine they have appropriated Ambition and Vanity to themselves. These noble Qualities flourish as notably in a Country Church, and Churchyard, as in the Drawing-Room, or in the Closet. Schemes have indeed been laid in the Vestry, which would hardly disgrace the Conclave. Here is a Ministry, and here is an Opposition. Here are Plots and Circumventions, Parties and Factions, equal to those which are to be found in Courts.

Nor are the Women here less practised in the highest Feminine Arts than their fair Superiors in Quality and Fortune. Here are Prudes and Coquettes. Here are Dressing and Ogling, Falshood, Envy, Malice, Scandal; in short, every Thing which is common to the most splendid Assembly, or politest Circle. Let those of high Life, therefore, no longer despise the Ignorance of their Inferiors; nor the Vulgar any longer rail at the Vices of their Betters.

Molly had seated herself some time before she was known by her Neighbours. And then a Whisper ran through the whole Congregation, 'Who is she?' But when she was discovered, such sneering, gigling, tittering, and laughing, ensued among the Women, that Mr. *Allworthy* was obliged to exert his Authority to preserve any Decency among them.

CHAPTER VIII

A Battle sung by the Muse in the Homerican *Stile, and which none but the classical Reader can taste.*

MR. *Western* had an Estate in this Parish; and as his House stood at little greater Distance from this Church than from his own, he very often came to divine Service here; and both he and the charming *Sophia* happened to be present at this Time.

Sophia was much pleased with the Beauty of the Girl, whom she pitied for her Simplicity, in having dressed herself in that Manner, as she saw the Envy which it had occasioned among her Equals. She no sooner came home, than she sent for the Gamekeeper, and ordered him to bring his Daughter to her; saying, She would provide for her in the Family, and might possibly place the Girl about her own Person, when her own Maid, who was now going away, had left her.

Poor *Seagrim* was thunderstruck at this; for he was no Stranger to the Fault in the Shape of his Daughter. He answered, in a stammering Voice, 'That he was afraid *Molly* would be too aukward to wait on her Ladyship, as she had never been at Service.' 'No matter for that,' says *Sophia*, 'she will soon improve. I am pleased with the Girl, and am resolved to try her.'

Black George now repaired to his Wife, on whose prudent Counsel he depended to extricate him out of this Dilemma; but when he came thither, he found his House in some Confusion. So great Envy had this Sack occasioned, that when Mr. *Allworthy* and the other Gentry were gone from Church, the Rage, which had hitherto been confined, burst into an Uproar, and, having vented itself at first in opprobrious Words, Laughs, Hisses, and Gestures, betook itself at last to certain missile Weapons; which, though from their plastic Nature they threatened neither the Loss of Life or of Limb, were however sufficiently dreadful to a well-dressed Lady. *Molly* had too much Spirit to bear this Treatment tamely. Having therefore——But hold, as we are diffident of our own Abilities, let us here invite a superior Power to our Assistance.

Ye Muses then, whoever ye are, who love to sing Battles, and principally thou, who whileom didst recount the Slaughter in those Fields where *Hudibras* and *Trulla* fought,[1] if thou wert not starved with thy Friend *Butler*,[2] assist me on this great Occasion. All things are not in the Power of all.[3]

As a vast Herd of Cows[4] in a rich Farmer's Yard, if, while they

[1] See Butler's *Hudibras*, I. iii. 769 ff.

[2] Even though Samuel Butler had in 1677 been granted a royal pension of £100 a year, the legend grew that he had been allowed to starve to death in a garret, and so in the eighteenth century Butler became the very type of the neglected genius. Erected in 1721, the monument to him in Westminster Abbey was inscribed with the following verses: 'The Poets Fate is here in Emblem shown:/ He asked for Bread and he received a Stone.' Among the innumerable contemporary allusions to the tradition, see Oldham's *Satire against Poetry*; Dryden's *Hind and the Panther*, iii. 247–50; and Bayle's *General Dictionary, Historical and Critical* (1734–41), s.v. 'Hudibras'. Earlier references in Fielding occur in *Eurydice Hiss'd* (1737), *The Champion* (27 November 1739), and 'Epitaph on Butler's Monument' (*Miscellanies*, 1743).

[3] Cf. Virgil's *Eclogues*, viii. 63. See below, pp. 414, 543.

[4] Molly's battle in the churchyard burlesques the *Iliad*, iv–v, Homer's account of the first battle between the Greek and Trojan armies. With the present paragraph compare, specifically, the *Iliad*, iv. 433–49, which describes the war-cry of the Trojans and introduces the conflict. Pope translates as follows:

> Not so the *Trojans*, from their Host ascends
> A gen'ral Shout that all the Region rends.

are milked, they hear their Calves at a Distance, lamenting the Robbery which is then committing, roar and bellow: So roared forth the *Somersetshire* Mob an Hallaloo, made up of almost as many Squawls, Screams, and other different Sounds, as there were Persons, or indeed Passions, among them: Some were inspired by Rage, others alarmed by Fear, and others had nothing in their Heads but the Love of Fun; but chiefly Envy, the Sister of *Satan*, and his constant Companion, rushed among the Crowd, and blew up the Fury of the Women; who no sooner came up to *Molly*, than they pelted her with Dirt and Rubbish.

Molly, having endeavoured in vain to make a handsome Retreat, faced about; and laying hold of ragged *Bess*, who advanced in the Front of the Enemy, she at one Blow felled her to the Ground. The whole Army of the Enemy (though near a hundred in Number) seeing the Fate of their General, gave back many Paces, and retired behind a new-dug Grave; for the Churchyard was the Field of Battle, where there was to be a Funeral that very Evening. *Molly* pursued her Victory, and catching up a Skull which lay on the Side of the Grave, discharged it with such Fury, that having hit a Taylor on the Head, the two Skulls sent equally forth a hollow Sound at their Meeting, and the Taylor took presently measure of his Length on the Ground, where the Skulls lay side by side, and it was doubtful which was the more valuable of the two. *Molly* then taking a Thigh Bone in her

As when the fleecy Flocks unnumber'd stand
In wealthy Folds, and wait the Milker's Hand,
The hollow Vales incessant Bleating fills,
The Lambs reply from all the neighb'ring Hills:
Such Clamours rose from various Nations round,
Mix'd was the Murmur, and confus'd the Sound.
Each Host now joins, and each a God inspires,
These *Mars* incites, and those *Minerva* fires.
Pale *Flight* around, and dreadful *Terror* reign;
And *Discord* raging bathes the purple Plain:
Discord! dire Sister of the slaught'ring Pow'r,
Small at her Birth, but rising ev'ry Hour,
While scarce the Skies her horrid Head can bound,
She stalks on Earth, and shakes the World around;
The Nations bleed, where-e'er her Steps she turns,
The Groan still deepens, and the Combat burns.
  Now Shield with Shield, with Helmet Helmet clos'd,
To Armour Armour, Lance to Lance oppos'd,
Host against Host with shadowy Squadrons drew,
The sounding Darts in Iron Tempests slew. . . . (iv. 490–511)

Hand,[1] fell in among the flying Ranks, and dealing her Blows
with great Liberality on either Side, overthrew the Carcass of
many a mighty Heroe and Heroine.

Recount, O Muse, the Names of those who fell on this fatal
Day. First *Jemmy Tweedle* felt on his hinder Head the direful
Bone. Him the pleasant Banks of sweetly winding *Stower* had
nourished,[2] where he first learnt the vocal Art, with which,
wandring up and down at Wakes and Fairs, he cheered the rural
Nymphs and Swains, when upon the Green they interweav'd the
sprightly Dance; while he himself stood fidling and jumping to
his own Music. How little now avails his Fiddle? He thumps the
verdant Floor with his Carcass. Next old *Echepole*,[3] the Sow-
gelder, received a Blow in his Forehead from our Amazonian
Heroine, and immediately fell to the Ground. He was a swinging
fat Fellow, and fell with almost as much Noise as a House. His
Tobacco-box dropt at the same Time from his Pocket, which
Molly took up as lawful Spoils. Then *Kate* of the Mill tumbled
unfortunately over a Tombstone, which catching hold of her un-
gartered Stocking, inverted the Order of Nature, and gave her
Heels the Superiority to her Head.[4] *Betty Pippin*, with young
Roger her Lover, fell both to the Ground. Where, O perverse

[1] Cf. Judges 15: 15-16—Samson's slaying a thousand Philistines with the jawbone of an
ass.
[2] Cf. *Iliad*, iv. 473-6—'Fair *Simoïsius*, whom his Mother bore/ Amid the Flocks on
silver *Simois*' Shore . . .' (Pope's trans., iv. 544-5).
[3] Cf. *Iliad*, iv. 457-66—the death of Echepolus:

> The bold *Antilochus* the Slaughter led,
> The first who strook a valiant *Trojan* dead:
> At great *Echepolus* the Lance arrives,
> Raz'd his high Crest, and thro' his Helmet drives,
> Warm'd in the Brain the brazen Weapon lies,
> And Shades Eternal settle o'er his Eyes.
> So sinks a Tow'r, that long Assaults had stood
> Of Force and Fire; its Walls besmear'd with Blood.
> Him, the bold Leader of th' *Abantian* Throng
> Seiz'd to despoil. . . .   (Pope's trans., iv. 522-31.)

[4] Cf. *Iliad*, v. 582-3, 585-6—the fate and posture of the fallen Mydon:

> . . . From his numb'd Hand the Iv'ry-studded Reins
> Dropt in the Dust are trail'd along the Plains.
> . . . He groans in Death, and pondrous sinks to Ground:
> Deep drove his Helmet in the Sands, and there
> The Head stood fix'd, the quiv'ring Legs in Air. . . .
>   (Pope's trans., v. 713-14, 716-18.)

Fate, she salutes the Earth, and he the Sky.[1] *Tom Freckle*,[2] the
Smith's Son, was the next Victim to her Rage. He was an ingen-
ious Workman, and made excellent Pattins; nay the very Pattin
with which he was knocked down was his own Workmanship.
Had he been at that Time singing Psalms in the Church, he
would have avoided a broken Head. Miss *Crow*, the Daughter of
a Farmer; *John Giddish*, himself a Farmer; *Nan Slouch*, *Esther
Codling*, *Will Spray*, *Tom Bennet*; the three Misses *Potter*, whose
Father keeps the Sign of the *Red Lion*; *Betty Chambermaid*, *Jack
Ostler*, and many others of inferior Note, lay rolling among the
Graves.

Not that the strenuous Arm of *Molly* reached all these; for
many of them in their Flight overthrew each other.

But now Fortune, fearing she had acted out of Character,
and had inclined too long to the same Side, especially as it was
the right Side, hastily turned about: For now Goody *Brown*,
whom *Zekiel Brown* caressed in his Arms; nor he alone, but half
the Parish besides; so famous was she in the Fields of *Venus*, nor
indeed less in those of *Mars*. The Trophies of both these, her
Husband always bore about on his Head and Face; for if ever
human Head did by its Horns display the amorous Glories of a
Wife, *Zekiel's* did; nor did his well-scratched Face less denote her
Talents (or rather Talons) of a different Kind.

No longer bore this Amazon the shameful Flight of her
Party. She stopt short, and calling aloud to all who fled, spoke as

---

[1] Cf. Virgil's *Aeneid*, ix. 444–5—where Nisus, slain, falls upon his dead friend Euryalus:
> Dying, he slew; and stagg'ring on the Plain,
> With swimming Eyes he sought his Lover slain:
> Then quiet on his bleeding Bosom fell;
> Content in Death, to be reveng'd so well.
>   (Dryden's trans., ix. 593–6.)

[2] Cf. *Iliad*, v. 59–64—the death of Phereclus:
> Next artful *Phereclus* untimely fell;
> Bold *Merion* sent him to the Realms of Hell.
> Thy Father's Skill, O *Phereclus*, was thine,
> The graceful Fabrick and the fair Design;
> For lov'd by *Pallas*, *Pallas* did impart
> To him the Shipwright's and the Builder's Art.
> Beneath his Hand the Fleet of *Paris* rose,
> The fatal Cause of all his Country's Woes,
> But he, the mystick Will of Heav'n unknown,
> Nor saw his Country's Peril, nor his own.
>   (Pope's trans., v. 75–84.)

follows:[1] 'Ye *Somersetshire* Men, or rather ye *Somersetshire* Women, are ye not ashamed, thus to fly from a single Woman; but if no other will oppose her, I myself and *Joan Top* here will have the Honour of the Victory.' Having thus said, she flew at *Molly Seagrim*, and easily wrenched the Thigh Bone from her Hand, at the same Time clawing off her Cap from her Head. Then laying hold of the Hair of *Molly*, with her Left Hand, she attacked her so furiously in the Face with the Right, that the Blood soon began to trickle from her Nose. *Molly* was not idle this while. She soon removed the Clout from the Head of Goody *Brown*, and then fastening on her Hair with one Hand, with the other she caused another bloody Stream to issue forth from the Nostrils of the Enemy.

When each of the Combatants had borne off sufficient Spoils of Hair from the Head of her Antagonist, the next Rage was against the Garments. In this Attack they exerted so much Violence, that in a very few Minutes, they were both naked to the middle.

It is lucky for the Women, that the Seat of Fistycuff-War is not the same with them as among Men; but though they may seem a little to deviate from their Sex, when they go forth to Battle, yet I have observed they never so far forget, as to assail the Bosoms of each other; where a few Blows would be fatal to most of them. This, I know, some derive from their being of a more bloody Inclination than the Males. On which Account they apply to the Nose, as to the Part whence Blood may most easily be drawn; but this seems a far-fetched, as well as ill-natured Supposition.

Goody *Brown* had great Advantage of *Molly* in this Particular; for the former had indeed no Breasts, her Bosom (if it may be so called) as well in Colour as in many other Properties, exactly resembling an antient Piece of Parchment, upon which any one might have drummed a considerable while, without doing her any great Damage.

Molly, beside her present unhappy Condition, was differently

---

[1] Cf. *Iliad*, v. 785–7—Stentor's hortatory speech to the Greeks: Hera
. . . shouts, in *Stentor's* sounding Voice, aloud:
Stentor the strong, endu'd with Brazen Lungs,
Whose Throat surpass'd the Force of fifty Tongues.
Inglorious *Argives!* to your Race a Shame,
And only Men in Figure and in Name!
(Pope's trans., v. 977–81.)

formed in those Parts, and might, perhaps, have tempted the Envy of *Brown* to give her a fatal Blow, had not the lucky Arrival of *Tom Jones* at this Instant put an immediate End to the bloody Scene.

This Accident was luckily owing to Mr. *Square*; for he, Master *Blifil*, and *Jones*, had mounted their Horses, after Church, to take the Air, and had ridden about a Quarter of a Mile, when *Square*, changing his Mind, (not idly, but for a Reason which we shall unfold as soon as we have Leisure) desired the young Gentlemen to ride with him another Way than they had at first purposed. This Motion being complied with, brought them of Necessity back again to the Church-yard.

Master *Blifil*, who rode first, seeing such a Mob assembled, and two Women in the Posture in which we left the Combatants, stopt his Horse to enquire what was the Matter. A Country Fellow, scratching his Head, answered him; 'I don't know Measter un't I; an't please your Honour, here hath been a Vight, I think, between Goody *Brown* and *Mol Seagrim*.' 'Who, who?' cries *Tom*; but without waiting for an Answer, having discovered the Features of his *Molly* through all the Discomposure in which they now were, he hastily alighted, turned his Horse loose, and leaping over the Wall, ran to her. She now, first bursting into Tears, told him how barbarously she had been treated. Upon which, forgetting the Sex of Goody *Brown*, or perhaps not knowing it, in his Rage; for, in reality, she had no feminine Appearance, but a Petticoat, which he might not observe, he gave her a Lash or two with his Horsewhip; and then flying at the Mob, who were all accused by *Molly*, he dealt his Blows so profusely on all Sides, that unless I would again invoke the Muse, (which the good-natured Reader may think a little too hard upon her, as she hath so lately been violently sweated) it would be impossible for me to recount the Horsewhipping of that Day.

Having scoured the whole Coast of the Enemy, as well as any of *Homer's* Heroes ever did, or as *Don Quixotte*,[1] or any Knight Errant in the World could have done, he returned to *Molly*, whom he found in a Condition, which must give both me and my Reader Pain, was it to be described here. *Tom* raved like a Madman, beat his Breast, tore his Hair, stamped on the Ground,

[1] For Fielding's opinion of Cervantes, see below, p. 686, n. 1.

and vowed the utmost Vengeance on all who had been concerned. He then pulled off his Coat, and buttoned it round her, put his Hat upon her Head, wiped the Blood from her Face as well as he could with his Handkerchief, and called out to the Servant to ride as fast as possible for a Side-saddle, or a Pillion, that he might carry her safe home.

Master *Blifil* objected to the sending away the Servant, as they had only one with them; but as *Square* seconded the Order of *Jones*, he was obliged to comply.

The Servant returned in a very short Time with the Pillion, and *Molly*, having collected her Rags as well as she could, was placed behind him. In which Manner she was carried home, *Square, Blifil,* and *Jones*, attending.

Here *Jones*, having received his Coat, given her a sly Kiss, and whispered her that he would return in the Evening, quitted his *Molly*, and rode on after his Companions.

CHAPTER IX

Containing Matter of no very peaceable Colour.

*M*OLLY had no sooner apparelled herself in her accustomed Rags, than her Sisters began to fall violently upon her; particularly her eldest Sister, who told her she was well enough served. 'How had she the Assurance to wear a Gown which young Madam *Western* had given to Mother! If one of us was to wear it, I think,' says she, 'I myself have the best Right; but I warrant you think it belongs to your Beauty. I suppose you think yourself more handsomer than any of us.' 'Hand her down the Bit of Glass from over the Cupboard,' cries another, 'I'd wash the Blood from my Face before I tauked of my Beauty.' 'You'd better have minded what the Parson says,' cries the eldest, 'and not a harkened after Men Voke.' 'Indeed, Child, and so she had,' says the Mother sobbing, 'she hath brought a Disgrace upon us all. She's the vurst of the Vamily that ever was a Whore.' 'You need not upbraid me with that, Mother,' cries *Molly*, 'you yourself was brought to-bed of Sister there within a Week after you was married.' 'Yes, Hussy,' answered the enraged Mother, 'so

I was, and what was the mighty Matter of that? I was made an honest Woman then; and if you was to be made an honest Woman, I should not be angry; but you must have to be doing with a Gentleman, you nasty Slut, you will have a Bastard, Hussy, you will; and that I defy any one to say of me.'

In this Situation *Black George* found his Family, when he came home for the Purpose before mentioned. As his Wife and three Daughters were all of them talking together, and most of them crying, it was some time before he could get an Opportunity of being heard; but as soon as such an Interval occurred, he acquainted the Company with what *Sophia* had said to him.

Goody *Seagrim* then began to revile her Daughter afresh. 'Here,' says she, 'you have brought us into a fine Quandary indeed. What will Madam say to that big Belly? Oh that ever I should live to see this Day.'

Molly answered with great Spirit, 'And what is this mighty Place which you have got for me, Father?' (for he had not well understood the Phrase used by *Sophia* of being about her Person) 'I suppose it is to be under the Cook; but I shan't wash Dishes for any Body. My Gentleman will provide better for me. See what he hath given me this Afternoon; he hath promised I shall never want Money; and you shan't want Money neither, Mother, if you will hold your Tongue, and know when you are well.' And so saying, she pulled out several Guineas, and gave her Mother one of them.

The good Woman no sooner felt the Gold within her Palm, than her Temper began (such is the Efficacy of that *Panacea*) to be mollified. 'Why Husband,' says she, 'would any but such a Blockhead as you not have enquired what Place this was before he had accepted it! Perhaps, as *Molly* says, it may be in the Kitchin, and truly I don't care my Daughter should be a Scullion Wench: For poor as I am, I am a Gentlewoman. And thof I was obliged, as my Father, who was a Clergyman, died worse than nothing, and so could not give me a Shilling of *Potion*, to undervalue myself, by marrying a poor Man, yet I would have you to know, I have a Spirit above all *them* Things. Marry come up, it would better become Madam *Western* to look at Home, and remember who her own Grandfather was. Some of my Family, for ought I know, might ride in their Coaches, when the Grandfathers of some Voke walked a-voot. I warrant she fancies she did a mighty Matter, when she sent us that old *Gownd*; some of my Family would not have picked up such Rags in the Street; but poor People are always trampled upon.——The Parish need not have been in such a Fluster with *Molly*.——You might have told them, Child, your Grandmother wore better Things new out of the Shop.'

'Well but, consider,' cried *George*, 'What Answer shall I make to Madam?' 'I don't know what Answer,' says she, 'You are always bringing your Family into one Quandary or other. Do you remember when you shot the Partridge, the Occasion of all our Misfortunes? Did not I advise you never to go into Squire *Western's* Manor? Did not I tell you many a good Year ago what would come of it? but you would have your own headstrong Ways; yes, you would, you Villain——'

Black George was, in the main, a peaceable kind of Fellow, and nothing *choleric, nor rash*, yet did he bear about him some thing of what the Antients called the *Irascible*, and which his Wife, if she had been endowed with much *Wisdom, would have feared.*[1] He had long experienced, that when the Storm grew very high Arguments were but Wind, which served rather to increase than to abate it. He was therefore seldom unprovided with a small Switch, a Remedy of wonderful Force, as he had often essayed, and which the Word Villain served as a Hint for his applying.

No sooner, therefore, had this Symptom appeared, than he had immediate Recourse to the said Remedy, which though, as it is usual in all very efficacious Medicines, it at first seemed to heighten and inflame the Disease, soon produced a total Calm, and restored the Patient to perfect Ease and Tranquility.

This is, however, a kind of Horse-medicine, which requires a very robust Constitution to digest, and is therefore proper only for the Vulgar, unless in one single Instance, *viz.* where Superiority of Birth breaks out; in which Case, we should not think it very improperly applied by any Husband whatever, if the Application was not, in itself so base, that, like certain Applications of the Physical Kind which need not be mentioned, it so much degrades and contaminates the Hand employed in it, that

---

[1] Cf. Hamlet to Laertes (v. i):

> For, though I am not splenitive and rash,
> Yet have I in me something dangerous,
> Which let thy wisdom fear.

no Gentleman should endure the Thought of any Thing so low and detestable.

The whole Family were soon reduced to a State of perfect Quiet: For the Virtue of this Medicine, like that of Electricity, is often communicated through one Person to many others, who are not touched by the Instrument. To say the Truth, as they both operate by Friction, it may be doubted whether there is not something analogous between them, of which Mr. *Freke*[1] would do well to enquire before he publishes the next Edition of his Book.

A Council was now called, in which, after many Debates, *Molly* still persisting that she would not go to Service, it was at length resolved, that Goody *Seagrim* herself should wait on Miss *Western*, and endeavour to procure the Place for her eldest Daughter, who declared great Readiness to accept it; but Fortune, who seems to have been an Enemy of this little Family, afterwards put a Stop to her Promotion.

CHAPTER X

A Story told by Mr. Supple, *the Curate. The Penetration of Squire* Western. *His great Love for his Daughter, and the Return to it made by her.*

THE next Morning *Tom Jones* hunted with Mr. *Western*, and was at his Return invited by that Gentleman to Dinner.

The lovely *Sophia* shone forth that Day with more Gaiety and Sprightliness than usual. Her Battery was certainly levelled at our Heroe; though, I believe, she herself scarce yet knew her own Intention; but if she had any Design of charming him, she now succeeded.

Mr. *Supple*, the Curate of Mr. *Allworthy's* Parish, made one of the Company. He was a good-natured worthy Man; but chiefly remarkable for his great Taciturnity at Table, though his Mouth was never shut at it. In short, he had one of the best

[1] See above, p. 86, n. 1. In his *Essay to Shew the Cause of Electricity*, Freke had attempted to explain 'Why a Company of unelectrify'd Persons, who are joined together by their holding each a Piece of iron Wire betwixt them, tho' they are ever so many, do all receive a violent Blow or Concussion on their Bodies, when one of them touches a Piece of electrify'd Iron' (pp. 36–7).

Appetites in the World. However, the Cloth was no sooner taken away, than he always made sufficient Amends for his Silence: For he was a very hearty Fellow; and his Conversation was often entertaining, never offensive.

At his first Arrival, which was immediately before the Entrance of the Roast-beef, he had given an Intimation that he had brought some News with him, and was beginning to tell, that he came that Moment from Mr. *Allworthy's*, when the Sight of the Roast-beef struck him dumb, permitting him only to say Grace, and to declare he must pay his Respect to the Baronet:[1] For so he called the Sirloin.

When Dinner was over, being reminded by *Sophia* of his News, he began as follows, 'I believe, Lady, your Ladyship observed a young Woman at Church yesterday at Even-song, who was drest in one of your outlandish Garments; I think I have seen your Ladyship in such a one. However, in the Country, such Dresses are

Rara avis in Terris, nigroque simillima Cycno,[2]

That is, Madam, as much as to say,

A rare Bird upon the Earth, and very like a black Swan.

'The Verse is in *Juvenal*: but to return to what I was relating. I was saying such Garments are rare Sights in the Country, and perchance too, it was thought the more rare, Respect being had to the Person who wore it, who, they tell me, is the Daughter of *Black George*, your Worship's Game-keeper, whose Sufferings I should have opined, might have taught him more Wit than to dress forth his Wenches in such gaudy Apparel. She created so much Confusion in the Congregation, that if Squire *Allworthy* had not silenced it, it would have interrupted the Service: For I was once about to stop in the Middle of the first Lesson. Howbeit, nevertheless, after Prayer was over, and I was departed home, this occasioned a Battle in the Church-yard, where, amongst other Mischief, the Head of a travelling Fidler was very much broken. This Morning the Fidler came to Squire *Allworthy* for a Warrant, and the Wench was brought before him. The Squire was inclined to have compounded Matters; when, lo! on a sudden, the

---

[1] A 'baron of beef' was 'a joint consisting of two sirloins left uncut at the backbone' (*OED*).

[2] Juvenal, *Satires*, vi. 165.

Wench appeared (I ask your Ladyship's Pardon) to be, as it were at the Eve of bringing forth a Bastard. The Squire demanded of her who was the Father; but she pertinaciously refused to make any Response. So that he was about to make her Mittimus to *Bridewel*, when I departed.'

'And is a Wench having a Bastard all your News, Doctor?' cries *Western*. 'I thought it might have been some public Matter, something about the Nation.'

'I am afraid it is too common, indeed,' answered the Parson, 'but I thought the whole Story all together deserved commemorating. As to National Matters, your Worship knows them best. My Concerns extend no farther than my own Parish.'

'Why ay,' says the Squire, 'I believe I do know a little of that Matter, as you say; but come, *Tommy*, drink about, the Bottle stands with you.'

Tom begged to be excused, for that he had particular Business; and getting up from Table, escaped the Clutches of the Squire who was rising to stop him, and went off with very little Ceremony.

The Squire gave him a good Curse at his Departure; and then turning to the Parson, he cried out, 'I smoke it, I smoke it. *Tom* is certainly the Father of this Bastard. Zooks, Parson, you remember how he recommended the Veather o'her to me—— d—n un, what a sly B—ch 'tis. Ay, ay, as sure as Twopence, *Tom* is the Veather of the Bastard.'

'I should be very sorry for that,' says the Parson. 'Why sorry,' cries the Squire, 'Where is the mighty Matter o't? What, I suppose, dost pretend that thee hast never got a Bastard? Pox! more good Luck's thine: for I warrant hast a done *therefore* many's the good Time and often.' 'Your Worship is pleased to be jocular,' answered the Parson, 'but I do not only animadvert on the Sinfulness of the Action, though that surely is to be greatly deprecated; but I fear his Unrighteousness may injure him with Mr. *Allworthy*. And truly I must say, though he hath the Character of being a little wild, I never saw any Harm in the young Man; nor can I say I have heard any, save what your Worship now mentions. I wish, indeed he was a little more regular in his Responses at Church; but altogether he seems

Ingenui vultus puer ingenuique pudoris.[1]

[1] Juvenal, *Satires*, xi. 154.

'That is a classical Line, young Lady, and being rendered into *English* is, A Lad of an ingenuous Countenance and of an ingenuous Modesty: For this was a Virtue in great Repute both among the *Latins* and *Greeks*. I must say the young Gentleman (for so I think I may call him, notwithstanding his Birth) appears to me a very modest, civil Lad, and I should be sorry that he should do himself any Injury in Squire *Allworthy's* Opinion.'

'Poogh!' says the Squire, 'Injury with *Allworthy*! Why *Allworthy* loves a Wench himself. Doth not all the Country know whose Son *Tom* is? You must talk to another Person in that Manner. I remember *Allworthy* at College.'

'I thought,' said the Parson, 'he had never been at the University.'

'Yes, yes, he was,' says the Squire, 'and many a Wench have we two had together. As arrant a Whoremaster as any within five Miles o'un. No, no. It will do'n no Harm with he, assure your self; nor with any Body else. Ask *Sophy* there.—You have not the worse Opinion of a young Fellow for getting a Bastard, have you, Girl? No, no, the Women will like un the better for't.'

This was a cruel Question to poor *Sophia*. She had observed *Tom's* Colour change at the Parson's Story; and that, with his hasty and abrupt Departure, gave her sufficient Reason to think her Father's Suspicion not groundless. Her Heart now, at once, discovered the great Secret to her, which it had been so long disclosing by little and little; and she found herself highly interested in this Matter. In such a Situation, her Father's malapert Question rushing suddenly upon her, produced some Symptoms which might have alarmed a suspicious Heart; but to do the Squire Justice, that was not his Fault. When she rose therefore from her Chair, and told him, a Hint from him was always sufficient to make her withdraw, he suffered her to leave the Room; and then with great Gravity of Countenance remarked, 'that it was better to see a Daughter over-modest, than over-forward;' a Sentiment which was highly applauded by the Parson.

There now ensued between the Squire and the Parson, a most excellent political Discourse, framed out of News-papers, and political Pamphlets; in which they made a Libation of four Bottles of Wine to the Good of their Country; and then, the Squire being fast asleep, the Parson lighted his Pipe, mounted his Horse, and rode home.

When the Squire had finished his Half-hour's Nap, he summoned his Daughter to her Harpsichord; but she begged to be excused that Evening, on Account of a violent Head-ach. This Remission was presently granted: For indeed she seldom had Occasion to ask him twice, as he loved her with such ardent Affection, that by gratifying her, he commonly conveyed the highest Gratification to himself. She was really what he frequently called her, his little Darling; and she well deserved to be so: For she returned all his Affection in the most ample Manner. She had preserved the most inviolable Duty to him in all Things; and this her Love made not only easy, but so delightful, that when one of her Companions laughed at her for placing so much Merit in such scrupulous Obedience, as that young Lady called it, *Sophia* answered, 'You mistake me, Madam, if you think I value myself upon this Account: For besides that I am barely discharging my Duty, I am likewise pleasing myself. I can truly say, I have no Delight equal to that of contributing to my Father's Happiness; and if I value myself, my Dear, it is on having this Power, and not on executing it.'

This was a Satisfaction, however, which poor *Sophia* was incapable of tasting this Evening. She therefore not only desired to be excused from her Attendance at the Harpsichord, but likewise begged that he would suffer her to absent herself from Supper. To this Request likewise the Squire agreed, though not without some Reluctance; for he scarce ever permitted her to be out of his Sight, unless when he was engaged with his Horses, Dogs, or Bottle. Nevertheless he yielded to the Desire of his Daughter, though the poor Man was, at the same Time, obliged to avoid his own Company, (if I may so express myself) by sending for a neighbouring Farmer to sit with him.

CHAPTER XI

The narrow Escape of Molly Seagrim*, with some Observations for which we have been forced to dive pretty deep into Nature.*

*T*OM *JONES* had ridden one of Mr. *Western's* Horses that Morning in the Chace: so that having no Horse of his own in the Squire's Stable, he was obliged to go home on Foot. This he did so expeditiously, that he ran upwards of three Miles within the half Hour.

Just as he arrived at Mr. *Allworthy's* outward Gate, he met the Constable and Company, with *Molly* in their Possession, whom they were conducting to that House where the inferior Sort of People may learn one good Lesson, *viz.* Respect and Deference to their Superiors. Since it must shew them the wide Distinction Fortune intends between those Persons who are to be corrected for their Faults, and those who are not; which Lesson, if they do not learn, I am afraid, they very rarely learn any other good Lesson, or improve their Morals, at the House of Correction.[1]

A Lawyer may, perhaps, think Mr. *Allworthy* exceeded his Authority a little in this Instance.[2] And, to say the Truth, I question, as here was no regular Information before him, whether his Conduct was strictly regular. However, as his Intention was truly upright, he ought to be excused in *Foro Conscientiæ*,[3] since so many arbitrary Acts are daily committed by Magistrates, who have not this Excuse to plead for themselves.

Tom was no sooner informed by the Constable, whither they were proceeding, (indeed he pretty well guessed it of himself) than he caught *Molly* in his Arms, and embracing her tenderly before them all, swore he would murder the first Man who offered to lay hold of her. He bid her dry her Eyes, and be comforted; for wherever she went, he would accompany her. Then turning to the Constable, who stood trembling with his Hat off, he desired him, in a very mild Voice, to return with him for a Moment only to his Father, (so he now called *Allworthy*) for he durst, he said, be assured, that when he had alledged what he had to say in her Favour, the Girl would be discharged.

The Constable, who, I make no Doubt, would have surrendered his Prisoner, had *Tom* demanded her, very readily consented to this Request. So back they all went into Mr. *Allworthy's* Hall;

---

[1] See above, p. 59, n. 1.

[2] Though the mother of a bastard child could be committed to the house of correction (see above, p. 40, n. 1), yet this could only be after she had been examined and the order of commitment signed by at least two justices, one being of the quorum. Furthermore, in order to prevent a possible miscarriage, it was unlawful for the justices to commit the woman, or even to summon her for examination, until one month after she had been delivered of the child. (See Barlow, *The Justice of the Peace* [1745], pp. 57–8, and Dalton, *The Country Justice* [1746], p. 34.)

[3] In a court of conscience. (See below, pp. 257.22, 676.24).

where *Tom* desired them to stay till his Return, and then went himself in Pursuit of the Good Man. As soon as he was found, *Tom* threw himself at his Feet, and having begged a patient Hearing, confessed himself to be the Father of the Child, of which *Molly* was then big. He entreated him to have Compassion on the poor Girl, and to consider, if there was any Guilt in the Case, it lay principally at his Door.

'If there is any Guilt in the Case!' answered *Allworthy* warmly, 'are you then so profligate and abandoned a Libertine, to doubt whether the breaking the Laws of God and Man, the corrupting and ruining a poor Girl, be Guilt? I own, indeed, it doth lie principally upon you, and so heavy it is, that you ought to expect it should crush you.'

'Whatever may be my Fate,' says *Tom*, 'let me succeed in my Intercessions for the poor Girl. I confess I have corrupted her; but whether she shall be ruined depends on you. For Heaven's Sake, Sir, revoke your Warrant, and do not send her to a Place which must unavoidably prove her Destruction.'

Allworthy bid him immediately call a Servant. *Tom* answered, there was no Occasion; for he had luckily met them at the Gate, and relying upon his Goodness, had brought them all back into his Hall, where they now waited his final Resolution, which, upon his Knees, he besought him might be in favour of the Girl; that she might be permitted to go home to her Parents, and not be exposed to a greater Degree of Shame and Scorn than must necessarily fall upon her. 'I know,' said he, 'that is too much. I know I am the wicked Occasion of it. I will endeavour to make Amends, if possible; and if you shall have hereafter the Goodness to forgive me, I hope I shall deserve it.'

Allworthy hesitated some Time, and at last said, 'Well, I will discharge my Mittimus.—You may send the Constable to me.' He was instantly called, discharged, and so was the Girl.

It will be believed, that Mr. *Allworthy* failed not to read *Tom* a very severe Lecture on this Occasion; but it is unnecessary to insert it here, as we have faithfully transcribed what he said to *Jenny Jones* in the first Book, most of which may be applied to the Men, equally with the Women. So sensible an Effect had these Reproofs on the young Man, who was no hardened Sinner, that he retired to his own Room, where he passed the Evening alone in much melancholy Contemplation.

Allworthy was sufficiently offended by this Transgression of *Jones*; for notwithstanding the Assertions of Mr. *Western*, it is certain this worthy Man had never indulged himself in any loose Pleasures with Women, and greatly condemned the Vice of Incontinence in others. Indeed, there is much Reason to imagine, that there was not the least Truth in what Mr. *Western* affirmed, especially as he laid the Scene of those Impurities at the University, where Mr. *Allworthy* had never been. In fact, the good Squire was a little too apt to indulge that Kind of Pleasantry which is generally called *Rodomontade*; but which may, with as much Propriety, be expressed by a much shorter Word; and, perhaps, we too often supply the Use of this little Monosyllable by others; since very much of what frequently passes in the World for Wit and Humour, should, in the strictest Purity of Language, receive that short Appellation, which, in Conformity to the well-bred Laws of Custom, I here suppress.

But whatever Detestation Mr. *Allworthy* had to this or to any other Vice, he was not so blinded by it, but that he could discern any Virtue in the guilty Person, as clearly, indeed, as if there had been no Mixture of Vice in the same Character. While he was angry, therefore, with the Incontinence of *Jones*, he was no less pleased with the Honour and Honesty of his Self-accusation. He began now to form in his Mind the same Opinion of this young Fellow which we hope our Reader may have conceived. And in ballancing his Faults with his Perfections, the latter seemed rather to preponderate.

It was to no Purpose, therefore, that *Thwackum*, who was immediately charged by Mr. *Blifil* with the Story, unbended all his Rancour against poor *Tom*. *Allworthy* gave a patient Hearing to these Invectives, and then answered coldly; 'That young Men of *Tom's* Complexion were too generally addicted to this Vice; but he believed that Youth was sincerely affected with what he had said to him on the Occasion, and he hoped he would not transgress again.' So that, as the Days of whipping were at an End, the Tutor had no other Vent but his own Mouth for his Gall, the usual poor Resource of impotent Revenge.

But *Square*, who was a less violent, was a much more artful Man; and as he hated *Jones* more, perhaps, than *Thwackum* himself did, so he contrived to do him more Mischief in the Mind of Mr. *Allworthy*.

The Reader must remember the several little Incidents of the Partridge, the Horse, and the Bible, which were recounted in the second Book. By all which *Jones* had rather improved than injured the Affection which Mr. *Allworthy* was inclined to entertain for him. The same, I believe, must have happened to him with every other Person who hath any Idea of Friendship, Generosity, and Greatness of Spirit; that is to say, who hath any Traces of Goodness in his Mind.

Square himself was not unacquainted with the true Impression which those several Instances of Goodness had made on the excellent Heart of *Allworthy*; for the Philosopher very well knew what Virtue was, though he was not always, perhaps, steady in its Pursuit; but as for *Thwackum*, from what Reason I will not determine, no such Thoughts ever entered into his Head. He saw *Jones* in a bad Light, and he imagined *Allworthy* saw him in the same, but that he was resolved, from Pride and Stubbornness of Spirit, not to give up the Boy whom he had once cherished, since, by so doing, he must tacitly acknowledge that his former Opinion of him had been wrong.

Square therefore embraced this Opportunity of injuring *Jones* in the tenderest Part, by giving a very bad Turn to all these before-mentioned Occurrences. 'I am sorry, Sir,' said he, 'to own I have been deceived as well as yourself. I could not, I confess, help being pleased with what I ascribed to the Motive of Friendship, though it was carried to an Excess, and all Excess is faulty, and vicious; but in this I made Allowance for Youth. Little did I suspect that the Sacrifice of Truth, which we both imagined to have been made to Friendship, was, in reality, a Prostitution of it to a depraved and debauched Appetite. You now plainly see whence all the seeming Generosity of this young Man to the Family of the Game-keeper proceeded. He supported the Father in order to corrupt the Daughter, and preserved the Family from starving, to bring one of them to Shame and Ruin. This is Friendship! this is Generosity! As Sir *Richard Steele* says,[1] Gluttons who give high Prices for Delicacies, are very worthy to be called generous. In short, I am resolved, from this Instance, never to give Way to the Weakness of Human Nature more, nor

---

[1] In *The Conscious Lovers* (1722), v. iii, Mr. Sealand scoffs when Indiana declares Bevil's generosity to her: 'Bounty! when Gluttons give high Prices for Delicates, they are prodigious Bountiful.'

to think any thing Virtue which doth not exactly quadrate with the unerring Rule of Right.'

The Goodness of *Allworthy* had prevented those Considerations from occurring to himself; yet were they too plausible to be absolutely and hastily rejected, when laid before his Eyes by another. Indeed what *Square* had said sunk very deeply into his Mind, and the Uneasiness which it there created was very visible to the other; though the good Man would not acknowledge this, but made a very slight Answer, and forcibly drove off the Discourse to some other Subject. It was well, perhaps, for poor *Tom*, that no such Suggestions had been made before he was pardoned; for they certainly stamped in the Mind of *Allworthy* the first bad Impression concerning *Jones*.

CHAPTER XII

Containing much clearer Matters; but which flowed from the same Fountain with those in the preceding Chapter.

THE Reader will be pleased, I believe, to return with me to *Sophia*. She passed the Night, after we saw her last, in no very agreeable Manner. Sleep befriended her but little, and Dreams less. In the Morning, when Mrs. *Honour* her Maid attended her, at the usual Hour, she was found already up and drest.

Persons who live two or three Miles Distance in the Country are considered as next Door Neighbours, and Transactions at the one House fly with incredible Celerity to the other. Mrs. *Honour*, therefore, had heard the whole Story of *Molly's* Shame; which she, being of a very communicative Temper, had no sooner entered the Apartment of her Mistress, than she began to relate in the following Manner:

'La Ma'am, what doth your La'ship think? the Girl that your La'ship saw at Church on *Sunday*, whom you thought so handsome; though you would not have thought her so handsome neither, if you had seen her nearer; but to be sure she hath been carried before the Justice for being big with Child. She seemed to me to look like a confident Slut; and to be sure she hath laid the Child to young Mr. *Jones*. And all the Parish says Mr.

Allworthy is so angry with young Mr. *Jones*, that he won't see him. To be sure, one can't help pitying the poor young Man, and yet he doth not deserve much Pity neither, for demeaning himself with such Kind of Trumpery. Yet he is so pretty a Gentleman, I should be sorry to have him turned out of Doors. I dares to swear the Wench was as willing as he; for she was always a forward Kind of Body. And when Wenches are so coming, young Men are not so much to be blamed neither; for to be sure they do no more than what is natural. Indeed it is beneath them to meddle with such dirty Draggle-tails, and whatever happens to them, it is good enough for them. And yet to be sure the vile Baggages are most in Fault. I wishes, with all my Heart, they were well to be whipped at the Cart's Tail; for it is Pity they should be the Ruin of a pretty young Gentleman; and no body can deny but that Mr. *Jones* is one of the most handsomest young Men that ever———'

She was running on thus, when *Sophia*, with a more peevish Voice than she had ever spoken to her in before, cried, 'Prithee why do'st thou trouble me with all this Stuff? What Concern have I in what Mr. *Jones* doth? I suppose you are all alike. And you seem to me to be angry it was not your own Case.'

'I, Ma'am!' answered Mrs. *Honour*, 'I am sorry your Ladyship should have such an Opinion of me. I am sure nobody can say any such thing of me. All the young Fellows in the World may go to the *Divil*, for me. Because I said he was a handsome Man! Every body says it as well as I———To be sure, I never thought as it was any Harm to say a young Man was handsome; but to be sure I shall never think him so any more now; for handsome is that handsome does. A Beggar Wench!———'

'Stop thy Torrent of Impertinence,' cries *Sophia*, 'and see whether my Father wants me at Breakfast.'

Mrs. *Honour* then flung out of the Room, muttering much to herself—of which—'Marry come up, I assure you,' was all that could be plainly distinguished.

Whether Mrs. *Honour* really deserved that Suspicion, of which her Mistress gave her a Hint, is a Matter which we cannot indulge our Reader's Curiosity by resolving. We will however make him Amends, in disclosing what passed in the Mind of *Sophia*.

The Reader will be pleased to recollect, that a secret Affection for Mr. *Jones* had insensibly stolen into the Bosom of this young

Lady. That it had there grown to a pretty great Height before she herself had discovered it. When she first began to perceive its Symptoms, the Sensations were so sweet and pleasing, that she had not Resolution sufficient to check or repel them; and thus she went on cherishing a Passion of which she never once considered the Consequences.

This Incident relating to *Molly*, first opened her Eyes. She now first perceived the Weakness of which she had been guilty; and though it caused the utmost Perturbation in her Mind, yet it had the Effect of other nauseous Physic, and for the Time expelled her Distemper. Its Operation indeed was most wonderfully quick; and in the short Interval, while her Maid was absent, so entirely removed all Symptoms, that when Mrs. *Honour* returned with a Summons from her Father, she was become perfectly easy, and had brought herself to a thorough Indifference for Mr. *Jones*.

The Diseases of the Mind do in almost every Particular imitate those of the Body. For which Reason, we hope, That learned Faculty, for whom we have so profound a Respect, will pardon us the violent Hands we have been necessitated to lay on several Words and Phrases,[1] which of Right belong to them, and without which our Descriptions must have been often unintelligible.

Now there is no one Circumstance in which the Distempers of the Mind bear a more exact Analogy to those which are called Bodily, than that Aptness which both have to a Relapse. This is plain, in the violent Diseases of Ambition and Avarice. I have known Ambition, when cured at Court by frequent Disappointments, (which are the only Physic for it) to break out again in a Contest for Foreman of the Grand Jury at an Assizes; and have heard of a Man who had so far conquered Avarice, as to give away many a Sixpence, that comforted himself, at last, on his Death-bed, by making a crafty and advantagious Bargain concerning his ensuing Funeral, with an Undertaker who had married his only Child.

In the Affair of Love, which out of strict Conformity with the Stoic Philosophy, we shall here treat as a Disease,[2] this Proneness

---

[1] Cf. *The Champion* (17 January 1739/40): 'every particular Profession seems to have laid violent Hands on, some certain Syllables which they use *ad Libitum* without conveying any Idea whatsoever.'

[2] For the stoic doctrine that the passions 'are but the diseases of Fools', see Anthony LeGrand, *Man without Passion: or, The Wise Stoick, According to the Sentiments of Seneca,*

to relapse is no less conspicuous. Thus it happened to poor *Sophia*; upon whom, the very next Time she saw young *Jones*, all the former Symptoms returned, and from that Time cold and hot Fits alternately seized her Heart.

The Situation of this young Lady was now very different from what it had ever been before. That Passion, which had formerly been so exquisitely delicious, became now a Scorpion in her Bosom. She resisted it therefore with her utmost Force, and summoned every Argument her Reason (which was surprizingly strong for her Age) could suggest, to subdue and expel it. In this she so far succeeded, that she began to hope from Time and Absence a perfect Cure. She resolved therefore to avoid *Tom Jones*, as much as possible; for which Purpose she began to conceive a Design of visiting her Aunt, to which she made no Doubt of obtaining her Father's Consent.

But Fortune, who had other Designs in her Head, put an immediate Stop to any such Proceeding, by introducing an Accident, which will be related in the next Chapter.

CHAPTER XIII

A dreadful Accident which befel Sophia. *The gallant Behaviour of* Jones, *and the more dreadful Consequence of that Behaviour to the young Lady; with a short Digression in Favour of the Female Sex.*

MR. *Western* grew every Day fonder and fonder of *Sophia*, insomuch that his beloved Dogs themselves almost gave Place to her in his Affections; but as he could not prevail on himself to abandon these, he contrived very cunningly to enjoy their Company, together with that of his Daughter, by insisting on her riding a hunting with him.

Sophia, to whom her Father's Word was a Law, readily complied with his Desires, though she had not the least Delight in a Sport, which was of too rough and masculine a Nature to suit with her Disposition. She had, however, another Motive, beside

trans. G. R. (1675). LeGrand is especially severe with those 'lascivious *Poets*' who refuse to 'learn from Reason that that Love whose frequent Victories you proclaim is but the destemper [*sic*] of Mad-men' (p. 135).

her Obedience, to accompany the old Gentleman in the Chace; for by her Presence she hoped in some Measure to restrain his Impetuosity, and to prevent him from so frequently exposing his Neck to the utmost Hazard.

The strongest Objection was that which would have formerly been an Inducement to her, namely, the frequent Meeting with young *Jones*, whom she had determined to avoid; but as the End of the hunting Season now approached, she hoped, by a short Absence with her Aunt, to reason herself entirely out of her unfortunate Passion; and had not any Doubt of being able to meet him in the Field the subsequent Season without the least Danger.

On the second Day of her Hunting, as she was returning from the Chace, and was arrived within a little Distance from Mr. *Western's* House, her Horse, whose mettlesome Spirit required a better Rider, fell suddenly to prancing and capering, in such a Manner, that she was in the most eminent Peril of falling. *Tom Jones*, who was at a little Distance behind, saw this, and immediately galloped up to her Assistance. As soon as he came up, he leapt from his own Horse, and caught hold of her's by the Bridle. The unruly Beast presently reared himself an End on his hind Legs, and threw his lovely Burthen from his Back, and *Jones* caught her in his Arms.

She was so affected with the Fright, that she was not immediately able to satisfy *Jones*, who was very sollicitous to know whether she had received any Hurt. She soon after, however, recovered her Spirits, assured him she was safe, and thanked him for the Care he had taken of her. *Jones* answered, 'If I have preserved you, Madam, I am sufficiently repaid; for I promise you, I would have secured you from the least Harm, at the Expence of a much greater Misfortune to myself, than I have suffered on this Occasion.'

'What Misfortune,' replied *Sophia*, eagerly, 'I hope you have come to no Mischief?'

'Be not concerned, Madam,' answered *Jones*, 'Heaven be praised, you have escaped so well, considering the Danger you was in. If I have broke my Arm, I consider it as a Trifle, in Comparison of what I feared upon your Account.'

Sophia then screamed out, 'Broke your Arm! Heaven forbid.'

'I am afraid I have, Madam,' says *Jones*, 'but I beg you will suffer me first to take Care of you. I have a Right-hand yet at your Service, to help you into the next Field, whence we have but a very little Walk to your Father's House.'

Sophia seeing his left Arm dangling by his Side, while he was using the other to lead her, no longer doubted of the Truth. She now grew much paler than her Fears for herself had made her before. All her Limbs were seized with a Trembling, insomuch that *Jones* could scarce support her; and as her Thoughts were in no less Agitation, she could not refrain from giving *Jones* a Look so full of Tenderness, that it almost argued a stronger Sensation in her Mind, than even Gratitude and Pity united can raise in the gentlest female Bosom, without the Assistance of a third more powerful Passion.

Mr. *Western*, who was advanced at some Distance when this Accident happened, was now returned, as were the rest of the Horsemen. *Sophia* immediately acquainted them with what had befallen *Jones*, and begged them to take Care of him. Upon which, *Western*, who had been much alarmed by meeting his Daughter's Horse without its Rider, and was now overjoyed to find her unhurt, cried out, 'I am glad it is no worse; if *Tom* hath broken his Arm, we will get a Joiner to mend un again.'

The Squire alighted from his Horse, and proceeded to his House on foot, with his Daughter and *Jones*. An impartial Spectator, who had met them on the Way, would, on viewing their several Countenances, have concluded *Sophia* alone to have been the Object of Compassion: For as to *Jones*, he exulted in having probably saved the Life of the young Lady, at the Price only of a broken Bone; and Mr. *Western*, though he was not unconcerned at the Accident which had befallen *Jones*, was, however, delighted in a much higher Degree with the fortunate Escape of his Daughter.

The Generosity of *Sophia's* Temper construed this Behaviour of *Jones* into great Bravery; and it made a deep Impression on her Heart: For certain it is, that there is no one Quality which so generally recommends Men to Women as this; proceeding, if we believe the common Opinion, from that natural Timidity of the Sex; which is, says Mr. *Osborne*,[1] so great, that a Woman is

---

[1] Francis Osborne (1592–1659) was something of a misogynist. Though the words Fielding attributes to him do not occur in Osborne's works, the sentiment may be illustrated from his most popular book, *Advice to a Son* (1656–8), wherein he remarks as follows on the folly of affecting false characters: it remains, Osborne writes, '*equally rare,*

'the most cowardly of all the Creatures God ever made.' A Sentiment more remarkable for its Bluntness, than for its Truth. *Aristotle*, in his Politics,[1] doth them, I believe, more Justice, when he says, 'The Modesty and Fortitude of Men differ from those Virtues in Women; for the Fortitude which becomes a Woman, would be Cowardice in a Man; and the Modesty which becomes a Man, would be Pertness in a Woman.' Nor is there, perhaps, more of Truth in the Opinion of those who derive the Partiality which Women are inclined to shew to the Brave, from this Excess of their Fear. Mr. *Bayle*[2] (I think, in his Article of *Helen*) imputes this, and with greater Probability, to their violent Love of Glory; for the Truth of which, we have the Authority of him, who, of all others, saw farthest into human Nature; and who introduces the Heroine of his Odyssey,[3] the great Pattern of matrimonial Love and Constancy, assigning the Glory of her Husband as the only Source of her Affection towards him.*

However this be, certain it is that the Accident operated very strongly on *Sophia*; and, indeed, after much Enquiry into the Matter, I am inclined to believe, that at this very Time, the

* The *English* Reader will not find this in the Poem: For the Sentiment is entirely left out in the Translation.

---

to find a *starched and Complemental Man wise*, as *a woman Valiant*: the most serious *Endeavours* of them both being to *captivate the ignorant Beholders*. And though this may pass but for a *blemish* in *Youth*, it becomes an *Ugly deformity* in *Age*: asserting their *Opinion* who have formerly thought *Apes* to be of the extraction of *Cham*, or some other *By-blow* of *Human Generation*, by their too near *approaching* towards the nature of *women*' (*Works*, 8th ed. [1682], pp. 147–8).

[1] Cf. *Politics*, I. v. 8.

[2] Pierre Bayle (1647–1706), French rationalist philosopher and author of the influential *Dictionnaire historique et critique* (1697–1702). The observation to which Fielding alludes occurs in Bayle's article on the Duke of Guise: 'It is granted that the Ladies love courageous men, and valiant admirers; but it's not because they are brave in all respects; it is rather on account of the exalted fame that is inseparable from bravery, and which reflects an honour on the mistresses of those who have acquired so great a renown. Therefore, when Women prefer Warriors to those of a peaceable profession, and Warriors of distinguished bravery to those who are otherwise, this arises more from pride than from lewdness. They think it is more glorious to captivate a man of exalted courage than to ensnare one of a pacifick disposition' (*A General Dictionary, Historical and Critical* [1734–41], v. 643, n. *o*). Bayle then cites the story of Paris and Helen, a circumstance which may explain Fielding's mistake in locating the passage. See also *Amelia* (1751; XII. iii).

[3] Cf. Penelope in the *Odyssey*, i. 343–4: 'So dear a head do I ever remember with longing, even my husband, whose fame [κλέος] is wide through Hellas and mid-Argos' (trans. A. T. Murray, Loeb Classical Library, 1919). For Pope's rendering of these lines, see his translation (1725–6), i. 437–40.

charming *Sophia* made no less Impression on the Heart of *Jones*; to say Truth, he had for some Time become sensible of the irresistible Power of her Charms.

CHAPTER XIV

The Arrival of a Surgeon. His Operations, and a long Dialogue between Sophia *and her Maid.*

WHEN they arrived in Mr. *Western's* Hall, *Sophia*, who had totter'd along with much Difficulty, sunk down in a Chair; but by the Assistance of Hartshorn and Water, she was prevented from fainting away, and had pretty well recovered her Spirits, when the Surgeon, who was sent for to *Jones*, appeared. Mr. *Western*, who imputed these Symptoms in his Daughter to her Fall, advised her to be presently blooded by way of Prevention. In this Opinion he was seconded by the Surgeon, who gave so many Reasons for bleeding, and quoted so many Cases where Persons had miscarried for want of it, that the Squire became very importunate, and indeed insisted peremptorily that his Daughter should be blooded.

Sophia soon yielded to the Commands of her Father, though entirely contrary to her own Inclinations: For she suspected, I believe, less Danger from the Fright, than either the Squire or the Surgeon. She then stretched out her beautiful Arm, and the Operator began to prepare for his Work.

While the Servants were busied in providing Materials; the Surgeon, who imputed the Backwardness which had appeared in *Sophia* to her Fears, began to comfort her with Assurances that there was not the least Danger; for no Accident, he said, could ever happen in Bleeding, but from the monstrous Ignorance of Pretenders to Surgery, which he pretty plainly insinuated was not at present to be apprehended. *Sophia* declared she was not under the least Apprehension; adding, 'if you open an Artery, I promise you I'll forgive you.' 'Will you,' cries *Western*, 'D—n me, if I will; if he does thee the least Mischief, d—n me, if I don't ha' the Heart's Blood o'un out.' The Surgeon assented to bleed her upon these Conditions, and then proceeded to his Operation, which he performed with as much Dexterity as he had promised; and with as much Quickness: For he took but little Blood from her, saying, it was much safer to bleed again and again, than to take away too much at once.

Sophia, when her Arm was bound up, retired: For she was not willing (nor was it, perhaps, strictly decent) to be present at the Operation on *Jones*. Indeed one Objection which she had to Bleeding, (tho' she did not make it) was the Delay which it would occasion to setting the broken Bone. For *Western*, when *Sophia* was concerned, had no Consideration, but for her; and as for *Jones* himself, he 'sat like Patience on a Monument smiling at Grief'.[1] To say the Truth, when he saw the Blood springing from the lovely Arm of *Sophia*, he scarce thought of what had happened to himself.

The Surgeon now ordered his Patient to be stript to his Shirt, and then entirely baring the Arm, he began to stretch and examine it, in such a Manner, that the Tortures he put him to, caused *Jones* to make several wry Faces; which the Surgeon observing, greatly wondered at, crying, 'What is the Matter, Sir? I am sure it is impossible I should hurt you.' And then holding forth the broken Arm, he began a long and very learned Lecture of Anatomy, in which simple and double Fractures were most accurately considered, and the several Ways in which *Jones* might have broken his Arm were discussed, with proper Annotations, shewing how many of these would have been better, and how many worse than the present Case.

Having at length finish'd his laboured Harangue, with which the Audience, tho' it had greatly raised their Attention and Admiration, were not much edified, as they really understood not a single Syllable of all he had said, he proceeded to Business, which he was more expeditious in finishing, than he had been in beginning.

Jones was then ordered into a Bed, which Mr. *Western* compelled him to accept at his own House, and Sentence of Water-Gruel was passed upon him.

Among the good Company which had attended in the Hall during the Bone-setting, Mrs. *Honour* was one; who being summoned to her Mistress as soon as it was over, and asked by her how the young Gentleman did, presently launched into extravagant Praises on the *Magnimity*, as she called it, of his Behaviour,

---

[1] *Twelfth Night*, II. iv—Viola describing to the Duke her 'sister's' silent love.

which, she said, 'was so charming in so pretty a Creature.' She then burst forth into much warmer Encomiums on the Beauty of his Person; enumerating many Particulars, and ending with the Whiteness of his Skin.

This Discourse had an Effect on *Sophia's* Countenance, which would not perhaps have escaped the Observance of the sagacious Waiting-woman, had she once looked her Mistress in the Face, all the Time she was speaking; but as a Looking-glass, which was most commodiously placed opposite to her, gave her an Opportunity of surveying those Features, in which, of all others, she took most Delight, so she had not once removed her Eyes from that amiable Object during her whole Speech.

Mrs. *Honour* was so entirely wrapped up in the Subject on which she exercised her Tongue, and the Object before her Eyes, that she gave her Mistress Time to conquer her Confusion; which having done, she smiled on her Maid, and told her, 'She was certainly in Love with this young Fellow.' 'I in Love, Madam!' answers she, 'upon my Word, Ma'am, I assure you, Ma'am, upon my Soul, Ma'am, I am not.' 'Why if you was,' cries her Mistress, 'I see no Reason that you should be ashamed of it; for he is certainly a pretty Fellow.'—'Yes, Ma'am,' answered the other, 'That he is, the most handsomest Man I ever saw in my Life. Yes, to be sure, that he is, and, as your Ladyship says, I don't know why I should be ashamed of loving him, though he is my Betters. To be sure gentle Folks are but Flesh and Blood no more than us Servants. Besides, as for Mr. *Jones*, thof Squire *Allworthy* hath made a Gentleman of him, he was not so good as myself by Birth: For thof I am a poor Body, I am an honest Person's Child, and my Father and Mother were married, which is more than some People can say, as high as they hold their Heads. Marry, come up! I assure you, my dirty Cousin! thof his Skin be so white, and to be sure, it is the most whitest that ever was seen, I am a Christian as well as he, and no-body can say that I am base born, my grand-father was a Clergyman,* and

---

* This is the second Person of low Condition whom we have recorded in this History, to have sprung from the Clergy. It is to be hoped such Instances will, in future Ages, when some Provision is made for the Families of the inferior Clergy, appear stranger than they can be thought at present.[1]

---

[1] From the time of *The Champion* (29 March, 5, 12, 19 April 1740) Fielding endeavoured in his writings to improve the condition of the inferior clergy and to remove from them and

would have been very angry, I believe, to have thought any of his Family should have taken up with *Molly Seagrim's* dirty Leavings.'

Perhaps *Sophia* might have suffered her Maid to run on in this Manner, from wanting sufficient Spirits to stop her Tongue, which the Reader may probably conjecture was no very easy Task: For, certainly there were some Passages in her Speech, which were far from being agreeable to the Lady. However, she now checked the Torrent, as there seemed no End of its Flowing. 'I wonder,' says she, 'at your Assurance in daring to talk thus of one of my Father's Friends. As to the Wench, I order you never to mention her Name to me. And, with Regard to the young Gentleman's Birth, those who can say nothing more to his Disadvantage, may as well be silent on that Head, as I desire you will be for the future.'

'I am sorry, I have offended your Ladyship,' answered Mrs. *Honour*, 'I am sure I hate *Molly Seagrim* as much as your Ladyship can, and as for abusing Squire *Jones*, I can call all the Servants in the House to witness, that whenever any Talk hath been about Bastards, I have always taken his Part: 'For which of you,' says I to the Footmen, 'would not be a Bastard, if he could, to be made a Gentleman of? and,' says I, 'I am sure he is a very fine Gentleman; and he hath one of the whitest Hands in the World:' For to be sure so he hath; 'and' says I, 'one of the sweetest temperedest, best naturedest Men in the World he is, and' says I, 'all the Servants and Neighbours all round the Country loves him.' And, to be sure, I could tell your Ladyship something, but that I am afraid it would offend you.'—'What could you tell me, *Honour*?' says *Sophia*. 'Nay, Ma'am, to be sure he meant nothing by it, therefore I would not have your Ladyship be offended.' —'Prithee tell me,' says *Sophia*,—'I will know it this Instant.' 'Why, Ma'am,' answered Mrs. *Honour*, 'he came into the Room, one Day last Week when I was at Work, and there lay your Ladyship's Muff on a Chair, and to be sure he put his Hands into it, that very Muff your Ladyship gave me but yesterday; 'La,' says I, 'Mr. *Jones*, you will stretch my Lady's Muff and

their families that 'contempt' which they suffered in large part because of their poverty. (See Battestin, *The Moral Basis of Fielding's Art*, ch. vii.) In 1748 he devoted several numbers of *The Jacobite's Journal* (23 April, 18, 25 June, 2, 9 July 1748) to urging the establishment 'of a charitable Provision for the Widows and Children of the poor Clergy', who, he declared, 'are, of all others, most the Objects of Compassion'. See also *The Covent-Garden Journal* (6 June 1752).

spoil it;' but he still kept his Hands in it, and then he kissed it—
to be sure, I hardly ever saw such a Kiss in my Life as he gave it.'
—'I suppose he did not know it was mine,' reply'd *Sophia*.
'Your Ladyship shall hear, Ma'am. He kissed it again and again,
and said it was the prettiest Muff in the World. 'La! Sir,' says I,
'you have seen it a hundred Times.'—'Yes, Mrs. *Honour*,' cry'd
he; 'but who can see any thing beautiful in the Presence of your
Lady but herself:' Nay, that's not all neither, but I hope your
Ladyship won't be offended, for to be sure he meant nothing:
One Day as your Ladyship was playing on the Harpsicord to my
Master, Mr. *Jones* was sitting in the next Room, and methought
he looked melancholy. 'La!' says I, 'Mr. *Jones*, what's the Matter?
A Penny for your Thoughts,' says I; 'Why, Hussy,' says he,
starting up from a Dream, 'what can I be thinking of when that
Angel your Mistress is playing?' And then squeezing me by the
Hand—'Oh! Mrs. *Honour*,' says he, 'how happy will that Man
be!'—and then he sighed; upon my Troth, his Breath is as sweet
as a Nosegay—but to be sure he meant no Harm by it. So I
hope your Ladyship will not mention a Word: For he gave me a
Crown never to mention it, and made me swear upon a Book, but
I believe, indeed, it was not the Bible.'

Till something of a more beautiful Red than Vermilion be
found out, I shall say nothing of *Sophia's* Colour on this Occasion. '*Ho—nour*,' says she, 'I—if you will not mention this any
more to me,—nor to any Body else, I will not betray you—I
mean I will not be angry; but I am afraid of your Tongue. Why,
my Girl, will you give it such Liberties?' 'Nay, Ma'am,' answered
she, 'to be sure, I would sooner cut out my Tongue than offend
your Ladyship—to be sure, I shall never mention a Word that
your Ladyship would not have me.'—'Why I would not have
you mention this any more,' said *Sophia*, 'for it may come to my
Father's Ears, and he would be angry with Mr. *Jones*; tho' I
really believe, as you say, he meant nothing. I should be very
angry myself if I imagined——' 'Nay, Ma'am,' says *Honour*,
'I protest I believe he meant nothing. I thought he talked as if
he was out of his Senses; nay, he said he believed he was beside
himself when he had spoken the Words. 'Ay, Sir,' says I, 'I
believe so too.' 'Yes,' says he, '*Honour*,—' but I ask your Ladyship's Pardon; I could tear my Tongue out for offending you.'
'Go on,' says *Sophia*, 'you may mention any thing you have not

told me before.' 'Yes, *Honour*,' says he, (this was some time after-wards when he gave me the Crown) 'I am neither such a Cox-comb, or such a Villain as to think of her, in any other *Delight*, but as my Goddess; as such I will always worship and adore her while I have Breath.' This was all, Ma'am, I will be sworn, to the best of my Remembrance; I was in a Passion with him, myself, till I found he meant no Harm.' 'Indeed, *Honour*,' says *Sophia*, 'I believe you have a real Affection for me; I was provoked the other Day when I gave you Warning; but if you have a Desire to stay with me, you shall.' 'To be sure, Ma'am,' answered Mrs. *Honour*, 'I shall never desire to part with your Ladyship. To be sure, I almost cried my Eyes out when you gave me Warning. It would be very ungrateful in me, to desire to leave your Lady-ship; because as why, I should never get so good a Place again. I am sure I would live and die with your Ladyship—for, as poor Mr. *Jones* said, happy is the Man——'

Here the Dinner-bell interrupted a Conversation which had wrought such an Effect on *Sophia*, that she was, perhaps, more obliged to her bleeding in the Morning, than she, at the time, had apprehended she should be. As to the present Situation of her Mind, I shall adhere to a Rule of *Horace*,[1] by not attempting to describe it, from Despair of Success. Most of my Readers will suggest it easily to themselves, and the few who cannot, would not understand the Picture, or at least would deny it to be natural, if ever so well drawn.

[1] *Ars Poetica*, 149–50: 'et quae / desperat tractata nitescere posse, relinquit' ('and what he fears he cannot make attractive with his touch he abandons'—trans. H. R. Fairclough, Loeb Classical Library, 1929).

BOOK V

Containing a Portion of Time, somewhat longer than Half a Year.

CHAPTER I

Of THE SERIOUS *in writing; and for what Purpose it is introduced.*

PERADVENTURE there may be no Parts in this prodigious Work which will give the Reader less Pleasure in the perusing, than those which have given the Author the greatest Pains in composing. Among these probably may be reckoned those initial Essays which we have prefixed to the historical Matter contained in every Book; and which we have determined to be essentially necessary to this kind of Writing, of which we have set ourselves at the Head.

For this our Determination we do not hold ourselves strictly bound to assign any Reason; it being abundantly sufficient that we have laid it down as a Rule necessary to be observed in all Prosai-comi-epic Writing. Who ever demanded the Reasons of that nice Unity of Time or Place¹ which is now established to be

---

¹ By the middle decades of the seventeenth century, the French critics, following certain hints in Aristotle and his Italian commentators, had established the doctrine of the dramatic unities as an essential article of neoclassical orthodoxy. To Aristotle's insistence upon the unity of dramatic action, the French added the unities of time and place. In order to achieve a heightened sense of verisimilitude in the drama, they required a close correspondence between dramatic time and place and the actual circumstances of representation in the theatre; the action of the play was to be narrowly limited to one specific locale and to a single day in the hero's life. Though formulated earlier by Richelieu and the French Academy, this rigidly mechanistic theory of dramatic imitation was firmly established by Boileau (*Art poétique*, 1674) and by such other influential critics as René Rapin (*Réflexions sur la poétique et les poètes*, 1674), Père Bossu (*Traité du poème épique*, 1675), and André Dacier (trans. Aristotle's *Poetics*, 1692).

In England the arguments of Crites and Lisideus in Dryden's *Essay of Dramatic Poesy* (1666) gave currency to these ideas, which were approved and rigorously applied to the drama by such critics as Thomas Rymer (*The Tragedies of the Last Age, Considered and Examined*, 1678), the Earl of Mulgrave (*An Essay upon Poetry*, 1682), Jeremy Collier (*A Short View of the Immorality and Prophaneness of the English Stage*, 1698), Charles Gildon (*Complete Art of Poetry*, 1718), John Dennis (*The Characters and Conduct of Sir John Edgar*, 1720), and Joseph Trapp (*Lectures on Poetry*, 1742). Although the theory was not effectively

so essential to dramatick Poetry? What Critick hath been ever asked why a Play may not contain two Days as well as one, or why the Audience (provided they travel like Electors, without any Expence) may not be wafted Fifty Miles as well as five! Hath any Commentator well accounted for the Limitation which an ancient Critic[1] hath set to the Drama, which he will have contain neither more nor less than five Acts; or hath any one living attempted to explain, what the modern Judges of our Theatres mean by that Word *low*; by which they have happily succeeded in banishing all Humour from the Stage,[2] and have made the Theatre as dull as a Drawing-Room? Upon all these Occasions, the World seems to have embraced a Maxim of our Law, viz. *Cuicunque in Arte sua perito credendum est:*[3] For it seems, perhaps, difficult to conceive that any one should have had enough of Impudence, to lay down dogmatical Rules in any Art or Science without the least Foundation. In such Cases, therefore, we are apt to conclude there are sound and good Reasons at the Bottom, tho' we are unfortunately not able to see so far.

Now, in Reality, the World have paid too great a Compliment to Critics, and have imagined them Men of much greater Profundity than they really are. From this Complaisance, the Critics have been emboldened to assume a Dictatorial Power, and have so far succeeded that they are now become the Masters, and have the Assurance to give Laws to those Authors, from whose Predecessors they originally received them.

exploded until Johnson's famous attack in the *Preface to Shakespeare* (1765), others besides Fielding had repudiated it much earlier. After Collier had condemned *The Relapse* for violating the unities of time and place—the action taking up most of a week and the setting being 'stroll'd Fifty Miles off' from London, where the play began—Farquhar rose to the defence in *A Discourse upon Comedy in Reference to the English Stage* (1702). Others who anticipated Fielding's liberal views include Sir Robert Howard (Prefaces to *Four New Plays* [1665] and *The Great Favourite* [1668]), Dryden (the arguments of Eugenius and Neander in *An Essay of Dramatic Poesy*, 1666), Leonard Welsted (*Dissertation concerning the Perfection of the English Language, the State of Poetry. &c.*, 1724).

1 Horace, *Ars Poetica*, 189. Though he may not have 'well accounted' for Horace's rule, the Earl of Roscommon offered the following explanation in a footnote to his translation: 'Plays of three Acts have the Defect which *Aristotle* finds in little Objects. The Sight is confounded, and they are either naked of, or loaded with Incidents. Plays of six or seven *Acts* would have the Defect of great Objects. The Spectators would lose the Idea of the whole, on Account of its excessive Bigness, wherefore the just Medium lies in the five *Acts*' (*Horace's Treatise Concerning the Art of Poetry* [Dublin, 1733], pp. 68–70).

2 See below, p. 638, n. 1.

3 'Whoever is skilled in his profession should be believed' (cf. *Coke upon Littleton*, 125a).

The Critic, rightly considered, is no more than the Clerk, whose Office it is to transcribe the Rules and Laws laid down by those great Judges, whose vast Strength of Genius hath placed them in the Light of Legislators in the several Sciences over which they presided. This Office was all which the Critics of old aspired to, nor did they ever dare to advance a Sentence, without supporting it by the Authority of the Judge from whence it was borrowed.

But in Process of Time, and in Ages of Ignorance, the Clerk began to invade the Power and assume the Dignity of his Master. The Laws of Writing were no longer founded on the Practice of the Author, but on the Dictates of the Critic. The Clerk became the Legislator, and those very peremptorily gave Laws, whose Business it was, at first, only to transcribe them.

Hence arose an obvious, and, perhaps, an unavoidable Error: For these Critics being Men of shallow Capacities, very easily mistook mere Form for Substance. They acted as a Judge would, who should adhere to the lifeless Letter of Law, and reject the Spirit. Little Circumstances which were, perhaps, accidental in a great Author, were, by these Critics, considered to constitute his chief Merit, and transmitted as Essentials to be observed by all his Successors. To these Encroachments, Time and Ignorance, the two great Supporters of Imposture, gave Authority; and thus, many Rules for good Writing have been established, which have not the least Foundation in Truth or Nature; and which commonly serve for no other Purpose than to curb and restrain Genius, in the same Manner, as it would have restrained the Dancing-master, had the many excellent Treatises on that Art,[1] laid it down as an essential Rule, that every Man must dance in Chains.

To avoid, therefore, all Imputation of laying down a Rule for Posterity, founded only on the Authority of *ipse dixit*; for which,

---

[1] Fielding's analogy may have been inspired by Pope's famous lines in the *Essay on Criticism* (1711), 362–3: 'True Ease in Writing comes from Art, not Chance, / As those move easiest who have learn'd to Dance.' (See also below, p. 740, n. 1.) From the time of Queen Anne, several dancing-masters published treatises disclosing the mysteries of this necessary social art. Among these were essays, based on the French of Rameau and Feuillet, by Messrs. Isaac, Siris, Pemberton, Weaver, and Tomlinson. For Fielding, however, the dancing-master *par excellence* was John Essex (see below, p. 741, n. 1), author of *A Treatis of Chorography* (1710) and *The Dancing-Master: or, The Whole Art and Mystery of Dancing Explained* (2nd ed., 1731).

to say the Truth, we have not the profoundest Veneration; we shall here wave the Privilege above contended for, and proceed to lay before the Reader, the Reasons which have induced us, to intersperse these several digressive Essays, in the Course of this Work.

And here we shall of Necessity be led to open a new Vein of Knowledge, which, if it hath been discovered, hath not, to our Remembrance, been wrought on by any antient or modern Writer. This Vein is no other than that of Contrast,[1] which runs through all the Works of the Creation, and may probably have a large Share in constituting in us the Idea of all Beauty, as well natural as artificial: For what demonstrates the Beauty and Excellence of any thing, but its Reverse? Thus the Beauty of Day, and that of Summer, is set off by the Horrors of Night and Winter. And I believe, if it was possible for a Man to have seen only the two former, he would have a very imperfect Idea of their Beauty.

But to avoid too serious an Air: Can it be doubted, but that the finest Woman in the World would lose all Benefit of her Charms, in the Eye of a Man who had never seen one of another Cast? The Ladies themselves seem so sensible of this, that they are all industrious to procure Foils; nay, they will become Foils to themselves; for I have observed, (at *Bath* particularly) that they endeavour to appear as ugly as possible in the Morning, in order to set off that Beauty which they intend to shew you in the Evening.

---

1 Far from opening a 'new Vein of Knowledge', Fielding here merely applies an old and quite familiar aesthetic principle to his own theory of prose fiction. Related ultimately to the classical notion of *concordia discors*, of cosmic harmony resulting from the reconciliation of opposite elements, the important role that variety and contrast play in the creation of beauty, both in nature and in art, had long been recognized by philosophers and aestheticians. (For thorough documentation of this point, see H. V. S. Ogden, 'The Principles of Variety and Contrast in Seventeenth Century Aesthetics, and Milton's Poetry', *JHI*, x [1949], 159–82. On the background of *concordia discors*, see Leo Spitzer, *Classical and Christian Ideas of World Harmony* [Baltimore, Md., 1963].) The 'World's Beauty', observed Shaftesbury, is 'founded thus *on Contrarietys*' ('The Moralists', I. iii; *Characteristicks*, 5th ed. [1732], ii. 214). And the same point was made more than a century earlier by Richard Ashley, who anticipated Fielding's own illustrations: 'we may say in all cases, that contraries when they are put neere one to the other, they appeare the more cleerely: Even as want maketh riches to be the more esteemed; and the obscuritie of darkenesse commendeth the cleernesse of light: The sweetnesse of the Springtime is more esteemed by the sharpnesse of Winter: the happinesse of peace, by the calamaties of warre; and faire weather after long rayne' (trans. of Louis LeRoy, *Of the Interchangeable Course or Variety of Things in the Whole World* [1594], fol. 6ʳ; quoted in Ogden, op. cit., p. 168).

Most Artists have this Secret in Practice, tho' some, perhaps, have not much studied the Theory. The Jeweller knows that the finest Brilliant requires a Foil; and the Painter, by the Contrast of his Figures, often acquires great Applause.

A great Genius among us, will illustrate this Matter fully. I cannot, indeed, range him under any general Head of common Artists, as he hath a Title to be placed among those

Inventas, qui vitam excoluere per Artes.[1]

Who by invented Arts have Life improv'd.

I mean here the Inventor of that most exquisite Entertainment, called the *English* Pantomime.[2]

This Entertainment consisted of two Parts, which the Inventor distinguished by the Names of *the Serious* and *the Comic*. The *Serious* exhibited a certain Number of Heathen Gods and Heroes, who were certainly the worst and dullest Company into which an Audience was ever introduced; and (which was a Secret

---

[1] *Aeneid,* vi. 663.

[2] John Rich (1682?–1761), from 1732 manager of the Covent-Garden Theatre. Rich was chiefly responsible for the great popularity of pantomimes and 'entertainments', in which he performed the part of Harlequin, astonishing audiences with spectacular tricks and stage effects. Thomas Davies provides an illuminating gloss on the present passage: 'Rich created a species of dramatic composition unknown to this, and, I believe, to any other country, which he called a pantomime. It consisted of two parts; one serious, and the other comic: by the help of gay scenes, fine habits, grand dances, appropriated music, and other decorations, he exhibited a story from Ovid's Metamorphosis, or some other fabulous history. Between the pauses or acts of this serious representation he interwove a comic fable consisting chiefly of the courtship of Harlequin and Columbine, with a variety of surprising adventures and tricks, which were produced by the magic wand of Harlequin; such as the sudden transformation of palaces and temples to huts and cottages; of men and women into wheel-barrows and joint-stools; of trees turned to houses; colonades to beds of tulips; and mechanics shops into serpents and ostriches' (*Memoirs of the Life of David Garrick, Esq.* [1780], i. 92).

In Fielding's *Tumble-Down Dick* (1736) Rich is brought on stage as Mr. Machine, declaring the 'serious Nature' of his Ovidian entertainment: 'This', he assures the doubtful Fustian, 'has been the Serious, Sir.—the Sublime. The Serious in an Entertainment, answers to the Sublime in Writing.' Rich persisted in his strategy of using 'the Serious' to heighten 'the Comic' part of his entertainments despite criticism from those who agreed with Fielding that the change effected was only in degrees of dullness: 'the friggling Tricks of Mr. *Merryman,* the Harlequin, have too much of the Sameness; and the grave poetic Part does well enough—to cloy, but not to invite'—such was the judgement of the anonymous author of *A Letter to a Certain Patentee* [1747], p. 9. Dullness, as Pope had shown in *The Dunciad* (iii. 252–64), was indeed the essential characteristic of Rich's pantomimes. For other references to Rich in Fielding's writings, see *Pasquin* (1736), v, *The Champion* (22 April, 3, 24 May 1740), *Joseph Andrews* (1742; I. vii), and *The Covent-Garden Journal* (11 January, 18 November 1752). See also below, p. 666, n. 1.

known to few) were actually intended so to be, in order to contrast the *Comic* Part of the Entertainment, and to display the Tricks of Harlequin to the better Advantage.

This was, perhaps, no very civil Use of such Personages; but the Contrivance was nevertheless ingenious enough, and had its Effect. And this will now plainly appear, if instead of *Serious* and *Comic*, we supply the Words *Duller* and *Dullest*; for the *Comic* was certainly duller than any thing before shewn on the Stage, and could be set off only by that superlative Degree of Dulness, which composed the *Serious*. So intolerably serious, indeed, were these Gods and Heroes, that Harlequin (tho' the *English* Gentleman of that Name is not at all related to the *French* Family, for he is of a much more serious Disposition)[1] was always welcome on the Stage, as he relieved the Audience from worse Company.

Judicious Writers have always practised this Art of Contrast, with great Success. I have been surprized that *Horace* should cavil at this Art in *Homer*; but indeed he contradicts himself in the very next Line.

> *Indignor quandoque bonus dormitat* Homerus,
> *Verum Opere in longo fas est obrepere Somnum.*[2]

> I grieve if e'er great *Homer* chance to sleep,
> Yet Slumbers on long Works have right to creep.

For we are not here to understand, as, perhaps, some have, that an Author actually falls asleep while he is writing. It is true that Readers are too apt to be so overtaken; but if the Work was as long as any of *Oldmixon*,[3] the Author himself is too well enter-

---

[1] Cf. Davies's observation that Rich's 'harlequinade' was 'very different from that which is seen at the opera comique in Paris, where harlequin and all the characters speak, and a kind of droll farce, full of ridiculous incidents, and certain bon mots, called naivetès, keep the audience in continual laughter' (op. cit., i. 91).

[2] *Ars Poetica*, 359–60. Even in the eighteenth century Fielding's reading 'opere in longo' was considered less correct, and less 'elegant', than 'operi longo'. (See Philip Francis, trans. *The Works of Horace*, 2nd ed. [1747], iv. 254–5.) The verse translation appears to be Fielding's own.

[3] John Oldmixon (1673–1742), commemorated for his dullness in *The Dunciad* (A, ii. 199–202; B, ii. 283–90), had an unhappy reputation as a 'laborious' poet, an injudicious critic, and a 'virulent Party-writer for hire'. Written from a Whig bias, his voluminous histories include *The Secret History of Europe* (1712–15), the *Critical History of England* (1724–6), and *The History of England* from the time of the Stuarts until the reign of George I (1729–35). Fielding apparently regarded him as the very type of the tedious, long-winded hackney author: see *Ovid's Art of Love Paraphrased* (1747) and *The Covent-Garden*

tained to be subject to the least Drowsiness. He is, as Mr. *Pope* observes,

Sleepless himself to give his Readers Sleep.[1]

To say the Truth, these soporific Parts are so many Scenes of *Serious* artfully interwoven, in order to contrast and set off the rest; and this is the true Meaning of a late facetious Writer,[2] who told the Public, that whenever he was dull, they might be assured there was a Design in it.

In this Light then, or rather in this Darkness, I would have the Reader to consider these initial Essays. And after this Warning, if he shall be of Opinion, that he can find enough of Serious in other Parts of this History, he may pass over these, in which we profess to be laboriously dull, and begin the following Books, at the second Chapter.

CHAPTER II

In which Mr. Jones *receives many friendly Visits during his Confinement; with some fine Touches of the Passion of Love, scarce visible to the naked Eye.*

*T*OM JONES had many Visitors during his Confinement, tho' some, perhaps, were not very agreeable to him. Mr. *Allworthy* saw him almost every Day; but tho' he pitied *Tom's* Sufferings, and greatly approved the gallant Behaviour which had occasioned them, yet he thought this was a favourable Opportunity to bring him to a sober Sense of his indiscreet Conduct; and that wholsome Advice for that Purpose, could never be applied at a more proper Season than at the present; when the Mind was softened by Pain and Sickness, and alarmed by Danger; and when its Attention was unembarrassed with those turbulent Passions, which engage us in the Pursuit of Pleasure.

Journal (11 January 1752); see also the parody of Oldmixon's histories in that journal (29 February 1752).

¹ *The Dunciad* (A), i. 92: 'While pensive Poets painful vigils keep, / Sleepless themselves, to give their readers sleep.'

² Sir Richard Steele (1672–1729) in *The Tatler*, No. 38 (7 July 1709): '*It is to be noted, That when any Part of this Paper appears dull, there is a Design in it*' (1728 ed.). Fielding, who acknowledged Steele as his model in the art of the periodical essay, was particularly fond of this passage: see *The Champion* (22 May 1740), *The Jacobite's Journal* (2 July 1748), and *The Covent-Garden Journal* (4 January 1752).

At all Seasons, therefore, when the good Man was alone with the Youth, especially when the latter was totally at Ease, he took Occasion to remind him of his former Miscarriages, but in the mildest and tenderest Manner, and only in order to introduce the Caution, which he prescribed for his future Behaviour; 'on which alone' he assured him, 'would depend his own Felicity, and the Kindness which he might yet promise himself to receive at the Hands of his Father by Adoption unless he should hereafter forfeit his Good Opinion: For as to what had past,' he said, 'it should be all forgiven and forgotten.' He, therefore, advised him 'to make a good Use of this Accident, that so in the End it might prove a Visitation for his own Good.'

Thwackum was likewise pretty assiduous in his Visits; and he too considered a sick Bed to be a convenient Scene for Lectures. His Stile, however, was more severe than Mr. *Allworthy's*: He told his Pupil, 'that he ought to look on his broken Limb as a Judgment from Heaven on his Sins. That it would become him to be daily on his Knees, pouring forth Thanksgivings that he had broken his Arm only, and not his Neck; which latter,' he said, 'was very probably reserved for some future Occasion, and that perhaps, not very remote. For his Part,' he said, 'he had often wondered some Judgment had not overtaken him before; but it might be perceived by this, that divine Punishments, tho' slow, are always sure.' Hence likewise he advised him 'to foresee, with equal Certainty, the greater Evils which were yet behind, and which were as sure as this, of overtaking him in his State of Reprobacy. These are,' said he, 'to be averted only by such a thorough and sincere Repentance, as is not to be expected or hoped for, from one so abandoned in his Youth, and whose Mind, I am afraid, is totally corrupted. It is my Duty, however, to exhort you to this Repentance, tho' I too well know all Exhortations will be vain and fruitless. But *liberavi Animam meam*.[1] I can accuse my own Conscience of no Neglect; tho' it is, at the same time, with the utmost Concern, I see you travelling on to certain Misery in this World, and to as certain Damnation in the next.

Square talked in a very different Strain: He said, 'such Accidents as a broken Bone were below the Consideration of a wise

---

[1] 'I have delivered my soul'—a familiar formula, evidently derived from Ezekiel 3: 19. Cf. Epistle 371 of St. Bernard of Clairvaux.

Man. That it was abundantly sufficient to reconcile the Mind to any of these Mischances, to reflect that they are liable to befal the wisest of Mankind, and are undoubtedly for the Good of the whole.' He said, 'it was a mere Abuse of Words, to call those Things Evils, in which there was no moral Unfitness; that Pain, which was the worst Consequence of such Accidents, was the most contemptible thing in the World;' with more of the like Sentences, extracted out of the Second Book of *Tully's* Tusculan *Questions*,[1] and from the Great Lord *Shaftesbury*.[2] In pronouncing these he was one Day so eager, that he unfortunately bit his Tongue; and in such a Manner, that it not only put an End to his Discourse, but created much Emotion in him, and caused him to mutter an Oath or two: But what was worst of all, this Accident gave *Thwackum*, who was present, and who held all such Doctrine to be heathenish and atheistical, an Opportunity to clap a Judgment on his Back. Now this was done with so malicious a Sneer, that it totally unhinged (if I may so say) the Temper of the Philosopher, which the Bite of his Tongue had somewhat ruffled; and as he was disabled from venting his Wrath at his Lips, he had possibly found a more violent Method of revenging himself, had not the Surgeon, who was then luckily in the Room, contrary to his own Interest, interposed, and preserved the Peace.

Mr. *Blifil* visited his Friend *Jones* but seldom, and never alone. This worthy young Man, however, professed much Regard for him, and as great Concern at his Misfortune; but cautiously avoided any Intimacy, lest, as he frequently hinted, it might

[1] Cf. Cicero, *Tusculan Disputations*, II. v. 14 ff. Cicero here rejects as a mere quibble Zeno's refusal to consider pain an evil, a term the latter reserved exclusively for base and immoral acts (II. xii. 29). Yet, Cicero continues, since 'disgrace is worse than pain, pain is clearly of no account . . . for either no virtue exists or all pain is to be despised' (II. xiii. 31—trans. J. E. King, Loeb Classical Library, 1927). As Fielding had remarked in his *Charge to the Jury* (1745), the contempt of pain was, of course, a fundamental tenet of the Stoic philosophers: in *Man without Passion: or, The Wise Stoick* (trans. G. R., 1675), Anthony LeGrand maintained '*That Tortures are not terrible but in opinion, and that Fools or Cowards only are affrighted at them*' (II. iii. 2). While in the stocks, Butler's Hudibras invokes this same stoic doctrine (Wilders ed., II. i. 183 ff.).

[2] Anthony Ashley Cooper (1671–1713), third Earl of Shaftesbury, whose *Characteristicks of Men, Manners, Opinions and Times* (1711) made him the most influential deist philosopher of the period. In 'An Inquiry concerning Virtue, or Merit' and 'The Moralists', Shaftesbury's constant theme is that 'there is no such thing as real ILL in the Universe, nothing ILL with respect to the Whole' (*Characteristicks*, 5th ed. [1732], ii. 9). The place of Shaftesburian ideas in Square's philosophy is discussed above, p. 124, n. See also the description of Mr. Wilson's club of '*Rule of Right-men*' in *Joseph Andrews* (1742; III. iii). For later references to Shaftesbury in *Tom Jones*, see below, pp. 398, n. 4; 736, n. 1.

contaminate the Sobriety of his own Character: For which Purpose, he had constantly in his Mouth that Proverb in which
Solomon speaks against Evil Communication.[1] Not that he was
so bitter as *Thwackum*; for he always expressed some Hopes of
Tom's Reformation; 'which,' he said, 'the unparalleled Goodness
shewn by his Uncle on this Occasion, must certainly effect, in
one not absolutely abandoned;' but concluded, 'if Mr. *Jones*
ever offends hereafter, I shall not be able to say a Syllable in his
Favour.'

As to Squire *Western*, he was seldom out of the Sick Room;
unless when he was engaged either in the Field, or over his Bottle.
Nay, he would sometimes retire hither to take his Beer, and it
was not without Difficulty, that he was prevented from forcing
Jones to take his Beer too: For no Quack ever held his Nostrum
to be a more general *Panacea*, than he did this; which, he said,
had more Virtue in it than was in all the Physic in an Apothecary's
Shop. He was, however, by much Entreaty, prevailed on to
forbear the Application of this Medicine; but from serenading
his Patient every Hunting Morning with the Horn under his
Window, it was impossible to withhold him; nor did he ever lay
aside that Hollow, with which he entered into all Companies,
when he visited *Jones*, without any Regard to the sick Person's
being at that Time either awake or asleep.

This boisterous Behaviour, as it meant no Harm, so happily it
effected none, and was abundantly compensated to *Jones*, as soon
as he was able to sit up, by the Company of *Sophia*, whom the
Squire then brought to visit him; nor was it, indeed, long before
Jones was able to attend her to the Harpsichord, where she would
kindly condescend, for Hours together, to charm him with the
most delicious Music, unless when the Squire thought proper to
interrupt her, by insisting on *Old Sir Simon*,[2] or some other of his
favourite Pieces.

Notwithstanding the nicest Guard which *Sophia* endeavoured
to set on her Behaviour, she could not avoid letting some Appearances now and then slip forth: For Love may again be likened

---

[1] As 'Orbilius' gleefully pointed out in his *Examen* (1749; pp. 44–5) of *Tom Jones*,
Fielding incorrectly identifies the source of the proverb, 'evil communications corrupt
good manners', which is found in St. Paul (1 Corinthians 15: 33) and Menander (*Thais*,
Fragment 2). Later, in *The Covent-Garden Journal* (4 February 1752), Fielding rectified
his mistake. See also below, p. 630.

[2] See above, p. 169, n. 3.

to a Disease in this, that when it is denied a Vent in one Part, it will certainly break out in another. What her Lips therefore concealed, her Eyes, her Blushes, and many little involuntary Actions, betrayed.

One Day when *Sophia* was playing on the Harpsichord, and *Jones* was attending, the Squire came into the Room, crying, 'There, *Tom*, I have had a Battle for thee below Stairs with thick Parson *Thwackum*.——He hath been a telling *Allworthy*, before my Face, that the broken Bone was a Judgment upon thee. D——n it, says I, how can that be? Did not he come by it in Defence of a young Woman? A Judgment indeed! Pox, if he never doth any thing worse, he will go to Heaven sooner than all the Parsons in the Country. He hath more reason to glory in it, than to be ashamed of it.' 'Indeed, Sir,' says *Jones*, 'I have no Reason for either; but if it preserved Miss *Western*, I shall always think it the happiest Accident of my Life.'——'And to gu,' said the Squire, 'to zet *Allworthy* against thee vor it.——D——n un, if the Parson had unt had his Petticuoats on, I should ha lent un a Flick; for I love thee dearly, my Boy, and d——n me if there is any thing in my Power which I won't do for thee. Sha't take thy Choice of all the Horses in my Stable to-morrow Morning, except only the *Chevalier*[1] and Miss *Slouch*.' *Jones* thanked him, but declined accepting the Offer.——'Nay,' added the Squire, 'Sha't ha the sorrel Mare that *Sophy* rode. She cost me fifty Guineas, and comes six Years old this Grass.' 'If she had cost me a thousand,' cries *Jones* passionately, 'I would have given her to the Dogs.' 'Pooh! pooh!' answered *Western*, 'what because she broke thy Arm. Shouldst forget and forgive. I thought hadst been more a Man than to bear Malice against a dumb Creature.'——Here *Sophia* interposed, and put an End to the Conversation, by desiring her Father's Leave to play to him; a Request which he never refused.

The Countenance of *Sophia* had undergone more than one Change during the foregoing Speeches; and probably she imputed the passionate Resentment which *Jones* had expressed against the Mare to a different Motive from that from which her Father had derived it. Her Spirits were at this Time in a visible Flutter; and she played so intolerably ill, that had not *Western* soon fallen asleep, he must have remarked it. *Jones*, however,

---

[1] The name of Western's favourite horse is doubtless in honour of the Pretender, James Francis Edward Stuart (1688–1766), known as the Chevalier de St. Georges.

who was sufficiently awake, and was not without an Ear any more than without Eyes, made some Observations; which being joined to all which the Reader may remember to have passed formerly, gave him pretty strong Assurances, when he came to reflect on the whole, that all was not well in the tender Bosom of *Sophia.* An Opinion which many young Gentlemen will, I doubt not, extremely wonder at his not having been well confirmed in long ago. To confess the Truth, he had rather too much Diffidence in himself, and was not forward enough in seeing the Advances of a young Lady; a Misfortune which can be cured only by that early Town Education, which is at present so generally in Fashion.

When these Thoughts had fully taken Possession of *Jones*, they occasioned a Perturbation in his Mind, which, in a Constitution less pure and firm than his, might have been, at such a Season, attended with very dangerous Consequences. He was truly sensible of the great Worth of *Sophia.* He extremely liked her Person, no less admired her Accomplishments, and tenderly loved her Goodness. In Reality, as he had never once entertained any Thought of possessing her, nor had ever given the least voluntary Indulgence to his Inclinations, he had a much stronger Passion for her than he himself was acquainted with. His Heart now brought forth the full Secret, at the same Time that it assured him the adorable Object returned his Affection.

CHAPTER III

Which all, who have no Heart, will think to contain much ado about nothing.

THE Reader will perhaps imagine, the Sensations which now arose in *Jones* to have been so sweet and delicious, that they would rather tend to produce a cheerful Serenity in the Mind, than any of those dangerous Effects which we have mentioned; but in fact, Sensations of this Kind, however delicious, are, at their first Recognition, of a very tumultuous Nature, and have very little of the Opiate in them. They were, moreover, in the present Case, embittered with certain Circumstances, which being mixed with sweeter Ingredients, tended altogether to compose a

Draught that might be termed *bitter-sweet*; than which, as nothing can be more disagreeable to the Palate, so nothing, in the metaphorical Sense, can be so injurious to the Mind.

For first, though he had sufficient Foundation to flatter himself in what he had observed in *Sophia*, he was not yet free from Doubt of misconstruing Compassion, or, at best, Esteem, into a warmer Regard. He was far from a sanguine Assurance that *Sophia* had any such Affection towards him, as might promise his Inclinations that Harvest, which, if they were encouraged and nursed, they would finally grow up to require. Besides, if he could hope to find no Bar to his Happiness from the Daughter, he thought himself certain of meeting an effectual Bar in the Father; who, though he was a Country Squire in his Diversions, was perfectly a Man of the World in whatever regarded his Fortune; had the most violent Affection for this only Daughter, and had often signified, in his Cups, the Pleasure he proposed in seeing her married to one of the richest Men in the County. *Jones* was not so vain and senseless a Coxcomb as to expect, from any Regard which *Western* had professed for him, that he would ever be induced to lay aside these Views of advancing his Daughter. He well knew that Fortune is generally the principal, if not the sole Consideration, which operates on the best of Parents in these Matters: For Friendship makes us warmly espouse the Interest of others; but it is very cold to the Gratification of their Passions. Indeed, to feel the Happiness which may result from this, it is necessary we should possess the Passion ourselves. As he had therefore no Hopes of obtaining her Father's Consent, so he thought to endeavour to succeed without it, and by such Means to frustrate the Great Point of Mr. *Western's* Life, was to make a very ill Use of his Hospitality, and a very ungrateful Return to the many little Favours received (however roughly) at his Hands. If he saw such a Consequence with Horror and Disdain, how much more was he shocked with what regarded Mr. *Allworthy*; to whom, as he had more than filial Obligations, so had he for him more than filial Piety. He knew the Nature of that good Man to be so averse to any Baseness or Treachery, that the least Attempt of such a Kind would make the sight of the guilty Person for ever odious to his Eyes, and his Name a detestable Sound in his Ears. The Appearance of such unsurmountable Difficulties was sufficient to have inspired him with Despair, however ardent his Wishes had been; but even these were controlled by Compassion for another Woman. The Idea of lovely *Molly* now intruded itself before him. He had sworn eternal Constancy in her Arms, and she had as often vowed never to outlive his deserting her. He now saw her in all the most shocking Postures of Death; nay, he considered all the Miseries of Prostitution to which she would be liable, and of which he would be doubly the Occasion; first by seducing, and then by deserting her; for he well knew the Hatred which all her Neighbours, and even her own Sisters, bore her, and how ready they would all be to tear her to Pieces. Indeed he had exposed her to more Envy than Shame, or rather to the latter by Means of the former: For many Women abused her for being a Whore, while they envied her her Lover and her Finery, and would have been themselves glad to have purchased these at the same Rate. The Ruin, therefore, of the poor Girl must, he foresaw, unavoidably attend his deserting her; and this Thought stung him to the Soul. Poverty and Distress seemed to him to give none a Right of aggravating those Misfortunes. The Meanness of her Condition did not represent her Misery as of little Consequence in his Eyes, nor did it appear to justify, or even to palliate, his Guilt, in bringing that Misery upon her. But why do I mention Justification; his own Heart would not suffer him to destroy a human Creature, who, he thought, loved him, and had to that Love sacrificed her Innocence. His own good Heart pleaded her Cause; not as a cold venal Advocate; but as one interested in the Event, and which must itself deeply share in all the Agonies its Owner brought on another.

When this powerful Advocate had sufficiently raised the Pity of *Jones*, by painting poor *Molly* in all the Circumstances of Wretchedness; it artfully called in the Assistance of another Passion, and represented the Girl in all the amiable Colours of Youth, Health, and Beauty; as one greatly the Object of Desire, and much the more so, at least to a good Mind, from being, at the same time, the Object of Compassion.

Amidst these Thoughts, poor *Jones* passed a long sleepless Night, and in the Morning the Result of the whole was to abide by *Molly*, and to think no more of *Sophia*.

In this virtuous Resolution he continued all the next Day till the Evening, cherishing the Idea of *Molly*, and driving *Sophia* from his Thoughts; but in the fatal Evening, a very trifling

Accident set all his Passions again on Float, and worked so total a Change in his Mind, that we think it decent to communicate it in a fresh Chapter.

CHAPTER IV

A little Chapter, in which is contained a little Incident.

AMONG other Visitants, who paid their Compliments to the young Gentleman in his Confinement, Mrs. *Honour* was one. The Reader, perhaps, when he reflects on some Expressions which have formerly dropt from her, may conceive that she herself had a very particular Affection for Mr. *Jones*; but, in reality, it was no such thing. *Tom* was a handsome young Fellow; and for that Species of Men Mrs. *Honour* had some Regard; but this was perfectly indiscriminate: For having been crossed in the Love which she bore a certain Nobleman's Footman, who had basely deserted her after a Promise of Marriage, she had so securely kept together the broken Remains of her Heart, that no Man had ever since been able to possess himself of any single Fragment. She viewed all handsome Men with that equal Regard and Benevolence, which a sober and virtuous Mind bears to all the Good.—She might, indeed, be called a Lover of Men, as *Socrates* was a Lover of Mankind, preferring one to another for corporeal, as he for mental Qualifications; but never carrying this Preference so far as to cause any Perturbation in the philosophical Serenity of her Temper.

The Day after Mr. *Jones* had that Conflict with himself, which we have seen in the preceding Chapter, Mrs. *Honour* came into his Room, and finding him alone, began in the following Manner: 'La, Sir, where do you think I have been? I warrants you, you would not guess in fifty Years; but if you did guess, to be sure, I must not tell you neither.' 'Nay, if it be something which you must not tell me,' said *Jones*, 'I shall have the Curiosity to enquire, and I know you will not be so barbarous to refuse me.' 'I don't know,' cries she, 'why I should refuse you neither, for that Matter; for to be sure you won't mention it any more. And for that Matter, if you knew where I have been, unless you knew what I have been about, it would not signify much. Nay, I don't see why it should be kept a Secret, for my Part; for to be sure she is the best Lady in the World.' Upon this, *Jones* began to beg earnestly to be let into this Secret, and faithfully promised not to divulge it. She then proceeded thus. 'Why, you must know, Sir, my young Lady sent me to enquire after *Molly Seagrim*, and to see whether the Wench wanted any thing; to be sure, I did not care to go, methinks; but Servants must do what they are ordered.—How could you undervalue yourself so, Mr. *Jones*?—So my Lady bid me go, and carry her some Linnen, and other Things.—She is too good. If such forward Sluts were sent to *Bridewell*, it would be better for them. I told my Lady, says I, Madam, Your La'ship is encouraging Idleness——' 'And was my *Sophia* so good?' says *Jones*.—'My *Sophia*! I assure you, marry come up,' answered *Honour*. 'And yet if you knew all.—Indeed, if I was as Mr. *Jones*, I should look a little higher than such Trumpery as *Molly Seagrim*.' 'What do you mean by these Words,' replied *Jones*, 'If I knew all?' 'I mean what I mean,' says *Honour*. 'Don't you remember putting your Hands in my Lady's Muff once? I vow I could almost find in my Heart to tell, if I was certain my Lady would never come to the Hearing on't.'—*Jones* then made several solemn Protestations. And *Honour* proceeded— 'then, to be sure, my Lady gave me that Muff; and afterwards, upon hearing what you had done——' 'Then you told her what I had done!' interrupted *Jones*. 'If I did, Sir,' answered she, 'you need not be angry with me. Many's the Man would have given his Head to have had my Lady told, if they had known—for, to be sure, the biggest Lord in the Land might be proud—but, I protest, I have a great Mind not to tell you.' *Jones* fell to Entreaties, and soon prevailed on her to go on thus. 'You must know then, Sir, that my Lady had given this Muff to me; but about a Day or two after I had told her the Story, she quarrels with her new Muff, and to be sure it is the prettiest that ever was seen. '*Honour*,' says she,—'this is an odious Muff;—it is too big for me,—I can't wear it—till I can get another, you must let me have my old one again, and you may have this in the room on't'—for she's a good Lady, and scorns to give a Thing and take a Thing, I promise you that. So to be sure I fetched it her back again, and, I believe, she hath worn it upon her Arm almost ever since, and I warrants hath given it many a Kiss when nobody hath seen her.'

Here the Conversation was interrupted by Mr. *Western* himself, who came to summon *Jones* to the Harpsichord; whither the poor young Fellow went all pale and trembling. This *Western* observed, but, on seeing Mrs. *Honour,* imputed it to a wrong Cause; and having given *Jones* a hearty Curse between Jest and Earnest, he bid him beat abroad, and not poach up the Game in his Warren.

Sophia looked this Evening with more than usual Beauty, and we may believe it was no small Addition to her Charms, in the Eye of Mr. *Jones,* that she now happened to have on her Right Arm this very Muff.

She was playing one of her Father's favourite Tunes, and he was leaning on her Chair, when the Muff fell over her Fingers, and put her out. This so disconcerted the Squire, that he snatched the Muff from her, and with a hearty Curse threw it into the Fire. *Sophia* instantly started up, and with the utmost Eagerness recovered it from the Flames.

Though this Incident will probably appear of little Consequence to many of our Readers, yet, trifling as it was, it had so violent an Effect on poor *Jones,* that we thought it our Duty to relate it. In reality, there are many little Circumstances too often omitted by injudicious Historians, from which Events of the utmost Importance arise.[1] The World may indeed be considered as a vast Machine,[2] in which the great Wheels are originally set in Motion by those which are very minute, and almost imperceptible to any but the strongest Eyes.

Thus, not all the Charms of the incomparable *Sophia*; not all the dazzling Brightness, and languishing Softness of her Eyes;

---

[1] Several passages in *Tom Jones* attest to Fielding's keen interest in the intricacies of historical causation: in life, and hence necessarily in those fictive 'histories' in which life is truly imitated, a perceptive observer may discern a 'nice Train of little Circumstances' (p. 916) working to complete the 'main Design' (p. 524). One historian whom Fielding would have exempted from the censure of being injudicious in this regard was Livy, who 'gives us so just a Detail of all the Circumstances that preceded and produced [an event]' (*The True Patriot,* 24 December 1745).

[2] The metaphor of the universe as a vast and intricate machine implying the existence of God, the supreme Artificer, was a commonplace in the period. With the present passage compare, among many possible examples, John Spencer, *A Discourse concerning Prodigies* (1665), sig. (A): '*to shew how many wheels in some great Engine, move in subordination to the production of some great work, were [not] to obscure and eclipse the art of the Artificer.*' The figure was a favourite with Robert Boyle and may be found as well in Henry More, John Ray, Isaac Barrow, John Tillotson, Samuel Clarke, and many others.

the Harmony of her Voice, and of her Person; not all her Wit, good Humour, Greatness of Mind, or Sweetness of Disposition, had been able so absolutely to conquer and enslave the Heart of poor *Jones*, as this little Incident of the Muff. Thus the Poet sweetly sings of *Troy*.

> ——*Captique dolis lachrymisque coacti*
> *Quos neque Tydides, nec Larissæus Achilles,*
> *Non anni domuere decem, non mille Carinæ.*[1]

> What *Diomede*, or *Thetis'* greater Son,
> A thousand Ships, nor ten Years Siege had done,
> False Tears, and fawning Words, the City won.
> DRYDEN.

The Citadel of *Jones* was now taken by Surprize. All those Considerations of Honour and Prudence, which our Heroe had lately with so much military Wisdom placed as Guards over the Avenues of his Heart, ran away from their Posts, and the God of Love marched in in Triumph.

CHAPTER V

A very long Chapter, containing a very great Incident.

BUT though this victorious Deity easily expelled his avowed Enemies from the Heart of *Jones*, he found it more difficult to supplant the Garrison which he himself had placed there. To lay aside all Allegory, the Concern for what must become of poor *Molly*, greatly disturbed and perplexed the Mind of the worthy Youth. The superior Merit of *Sophia*, totally eclipsed, or rather extinguished all the Beauties of the poor Girl; but Compassion instead of Contempt succeeded to Love. He was convinced the Girl had placed all her Affections, and all her Prospect of future Happiness in him only. For this he had, he knew, given sufficient Occasion, by the utmost Profusion of Tenderness towards her: A Tenderness which he had taken every Means to persuade her he would always maintain. She, on her Side, had assured him of her firm Belief in his Promise, and had with the most solemn

---

[1] *Aeneid*, ii. 196–8, with reference to the Trojan horse. The verse translation is Dryden's (ii. 261–3).

Vows declared, that on his fulfilling, or breaking these Promises, it depended, whether she should be the happiest, or the most miserable of Womankind. And to be the Author of this highest Degree of Misery to a human Being, was a Thought on which he could not bear to ruminate a single Moment. He considered this poor Girl as having sacrificed to him every Thing in her little Power; as having been at her own Expence the Object of his Pleasure; as sighing and languishing for him even at that very Instant. Shall then, says he, my Recovery, for which she hath so ardently wished; shall my Presence which she hath so eagerly expected, instead of giving her that Joy with which she hath flattered herself, cast her at once down into Misery and Dispair? Can I be such a Villain? Here, when the Genius of poor *Molly* seem'd triumphant, the Love of *Sophia* towards him, which now appeared no longer dubious, rushed upon his Mind, and bore away every Obstacle before it.

At length it occurred to him, that he might possibly be able to make *Molly* amends another Way; namely, by giving her a Sum of Money. This nevertheless, he almost despaired of her accepting, when he recollected the frequent and vehement Assurances he had received from her, that the World put in Ballance with him, would make her no Amends for his Loss. However, her extreme Poverty, and chiefly her egregious Vanity, (somewhat of which hath been already hinted to the Reader) gave him some little Hope, that notwithstanding all her avowed Tenderness, she might in Time be brought to content herself with a Fortune superiour to her Expectation, and which might indulge her Vanity, by setting her above all her Equals. He resolved therefore, to take the first Opportunity of making a Proposal of this Kind.

One Day accordingly, when his Arm was so well recovered, that he could walk easily with it slung in a Sash, he stole forth, at a Season when the Squire was engaged in his Field Exercises, and visited his Fair one. Her Mother and Sisters, whom he found taking their Tea, informed him first that *Molly* was not at Home; but afterwards, the eldest Sister acquainted him with a malicious Smile, that she was above Stairs a-bed. *Tom* had no Objection to this Situation of his Mistress, and immediately ascended the Ladder which led towards her Bed-Chamber; but when he came to the Top, he, to his great Surprize, found the Door fast; nor

...ie for some Time obtain any Answer from within; for ..., as she herself afterwards informed him, was fast asleep.

The Extremes of Grief and Joy have been remarked to produce very similar Effects;[1] and when either of these rushes on us by Surprize, it is apt to create such a total Perturbation and Confusion, that we are often thereby deprived of the Use of all our Faculties. It cannot therefore be wondered at, that the unexpected Sight of Mr. *Jones* should so strongly operate on the Mind of *Molly*, and should overwhelm her with such Confusion, that for some Minutes she was unable to express the great Raptures, with which the Reader will suppose she was affected on this Occasion. As for *Jones*, he was so entirely possessed, and as it were enchanted by the Presence of his beloved Object, that he for a while forgot *Sophia*, and consequently the principal Purpose of his Visit.

This, however, soon recurred to his Memory; and after the first Transports of their Meeting were over, he found Means by Degrees to introduce a Discourse on the fatal Consequences which must attend their Amour, if Mr. *Allworthy*, who had strictly forbidden him ever seeing her more, should discover that he still carried on this Commerce. Such a Discovery, which his Enemies gave him Reason to think would be unavoidable, must, he said, end in his Ruin, and consequently in hers. Since, therefore, their hard Fates had determined that they must separate, he advised her to bear it with Resolution, and swore he would never omit any Opportunity through the Course of his Life, of shewing her the Sincerity of his Affection, by providing for her in a Manner beyond her utmost Expectation, or even beyond her Wishes, if ever that should be in his Power; concluding, at last, that she might soon find some Man who would marry her, and who would make her much happier than she could be by leading a disreputable Life with him.

Molly remained a few Moments in Silence, and then bursting into a Flood of Tears, she began to upbraid him in the following Words. 'And is this your Love for me, to forsake me in this Manner, now you have ruined me? How often, when I have told you that all Men are false and Perjury alike, and grow tired of us as soon as ever they have had their wicked Wills of us, how often have you sworn you would never forsake me? And can

[1] See above, p. 44, n. 1.

you be such a perjury Man after all? What signifies all the
Riches in the World to me without you, now you have gained my
Heart, so you have—you have—? Why do you mention another
Man to me? I can never love any other Man as long as I live.
All other Men are nothing to me. If the greatest Squire in all the
Country would come a suiting to me to-morrow, I would not
give my Company to him. No, I shall always hate and despise the
whole Sex for your Sake——'

She was proceeding thus, when an Accident put a Stop to her
Tongue, before it had run out half its Career. The Room, or
rather Garret, in which *Molly* lay, being up one Pair of Stairs,
that is to say, at the Top of the House, was of a sloping Figure,
resembling the great *Delta* of the *Greeks*. The *English* Reader
may, perhaps, form a better Idea of it, by being told, that it was
impossible to stand upright any where but in the Middle. Now,
as this Room wanted the Conveniency of a Closet, *Molly* had, to
supply that Defect, nailed up an old Rug against the Rafters of
the House, which enclosed a little Hole where her best Apparel,
such as the Remains of that Sack which we have formerly mentioned, some Caps, and other Things with which she had lately
provided herself, were hung up and secured from the Dust.

This inclosed Place exactly fronted the Foot of the Bed, to
which, indeed, the Rug hung so near, that it served, in a Manner,
to supply the Want of Curtains. Now, whether *Molly* in the
Agonies of her Rage, pushed this Rug with her Feet; or, *Jones*
might touch it; or whether the Pin or Nail gave way of its own
Accord, I am not certain; but as *Molly* pronounced those last
Words, which are recorded above, the wicked Rug got loose from
its Fastning, and discovered every thing hid behind it; where
among other female Utensils appeared—(with Shame I write it,
and with Sorrow will it be read)—the Philosopher *Square*, in a
Posture (for the Place would not near admit his standing upright) as ridiculous as can possibly be conceived.

The Posture, indeed, in which he stood, was not greatly unlike that of a Soldier who is tyed Neck and Heels; or rather resembling the Attitude in which we often see Fellows in the public
Streets of *London*, who are not suffering but deserving Punishment by so standing. He had a Night-cap belonging to *Molly*
on his Head, and his two large Eyes, the Moment the Rug fell,
stared directly at *Jones*; so that when the Idea of Philosophy was

added to the Figure now discovered, it would have been very difficult for any Spectator to have refrained from immoderate Laughter.

I question not but the Surprize of the Reader will be here equal to that of *Jones*; as the Suspicions which must arise from the Appearance of this wise and grave Man in such a Place, may seem so inconsistent with that Character, which he hath, doubtless, maintained hitherto, in the Opinion of every one.

But to confess the Truth, this Inconsistency is rather imaginary than real. Philosophers are composed of Flesh and Blood as well as other human Creatures; and however sublimated and refined the Theory of these may be, a little practical Frailty is as incident to them as to other Mortals. It is, indeed, in Theory only and not in Practice, as we have before hinted, that consists the Difference: For tho' such great Beings think much better and more wisely, they always act exactly like other Men. They know very well how to subdue all Appetites and Passions, and to despise both Pain and Pleasure; and this Knowledge affords much delightful Contemplation, and is easily acquired; but the Practice would be vexatious and troublesome; and, therefore, the same Wisdom which teaches them to know this, teaches them to avoid carrying it into Execution.

Mr. *Square* happened to be at Church, on that *Sunday* when, as the Reader may be pleased to remember, the Appearance of *Molly* in her Sack had caused all that Disturbance. Here he first observed her and was so pleased with her Beauty, that he prevailed with the young Gentlemen to change their intended Ride that Evening, that he might pass by the Habitation of *Molly*, and, by that Means, might obtain a second Chance of seeing her. This Reason, however, as he did not at that time mention to any, so neither did we think proper to communicate it then to the Reader.

Among other Particulars which constituted the Unfitness of Things in Mr. *Square's* Opinion, Danger and Difficulty were two. The Difficulty, therefore, which he apprehended there might be in corrupting this young Wench, and the Danger which would accrue to his Character on the Discovery, were such strong Dissuasives, that it is probable, he at first intended to have contented himself with the pleasing Ideas which the Sight of Beauty furnishes us with. These the gravest Men, after a full Meal of serious Meditation, often allow themselves by Way of Desert: For which Purpose, certain Books and Pictures find their Way into the most private Recesses of their Study, and a certain liquorish Part of natural Philosophy is often the principal Subject of their Conversation.

But when the Philosopher heard a Day or two afterwards, that the Fortress of Virtue had already been subdued, he began to give a larger Scope to his Desires. His Appetite was not of that squeamish Kind which cannot feed on a Dainty because another hath tasted it. In short, he liked the Girl the better for the Want of that Chastity, which, if she had possessed it, must have been a Bar to his Pleasures; he pursued, and obtained her.

The Reader will be mistaken, if he thinks *Molly* gave *Square* the Preference to her younger Lover: On the contrary, had she been confined to the Choice of one only, *Tom Jones* would, undoubtedly, have been, of the two, the victorious Person. Nor was it solely the Consideration that two are better than one (tho' this had its proper Weight) to which Mr. *Square* owed his Success; the Absence of *Jones* during his Confinement was an unlucky Circumstance; and in that Interval, some well chosen Presents from the Philosopher so softened and unguarded the Girl's Heart, that a favourable Opportunity became irresistable, and *Square* triumphed over the poor Remains of Virtue which subsisted in the Bosom of *Molly*.

It was now about a Fortnight since this Conquest, when *Jones* paid the above-mentioned Visit to his Mistress, at a time when she and *Square* were in Bed together. This was the true Reason why the Mother denied her as we have seen; for as the old Woman shared in the Profits arising from the Iniquity of her Daughter, she encouraged and protected her in it to the utmost of her Power; but such was the Envy and Hatred which the eldest Sister bore towards *Molly*, that, notwithstanding she had some Part of the Booty, she would willingly have parted with this to ruin her Sister, and spoil her Trade. Hence she had acquainted *Jones* with her being above Stairs in Bed, in Hopes that he might have caught her in *Square's* Arms. This, however, *Molly* found Means to prevent, as the Door was fastned; which gave her an Opportunity of conveying her Lover behind that Rug or Blanket where he now was unhappily discovered.

Square no sooner made his Appearance than *Molly* flung

herself back in her Bed, cried out she was undone, and abandoned herself to Despair. This poor Girl, who was yet but a Novice in her Business, had not arrived to that Perfection of Assurance which helps off a Town Lady in any Extremity; and either prompts her with an Excuse, or else inspires her to brazen out the Matter with her Husband; who from Love of Quiet, or out of Fear of his Reputation, and sometimes, perhaps, from Fear of the Gallant, who, like Mr. *Constant* in the Play,[1] wears a Sword, is glad to shut his Eyes, and contented to put his Horns in his Pocket: *Molly*, on the contrary, was silenced by this Evidence, and very fairly gave up a Cause which she had hitherto maintained with so many Tears, and with such solemn and vehement Protestations of the purest Love and Constancy.

As to the Gentleman behind the Arras, he was not in much less Consternation. He stood for a while motionless, and seemed equally at a Loss what to say, or whither to direct his Eyes. *Jones*, tho' perhaps the most astonished of the three, first found his Tongue; and, being immediately recovered from those uneasy Sensations, which *Molly* by her Upbraidings had occasioned, he burst into a loud Laughter, and then saluting Mr. *Square*, advanced to take him by the Hand, and to relieve him from his Place of Confinement.

Square, being now arrived in the Middle of the Room, in which Part only he could stand upright, looked at *Jones* with a very grave Countenance, and said to him, 'Well, Sir, I see you enjoy this mighty Discovery, and, I dare swear, taste great Delight in the Thoughts of exposing me; but if you will consider the Matter fairly, you will find you are yourself only to blame. I am not guilty of corrupting Innocence. I have done nothing for which that Part of the World which judges of Matters by the Rule of Right will condemn me. Fitness is governed by the Nature of Things, and not by Customs, Forms, or municipal Laws. Nothing is, indeed, unfit which is not unnatural.' 'Well reasoned, old Boy,' answered *Jones*; 'but why dost thou think I should desire to expose thee? I promise thee, I was never better pleased with thee in my Life; and unless thou hast a Mind to discover it thyself, this Affair may remain a profound Secret

---

[1] In Vanbrugh's *The Provok'd Wife* (1697). When discovered in an intrigue with Lady Brute (v. ii), Constant hopes her husband will be assured that their relationship was innocent: 'If not—I wear a Sword, Sir, and so good b'uy to you' (1710 ed.).

for me.' 'Nay, Mr. *Jones*,' replied *Square*, 'I would not be thought to undervalue Reputation. Good Fame is a Species of the K A L O N[1] and it is by no Means fitting to neglect it. Besides to murder one's own Reputation, is a kind of Suicide, a detestable and odious Vice. If you think proper, therefore, to conceal any Infirmity of mine; (for such I may have, since no Man is perfectly perfect) I promise you I will not betray myself. Things may be fitting to be done, which are not fitting to be boasted of: for by the perverse Judgment of the World, That often becomes the Subject of Censure, which is, in Truth, not only innocent but laudable.' 'Right!' cries *Jones*, 'what can be more innocent than the Indulgence of a natural Appetite? or what more laudable than the Propagation of our Species?' 'To be serious with you,' answered *Square*, 'I profess they always appeared so to me.' 'And yet,' said *Jones*, 'you was of a different Opinion when my Affair with this Girl was first discovered.' 'Why, I must confess,' says *Square*, 'as the Matter was misrepresented to me by that Parson *Thwackum*, I might condemn the Corruption of Innocence: It was that, Sir, it was that—and that—: For you must know, Mr. *Jones*, in the Consideration of Fitness, very minute Circumstances, Sir, very minute Circumstances cause great Alteration.'—'Well,' cries *Jones*, 'be that as it will, it shall be your own Fault, as I have promised you, if you ever hear any more of this Adventure. Behave kindly to the Girl, and I will never open my Lips concerning the Matter to any one. And, *Molly*, do you be faithful to your Friend, and I will not only forgive your Infidelity to me; but will do you all the Service I can.' So saying, he took a hasty Leave, and slipping down the Ladder, retired with much Expedition.

Square was rejoyced to find this Adventure was likely to have no worse Conclusion; and as for *Molly*, being recovered from her Confusion, she began at first to upbraid *Square* with having been the Occasion of her Loss of *Jones*; but that Gentleman soon found the Means of mitigating her Anger, partly by Caresses, and partly by a small Nostrum from his Purse, of wonderful and approved Efficacy in purging off the ill Humours of the Mind, and in restoring it to a good Temper.

---

[1] Cf. Bishop Berkeley's definition in *Alciphron: or, The Minute Philosopher* (1732): 'Doubtless there is a beauty of the mind, a charm in virtue, a symmetry and proportion in the moral world. This moral beauty was known to the ancients by the name of *honestum*, or τὸ καλόν' (Fraser ed., *Works* [1901], ii. 127).

She then poured forth a vast Profusion of Tenderness towards her new Lover; turned all she had said to *Jones*, and *Jones* himself into Ridicule, and vowed, tho' he once had the Possession of her Person, that none but *Square* had ever been Master of her Heart.

CHAPTER VI

By comparing which with the former, the Reader may possibly correct some Abuse which he hath formerly been guilty of, in the Application of the Word LOVE.

THE Infidelity of *Molly*, which *Jones* had now discovered, would, perhaps, have vindicated a much greater Degree of Resentment than he expressed on the Occasion; and if he had abandoned her directly from that Moment, very few, I believe, would have blamed him.

Certain, however, it is, that he saw her in the Light of Compassion; and tho' his Love to her was not of that Kind which could give him any great Uneasiness at her Inconstancy, yet was he not a little shocked on reflecting that he had himself originally corrupted her Innocence; for to this Corruption he imputed all the Vice, into which she appeared now so likely to plunge herself.

This Consideration gave him no little Uneasiness, till *Betty*, the eldest Sister, was so kind some time afterwards entirely to cure him by a Hint, that one *Will Barnes*, and not himself, had been the first Seducer of *Molly*; and that the little Child, which he had hitherto so certainly concluded to be his own, might very probably have an equal Title at least, to claim *Barnes* for its Father.

Jones eagerly pursued this Scent when he had first received it; and in a very short Time was sufficiently assured that the Girl had told him Truth, not only by the Confession of the Fellow, but, at last, by that of *Molly* herself.

This *Will Barnes* was a Country Gallant, and had acquired as many Trophies of this Kind as any Ensign or Attorney's Clerk in the Kingdom. He had, indeed, reduced several Women to a State of utter Profligacy, had broke the Hearts of some, and had the Honour of occasioning the violent Death of one poor Girl, who had either drowned herself, or, what was rather more probable, had been drowned by him.

Among other of his Conquests, this Fellow had triumphed over the Heart of *Betty Seagrim*. He had made love to her long before *Molly* was grown to be a fit Object of that Pastime; but had afterwards deserted her, and applied to her Sister, with whom he had almost immediate Success. Now *Will* had, in reality, the sole Possession of *Molly's* Affection, while *Jones* and *Square* were almost equally Sacrifices to her Interest, and to her Pride.

Hence had grown that implacable Hatred which we have before seen raging in the Mind of *Betty*; though we did not think it necessary to assign this Cause sooner, as Envy itself alone was adequate to all the Effects we have mentioned.

Jones was become perfectly easy by Possession of this Secret with Regard to *Molly*; but as to *Sophia*, he was far from being in a State of Tranquility; nay, indeed, he was under the most violent Perturbation: His Heart was now, if I may use the Metaphor, entirely evacuated, and *Sophia* took absolute Possession of it. He loved her with an unbounded Passion, and plainly saw the tender Sentiments she had for him; yet could not this Assurance lessen his Despair of obtaining the Consent of her Father, nor the Horrors which attended his Pursuit of her by any base or treacherous Method.

The Injury which he must thus do to Mr. *Western*, and the Concern which would accrue to Mr. *Allworthy*, were Circumstances that tormented him all Day, and haunted him on his Pillow at Night. His Life was a constant Struggle between Honour and Inclination, which alternately triumphed over each other in his Mind. He often resolved, in the Absence of *Sophia*, to leave her Father's House, and to see her no more; and as often, in her Presence, forgot all those Resolutions, and determined to pursue her at the Hazard of his Life, and at the Forfeiture of what was much dearer to him.

This Conflict began soon to produce very strong and visible Effects: For he lost all his usual Sprightliness and Gaiety of Temper, and became not only melancholy when alone, but dejected and absent in Company; nay, if ever he put on a forced Mirth, to comply with Mr. *Western's* Humour, the Constraint appeared so plain, that he seemed to have been giving the strongest Evidence of what he endeavoured to conceal by such Ostentation.

It may, perhaps, be a Question, whether the Art which he used to conceal his Passion, or the Means which honest Nature employed to reveal it, betrayed him most: For while Art made him more than ever reserved to *Sophia*, and forbad him to address any of his Discourse to her; nay, to avoid meeting her Eyes, with the utmost Caution; Nature was no less busy in counterplotting him. Hence, at the Approach of the young Lady, he grew pale; and if this was sudden, started. If his Eyes accidentally met hers, the Blood rushed into his Cheeks, and his Countenance became all over Scarlet. If common Civility ever obliged him to speak to her, as to drink her Health at Table, his Tongue was sure to faulter. If he touched her his Hand, nay his whole Frame trembled. And if any Discourse tended, however remotely, to raise the Idea of Love, an involuntary Sigh seldom failed to steal from his Bosom. Most of which Accidents Nature was wonderfully industrious to throw daily in his Way.

All these Symptoms escaped the Notice of the Squire; but not so of *Sophia*. She soon perceived these Agitations of Mind in *Jones*, and was at no Loss to discover the Cause; for indeed she recognized it in her own Breast. And this Recognition is, I suppose, that Sympathy which hath been so often noted in Lovers, and which will sufficiently account for her being so much quicker-sighted than her Father.

But, to say the Truth, there is a more simple and plain Method of accounting for that prodigious Superiority of Penetration which we must observe in some Men over the rest of the human Species, and one which will serve not only in the Case of Lovers, but of all others. From whence is it that the Knave is generally so quick-sighted to those Symptoms and Operations of Knavery which often dupe an honest Man of a much better Understanding? There surely is no general Sympathy among Knaves, nor have they, like Free Masons, any common Sign of Communication.[1] In reality, it is only because they have the same thing in their Heads, and their Thoughts are turned the same Way. Thus, that *Sophia* saw, and that *Western* did not see the plain Symptoms of Love in *Jones* can be no Wonder, when we con-

---

[1] See above, p. 85, n. 1. For the signs to which Fielding refers, see *The Secret History of the Free-Masons. . . . With a Short Dictionary of private Signs, or Signals* (2nd ed., 1725).

sider that the Idea of Love never entered into the Head of the
Father, whereas the Daughter, at present, thought of nothing
else.

When *Sophia* was well satisfied of the violent Passion which
tormented poor *Jones*, and no less certain that she herself was its
Object, she had not the least Difficulty in discovering the true
Cause of his present Behaviour. This highly endeared him to her,
and raised in her Mind two of the best Affections which any
Lover can wish to raise in a Mistress. These were Esteem and
Pity; for sure the most outragiously rigid among her Sex will
excuse her pitying a Man, whom she saw miserable on her own
Account; nor can they blame her for esteeming one who visibly
from the most honourable Motives, endeavoured to smother a
Flame in his own Bosom, which, like the famous *Spartan* Theft,[1]
was preying upon, and consuming his very Vitals. Thus his
Backwardness, his Shunning her, his Coldness and his Silence,
were the forwardest, the most diligent, the warmest, and most
eloquent Advocates; and wrought so violently on her sensible and
tender Heart, that she soon felt for him all those gentle Sensations
which are consistent with a virtuous and elevated female Mind—
In short, all which Esteem, Gratitude and Pity, can inspire in
such, towards an agreeable Man—Indeed, all which the nicest
Delicacy can allow—In a Word,—she was in Love with him to
Distraction.

One Day, this young Couple accidentally met in the Garden,
at the End of two Walks, which were both bounded by that
Canal in which *Jones* had formerly risqued drowning to retrieve
the little Bird that *Sophia* had there lost.

This Place had been of late much frequented by *Sophia*. Here
she used to ruminate, with a Mixture of Pain and Pleasure, on
an Incident, which, however trifling in itself, had possibly sown
the first Seeds of that Affection which was now arrived to such
Maturity in her Heart.

Here then this young Couple met. They were almost close
together before either of them knew any Thing of the other's
Approach. A By-stander would have discovered sufficient Marks

[1] See Plutarch, *Life of Lycurgus*, xviii. 1: a Spartan youth who had stolen a fox and
concealed it under his cloak, suffered the animal to tear out his bowels rather than have
the theft discovered. Fielding alludes to the story again in *The Covent-Garden Journal*
(22 August 1752).

of Confusion, in the Countenance of each; but they felt it too much themselves to make any Observation. As soon as *Jones* had a little recovered his first Surprize, he accosted the young Lady with some of the ordinary Forms of Salutation, which she in the same Manner returned, and their Conversation began, as usual, on the delicious Beauty of the Morning. Hence they past to the Beauty of the Place, on which *Jones* launched forth very high Encomiums. When they came to the Tree whence he had formerly tumbled into the Canal, *Sophia* could not help reminding him of that Accident, and said, 'I fancy, Mr. *Jones*, you have some little shuddering when you see that Water.' 'I assure you, Madam,' answered *Jones*, 'the Concern you felt at the Loss of your little Bird, will always appear to me the highest Circumstance in that Adventure. Poor little *Tommy*, there is the Branch he stood upon. How could the little Wretch have the Folly to fly away from that State of Happiness in which I had the Honour to place him? His Fate was a just Punishment for his Ingratitude.' 'Upon my Word, Mr. *Jones*,' said she, 'your Gallantry very narrowly escaped as severe a Fate. Sure, the Remembrance must affect you.' 'Indeed, Madam,' answered he, 'if I have any Reason to reflect with Sorrow on it, it is, perhaps, that the Water had not been a little deeper, by which I might have escaped many bitter Heart-achs, that Fortune seems to have in Store for me.' 'Fie, Mr. *Jones*,' replied *Sophia*, 'I am sure you cannot be in Earnest now. This affected Contempt of Life is only an Excess of your Complaisance to me. You would endeavour to lessen the Obligation of having twice ventured it for my Sake. Beware the third Time.'—She spoke these last Words with a Smile and a Softness inexpressible. *Jones* answered with a Sigh, 'He feared it was already too late for Caution,'—and then looking tenderly and stedfastly on her, he cry'd, 'Oh! Miss *Western*, —Can you desire me to live? Can you wish me so ill?'—*Sophia* looking down on the Ground, answered with some Hesitation, 'Indeed, Mr. *Jones*, I do not wish you ill.'—'Oh! I know too well that heavenly Temper,' cries *Jones*, 'that divine Goodness which is beyond every other Charm.' 'Nay, now,' answered she, 'I understand you not.—I can stay no longer,—I——.' 'I would not be understood,' cries he, 'nay, I can't be understood. I know not what I say. Meeting you here so unexpectedly—I have been unguarded—for Heaven's Sake pardon me, if I have said any Thing to offend you—I did not mean it—indeed, I would rather have died—nay, the very Thought would kill me.' 'You surprize me,' answered she,—'How can you possibly think you have offended me?' 'Fear, Madam,' says he, 'easily runs into Madness; and there is no Degree of Fear like that which I feel of offending you. How can I speak then? Nay don't look angrily at me, one Frown will destroy me.—I mean nothing—Blame my Eyes, or blame those Beauties—What am I saying? Pardon me if I have said too much. My Heart overflowed. I have struggled with my Love to the utmost, and have endeavoured to conceal a Fever which preys on my Vitals, and will, I hope, soon make it impossible for me ever to offend you more.'

Mr. *Jones* now fell a trembling as if he had been shaken with the Fit of an Ague. *Sophia*, who was in a Situation not very different from his, answered in these Words: 'Mr. *Jones*, I will not affect to misunderstand you; indeed I understand you too well; but for Heaven's Sake, if you have any Affection for me, let me make the best of my way into the House. I wish I may be able to support myself thither.'

Jones, who was hardly able to support himself, offered her his Arm, which she condescended to accept, but begged he would not mention a Word more to her of this Nature at present. He promised he would not, insisting only on her Forgiveness of what Love, without the Leave of his Will, had forced from him: This, she told him, he knew how to obtain by his future Behaviour; and thus this young Pair tottered and trembled along, the Lover not once daring to squeeze the Hand of his Mistress, tho' it was locked in his.

Sophia immediately retired to her Chamber, where Mrs. *Honour* and the Hartshorn were summoned to her Assistance. As to poor *Jones*, the only Relief to his distempered Mind, was an unwelcome Piece of News, which, as it opens a Scene of a different Nature from those in which the Reader hath lately been conversant, will be communicated to him in the next Chapter.

CHAPTER VII

In which Mr. Allworthy *appears on a Sick-Bed.*

MR. *Western* was become so fond of *Jones*, that he was unwilling to part with him, tho' his Arm had been long since cured; and *Jones*, either from the Love of Sport, or from some other Reason, was easily persuaded to continue at his House, which he did sometimes for a Fortnight together without paying a single Visit at Mr. *Allworthy's*; nay, without ever hearing from thence.

Mr. *Allworthy* had been for some Days indisposed with a Cold, which had been attended with a little Fever. This he had, however, neglected, as it was usual with him to do all Manner of Disorders which did not confine him to his Bed, or prevent his several Faculties from performing their ordinary Functions. A Conduct which we would by no Means be thought to approve or recommend to Imitation: For surely the Gentlemen of the *Æsculapian* Art are in the Right in advising, that the Moment the Disease is entered at one Door, the Physician should be introduced at the other; what else is meant by that old Adage: *Venienti occurrite Morbo?*[1] 'Oppose a Distemper at its first Approach.' Thus the Doctor and the Disease meet in fair and equal Conflict; whereas, by giving Time to the latter, we often suffer him to fortify and entrench himself, like a *French* Army;[2] so that the learned Gentleman finds it very difficult, and sometimes impossible to come at the Enemy. Nay sometimes by gaining Time, the Disease applies to the *French* military Politics,[3] and corrupts Nature over to his Side, and then all the Powers of Physick must arrive too late. Agreeable to these Observations was, I remember, the Complaint of the great Doctor *Misaubin*,[4]

[1] Persius, *Satires*, iii. 64.

[2] A correspondent in *The Jacobite's Journal* (26 December 1747) repeated the widespread opinion that the success of France in the War of the Austrian Succession was attributable in part to the skill of her military engineers, 'the greatest . . . which perhaps the World hath produced'. Fielding offered a similar appraisal in *A Dialogue between a Gentleman of London . . . and an honest Alderman* (1747). See below, p. 266.

[3] This was one popular explanation for the ineffectual conduct of the Dutch in the war with France: the English believed that Dutch legislators had been bribed into pressing for a Treaty of Neutrality (see below, p. 333, n. 1), and that the governors of certain fortified towns in Flanders had been paid to capitulate without a struggle (see below, p. 513, n. 1).

[4] The French physician John Misaubin (d. 1734) settled in London to practise medicine. Though a duly licensed member of the College of Physicians (1719), Misaubin's faith in

who used very pathetically to lament the late Applications which were made to his Skill: Saying, 'Bygar, me believe my Pation take me for de Undertaker: For dey never send for me till de Physicion have kill dem.'

Mr. *Allworthy's* Distemper, by Means of this Neglect, gained such Ground, that when the Increase of his Fever obliged him to send for Assistance, the Doctor at his first Arrival shook his Head, wished he had been sent for sooner, and intimated that he thought him in very imminent Danger. Mr. *Allworthy*, who had settled all his Affairs in this World, and was as well prepared, as it is possible for human Nature to be, for the other, received this Information with the utmost Calmness and Unconcern. He could, indeed, whenever he laid himself down to Rest, say with *Cato* in the tragical Poem,[1]

> ——*Let Guilt or Fear*
> *Disturb Man's Rest,* Cato *knows neither of them;*
> *Indifferent in his Choice, to sleep or die.*

In Reality, he could say this with ten times more Reason and Confidence than *Cato*, or any other proud Fellow among the ancient or modern Heroes: For he was not only devoid of Fear; but might be considered as a faithful Labourer, when at the End of Harvest, he is summoned to receive his Reward at the Hands of a bountiful Master.[2]

The good Man gave immediate Orders for all his Family to be summoned round him. None of these were then abroad, but Mrs.

the infallible efficacy of his pills, together with his foreign speech and arrogant manner, made him the target of ridicule. Hogarth satirized him on several occasions, in Plate V of *The Harlot's Progress* (1732), for example, and in another print in which Misaubin is shown pointing to the monument of one recently deceased and offering the belated advice, 'Prenez des Pilules, prenez des Pilules.' (See Print 1987, *A Catalogue of Prints and Drawings in the British Museum*, vol. ii, 1689–1733 [1873]; see also Print 1986.) Fielding's *The Mock Doctor* (1732) is ironically dedicated to Misaubin, who though others might call him 'an illiterate Empirick', deserves the warmest praise for inventing 'that *Little Pill*', an 'invaluable Remedy, to which so many owe their Health, their Pleasure, nay the very Preservation of their Being'. In the play itself, Gregory is made to impersonate Misaubin when he poses as a French physician, urging Dorcas to 'taka de Peel; me sal give you de litle Peel dat sal cure you'. For a later reference to Misaubin in *Tom Jones*, see below, p. 688.

1 Addison's *Cato. A Tragedy* (1713), v. i.

2 Cf. Matthew 20: 1–16. With Fielding's application of this parable in the present context, compare Bishop Hoadly's sermon xviii, 'The Parable of the Labourers in the Vineyard, explained: together with the great Danger of delaying Amendment' (*Works*, ed. John Hoadly [1773], iii. 611–19).

Blifil, who had been some Time in *London*, and Mr. *Jones*, whom the Reader hath just parted from at Mr. *Western's* and who received this Summons just as *Sophia* had left him.

The News of Mr. *Allworthy's* Danger (for the Servant told him he was dying) drove all Thoughts of Love out of his Head. He hurried instantly into the Chariot which was sent for him, and ordered the Coachman to drive with all imaginable Haste; nor did the Idea of *Sophia*, I believe, once occur to him on the Way.

And now, the whole Family, namely, Mr. *Blifil*, Mr. *Jones*, Mr. *Thwackum*, Mr. *Square*, and some of the Servants (for such were Mr. *Allworthy's* Orders) being all assembled round his Bed, the good Man sat up in it, and was beginning to speak, when *Blifil* fell to blubbering; and began to express very loud and bitter Lamentations. Upon this Mr. *Allworthy* shook him by the Hand, and said, 'Do not sorrow thus, my dear Nephew, at the most ordinary of all human Occurrences. When Misfortunes befal our Friends we are justly grieved: For those are Accidents which might often have been avoided, and which may seem to render the Lot of one Man, more peculiarly unhappy than that of others; but Death is certainly unavoidable, and is that common Lot, in which alone the Fortunes of all Men agree; nor is the Time when this happens to us very material. If the wisest of Men hath compared Life to a Span,[1] surely we may be allowed to consider it as a Day. It is my Fate to leave it in the Evening; but those who are taken away earlier, have only lost a few Hours, at the best little worth lamenting, and much oftner Hours of Labour and Fatigue, of Pain and Sorrow. One of the *Roman* Poets,[2] I remember, likens our leaving Life to our Departure from a Feast. A Thought which hath often occurred to me, when I have seen Men struggling to protract an Entertainment, and to enjoy the Company of their Friends a few Moments longer. Alas! how short is the most protracted of such Enjoyments! How immaterial the Difference between him who retires the soonest, and him who stays the latest! This is seeing Life in the best View, and this

---

[1] Cf. Psalm 39 as rendered in *The Book of Common Prayer*, where it is part of the liturgy for the Burial of the Dead: 'Behold, thou hast made my days as it were a span long.' Cf. *Amelia* (1751; VIII. x) and 'Of the Remedy of Affliction for the Loss of Our Friends' (1743), where Fielding attributes the saying to Solomon.

[2] Cf. Lucretius, *De Rerum Natura*, iii. 938–9: 'Why not like a banqueter fed full of life, withdraw with contentment and rest in peace' (trans. W. H. D. Rouse, Loeb Classical Library, 1924). The figure is repeated by Horace, *Satires*, I. i. 118; *Epistles*, II. ii. 215.

Unwillingness to quit our Friends is the most amiable Motive, from which we can derive the Fear of Death; and yet the longest Enjoyment which we can hope for of this Kind is of so trivial a Duration, that it is to a wise Man truly contemptible. Few Men, I own, think in this Manner: for, indeed, few Men think of Death till they are in its Jaws. However gigantic and terrible an Object this may appear when it approaches them, they are nevertheless incapable of seeing it at any Distance; nay, tho' they have been ever so much alarmed and frightned when they have apprehended themselves in Danger of dying, they are no sooner cleared from this Apprehension than even the Fears of it are erased from their Minds. But alas! he who escapes from Death is not pardoned, he is only reprieved, and reprieved to a short Day.

'Grieve, therefore, no more, my dear Child, on this Occasion; an Event which may happen every Hour, which every Element, nay almost every Particle of Matter that surrounds us is capable of producing, and which must and will most unavoidably reach us all at last, ought neither to occasion our Surprize, nor our Lamentation.

'My Physician having acquainted me (which I take very kindly of him) that I am in Danger of leaving you all very shortly, I have determined to say a few Words to you at this our Parting, before my Distemper, which I find grows very fast upon me, puts it out of my Power.

'But I shall waste my Strength too much.—I intended to speak concerning my Will, which tho' I have settled long ago, I think proper to mention such Heads of it as concern any of you, that I may have the Comfort of perceiving you are all satisfied with the Provision I have there made for you.

'Nephew *Blifil*, I leave you the Heir to my whole Estate, except only 500 *l.* a Year which is to revert to you after the Death of your Mother, and except one other Estate of 500 *l.* a Year, and the Sum of 6000 *l.* which I have bestowed in the following Manner.

'The Estate of 500 *l.* a Year I have given to you, Mr. *Jones*. And as I know the Inconvenience which attends the Want of ready Money, I have added 1000 *l.* in Specie. In this I know not whether I have exceeded, or fallen short of your Expectation. Perhaps you will think I have given you too little, and the World will be as ready to condemn me for giving you too much; but the latter Censure I despise, and as to the former, unless you should entertain that common Error, which I have often heard in my Life pleaded as an Excuse for a total Want of Charity; namely, that instead of raising Gratitude by voluntary Acts of Bounty, we are apt to raise Demands, which of all others are the most boundless and most difficult to satisfy——Pardon me the bare Mention of this, I will not suspect any such Thing.'

Jones flung himself at his Benefactor's Feet, and taking eagerly hold of his Hand, assured him, his Goodness to him, both now, and all other Times, had so infinitely exceeded not only his Merit, but his Hopes, that no Words could express his Sense of it. 'And I assure you, Sir,' said he, 'your present Generosity hath left me no other Concern than for the present melancholy Occasion.—Oh, my Friend! my Father!' Here his Words choaked him, and he turned away to hide a Tear which was starting from his Eyes.

Allworthy then gently squeezed his Hand, and proceeded thus. 'I am convinced, my Child, that you have much Goodness, Generosity and Honour in your Temper; if you will add Prudence[1] and Religion to these, you must be happy: For the three former Qualities, I admit, make you worthy of Happiness, but they are the latter only which will put you in Possession of it.

'One thousand Pound I have given to you Mr. *Thwackum*; a Sum, I am convinced, which greatly exceeds your Desires as well as your Wants. However, you will receive it as a Memorial of my Friendship; and whatever Superfluities may redound to you, that Piety which you so rigidly maintain, will instruct you how to dispose of them.

'A like Sum, Mr. *Square*, I have bequeathed to you. This, I hope, will enable you to pursue your Profession with better Success than hitherto. I have often observed with Concern, that Distress is more apt to excite Contempt than Commiseration, especially among Men of Business, with whom Poverty is understood to indicate Want of Ability. But the little I have been able to leave you, will extricate you from those Difficulties with which you have formerly struggled, and then I doubt not but you will meet with sufficient Prosperity to supply what a Man of your Philosophical Temper will require.

'I find myself growing faint, so I shall refer you to my Will for

---

[1] See above, p. 36, n. 1.

my Disposition of the Residue. My Servants will there find some Tokens to remember me by, and there are a few Charities which, I trust, my Executors will see faithfully performed. Bless you all. I am setting out a little before you———'

Here a Footman came hastily into the Room, and said there was an Attorney from *Salisbury*, who had a particular Message, which he said he must communicate to Mr. *Allworthy* himself: That he seemed in a violent Hurry, and protested he had so much Business to do, that if he could cut himself into four Quarters, all would not be sufficient.

'Go, Child,' said *Allworthy* to *Blifil*, 'see what the Gentleman wants. I am not able to do any Business now, nor can he have any with me, in which you are not at present more concerned than myself. Besides I really am—I am incapable of seeing any one at present, or of any longer Attention.' He then saluted them all, saying, perhaps he should be able to see them again, but he should be now glad to compose himself a little, finding that he had too much exhausted his Spirits in Discourse.

Some of the Company shed Tears at their Parting; and even the Philosopher *Square* wiped his Eyes, *albeit unused to the melting Mood*. As to Mrs. *Wilkins*, she dropt her Pearls as fast *as the Arabian Trees their Medicinal Gums*;[1] for this was a Ceremonial which that Gentlewoman never omitted on a proper Occasion.

After this Mr. *Allworthy* again laid himself down on his Pillow, and endeavoured to compose himself to Rest.

CHAPTER VIII

Containing Matter rather natural than pleasing.

BESIDES Grief for her Master, there was another Source for that briny Stream which so plentifully rose above the two mountainous Cheek Bones of the House-keeper. She was no sooner retired, than she began to mutter to herself in the following pleasant Strain. 'Sure Master might have made some Difference, methinks, between me and the other Servants. I suppose

---

1 Cf. *Othello*, v. ii:		. . . of one whose subdu'd eyes,
							Albeit unused to the melting mood,
							Drop tears as fast as the Arabian trees
							Their med'cinable gum.

he hath left me Mourning; but, i-fackins! if that be all, the Devil shall wear it for him for me. I'd have his Worship know I am no Beggar. I have saved five hundred Pound in his Service, and after all to be used in this Manner. It is a fine Encouragement to Servants to be honest; and to be sure, if I have taken a little Something now and then, others have taken ten times as much; and now we are all put in a Lump together. If so be that it be so, the Legacy may go to the Devil with him that gave it. No, I won't give it up neither, because that will please some Folks. No, I'll buy the gayest Gown I can get, and dance over the old Curmudgeon's Grave in it. This is my Reward for taking his Part so often, when all the Country have cried Shame of him for breeding up his Bastard in that Manner; but he is going now where he must pay for all. It would have becomed him better to have repented of his Sins on his Death-bed, than to glory in them, and give away his Estate out of his own Family to a mis-begotten Child. Found in his Bed, forsooth! A pretty Story! Ay, ay, those that hide know where to find. Lord forgive him, I warrant he hath many more Bastards to answer for, if the Truth was known. One Comfort is, they will all be known where he is a going now. 'The Servants will find some Token to remember me by.' Those were the very Words, I shall never forget them, if I was to live a thousand Years. Ay, ay, I shall remember you for huddling me among the Servants. One would have thought he might have mentioned my Name as well as that of *Square*; but he is a Gentleman forsooth, though he had not Clothes to his Back when he came hither first. Marry come up with such Gentlemen! though he hath lived here this many Years, I don't believe there is *arrow* Servant in the House ever saw the Colour of his Money. The Devil shall wait upon such a Gentleman for me.' Much more of the like kind she muttered to herself; but this Taste shall suffice to the Reader.

Neither *Thwackum* nor *Square* were much better satisfied with their Legacies. Tho' they breathed not their Resentment so loud, yet from the Discontent which appeared in their Countenances, as well as from the following Dialogue, we collect that no great Pleasure reigned in their Minds.

About an Hour after they had left the sick Room, *Square* met *Thwackum* in the Hall, and accosted him thus, 'Well, Sir, have you heard any News of your Friend since we parted from him?'

'If you mean Mr. *Allworthy*,' answered *Thwackum*, 'I think you might rather give him the Appellation of your Friend: For he seems to me to have deserved that Title.' 'The Title is as good on your Side,' replied *Square*, 'for his Bounty, such as it is, hath been equal to both.' 'I should not have mentioned it first,' cries *Thwackum*, 'but since you begin, I must inform you I am of a different Opinion. There is a wide Distinction between voluntary Favours and Rewards. The Duty I have done in his Family, and the Care I have taken in the Education of his two Boys, are Services for which some Men might have expected a greater Return. I would not have you imagine I am therefore dissatisfied; for St. *Paul* hath taught me[1] to be content with the little I have. Had the Modicum been less, I should have known my Duty. But though the Scripture obliges me to remain contented, it doth not enjoin me to shut my Eyes to my own Merit, nor restrain me from seeing, when I am injured by an unjust Comparison.' 'Since you provoke me,' returned *Square*, 'that Injury is done to me: Nor did I ever imagine Mr. *Allworthy* had held my Friendship so light, as to put me in Ballance with one who received his Wages: I know to what it is owing; it proceeds from those narrow Principles which you have been so long endeavouring to infuse into him, in Contempt of every Thing which is great and noble. The Beauty and Loveliness of Friendship is too strong for dim Eyes, nor can it be perceived by any other Medium, than that unerring Rule of Right which you have so often endeavoured to ridicule, that you have perverted your Friend's Understanding.' 'I wish,' cries *Thwackum*, in a Rage, 'I wish for the Sake of his Soul, your damnable Doctrines have not perverted his Faith. It is to this, I impute his present Behaviour so unbecoming a Christian. Who but an Atheist could think of leaving the World without having first made up his Account? without confessing his Sins, and receiving that Absolution which he knew he had one in the House duly authorised to give him? He will feel the Want of these Necessaries when it is too late. When he is arrived at that Place where there is Wailing and Gnashing of Teeth.[2] It is then he will find in what mighty Stead that Heathen Goddess, that Virtue which you and all other Deists of the Age adore, will stand him. He will then summon his Priest when there is none to be found,

---

[1] Cf. Philippians 4: 11, 1 Timothy 6: 6–8, Hebrews 13: 5.
[2] Cf. Matthew 8: 12, 13: 42, 50, etc.

and will lament the Want of that Absolution, without which no Sinner can be safe.' 'If it be so material,' says *Square*, 'Why don't you present it him of your own Accord?' 'It hath no Virtue,' cries *Thwackum*, 'but to those who have sufficient Grace to require it. But why do I talk thus to a Heathen and an Unbeliever? It is you that taught him this Lesson, for which you have been well rewarded in this World, as I doubt not your Disciple will soon be in the other.' 'I know not what you mean by Reward,' said *Square*, 'but if you hint at that pitiful Memorial of our Friendship, which he hath thought fit to bequeath me, I despise it, and nothing but the unfortunate Situation of my Circumstances should prevail on me to accept it.'

The Physician now arrived, and began to enquire of the two Disputants, *How we all did above Stairs?* 'In a miserable Way,' answered *Thwackum*. 'It is no more than I expected,' cries the Doctor; 'but pray what Symptoms have appeared since I left you?' 'No good ones, I am afraid,' replied *Thwackum*, 'after what past at our Departure, I think there were little Hopes.' The bodily Physician, perhaps, misunderstood the Curer of Souls, and before they came to an Explanation, Mr. *Blifil* came to them with a most melancholy Countenance, and acquainted them that he brought sad News: For that his Mother was dead at *Salisbury*. That she had been seized on the Road home with the Gout in her Head and Stomach, which had carried her off in a few Hours. 'Goodlack-a-day,' says the Doctor. 'One cannot answer for Events; but I wish I had been at Hand to have been called in. The Gout is a Distemper which it is difficult to treat, yet I have been remarkably successful in it.' *Thwackum* and *Square* both condoled with Mr. *Blifil* for the Loss of his Mother, which the one advised him to bear like a Man, and the other like a Christian. The young Gentleman said, he knew very well we were all mortal, and he would endeavour to submit to his Loss, as well as he could. That he could not, however, help complaining a little against the peculiar Severity of his Fate, which brought the News of so great a Calamity to him by Surprize, and that at a Time when he hourly expected the severest Blow he was capable of feeling from the Malice of Fortune. He said, the present Occasion would put to the Test those excellent Rudiments, which he had learnt from Mr. *Thwackum* and Mr. *Square*, and it would be entirely owing to them, if he was enabled to survive such Misfortunes.

It was now debated whether Mr. *Allworthy* should be informed of the Death of his Sister: This the Doctor violently op-
posed, in which, I believe, the whole College will agree with him;
but Mr. *Blifil* said he had received such positive and repeated
Orders from his Uncle never to keep any Secret from him, for
Fear of the Disquietude which it might give him, that he durst
not think of Disobedience, whatever might be the Consequence.
He said, for his Part, considering the religious and philosophic
Temper of his Uncle, he could not agree with the Doctor in his
Apprehensions. He was therefore resolved to communicate it to
him: For if his Uncle recovered (as he heartily prayed he might)
he knew he would never forgive an Endeavour to keep a Secret
of this Kind from him.

The Physician was forced to submit to these Resolutions which
the two other learned Gentlemen very highly commended. So
together moved Mr. *Blifil* and the Doctor towards the sick Room;
where the Physician first entered, and approached the Bed, in
order to feel his Patient's Pulse, which he had no sooner done,
than he declared he was much better, that the last Application
had succeeded to a Miracle, and had brought the Fever to inter-
mit. So that, he said, there appeared now to be as little Danger
as he had before apprehended there were Hopes.

To say the Truth, Mr. *Allworthy's* Situation had never been
so bad, as the great Caution of the Doctor had represented it;
but as a wise General never despises his Enemy, however inferior that Enemy's Force may be, so neither doth a wise Physician
ever despise a Distemper, however inconsiderable. As the former
preserves the same strict Discipline, places the same Guards,
and employs the same Scouts, tho' the Enemy be never so
weak; so the latter maintains the same Gravity of Countenance,
and shakes his Head with the same significant Air, let the Distemper be never so trifling. And both, among many other good
ones, may assign this solid Reason for their Conduct, that by
these Means the greater Glory redounds to them if they gain
the Victory, and the less Disgrace if by any unlucky Accident
they should happen to be conquered.

Mr. *Allworthy* had no sooner lifted up his Eyes, and thanked
Heaven for these Hopes of his Recovery, than Mr. *Blifil* drew
near with a very dejected Aspect, and having applied his
Handkerchief to his Eye, either to wipe away his Tears,

or to do as *Ovid* somewhere expresses himself on another Occasion,[1]

Si nullus erit, tamen excute nullum.

If there be none, then wipe away that none.

he communicated to his Uncle what the Reader hath been just before acquainted with.

Allworthy received the News with Concern, with Patience, and with Resignation. He dropt a tender Tear, then composed his Countenance, and at last cried, 'The Lord's Will be done in every Thing.'

He now enquired for the Messenger; but *Blifil* told him, it had been impossible to detain him a Moment; for he appeared by the great Hurry he was in to have some Business of Importance on his Hands: That he complained of being hurried, and driven and torn out of his Life, and repeated many Times, that if he could divide himself into four Quarters, he knew how to dispose of every one.

Allworthy then desired *Blifil* to take Care of the Funeral. He said, he would have his Sister deposited in his own Chapel; and as to the Particulars, he left them to his own Discretion, only mentioning the Person whom he would have employed on this Occasion.

CHAPTER IX

Which, among other Things, may serve as a Comment on that Saying of Æschines,[2] *that* DRUNKENNESS SHEWS THE MIND OF A MAN, AS A MIRROUR REFLECTS HIS PERSON.

THE Reader may, perhaps, wonder at hearing nothing of Mr. *Jones* in the last Chapter. In fact, his Behaviour was so different from that of the Persons there mentioned, that we chose not to confound his Name with theirs.

---

[1] *Ars Amatoria,* i. 151: 'si nullus erit pulvis, tamen excute nullum.' Ovid advises the lover to affect a tender concern for his mistress, in this instance by pretending to brush away a fleck of dust from her garment.

[2] Aeschines (*c.* 390–330 B.C.), the famous Athenian orator and rival of Demosthenes. As in Stobæus, however, whose anthology of Greek aphorisms Fielding knew (see below, p. 257, n. 1), the saying should be attributed to Aeschylus (*Fragments,* 221 [393]): *Aes formæ speculum est, vinum mentis*: bronze is a mirror of the person, wine of the mind. (See

When the good Man had ended his Speech, *Jones* was the last who deserted the Room. Thence he retired to his own Apartment, to give Vent to his Concern; but the Restlessness of his Mind would not suffer him to remain long there; he slipped softly, therefore, to *Allworthy's* Chamber Door, where he listened a considerable Time without hearing any Kind of Motion within, unless a violent snoring, which at last his Fears misrepresented as Groans. This so alarmed him, that he could not forbear entering the Room; where he found the good Man in the Bed in a sweet composed Sleep, and his Nurse snoring in the abovementioned hearty Manner, at the Bed's-Feet. He immediately took the only Method of silencing this thorough Bass, whose Music he feared might disturb Mr. *Allworthy*; and then sitting down by the Nurse, he remained motionless till *Blifil* and the Doctor came in together, and waked the sick Man; in order that the Doctor might feel his Pulse, and that the other might communicate to him that Piece of News, which, had *Jones* been apprized of it, would have had great Difficulty of finding its Way to Mr. *Allworthy's* Ear at such a Season.

When he first heard *Blifil* tell his Uncle this Story, *Jones* could hardly contain the Wrath which kindled in him at the other's Indiscretion, especially as the Doctor shook his Head, and declared his Unwillingness to have the Matter mentioned to his Patient. But as his Passion did not so far deprive him of all Use of his Understanding, as to hide from him the Consequences which any violent Expressions towards *Blifil* might have on the Sick, this Apprehension stilled his Rage, at the present; and he grew afterwards so satisfied with finding that this News had, in fact, produced no Mischief, that he suffered his Anger to die in his own Bosom, without ever mentioning it to *Blifil*.

The Physician dined that Day at Mr. *Allworthy's*; and having after Dinner visited his Patient, he returned to the Company, and told them, that he had now the Satisfaction to say, with

John Stobæus, *Sententiæ ex Thesauris Græcorum Delectæ* [Aureliæ Allobrogum, 1609], sermo xviii, 'De Incontinentia', p. 164.) Nevertheless, considering the context, Fielding may have wished to recall Aeschines. In *De Falsa Legatione*, Demosthenes called attention to his rival's drunken behaviour at a banquet in Macedonia, during which Aeschines was said to have cruelly abused a young woman who refused to drink with him: if the girl had not been rescued, Demosthenes declared, 'she would have perished, the victim of a drunken orgy, for the drunkenness of this blackguard is something terrible' (198—trans. C. A. and J. H. Vince, Loeb Classical Library, 1926).

Assurance, that his Patient was out of all Danger: That he had brought his Fever to a perfect Intermission, and doubted not by throwing in the Bark¹ to prevent its Return.

This Account so pleased *Jones*, and threw him into such immoderate Excess of Rapture, that he might be truly said to be drunk with Joy. An Intoxication which greatly forwards the Effects of Wine; and as he was very free too with the Bottle on this Occasion, (for he drank many Bumpers to the Doctor's Health, as well as to other Toasts) he became very soon literally drunk.

Jones had naturally violent animal Spirits. These being set on Float, and augmented by the Spirit of Wine, produced most extravagant Effects. He kissed the Doctor, and embraced him with the most passionate Endearments; swearing that, next to Mr. *Allworthy* himself, he loved him 'of all Men living.' 'Doctor,' added he, 'you deserve a Statue to be erected to you at the public Expence, for having preserved a Man, who is not only the Darling of all good Men who know him, but a Blessing to Society, the Glory of his Country, and an Honour to Human Nature. D—n me if I don't love him better than my own Soul.'

'More shame for you,' cries *Thwackum*. 'Though I think you have reason to love him, for he hath provided very well for you. And, perhaps, it might have been better for some Folks, that he had not lived to see just Reason of revoking his Gift.'

Jones now, looking on *Thwackum* with inconceivable Disdain, answered, 'And doth thy mean Soul imagine that any such Considerations could weigh with me? No, let the Earth open and swallow her own Dirt (if I had Millions of Acres I would say it) rather than swallow up my dear glorious Friend.'

> *Quis Desiderio sit Pudor aut modus*
> *Tam chari Capitis?**²

The Doctor now interposed, and prevented the Effects of a Wrath which was kindling between *Jones* and *Thwackum*; after

---

* 'What Modesty, or Measure, can set Bounds to our Desire of so dear a Friend!' The Word *Desiderium* here cannot be easily translated. It includes our Desire of enjoying our Friend again, and the Grief which attends that Desire.

---

¹ The bark of the Cinchona tree, from which quinine is derived.
² Horace, *Odes*, I. xxiv. 1–2. The ode is addressed to Virgil on the death of their mutual friend, Quintilius.

which the former gave a Loose to Mirth, sang two or three amorous Songs, and fell into every frantic Disorder which un-bridled Joy is apt to inspire; but so far was he from any Dis-position to quarrel, that he was ten times better humoured, if possible, than when he was sober.

To say Truth, nothing is more erroneous than the common Observation, That Men who are ill-natured and quarrelsome when they are drunk, are very worthy Persons when they are sober: For Drink, in reality, doth not reverse Nature, or create Passions in Men, which did not exist in them before.[1] It takes away the Guard of Reason, and consequently forces us to produce those Symptoms, which many, when sober, have Art enough to conceal. It heightens and inflames our Passions (generally indeed that Passion which is uppermost in our Mind) so that the angry Temper, the amorous, the generous, the good-humoured, the avaricious, and all other Dispositions of Men, are in their Cups heightened and exposed.

And yet as no Nation produces so many drunken Quarrels, especially among the lower People, as *England*; (for, indeed, with them, to drink and to fight together are almost synonimous Terms) I would not, methinks, have it thence concluded that the *English* are the worst-natured People alive. Perhaps the Love of Glory only is at the Bottom of this; so that the fair Conclusion seems to be, that our Countrymen have more of that Love, and more of Bravery, than any other Plebeians. And this the rather, as there is seldom any thing ungenerous, unfair, or ill-natured, exercised on those Occasions: Nay, it is common for the Com-batants to express Good-will for each other, even at the Time of the Conflict; and as their drunken Mirth generally ends in a Battle, so do most of their Battles end in Friendship.

But to return to our History. Tho' *Jones* had shewn no Design of giving Offence, yet Mr. *Blifil* was highly offended at a Be-haviour which was so inconsistent with the sober and prudent Reserve of his own Temper. He bore it too with the greater Impatience, as it appeared to him very indecent at this Season; 'when,' as he said, 'the House was a House of Mourning, on the Account of his dear Mother; and if it had pleased Heaven to give them some Prospect of Mr. *Allworthy's* Recovery, it

---

[1] Cf. Seneca 'On Drunkenness', *Epistulae Morales*, lxxxiii. 19–20, and *Spectator*, No. 569 (19 July 1712).

would become them better to express the Exultations of their
Hearts in Thanksgiving than in Drunkenness and Riots; which
were properer Methods to encrease the divine Wrath, than to
avert it.' *Thwackum*, who had swallowed more Liquor than *Jones*,
but without any ill Effect on his Brain, seconded the pious
Harangue of *Blifil*; but *Square*, for Reasons which the Reader
may probably guess, was totally silent.

Wine had not so totally overpowered *Jones*, as to prevent his
recollecting Mr. *Blifil's* Loss, the Moment it was mentioned. As
no Person, therefore, was more ready to confess and condemn
his own Errors, he offered to shake Mr. *Blifil* by the Hand, and
begged his Pardon, saying, 'His excessive Joy for Mr. *Allworthy's*
Recovery had driven every other Thought out of his Mind.'

Blifil scornfully rejected his Hand; and, with much Indignation, answered, 'It was little to be wondered at, if tragical Spectacles made no Impressions on the Blind; but, for his Part, he
had the Misfortune to know who his Parents were, and consequently must be affected with their Loss.'

Jones, who, notwithstanding his good Humour, had some
Mixture of the irascible in his Constitution, leaped hastily from
his Chair, and catching hold of *Blifil's* Collar, cried out, 'D——n
you for a Rascal, do you insult me with the Misfortune of my
Birth?' He accompanied these Words with such rough Actions,
that they soon got the better of Mr. *Blifil's* peaceful Temper;
and a Scuffle immediately ensued, which might have produced
Mischief, had it not been prevented by the Interposition of
Thwackum and the Physician; for the Philosophy of *Square*
rendered him superior to all Emotions, and he very calmly
smoaked his Pipe, as was his Custom in all Broils, unless
when he apprehended some Danger of having it broke in his
Mouth.

The Combatants being now prevented from executing present
Vengeance on each other, betook themselves to the common
Resources of disappointed Rage, and vented their Wrath in
Threats and Defiance. In this kind of Conflict, Fortune, which,
in the personal Attack, seemed to incline to *Jones*, was now
altogether as favourable to his Enemy.

A Truce, nevertheless, was at length agreed on, by the Mediation of the neutral Parties, and the whole Company again sat
down at the Table; where *Jones* being prevailed on to ask Pardon,

and *Blifil* to give it, Peace was restored, and every thing seemed in *Statu quo.*

But though the Quarrel was, in all Appearance, perfectly re-conciled, the Good-humour which had been interrupted by it, was by no means restored. All Merriment was now at an End, and the subsequent Discourse consisted only of grave Relations of Matters of Fact, and of as grave Observations upon them. A Species of Conversation, in which, though there is much of Dignity and Instruction, there is but little Entertainment. As we presume, therefore, to convey only this last to the Reader, we shall pass by whatever was said, till the rest of the Company having, by Degrees, dropped off, left only *Square* and the Physician together; at which Time the Conversation was a little heightened by some Comments on what had happened between the two young Gentlemen; both of whom the Doctor declared to be no better than Scoundrels; to which Appellation the Philosopher, very sagaciously shaking his Head, agreed.

CHAPTER X

Shewing the Truth of many Observations of Ovid,[1] *and of other more grave Writers, who have proved, beyond Contradiction, that Wine is often the Fore-runner of Incontinency.*

*J*ONES retired from the Company, in which we have seen him engaged, into the Fields, where he intended to cool himself by a Walk in the open Air, before he attended Mr. *Allworthy.* There, whilst he renewed those Meditations on his dear *Sophia,* which the dangerous Illness of his Friend and Benefactor had for some time interrupted, an Accident happened, which with Sorrow we relate, and with Sorrow, doubtless, will it be read; however, that historic Truth to which we profess so inviolable an Attachment, obliges us to communicate it to Posterity.

It was now a pleasant Evening in the latter End of *June,*[2] when our Heroe was walking in a most delicious Grove, where

[1] Cf. *Ars Amatoria,* i. 237.

[2] In revising the novel Fielding overlooked this vestige of an original time-scheme: in VII. xi, a point in the narrative just three weeks later, the time is given as November 1745. See below, p. 368, n. 1, and the General Introduction, pp. xxxvii ff.

the gentle Breezes fanning the Leaves, together with the sweet Trilling of a murmuring Stream, and the melodious Notes of Nightingales formed all together the most enchanting Harmony. In this Scene, so sweetly accommodated to Love, he meditated on his dear *Sophia*. While his wanton Fancy roved unbounded over all her Beauties, and his lively Imagination painted the charming Maid in various ravishing Forms, his warm Heart melted with Tenderness, and at length throwing himself on the Ground by the Side of a gently murmuring Brook, he broke forth into the following Ejaculation.

'O *Sophia*, would Heaven give thee to my Arms, how blest would be my Condition! Curst be that Fortune which sets a Distance between us. Was I but possessed of thee, one only Suit of Rags thy whole Estate, is there a Man on Earth whom I would envy! How contemptible would the brightest *Circassian* Beauty, drest in all the Jewels of the *Indies*, appear to my Eyes! But why do I mention another Woman? could I think my Eyes capable of looking at any other with Tenderness, these Hands should tear them from my Head. No, my *Sophia*, if cruel Fortune separates us for ever, my Soul shall doat on thee alone. The chastest Constancy will I ever preserve to thy Image. Tho' I should never have Possession of thy charming Person, still shalt thou alone have Possession of my Thoughts, my Love, my Soul. Oh! my fond Heart is so wrapt in that tender Bosom, that the brightest Beauties would for me have no Charms, nor would a Hermit be colder in their Embraces. *Sophia, Sophia* alone shall be mine. What Raptures are in that Name! I will engrave it on every Tree.'

At these Words he started up, and beheld—not his *Sophia*—no, nor a *Circassian* Maid richly and elegantly attired for the Grand Signior's Seraglio. No; without a Gown, in a Shift that was somewhat of the coarsest, and none of the cleanest, bedewed likewise with some odoriferous Effluvia, the Produce of the Day's Labour, with a Pitch-fork in her Hand, *Molly Seagrim* approached. Our Heroe had his Pen-knife in his Hand, which he had drawn for the before-mentioned Purpose, of carving on the Bark; when the Girl coming near him cry'd out with a Smile, 'You don't intend to kill me, Squire, I hope!' 'Why should you think I would kill you?' answered *Jones*. 'Nay,' replied she, 'after your cruel Usage of me when I saw you last, killing me would, perhaps, be too great Kindness for me to expect.'

Here ensued a Parly, which, as I do not think myself obliged to relate it, I shall omit. It is sufficient that it lasted a full Quarter of an Hour, at the Conclusion of which they retired into the thickest Part of the Grove.

Some of my Readers may be inclined to think this Event unnatural. However, the Fact is true; and, perhaps, may be sufficiently accounted for, by suggesting that *Jones* probably thought one Woman better than none, and *Molly* as probably imagined two Men to be better than one. Besides the before-mentioned Motive assigned to the present Behaviour of *Jones*, the Reader will be likewise pleased to recollect in his Favour, that he was not at this Time perfect Master of that wonderful Power of Reason, which so well enables grave and wise Men to subdue their unruly Passions, and to decline any of these prohibited Amusements. Wine now had totally subdued this Power in *Jones*. He was, indeed, in a Condition, in which if Reason had interposed, tho' only to advise, she might have received the Answer which one *Cleostratus*[1] gave many Years ago to a silly Fellow, who asked him if he was not ashamed to be drunk? 'Are not you,' said *Cleostratus*, 'ashamed to admonish a drunken Man?'—To say the Truth, in a Court of Justice, Drunkenness must not be an Excuse,[2] yet in a Court of Conscience it is greatly so; and therefore *Aristotle*, who commends the Laws of *Pittacus*,[3] by which drunken Men received double Punishment for their Crimes, allows there is more of Policy than Justice in that Law. Now, if there are any Transgressions pardonable from Drunkenness, they are certainly such as Mr. *Jones* was at present guilty of; on which Head I could pour forth a vast Profusion of Learning, if I imagined it would either entertain my Reader, or teach him any Thing more than he knows already. For his Sake, therefore, I shall keep my Learning to myself, and return to my History.

---

[1] The only source for this anecdote appears to be Stobæus' anthology, sermo xxxiv, 'De Tempestiva Oratione': *'Cleostratus ei qui dixerat, nö te pudet ebrietatis? respondit: Te verò non pudet ebrium admonere?'* (*Sententiæ ex Thesauris Græcorum Delectæ* [Aureliæ Allobrogum, 1609], p. 215; Fielding owned a copy of this edition.)

[2] In fact, drunkenness was legally considered to be an aggravation of the offence. (See Wood, *Institutes*, 7th ed. [1745], p. 14.)

[3] *Politics*, II. ix. 9. Pittacus of Mytilene (c. 650–570 B.C.), one of the 'Seven Sages' of Greece. Referring to this law in *An Enquiry into the Causes of the late Increase of Robbers* (1751), section ii ('Of Drunkenness'), Fielding remarked that he did not know 'a more excellent Institution'.

It hath been observed, that Fortune seldom doth Things by Halves. To say Truth, there is no End to her Freaks whenever she is disposed to gratify or displease. No sooner had our Heroe retired with his *Dido*, but

> *Speluncam* Blifil, *Dux et Divinus eandem*
> *Deveniunt.*———[1]

the Parson and the young Squire, who were taking a serious Walk, arrived at the Stile which leads into the Grove, and the latter caught a View of the Lovers, just as they were sinking out of Sight.

Blifil knew *Jones* very well, tho' he was at above a hundred Yards Distance, and he was as positive to the Sex of his Companion, tho' not to the individual Person. He started; blessed himself, and uttered a very solemn Ejaculation.

Thwackum express'd some Surprize at these sudden Emotions, and asked the Reason of them. To which *Blifil* answered, 'he was certain he had seen a Fellow and Wench retire together among the Bushes, which he doubted not was with some wicked Purpose.' As to the Name of *Jones* he thought proper to conceal it, and why he did so must be left to the Judgment of the sagacious Reader: For we never chuse to assign Motives to the Actions of Men, when there is any possibility of our being mistaken.

The Parson, who was not only strictly chaste in his own Person, but a great Enemy to the opposite Vice in all others, fired at this Information. He desired Mr. *Blifil* to conduct him immediately to the Place, which as he approached, he breathed forth Vengeance mixed with Lamentations; nor did he refrain from casting some oblique Reflections on Mr. *Allworthy*; insinuating that the Wickedness of the Country was principally owing to the Encouragement he had given to Vice, by having exerted such Kindness to a Bastard, and by having mitigated that just and wholsome Rigour of the Law, which allots a very severe Punishment to loose Wenches.

The Way, through which our Hunters were to pass in Pursuit of their Game, was so beset with Briars, that it greatly obstructed their Walk, and caused, besides, such a rustling that *Jones* had

---

1 Fielding parodies the *Aeneid*, iv. 165–6. In a shower of rain Dido and Aeneas take shelter in a cave, where they consummate their love: 'speluncam Dido dux et Troianus eandem / deveniunt' ('To the same cave come Dido and the Trojan chief'—trans. H. R. Fairclough, Loeb Classical Library, 1916).

sufficient Warning of their Arrival, before they could surprize him; nay, indeed, so incapable was *Thwackum* of concealing his Indignation, and such Vengeance did he mutter forth every Step he took, that this alone must have abundantly satisfied *Jones*, that he was (to use the Language of Sportsmen) *found sitting*.

CHAPTER XI

In which a Simile in Mr. Pope's *Period of a Mile,*[1] *introduces as bloody a Battle as can possibly be fought, without the Assistance of Steel or cold* Iron.

AS in the Season of RUTTING[2] (an uncouth Phrase, by which the Vulgar denote that gentle Dalliance, which in the well-wooded Forest* of *Hampshire*, passes between Lovers of the Ferine Kind) if while the lofty crested Stag meditates the amorous Sport, a Couple of Puppies, or any other Beasts of hostile Note, should wander so near the Temple of *Venus Ferina*, that the fair Hind should shrink from the Place, touched with that Somewhat, either of Fear or Frolic, of Nicety or Skittishness, with which Nature hath bedecked all Females, or hath, at least, instructed them how to put it on; lest, thro' the Indelicacy of Males, the *Samean* Mysteries[3] should be pryed into by un-hallowed Eyes: For at the Celebration of these Rites, the female

---

* This is an ambiguous Phrase, and may mean either a Forest well clothed with Wood, or well stript of it.[4]

---

[1] In *The Fourth Satire of Dr. John Donne, Dean of St. Paul's, Versifyed* (1733), l. 73, Pope alludes to Bishop Hoadly's long-windedness. When asked which writers he most esteems, the speaker replies: '*Swift*, for closer Style, / And Ho[*adl*]y for a Period of a Mile.'

[2] With Fielding's account of the behaviour of stags in 'rutting' season (usually mid-September until mid-November), compare *The Gentleman's Recreation*, 6th ed. (1721), pp. 7, 52–4.

[3] Samos, an island in the Ionian Sea, was sacred to Juno, queen of the gods, whose function it was to preside over marriage and childbirth.

[4] The New Forest—of which Fielding's patron, the Duke of Bedford, was Warden (see above, p. 5, n. 1)—had fallen into decay under the Stuarts, who liberally awarded timber privileges to their favourites. In 1693, recognizing that 'the Forest was in danger of being destroyed', William III authorized the planting of 6,000 acres, but the devastation continued virtually unchecked until the last decade of the eighteenth century. (See J. R. Wise, *The New Forest: Its History and its Scenery* [1863], pp. 43–5.)

Priestess cries out with her in *Virgil* (who was then probably hard at Work on such Celebration)

——*Procul, O procul este, profani;*
Proclamat Vates, totoque absistite Luco.[1]

——Far hence be Souls prophane,
The Sibyl cry'd, and from the Grove abstain.

DRYDEN.

If, I say, while these sacred Rites, which are in common to *Genus omne Animantium*,[2] are in Agitation between the Stag and his Mistress, any hostile Beasts should venture too near, on the first Hint given by the frighted Hind, fierce and tremendous rushes forth the Stag to the Entrance of the Thicket; there stands he Centinel over his Love, stamps the Ground with his Foot, and with his Horns brandished aloft in Air, proudly provokes the apprehended Foe to Combat.

Thus, and more terrible, when he perceived the Enemy's Approach, leap'd forth our Heroe. Many a Step advanced he forwards, in order to conceal the trembling Hind, and, if possible, to secure her Retreat. And now *Thwackum* having first darted some livid Lightning from his fiery Eyes, began to thunder forth, 'Fie upon it! Fie upon it! Mr. *Jones*. Is it possible you should be the Person!' 'You see,' answered *Jones*, 'it is possible I should be here.' 'And who,' said *Thwackum*, 'is that wicked Slut with you?' 'If I have any wicked Slut with me,' cries *Jones*, 'it is possible I shall not let you know who she is.' 'I command you to tell me immediately,' says *Thwackum*, 'and I would not have you imagine, young Man, that your Age, tho' it hath somewhat abridged the Purpose of Tuition, hath totally taken away the Authority of the Master. The Relation of the Master and Scholar is indelible, as, indeed, all other Relations are: For they all derive their Original from Heaven. I would have you think yourself, therefore, as much obliged to obey me now, as when I taught you your first Rudiments.' 'I believe you would,' cries *Jones*, 'but that will not happen, unless you had the same Birchen Argument to convince me.' 'Then I must tell you plainly,' said *Thwackum*, 'I am resolved

---

[1] *Aeneid*, vi. 258–9—as dogs howl and other ominous signs occur, the Cumaean Sibyl speaks these lines at the entrance to the underworld. For the translation, see Dryden's *Aeneis*, vi. 368–9.
[2] 'The whole race of living creatures.'

to discover the wicked Wretch.' 'And I must tell you plainly,' returned *Jones*, 'I am resolved you shall not.' *Thwackum* then offered to advance, and *Jones* laid hold of his Arms; which Mr. *Blifil* endeavoured to rescue, declaring 'he would not see his old Master insulted.'

Jones now finding himself engaged with two, thought it necessary to rid himself of one of his Antagonists as soon as possible. He, therefore, applied to the weakest first; and letting the Parson go, he directed a Blow at the young Squire's Breast, which luckily taking Place, reduced him to measure his Length on the Ground.

Thwackum was so intent on the Discovery, that the Moment he found himself at Liberty, he stept forward directly into the Fern, without any great Consideration of what might, in the mean Time, befal his Friend; but he had advanced a very few Paces into the Thicket, before *Jones* having defeated *Blifil*, overtook the Parson, and dragged him backward by the Skirt of his Coat.

This Parson had been a Champion in his Youth, and had won much Honour by his Fist, both at School and at the University. He had now, indeed, for a great Number of Years, declined the Practice of that noble Art; yet was his Courage full as strong as his Faith, and his Body no less strong than either. He was moreover, as the Reader may, perhaps, have conceived, somewhat irascible in his Nature. When he looked back, therefore, and saw his Friend stretched out on the Ground, and found himself at the same Time so roughly handled by one who had formerly been only passive in all Conflicts between them, (a Circumstance which highly aggravated the whole) his Patience at length gave Way; he threw himself into a Posture of Offence, and collecting all his Force, attacked *Jones* in the Front, with as much Impetuosity as he had formerly attacked him in the Rear.

Our Heroe received the Enemy's Attack with the most undaunted Intrepidity, and his Bosom resounded with the Blow. This he presently returned with no less Violence, aiming likewise at the Parson's Breast; but he dextrously drove down the Fist of *Jones*, so that it reached only his Belly, where two Pounds of Beef and as many of Pudding were then deposited, and whence consequently no hollow Sound could proceed. Many lusty Blows, much more pleasant as well as easy to have seen, than to read or describe, were given on both Sides; at last a violent Fall in which *Jones* had thrown his Knees into *Thwackum's* Breast, so weakened the latter, that Victory had been no longer dubious, had not *Blifil*, who had now recovered his Strength, again renewed the Fight, and, by engaging with *Jones*, given the Parson a Moment's Time to shake his Ears, and to regain his Breath.

And now both together attacked our Heroe, whose Blows did not retain that Force with which they had fallen at first; so weakened was he by his Combat with *Thwackum*: For tho' the Pedagogue chose rather to play *Solos* on the human Instrument, and had been lately used to those only, yet he still retained enough of his ancient Knowledge to perform his Part very well in a *Duet*.

The Victory, according to modern Custom, was like to be decided by Numbers,[1] when, on a sudden, a fourth Pair of Fists appeared in the Battle, and immediately paid their Compliments to the Parson; the Owner of them, at the same Time, crying out, 'Are not you ashamed and be d—nd to you, to fall two of you upon one?'

The Battle, which was of the Kind, that for Distinction's Sake is called R O Y A L,[2] now raged with the utmost Violence during a few Minutes; till *Blifil* being a second Time laid sprawling by *Jones*, *Thwackum* condescended to apply for Quarter to his new Antagonist, who was now found to be Mr. *Western* himself: For in the Heat of the Action none of the Combatants had recognized him.

In Fact, that honest Squire, happening in his Afternoon's Walk with some Company, to pass through the Field where the bloody Battle was fought, and having concluded from seeing three Men engaged, that two of them must be on a Side, he hastened from his Companions, and with more Gallantry than Policy, espoused the Cause of the weaker Party. By which generous Pro-

---

[1] Fielding's constant theme during the disastrous war with France was that the French owed their victories not to the greater courage of their soldiers, but to their superiority in numbers. In *The True Patriot* (10 December 1745) and *A Dialogue between a Gentleman of London . . . and an honest Alderman* (1747) he put the ratio of French to Allied troops at three to one. Particularly relevant here, in view of the allusion which introduces the succeeding paragraph, is Fielding's facetious account in *The True Patriot* (28 January–4 February 1746, under 'Foreign History'), comparing the commencement of hostilities in the Low Countries to a 'Cock-Match'. After noting that 'one Lewis the Fifteenth, a great Cock-Merchant, threatens to bring above 200,000 Head into the Pit, on the other Side', he concludes: '*N. B.* It is imagined most of the French are Shack-bags, and only depend on the Superiority of their Numbers, as there are to be several Battles Royal.' See also below, p. 679.

[2] In cock-fighting, a general battle between several combinations of birds. See above, n. 1.

ceeding, he very probably prevented Mr. *Jones* from becoming a Victim to the Wrath of *Thwackum*, and to the pious Friendship which *Blifil* bore his old Master: For besides the Disadvantage of such Odds, *Jones* had not yet sufficiently recovered the former Strength of his broken Arm. This Reinforcement, however, soon put an End to the Action, and *Jones* with his Ally obtained the Victory.

CHAPTER XII

In which is seen a more moving Spectacle, than all the Blood in the Bodies of Thwackum *and* Blifil *and of Twenty other such, is capable of producing.*

THE rest of Mr. *Western's* Company were now come up, being just at the Instant when the Action was over. These were the honest Clergyman, whom we have formerly seen at Mr. *Western's* Table; Mrs. *Western* the Aunt of *Sophia*; and lastly, the lovely *Sophia* herself.

At this Time, the following was the Aspect of the bloody Field. In one Place, lay on the Ground, all pale and almost breathless, the vanquished *Blifil*. Near him stood the Conqueror *Jones*, almost covered with Blood, part of which was naturally his own, and part had been lately the Property of the Reverend Mr. *Thwackum*. In a third Place stood the said *Thwackum*, like King *Porus*,[1] sullenly submitting to the Conqueror. The last Figure in the Piece was *Western the Great*, most gloriously forbearing the vanquished Foe.

---

[1] The story of Alexander's victory over Porus (326 B.C.), the Indian king, is told in Plutarch, *Life of Alexander*, lx, and in Arrian, *Anabasis of Alexander*, v. viii ff. Fielding's mock-heroic description of this bloody scene recalls one of the most celebrated historical *tableaux* of the period: Plate VI of Charles LeBrun's magnificent series depicting the victories of Alexander. (See Plate 6.) Done in 1661–8 at the command of Louis XIV, LeBrun's paintings now hang in the Louvre. Copies of the official engravings by the Audrans were commissioned in England and published by Carington Bowles (British Museum Print Room: C. 293*). The series was much admired: see, for example, Farquhar's *Beaux' Stratagem* (1707), iv, and Charles Gildon, *The Complete Art of Poetry* (1718), i. 230. When Louis Laguerre was commissioned to commemorate Marlborough's victories over the French, he looked to LeBrun's *tableaux* for a model (see M. Whinney and O. Millar, *English Art, 1625–1744* [Oxford, 1957], pp. 305–6). King Porus also figured prominently in several operas based on Metastasio's libretto, *Alessandro nelle Indie*; one of these, with music by Lampugnani, was produced in London in 1746.

Blifil, in whom there was little Sign of Life, was at first the principal Object of the Concern of every one, and particularly of Mrs. *Western*, who had drawn from her Pocket a Bottle of Hartshorn, and was herself about to apply it to his Nostrils; when on a sudden the Attention of the whole Company was diverted from poor *Blifil*, whose Spirit, if it had any such Design, might have now taken an Opportunity of stealing off to the other World, without any Ceremony.

For now a more melancholy and a more lovely Object lay motionless before them. This was no other than the charming *Sophia* herself, who, from the Sight of Blood, or from Fear for her Father, or from some other Reason, had fallen down in a Swoon, before any one could get to her Assistance.

Mrs. *Western* first saw her, and screamed. Immediately two or three Voices cried out, 'Miss *Western* is dead.' Hartshorn, Water; every Remedy was called for, almost at one and the same Instant.

The Reader may remember, that in our Description of this Grove, we mentioned a murmuring Brook, which Brook did not come there, as such gentle Streams flow through vulgar Romances, with no other Purpose than to murmur. No; Fortune had decreed to enoble this little Brook with a higher Honour than any of those which wash the Plains of *Arcadia*, ever deserved.

Jones was rubbing *Blifil's* Temples: For he began to fear he had given him a Blow too much, when the Words, Miss *Western* and *Dead*, rushed at once on his Ear. He started up, left *Blifil* to his Fate, and flew to *Sophia*, whom, while all the rest were running against each other backward and forward looking for Water in the dry Paths, he caught up in his Arms, and then ran away with her over the Field to the Rivulet above-mentioned; where, plunging himself into the Water, he contrived to besprinkle her Face, Head, and Neck very plentifully.

Happy was it for *Sophia*, that the same Confusion which prevented her other Friends from serving her, prevented them likewise from obstructing *Jones*. He had carried her half ways before they knew what he was doing, and he had actually restored her to Life before they reached the Water-side: She stretched out her Arms, opened her Eyes, and cried, 'Oh, Heavens!' just as her Father, Aunt and the Parson came up.

Jones, who had hitherto held this lovely Burthen in his Arms, now relinquished his Hold; but gave her at the same Instant a tender Caress, which, had her Senses been then perfectly restored, could not have escaped her Observation. As she expressed, therefore, no Displeasure at this Freedom, we suppose she was not sufficiently recovered from her Swoon at the Time.

This tragical Scene was now converted into a sudden Scene of Joy. In this, our Heroe was, most certainly, the principal Character: For as he probably felt more extatic Delight in having saved *Sophia*, than she herself received from being saved; so neither were the Congratulations paid to her, equal to what were conferred on *Jones*, especially by Mr. *Western* himself, who, after having once or twice embraced his Daughter, fell to hugging and kissing *Jones*. He called him the Preserver of *Sophia*, and declared there was nothing, except her, or his Estate, which he would not give him; but upon Recollection, he afterwards excepted his Fox-hounds, the *Chevalier*, and Miss *Slouch* (for so he called his favourite Mare).

All Fears for *Sophia* being now removed, *Jones* became the Object of the Squire's Consideration. 'Come, my Lad,' says *Western*, 'D'*off* thy *Quoat* and wash thy *Feace*: For *att* in a devilish Pickle, I promise thee. Come, come, wash thyself, and *shat* go *Huome* with me; and *wel zee* to *vind* thee another *Quoat*.'

Jones immediately complied; threw off his Coat, went down to the Water, and washed both his Face and Bosom: For the latter was as much exposed, and as bloody as the former: But tho' the Water could clear off the Blood, it could not remove the black and blue Marks which *Thwackum* had imprinted on both his Face and Breast, and which, being discerned by *Sophia*, drew from her a Sigh, and a Look full of inexpressible Tenderness.

Jones receiv'd this full in his Eyes, and it had infinitely a stronger Effect on him than all the Contusions which he had received before. An Effect, however, widely different; for so soft and balmy was it, that, had all his former Blows been Stabs, it would for some Minutes have prevented his feeling their Smart.

The Company now moved backwards, and soon arrived where *Thwackum* had got Mr. *Blifil* again on his Legs. Here we cannot suppress a pious Wish, that all Quarrels were to be decided by those Weapons only, with which Nature, knowing what is proper for us, hath supplied us; and that cold Iron was to be used in digging no Bowels, but those of the Earth. Then would War,

the Pastime of Monarchs, be almost inoffensive, and Battles between great Armies might be fought at the particular Desire of
several Ladies of Quality; who, together with the Kings themselves, might be actual Spectators of the Conflict. Then might the
Field be this Moment well strewed with human Carcasses, and
the next, the dead Men, or infinitely the greatest Part of them,
might get up, like Mr. *Bayes's* Troops,[1] and march off either at
the Sound of a Drum or Fiddle, as should be previously agreed on.

I would avoid, if possible, treating this Matter ludicrously,
lest grave Men and Politicians, whom I know to be offended at a
Jest, may cry Pish at it; but, in reality, might not a Battle be as
well decided by the greater Number of broken Heads, bloody
Noses, and black Eyes, as by the greater Heaps of mangled and
murdered human Bodies? Might not Towns be contended for
in the same Manner? Indeed, this may be thought too detrimental
a Scheme to the *French* Interest, since they would thus lose the
Advantage they have over other Nations, in the Superiority of
their Engineers:[2] But when I consider the Gallantry and Generosity of that People, I am persuaded they would never decline
putting themselves upon a Par with their Adversary; or, as the
Phrase is, *making themselves his Match.*

But such Reformations are rather to be wished than hoped for;
I shall content myself, therefore, with this short Hint, and return
to my Narrative.

Western began now to enquire into the original Rise of this
Quarrel. To which neither *Blifil* nor *Jones* gave any Answer;
but *Thwackum* said surlily, 'I believe, the Cause is not far off;
if you beat the Bushes well you may find her.' 'Find her!' replied
Western, 'what, have you been fighting for a Wench?' 'Ask the
Gentleman in his Wastecoat there,' said *Thwackum*, 'he best
knows.' 'Nay, then,' cries *Western*, 'it is a Wench certainly.—
Ah, *Tom*, *Tom*; thou art a liquorish Dog—but come, Gentlemen,
be all Friends, and go home with me, and make final Peace over
a Bottle.' 'I ask your Pardon, Sir,' says *Thwackum*, 'it is no such
slight Matter for a Man of my Character to be thus injuriously
treated, and buffetted by a Boy; only because I would have done

---

[1] Cf. *The Rehearsal* (1671), II. v—a hilarious burlesque of heroic drama by the Duke of
Buckingham and others. Though fallen in battle, the soldiers in Bayes's play rise up 'at a
certain Note . . . in *Effaut flat*, and fall a Dancing'.

[2] See above, p. 240, n. 2.

my Duty, in endeavouring to detect and bring to Justice a wanton
Harlot; but, indeed, the principal Fault lies in Mr. *Allworthy* and
yourself: For, if you put the Laws in Execution, as you ought to
do, you would soon rid the Country of these Vermin.'

'I would as soon rid the Country of Foxes,' cries *Western*. 'I
think we ought to encourage the recruiting those Numbers which
we are every Day losing in the War:[1] But where is she?—Prithee,
Tom, shew me.' He then began to beat about, in the same
Language, and in the same Manner, as if he had been beating for
a Hare, and at last cried out, 'Soho![2] Puss is not far off. Here's her
Form, upon my Soul; I believe I may cry *stole away*.' And indeed
so he might, for he had now discovered the Place whence the
poor Girl had, at the Beginning of the Fray, *stolen away*, upon
as many Feet as a Hare generally uses in travelling.

Sophia now desired her Father to return home; saying, she
found herself very faint, and apprehended a Relapse. The Squire
immediately complied with his Daughter's Request (for he was
the fondest of Parents). He earnestly endeavoured to prevail with
the whole Company to go and sup with him; but *Blifil* and
Thwackum absolutely refused; the former saying, There were
more Reasons than he could then mention, why he must decline
this Honour; and the latter declaring (perhaps rightly) that it
was not proper for a Person of his Function to be seen at any
Place in his present Condition.

Jones was incapable of refusing the Pleasure of being with his
Sophia. So on he marched with Squire *Western* and his Ladies,
the Parson bringing up the Rear. This had, indeed, offered to
tarry with his Brother *Thwackum*, professing, his Regard for the
Cloth would not permit him to depart; but *Thwackum* would not
accept the Favour, and, with no great Civility, pushed him after
Mr. *Western*.

Thus ended this bloody Fray; and thus shall end the fifth
Book of this History.

---

[1] The War of the Austrian Succession (1740–8), in which Britain, Austria, and Holland
were allied against Prussia (until 1745), France, Spain, and Bavaria. For Britain virtually
the only bright moment of the conflict was the early victory over the French at Dettingen
(June 1743). After war between France and England was formally declared in March 1744,
massive French armies invaded the Netherlands and defeated the Allied forces repeatedly in
a series of disastrous engagements, most notably at Fontenoy (May 1745).

[2] The huntsman's cry when a hare ('Puss') has been started.

BOOK VI

Containing about three Weeks.

CHAPTER I

Of Love.

IN our last Book we have been obliged to deal pretty much with the Passion of Love; and, in our succeeding Book, shall be forced to handle this Subject still more largely. It may not, therefore, in this Place, be improper to apply ourselves to the Examination of that modern Doctrine, by which certain Philosophers, among many other wonderful Discoveries, pretend to have found out, that there is no such Passion in the human Breast.

Whether these Philosophers be the same with that surprizing Sect, who are honourably mentioned by the late Dr. *Swift*;[1] as having, by the mere Force of Genius alone, without the least Assistance of any Kind of Learning, or even Reading, discovered that profound and invaluable Secret, That there is no G——: or whether they are not rather the same with those who, some Years since, very much alarmed the World, by shewing that there were no such things as Virtue or Goodness really existing in Human Nature, and who deduced our best Actions from Pride,[2] I will

---

[1] See *An Argument to prove, That the Abolishing of Christianity in England, May, as Things now Stand, be attended with some Inconveniencies, and perhaps, not produce those many good Effects proposed thereby* (1711). Attacking the Free-thinkers, Swift ironically deplored the curtailment of 'Liberty of Conscience' by the Church. In evidence he cited the 'severe Instance' of two officers, 'young Gentlemen of great Hopes, bright Wit, and profound Judgment, who upon a thorough Examination of Causes and Effects, and by the meer Force of natural Abilities, without the least Tincture of Learning; having made a Discovery, that there was no God, and generously communicating their Thoughts for the Good of the Publick; were some Time ago, by an unparalleled Severity, and upon I know not what *obsolete* Law, broke only for *Blasphemy*' (H. Davis [ed.], *Bickerstaff Papers and Pamphlets on the Church* [Oxford, 1957], p. 28).

[2] Throughout his career as novelist and journalist, Fielding warmly denounced the views of those 'Political Philosophers' who followed Hobbes (*Leviathan*, 1651) in representing human nature as 'depraved, and totally bad' (*The Champion*, 22 January 1739/40). Among these, La Rochefoucauld (*Sentences et maximes de morale*, 1664) and Esprit (*La Fausseté des vertus humaines*, 1678) traced all human actions, even those of pity and love, to self-interested motives. In Fielding's own century the most notorious exponent of this cynical doctrine was Bernard Mandeville (1670–1733), who in several essays in *The Fable of*

not here presume to determine. In reality, I am inclined to suspect, that all these several Finders of Truth are the very identical Men, who are by others called the *Finders of Gold*.[1] The Method used in both these Searches after Truth and after Gold, being, indeed, one and the same; *viz.* the searching, rummaging, and examining into a nasty Place; indeed, in the former Instances, into the nastiest of all Places, A BAD MIND.

But though, in this Particular, and perhaps in their Success, the Truth-finder, and the Gold-finder, may very properly be compared together; yet in Modesty, surely, there can be no Comparison between the two; for who ever heard of a Gold-finder that had the Impudence or Folly to assert, from the ill Success of his Search, that there was no such thing as Gold in the World? Whereas the Truth-finder, having raked out that *Jakes* his own Mind, and being there capable of tracing no Ray of Divinity, nor any thing virtuous, or good, or lovely, or loving, very fairly, honestly, and logically concludes, that no such things exist in the whole Creation.[2]

To avoid, however, all Contention, if possible, with these Philosophers, if they will be called so; and to shew our own Disposition to accommodate Matters peaceably between us, we shall here make them some Concessions, which may possibly put an End to the Dispute.

the Bees (1714–34) dedicated himself to refuting Shaftesbury and to elaborating the proposition that 'the nearer we search into human Nature, the more we shall be convinced, that the Moral Virtues are the Political Offspring which Flattery begot upon Pride' ('An Enquiry into the Origin of Moral Virtue' [1714]; ed. F. B. Kaye [Oxford, 1924], i. 51). Accordingly, Fielding's sharpest criticism of this school was generally directed at 'that charming Fellow *Mandevil*', as Miss Matthews calls him in *Amelia* (1751; III. v): 'I hope you do not agree with *Mandevil* neither [Booth replies], who hath represented human Nature as a Picture of the highest Deformity. He hath left out of his System the best Passion which the Mind can possess, and attempts to derive the Effects or Energies of that Passion, from the base Impulses of Pride or Fear. Whereas, it is as certain that Love exists in the Mind of Man, as that its opposite Hatred doth, and the same Reasons will equally prove the Existence of the one as the Existence of the other.' See also *The Covent-Garden Journal* (14 March 1752), where 'Iago' agrees with 'that very wise Writer Dr. Mandevil' in tracing benevolence to motives of vanity.

[1] A slang phrase applied to those who cleaned out latrines. (See *The Champion*, 31 May 1740.)

[2] Thus Fielding usually explained and dismissed the arguments for universal depravity advanced by Whitefield and the Calvinists on the one hand (see above, pp. 79, n. 4; 96, n. 2) and by Hobbes and Mandeville on the other. See, for example, *The Champion* (11 December 1739), the Preface to the *Miscellanies* and 'An Essay on Conversation' (1743), *The True Patriot* (18–25 February 1746), and *Tom Jones*, below, p. 486.

First, we will grant that many Minds, and perhaps those of the Philosophers, are entirely free from the least Traces of such a Passion.

Secondly, That what is commonly called Love, namely, the Desire of satisfying a voracious Appetite with a certain Quantity of delicate white human Flesh, is by no Means that Passion for which I here contend. This is indeed more properly Hunger; and as no Glutton is ashamed to apply the Word Love to his Appetite, and to say he L O V E S such and such Dishes; so may the Lover of this Kind, with equal Propriety say, he H U N G E R S after such and such Women.

Thirdly, I will grant, which I believe will be a most acceptable Concession, that this Love for which I am an Advocate, though it satisfies itself in a much more delicate Manner, doth nevertheless seek its own Satisfaction as much as the grossest of all our Appetites.

And, Lastly, That this Love when it operates towards one of a different Sex, is very apt, towards its complete Gratification, to call in the Aid of that Hunger which I have mentioned above; and which it is so far from abating, that it heightens all its Delights to a Degree scarce imaginable. by those who have never been susceptible of any other Emotions, than what have proceeded from Appetite alone.

In return to all these Concessions, I desire of the Philosophers to grant, that there is in some (I believe in many) human Breasts, a kind and benevolent Disposition, which is gratified by contributing to the Happiness of others.[1] That in this Gratification alone, as in Friendship, in parental and filial Affection, as indeed in general Philanthropy, there is a great and exquisite Delight. That if we will not call such Disposition Love, we have no Name for it. That though the Pleasures arising from such pure Love may be heightened and sweetened by the Assistance of amorous Desires, yet the former can subsist alone, nor are they destroyed by the Intervention of the latter. Lastly, That Esteem and Gratitude are the proper Motives to Love, as Youth and Beauty are to Desire; and therefore though such Desire may naturally cease, when Age or Sickness overtakes its Object, yet these can have no Effect on Love, nor ever shake or remove from a good Mind, that Sensation or Passion which hath Gratitude and Esteem for its Basis.

[1] See above, p. 39, n. 1.

To deny the Existence of a Passion of which we often see manifest Instances, seems to be very strange and absurd; and can indeed proceed only from that Self-Admonition which we have mentioned above: But how unfair is this? Doth the Man who recognizes in his own Heart no Traces of Avarice or Ambition, conclude therefore, that there are no such Passions in Human Nature? Why will we not modestly observe the same Rule in judging of the Good, as well as the Evil of others? Or why, in any Case, will we, as *Shakespear* phrases it, 'put the World in our own Person?'[1]

Predominant Vanity is, I am afraid, too much concerned here. This is one Instance of that Adulation which we bestow on our own Minds, and this almost universally. For there is scarce any Man, how much soever he may despise the Character of a Flatterer, but will condescend in the meanest Manner to flatter himself.[2]

To those, therefore, I apply for the Truth of the above Observations, whose own Minds can bear Testimony to what I have advanced.

Examine your Heart, my good Reader, and resolve whether you do believe these Matters with me. If you do, you may now proceed to their Exemplification in the following Pages; if you do not, you have, I assure you, already read more than you have understood; and it would be wiser to pursue your Business, or your Pleasures (such as they are) than to throw away any more of your Time in reading what you can neither taste nor comprehend. To treat of the Effects of Love to you, must be as absurd as to discourse on Colours to a Man born blind; since possibly your Idea of Love may be as absurd as that which we are told such blind Man once entertained of the Colour Scarlet: that Colour seemed to him to be very much like the Sound of a Trumpet;[3]

---

[1] From Benedick's speech in *Much Ado about Nothing* (II. i): 'It is the base (though bitter) disposition of Beatrice that puts the world into her person. . . .'

[2] Cf. 'Of True Greatness' (1741), ll. 43–4: 'Disdaining outward Flatterers to win,/ Dost thou not feed a Flatterer within?'

[3] Cf. Steele in *Tatler*, No. 227 (19–21 September 1710): 'A man cannot have an idea of perfection in another which he was never sensible of in himself. Mr. Locke tells us, that upon asking a blind man, what he thought scarlet was, he answered, that he believed it was like the sound of a trumpet. He was forced to form his conceptions of ideas which he had not by those which he had' (G. A. Aitken, ed. [1899], iv. 166). For the passage from Locke's *Essay concerning Human Understanding*, see above, p. 152, n. 2.

and Love probably may, in your Opinion, very greatly resemble a Dish of Soup, or a Sir-loin of Roast-beef.

CHAPTER II

The Character of Mrs. Western. *Her great Learning and Know-ledge of the World, and an Instance of the deep Penetration which she derived from those Advantages.*

THE Reader hath seen Mr. *Western*, his Sister and Daughter, with young *Jones*, and the Parson, going together to Mr. *Western's* House, where the greater Part of the Company spent the Evening with much Joy and Festivity. *Sophia* was indeed the only grave Person: For as to *Jones*, though Love had now gotten entire Possession of his Heart, yet the pleasing Reflection on Mr. *Allworthy's* Recovery, and the Presence of his Mistress, joined to some tender Looks which she now and then could not refrain from giving him, so elevated our Heroe, that he joined the Mirth of the other three, who were perhaps as good-humoured People as any in the World.

Sophia retained the same Gravity of Countenance the next Morning at Breakfast; whence she retired likewise earlier than usual, leaving her Father and Aunt together. The Squire took no Notice of this Change in his Daughter's Disposition. To say the Truth, though he was somewhat of a Politician, and had been twice a Candidate in the Country Interest[1] at an Election, he was a Man of no great Observation. His Sister was a Lady of a different Turn. She had lived about the Court, and had seen the World. Hence she had acquired all that Knowledge which the said World usually communicates; and was a perfect Mistress of Manners, Customs, Ceremonies, and Fashions; nor did her Erudition stop here. She had considerably improved her Mind by Study; she had not only read all the modern Plays, Operas,

---

[1] The Country Interest, or Country Party, was the name assumed by those Tories who opposed the Pelham administration (formed December 1744), affecting to champion the best interests of the country as a whole by resisting the selfish schemes of Whig placemen and pensioners at Court. A staunch defender of the Pelham government, Fielding's views of 'the Country Party, as it is absurdly called', are presented at length in the electioneering pamphlet, *A Dialogue between a Gentleman of London, Agent for Two Court Candidates, and an Honest Alderman of the Country Party* (June 1747).

Oratorios, Poems and Romances; in all which she was a Critic; but had gone thro' *Rapin's* History of *England*,[1] *Eachard's Roman History*,[2] and many *French Memoires pour servir a l'Histoire*;[3] to these she had added most of the political Pamphlets and Journals, published within the last twenty Years. From which she had attained a very competent Skill in Politics, and could discourse very learnedly on the Affairs of *Europe*. She was moreover excellently well skilled in the Doctrine of Amour, and knew better than any body who and who were together: A Knowledge which she the more easily attained, as her Pursuit of it was never diverted by any Affairs of her own; for either she had no Inclinations, or they had never been sollicited; which last is indeed very probable: For her masculine Person, which was near six Foot high, added to her Manner and Learning, possibly prevented the other Sex from regarding her, notwithstanding her Petticoats, in the Light

---

[1] *Histoire d'Angleterre* (1723–5) by the French Huguenot, Paul de Rapin de Thoyras (1661–1725), who came to England in 1688 with William of Orange. Nicholas Tindal translated the work into English (1726–31) and continued it to include the period from the Revolution to the accession of George II (1745–7). Written from the Whig point of view, Rapin's history came under attack from Tory writers who resented its representation of the Stuart kings: see, for example, Thomas Salmon, *The History of Great Britain and Ireland . . . With a Preface, wherein the Partiality of Mons. Rapin, and some other Republican Historians, is Demonstrated* (2nd ed., 1725); anon., *A Vindication of the Royal Family of the Stuarts, from the Aspersions Cast on them by Monsieur Rapin, Mr. Oldmixon, and Others* (1734); and Thomas Carte, *A Defence of English History against the Misrepresentations of M. Rapin de Thoyras* (1734). Though in *Joseph Andrews* (1742; III. i) Fielding ridiculed Rapin's work along with other partisan histories, in *A Charge Delivered to the Grand Jury* (1749) he referred to it approvingly. See also *The Champion* (13 September 1740) and *The Covent-Garden Journal* (28 October 1752).

[2] *The Roman History* (vols. i–ii, 1695–8) by Laurence Echard (*c.* 1670–1730). This work was continued by other hands and went through numerous editions. Among serious readers, however, it was considered a most imperfect performance: in the Preface to his own Roman history (1738) Fielding's friend Nathaniel Hooke (see below, p. 794, n. 2) observed that Echard's work, 'though very useful for school-boys, has been thought by persons of riper age and more curiosity, too dry, too brief and unsatisfactory' (i. A3ᵛ); and Goldsmith was even more severe (*The Roman History* [1769], I. iii). In *A Journey from This World to the Next* (1743; I. ix) Fielding has Livy himself express his contempt for Echard's work, and later in *Tom Jones* (see below, p. 421) Echard's second volume turns up in the library of Partridge, not a very reliable guide in scholarly matters.

[3] A formula often used in the titles of French works: e.g. C. Perrault, *Mémoires pour servir à l'histoire naturelle des animaux* (1671); W. Theylis, *Mémoires pour servir à l'histoire de Charles XII., roi de Suède* (1722); G. de Lamberty, *Mémoires pour servir à l'histoire du XVIIIᵉ siècle* (2nd ed., 1731); etc. In *An Attempt towards a Natural History of the Hanover Rat* (1744) Fielding facetiously alludes to one such work, *Mémoires pour servir à l'histoire des insectes* by René A. F. de Réaumur (6 vols., Paris, 1734–42); he also probably knew *Mémoires pour servir à l'histoire d'un genre de polypes* (Leyden, 1744) by A. Trembley, the author and the subject ridiculed in *Some Papers Proper to be Read before the Royal Society* (1743).

of a Woman. However, as she had considered the Matter scienti-
fically, she perfectly well knew, though she had never practised
them, all the Arts which fine Ladies use when they desire to
give Encouragement, or to conceal Liking, with all the long
Appendage of Smiles, Ogles, Glances, &c. as they are at present
practised in the Beau-monde. To sum the whole, no Species of
Disguise or Affectation had escaped her Notice; but as to the
plain simple Workings of honest Nature, as she had never seen
any such, she could know but little of them.

By means of this wonderful Sagacity, Mrs. *Western* had now,
as she thought, made a Discovery of something in the Mind of
Sophia. The first Hint of this she took from the Behaviour of the
young Lady in the Field of Battle; and the Suspicion which she
then conceived, was greatly corroborated by some Observations
which she had made that Evening, and the next Morning. However, being greatly cautious to avoid being found in a Mistake,
she carried the Secret a whole Fortnight in her Bosom, giving
only some oblique Hints, by Simperings, Winks, Nods, and now
and then dropping an obscure Word, which indeed sufficiently
alarmed *Sophia*, but did not at all affect her Brother.

Being at length, however, thoroughly satisfied of the Truth of
her Observation, she took an Opportunity, one Morning, when
she was alone with her Brother, to interrupt one of his Whistles
in the following Manner.

'Pray, Brother, have you not observed something very extraordinary in my Niece lately?' 'No, not I,' answered *Western*;
'Is any thing the Matter with the Girl?' 'I think there is,' replies
she, 'and something of much Consequence too.' 'Why she doth
not complain of any Thing,' cries *Western*, 'and she hath had the
Small Pox.' 'Brother,' returned she, 'Girls are liable to other
Distempers besides the Small Pox, and sometimes possibly to
much worse.' Here *Western* interrupted her with much Earnestness, and begged her, if any thing ailed his Daughter, to acquaint
him immediately, adding, 'she knew he loved her more than his
own Soul, and that he would send to the World's End for the
best Physician to her.' 'Nay, nay,' answered she, smiling, 'the
Distemper is not so terrible; but I believe, Brother, you are convinced I know the World, and I promise you I was never more
deceived in my Life, if my Niece be not most desperately in
Love.' 'How! in Love,' cries *Western*, in a Passion, 'in Love

without acquainting me! I'll disinherit her, I'll turn her out of
Doors, stark naked, without a Farthing. Is all my Kindness vor
'ur, and vondness o'ur come to this, to fall in Love without asking me Leave!' 'But you will not,' answered Mrs. *Western*, 'turn
this Daughter, whom you love better than your own Soul, out of
Doors, before you know whether you shall approve her Choice.
Suppose she should have fixed on the very Person whom you
yourself would wish, I hope you would not be angry then.'
'No, no,' cries *Western*, 'that would make a Difference. If she
marries the Man I would ha' her, she may love whom she pleases,
I shan't trouble my Head about that.' 'That is spoken,' answered
the Sister, 'like a sensible Man, but I believe the very Person
she hath chosen, would be the very Person you would chuse for
her. I will disclaim all Knowledge of the World if it is not so;
and I believe, Brother, you will allow I have some.' 'Why lookee,
Sister,' said *Western*, 'I do believe you have as much as any
Woman; and to be sure those are Women's Matters. You know
I don't love to hear you talk about Politics, they belong to us,
and Petticoats should not meddle: But come, Who is the Man?'
'Marry!' said she, 'you may find him out yourself, if you please.
You who are so great a Politician can be at no great Loss. The
Judgment which can penetrate into the Cabinets of Princes, and
discover the secret Springs which move the great State Wheels
in all the political Machines of *Europe*, must surely, with very little
Difficulty find out what passes in the rude uninformed Mind of a
Girl.' 'Sister,' cries the Squire, 'I have often warned you not to
talk the Court Gibberish to me. I tell you, I don't understand
the Lingo; but I can read a Journal, or the *London Evening-
Post*.[1] Perhaps indeed, there may be now and tan a Verse which
I can't make much of, because half the Letters are left out;[2] yet

---

[1] Founded in 1727, *The London Evening-Post* was one of the principal Opposition organs
of the period; from 1737 it had been under the editorship of John Meres (1698–1761),
printer and journalist of barely concealed Jacobite tendencies. Not surprisingly, therefore,
the paper became a prime target for Fielding's satire in *The Jacobite's Journal*, where it is
called 'the worst News-Paper that I believe was ever published': 'To spread Libels three
Times a Week over the whole Island, representing the Ministry as a Set of Persons who are
Enemies to the Public, and who are engaged in a Conspiracy to betray the Interest of their
Country; and, indeed, their Country itself, into the Hands of its Enemies, must produce, in
Time, very mischievous Consequences' (24 September 1748).

[2] Political journalists, and other authors who wished to escape prosecution for libel,
customarily deleted the vowels when printing the names of their victims. In *The Jacobite's
Journal* (5 December 1747) Fielding called this practice 'emvowelling' and he parodied

I know very well what is meant by that, and that our Affairs don't go so well as they should do, because of Bribery and Corruption.' 'I pity your Country Ignorance from my Heart,' cries the Lady. 'Do you?' answered *Western*, 'and I pity your Town Learning, I had rather be any Thing than a Courtier, and a Presbyterian, and a *Hannoverian* too, as some People, I believe, are.' 'If you mean me,' answered she, 'you know I am a Woman, Brother; and it signifies nothing what I am. Besides———' 'I do know you are a Woman,' cries the Squire, 'and it's well for thee, that art one; if hadst been a Man, I promise thee I had lent thee a *Flick* long ago.' 'Ay there,' said she, 'in that *Flick* lies all your fancied Superiority. Your Bodies, and not your Brains, are stronger than ours. Believe me, it is well for you that you are able to beat us, or such is the Superiority of our Understanding, we should make all of you what the brave, and wise, and witty, and polite are already,—our Slaves.' 'I am glad I know your Mind,' answered the Squire, 'but we'll talk more of this Matter another Time. At present, do tell me what Man is it you mean about my Daughter.' 'Hold a Moment,' said she, 'while I digest that sovereign Contempt I have for your Sex; or else I ought to be angry too with you. There— I have made a Shift to gulp it down. And now, good politic Sir, what think you of Mr. *Blifil*? Did she not faint away on seeing him lie breathless on the Ground? Did she not, after he was recovered, turn pale again the Moment we came up to that Part of the Field where he stood? And pray what else should be the Occasion of all her Melancholy that Night at Supper, the next Morning, and indeed ever since?' ''Fore *George*!' cries the Squire, 'now you mind me on't, I remember it all. It is certainly so, and I am glad on't with all my Heart. I knew *Sophy* was a good Girl, and would not fall in Love to make me angry. I was never more rejoiced in my Life: For nothing can lie so handy together as our two Estates. I had this

the absurd lengths to which Meres had carried it in *The London Evening-Post*: 'In this Dress [i.e. the tartan of the Jacobites] I intend to abuse the ✳ ✳ ✳, and the ✳ ✳ ✳, and the ✳ ✳ ✳. I intend to lash not only the M——stry, but EVERY MAN who *hath* any P—ce or P—ns—n from the G–v–rnm–nt, or who is *intrusted* with *any Degree of Power* or *Trust* under it, let his R–nk be never so *high*, his F–rt–n– never so *great*, or his Ch–r–ct–r never so *good*. For this Purpose I have provided myself with a vast Quantity of *Italian* Letter, and Astericks of all Sorts: And as for all the Words which I *embowel*, or rather *emvowel*, I will never so mangle them, but they shall be all as well known as if they retained every Vowel in them. This I promise my Readers, that when I have any Meaning, they shall understand it.' (See also the *Journal* for 11 June, 27 August 1748.)

Matter in my Head some Time ago; for certainly the two Estates are in a Manner joined together in Matrimony already, and it would be a thousand Pities to part them. It is true indeed, there be larger Estates in the Kingdom, but not in this County, and I had rather bate something, than marry my Daughter among Strangers and Foreigners. Besides most o' zuch great Estates be in the Hands of Lords, and I heate the very Name of *themmun*. Well but, Sister, what would you advise me to do: For I tell you Women know these Matters better than we do?' 'O, your humble Servant, Sir,' answered the Lady, 'we are obliged to you for allowing us a Capacity in any Thing. Since you are pleased then, most politic Sir, to ask my Advice, I think you may propose the Match to *Allworthy* yourself. There is no Indecorum in the Proposal's coming from the Parent of either Side. King *Alcinous*, in Mr. *Pope's* Odyssey,[1] offers his Daughter to *Ulysses*. I need not caution so politic a Person not to say that your Daughter is in Love; that would indeed be against all Rules.' 'Well,' said the Squire, 'I will propose it; but I shall certainly, lend un a *Flick*, if he should refuse me.' 'Fear not,' cries Mrs. *Western*, 'the Match is too advantageous to be refused.' 'I don't know that,' answered the Squire, '*Allworthy* is a queer B—ch, and Money hath no Effect o'un.' 'Brother,' said the Lady, 'your Politics astonish me. Are you really to be imposed on by Professions? Do you think Mr. *Allworthy* hath more Contempt for Money than other Men, because he professes more. Such Credulity would better become one of us weak Women, than that wise Sex which Heaven hath formed for Politicians. Indeed, Brother, you would make a fine Plenipo to negotiate with the *French*. They would soon persuade you, that they take Towns out of mere defensive Principles.' 'Sister,' answered the Squire, with much Scorn, 'Let your Friends at Court answer for the Towns taken; as you are a Woman, I shall lay no Blame upon you: For I suppose they are wiser than to trust Women with Secrets.' He accompanied this with so sarcastical a Laugh, that Mrs. *Western* could bear no longer. She had been all this Time fretted in a tender Part (for she was indeed very deeply skilled in these Matters, and very violent in them) and therefore burst forth in a Rage, declared her Brother to be both a Clown and a Blockhead, and that she would stay no longer in his House.

[1] See Pope's *Odyssey* (1725–6), vii. 395–402.

The Squire, tho', perhaps, he had never read *Machiavel*,[1] was, however, in many Points, a perfect Politician. He strongly held all those wise Tenets, which are so well inculcated in that Politico-Peripatetic School of *Exchange-Alley*.[2] He knew the just Value and only Use of Money, *viz.* to lay it up. He was likewise well skilled in the exact Value of Reversions,[3] Expectations, *&c.* and had often considered the Amount of his Sister's Fortune, and the Chance which he or his Posterity had of inheriting it. This he was infinitely too wise to sacrifice to a trifling Resentment. When he found, therefore, he had carried Matters too far, he began to think of reconciling them; which was no very difficult Task, as the Lady had great Affection for her Brother, and still greater for her Niece; and tho' too susceptible of an Affront offered to her Skill in Politics, on which she much valued herself, was a Woman of a very extraordinary good and sweet Disposition.

Having first, therefore, laid violent Hands on the Horses, for whose Escape from the Stable no Place but the Window was left open; he next applied himself to his Sister, softened and soothed her, by unsaying all he had said, and by Assertions directly contrary to those which had incensed her. Lastly, he summoned the Eloquence of *Sophia* to his Assistance, who, besides a most graceful and winning Address, had the Advantage of being heard with great Favour and Partiality by her Aunt.

The Result of the whole was a kind Smile from Mrs. *Western*, who said, 'Brother, you are absolutely a perfect *Croat*;[4] but as those have their Use in the Army of the Empress Queen, so you likewise have some good in you. I will therefore once more sign a Treaty of Peace with you, and see that you do not infringe it on your Side; at least, as you are so excellent a Politician, I may expect you will keep your Leagues like the *French*,[5] till your Interest calls upon you to break them.'

[1] Niccolo di Bernardo dei Machiavelli (1469–1527), Florentine statesman and author of *Il Principe* (1513), the work which earned him his reputation as the master of unscrupulous power politics.

[2] A play on the so-called Peripatetic school of philosophy founded by Aristotle at the Lyceum. The coffee-houses in Exchange Alley, near the Royal Exchange, were a favourite resort of bankers, merchants, stock-jobbers, and speculators of all sorts.

[3] See below, p. 748, n. 1; also above, p. 109.10.

[4] In October 1740 Maria Theresa (1717–80) had become Queen of Hungary and ruler of the Austrian empire. Irregular Croatian troops in her army harassed Frederick of Prussia when he invaded Bohemia in 1744 and forced him to withdraw.

[5] Among their other grievances against France, Englishmen accused her of 'breaking the

CHAPTER III

Containing two Defiances to the Critics.

THE Squire having settled Matters with his Sister, as we have seen in the last Chapter, was so greatly impatient to communicate the Proposal to *Allworthy*, that Mrs. *Western* had the utmost Difficulty to prevent him from visiting that Gentleman in his Sickness, for this Purpose.

Mr. *Allworthy* had been engaged to dine with Mr. *Western* at the Time when he was taken ill. He was, therefore, no sooner discharged out of the Custody of Physic, but he thought (as was usual with him on all Occasions, both the highest and the lowest) of fulfilling his Engagement.

In the Interval between the Time of the Dialogue in the last Chapter, and this Day of public Entertainment, *Sophia* had, from certain obscure Hints thrown out by her Aunt, collected some Apprehension that the sagacious Lady suspected her Passion for *Jones*. She now resolved to take this Opportunity of wiping out all such Suspicion, and for that Purpose to put an entire Constraint on her Behaviour.

First, she endeavoured to conceal a throbbing melancholy Heart with the utmost Sprightliness in her Countenance, and the highest Gayety in her Manner. Secondly, she addressed her whole Discourse to Mr. *Blifil*, and took not the least Notice of poor *Jones* the whole Day.

The Squire was so delighted with this Conduct of his Daughter, that he scarce eat any Dinner, and spent almost his whole Time in watching Opportunities of conveying Signs of his Approbation by Winks and Nods to his Sister; who was not at first altogether so pleased with what she saw as was her Brother.

Faith of All the Treaties she had made with All the Powers which she is now at War with' (*The General Advertiser*, 30 August 1746). Meant as a warning to the Allied ministers gathering at Breda for peace talks, a poem entitled 'King William's Advice' was published in *The General Advertiser* for 5 December 1746 to elaborate the point:

> As Spiders Nets and Cobwebs weave
> To catch a Prize and Flies deceive,
> So *Frenchmen* fine-spun Treaties make
> To hamper Dupes, then Bargains break—

In recent memory, the writer recalls, the French '*Proteus*' had violated the provisions of the Treaty of Utrecht and the Pragmatic Sanction.

In short, *Sophia* so greatly overacted her Part, that her Aunt was at first staggered, and began to suspect some Affectation in her Niece; but as she was herself a Woman of Great Art, so she soon attributed this to extreme Art in *Sophia*. She remembered the many Hints she had given her Niece concerning her being in Love, and imagined the young Lady had taken this Way to rally her out of her Opinion, by an overacted Civility; a Notion that was greatly corroborated by the excessive Gaiety with which the whole was accompanied. We cannot here avoid remarking that this Conjecture would have been better founded, had *Sophia* lived ten Years in the Air of *Grosvenor-square*, where young Ladies do learn a wonderful Knack of rallying and playing with that Passion, which is a mighty serious Thing in Woods and Groves a hundred Miles distant from *London*.

To say the Truth, in discovering the Deceit of others, it matters much that our own Art be wound up, if I may use the Expression, in the same Key with theirs: For very artful Men sometimes miscarry by fancying others wiser, or in other Words, greater Knaves than they really are. As this Observation is pretty deep, I will illustrate it by the following short Story. Three Countrymen were pursuing a *Wiltshire* Thief through *Brentford*. The simplest of them seeing the *Wiltshire House* written under a Sign, advised his Companions to enter it, for there most probably they would find their Countryman. The second, who was wiser, laughed at this Simplicity; but the third, who was wiser still, answered, 'Let us go in, however, for he may think we should not suspect him of going amongst his own Countrymen.' They accordingly went in and searched the House, and by that Means missed overtaking the Thief, who was at that Time, but a little ways before them; and who, as they all knew, but had never once reflected, could not read.

The Reader will pardon a Digression in which so invaluable a Secret is communicated, since every Gamester will agree how necessary it is to know exactly the Play of another, in order to countermine him. This will, moreover, afford a Reason why the wiser Man, as is often seen, is the Bubble of the weaker, and why many simple and innocent Characters are so generally misunderstood and misrepresented; but what is most material, this will account for the Deceit which *Sophia* put on her politic Aunt.

Dinner being ended, and the Company retired into the Garden,

Mr. *Western*, who was thoroughly convinced of the Certainty of what his Sister had told him, took Mr. *Allworthy* aside, and very bluntly proposed a Match between *Sophia* and young Mr. *Blifil*.

Mr. *Allworthy* was not one of those Men, whose Hearts flutter at any unexpected and sudden Tidings of worldly Profit. His Mind was, indeed, tempered with that Philosophy which becomes a Man and a Christian. He affected no absolute Superiority to all Pleasure and Pain, to all Joy and Grief; but was not at the same time to be discomposed and ruffled by every accidental Blast; by every Smile or Frown of Fortune. He received, therefore, Mr. *Western's* Proposal without any visible Emotion, or without any Alteration of Countenance. He said, the Alliance was such as he sincerely wished; then launched forth into a very just Encomium on the young Lady's Merit; acknowledged the Offer to be advantageous in Point of Fortune; and after thanking Mr. *Western* for the good Opinion he had profess'd of his Nephew, concluded, that if the young People liked each other, he should be very desirous to complete the Affair.

Western was a little disappointed at Mr. *Allworthy's* Answer; which was not so warm as he expected. He treated the Doubt whether the young People might like one another with great Contempt; saying, 'That Parents were the best Judges of proper Matches for their Children; that, for his Part, he should insist on the most resigned Obedience from his Daughter; and if any young Fellow could refuse such a Bedfellow, he was his humble Servant, and hoped there was no Harm done.'

Allworthy endeavoured to soften this Resentment by many Elogiums on *Sophia*; declaring, he had no doubt but that Mr. *Blifil* would very gladly receive the Offer; but all was ineffectual, he could obtain no other Answer from the Squire but—'I say no more—I humbly hope there's no Harm done—that's all.' Which Words he repeated, at least, a hundred Times before they parted.

Allworthy was too well acquainted with his Neighbour to be offended at this Behaviour; and tho' he was so averse to the Rigour which some Parents exercise on their Children in the Article of Marriage, that he had resolved never to force his Nephew's Inclinations, he was nevertheless much pleased with the Prospect of this Union: For the whole Country resounded the Praises of *Sophia*, and he had himself greatly admired the uncommon Endowments of both her Mind and Person. To which, I believe we may add, the Consideration of her vast Fortune, which, tho' he was too sober to be intoxicated with it, he was too sensible to despise.

And here, in Defiance of all the barking Critics in the World, I must and will introduce a Digression concerning true Wisdom,[1] of which Mr. *Allworthy* was in Reality as great a Pattern as he was of Goodness.

True Wisdom then, notwithstanding all which Mr. *Hogarth's* poor Poet[2] may have writ against Riches, and in Spite of all which any rich, well-fed Divine may have preached against Pleasure, consists not in the Contempt of either of these. A Man may have as much Wisdom in the Possession of an affluent Fortune, as any Beggar in the Streets; or may enjoy a handsome Wife or a hearty Friend, and still remain as wise as any sour Popish Recluse, who buries all his social Faculties, and starves his Belly while he well lashes his Back.

To say Truth, the wisest Man is the likeliest to possess all worldly Blessings in an eminent Degree: For as that Moderation which Wisdom prescribes is the surest Way to useful Wealth; so can it alone qualify us to taste many Pleasures. The wise Man gratifies every Appetite and every Passion, while the Fool sacrifices all the rest to pall and satiate one.

---

[1] In developing the argument that true wisdom comprehends the temperate enjoyment of both riches and pleasure, Fielding owes most to Seneca, *De Vita Beata*, esp. xxi. 3 ff. With the remarks to follow, compare also *The Champion* (24 January 1739/40), where Fielding had insisted that 'Virtue is not that coy, nor that cruel Mistress she is represented. Nor is she of that morose and rigid Nature, which some mistake her to be':

'Virtue forbids not the satisfying our Appetites, Virtue forbids us only to glut and destroy them. The temperate Man tastes and relishes Pleasure in a Degree infinitely superior to that of the voluptuous. . . . The Sot soon ceases to enjoy his Wine, the Glutton his Dainties, and the Libertine his Women. The temperate Man enjoys all in the highest Degree, and indeed with the greatest Variety: For human nature will not suffice for an Excess in every Passion, and wherever one runs away with a Man, we may generally observe him sacrificing all the rest to the Enjoyment of that alone. The virtuous and temperate Man only hath Inclination, hath Strength; and . . . hath Opportunity to enjoy all his Passions.

'Poverty is so far from being enjoined us by Virtue, that Parsimony, which she expresly prescribes, is a certain Way to Wealth.'

[2] See Hogarth's *The Distressed Poet*, in the revised version of which (1740) the poet, in the midst of abject poverty, is shown composing a work entitled, 'Riches: a Poem'. Fielding was particularly amused by this piece of irony, to which he also refers in a footnote to *The Vernoniad* (1741) and in *The Jacobite's Journal* (9 July 1748, under 'Domestic News'). For other refrences to Hogarth, see above, p. 66, n. 1.

It may be objected, that very wise Men have been notoriously avaricious. I answer, not wise in that Instance. It may likewise be said, that the wisest Men have been in their Youth, immoderately fond of Pleasure. I answer, they were not wise then.

Wisdom, in short, whose Lessons have been represented as so hard to learn by those who never were at her School, only teaches us to extend a simple Maxim universally known and followed even in the lowest Life, a little farther than that Life carries it. And this is not to buy at too dear a Price.

Now, whoever takes this Maxim abroad with him into the grand Market of the World, and constantly applies it to Honours, to Riches, to Pleasures, and to every other Commodity which that Market affords, is, I will venture to affirm, a wise Man; and must be so acknowledged in the worldly Sense of the Word: For he makes the best of Bargains, since in Reality he purchases every Thing at the Price only of a little Trouble, and carries home all the good Things I have mentioned, while he keeps his Health, his Innocence, and his Reputation, the common Prices which are paid for them by others, entire and to himself.

From this Moderation, likewise, he learns two other Lessons, which complete his Character. First, never to be intoxicated when he hath made the best Bargain, nor dejected when the Market is empty, or when its Commodities are too dear for his Purchase.

But I must remember on what Subject I am writing, and not trespass too far on the Patience of a good-natured Critic. Here therefore I put an End to the Chapter.

CHAPTER IV

Containing sundry curious Matters.

AS soon as Mr. *Allworthy* returned home, he took Mr. *Blifil* apart, and after some Preface, communicated to him the Proposal which had been made by Mr. *Western*, and, at the same Time, informed him how agreeable this Match would be to himself.

The Charms of *Sophia* had not made the least Impression on *Blifil*; not that his Heart was pre-engaged; neither was he totally insensible of Beauty, or had any Aversion to Women; but his Appetites were, by Nature, so moderate, that he was able by Philosophy or by Study, or by some other Method, easily to subdue them; and as to that Passion which we have treated of in the first Chapter of this Book, he had not the least Tincture of it in his whole Composition.

But tho' he was so entirely free from that mixed Passion, of which we there treated, and of which the Virtues and Beauty of *Sophia* formed so notable an Object; yet was he altogether as well furnished with some other Passions, that promised themselves very full Gratification in the young Lady's Fortune. Such were Avarice and Ambition, which divided the Dominion of his Mind between them.[1] He had more than once considered the Possession of this Fortune as a very desirable Thing, and had entertained some distant Views concerning it: But his own Youth and that of the young Lady, and indeed principally a Reflection that Mr. *Western* might marry again, and have more Children, had restrained him from too hasty or eager a Pursuit.

This last and most material Objection was now in great Measure removed, as the Proposal came from Mr. *Western* himself. *Blifil*, therefore, after a very short Hesitation, answered Mr. *Allworthy*, that Matrimony was a Subject on which he had not yet thought: But that he was so sensible of his friendly and fatherly Care, that he should in all Things submit himself to his Pleasure.

Allworthy was naturally a Man of Spirit, and his present Gravity arose from true Wisdom and Philosophy, not from any original Phlegm in his Disposition: For he had possessed much Fire in his Youth, and had married a beautiful Woman for Love. He was not, therefore, greatly pleased with this cold Answer of his Nephew; nor could he help launching forth into the Praises of *Sophia*, and expressing some Wonder that the Heart of a young Man could be impregnable to the force of such Charms, unless it was guarded by some prior Affection.

Blifil assured him he had no such Guard; and then proceeded

---

[1] In the humanist tradition, avarice and ambition were regarded as the summarizing vices of human nature, complementary passions exemplifying negative and positive excess: e.g. Aristotle, *Politics*, II. vi. 19, and Horace, *Satires*, I. iv. 25–6. Discussing worldly wisdom in *The Covent-Garden Journal* (4 November 1752), Fielding quotes the verses from Horace and declares that 'Avarice and Ambition' are 'the two great Characteristics of this Wisdom'.

to discourse so wisely and religiously on Love and Marriage, that he would have stopt the Mouth of a Parent much less devoutly inclined than was his Uncle. In the End, the good Man was satisfied, that his Nephew, far from having any Objections to *Sophia*, had that Esteem for her, which in sober and virtuous Minds is the sure Foundation of Friendship and Love. And as he doubted not but the Lover would, in a little Time, become altogether as agreeable to his Mistress, he foresaw great Happiness arising to all Parties by so proper and desirable a Union. With Mr. *Blifil's* Consent, therefore, he wrote the next Morning to Mr. *Western*, acquainting him that his Nephew had very thankfully and gladly received the Proposal, and would be ready to wait on the young Lady, whenever she should be pleased to accept his Visit.

Western was much pleased with this Letter, and immediately returned an Answer; in which, without having mentioned a Word to his Daughter, he appointed that very Afternoon for opening the Scene of Courtship.

As soon as he had dispatched this Messenger, he went in Quest of his Sister, whom he found reading and expounding the Gazette[1] to Parson *Supple*. To this Exposition he was obliged to attend near a Quarter of an Hour, tho' with great Violence to his natural Impetuosity, before he was suffered to speak. At length, however, he found an Opportunity of acquainting the Lady, that he had Business of great Consequence to impart to her; to which she answered, 'Brother, I am entirely at your Service. Things look so well in the North[2] that I was never in a better Humour.'

---

[1] Established in 1666, *The London Gazette* was the official government newspaper, published three times a week with extraordinary issues for important news. From 1741 until his death the editor was Edward Weston (1703–70). Despite the paper's official connection with the Pelham administration, which he himself supported, Fielding in *The True Patriot* repeatedly denounced the editors of the *Gazette* for incompetency and for the selfish exploitation, during a time of national crisis, of the office entrusted to them. The reasons for his disapproval are set forth by a correspondent to *The True Patriot* (24 December 1745); the letter, though asserting the innocence of the Administration itself, roundly condemns the editors of the *Gazette* for their corrupt practices: 'A Paper said to be *published by Authority* has of late been so *prolix*, so *unintelligible*, so *excessive dear* [price 2*d.*], the *Publication* of it so *unreasonably retarded*, and in short been so much made a JOB of, as the Phrase is, that it gives just Offence to every honest Man'. See also *The True Patriot* (7, 21 January, 28 January–4 February, 15–22 April 1746).

[2] In the political jargon of the age, 'the North' signified Sweden, Denmark, Prussia, and Russia. In *The True Patriot* (18–25 March 1746, under 'Foreign History') Fielding was

The Parson then withdrawing, *Western* acquainted her with all which had passed, and desired her to communicate the Affair to *Sophia*, which she readily and chearfully undertook; tho' perhaps her Brother was a little obliged to that agreeable Northern Aspect which had so delighted her, that he heard no Comment on his Proceedings: for they were certainly somewhat too hasty and violent.

CHAPTER V

In which is related what passed between Sophia *and her Aunt.*

SOPHIA was in her Chamber reading, when her Aunt came in. The Moment she saw Mrs. *Western*, she shut the Book with so much Eagerness, that the good Lady could not forbear asking her, What Book that was which she seemed so much afraid of shewing. 'Upon my Word, Madam,' answered *Sophia*, 'it is a Book which I am neither ashamed nor afraid to own I have read. It is the Production of a young Lady of Fashion,[1] whose good Understanding, I think, doth Honour to her Sex, and whose good Heart is an Honour to Human Nature.' Mrs. *Western* then took up the Book, and immediately after threw it down, saying—'Yes, the Author is of a very good Family; but she is not much among People one knows. I have never read it; for the best Judges say, there is not much in it.' 'I dare not, Madam, set up my own Opinion,' says *Sophia*, 'against the best Judges, but there appears to me a great deal of human Nature in it; and in many Parts, so much true Tenderness and Delicacy, that it hath cost me many a Tear.' 'Ay, and do you love to cry then?' says the Aunt. 'I love a tender Sensation,' answered the Niece, 'and would pay the Price of a Tear for it at any Time.' 'Well, but

encouraged by the fact that internal disputes among these countries prevented them from combining their forces, and thereby upsetting the balance of power.

[1] The book is very probably *The Adventures of David Simple* (1744) by Fielding's sister Sarah (1710–68). In the Preface he contributed to the second edition (July 1744) Fielding remarked that the novel had been unjustly criticized by those who thereby only revealed their own 'Folly, Meanness and Malevolence'. Like Sophia he praised the work for 'a vast Penetration into human Nature' and for the 'Sentiments', which 'are in general extremely delicate'. And like Sophia he further observed that 'a short Communication with her own Heart, will leave the Author of this Book very little to seek abroad of all the Good which is to be found in Human Nature'.

shew me,' said the Aunt, 'what was you reading when I came in; there was something very tender in that, I believe, and very loving too. You blush, my dear *Sophia*. Ah! Child, you should read Books, which would teach you a little Hypocrisy, which would instruct you how to hide your Thoughts a little better.' 'I hope, Madam,' answered *Sophia*, 'I have no Thoughts which I ought to be ashamed of discovering.' 'Ashamed! no,' cries the Aunt, 'I don't think you have any Thoughts which you ought to be ashamed of, and yet, Child, you blushed just now when I mentioned the Word *Loving*. Dear *Sophy*, be assured you have not one Thought which I am not well acquainted with; as well, Child, as the *French* are with our Motions, long before we put them in Execution. Did you think, Child, because you have been able to impose upon your Father, that you could impose upon me? Do you imagine I did not know the Reason of your over-acting all that Friendship for Mr. *Blifil* yesterday? I have seen a little too much of the World, to be so deceived. Nay, nay, do not blush again. I tell you it is a Passion you need not be ashamed of. —It is a Passion I myself approve, and have already brought your Father into the Approbation of it. Indeed, I solely consider your Inclination; for I would always have that gratified, if possible, though one may sacrifice higher Prospects. Come, I have News which will delight your very Soul. Make me your Confident, and I will undertake you shall be happy to the very Extent of your Wishes.' 'La, Madam,' says *Sophia*, looking more foolishly than ever she did in her Life, 'I know not what to say—— Why, Madam, should you suspect?'—'Nay, no Dishonesty,' returned Mrs. *Western*. 'Consider, you are speaking to one of your own Sex, to an Aunt, and I hope you are convinced you speak to a Friend. Consider, you are only revealing to me what I know already, and what I plainly saw yesterday through that most artful of all Disguises, which you had put on, and which must have deceived any one who had not perfectly known the World. Lastly, consider it is a Passion which I highly approve.' 'La, Madam,' says *Sophia*, 'you come upon one so unawares, and on a sudden. To be sure, Madam, I am not blind—and certainly, if it be a Fault to see all human Perfections assembled together—— But is it possible my Father and you, Madam, can see with my Eyes?' 'I tell you,' answered the Aunt, 'we do entirely approve; and this very Afternoon your Father hath appointed for you to receive your Lover.' 'My Father, this Afternoon!' cries *Sophia*, with the Blood starting from her Face.'—'Yes, Child,' said the Aunt, 'this Afternoon. You know the Impetuosity of my Brother's Temper. I acquainted him with the Passion which I first discovered in you that Evening when you fainted away in the Field. I saw it in your Fainting. I saw it immediately upon your Recovery. I saw it that Evening at Supper, and the next Morning at Breakfast: (you know, Child, I have seen the World). Well, I no sooner acquainted my Brother; but he immediately wanted to propose it to *Allworthy*. He proposed it Yesterday, *Allworthy* consented, (as to be sure he must with Joy) and this Afternoon, I tell you, you are to put on all your best Airs.' 'This Afternoon!' cries *Sophia*. 'Dear Aunt, you frighten me out of my Senses.' 'O, my Dear,' said the Aunt, 'you will soon come to yourself again; for he is a charming young Fellow, that's the Truth on't.' 'Nay, I will own,' says *Sophia*, 'I know none with such Perfections. So brave, and yet so gentle; so witty, yet so inoffensive; so humane, so civil, so genteel, so handsome! What signifies his being base born, when compared with such Qualifications as these?' 'Base born! what do you mean,' said the Aunt, 'Mr. *Blifil* base born!' *Sophia* turned instantly pale at this Name, and faintly repeated it. Upon which the Aunt cried, 'Mr. *Blifil*, ay Mr. *Blifil*, of whom else have we been talking?' 'Good Heavens,' answered *Sophia*, ready to sink, 'of Mr. *Jones*, I thought; I am sure I know no other who deserves——' 'I protest,' cries the Aunt, 'you frighten me in your Turn. Is it Mr. *Jones*, and not Mr. *Blifil*, who is the Object of your Affection?' 'Mr. *Blifil*!' repeated *Sophia*. 'Sure it is impossible you can be in earnest; if you are, I am the most miserable Woman alive.' Mrs. *Western* now stood a few Moments silent, while Sparks of fiery Rage flashed from her Eyes. At length, collecting all her Force of Voice, she thundered forth in the following articulate Sounds:

'And is it possible you can think of disgracing your Family by allying yourself to a Bastard? Can the Blood of the *Westerns* submit to such Contamination! If you have not Sense sufficient to restrain such monstrous Inclinations, I thought the Pride of our Family would have prevented you from giving the least Encouragement to so base an Affection; much less did I imagine you would ever have had the Assurance to own it to my Face.'

'Madam,' answered *Sophia*, trembling, 'what I have said you have extorted from me. I do not remember to have ever mentioned the Name of Mr. *Jones*, with Approbation, to any one before; nor should I now, had I not conceived he had had your Approbation. Whatever were my Thoughts of that poor unhappy young Man, I intended to have carried them with me to my Grave.— To that Grave where only now, I find, I am to seek Repose.'— Here she sunk down in her Chair, drowned in her Tears, and, in all the moving Silence of unutterable Grief, presented a Spectacle which must have affected almost the hardest Heart.

All this tender Sorrow, however, raised no Compassion in her Aunt. On the contrary, she now fell into the most violent Rage.— 'And I would rather,' she cried, in a most vehement Voice, 'follow you to your Grave, than I would see you disgrace yourself and your Family by such a Match. O Heavens! could I have ever suspected that I should live to hear a Niece of mine declare a Passion for such a Fellow? You are the first—yes, Miss *Western*, you are the first of your Name who ever entertained so groveling a Thought. A Family so noted for the Prudence of its Women——' Here she run on a full Quarter of an Hour, till having exhausted her Breath rather than her Rage, she concluded with threatening to go immediately and acquaint her Brother.

Sophia then threw herself at her Feet, and laying hold of her Hands, begged her, with Tears, to conceal what she had drawn from her; urging the Violence of her Father's Temper, and protesting that no Inclinations of hers should ever prevail with her to do any thing which might offend him.

Mrs. *Western* stood a Moment looking at her, and then having recollected herself, said, 'that on one Consideration only she would keep the Secret from her Brother; and this was, that *Sophia* should promise to entertain Mr. *Blifil* that very Afternoon as her Lover, and to regard him as the Person who was to be her Husband.'

Poor *Sophia* was too much in her Aunt's Power to deny her any thing positively; she was obliged to promise that she would see Mr. *Blifil*, and be as civil to him as possible; but begged her Aunt that the Match might not be hurried on. She said, 'Mr. *Blifil* was by no means agreeable to her, and she hoped her Father would be prevailed on not to make her the most wretched of Women.'

Mrs. *Western* assured her, 'that the Match was entirely agreed upon, and that nothing could or should prevent it.' 'I must own,' said she, 'I looked on it as on a Matter of Indifference; nay, perhaps, had some Scruples about it before, which were actually got over by my thinking it highly agreeable to your own Inclinations; but now I regard it as the most eligible Thing in the World; nor shall there be, if I can prevent it, a Moment of Time lost on the Occasion.'

Sophia replied, 'Delay at least, Madam, I may expect from both your Goodness and my Father's. Surely you will give me Time to endeavour to get the better of so strong a Disinclination as I have at present to this Person.'

The Aunt answered, 'She knew too much of the World to be so deceived; that as she was sensible another Man had her Affections, she should persuade Mr. *Western* to hasten the Match as much as possible. It would be bad Politics indeed,' added she, 'to protract a Siege when the Enemy's Army is at Hand, and in Danger of relieving it. No, no, *Sophy*,' said she, 'as I am convinced you have a violent Passion, which you can never satisfy with Honour, I will do all I can to put your Honour out of the Care of your Family: For when you are married those Matters will belong only to the Consideration of your Husband. I hope, Child, you will always have Prudence enough to act as becomes you; but if you should not, Marriage hath saved many a Woman from Ruin.'

Sophia well understood what her Aunt meant; but did not think proper to make her an Answer. However, she took a Resolution to see Mr. *Blifil*, and to behave to him as civilly as she could: For on that Condition only she obtained a Promise from her Aunt to keep secret the Liking which her ill Fortune, rather than any Scheme of Mrs. *Western*, had unhappily drawn from her.

CHAPTER VI

Containing a Dialogue between Sophia *and Mrs.* Honour, *which may a little relieve those tender Affections which the foregoing Scene may have raised in the Mind of a good-natur'd Reader.*

MRS. *Western* having obtained that Promise from her Niece which we have seen in the last Chapter, withdrew, and presently after arrived Mrs. *Honour*. She was at Work in a neighbouring Apartment, and had been summoned to the Key-hole by some Vociferation in the preceding Dialogue, where she had continued during the remaining Part of it. At her Entry into the Room, she found *Sophia* standing motionless, with the Tears trickling from her Eyes. Upon which she immediately ordered a proper Quantity of Tears into her own Eyes, and then began, 'O Gemini, my dear Lady, what is the Matter?' 'Nothing,' cries *Sophia*. 'Nothing! O dear Madam,' answers Mrs. *Honour*, 'you must not tell me that, when your Ladyship is in this Taking, and when there hath been such a *Preamble* between your Lady-ship and Madam *Western*.' 'Don't teaze me,' cries *Sophia*, 'I tell you nothing is the Matter.—Good Heavens! Why was I born!'— 'Nay, Madam,' says Mrs. *Honour*, 'you shall never persuade me, that your La'ship can lament yourself so for nothing. To be sure, I am but a Servant; but to be sure I have been always faithful to your Ladyship, and to be sure I would serve your La'ship with my Life.' 'My dear *Honour*,' says *Sophia*, ''tis not in thy Power to be of any Service to me. I am irretrievably undone.' 'Heaven forbid,' answered the Waiting-woman; 'but if I can't be of any Service to you, pray tell me, Madam, it will be some Comfort to me to know; Pray, dear Ma'am, tell me what's the Matter.' 'My Father,' cries *Sophia*, 'is going to marry me to a Man I both despise and hate.' 'O, dear Ma'am,' answered the other, 'Who is this wicked Man? for to be sure he is very bad, or your La'ship would not despise him.' 'His Name is Poison to my Tongue,' replied *Sophia*, 'thou wilt know it too soon.' Indeed, to confess the Truth, she knew it already, and therefore was not very inquisitive as to that Point. She then proceeded thus: 'I don't pretend to give your La'ship Advice, *whereof* your La'ship knows much better than I can pretend to, being but a Servant; but, i-fackins! no Father in *England* should marry me against my Consent. And to be sure, the Squire is so good, that if he did but know your La'ship despises and hates the young Man, to be sure he would not desire you to marry him. And if your La'ship would but give me Leave to tell my Master so—— To be sure, it would be more properer to come from your own Mouth; but as your La'ship doth not care to foul your Tongue with his nasty Name.' 'You are mistaken, *Honour*,' says *Sophia*, 'my Father was determined before he ever thought fit to mention it to me.' 'More Shame for him,' cries *Honour*, 'you are to go to Bed to him, and not Master. And thof a Man may be a very proper Man, yet every Woman mayn't think him handsome alike. I am sure my Master would never act in this Manner of his own Head. I wish some People would trouble themselves only with what belongs to them; they would not, I believe, like to be served so, if it was their own Case: For tho' I am a Maid, I can easily believe as how all Men are not equally agreeable. And what signifies your La'ship having so great a Fortune, if you can't please yourself with the Man you think most handsomest? Well, I say nothing, but to be sure it is Pity some Folks had not been better born; nay, as for that Matter, I should not mind it my self: But then there is not so much Money, and what of that, your La'ship hath Money enough for both; and where can your La'ship bestow your Fortune better? For to be sure every one must allow, that he is the most handsomest, charmingest, finest, tallest, properest Man in the World.' 'What do you mean by running on in this Manner to me?' cries *Sophia*, with a very grave Countenance. 'Have I ever given any Encouragement for these Liberties?' 'Nay, Ma'am, I ask Pardon, I meant no Harm,' answered she, 'but to be sure the poor Gentleman hath run in my Head ever since I saw him this Morning.—To be sure, if your Ladyship had but seen him just now, you must have pitied him. Poor Gentleman! I wishes some Misfortune hath not happened to him: For he hath been walking about with his Arms a-cross, and looking so melancholy[1] all this Morning; I vow and protest it made me almost cry to see him.' 'To see whom?' says *Sophia*. 'Poor Mr. *Jones*,' answered *Honour*. 'See him! Why, where did you see him?' cries *Sophia*. 'By the Canal, Ma'am,' says *Honour*. 'There

---

[1] Walking about alone with his arms folded, Jones expresses his melancholy according to stylized Renaissance conventions depicting the 'Inamorato' or 'Malcontent'. The iconographic tradition appears in a panel representing the 'Inamorato' from the frontispiece of Burton's *Anatomy of Melancholy* (1621). On the stage, several of Shakespeare's love-sick heroes strike a similar attitude—Valentine, for instance, whose passion is therefore easily recognized by Speed (*Two Gentlemen of Verona*, II. i):

Val. Why, how know you that I am in love?

Speed. Marry, sir, by these special old marks; first, you have learned, like Sir Protheus, to wreath your arms like a malecontent—to walk alone like one that had the pestilence....

Cf. also *Love's Labour's Lost* (III. i), where Berowne describes Cupid as 'Regent of love-rimes, Lord of folded arms'. This conventional posture of the melancholy man is attributed to Ferdinand in *The Tempest* (I. ii) and to Brutus in *Julius Caesar* (II. i). Portia's description of Brutus' behaviour in his grief is especially close to Honour's representation of Jones: 'You . . . walk'd about, / Musing, and sighing, with your arms across . . . .'

he hath been walking all this Morning, and at last there he laid himself down; I believe he lies there still. To be sure, if it had not been for my Modesty, being a Maid as I am, I should have gone and spoke to him. Do, Ma'am, let me go and see, only for a Fancy, whether he is there still.' 'Pugh!' says *Sophia*, 'There! no, no, what should he do there? He is gone before this Time to be sure. Besides, why—what—why should you go to see?—Besides, I want you for something else. Go, fetch me my Hat and Gloves. I shall walk with my Aunt in the Grove before Dinner.' *Honour* did immediately as she was bid, and *Sophia* put her Hat on; when looking in the Glass, she fancied the Ribbon with which her Hat was tied, did not become her, and so sent her Maid back again for a Ribbon of a different Colour; and then giving Mrs. *Honour* repeated Charges not to leave her Work on any Account, as she said it was in violent Haste, and must be finished that very Day, she muttered something more about going to the Grove, and then sallied out the contrary Way, and walked as fast as her tender trembling Limbs could carry her, directly towards the Canal.

Jones had been there, as Mrs. *Honour* had told her: He had indeed spent two Hours there that Morning in melancholy Contemplation on his *Sophia*, and had gone out from the Garden at one Door, the Moment she entered it at another. So that those unlucky Minutes which had been spent in changing the Ribbons, had prevented the Lovers from Meeting at this Time. A most unfortunate Accident, from which my fair Readers will not fail to draw a very wholesome Lesson. And here I strictly forbid all Male Critics to intermeddle with a Circumstance, which I have recounted only for the Sake of the Ladies, and upon which they only are at Liberty to comment.

CHAPTER VII

A Picture of formal Courtship in Miniature, as it always ought to be drawn, and a Scene of a tenderer Kind, painted at full Length.

IT was well remarked by one, (and perhaps by more) that Misfortunes do not come single. This wise Maxim was now verified by *Sophia*, who was not only disappointed of seeing the

Man she loved; but had the Vexation of being obliged to dress herself out, in order to receive a Visit from the Man she hated.

That Afternoon, Mr. *Western*, for the first Time, acquainted his Daughter with his Intention; telling her, he knew very well that she had heard it before from her Aunt. *Sophia* looked very grave upon this, nor could she prevent a few Pearls from stealing into her Eyes. 'Come, come,' says *Western*, 'none of your Maidenish Airs; I know all; I assure you, Sister hath told me all.'

'Is it possible,' says *Sophia*, 'that my Aunt can have betrayed me already?' 'Ay, ay,' says *Western*, 'betrayed you! ay. Why, you betrayed yourself yesterday at Dinner. You shewed your Fancy very plainly, I think. But you young Girls never know what you would be at. So you cry because I am going to marry you to the Man you are in Love with! Your Mother, I remember, whimpered and whined just in the same Manner; but it was all over within twenty-four Hours after we were married: Mr. *Blifil* is a brisk young Man, and will soon put an End to your Squeamishness. Come, chear up, chear up, I expect un every Minute.'

Sophia was now convinced that her Aunt had behaved honourably to her; and she determined to go through that disagreeable Afternoon with as much Resolution as possible, and without giving the least Suspicion in the World to her Father.

Mr. *Blifil* soon arrived; and Mr. *Western* soon after withdrawing, left the young Couple together.

Here a long Silence of near a Quarter of an Hour ensued: For the Gentleman who was to begin the Conversation had all that unbecoming Modesty which consists in Bashfulness. He often attempted to speak, and as often suppressed his Words just at the very Point of Utterance. At last out they broke in a Torrent of far-fetched and high-strained Compliments, which were answered, on her Side, by downcast Looks, half Bows and civil Monosyllables. *Blifil* from his Inexperience in the Ways of Women, and from his Conceit of himself, took this Behaviour for a modest Assent to his Courtship; and when to shorten a Scene which she could no longer support, *Sophia* rose up and left the Room, he imputed that too, merely to Bashfulness, and comforted himself, that he should soon have enough of her Company.

He was indeed perfectly well satisfied with his Prospect of Success: For as to that entire and absolute Possession of the

Heart of his Mistress, which romantic Lovers require, the very
Idea of it never entered his Head. Her Fortune and her Person
were the sole Objects of his Wishes, of which he made no Doubt
soon to obtain the absolute Property; as Mr. *Western's* Mind was
so earnestly bent on the Match; and as he well knew the strict
Obedience which *Sophia* was always ready to pay to her Father's
Will, and the greater still which her Father would exact, if there
was Occasion. This Authority, therefore, together with the
Charms which he fancied in his own Person and Conversation,
could not fail, he thought, of succeeding with a young Lady,
whose Inclinations, were, he doubted not, entirely disengaged.

Of *Jones* he certainly had not even the least Jealousy; and I
have often thought it wonderful that he had not. Perhaps he
imagined the Character which *Jones* bore all over the Country,
(how justly let the Reader determine) of being one of the wildest
Fellows in *England*, might render him odious to a Lady of the
most exemplary Modesty. Perhaps his Suspicions might be
laid asleep by the Behaviour of *Sophia*, and of *Jones* himself,
when they were all in Company together. Lastly, and indeed
principally, he was well assured there was not another Self in
the Case. He fancied that he knew *Jones* to the Bottom, and had
in reality a great Contempt for his Understanding, for not being
more attached to his own Interest. He had no Apprehension that
Jones was in Love with *Sophia*; and as for any lucrative Motives,
he imagined they would sway very little with so silly a Fellow.
Blifil, moreover, thought the Affair of *Molly Seagrim* still went on,
and indeed believed it would end in Marriage: For *Jones* really
loved him from his Childhood, and had kept no Secret from him,
till his Behaviour on the Sickness of Mr. *Allworthy* had entirely
alienated his Heart; and it was by means of the Quarrel which
had ensued on this Occasion, and which was not yet reconciled,
that Mr. *Blifil* knew nothing of the Alteration which had happened in the Affection which *Jones* had formerly borne towards
Molly.

From these Reasons, therefore, Mr. *Blifil* saw no Bar to his
Success with *Sophia*. He concluded, her Behaviour was like that
of all other young Ladies on a first Visit from a Lover, and it had
indeed entirely answered his Expectations.

Mr. *Western* took Care to way-lay the Lover at his Exit from
his Mistress. He found him so elevated with his Success, so

enamoured with his Daughter, and so satisfied with her Reception of him, that the old Gentleman began to caper and dance about his Hall, and by many other antic Actions, to express the Extravagance of his Joy: For he had not the least Command over any of his Passions; and that which had at any Time the Ascendant in his Mind, hurried him to the wildest Excesses.

As soon as *Blifil* was departed, which was not till after many hearty Kisses and Embraces bestowed on him by *Western*, the good Squire went instantly in Quest of his Daughter, whom he no sooner found than he poured forth the most extravagant Raptures, bidding her chuse what Clothes and Jewels she pleased; and declaring that he had no other Use for Fortune but to make her happy. He then caressed her again and again with the utmost Profusion of Fondness, called her by the most endearing Names, and protested she was his only Joy on Earth.

Sophia perceiving her Father in this Fit of Affection, which she did not absolutely know the Reason of, (for Fits of Fondness were not unusual to him, tho' this was rather more violent than ordinary) thought she should never have a better Opportunity of disclosing herself than at present; as far at least, as regarded Mr. *Blifil*; and she too-well foresaw the Necessity which she should soon be under of coming to a full Explanation. After having thanked the Squire, therefore, for all his Professions of Kindness, she added, with a Look full of inexpressible Softness, 'And is it possible my Papa can be so good to place all his Joy in his *Sophy's* Happiness?' which *Western* having confirmed by a great Oath, and a Kiss; she then laid hold of his Hand, and falling on her Knees, after many warm and passionate Declarations of Affection and Duty, she begged him 'not to make her the most miserable Creature on Earth, by forcing her to marry a Man whom she detested.' 'This I entreat of you, dear Sir,' said she, 'for your Sake as well as my own, since you are so very kind to tell me your Happiness depends on mine.' 'How! what!' says *Western*, staring wildly. 'O Sir,' continued she, 'not only your poor *Sophy's* Happiness; her very Life, her Being depends upon your granting her Request. I cannot live with Mr. *Blifil*. To force me into this Marriage, would be killing me.' 'You can't live with Mr. *Blifil*!' says *Western*. 'No, upon my Soul I can't,' answered *Sophia*. 'Then die and be d—ned,' cries he, spurning her from him. 'Oh! Sir,' cries *Sophia*, catching hold of the Skirt of his

Coat, 'take Pity on me, I beseech you. Don't look, and say such cruel—— Can you be unmoved while you see your *Sophy* in this dreadful Condition? Can the best of Fathers break my Heart? Will he kill me by the most painful, cruel, lingering Death?' 'Pooh! Pooh!' cries the Squire, 'all Stuff and Nonsense, all maidenish Tricks. Kill you indeed! Will Marriage kill you?'— 'Oh! Sir,' answered *Sophia*, 'such a Marriage is worse than Death.— He is not even indifferent, I hate and detest him.'— 'If you detest un never so much,' cries *Western*, 'you shall ha' un.' This he bound by an Oath too shocking to repeat, and after many violent Asseverations, concluded in these Words. 'I am resolved upon the Match, and unless you consent to it, I will not give you a Groat, not a single Farthing; no, tho' I saw you expiring with Famine in the Street, I would not relieve you with a Morsel of Bread. This is my fixed Resolution, and so I leave you to consider on it.' He then broke from her with such Violence, that her Face dashed against the Floor, and he burst directly out of the Room, leaving poor *Sophia* prostrate on the Ground.

When *Western* came into the Hall, he there found *Jones*; who seeing his Friend looking wild, pale, and almost breathless, could not forbear enquiring the Reason of all these melancholy Appearances. Upon which the Squire immediately acquainted him with the whole Matter, concluding with bitter Denunciations against *Sophia*, and very pathetic Lamentations of the Misery of all Fathers who are so unfortunate to have Daughters.

Jones, to whom all the Resolutions which had been taken in Favour of *Blifil* were yet a Secret, was at first almost struck dead with this Relation; but recovering his Spirits a little, mere Despair, as he afterwards said, inspired him to mention a Matter to Mr. *Western*, which seemed to require more Impudence than a human Forehead was ever gifted with. He desired Leave to go to *Sophia*, that he might endeavour to obtain her Concurrence with her Father's Inclinations.

If the Squire had been as quick-sighted, as he was remarkable for the contrary, Passion might at present very well have blinded him. He thanked *Jones* for offering to undertake the Office, and said, '*Go, go*, prithee, try what can'st do;' and then swore many execrable Oaths that he would turn her out of Doors unless she consented to the Match.

CHAPTER VIII

The Meeting between Jones *and* Sophia.

JONES departed instantly in Quest of *Sophia*, whom he found just risen from the Ground where her Father had left her, with the Tears trickling from her Eyes, and the Blood running from her Lips. He presently ran to her, and with a Voice full at once of Tenderness and Terrour, cried, 'O my *Sophia*, what means this dreadful Sight!'—She looked softly at him for a Moment before she spoke, and then said, 'Mr. *Jones*, for Heaven's Sake, how came you here?—Leave me, I beseech you, this Moment.' 'Do not,' says he, 'impose so harsh a Command upon me—my Heart bleeds faster than those Lips. O *Sophia*, how easily could I drain my Veins to preserve one Drop of that dear Blood.' 'I have too many Obligations to you already,' answered she, 'for sure you meant them such.'—Here she looked at him tenderly almost a Minute, and then bursting into an Agony, cried,—'O Mr. *Jones*,—why did you save my Life?—my Death would have been happier for us both.'—'Happier for us both!' cried he, 'Could Racks or Wheels kill me so painfully as *Sophia's*! —I cannot bear the dreadful Sound.—Do I live but for her?'— Both his Voice and Look were full of inexpressible Tenderness when he spoke these Words, and at the same Time he laid gently hold on her Hand, which she did not withdraw from him; to say the Truth, she hardly knew what she did or suffered. A few Moments now passed in Silence between these Lovers, while his Eyes were eagerly fixed on *Sophia*, and hers declining towards the Ground; at last she recovered Strength enough to desire him again to leave her; for that her certain Ruin would be the Consequence of their being found together; adding,—'O Mr. *Jones*, you know not, you know not what hath passed this cruel Afternoon.' 'I know all, my *Sophia*,' answered he; 'your cruel Father hath told me all, and he himself hath sent me hither to you.' 'My Father sent you to me!' replied she, 'sure you dream.' 'Would to Heaven,' cries he, 'it was but a Dream. O *Sophia*, your Father hath sent me to you, to be an Advocate for my odious Rival, to solicite you in his Favour.—I took any Means to get Access to you.—O speak to me, *Sophia*, comfort my bleeding Heart. Sure no one ever loved, ever doated like me. Do not unkindly with-hold this dear, this soft, this gentle Hand.—One Moment, perhaps, tears you for ever from me.— Nothing less than this cruel Occasion could, I believe, have ever conquered the Respect and Awe, with which you have inspired me.' She stood a Moment silent and covered with Confusion, then lifting up her Eyes gently towards him, she cried, 'What would Mr. *Jones* have me say?' 'O do but promise,' cries he, 'that you never will give yourself to *Blifil*.' 'Name not,' answered she, 'the detested Sound. Be assured I never will give him what is in my Power to with-hold from him.' 'Now then,' cries he, 'while you are so perfectly kind, go a little farther, and add that I may hope.'— 'Alas,' says she, 'Mr. *Jones*, whither will you drive me? What Hope have I to bestow? You know my Father's Intentions.'— 'But I know,' answered he, 'your Compliance with them cannot be compelled.' 'What,' says she, 'must be the dreadful Consequence of my Disobedience? My own Ruin is my least Concern. I cannot bear the Thoughts of being the Cause of my Father's Misery.' 'He is himself the Cause,' cries *Jones*, 'by exacting a Power over you which Nature hath not given him. Think on the Misery which I am to suffer, if I am to lose you, and see on which Side Pity will turn the Ballance.' 'Think of it!' replied she, 'can you imagine I do not feel the Ruin which I must bring on you, should I comply with your Desire?—It is that Thought which gives me Resolution to bid you fly from me for ever, and avoid your own Destruction.' 'I fear no Destruction,' cries he, 'but the Loss of *Sophia*; if you would save me from the most bitter Agonies, recall that cruel Sentence.—Indeed, I can never part with you, indeed I cannot.'

The Lovers now stood both silent and trembling, *Sophia* being unable to with-draw her Hand from *Jones*, and he almost as unable to hold it; when the Scene, which I believe some of my Readers will think had lasted long enough, was interrupted by one of so different a Nature, that we shall reserve the Relation of it for a different Chapter.

CHAPTER IX

Being of a much more tempestuous Kind than the former.

BEFORE we proceed with what now happened to our Lovers, it may be proper to recount what had past in the Hall, during their tender Interview.

Soon after *Jones* had left Mr. *Western* in the Manner above-mentioned, his Sister came to him; and was presently informed of all that had past between her Brother and *Sophia*, relating to *Blifil*.

This Behaviour in her Niece, the good Lady construed to be an absolute Breach of the Condition, on which she had engaged to keep her Love for Mr. *Jones* a Secret. She considered herself, therefore, at full Liberty to reveal all she knew to the Squire, which she immediately did in the most explicit Terms, and without any Ceremony or Preface.

The Idea of a Marriage between *Jones* and his Daughter, had never once entered into the Squire's Head, either in the warmest Minutes of his Affection towards that young Man, or from Suspicion, or on any other Occasion. He did indeed consider a Parity of Fortune and Circumstances, to be physically as necessary an ingredient in Marriage, as Difference of Sexes, or any other Essential; and had no more Apprehension of his Daughter's falling in Love with a poor Man, than with any Animal of a different Species.

He became, therefore, like one Thunder-struck at his Sister's Relation. He was, at first, incapable of making any Answer, having been almost deprived of his Breath by the Violence of the Surprize. This, however, soon returned, and, as is usual in other Cases after an Intermission, with redoubled Force and Fury.

The first Use he made of the Power of Speech, after his Recovery from the sudden Effects of his Astonishment, was to discharge a round Volley of Oaths and Imprecations. After which he proceeded hastily to the Apartment, where he expected to find the Lovers, and murmured, or indeed, rather roared forth Intentions of Revenge every Step he went.

As when two Doves, or two Wood-pigeons, or as when *Strephon* and *Phillis* (for that comes nearest to the Mark) are retired into some pleasant solitary Grove, to enjoy the delightful Conversation of Love; that bashful Boy who cannot speak in

Public, and is never a good Companion to more than two at a Time. Here while every Object is serene, should hoarse Thunder burst suddenly through the shattered Clouds, and rumbling roll along the Sky, the frightened Maid starts from the mossy Bank or verdant Turf; the pale Livery of Death succeeds the red Regimentals in which Love had before drest her Cheeks; Fear shakes her whole Frame, and her Lover scarce supports her trembling, tottering Limbs.

Or as when two Gentlemen, Strangers to the wonderous Wit of the Place, are cracking a Bottle together at some Inn or Tavern at *Salisbury*, if the great *Dowdy*[1] who acts the Part of a Madman, as well as some of his Setters-on do that of a Fool, should rattle his Chains, and dreadfully hum forth the grumbling Catch along the Gallery; the frighted Strangers stand aghast, scared at the horrid Sound, they seek some Place of Shelter from the approaching Danger, and if the well-barred Windows did admit their Exit, would venture their Necks to escape the threatning Fury now coming upon them.

So trembled poor *Sophia*, so turned she pale at the Noise of her Father, who in a Voice most dreadful to hear, came on swearing, cursing and vowing the Destruction of *Jones*. To say the Truth, I believe the Youth himself would, from some prudent Considerations, have preferred another Place of Abode at this Time, had his Terrour on *Sophia's* Account given him Liberty to reflect a Moment on what any otherways concerned himself, than as his Love made him partake whatever affected her.

[1] Daniel Pearce (d. 1762), one of the Corporation mace-bearers in Salisbury. An obituary appearing in *Lloyd's Evening Post, and British Chronicle* (18–20 January 1762) identifies Fielding's allusion and supplies the following account of Pearce's antics as a practical joker:

'The Demerit of this man, known by the name of *Dowdy*, consisted in assuming the tatter'd garment, decorations of straw, rattling chains, visage stained with blood, and deportment of the most desperate lunatic; in which he was assisted by a frightful tone of voice and articulation (which he could modulate, for the pastime of those who put him on this barbarous sport, to increase or decrease, at pleasure, the terror of its object): he had a peculiar genius for this part, so as to fill the boldest with real fear, and hunt them to and fro, thro' windows, up chimneys, and even over the tops of houses, to escape the fury of a supposed raving, mischievous Bedlamite, intent on their destruction. . . . Mr. Pearce (except in the exercise of this piece of false humour) was a pacifick and civil man; and, it is said, has sometimes, after he had thrown off his disguise, and the person attacked has been made sensible of the cruel joke put upon him, officiously tendered his service, and gone about with him in pretended search after the madman, in order to correct his insolence, or bring him to justice.'

And now the Squire having burst open the Door, beheld an Object which instantly suspended all his Fury against *Jones*; this was the ghastly Appearance of *Sophia*, who had fainted away in her Lover's Arms. This tragical Sight Mr. *Western* no sooner beheld, than all his Rage forsook him, he roared for Help with his utmost Violence; ran first to his Daughter, then back to the Door, calling for Water, and then back again to *Sophia*, never considering in whose Arms she then was, nor, perhaps, once re-collecting that there was such a Person in the World as *Jones*: For, indeed, I believe, the present Circumstances of his Daughter were now the sole Consideration which employed his Thoughts.

Mrs. *Western* and a great Number of Servants soon came to the Assistance of *Sophia*, with Water, Cordials, and every Thing necessary on those Occasions. These were applied with such Success, that *Sophia* in a very few Minutes began to recover, and all the Symptoms of Life to return. Upon which she was presently led off by her own Maid and Mrs. *Western*; nor did that good Lady depart without leaving some wholsome Admonitions with her Brother, on the dreadful Effects of his Passion, or, as she pleased to call it, Madness.

The Squire, perhaps, did not understand this good Advice, as it was delivered in obscure Hints, Shrugs, and Notes of Admiration; at least, if he did understand it, he profited very little by it: For no sooner was he cured of his immediate Fears for his Daughter, than he relapsed into his former Frenzy, which must have produced an immediate Battle with *Jones*, had not Parson *Supple*, who was a very strong Man, been present, and by mere Force restrained the Squire from Acts of Hostility.

The Moment *Sophia* was departed, *Jones* advanced in a very suppliant Manner to Mr. *Western*, whom the Parson held in his Arms, and begged him to be pacify'd; for that while he continued in such a Passion it would be impossible to give him any Satisfaction.

'I wull have Satisfaction o' thee,' answered the Squire, 'so doff thy Clothes. *At unt* half a Man, and I'll lick thee as well as wast ever licked in thy Life.' He then bespattered the Youth with Abundance of that Language, which passes between Country Gentlemen who embrace opposite Sides of the Question; with frequent Applications to him to salute that Part which is generally introduced into all Controversies, that arise among the lower

Orders of the *English* Gentry, at Horse-races, Cock-matches, and other public Places. Allusions to this Part are likewise often made for the Sake of the Jest. And here, I believe, the Wit is generally misunderstood. In Reality, it lies in desiring another to kiss your A— for having just before threatened to kick his: For I have observed very accurately, that no one ever desires you to kick that which belongs to himself, nor offers to kiss this Part in another.

It may likewise seem surprizing, that in the many thousand kind Invitations of this Sort, which every one who hath conversed with Country Gentlemen, must have heard, no one, I believe, hath ever seen a single Instance where the Desire hath been complied with. A great Instance of their Want of Politeness: For in Town, nothing can be more common than for the finest Gentlemen to perform this Ceremony every Day to their Superiors, without having that Favour once requested of them.

To all such Wit, *Jones* very calmly answered, 'Sir, this Usage, may, perhaps, cancel every other Obligation you have conferred on me; but there is one you can never cancel; nor will I be provoked by your Abuse, to lift my Hand against the Father of *Sophia*.'

At these Words, the Squire grew still more outrageous than before; so that the Parson begged *Jones* to retire, saying, 'You behold, Sir, how he waxeth Wroth at your Abode here; therefore, let me pray you not to tarry any longer. His Anger is too much kindled for you to commune with him at present. You had better, therefore, conclude your Visit, and refer what Matters you have to urge in your Behalf, to some other Opportunity.'

Jones accepted this Advice with Thanks, and immediately departed. The Squire now regained the Liberty of his Hands, and so much Temper as to express some Satisfaction in the Restraint which had been laid upon him; declaring that he should certainly have beat his Brains out; and adding, 'It would have vexed one confoundedly to have been hanged for such a Rascal.'

The Parson now began to triumph in the Success of his Peace-making Endeavours, and proceeded to read a Lecture against Anger, which might, perhaps, rather have tended to raise than to quiet that Passion in some hasty Minds. This Lecture he enriched with many valuable Quotations from the Antients, particularly from *Seneca*;[1] who hath, indeed, so well handled this

---

[1] Cf. Seneca's *Moral Essays*, iii ('Ad Novatum de Ira').

Passion, that none but a very angry Man can read him without great Pleasure and Profit. The Doctor concluded this Harangue with the famous Story of *Alexander* and *Clytus*;[1] but as I find that entered in my Common-Place under Title Drunkenness, I shall not insert it here.

The Squire took no Notice of this Story, nor, perhaps, of any Thing he said: For he interrupted him before he had finished by calling for a Tankard of Beer; observing (which is, perhaps, as true as any Observation on this Fever of the Mind) *that Anger makes a Man dry.*

No sooner had the Squire swallowed a large Draught than he renewed the Discourse on *Jones*, and declared a Resolution of going the next Morning early to acquaint Mr. *Allworthy.* His Friend would have dissuaded him from this, from the mere Motive of Good-nature; but his Dissuasion had no other Effect, than to produce a large Volley of Oaths and Curses, which greatly shocked the pious Ears of *Supple*; but he did not dare to remonstrate against a Privilege, which the Squire claimed as a free-born *Englishman.* To say Truth, the Parson submitted to please his Palate at the Squire's Table, at the Expence of suffering now and then this Violence to his Ears. He contented himself with thinking he did not promote this evil Practice, and that the Squire would not swear an Oath the less if he never entered within his Gates. However, tho' he was not guilty of ill Manners by rebuking a Gentleman in his own House, he paid him off obliquely in the Pulpit; which had not, indeed, the good Effect of working a Reformation in the Squire himself, yet it so far operated on his Conscience, that he put the Laws[2] very severely in Execution against others, and the Magistrate was the only Person in the Parish who could swear with Impunity.

[1] Cf. Plutarch's *Life of Alexander*, l–li; and Arrian, *Anabasis of Alexander*, IV. viii. Alexander killed his friend Cleitus for insulting him during a drunken quarrel (328 B.C.).

[2] That Fielding deplored what he called the 'detestable Crime' of 'profane Cursing and Swearing' is clear from *A Charge Delivered to the Grand Jury* (1749), in which he discusses the statutes designed to punish offenders and exhorts magistrates and peace-officers to enforce them. The most recent of these laws had been passed in 1746.

CHAPTER X

In which Mr. Western *visits Mr.* Allworthy.

MR. *Allworthy* was now retired from Breakfast with his Nephew, well satisfied with the Report of the young Gentleman's successful Visit to *Sophia* (for he greatly desired the Match, more on Account of the young Lady's Character than of her Riches) when Mr. *Western* broke abruptly in upon them, and without any Ceremony began as follows.

'There, you have done a fine Piece of Work truly. You have brought up your Bastard to a fine Purpose; not that I believe you have had any Hand in it neither, that is, as a Man may say, designedly; but there is a fine Kettle of Fish made on't up at our House.' 'What can be the Matter, Mr. *Western?*' said *Allworthy.* 'O Matter *enow* of all Conscience; my Daughter hath fallen in Love with your Bastard, that's all, but I won't *ge* her a *Hapenny*, not the Twentieth Part of a Brass *Varden.* I always thought what would come o' breeding up a Bastard like a Gentleman, and letting *un* come about to *Vok's* Houses. It's well *vor un* I could not get *at un*, I'd *a licked un*, I'd a spoil'd his Caterwauling, I'd a taught the Son of a Whore to meddle with Meat for his Master. He shan't ever have a Morsel of Meat of mine, or a *Varden* to buy it: If she will *ha un*, one Smock shall be her Portion. I'll sooner *ge* my *Esteate* to the *zinking* Fund,[1] that it may be sent to *Hannover* to corrupt our Nation with.' 'I am heartily sorry,' cries *Allworthy.* 'Pox o' your Sorrow,' says *Western*, 'it will do me Abundance of Good, when I have lost my only Child, my poor *Sophy*, that was the Joy of my Heart, and all the Hope and Comfort of my Age; but I am resolved I will turn her out o' Doors, she shall beg and starve and rot in the Streets. Not one *Hapenny*, not a *Hapenny* shall she ever *hae* o' mine. The Son of a Bitch was always good at finding a Hare sitting; an' be rotted to'n, I little thought what Puss he was looking after; but it shall be the worst he ever *vound* in his Life. She shall be no better than

---

[1] Established by Walpole in 1717, the Sinking Fund was created from 'the *Surplusses* of the *Aggregate, South-Sea,* and *general Funds*' and was originally intended 'to *sink* or discharge the *National Debts*' (see *An Essay on the Sinking Fund* [1736], p. 9). As the expense of government rose, however, this money was appropriated for other purposes. Since 1742 the Opposition had made a special issue of the use of the fund to maintain the Hanoverian troops (see below, p. 321, n. 2).

Carrion; the Skin o'er is all he shall *ha*, and *zu* you may tell *un*.'
'I am in Amazement,' cries *Allworthy*, 'at what you tell me, after
what passed between my Nephew and the young Lady no longer
ago than Yesterday.' 'Yes, Sir,' answered *Western*, 'it was after
what passed between your Nephew and she that the whole Matter
came out. Mr. *Blifil* there was no sooner gone than the Son of
a Whore came lurching about the House. Little did I think when
I used to love him for a Sportsman, that he was all the while
a poaching after my Daughter.' 'Why, truly,' says *Allworthy*,
'I could wish you had not given him so many Opportunities with
her; and you will do me the Justice to acknowledge, that I have
always been averse to his staying so much at your House, tho'
I own I had no Suspicion of this Kind.' 'Why, Zounds!' cries
Western, 'who could have thought it? What the Devil had she
to do wi'n? He did not come there a courting to her, he came
there a hunting with me.' 'But was it possible,' says *Allworthy*,
'that you should never discern any Symptoms of Love between
them, when you have seen them so often together?' 'Never in
my Life, as I hope to be saved,' cries *Western*. 'I never so much
as zeed him kiss her in all my Life; and so far from courting her,
he used rather to be more silent when she was in Company than
at any other Time: And as for the Girl, she was always less civil
to'n than to any young Man that came to the House. As to that
Matter, I am not more easy to be deceived than another, I would
not have you think I am, Neighbour.' *Allworthy* could scarce
refrain Laughter at this; but he resolved to do a Violence to
himself: For he perfectly well knew Mankind, and had too much
good Breeding and good Nature to offend the Squire in his
present Circumstances. He then asked *Western* what he would
have him do upon this Occasion. To which the other answered,
'That he would have him keep the Rascal away from his House,
and that he would go and lock up the Wench: For he was resolved
to make her marry Mr. *Blifil* in Spite of her Teeth.' He then
shook *Blifil* by the Hand, and swore he would have no other Son-
in-law. Presently after which he took his Leave, saying, his
House was in such Disorder, that it was necessary for him to
make Haste home, to take care his Daughter did not give him
the Slip; and as for *Jones*, he swore if he caught him at his House,
he would qualify him to run for the Gelding's Plate.

When *Allworthy* and *Blifil* were again left together, a long

Silence ensued between them; all which Interval the young Gentle-man filled up with Sighs, which proceeded partly from Disap-pointment, but more from Hatred: For the Success of *Jones* was much more grievous to him, than the Loss of *Sophia*.

At length his Uncle asked him what he was determined to do, and he answered in the following Words. 'Alas, Sir, can it be a Question what Step a Lover will take, when Reason and Passion point different Ways? I am afraid it is too certain he will, in that Dilemma, always follow the latter. Reason dictates to me, to quit all Thoughts of a Woman who places her Affections on another; my Passion bids me hope she may, in Time, change her Inclinations in my Favour. Here, however, I conceive an Objection may be raised, which if it could not fully be answered, would totally deter me from any further Pursuit. I mean the In-justice of endeavouring to supplant another, in a Heart of which he seems already in Possession; but the determined Resolution of Mr. *Western* shews, that in this Case, I shall by so doing, promote the Happiness of every Party; not only that of the Parent, who will thus be preserved from the highest Degree of Misery, but of both the others, who must be undone by this Match. The Lady, I am sure, will be undone in every Sense: For besides the Loss of most Part of her own Fortune, she will be not only married to a Beggar, but the little Fortune which her Father cannot with-hold from her, will be squandered on that Wench, with whom I know he yet converses.—Nay, that is a Trifle: For I know him to be one of the worst Men in the World: For had my dear Uncle known what I have hitherto endeavoured to conceal, he must have long since abandoned so profligate a Wretch.' 'How,' said *Allworthy*, 'hath he done any Thing worse than I already know? Tell me, I beseech you.' 'No,' replied *Blifil*, 'it is now past, and perhaps he may have repented of it.' 'I command you on your Duty,' said *Allworthy*, 'to tell me what you mean.' 'You know, Sir,' says *Blifil*, 'I never disobeyed you; but I am sorry I mentioned it, since it may now look like Revenge, whereas, I thank Heaven, no such Motive ever entered my Heart; and if you oblige me to discover it, I must be his Petitioner to you for your Forgiveness.' 'I will have no Conditions,' answered *Allworthy*, 'I think I have shewn Tenderness enough towards him, and more, perhaps, than you ought to thank me for.' 'More, indeed, I fear than he deserved,' cries *Blifil*, 'for in the very Day of your utmost Danger, when myself and all the Family were in Tears, he filled the House with Riot and Debauchery. He drank and sung and roared, and when I gave him a gentle Hint of the Indecency of his Actions, he fell into a violent Passion, swore many Oaths, called me Rascal, and struck me.' 'How!' cries *Allworthy*, 'did he dare to strike you?' 'I am sure,' cries *Blifil*, 'I have forgiven him that long ago. I wish I could so easily forget his Ingratitude to the best of Benefactors; and yet, even that, I hope you will forgive him, since he must have certainly been possessed with the Devil: For that very Evening, as Mr. *Thwackum* and myself were taking the Air in the Fields, and exulting in the good Symptoms which then first began to discover themselves, we unluckily saw him engaged with a Wench in a Manner not fit to be mentioned. Mr. *Thwackum*, with more Boldness than Prudence, advanced to rebuke him, when, (I am sorry to say it) he fell upon the worthy Man, and beat him so outragiously, that I wish he may have yet recovered the Bruises. Nor was I without my Share of the Effects of his Malice, while I endeavoured to protect my Tutor: But that I have long forgiven, nay I prevailed with Mr. *Thwackum* to forgive him too, and not to inform you of a Secret which I feared might be fatal to him. And now, Sir, since I have unadvisedly dropped a Hint of this Matter, and your Commands have obliged me to discover the whole, let me intercede with you for him.' 'O Child,' said *Allworthy*, 'I know not whether I should blame or applaud your Goodness, in concealing such Villany a Moment; but where is Mr. *Thwackum?* Not that I want any Confirmation of what you say; but I will examine all the Evidence of this Matter, to justify to the World the Example I am resolved to make of such a Monster.'

Thwackum was now sent for, and presently appeared. He corroborated every Circumstance which the other had deposed. Nay, he produced the Record upon his Breast, where the Handwriting of Mr. *Jones* remained very legible in black and blue. He concluded with declaring to Mr. *Allworthy*, that he should have long since informed him of this Matter, had not Mr. *Blifil*, by the most earnest Interpositions, prevented him. 'He is,' says he, 'an excellent Youth; though such Forgiveness of Enemies is carrying the Matter too far.'

In reality, *Blifil* had taken some Pains to prevail with the Parson, and to prevent the Discovery at that Time; for which he had many Reasons. He knew that the Minds of Men are apt to be softened and relaxed from their usual Severity by Sickness. Besides, he imagined that if the Story was told when the Fact was so recent, and the Physician about the House, who might have unravelled the real Truth, he should never be able to give it the malicious Turn which he intended. Again, he resolved to hoard up this Business, till the Indiscretion of *Jones* should afford some additional Complaints; for he thought the joint Weight of many Facts falling upon him together, would be the most likely to crush him; and he watched therefore some such Opportunity as that, with which Fortune had now kindly presented him. Lastly, by prevailing with *Thwackum* to conceal the Matter for a Time, he knew he should confirm an Opinion of his Friendship to *Jones*, which he had greatly laboured to establish in Mr. *Allworthy*.

CHAPTER XI

A short Chapter; but which contains sufficient Matter to affect the good-natured Reader.

IT was Mr. *Allworthy's* Custom never to punish any one, not even to turn away a Servant, in a Passion.[1] He resolved, therefore, to delay passing Sentence on *Jones* till the Afternoon.

The poor young Man attended at Dinner, as usual; but his Heart was too much loaded to suffer him to eat. His Grief too was a good deal aggravated by the unkind Looks of Mr. *Allworthy*; whence he concluded that *Western* had discovered the whole Affair between him and *Sophia*: But as to Mr. *Blifil's* Story, he had not the least Apprehension; for of much the greater Part he was entirely innocent, and for the Residue, as he had forgiven and forgotten it himself, so he suspected no Remembrance on the other Side. When Dinner was over, and the Servants departed,

---

[1] In his temperate refusal to inflict punishment when he is angry, Allworthy imitates the example of Plato, about whom Diogenes Laertius records the following anecdote: 'One day, when Xenocrates had come in, Plato asked him to chastise his slave, since he was unable to do it himself because he was in a passion. Further, it is alleged that he said to one of his slaves, "I would have given you a flogging, had I not been in a passion"' (*Lives of Eminent Philosophers*, iii. 38–9; trans. R. D. Hicks, Loeb Classical Library, 1925). Cf. also Cicero, *De Officiis*, I. xxv. 89, and Seneca, *De Ira*, I. xv. 3, where the story is told of Socrates.

Mr. *Allworthy* began to harangue. He set forth, in a long Speech, the many Iniquities of which *Jones* had been guilty, particularly those which this Day had brought to light, and concluded by telling him, 'that unless he could clear himself of the Charge, he was resolved to banish him from his Sight for ever.'

Many Disadvantages attended poor *Jones* in making his Defence; nay, indeed he hardly knew his Accusation: For as Mr. *Allworthy*, in recounting the Drunkenness, *&c.* while he lay ill, out of Modesty sunk every thing that related particularly to himself, which indeed principally constituted the Crime, *Jones* could not deny the Charge. His Heart was, besides, almost broken already, and his Spirits were so sunk, that he could say nothing for himself; but acknowledged the whole, and, like a Criminal in Despair, threw himself upon Mercy; concluding, 'That tho' he must own himself guilty of many Follies and Inadvertencies, he hoped he had done nothing to deserve what would be to him the greatest Punishment in the World.'

Allworthy answered, 'that he had forgiven him too often already, in Compassion to his Youth, and in Hopes of his Amendment: That he now found he was an abandoned Reprobate, and such as it would be criminal in any one to support and encourage. Nay,' said Mr. *Allworthy* to him, 'your audacious Attempt to steal away the young Lady, calls upon me to justify my own Character in punishing you. The World, who have already censured the Regard I have shewn for you, may think, with some Colour at least of Justice, that I connive at so base and barbarous an Action. An Action of which you must have known my Abhorrence, and which, had you had any Concern for my Ease and Honour, as well as for my Friendship, you would never have thought of undertaking. Fie upon it, young Man! indeed there is scarce any Punishment equal to your Crimes, and I can scarce think myself justifiable in what I am now going to bestow on you. However, as I have educated you like a Child of my own, I will not turn you naked into the World. When you open this Paper, therefore, you will find something which may enable you, with Industry, to get an honest Livelihood; but if you employ it to worse Purposes, I shall not think myself obliged to supply you farther, being resolved, from this Day forward, to converse no more with you on any Account. I cannot avoid saying, There is no Part of your Conduct which I resent more than your ill

Treatment of that good young Man (meaning *Blifil*) who hath behaved with so much Tenderness and Honour towards you.'

These last Words were a Dose almost too bitter to be swallowed. A Flood of Tears now gushed from the Eyes of *Jones*, and every Faculty of Speech and Motion seemed to have deserted him. It was some Time before he was able to obey *Allworthy's* peremptory Commands of departing; which he at length did, having first kissed his Hands with a Passion difficult to be affected, and as difficult to be described.

The Reader must be very weak, if when he considers the Light in which *Jones* then appeared to Mr. *Allworthy*, he should blame the Rigour of his Sentence. And yet all the Neighbourhood, either from this Weakness, or from some worse Motive, condemned this Justice and Severity as the highest Cruelty. Nay, the very Persons who had before censured the good Man for the Kindness and Tenderness shewn to a Bastard (his own, according to the general Opinion) now cried out as loudly against turning his own Child out of Doors. The Women especially were unanimous in taking the Part of *Jones*, and raised more Stories on the Occasion, than I have room, in this Chapter, to set down.

One thing must not be omitted, that in their Censures on this Occasion, none ever mentioned the Sum contained in the Paper which *Allworthy* gave *Jones*, which was no less than Five hundred Pounds; but all agreed that he was sent away Pennyless, and some said, naked from the House of his inhuman Father.

CHAPTER XII

Containing Love Letters, &c.

JONES was commanded to leave the House immediately, and told, that his Clothes and every thing else should be sent to him whithersoever he should order them.

He accordingly set out, and walked above a Mile, not regarding, and indeed scarce knowing whither he went. At length a little Brook obstructing his Passage, he threw himself down by the Side of it; nor could he help muttering with some little Indignation, 'Sure my Father will not deny me this Place to rest in?'

Here he presently fell into the most violent Agonies, tearing his Hair from his Head, and using most other Actions which generally accompany Fits of Madness, Rage, and Despair.

When he had in this Manner vented the first Emotions of Passion, he began to come a little to himself. His Grief now took another Turn, and discharged itself in a gentler Way, till he became at last cool enough to reason with his Passion, and to consider what Steps were proper to be taken in his deplorable Condition.

And now the great Doubt was how to act with regard to *Sophia*. The Thoughts of leaving her almost rent his Heart asunder; but the Consideration of reducing her to Ruin and Beggary still racked him, if possible, more; and if the violent Desire of possessing her Person could have induced him to listen one Moment to this Alternative, still he was by no means certain of her Resolution to indulge his Wishes at so high an Expence. The Resentment of Mr. *Allworthy*, and the Injury he must do to his Quiet, argued strongly against this latter; and lastly, the apparent Impossibility of his Success, even if he would sacrifice all these Considerations to it, came to his Assistance; and thus Honour at last, backed with Despair, with Gratitude to his Benefactor, and with real Love to his Mistress, got the better of burning Desire, and he resolved rather to quit *Sophia*, than to pursue her to her Ruin.

It is difficult for any who have not felt it, to conceive the glowing Warmth which filled his Breast, on the first Contemplation of this Victory over his Passion. Pride flattered him so agreeably, that his Mind perhaps enjoyed perfect Happiness; but this was only momentary, *Sophia* soon returned to his Imagination, and allayed the Joy of his Triumph with no less bitter Pangs than a good-natured General must feel when he surveys the bleeding Heaps, at the Price of whose Blood he hath purchased his Laurels; for thousands of tender Ideas lay murdered before our Conqueror.

Being resolved, however, to pursue the Paths of this Giant Honour, as the gigantic Poet *Lee* calls it,[1] he determined to

---

[1] Nathaniel Lee (1653 ?–92), whose bombastic dramas Fielding had earlier burlesqued in *The Tragedy of Tragedies* (1731). The phrase is from Varanes's speech in *Theodosius: or, The Force of Love* (1680), II. i: 'As to the World thy Judgment soars above me, / And I am dar'd with this Gigantick Honour' (1725 ed.).

write a farewel Letter to *Sophia*; and accordingly proceeded to a House not far off, where, being furnished with proper Materials, he wrote as follows:

MADAM,

'WHEN you reflect on the Situation in which I write, I am sure your Good-nature will pardon any Inconsistency or Absurdity which my Letter contains; for every thing here flows from a Heart so full, that no Language can express its Dictates.

'I have resolved, Madam, to obey your Commands, in flying for ever from your dear, your lovely Sight. Cruel indeed those Commands are; but it is a Cruelty which proceeds from Fortune, not from my *Sophia*. Fortune hath made it necessary, necessary to your Preservation, to forget there ever was such a Wretch as I am.

'Believe me, I would not hint all my Sufferings to you, if I imagined they could possibly escape your Ears. I know the Goodness and Tenderness of your Heart, and would avoid giving you any of those Pains which you always feel for the Miserable. O let nothing which you shall hear of my hard Fortune cause a Moment's Concern; for after the Loss of you, every thing is to me a Trifle.

'O my *Sophia*! it is hard to leave you; it is harder still to desire you to forget me; yet the sincerest Love obliges me to both. Pardon my conceiving that any Remembrance of me can give you Disquiet; but if I am so gloriously wretched, sacrifice me every Way to your Relief. Think I never loved you; or think truly how little I deserve you; and learn to scorn me for a Presumption which can never be too severely punished.—I am unable to say more.—May Guardian Angels protect you for ever.'

He was now searching his Pockets for his Wax, but found none, nor indeed any thing else, therein; for in Truth he had, in his frantic Disposition, tossed every thing from him, and, amongst the rest, his Pocket-book, which he had received from Mr. *Allworthy*, which he had never opened, and which now first occurred to his Memory.

The House supplied him with a Wafer for his present Purpose, with which having sealed his Letter, he returned hastily towards the Brook Side, in order to search for the Things which he had there lost. In his Way he met his old Friend *Black George*, who heartily condoled with him on his Misfortune; for this had already reached his Ears, and indeed those of all the Neighbour-hood.

Jones acquainted the Game-keeper with his Loss, and he as readily went back with him to the Brook, where they searched every Tuft of Grass in the Meadow, as well where *Jones* had not been, as where he had been; but all to no Purpose, for they found nothing: For indeed, though the Things were then in the Meadow, they omitted to search the only Place where they were deposited; to wit, in the Pockets of the said *George*; for he had just before found them, and being luckily apprized of their Value, had very carefully put them up for his own Use.

The Game-keeper having exerted as much Diligence in Quest of the lost Goods, as if he had hoped to find them, desired Mr. *Jones* to recollect if he had been in no other Place; 'For sure,' said he, 'if you had lost them here so lately, the Things must have been here still; for this is a very unlikely Place for any one to pass by;' and indeed it was by great Accident that he himself had passed through that Field, in order to lay Wires for Hares, with which he was to supply a Poulterer at *Bath* the next Morning.

Jones now gave over all Hopes of recovering his Loss, and almost all Thoughts concerning it, and turning to *Black George*, asked him earnestly, If he would do him the greatest Favour in the World.

George answered, with some Hesitation, 'Sir, you know you may command me whatever is in my Power, and I heartily wish it was in my Power to do you any Service.' In fact, the Question staggered him; for he had, by selling Game, amassed a pretty good Sum of Money in Mr. *Western's* Service, and was afraid that *Jones* wanted to borrow some small Matter of him; but he was presently relieved from his Anxiety, by being desired to convey a Letter to *Sophia*, which with great Pleasure he promised to do. And indeed, I believe there are few Favours which he would not have gladly conferred on Mr. *Jones*; for he bore as much Gratitude towards him as he could, and was as honest as Men who love Money better than any other Thing in the Universe generally are.

Mrs. *Honour* was agreed by both to be the proper Means by which this Letter should pass to *Sophia*. They then separated; the Game-keeper returned home to Mr. *Western's*, and *Jones* walked to an Alehouse at half a Mile's Distance, to wait for his Messenger's Return.

George no sooner came home to his Master's House, than he met with Mrs. *Honour*; to whom, having first sounded her with a few previous Questions, he delivered the Letter for her Mistress, and received at the same Time another from her for Mr. *Jones*; which *Honour* told him she had carried all that Day in her Bosom, and began to despair of finding any Means of delivering it.

The Game-keeper returned hastily and joyfully to *Jones*, who having received *Sophia's* Letter from him, instantly withdrew, and eagerly breaking it open, read as follows:

Sir,

'It is impossible to express what I have felt since I saw you. Your submitting, on my Account, to such cruel Insults from my Father, lays me under an Obligation I shall ever own. As you know his Temper, I beg you will, for my Sake, avoid him. I wish I had any Comfort to send you; but believe this, that nothing but the last Violence shall ever give my Hand or Heart where you would be sorry to see them bestowed.'

Jones read this Letter a hundred Times over, and kissed it a hundred Times as often. His Passion now brought all tender Desires back into his Mind. He repented that he had writ to *Sophia* in the Manner we have seen above; but he repented more that he had made use of the Interval of his Messenger's Absence to write and dispatch a Letter to Mr. *Allworthy*, in which he had faithfully promised and bound himself to quit all Thoughts of his Love. However, when his cool Reflections returned, he plainly perceived that his Case was neither mended nor altered by *Sophia's* Billet, unless to give him some little Glimpse of Hope from her Constancy, of some favourable Accident hereafter. He therefore resumed his Resolution, and taking leave of *Black George*, set forward to a Town about five Miles distant,[1] whither he had desired Mr. *Allworthy*, unless he pleased to revoke his Sentence, to send his Things after him.

[1] Probably Wells.

CHAPTER XIII

The Behaviour of Sophia *on the present Occasion; which none of her
Sex will blame, who are capable of behaving in the same Manner.
And the Discussion of a knotty Point in the Court of Conscience.*

SOPHIA had passed the last twenty-four Hours in no very
desirable Manner. During a large Part of them she had been
entertained by her Aunt, with Lectures of Prudence, recommending to her the Example of the polite World, where Love (so the
good Lady said) is at present entirely laughed at, and where
Women consider Matrimony, as Men do Offices of public
Trust, only as the Means of making their Fortunes, and of
advancing themselves in the World. In commenting on which
Text Mrs. *Western* had displayed her Eloquence during several
Hours.

These sagacious Lectures, though little suited either to the
Taste or Inclination of *Sophia*, were, however, less irksome to her
than her own Thoughts, that formed the Entertainment of the
Night, during which she never once closed her Eyes.

But though she could neither sleep nor rest in her Bed, yet,
having no Avocation from it, she was found there by her Father
at his Return from *Allworthy's*, which was not till past Ten o'
Clock in the Morning. He went directly up to her Apartment,
opened the Door, and seeing she was not up—cried—'Oh! you
are safe then, and I am resolved to keep you so.' He then locked
the Door, and delivered the Key to *Honour*, having first given her
the strictest Charge, with great Promises of Rewards for her
Fidelity, and most dreadful Menaces of Punishment, in case she
should betray her Trust.

Honour's Orders were not to suffer her Mistress to come out of
her Room without the Authority of the Squire himself, and to
admit none to her but him and her Aunt; but she was herself to
attend her with whatever *Sophia* pleased, except only Pen, Ink,
and Paper, of which she was forbidden the Use.

The Squire ordered his Daughter to dress herself and attend
him at Dinner; which she obeyed; and having sat the usual Time,
was again conducted to her Prison.

In the Evening, the Goaler *Honour* brought her the Letter

which she received from the Game-keeper.[1] *Sophia* read it very
attentively twice or thrice over, and then threw herself upon the
Bed, and burst into a Flood of Tears. Mrs. *Honour* expressed
great Astonishment at this Behaviour in her Mistress; nor could
she forbear very eagerly begging to know the Cause of this
Passion. *Sophia* made her no Answer for some Time, and then
starting suddenly up, caught her Maid by the Hand, and cried,
'O *Honour*! I am undone.' 'Marry forbid,' cries *Honour*, 'I
wish the Letter had been burnt before I had brought it to your
La'ship. I'm sure I thought it would have comforted your
La'ship, or I would have seen it at the Devil before I would have
touch'd it.' '*Honour*,' says *Sophia*, 'you are a good Girl, and it is
vain to attempt concealing longer my Weakness from you; I
have thrown away my Heart on a Man who hath forsaken me.'
'And is Mr. *Jones*,' answered the Maid, 'such a Perfidy Man?'
'He hath taken his Leave of me,' says *Sophia*, 'for ever in that
Letter. Nay, he hath desired me to forget him. Could he have
desired that, if he had loved me? Could he have borne such a
Thought? could he have written such a Word?' 'No certainly,
Ma'am,' cries *Honour*, 'and to be sure, if the best Man in *England*
was to desire me to forget him, I'd take him at his Word. Marry
come up! I am sure your La'ship hath done him too much Honour
ever to think on him. A young Lady who may take her Choice
of all the young Men in the Country. And to be sure, if I may
be so presumptious as to offer my poor Opinion, there is young
Mr. *Blifil*, who besides that he is come of honest Parents, and will
be one of the greatest Squires all hereabouts, he is to be sure, in
my poor Opinion, a more handsomer, and a more politer Man by
half; and besides, he is a young Gentleman of a sober Character,
and who may defy any of the Neighbours to say black is his
Eye:[2] He follows no dirty Trollops, nor can any Bastards be
laid at his Door. Forget him indeed! I thank Heaven I myself

---

[1] Sophia's situation at this point in the novel recalls that of Shakespeare's heroine in
Romeo and Juliet. As Juliet loves Romeo but is intended by her family for Paris, so Sophia
loves Jones while her family arranges her marriage to Blifil. With the present scene between
Honour and Sophia compare, in particular, *Romeo and Juliet* (III. ii): when the Nurse
brings news that Romeo has been banished for killing Tybalt, Juliet at first condemns her
faithless lover, then reproves her companion for echoing her sentiments (see below, p. 318,
n. 1).

[2] A proverbial expression meaning to find fault with. (See W. G. Smith and P. Harvey,
Oxford Dictionary of English Proverbs, 2nd ed. [Oxford, 1948], p. 48.)

am not so much at my last Prayers, as to suffer any Man to bid
me forget him twice. If the best He that wears a Head was for to
go for to offer for to say such an affronting Word to me, I would
never give him my Company afterwards, if there was another
young Man in the Kingdom. And as I was a saying, to be sure,
there is young Mr. *Blifil*——' 'Name not his detested Name,'
cries *Sophia*. 'Nay, Ma'am,' says *Honour*, 'if your La'ship doth
not like him, there be more jolly handsome young Men that
would court your La'ship, if they had but the least Encouragement. I don't believe there is arrow young Gentleman in this
Country, or in the next to it, that if your La'ship was but to
look as if you had a Mind to him, would not come about to make
his Offers directly.' 'What a Wretch dost thou imagine me,'
cries *Sophia*, 'by affronting my Ears with such Stuff! I detest all
Mankind.' 'Nay, to be sure, Ma'am,' answered *Honour*, 'your
La'ship hath had enough to give you a Surfeit of them. To be
used ill by such a poor beggarly bastardly Fellow.' 'Hold your
blasphemous Tongue,'[1] cries *Sophia*, 'how dare you mention his
Name with Disrespect before me? He use me ill? No, his poor
bleeding Heart suffered more when he writ the cruel Words,
than mine from reading them. O! he is all heroic Virtue, and
angelic Goodness. I am ashamed of the Weakness of my own
Passion, for blaming what I ought to admire.—O *Honour*! it is
my Good only which he consults. To my Interest he sacrifices
both himself and me.—The Apprehension of ruining me hath
driven him to Despair.' 'I am very glad,' says *Honour*, 'to hear
your La'ship takes that into your Consideration: for to be sure,
it must be nothing less than Ruin, to give your Mind to one that
is turned out of Doors, and is not worth a Farthing in the World.'
'Turned out of Doors!' cries *Sophia* hastily, 'how! what dost thou
mean?' 'Why, to be sure, Ma'am, my Master no sooner told
Squire *Allworthy* about Mr. *Jones* having offered to make Love
to your Ladyship, than the Squire stripped him stark naked, and
turned him out of Doors.' 'Ha!' says *Sophia*, 'have I been the

---

[1] Cf. Juliet to the Nurse, *Romeo and Juliet* (III. ii):

> Blistered be thy tongue
> For such a wish! He was not born to shame.
> Upon his brow shame is asham'd to sit;
> For 'tis a throne where honour may be crown'd
> Sole monarch of the universal earth.
> O, what a beast was I to chide at him!

cursed, wretched Cause of his Destruction?—Turn'd naked out of Doors! Here, *Honour*, take all the Money I have; take the Rings from my Fingers.—Here my Watch, carry him all.— Go, find him immediately.' 'For Heaven's Sake, Ma'am,' answered Mrs. *Honour*, 'do but consider, if my Master should miss any of these Things, I should be made to answer for them. Therefore let me beg your Ladyship not to part with your Watch and Jewels. Besides the Money, I think, is enough of all Conscience; and as for that, my Master can never know any thing of the Matter.' 'Here then,' cries *Sophia*, 'take every Farthing I am worth, find him out immediately and give it him. Go, go, lose not a Moment.'

Mrs. *Honour* departed according to Orders, and finding *Black George* below Stairs, delivered him the Purse which contained Sixteen Guineas, being indeed the whole Stock of *Sophia*: For tho' her Father was very liberal to her, she was much too generous herself to be rich.

Black George having received the Purse, set forward towards the Alehouse; but in the Way a Thought occurred to him, whether he should not detain this Money likewise. His Conscience, however, immediately started at this Suggestion, and began to upbraid him with Ingratitude to his Benefactor. To this his Avarice answered, 'That his Conscience should have considered that Matter before, when he deprived poor *Jones* of his 500 *l*. That having quietly acquiesced in what was of so much greater Importance, it was absurd, if not downright Hypocrisy, to affect any Qualms at this Trifle.' In return to which, Conscience, like a good Lawyer, attempted to distinguish between an absolute Breach of Trust, as here where the Goods were delivered, and a bare Concealment of what was found, as in the former Case.[1] Avarice presently treated this with Ridicule, called it a Distinction without a Difference, and absolutely insisted, that when once all Pretensions of Honour and Virtue were given up in any one Instance, that there was no Precedent for resorting to them upon a second Occasion. In short, poor Conscience had certainly been defeated in the

---

[1] A casuist might thus distinguish between these points in a 'court of conscience'. In a court of law, however, if an 'action of trover' were brought against Black George by the rightful owners, he would be compelled to restore to the plaintiffs both the bank-notes and the guineas. (See below, p. 632, n. 2, and p. 947, where Lawyer Dowling advises Allworthy to prosecute George in this way.)

Argument, had not Fear stept in to her Assistance, and very strenuously urged, that the real Distinction between the two Actions, did not lie in the different Degrees of Honour, but of Safety: For that the secreting the 500 *l.* was a Matter of very little Hazard; whereas the detaining the Sixteen Guineas was liable to the utmost Danger of Discovery.

By this friendly Aid of Fear, Conscience obtained a compleat Victory in the Mind of *Black George*, and after making him a few Compliments on his Honesty, forced him to deliver the Money to *Jones.*

CHAPTER XIV

A short Chapter, containing a short Dialogue between Squire Western *and his Sister.*

MRS. *Western* had been engaged abroad all that Day. The Squire met her at her Return home; and when she enquired after *Sophia*, he acquainted her that he had secured her safe enough. 'She is locked up in Chamber,' cries he, 'and *Honour* keeps the Key.' As his Looks were full of prodigious Wisdom and Sagacity when he gave his Sister this Information, it is probable he expected much Applause from her for what he had done; but how was he disappointed, when with a most disdainful Aspect, she cry'd, 'Sure, Brother, you are the weakest of all Men. Why will you not confide in me for the Management of my Niece? Why will you interpose? You have now undone all that I have been spending my Breath in order to bring about. While I have been endeavouring to fill her Mind with Maxims of Prudence, you have been provoking her to reject them. *English* Women, Brother, I thank Heaven, are no Slaves. We are not to be locked up like the *Spanish* and *Italian* Wives. We have as good a Right to Liberty as yourselves. We are to be convinced by Reason and Persuasion only, and not governed by Force. I have seen the World, Brother, and know what Arguments to make Use of; and if your Folly had not prevented me, should have prevailed with her to form her Conduct by those Rules of Prudence and Discretion which I formerly taught her.' 'To be sure,' said the Squire, 'I am always in the Wrong.' 'Brother,' answered the

Lady, 'you are not in the Wrong, unless when you meddle with Matters beyond your Knowledge. You must agree, that I have seen most of the World; and happy had it been for my Niece, if she had not been taken from under my Care. It is by living at home with you that she hath learnt romantic Notions of Love and Nonsense.' 'You don't imagine, I hope,' cries the Squire, 'that I have taught her any such Things.' 'Your Ignorance, Brother,' returned she, 'as the great *Milton* says, almost subdues my Patience.'* 'D——n *Milton*,' answered the Squire, 'if he had the Impudence to say so to my Face, I'd lend him a Douse, thof he was never so great a Man. Patience! an you come to that, Sister, I have more Occasion of Patience, to be used like an over-grown School-boy as I am by you. Do you think no one hath any Understanding, unless he hath been about at Court? Pox! the World is come to a fine Pass indeed, if we are all Fools, except a Parcel of Roundheads and *Hannover* Rats. Pox! I hope the Times are a coming that we shall make Fools of them, and every Man shall enjoy his own. That's all, Sister, and every Man shall enjoy his own.[1] I hope to *zee* it, Sister, before the *Hannover* Rats have eat up all our Corn,[2] and left us nothing but Turneps[3] to feed

* The Reader may perhaps subdue his own Patience, if he searches for this in *Milton*.

---

[1] 'The King shall enjoy his own again' was a Jacobite song.

[2] Formulated in July 1742, the government's policy of subsidizing large numbers of Hanoverian troops to fight in the Pragmatic army soon became the most controversial issue of the period. While in Opposition, Fielding's friends Lyttelton, Pitt, Dodington, and Chesterfield were outspoken critics of the measure, and, ironically enough, in November 1744 Fielding himself had anticipated Squire Western's strictures in the satirical pamphlet, *An Attempt towards a Natural History of the Hanover Rat*: these 'Vermin', he declared, 'are become the Plague and Terror of the Nation'; 'they are now to be found in every Man's Ground in the Kingdom, seeking what they can devour.' When, however, on the strength of such criticism his friends rose to power the following month, their attitude toward the Hanoverian question changed completely; from opposing the policy, they became its staunchest advocates. (See J. B. Owen, *The Rise of the Pelhams* [1957], chs. iv–vii.) Thereafter, as the principal spokesman for the new administration, Fielding undertook to defend the very measures he had formerly ridiculed. In *The Jacobite's Journal* (13 February 1748), for instance, he anticipated the satire of Western by printing a letter from 'Humphry Gubbins', a blustering, illiterate Tory squire who urges the editor to give the Ministry 'zum *Stingers*' about *Forreners*; and don't forget HANNOVER RATS; for I promise you I've a zeed um, and larger Rats they be than ever were a zeed in *England*, till of late Years'. (See the similar letter from 'George Trott' in the *Journal* for 30 January 1748.)

[3] In the political satires of this period, Hanover was often referred to as the 'Turnip garden'. Occasioned by Parliament's decision in 1742 to retain the Hanoverian troops in British pay, one print, entitled 'The H[anove]r T[urni]p Man come again', depicts one of these soldiers holding a bunch of turnips and exclaiming, 'By G-d these Turnips are dear'.

upon.' 'I protest, Brother,' cries she, 'you are now got beyond my Understanding. Your Jargon of Turneps and *Hannover Rats*, is to me perfectly unintelligible.' 'I believe,' cries he, 'you don't care to hear o'em; but the Country Interest[1] may succeed one Day or other for all that.' 'I wish,' answered the Lady, 'you would think a little of your Daughter's Interest: For believe me, she is in greater Danger than the Nation.' 'Just now,' said he, 'you chid me for thinking on her, and would ha' her left to you.' 'And if you will promise to interpose no more,' answered she, 'I will, out of my Regard to my Niece, undertake the Charge.' 'Well, do then,' said the Squire, 'for you know I always agreed, that Women are the properest to manage Women.'

Mrs. *Western* then departed, muttering something with an Air of Disdain, concerning Women and the Management of the Nation. She immediately repaired to *Sophia's* Apartment, who was now, after a Day's Confinement released again from her Captivity.

The End of the Second Volume.

(See Print No. 2578, *Catalogue of Prints and Drawings in the British Museum*, Division I, Political and Personal Satires, iii [1734–*c.* 1750], edd. F. G. Stephens and E. Hawkins, 1877.)

[1] See above, p. 272, n. 1.

BOOK VII

Containing three Days.

CHAPTER I

A Comparison between the World and the Stage.

THE World hath been often compared to the Theatre;[1] and many grave Writers, as well as the Poets, have considered human Life as a great Drama, resembling, in almost every Particular, those scenical Representations, which *Thespis*[2] is first reported to have invented, and which have been since received with so much Approbation and Delight in all polite Countries.

This Thought hath been carried so far, and is become so general, that some Words proper to the Theatre, and which were, at first, metaphorically applied to the World, are now indiscriminately and literally spoken of both: Thus Stage and Scene are by common Use grown as familiar to us, when we speak of Life in general, as when we confine ourselves to dramatic Performances; and when Transactions behind the Curtain are

---

[1] For a discussion of this commonplace and its significance within the Christian humanist tradition, see Aubrey L. Williams, *Pope's 'Dunciad': A Study of its Meaning* (1955), ch. iv, esp. pp. 94 ff., and his article, 'Poetical Justice, the Contrivances of Providence, and the Works of William Congreve', *ELH*, xxxv (1968), 540–65, esp. pp. 547–53. The *locus classicus* is Epictetus: 'Remember, that the World is a Theatre, and that your Part in this Play of Life is determined by the Poet: Upon him it must depend, whether you shall act a long or a short one; whether your Character shall be high or low: If therefore he assign you that of a Beggar, take care to humour it well; if a Cripple, or a Prince, or a private obscure Man, or whatever it be, make the best of it: For consider, that the playing of the Part assigned you commendably, depends upon your self. This is your Business; but the giving out of the Parts, and choosing the Actors, is not yours, but another Person's.' (George Stanhope, trans. *Epictetus His Morals, With Simplicius His Comment* [1694], p. 193.) The point of this comparison, as Simplicius remarks, is to enforce the lesson that man's duty is to accept the part that Providence has assigned him and to act it well. To a degree anticipating Fielding's later development of the metaphor in this chapter, Simplicius points out that, like the audience in the theatre, those who behold this spectacle of life reserve their applause not for the part assigned us but for the manner of our acting it.

In *The Champion* (19 August 1740) Fielding, at some length, had presented a similar analogy between the world and the stage. For a contemporary treatment of this figure with which he was certainly acquainted, see James Harris, 'Concerning Happiness', *Three Treatises* (1744), pp. 210–11, 333–4 (Note liii).

[2] See Horace, *Ars Poetica*, 275–7.

mentioned, *St. James's* is more likely to occur to our Thoughts than *Drury-Lane*.

It may seem easy enough to account for all this, by reflecting that the theatrical Stage is nothing more than a Representation, or, as *Aristotle* calls it,[1] an Imitation of what really exists; and hence, perhaps, we might fairly pay a very high Compliment to those, who by their Writings or Actions have been so capable of imitating Life, as to have their Pictures, in a Manner confounded with, or mistaken for the Originals.

But, in Reality, we are not so fond of paying Compliments to these People, whom we use as Children frequently do the Instruments of their Amusement; and have much more Pleasure in hissing and buffeting them, than in admiring their Excellence. There are many other Reasons which have induced us to see this Analogy between the World and the Stage.

Some have considered the larger Part of Mankind in the Light of Actors, as personating Characters no more their own, and to which, in Fact, they have no better Title, than the Player hath to be in Earnest thought the King or Emperor whom he represents. Thus the Hypocrite may be said to be a Player; and indeed the *Greeks* called them both by one and the same Name.[2]

The Brevity of Life hath likewise given Occasion to this Comparison. So the immortal *Shakespear*:[3]

> ——*Life's a poor Player,*
> *That struts and frets his Hour upon the Stage,*
> *And then is heard no more.*

For which hackneyed Quotation, I will make the Reader Amends by a very noble one, which few, I believe, have read. It is taken from a Poem called the DEITY,[4] published about nine Years ago, and long since buried in Oblivion. A Proof that good Books no more than good Men do always survive the bad.

---

[1] Cf. *Poetics*, i. 2, xxv. 2.

[2] The Greek word ὑποκριτής signifies both a dissembler and an actor on the stage.

[3] *Macbeth*, v. v.

[4] *Deity* by Samuel Boyse (1708–May 1749), a poem on the attributes of God done vaguely in the manner of Pope's *Essay on Man*. It is pleasant to note that Fielding's 'puff' in *Tom Jones*, together with James Hervey's praise in his *Meditations and Contemplations* (1746), was instrumental in rescuing *Deity* from 'Oblivion'—as one may infer from the advertisements announcing publication of a second edition on 6 March 1749 (see *The*

From thee* all human Actions take their Springs,
The Rise of Empires, and the Fall of Kings!
See the VAST THEATRE OF TIME *display'd,*
While o'er the Scene succeeding Heroes tread!
With Pomp the shining Images succeed,
What Leaders triumph, and what Monarchs bleed!
Perform the Parts thy Providence assign'd,
Their Pride, their Passions to thy Ends inclin'd:
A while they glitter in the Face of Day,
Then at thy Nod the Phantoms pass away;
No Traces left of all the busy Scene,
*But that Remembrance says—*THE THINGS HAVE BEEN!

In all these, however, and in every other Similitude of Life to the Theatre, the Resemblance hath been always taken from the Stage only. None, as I remember, have at all considered the Audience at this great Drama.

But as Nature often exhibits some of her best Performances to a very full House; so will the Behaviour of her Spectators no less admit the above-mentioned Comparison than that of her Actors. In this vast Theatre of Time are seated the Friend and the Critic; here are Claps and Shouts, Hisses and Groans; in short, every Thing which was ever seen or heard at the Theatre Royal.

Let us examine this in one Example: For Instance, in the Behaviour of the great Audience on that Scene which Nature was pleased to exhibit in the 12th Chapter of the preceding Book, where she introduced *Black George* running away with the 500 *l.* from his Friend and Benefactor.

* The DEITY.

General Advertiser, 6–8 March 1749). A third edition appeared in 1752 and thereafter the poem was frequently anthologized.

Fielding, in fact, had admired Boyse's poem when it was originally published in February 1740 (the title-page reads 1739). In a 'Literary Article' in *The Champion* (12 February 1739/40) he wrote: 'Last Week a Poem was publish'd, with the simple but all-comprehensive Title of *Deity*; which, 'tis presum'd, will excite but little Curiosity, and therefore, will be but little read: Not that it does not deserve a Reading, or will not afford a serious Mind a very elevated Entertainment,—but because few Readers can be entertain'd with what is serious, or care to be made so themselves. 'Tis divided into as many Sections, as we ascribe attributes to the Godhead: is wrote in a clear and elegant Stile, the versification smooth and flowing, but by being cramp'd within almost perpetual Distichs, allows very little Variety of Cadence, and Period: And that it is not void of the Sublime, let the following Passage demonstrate.' He then quotes from *Deity*, section viii ('Providence'), 615–26—the identical passage reprinted in *Tom Jones*.

Those who sat in the World's upper Gallery,[1] treated that Incident, I am well convinced, with their usual Vociferation; and every Term of scurrilous Reproach was most probably vented on that Occasion.

If we had descended to the next Order of Spectators, we should have found an equal Degree of Abhorrence, tho' less of Noise and Scurrility; yet here the good Women gave *Black George* to the Devil, and many of them expected every Minute that the cloven-footed Gentleman would fetch his own.

The Pit, as usual, was no doubt divided: Those who delight in heroic Virtue and perfect Character, objected to the producing such Instances of Villainy, without punishing them very severely for the Sake of Example.[2] Some of the Author's Friends, cry'd— 'Look'e, Gentlemen, the Man is a Villain; but it is Nature for all that.' And all the young Critics of the Age, the Clerks, Apprentices, &c. called it Low, and fell a Groaning.

As for the Boxes, they behaved with their accustomed Politeness. Most of them were attending to something else. Some of those few who regarded the Scene at all, declared he was a bad Kind of Man; while others refused to give their Opinion till they had heard that of the best Judges.

---

[1] A useful gloss on Fielding's characterization of the four classes of theatre-goers is the following passage from *The Tricks of the Town laid open: or, A Companion for Country Gentlemen,* 2nd ed. (1747), letter vii: 'In our Playhouses at *London,* besides an Upper-Gallery for Footmen, Coachmen, Mendicants, &c. we have three other different and distinct Classes; the first is called the *Boxes,* where there is one peculiar to the King and Royal Family, and the rest for the Persons of Quality, and for the Ladies and Gentlemen of the highest Rank.... The second is call'd the *Pit,* where sit the *Judges, Wits* and *Censurers,* or rather the *Censurers without either Wit or Judgment.* These are the *Bully-Judges,* that *damn and sink the Play at a venture;* 'tis no matter whether it be good or bad, but 'tis a *Play,* and *they are the Judges,* and so it must be *damn'd, curs'd, and censur'd* in Course; in common with these sit the *Squires, Sharpers, Beaus, Bullies* and *Whores,* and here and there an extravagant *Male* and *Female Cit.* The third is distinguished by the Title of the *Middle Gallery,* where the Citizens Wives and Daughters, together with the *Abigails,* Serving-men, Journey-men and Apprentices commonly take their Places; and now and then some desponding Mistresses and superannuated Poets' (pp. 27–8). In 1748 the prices for the four seating areas were: boxes 5*s.,* pit 3*s.,* first [or middle] gallery 2*s.,* upper gallery 1*s.*

[2] On the differing attitudes toward the dramatic rule of poetic justice in the period, see Richard H. Tyre, 'Versions of Poetic Justice in the Early Eighteenth Century', *SP,* liv (1957), 29–44. Those who believed that in drama virtue should be invariably rewarded and vice punished for the sake of the moral lesson included Dryden's Eugenius, Rymer, Tate, Temple, Dennis, and Blackmore. Fielding, however, would seem here to side with Addison in considering this an unnatural and 'ridiculous Doctrine in modern Criticism' (*Spectator,* No. 40 [16 April 1711]).

Now we, who are admitted behind the Scenes of this great Theatre of Nature, (and no Author ought to write any Thing besides Dictionaries and Spelling-Books[1] who hath not this Privilege) can censure the Action, without conceiving any absolute Detestation of the Person, whom perhaps Nature may not have designed to act an ill Part in all her Dramas: For in this Instance, Life most exactly resembles the Stage, since it is often the same Person who represents the Villain and the Heroe; and he who engages your Admiration To-day, will probably attract your Contempt To-Morrow. As *Garrick*,[2] whom I regard in Tragedy to be the greatest Genius the World hath ever produced, sometimes condescends to play the Fool; so did *Scipio* the Great and *Lælius* the Wise, according to *Horace*,[3] many Years ago: nay, *Cicero* reports them to have been 'incredibly childish.'[4]—These, it is true play'd the Fool, like my Friend *Garrick*, in Jest only; but

---

[1] If a specific reference is intended, it is doubtless to Nathan Bailey (see below, p. 333, n. 2), author of *Dictionarium Britannicum: or a more Compleat Universal Etymological English Dictionary* (1721, 1736, and many other editions), *An Orthographical Dictionary* (1727), and *An Introduction to the English Tongue: Being a Spelling Book . . . For the Use of Schools* (1726). For other allusions to Bailey in Fielding's writings, see *The Champion* (14 February 1739/40, 17 May 1740) and *The Covent-Garden Journal* (18 February 1752). In 1755 Bailey's dictionary, of course, would be superseded by Johnson's, the *Plan* of which, addressed to Lord Chesterfield, was published in August 1747. With Fielding's low opinion of the abilities of lexicographers, compare Johnson's introductory remarks, regretting that the work in which he was engaged 'is generally considered as drudgery for the blind, as the proper toil of artless industry; a task that requires neither the light of learning, nor the activity of genius, but may be successfully performed without any higher quality than that of bearing burthens with dull patience, and beating the track of the alphabet with sluggish resolution'. Of 'all the candidates for literary praise', Johnson continued, 'the unhappy lexicographer holds the lowest place'.

[2] David Garrick (1717–79), the brilliant actor who in 1747 became patentee of the Drury-Lane Theatre. Fielding and Garrick were the closest of friends. From the *Miscellanies* (1743) to *The Covent-Garden Journal* (1752) Fielding's writings abound in extravagant compliments to the man he esteemed 'the best Actor the World could have ever produced' (see the *Journal* for 11 January 1752). Garrick's most popular comic roles included Bayes, Abel Drugger, Costar Pearmain, Fondlewife, and Sir John Brute. Some critics, however, were sufficiently dour to object to his donning the sock. On 18 January 1742 the Rev. Mr. Newton wrote to Garrick complaining: 'You . . . strangely demean yourself in acting any thing that is low and little. . . . If I was an actor surely I would rather wish to be a Raphael than a Hogarth; or if I was a poet, I would choose infinitely rather to be a Milton than a Hudibras' (quoted in A. H. Scouten, *The London Stage, 1660–1800*, Part III: 1729–47 [Carbondale, Ill., 1961], p. 959). For other allusions to Garrick in *Tom Jones*, see below, pp. 493, 853.

[3] *Satires*, II. i. 71–4. Scipio Africanus Minor (*c.* 185–129 B.C.) and Caius Laelius Sapiens (b. *c.* 186 B.C.).

[4] *De Oratore*, II. vi. See also *Joseph Andrews* (1742; III. vii).

several eminent Characters have, in numberless Instances of their Lives, played the Fool egregiously in Earnest; so far as to render it a Matter of some Doubt, whether their Wisdom or Folly was predominant; or whether they were better intitled to the Applause or Censure, the Admiration or Contempt, the Love or Hatred of Mankind.

Those Persons, indeed, who have passed any Time behind the Scenes of this great Theatre, and are thoroughly acquainted not only with the several Disguises which are there put on, but also with the fantastic and capricious Behaviour of the Passions¹ who are the Managers and Directors of this Theatre, (for as to Reason the Patentee, he is known to be a very idle Fellow, and seldom to exert himself) may most probably have learned to understand the famous *Nil admirari* of *Horace*,² or in the *English* Phrase, *To stare at nothing*.

A single bad Act no more constitutes a Villain in Life, than a single bad Part on the Stage. The Passions, like the Managers of

---

¹ To explain the actions of men and the apparent variety in their characters, Fielding resorted to the familiar psychological theory of the passions—a theory most memorably expressed in Pope's *Epistle to Cobham* (1734) and in Epistle II of the *Essay on Man* (1733–4). (See Bertrand A. Goldgar, 'Pope's Theory of the Passions: The Background of Epistle II of the *Essay on Man*', *PQ*, xli [1962], 730–43.) Accordingly, in the poem 'To John Hayes, Esq;' (1743) Fielding remarked in individual men

> How Passions blended on each other fix,
> How Vice with Virtues, Faults with Graces mix;
> How Passions opposite, as sour to sweet,
> Shall in one Bosom at one Moment meet.

Yet in Fielding's view, as in Pope's, a man's actions are generally determined by the impulses of one master passion that dominates the rest: thus Black George, the example of the present chapter, is said to be 'honest' enough when his better nature is not subdued by his love of money (VI. xii), and Fielding's other characters—from Lady Booby and Peter Pounce to Miss Matthews and Colonel James—similarly reveal the dominion of Lust or Avarice or Vanity in their minds. Both the cogency of this theory and its dangerous consequences to the moralist who embraces it too casually and uncritically are presented at length in the story of Captain Booth in *Amelia* (1751), whose belief that men act solely from the impulses of a dominant passion betrays him into the philosophical error of fatalism. The lesson that Booth finally learns had been stated earlier in *The Champion* (2 February 1739/40), where Fielding recommended 'that glorious Precept *vince teipsum*', the necessity for the individual, by reason and the will, to direct and order the passions. As he put it in the introductory chapter to *Amelia* (1751), only by the proper exercise of 'Prudence' (see above, p. 36, n. 1) may we escape the miseries in which we involve ourselves by 'following the blind Guidance of a predominant Passion'. (For discussions of Fielding's theory of the passions, see Battestin, *The Moral Basis of Fielding's Art* [1959], pp. 58–60, and Miller, *Essays on Fielding's 'Miscellanies'* [1961], pp. 113–18.)

² *Epistles*, I. vi. 1.

a Playhouse, often force Men upon Parts, without consulting their Judgement, and sometimes without any Regard to their Talents. Thus the Man, as well as the Player, may condemn what he himself acts; nay, it is common to see Vice sit as awkwardly on some Men, as the Character of *Iago* would on the honest Face of Mr. *William Mills*.[1]

Upon the whole then, the Man of Candour, and of true Understanding, is never hasty to condemn. He can censure an Imperfection, or even a Vice, without Rage against the guilty Party. In a Word, they are the same Folly, the same Childishness, the same Ill-breeding, and the same Ill-nature, which raise all the Clamours and Uproars both in Life, and on the Stage. The worst of Men generally have the Words *Rogue* and *Villain* most in their Mouths, as the lowest of all Wretches are the aptest to cry out *low* in the Pit.

---

[1] Fielding was especially fond of '*Honest Billy Mills*' (d. 17 April 1750), a good man if no very good actor. He paid him an early compliment in *Joseph Andrews* (1742; I. viii), and later, when Mills and his family had fallen upon hard times, Fielding devoted space in *The Jacobite's Journal* (23 April 1748) to urging attendance at a benefit performance for him at Drury Lane. Perhaps, as Oliver Ferguson has proposed (*PQ*, xliii [1964], 73–8), Mills in the role of Claudius is the victim of Partridge's 'vile encomium' in *Tom Jones* (XVI. v; see below, p. 855, n. 2).

Implicit in the present passage, moreover, may well be a facetious allusion to another actor friend of Fielding's, Charles Macklin (1699–1797). Macklin's 'good long, dismal, mercy-begging Face', as he himself called it in the Prologue to *The Wedding Day* (1743), was a standing jest in theatrical circles; to the player in *Joseph Andrews* (III. x), for example, he is an 'ill-looked Dog'. Early in 1747 Macklin became the focus of a critical controversy concerning his facial qualifications to play the role of Iago—not that, like Mills, his face was too 'honest', but that, on the contrary, the marks of the villain were so indelibly stamped on his countenance that the audience could not believe in him as 'honest Iago', the fair-seeming hypocrite. In *A Treatise on the Passions, So far as they regard the Stage* (February 1747), Samuel Foote defended Macklin against his detractors: 'Let us now proceed to examine whether Mr. *Macklin* is happy in looking this Character [i.e. Iago]. I think it is generally agreed that his Muscles are luckily formed for marking the Villain; but it has been objected, that Nature has denied him the Advantage of expressing the open, sincere, honest Man; or, in other Words, of playing the Hypocrite well in this Part'; but, Foote generously noted, 'let *Macklin*'s Visage be ever so unfortunate, I am sure he has the Art of looking more like a Rogue at one Time than another' (p. 38). Unconvinced, one 'J. T.' replied: '*M[acklin]* has such a strong Stamp of the Villian [*sic*] imprinted in his Countenance, even when he endeavours to appear honest; that we can't help thinking it a Weakness in *Othello* to have any Concerns with him at all' (*A Letter of Compliment to the ingenious Author of a Treatise on the Passions* [March 1747], p. 27).

CHAPTER II

Containing a Conversation which Mr. Jones *had with himself.*

JONES received his Effects from Mr. *Allworthy's* early in the Morning, with the following Answer to his Letter.

Sir,

'I am commanded by my Uncle to acquaint you, that as he did not proceed to those Measures he had taken with you, without the greatest Deliberation, and after the fullest Evidence of your Unworthiness, so will it be always out of your Power to cause the least Alteration in his Resolution. He expresses great Surprize at your Presumption in saying, you have resigned all Pretensions to a young Lady, to whom it is impossible you should ever have had any, her Birth and Fortune having made her so infinitely your superior. Lastly, I am commanded to tell you, that the only Instance of your Compliance with my Uncle's Inclinations, which he requires, is, your immediately quitting this Country. I cannot conclude this without offering you my Advice, as a Christian, that you would seriously think of amending your Life; that you may be assisted with Grace so to do, will be always the Prayer of

Your Humble Servant,

W. Blifil.'

Many contending Passions were raised in our Heroe's Mind by this Letter; but the Tender prevailed at last over the Indignant and Irascible, and a Flood of Tears came seasonably to his Assistance, and possibly prevented his Misfortunes from either turning his Head, or bursting his Heart.

He grew, however, soon ashamed of indulging this Remedy; and starting up, he cried, 'Well then, I will give Mr. *Allworthy* the only Instance he requires of my Obedience. I will go this Moment—but whither?—why, let Fortune direct; since there is no other who thinks it of any Consequence what becomes of this wretched Person, it shall be a Matter of equal Indifference to myself. Shall I alone regard what no other?—Ha! have I not Reason to think there is another?—One whose Value is above that of the whole World!—I may, I must imagine my *Sophia* is not indifferent to what becomes of me. Shall I then leave this only

Friend—and such a Friend? Shall I not stay with her?—Where? How can I stay with her? Have I any Hopes of ever seeing her, tho' she was as desirous as myself, without exposing her to the Wrath of her Father? And to what Purpose? Can I think of soliciting such a Creature to consent to her own Ruin? Shall I indulge any Passion of mine at such a Price?—Shall I lurk about this Country like a Thief, with such Intentions?—No, I disdain, I detest the Thought. Farewel, *Sophia*; farewel most lovely, most beloved——' Here Passion stopped his Mouth, and found a Vent at his Eyes.

And now, having taken a Resolution to leave the Country, he began to debate with himself whither he should go. *The World*, as *Milton* phrases it,[1] *lay all before him*; and *Jones*, no more than *Adam*, had any Man to whom he might resort for Comfort or Assistance. All his Acquaintance were the Acquaintance of Mr. *Allworthy*, and he had no reason to expect any Countenance from them, as that Gentleman had with-drawn his Favour from him. Men of great and good Characters should indeed be very cautious how they discard their Dependents; for the Consequence to the unhappy Sufferer is being discarded by all others.

What Course of Life to pursue, or to what Business to apply himself, was a second Consideration; and here the Prospect was all a melancholy Void. Every Profession, and every Trade, required Length of Time, and what was worse, Money; for Matters are so constituted, that 'Nothing out of Nothing'[2] is not a truer Maxim in Physics than in Politics; and every Man who is greatly destitute of Money, is on that Account entirely excluded from all Means of acquiring it.

At last the Ocean, that hospitable Friend to the Wretched, opened her capacious Arms to receive him; and he instantly resolved to accept her kind Invitation. To express myself less figuratively, he determined to go to Sea.

This Thought indeed no sooner suggested itself, than he eagerly embraced it; and having presently hired Horses, he set out for *Bristol* to put it in Execution.

---

[1] *Paradise Lost*, xii. 646–7. Adam and Eve having been banished from Eden, Milton writes: 'The World was all before them, where to choose'/ Thir place of rest, and Providence thir guide.'

[2] *Ex nihilo nihil fit*—a maxim found in Aristotle, *Physica* (I. iv. 2–3) and *Metaphysica* (III. iv. 4), Lucretius *De Rerum Natura* (i. 155–6), and elsewhere. Fielding plays with the idea in his 'Essay on Nothing' (1743), section i.

But before we attend him on this Expedition, we shall resort a while to Mr. *Western's*, and see what farther happened to the charming *Sophia*.

CHAPTER III

Containing several Dialogues.

THE Morning in which Mr. *Jones* departed, Mrs. *Western* summoned *Sophia* into her Apartment, and having first acquainted her that she had obtained her Liberty of her Father, she proceeded to read her a long Lecture on the Subject of Matrimony; which she treated not as a romantic Scheme of Happiness arising from Love, as it hath been described by the Poets; nor did she mention any of those Purposes for which we are taught by Divines to regard it as instituted by sacred Authority; she considered it rather as a Fund in which prudent Women deposite their Fortunes to the best Advantage, in order to receive a larger Interest for them, than they could have elsewhere.

When Mrs. *Western* had finished, *Sophia* answered, 'that she was very incapable of arguing with a Lady of her Aunt's superior Knowledge and Experience, especially on a Subject which she had so very little considered, as this of Matrimony.'

'Argue with me, Child!' replied the other, 'I do not indeed expect it. I should have seen the World to very little Purpose truly, if I am to argue with one of your Years. I have taken this Trouble, in order to instruct you. The ancient Philosophers, such as *Socrates*, *Alcibiades*,[1] and others, did not use to argue with their Scholars. You are to consider me, Child, as *Socrates*, not asking your Opinion, but only informing you of mine.' From which last Words the Reader may possibly imagine, that this Lady had read no more of the Philosophy of *Socrates*, than she had of that of *Alcibiades*; and indeed we cannot resolve his Curiosity as to this Point.

'Madam,' cries *Sophia*, 'I have never presumed to controvert

---

[1] Though he appears with Socrates in the *Symposium* and in the dialogue which bears his name, Alcibiades (b. *c.* 450 B.C.) was of course not a philosopher, but an Athenian general and politician. Nor is Mrs. Western any better acquainted with the Socratic method, in which a series of easily answered questions leads to a foregone conclusion.

any Opinion of yours, and this Subject, as I said, I have never yet thought of, and perhaps never may.'

'Indeed, *Sophy*,' replied the Aunt, 'this Dissimulation with me is very foolish. The *French* shall as soon persuade me, that they take foreign Towns in Defence only of their own Country, as you can impose on me to believe you have never yet thought seriously of Matrimony. How can you, Child, affect to deny that you have considered of contracting an Alliance, when you so well know I am acquainted with the Party with whom you desire to contract it. An Alliance as unnatural, and contrary to your Interest, as a separate League with the *French* would be to the Interest of the *Dutch*![1] But however, if you have not hitherto considered of this Matter, I promise you it is now high Time; for my Brother is resolved immediately to conclude the Treaty with Mr. *Blifil*; and indeed I am a sort of Guarantee in the Affair, and have promised your Concurrence.'

'Indeed, Madam,' cries *Sophia*, 'this is the only Instance in which I must disobey both yourself and my Father. For this is a Match which requires very little Consideration in me to refuse.'

'If I was not as great a Philosopher as *Socrates* himself,' returned Mrs. *Western*, 'you would overcome my Patience. What Objection can you have to the young Gentleman?'

'A very solid Objection, in my Opinion,' says *Sophia*,—'I hate him.'

'Will you never learn a proper Use of Words?' answered the Aunt. 'Indeed Child, you should consult *Bailey's Dictionary*.[2] It is

---

[1] Until France actually invaded Flanders in April 1747—an event which led to the election of William as Stadtholder of the United Provinces and to a stiffening of their resistance in the war—the Dutch had been openly negotiating toward a separate peace with France that would allow them to withdraw from the conflict. The French had made overtures to this purpose as early as July 1742, and in the autumn of 1745 a congress was proposed to arrange the treaty. (See Jean Rousset, *Relation historique de la grande révolution arrivée dans la république des Provinces-Unies* [Amsterdam, 1747]; also the anonymous work, *Considerations on the Conduct of the Dutch* [1745].) In England, naturally, the Dutch neutralist policy was regarded with a mixture of resentment and apprehension. In *The True Patriot* it was the subject of several articles, the intent of which was to advise the Dutch that their own interest and self-respect should dissuade them from purchasing a temporary peace at the price of becoming a mere province of France (see, for example, the numbers for 18–25 March, 25 March–1 April 1746, under 'Foreign History').

[2] Nathan or Nathaniel Bailey (d. 1742), author of *Dictionarium Britannicum: Or a Compleat Universal Etymological English Dictionary* (1721). (See above, p. 327, n. 1.) In her insistence on the 'proper Use of Words' Mrs. Western may recall Bailey's Preface: 'Words are those Vehicles or Channels by the which the Knowledge of Things is convey'd to our

impossible you should hate a Man from whom you have received no Injury. By Hatred, therefore, you mean no more than Dislike, which is no sufficient Objection against your marrying of him. I have known many Couples, who have entirely disliked each other, lead very comfortable, genteel Lives. Believe me, Child, I know these Things better than you. You will allow me, I think, to have seen the World, in which I have not an Acquaintance who would not rather be thought to dislike her Husband, than to like him. The contrary is such out-of-Fashion romantic Nonsense, that the very Imagination of it is shocking.'

'Indeed Madam,' replied *Sophia*, 'I shall never marry a Man I dislike. If I promise my Father never to consent to any Marriage contrary to his Inclinations, I think I may hope he will never force me into that State contrary to my own.'

'Inclinations!' cries the Aunt, with some Warmth. 'Inclinations! I am astonished at your Assurance. A young Woman of your Age, and unmarried, to talk of Inclinations! But whatever your Inclinations may be, my Brother is resolved; nay, since you talk of Inclinations, I shall advise him to hasten the Treaty. Inclinations!'

Sophia then flung herself upon her Knees, and Tears began to trickle from her shining Eyes. She entreated her Aunt 'to have Mercy upon her, and not to resent so cruelly her Unwillingness to make herself miserable;' often urging, 'that she alone was concerned, and that her Happiness only was at Stake.'

As a Bailiff, when well authorised by his Writ, having possessed himself of the Person of some unhappy Debtor, views all his Tears without Concern: In vain the wretched Captive attempts to raise Compassion; in vain the tender Wife bereft of her Companion, the little prattling Boy, or frighted Girl, are mentioned as Inducements to Reluctance. The noble Bumtrap, blind

Understandings and therefore, upon a right Apprehension of the Meaning of them, depends the Rectitude of those Ideas or Notions that we receive by hearing or reading. Therefore in Order to furnish our Minds with just and adequate Ideas, either of the Things, Matters, or Facts; Words must be apprehended in their proper Sense and Meaning, either in receiving from or communicating to others: For if the Words either of a Speaker or Writer, tho' ever so Apposite to the Matter be taken or understood in a wrong Sense, they will necessarily form wrong Conceptions concerning the Thing spoken or written of; and if we our selves use Words in an improper Sense, this will cause a Confusion in the Understanding of the Hearer and render our Discourse both unintelligible and useless' (2nd ed., 1736; Sig. a1^r). In this edition Bailey defines 'A HATELING' as 'a hated Person, or one who deserves to be hated'.

and deaf to every Circumstance of Distress, greatly rises above all the Motives to Humanity, and into the Hands of the Goaler resolves to deliver his miserable Prey.

Not less blind to the Tears, or less deaf to every Entreaty of *Sophia* was the politic Aunt, nor less determined was she to deliver over the trembling Maid into the Arms of the Goaler *Blifil*. She answered with great Impetuosity, 'So far, Madam, from your being concerned alone, your Concern is the least, or surely the least important. It is the Honour of your Family which is concerned in this Alliance; you are only the Instrument. Do you conceive, Mistress, that in an Intermarriage between Kingdoms, as when a Daughter of *France* is married into *Spain*,[1] the Princess herself is alone considered in the Match? No, it is a Match between two Kingdoms, rather than between two Persons. The same happens in great Families, such as ours. The Alliance between the Families is the principal Matter. You ought to have a greater Regard for the Honour of your Family, than for your own Person; and if the Example of a Princess cannot inspire you with these noble Thoughts, you cannot surely complain at being used no worse than all Princesses are used.'

'I hope, Madam,' cries *Sophia*, with a little Elevation of Voice, 'I shall never do any Thing to dishonour my Family; but as for Mr. *Blifil*, whatever may be the Consequence, I am resolved against him, and no Force shall prevail in his Favour.'

Western, who had been within hearing during the greater Part of the preceding Dialogue, had now exhausted all his Patience; he therefore entered the Room in a violent Passion, crying, 'D—n me then if *shatunt* ha' un, d—n me if *shatunt*, that's all—— that's all—— D—n me if *shatunt*.'

Mrs. *Western* had collected a sufficient Quantity of Wrath for the Use of *Sophia*; but she now transferred it all to the Squire. 'Brother,' said she, 'it is astonishing that you will interfere in a Matter which you had totally left to my Negotiation. Regard to my Family hath made me take upon myself to be the mediating Power, in order to rectify those Mistakes in Policy which you

---

[1] In August 1739, shortly after her twelfth birthday, Louise Elizabeth, daughter of Louis XV, was married by proxy to Don Philip, son of Philip V of Spain. Commenting on this political marriage, a correspondent in *The General Advertiser* (3 February 1748) noted that 'a Daughter of France is little set by, if a Provision for her any Way interferes with the Aggrandizement of the Monarchy. To this single Point, all the Maxims taught at Versailles have a Tendency, either directly or indirectly, openly or covertly'.

have committed in your Daughter's Education. For, Brother, it is you; it is your preposterous Conduct which hath eradicated all the Seeds that I had formerly sown in her tender Mind.—It is you yourself who have taught her Disobedience.'—'Blood!' cries the Squire, foaming at the Mouth, 'you are enough to conquer the Patience of the Devil! Have I ever taught my Daughter Disobedience?—Here she stands; Speak honestly, Girl, did ever I bid you be disobedient to me? Have not I done every thing to humour, and to gratify you, and to make you obedient to me? And very obedient to me she was when a little Child, before you took her in Hand and spoiled her, by filling her Head with a Pack of Court Notions.—Why—why—why—did not I over-hear you telling her she must behave like a Princess? You have made a Whig of the Girl; and how should her Father, or any body else, expect any Obedience from her?' 'Brother,' answered Mrs. *Western*, with an Air of great Disdain, 'I cannot express the Contempt I have for your Politics of all Kinds; but I will appeal likewise to the young Lady herself, whether I have ever taught her any Principles of Disobedience. On the contrary, Niece, have I not endeavoured to inspire you with a true Idea of the several Relations in which a human Creature stands in Society? Have I not taken infinite Pains to shew you, that the Law of Nature hath injoined a Duty on Children to their Parents? Have I not told you what *Plato* says on that Subject?[1]—A Subject on which you was so notoriously ignorant when you came first under my Care, that I verily believe you did not know the Relation between a Daughter and a Father.' ' 'Tis a Lie,' answered *Western*. 'The Girl is no such Fool, as to live to eleven Years old without knowing that she was her Father's Relation.' 'O more than Gothic Ignorance,' answered the Lady.—'And as for your Manners, Brother, I must tell you, they deserve a Cane.' 'Why then you may gi' it me, if you think you are able,' cries the Squire; 'nay, I suppose your Niece there will be ready enough to help you.' 'Brother,' said Mrs. *Western*, 'tho' I despise you beyond Expression, yet I shall

---

1 Cf. *Laws*, iv. 717b–e. Pufendorf, along with Grotius the principal modern authority on the 'law of nature' (see above, p. 161, n. 1), quotes this passage when discussing 'pater-nal Power ' in *Of the Law of Nature and Nations* (1672), VI. ii (see B. Kennett, trans., 4th ed. [1729], p. 609). In sec. xiv, Pufendorf states that, after carefully weighing the advice of their parents concerning a marriage partner, children who are of age have the right to marry against their parents' wishes, at the risk, however, of being disowned and disin-herited (ibid., pp. 612–13).

endure your Insolence no longer; so I desire my Coach may be got ready immediately, for I am resolved to leave your House this very Morning.' 'And a good Riddance too,' answered he; 'I can bear your Insolence no longer, an you come to that. Blood! it is almost enough of itself, to make my Daughter undervalue my Sense, when she hears you telling me every Minute you despise me.' 'It is impossible, it is impossible,' cries the Aunt, 'no one can undervalue such a Boor.' 'Boar,' answered the Squire, 'I am no Boar; no, nor Ass; no, nor Rat neither, Madam. Remember that —I am no Rat. I am a true *Englishman*, and not of your *Hannover* Breed, that have eat up the Nation.'[1] 'Thou art one of those wise Men,' cries she, 'whose nonsensical Principles have undone the Nation; by weakening the Hands of our Government at home, and by discouraging our Friends, and encouraging our Enemies abroad.' 'Ho! are you come back to your Politics,' cries the Squire, 'as for those I despise them as much as I do a F—t.' Which last Word he accompanied and graced with the very Action, which, of all others, was the most proper to it. And whether it was this Word, or the Contempt exprest for her Politics, which most affected Mrs. *Western*, I will not determine; but she flew into the most violent Rage, uttered Phrases improper to be here related, and instantly burst out of the House. Nor did her Brother or her Niece think proper either to stop or to follow her: For the one was so much possessed by Concern, and the other by Anger, that they were rendered almost motionless.

The Squire, however, sent after his Sister the same Holla which attends the Departure of a Hare, when she is first started before the Hounds. He was indeed a great Master of this Kind of Vociferation, and had a Holla proper for most Occasions in Life.

Women who, like Mrs. *Western*, know the World, and have applied themselves to Philosophy and Politics, would have immediately availed themselves of the present Disposition of Mr. *Western's* Mind; by throwing in a few artful Compliments to his Understanding at the Expence of his absent Adversary; but poor *Sophia* was all Simplicity. By which Word we do not intend to insinuate to the Reader, that she was silly, which is generally understood as a synonimous Term with simple: For she was indeed a most sensible Girl, and her Understanding was of the first Rate; but she wanted all that useful Art which Females

[1] See above, p. 321, n. 2.

convert to so many good Purposes in Life, and which, as it rather arises from the Heart, than from the Head, is often the Property of the silliest of Women.

CHAPTER IV

A Picture of a Country Gentlewoman taken from the Life.

MR. *Western* having finished his Holla, and taken a little Breath, began to lament, in very pathetic Terms, the unfortunate Condition of Men, who are, says he, always *whipt in* by the Humours of some d—nd B—— or other. I think I was *hard run* enough by your Mother for one Man; but after giving her a *Dodge*, here's another B—— follows me upon the *Foil*;[1] but curse my Jacket if I will be *run down* in this Manner by any o'um.

Sophia never had a single Dispute with her Father, till this unlucky Affair of *Blifil*, on any Account, except in Defence of her Mother, whom she had loved most tenderly, though she lost her in the eleventh Year of her Age. The Squire, to whom that poor Woman had been a faithful upper Servant all the Time of their Marriage, had returned that Behaviour, by making what the World calls a good Husband. He very seldom swore at her (perhaps not above once a Week) and never beat her: She had not the least Occasion for Jealousy, and was perfect Mistress of her Time: for she was never interrupted by her Husband, who was engaged all the Morning in his Field Exercises, and all the Evening with Bottle Companions. She scarce indeed ever saw him but at Meals; where she had the Pleasure of carving those Dishes which she had before attended at the Dressing. From these Meals she retired about five Minutes after the other Servants, having only stayed to drink the King over the Water.[2] Such were, it seems, Mr. *Western's* Orders: For it was a Maxim with him, that Women should come in with the first Dish, and go out after the first Glass. Obedience to these Orders was perhaps no difficult Task: For the Conversation (if it may be called so) was

---

[1] The track of a hunted animal.

[2] A favourite Jacobite toast—in reference to the Old Pretender, James Francis Edward Stuart (1688–1766), in exile in France.

seldom such as could entertain a Lady. It consisted chiefly of Hollowing, Singing, Relations of sporting Adventures, B—d—y, and Abuse of Women and of the Government.

These, however, were the only Seasons when Mr. *Western* saw his Wife: For when he repaired to her Bed, he was generally so drunk that he could not see; and in the sporting Season he always rose from her before it was light. Thus was she perfect Mistress of her Time; and had besides a Coach and four usually at her Command; tho' unhappily indeed the Badness of the Neighbourhood, and of the Roads, made this of little Use: For none who had set much Value on their Necks would have passed through the one, or who had set any Value on their Hours, would have visited the other. Now to deal honestly with the Reader, she did not make all the Return expected to so much Indulgence: For she had been married against her Will, by a fond Father, the Match having been rather advantageous on her Side: For the Squire's Estate was upwards of 3000 *l.* a Year, and her Fortune no more than a bare 8000 *l.* Hence perhaps she had contracted a little Gloominess of Temper: For she was rather a good Servant than a good Wife; nor had she always the Gratitude to return the extraordinary Degree of roaring Mirth, with which the Squire received her, even with a good-humoured Smile. She would, moreover, sometimes interfere with Matters which did not concern her, as the violent Drinking of her Husband, which in the gentlest Terms she would take some of the few Opportunities he gave her of remonstrating against. And once in her Life she very earnestly entreated him to carry her for two Months to *London*, which he peremptorily denied; nay, was angry with his Wife for the Request ever after, being well assured, that all the Husbands in *London* are Cuckolds.

For this last, and many other good Reasons, *Western* at length heartily hated his Wife; and as he never concealed this Hatred before her Death, so he never forgot it afterwards; but when any Thing in the least soured him, as a bad scenting Day, or a Distemper among his Hounds, or any other such Misfortune, he constantly vented his Spleen by Invectives against the Deceased; saying,—'If my Wife was alive now, she would be glad of this.'

These Invectives he was especially desirous of throwing forth before *Sophia*: For as he loved her more than he did any other, so he was really jealous that she had loved her Mother better than him. And this Jealousy *Sophia* seldom failed of heightening on these Occasions: For he was not contented with violating her Ears with the Abuse of her Mother; but endeavoured to force an explicit Approbation of all this Abuse, with which Desire he never could prevail upon her by any Promise or Threats to comply.

Hence some of my Readers will, perhaps, wonder that the Squire had not hated *Sophia* as much as he had hated her Mother; but I must inform them, that Hatred is not the Effect of Love, even through the Medium of Jealousy. It is, indeed, very possible for jealous Persons to kill the Objects of their Jealousy, but not to hate them. Which Sentiment being a pretty hard Morsel, and bearing something of the Air of a Paradox, we shall leave the Reader to chew the Cud upon it to the End of the Chapter.

CHAPTER V

The generous Behaviour of Sophia *towards her Aunt.*

SOPHIA kept Silence during the foregoing Speech of her Father, nor did she once answer otherwise than with a Sigh; but as he understood none of the Language, or as he called it, Lingo of the Eyes, so he was not satisfied without some further Approbation of his Sentiments; which he now demanded of his Daughter; telling her, in the usual Way, 'he expected she was ready to take the Part of every Body against him, as she had always done that of the B—— her Mother.' *Sophia* remaining still silent, he cry'd out, 'What art dumb? why dost unt speak. Was not thy Mother a d—d B—— to me? Answer me that. What, I suppose, you despise your Father too, and don't think him good enough to speak to?'

'For Heaven's Sake, Sir,' answered *Sophia*, 'do not give so cruel a Turn to my Silence. I am sure I would sooner die than be guilty of any Disrespect towards you; but how can I venture to speak, when every Word must either offend my dear Papa, or convict me of the blackest Ingratitude as well as Impiety to the Memory of the best of Mothers: For such, I am certain my Mamma was always to me?'

'And your Aunt, I suppose, is the best of Sisters too!' replied

the Squire. 'Will you be so kind as to allow that she is a B——?
I may fairly insist upon that, I think.'

'Indeed, Sir,' says *Sophia*, 'I have great Obligations to my
Aunt. She hath been a second Mother to me.'

'And a second Wife to me too,' returned *Western*; 'so you will
take her Part too! You won't confess that she hath acted the
Part of the vilest Sister in the World?'

'Upon my Word, Sir,' cries *Sophia*, 'I must belie my Heart
wickedly if I did. I know my Aunt and you differ very much in
your Ways of thinking; but I have heard her a thousand Times
express the greatest Affection for you; and I am convinced so far
from her being the worst Sister in the World, there are very few
who love a Brother better.'

'The *English* of all which is,' answered the Squire, 'that I am
in the wrong. Ay, certainly. Ay, to be sure the Woman is in the
Right, and the Man in the Wrong always.'

'Pardon me, Sir,' cries *Sophia*, 'I do not say so.'

'What don't you say?' answered the Father, 'you have the
Impudence to say she's in the Right; doth it not follow then of
Course that I'm in the wrong? And perhaps I am in the wrong to
suffer such a Presbyterian *Hannoverian* B—— to come into my
House. She may 'dite me of a Plot for any Thing I know, and
give my Estate to the Government.'[1]

'So far, Sir, from injuring you or your Estate,' says *Sophia*, 'if
my Aunt had died Yesterday, I am convinced she would have
left you her whole Fortune.'

Whether *Sophia* intended it or no, I shall not presume to assert;
but certain it is, these last Words penetrated very deep into the
Ears of her Father, and produced a much more sensible Effect
than all she had said before. He received the Sound with much
the same Action as a Man receives a Bullet in his Head. He
started, staggered and turned pale. After which he remained
silent above a Minute, and then began in the following hesitating
Manner. 'Yesterday! she would have left me her Esteate Yesterday! would she? Why Yesterday of all the Days in the Year? I

---

[1] The forfeiture of one's estate had long been the penalty for high treason. (See Wood,
Institutes, 7th ed. [1745], p. 679.) In April 1744, however—war with France having been
declared and the nation fearing an invasion in support of the Jacobites—Parliament passed
a bill making it treasonable to correspond with the sons of the Pretender and, according to
the terms of an amendment proposed by Lord Hardwicke (see above, p. 172, n. 2), making
forfeiture the penalty for such correspondence.

suppose if she dies To-morrow she will leave it to somebody else, and perhaps out of the Vamily!' 'My Aunt, Sir,' cries *Sophia*, 'hath very violent Passions, and I can't answer what she may do under their Influence.'

'You can't!' returned the Father, 'and pray who hath been the Occasion of putting her into those violent Passions? Nay, who hath actually put her into them? Was not you and she hard at it before I came into the Room? Besides, was not all our Quarrel about you? I have not quarreled with Sister this many Years but upon your Account; and now you would throw the whole Blame upon me, as thof I should be the Occasion of her leaving the Esteate out o' the Vamily. I could have expected no better indeed, this is like the Return you make to all the rest of my Fondness.'

'I beseech you then,' cries *Sophia*, 'upon my Knees I beseech you, if I have been the unhappy Occasion of this Difference, that you will endeavour to make it up with my Aunt, and not suffer her to leave your House in this violent Rage of Anger: She is a very good-natured Woman, and a few civil Words will satisfy her.—Let me intreat you, Sir.'

'So I must go and ask Pardon for your Fault, must I?' answered *Western*. 'You have lost the Hare, and I must draw every Way to find her again? Indeed if I was certain——' Here he stopt, and *Sophia* throwing in more Entreaties, at length prevailed upon him; so that after venting two or three bitter sarcastical Expressions against his Daughter, he departed as fast as he could to recover his Sister, before her Equipage could be gotten ready.

Sophia then returned to her Chamber of Mourning, where she indulged herself (if the Phrase may be allowed me) in all the Luxury of tender Grief. She read over more than once the Letter which she had received from *Jones*; her Muff too was used on this Occasion; and she bathed both these, as well as herself, with her Tears. In this Situation, the friendly Mrs. *Honour* exerted her utmost Abilities to comfort her afflicted Mistress. She ran over the Names of many young Gentlemen; and having greatly commended their Parts and Persons, assured *Sophia* that she might take her Choice of any. These Methods must have certainly been used with some Success in Disorders of the like Kind, or so skilful a Practitioner as Mrs. *Honour* would never have ventured to apply them; nay, I have heard that the College of Chambermaids hold them to be as sovereign Remedies as any in the female Dispensary; but whether it was that *Sophia's* Disease differed inwardly, from those Cases with which it agreed in external Symptoms, I will not assert; but, in Fact, the good Waiting-woman did more Harm than Good, and at last so incensed her Mistress (which was no easy Matter) that with an angry Voice she dismissed her from her Presence.

CHAPTER VI

Containing great Variety of Matter.

THE Squire overtook his Sister just as she was stepping into the Coach, and partly by Force and partly by Solicitations, prevailed upon her to order her Horses back into their Quarters. He succeeded in this Attempt without much Difficulty: For the Lady was, as we have already hinted, of a most placable Disposition, and greatly loved her Brother, tho' she despised his Parts, or rather his little Knowledge of the World.

Poor *Sophia*, who had first set on Foot this Reconciliation, was now made the Sacrifice to it. They both concurred in their Censures on her Conduct; jointly declared War against her; and directly proceeded to Counsel, how to carry it on in the most vigorous Manner. For this Purpose, Mrs. *Western* proposed not only an immediate Conclusion of the Treaty with *Allworthy*; but as immediately to carry it into Execution; saying, 'That there was no other Way to succeed with her Niece but by violent Methods, which she was convinced *Sophia* had not sufficient Resolution to resist. By violent,' says she, 'I mean rather, hasty Measures: For as to Confinement or absolute Force, no such Things must or can be attempted. Our Plan must be concerted for a Surprize, and not for a Storm.'

These Matters were resolved on, when Mr. *Blifil* came to pay a Visit to his Mistress. The Squire no sooner heard of his Arrival, than he stept aside, by his Sister's Advice, to give his Daughter Orders for the proper Reception of her Lover; which he did with the most bitter Execrations and Denunciations of Judgment on her Refusal.

The Impetuosity of the Squire bore down all before him; and *Sophia*, as her Aunt very wisely foresaw, was not able to resist him. She agreed, therefore, to see *Blifil*, tho' she had scarce

Spirits or Strength sufficient to utter her Assent. Indeed, to give a peremptory Denial to a Father whom she so tenderly loved, was no easy Task. Had this Circumstance been out of the Case, much less Resolution than what she was really Mistress of, would, perhaps, have served her; but it is no unusual Thing to ascribe those Actions entirely to Fear, which are in a great Measure produced by Love.

In Pursuance, therefore, of her Father's peremptory Command, *Sophia* now admitted Mr. *Blifil's* Visit. Scenes, like this, when painted at large, afford, as we have observed, very little Entertainment to the Reader. Here, therefore, we shall strictly adhere to a Rule of *Horace*;[1] by which Writers are directed to pass over all those Matters, which they despair of placing in a shining Light. A Rule, we conceive, of excellent Use as well to the Historian as to the Poet; and which, if followed, must, at least, have this good Effect, that many a great Evil (for so all great Books are called) would thus be reduced to a small one.

It is possible the great Art used by *Blifil* at this Interview, would have prevailed on *Sophia* to have made another Man in his Circumstances her Confident, and to have revealed the whole Secret of her Heart to him; but she had contracted so ill an Opinion of this young Gentleman, that she was resolved to place no Confidence in him: For Simplicity, when set on its Guard, is often a Match for Cunning. Her Behaviour to him, therefore, was entirely forced, and indeed such as is generally prescribed to Virgins upon the second formal Visit from one who is appointed for their Husband.

But tho' *Blifil* declared himself to the Squire perfectly satisfied with his Reception; yet that Gentleman, who in Company with his Sister had overheard all, was not so well pleased. He resolved, in Pursuance of the Advice of the sage Lady, to push Matters as forward as possible; and addressing himself to his intended Son-in-Law in the hunting Phrase, he cry'd after a loud Holla, 'Follow her, Boy, follow her; run in, run in, that's it, Honeys. Dead, dead, dead.—Never be bashful, nor stand shall I, shall I? —*Allworthy* and I can finish all Matters between us this Afternoon, and let us ha' the Wedding To-morrow.'

Blifil having conveyed the utmost Satisfaction into his Countenance, answered, 'As there is nothing, Sir, in this World, which

---

[1] See above, p. 208, n. 1.

I so eagerly desire as an Alliance with your Family, except my Union with the most amiable and deserving *Sophia*, you may easily imagine how impatient I must be to see myself in Possession of my two highest Wishes. If I have not therefore importuned you on this Head, you will impute it only to my Fear of offending the Lady, by endeavouring to hurry on so blessed an Event, faster than a strict Compliance with all the Rules of Decency and Decorum will permit. But if by your Interest, Sir, she might be induced to dispence with any Formalities——'

'Formalities! with a Pox!' answered the Squire, 'Pooh, all Stuff and Nonsense. I tell thee, she shall ha' thee To-morrow; you will know the World better hereafter, when you come to my Age. Women never gi' their Consent, Man, if they can help it, 'tis not the Fashion. If I had staid for her Mother's Consent, I might have been a Batchelor to this Day.—To her, to her, co to her, that's it, you jolly Dog. I tell thee shat ha' her To-morrow Morning.'

Blifil suffered himself to be overpowered by the forcible Rhetoric of the Squire; and it being agreed that *Western* should close with *Allworthy* that very Afternoon, the Lover departed home, having first earnestly begged that no Violence might be offered to the Lady by this Haste, in the same Manner as a Popish Inquisitor begs the Lay Power to do no Violence to the Heretic, delivered over to it, and against whom the Church hath passed Sentence.

And to say the Truth, *Blifil* had passed Sentence against *Sophia*; for however pleased he had declared himself to *Western*, with his Reception, he was by no means satisfied, unless it was that he was convinced of the Hatred and Scorn of his Mistress; and this had produced no less reciprocal Hatred and Scorn in him. It may, perhaps, be asked, Why then did he not put an immediate End to all further Courtship? I answer, for that very Reason, as well as for several others equally good, which we shall now proceed to open to the Reader.

Tho' Mr. *Blifil* was not of the Complexion of *Jones*, nor ready to eat every Woman he saw, yet he was far from being destitute of that Appetite which is said to be the common Property of all Animals. With this, he had likewise that distinguishing Taste, which serves to direct Men in their Choice of the Objects, or Food of their several Appetites; and this taught him to consider

Sophia as a most delicious Morsel, indeed to regard her with the same Desires which an Ortolan inspires into the Soul of an Epicure. Now the Agonies which affected the Mind of *Sophia* rather augmented than impaired her Beauty; for her Tears added Brightness to her Eyes, and her Breasts rose higher with her Sighs. Indeed no one hath seen Beauty in its highest Lustre, who hath never seen it in Distress. *Blifil* therefore looked on this human Ortolan with greater Desire than when he viewed her last; nor was his Desire at all lessened by the Aversion which he discovered in her to himself. On the contrary, this served rather to heighten the Pleasure he proposed in rifling her Charms, as it added Triumph to Lust; nay, he had some further Views, from obtaining the absolute Possession of her Person, which we detest too much even to mention; and Revenge itself was not without its Share in the Gratifications which he promised himself. The rivalling poor *Jones*, and supplanting him in her Affections, added another Spur to his Pursuit, and promised another additional Rapture to his Enjoyment.

Besides all these Views, which to some scrupulous Persons may seem to savour too much of Malevolence, he had one Prospect, which few Readers will regard with any great Abhorrence. And this was the Estate of Mr. *Western*; which was all to be settled on his Daughter and her Issue; for so extravagant was the Affection of that fond Parent, that provided his Child would but consent to be miserable with the Husband he chose, he cared not at what Price he purchased him.

For these Reasons Mr. *Blifil* was so desirous of the Match, that he intended to deceive *Sophia*, by pretending Love to her; and to deceive her Father and his own Uncle, by pretending he was beloved by her. In doing this, he availed himself of the Piety of *Thwackum*, who held, that if the End proposed was religious (as surely Matrimony is) it mattered not how wicked were the Means. As to other Occasions, he used to apply the Philosophy of *Square*, which taught, that the End was immaterial, so that the Means were fair and consistent with moral Rectitude. To say Truth, there were few Occurrences in Life on which he could not draw Advantage from the Precepts of one or other of those great Masters.

Little Deceit was indeed necessary to be practised on Mr. *Western*; who thought the Inclinations of his Daughter of as little Consequence, as *Blifil* himself conceived them to be; but as the Sentiments of Mr. *Allworthy* were of a very different Kind, so it was absolutely necessary to impose on him. In this, however, *Blifil* was so well assisted by *Western*, that he succeeded without Difficulty: For as Mr. *Allworthy* had been assured by her Father, that *Sophia* had a proper Affection for *Blifil*, and that all which he had suspected concerning *Jones*, was entirely false, *Blifil* had nothing more to do, than to confirm these Assertions; which he did with such Equivocations, that he preserved a Salvo for his Conscience; and had the Satisfaction of conveying a Lie to his Uncle, without the Guilt of telling one. When he was examined touching the Inclinations of *Sophia*, by *Allworthy*, who said, 'he would, on no Account, be accessary to forcing a young Lady into a Marriage contrary to her own Will,' he answered, 'That the real Sentiments of young Ladies were very difficult to be understood; that her Behaviour to him was full as forward as he wished it, and that if he could believe her Father, she had all the Affection for him which any Lover could desire. As for *Jones*,' said he, 'whom I am loth to call Villain, tho' his Behaviour to you, Sir, sufficiently justifies the Appellation, his own Vanity, or perhaps some wicked Views, might make him boast of a Falshood; for if there had been any Reality in Miss *Western's* Love to him, the Greatness of her Fortune would never have suffered him to desert her, as you are well informed he hath. Lastly, Sir, I promise you I would not myself, for any Consideration, no not for the whole World, consent to marry this young Lady, if I was not persuaded she had all the Passion for me which I desire she should have.'

This excellent Method of conveying a Falshood with the Heart only, without making the Tongue guilty of an Untruth, by the Means of Equivocation and Imposture, hath quieted the Conscience of many a notable Deceiver; and yet when we consider that it is Omniscience on which these endeavour to impose, it may possibly seem capable of affording only a very superficial Comfort; and that this artful and refined Distinction between communicating a Lie, and telling one, is hardly worth the Pains it costs them.

Allworthy was pretty well satisfied with what Mr. *Western* and Mr. *Blifil* told him; and the Treaty was now, at the End of two Days, concluded. Nothing then remained previous to the Office of the Priest, but the Office of the Lawyers, which threatened to take up so much Time, that *Western* offered to bind himself by all Manner of Covenants, rather than defer the Happiness of the young Couple. Indeed he was so very earnest and pressing, that an indifferent Person might have concluded he was more a Principal in this Match than he really was: But this Eagerness was natural to him on all Occasions; and he conducted every Scheme he undertook in such a Manner, as if the Success of that alone was sufficient to constitute the whole Happiness of his Life.

The joint Importunities of both Father and Son-in-law would probably have prevailed on Mr. *Allworthy*, who brooked but ill any Delay of giving Happiness to others, had not *Sophia* herself prevented it, and taken Measures to put a final End to the whole Treaty, and to rob both Church and Law of those Taxes[1] which these wise Bodies have thought proper to receive from the Propagation of the human Species, in a lawful Manner. Of which in the next Chapter.

CHAPTER VII

A strange Resolution of Sophia, *and a more strange Stratagem of* Mrs. Honour.

THO' Mrs. *Honour* was principally attached to her own Interest, she was not without some little Attachment to *Sophia*. To say Truth, it was very difficult for any one to know that young Lady without loving her. She no sooner, therefore, heard a Piece of News, which she imagined to be of great Importance to her Mistress, than quite forgetting the Anger which she had conceived two Days before, at her unpleasant Dismission from *Sophia's* Presence, she ran hastily to inform her of this News.

The Beginning of her Discourse was as abrupt as her Entrance into the Room. 'O dear Ma'am,' says she, 'what doth your La'ship think? To be sure, I am frightened out of my Wits; and yet I thought it my Duty to tell your La'ship, tho' perhaps it may

---

[1] Fielding refers to the lawyer's charges for drawing up the jointure (or settlement of property upon the woman in consideration of marriage) and to the cost of the marriage licence, for which the King received a tax of five shillings levied on the parchment and the Church a fee of one shilling.

make you angry, for we Servants don't always know what will make our Ladies angry; for to be sure, every thing is always laid to the Charge of a Servant. When our Ladies are out of Humour, to be sure, we must be scolded; and to be sure I should not wonder if your La'ship should be out of Humour; nay, it must surprize you certainly, ay, and shock you too.'—'Good *Honour!* let me know it without any longer Preface,' says *Sophia*; 'there are few Things, I promise you, which will surprize, and fewer which will shock me.' 'Dear Ma'am,' answered *Honour*, 'to be sure, I overheard my Master talking to Parson *Supple* about getting a Licence this very Afternoon; and to be sure I heard him say your La'ship should be married To-morrow Morning.' *Sophia* turned pale at these Words, and repeated eagerly, 'To-morrow Morning!' —'Yes, Madam,' replied the trusty Waiting-woman, 'I will take my Oath I heard my Master say so.' '*Honour*,' says *Sophia*, 'you have both surprized and shocked me to such a Degree, that I have scarce any Breath or Spirits left. What is to be done in my dreadful Situation?' 'I wish I was able to advise your La'ship,' says she. 'Do, advise me,' cries *Sophia*, 'pray, dear *Honour* advise me. Think what you would attempt if it was your own Case.' 'Indeed, Ma'am,' cries *Honour*, 'I wish your La'ship and I could change Situations; that is, I mean, without hurting your La'ship, for to be sure I don't wish you so bad as to be a Servant; but because that if so be it was my Case, I should find no Manner of Difficulty in it; for in my poor Opinion, young Squire *Blifil* is a charming, sweet, handsome Man.'—'Don't mention such Stuff,' cries *Sophia*.—'Such Stuff,' repeated *Honour*, 'why there—— Well, to be sure, what's one Man's Meat is another Man's Poison, and the same is altogether as true of Women.' '*Honour*,' says *Sophia*, 'rather than submit to be the Wife of that contemptible Wretch, I would plunge a Dagger into my Heart.' 'O lud, Ma'm,' answered the other, 'I am sure you frighten me out of my Wits now. Let me beseech your La'ship not to suffer such wicked Thoughts to come into your Head. O lud, to be sure I tremble every Inch of me. Dear Ma'm, consider—that to be denied Christian Burial, and to have your Corpse buried in the Highway, and a Stake drove through you, as Farmer *Halfpenny* was served at *Ox-Cross*,[1] and, to be sure, his Ghost hath walked there ever

---

[1] On the laws and customs relating to the treatment and burial of the bodies of suicides, see Edmund Gibson, *Codex Juris Ecclesiastici Anglicani* (1713), i. 540–1; Giles Jacob, *New*

since; for several People have seen him. To be sure it can be nothing but the Devil which can put such wicked Thoughts into the Head of any body; for certainly it is less wicked to hurt all the World than one's own dear Self, and so I have heard said by more Parsons than one. If your La'ship hath such a violent Aversion, and hates the young Gentleman so very bad, that you can't bear to think of going into Bed to him; for to be sure there may be such Antipathies in Nature, and one had lieverer touch a Toad than the Flesh of some People——'

Sophia had been too much wrapped in Contemplation to pay any great Attention to the foregoing excellent Discourse of her Maid; interrupting her therefore, without making any Answer to it, she said, '*Honour*, I am come to a Resolution. I am determined to leave my Father's House this very Night; and if you have the Friendship for me which you have often professed, you will keep me Company.' 'That I will, Ma'm, to the World's End,' answered *Honour*; 'but I beg your La'ship to consider the Consequence before you undertake any rash Action. Where can your La'ship possibly go?' 'There is,' replied *Sophia*, 'a Lady of Quality in *London*, a Relation of mine, who spent several Months with my Aunt in the Country; during all which Time she treated me with great Kindness, and expressed so much Pleasure in my Company, that she earnestly desired my Aunt to suffer me to go with her to *London*. As she is a Woman of very great Note, I shall easily find her out, and I make no Doubt of being very well and kindly received by her.' 'I would not have your La'ship too confident of that,' cries *Honour*; 'for the first Lady I lived with used to invite People very earnestly to her House; but if she heard afterwards they were coming, she used to get out of the Way. Besides, tho' this Lady would be very glad to see your La'ship, as to be sure any body would be glad to see your La'ship, yet when she hears your La'ship is run away from my Master——'

'You are mistaken, *Honour*,' says *Sophia*, 'she looks upon the Authority of a Father in a much lower Light than I do; for she pressed me violently to go to *London* with her, and when I

Law Dictionary, 4th ed. (1739), s.v. 'felo de se'; and Michael Dalton, *The Country Justice* (1746), p. 327. A case very similar to that of 'Farmer *Halfpenny*' was reported in *The General Advertiser* (Monday, 16 February 1746/7): 'Friday last in the Afternoon, a Woman, about forty Years of Age, who was found last Tuesday to have poison'd herself at her Lodgings at Hatton Wall, was buried, and a Stake drove thro' her Body, in the Cross-Road at the Bottom of Hatton-Garden, leading to Hockley in the Hole'.

refused to go without my Father's Consent, she laughed me to Scorn, called me silly Country Girl, and said I should make a pure loving Wife, since I could be so dutiful a Daughter. So I have no Doubt but she will both receive me, and protect me too, till my Father, finding me out of his Power, can be brought to some Reason.'

'Well but, Ma'm,' answered *Honour*, 'how doth your La'ship think of making your Escape? Where will you get any Horses or Conveyance? for as for your own Horse, as all the Servants know a little how Matters stand between my Master and your La'ship, *Robin* will be hanged before he will suffer it to go out of the Stable without my Master's express Orders.' 'I intend to escape,' said *Sophia*, 'by walking out of the Doors when they are open. I thank Heaven my Legs are very able to carry me. They have supported me many a long Evening, after a Fiddle, with no very agreeable Partner; and surely they will assist me in running from so detestable a Partner for Life.' 'O Heavens, Ma'm, doth your La'ship know what you are saying?' cries *Honour*, 'would you think of walking about the Country by Night and alone?' 'Not alone,' answered the Lady, 'you have promised to bear me Company.' 'Yes, to be sure,' cries *Honour*, 'I will follow your La'ship through the World; but your La'ship had almost as good be alone; for I shall not be able to defend you, if any Robbers, or other Villains, should meet with you. Nay, I should be in as horrible a Fright as your La'ship; for to be certain, they would ravish us both. Besides, Ma'm, consider how cold the Nights are now,[1] we shall be frozen to Death.' 'A good brisk Pace,' answered *Sophia*, 'will preserve us from the Cold; and if you cannot defend me from a Villain, *Honour*, I will defend you; for I will take a Pistol with me. There are two always charged in the Hall.' 'Dear Ma'm, you frighten me more and more,' cries *Honour*, 'sure your La'ship would not venture to fire it off! I had rather run any Chance, than your La'ship should do that.' 'Why so?' says

[1] The first clear indication that Fielding has discarded an earlier time-scheme for his central narrative. In Book v, chapter x, Jones's amorous encounter with Molly Seagrim is said to have taken place on 'a pleasant Evening in the latter End of *June*'. According to the plan of Book vi, however, this episode occurred just three weeks before Jones was expelled from 'Paradise Hall', and on the evening of the day following that sad event Jones finds himself at Hambrook (VII. xi), where he joins the King's soldiers marching north to oppose the advance of the Jacobite rebels. At this point in the narrative, the action is clearly set in late November 1745 (see below, p. 368, n. 1).

Sophia, smiling; 'would not you, *Honour*, fire a Pistol at any one who should attack your Virtue?' 'To be sure, Ma'm,' cries *Honour*, 'one's Virtue is a dear Thing, especially to us poor Servants; for it is our Livelihood, as a Body may say, yet I mortally hate Fire-arms; for so many Accidents happen by them.' 'Well, well,' says *Sophia*, 'I believe I may ensure your Virtue at a very cheap Rate, without carrying any Arms with us; for I intend to take Horses at the very first Town we come to, and we shall hardly be attacked in our Way thither. Look'ee, *Honour*, I am resolved to go, and if you will attend me, I promise you I will reward you to the very utmost of my Power.'

This last Argument had a stronger Effect on *Honour* than all the preceding. And since she saw her Mistress so determined, she desisted from any further Dissuasions. They then entered into a Debate on Ways and Means of executing their Project. Here a very stubborn Difficulty occurred, and this was the Removal of their Effects, which was much more easily got over by the Mistress than by the Maid: For when a Lady hath once taken a Resolution to run to a Lover, or to run from him, all Obstacles are considered as Trifles. But *Honour* was inspired by no such Motive; she had no Raptures to expect, nor any Terrors to shun, and besides the real Value of her Clothes, in which consisted a great Part of her Fortune, she had a capricious Fondness for several Gowns, and other Things; either because they became her, or because they were given her by such a particular Person; because she had bought them lately, or because she had had them long; or for some other Reasons equally good; so that she could not endure the Thoughts of leaving the poor Things behind her exposed to the Mercy of *Western*, who, she doubted not, would in his Rage make them suffer Martyrdom.

The ingenious Mrs. *Honour* having applied all her Oratory to dissuade her Mistress from her Purpose, when she found her positively determined, at last started the following Expedient to remove her Clothes, *viz.* to get herself turned out of Doors that very Evening. *Sophia* highly approved this Method, but doubted how it might be brought about. 'Oh! Ma'm,' cries *Honour*, 'your La'ship may trust that to me; we Servants very well know how to obtain this Favour of our Masters and Mistresses; tho' sometimes indeed where they owe us more Wages than they can readily pay, they will put up with all our Affronts, and will hardly take any

Warning we can give them; but the Squire is none of those; and since your La'ship is resolved upon setting out to Night, I warrant I get discharged this Afternoon.' It was then resolved that she should pack up some Linnen, and a Night-gown for *Sophia*, with her own Things; and as for all her other Clothes, the young Lady abandoned them with no more Remorse than the Sailor feels when he throws over the Goods of others in order to save his own Life.

CHAPTER VIII

Containing Scenes of Altercation, of no very uncommon Kind.

MRS. *Honour* had scarce sooner parted from her young Lady, than something, (for I would not, like the old Woman in *Quivedo*,[1] injure the Devil by any false Accusation, and possibly he might have no Hand in it) but something, I say, suggested itself to her, that by sacrificing *Sophia* and all her Secrets to Mr. *Western*, she might probably make her Fortune. Many Considerations urged this Discovery. The fair Prospect of a handsome Reward for so great and acceptable a Service to the Squire, tempted her Avarice; and again, the Danger of the Enterprize she had undertaken; the Uncertainty of its Success; Night, Cold, Robbers, Ravishers, all alarmed her Fears. So forcibly did all these operate upon her, that she was almost determined to go directly to the Squire, and to lay open the whole Affair. She was, however, too upright a Judge to decree on one Side before she had heard the other. And here, first, a Journey to *London* appeared very strongly in Support of *Sophia*. She eagerly longed to see a Place in which she fancied Charms short only of those which a raptured Saint imagines in Heaven. In the next Place, as she knew *Sophia* to have much more Generosity than her Master, so her Fidelity promised her a greater Reward than she could gain by Treachery. She then cross-examined all the Articles which had raised her Fears on the other Side, and found, on fairly

---

[1] The well-known Spanish satirist, Francisco Gomez de Quevedo (1580–1645). The allusion may be to the seventh of Quevedo's *Visions*, in which 'an *old Bawd* of a *Gouvernante*' fans the flames of rebellion in hell, threatening, though in vain, to depose the devil. (See Sir Roger L'Estrange, trans., 10th ed. [1708].) For an earlier reference to Quevedo, see *The Champion* (27 December 1739).

sifting the Matter, that there was very little in them. And now both Scales being reduced to a pretty even Ballance, her Love to her Mistress being thrown into the Scale of her Integrity, made that rather preponderate, when a Circumstance struck upon her Imagination, which might have had a dangerous Effect, had its whole Weight been fairly put into the other Scale. This was the Length of Time which must intervene before *Sophia* would be able to fulfil her Promises; for tho' she was intitled to her Mother's Fortune, at the Death of her Father, and to the Sum of 3000 *l.* left her by an Uncle when she came of Age; yet these were distant Days, and many Accidents might prevent the intended Generosity of the young Lady, whereas the Rewards she might expect from Mr. *Western* were immediate. But while she was pursuing this Thought, the good Genius of *Sophia*, or that which presided over the Integrity of Mrs. *Honour*, or perhaps mere Chance, sent an Accident in her Way, which at once preserved her Fidelity, and even facilitated the intended Business.

Mrs. *Western's* Maid claimed great Superiority over Mrs. *Honour*, on several Accounts. First, her Birth was higher: For her great Grand-mother by the Mother's Side was a Cousin, not far removed, to an *Irish* Peer. Secondly, her Wages were greater. And lastly, she had been at *London*, and had of Consequence seen more of the World. She had always behaved, therefore, to Mrs. *Honour* with that Reserve, and had always exacted of her those Marks of Distinction, which every Order of Females preserves and requires in Conversation with those of an inferior Order. Now as *Honour* did not at all Times agree with this Doctrine; but would frequently break in upon the Respect which the other demanded, Mrs. *Western's* Maid was not at all pleased with her Company: Indeed, she earnestly longed to return home to the House of her Mistress, where she domineered at Will over all the other Servants. She had been greatly, therefore, disappointed in the Morning when Mrs. *Western* had changed her Mind on the very Point of Departure, and had been in what is vulgarly called, a glouting Humour ever since.

In this Humour, which was none of the sweetest, she came into the Room where *Honour* was debating with herself, in the Manner we have above related. *Honour* no sooner saw her, than she addressed her in the following obliging Phrase. 'Soh! Madam, I find we are to have the Pleasure of your Company longer, which

I was afraid the Quarrel between my Master and your Lady would have robbed us of.' 'I don't know, Madam,' answered the other, 'who you mean by We and Us. I assure you I do not look on any of the Servants in this House to be proper Company for me. I am Company, I hope, for their Betters every Day in the Week. I do not speak on your Account, Mrs. *Honour*; for you are a civilized young Woman; and when you have seen a little more of the World, I should not be ashamed to walk with you in *St. James's* Park.' 'Hoity! toity!' cries *Honour*, 'Madam is in her Airs, I protest. Mrs. *Honour* forsooth! sure, Madam, you might call me by my Sir-name;[1] for tho' my Lady calls me *Honour*, I have a Sir-name as well as other Folks. Ashamed to walk with me, quotha! Marry, as good as yourself I hope.' 'Since you make such a Return to my Civility,' said the other, 'I must acquaint you, Mrs. *Honour*, that you are not so good as me. In the Country indeed one is obliged to take up with all kind of Trumpery, but in Town I visit none but the Women of Women of Quality. Indeed, Mrs. *Honour*, there is some Difference, I hope, between you and me.' 'I hope so too,' answered *Honour*, 'there is some Difference in our Ages, and—I think in our Persons.' Upon speaking which last Words, she strutted by Mrs. *Western's* Maid with the most provoking Air of Contempt; turning up her Nose, tossing her Head, and violently brushing the Hoop of her Competitor with her own. The other Lady put on one of her most malicious Sneers, and said, 'Creature! you are below my Anger; and it is beneath me to give ill Words to such an audacious saucy Trollop; but, Hussy, I must tell you, your Breeding shews the Meanness of your Birth as well as of your Education; and both very properly qualify you to be the mean serving Woman of a Country Girl.' 'Don't abuse my Lady,' cries *Honour*, 'I won't take that of you; she's as much better than yours as she is younger, and ten thousand Times more handsomer.'

Here ill Luck, or rather good Luck, sent Mrs. *Western* to see her Maid in Tears, which began to flow plentifully at her Approach; and of which being asked the Reason by her Mistress, she presently acquainted her, that her Tears were occasioned by the rude Treatment of that Creature there, meaning *Honour*. 'And, Madam,' continued she, 'I could have despised all she said to me; but she hath had the Audacity to affront your Ladyship,

[1] i.e. Blackmore (see Honour's letter in xv. x).

and to call you ugly.—Yes, Madam, she called you ugly old Cat to my Face. I could not bear to hear your Ladyship called ugly.'—'Why do you repeat her Impudence so often?' said Mrs. *Western*. And then turning to Mrs. *Honour*, she asked her 'how she had the Assurance to mention her Name with Disrespect?' 'Disrespect Madam!' answered *Honour*, 'I never mentioned your Name at all. I said somebody was not as handsome as my Mistress, and to be sure you know that as well as I.' 'Hussy,' replied the Lady, 'I will make such a saucy Trollop as yourself, know that I am not a proper Subject of your Discourse. And if my Brother doth not discharge you this Moment, I will never sleep in his House again. I will find him out and have you discharged this Moment.' 'Discharged!' cries *Honour*, 'and suppose I am, there are more Places in the World than one. Thank Heaven, good Servants need not want Places; and if you turn away all who do not think you handsome, you will want Servants very soon, let me tell you that.'

Mrs. *Western* spoke, or rather thundered in Answer; but as she was hardly articulate, we cannot be very certain of the identical Words: We shall, therefore, omit inserting a Speech, which, at best, would not greatly redound to her Honour. She then departed in Search of her Brother, with a Countenance so full of Rage, that she resembled one of the Furies rather than a human Creature.

The two Chambermaids being again left alone, began a second Bout at Altercation, which soon produced a Combat of a more active Kind. In this the Victory belonged to the Lady of inferior Rank, but not without some Loss of Blood, of Hair, and of Lawn and Muslin.

CHAPTER IX

The wise Demeanour of Mr. Western in the Character of a Magistrate. A Hint to Justices of Peace, concerning the necessary Qualifications of a Clerk; with extraordinary Instances of paternal Madness, and filial Affection.

LOGICIANS sometimes prove too much by an Argument, and Politicians often overreach themselves in a Scheme. Thus had it like to have happened to Mrs. *Honour*, who instead of recovering the rest of her Clothes, had like to have stopped even

those she had on her Back from escaping: For the Squire no
sooner heard of her having abused his Sister, than he swore
twenty Oaths he would send her to *Bridewell*.[1]

Mrs. *Western* was a very good-natured Woman, and ordinarily
of a forgiving Temper. She had lately remitted the Trespass of a
Stage-coach Man, who had overturned her Post-chaise into a
Ditch; nay, she had even broken the Law in refusing to prosecute
a High-way-man who had robbed her,[2] not only of a Sum of
Money, but of her Ear-rings; at the same Time d—ning her,
and saying, 'such handsome B—s as you, don't want Jewels to
set them off, and be d—nd to you.' But now, so uncertain are our
Tempers, and so much do we at different Times differ from our-
selves, she would hear of no Mitigation; nor could all the affected
Penitence of *Honour*, nor all the Entreaties of *Sophia* for her own
Servant, prevail with her to desist from earnestly desiring her
Brother to execute Justiceship (for it was indeed a Syllable more
than Justice) on the Wench.

But luckily the Clerk had a Qualification, which no Clerk to a
Justice of Peace ought ever to be without, namely, some Understanding in the Law of this Realm. He therefore whispered in the
Ear of the Justice, that he would exceed his Authority by committing the Girl to *Bridewell*, as there had been no Attempt to
break the Peace; 'for I am afraid, Sir,' says he, 'you cannot legally
commit any one to *Bridewell* only for Ill-breeding.'

In Matters of high Importance, particularly in Cases relating
to the Game, the Justice was not always attentive to these
Admonitions of his Clerk: For, indeed, in executing the Laws
under that Head, many Justices of Peace suppose they have a
large discretionary Power. By Virtue of which, under the Notion
of searching for, and taking away Engines for the Destruction
of the Game,[3] they often commit Trespasses, and sometimes
Felony at their Pleasure.

[1] See above, p. 59, n. 1.

[2] Because of the injury to both the public and the Crown, a person refusing to levy 'Hue
and Cry' against a felon who had robbed him was liable to be fined and imprisoned. (See
Jacob, *New Law-Dictionary*, 4th ed. [1739], s.v. 'Hue and Cry'; and Wood, *Institutes*, 7th
ed. [1745], p. 393.) In *An Enquiry into the Causes of the late Increase of Robbers* (1751),
section viii, Fielding put the case as follows: 'Robbery is an Offence not only against the
Party robbed, but against the Public, who are therefore entitled to Prosecution; and he who
prevents or stifles such the Prosecution, is no longer an innocent Man, but guilty of a
high Offence against the Public Good.'

[3] According to the Game Laws, only those persons having an estate valued at £100 per

But this Offence was not of quite so high a Nature, nor so dangerous to the Society. Here, therefore, the Justice behaved with some Attention to the Advice of his Clerk: For, in Fact, he had already had two Informations exhibited against him in the King's-Bench,[1] and had no Curiosity to try a third.

The Squire, therefore, putting on a most wise and significant Countenance, after a Preface of several Hum's and Ha's, told his Sister, that upon more mature Deliberation, he was of Opinion that 'as there was no breaking up of the Peace, such as the Law,' says he, 'calls breaking open a Door, or breaking a Hedge, or breaking a Head; or any such Sort of Breaking; the Matter did not amount to a felonious Kind of a Thing, nor Trespasses nor Damages, and, therefore, there was no Punishment in the Law for it.'

Mrs. *Western* said, 'she knew the Law much better; that she had known Servants very severely punished for affronting their Masters; and then named a certain Justice of the Peace in *London*, who,' she said, 'would commit a Servant to *Bridewell*, at any Time when a Master or Mistress desired it.'

'Like enough,' cries the Squire, 'it may be so in *London*; but the Law is different in the Country.' Here followed a very learned Dispute between the Brother and Sister concerning the Law, which we would insert, if we imagined many of our Readers could understand it. This was, however, at length referred by both Parties to the Clerk, who decided it in Favour of the Magistrate; and Mrs. *Western* was, in the End, obliged to content herself with the Satisfaction of having *Honour* turned away; to which *Sophia* herself very readily and chearfully consented.

Thus Fortune, after having diverted herself, according to Custom, with two or three Frolicks, at last disposed all Matters to the Advantage of our Heroine; who, indeed, succeeded admirably well in her Deceit, considering it was the first she had ever practised. And, to say the Truth, I have often concluded, that the honest Part of Mankind would be much too hard for

year were eligible to possess guns, dogs, or other 'Engines for taking of the Game'. Justices could issue warrants to game-keepers authorizing them to search the houses of those suspected of violating this law and to seize such guns, dogs, etc. (See Wood, *Institutes*, 7th ed. [1745], p. 461.)

[1] Justices of the peace were appointed by the Lord Chancellor in the King's name. Their authority, if abused, was revocable. (See Theodore Barlow, *The Justice of the Peace: A Treatise Containing the Power and Duty of that Magistrate* [1745], pp. ix–x, xv.)

the knavish, if they could bring themselves to incur the Guilt, or thought it worth their while to take the Trouble.

Honour acted her Part to the utmost Perfection. She no sooner saw herself secure from all Danger of *Bridewell*, a Word which had raised most horrible Ideas in her Mind, than she resumed those Airs which her Terrours before had a little abated; and laid down her Place, with as much Affectation of Content, and indeed of Contempt, as was ever practised at the Resignation of Places of much greater Importance. If the Reader pleases, therefore, we chuse rather to say she resigned—which hath, indeed, been always held a synonimous Expression with being turned out, or turned away.

Mr. *Western* ordered her to be very expeditious in packing: For his Sister declared she would not sleep another Night under the same Roof with so impudent a Slut. To work therefore she went, and that so earnestly, that every Thing was ready early in the Evening; when having received her Wages, away packed she Bag and Baggage, to the great Satisfaction of every one, but of none more than of *Sophia*; who, having appointed her Maid to meet her at a certain Place not far from the House, exactly at the dreadful and ghostly Hour of Twelve, began to prepare for her own Departure.

But first she was obliged to give two painful Audiences, the one to her Aunt, and the other to her Father. In these Mrs. *Western* herself began to talk to her in a more peremptory Stile than before; but her Father treated her in so violent and outragious a Manner, that he frightened her into an affected Compliance with his Will, which so highly pleased the good Squire, that he changed his Frowns into Smiles, and his Menaces into Promises; he vowed his whole Soul was wrapped in hers, that her Consent (for so he construed the Words, *You know, Sir, I must not, nor can refuse to obey any absolute Command of yours*) had made him the happiest of Mankind. He then gave her a large Bank-bill to dispose of in any Trinkets she pleased, and kissed and embraced her in the fondest Manner, while Tears of Joy trickled from those Eyes, which a few Moments before had darted Fire and Rage against the dear Object of all his Affection.

Instances of this Behaviour in Parents are so common, that the Reader, I doubt not, will be very little astonished at the whole Conduct of Mr. *Western*. If he should, I own I am not able to account for it; since that he loved his Daughter most tenderly, is, I think, beyond Dispute. So indeed have many others, who have rendered their Children most compleatly miserable by the same Conduct; which, tho' it is almost universal in Parents, hath always appeared to me to be the most unaccountable of all the Absurdities, which ever entered into the Brain of *that strange prodigious Creature Man.*[1]

The latter Part of Mr. *Western's* Behaviour had so strong an Effect on the tender Heart of *Sophia*, that it suggested a Thought to her, which not all the Sophistry of her politic Aunt, nor all the Menaces of her Father had ever once brought into her Head. She reverenced her Father so piously, and loved him so passionately, that she had scarce ever felt more pleasing Sensations, than what arose from the Share she frequently had of contributing to his Amusement; and sometimes, perhaps, to higher Gratifications; for he never could contain the Delight of hearing her commended, which he had the Satisfaction of hearing almost every Day of her Life. The Idea, therefore, of the immense Happiness she should convey to her Father by her Consent to this Match, made a strong Impression on her Mind. Again, the extreme Piety of such an Act of Obedience, worked very forcibly, as she had a very deep Sense of Religion. Lastly, when she reflected how much she herself was to suffer, being indeed to become little less than a Sacrifice, or a Martyr, to filial Love and Duty, she felt an agreeable Tickling in a certain little Passion, which tho' it bears no immediate Affinity either to Religion or Virtue, is often so kind as to lend great Assistance in executing the Purposes of both.

Sophia was charmed with the Contemplation of so heroic an Action, and began to compliment herself with much premature Flattery, when *Cupid*, who lay hid in her Muff, suddenly crept out, and, like *Punchinello* in a Puppet-shew,[2] kicked all out before him. In Truth (for we scorn to deceive our Reader, or to vindi-

---

[1] Cf. Rochester's *Satyr against Mankind* (1679), l. 2.

[2] Punch, the rowdy hero of the English puppet theatre, ultimately derives from the Italian Pulcinella (or Punchinello), introduced into England shortly after the Restoration. (See George Speaight, *The History of the English Puppet Theatre* [1955], ch. v and p. 219.) Fielding so much admired the droll, satiric exploits of Punch and his wife Joan that in the spring of 1748 he sought to revive interest in them by conducting his own puppet theatre under the name of 'Madame de la Nash'. (See the General Introduction, p. xxxi–xxxii.) Later in *Tom Jones* (XII. v) he constructs an entire episode around his hero's chance encounter with a travelling puppet-master.

cate the Character of our Heroine, by ascribing her Actions to supernatural Impulse) the Thoughts of her beloved *Jones*, and some Hopes (however distant) in which he was very particularly concerned, immediately destroyed all which filial Love, Piety and Pride had, with their joint Endeavours, been labouring to bring about.

But before we proceed any farther with *Sophia*, we must now look back to Mr. *Jones*.

CHAPTER X

Containing several Matters natural enough perhaps, but Low.

THE Reader will be pleased to remember, that we left Mr. *Jones* in the Beginning of this Book, on his Road to *Bristol*; being determined to seek his Fortune at Sea, or rather, indeed, to fly away from his Fortune on Shore.

It happened, (a Thing not very unusual) that the Guide who undertook to conduct him on his Way, was unluckily unacquainted with the Road; so that having missed his right Track, and being ashamed to ask Information, he rambled about backwards and forwards, till Night came on, and it began to grow dark. *Jones* suspecting what had happened, acquainted the Guide with his Apprehensions; but he insisted on it, that they were in the right Road, and added, it would be very strange if he should not know the Road to *Bristol*; tho', in Reality, it would have been much stranger if he had known it, having never past through it in his Life before.

Jones had not such implicit Faith in his Guide; but that on their Arrival at a Village,[1] he enquired of the first Fellow he saw, whether they were in the Road to *Bristol*. 'Whence did you come?' cries the Fellow. 'No Matter,' says *Jones*, a little hastily, 'I want to know if this be the Road to *Bristol*.' 'The Road to *Bristol*!' cries the Fellow, scratching his Head, 'Why, Master, I believe you will hardly get to *Bristol* this Way to Night.' 'Prithee, Friend, then,' answered *Jones*, 'do tell us which is the Way.'—'Why, Measter,' cries the Fellow, 'you must be come out of your Road

[1] The village, as Fielding later reveals (p. 562), is Hambrook, about five miles north-east of Bristol on the road to Gloucester.

the Lord knows whither: For thick Way goeth to *Glocester*.'
'Well, and which Way goes to *Bristol*,' said *Jones*. 'Why, you be
going away from *Bristol*,' answered the Fellow.'—'Then,' said
Jones, 'we must go back again.' 'Ay, you must,' said the Fellow.
'Well, and when we come back to the Top of the Hill, which
Way must we take?' 'Why you must keep the strait Road.' 'But I
remember there are two Roads, one to the Right and the other to
the Left.' 'Why you must keep the right-hand Road, and then
gu strait vorwards; only remember to turn first to your Right, and
then to your Left again, and then to your Right; and that brings
you to the Squire's, and then you must keep strait vorwards, and
turn to the Left.'

Another Fellow now came up, and asked which Way the
Gentlemen were going?—of which being informed by *Jones*, he
first scratched his Head, and then leaning upon a Pole he had in
his Hand, began to tell him, 'That he must keep the Right-hand
Road for about a Mile or a Mile and half or zuch a Matter, and
then he must turn short to the Left, which would bring him
round by Measter *Jin Bearnes's*.' 'But which is Mr. *John
Bearnes's*,' says *Jones*. 'O Lord,' cries the Fellow, 'why don't you
know Measter *Jin Bearnes*? Whence then did you come?'

These two Fellows had almost conquered the Patience of
Jones, when a plain well-looking Man (who was indeed a Quaker)
accosted him thus: 'Friend, I perceive thou hast lost thy Way,
and if thou wilt take my Advice thou wilt not attempt to find it to
Night. It is almost dark, and the Road is difficult to hit; besides
there have been several Robberies committed lately between this
and *Bristol*. Here is a very creditable good House just by, where
thou may'st find good Entertainment for thyself and thy Cattle
till Morning.' *Jones*, after a little Persuasion, agreed to stay in
this Place till the Morning, and was conducted by his Friend to
the Public-House.

The Landlord, who was a very civil Fellow, told *Jones*, 'he
hoped he would excuse the Badness of his Accommodation: For
that his Wife was gone from home, and had locked up almost
every Thing, and carried the Keys along with her.' Indeed, the
Fact was, that a favourite Daughter of hers was just married, and
gone, that Morning, home with her Husband; and that she and
her Mother together, had almost stript the poor Man of all his
Goods, as well as Money: For tho' he had several Children, this

Daughter only, who was the Mother's Favourite, was the Object of her Consideration; and to the Humour of this one Child, she would, with Pleasure, have sacrificed all the rest, and her Husband into the Bargain.

Tho' *Jones* was very unfit for any Kind of Company, and would have preferred being alone, yet he could not resist the Importunities of the honest Quaker; who was the more desirous of sitting with him, from having remarked the Melancholy which appeared both in his Countenance and Behaviour; and which the poor Quaker thought his Conversation might in some Measure relieve.

After they had past some Time together, in such a Manner that my honest Friend might have thought himself at one of his Silent-Meetings, the Quaker began to be moved by some Spirit or other, probably that of Curiosity; and said, 'Friend, I perceive some sad Disaster hath befallen thee; but, pray be of Comfort. Perhaps thou hast lost a Friend. If so, thou must consider we are all mortal. And why should'st thou grieve, when thou knowest thy Grief will do thy Friend no Good. We are all born to Affliction. I myself have my Sorrows as well as thee, and most probably greater Sorrows. Tho' I have a clear Estate of a 100 *l.* a Year, which is as much as I want, and I have a Conscience, I thank the Lord, void of Offence. My Constitution is sound and strong, and there is no Man can demand a Debt of me, nor accuse me of an Injury—yet, Friend, I should be concerned to think thee as miserable as myself.'

Here the Quaker ended with a deep Sigh; and *Jones* presently answered, 'I am very sorry, Sir, for your Unhappiness, whatever is the Occasion of it.' 'Ah! Friend,' replyed the Quaker, 'one only Daughter is the Occasion. One who was my greatest Delight upon Earth, and who within this Week is run away from me, and is married against my Consent. I had provided her a proper Match, a sober Man, and one of Substance; but she, forsooth would chuse for herself, and away she is gone with a young Fellow not worth a Groat. If she had been dead, as I suppose thy Friend is, I should have been happy!' 'That is very strange, Sir,' said *Jones*. 'Why, would it not be better for her to be dead, than to be a Beggar?' replied the Quaker: 'For, as I told you, the Fellow is not worth a Groat; and surely she cannot expect that I shall ever give her a Shilling. No, as she hath married for Love, let her live on Love if she can; let her carry her Love to Market, and see whether any one will change it into Silver, or even into Halfpence.' 'You know your own Concerns best, Sir,' said *Jones*. 'It must have been,' continued the Quaker, 'a long premeditated Scheme to cheat me: For they have known one another from their Infancy; and I always preached to her against Love —and told her a thousand Times over, it was all Folly and Wickedness. Nay, the cunning Slut pretended to hearken to me, and to despise all Wantonness of the Flesh; and yet, at last, broke out at a Window two Pair of Stairs: For I began, indeed, a little to suspect her, and had locked her up carefully, intending the very next Morning to have married her up to my Liking. But she disappointed me within a few Hours, and escaped away to the Lover of her own chusing, who lost no Time: For they were married and beded, and all within an Hour.

'But it shall be the worst Hour's Work for them both that ever they did, for they may starve, or beg, or steal together for me. I will never give either of them a Farthing.' Here *Jones* starting up, cry'd, 'I really must be excused, I wish you would leave me.' 'Come, come, Friend,' said the Quaker, 'don't give Way to Concern. You see there are other People miserable, besides yourself.' 'I see there are Madmen and Fools and Villains in the World,' cries *Jones*.—'But let me give you a Piece of Advice; send for your Daughter and Son-in-law home, and don't be yourself the only Cause of Misery to one you pretend to love.' 'Send for her and her Husband home!' cries the Quaker loudly, 'I would sooner send for the two greatest Enemies I have in the World!' 'Well, go home yourself, or where you please,' said *Jones*: 'For I will sit no longer in such Company.'—'Nay, Friend,' answered the Quaker, 'I scorn to impose my Company on any one.' He then offered to pull Money from his Pocket, but *Jones* pushed him with some Violence out of the Room.

The Subject of the Quaker's Discourse had so deeply affected *Jones*, that he stared very wildly all the Time he was speaking. This the Quaker had observed, and this, added to the rest of his Behaviour, inspired honest *Broadbrim* with a Conceit, that his Companion was, in Reality, out of his Senses. Instead of resenting the Affront, therefore, the Quaker was moved with Compassion for his unhappy Circumstances; and having communicated his Opinion to the Landlord, he desired him to take great Care of his Guest, and to treat him with the highest Civility.

'Indeed,' says the Landlord, 'I shall use no such Civility towards him: For it seems, for all his laced Waistcoat there, he is no more a Gentleman than myself; but a poor Parish Bastard bred up at a great Squire's about 30 Miles off, and now turned out of Doors (not for any Good to be sure.) I shall get him out of my House as soon as possible. If I do lose my Reckoning, the first Loss is always the best. It is not above a Year ago that I lost a Silver-spoon.'

'What, dost thou talk of a Parish Bastard, *Robin*?' answered the Quaker. 'Thou must certainly be mistaken in thy Man.'

'Not at all,' replied *Robin*, 'the Guide, who knows him very well, told it me.' For, indeed, the Guide had no sooner taken his Place at the Kitchin-Fire, than he acquainted the whole Company with all he knew, or had ever heard concerning *Jones*.

The Quaker was no sooner assured by this Fellow of the Birth and low Fortune of *Jones*, than all Compassion for him vanished; and the honest, plain Man went home fired with no less Indignation than a Duke would have felt at receiving an Affront from such a Person.

The Landlord himself conceived an equal Disdain for his Guest; so that when *Jones* rung the Bell in order to retire to Bed, he was acquainted that he could have no Bed there. Besides Disdain of the mean Condition of his Guest, *Robin* entertained violent Suspicion of his Intentions, which were, he supposed, to watch some favourable Opportunity of robbing the House. In reality, he might have been very well eased of these Apprehensions by the prudent Precautions of his Wife and Daughter, who had already removed every thing which was not fixed to the Freehold; but he was by Nature suspicious, and had been more particularly so since the Loss of his Spoon. In short, the Dread of being robbed, totally absorbed the comfortable Consideration that he had nothing to lose.

Jones being assured that he could have no Bed, very contentedly betook himself to a great Chair made with Rushes, when Sleep, which had lately shunned his Company in much better Apartments, generously paid him a Visit in his humble Cell.

As for the Landlord, he was prevented by his Fears from retiring to Rest. He returned therefore to the Kitchen-Fire, whence he could survey the only Door which opened into the Parlour, or rather Hole, where *Jones* was seated; and as for the Window to that Room, it was impossible for any Creature larger than a Cat to have made his Escape through it.

CHAPTER XI

The Adventure of a Company of Soldiers.

THE Landlord having taken his Seat directly opposite to the Door of the Parlour, determined to keep Guard there the whole Night. The Guide and another Fellow remained long on Duty with him, tho' they neither knew his Suspicions, nor had any of their own. The true Cause of their watching did indeed, at length, put an End to it; for this was no other than the Strength and Goodness of the Beer, of which having tippled a very large Quantity, they grew at first very noisy and vociferous, and afterwards fell both asleep.

But it was not in the Power of Liquor to compose the Fears of *Robin*. He continued still waking in his Chair, with his Eyes fixed stedfastly on the Door which led into the Apartment of Mr. *Jones*, till a violent Thundering at his outward Gate called him from his Seat, and obliged him to open it; which he had no sooner done, than his Kitchen was immediately full of Gentlemen in red Coats, who all rushed upon him in as tumultuous a Manner, as if they intended to take his little Castle by Storm.

The Landlord was now forced from his Post to furnish his numerous Guests with Beer, which they called for with great Eagerness; and upon his second or third Return from the Cellar, he saw Mr. *Jones* standing before the Fire in the midst of the Soldiers; for it may easily be believed, that the Arrival of so much good Company should put an End to any Sleep, unless that from which we are to be awakened only by the last Trumpet.

The Company having now pretty well satisfied their Thirst, nothing remained but to pay the Reckoning, a Circumstance often productive of much Mischief and Discontent among the inferior Rank of Gentry; who are apt to find great Difficulty in assessing the Sum, with exact Regard to distributive Justice, which directs, that every Man shall pay according to the Quantity which he drinks. This Difficulty occurred upon the present Occasion; and it was the greater, as some Gentlemen had, in their extreme Hurry, marched off, after their first Draught, and had entirely forgot to contribute any thing towards the said Reckoning.

A violent Dispute now arose, in which every Word may be said to have been deposed upon Oath; for the Oaths were at least equal to all the other Words spoken. In this Controversy, the whole Company spoke together, and every Man seemed wholly bent to extenuate the Sum which fell to his Share; so that the most probable Conclusion which could be foreseen, was, that a large Portion of the Reckoning would fall to the Landlord's Share to pay, or (what is much the same thing) would remain unpaid.

All this while Mr. *Jones* was engaged in Conversation with the Serjeant; for that Officer was entirely unconcerned in the present Dispute, being privileged, by immemorial Custom, from all Contribution.

The Dispute now grew so very warm, that it seemed to draw towards a military Decision, when *Jones* stepping forward, silenced all their Clamours at once, by declaring that he would pay the whole Reckoning, which indeed amounted to no more than three Shillings and Four-pence.

This Declaration procured *Jones* the Thanks and Applause of the whole Company. The Terms honourable, noble, and worthy Gentleman, resounded through the Room; nay, my Landlord himself began to have a better Opinion of him, and almost to disbelieve the Account which the Guide had given.

The Serjeant had informed Mr. *Jones*, that they were marching against the Rebels, and expected to be commanded by the glorious Duke of *Cumberland*.[1] By which the Reader may

---

[1] William Augustus (1726–65), Duke of Cumberland, the youngest son of George II. Before his twentieth year Cumberland, though no very brilliant strategist, had distinguished himself for courage and daring at the battles of Dettingen (1743) and Fontenoy (1745), and in April 1746 he put an end to the Jacobite uprising by defeating the rebel forces at Culloden. His severity in dealing with the rebel clansmen earned him the name of 'Billy the Butcher', but Fielding never mentions him except in the most laudatory terms: after the decisive victory at Culloden, Fielding in two numbers of *The True Patriot* (22–29 April, 29 April–6 May 1746) praises 'the Glorious Duke of CUMBERLAND, that *Fulmen Belli*' and contrasts his bravery in battle with the cowardice of his rival, Charles Edward Stuart. See also *Ovid's Art of Love Paraphrased* (1747) and *An Enquiry into the Causes of the late Increase of Robbers* (1751), section ii, where Cumberland is ranked with Edward, Henry, and Marlborough as the greatest of British generals.

perceive (a Circumstance which we have not thought necessary to communicate before) that this was the very Time when the late Rebellion was at the highest; and indeed the Banditti were now marched into *England*, intending, as it was thought, to fight the King's Forces, and to attempt pushing forward to the Metropolis.[1]

Jones had some Heroic Ingredients in his Composition, and was a hearty Well-wisher to the glorious Cause of Liberty, and of the Protestant Religion. It is no wonder, therefore, that in Circumstances which would have warranted a much more romantic and wild Undertaking, it should occur to him to serve as a Volunteer in this Expedition.

Our commanding Officer had said all in his Power to encourage and promote this good Disposition, from the first Moment he had been acquainted with it. He now proclaimed the noble Resolution aloud, which was received with great Pleasure by the whole Company, who all cried out, 'God bless King *George*, and your Honour;' and then added, with many Oaths, 'We will stand by you both to the last Drops of our Blood.'

The Gentleman, who had been all Night tippling at the Ale-house, was prevailed on by some Arguments which a Corporal had put into his Hand, to undertake the same Expedition. And now the Portmanteau belonging to Mr. *Jones* being put up in the Baggage-cart, the Forces were about to move forwards; when the Guide, stepping up to *Jones*, said, 'Sir, I hope you will consider that the Horses have been kept out all Night, and we have travel-led a great ways out of our Way.' *Jones* was surprized at the Impudence of this Demand, and acquainted the Soldiers with the Merits of his Cause, who were all unanimous in condemning the

---

[1] Though it is questionable that Fielding intended his readers to date the events of his narrative quite so precisely, the allusions in this paragraph fix the time of Jones's brief stay in Hambrook as late November 1745. The rebel army had crossed the Tweed into England on 6 November, advancing southward, steadily and virtually unopposed, until they reached Derby on 4 December; from Derby two days later, having decided not to engage the King's forces, they began their long retreat into Scotland. Cumberland's appointment as commander of the forces was not announced, however, until 23 November; he set out for Lichfield, his headquarters, on the 26th, arriving there the following evening. (See *The London Gazette*, 19–23, 23–6, 26–30 November 1745.) Finally, if there is truth in the somewhat extravagant hypothesis that Fielding consulted an almanac before making the full moon rise at 5.00 p.m. at Gloucester (VIII. ix; see below, p. 435, n. 1), then the time of the present chapter, the events of which take place four days earlier, may be precisely fixed as 25 November 1745.

Guide for his Endeavours to put upon a Gentleman. Some said, he ought to be tied Neck and Heels; others, that he deserved to run the Gauntlope; and the Serjeant shook his Cane at him, and wished he had him under his Command, swearing heartily he would make an Example of him.

Jones contented himself, however, with a negative Punishment, and walked off with his new Comrades, leaving the Guide to the poor Revenge of cursing and reviling him, in which latter the Landlord joined, saying, 'Ay, ay, he is a pure one, I warrant you. A pretty Gentleman, indeed, to go for a Soldier. He shall wear a laced Waistcoat truly. It is an old Proverb and a true one, all is not Gold that glisters. I am glad my House is well rid of him.'

All that Day the Serjeant and the young Soldier marched together; and the former, who was an arch Fellow, told the latter many entertaining Stories of his Campaigns, tho' in Reality he had never made any; for he was but lately come into the Service, and had, by his own Dexterity, so well ingratiated himself with his Officers, that he had promoted himself to a Halberd,[1] chiefly indeed by his Merit in recruiting, in which he was most excellently well skilled.

Much Mirth and Festivity passed among the Soldiers during their March. In which the many Occurrences that had passed at their last Quarters were remembered, and every one, with great Freedom, made what Jokes he pleased on his Officers, some of which were of the coarser Kind, and very near bordering on Scandal. This brought to our Heroe's Mind the Custom which he had read of among the *Greeks* and *Romans*,[2] of indulging, on certain Festivals and solemn Occasions, the Liberty to Slaves, of using an uncontrouled Freedom of Speech towards their Masters.

Our little Army, which consisted of two Companies of Foot, were now arrived at the Place[3] where they were to halt that Evening. The Serjeant then acquainted his Lieutenant, who was the commanding Officer, that they had picked up two Fellows in that Day's March; one of which, he said, was as fine a Man as ever he saw (meaning the Tippler) for that he was near six Feet,

---

[1] This ancient weapon denoted the rank of sergeant.

[2] The Saturnalia, a Roman religious festival held in December, was an occasion for debauchery and licentiousness, when slaves and servants were permitted to behave disrespectfully toward their masters. Cf. Lucian, *Saturnalia*, 'A Conversation with Cronos' 5–18.

[3] Possibly Cambridge, a village about ten miles south-west of Gloucester.

well-proportioned, and strongly limbed; and the other, (meaning *Jones*) would do well enough for the rear Rank.

The new Soldiers were now produced before the Officer, who having examined the six Foot Man, he being first produced, came next to survey *Jones*; at the first Sight of whom, the Lieutenant could not help shewing some Surprize; for, besides that he was very well dressed, and was naturally genteel, he had a remarkable Air of Dignity in his Look, which is rarely seen among the Vulgar, and is indeed not inseparably annexed to the Features of their Superiors.

'Sir,' said the Lieutenant, 'my Serjeant informed me, that you are desirous of enlisting in the Company I have at present under my Command; if so, Sir, we shall very gladly receive a Gentleman who promises to do much Honour to the Company, by bearing Arms in it.'

Jones answered: 'That he had not mentioned any thing of enlisting himself; that he was most zealously attached to the glorious Cause for which they were going to fight, and was very desirous of serving as a Volunteer;' concluding with some Compliments to the Lieutenant, and expressing the great Satisfaction he should have in being under his Command.

The Lieutenant returned his Civility, commended his Resolution, shook him by the Hand, and invited him to dine with himself and the rest of the Officers.

CHAPTER XII

The Adventure of a Company of Officers.

THE Lieutenant, whom we mentioned in the preceding Chapter, and who commanded this Party, was now near sixty Years of Age. He had entered very young into the Army, and had served in the Capacity of an Ensign at the Battle of *Tannieres*;[1] here he had received two Wounds, and had so well

---

[1] On 11 September 1709 Marlborough won a bloody victory over the French in the Battle of Malplaquet, sometimes called the Battle of Taisnières after the wood in which the enemy's left flank was strongly entrenched. (See *Relation de la campagne de Tannières* [The Hague, 1710].)

distinguished himself, that he was by the Duke of *Marlborough*[1] advanced to be a Lieutenant, immediately after that Battle.[2]

In this Commission he had continued ever since, *viz.* near forty Years; during which Time he had seen vast Numbers preferred over his Head, and had now the Mortification to be commanded by Boys, whose Fathers were at Nurse when he first entered into the Service.

Nor was this ill Success in his Profession solely owing to his having no Friends among the Men in Power. He had the Misfortune to incur the Displeasure of his Colonel, who for many Years continued in the Command of this Regiment. Nor did he owe the implacable Ill-will which this Man bore him to any Neglect or Deficiency as an Officer, nor indeed to any Fault in himself; but solely to the Indiscretion of his Wife, who was a very beautiful Woman, and who, tho' she was remarkably fond of her Husband, would not purchase his Preferment at the Expence of certain Favours which the Colonel required of her.

The poor Lieutenant was more peculiarly unhappy in this, that while he felt the Effects of the Enmity of his Colonel, he neither knew, nor suspected, that he really bore him any; for he could not suspect an Ill-will for which he was not conscious of giving any Cause; and his Wife, fearing what her Husband's nice Regard to his Honour might have occasioned, contented herself with preserving her Virtue, without enjoying the Triumphs of her Conquest.

This unfortunate Officer (for so I think he may be called) had many good Qualities, besides his Merit in his Profession; for he was a religious, honest, good-natured Man; and had behaved so well in his Command, that he was highly esteemed and beloved, not only by the Soldiers of his own Company; but by the whole Regiment.

[1] John Churchill (1650–1722), first Duke of Marlborough, victorious commander of the British forces against France, 1702–11. In frequent references to the controversial hero of the Whigs, Fielding, whose father had served under Marlborough at Blenheim and whose mother was a distant relation of the Churchills, was adulatory. In *A Proper Answer to a late Scurrilous Libel* (1747) he summed up his feelings by referring to 'the unparalell'd [*sic*] Successes of our Arms, under the Conduct of the Great, the Protestant, the Whig Duke of *Marlborough*'. In April 1742 Fielding published his *Full Vindication of the Dutchess Dowager of Marlborough*, written in behalf of Sarah, Marlborough's widow.

[2] The honest lieutenant whose career Fielding briefly describes in these paragraphs is an adumbration of Bob Bound in *Amelia* (x. ix), though the reasons for his lack of preferment more particularly foreshadow Booth's own situation.

The other Officers who marched with him were a *French* Lieutenant, who had been long enough out of *France* to forget his own Language, but not long enough in *England* to learn ours, so that he really spoke no Language at all, and could barely make himself understood, on the most ordinary Occasions. There were likewise two Ensigns, both very young Fellows; one of whom had been bred under an Attorney, and the other was Son to the Wife of a Nobleman's Butler.

As soon as Dinner was ended, *Jones* informed the Company of the Merriment which had passed among the Soldiers upon their March; 'and yet,' says he, 'notwithstanding all their Vociferation, I dare swear they will behave more like *Grecians* than *Trojans* when they come to the Enemy.' '*Grecians* and *Trojans*!' says one of the Ensigns, 'who the Devil are they? I have heard of all the Troops in *Europe*, but never of any such as these.'

'Don't pretend to more Ignorance than you have, Mr. *Northerton*,' said the worthy Lieutenant, 'I suppose you have heard of the *Greeks* and *Trojans*, tho', perhaps, you never read *Pope's Homer*; who, I remember, now the Gentleman mentions it, compares the March of the *Trojans* to the Cackling of Geese, and greatly commends the Silence of the *Grecians*.[1] And upon my Honour, there is great Justice in the Cadet's Observation.'

'Begar, me remember dem ver well,' said the *French* Lieutenant, 'me ave read dem at School in dans Madam *Daciere*,[2] des *Greek*, des *Trojan*, dey fight for von Woman—ouy, ouy, me ave read all dat.'

'D——n *Homo* with all my Heart,' says *Northerton*, 'I have the Marks of him in my A—— yet. There's *Thomas*[3] of our Regi-

---

[1] Pope's *Iliad*, iii. 1–13—though Pope compares the motions of the Trojan army to a flight of cranes, not geese.

[2] Anne Lefèvre Dacier (*c.* 1654–1720), celebrated French bluestocking and wife of the critic André Dacier (see below, pp. 396, n. 1; 569, n. 3). Her translation of the *Iliad* appeared in 1711, the *Odyssey* in 1716. Though Fielding feared that learning in women was not conducive to domestic harmony—consider the examples of Jenny Jones (I. vi) and Mrs. Bennet in *Amelia* (1751)—he was nevertheless a great admirer of Mme Dacier and her works. In *A Journey from This World to the Next* (1743; I. viii), for instance, he introduces her in Elysium sitting on Homer's lap. For other references, see *The Champion* (4 December 1739), *Joseph Andrews* (1742; III. ii), *Plutus* (1742), *Amelia* (VI. vii, VIII. v, X. i), and *The Covent-Garden Journal* (8 February, 21 October 1752).

[3] Some readers identified this literate soldier with a certain Captain Lewis Thomas (of the Fourth, or King's Own, Regiment), an avid reader who amused his fellow officers by going about with a copy of Homer in his pocket. (See Thomas's letter to Welbore Ellis, written from Carlisle, 3 April 1749; quoted by J. P. Feil, *PQ*, xxxix [1960], 508–10.)

ment, always carries a *Homo* in his Pocket: D——n me if ever I come at it, if I don't burn it. And there's *Corderius*,[1] another d——n'd Son of a Whore that hath got me many a Flogging.'

'Then you have been at School, Mr. *Northerton?*' said the Lieutenant.

'Ay d——n me have I,' answered he, 'the Devil take my Father for sending me thither. The old Put wanted to make a Parson of me, but d——n me, thinks I to myself, I'll nick you there, old Cull: The Devil a Smack of your Nonsense, shall you ever get into me. There's *Jemmy Oliver* of our Regiment, he narrowly escaped being a Pimp too; and that would have been a thousand Pities: For d——n me if he is not one of the prettiest Fellows in the whole World; but he went farther than I with the old Cull: For *Jemmy* can neither write nor read.'

'You give your Friend a very good Character,' said the Lieutenant, 'and a very deserved one, I dare say; but prithee, *Northerton*, leave off that foolish as well as wicked Custom of swearing: For you are deceived, I promise you, if you think there is Wit or Politeness in it. I wish too, you would take my Advice, and desist from abusing the Clergy. Scandalous Names and Reflections cast on any Body of Men, must be always unjustifiable;[2] but especially so, when thrown on so sacred a Function: For to abuse the Body is to abuse the Function itself; and I leave to you to judge how inconsistent such Behaviour is in Men, who are going to fight in Defence of the Protestant Religion.'

Mr. *Adderley*, which was the Name of the other Ensign, had sat hitherto kicking his Heels and humming a Tune, without seeming to listen to the Discourse; he now answered, '*O Monsieur, on ne parle pas de la Religion dans la Guerre.*'[3] 'Well said,

---

Though Thomas denied that he was 'in the least known to Mr. Fielding', the two men did have at least one acquaintance in common: Mrs. Whitefield of the Bell Inn, Gloucester (see below, p. 430, n. 1).

[1] The Latin name of Mathurin Cordier (1479–1564), a French-Protestant pedagogue whose best-known work, *Colloquiorum scholasticorum libri quatuor* (1563), was translated into English by Charles Hoole (1657) and John Clarke (1718), among others. The *Colloquies* of Corderius went through numerous editions and was widely used by schoolboys.

[2] Cf. Fielding's 'Apology for the Clergy' in *The Champion* (29 March, 5, 12, 19 April 1740), which begins: 'There is nothing so unjustifiable as the general Abuse of any Nation or Body of Men . . .'; also 'An Essay on Conversation' (1743).

[3] That the ensign should choose to express this sentiment in French is apt enough during a time of war with France, when the perfidy of the enemy was generally deplored in England. Perhaps, however, Fielding recalls the views of such French generals as the

Jack,' cries *Northerton*, 'if la Religion was the only Matter, the Parsons should fight their own Battles for me.'

'I don't know, Gentlemen,' says *Jones*, 'what may be your Opinion; but I think no Man can engage in a nobler Cause than that of his Religion; and I have observed in the little I have read of History, that no Soldiers have fought so bravely, as those who have been inspired with a religious Zeal: For my own Part, tho' I love my King and Country, I hope, as well as any Man in it, yet the Protestant Interest is no small Motive to my becoming a Volunteer in the Cause.'

Northerton now winked on *Adderley*, and whispered to him slily, 'Smoke the Prig, *Adderley*, smoke him.' Then turning to *Jones*, said to him, 'I am very glad, Sir, you have chosen our Regiment to be a Volunteer in: For if our Parson should at any Time take a Cup too much, I find you can supply his Place. I presume, Sir, you have been at the University, may I crave the Favour to know what College?'

'Sir,' answered *Jones*, 'so far from having been at the University, I have even had the Advantage of yourself: for I was never at School.'

'I presumed,' cries the Ensign, 'only upon the Information of your great Learning.'—'Oh! Sir,' answered *Jones*, 'it is as possible for a Man to know something without having been at School; as it is to have been at School and to know nothing.'

'Well said, young Volunteer,' cries the Lieutenant, 'upon my Word, *Northerton*, you had better let him alone, for he will be too hard for you.'

Northerton did not very well relish the Sarcasm of *Jones*; but he thought the Provocation was scarce sufficient to justify a Blow, or a Rascal, or Scoundrel, which were the only Repartees that

---

Marquis of Pescayre and Cipierre, recorded in Brantome's *Les Vies des hommes illustres et grands capitaines estrangers de son temps* (Leyden, 1699), i. 132–3, and given additional currency in the notes to Bayle's *General Dictionary, Historical and Critical*, iv (1736), s.v. 'Cipierre'. Having been reproved by the papal legate for the disorderly conduct of his troops in Lombardy, Pescayre replied: 'Monsieur le Legat, il n'y a point de chose plus difficile à ceux qui exercent la guerre que de servir en un mesme temps & avec esgale discipline à Mars & à Christ, parce que l'usage de la guerre en cette corruption de Milice est du tout contraire à la justice & à la Religion.' Similarly, the Cardinal of Ferrara having objected that the troops fighting the heretics at Orleans should behave like true believers and abstain from eating meat during Lent, Cipierre answered: 'Monsieur ne pensez pas regler nos gens de guerre comme vos gens d'Eglise car autre chose est de servir Dieu & servir la guerre. . . .'

suggested themselves. He was, therefore, silent at present; but resolved to take the first Opportunity of returning the Jest by Abuse.

It now came to the Turn of Mr. *Jones* to give a Toast, as it is called; who could not refrain from mentioning his dear *Sophia*. This he did the more readily, as he imagined it utterly impossible, that any one present should guess the Person he meant.

But the Lieutenant, who was the Toast-master, was not contented with *Sophia* only. He said, he must have her Sir-name; upon which *Jones* hesitated a little, and presently after named Miss *Sophia Western*. Ensign *Northerton* declared, he would not drink her Health, in the same Round with his own Toast, unless somebody would vouch for her. 'I knew one *Sophy Western*,' says he, 'that was lain-with by Half the young Fellows at *Bath*; and, perhaps, this is the same Woman.' *Jones* very solemnly assured him of the contrary; asserting that the young Lady he named was one of great Fashion and Fortune. 'Ay, ay,' says the Ensign, 'and so she is, d—n me it is the same Woman, and I'll hold Half a Dozen of *Burgundy*, *Tom French* of our Regiment brings her into Company with us at any Tavern in *Bridges-street*.'[1] He then proceeded to describe her Person exactly, (for he had seen her with her Aunt) and concluded with saying, 'That her Father had a great Estate in *Somersetshire*.'

The Tenderness of Lovers can ill brook the least jesting with the Names of their Mistresses. However, *Jones*, tho' he had enough of the Lover and of the Heroe too in his Disposition, did not resent these Slanders as hastily as, perhaps, he ought to have done. To say the Truth, having seen but little of this Kind of Wit, he did not readily understand it, and for a long Time imagined Mr. *Northerton* had really mistaken his Charmer for some other. But now turning to the Ensign with a stern Aspect, he said, 'Pray, Sir, chuse some other Subject for your Wit: For I promise you I will bear no jesting with this Lady's Character.' 'Jesting,' cries the other, 'd—n me if ever I was more in Earnest in my Life. *Tom French* of our Regiment had both her and her

---

[1] The most notorious street in the most disreputable district of London, the Hundred of Drury, which, according to Ned Ward's calculations, contained no fewer than 107 brothels. Here were 'the Gates of *Sodom* . . . the Jakes of the Town'. (See *A View of London and Westminster: or, The Town Spy* [1725], i. 13–14, ii. 48.) Bridges Street is the scene of Jonathan Wild's amorous adventure with the prostitute, Molly Straddle (II. iii).

Aunt at *Bath*.' 'Then I must tell you in Earnest,' cries *Jones*, 'that you are one of the most impudent Rascals upon Earth.'

He had no sooner spoken these Words, than the Ensign, together with a Volley of Curses, discharged a Bottle full at the Head of *Jones*, which hitting him a little above the right Temple, brought him instantly to the Ground.

The Conqueror perceiving the Enemy to lie motionless before him, and Blood beginning to flow pretty plentifully from his Wound, began now to think of quitting the Field of Battle, where no more Honour was to be gotten; but the Lieutenant interposed, by stepping before the Door, and thus cut off his Retreat.

Northerton was very importunate with the Lieutenant for his Liberty; urging the ill Consequences of his Stay, asking him, what he could have done less! 'Zounds!' says he, 'I was but in Jest with the Fellow. I never heard any Harm of Miss *Western* in my Life.' 'Have not you?' said the Lieutenant, 'then you richly deserve to be hanged, as well for making such Jests, as for using such a Weapon. You are my Prisoner, Sir; nor shall you stir from hence, till a proper Guard comes to secure you.'

Such an Ascendant had our Lieutenant over this Ensign, that all that Fervency of Courage which had levelled our poor Heroe with the Floor, would scarce have animated the said Ensign to have drawn his Sword against the Lieutenant, had he then one dangling at his Side; but all the Swords being hung up in the Room, were, at the very Beginning of the Fray, secured by the *French* Officer. So that Mr. *Northerton* was obliged to attend the final Issue of this Affair.

The *French* Gentleman and Mr. *Adderley*, at the Desire of their Commanding-Officer, had raised up the Body of *Jones*; but as they could perceive but little (if any) Sign of Life in him, they again let him fall. *Adderley* damning him for having blooded his Waistcoat; and the *Frenchman* declaring, 'Begar me no tush de Engliseman de mort, me ave heard de Englise Ley, Law, what you call, hang up de Man dat tush him last.'[1]

When the good Lieutenant applied himself to the Door, he applied himself likewise to the Bell; and the Drawer immediately

[1] Careful search of the laws pertaining to murder and presumptive evidence has failed to disclose any such curious provision, to which the lawyer in *Joseph Andrews* (1742; I. xii) also alludes.

attending, he dispatched him for a File of Musqueteers and a Surgeon. These Commands, together with the Drawer's Report of what he had himself seen, not only produced the Soldiers, but presently drew up the Landlord of the House, his Wife and Servants, and, indeed, every one else, who happened, at that Time, to be in the Inn.

To describe every Particular, and to relate the whole Conversation of the ensuing Scene, is not within my Power, unless I had forty Pens, and could, at once, write with them all together, as the Company now spoke. The Reader must, therefore, content himself with the most remarkable Incidents, and perhaps he may very well excuse the rest.

The first Thing done, was securing the Body of *Northerton*, who being delivered into the Custody of six Men with a Corporal at their Head, was by them conducted from a Place which he was very willing to leave, but it was unluckily to a Place whither he was very unwilling to go. To say the Truth, so whimsical are the Desires of Ambition, the very Moment this Youth had attained the above-mentioned Honour, he would have been well contented to have retired to some Corner of the World, where the Fame of it should never have reached his Ears.

It surprizes us, and so, perhaps, it may the Reader, that the Lieutenant, a worthy and good Man, should have applied his chief Care, rather to secure the Offender, than to preserve the Life of the wounded Person. We mention this Observation, not with any View of pretending to account for so odd a Behaviour, but lest some Critic should hereafter plume himself on discovering it. We would have these Gentlemen know we can see what is odd in Characters as well as themselves, but it is our Business to relate Facts as they are; which when we have done, it is the Part of the learned and sagacious Reader to consult that original Book of Nature, whence every Passage in our Work is transcribed, tho' we quote not always the particular Page for its Authority.

The Company which now arrived were of a different Disposition. They suspended their Curiosity concerning the Person of the Ensign, till they should see him hereafter in a more engaging Attitude. At present, their whole Concern and Attention were employed about the bloody Object on the Floor; which being placed upright in a Chair, soon began to discover some Symptoms of Life and Motion. These were no sooner perceived by the Company (for *Jones* was, at first, generally concluded to be dead) than they all fell at once to prescribing for him: (For as none of the physical Order was present, every one there took that Office upon him.)

Bleeding was the unanimous Voice of the whole Room; but unluckily there was no Operator at hand: Every one then cry'd, 'Call the Barber;' but none stirred a Step. Several Cordials were likewise prescribed in the same ineffective Manner; till the Landlord ordered up a Tankard of strong Beer, with a Toast, which he said was the best Cordial in *England*.

The Person principally assistant on this Occasion, indeed the only one who did any Service, or seemed likely to do any, was the Landlady. She cut off some of her Hair, and applied it to the Wound to stop the Blood. She fell to chafing the Youth's Temples with her Hand; and having exprest great Contempt for her Husband's Prescription of Beer, she dispatched one of her Maids to her own Closet for a Bottle of Brandy, of which, as soon as it was brought, she prevailed upon *Jones*, who was just returned to his Senses, to drink a very large and plentiful Draught.

Soon afterwards arrived the Surgeon, who having viewed the Wound, having shaken his Head, and blamed every Thing which was done, ordered his Patient instantly to Bed; in which Place, we think proper to leave him, some Time, to his Repose, and shall here, therefore, put an End to this Chapter.

CHAPTER XIII

Containing the great Address of the Landlady; the great Learning of a Surgeon; and the solid Skill in Casuistry of the worthy Lieutenant.

WHEN the wounded Man was carried to his Bed, and the House began again to clear up from the Hurry which this Accident had occasioned; the Landlady thus addressed the commanding Officer. 'I am afraid, Sir,' said she, 'this young Man did not behave himself as well as he should do to your Honours; and if he had been killed, I suppose he had had but his *Desarts*; to be sure, when Gentlemen admit inferior *Parsons* into their Company, they *oft* to keep their Distance; but, as my first Husband used to say, few of em know how to do it. For my own Part, I am sure, I should not have suffered any Fellows to *include* themselves into Gentlemen's Company: but I *thoft* he had been an Officer himself, till the Serjeant told me he was but a Recruit.'

'Landlady,' answered the Lieutenant, 'you mistake the whole Matter. The young Man behaved himself extremely well, and is, I believe, a much better Gentleman than the Ensign, who abused him. If the young Fellow dies, the Man who struck him will have most Reason to be sorry for it: For the Regiment will get rid of a very troublesome Fellow, who is a Scandal to the Army; and if he escapes from the Hands of Justice, blame me, Madam, that's all.'

'Ay! Ay! good Lack-a-day!' said the Landlady, 'who could have *thoft* it? Ay, ay, ay, I am satisfied your Honour will see Justice done; and to be sure it *oft* to be to every one. Gentlemen *oft* not to kill poor Folks without answering for it. A poor Man hath a Soul to be saved as well as his Betters.'

'Indeed, Madam,' said the Lieutenant, 'you do the Volunteer wrong; I dare swear he is more of a Gentleman than the Officer.'

'Ay,' cries the Landlady, 'why look you there now: Well, my first Husband was a wise Man; he used to say, you can't always know the Inside by the Outside. Nay, that might have been well enough too: For I never *saw'd* him till he was all over blood. Who would have *thoft* it! mayhap, some young Gentleman crossed in Love. Good Lack-a-day! if he should die, what a Concern it will be to his Parents! Why sure the Devil must possess the wicked Wretch to do such an Act. To be sure, he is a Scandal to the Army, as your Honour says: For most of the Gentlemen of the Army that ever I saw, are quite different Sort of People, and look as if they would scorn to spill any Christian Blood as much as any Men. I mean, that is, in a civil Way, as my first Husband used to say. To be sure, when they come into the Wars, there must be Blood-shed; but that they are not to be blamed for. The more of our Enemies they kill there, the better; and I wish, with all my Heart, they could kill every Mother's Son of them.'

'O fie! Madam,' said the Lieutenant smiling, 'ALL is rather too bloody-minded a Wish.'

'Not at all, Sir,' answered she, 'I am not at all bloody-minded, only to our Enemies, and there is no Harm in that. To be sure it is natural for us to wish our Enemies dead, that the Wars may be at an End, and our Taxes be lowered: For it is a dreadful Thing to pay as we do. Why now there is above forty Shillings for Window-lights,[1] and yet we have stopt up all we could; we have almost blinded the House I am sure: Says I to the Exciseman, says I, I think you *oft* to favour us, I am sure we are very good Friends to the Government; and so we are for *sartain*: For we pay a Mint of Money to 'um. And yet I often think to myself, the Government doth not imagine itself more obliged to us, than to those that don't pay 'um a Farthing. Ay, ay; it is the Way of the World.'

She was proceeding in this Manner, when the Surgeon entered the Room. The Lieutenant immediately asked how his Patient did? But he resolved him only by saying, 'Better, I believe, than he would have been by this Time, if I had not been called; and even as it is, perhaps it would have been lucky if I could have been called sooner.' 'I hope, Sir,' said the Lieutenant, 'the Skull is not fractured.' 'Hum,' cries the Surgeon, 'Fractures are not always the most dangerous Symptoms. Contusions and Lacerations are often attended with worse Phænomena, and with more fatal Consequences than Fractures. People who know nothing of the Matter conclude, if the Skull is not fractured, all is well; whereas, I had rather see a Man's Skull broke all to Pieces, than some Contusions I have met with.' 'I hope,' says the Lieutenant, 'there are no such Symptoms here.' 'Symptoms,' answered the Surgeon, 'are not always regular nor constant. I have known very unfavourable Symptoms in the Morning change to favourable ones at Noon, and return to unfavourable again at Night. Of Wounds,

---

[1] According to the time-scheme established in VII. xi (see above, p. 368, n. 1), the landlady's complaint against the window tax is anachronistic. Though a window tax had been in effect since 1696, until 25 March 1747 the maximum yearly charge to the householder had been limited to 20*s*. On that date a new law (20 George II, cap. 3) levied a tax on 'every Window or Light, in every Dwelling-house', the rates being scaled so as to fall most heavily on the rich: houses having from 10 to 14 windows paid 6*d*. per window per year; for houses having from 15 to 19 windows the rate was 9*d*.; and for those having 20 or more windows, 1*s*. For the most part public opinion approved this more equitable tax. (See the articles from *The Westminster Journal* and *The Craftsman* reprinted in *The Gentleman's Magazine*, xvi [March 1746], 150–2, and xvii [February 1747], 72–3.) But there were those who preferred to seal up their windows rather than pay it. Such is 'Humphry Gubbins', the intransigent Tory of *The Jacobite's Journal* (13 February 1748), who writes to protest against the new law: 'I put out one haf of my Windows last Year, and if there comes another Ile put out t'other haf.—D—n me a Man may drink in the Dark, and mayhap he may then be the buolder in toasting honest Healths.' See also the poem, 'On a Quaker's stopping up more than half his windows, in pursuance of the late tax on lights', *The British Magazine*, ii (April 1747), 176.

indeed, it is rightly and truly said, *Nemo repente fuit turpissimus.*[1] I was once, I remember, called to a Patient, who had received a violent Contusion in his Tibia, by which the exterior Cutis was lacerated, so that there was a profuse sanguinary Discharge; and the interior Membranes were so divellicated, that the Os or Bone very plainly appeared through the Aperture of the Vulnus or Wound. Some febrile Symptoms intervening at the same Time, (for the Pulse was exuberant and indicated much Phlebotomy) I apprehended an immediate Mortification. To prevent which I presently made a large Orifice in the Vein of the left Arm, whence I drew twenty Ounces of Blood; which I expected to have found extremely sizy and glutinous, or indeed coagulated, as it is in pleuritic Complaints; but, to my Surprize, it appeared rosy and florid, and its Consistency differed little from the Blood of those in perfect Health. I then applied a Fomentation to the Part, which highly answered the Intention, and after three or four Times dressing, the Wound began to discharge a thick Pus or Matter, by which Means the Cohesion—but perhaps I do not make myself perfectly well understood.' 'No really,' answered the Lieutenant, 'I cannot say I understand a Syllable.' 'Well, Sir,' said the Surgeon, 'then I shall not tire your Patience; in short, within six Weeks, my Patient was able to walk upon his Legs, as perfectly as he could have done before he received the Contusion.' 'I wish, Sir,' said the Lieutenant, 'you would be so kind only to inform me, whether the Wound this young Gentleman hath had the Misfortune to receive is likely to prove mortal?' 'Sir,' answered the Surgeon, 'to say whether a Wound will prove mortal or not at first Dressing, would be very weak and foolish Presumption: We are all mortal, and Symptoms often occur in a Cure which the greatest of our Profession could never foresee.'— 'But do you think him in Danger?' says the other. 'In Danger! ay, surely,' cries the Doctor, 'who is there among us, who in the most perfect Health can be said not to be in Danger? Can a Man, therefore, with so bad a Wound as this be said to be out of Danger? All I can say, at present, is, that it is well I was called as I was, and perhaps it would have been better if I had been called sooner. I will see him again early in the Morning, and in the mean Time let him be kept extremely quiet, and drink liberally of

---

[1] Juvenal, *Satires,* ii. 83: 'no one reaches the depths of turpitude all at once'—trans. G. G. Ramsay, Loeb Classical Library, 1928.

Water-Gruel.' 'Won't you allow him Sack-whey?'[1] said the Land-lady. 'Ay, ay, Sack-whey,' cries the Doctor, 'if you will, provided it be very small.' 'And a little Chicken-broth too?' added she.— 'Yes, yes, Chicken-broth,' said the Doctor, 'is very good.' 'May'nt I make him some Jellies too?' said the Landlady. 'Ay, ay,' answered the Doctor, 'Jellies are very good for Wounds, for they promote Cohesion.' And, indeed, it was lucky she had not named Soop or high Sauces, for the Doctor would have complied, rather than have lost the Custom of the House.

The Doctor was no sooner gone, than the Landlady began to trumpet forth his Fame to the Lieutenant, who had not, from their short Acquaintance, conceived quite so favourable an Opinion of his physical Abilities, as the good Woman, and all the Neighbourhood entertained; (and perhaps very rightly) for tho' I am afraid the Doctor was a little of a Coxcomb, he might be nevertheless very much of a Surgeon.

The Lieutenant having collected from the learned Discourse of the Surgeon, that Mr. *Jones* was in great Danger, gave Orders for keeping Mr. *Northerton* under a very strict Guard, designing in the Morning to attend him to a Justice of Peace, and to commit the conducting the Troops to *Gloucester* to the *French* Lieutenant, who, tho' he could neither read, write, nor speak any Language, was, however, a good Officer.

In the Evening our Commander sent a Message to Mr. *Jones*, that if a Visit would not be troublesome he would wait on him. This Civility was very kindly and thankfully received by *Jones*, and the Lieutenant accordingly went up to his Room, where he found the wounded Man much better than he expected; nay, *Jones* assured his Friend, that if he had not received express Orders to the contrary from the Surgeon, he should have got up long ago: For he appeared to himself to be as well as ever, and felt no other Inconvenience from his Wound but an extreme Soreness on that Side of his Head.

'I should be very glad,' quoth the Lieutenant, 'if you was as well as you fancy yourself: For then you could be able to do yourself Justice immediately; for when a Matter can't be made up, as in a Case of a Blow, the sooner you take him out the better; but I am afraid you think yourself better than you are, and he would have too much Advantage over you.'

---

[1] A hot drink of sherry (half a glass), milk (half a pint), and sugar. See also below, p. 536.

'I'll try, however,' answered *Jones*, 'if you please, and will be so kind to lend me a Sword: For I have none here of my own.'

'My Sword is heartily at your Service, my dear Boy,' cries the Lieutenant, kissing him, 'you are a brave Lad, and I love your Spirit; but I fear your Strength: For such a Blow, and so much Loss of Blood, must have very much weakened you; and tho' you feel no Want of Strength in your Bed, yet you most probably would after a Thrust or two. I can't consent to your taking him out To-night; but I hope you will be able to come up with us before we get many Days March advance; and I give you my Honour you shall have Satisfaction, or the Man who hath injured you shan't stay in our Regiment.'

'I wish,' said *Jones*, 'it was possible to decide this Matter To-night; now you have mentioned it to me, I shall not be able to rest.'

'O never think of it,' returned the other, 'a few Days will make no Difference. The Wounds of Honour are not like those in your Body. They suffer nothing by the Delay of Cure. It will be altogether as well for you, to receive Satisfaction a Week hence as now.'

'But suppose,' says *Jones*, 'I should grow worse, and die of the Consequences of my present Wound.'

'Then your Honour,' answered the Lieutenant, 'will require no Reparation at all. I myself will do Justice to your Character, and testify to the World your Intention to have acted properly, if you had recovered.'

'Still,' replied *Jones*, 'I am concerned at the Delay. I am almost afraid to mention it to you who are a Soldier; but tho' I have been a very wild young Fellow, still in my most serious Moments, and at the Bottom, I am really a Christian.'

'So am I too, I assure you,' said the Officer: 'And so zealous a one, that I was pleased with you at Dinner for taking up the Cause of your Religion; and I am a little offended with you now, young Gentleman, that you should express a Fear of declaring your Faith before any one.'

'But how terrible must it be,' cries *Jones*, 'to any one who is really a Christian, to cherish Malice in his Breast, in Opposition to the Command of him who hath expressly forbid it?[1] How can I

---

[1] See above, p. 52, n. 1. Like Steele and Richardson, Fielding condemned what he called 'the present abominable Custom of Duelling' (*The Covent-Garden Journal,*

bear to do this on a sick Bed? Or how shall I make up my Account, with such an Article as this in my Bosom against me?'

'Why I believe there is such a Command,' cries the Lieutenant; 'but a Man of Honour can't keep it. And you must be a Man of Honour, if you will be in the Army. I remember I once put the Case to our Chaplain over a Bowl of Punch, and he confessed there was much Difficulty in it; but he said, he hoped there might be a Latitude granted to Soldiers in this one Instance; and to be sure it is our Duty to hope so: For who would bear to live without his Honour? No, no, my dear Boy, be a good Christian as long as you live; but be a Man of Honour too, and never put up an Affront; not all the Books, nor all the Parsons in the World, shall ever persuade me to that. I love my Religion very well, but I love my Honour more. There must be some Mistake in the wording the Text, or in the Translation, or in the understanding it, or somewhere or other. But however that be, a Man must run the Risque, for he must preserve his Honour. So compose yourself To-night, and I promise you, you shall have an Opportunity of doing yourself Justice.' Here he gave *Jones* a hearty Buss, shook him by the Hand, and took his Leave.

But tho' the Lieutenant's Reasoning was very satisfactory to himself, it was not entirely so to his Friend. *Jones* therefore having revolved this Matter much in his Thoughts, at last came to a Resolution, which the Reader will find in the next Chapter.

CHAPTER XIV

A most dreadful Chapter indeed; and which few Readers ought to venture upon in an Evening, especially when alone.

JONES swallowed a large Mess of Chicken, or rather Cock, Broth, with a very good Appetite, as indeed he would have done the Cock it was made of, with a Pound of Bacon into the

7 January 1752; see Dudden, ii. 833, n. 1). Absurdly and in direct defiance of the precepts of morality and religion, *honour* in the 'Modern Glossary' had become synonymous with *duelling* (*The Covent-Garden Journal*, 14 January 1752)—a fact demonstrated at length in the character of Colonel Bath in *Amelia* (1751). Indeed, the irreconcilable opposition between Christian principles and the modern code of honour is a recurrent theme of that novel (see esp. IX. iii, XII. iii). See also the exchange between Valentine and Veromil in *The Temple Beau* (1730), II. xii. For the treatment of this theme by a divine whom Fielding greatly admired, see Robert South's sermon, 'The Fatal Influence of Words and Names Falsely Applied' (*Sermons Preached upon Several Occasions* [1865], i. 554–5).

Bargain; and now, finding in himself no Deficiency of either Health or Spirit, he resolved to get up and seek his Enemy.

But first he sent for the Serjeant, who was his first Acquaintance among these military Gentlemen. Unluckily that worthy Officer having, in a literal Sense, taken his Fill of Liquor, had been some Time retired to his Bolster, where he was snoring so loud, that it was not easy to convey a Noise in at his Ears capable of drowning that which issued from his Nostrils.

However, as *Jones* persisted in his Desire of seeing him, a vociferous Drawer at length found Means to disturb his Slumbers, and to acquaint him with the Message. Of which the Serjeant was no sooner made sensible, than he arose from his Bed, and having his Clothes already on, immediately attended. *Jones* did not think fit to acquaint the Serjeant with his Design, tho' he might have done it with great Safety; for the Halberdier was himself a Man of Honour, and had killed his Man. He would therefore have faithfully kept this Secret, or indeed any other which no Reward was published for discovering. But as *Jones* knew not those Virtues in so short an Acquaintance, his Caution was perhaps prudent and commendable enough.

He began therefore by acquainting the Serjeant, that as he was now entered into the Army, he was ashamed of being without what was perhaps the most necessary Implement of a Soldier, namely, a Sword; adding, that he should be infinitely obliged to him if he could procure one. 'For which,' says he, 'I will give you any reasonable Price. Nor do I insist upon its being Silver-hilted, only a good Blade, and such as may become a Soldier's Thigh.'

The Serjeant, who well knew what had happened, and had heard that *Jones* was in a very dangerous Condition, immediately concluded, from such a Message, at such a Time of Night, and from a Man in such a Situation, that he was light-headed. Now as he had his Wit (to use that Word in its common Signification) always ready, he bethought himself of making his Advantage of this Humour in the sick Man. 'Sir,' says he, 'I believe I can fit you. I have a most excellent Piece of Stuff by me. It is not indeed Silver-hilted, which, as you say, doth not become a Soldier; but the Handle is decent enough, and the Blade one of the best in *Europe*.—It is a Blade that—a Blade that—— In short, I will fetch it you this Instant, and you shall see it and handle it.—I am glad to see your Honour so well with all my Heart.'

Being instantly returned with the Sword, he delivered it to *Jones*, who took it and drew it; and then told the Serjeant it would do very well, and bid him name his Price.

The Serjeant now began to harangue in Praise of his Goods. He said (nay he swore very heartily) 'that the Blade was taken from a *French* Officer of very high Rank, at the Battle of *Dettingen*.[1] I took it myself,' says he, 'from his Side, after I had knocked him o' the Head. The Hilt was a golden one. That I sold to one of our fine Gentlemen; for there are some of them, an't please your Honour, who value the Hilt of a Sword more than the Blade.'

Here the other stopped him, and begged him to name a Price. The Serjeant, who thought *Jones* absolutely out of his Senses, and very near his End, was afraid, lest he should injure his Family by asking too little.—However, after a Moment's Hesitation, he contented himself with naming twenty Guineas, and swore he would not sell it for less to his own Brother.

'Twenty Guineas!' says *Jones*, in the utmost Surprize, 'sure you think I am mad, or that I never saw a Sword in my Life. Twenty Guineas indeed! I did not imagine you would endeavour to impose upon me.—Here, take the Sword—— No, now I think on't, I will keep it myself, and shew it your Officer in the Morning, acquainting him, at the same Time, what a Price you asked me for it.'

The Serjeant, as we have said, had always his Wit (*in sensu prædicto*)[2] about him, and now plainly saw that *Jones* was not in the Condition he had apprehended him to be; he now, therefore, counterfeited as great Surprize as the other had shewn, and said, 'I am certain, Sir, I have not asked you so much out of the way. Besides, you are to consider, it is the only Sword I have, and I must run the Risque of my Officer's Displeasure, by going without one myself. And truly, putting all this together, I don't think twenty Shillings was so much out of the Way.'

'Twenty Shillings!' cries *Jones*, 'why you just now asked me twenty Guineas.' 'How!' cries the Serjeant.—'Sure your Honour must have mistaken me; or else I mistook myself—and indeed I am but half awake.—Twenty Guineas indeed! no wonder your Honour flew into such a Passion. I say twenty Guineas too.—No,

---

[1] The Battle of Dettingen (15 June 1743), in which George II led the Pragmatic Army to victory over the French, marked the zenith of British fortunes in the Continental war.
[2] 'In the sense aforementioned'.

no, I meant twenty Shillings, I assure you. And when your
Honour comes to consider every thing, I hope you will not think
that so extravagant a Price. It is indeed true, you may buy a
Weapon which looks as well for less Money. But——'

Here *Jones* interrupted him, saying, 'I will be so far from
making any Words with you, that I will give you a Shilling more
than your Demand.' He then gave him a Guinea, bid him return
to his Bed, and wished him a good March; adding, he hoped to
overtake them before the Division reached *Worcester*.

The Serjeant very civilly took his Leave, fully satisfied with his
Merchandize, and not a little pleased with his dextrous Recovery
from that false Step into which his Opinion of the Sick Man's
Light-headedness had betrayed him.

As soon as the Serjeant was departed, *Jones* rose from his Bed,
and dressed himself entirely, putting on even his Coat, which, as
its Colour was white, shewed very visibly the Streams of Blood
which had flowed down it; and now, having grasped his new-
purchased Sword in his Hand, he was going to issue forth, when
the Thought of what he was about to undertake laid suddenly
hold of him, and he began to reflect that in a few Minutes he
might possibly deprive a human Being of Life, or might lose his
own. 'Very well,' said he, 'and in what Cause do I venture my
Life? Why, in that of my Honour. And who is this human
Being? A Rascal who hath injured and insulted me without
Provocation. But is not Revenge forbidden by Heaven?—Yes,
but it is enjoined by the World. Well, but shall I obey the World
in Opposition to the express Commands of Heaven? Shall I
incur the divine Displeasure rather than be called—Ha—
Coward—Scoundrel?—I'll think no more, I am resolved and
must fight him.'

The Clock had now struck Twelve, and every one in the House
were in their Beds, except the Centinel who stood to guard
Northerton, when *Jones* softly opening his Door, issued forth in
Pursuit of his Enemy, of whose Place of Confinement he had
received a perfect Description from the Drawer. It is not easy to
conceive a much more tremendous Figure than he now exhibited.
He had on, as we have said, a light-coloured Coat, covered with
Streams of Blood. His Face, which missed that very Blood, as
well as twenty Ounces more drawn from him by the Surgeon, was
pallid. Round his Head was a Quantity of Bandage, not unlike a

Turban. In the right Hand he carried a Sword, and in the left a Candle. So that the bloody *Banquo*[1] was not worthy to be compared to him. In Fact, I believe a more dreadful Apparition was never raised in a Church-yard, nor in the Imagination of any good People met in a Winter Evening over a Christmas Fire in *Somersetshire*.

When the Centinel first saw our Heroe approach, his Hair began gently to lift up his Grenadier Cap; and in the same Instant his Knees fell to Blows with each other. Presently his whole Body was seized with worse than an Ague Fit. He then fired his Piece, and fell flat on his Face.

Whether Fear or Courage was the Occasion of his Firing, or whether he took Aim at the Object of his Terror, I cannot say. If he did, however, he had the good Fortune to miss his Man.

Jones seeing the Fellow fall, guessed the Cause of his Fright, at which he could not forbear smiling, not in the least reflecting on the Danger from which he had just escaped. He then passed by the Fellow, who still continued in the Posture in which he fell, and entered the Room where *Northerton*, as he had heard, was confined. Here, in a solitary Situation, he found—an empty Quart Pot standing on the Table, on which some Beer being spilt, it looked as if the Room had lately been inhabited; but at present it was entirely vacant.

Jones then apprehended it might lead to some other Apartment; but, upon searching all round it, he could perceive no other Door than that at which he entered, and where the Centinel had been posted. He then proceeded to call *Northerton* several Times by his Name; but no one answered; nor did this serve to any other Purpose than to confirm the Centinel in his Terrors, who was now convinced that the Volunteer was dead of his Wounds, and that his Ghost was come in Search of the Murtherer: He now lay in all the Agonies of Horror, and I wish, with all my Heart, some of those Actors, who are hereafter to represent a Man frighted out of his Wits, had seen him, that they might be taught to copy Nature instead of performing several antic Tricks and Gestures, for the Entertainment and Applause of the Galleries.

Perceiving the Bird was flown, at least despairing to find him, and rightly apprehending that the Report of the Firelock would alarm the whole House, our Heroe now blew out his Candle, and

---

[1] *Macbeth*, III. iv, IV. i.

gently stole back again to his Chamber, and to his Bed: Whither he would not have been able to have gotten undiscovered, had any other Person been on the same Stair-case, save only one Gentleman who was confined to his Bed by the Gout; for before he could reach the Door to his Chamber, the Hall where the Centinel had been posted was half full of People. Some in their Shirts, and others not half drest, all very earnestly enquiring of each other, what was the Matter?

The Soldier was now found lying in the same Place and Posture in which we just now left him. Several immediately applied themselves to raise him, and some concluded him dead: But they presently saw their Mistake; for he not only struggled with those who laid their Hands on him, but fell a roaring like a Bull. In reality, he imagined so many Spirits or Devils were handling him; for his Imagination being possessed with the Horror of an Apparition, converted every Object he saw or felt, into nothing but Ghosts and Spectres.

At length he was overpowered by Numbers, and got upon his Legs; when Candles being brought, and seeing two or three of his Comrades present, he came a little to himself; but when they asked him what was the Matter? he answered, 'I am a dead Man, that's all, I'm a dead Man. I can't recover it. I have seen him.' 'What hast thou seen, *Jack*,' says one of the Soldiers. 'Why, I have seen the young Volunteer that was killed Yesterday.' He then imprecated the most heavy Curses on himself, if he had not seen the Volunteer, all over Blood, vomiting Fire out of his Mouth and Nostrils, pass by him into the Chamber where Ensign *Northerton* was, and then seizing the Ensign by the Throat, fly away with him in a Clap of Thunder.

This Relation met with a gracious Reception from the Audience. All the Women present believed it firmly, and prayed Heaven to defend them from Murther. Amongst the Men too, many had Faith in the Story; but others turned it into Derision and Ridicule; and a Serjeant who was present, answered very coolly: 'Young Man, you will hear more of this for going to sleep, and dreaming on your Post.'

The Soldier replied, 'You may punish me if you please; but I was as broad awake as I am now; and the Devil carry me away, as he hath the Ensign, if I did not see the dead Man, as I tell you, with Eyes as big and as fiery as two large Flambeaux.'

The Commander of the Forces, and the Commander of the House, were now both arrived: For the former being awake at the Time, and hearing the Centinel fire his Piece, thought it his Duty to rise immediately, tho' he had no great Apprehensions of any Mischief; whereas the Apprehensions of the latter were much greater, lest her Spoons and Tankards should be upon the March, without having received any such Orders from her.

Our poor Centinel, to whom the Sight of this Officer was not much more welcome than the Apparition, as he thought it, which he had seen before, again related the dreadful Story, and with many Additions of Blood and Fire: But he had the Misfortune to gain no Credit with either of the last-mentioned Persons; for the Officer, tho' a very religious Man, was free from all Terrors of this Kind; besides, having so lately left *Jones* in the Condition we have seen, he had no Suspicion of his being dead. As for the Landlady, tho' not over religious, she had no kind of Aversion to the Doctrine of Spirits; but there was a Circumstance in the Tale which she well knew to be false, as we shall inform the Reader presently.

But whether *Northerton* was carried away in Thunder or Fire, or in whatever other Manner he was gone; it was now certain, that his Body was no longer in Custody. Upon this Occasion, the Lieutenant formed a Conclusion not very different from what the Serjeant is just mentioned to have made before, and immediately ordered the Centinel to be taken Prisoner. So that, by a strange Reverse of Fortune (tho' not very uncommon in a military Life) the Guard became the guarded.

CHAPTER XV

The Conclusion of the foregoing Adventure.

BESIDES the Suspicion of Sleep, the Lieutenant harboured another, and worse Doubt, against the poor Centinel, and this was that of Treachery: For as he believed not one Syllable of the Apparition, so he imagined the whole to be an Invention, formed only to impose upon him, and that the Fellow had, in Reality, been bribed by *Northerton* to let him escape. And this he imagined the rather, as the Fright appeared to him, the more unnatural in one who had the Character of as brave and bold a Man as any in the Regiment, having been in several Actions, having received several Wounds, and, in a Word, having behaved himself always like a good and valiant Soldier.

That the Reader, therefore, may not conceive the least ill Opinion of such a Person, we shall not delay a Moment in rescuing his Character from the Imputation of this Guilt.

Mr. *Northerton* then, as we have before observed, was fully satisfied with the Glory which he had obtained from this Action. He had, perhaps, seen, or heard, or guessed, that Envy is apt to attend Fame. Not that I would here insinuate, that he was heathenishly inclined to believe in, or to worship, the Goddess *Nemesis*; for, in fact, I am convinced he never heard of her Name. He was, besides, of an active Disposition, and had a great Antipathy to those close Winter Quarters in the Castle of *Gloucester*, for which a Justice of Peace might possibly give him a Billet. Nor was he moreover free from some uneasy Meditations on a certain wooden Edifice, which I forbear to name, in Conformity to the Opinion of Mankind, who, I think, rather ought to honour than to be ashamed of this Building, as it is, or at least might be made, of more Benefit to Society than almost any other public Erection. In a Word, to hint at no more Reasons for his Conduct, Mr. *Northerton* was desirous of departing that Evening, and nothing remained for him but to contrive the *Quomodo*, which appeared to be a Matter of some Difficulty.

Now this young Gentleman, tho' somewhat crooked in his Morals, was perfectly strait in his Person, which was extremely strong and well made. His Face too was accounted handsome by the Generality of Women, for it was broad and ruddy, with tolerably good Teeth. Such Charms did not fail making an Impression on my Landlady, who had no little Relish for this kind of Beauty. She had, indeed, a real Compassion for the young Man; and hearing from the Surgeon that Affairs were like to go ill with the Volunteer, she suspected they might hereafter wear no benign Aspect with the Ensign. Having obtained, therefore, leave to make him a Visit, and finding him in a very melancholy Mood, which she considerably heightened, by telling him there were scarce any Hopes of the Volunteer's Life, she proceeded to throw forth some Hints, which the other readily and eagerly taking up, they soon came to a right Understanding; and it was at length agreed, that the Ensign should, at a certain Signal, ascend the Chimney, which communicating very soon with that of the Kitchen, he might there again let himself down; for which she would give him an Opportunity, by keeping the Coast clear.

But lest our Readers, of a different Complexion, should take this Occasion of too hastily condemning all Compassion as a Folly, and pernicious to Society, we think proper to mention another Particular, which might possibly have some little Share in this Action. The Ensign happened to be at this Time possessed of the Sum of fifty Pounds, which did indeed belong to the whole Company: For the Captain having quarreled with his Lieutenant, had entrusted the Payment of his Company to the Ensign. This Money, however, he thought proper to deposite in my Landlady's Hand, possibly by way of Bail or Security that he would hereafter appear and answer to the Charge against him; but whatever were the Conditions, certain it is, that she had the Money, and the Ensign his Liberty.

The Reader may, perhaps, expect, from the compassionate Temper of this good Woman, that when she saw the poor Centinel taken Prisoner for a Fact of which she knew him innocent, she should immediately have interposed in his Behalf; but whether it was that she had already exhausted all her Compassion in the above-mentioned Instance, or that the Features of this Fellow, tho' not very different from those of the Ensign, could not raise it, I will not determine; but far from being an Advocate for the present Prisoner, she urged his Guilt to his Officer, declaring with uplifted Eyes and Hands, that she would not have had any Concern in the Escape of a Murderer for all the World.

Every thing was now once more quiet; and most of the Company returned again to their Beds; but the Landlady, either from the natural Activity of her Disposition, or from her Fear for her Plate, having no Propensity to sleep, prevailed with the Officers, as they were to march within little more than an Hour, to spend that Time with her over a Bowl of Punch.

Jones had lain awake all this while, and had heard great Part of the Hurry and Bustle that had passed, of which he had now some Curiosity to know the Particulars. He therefore applied to his Bell, which he rung at least twenty Times without any Effect; for my Landlady was in such high Mirth with her Company, that no Clapper could be heard there but her own, and the Drawer and

Chambermaid, who were sitting together in the Kitchen, (for neither durst he sit up, nor she lie in Bed alone) the more they heard the Bell ring, the more they were frightened, and, as it were, nailed down in their Places.

At last, at a lucky Interval of Chat, the Sound reached the Ears of our good Landlady, who presently sent forth her Summons, which both her Servants instantly obeyed. '*Joo*,' says the Mistress, 'don't you hear the Gentleman's Bell ring? why don't you go up?' 'It is not my Business,' answered the Drawer, 'to wait upon the Chambers. It is *Betty* Chambermaid's!' 'If you come to that,' answered the Maid, 'it is not my Business to wait upon Gentlemen. I have done it, indeed, sometimes; but the Devil fetch me if ever I do again, since you make your Preambles about it.' The Bell still ringing violently, their Mistress fell into a Passion, and swore, if the Drawer did not go up immediately, she would turn him away that very Morning. 'If you do, Madam,' says he, 'I can't help it. I won't do another Servant's Business.' She then applied herself to the Maid, and endeavoured to prevail by gentle Means; but all in vain, *Betty* was as inflexible as *Joo*. Both insisted it was not their Business, and they would not do it.

The Lieutenant then fell a laughing, and said, 'Come, I will put an End to this Contention;' and then turning to the Servants, commended them for their Resolution, in not giving up the Point; but added, he was sure, if one would consent to go, the other would. To which Proposal they both agreed in an Instant, and accordingly went up very lovingly and close together. When they were gone, the Lieutenant appeased the Wrath of the Landlady, by satisfying her why they were both so unwilling to go alone.

They returned soon after, and acquainted their Mistress, that the sick Gentleman was so far from being dead, that he spoke as heartily as if he was well; and that he gave his Service to the Captain, and should be very glad of the Favour of seeing him before he marched.

The good Lieutenant immediately complied with his Desires, and sitting down by his Bed-side, acquainted him with the Scene which had happened below, concluding with his Intentions to make an Example of the Centinel.

Upon this, *Jones* related to him the whole Truth, and earnestly begged him not to punish the poor Soldier, 'who, I am confident,' says he, 'is as innocent of the Ensign's Escape, as he is of forging any Lie, or of endeavouring to impose on you.'

The Lieutenant hesitated a few Moments, and then answered: 'Why, as you have cleared the Fellow of one Part of the Charge, so it will be impossible to prove the other; because he was not the only Centinel. But I have a good mind to punish the Rascal for being a Coward. Yet who knows what Effect the Terror of such an Apprehension may have; and to say the Truth, he hath always behaved well against an Enemy. Come, it is a good Thing to see any Sign of Religion in these Fellows; so I promise you he shall be set at liberty when we march. But hark, the General beats. My dear Boy, give me another Buss. Don't discompose nor hurry yourself; but remember the Christian Doctrine of Patience, and I warrant you will soon be able to do yourself Justice, and to take an honourable Revenge on the Fellow who hath injured you.' The Lieutenant then departed, and *Jones* endeavoured to compose himself to Rest.

BOOK VIII

Containing above two Days.

CHAPTER I

A wonderful long Chapter concerning the Marvellous; being much the longest of all our introductory Chapters.

AS we are now entering upon a Book, in which the Course of our History will oblige us to relate some Matters of a more strange and surprizing Kind than any which have hitherto occurred, it may not be amiss in the prolegomenous, or introductory Chapter, to say something of that Species of Writing which is called the Marvellous[1]. To this we shall, as well for the

---

[1] Throughout this chapter Fielding applies to his own 'new species of writing' the familiar assumptions and arguments of neoclassical criticism of the epic. Drawing upon Aristotle (*Poetics*, ix, xxiv. 15–17, 19), the French critics had distinguished two contrary elements in 'the Fable' of the heroic poem: these were 'the Probable' ('la Vraisemblance')—the representation of such characters and actions as conform to the commonly received notions of human behaviour and therefore do not strain the credulity of the reader; and 'the Marvellous' ('l'Admirable')—the representation of such characters, actions and circumstances as contradict normal human experience and the ordinary course of nature. (Among the chief expositors of this distinction were Rapin, *Reflections on Aristotle's Treatise of Poesie*, trans. Rymer [1674], Pt. I, sec. xxii–xxiv and Pt. II, sec. xii; Le Bossu, *Traité du poëme épique* [Paris, 1675], Bk. III, chs. vii–viii; and André Dacier in the remarks to his translation of the *Poetics* [Paris, 1692].) By adhering to the rule of probability alone, a fable becomes worthy of the reader's belief, but it is likely to be dull; by containing too much of the marvellous, it may surprise and entertain, but it will do so to no purpose, since the reader will dismiss the performance as mere fantasy.

The province of the poet, moreover, differs from that of the historian or the romance writer. Truth, the recording of things as they actually are, is the business of the historian, who on occasion must therefore deal in matters stranger than fiction, relating what is possible to occur but not probable. The marvellous, freely indulged, is the stuff of romance. But the probable is the special concern of the poet, whose aim is to represent not what *did* happen or what possibly *might* happen, but what *should* happen; the poet deals not in particular facts, but in universal and general truths, and he prefers, as Aristotle expressed it, 'what is convincing though impossible' to 'what is possible and unconvincing' (*Poetics*, xxiv. 19). The theory and the ideal were summarized by Addison in *The Spectator*, no. 315 (1 March 1712):

'. . . the Fable of an Epic Poem should abound in Circumstances that are both credible and astonishing; or as the *French* Critics chuse to phrase it, the Fable should be filled with the Probable and the Marvellous. . . . If the Fable is only Probable, it differs

Sake of ourselves, as of others, endeavour to set some certain Bounds; and indeed nothing can be more necessary, as Criticks* of different Complexions are here apt to run into very different Extremes; for while some are, with M. *Dacier*,[1] ready to allow, that the same Thing which is impossible may be yet probable,† others have so little Historic or Poetic Faith, that they believe nothing to be either possible or probable, the like to which hath not occurred to their own Observation.

First then, I think, it may very reasonably be required of every

---

* By this Word here, and in most other Parts of our Work, we mean every Reader in the World.

† It is happy for M. *Dacier* that he was not an *Irishman*.[2]

---

nothing from a true History; if it is only Marvellous, it is no better than a Romance. The great Secret therefore of Heroic Poetry is to relate such Circumstances, as may produce in the Reader at the same time both Belief and Astonishment.'

For a comprehensive discussion of the subject, see H. T. Swedenberg, Jr., *The Theory of the Epic in England, 1650–1800* (Berkeley and Los Angeles, Cal., 1944), ch. x.

[1] André Dacier (1651–1722), husband of Mme Dacier (see above, p. 372, n. 2), in *La Poëtique d'Aristote traduite en françois avec des remarques* (Paris, 1692), commenting upon *Poetics*, xxv. 31 (xxiv. 19 in the Loeb Classical Library edition). In his 'Observations on the Tenth Book' of the *Odyssey*—to which Fielding alludes in the following paragraph (see below, p. 397, n. 1)—Broome explains the passage in Dacier as follows: 'How are these incredible stories to be reduc'd into the bounds of probability? 'tis true, the Marvellous ought to be used in Epic Poetry; but ought it to transgress all power of belief? *Aristotle* in his *Art of Poetry* lays down a rule to justifie these incidents: *A Poet*, says that Author, *ought to prefer things impossible, provided they are probable, before things possible, that are nevertheless incredible.* . . . This rule is not without obscurity; but Monsieur *Dacier* has explain'd it in his Annotations upon that Author: A thing may be impossible, and yet probable: Thus when the Poet introduces a Deity, any incident humanly impossible receives a full probability by being ascribed to the skill and power of a God' (Pope's *Odyssey* [1725]). Fielding compliments Dacier later in *Tom Jones*, p. 569.

[2] The Irish were noted for the sort of self-contradictory assertion (later called an 'Irish bull') which Fielding here remarks in Dacier. (See A. M. Hyamson, *Dictionary of English Phrases* [1922], s.v. 'Bull', and E. Partridge, *Dictionary of Slang and Unconventional English* [1961].) Thus in x. ii, Mr. Fitzpatrick declares that he would have caught up with his errant wife, 'if I had not found her gone just as I came up with her'; and in the same chapter, Mr. MacLachlan is equally muddled as he assures his compatriot that Mrs. Waters is not his wife: 'don't I see that the Lady, whom the Gentleman who stands here in his Shirt is lying in Bed with, is none of her?' The point of Fielding's footnote seems to be that, if Dacier had been an Irishman, his paradox would have been dismissed as such another logical blunder. It may also be worth noting that in *The Champion* (29 January 1739/40) Fielding had associated Irishmen with French pedagogues for the reason that they were both adepts in the 'Science' of 'Impudence', the latter pretending to more knowledge than they possessed. For a discussion of contemporary opinions of the Irish character, see *A Modest Argument, Pro and Con, Enquiring into the Causes Why Base and Mean Actions should be Committed by the Irish in particular, more than any other Nation* (1731). See also below, pp. 601, n. 1; 828.

Writer, that he keeps within the Bounds of Possibility; and still remembers that what it is not possible for Man to perform, it is scarce possible for Man to believe he did perform. This Conviction, perhaps, gave Birth to many Stories of the antient Heathen Deities (for most of them are of poetical Original). The Poet, being desirous to indulge a wanton and extravagant Imagination, took Refuge in that Power, of the Extent of which his Readers were no Judges, or rather which they imagined to be infinite, and consequently they could not be shocked at any Prodigies related of it. This hath been strongly urged in Defence of *Homer's* Miracles; and it is, perhaps, a Defence; not, as Mr. *Pope* would have it,[1] because *Ulysses* told a Set of foolish Lies to the *Phæacians*, who were a very dull Nation; but because the Poet himself wrote to Heathens, to whom poetical Fables were Articles of Faith.[2] For my own Part, I must confess, so compassionate is my Temper, I wish *Polypheme*[3] had confined himself to his Milk Diet, and preserved his Eye; nor could *Ulysses* be much more concerned than myself, when his Companions were turned into Swine by *Circe*,[4] who shewed, I think, afterwards, too much Regard for Man's Flesh to be supposed capable of converting it into Bacon. I wish, likewise, with all my Heart, that *Homer* could have known the Rule prescribed by *Horace*,[5] to introduce

[1] Though found in Pope's *Odyssey*, the passage to which Fielding alludes is by William Broome (1689–1745), who merely repeated Dacier's interpretation (see *La Poëtique d'Aristote* [Paris, 1692], p. 408). In his 'Observations on the Tenth Book' of the *Odyssey*, Broome explains how Homer shrewdly brought such marvellous episodes as those of Circe and Polyphemus 'within the degrees' of probability: 'he makes *Ulysses* relate them before a credulous and ignorant assembly; he lets us into the character of the *Phæacians*, by saying they were a very dull nation, in the sixth book,

Where never Science rear'd her laurel'd Head.

It is thus the Poet gives probability to his fables, by reciting them to a people who believ'd them, and who thro' a laziness of life were fond of romantic stories; he adapts himself to his audience. . . .'

[2] According to Aristotle (cf. *Poetics*, xxiv. 19), the inclusion of fabulous episodes in a fiction could be justified if the poet's audience believed them to be true. Thus Addison observed that 'a *well chosen* Fable' must relate 'such things as have really happened, or at least . . . such things as have happen'd according to the received Opinions of Mankind', and he proceeded to illustrate this principle by reference to the extraordinary episodes of *Paradise Lost*, which, 'though they are very astonishing in themselves, are not only credible, but actual Points of Faith'. (*Spectator*, No. 315 [1 March 1712].)

[3] *Odyssey*, ix.   [4] Ibid., x.

[5] *Ars Poetica*, 191–2: 'nec deus intersit, nisi dignus vindice nodus/ inciderit' ('And let no god intervene, unless a knot come worthy of such a deliverer'—trans. H. R. Fairclough, Loeb Classical Library, 1929). See *Jonathan Wild* (1743), II. xii, where Fielding quotes this passage and comments upon it. See also *Tom Jones*, pp. 512; 876, n. 1.

supernatural Agents as seldom as possible. We should not then have seen his Gods coming on trivial Errands, and often behaving themselves so as not only to forfeit all Title to Respect, but to become the Objects of Scorn and Derision.¹ A Conduct which must have shocked the Credulity of a pious and sagacious Heathen; and which could never have been defended, unless by agreeing with a Supposition to which I have been sometimes almost inclined, that this most glorious Poet, as he certainly was, had an Intent to burlesque the superstitious Faith of his own Age and Country.

But I have rested too long on a Doctrine which can be of no Use to a Christian Writer: For as he cannot introduce into his Works any of that heavenly Host which make a Part of his Creed;² so is it horrid Puerility to search the Heathen Theology for any of those Deities who have been long since dethroned from their Immortality.³ Lord *Shaftesbury* observes,⁴ that nothing

---

¹ Cf. Longinus' complaint that Homer's representation of the pranks and passions of the gods was 'utterly irreligious' and a violation of poetic decorum (*On the Sublime*, ix. 7— trans. W. H. Fyfe, Loeb Classical Library, 1927). Later critics, such as Sir Richard Blackmore, similarly regretted that in his irreverent treatment of the gods Homer had debased the dignity of the epic by admitting into his poem 'such Strains as have an Air of Raillery and Burlesque': 'And as by introducing into Heaven Farce and Buffoonery, an improper Place for such Diversion, he has broken in upon the Congruity and Decency which should always be preserv'd in the Characters, so he transgresses the Rule, that banishes in general from Heroick Works, all comick Manners, witty Conceits and Ridicule . . .' (*Essays upon Several Subjects*, i [1716], 75–6).

² A majority of critics followed Boileau (*L'Art poétique* [1674], iii. 199–204) in opposing the use of Christian 'machines' in the epic, despite the formidable example of Milton and the authority of those such as Dryden and Addison who approved his practice. Dennis was particularly adamant on this point, invoking Boileau's argument: 'That the Terrible Mysteries of the Christian Faith are not capable of delightful Ornaments. That the Gospel offers nothing to us but Repentance on the one side, or Eternal Torments on the other, and that the Criminal mixture of Poetical Fictions gives a Fabulous Air, even to its most Sacred Truths.' ('Remarks on *Prince Arthur*' [1696], in *Critical Works*, ed. E. N. Hooker, i [1939], 53; and 'Observations on the *Paradise Lost* of Milton' [1721], ibid., ii [1943], 228–9.) For a thorough discussion of the subject, see H. T. Swedenberg, op. cit., ch. xi.

³ Though the critics disagreed about the propriety of Christian machinery in a modern epic, they were unanimous in condemning the use of mythological deities. With Fielding's phrasing, compare Addison's in *Spectator*, No. 523 (30 October 1712): '*Virgil* and *Homer* might compliment their Heroes, by interweaving the Actions of Deities with their Atchievements; but for a Christian Author to write in the Pagan Creed . . . would be downright Puerility, and unpardonable in a Poet that is past Sixteen.'

⁴ In 'A Letter concerning Enthusiasm', section 1. On the poetic practice of invoking the Muse, Shaftesbury (see above, p. 217, n. 2) addresses Lord Somers: 'You must certainly have observ'd our Poets under a remarkable Constraint, when oblig'd to assume this

is more cold than the Invocation of a Muse by a Modern; he might have added that nothing can be more absurd. A modern may with much more Elegance invoke a Ballad, as some have thought *Homer* did,[1] or a Mug of Ale with the Author of *Hudibras*;[2] which latter may perhaps have inspired much more Poetry as well as Prose, than all the Liquors of *Hippocrene* or *Helicon*.

The only supernatural Agents which can in any Manner be allowed to us Moderns are Ghosts;[3] but of these I would advise an Author to be extremely sparing. These are indeed like Arsenic, and other dangerous Drugs in Physic, to be used with the utmost Caution; nor would I advise the Introduction of them at all in those Works, or by those Authors to which, or to whom a Horse-Laugh in the Reader, would be any great Prejudice or Mortification.

Character: and you have wonder'd, perhaps, why that Air of *Enthusiasm*, which sits so gracefully with an Antient, shou'd be so spiritless and aukard [*sic*] in a Modern' (*Characteristicks*, 5th ed. [1732], i. 4). In *Ovid's Art of Love Paraphrased* (1747) Fielding had expressed the view that his author's invocation of Venus was 'a manifest Burlesque' of a silly convention. Referring to this same passage from Shaftesbury, he continued: 'For my own part, I must confess, I cannot perceive *that graceful Air of Enthusiasm* which a noble Author observes in the Invocation of the Antients; many of them indeed seem to have been too apparently in jest, to endeavour to impose on their Readers, and in reality to apply to the Muses with less Devotion than our modern Poets, many of whom perhaps believe as much in those Deities as in any other.'

[1] Richard Bentley (1662–1742), the brilliant if controversial classicist, was the principal advocate of the view that Homer 'wrote a sequel of Songs and Rhapsodies, to be sung by himself for small earnings and good cheer, at Festivals and other days of Merriment; the *Ilias* he made for the Men, and the *Odysseis* for the other Sex. These loose Songs were not collected together in the form of an Epic Poem till *Pisistratus's* Time, above 500 years after.' (Bentley, 'Remarks upon a Late Discourse of Free-Thinking' [1713], in *Enchiridion Theologicum* [Oxford, 1792], v. 94.) Fielding had earlier ridiculed the theory in *Joseph Andrews* (1742; II. i), and in *A Journey from This World to the Next* (1743; I. viii) Homer himself finds it preposterous.

[2] See above, p. 151, n. 1.

[3] In his essay 'Of Heroique Playes' prefixed to *The Conquest of Granada* (1672), Dryden had defended the use of 'Spirits, or Spectres' in heroic poetry, citing the examples of Virgil, Ariosto, Tasso, and Spenser:

'. . . I dare farther affirm that the whole Doctrine of separated beings, whether those Spirits are incorporeal substances, (which Mr. *Hobbs*, with some reason thinks to imply a contradiction,) or that they are a thinner and more Aerial sort of bodies (as some of the Fathers have conjectur'd) may better be explicated by Poets, than by Philosophers or Divines. . . .

'Some men think they have rais'd a great argument against the use of Spectres and Magique in Heroique Poetry, by saying, They are unnatural: but, whether they or I believe there are such things, is not material, 'tis enough that, for ought we know, they may be in Nature: and what ever is or may be, is not, properly, unnatural.' (Sig. a4)

As for Elves and Fairies, and other such Mummery,[1] I purposely omit the Mention of them, as I should be very unwilling to confine within any Bounds those surprizing Imaginations, for whose vast Capacity the Limits of human Nature are too narrow; whose Works are to be considered as a new Creation; and who have consequently just Right to do what they will with their own.

Man therefore is the highest Subject (unless on very extraordinary Occasions indeed) which presents itself to the Pen of our Historian, or of our Poet; and in relating his Actions, great Care is to be taken, that we do not exceed the Capacity of the Agent we describe.

Nor is Possibility alone sufficient to justify us, we must keep likewise within the Rules of Probability. It is, I think, the Opinion of *Aristotle*; or if not, it is the Opinion of some wise Man, whose Authority will be as weighty, when it is as old; 'that it is no Excuse for a Poet who relates what is incredible, that the thing related is really Matter of Fact.'[2] This may perhaps be allowed true with regard to Poetry, but it may be thought impracticable to extend it to the Historian: For he is obliged to record Matters as he finds them;[3] though they may be of so extraordinary a Nature, as will require no small Degree of historical Faith to swallow them. Such was the successless Armament of *Xerxes*, described by *Herodotus*,[4] or the successful

---

[1] Fielding's disdainful repudiation of the fantastic and preternatural as proper subjects for fiction reflects the usual critical response to the epic narratives of Ariosto, Tasso, and Spenser, who, straining to astonish their readers with marvellous adventures, entirely disregarded the rules of probability. Spenser, Rymer had complained, 'suffer'd himself to be misled by *Ariosto*; with whom blindly rambling on *marvellous* Adventures, he makes no Conscience of *Probability*. All is fanciful and chimerical, without any Uniformity, without any Foundation in Truth; his Poem is perfect *Fairy-Land*' (Preface to Rapin's *Reflexions on Aristotle's Treatise of Poesy*, in *The Whole Critical Works of Monsieur Rapin*, 3rd ed. [1731], ii. 114). See also Davenant, *Discourse upon Gondibert* (1650), pp. 10–13; Shaftesbury, 'Advice to an Author', in *Characteristicks*, 5th ed. (1732), i. 344–7; and Blackmore, *Essays upon Several Subjects*, i (1716), 31–3. With the language of the present paragraph, compare *Joseph Andrews* (1742; III. i), where Fielding satirizes 'those Persons of surprising Genius, the Authors of immense Romances, or the modern Novel and *Atalantis* Writers; who without any Assistance from Nature or History, record Persons who never were, or will be, and Facts which never did nor possibly can happen: Whose Heroes are of their own Creation, and their Brains the Chaos whence all their Materials are collected'.

[2] Cf. *Poetics*, xxiv. 19: 'What is convincing though impossible should always be preferred to what is possible and unconvincing' (trans. W. H. Fyfe, Loeb Classical Library, 1927). [3] Cf. *Poetics*, ix. 1–3.

[4] Herodotus, *History*, vii. 20–1 and *passim*—relating the preparations of Xerxes' armies for the invasion of Greece.

Expedition of *Alexander* related by *Arrian*.[1] Such of later Years was the Victory of *Agincourt* obtained by *Harry* the Fifth,[2] or that of *Narva*, won by *Charles* the Twelfth of *Sweden*.[3] All which Instances, the more we reflect on them, appear still the more astonishing.

Such Facts, however, as they occur in the Thread of the Story; nay, indeed, as they constitute the essential Parts of it, the Historian is not only justifiable in recording as they really happened; but indeed would be unpardonable, should he omit or alter them. But there are other Facts not of such Consequence nor so necessary, which tho' ever so well attested, may nevertheless be sacrificed to Oblivion in Complaisance to the Scepticism of a Reader. Such is that memorable Story of the Ghost of *George Villers*,[4] which might with more Propriety have been made a Present of to Dr. *Drelincourt*,[5] to have kept the Ghost of Mrs. *Veale* Company, at the Head of his Discourse upon Death, than have been introduced into so solemn a Work as the History of the Rebellion.

To say the Truth, if the Historian will confine himself to what really happened, and utterly reject any Circumstance, which, tho' never so well attested, he must be well assured is false, he will

---

[1] Arrian's *Anabasis* recounts the campaigns of Alexander in seven books.

[2] The battle of Agincourt (1415), in which the English bowmen defeated a much larger force of French knights.

[3] On 20 November 1700, Charles XII defeated a powerful Russian army that had laid siege to Narva. For an account of this battle, 'which will be always famous in history', see Gustavus Adlerfeld, *The Military History of Charles XII. King of Sweden* (1740), i. 50–7—a translation from the French in which Fielding assisted.

[4] The story is told in *The True Historical Narrative of the Rebellion and Civil Wars in England* (1702–4), Book I, by Edward Hyde (1609–74), Earl of Clarendon—a work which Fielding had earlier ridiculed for its 'Tory' bias (see *Joseph Andrews* [1742; III. i]). Clarendon relates that some six months before the Duke of Buckingham was assassinated in 1628, the ghost of his father, Sir George Villiers, appeared three times to a royal officer at Windsor Castle, telling the man to warn Buckingham that unless he courted popular favour, he would soon die. With the present passage, compare Hogarth's 'Credulity, Superstition, and Fanaticism' (1762), in which two of the three ghostly figures decorating the pulpit of the enthusiastical preacher are those of George Villiers and Mrs. Veale (see below, n. 5).

[5] Charles Drelincourt (1595–1669), a French Protestant clergyman and author of several pious works. His *Consolations* (1669) was translated into English in 1675 under the title, *The Christian's Defence Against the Fears of Death*. To the fourth edition (1706) was prefixed Defoe's 'True Relation of the Apparition of one Mrs. Veale, the next Day after her Death, to one Mrs. Bargrave, at Canterbury, the 8th of September, 1705'—the ghost of Mrs. Veale having recommended Drelincourt's book as 'the best . . . on that Subject, ever wrote'.

sometimes fall into the Marvellous, but never into the Incredible. He will often raise the Wonder and Surprize of his Reader, but never that incredulous Hatred mentioned by *Horace*.[1] It is by falling into Fiction therefore, that we generally offend against this Rule, of deserting Probability, which the Historian seldom if ever quits, till he forsakes his Character, and commences a Writer of Romance. In this, however, those Historians who relate publick Transactions, have the Advantage of us who confine ourselves to Scenes of private Life. The Credit of the former is by common Notoriety supported for a long Time; and public Records, with the concurrent Testimony of many Authors bear Evidence to their Truth in future Ages. Thus a *Trajan* and an *Antoninus*, a *Nero* and a *Caligula*,[2] have all met with the Belief of Posterity; and no one doubts but that Men so very good, and so very bad, were once the Masters of Mankind.

But we who deal in private Character, who search into the most retired Recesses, and draw forth Examples of Virtue and Vice, from Holes and Corners of the World, are in a more dangerous Situation. As we have no publick Notoriety, no concurrent Testimony, no Records to support and corroborate what we deliver, it becomes us to keep within the Limits not only of Possibility, but of Probability too; and this more especially in painting what is greatly good and amiable. Knavery and Folly, though never so exorbitant, will more easily meet with Assent; for Ill-nature adds great Support and Strength to Faith.

Thus we may, perhaps, with little Danger relate the History of *Fisher*;[3] who having long owed his Bread to the Generosity of Mr.

---

[1] *Ars Poetica*, 188: 'incredulus odi.'

[2] Trajan (ruled A.D. 98–117) and either Antoninus Pius (138–61) or Marcus Aurelius Antoninus (161–80)—probably the latter (see below, p. 406.1)—are mentioned as excellent Roman emperors, in contrast to Nero (54–68) and Caligula (37–41).

[3] On the night of 10 April 1727 Henry Fisher (b. *c.* 1704), an attorney, murdered and robbed his benefactor, one Widdrington Darby, clerk of the Prothonotary's Office in Hare-Court, the Inner Temple. Though arrested some three weeks later and committed to Newgate, Fisher escaped on 17 May, the day before his trial, in the company of the notorious criminal, Roger Johnson. He fled to the Continent, where he remained at large. Fisher's villainy was not soon forgotten (see, for example, the facetious item in *The General Advertiser* [4 February 1746/7], listing him among the Pretender's retinue in Scotland); but Fielding's circumstantial knowledge of a crime committed more than twenty years earlier may be owing to his friendship with Richard Willoughby (see below, p. 458, n. 1), who was living at the time in Southampton Buildings, where Fisher, too, resided. Fisher's guilt was discovered when 'Mr. Willoughby, his Landlord, a Gentleman of Worth and Reputation', became suspicious and caused his apartment to be searched. (For details of the

Derby, and having one Morning received a considerable Bounty from his Hands, yet in order to possess himself of what remained in his Friend's Scrutore, concealed himself in a public Office of the Temple, through which there was a Passage into Mr. *Derby's* Chambers. Here he overheard Mr. *Derby* for many Hours solacing himself at an Entertainment which he that Evening gave his Friends, and to which *Fisher* had been invited. During all this Time, no tender, no grateful Reflections arose to restrain his Purpose; but when the poor Gentleman had let his Company out through the Office, *Fisher* came suddenly from his lurking Place, and walking softly behind his Friend into his Chamber, discharged a Pistol Ball into his Head. This may be believed, when the Bones of *Fisher* are as rotten as his Heart. Nay, perhaps, it will be credited that the Villain went two Days afterwards with some young Ladies to the Play of *Hamlet*;[1] and with an unaltered Countenance heard one of the Ladies, who little suspected how near she was to the Person, cry out, Good God! if the Man that murdered Mr. *Derby* was now present! Manifesting in this a more seared and callous Conscience than even *Nero* himself; of whom we are told by *Suetonius*, 'that the Consciousness of his Guilt after the Death of his Mother became immediately intolerable, and so continued; nor could all the Congratulations of the Soldiers, of the Senate, and the People, allay the Horrors of his Conscience.'[2]

But now, on the other hand, should I tell my Reader, that I had known a Man[3] whose penetrating Genius had enabled him to raise a large Fortune in a Way where no Beginning was chaulked out to him: That he had done this with the most perfect Preservation of his Integrity, and not only without the least Injustice or Injury to any one individual Person, but with the highest Advantage to Trade, and a vast Increase of the public Revenue: That he had expended one Part of the Income of this Fortune in

crime, which Fielding accurately describes, see the accounts in *The Weekly Journal: or, The British Gazetteer*, 15, 29 April, 6, 13, 20 May 1727; also *The British Journal* and *The London Journal* for these dates; and *The London Gazette*, 11–15, 25–9 April, 16–20 May 1727. See also *A Full and Particular Account of the Life and Notorious Transactions of Roger Johnson* [1740], pp. 20–1.)

[1] The only performance of *Hamlet* between the time of the murder and Fisher's arrest was at Drury Lane, 15 April 1727.

[2] Suetonius, *The Lives of the Cæsars*, VI. xxxiv. 4.

[3] Ralph Allen (see above, p. 4, n. 1).

discovering a Taste superior to most, by Works where the highest
Dignity was united with the purest Simplicity, and another Part
in displaying a Degree of Goodness superior to all Men, by Acts
of Charity to Objects whose only Recommendations were their
Merits, or their Wants: That he was most industrious in searching after Merit in Distress, most eager to relieve it, and then as
careful (perhaps too careful) to conceal what he had done: That
his House, his Furniture, his Gardens, his Table, his private
Hospitality, and his public Beneficence all denoted the Mind
from which they flowed, and were all intrinsically rich and noble,
without Tinsel, or external Ostentation: That he filled every
Relation in Life with the most adequate Virtue: That he was most
piously religious to his Creator, most zealously loyal to his
Sovereign; a most tender Husband to his Wife, a kind Relation,
a munificent Patron, a warm and firm Friend, a knowing and
a chearful Companion, indulgent to his Servants, hospitable to
his Neighbours, charitable to the Poor, and benevolent to all
Mankind. Should I add to these the Epithets of wise, brave,
elegant, and indeed every other amiable Epithet in our Language,
I might surely say,

> ——*Quis credet? nemo Hercule! nemo;*
> *Vel duo, vel nemo.*[1]

And yet I know a Man who is all I have here described. But a
single Instance (and I really know not such another) is not
sufficient to justify us, while we are writing to thousands who
never heard of the Person, nor of any Thing like him. Such
Raræ Aves[2] should be remitted to the Epitaph-Writer,[3] or to some
Poet, who may condescend to hitch him in a Distich, or to slide
him into a Rhime with an Air of Carelessness and Neglect,
without giving any Offence to the Reader.[4]

---

1 'Who will believe it? No one, by Hercules! no one; maybe one or two, maybe no one'—
slightly altered from Persius, *Satires*, i. 2–3.

2 See above, p. 188, n. 2.

3 See above, p. 114, n. 1.

4 The phrasing echoes Pope in *The First Satire of the Second Book of Horace Imitated*
(1733), 77–9: 'Who-e'er offends, at some unlucky Time/ Slides into Verse, and hitches in a
Rhyme,/ Sacred to Ridicule!' Thus Pope had protested that his satire was discriminating
and judicious, punishing only those who deserved castigation. But, Fielding here implies,
when Pope came to praise his good friend Ralph Allen, his method was similarly 'to hitch
him in a Distich'—the famous, but almost insultingly inadequate tribute of the *Epilogue to
the Satires. Dialogue I* (1738), 135–6: 'Let humble ALLEN, with an aukward Shame,/ Do
good by stealth, and blush to find it Fame.' (See the Dedication, p. 6, where Fielding

In the last Place, the Actions should be such as may not only be within the Compass of human Agency, and which human Agents may probably be supposed to do; but they should be likely for the very Actors and Characters themselves to have performed: For what may be only wonderful and surprizing in one Man, may become improbable, or indeed impossible, when related of another.

This last Requisite is what the dramatic Critics call Conservation of Character,[1] and it requires a very extraordinary Degree of Judgment, and a most exact Knowledge of human Nature.

It is admirably remarked by a most excellent Writer,[2] That Zeal can no more hurry a Man to act in direct Opposition to itself, than a rapid Stream can carry a Boat against its own Current. I will venture to say, that for a Man to act in direct Contradiction to the Dictates of his Nature, is, if not impossible, as improbable and as miraculous as any Thing which can well be conceived.

quotes from this couplet.) Prompted by Pope's condescension to Allen, the sarcasm in this passage is a rare exception to the laudatory tenor of Fielding's other public allusions to the poet, whom he greatly admired. For the most part, he regarded Pope as 'a Genius of the highest Rank' (see below, p. 406), yet it is clear from his early unpublished verses that Fielding sometimes found the poet's spitefulness and pride offensive. (See I. Grundy, 'New Verse by Henry Fielding', *PMLA*, lxxxvii [1972], 213-45.)

[1] Cf. Aristotle, *Poetics*, xv. 4, and Horace, *Ars Poetica*, 119-27. The rule stipulated that a dramatic character, if drawn from history or tradition, must be represented throughout in a manner consistent with the expectations of the audience; if invented by the author, the character must be self-consistent or, according to Horace, must be 'kept to the end even as it came forth at the first' (trans. H. R. Fairclough, Loeb Classical Library, 1929). Fielding's phrase echoes Boileau: 'Conservez à chacun son propre caractère' (*L'Art poétique*, ed. D. N. Smith [Cambridge, 1931], iii. 112). In *Jonathan Wild* (1743; IV. xiv) Fielding designed the final act of his hero's life—Wild on the gallows having picked the parson's pocket of a bottle-screw—'to shew the most admirable Conservation of Character . . . to the last moment'.

[2] George Lyttelton (see above, p. 3, n. 1) in *Observations on the Conversion and Apostleship of St. Paul* (May 1747): 'The power of imagination in enthusiastical minds is no doubt very strong, but always acts in conformity to the opinions imprinted upon it at the time of its working, and can no more act against them, than a rapid river can carry a boat against the current of its own stream' (*Works*, ed. G. E. Ayscough [1774], p. 316). In context this is Lyttelton's crucial argument to prove that St. Paul's conversion on the road to Damascus was a true miracle and, consequently, that Christianity itself is a divine revelation: since, Lyttelton maintains, Paul set out on his journey not only disbelieving the Christian faith but intending to persecute its followers, his sudden transformation from infidel to believer cannot be explained by reference to natural causes. For another compliment to Lyttelton as 'a Master of Style, as of every other Excellence', see Fielding's Preface to his sister's *Familiar Letters between the Principal Characters in David Simple* (1747). Later in *Tom Jones* (XVIII. iv) Lyttelton's *Observations* is part of the background of Square's conversion (see below, p. 952, n. 2).

Should the best Parts of the Story of *Marcus Antoninus* be ascribed to *Nero*, or should the worst Incidents of *Nero's* Life be imputed to *Antoninus*, what would be more shocking to Belief than either Instance; whereas both these being related of their proper Agent, constitute the Truly Marvellous.

Our modern Authors of Comedy have fallen almost universally into the Error here hinted at: Their Heroes generally are notorious Rogues, and their Heroines abandoned Jades, during the first four Acts; but in the fifth, the former become very worthy Gentlemen, and the latter, Women of Virtue and Discretion: Nor is the Writer often so kind as to give himself the least Trouble, to reconcile or account for this monstrous Change and Incongruity. There is, indeed, no other Reason to be assigned for it, than because the Play is drawing to a Conclusion; as if it was no less natural in a Rogue to repent in the last Act of a Play, than in the last of his Life; which we perceive to be generally the Case at *Tyburn*,[1] a Place which might, indeed, close the Scene of some Comedies with much Propriety, as the Heroes in these are most commonly eminent for those very Talents which not only bring Men to the Gallows, but enable them to make an heroic Figure when they are there.

Within these few Restrictions, I think, every Writer may be permitted to deal as much in the Wonderful as he pleases; nay, if he thus keeps within the Rules of Credibility, the more he can surprize the Reader, the more he will engage his Attention, and the more he will charm him. As a Genius of the highest Rank observes in his 5th Chapter of the *Bathos*, 'The great Art of all Poetry is to mix Truth with Fiction; in order to join the Credible with the Surprizing.'[2]

For though every good Author will confine himself within the

---

[1] The place of public execution in London. Until 1759 the gallows was a permanent structure situated on Tyburn Road near what is now Marble Arch. Fielding's comparison between the theatre and the scene at Tyburn (see also below, p. 875) was not as far-fetched as it may seem. 'Hanging days', which occurred eight times a year, were rowdy and festive occasions. Stands were erected and large crowds gathered to witness the spectacle and to hear the last confessions of the condemned. For a contemporary description of a typical hanging-day at Tyburn—'The Tragic-Comedy of the *Dark Leap*', as the writer calls it—see *A Trip from St. James's to the Royal Exchange* (1744), pp. 42–50. In *An Enquiry into the Causes of the Late Increase of Robbers* (1751), section xi, Fielding condemned this custom of turning so serious an occasion into an entertaining holiday for the mob.

[2] Pope's *Peri Bathous: or, Martinus Scriblerus His Treatise of the Art of Sinking in Poetry* (1728), ch. v.

Bounds of Probability, it is by no means necessary that his Characters, or his Incidents, should be trite, common, or vulgar; such as happen in every Street, or in every House, or which may be met with in the home Articles of a News-paper. Nor must he be inhibited from shewing many Persons and Things, which may possibly have never fallen within the Knowledge of great Part of his Readers. If the Writer strictly observes the Rules abovementioned, he hath discharged his Part; and is then intitled to some Faith from his Reader, who is indeed guilty of critical Infidelity if he disbelieves him. For want of a Portion of such Faith, I remember the Character of a young Lady of Quality,[1] which was condemned on the Stage for being unnatural, by the unanimous Voice of a very large Assembly of Clerks and Apprentices; tho' it had the previous Suffrages of many Ladies of the first Rank; one of whom very eminent for her Understanding, declared it was the Picture of half the young People of her Acquaintance.

CHAPTER II

In which the Landlady pays a Visit to Mr. Jones.

WHEN *Jones* had taken Leave of his Friend the Lieutenant, he endeavoured to close his Eyes, but all in vain; his Spirits were too lively and wakeful to be lulled to Sleep. So having amused, or rather tormented himself with the Thoughts of his *Sophia*, till it was open Day-light, he called for some Tea; upon which Occasion my Landlady herself vouchsafed to pay him a Visit.

This was indeed the first Time she had seen him, or at least had taken any Notice of him; but as the Lieutenant had assured her that he was certainly some young Gentleman of Fashion, she now determined to shew him all the Respect in her Power: for, to speak truly, this was one of those Houses where Gentlemen, to use the Language of Advertisements, meet with civil Treatment for their Money.

---

[1] Probably Lady Charlotte in Fielding's own play, *The Modern Husband* (1732), which was hissed the night of its first performance at Drury Lane. The person who approved the characterization is likely to have been Fielding's cousin, Lady Mary Wortley Montagu (1689–1762), to whom he had submitted the manuscript for criticism.

She had no sooner begun to make his Tea, than she likewise began to discourse. 'La! Sir,' said she, 'I think it is great Pity that such a pretty young Gentleman should undervalue himself so, as to go about with these Soldier Fellows. They call themselves Gentlemen, I warrant you; but, as my first Husband used to say, they should remember it is we that pay them. And to be sure it is very hard upon us to be obliged to pay them, and to keep 'em too, as we Publicans are.[1] I had twenty of 'um last Night, besides Officers; nay, for matter o' that, I had rather have the Soldiers than Officers: For nothing is ever good enough for those Sparks; and I am sure if you was to see the Bills; La, Sir, it is nothing. I have had less Trouble, I warrant you, with a good Squire's Family, where we take forty or fifty Shillings of a Night, besides Horses. And yet I warrants me, there is *narrow* a one of all those Officer Fellows, but looks upon himself to be as good as *arrow* a Squire of 500 *l.* a Year. To be sure it doth me Good to hear their Men run about after 'um, crying your Honour, and your Honour. Marry come up with such Honour, and an Ordinary at a Shilling a Head. Then there's such Swearing among 'um, to be sure, it frightens me out o' my Wits, I thinks nothing can ever prosper with such wicked People. And here one of 'um has used you in so barbarous a Manner. I thought indeed how well the rest would secure him; they all hang together; for if you had been in Danger of Death, which I am glad to see you are not, it would have been all as one to such wicked People. They would have let the Murderer go. Laud have Mercy upon 'um, I would not have such a Sin to answer for, for the whole World. But tho' you are likely, with the Blessing to recover, there is Laa for him yet, and if you will employ Lawyer *Small,* I darest be sworn he'll make the Fellow fly the Country for him; tho' perhaps he'll have fled the Country before; for it is here To-day and gone To-morrow with such Chaps. I hope, however, you will learn more Wit for the future, and return back to your Friends; I warrant they are all miserable for your Loss; and if they was but to know what had happened. La, my seeming! I would not for the World they should. Come, come, we know very well what all the Matter is;

---

1 According to the annual statute against Mutiny and Desertion, the keepers of inns and ale-houses were required to provide food and lodging for the Army at a rate *per diem* of 4*d.* for a foot-soldier and 1*s.* for a commissioned officer below the rank of captain. (See Barlow, *The Justice of the Peace* [1745], s.v. 'Soldiers'.)

but if one won't, another will, so pretty a Gentleman need never want a Lady. I am sure if I was as you, I would see the finest She that ever wore a Head hanged, before I would go for a Soldier for her.—Nay, don't blush so; (for indeed he did to a violent Degree) why, you thought, Sir, I knew nothing of the Matter, I warrant you, about Madam *Sophia*.' 'How,' says *Jones*, starting up, 'do you know my *Sophia*?' 'Do I? ay marry,' cries the Land-lady, 'many's the Time hath she lain in this House.' 'With her Aunt, I suppose,' says *Jones*.—'Why there it is now,' cries the Landlady. 'Ay, ay, ay, I know the old Lady very well. And a sweet young Creature is Madam *Sophia*, that's the Truth on't.' 'A sweet Creature!' cries *Jones*, 'Oh Heavens!

> *Angels are painted fair to look like her.*
> *There's in her all that we believe of Heaven,*
> *Amazing Brightness, Purity and Truth,*
> *Eternal Joy, and everlasting Love.*[1]

'And could I ever have imagined that you had known my *Sophia*.' 'I wish,' says the Landlady, 'you knew half so much of her. What would you have given to have sat by her Bed-side? What a delicious Neck she hath! Her lovely Limbs have stretched themselves in that very Bed you now lie in.' 'Here!' cries *Jones*, 'hath *Sophia* ever lain here?'—'Ay, ay, here; there; in that very Bed,' says the Landlady, 'where I wish you had her this Moment; and she may wish so too, for any thing I know to the contrary: For she hath mentioned your Name to me.'—'Ha,' cries he, 'did she ever mention her poor *Jones*?—You flatter me now, I can never believe so much.' 'Why then,' answered she, 'as I hope to be sav'd, and may the Devil fetch me, if I speak a Syllable more than the Truth. I have heard her mention Mr. *Jones*; but in a civil and modest Way, I confess; yet I could perceive she thought a great deal more than she said.' 'O my dear Woman,' cries *Jones*, 'her Thoughts of me I shall never be worthy of. O she is all Gentleness, Kindness, Goodness. Why was such a Rascal as I born, ever to give her soft Bosom a Moment's Uneasiness? Why am I cursed? I, who would undergo all the Plagues and Miseries which any Dæmon ever invented for Mankind, to procure her any Good; nay, Torture itself could not be Misery to me, did I

[1] Jones applies to Sophia, Jaffeir's apostrophe to woman in Otway's *Venice Preserv'd* (1682), I. i.

but know that she was happy.' 'Why look you there now,' says the Landlady, 'I told her you was a constant Lovier.' 'But pray, Madam, tell me when or where you knew any thing of me; for I never was here before, nor do I remember ever to have seen you.' 'Nor is it possible you should,' answered she, 'for you was a little Thing when I had you in my Lap at the Squire's.'—'How, the Squire's,' says *Jones*, 'what do you know that great and good Mr. *Allworthy* then?' 'Yes, marry do I,' says she; 'Who in the Country doth not?'—'The Fame of his Goodness indeed,' answered *Jones*, 'must have extended farther than this; but Heaven only can know him, can know that Benevolence which it copied from itself, and sent upon Earth as its own Pattern. Mankind are as ignorant of such divine Goodness, as they are unworthy of it; but none so unworthy of it as myself. I who was raised by him to such a Height; taken in, as you must well know, a poor base-born Child, adopted by him, and treated as his own Son to dare by my Follies to disoblige him, to draw his Vengeance upon me. Yes, I deserve it all: For I will never be so ungrateful as ever to think he hath done an Act of Injustice by me. No, I deserve to be turned out of Doors, as I am. And now, Madam,' says he, 'I believe you will not blame me for turning Soldier, especially with such a Fortune as this in my Pocket.' At which Words he shook a Purse which had but very little in it, and which still appeared to the Landlady to have less.

My good Landlady was, (according to vulgar Phrase) struck all of a Heap by this Relation. She answered coldly, 'That to be sure People were the best Judges what was most proper for their Circumstances.—But hark,' says she, 'I think I hear some body call. Coming! coming! the Devil's in all our Volk, nobody hath any Ears. I must go down Stairs, if you want any more Breakfast, the Maid will come up. Coming!' At which Words, without taking any Leave, she flung out of the Room: For the lower Sort of People are very tenacious of Respect; and tho' they are contented to give this *gratis* to Persons of Quality, yet they never confer it on those of their own Order, without taking Care to be well paid for their Pains.

CHAPTER III

In which the Surgeon makes his second Appearance.

BEFORE we proceed any farther, that the Reader may not be mistaken in imagining the Landlady knew more than she did, nor surprized that she knew so much, it may be necessary to inform him, that the Lieutenant had acquainted her that the Name of *Sophia* had been the Occasion of the Quarrel; and as for the rest of her Knowledge, the sagacious Reader will observe how she came by it in the preceding Scene. Great Curiosity was indeed mixed with her Virtues; and she never willingly suffered any one to depart from her House without enquiring as much as possible into their Names, Families and Fortunes.

She was no sooner gone, than *Jones*, instead of animadverting on her Behaviour, reflected that he was in the same Bed, which he was informed had held his dear *Sophia*. This occasioned a thousand fond and tender Thoughts, which we would dwell longer upon, did we not consider that such kind of Lovers will make a very inconsiderable Part of our Readers.

In this Situation the Surgeon found him, when he came to dress his Wound. The Doctor, perceiving, upon Examination, that his Pulse was disordered, and hearing that he had not slept, declared that he was in great Danger: For he apprehended a Fever was coming on; which he would have prevented by Bleeding, but *Jones* would not submit, declaring he would lose no more Blood; and 'Doctor,' says he, 'if you will be so kind only to dress my Head, I have no Doubt of being well in a Day or two.'

'I wish,' answered the Surgeon, 'I could assure your being well in a Month or two. Well, indeed! No, no, People are not so soon well of such Contusions; but, Sir, I am not at this Time of Day to be instructed in my Operations by a Patient, and I insist on making a Revulsion[1] before I dress you.'

Jones persisted obstinately in his Refusal, and the Doctor at last yielded; telling him at the same Time, that he would not be answerable for the ill Consequence, and hoped he would do him the Justice to acknowledge that he had given him a contrary Advice; which the Patient promised he would.

---

[1] In medicine, the withdrawal of an inflammation from a diseased part of the body by operating upon another part—in this instance, by bleeding.

The Doctor retired into the Kitchen, where, addressing himself to the Landlady, he complained bitterly of the undutiful Behaviour of his Patient, who would not be blooded, though he was in a Fever.

'It is an eating Fever then,' says the Landlady: 'For he hath devoured two swinging buttered Toasts this Morning for Breakfast.'

'Very likely,' says the Doctor, 'I have known People eat in a Fever; and it is very easily accounted for; because the Acidity occasioned by the febrile Matter, may stimulate the Nerves of the Diaphragm, and thereby occasion a Craving, which will not be easily distinguishable from a natural Appetite; but the Aliment will not be concreted, nor assimilated into Chyle, and so will corrode the vascular Orifices, and thus will aggravate the febrific Symptoms. Indeed I think the Gentleman in a very dangerous Way, and, if he is not blooded, I am afraid will die.'

'Every Man must die some Time or other,' answered the good Woman; 'it is no Business of mine. I hope, Doctor, you would not have me hold him while you bleed him.—But, harkee, a Word in your Ear, I would advise you before you proceed too far, to take care who is to be your Paymaster.'

'Paymaster!' said the Doctor, staring, 'why, I've a Gentleman under my Hands, have I not?'

'I imagined so as well as you,' said the Landlady; 'but as my first Husband used to say, every Thing is not what it looks to be. He is an arrant Scrub, I assure you. However, take no Notice that I mentioned any thing to you of the Matter; but I think People in Business *oft* always to let one another know such Things.'

'And have I suffered such a Fellow as this,' cries the Doctor, in a Passion, 'to instruct me? Shall I hear my Practice insulted by one who will not pay me! I am glad I have made this Discovery in Time. I will see now whether he will be blooded or no.' He then immediately went up Stairs, and flinging open the Door of the Chamber with much Violence, awaked poor *Jones* from a very sound Nap, into which he was fallen, and what was still worse, from a delicious Dream concerning *Sophia*.

'Will you be blooded or no?' cries the Doctor, in a Rage. 'I have told you my Resolution already,' answered *Jones*, 'and I wish with all my Heart you had taken my answer: For you have awaked me out of the sweetest Sleep which I ever had in my Life.'

'Ay, ay,' cries the Doctor, 'many a Man hath dosed away his Life. Sleep is not always good, no more than Food; but remember I demand of you, for the last Time, will you be blooded?' 'I answer you for the last Time,' said *Jones*, 'I will not.' 'Then I wash my Hands of you,' cries the Doctor, 'and I desire you to pay me for the Trouble I have had already. Two Journeys at 5*s*. each, two Dressings at 5*s*. more, and half a Crown for Phlebotomy.' 'I hope,' said *Jones*, 'you don't intend to leave me in this Condition.' 'Indeed but I shall,' said the other. 'Then,' said *Jones*, 'you have used me rascally, and I will not pay you a Farthing.' 'Very well,' cries the Doctor, 'the first Loss is the best. What a Pox did my Landlady mean by sending for me to such Vagabonds?' At which Words he flung out of the Room, and his Patient turning himself about, soon recovered his Sleep; but his Dream was unfortunately gone.

CHAPTER IV

In which is introduced one of the pleasantest Barbers that was ever recorded in History, the Barber of Bagdad,[1] *or he in* Don Quixotte[2] *not excepted.*

THE Clock had now struck Five, when *Jones* awaked from a Nap of seven Hours, so much refreshed, and in such perfect Health and Spirits, that he resolved to get up and dress himself: for which Purpose he unlocked his Portmanteau, and took out clean Linnen, and a Suit of Cloaths; but first he slipt on a Frock, and went down into the Kitchen to bespeak something that might pacify certain Tumults he found rising within his Stomach.

Meeting the Landlady, he accosted her with great Civility, and asked 'what he could have for Dinner.' 'For Dinner!' says she, 'it is an odd Time a Day to think about Dinner. There is nothing drest in the House, and the Fire is almost out.' 'Well but,' says he, 'I must have something to eat, and it is almost indifferent to

---

[1] The barber of Baghdad is introduced in Vol. ii of *The Arabian Nights* (English trans. 1706, from the French of Antoine Galland). Though an incessant prattler and a boaster who represents himself as something of a universal genius, he goes by 'the honourable Title of Silent'.

[2] Nicholas, introduced in *Don Quixote* (Motteux-Ozell version), Pt. i, Bk. i, ch. 5. For Fielding's opinion of Cervantes, see below, p. 686, n. 1.

me what: For to tell you the Truth, I was never more hungry in my Life.' 'Then,' says she, 'I believe there is a Piece of cold Buttock and Carrot, which will fit you.'—'Nothing better,' answered *Jones*, 'but I should be obliged to you, if you would let it be fried.' To which the Landlady consented, and said smiling, 'she was glad to see him so well recovered:' For the Sweetness of our Heroe's Temper was almost irresistable; besides, she was really no ill-humoured Woman at the Bottom; but she loved Money so much, that she hated every Thing which had the Semblance of Poverty.

Jones now returned in order to dress himself, while his Dinner was preparing, and was, according to his Orders, attended by the Barber.

This Barber, who went by the Name of little *Benjamin*, was a Fellow of great Oddity and Humour, which had frequently led him into small Inconveniencies, such as Slaps in the Face, Kicks in the Breech, broken Bones, &c. For every one doth not understand a Jest; and those who do, are often displeased with being themselves the Subjects of it. This Vice was, however, incurable in him; and though he had often smarted for it, yet if ever he conceived a Joke, he was certain to be delivered of it, without the least Respect of Persons, Time, or Place.

He had a great many other Particularities in his Character, which I shall not mention, as the Reader will himself very easily perceive them, on his farther Acquaintance with this extraordinary Person.

Jones being impatient to be drest, for a Reason which may easily be imagined, thought the Shaver was very tedious in preparing his Suds, and begged him to make Haste; to which the other answered, with much Gravity: For he never discomposed his Muscles on any Account. '*Festina lente*[1] is a Proverb which I learnt long before I ever touched a Razor.' 'I find, Friend, you are a Scholar,' replied *Jones*. 'A poor one,' said the Barber, '*non omnia possumus omnes*.'[2] 'Again!' said *Jones*; 'I fancy you are good at capping Verses.'[3] 'Excuse me, Sir,' said the Barber, '*non tanto*

---

[1] 'Make haste slowly'—a favourite maxim of Augustus Caesar, according to Suetonius, and also of Erasmus. (See King's *Classical Quotations*, 1887.)

[2] See above, p. 178, n. 3.

[3] A contest in which each participant tries to 'cap' a classical verse quoted by his opponent with another beginning with the last letter of the verse his rival has used. For an example, see *Joseph Andrews* (1742; II. xi).

me dignor honore.[1] And then proceeding to his Operation, 'Sir,' said he, 'since I have dealt in Suds, I could never discover more than two Reasons for shaving, the one is to get a Beard, and the other to get rid of one. I conjecture, Sir, it may not be long since you shaved, from the former of these Motives. Upon my Word you have had good Success, for one may say of your Beard, that it is *Tondenti gravior.*[2] 'I conjecture,' says *Jones,* 'that thou art a very comical Fellow.' 'You mistake me widely, Sir,' said the Barber, 'I am too much addicted to the Study of Philosophy, *Hinc illæ Lacrymæ,*[3] Sir, that's my Misfortune. Too much Learning hath been my Ruin.' 'Indeed,' says *Jones,* 'I confess, Friend, you have more Learning than generally belongs to your Trade; but I can't see how it can have injured you.' 'Alas, Sir,' answered the Shaver, 'my Father disinherited me for it. He was a Dancing-Master; and because I could read, before I could dance, he took an Aversion to me, and left every Farthing among his other Children.—Will you please to have your Temples—— O la! I ask your Pardon, I fancy there is *Hiatus in manuscriptis.* I heard you was going to the Wars: but I find it was a Mistake.' 'Why do you conclude so?' says *Jones.* 'Sure, Sir,' answered the Barber, 'you are too wise a Man to carry a broken Head thither; for that would be carrying Coals to *Newcastle.*'

'Upon my Word,' cries *Jones,* 'thou art a very odd Fellow, and I like thy Humour extremely; I shall be very glad if thou wilt come to me after Dinner, and drink a Glass with me; I long to be better acquainted with thee.'

'O dear Sir,' said the Barber, 'I can do you twenty times as great a Favour, if you will accept of it.' 'What is that, my Friend,' cries *Jones.* 'Why, I will drink a Bottle with you, if you please; for I dearly love Good-nature, and as you have found me out to be a comical Fellow, so I have no Skill in Physiognomy, if you are not one of the best-natured Gentlemen in the Universe.' *Jones* now walked down Stairs neatly drest, and perhaps the fair *Adonis* was not a lovelier Figure; and yet he had no Charms for my Land-lady: For as that good Woman did not resemble *Venus* at all in her

[1] 'I do not deem myself worthy of so much honour.' Cf. Virgil, *Aeneid,* i. 335: 'haud equidem tali me dignor honore.' See below, p. 419, n. 2.
[2] 'Troublesome to the one shaving.'
[3] 'Hence proceed all those tears'—a proverbial expression found, for example, in Terence *Andria* (I. i) and Horace, *Epistles* (I. xix. 41).

Person, so neither did she in her Taste.[1] Happy had it been for *Nancy* the Chambermaid, if she had seen with the Eyes of her Mistress; for that poor Girl fell so violently in love with *Jones* in five Minutes, that her Passion afterwards cost her many a Sigh. This *Nancy* was extremely pretty, and altogether as coy; for she had refused a Drawer, and one or two young Farmers in the Neighbourhood, but the bright Eyes of our Heroe thawed all her Ice in a Moment.

When *Jones* returned to the Kitchen, his Cloth was not yet laid; nor indeed was there any Occasion it should, his Dinner remaining in *Statu quo*, as did the Fire which was to dress it. This Disappointment might have put many a philosophical Temper into a Passion; but it had no such Effect on *Jones*. He only gave the Landlady a gentle Rebuke, saying, 'Since it was so difficult to get it heated, he would eat the Beef cold.' But now the good Woman, whether moved by Compassion, or by Shame, or by whatever other Motive, I cannot tell, first gave her Servants a round Scold for disobeying the Orders which she had never given, and then bidding the Drawer lay a Napkin in the Sun, she set about the Matter in good earnest, and soon accomplished it.

This Sun, into which *Jones* was now conducted, was truly named as *Lucus a non lucendo*;[2] for it was an Apartment into which the Sun had scarce ever looked. It was indeed the worst Room in the House; and happy was it for *Jones* that it was so. However, he was now too hungry to find any Fault; but having once satisfied his Appetite, he ordered the Drawer to carry a Bottle of Wine into a better Room, and expressed some Resentment at having been shewn into a Dungeon.

The Drawer having obeyed his Commands, he was, after some Time, attended by the Barber; who would not indeed have suffered him to wait so long for his Company, had he not been listening in the Kitchen to the Landlady, who was entertaining a Circle that she had gathered round her with the History of poor *Jones*, Part of which she had extracted from his own Lips, and the other Part was her own ingenious Composition; 'for,' she said, 'he was a poor Parish Boy, taken into the House of Squire

---

[1] Cf. Ovid, *Metamorphoses*, x. 520–59, 708–39.

[2] 'A grove is so called from its not giving light'—found in Quintilian as an example of 'the derivation of certain words from their opposites' (*Institutio Oratoria*, I. vi. 34—trans. H. E. Butler, Loeb Classical Library, 1920). See also *The Covent-Garden Journal* (9 May 1752).

Allworthy, where he was bred up as an Apprentice, and now turned out of Doors for his Misdeeds, particularly for making Love to his young Mistress, and probably for robbing the House; for how else should he come by the little Money he hath. And this,' says she, 'is your Gentleman, forsooth.' 'A Servant of Squire *Allworthy*!' says the Barber, 'what's his Name?' —'Why he told me his Name was *Jones*,' says she, 'perhaps he goes by a wrong Name. Nay, and he told me too, that the Squire had maintained him as his own Son, *thof* he had quarrelled with him now.' 'And if his Name be *Jones*, he told you the Truth,' said the Barber; 'for I have Relations who live in that Country, nay, and some People say he is his Son.' 'Why doth he not go by the Name of his Father?' 'I can't tell that,' said the Barber, 'many People's Sons don't go by the Name of their Father.' 'Nay,' said the Landlady, 'if I thought he was a Gentleman's Son, *thof* he was a Bye Blow, I should behave to him in anotherguess Manner; for many of these Bye Blows come to be great Men; and, as my poor first Husband used to say, Never affront any Customer that's a Gentleman.'

CHAPTER V

A Dialogue between Mr. Jones *and the Barber.*

THIS Conversation passed partly while *Jones* was at Dinner in his Dungeon, and partly while he was expecting the Barber in the Parlour. And, as soon as it was ended, Mr. *Benjamin*, as we have said, attended him, and was very kindly desired to sit down. *Jones* then filling out a Glass of Wine, drank his Health by the Appellation of *Doctissime Tonsorum*.[1] '*Ago tibi Gratias, Domine*,'[2] said the Barber, and then looking very stedfastly at *Jones*, he said, with great Gravity, and with a seeming Surprize, as if he had recollected a Face he had seen before, 'Sir, may I crave the Favour to know if your Name is not *Jones*?' To which the other answered, That it was. '*Proh Deum atque Hominum Fidem*,'[3]

---

[1] 'Most learned of barbers.'
[2] 'I give you thanks, master.'
[3] Terence, *Andria*, I. v: 'O, by the faith of gods and men!' See below, p. 419, n. 2.

says the Barber, 'how strangely Things come to pass. Mr. *Jones*, I am your most obedient Servant. I find you do not know me, which indeed is no Wonder, since you never saw me but once, and then you was very young. Pray, Sir, how doth the good Squire *Allworthy?* How doth *Ille optimus omnium Patronus?*'¹ 'I find,' said *Jones*, 'you do indeed know me; but I have not the like Happiness of recollecting you.'—'I do not wonder at that,' cries *Benjamin*; 'but I am surprized I did not know you sooner, for you are not in the least altered. And pray, Sir, may I without Offence enquire whither you are travelling this Way?' 'Fill the Glass, Mr. Barber,' said *Jones*, 'and ask no more Questions.' 'Nay, Sir,' answered *Benjamin*, 'I would not be troublesome; and I hope you don't think me a Man of an impertinent Curiosity, for that is a Vice which nobody can lay to my Charge; but I ask Pardon, for when a Gentleman of your Figure travels without his Servants, we may suppose him to be, as we say, in *Casu incognito*,² and perhaps I ought not to have mentioned your Name.' 'I own,' says *Jones*, 'I did not expect to have been so well known in this Country as I find I am, yet, for particular Reasons, I shall be obliged to you if you will not mention my Name to any other Person, till I am gone from hence.' '*Pauca Verba*,'³ answered the Barber; 'and I wish no other here knew you but myself; for some People have Tongues; but I promise you I can keep a Secret. My Enemies will allow me that Virtue.' 'And yet that is not the Characteristic of your Profession, Mr. Barber,' answered *Jones*. 'Alas, Sir,' replied *Benjamin*, '*Non si male nunc et olim sic erit.*⁴ I was not born nor bred a Barber, I assure you. I have spent most of my Time among Gentlemen, and tho' I say it, I understand something of Gentility. And if you had thought me as worthy of your Confidence as you have some other People, I should have shewn you I could have kept a Secret better. I should not have degraded your Name in a public Kitchen; for indeed, Sir, some People have not used you well; for besides making a public Proclamation of what you told them of a Quarrel between your-

---

¹ 'That best patron of all.' Cf. Catullus, *Poems* xlix, 7. See below, p. 419, n. 2.

² 'Some unknown misfortune', with a pun perhaps—since Partridge was once a school-master—on *casus* in the grammatical sense of *case*.

³ 'Few words.' Cf. Lucan, *Pharsalia*, ix. 188–9, and Sir Hugh Evans in *The Merry Wives of Windsor*, I. i: 'Pauca verba, Sir John; goot worts.'

⁴ Horace, *Odes*, II. x. 17–18: 'If we fare ill today, 'twill not be ever so' (trans. C. E. Bennett, Loeb Classical Library, 1914).

self and Squire *Allworthy*, they added Lies of their own, Things which I knew to be Lies.' 'You surprize me greatly,' cries *Jones*. 'Upon my Word, Sir,' answered *Benjamin*, 'I tell the Truth, and I need not tell you my Landlady was the Person. I am sure it moved me to hear the Story, and I hope it is all false; for I have a great Respect for you, I do assure you I have, and have had, ever since the Good-nature you shewed to *Black George*, which was talked of all over the Country, and I received more than one Letter about it. Indeed it made you beloved by every body. You will pardon me, therefore; for it was real Concern at what I heard made me ask any Questions; for I have no impertinent Curiosity about me; but I love Good-nature, and thence became *Amoris abundantia erga Te*.'[1]

Every Profession of Friendship easily gains Credit with the Miserable; it is no wonder, therefore, if *Jones*, who, besides his being miserable, was extremely open-hearted, very readily believed all the Professions of *Benjamin*, and received him into his Bosom. The Scraps of *Latin*, some of which *Benjamin* applied properly enough, tho' it did not savour of profound Literature,[2] seemed yet to indicate something superior to a common Barber, and so indeed did his whole Behaviour. *Jones* therefore believed the Truth of what he had said, as to his Original and Education, and at length, after much Entreaty, he said, 'Since you have heard, my Friend, so much of my Affairs, and seem so desirous to know the Truth, if you will have Patience to hear it, I will inform you of the whole.' 'Patience,' cries *Benjamin*, 'that I will, if the Chapter was never so long, and I am very much obliged to you for the Honour you do me.'

Jones now began, and related the whole History, forgetting only a Circumstance or two, namely, every thing which passed on that Day in which he had fought with *Thwackum*, and ended with his Resolution to go to Sea, till the Rebellion in the North had

---

[1] 'An abundance of love towards you'—cf. Cicero, *Ad Familiares*, I. ix. I.

[2] For the most part, Partridge's 'Scraps of *Latin*' are either proverbial expressions or they were used as illustrative examples in William Lily's grammar, the standard textbook of the period. The verses from Virgil (p. 415, n. 1) and Terence (p. 417, n. 3), for instance, may be found in *A Short Introduction to Grammar* [1720], pp. 154, 171, and *Lily's Rules Construed* [1720], pp. 64, 88. These verses, together with the quotation from Catullus (p. 418, n. 1), also appear in the Eton Latin grammar, based on Lily, with which Fielding would have been thoroughly acquainted (see *An Introduction to the Latin Tongue, for the Use of Youth* [Eton, 1758], pp. 88 and 153, 96, 106, and 175).

made him change his Purpose, and had brought him to the Place where he then was.

Little *Benjamin*, who had been all Attention, never once interrupted the Narrative; but when it was ended, he could not help observing, that there must be surely something more invented by his Enemies, and told Mr. *Allworthy* against him, or so good a Man would never have dismissed one he had loved so tenderly, in such a Manner. To which *Jones* answered, 'He doubted not but such villanous Arts had been made use of to destroy him.'

And surely it was scarce possible for any one to have avoided making the same Remark with the Barber; who had not, indeed, heard from *Jones* one single Circumstance upon which he was condemned; for his Actions were not now placed in those injurious Lights, in which they had been misrepresented to *Allworthy*: Nor could he mention those many false Accusations which had been from time to time preferred against him to *Allworthy*; for with none of these he was himself acquainted. He had likewise, as we have observed, omitted many material Facts in his present Relation. Upon the whole, indeed, every thing now appeared in such favourable Colours to *Jones*, that Malice itself would have found it no easy Matter to fix any Blame upon him.

Not that *Jones* desired to conceal or to disguise the Truth; nay, he would have been more unwilling to have suffered any Censure to fall on Mr. *Allworthy* for punishing him, than on his own Actions for deserving it; but, in Reality, so it happened, and so it always will happen: For let a Man be never so honest, the Account of his own Conduct will, in Spite of himself, be so very favourable, that his Vices will come purified through his Lips, and, like foul Liquors well strained, will leave all their Foulness behind. For tho' the Facts themselves may appear, yet so different will be the Motives, Circumstances, and Consequences, when a Man tells his own Story, and when his Enemy tells it, that we scarce can recognize the Facts to be one and the same.

Tho' the Barber had drank down this Story with greedy Ears, he was not yet satisfied. There was a Circumstance behind, which his Curiosity, cold as it was, most eagerly longed for. *Jones* had mentioned the Fact of his Amour, and of his being the Rival of *Blifil*, but had cautiously concealed the Name of the young

Lady. The Barber therefore, after some Hesitation, and many Hums and Ha's, at last begged Leave to crave the Name of the Lady, who appeared to be the principal Cause of all this Mischief. *Jones* paused a Moment, and then said, 'Since I have trusted you with so much, and since, I am afraid, her Name is become too public already on this Occasion, I will not conceal it from you. Her Name is *Sophia Western*.'

'*Proh Deum atque Hominum Fidem*!¹ Squire *Western* hath a Daughter grown a Woman!' 'Ay, and such a Woman,' cries *Jones*, 'that the World cannot match. No Eye ever saw any thing so beautiful; but that is her least Excellence. Such Sense, such Goodness! O I could praise her for ever, and yet should omit half her Virtues.' 'Mr. *Western* a Daughter grown up!' cries the Barber, 'I remember the Father a Boy; well, *Tempus edax Rerum*.'²

The Wine being now at an End, the Barber pressed very eagerly to be his Bottle; but *Jones* absolutely refused, saying, 'He had already drank more than he ought; and that he now chose to retire to his Room, where he wished he could procure himself a Book.' 'A Book!' cries *Benjamin*, 'what Book would you have? *Latin* or *English*? I have some curious Books in both Languages. Such as *Erasmi Colloquia*, *Ovid de Tristibus*, *Gradus ad Parnassum*;³ and in *English* I have several of the best Books, tho' some of them are a little torn; but I have a great Part of *Stowe's* Chronicle;⁴ the sixth Volume of *Pope's Homer*;⁵ the third Volume of the Spectator; the second Volume of *Echard's Roman* History;⁶ the Craftsman;⁷

---

¹ See above, p. 417, n. 3.

² Ovid, *Metamorphoses*, xv. 234: 'O Time, devourer of things.' An example in *A Short Introduction to Grammar* [1720], p. 141; *Lily's Rules Construed* [1720], p. 43; and the Eton Latin grammar (1758), p. 84. See also below, p. 471.

³ These three Latin works were widely used as texts for schoolboys. Erasmus's *Colloquia* was first published in 1516. *Gradus ad Parnassum* (1686) is a collection of synonyms, epithets, and phrases from the classical poets; the young Jonathan Wild pilfers a copy of this book while at school (1743; I. iii).

⁴ *The Chronicles of England from Brute unto this present yeare of Christ*, 1580, by the well-known historian and antiquary, John Stow (1525?–1605).

⁵ This would be the final volume of the *Iliad*, originally published in 1720.

⁶ See above, p. 273, n. 2. Vol. ii of this work related the history of Rome 'from the Settlement of the Empire by Augustus Cæsar, to the Removal of the Imperial Seat by Constantine the Great'.

⁷ Founded originally to oppose Walpole, *The Craftsman* (1726–50) was the principal 'Tory' journal of the period. The earlier numbers were reprinted in book form in 14 vols. (1731–7).

Robinson Crusoe;[1] *Thomas a Kempis*,[2] and two Volumes of *Tom Brown's* Works.'[3]

'Those last,' cries *Jones*, 'are Books I never saw, so if you please to lend me one of those Volumes.' The Barber assured him he would be highly entertained; for he looked upon the Author to have been one of the greatest Wits that ever the Nation produced. He then stepped to his House, which was hard by, and immediately returned, after which, the Barber having received very strict Injunctions of Secrecy from *Jones*, and having sworn inviolably to maintain it, they separated; the Barber went home, and *Jones* retired to his Chamber.

CHAPTER VI

In which more of the Talents of Mr. Benjamin *will appear, as well as who this extraordinary Person was.*

IN the Morning *Jones* grew a little uneasy at the Desertion of his Surgeon, as he apprehended some Inconvenience, or even Danger, might attend the not Dressing his Wound; he enquired therefore of the Drawer what other Surgeons were to be met with in that Neighbourhood. The Drawer told him there was one not far off; but he had known him often refuse to be concerned after another had been sent for before him; 'but, Sir,' says he, 'if you will take my Advice, there is not a Man in the Kingdom can do your Business better than the Barber who was with you last Night.

---

[1] Though he remarked on its great vogue, Fielding seems to have considered Defoe's *Robinson Crusoe* (1719) an inferior form of popular literature. (See *The Jacobite's Journal*, 27 February 1748; also *The Champion*, 20 March 1739/40.)

[2] Thomas à Kempis—Thomas Haemmerlein or Hemercker of Kempen (1380–1471)— was an Augustinian monk and the supposed author of the *Imitation of Christ* (1441). He was also a favourite of Joseph Andrews (1742; I. iii).

[3] Tom Brown (1663–1704), hackney journalist, satirist, and translator. Three volumes of his *Works* appeared in 1707; two more were added in 1720. In dedicating Brown's works to the Duke of Ormonde, Dr. James Drake flatly declared that '*all men of sense and learning admir'd the comic stile of Mr.* BROWN, *in which no man yet has equall'd him*', and he concluded this modest appraisal by asserting that his author, if not 'one of our best poets . . . was undeniably one of our greatest genius's' (*Works*, 8th ed. [1744], i. iv, xii). For the most part, however, Brown's admirers were limited to the likes of Dr. Drake, Swift's Simon Wagstaff, and Partridge. To Fielding, Brown was in a class with Tom D'Urfey—mere 'Scriblers' whose popularity attested to the lack of literary judgement in '*this tasteless, silly Town*' (*The Covent-Garden Journal*, 4 February 1752).

We look upon him to be one of the ablest Men at a Cut in all this Neighbourhood. For tho' he hath not been here above three Months, he hath done several great Cures.'

The Drawer was presently dispatched for little *Benjamin*, who being acquainted in what Capacity he was wanted, prepared himself accordingly, and attended; but with so different an Air and Aspect from that which he wore when his Bason was under his Arm, that he could scarce be known to be the same Person.

'So, Tonsor,' says *Jones*, 'I find you have more Trades than one; how came you not to inform me of this last Night?' 'A Surgeon,' answered *Benjamin*, with great Gravity, 'is a Profession, not a Trade. The Reason why I did not acquaint you last Night that I professed this Art, was that I then concluded you was under the Hands of another Gentleman, and I never love to interfere with my Brethren in their Business. *Ars omnibus communis*;[1] but now, Sir, if you please, I will inspect your Head, and when I see into your Skull, I will give my Opinion of your Case.'

Jones had no great Faith in this new Professor; however he suffered him to open the Bandage, and to look at his Wound, which as soon as he had done, *Benjamin* began to groan and shake his Head violently. Upon which *Jones*, in a peevish Manner, bid him not play the Fool, but tell him in what Condition he found him. 'Shall I answer you as a Surgeon, or a Friend?' said *Benjamin*. 'As a Friend, and seriously,' said *Jones*. 'Why then, upon my Soul,' cries *Benjamin*, 'it would require a great deal of Art to keep you from being well after a very few Dressings; and if you will suffer me to apply some Salve of mine, I will answer for the Success.' *Jones* gave his Consent, and the Plaister was applied accordingly.

'There, Sir,' cries *Benjamin*, 'now I will, if you please, resume my former Self; but a Man is obliged to keep up some Dignity in his Countenance whilst he is performing these Operations, or the World will not submit to be handled by him. You can't imagine, Sir, of how much Consequence a grave Aspect is to a grave Character. A Barber may make you laugh, but a Surgeon ought rather to make you cry.'

'Mr. *Barber*, or Mr. *Surgeon*, or Mr. *Barber-Surgeon*,' said *Jones*.—'O dear Sir,' answered *Benjamin*, interrupting him,

---

[1] 'The art is common to all'—perhaps a play on '*mors omnibus communis*' (see below, p. 629, n. 2).

'*Infandum Regina jubes renovare Dolorem.*[1] You recal to my Mind
that cruel Separation of the united Fraternities,[2] so much to the
Prejudice of both Bodies, as all Separations must be, according to
the old Adage, *Vis unita fortior*;[3] which to be sure there are not
wanting some of one or of the other Fraternity who are able to
construe. What a Blow was this to me who unite both in my own
Person.'—'Well, by whatever Name you please to be called,'
continued *Jones*, 'you certainly are one of the oddest, most
comical Fellows I ever met with, and must have something very
surprizing in your Story, which you must confess I have a Right
to hear.' 'I do confess it,' answered *Benjamin*, 'and will very
readily acquaint you with it, when you have sufficient Leisure;
for I promise you it will require a good deal of Time.' *Jones* told
him, He could never be more at Leisure than at present. 'Well
then,' said *Benjamin*, 'I will obey you; but first I will fasten the
Door, that none may interrupt us.' He did so, and then advancing
with a solemn Air to *Jones*, said; 'I must begin by telling you,
Sir, that you yourself have been the greatest Enemy I ever had.'
Jones was a little startled at this sudden Declaration. 'I your
Enemy, Sir!' says he, with much Amazement, and some Sternness in his Look. 'Nay, be not angry,' said *Benjamin*, 'for I
promise you I am not. You are perfectly innocent of having intended me any Wrong; for you was then an Infant; but I shall,
I believe, unriddle all this the Moment I mention my Name. Did
you never hear, Sir, of one *Partridge*, who had the Honour of
being reputed your Father, and the Misfortune of being ruined
by that Honour?' 'I have indeed heard of that *Partridge*,' says
Jones, 'and have always believed myself to be his Son.' 'Well,
Sir,' answered *Benjamin*, 'I am that *Partridge*; but I here absolve
you from all filial Duty; for I do assure you you are no Son of
mine.' 'How,' replied *Jones*, 'and is it possible that a false
Suspicion should have drawn all the ill Consequences upon you,

---

[1] Virgil, *Aeneid*, ii. 3: 'Beyond all words, O queen, is the grief thou bidst me revive'
(trans. H. R. Fairclough, Loeb Classical Library, 1916)—Aeneas to Dido, as he begins
the story of the destruction of Troy. This is Partridge's favourite quotation; see also
pp. 438, 628, 752.

[2] The barbers and surgeons of London had been united in one corporation since the time
of Henry VIII. By 18 George II, cap. 15 ('An Act for making the Surgeons of *London* and
the Barbers of *London* Two Separate and Distinct Corporations'), this union was dissolved,
effective 24 June 1745. Fielding's friend John Ranby (see pp. 112, n. 2; 468, n. 1; 911,
n. 1) was appointed governor of the new Company of Surgeons.

[3] 'Strength united is more powerful'—a proverbial expression.

with which I am too well acquainted?' 'It is possible,' cries
Benjamin, 'for it is so; but tho' it is natural enough for Men to
hate even the innocent Causes of their Sufferings, yet I am of a
different Temper. I have loved you ever since I heard of your
Behaviour to *Black George*, as I told you; and I am convinced,
from this extraordinary Meeting, that you are born to make me
Amends for all I have suffered on that Account. Besides, I
dreamt, the Night before I saw you, that I stumbled over a
Stool without hurting myself; which plainly shewed me something good was towards me; and last Night I dreamt again, that I
rode behind you on a Milk white Mare, which is a very excellent
Dream,[1] and betokens much good Fortune, which I am resolved
to pursue, unless you have the Cruelty to deny me.'

'I should be very glad, Mr. *Partridge*,' answered *Jones*, 'to
have it in my Power to make you Amends for your Sufferings on
my Account; tho' at present I see no Likelihood of it; however,
I assure you I will deny you nothing which is in my Power to
grant.'

'It is in your Power sure enough,' replied *Benjamin*, 'for I
desire nothing more than Leave to attend you in this Expedition.
Nay, I have so entirely set my Heart upon it, that if you should
refuse me, you will kill both a Barber and a Surgeon in one
Breath.'

Jones answered smiling, That he should be very sorry to be the
Occasion of so much Mischief to the Public. He then advanced
many prudential Reasons, in order to dissuade *Benjamin* (whom
we shall hereafter call *Partridge*) from his Purpose; but all were in
vain. *Partridge* relied strongly on his Dream of the milk-white
Mare. 'Besides, Sir,' says he, 'I promise you, I have as good an
Inclination to the Cause, as any Man can possibly have; and go I
will, whether you admit me to go in your Company or not.'

Jones, who was as much pleased with *Partridge*, as *Partridge*
could be with him, and who had not consulted his own Inclination, but the Good of the other in desiring him to stay behind;

---

[1] A number of fortune-telling manuals purporting to explain the significance of dreams
were circulating in the mid-eighteenth century: e.g. *The High German Fortune-Teller;
Dreams and Moles with their Interpretation and Signification . . . by a Fellow of the Royal
Society, and a true Lover of Learning*; and the *New and Well Experienced Fortune Book*.
Appropriately enough, the authors of this last pamphlet were 'Partridge and Flamsted'.
The omens in Partridge's dreams are among those explained in a twentieth-century descen-
dant of such compilations, *The Mystic Dream Book* [1933].

when he found his Friend so resolute, at last gave his Consent; but then recollecting himself, he said, 'Perhaps, Mr. *Partridge*, you think I shall be able to support you, but I really am not;' and then taking out his Purse, he told out nine Guineas, which he declared were his whole Fortune.

Partridge answered, 'that his Dependance was only on his future Favour: For he was thoroughly convinced he would shortly have enough in his Power. At present, Sir,' said he, 'I believe I am rather the richer Man of the two; but all I have is at your Service, and at your Disposal. I insist upon your taking the whole, and I beg only to attend you in the Quality of your Servant, *Nil desperandum est Teucro duce et auspice Teucro*;'[1] But to this generous Proposal concerning the Money, *Jones* would by no means submit.

It was resolved to set out the next Morning; when a Difficulty arose concerning the Baggage, for the Portmanteau of Mr. *Jones* was too large to be carried without a Horse.

'If I may presume to give my Advice,' says *Partridge*, 'this Portmanteau, with every Thing in it, except a few Shirts, should be left behind. Those I shall be easily able to carry for you, and the rest of your Clothes will remain very safely locked up in my House.'

This Method was no sooner proposed than agreed when the Barber departed, in order to prepare every Thing for his intended Expedition.

CHAPTER VII

Containing better Reasons than any which have yet appeared for the Conduct of Partridge; *an Apology for the Weakness of* Jones; *and some farther Anecdotes concerning my Landlady.*

THOUGH *Partridge* was one of the most superstitious of Men, he would hardly, perhaps, have desired to accompany *Jones* on his Expedition merely from the Omens of the Joint-stool, and white Mare, if his Prospect had been no better than to have shared the Plunder gained in the Field of Battle. In Fact, when *Partridge* came to ruminate on the Relation he had heard

---

[1] Slightly altered (Partridge adds *est*) from Horace, *Odes*, I. vii. 27: 'Nothing is to be despaired of under Teucer's leadership and Teucer's auspices.'

from *Jones*, he could not reconcile to himself, that Mr. *Allworthy* should turn his Son (for so he most firmly believed him to be) out of Doors, for any Reason which he had heard assigned. He concluded therefore, that the whole was a Fiction, and that *Jones*, of whom he had often from his Correspondents heard the wildest Character, had in reality run away from his Father. It came into his Head, therefore, that if he could prevail with the young Gentleman to return back to his Father, he should by that Means render a Service to *Allworthy*, which would obliterate all his former Anger; nay, indeed he conceived that very Anger was counterfeited, and that *Allworthy* had sacrificed him to his own Reputation. And this Suspicion, indeed, he well accounted for, from the tender Behaviour of that excellent Man to the Foundling Child; from his great Severity to *Partridge*, who knowing himself to be innocent, could not conceive that any other should think him guilty; lastly, from the Allowance which he had privately received long after the Annuity had been publickly taken from him; and which he looked upon as a kind of Smart-money, or rather by way of Atonement for Injustice: For it is very uncommon, I believe, for Men to ascribe the Benefactions they receive to pure Charity, when they can possibly impute them to any other Motive. If he could by any Means, therefore, persuade the young Gentleman to return home, he doubted not but that he should again be received into the Favour of *Allworthy*, and well rewarded for his Pains; nay, and should be again restored to his native Country; a Restoration which *Ulysses* himself never wished more heartily than poor *Partridge*.

As for *Jones*, he was well satisfied with the Truth of what the other had asserted, and believed that *Partridge* had no other Inducements but Love to him, and Zeal for the Cause. A blameable Want of Caution, and Diffidence in the Veracity of others, in which he was highly worthy of Censure. To say the Truth, there are but two Ways by which Men become possessed of this excellent Quality. The one is from long Experience, and the other is from Nature; which last, I presume, is often meant by Genius, or great natural Parts; and it is infinitely the better of the two, not only as we are Masters of it much earlier in Life, but as it is much more infallible and conclusive: For a Man who hath been imposed on by ever so many, may still hope to find others more honest; whereas he who receives certain necessary

Admonitions from within, that this is impossible, must have very little Understanding indeed, if he ever renders himself liable to be once deceived. As *Jones* had not this Gift from Nature, he was too young to have gained it by Experience; for at the diffident Wisdom which is to be acquired this Way, we seldom arrive till very late in Life; which is perhaps the Reason why some old Men are apt to despise the Understandings of all those who are a little younger than themselves.

Jones spent most Part of the Day in the Company of a new Acquaintance. This was no other than the Landlord of the House, or rather the Husband of the Landlady. He had but lately made his Descent down Stairs, after a long Fit of the Gout, in which Distemper he was generally confined to his Room during one half of the Year; and during the rest, he walked about the House, smoaked his Pipe, and drank his Bottle with his Friends, without concerning himself in the least with any Kind of Business. He had been bred, as they call it, a Gentleman, that is, bred up to do nothing, and had spent a very small Fortune, which he inherited from an industrious Farmer his Uncle, in Hunting, Horse-racing, and Cock-fighting, and had been married by my Landlady for certain Purposes which he had long since desisted from answering: for which she hated him heartily. But as he was a surly Kind of Fellow, so she contented herself with frequently upbraiding him by disadvantageous Comparisons with her first Husband, whose Praise she had eternally in her Mouth; and as she was for the most part Mistress of the Profit, so she was satisfied to take upon herself the Care and Government of the Family, and after a long successless Struggle, to suffer her Husband to be Master of himself.

In the Evening when *Jones* retired to his Room, a small Dispute arose between this fond Couple concerning him. 'What,' says the Wife, 'you have been tipling with the Gentleman! I see.' 'Yes,' answered the Husband, 'we have cracked a Bottle together, and a very Gentleman-like Man he is, and hath a very pretty Notion of Horse-flesh. Indeed he is young, and hath not seen much of the World: For I believe he hath been at very few Horse-races.' 'O ho! he is one of your Order, is he?' replies the Landlady, 'he must be a Gentleman to be sure, if he is a Horse-racer. The Devil fetch such Gentry, I am sure I wish I had never seen any of them. I have Reason to love Horse-racers truly.'

'That you have,' says the Husband; 'for I was one you know.' 'Yes,' answered she, 'You are a pure one indeed. As my first Husband used to say, I may put all the Good I have ever got by you in my Eyes, and see never the worse.' 'D—n your first Husband,' cries he.—'Don't d—n a better Man than yourself,' answered the Wife, 'if he had been alive, you durst not have done it.' 'Then you think,' says he, 'I have not so much Courage as yourself: For you have d—n'd him often in my Hearing.' 'If I did,' says she, 'I have repented of it many's the good Time and oft. And if he was so good to forgive me a Word spoken in Haste, or so, it doth not become such a one as you to *twitter* me. He was a Husband to me, he was; and if ever I did make use of an ill Word or so in a Passion; I never called him Rascal, I should have told a Lie, if I had called him Rascal.' Much more she said, but not in his Hearing: For having lighted his Pipe, he staggered off as fast as he could. We shall therefore transcribe no more of her Speech, as it approached still nearer and nearer to a Subject too indelicate to find any Place in this History.

Early in the Morning, *Partridge* appeared at the Bedside of *Jones*, ready equipped for the Journey, with his Knapsack at his Back. This was his own Workmanship; for besides his other Trades, he was no indifferent Taylor. He had already put up his whole Stock of Linnen in it, consisting of four Shirts, to which he now added eight for Mr. *Jones*, and then packing up the Portmanteau, he was departing with it towards his own House, but was stopt in his Way by the Landlady, who refused to suffer any Removals till after the Payment of the Reckoning.

The Landlady was, as we have said, absolute Governess in these Regions; it was therefore necessary to comply with her Rules, so the Bill was presently writ out, which amounted to a much larger Sum than might have been expected, from the Entertainment which *Jones* had met with; but here we are obliged to disclose some Maxims, which Publicans hold to be the grand Mysteries of their Trade. The first is, if they have any Thing good in their House (which indeed very seldom happens) to produce it only to Persons who travel with great Equipages. Secondly, To charge the same for the very worst Provisions, as if they were the best. And, lastly, if any of their Guests call but for little, to make them pay a double Price for every Thing they have; so that the Amount by the Head may be much the same.

The Bill being made and discharged, *Jones* set forward with *Partridge* carrying his Knapsack; nor did the Landlady condescend to wish him a good Journey: for this was, it seems, an Inn frequented by People of Fashion; and I know not whence it is, but all those who get their Livelihood by People of Fashion, contract as much Insolence to the rest of Mankind, as if they really belonged to that Rank themselves.

CHAPTER VIII

Jones arrives at Gloucester, *and goes to the* Bell; *the Character of that House, and of a Petty-fogger, which he there meets with.*

MR. *Jones*, and *Partridge*, or *Little Benjamin*, (which Epithet of *Little* was perhaps given him ironically, he being in reality near six Feet high) having left their last Quarters in the Manner before described, travelled on to *Gloucester* without meeting any Adventure worth relating.

Being arrived here, they chose for their House of Entertainment the Sign of the *Bell*, an excellent House indeed, and which I do most seriously recommend to every Reader who shall visit this ancient City. The Master of it is Brother to the great Preacher *Whitefield*;[1] but is absolutely untainted with the pernicious Principles of Methodism, or of any other heretical Sect. He is indeed a very honest plain Man, and in my Opinion,

---

[1] For Fielding's views on George Whitefield and Methodism, see pp. 63, n. 1; 79, n. 4; 93, n. 1; 96, n. 2; 929, n. 1. Whitefield grew up in the Bell—'an excellent House indeed', as Fielding calls it, which continues to prosper at the present day—and until shortly after his brother Richard's marriage in 1729, he had intended to help manage the inn; but he quarrelled with his new sister-in-law and left the household. (See *A Short Account of God's Dealings with the Reverend Mr. George Whitefield* [1740].) Not everyone who knew her shared Fielding's fondness for this woman, Elizabeth Whitefield (d. 7 August 1755). Having read the passage in *Tom Jones*—a book which he otherwise very much admired—Captain Lewis Thomas (see above, p. 372, n. 3) wrote to Welbore Ellis on 3 April 1749, expressing his own opinion of Mrs. Whitefield's character:

'I breakfasted two or three times with Mrs Whitfield, we talk'd of nothing but gayety & Assemblies; she let me into a Short History of her Lovers, & told me ye conquests she had made when Younger, & if I might put any faith in her own Commentaries, she had had as many occasions of triumph as Julius Caesar; in short I went away extremely disgusted with the Folly & behaviour of my Coquet Landlady.

'How ye Devil came it into Fielding's head to praise this Woman so exuberantly? If I was Master of the Bell Inn, I vow I should be absolutely Jealous.' (See J. P. Feil, *PQ*, xxxix [1960], 508–10.)

not likely to create any Disturbance either in Church or State. His Wife hath, I believe, had much Pretension to Beauty, and is still a very fine Woman. Her Person and Deportment might have made a shining Figure in the politest Assemblies; but though she must be conscious of this, and many other Perfections, she seems perfectly contented with, and resigned to that State of Life to which she is called; and this Resignation is entirely owing to the Prudence and Wisdom of her Temper: For she is at present as free from any methodistical Notions as her Husband. I say at present: For she freely confesses that her Brother's Documents made at first some Impression upon her, and that she had put herself to the Expence of a long Hood, in order to attend the extraordinary Emotions of the Spirit; but having found during an Experiment of three Weeks, no Emotions, she says, worth a Farthing, she very wisely laid by her Hood, and abandoned the Sect. To be concise, she is a very friendly, good-natured Woman, and so industrious to oblige, that the Guests must be of a very morose Disposition who are not extremely well satisfied in her House.

Mrs. *Whitefield* happened to be in the Yard when *Jones* and his Attendant marched in. Her Sagacity soon discovered in the Air of our Heroe something which distinguished him from the Vulgar. She ordered her Servants, therefore, immediately to shew him into a Room, and presently afterwards invited him to Dinner with herself; which Invitation he very thankfully accepted: For indeed much less agreeable Company than that of Mrs. *Whitefield*, and a much worse Entertainment than she had provided, would have been welcome, after so long fasting, and so long a Walk.

Besides Mr. *Jones* and the good Governess of the Mansion, there sat down at Table an Attorney of *Salisbury*, indeed the very same who had brought the News of Mrs. *Blifil's* Death to Mr. *Allworthy*, and whose Name, which, I think, we did not before mention, was *Dowling*; there was likewise present another Person, who stiled himself a Lawyer, and who lived somewhere near *Lidlinch*[1] in *Somersetshire*. This Fellow, I say, stiled himself a Lawyer, but was indeed a most vile Petty-fogger, without Sense or Knowledge of any Kind; one of those who may be termed Train-bearers to the Law; a Sort of Supernumeraries in the

---

[1] The village of Lydlinch is actually situated in Dorset, four miles from the Somerset border.

Profession, who are the Hackneys of Attornies, and will ride more Miles for half a Crown, than a Post-boy.

During the time of Dinner, the *Somersetshire* Lawyer recollected the Face of *Jones*, which he had seen at Mr. *Allworthy's*: For he had often visited in that Gentleman's Kitchen. He therefore took Occasion to enquire after the good Family there, with that Familiarity which would have become an intimate Friend or Acquaintance of Mr. *Allworthy*; and indeed he did all in his Power to insinuate himself to be such, though he had never had the Honour of speaking to any Person in that Family higher than the Butler. *Jones* answered all his Questions with much Civility, though he never remembered to have seen the Petty-fogger before, and though he concluded from the outward Appearance and Behaviour of the Man, that he usurped a Freedom with his Betters, to which he was by no means intitled.

As the Conversation of Fellows of this Kind, is of all others the most detestable to Men of any Sense, the Cloth was no sooner removed than Mr. *Jones* withdrew, and a little barbarously left poor Mrs. *Whitefield* to do a Pennance, which I have often heard Mr. *Timothy Harris*,[1] and other Publicans of good Taste, lament as the severest Lot annexed to their Calling, namely, that of being obliged to keep Company with their Guests.

Jones had no sooner quitted the Room, than the Petty-fogger, in a whispering Tone, asked Mrs. *Whitefield*, 'if she knew who that fine Spark was?' She answered, 'she had never seen the Gentleman before.' 'The Gentleman, indeed!' replied the Petty-fogger, 'a pretty Gentleman truly! Why, he's the Bastard of a Fellow who was hanged for Horse-stealing. He was dropt at Squire *Allworthy's* Door, where one of the Servants found him in a Box so full of Rain-water, that he would certainly have been drowned, had he not been reserved for another Fate.' 'Ay, ay, you need not mention it, I protest, we understand what that Fate is very well,' cries *Dowling*, with a most facetious Grin. 'Well,' continued the other, 'the Squire ordered him to be taken in: For he is a timborsome Man every Body knows, and was afraid of drawing himself into a Scrape, and there the Bastard was bred up,

1 Timothy Harris (d. October 1748), keeper of the Red Lion at Egham, Surrey, whom Fielding had earlier complimented in *Joseph Andrews* (I. xi). (See his death notice, 20 October 1748: Roll for the Manor of Staines in the County of Middlesex, 1743–8. Acc. 801. And his will, proved 16 November 1748: Prerogative Court of Canterbury. Strahan, Folio 329.)

and fed and cloathified all to the World like any Gentleman; and
there he got one of the Servant Maids with Child, and persuaded
her to swear it to the Squire himself; and afterwards he broke the
Arm of one Mr. *Thwackum* a Clergyman, only because he reprimanded him for following Whores; and afterwards he snapt a
Pistol at Mr. *Blifil* behind his Back; and once when Squire
Allworthy was sick, he got a Drum, and beat it all over the House,
to prevent him from sleeping: And twenty other Pranks he hath
played, for all which, about four or five Days ago, just before I left
the Country, the Squire strip'd him stark naked, and turned him
out of Doors.'

'And very justly too, I protest,' cries *Dowling*, 'I would turn
my own Son out of Doors, if he was guilty of half as much. And
pray what is the Name of this pretty Gentleman?'

'The Name o'un!' answered Petty-fogger, 'why, he is a called
Thomas Jones.'

'*Jones*!' answered *Dowling*, a little eagerly, 'what, Mr. *Jones*
that lived at Mr. *Allworthy's*! was that the Gentleman that dined
with us?' 'The very same,' said the other. 'I have heard of the
Gentleman,' cries *Dowling*, 'often; but I never heard any ill
Character of him.' 'And I am sure,' says Mrs. *Whitefield*, 'if half
what this Gentleman hath said be true, Mr. *Jones* hath the most
deceitful Countenance I ever saw; for sure his Looks promise
something very different; and I must say, for the little I have seen
of him, he is as civil a well-bred Man as you would wish to
converse with.'

Petty-fogger calling to mind that he had not been sworn, as he
usually was, before he gave his Evidence, now bound what he had
declared with so many Oaths and Imprecations, that the Lady's
Ears were shocked, and she put a Stop to his swearing, by
assuring him of her Belief. Upon which he said, 'I hope, Madam,
you imagine I would scorn to tell such Things of any Man, unless
I knew them to be true. What Interest have I in taking away
the Reputation of a Man who never injured me? I promise you
every Syllable of what I have said is Fact, and the whole Country
knows it.'

As Mrs. *Whitefield* had no Reason to suspect that the
Petty-fogger had any Motive or Temptation to abuse *Jones*, the
Reader cannot blame her for believing what he so confidently
affirmed with many Oaths. She accordingly gave up her Skill in

Physiognomy, and henceforwards conceived so ill an Opinion of her Guest, that she heartily wished him out of her House.

This Dislike was now farther encreased by a Report which Mr. *Whitefield* made from the Kitchen, where *Partridge* had informed the Company, 'That tho' he carried the Knapsack, and contented himself with staying among Servants, while *Tom Jones* (as he called him) was regaling in the Parlour, he was not his Servant, but only a Friend and Companion, and as good a Gentleman as Mr. *Jones* himself.'

Dowling sat all this while silent, biting his Fingers, making Faces, grinning, and looking wonderfully arch; at last he opened his Lips, and protested that the Gentleman looked like another Sort of Man. He then called for his Bill with the utmost Haste, declared he must be at *Hereford* that Evening, lamented his great Hurry of Business, and wished he could divide himself into twenty Pieces, in order to be at once in twenty Places.

The Petty-fogger now likewise departed, and then *Jones* desired the Favour of Mrs. *Whitefield's* Company to drink Tea with him; but she refused, and with a Manner so different from that with which she had received him at Dinner, that it a little surprized him. And now he soon perceived her Behaviour totally changed; for instead of that natural Affability which we have before celebrated, she wore a constrained Severity on her Countenance, which was so disagreeable to Mr. *Jones*, that he resolved, however late, to quit the House that Evening.

He did indeed account somewhat unfairly for this sudden Change; for besides some hard and unjust Surmises concerning female Fickleness and Mutability,[1] he began to suspect that he owed this Want of Civility to his Want of Horses, a Sort of Animals which, as they dirty no Sheets, are thought, in Inns, to pay better for their Beds than their Riders, and are therefore considered as the more desirable Company; but Mrs. *Whitefield*, to do her Justice, had a much more liberal Way of thinking. She was perfectly well-bred, and could be very civil to a Gentleman, tho' he walked on Foot: In Reality, she looked on our Heroe as a sorry Scoundrel, and therefore treated him as such, for which not even *Jones* himself, had he known as much as the Reader, could have blamed her; nay, on the contrary, he must have approved her Conduct, and have esteemed her the more for the Disrespect

---

[1] Cf. Virgil, *Aeneid*, iv. 569–70: 'varium et mutabile semper/ femina.'

shewn towards himself. This is indeed a most aggravating Circumstance which attends depriving Men unjustly of their Reputation; for a Man who is conscious of having an ill Character, cannot justly be angry with those who neglect and slight him; but ought rather to despise such as affect his Conversation, unless where a perfect Intimacy must have convinced them that their Friend's Character hath been falsely and injuriously aspersed.

This was not, however, the Case of *Jones*; for as he was a perfect Stranger to the Truth, so he was with good Reason offended at the Treatment he received. He therefore paid his Reckoning and departed, highly against the Will of Mr. *Partridge*, who having remonstrated much against it to no Purpose, at last condescended to take up his Knapsack, and to attend his Friend.

CHAPTER IX

Containing several Dialogues between Jones *and* Partridge, *concerning Love, Cold, Hunger, and other Matters; with the lucky and narrow Escape of* Partridge, *as he was on the very Brink of making a fatal Discovery to his Friend.*

THE Shadows began now to descend larger from the high Mountains: The feather'd Creation had betaken themselves to their Rest. Now the highest Order of Mortals were sitting down to their Dinners, and the lowest Order to their Suppers. In a Word, the Clock struck five just as Mr. *Jones* took his Leave of *Gloucester*; an Hour at which (as it was now Midwinter) the dirty Fingers of Night would have drawn her sable Curtain over the Universe, had not the Moon forbid her, who now with a Face as broad and as red as those of some jolly Mortals, who, like her, turn Night into Day, began to rise from her Bed,[1] where she had

---

[1] Since the time of Tom's 'mid-winter' journey is late November 1745 (see above, p. 368, n. 1), the circumstance of the full moon's rising at Gloucester at 5.00 p.m. has led to the theory that Fielding consulted an almanac when plotting the chronology of his novel. (See F. S. Dickson, *N & Q*, 11th Ser., ix [30 May 1914], 425–6, and *The Library*, 3rd Ser., viii [1917], 218–24.) According to this hypothesis, the precise date of Tom's departure from Gloucester is 29 November 1745. From this assumption it is possible to assign specific dates to the events of the narrative from the time (22 November) Western proposes a match between Sophia and Blifil (VI. iii) to the time when Tom and Sophia marry (24 December) and, two days later, retire to the country (26 December). At least one contemporary reader

slumbred away the Day, in order to sit up all Night. *Jones* had not travelled far before he paid his Compliments to that beautiful Planet, and turning to his Companion, asked him, If he had ever beheld so delicious an Evening. *Partridge* making no ready Answer to his Question, he proceeded to comment on the Beauty of the Moon, and repeated some Passages from *Milton*,[1] who hath certainly excelled all other Poets in his Description of the heavenly Luminaries. He then told *Partridge* the Story from the *Spectator*,[2] of two Lovers who had agreed to entertain themselves when they were at a great Distance from each other, by repairing, at a certain fixed Hour, to look at the Moon; thus pleasing themselves with the Thought that they were both employed in contemplating the same Object at the same Time. 'Those Lovers,' added he, 'must have had Souls truly capable of feeling all the Tenderness of the sublimest of all human Passions.' 'Very probably,' cries *Partridge*, 'but I envy them more if they had Bodies incapable of feeling cold; for I am almost frozen to Death, and am very much afraid I shall lose a Piece of my Nose before we get to another House of Entertainment. Nay, truly, we may well expect some Judgment should happen to us for our Folly in running away so by Night from one of the most excellent Inns I ever set my Foot into. I am sure I never saw more good Things in my Life, and

seems to have sensed this chronology when, in a clumsy poem, he referred to the Christmas season as the time when 'F[IE]LD[IN]G's *Heroes* timely *hang*—or *marry*.' (See '*At* [*sic*] String *of* SIMILIES, *in the true* CHRISTMAS, Frigid, *or* F[IE]LDINGIAN STILE', *London Evening-Post*, 21–3 December 1749.)

In general, however, the evidence is against Fielding's having attempted to make the action of his central narrative conform to calendar time. If, for instance, we are meant to understand that Tom Jones's marriage takes place on Christmas Eve, it is odd that Fielding should avoid any mention of the fact. And there are other anomalies. Originally, it appears, Fielding thought of Allworthy's illness as occurring in June, not in early November (v. x, p. 255). By VII. vii, however, when Honour complains of the freezing nights, the 'mid-winter' time-scheme is clearly suggested, and by VII. xi, as we have seen, it is firmly established (see p. 368, n. 1). Yet even from this point there is no reason to believe that Fielding has begun to follow almanac and calendar. In IX. vii—the events of which, according to Dickson's chronology, would be placed on 30 November—the moon is said to be shining brightly long after it had set (see p. 521, n. 1); and in XIII. ix—according to Dickson, 15 December—Sophia is made to attend a play on a Sunday. (See also, pp. 729, n. 1; 853, n. 1.)

   1 Cf. *Paradise Lost*, i. 286–91, iv. 605–9, viii. 140–8.

   2 In *The Spectator*, No. 241 (6 December 1711), Addison recalls the story from 'one of *Scudery's* Romances' of a couple who, while separated, set aside a certain time each day to think of one another. The amiable function of the moon in uniting these lovers is, however, Fielding's own contribution.

the greatest Lord in the Land cannot live better in his own House than he may there. And to forsake such a House, and go a rambling about the Country, the Lord knows whither, *per devia rura viarum*,[1] I say nothing, for my Part; but some People might not have Charity enough to conclude we were in our sober Senses.' 'Fie upon it, Mr. *Partridge*,' says *Jones*, 'have a better Heart; consider you are going to face an Enemy, and are you afraid of facing a little Cold? I wish, indeed, we had a Guide to advise which of these Roads we should take.'[2] 'May I be so bold,' says *Partridge*, 'to offer my Advice: *Interdum Stultus opportuna loquitur.*'[3] 'Why, which of them,' cries *Jones*, 'would you recommend?' 'Truly neither of them,' answered *Partridge*. 'The only Road we can be certain of finding, is the Road we came. A good hearty Pace will bring us back to *Gloucester* in an Hour; but if we go forward, the Lord *Harry* knows when we shall arrive at any Place; for I see at least fifty Miles before me, and no House in all the Way.' 'You see, indeed, a very fair Prospect,' says *Jones*, 'which receives great additional Beauty from the extreme Lustre of the Moon. However, I will keep the Left-hand Track, as that seems to lead directly to those Hills,[4] which we were informed lie not far from *Worcester*. And here, if you are inclined to quit me, you may, and return back again; but for my Part, I am resolved to go forward.'

'It is unkind in you, Sir,' says *Partridge*, 'to suspect me of any such Intention. What I have advised hath been as much on your Account as on my own; but since you are determined to go on, I am as much determined to follow. *I præ, sequar te.*'[5]

They now travelled some Miles without speaking to each other, during which Suspence of Discourse *Jones* often sighed, and *Partridge* groaned as bitterly, tho' from a very different Reason. At length *Jones* made a full Stop, and turning about, cries, 'Who knows, *Partridge*, but the loveliest Creature in the Universe may have her Eyes now fixed on that very Moon which I behold at this Instant!' 'Very likely, Sir,' answered *Partridge*, 'and if my Eyes were fixed on a good Surloin of Roast Beef, the

---

[1] 'Through country by-roads.' Cf. Ovid, *Metamorphoses*, i. 676: 'per devia rura capellas'.

[2] The travellers have probably reached the fork in the road at Corse, some five miles north-west of Gloucester.

[3] 'Sometimes a fool speaks opportunely'—proverbial.

[4] The Malverns.

[5] Terence, *Andria*, I. i. 172: 'you go first, I will follow you.'

Devil might take the Moon and her Horns into the Bargain.'
'Did ever *Tramontane*[1] make such an Answer?' cries *Jones*.
'Prithee, *Partridge*, wast thou never susceptible of Love in thy
Life, or hath Time worn away all the Traces of it from thy
Memory?' 'Alack-a-day,' cries *Partridge*, 'well would it have been
for me if I had never known what Love was. *Infandum Regina
jubes renovare Dolorem*.[2] I am sure I have tasted all the Tenderness
and Sublimities and Bitternesses of the Passion.' 'Was your
Mistress unkind then?' says *Jones*. 'Very unkind indeed, Sir,'
answered *Partridge*; 'for she married me, and made one of the
most confounded Wives in the World. However, Heaven be
praised, she's gone, and if I believed she was in the Moon,
according to a Book I once read, which teaches that to be the
Receptacle of departed Spirits,[3] I would never look at it for fear of
seeing her; but I wish, Sir, that the Moon was a Looking-glass
for your Sake, and that Miss *Sophia Western* was now placed
before it.' 'My dear *Partridge*,' cries *Jones*, 'what a Thought was
there! A Thought which I am certain could never have entered
into any Mind but that of a Lover. O *Partridge*, could I hope once
again to see that Face; but, alas! all those golden Dreams are
vanished for ever, and my only Refuge from future Misery is to
forget the Object of all my former Happiness.' 'And do you really
despair of ever seeing Miss *Western* again?' answered *Partridge*;
'if you will follow my Advice, I will engage you shall not only see
her, but have her in your Arms.' 'Ha! do not awaken a Thought
of that Nature,' cries *Jones*. 'I have struggled sufficiently to
conquer all such Wishes already.' 'Nay,' answered *Partridge*, 'if
you do not wish to have your Mistress in your Arms, you are a
most extraordinary Lover indeed.' 'Well, well,' says *Jones*, 'let us
avoid this Subject; but pray what is your Advice?' 'To give it you
in the military Phrase then,' says *Partridge*, 'as we are Soldiers;
"To the Right about." Let us return the Way we came, we may
yet reach *Gloucester* to Night, tho' late; whereas if we proceed,

---

[1] Originally an Italian expression applied to foreigners beyond the Alps, with the
connotation 'uncouth, unpolished, barbarous' (*OED*). Steele was fond of the word (see the
epilogue to *The Tender Husband* [1703] and *Tatler*, No. 222 [9 September 1710]), and
Fielding had used it earlier in *The Miser* (1733), II. iii. See also below, p. 806, n. 2.

[2] See above, p. 424, n. 1.

[3] Cf. Plutarch, 'Concerning the Face which Appears in the Orb of the Moon', *Moralia*,
943–4. For a thorough discussion of the subject, see Marjorie Nicolson, *A World in the
Moon*, Smith College Studies in Modern Languages, xvii (1935–6).

we are likely, for ought I see, to ramble about for ever without coming either to House or Home.' 'I have already told you my Resolution is to go on,' answered *Jones*; 'but I would have you go back. I am obliged to you for your Company hither, and I beg you to accept a Guinea as a small Instance of my Gratitude, Nay, it would be cruel in me to suffer you to go any farther; for, to deal plainly with you, my chief End and Desire is a glorious Death in the Service of my King and Country.' 'As for your Money,' replied *Partridge*, 'I beg, Sir, you will put it up; I will receive none of you at this Time; for at present I am, I believe, the richer Man of the two. And as your Resolution is to go on, so mine is to follow you if you do. Nay, now my Presence appears absolutely necessary to take Care of you, since your Intentions are so desperate, for I promise you my Views are much more prudent: As you are resolved to fall in Battle, if you can, so I am resolved as firmly to come to no Hurt if I can help it. And indeed I have the Comfort to think there will be but little Danger; for a popish Priest told me the other Day, the Business would soon be over, and he believed without a Battle.' 'A popish Priest,' cries *Jones*, 'I have heard, is not always to be believed when he speaks in Behalf of his Religion.' 'Yes, but so far,' answered the other, 'from speaking in Behalf of his Religion, he assured me, the Catholicks did not expect to be any Gainers by the Change; for that Prince *Charles* was as good a Protestant as any in *England*; and that nothing but Regard to Right made him and the rest of the popish Party to be *Jacobites*.'[1] 'I believe him to be as much a Protestant as I believe he hath any Right,' says *Jones*, 'and I make

---

[1] Like Addison before him (e.g. *Freeholder*, No. 14 [6 February 1716]), Fielding scoffed at the credulity of those who subscribed to the 'Mysteries' of the Jacobite creed, all of which were 'infinitely above the Reach of human Reason'. Partridge cherishes one of the most preposterous of these, as set forth in *The Jacobite's Journal* for 19 December 1747: namely, 'That a Popish Prince may be the Defender of a Protestant Church'. With Partridge's views, compare the belief of 'a Female Jacobite' in the *Journal* for 2 January 1748: 'That this P[retender] is deprived of his Right in the same manner as a private Person would be, who was violently turned out of his Estate. That he is protected and assisted by all the Popish Powers in *Europe*, only out of Compassion; and that he, and all his Family, tho' born and bred at *Rome*, are true, good *Englishmen* in their Hearts, &c., &c., &c.' Variations on this theme are heard in most of Fielding's writings of the period: besides many other numbers of *The Jacobite's Journal*, see, for instance, *A Serious Address to the People of Great Britain* (1745), *A Dialogue between the Devil, the Pope and the Pretender* (1745), *The True Patriot* (8–15 April, 27 May–3 June 1746), *A Dialogue between a Gentleman of London . . . and an honest Alderman of the Country Party* (1747), and *A Proper Answer to a late scurrilous Libel* (1747).

no Doubt of our Success, but not without a Battle. So that I am not so sanguine as your Friend the popish Priest.' 'Nay, to be sure, Sir,' answered *Partridge*, 'all the Prophecies I have ever read, speak of a great deal of Blood to be spilt in the Quarrel, and the Miller with three Thumbs, who is now alive, is to hold the Horses of three Kings, up to his Knees in Blood.[1] Lord have Mercy upon us all, and send better Times!' 'With what Stuff and Nonsense hast thou filled thy Head?' answered *Jones*. 'This too, I suppose, comes from the popish Priest. Monsters and Prodigies are the proper Arguments to support monstrous and absurd Doctrines. The Cause of King *George* is the Cause of Liberty and true Religion. In other Words, it is the Cause of common Sense,

---

[1] In *The Freeholder*, No. 24 (12 March 1716), Addison had ridiculed the superstitions of the Jacobites, who, having despaired of all natural means of overthrowing the government, had been 'reduced to the poor Comfort of Prodigies and old Women's Fables. . . . Nay, I have been lately shewn a written Prophecy that is handed among them with great Secresy, by which it appears their chief Reliance at present is upon a *Cheshire* Miller that was born with two Thumbs upon one hand'. After the '45, Fielding adopted a similar strategy, describing the Jacobites as 'the most superstitious of all People': 'In the worst of Times, and when their Hopes have seemed to lose all Foundations, a River having too much or too little Water in it, a Man born with an extraordinary Member, an Eclipse, a Comet, an Aurora Borealis, or any such ordinary or extraordinary Phenomenon, is sufficient to support their drooping Spirits, and is interpreted to be a Fore-runner of him they look for' (*Jacobite's Journal*, 21 May 1748). In the *Journal* for 27 February 1748 he had facetiously reported several prodigies in the Jacobite county of Staffordshire, where 'there are at present several Millars with two Thumbs'.

As usual during times of national crisis, the '45 prompted the publication of numerous pamphlets reporting the predictions of such woeful prognosticators as Mother Shipton, John Saltmarsh, Thomas Rymer, 'Marvellous Merlin', Thomas Newans, and many others. The most popular of these, to which Addison alludes in *The Freeholder*, was Robert Nixon's *Cheshire Prophecy at Large* (15th ed., 1745), with a commentary by John Oldmixon. Nixon, 'a kind of *Idiot*' who lived during the reign of James I, prophesied that a Cheshire miller with two heels would deliver England from foreign invaders (p. 3), that '*A Boy shall be born with three Thumbs, and shall hold three Kings Horses, while* England *shall three Times be Won and Lost in one Day*' (p. 4), and that a great battle would be fought upon London Bridge, 'which would be so Bloody, that People should ride in *London* Streets up to their Horses Bellies in Blood' (pp. 9–10). In a letter included in this volume, one William Ewers pointed out Addison's mistake in giving the miller two thumbs rather than the two heels Nixon endowed him with (p. 21). A good Whig, Oldmixon of course took care to ridicule such superstitions, turning them to the advantage of the Hanoverian cause and, appropriately enough in the present context, comparing them with the predictions of John Partridge, the victim of Swift's Bickerstaff papers. Though Fielding certainly knew of this work, he may have had Partridge recall the Norfolk prophecies of Mother Shipton, one version of which, according to Walter Rye, tells 'how a wondrous Londoner, a miller by trade, with three thumbs on one hand, is to hold the three kings' horses' in battle, 'when the blood is to run so thickly as to clot by the wayside . . .' (Introduction, *Tourist's Guide to the County of Norfolk* [1879], p. 19).

my Boy, and I warrant you will succeed, tho' *Briareus* himself[1]
was to rise again with his hundred Thumbs, and to turn Miller.'
Partridge made no Reply to this. He was indeed cast into the
utmost Confusion by this Declaration of *Jones*. For to inform the
Reader of a Secret, which we had no proper Opportunity of
revealing before, *Partridge* was in Truth a *Jacobite*, and had concluded that *Jones* was of the same Party, and was now proceeding
to join the Rebels. An Opinion which was not without Foundation. For the tall long-sided Dame, mentioned by *Hudibras*;[2]
that many-eyed, many-tongued, many-mouthed, many-eared
Monster of *Virgil*,[3] had related the Story of the Quarrel between
Jones and the Officer, with her usual Regard to Truth. She had
indeed changed the Name of *Sophia* into that of the Pretender,
and had reported, that drinking his Health was the Cause for
which *Jones* was knocked down. This *Partridge* had heard, and
most firmly believed. 'Tis no Wonder, therefore, that he had
thence entertained the above-mentioned Opinion of *Jones*; and
which he had almost discovered to him before he found out his
own Mistake. And at this the Reader will be the less inclined to
wonder, if he pleases to recollect the doubtful Phrase in which
Jones first communicated his Resolution to Mr. *Partridge*; and,
indeed, had the Words been less ambiguous, *Partridge* might
very well have construed them as he did; being persuaded, as he
was, that the whole Nation were of the same Inclination in their
Hearts: Nor did it stagger him that *Jones* had travelled in the
Company of Soldiers; for he had the same Opinion of the Army
which he had of the rest of the People.

   But however well affected he might be to *James* or *Charles*,[4] he
was still much more attached to *Little Benjamin* than to either;
for which Reason he no sooner discovered the Principles of his
Fellow-traveller, than he thought proper to conceal, and outwardly to give up his own to the Man on whom he depended for the

   [1] In Greek mythology, a giant with one hundred hands who helped the gods in their
war with the Titans.
   [2] *Hudibras*, II. i. 45–6: 'There is a Tall Long-sided Dame,/ (But wondrous light)
ycleped *Fame*.'
   [3] *Aeneid*, iv. 181–3, describing Fame—'a monster awful and huge, who for the many
feathers in her body has as many watchful eyes below—wondrous to tell—as many tongues,
as many sounding mouths, as many pricked-up ears' (trans. H. R. Fairclough, Loeb
Classical Library, 1916).
   [4] The 'Old Pretender', James Francis Edward Stuart (1688–1766), and his son Charles
(1720–88), the 'Young Pretender'.

making his Fortune, since he by no means believed the Affairs of *Jones* to be so desperate as they really were with Mr. *Allworthy*; for as he had kept a constant Correspondence with some of his Neighbours since he left that Country, he had heard much, indeed more than was true, of the great Affection Mr. *Allworthy* bore this young Man, who, as *Partridge* had been instructed, was to be that Gentleman's Heir, and whom, as we have said, he did not in the least doubt to be his Son.

He imagined, therefore, that whatever Quarrel was between them, it would be certainly made up at the Return of Mr. *Jones*; an Event from which he promised great Advantages, if he could take this Opportunity of ingratiating himself with that young Gentleman; and if he could by any Means be instrumental in procuring his Return, he doubted not, as we have before said, but it would as highly advance him in the Favour of Mr. *Allworthy*.

We have already observed, that he was a very good-natured Fellow, and he hath himself declared the violent Attachment he had to the Person and Character of *Jones*; but possibly the Views which I have just before mentioned, might likewise have some little Share in prompting him to undertake this Expedition, at least in urging him to continue it, after he had discovered, that his Master and himself, like some prudent Fathers and Sons, tho' they travelled together in great Friendship, had embraced opposite Parties. I am led into this Conjecture, by having remarked, that tho' Love, Friendship, Esteem, and such like, have very powerful Operations in the human Mind; Interest, however, is an Ingredient seldom omitted by wise Men, when they would work others to their own Purposes. This is indeed a most excellent Medicine, and like *Ward's* Pill,[1] flies at once to the particular Part of the Body on which you desire to operate, whether it be the Tongue, the Hand, or any other Member, where it scarce ever fails of immediately producing the desired Effect.

---

1 Joshua 'Spot' Ward (1685–1761), the well-known empiric, claimed that his 'Pill and Drop' were universal nostrums. They were in fact virulent preparations of antimony and arsenic which killed as many people as they cured. Nevertheless, he was a generous man who dispensed his medicine gratis to the poor and he enjoyed the favour of some of the most influential members of the aristocracy. For these reasons he was especially exempted from the act of 1748 which prohibited all but duly licensed apothecaries from preparing medicines. In pleading Ward's case at that time a writer in *The London Evening-Post* (3–5 May 1748) compared him to the Man of Ross as a paragon of charity.

From the time he began to practise, Ward was the target of ridicule, by Pope, for in-

CHAPTER X

In which our Travellers meet with a very extraordinary Adventure.

JUST as *Jones* and his Friend came to the End of their Dialogue
in the preceding Chapter, they arrived at the Bottom of a very
steep Hill. Here *Jones* stopt short, and directing his Eyes upwards, stood for a while silent. At length he called to his Companion, and said, '*Partridge*, I wish I was at the Top of this Hill;
it must certainly afford a most charming Prospect, especially by
this Light: For the solemn Gloom which the Moon casts on all
Objects, is beyond Expression beautiful, especially to an Imagination which is desirous of cultivating melancholy Ideas.' 'Very
probably,' answered *Partridge*; 'but if the Top of the Hill be
properest to produce melancholy Thoughts, I suppose the Bottom
is the likeliest to produce merry ones, and these I take to be much
the better of the two. I protest you have made my Blood run cold
with the very mentioning the Top of that Mountain; which
seems to me to be one of the highest in the World. No, no, if we
look for any thing, let it be for a Place under Ground, to screen
ourselves from the Frost.'—'Do so,' said *Jones*, 'let it be but
within Hearing of this Place, and I will hollow to you at my
Return back.' 'Surely, Sir, you are not mad,' said *Partridge*.
'Indeed I am,' answered *Jones*, 'if ascending this Hill be Madness:
But as you complain so much of the Cold already, I would have
you stay below. I will certainly return to you within an Hour.'
'Pardon me, Sir,' cries *Partridge*, 'I have determined to follow you
where-ever you go.' Indeed he was now afraid to stay behind; for
tho' he was Coward enough in all Respects, yet his chief Fear was
that of Ghosts, with which the present Time of Night, and the
Wildness of the Place, extremely well suited.

At this Instant *Partridge* espied a glimmering Light through
some Trees, which seemed very near to them. He immediately

stance, in the *Imitations of Horace*, Epistles I. vi. 56 (1738), II. i. 182 (1737), and by Hogarth
in Plate V of the *Harlot's Progress* (1732). After several incidental satires of Ward—e.g.
The Champion (28 February 1739/40, 26 August 1740) and *A Journey from This World to
the Next* (1743), I. iii—Fielding towards the end of his life submitted to be treated by him.
There is a complimentary reference to Ward's pill in *Amelia* (1751), VIII. ix, and in *The
Journal of a Voyage to Lisbon* (1755) Fielding gratefully acknowledged his 'Obligations' to
the man who had cared for him during his final illness.

cried out in a Rapture, 'Oh, Sir! Heaven hath at last heard my Prayers, and hath brought us to a House; perhaps it may be an Inn. Let me beseech you, Sir, if you have any Compassion either for me or yourself, do not despise the Goodness of Providence, but let us go directly to yon Light. Whether it be a Public-house or no, I am sure if they be Christians that dwell there, they will not refuse a little House-room to Persons in our miserable Condition.' *Jones* at length yielded to the earnest Supplications of *Partridge*, and both together made directly towards the Place whence the Light issued.

They soon arrived at the Door of this House or Cottage: For it might be called either, without much Impropriety. Here *Jones* knocked several Times without receiving any Answer from within; at which *Partridge*, whose Head was full of nothing but of Ghosts, Devils, Witches, and such like, began to tremble, crying, 'Lord have Mercy upon us, sure the People must be all dead. I can see no Light neither now, and yet I am certain I saw a Candle burning but a Moment before.—Well! I have heard of such Things.'—'What hast thou heard of,' said *Jones*. 'The People are either fast asleep, or probably as this is a lonely Place, are afraid to open their Door. He then began to vociferate pretty loudly, and at last an old Woman opening an upper Casement, asked 'who they were, and what they wanted?' *Jones* answered, 'they were Travellers who had lost their Way, and having seen a Light in the Window, had been led thither in Hopes of finding some Fire to warm themselves.' 'Whoever you are,' cries the Woman, 'you have no Business here; nor shall I open the Door to any body at this Time of Night.' *Partridge*, whom the Sound of a human Voice had recovered from his Fright, fell to the most earnest Supplications to be admitted for a few Minutes to the Fire, saying, 'he was almost dead with the Cold,' to which Fear had indeed contributed equally with the Frost. He assured her, that the Gentleman who spoke to her, was one of the greatest Squires in the Country, and made use of every Argument save one, which *Jones* afterwards effectually added, and this was the Promise of Half a Crown. A Bribe too great to be resisted by such a Person, especially as the genteel Appearance of *Jones*, which the Light of the Moon plainly discovered to her, together with his affable Behaviour, had entirely subdued those Apprehensions of Thieves which she had at first conceived. She agreed, therefore, at last to let them in, where *Partridge*, to his infinite Joy, found a good Fire ready for his Reception.

The poor Fellow, however, had no sooner warmed himself, than those Thoughts which were always uppermost in his Mind, began a little to disturb his Brain. There was no Article of his Creed in which he had a stronger Faith, than he had in Witchcraft, nor can the Reader conceive a Figure more adapted to inspire this Idea, than the old Woman who now stood before him. She answered exactly to that Picture drawn by *Otway* in his *Orphan*.[1] Indeed if this Woman had lived in the Reign of *James* the First,[2] her Appearance alone would have hanged her, almost without any Evidence.

Many Circumstances likewise conspired to confirm *Partridge* in his Opinion. Her living, as he then imagined, by herself in so lonely a Place; and in a House, the Outside of which seemed much too good for her; but its Inside was furnished in the most neat and elegant Manner. To say the Truth, *Jones* himself was not a little surprized at what he saw: For, besides the extraordinary Neatness of the Room, it was adorned with a great Number of

---

[1] In *The Orphan: or, The Unhappy Marriage* (1680) by Thomas Otway (1651–85) Chamont meets a witch who warns him of danger to his sister Mònimia (see also below p. 589):

> I spy'd a wrinkled Hagg, with Age grown double,
> Picking dry Sticks, and mumbling to her self;
> Her Eyes with scalding Rheum were gall'd and red;
> Cold Palsie shook her Head, her Hands seem'd wither'd,
> And on her crooked Shoulders had she wrapt
> The tatter'd Remnant of an old strip'd Hanging,
> Which serv'd to keep her Carkass from the Cold;
> So there was nothing of a-piece about her:
> Her lower Weeds were all o'er coursely patch'd
> With diff'rent colour'd Rags, black, red, white, yellow
> And seem'd to speak variety of Wretchedness. . . . (II. i, 1712 ed.)

The speech is quoted in *Spectator*, No. 117 (14 July 1711).

[2] James VI of Scotland (1566–1625) succeeded Elizabeth in 1603, becoming James I of England. In 1597 he had written *Demonology*, a tract against witches, and immediately upon his accession to the throne of England, Parliament passed the 'Act against Conjuration, Witchcraft, and dealing with evil and wicked Spirits' (1 James I, cap. 12), by which witches were condemned as felons without benefit of clergy. This statute was repealed by 9 George II, cap. 5 (1736). To Fielding, of course, such superstitious doctrines were characteristic of the Stuart monarchy, whose 'tyrannical Proceedings' he deplored. (See, for example, the *Charge Delivered to the Grand Jury* [1749] and *The Jacobite's Journal* [20 February 1748].) In the *Journal of a Voyage to Lisbon* (1755) he contrasted the practice of former times, when Sir Matthew Hale hanged witches, to the enlightened attitude of the Hanoverian period, as exemplified in the Act of 1736.

Nick-nacks, and Curiosities, which might have engaged the Attention of a Virtuoso.

While *Jones* was admiring these Things, and *Partridge* sat trembling with the firm Belief that he was in the House of a Witch, the old Woman said, 'I hope, Gentlemen, you will make what Haste you can; for I expect my Master presently, and I would not for double the Money he should find you here.' 'Then you have a Master,' cries *Jones*; 'indeed you will excuse me, good Woman, but I was surprized to see all those fine Things in your House.' 'Ah, Sir!' said she, 'if the twentieth Part of these Things were mine, I should think myself a rich Woman; but pray, Sir, do not stay much longer: For I look for him in every Minute.'—'Why sure he would not be angry with you,' said *Jones*, 'for doing a common Act of Charity.' 'Alack-a-day, Sir,' said she, 'he is a strange Man, not at all like other People. He keeps no Company with any Body, and seldom walks out but by Night, for he doth not care to be seen; and all the Country People are as much afraid of meeting him; for his Dress is enough to frighten those who are not used to it. They call him, *The Man of the Hill* (for there he walks by Night) and the Country People are not, I believe, more afraid of the Devil himself. He would be terribly angry if he found you here.' 'Pray, Sir,' says *Partridge*, 'don't let us offend the Gentleman, I am ready to walk, and was never warmer in my Life.—Do, pray Sir, let us go—here are Pistols over the Chimney; who knows whether they be charged or no, or what he may do with them.' 'Fear nothing, *Partridge*,' cries *Jones*, 'I will secure thee from Danger.'—'Nay, for Matter o' that, he never doth any Mischief,' said the Woman; 'but to be sure it is necessary he should keep some Arms for his own Safety; for his House hath been beset more than once, and it is not many Nights ago, that we thought, we heard Thieves about it: for my own Part, I have often wondered that he is not murdered by some Villain or other, as he walks out by himself at such Hours; but then, as I said, the People are afraid of him, and besides they think, I suppose, he hath nothing about him worth taking.' 'I should imagine, by this Collection of Rarities,' cries *Jones*, 'that your Master had been a Traveller.' 'Yes, Sir,' answered she, 'he hath been a very great one; there be few Gentlemen that know more of all Matters than he; I fancy he hath been crost in Love, or whatever it is, I know not, but I have lived with him above these thirty Years, and in all that Time he hath hardly spoke to six living People.' She then again solicited their Departure, in which she was backed by *Partridge*; but *Jones* purposely protracted the time: For his Curiosity was greatly raised to see this extraordinary Person. Tho' the old Woman, therefore, concluded every one of her Answers with desiring him to be gone, and *Partridge* proceeded so far as to pull him by the Sleeve, he still continued to invent new Questions, till the old Woman with an affrighted Countenance, declared she heard her Master's Signal; and at the same Instant more than one Voice was heard without the Door, crying, 'D—n your Blood, shew us your Money this Instant. Your Money, you Villain, or we will blow your Brains about your Ears.'

'O, good Heaven!' cries the old Woman. 'Some Villains, to be sure, have attacked my Master. O la! what shall I do? what shall I do?' 'How,' cries *Jones*, 'how—— Are these Pistols loaded?' 'O, Good Sir, there is nothing in them, indeed—O, pray don't murder us, Gentlemen' (for in reality she now had the same Opinion of those within, as she had of those without.) *Jones* made her no Answer; but snatching an old Broad-sword[1] which hung in the Room, he instantly sallied out, where he found the old Gentleman struggling with two Ruffians, and begging for Mercy. *Jones* asked no Questions, but fell so briskly to work with his Broad-sword, that the Fellows immediately quitted their Hold, and without offering to attack our Heroe, betook themselves to their Heels, and made their Escape; for he did not attempt to pursue them, being contented with having delivered the old Gentleman; and indeed he concluded he had pretty well done their Business: For both of them, as they ran off, cried out with bitter Oaths, that they were dead Men.

Jones presently ran to lift up the old Gentleman, who had been thrown down in the Scuffle, expressing at the same Time great Concern, lest he should have received any Harm from the Villains. The old Man stared a Moment at *Jones*, and then cried, —'No, Sir, no, I have very little Harm, I thank you. Lord have Mercy upon me.' 'I see, Sir,' said *Jones*, 'you are not free from Apprehensions even of those who have had the Happiness to be your Deliverers; nor can I blame any Suspicions which you may

---

[1] Fielding apparently forgets that in VII. xiv Jones had acquired his own sword, with which he later defends himself against Fitzpatrick (XVI. x).

have; but indeed, you have no real Occasion for any; here are none but your Friends present. Having mist our Way this cold Night, we took the Liberty of warming ourselves at your Fire, whence we were just departing when we heard you call for Assistance, which I must say, Providence alone seems to have sent you.'—'Providence indeed,' cries the old Gentleman, 'if it be so.'—'So it is, I assure you,' cries *Jones*, 'here is your own Sword, Sir. I have used it in your Defence, and I now return it into your own Hand.' The old Man having received the Sword, which was stained with the Blood of his Enemies, looked stedfastly at *Jones* during some Moments, and then with a Sigh, cried out, 'You will pardon me, young Gentleman, I was not always of a suspicious Temper, nor am I a Friend to Ingratitude.' 'Be thankful then,' cries *Jones*, 'to that Providence to which you owe your Deliverance; as to my Part, I have only discharged the common Duties of Humanity, and what I would have done for any Fellow Creature in your Situation.' 'Let me look at you a little longer,' cries the old Gentleman.—'You are a human Creature then?— Well, perhaps, you are. Come, pray walk into my little Hutt. You have been my Deliverer indeed.'

The old Woman was distracted between the Fears which she had of her Master, and for him; and *Partridge* was, if possible, in a greater Fright. The former of these, however, when she heard her Master speak kindly to *Jones*, and perceived what had happened, came again to herself; but *Partridge* no sooner saw the Gentleman, than the Strangeness of his Dress infused greater Terrors into that poor Fellow, than he had before felt either from the strange Description which he had heard, or from the Uproar which had happened at the Door.

To say the Truth, it was an Appearance which might have affected a more constant Mind than that of Mr. *Partridge*. This Person was of the tallest Size, with a long Beard as white as Snow. His Body was cloathed with the Skin of an Ass, made something into the Form of a Coat.[1] He wore likewise Boots on his Legs, and a Cap on his Head, both composed of the Skin of some other Animals.

---

[1] This peculiarity of dress recalls Lucian's Timon, who also appears clothed in a coat of skins. Like Timon, too, the Man of the Hill has fled from society, his misanthropy caused by the treachery and ingratitude of his friends. (A. M. Harmon, trans. *Lucian*, vol. ii [Loeb Classical Library, 1915].)

As soon as the old Gentleman came into his House, the old Woman began her Congratulations on his happy Escape from the Ruffians. 'Yes,' cried he, 'I have escaped indeed, Thanks to my Preserver.' 'O the Blessing on him,' answered she, 'he is a good Gentleman, I warrant him. I was afraid your Worship would have been angry with me for letting him in; and to be certain I should not have done it, had not I seen by the Moonlight, that he was a Gentleman, and almost frozen to Death. And to be certain it must have been some good Angel that sent him hither, and tempted me to do it.'

'I am afraid, Sir,' said the old Gentleman to *Jones*, 'that I have nothing in this House which you can either eat or drink, unless you will accept a Dram of Brandy; of which I can give you some most excellent, and which I have had by me these thirty Years.' *Jones* declined this Offer in a very civil and proper Speech, and then the other asked him 'Whither he was travelling when he mist his Way;' saying, 'I must own myself surprized to see such a Person as you appear to be journeying on Foot at this Time of Night. I suppose, Sir, you are a Gentleman of these Parts: for you do not look like one who is used to travel far without Horses.'

'Appearances,' cried *Jones*, 'are often deceitful; Men sometimes look like what they are not. I assure you, I am not of this Country, and whither I am travelling, in reality I scarce know myself.'

'Whoever you are, or whithersoever you are going,' answered the old Man, 'I have Obligations to you which I can never return.'

'I once more,' replied *Jones*, 'affirm, that you have none: For there can be no Merit in having hazarded that in your Service on which I set no Value. And nothing is so contemptible in my Eyes as Life.'

'I am sorry, young Gentleman,' answered the Stranger, 'that you have any Reason to be so unhappy at your Years.'

'Indeed I am, Sir,' answered *Jones*, 'the most unhappy of Mankind.'—'Perhaps you have had a Friend, or a Mistress,' replied the other. 'How could you,' cries *Jones*, 'mention two Words sufficient to drive me to Distraction?' 'Either of them are enough to drive any Man to Distraction,' answered the old Man. 'I enquire no farther, Sir. Perhaps my Curiosity hath led me too far already.'

'Indeed, Sir,' cries *Jones*, 'I cannot censure a Passion, which I feel at this Instant in the highest Degree. You will pardon me, when I assure you, that every Thing which I have seen or heard since I first entered this House, hath conspired to raise the greatest Curiosity in me. Something very extraordinary must have determined you to this Course of Life, and I have reason to fear your own History is not without Misfortunes.'

Here the old Gentleman again sighed, and remained silent for some Minutes; at last, looking earnestly on *Jones*, he said, 'I have read that a good Countenance is a Letter of Recommendation;[1] if so, none ever can be more strongly recommended than yourself. If I did not feel some Yearnings towards you from another Consideration, I must be the most ungrateful Monster upon Earth; and I am really concerned it is no otherwise in my Power, than by Words, to convince you of my Gratitude.'

Jones after a Moment's Hesitation, answered, 'That it was in his Power by Words to gratify him extremely. I have confest a Curiosity,' said he, 'Sir; need I say how much obliged I should be to you, if you would condescend to gratify it? Will you suffer me therefore to beg, unless any Consideration restrains you, that you would be pleased to acquaint me what Motives have induced you thus to withdraw from the Society of Mankind, and to betake yourself to a Course of Life to which it sufficiently appears you were not born?'

'I scarce think myself at Liberty to refuse you any thing, after what hath happened,' replied the old Man, 'If you desire therefore to hear the Story of an unhappy Man, I will relate it to you. Indeed you judge rightly, in thinking there is commonly something extraordinary in the Fortunes of those who fly from Society: For however it may seem a Paradox, or even a Contradiction, certain it is that great Philanthropy chiefly inclines us to avoid and detest Mankind; not on Account so much of their private and selfish Vices, but for those of a relative Kind; such as Envy, Malice, Treachery, Cruelty, with every other Species of Malevolence. These are the Vices which true Philanthropy abhors, and

---

[1] A proverbial expression attributed to Aristotle in Diogenes Laertius, *Lives of Eminent Philosophers*, v. xviii: 'Beauty he declared to be a greater recommendation than any letter of introduction' (trans. R. D. Hicks, Loeb Classical Library, 1925). Fielding's phrasing is especially close to Addison's, *Spectator*, No. 221 (13 November 1711). See also 'An Essay on the Knowledge of the Characters of Men' (1743) and *Amelia* (1751), IX. v.

which rather than see and converse with, she avoids Society itself. However, without a Compliment to you, you do not appear to me one of those whom I should shun or detest; nay, I must say, in what little hath dropt from you, there appears some Parity in our Fortunes; I hope however yours will conclude more successfully.'

Here some Compliments passed between our Heroe and his Host, and then the latter was going to begin his History, when *Partridge* interrupted him. His Apprehensions had now pretty well left him; but some Effects of his Terrors remained; he therefore reminded the Gentleman of that excellent Brandy which he had mentioned. This was presently brought, and *Partridge* swallowed a large Bumper.

The Gentleman then, without any farther Preface, began as you may read in the next Chapter.

CHAPTER XI

In which the Man of the Hill begins to relate his History.

'I WAS born in a Village of *Somersetshire*, called *Mark*, in the Year 1657; my Father was one of those whom they call Gentlemen Farmers. He had a little Estate of about 300 *l.* a Year of his own, and rented another Estate of near the same Value. He was prudent and industrious, and so good a Husbandman, that he might have led a very easy and comfortable Life, had not an arrant Vixen of a Wife soured his domestic Quiet. But tho' this Circumstance perhaps made him miserable, it did not make him poor: For he confined her almost entirely at Home, and rather chose to bear eternal Upbraidings in his own House, than to injure his Fortune by indulging her in the Extravagancies she desired abroad.

'By this *Xantippe* (so was the Wife of *Socrates* called, said *Partridge*)—By this *Xantippe* he had two Sons, of which I was the younger. He designed to give us both good Educations; but my elder Brother, who, unhappily for him, was the Favourite of my Mother, utterly neglected his Learning; insomuch that after having been five or six Years at School with little or no Improvement, my Father being told by his Master, that it would be to no

Purpose to keep him longer there, at last complied with my Mother in taking him home from the Hands of that Tyrant, as she called his Master; though indeed he gave the Lad much less Correction than his Idleness deserved, but much more, it seems, than the young Gentleman liked, who constantly complained to his Mother of his severe Treatment, and she as constantly gave him a Hearing.'

'Yes, yes,' cries *Partridge*, 'I have seen such Mothers; I have been abused myself by them, and very unjustly; such Parents deserve Correction as much as their Children.'

Jones chid the Pedagogue for this Interruption, and then the Stranger proceeded. 'My Brother now at the Age of fifteen, bid adieu to all Learning, and to every Thing else but to his Dog and Gun, with which latter he became so expert, that, though perhaps you may think it incredible, he could not only hit a standing Mark with great Certainty; but hath actually shot a Crow as it was flying in the Air. He was likewise excellent at finding a Hare sitting, and was soon reputed one of the best Sportsmen in the Country. A Reputation which both he and his Mother enjoyed as much as if he had been thought the finest Scholar.

'The Situation of my Brother made me at first think my Lot the harder, in being continued at School; but I soon changed my Opinion; for as I advanced pretty fast in Learning, my Labours became easy, and my Exercise so delightful, that Holidays were my most unpleasant Time: For my Mother, who never loved me, now apprehending that I had the greater Share of my Father's Affection, and finding, or at least thinking, that I was more taken Notice of by some Gentlemen of Learning, and particularly by the Parson of the Parish, than my Brother, she now hated my Sight, and made Home so disagreeable to me, that what is called by Schoolboys Black Monday, was to me the whitest in the whole Year.

'Having, at length, gone through the School at *Taunton*, I was thence removed to *Exeter* College in *Oxford*,[1] where I remained

---

[1] The mention of these institutions may well be meant as a compliment to Fielding's academic friends, the Uptons. James Upton (1670–1749), master at Eton during the period of Fielding's education there, became headmaster of the Taunton grammar school in 1730. His son John (1707–60) was born at Taunton and was a Fellow of Exeter College, Oxford. For a probable allusion to the latter's *Critical Observations on Shakespeare* (1746), see below, p. 524, n. 1. Although Fielding nowhere explicitly refers to the Uptons in his published writings, they had a close mutual friend in James Harris of Salisbury (see

four Years; at the End of which an Accident took me off entirely from my Studies, and hence I may truly date the Rise of all which happened to me afterwards in Life.

'There was at the same College with myself one Sir *George Gresham*, a young Fellow who was intitled to a very considerable Fortune; which he was not, by the Will of his Father, to come into full Possession of till he arrived at the Age of Twenty-five. However, the Liberality of his Guardians gave him little Cause to regret the abundant Caution of his Father: for they allowed him Five hundred Pound a Year while he remained at the University, where he kept his Horses and his Whore, and lived as wicked and as profligate a Life, as he could have done, had he been never so entirely Master of his Fortune; for besides the Five hundred a Year which he received from his Guardians, he found Means to spend a thousand more. He was above the Age of Twenty-one, and had no Difficulty in gaining what Credit he pleased.

'This young Fellow, among many other tolerable bad Qualities, had one very diabolical. He had a great Delight in destroying and ruining the Youth of inferior Fortune, by drawing them into Expences which they could not afford so well as himself; and the better, and worthier, and soberer, any young Man was, the greater Pleasure and Triumph had he in his Destruction. Thus acting the Character which is recorded of the Devil, and going about seeking whom he might devour.[1]

'It was my Misfortune to fall into an Acquaintance and Intimacy with this Gentleman. My Reputation of Diligence in my Studies made me a desirable Object of his mischievous Intention; and my own Inclination made it sufficiently easy for him to effect his Purpose; for tho' I had applied myself with much Industry to Books, in which I took great Delight, there were other Pleasures in which I was capable of taking much greater; for I was high-mettled, had a violent Flow of animal Spirits, was a little ambitious, and extremely amorous.

'I had not long contracted an Intimacy with Sir *George*, before I became a Partaker of all his Pleasures; and when I was once

Harris's *Three Treatises* [1744], p. 286, and *Upon the Rise and Progress of Criticism* [1752], pp. 20–1 n.); moreover, the friendship between the Uptons and the Fieldings may be inferred from Ursula Fielding's letter of 25 October 1748 (see J. P. de Castro, *N & Q*, clxxviii [9 March 1940], 164–7).

[1] 1 Peter 5: 8: 'Be sober, be vigilant; because your adversary the devil, as a roaring lion, walketh about, seeking whom he may devour'.

entered on that Scene, neither my Inclination, nor my Spirit, would suffer me to play an Under-Part. I was second to none of the Company in any Acts of Debauchery; nay, I soon distinguished myself so notably in all Riots and Disorders, that my Name generally stood first in the Roll of Delinquents, and instead of being lamented as the unfortunate Pupil of Sir *George*, I was now accused as the Person who had misled and debauched that hopeful young Gentleman; for tho' he was the Ring-leader and Promoter of all the Mischief, he was never so considered. I fell at last under the Censure of the Vice-Chancellor, and very narrowly escaped Expulsion.

'You will easily believe, Sir, that such a Life as I am now describing must be incompatible with my further Progress in Learning; and that in Proportion as I addicted myself more and more to loose Pleasure, I must grow more and more remiss in Application to my Studies. This was truly the Consequence; but this was not all. My Expences now greatly exceeded not only my former Income, but those Additions which I extorted from my poor generous Father, on Pretences of Sums being necessary for preparing for my approaching Degree of Batchelor of Arts. These Demands, however, grew at last so frequent and exorbitant, that my Father, by slow Degrees, opened his Ears to the Accounts which he received from many Quarters of my present Behaviour, and which my Mother failed not to eccho very faithfully and loudly; adding, "Ay, this is the fine Gentleman, the Scholar who doth so much Honour to his Family, and is to be the Making of it. I thought what all this Learning would come to. He is to be the Ruin of us all, I find, after his elder Brother hath been denied Necessaries for his Sake, to perfect his Education forsooth, for which he was to pay us such Interest; I thought what the Interest would come to;" with much more of the same Kind; but I have, I believe, satisfied you with this Taste.

'My Father, therefore, began now to return Remonstrances, instead of Money, to my Demands, which brought my Affairs, perhaps a little sooner to a Crisis; but had he remitted me his whole Income, you will imagine it could have sufficed a very short Time to support one who kept Pace with the Expences of Sir *George Gresham*.

'It is more than possible, that the Distress I was now in for

Money, and the Impracticability of going on in this Manner, might have restored me at once to my Senses, and to my Studies, had I opened my Eyes, before I became involved in Debts, from which I saw no Hopes of ever extricating myself. This was indeed the great Art of Sir *George*, and by which he accomplished the Ruin of many, whom he afterwards laughed at as Fools and Coxcombs, for vying, as he called it, with a Man of his Fortune. To bring this about, he would now and then advance a little Money himself, in order to support the Credit of the unfortunate Youth with other People; till, by Means of that very Credit, he was irretrievably undone.

'My Mind being, by these Means, grown as desperate as my Fortune, there was scarce a Wickedness which I did not meditate, in order for my Relief. Self-murder itself became the Subject of my serious Deliberation; and I had certainly resolved on it, had not a more shameful, tho' perhaps less sinful, Thought, expelled it from my Head.' Here he hesitated a Moment, and then cried out, 'I protest, so many Years have not washed away the Shame of this Act, and I shall blush while I relate it.' *Jones* desired him to pass over any thing that might give him Pain in the Relation; but *Partridge* eagerly cried out, 'O pray, Sir, let us hear this, I had rather hear this than all the rest; as I hope to be saved, I will never mention a Word of it.' *Jones* was going to rebuke him, but the Stranger prevented it by proceeding thus. 'I had a Chum, a very prudent, frugal young Lad, who, tho' he had no very large Allowance, had by his Parsimony heaped up upwards of forty Guineas, which I knew he kept in his Escritore. I took therefore an Opportunity of purloining his Key from his Breeches Pocket while he was asleep, and thus made myself Master of all his Riches. After which I again conveyed his Key into his Pocket, and counterfeiting Sleep, tho' I never once closed my Eyes, lay in Bed till after he arose and went to Prayers, an Exercise to which I had long been unaccustomed.

'Timorous Thieves, by extreme Caution, often subject themselves to Discoveries, which those of a bolder Kind escape. Thus it happened to me; for had I boldly broke open his Escritore, I had, perhaps, escaped even his Suspicion; but as it was plain that the Person who robbed him had possessed himself of his Key, he had no Doubt, when he first missed his Money, but that his Chum was certainly the Thief. Now as he was of a fearful Disposition, and much my Inferior in Strength, and, I believe, in Courage, he did not dare to confront me with my Guilt, for fear of worse bodily Consequences which might happen to him. He repaired therefore immediately to the Vice-Chancellor, and, upon swearing to the Robbery, and to the Circumstances of it, very easily obtained a Warrant against one who had now so bad a Character through the whole University.

'Luckily for me I lay out of the College the next Evening; for that Day I attended a young Lady in a Chaise to *Whitney*, where we staid all Night; and in our Return the next Morning to *Oxford*, I met one of my Cronies, who acquainted me with sufficient News concerning myself to make me turn my Horse another Way.'

'Pray Sir, did he mention any thing of the Warrant?' said *Partridge*. But *Jones* begged the Gentleman to proceed without regarding any impertinent Questions; which he did as follows.

'Having now abandoned all Thoughts of returning to *Oxford*, the next Thing which offered itself was a Journey to *London*. I imparted this Intention to my female Companion, who at first remonstrated against it, but upon producing my Wealth, she immediately consented. We then struck across the Country into the great *Cirencester* Road,[1] and made such Haste, that we spent the next Evening (save one) in *London*.

'When you consider the Place where I now was, and the Company with whom I was, you will, I fancy, conceive that a very short Time brought me to an End of that Sum of which I had so iniquitously possessed myself.

'I was now reduced to a much higher Degree of Distress than before; the Necessaries of Life began to be numbred among my Wants; and what made my Case still the more grievous, was, that my Paramour, of whom I was now grown immoderately fond, shared the same Distresses with myself. To see a Woman you love in Distress; to be unable to relieve her, and at the same Time to reflect that you have brought her into this Situation, is, perhaps, a Curse of which no Imagination can represent the Horrors to those who have not felt it.' 'I believe it from my Soul,' cries *Jones*, 'and I pity you from the Bottom of my Heart.' He then took two or three disorderly Turns about the Room, and at last begged

---

[1] This road ran between Gloucester and London, passing through Cirencester, Abingdon, Dorchester, Henley, Maidenhead, and Brentford. (See John Ogilby, *Britannia* [1675].)

Pardon, and flung himself into his Chair, crying, 'I thank Heaven I have escaped that.'

'This Circumstance,' continued the Gentleman, 'so severely aggravated the Horrors of my present Situation, that they became absolutely intolerable. I could with less Pain endure the raging of my own natural unsatisfied Appetites, even Hunger or Thirst, than I could submit to leave ungratified the most whimsical Desires of a Woman, on whom I so extravagantly doated, that tho' I knew she had been the Mistress of half my Acquaintance, I firmly intended to marry her. But the good Creature was unwilling to consent to an Action which the World might think so much to my Disadvantage. And as, possibly, she compassionated the daily Anxieties which she must have perceived me suffer on her Account, she resolved to put an End to my Distress. She soon, indeed, found Means to relieve me from my troublesome and perplexed Situation: For while I was distracted with various Inventions to supply her with Pleasures, she very kindly— betrayed me to one of her former Lovers at *Oxford*, by whose Care and Diligence I was immediately apprehended and committed to Goal.

'Here I first began seriously to reflect on the Miscarriages of my former Life; on the Errors I had been guilty of; on the Misfortunes which I had brought on myself; and on the Grief which I must have occasioned to one of the best of Fathers. When I added to all these the Perfidy of my Mistress, such was the Horror of my Mind, that Life, instead of being longer desirable, grew the Object of my Abhorrence, and I could have gladly embraced Death, as my dearest Friend, if it had offered itself to my Choice unattended by Shame.

'The Time of the Assizes soon came, and I was removed by *Habeas Corpus* to *Oxford*, where I expected certain Conviction and Condemnation; but, to my great Surprize, none appeared against me, and I was, at the End of the Sessions, discharged for Want of Prosecution. In short, my Chum had left *Oxford*, and whether from Indolence, or from what other Motive, I am ignorant, had declined concerning himself any farther in the Affair.'

'Perhaps,' cries *Partridge*, 'he did not care to have your Blood upon his Hands, and he was in the right on't. If any Person was to be hanged upon my Evidence, I should never be able to lie alone afterwards, for Fear of seeing his Ghost.'

'I shall shortly doubt, *Partridge*,' says *Jones*, 'whether thou art more brave or wise.' 'You may laugh at me, Sir, if you please,' answered *Partridge*, 'but if you will hear a very short Story which I can tell, and which is most certainly true, perhaps you may change your Opinion. In the Parish where I was born——' Here *Jones* would have silenced him, but the Stranger interceded that he might be permitted to tell his Story, and in the mean time promised to recollect the Remainder of his own.

Partridge then proceeded thus. 'In the Parish where I was born, there lived a Farmer whose Name was *Bridle*, and he had a Son named *Francis*, a good hopeful young Fellow; I was at the Grammar School with him, where I remember he was got into *Ovid's Epistles*, and he could construe you three Lines together sometimes without looking into a Dictionary. Besides all this, he was a very good Lad, never missed Church o' Sundays, and was reckoned one of the best Psalm-Singers in the whole Parish. He would indeed now and then take a Cup too much, and that was the only Fault he had.'—'Well, but come to the Ghost,' cries *Jones*. 'Never fear, Sir, I shall come to him soon enough,' answered *Partridge*. 'You must know then, that Farmer *Bridle* lost a Mare, a sorrel one to the best of my Remembrance, and so it fell out, that this young *Francis* shortly afterward being at a Fair at *Hindon*, and as I think it was on—I can't remember the Day; and being as he was, what should he happen to meet, but a Man upon his Father's Mare. *Frank* called out presently, Stop Thief; and it being in the Middle of the Fair, it was impossible, you know, for the Man to make his Escape. So they apprehended him, and carried him before the Justice, I remember it was Justice *Willoughby* of *Noyle*,[1] a very worthy good Gentleman, and he committed him to Prison, and bound *Frank* in a Recognizance,[2] I think they call it, a hard Word compounded of *re* and

---

[1] Richard Willoughby (*c.* 1703–62) of West Knoyle, Wilts.—a village about three miles west of Hindon. His family, many of whom were lawyers, had long resided in West Knoyle, but Willoughby sold the estate soon after he inherited it in 1731. At that time he was living at Southampton Buildings, London (see *The Gentleman's Magazine*, i [January 1731], 32) —a circumstance which, four years earlier, seems to have involved him as a principal witness in the Darby murder case (see above, p. 402, n. 3). Willoughby's name appears among the subscribers to Fielding's *Miscellanies* (1743). For the tradition (which is certainly correct) that Richard Willoughby is the person Fielding meant to compliment in the present passage, see Sir Richard Colt Hoare, *The History of Modern Wiltshire. Hundred of Mere* (1822), p. 41.

[2] '*A Recognizance* is a Bond of Record acknowledged to the King, upon Condition to

cognosco, but it differs in its Meaning from the Use of the Simple, as many other Compounds do. Well, at last, down came my Lord Justice *Page*[1] to hold the Assizes, and so the Fellow was had up, and *Frank* was had up for a Witness. To be sure I shall never forget the Face of the Judge, when he began to ask him what he had to say against the Prisoner. He made poor *Frank* tremble and shake in his Shoes. "Well, you Fellow," says my Lord, "what have you to say? Don't stand humming and hawing, but speak out;" but however he soon turned altogether as civil to *Frank*, and began to thunder at the Fellow; and when he asked him, if he had any Thing to say for himself, the Fellow said he had found the Horse. "Ay!" answered the Judge, "thou art a lucky Fellow; I have travelled the Circuit these forty Years, and never found a Horse in my Life; but I'll tell thee what, Friend, thou wast more lucky than thou didst know of: For thou didst not only find a Horse; but a Halter too, I promise thee." To be sure I shall never forget the Word. Upon which every Body fell a laughing, as how could they help it. Nay, and twenty other Jests he made which I can't remember now. There was something about his Skill in Horse-Flesh, which made all the Folks laugh. To be certain the Judge must have been a very brave Man, as well as a Man of much Learning. It is indeed charming Sport to hear Trials upon Life and Death. One Thing I own I thought a little hard, that the Prisoner's Counsel was not suffered to speak for him, though he desired only to be heard one very short Word; but my Lord would not hearken to him, though he suffered a Counsellor to talk against him for above half an Hour. I thought it hard, I own, that there should be so many of them; my Lord,

pay a certain Sum of Money if the Condition is not performed; as to appear at the Assises or Quarter-Sessions, to be of the Good Behaviour, &c.' (Wood's *Institutes*, 7th ed. [1745], p. 84). As a commissioner of the peace, Willoughby's function was only to commit the prisoner to stand trial and to bind over the witness. The actual trial would have taken place at the Salisbury Assizes. (See J. P. de Castro, *N & Q*, 11th Ser., x [26 September 1914], 253.)

[1] Sir Francis Page (1661 ?–1741), known as 'the hanging judge', was notorious for his coarseness and brutality while on the bench. Pope satirized him in several poems: e.g. *Imitations of Horace, Satires II. i* (1733), 82, and *The Dunciad*, iv (1742), 30. The last time Page presided over the Western Circuit during the Summer Assizes was in 1739. Bishop Douglas of Salisbury was once present when an innocent man was brought before Page to stand trial for horsestealing. As soon as he saw the prisoner, the judge exclaimed: 'A very ill-looking Fellow; I have no doubt of his guilt'. Happily, however, the trial ended in an acquittal. (See John Butt, ed. Pope's *Imitations of Horace*, Twickenham Edition, 2nd ed., iv [1953], 376.)

and the Court, and the Jury, and the Counsellors, and the
Witnesses all upon one poor Man, and he too in Chains. Well,
the Fellow was hanged, as to be sure it could be no otherwise, and
poor *Frank* could never be easy about it. He never was in the
dark alone, but he fancied he saw the Fellow's Spirit.' 'Well, and
is this thy Story?' cries *Jones*. 'No, no,' answer'd *Partridge*, 'O
Lord have Mercy upon me,—I am just now coming to the
Matter; for one Night, coming from the Alehouse in a long
narrow dark Lane, there he ran directly up against him, and the
Spirit was all in white and fell upon *Frank*, and *Frank* who is a
sturdy Lad, fell upon the Spirit again, and there they had a
Tussel together, and poor *Frank* was dreadfully beat; indeed he
made a shift at last to crawl Home, but what with the beating, and
what with the Fright, he lay ill above a Fortnight; and all this is
most certainly true, and the whole Parish will bear Witness to it.'

The Stranger smiled at this Story, and *Jones* burst into a loud
Fit of Laughter, upon which *Partridge* cried, 'Ay, you may laugh,
Sir, and so did some others, particularly a Squire, who is thought
to be no better than an Atheist; who forsooth, because there was
a Calf with a white Face found dead in the same Lane the next
Morning, would fain have it, that the Battle was between *Frank*
and that, as if a Calf would set upon a Man. Besides, *Frank* told
me he knew it to be a Spirit, and could swear to him in any Court
in Christendom, and he had not drank above a Quart or two, or
such a Matter of Liquor at the time. Lud have Mercy upon us,
and keep us all from dipping our Hands in Blood, I say.'

'Well, Sir,' said *Jones* to the Stranger, 'Mr. *Partridge* hath
finished his Story, and I hope will give you no future Interruption, if you will be so kind to proceed.' He then resumed his
Narration; but as he hath taken Breath for a while, we think
proper to give it to our Reader, and shall therefore put an End to
this Chapter.

CHAPTER XII

In which the Man of the Hill continues his History.

'I HAD now regained my Liberty,' said the Stranger,'but I had
lost my Reputation; for there is a wide Difference between
the Case of a Man who is barely acquitted of a Crime in a Court of

Justice, and of him who is acquitted in his own Heart, and in the Opinion of the People. I was conscious of my Guilt, and ashamed to look any one in the Face, so resolved to leave *Oxford* the next Morning, before the Daylight discovered me to the Eyes of any Beholders.

'When I had got clear of the City, it first entered into my Head to return Home to my Father, and endeavour to obtain his Forgiveness; but as I had no Reason to doubt his Knowledge of all which had past, and as I was well assured of his great Aversion to all Acts of Dishonesty, I could entertain no Hopes of being received by him, especially since I was too certain of all the good Offices in the Power of my Mother: Nay, had my Father's Pardon been as sure, as I conceived his Resentment to be, I yet question whether I could have had the Assurance to behold him, or whether I could, upon any Terms, have submitted to live and converse with those, who, I was convinced, knew me to have been guilty of so base an Action.

'I hastened therefore back to *London*, the best Retirement of either Grief or Shame, unless for Persons of a very public Character; for here you have the Advantage of Solitude without its Disadvantage, since you may be alone and in Company at the same Time; and while you walk or sit unobserved, Noise, Hurry, and a constant Succession of Objects, entertain the Mind, and prevent the Spirits from preying on themselves, or rather on Grief or Shame, which are the most unwholesome Diet in the World; and on which (though there are many who never taste either but in public) there are some who can feed very plentifully, and very fatally when alone.

'But as there is scarce any human Good without its concomitant Evil, so there are People who find an Inconvenience in this unobserving Temper of Mankind; I mean Persons who have no Money; for as you are not put out of Countenance, so neither are you cloathed or fed by those who do not know you. And a Man may be as easily starved in *Leadenhall* Market[1] as in the Desarts of *Arabia*.

'It was at present my Fortune to be destitute of that great Evil, as it is apprehended to be by several Writers, who I suppose were overburthened with it, namely, Money.' 'With Submission,

---

[1] Located in the City of London, Leadenhall was one of the largest provision markets in Europe.

Sir,' said *Partridge*, 'I do not remember any Writers who have called it *Malorum*; but *Irritamenta Malorum. Effodiuntur opes irritamenta Malorum.*[1] 'Well, Sir,' continued the Stranger, 'whether it be an Evil, or only the Cause of Evil, I was entirely void of it, and at the same Time of Friends, and as I thought of Acquaintance; when one Evening as I was passing through the *Inner Temple*, very hungry and very miserable, I heard a Voice on a sudden haling me with great Familiarity by my Christian Name; and upon my turning about, I presently recollected the Person who so saluted me, to have been my Fellow Collegiate, one who had left the University above a Year, and long before any of my Misfortunes had befallen me. This Gentleman, whose Name was *Watson*, shook me heartily by the Hand, and expressing great Joy at meeting me, proposed our immediately drinking a Bottle together. I first declined the Proposal, and pretended Business; but as he was very earnest and pressing, Hunger at last overcame my Pride, and I fairly confessed to him I had no Money in my Pocket; yet not without framing a Lie for an Excuse, and imputing it to my having changed my Breeches that Morning. Mr. *Watson* answered, "I thought, *Jack*, you and I had been too old Acquaintance for you to mention such a Matter." He then took me by the Arm and was pulling me along; but I gave him very little Trouble, for my own Inclinations pulled me much stronger than he could do.

'We then went into the Friars,[2] which you know is the Scene of all Mirth and Jollity. Here when we arrived at the Tavern,[3] Mr. *Watson* applied himself to the Drawer only, without taking the least Notice of the Cook; for he had no Suspicion but that I

---

[1] Ovid, *Metamorphoses*, i. 140: 'riches, the incitement to crime, are sought by digging'.

[2] The familiar name for the Blackfriars, the precinct situated between Ludgate Hill and the Thames, a few minutes' walk eastward from the Inner Temple. The district had been formerly occupied by the Dominicans or Black Friars, but after the dissolution of the monasteries by Henry VIII it became a retreat for disreputable persons of all kinds—thieves, sharpers, fences, prostitutes.

[3] The story of the Man of the Hill's experiences among the gamblers and confidence men of London should be viewed in the context of an extensive contemporary literature exposing the follies and vices of the town, many of these fugitive works being designed as cautionary guides for the naïve visitor from the country. Ned Ward's *London Spy* (1698-1709) is perhaps the best-known example, but with the present chapter compare, in particular, *The Tricks of the Town Laid Open; or, a Companion for Country Gentlemen* (1747), esp. letter xi, 'In which the Humours of the *Groom Porter's*, and the Tricks and Cheats of *Ordinaries*, and other *Gaming-houses* are briefly exposed'.

had dined long since. However, as the Case was really otherwise, I forged another Falshood, and told my Companion, I had been at the further End of the City on Business of Consequence, and had snapt up a Mutton Chop in Haste, so that I was again hungry, and wished he would add a Beef Steak to his Bottle.' 'Some People,' cries *Partridge*, 'ought to have good Memories, or did you find just Money enough in your Breeches to pay for the Mutton Chop?' 'Your Observation is right,' answered the Stranger, 'and I believe such Blunders are inseparable from all dealing in Untruth.—But to proceed—I began now to feel myself extremely happy. The Meat and Wine soon revived my Spirits to a high Pitch, and I enjoyed much Pleasure in the Conversation of my old Acquaintance, the rather, as I thought him entirely ignorant of what had happened at the University since his leaving it.

'But he did not suffer me to remain long in this agreeable Delusion; for taking a Bumper in one Hand, and holding me by the other, "Here, my Boy," cries he, "here's wishing you Joy of your being so honourably acquitted of that Affair laid to your Charge." I was Thunderstruck with Confusion at those Words, which *Watson* observing, proceeded thus—"Nay, never be ashamed, Man; thou hast been acquitted, and no one now dares call thee guilty; but prithee do tell me, who am thy Friend, I hope thou didst really rob him; for rat me if it was not a meritorious Action to strip such a sneaking pitiful Rascal, and instead of the Two hundred Guineas, I wish you had taken as many thousand. Come, come, my Boy, don't be shy of confessing to me, you are not now brought before one of the Pimps. D——n me, if I don't honour you for it; for, as I hope for Salvation, I would have made no manner of Scruple of doing the same Thing."

'This Declaration a little relieved my Abashment, and as Wine had now somewhat opened my Heart, I very freely acknowledged the Robbery, but acquainted him that he had been misinformed as to the Sum taken, which was little more than a fifth Part of what he had mentioned.

' "I am sorry for it with all my Heart," quoth he, "and I wish thee better Success another Time. Tho' if you will take my Advice, you shall have no Occasion to run any such Risque. Here," said he, (taking some Dice out of his Pocket) "here's the Stuff. Here are the Implements; here are the little

Doctors[1] which cure the Distempers of the Purse. Follow but my Counsel, and I will shew you a Way to empty the Pockets of a *Queer Cull*,[2] without any Danger of the *Nubbing Cheat*." '[3]

'*Nubbing Cheat*,' cries *Partridge*, 'Pray, Sir, what is that?'

'Why that, Sir,' says the Stranger, 'is a Cant Phrase for the Gallows; for as Gamesters differ little from Highwaymen in their Morals, so do they very much resemble them in their Language.

'We had now each drank our Bottle, when Mr. *Watson* said, the Board was sitting, and that he must attend, earnestly pressing me, at the same Time, to go with him and try my Fortune. I answered, He knew that was at present out of my Power, as I had informed him of the Emptiness of my Pocket. To say the Truth, I doubted not, from his many strong Expressions of Friendship, but that he would offer to lend me a small Sum for that Purpose; but he answered, "Never mind that, Man, e'en boldly run a Levant;[4] (*Partridge* was going to enquire the Meaning of that Word; but *Jones* stopped his Mouth) but be circumspect as to the Man. I will tip you the proper Person, which may be necessary, as you do not know the Town, nor can distinguish a Rum Cull[5] from a Queer one."

'The Bill was now brought, when *Watson* paid his Share, and was departing. I reminded him, not without blushing, of my having no Money. He answered, "That signifies nothing, score it behind the Door, or make a bold Brush,[6] and take no Notice.— Or—stay," says he, "I will go down Stairs first, and then do you take up my Money, and score the whole Reckoning at the Bar, and I will wait for you at the Corner." I expressed some Dislike at this, and hinted my Expectations that he would have deposited

---

[1] Watson's low-life jargon, like that of Jonathan Wild (I. v, xiii), may be illustrated from *A New Canting Dictionary: Comprehending All the Terms, Antient and Modern, Used in the Several Tribes of Gypsies, Beggars, Shoplifters, Highwaymen, Foot-Pads, and all other Clans of Cheats and Villains* (1725). An 'Implement' is a 'Tool' or 'Property' which may be 'easily engag'd in any (tho' difficult and dangerous) Enterprize'. A 'Doctor' is 'a false Die that will run but two or three Chances'.

[2] 'Cull' is the cant word for 'a Man, either Honest, or otherwise'. A 'queer cull', however, is 'a Fop, or Fool, a Codshead' (*New Canting Dictionary*).

[3] As Fielding explains in a footnote to *Jonathan Wild* (IV. ii), these are cant terms for 'hanging' and the 'gallows'.

[4] To make a bet with the intention of absconding if it is lost. (See *OED*, which cites this passage in *Tom Jones*.)

[5] According to the *New Canting Dictionary*, 'a rich Fool, that can be easily *bit*, or cheated by any body'.

[6] To 'brush' is 'to flee, or run away' (*New Canting Dictionary*).

the whole; but he swore he had not another Sixpence in his Pocket.

'He then went down, and I was prevailed on to take up the Money and follow him, which I did close enough to hear him tell the Drawer the Reckoning was upon the Table. The Drawer passed by me up Stairs; but I made such Haste into the Street, that I heard nothing of his Disappointment, nor did I mention a Syllable at the Bar, according to my Instructions.

'We now went directly to the Gaming-Table, where Mr. *Watson*, to my Surprize, pulled out a large Sum of Money, and placed it before him, as did many others; all of them, no doubt, considering their own Heaps as so many decoy Birds, which were to entice and draw over the Heaps of their Neighbours.

'Here it would be tedious to relate all the Freaks which Fortune, or rather the Dice, played in this her Temple. Mountains of Gold were in a few Moments reduced to nothing at one Part of the Table, and rose as suddenly in another. The Rich grew in a Moment poor, and the Poor as suddenly became rich; so that it seemed a Philosopher could no where have so well instructed his Pupils in the Contempt of Riches, at least he could no where have better inculcated the Incertainty of their Duration.

'For my own Part, after having considerably improved my small Estate, I at last entirely demolished it. Mr. *Watson* too, after much Variety of Luck, rose from the Table in some Heat, and declared he had lost a cool hundred, and would play no longer. Then coming up to me, he asked me to return with him to the Tavern; but I positively refused, saying, I would not bring myself a second Time into such a Dilemma, and especially as he had lost all his Money, and was now in my own Condition.' "Pooh," says he, "I have just borrowed a couple of Guineas of a Friend; and one of them is at your Service." He immediately put one of them into my Hand, and I no longer resisted his Inclination.

'I was at first a little shocked at returning to the same House whence we had departed in so unhandsome a Manner; but when the Drawer, with very civil Address, told us, "he believed we had forgot to pay our Reckoning," I became perfectly easy, and very readily gave him a Guinea, bid him pay himself, and acquiesced in the unjust Charge which had been laid on my Memory.

'Mr. *Watson* now bespoke the most extravagant Supper he could well think of, and tho' he had contented himself with

simple Claret before, nothing now but the most precious Burgundy would serve his Purpose.

'Our Company was soon encreased by the Addition of several
Gentlemen from the Gaming-Table; most of whom, as I afterwards found, came not to the Tavern to drink, but in the Way of
Business: For the true Gamesters pretended to be ill, and refused
their Glass, while they plied heartily two young Fellows, who were
to be afterwards pillaged, as indeed they were without Mercy.
Of this Plunder I had the good Fortune to be a Sharer, tho' I was
not yet let into the Secret.

'There was one remarkable Accident attended this Tavern
Play; for the Money, by Degrees, totally disappeared, so that
tho' at the Beginning the Table was half covered with Gold, yet
before the Play ended, which it did not till the next Day, being
Sunday, at Noon, there was scarce a single Guinea to be seen on
the Table; and this was the stranger, as every Person present
except myself declared he had lost; and what was become of the
Money, unless the Devil himself carried it away, is difficult to
determine.'

'Most certainly he did,' says *Partridge*, 'for evil Spirits can
carry away any thing without being seen, tho' there were never so
many Folk in the Room; and I should not have been surprized if
he had carried away all the Company of a Set of wicked Wretches,
who were at play in Sermon-time. And I could tell you a true
Story, if I would, where the Devil took a Man out of Bed from
another Man's Wife, and carried him away through the Key-hole
of the Door. I've seen the very House where it was done, and no
Body hath lived in it these thirty Years.'

Tho' *Jones* was a little offended by the Impertinence of
Partridge, he could not however avoid smiling at his Simplicity.
The Stranger did the same, and then proceeded with his Story,
as will be seen in the next Chapter.

CHAPTER XIII

In which the foregoing Story is farther continued.

'MY Fellow Collegiate had now entered me in a new Scene of
Life. I soon became acquainted with the whole Fraternity
of Sharpers, and was let into their Secrets. I mean into the Know-

ledge of those gross Cheats which are proper to impose upon the raw and unexperienced: For there are some Tricks of a finer Kind, which are known only to a few of the Gang, who are at the Head of their Profession; a Degree of Honour beyond my Expectation; for Drink, to which I was immoderately addicted, and the natural Warmth of my Passions, prevented me from arriving at any great Success in an Art, which requires as much Coolness as the most austere School of Philosophy.

'Mr. _Watson_, with whom I now lived in the closest Amity, had unluckily the former Failing to a very great Excess; so that instead of making a Fortune by his Profession, as some others did, he was alternately rich and poor, and was often obliged to surrender to his cooler Friends over a Bottle which they never tasted, that Plunder that he had taken from Culls at the public Table.

'However, we both made a Shift to pick up an uncomfortable Livelihood, and for two Years I continued of the Calling, during which Time I tasted all the Varieties of Fortune; sometimes flourishing in Affluence, and at others being obliged to struggle with almost incredible Difficulties. To-day wallowing in Luxury, and To-morrow reduced to the coarsest and most homely Fare. My fine Clothes being often on my Back in the Evening, and at the Pawnshop the next Morning.

'One Night as I was returning Pennyless from the Gaming-table, I observed a very great Disturbance, and a large Mob gathered together in the Street. As I was in no Danger from Pick-pockets, I ventured into the Croud, where, upon Enquiry, I found that a Man had been robbed and very ill used by some Ruffians. The wounded Man appeared very bloody, and seemed scarce able to support himself on his Legs. As I had not therefore been deprived of my Humanity by my present Life and Conversation, tho' they had left me very little of either Honesty or Shame, I immediately offered my Assistance to the unhappy Person, who thankfully accepted it, and putting himself under my Conduct, begged me to convey him to some Tavern, where he might send for a Surgeon, being, as he said, faint with Loss of Blood. He seemed indeed highly pleased at finding one who appeared in the Dress of a Gentleman: For as to all the rest of the Company present, their Outside was such that he could not wisely place any Confidence in them.

'I took the poor Man by the Arm, and led him to the Tavern where we kept our Rendezvous, as it happened to be the nearest at Hand. A Surgeon happening luckily to be in the House, immediately attended, and applied himself to dressing his Wounds, which I had the Pleasure to hear were not likely to be mortal.

'The Surgeon having very expeditiously and dextrously finished his Business, began to enquire in what Part of the Town the wounded Man lodged; who answered, "That he was come to Town that very Morning; that his Horse was at an Inn in *Piccadilly*, and that he had no other Lodging, and very little or no Acquaintance in Town."

'This Surgeon, whose Name I have forgot, tho' I remember it began with an *R*,[1] had the first Character in his Profession, and was Serjeant-Surgeon to the King. He had moreover many good Qualities, and was a very generous, good-natured Man, and ready to do any Service to his Fellow-Creatures. He offered his Patient the Use of his Chariot to carry him to his Inn, and at the same Time whispered in his Ear, "That if he wanted any Money, he would furnish him."

'The poor Man was not now capable of returning Thanks for this generous Offer: For having had his Eyes for some Time stedfastly on me, he threw himself back in his Chair, crying, O, my Son! my Son! and then fainted away.

'Many of the People present imagined this Accident had happened through his Loss of Blood; but I, who at the same Time began to recollect the Features of my Father, was now confirmed in my Suspicion, and satisfied that it was he himself who

---

[1] Though an anachronism, Fielding here certainly means to compliment his friend John Ranby (1703–73), who had been appointed Sergeant-Surgeon to George II in 1740 and Principal Sergeant-Surgeon in 1742. In 1745, the year in which he became involved in the medical controversy concerning the cause of Walpole's death (see above, p. 112, n. 2), Ranby was named governor of the newly created Company of Surgeons (see above, p. 424, n. 2). In *Amelia* (1751; v. vi) it is doubtless Ranby who is complimented as 'the most eminent Surgeon in the Kingdom, or perhaps in the World'. He advised Fielding during his final illness (see the *Journal of a Voyage to Lisbon*, 1755) and after the novelist's death in 1754, succeeded him as tenant of the farm at Fordhook, Ealing (see J. P. de Castro, *N & Q*, 12th Ser., ii [1 July 1916], 11). Later in *Tom Jones* (p. 911) Ranby attends Fitzpatrick after the latter has been wounded in his duel with Jones.

It has been proposed that the present passage alludes to Etienne Ronjat, who became Sergeant-Surgeon to William III in the 1690s. (See B. L. Greenberg, *N & Q*, N.S., ix [December 1962], 456–7.) But there is no evidence that Fielding knew of Ronjat, and, since this episode in the Man of the Hill's narrative is set some four years before Monmouth's Rebellion in 1685, this identification would in no way rectify the anachronism.

appeared before me. I presently ran to him, raised him in my Arms, and kissed his cold Lips with the utmost Eagerness. Here I must draw a Curtain over a Scene which I cannot describe: For though I did not lose my Being, as my Father for a while did, my Senses were however so overpowered with Affright and Surprize, that I am a Stranger to what past during some Minutes, and indeed till my Father had again recovered from his Swoon, and I found myself in his Arms, both tenderly embracing each other, while the Tears trickled a-pace down the Cheeks of each of us.

'Most of those present seemed affected by this Scene, which we, who might be considered as the Actors in it, were desirous of removing from the Eyes of all Spectators, as fast as we could; my Father therefore accepted the kind Offer of the Surgeon's Chariot, and I attended him in it to his Inn.

'When we were alone together, he gently upbraided me with having neglected to write to him during so long a Time, but entirely omitted the Mention of that Crime which had occasioned it. He then informed me of my Mother's Death, and insisted on my returning Home with him, saying, "That he had long suffered the greatest Anxiety on my Account; that he knew not whether he had most feared my Death, or wished it; since he had so many more dreadful Apprehensions for me. At last," he said, "a neighbouring Gentleman, who had just recovered a Son from the same Place, informed him where I was, and that to reclaim me from this Course of Life, was the sole Cause of his Journey to *London*." He thanked Heaven he had succeeded so far as to find me out by Means of an Accident which had like to have proved fatal to him; and had the Pleasure to think he partly owed his Preservation to my Humanity, with which he profest himself to be more delighted than he should have been with my filial Piety, if I had known that the Object of all my Care was my own Father.

'Vice had not so depraved my Heart, as to excite in it an Insensibility of so much paternal Affection, tho' so unworthily bestowed. I presently promised to obey his Commands in my return Home with him as soon as he was able to travel, which indeed he was in a very few Days, by the Assistance of that excellent Surgeon who had undertaken his Cure.

'The Day preceding my Father's Journey (before which Time I scarce ever left him) I went to take my Leave of some of my most intimate Acquaintance, particularly of Mr. *Watson*, who dissuaded me from burying myself, as he called it, out of a simple Compliance with the fond Desires of a foolish old Fellow. Such Solicitations, however, had no Effect, and I once more saw my own Home. My Father now greatly solicited me to think of Marriage; but my Inclinations were utterly averse to any such Thoughts. I had tasted of Love already, and perhaps you know the extravagant Excesses of that most tender and most violent Passion.' Here the old Gentleman paused, and looked earnestly at *Jones*; whose Countenance within a Minute's Space displayed the Extremities of both red and white. Upon which the old Man, without making any Observations, renewed his Narrative.

'Being now provided with all the Necessaries of Life, I betook myself once again to Study, and that with a more inordinate Application that I had ever done formerly. The Books which now employed my Time solely, were those, as well ancient as modern, which treat of true Philosophy, a Word, which is by many thought to be the Subject only of Farce and Ridicule. I now read over the Works of *Aristotle* and *Plato*, with the rest of those inestimable Treasures which ancient *Greece* had bequeathed to the World.

'These Authors, though they instructed me in no Science by which Men may promise to themselves to acquire the least Riches, or worldly Power, taught me, however, the Art of despising the highest Acquisitions of both. They elevate the Mind, and steel and harden it against the capricious Invasions of Fortune. They not only instruct in the Knowledge of Wisdom, but confirm Men in her Habits, and demonstrate plainly, that this must be our Guide, if we propose ever to arrive at the greatest worldly Happiness; or to defend ourselves with any tolerable Security against the Misery which every where surrounds and invests us.

'To this I added another Study, compared to which all the Philosophy taught by the wisest Heathens is little better than a Dream, and is indeed as full of Vanity as the silliest Jester ever pleased to represent it.[1] This is that divine Wisdom which is

---

[1] The Man of the Hill's insistence on the superior wisdom of Christian to heathen philosophy, the former being infallibly based upon divine revelation, has a place in a long tradition of Christian apologetics which, in the seventeenth and eighteenth centuries, came to be directed chiefly against the threat of deism. See, for example, Swift's sermon, 'The Excellency of Christianity, in Opposition to Heathen Philosophy' (upon 1 Corinthians 3: 19: 'The wisdom of this world is foolishness with God'), and the discussion by Louis Landa, ed. Swift's *Irish Tracts, 1720–1723, and Sermons* (Oxford, 1948), pp. 111–14. Fielding returns to this theme in XVIII. iv, as he presents the conversion of the deist Square.

alone to be found in the Holy Scriptures: for they impart to us the Knowledge and Assurance of Things much more worthy our Attention, than all which this World can offer to our Acceptance. Of Things which Heaven itself hath condescended to reveal to us, and to the smallest Knowledge of which the highest human Wit unassisted could never ascend. I began now to think all the Time I had spent with the best Heathen Writers, was little more than Labour lost: For however pleasant and delightful their Lessons may be, or however adequate to the right Regulation of our Conduct with Respect to this World only, yet when compared with the Glory revealed in Scripture, their highest Documents will appear as trifling, and of as little Consequence as the Rules by which Children regulate their childish little Games and Pastime. True it is, that Philosophy makes us wiser, but Christianity makes us better Men. Philosophy elevates and steels the Mind, Christianity softens and sweetens it. The Former makes us the Objects of human Admiration, the Latter of Divine Love. That insures us a temporal, but this an eternal Happiness.—But I am afraid I tire you with my Rhapsody.'

'Not at all,' cries *Partridge*, 'Lud forbid we should be tired with good Things.'

'I had spent,' continued the Stranger, 'about four Years in the most delightful Manner to myself, totally given up to Contemplation, and entirely unembarrassed with the Affairs of the World, when I lost the best of Fathers, and one whom I so entirely loved, that my Grief at his Loss exceeds all Description. I now abandoned my Books, and gave myself up for a whole Month to the Efforts of Melancholy and Despair. Time, however, the best Physician of the Mind, at length brought me Relief.' 'Ay, ay, *Tempus edax Rerum*,'[1] said *Partridge*. 'I then,' continued the Stranger, 'betook myself again to my former Studies, which I may say perfected my Cure: For Philosophy and Religion may be called the Exercises of the Mind, and when this is disordered they are as wholesome as Exercise can be to a distempered Body. They do indeed produce similar Effects with Exercise: For they strengthen and confirm the Mind; till Man becomes, in the noble Strain of *Horace*,

Fortis, et in seipso totus teres atque rotundus,

[1] See above, p. 421, n. 2.

Externi ne quid valeat per læve morari:
In quem manca ruit semper Fortuna.————*1

Here *Jones* smiled at some Conceit which intruded itself into his Imagination; but the Stranger, I believe, perceived it not, and proceeded thus.

'My Circumstances were now greatly altered by the Death of that best of Men: For my Brother, who was now become Master of the House, differed so widely from me in his Inclinations, and our Pursuits in Life had been so very various, that we were the worst of Company to each other; but what made our living together still more disagreeable, was the little Harmony which could subsist between the few who resorted to me, and the numerous Train of Sportsmen who often attended my Brother from the Field to the Table: For such Fellows, besides the Noise and Nonsense with which they persecute the Ears of sober Men, endeavour always to attack them with Affronts and Contempt. This was so much the Case, that neither I myself, nor my Friends, could ever sit down to a Meal with them, without being treated with Derision, because we were unacquainted with the Phrases of Sportsmen. For Men of true Learning, and almost universal Knowledge, always compassionate the Ignorance of others: but Fellows who excel in some little, low, contemptible Art, are always certain to despise those who are unacquainted with that Art.

'In short, we soon separated, and I went by the Advice of a Physician to drink the *Bath* Waters: For my violent Affliction,

---

* Firm in himself, who on himself relies,
　Polish'd and round, who runs his proper Course,
　And breaks Misfortunes with superior Force.
　　　　　　　　　　　Mr. FRANCIS.[2]

---

　¹ *Satires*, II. vii. 86–8. Later in the novel (pp. 760–1) Fielding's own ironic paraphrase of this passage reveals the reason for Jones's good-humoured disapproval of the Man of the Hill's stoical self-sufficiency. Jones, Fielding remarks, 'had all that Weakness which is called Compassion, and which distinguishes this imperfect Character from that noble Firmness of Mind, which rolls a Man, as it were, within himself, and, like a polished Bowl, enables him to run through the World, without once being stopped by the Calamities which happen to others'. Cf. also 'Of the Remedy of Affliction for the Loss of Our Friends' (1743).

　² Philip Francis (*c.* 1708–73), whose verse translation of Horace began to be published by Andrew Millar in 1746. Fielding frequently quotes from this work: e.g. *Tom Jones* (pp. 489, 570, 660) and *The Jacobite's Journal* (12 March, 15 October 1748).

added to a sedentary Life, had thrown me into a kind of paralytic
Disorder, for which those Waters are accounted an almost
certain Cure.[1] The second Day after my Arrival, as I was
walking by the River, the Sun shone so intensely hot (tho' it was
early in the Year) that I retired to the Shelter of some Willows,
and sat down by the River-side. Here I had not been seated long
before I heard a Person on the other Side the Willows, sighing
and bemoaning himself bitterly. On a sudden, having uttered a
most impious Oath, he cried, "I am resolved to bear it no longer,"
and directly threw himself into the Water. I immediately started,
and ran towards the Place, calling at the same Time as loudly as
I could for Assistance. An Angler happened luckily to be a
fishing a little below me, tho' some very high Sedge had hid him
from my Sight. He immediately came up, and both of us together, not without some Hazard of our Lives, drew the Body to
the Shore. At first we perceived no Sign of Life remaining; but
having held the Body up by the Heels (for we soon had Assistance
enough) it discharged a vast Quantity of Water at the Mouth,
and at length began to discover some Symptoms of Breathing,
and a little afterwards to move both its Hands and its Legs.

'An Apothecary, who happened to be present among others,
advised that the Body, which seemed now to have pretty well
emptied itself of Water, and which began to have many con-
vulsive Motions, should be directly taken up, and carried into a
warm Bed. This was accordingly performed, the Apothecary and
myself attending.

'As we were going towards an Inn, for we knew not the
Man's Lodgings, luckily a Woman met us, who, after some
violent Screaming, told us, that the Gentleman lodged at her
House.

'When I had seen the Man safely deposited there, I left him to
the Care of the Apothecary, who, I suppose, used all the right
Methods with him; for the next Morning I heard he had perfectly recovered his Senses.

'I then went to visit him, intending to search out as well as I
could the Cause of his having attempted so desperate an Act, and

---

[1] On the supposed efficacy of the Bath waters in curing such muscular disorders as
'Palsies, and the nervous *Atrophy* of the Limbs', see Dr. George Cheyne's *Account of the
Nature and Quality of Bath-Waters*, 8th ed. (1737), sec. xliv. On Cheyne, see below, p. 605,
n. 1.

to prevent as far as I was able, his pursuing such wicked Intentions for the future. I was no sooner admitted into his Chamber, than we both instantly knew each other; for who should this Person be, but my good Friend Mr. *Watson*! Here I will not trouble you with what past at our first Interview: For I would avoid Prolixity as much as possible.' 'Pray let us hear all,' cries *Partridge*, 'I want mightily to know what brought him to *Bath*.'

'You shall hear every Thing material,' answered the Stranger; and then proceeded to relate what we shall proceed to write, after we have given a short breathing Time to both ourselves and the Reader.

CHAPTER XIV

In which the Man of the Hill concludes his History.

'MR. *Watson*,' continued the Stranger, 'very freely acquainted me, that the unhappy Situation of his Circumstances, occasioned by a Tide of Ill-Luck, had in a Manner forced him to a Resolution of destroying himself.

'I now began to argue very seriously with him, in Opposition to this Heathenish, or indeed Diabolical Principle of the Lawfulness of Self-Murder; and said every Thing which occurred to me on the Subject; but to my great Concern, it seemed to have very little Effect on him. He seemed not at all to repent of what he had done, and gave me Reason to fear, he would soon make a second Attempt of the like horrible Kind.

'When I had finished my Discourse, instead of endeavouring to answer my Arguments, he looked me stedfastly in the Face, and with a Smile said, "You are strangely altered, my good Friend, since I remember you. I question whether any of our Bishops could make a better Argument against Suicide than you have entertained me with, but unless you can find Somebody who will lend me a cool Hundred, I must either hang, or drown, or starve; and in my Opinion the last Death is the most terrible of the three."

'I answered him very gravely, that I was indeed altered since I had seen him last. That I had found Leisure to look into my Follies, and to repent of them. I then advised him to pursue the

same Steps; and at last concluded with an Assurance, that I
myself would lend him a hundred Pound, if it would be of any
Service to his Affairs, and he would not put it into the Power of a
Die to deprive him of it.

'Mr. *Watson*, who seemed almost composed in Slumber by the
former Part of my Discourse, was roused by the latter. He seized
my Hand eagerly, gave me a thousand Thanks, and declared
I was a Friend indeed; adding, that he hoped I had a better
Opinion of him, than to imagine he had profited so little by
Experience, as to put any Confidence in those damned Dice,
which had so often deceived him. "No, no," cries he, "let me but
once handsomely be set up again, and if ever Fortune makes a
broken Merchant of me afterwards, I will forgive her."

'I very well understood the Language of *setting up*, and *broken
Merchant*. I therefore said to him with a very grave Face, "Mr.
Watson, you must endeavour to find out some Business, or
Employment, by which you may procure yourself a Livelihood;
and I promise you, could I see any Probability of being repaid
hereafter, I would advance a much larger Sum than what you
have mentioned, to equip you in any fair and honourable Calling;
but as to Gaming, besides the Baseness and Wickedness of making
it a Profession, you are really, to my own Knowledge, unfit for it,
and it will end in your certain Ruin."

' "Why now, that's strange," answered he, "neither you, nor
any of my Friends, would ever allow me to know any Thing of
the Matter, and yet, I believe I am as good a Hand at every
Game as any of you all; and I heartily wish I was to play with you
only for your whole Fortune; I should desire no better Sport, and
I would let you name your Game into the Bargain; but come, my
dear Boy, have you the Hundred in your Pocket?"

'I answered, I had only a Bill for 50 *l.* which I delivered him,
and promised to bring him the rest next Morning; and after
giving him a little more Advice, took my Leave.

'I was indeed better than my Word: For I returned to him that
very Afternoon. When I entered the Room, I found him sitting
up in his Bed at Cards with a notorious Gamester. This Sight,
you will imagine, shocked me not a little; to which I may
add the Mortification of seeing my Bill delivered by him to
his Antagonist, and thirty Guineas only given in Exchange
for it.

'The other Gamester presently quitted the Room, and then *Watson* declared he was ashamed to see me; "but," says he, "I find Luck runs so damnably against me, that I will resolve to leave off Play for ever. I have thought of the kind Proposal you made me ever since, and I promise you there shall be no Fault in me, if I do not put it in Execution."

'Though I had no great Faith in his Promises, I produced him the Remainder of the Hundred in Consequence of my own; for which he gave me a Note, which was all I ever expected to see in Return for my Money.

'We were prevented from any further Discourse at present, by the Arrival of the Apothecary, who with much Joy in his Countenance, and without even asking his Patient how he did, proclaimed there was great News arrived in a Letter to himself, which he said would shortly be public, "that the Duke of *Monmouth*[1] was landed in the West with a vast Army of *Dutch*, and that another vast Fleet hovered over the Coast of *Norfolk*, and was to make a Descent there, in order to favour the Duke's Enterprize with a Diversion on that Side."

'This Apothecary was one of the greatest Politicians of his Time. He was more delighted with the most paultry Packet, than with the best Patient; and the highest Joy he was capable of, he received from having a Piece of News in his Possession an Hour or two sooner than any other Person in the Town. His Advices, however, were seldom authentic; for he would swallow almost any thing as a Truth, a Humour which many made use of to impose upon him.

'Thus it happened with what he at present communicated; for it was known within a short Time afterwards, that the Duke was

---

1 James Scott (1649–85), Duke of Monmouth and Buccleuch, was the natural son of Charles II. He hoped to become King of England upon the death of his father and to this end associated himself with the Whig-Protestant interest which in 1679 and 1680, under the leadership of the first Earl of Shaftesbury, attempted unsuccessfully to pass a bill excluding the Catholic Duke of York from the throne. When York succeeded Charles as James II in 1685, Monmouth returned from exile in Holland intending to seize the throne by force. With 150 attendants he landed at Lyme, Dorset, on 11 June; his army soon grew to several thousand, drawing strength from the large nonconformist population of the West Country. After some early successes the rebels were crushed at Sedgemoor, near Bridgwater, and in the following days the fugitives were ruthlessly hunted down and executed. Monmouth himself was beheaded. In Fielding's opinion, the severity with which James suppressed the rebellion was 'inhuman and unparallel'd', the action of 'a Bigot and . . . a Tyrant' (see *A Serious Address to the People of Great Britain* [1745]).

really landed; but that his Army consisted only of a few Attendants; and as to the Diversion in *Norfolk*, it was entirely false.

'The Apothecary staid no longer in the Room, than while he
acquainted us with his News; and then, without saying a Syllable
to his Patient on any other Subject, departed to spread his
Advices all over the Town.

'Events of this Nature in the Public are generally apt to eclipse
all private Concerns. Our Discourse, therefore, now became
entirely political. For my own Part, I had been for some Time
very seriously affected with the Danger to which the Protestant
Religion was so visibly exposed, under a Popish Prince; and
thought the Apprehension of it alone sufficient to justify that
Insurrection: For no real Security can ever be found against the
persecuting Spirit of Popery, when armed with Power, except the
depriving it of that Power, as woeful Experience presently
shewed. You know how King *James* behaved after getting the
better of this Attempt; how little he valued either his Royal
Word, or Coronation-Oath, or the Liberties and Rights of his
People. But all had not the Sense to foresee this at first; and
therefore the Duke of *Monmouth* was weakly supported; yet all
could feel when the Evil came upon them; and therefore all
united, at last, to drive out that King, against whose Exclusion a
great Party among us had so warmly contended, during the
Reign of his Brother, and for whom they now fought with such
Zeal and Affection.'

'What you say,' interrupted *Jones*, 'is very true; and it has
often struck me, as the most wonderful thing I ever read of in
History, that so soon after this convincing Experience, which
brought our whole Nation to join so unanimously in expelling
King *James*, for the Preservation of our Religion and Liberties,
there should be a Party among us mad enough to desire the
placing his Family again on the Throne.' 'You are not in Earnest!'
answered the old Man; 'there can be no such Party. As bad as an
Opinion as I have of Mankind, I cannot believe them infatuated
to such a Degree! There may be some hot-headed Papists led by
their Priests to engage in this desperate Cause, and think it a
Holy War; but that Protestants, that Members of the Church of
England should be such Apostates, such *Felos de se*,[1] I cannot

---

[1] 'Felons to themselves', the legal phrase for suicides. Cf. *The True Patriot* (27 May–
3 June 1746), where Fielding declares that, after having experienced the tyranny of

believe it; no, no, young Man, unacquainted as I am with what has past in the World for these last thirty Years, I cannot be so imposed upon as to credit so foolish a Tale: But I see you have a Mind to sport with my Ignorance.' 'Can it be possible,' replied *Jones*, 'that you have lived so much out of the World as not to know, that during that Time there have been two Rebellions in favour of the Son of King *James*,[1] one of which is now actually raging in the very Heart of this Kingdom?' At these Words the old Gentleman started up, and, in a most solemn Tone of Voice conjured *Jones* by his Maker to tell him, if what he said was really true: Which the other as solemnly affirming, he walked several Turns about the Room, in a profound Silence, then cried, then laughed, and, at last, fell down on his Knees, and blessed God, in a loud Thanksgiving-Prayer, for having delivered him from all Society with Human Nature, which could be capable of such monstrous Extravagances. After which being reminded by *Jones*, that he had broke off his Story, he resumed it again, in this Manner.

'As Mankind, in the Days I was speaking of, was not yet arrived to that Pitch of Madness which I find they are capable of now, and which, to be sure, I have only escaped by living alone, and at a Distance from the Contagion, there was a considerable Rising in favour of *Monmouth*, and my Principles strongly inclining me to take the same Part, I determined to join him, and Mr. *Watson*, from different Motives concurring in the same Resolution, (for the Spirit of a Gamester will carry a Man as far upon such an Occasion as the Spirit of Patriotism) we soon provided ourselves with all Necessaries, and went to the Duke at *Bridgwater*. The unfortunate Event of this Enterprize you are, I conclude, as well acquainted with as myself. I escaped, together with Mr. *Watson*, from the Battle at *Sedgemore*, in which Action I received a slight Wound. We rode near forty Miles together on the *Exeter* Road, and then abandoning our Horses, scrambled as well as we could through the Fields and Bye-Roads, till we

---

James II, any Protestant who supports the Pretender's cause is guilty of idiocy: 'Nay, such Men may be said to participate of the Guilt to which they become the Objects. They are in a manner *Felo's de se*, and may more properly be said to impose on themselves, than to be imposed on by others'.

[1] The Jacobite uprisings in 1715 and 1745.

arrived at a little wild Hut on a Common, where a poor old Woman took all the Care of us she could, and dressed my Wound with Salve, which quickly healed it.'

'Pray, Sir, where was the Wound,' says *Partridge.* The Stranger satisfied him it was in his Arm, and then continued his Narrative. 'Here, Sir,' said he, 'Mr. *Watson* left me the next Morning, in order, as he pretended, to get us some Provision from the Town of *Cullumpton*;[1] but—can I relate it? or can you believe it?—This Mr. *Watson*, this Friend, this base, barbarous, treacherous Villain, betrayed me to a Party of Horse belonging to King *James*, and, at his Return, delivered me into their Hands.

'The Soldiers, being six in Number, had now seized me, and were conducting me to *Taunton* Goal; but neither my present Situation, nor the Apprehensions of what might happen to me, were half so irksome to my Mind, as the Company of my false Friend, who, having surrendered himself, was likewise considered as a Prisoner, tho' he was better treated, as being to make his Peace at my Expence. He at first endeavoured to excuse his Treachery; but when he received nothing but Scorn and Upbraiding from me, he soon changed his Note, abused me as the most atrocious and malicious Rebel, and laid all his own Guilt to my Charge, who, as he declared, had solicited, and even threatened him, to make him take up Arms against his gracious, as well as lawful, Sovereign.

'This false Evidence, (for, in Reality, he had been much the forwarder of the two) stung me to the Quick, and raised an Indignation scarce conceivable by those who have not felt it. However, Fortune at length took Pity on me; for as we were got a little beyond *Wellington*,[2] in a narrow Lane, my Guards received a false Alarm, that near fifty of the Enemy were at hand, upon which they shifted for themselves, and left me and my Betrayer to do the same. That Villain immediately ran from me, and I am glad he did, or I should have certainly endeavoured, though I had no Arms, to have executed Vengeance on his Baseness.

'I was now once more at Liberty, and immediately withdrawing from the Highway into the Fields, I travelled on, scarce knowing which Way I went, and making it my chief Care to avoid all public Roads, and all Towns, nay, even the most

---

[1] A market town in Devon, twelve miles north-east of Exeter.
[2] A market town in Somerset, six miles from Taunton on the Exeter road.

homely Houses; for I imagined every human Creature whom I saw, desirous of betraying me.

'At last, after rambling several Days about the Country, during which the Fields afforded me the same Bed, and the same Food, which Nature bestows on our Savage Brothers of the Creation, I at length arrived at this Place, where the Solitude and Wildness of the Country invited me to fix my Abode. The first Person with whom I took up my Habitation was the Mother of this old Woman, with whom I remained concealed, till the News of the glorious Revolution[1] put an End to all my Apprehensions of Danger, and gave me an Opportunity of once more visiting my own Home, and of enquiring a little into my Affairs, which I soon settled as agreeably to my Brother as to myself; having resigned every thing to him, for which he paid me the Sum of a thousand Pound, and settled on me an Annuity for Life.

'His Behaviour in this last Instance, as in all others, was selfish and ungenerous. I could not look on him as my Friend, nor indeed did he desire that I should; so I presently took my Leave of him, as well as of my other Acquaintance; and from that Day to this my History is little better than a Blank.'

'And is it possible, Sir,' said *Jones*, 'that you can have resided here, from that Day to this?' 'O no, Sir,' answered the Gentleman, 'I have been a great Traveller, and there are few Parts of *Europe* with which I am not acquainted.' 'I have not, Sir,' cried *Jones*, 'the Assurance to ask it of you now. Indeed it would be cruel, after so much Breath as you have already spent. But you will give me Leave to wish for some further Opportunity of hearing the excellent Observations, which a Man of your Sense and Knowledge of the World must have made in so long a Course of Travels.' 'Indeed, young Gentleman,' answered the Stranger, 'I will endeavour to satisfy your Curiosity on this Head likewise, as far as I am able.' *Jones* attempted fresh Apologies, but was prevented; and while he and *Partridge* sat with greedy and impatient Ears, the Stranger proceeded as in the next Chapter.

---

[1] The deposition of James II in 1688 was precipitated both by his own absolutist policies in the interest of re-establishing Catholicism as the national religion and by the birth of his son and heir on 20 June. William of Orange landed in England with his army in November.

CHAPTER XV

A brief History of Europe. *And a curious Discourse between Mr.* Jones *and the Man of the Hill.*

'IN *Italy* the Landlords are very silent. In *France* they are more talkative, but yet civil. In *Germany* and *Holland* they are generally very impertinent. And as for their Honesty, I believe it is pretty equal in all those Countries. The *Laquais a Louage*[1] are sure to lose no Opportunity of cheating you: And as for the Postilions, I think they are pretty much alike all the World over. These, Sir, are the Observations on Men which I made in my Travels, for these were the only Men I ever conversed with. My Design when I went abroad, was to divert myself by seeing the wondrous Variety of Prospects, Beasts, Birds, Fishes, Insects, and Vegetables, with which God hath been pleased to enrich the several Parts of this Globe.[2] A Variety, which as it must give great Pleasure to a contemplative Beholder, so doth it admirably display the Power

[1] Manservants for hire by travellers.

[2] Throughout this chapter the Man of the Hill—like Pope in the *Essay on Man* (1733–4)—echoes the orthodox cosmological theories of the period. Such works as Ralph Cudworth's *True Intellectual System of the Universe* (1678), John Ray's *The Wisdom of God Manifested in the Works of the Creation* (1691), and William Derham's *Physico-* (1713) *and Astro-Theology* (1715) attempted to demonstrate the being and attributes of the Deity by analysing the order apparent in the universe, its fullness and variety, its nice gradations and coherency. Barrow, Tillotson, Clarke, and many other rationalist divines expounded this doctrine from the pulpit, and it was popularized by Addison in *The Spectator* (No. 519 [20 October 1712]) and by such poets as Blackmore, Thomson, Boyse (see above, p. 324, n. 4), Young, and Smart. The classic study of this idea is A. O. Lovejoy, *The Great Chain of Being* (Cambridge, Mass., 1936); see also W. P. Jones, *The Rhetoric of Science* (Berkeley, Cal., 1966).

Like Pope—who, Fielding remarked, '*taught me a System of Philosophy in* English *Numbers*' (see the Preface to *Plutus* [1742])—the Man of the Hill, 'Expatiate[s] free o'er all this scene of Man' (i. 5), contemplating the 'Vast chain of being' from the heavens to the lower creation: 'Beast, bird, fish, insect! what no eye can see' (i. 239). (This language is partly echoed in the passage above.) But whereas Pope concludes that 'Heav'n's design' is not broken by the turpitude even of 'a Borgia, or a Catiline' (i. 155–6), the Man of the Hill asserts that the Creator is dishonoured by the immorality of mankind. In this respect the lesson of the *Essay on Man* is one to which Fielding would have subscribed:

> From pride, from pride, our very reas'ning springs;
> Account for moral as for nat'ral things:
> Why charge we Heav'n in those, in these acquit?
> In both, to reason right is to submit. . . .
> But ALL subsists by elemental strife;
> And Passions are the elements of Life.
> The gen'ral ORDER, since the whole began,
> Is kept in Nature, and is kept in Man. (i. 161–4, 169–72)

and Wisdom and Goodness of the Creator. Indeed, to say the Truth, there is but one Work in his whole Creation that doth him any Dishonour, and with that I have long since avoided holding any Conversation.'

'You will pardon me,' cries *Jones*, 'but I have always imagined, that there is in this very Work you mention, as great Variety as in all the rest; for besides the Difference of Inclination, Customs and Climates have, I am told, introduced the utmost Diversity into Human Nature.' 'Very little indeed,' answered the other; 'those who travel in order to acquaint themselves with the different Manners of Men, might spare themselves much Pains, by going to a Carnival at *Venice*; for there they will see at once all which they can discover in the several Courts of *Europe*. The same Hypocrisy, the same Fraud; in short, the same Follies and Vices, dressed in different Habits. In *Spain* these are equipped with much Gravity; and in *Italy*, with vast Splendor. In *France*, a Knave is dressed like a Fop; and in the Northern Countries, like a Sloven. But Human Nature is every where the same, every where the Object of Detestation and Scorn.'

'As for my own Part, I past through all these Nations, as you perhaps may have done through a Croud at a Shew, jostling to get by them, holding my Nose with one Hand, and defending my Pockets with the other, without speaking a Word to any of them, while I was pressing on to see what I wanted to see, which, however entertaining it might be in itself, scarce made me Amends for the Trouble the Company gave me.'

'Did not you find some of the Nations among which you travelled, less troublesome to you than others?' said *Jones*. 'O yes,' replied the old Man, 'the *Turks* were much more tolerable to me than the *Christians*. For they are Men of profound Taciturnity, and never disturb a Stranger with Questions. Now and then indeed they bestow a short Curse upon him, or spit in his Face as he walks the Streets, but then they have done with him, and a Man may live an Age in their Country without hearing a Dozen Words from them. But of all the People I ever saw, Heaven defend me from the *French*. With their damned Prate and Civilities, and doing the Honour of their Nation to Strangers, (as they are pleased to call it)[1] but indeed setting forth their own

---

[1] An idiom meaning to receive a guest or visitor according to the rules of politeness, as in Molière's *L'Avare*, III: 'Je vais faire pour vous, mon père, les honneurs de votre logis'.

Vanity; they are so troublesome, that I had infinitely rather pass my Life with the *Hottentots*, than set my Foot in *Paris* again. They are a nasty People, but their Nastiness is mostly *without*, whereas in *France*, and some other Nations that I won't name, it is all *within*, and makes them stink much more to my Reason than that of *Hottentots* does to my Nose.

'Thus, Sir, I have ended the History of my Life; for as to all that Series of Years, during which I have lived retired here, it affords no Variety to entertain you, and may be almost considered as one Day. The Retirement has been so compleat, that I could hardly have enjoyed a more absolute Solitude in the Deserts of the *Thebais*,[1] than here in the midst of this populous Kingdom. As I have no Estate, I am plagued with no Tenants or Stewards; my Annuity is paid me pretty regularly, as indeed it ought to be, for it is much less than what I might have expected, in Return for what I gave up. Visits I admit none, and the old Woman who keeps my House knows, that her Place entirely depends upon her saving me all the Trouble of buying the Things that I want, keeping off all Sollicitation or Business from me, and holding her Tongue whenever I am within hearing. As my Walks are all by Night, I am pretty secure in this wild, unfrequented Place from meeting any Company. Some few Persons I have met by Chance, and sent them Home heartily frighted, as from the Oddness of my Dress and Figure they took me for a Ghost or a Hobgoblin. But what has happened to Night shews, that even here I cannot be safe from the Villany of Men; for without your Assistance I had not only been robbed, but very probably murdered.'

Jones thanked the Stranger for the Trouble he had taken in relating his Story, and then expressed some Wonder how he could possibly endure a Life of such Solitude; 'in which,' says he, 'you may well complain of the Want of Variety. Indeed I am astonished how you have filled up, or rather killed, so much of your Time.'

'I am not at all surprized,' answered the other, 'that to one whose Affections and Thoughts are fixed on the World, my Hours should appear to have wanted Employment in this Place; but there is one single Act, for which the whole Life of Man is infinitely too short. What Time can suffice for the Contemplation

---

[1] In ancient geography, the domain of Thebes in Upper Egypt and the place of origin of Christian monasticism.

and Worship of that glorious, immortal, and eternal Being, among the Works of whose stupendous Creation, not only this Globe, but even those numberless Luminaries which we may here behold spangling all the Sky, tho' they should many of them be Suns lighting different Systems of Worlds,[1] may possibly appear but as a few Atoms, opposed to the whole Earth which we inhabit? Can a Man who, by Divine Meditations, is admitted, as it were, into the Conversation of this ineffable, incomprehensible Majesty, think Days, or Years, or Ages, too long, for the Continuance of so ravishing an Honour? Shall the trifling Amusements, the palling Pleasures, the silly Business of the World, roll away our Hours too swiftly from us; and shall the Pace of Time seem sluggish to a Mind exercised in Studies so high, so important, and so glorious! As no Time is sufficient, so no Place is improper for this great Concern. On what Object can we cast our Eyes, which may not inspire us with Ideas of his Power, of his Wisdom, and of his Goodness? It is not necessary, that the rising Sun should dart his fiery Glories over the Eastern Horizon; nor that the boisterous Winds should rush from their Caverns, and shake the lofty Forest; nor that the opening Clouds should pour their Deluges on the Plains: It is not necessary, I say, that any of these should proclaim his Majesty; there is not an Insect, not a Vegetable, of so low an Order in the Creation, as not to be honoured with bearing Marks of the Attributes of its great Creator; Marks not only of his Power, but of his Wisdom and Goodness. Man alone, the King of this Globe, the last and greatest Work of the Supreme Being, below the Sun; Man alone hath basely dishonoured his own Nature, and by Dishonesty, Cruelty, Ingratitude, and Treachery, hath called his Maker's Goodness in Question, by puzzling us to account how a benevolent Being should form so foolish, and so vile an Animal. Yet this is the Being from whose Conversation you think, I suppose, that I have been unfortunately restrained; and without

---

[1] Fontenelle's influential treatise, *Entretiens sur la pluralité des mondes* (1686), helped to disseminate the belief that the universe contained innumerable planetary systems and inhabited worlds. In his *Astro-Theology* (1715) Derham explained this 'New Systeme', which 'supposeth that there are many other Systemes of *Suns* and *Planets*, besides that in which we have our residence: namely, that every Fixt Star is a Sun, and encompassed with a Systeme of Planets, both Primary and Secondary, as well as ours'. Addison accepts this theory in *The Spectator* (No. 519 [20 October 1712]), as does Pope in the *Essay on Man* (i. 21–7). For a full discussion see Lovejoy, *The Great Chain of Being* (1936), pp. 130–42.

whose blessed Society, Life, in your Opinion, must be tedious and insipid.'

'In the former Part of what you said,' replied *Jones*, 'I most heartily and readily concur; but I believe, as well as hope, that the Abhorrence which you express for Mankind, in the Conclusion, is much too general. Indeed you here fall into an Error, which, in my little Experience, I have observed to be a very common one, by taking the Character of Mankind from the worst and basest among them; whereas indeed, as an excellent Writer observes,[1] nothing should be esteemed as characteristical of a Species, but what is to be found among the best and most perfect Individuals of that Species. This Error, I believe, is generally committed by those who, from Want of proper Caution in the Choice of their Friends and Acquaintance, have suffered Injuries from bad and worthless Men; two or three Instances of which are very unjustly charged on all Human Nature.'

'I think I had Experience enough of it,' answered the other. 'My first Mistress, and my first Friend, betrayed me in the basest Manner, and in Matters which threatened to be of the worst of Consequences, even to bring me to a shameful Death.'

'But you will pardon me,' cries *Jones*, 'if I desire you to reflect who that Mistress, and who that Friend were. What better, my good Sir, could be expected in Love derived from the Stews, or in Friendship first produced and nourished at the Gaming-Table! To take the Characters of Women from the former Instance, or of Men from the latter, would be as unjust as to assert, that Air is a nauseous and unwholesome Element, because we find it so in a Jakes. I have lived but a short Time in the World, and yet have known Men worthy of the highest Friendship, and Women of the highest Love.'

'Alas! young Man,' answered the Stranger; 'you have lived, you confess, but a very short Time in the World; I was somewhat older than you when I was of the same Opinion.'

'You might have remained so still,' replies *Jones*, 'if you had not been unfortunate, I will venture to say incautious in the placing your Affections. If there was indeed much more

---

[1] Cf. Cicero, *Tusculan Disputations*, I. xiv. 32: 'num dubitas quin specimen naturae capi deceat ex optima quaque natura?' ('Can you doubt that properly our ideal of human nature should be formed from the finest natures we meet with?'—trans. J. E. King, Loeb Classical Library, 1927). In a general way, this assumption also underlies the ethical philosophy of Shaftesbury and the Latitudinarian divines.

Wickedness in the World than there is, it would not prove such general Assertions against Human Nature, since much of this arrives by mere Accident, and many a Man who commits Evil, is not totally bad and corrupt in his Heart. In Truth, none seem to have any Title to assert Human Nature to be necessarily and universally evil, but those whose own Minds afford them one Instance of this natural Depravity;[1] which is not, I am convinced, your Case.'

'And such,' said the Stranger, 'will be always the most backward to assert any such thing. Knaves will no more endeavour to persuade us of the Baseness of Mankind, than a Highwayman will inform you that there are Thieves on the Road. This would indeed be a Method to put you on your Guard, and to defeat their own Purposes. For which Reason tho' Knaves, as I remember, are very apt to abuse particular Persons; yet they never cast any Reflection on Human Nature in general.' The old Gentleman spoke this so warmly, that as *Jones* despaired of making a Convert, and was unwilling to offend, he returned no Answer.

The Day now began to send forth its first Streams of Light, when *Jones* made an Apology to the Stranger for having staid so long, and perhaps detained him from his Rest. The Stranger answered, 'He never wanted Rest less than at present; for that Day and Night were indifferent Seasons to him, and that he commonly made use of the former for the Time of his Repose, and of the latter for his Walks and Lucubrations. However,' said he, 'it is now a most lovely Morning, and if you can bear any longer to be without your own Rest or Food, I will gladly entertain you with the Sight of some very fine Prospects, which I believe you have not yet seen.'

Jones very readily embraced this Offer, and they immediately set forward together from the Cottage. As for *Partridge*, he had fallen into a profound Repose, just as the Stranger had finished his Story; for his Curiosity was satisfied, and the subsequent Discourse was not forcible enough in its Operation to conjure down the Charms of Sleep. *Jones* therefore left him to enjoy his Nap; and as the Reader may perhaps be, at this Season, glad of the same Favour, we will here put an End to the Eighth Book of our History.

---

[1] See above, p. 269, n. 2.

BOOK IX

Containing twelve Hours.

CHAPTER I

Of those who lawfully may, and of those who may not write such
Histories as this.

AMONG other good Uses for which I have thought proper to
institute these several introductory Chapters, I have considered them as a Kind of Mark or Stamp, which may hereafter
enable a very indifferent Reader to distinguish, what is true and
genuine in this historic Kind of Writing, from what is false and
counterfeit. Indeed it seems likely that some such Mark may
shortly become necessary, since the favourable Reception which
two or three Authors have lately procured for their Works of this
Nature from the Public,[1] will probably serve as an Encouragement to many others to undertake the like. Thus a Swarm of foolish
Novels, and monstrous Romances will be produced, either to the
great impoverishing of Booksellers, or to the great Loss of Time,
and Depravation of Morals in the Reader; nay, often to the
spreading of Scandal and Calumny, and to the Prejudice of the
Characters of many worthy and honest People.

I question not but the ingenious Author of the Spectator[2] was
principally induced to prefix *Greek* and *Latin* Mottos to every

---

[1] Probably an allusion to Richardson's *Clarissa*, which began to be published in December 1747, and to Smollett's first novel, *Roderick Random*, which appeared in January 1748
with a second edition in April. Though Fielding had earlier ridiculed *Pamela* (1740), he
had a high regard for Richardson's second novel: in *The Jacobite's Journal* (2 January,
5 March 1748) he published two letters in praise of *Clarissa*, and before the year was out he
had written personally to congratulate Richardson on his book (see the letter of 15 October
1748). That his admiration for the novel was not unqualified, however, is suggested later in
Tom Jones (see pp. 793, 850) where he implicitly invites the reader to compare the sentiments and conduct of Sophia with those of Clarissa. Fielding's opinion of Smollett's novel
is recorded in *The Covent-Garden Journal* (7 January 1752): 'This Rodorick, in a former
Skirmish with the People called Critics, had owed some slight Success more to the Weakness
of the Critics, than to any Merit of his own.'

[2] In *Spectator*, No. 221 (13 November 1711), Addison discusses the mottoes to his papers,
but he does not give Fielding's explanation for them.

Paper from the same Consideration of guarding against the Pursuit of those Scribblers, who, having no Talents of a Writer but what is taught by the Writing-master, are yet nowise afraid nor ashamed to assume the same Titles with the greatest Genius, than their good Brother in the Fable was of braying in the Lion's Skin.¹

By the Device therefore of his Motto, it became impracticable for any Man to presume to imitate the Spectators, without understanding at least one Sentence in the learned Languages. In the same Manner I have now secured myself from the Imitation of those who are utterly incapable of any Degree of Reflection, and whose Learning is not equal to an Essay.

I would not be here understood to insinuate, that the greatest Merit of such historical Productions can ever lie in these introductory Chapters; but, in Fact, those Parts which contain mere Narrative only, afford much more Encouragement to the Pen of an Imitator, than those which are composed of Observation and Reflection. Here I mean such Imitators as *Rowe* was of *Shakespear*,² or as *Horace* hints³ some of the *Romans* were of *Cato*, by bare Feet and sour Faces.

To invent good Stories, and to tell them well, are possibly very rare Talents, and yet I have observed few Persons who have scrupled to aim at both; and if we examine the Romances and Novels with which the World abounds, I think we may fairly conclude, that most of the Authors would not have attempted to shew their Teeth (if the Expression may be allowed me) in any other Way of Writing; nor could indeed have strung together a dozen Sentences on any other Subject whatever. *Scribimus*

¹ The fable of the ass who disguised himself in a lion's skin only to be discovered by his voice and ears is included in Sir Roger L'Estrange, *Fables of Æsop and Other Eminent Mythologists*, 5th ed. (1708), No. 224. It is there attributed to Avianus. In the present context Fielding may wish to recall the lion's head that Addison erected at Button's Coffeehouse to serve as a depository for contributions to *The Guardian*. In No. 134 (14 August 1713) Addison lamented that by pouring ribaldry and scandal down the lion's throat, his correspondents 'have made a very Ass of him' (1747 ed., ii. 275).

² Nicholas Rowe (1674–1718), poet laureate, dramatist, and editor of Shakespeare's plays (1709). His tragedy of *Jane Shore* (1714), according to the title-page, was 'Written in Imitation of Shakespear's Style', but in Fielding's opinion Rowe produced only 'Fustian'. (See letter xl of Sarah Fielding's *Familiar Letters* [1747].)

³ In discussing the subject of literary imitation in *Epistles*, I. xix, Horace, by way of analogy, asks: 'What if a man were to ape Cato with grim and savage look, with bare feet and the cut of a scanty gown, would he thus set before us Cato's virtue and morals?' (lines 12–14—trans. H. R. Fairclough, Loeb Classical Library, 1926).

indocti doctique passim, *[1] may be more truly said of the Historian and Biographer, than of any other Species of Writing: For all the Arts and Sciences (even Criticism itself) require some little Degree of Learning and Knowledge. Poetry indeed may perhaps be thought an Exception; but then it demands Numbers, or something like Numbers; whereas to the Composition of Novels and Romances, nothing is necessary but Paper, Pens and Ink, with the manual Capacity of using them. This, I conceive, their Productions shew to be the Opinion of the Authors themselves; and this must be the Opinion of their Readers, if indeed there be any such.

Hence we are to derive that universal Contempt, which the World, who always denominate the Whole from the Majority, have cast on all historical Writers, who do not draw their Materials from Records.[2] And it is the Apprehension of this Contempt, that hath made us so cautiously avoid the Term Romance, a Name with which we might otherwise have been well enough contented. Though as we have good Authority for all our Characters, no less indeed than the vast authentic Doomsday-Book of Nature, as is elsewhere hinted, our Labours have sufficient Title to the Name of History. Certainly they deserve some Distinction from those Works, which one of the wittiest of Men regarded only as proceeding from a Pruritus,[3] or indeed rather from a Looseness of the Brain.

> *   ——Each desperate Blockhead dares to write,
>   Verse is the Trade of every living Wight.
>   FRANCIS.

---

[1] Horace, *Epistles,* II. i. 117: 'scribimus indocti doctique poemata passim' ('but, skilled or unskilled, we scribble poetry, all alike'—trans. H. R. Fairclough, Loeb Classical Library, 1926). On Francis and his translation, see above, p. 472, n. 2.

[2] To distinguish his own 'Species of Writing' from the scandal-mongering novels of Mrs. Manley or the fantastic productions of the French romance-writers, Fielding had earlier defined *Joseph Andrews* as a kind of biography or history, or as 'a Comic Romance' or 'Comic Epic-Poem in Prose' (see the Preface and I. i, III. i). In III. i of that work he developed the distinction between himself and Cervantes, who were historians 'of the World in general', and the authors of the histories of particular eras and countries, whom he preferred to call 'Chorographers' or 'Topographers'.

[3] Cf. Martinus Scriblerus, *Peri Bathous: The Art of Sinking in Poetry,* ch. iii ('*The Necessity of the* Bathos, *Physically consider'd*'): 'Therefore is the Desire of Writing properly term'd *Pruritus,* the *Titillation of the Generative Faculty of the Brain . . .*' This work, which comprised the final volume of *Miscellanies* (1727) by Swift, Pope, and Arbuthnot, is now generally attributed to Pope; but Fielding may have supposed Swift to be the author.

But besides the Dishonour which is thus cast on one of the most useful as well as entertaining of all Kinds of Writing, there is just Reason to apprehend, that by encouraging such Authors, we shall propagate much Dishonour of another Kind; I mean to the Characters of many good and valuable Members of Society: For the dullest Writers, no more than the dullest Companions, are always inoffensive. They have both enough of Language to be indecent and abusive. And surely if the Opinion just above cited be true, we cannot wonder, that Works so nastily derived should be nasty themselves, or have a Tendency to make others so.

To prevent therefore for the future, such intemperate Abuses of Leisure, of Letters, and of the Liberty of the Press, especially as the World seems at present to be more than usually threatned with them, I shall here venture to mention some Qualifications, every one of which are in a pretty high Degree necessary to this Order of Historians.

The first is Genius, without a full Vein of which, no Study, says *Horace*,[1] can avail us. By Genius I would understand that Power, or rather those Powers of the Mind, which are capable of penetrating into all Things within our Reach and Knowledge, and of distinguishing their essential Differences.[2] These are no other

---

[1] *Ars Poetica*, 409–10: 'ego nec studium sine divite vena, / nec rude quid prosit video ingenium.'

[2] Fielding's synthesis of *invention* (or what others among his contemporaries often called 'wit') and *judgment* as the correlative attributes of genius places him on the side of such critics as Quintilian and La Rochefoucauld. Quintilian, for example, disagreed with those who would separate judgement from invention in the creative process 'on the ground that it is necessary first to *invent* and then to *exercise our judgment*. For my part,' he asserts, 'I do not believe that *invention* can exist apart from *judgment*, since we do not say that a speaker has *invented* inconsistent, two-edged or foolish arguments, but merely that he has failed to avoid them' (*Institutio Oratoria*, III. iii. 5–6; trans. H. E. Butler, Loeb Classical Library, 1921–2). This, too, is the view of La Rochefoucauld, whose phrasing recalls Fielding's own: 'The making a Difference between Wit and Judgment, is a Vulgar Error. Judgment is nothing else but the exceeding Brightness of Wit, which, like Light, pierces [i.e., *pénètre*] into the very Bottom of Things, observes all that ought to be observed there, and discovers what seemed to be past any bodies finding out: From whence we must conclude, that the Energy and Extension of this Light of the Wit, is the very Thing that produces all those Effects, usually ascribed to the Judgment' (*Moral Maxims and Reflections*, 2nd ed. [1706], Maxim 98). The following discussions of the relationship between wit and judgement in Pope are useful in the present context: E. N. Hooker, 'Pope on Wit: The *Essay on Criticism*', in *The Seventeenth Century: Studies in the History of English Thought and Literature from Bacon to Pope*, by R. F. Jones, *et al.* (Stanford, Cal., 1951), pp. 225–46; and the Introduction to the Twickenham Edition of Pope's *Essay on Criticism*, edd. E. Audra and A. Williams (1961). Cf. Fielding's earlier account of the complementary functions of 'Judgment' and 'Sagacity' in *The True Patriot* (24 December 1745).

than Invention and Judgment; and they are both called by the
collective Name of Genius, as they are of those Gifts of Nature
which we bring with us into the World. Concerning each of
which many seem to have fallen into very great Errors: For by
Invention, I believe, is generally understood a creative Faculty;
which would indeed prove most Romance-Writers to have the
highest Pretensions to it; whereas by Invention is really meant no
more, (and so the Word signifies) than Discovery, or finding
out; or to explain it at large, a quick and sagacious Penetration
into the true Essence of all the Objects of our Contemplation.
This, I think, can rarely exist without the Concomitancy of
Judgment: For how we can be said to have discovered the true
Essence of two Things, without discerning their Difference,
seems to me hard to conceive; now this last is the undisputed
Province of Judgment,[1] and yet some few Men of Wit[2] have
agreed with all the dull Fellows in the World, in representing
these two to have been seldom or never the Property of one and
the same Person.

But tho' they should be so, they are not sufficient for our
Purpose without a good Share of Learning; for which I could
again cite the Authority of *Horace*,[3] and of many others, if any
was necessary to prove that Tools are of no Service to a Workman, when they are not sharpened by Art, or when he wants
Rules to direct him in his Work, or hath no Matter to work upon.
All these Uses are supplied by Learning: For Nature can only
furnish us with Capacity, or, as I have chose to illustrate it, with

---

[1] Cf. Locke's *Essay concerning Human Understanding*, II. xi. 2—a passage from which
Fielding had quoted in *The True Patriot* (24 December 1745): 'If in having our *Ideas* in the
Memory ready at hand, consists Quickness of Parts; in this of having them unconfused,
and being able nicely to distinguish one Thing from another, where there is but the least
Difference, consists, in a great measure, the Exactness of Judgment, and Clearness of
Reason, which is to be observed in one Man above another. And hence, perhaps, may be
given some Reason of that common Observation, That Men who have a great deal of Wit,
and prompt Memories, have not always the clearest Judgment, or deepest Reason. For
Wit lying most in the Assemblage of *Ideas*, and putting those together with Quickness and
Variety, wherein can be found any Resemblance or Congruity, thereby to make up pleasant
Pictures, and agreeable Visions in the Fancy: *Judgment* on the contrary, lies quite on the
other Side, in separating carefully, one from another, *Ideas* wherein can be found the least
Difference, thereby to avoid being misled by Similitude, and by Affinity to take one Thing
for another' (12th ed. [1741], i. 117).

[2] Locke, for one (see preceding note), and for another, Addison, who in *The Spectator*,
No. 62 (11 May 1711), agrees with his opinion that wit and judgement 'are not always the
Talents of the same Person'.   [3] Cf. *Ars Poetica*, 408–18.

the Tools of our Profession; Learning must fit them for Use, must direct them in it; and lastly, must contribute, Part at least, of the Materials. A competent Knowledge of History and of the *Belles Lettres*, is here absolutely necessary; and without this Share of Knowledge at least, to affect the Character of an Historian, is as vain as to endeavour at building a House without Timber or Mortar, or Brick or Stone. *Homer* and *Milton*,[1] who, though they added the Ornament of Numbers to their Works, were both Historians of our Order, were Masters of all the Learning of their Times.

Again, there is another Sort of Knowledge beyond the Power of Learning to bestow, and this is to be had by Conversation.[2] So necessary is this to the understanding the Characters of Men, that none are more ignorant of them than those learned Pedants, whose Lives have been entirely consumed in Colleges, and among Books: For however exquisitely Human Nature may have been described by Writers, the true practical System can be learnt only in the World. Indeed the like happens in every other Kind of Knowledge. Neither Physic, nor Law, are to be practically known from Books. Nay, the Farmer, the Planter, the Gardener, must perfect by Experience what he hath acquired the Rudiments of by Reading. How accurately soever the ingenious Mr. *Miller*[3]

---

[1] On Homer's reputation for learning, see, for example, 'An Essay on the Life, Writings and Learning, of Homer', section iii, prefixed to Pope's *Iliad* (1715). According to Rapin, Homer was 'the first Founder of all Arts and Sciences, and the Pattern of the wise Men in all Ages' ('Reflections on Aristotle's Treatise of Poesie', trans. Thomas Rymer, in Rapin's *Whole Critical Works*, 3rd ed. [1731], ii. 138). For Fielding's similar opinion, see *The True Patriot* (24 December 1745). In that journal for 5 November 1745 he described *Paradise Lost* as 'the best Poem which perhaps [the World] hath ever seen'.

[2] Cf. *Ars Poetica*, 156–7, 317–18.

[3] Philip Miller (1691–1771), F.R.S., gardener to the Company of Apothecaries at the Botanic Garden, Chelsea, and author of *The Gardeners Dictionary*, 2 vols. (1731, 1739). He was the best horticulturalist of his time and his *Dictionary* went through eight editions during his lifetime. To Fielding, Miller's work, which is an exhaustive description of the various species and uses of plants with a prefatory account of the history of gardening from Eden, may have seemed to comprise an amusing analogue to his own fictional anatomy of 'Human Nature'. In Miller's Preface, at least, Fielding would have found two passages relevant to his own themes in the present chapter. Miller, too, emphasized the need for practical experience in the art of gardening: 'to what Purpose is it, to a Person who wants to know the exact Method of propagating any particular Plant, to read over a fine Theory of *Gardening*, without ever entering into the necessary Instructions how he must proceed: And this is too often the Fault in many Books on this Subject; most of which have been wrote by Persons only skilful in the *Theory*, and therefore can't be suppos'd capable of instructing others in the *Practice*, that being what they themselves are unacquainted with' (1. x). And like Fielding, who began this chapter with reflections on incompetent imitators

may have described the Plant, he himself would advise his Disciple to see it in the Garden. As we must perceive, that after the nicest Strokes of a *Shakespear*, or a *Johnson*, of a *Wycherly*, or an *Otway*, some Touches of Nature will escape the Reader, which the judicious Action of a *Garrick*, of a *Cibber*, or a *Clive*,*[1] can convey to him; so on the real Stage, the Character shews himself in a stronger and bolder Light, than he can be described. And if this be the Case in those fine and nervous Descriptions, which great Authors themselves have taken from Life, how much more strongly will it hold when the Writer himself takes his Lines not from Nature, but from Books! Such Characters are

* There is a peculiar Propriety in mentioning this great Actor, and these two most justly celebrated Actresses in this Place; as they have all formed themselves on the Study of Nature only; and not on the Imitation of their Predecessors.[2] Hence they have been able to excel all who have gone before them; a Degree of Merit which the servile Herd of Imitators can never possibly arrive at.

---

of the novelist's art, applying the fable of the ass in the lion's skin, so Miller castigated those authors on gardening who were no better than ignorant plagiarists of their predecessors: these impostors, however, have 'manifested, how unable the assum'd Skin of the Lyon, has been to conceal those Ears, which are the peculiar Diagnostic of a much more servile and ignoble Creature' (I. xi). For another allusion to Miller, see the notes to *Ovid's Art of Love Paraphrased* (1747).

1 With the new theatrical season of 1747, these three fine performers were together for the first time at Drury Lane, Mrs. Cibber having joined the company after Garrick became patentee. On Garrick, see above, pp. 327, n. 2, and 853. Susannah Arne Cibber (1714–66) was unhappily married to Colley Cibber's son Theophilus. Handel admired her singing voice and as an actress she distinguished herself in tragedy. For Fielding's compliments to her, see *The Jacobite's Journal* (6, 13 February 1748), *Amelia* (1751), v. viii. and *The Covent-Garden Journal* (11 January 1752). Catherine 'Kitty' Clive (1711–85) was also a pleasing singer and in comedy the finest actress of her time—such, at least, was the opinion of Samuel Foote (*The Roman and English Comedy Consider'd and Compar'd* [1747], p. 41) and of Fielding himself (letter xl of Sarah Fielding's *Familiar Letters* [1747] and *The Jacobite's Journal* [30 January 1748]). In the late 1740s, however, Mrs. Clive's fortunes appear to have declined. One writer observed that she, though once 'esteem'd the Phænix [*sic*] of the Age, seems now to be of little Consequence; her Laurels are all wither'd; her Friends grown cold; and the repeated Acclamations that us'd to welcome her Appearance, are now no more' (J. T., *A Letter of Compliment to the ingenious Author of a Treatise on the Passions* [1747 ?], p. 33). Fielding, at least, who had been among the first to recognize her abilities and who had dedicated to her the published version of *The Intriguing Chambermaid* (1734), never ceased to praise her: besides the complimentary references already cited, see, for example, *Joseph Andrews* (1742), III. x; *Amelia*, I. vi, where she is said to be to acting what Shakespeare is to poetry and Hogarth to painting; and *The Covent-Garden Journal* (11 January 1752).

2 Cf. *The Jacobite's Journal* (6 February 1748), where Fielding similarly declares 'That the Business of an Actor, as well as of a Writer, is to copy Nature, and not to imitate the Excellencies of their Predecessors: That Mr. *Garrick*, Mr. *Quin*, Mrs. *Cibber*, Mrs. *Clive*, and Mrs. *Woffington*, are all, in their several Capacities, Examples of this Merit'.

only the faint Copy of a Copy, and can have neither the Justness nor Spirit of an Original.

Now this Conversation in our Historian must be universal, that is, with all Ranks and Degrees of Men: For the Knowledge of what is called High-Life, will not instruct him in low, nor *e converso*, will his being acquainted with the inferior Part of Mankind, teach him the Manners of the superior. And though it may be thought that the Knowledge of either may sufficiently enable him to describe at least that in which he hath been conversant; yet he will even here fall greatly short of Perfection: for the Follies of either Rank do in reality illustrate each other. For Instance, the Affectation of High-life appears more glaring and ridiculous from the Simplicity of the Low; and again the Rudeness and Barbarity of this latter, strikes with much stronger Ideas of Absurdity, when contrasted with, and opposed to the Politeness which controuls the former. Besides, to say the Truth, the Manners of our Historian will be improved by both these Conversations: For in the one he will easily find Examples of Plainness, Honesty, and Sincerity; in the other of Refinement, Elegance, and a Liberality of Spirit; which last Quality I myself have scarce ever seen in Men of low Birth and Education.

Nor will all the Qualities I have hitherto given my Historian avail him, unless he have what is generally meant by a good Heart, and be capable of feeling. The Author who will make me weep, says *Horace*,[1] must first weep himself. In reality, no Man can paint a Distress well, which he doth not feel while he is painting it; nor do I doubt, but that the most pathetic and affecting Scenes have been writ with Tears. In the same Manner it is with the Ridiculous. I am convinced I never make my Reader laugh heartily, but where I have laughed before him, unless it should happen at any Time, that instead of laughing with me, he should be inclined to laugh at me. Perhaps this may have been the Case at some Passages in this Chapter, from which Apprehension I will here put an End to it.

---

[1] *Ars Poetica*, 102–3: 'si vis me flere, dolendum est/ primum ipsi tibi.' On the requirement that a good author must first be a good man, see also Quintilian, *Institutio Oratoria*, i (Preface), 9–14.

CHAPTER II

Containing a very surprizing Adventure indeed, which Mr. Jones
met with in his Walk with the Man of the Hill.

*A*URORA now first opened her Casement, *anglicè*, the Day
began to break, when *Jones* walked forth in Company with
the Stranger, and mounted *Mazard-Hill*;[1] of which they had no
sooner gained the Summit, than one of the most noble Prospects
in the World presented itself to their View, and which we would
likewise present to the Reader; but for two Reasons. *First*, We
despair of making those who have seen this Prospect, admire our
Description. *Secondly*, We very much doubt whether those, who
have not seen it, would understand it.

Jones stood for some Minutes fixed in one Posture, and directing his Eyes towards the South; upon which the old Gentleman
asked, What he was looking at with so much Attention? 'Alas,
Sir,' answered he, with a Sigh, 'I was endeavouring to trace out
my own Journey hither. Good Heavens! what a Distance is
Gloucester from us! What a vast Tract of Land must be between
me and my own Home.' 'Ay, ay, young Gentleman,' cries the
other, 'and, by your Sighing, from what you love better than your
own Home, or I am mistaken. I perceive now the Object of your
Contemplation is not within your Sight, and yet I fancy you have
a Pleasure in looking that Way.' *Jones* answered with a Smile, 'I
find, old Friend, you have not yet forgot the Sensations of your
Youth.—I own my Thoughts were employed as you have guessed.'

They now walked to that Part of the Hill which looks to the
North West, and which hangs over a vast and extensive Wood.
Here they were no sooner arrived, than they heard at a Distance
the most violent Skreams of a Woman, proceeding from the
Wood below them. *Jones* listened a Moment, and then, without
saying a Word to his Companion (for indeed the Occasion seemed
sufficiently pressing) ran, or rather slid, down the Hill, and
without the least Apprehension or Concern for his own Safety,
made directly to the Thicket whence the Sound had issued.

[1] Apparently a fictitious name, but Fielding probably has in mind the Worcestershire
Beacon, the highest peak (1,394 ft.) of the Malverns and famous for its prospect of fourteen
counties. From this vantage point Gloucester is in full view to the south and, in the
eighteenth century, the dense woods of Malvern Chace extended to the north-west.

He had not entered far into the Wood before he beheld a most shocking Sight indeed, a Woman stript half naked, under the Hands of a Ruffian, who had put his Garter round her Neck, and was endeavouring to draw her up to a Tree. *Jones* asked no Questions at this Interval; but fell instantly upon the Villain, and made such good Use of his trusty Oaken Stick, that he laid him sprawling on the Ground, before he could defend himself, indeed almost before he knew he was attacked; nor did he cease the Prosecution of his Blows, till the Woman herself begged him to forbear, saying, She believed he had sufficiently done his Business.

The poor Wretch then fell upon her Knees to *Jones*, and gave him a thousand Thanks for her Deliverance: He presently lifted her up, and told her he was highly pleased with the extraordinary Accident which had sent him thither for her Relief, where it was so improbable she should find any; adding, that Heaven seemed to have designed him as the happy Instrument of her Protection. 'Nay,' answered she, 'I could almost conceive you to be some good Angel; and to say the Truth, you look more like an Angel than a Man, in my Eye.' Indeed he was a charming Figure, and if a very fine Person, and a most comely Set of Features, adorned with Youth, Health, Strength, Freshness, Spirit and Good-Nature, can make a Man resemble an Angel, he certainly had that Resemblance.

The redeemed Captive had not altogether so much of the human-angelic Species; she seemed to be, at least, of the middle Age, nor had her Face much Appearance of Beauty; but her Cloaths being torn from all the upper Part of her Body, her Breasts, which were well formed, and extremely white, attracted the Eyes of her Deliverer, and for a few Moments they stood silent, and gazing at each other; till the Ruffian on the Ground beginning to move, *Jones* took the Garter which had been intended for another Purpose, and bound both his Hands behind him. And now, on contemplating his Face, he discovered, greatly to his Surprize, and perhaps not a little to his Satisfaction, this very Person to be no other than Ensign *Northerton*. Nor had the Ensign forgotten his former Antagonist, whom he knew the Moment he came to himself. His Surprize was equal to that of *Jones*; but I conceive his Pleasure was rather less on this Occasion.

Jones helped *Northerton* upon his Legs, and then looking him stedfastly in the Face, 'I fancy, Sir,' said he, 'you did not expect to meet me any more in this World, and I confess I had as little Expectation to find you here. However, Fortune, I see, hath brought us once more together, and hath given me Satisfaction for the Injury I have received, even without my own Knowledge.'

'It is very much like a Man of Honour indeed,' answered *Northerton*, 'to take Satisfaction by knocking a Man down behind his Back. Neither am I capable of giving you Satisfaction here, as I have no Sword; but if you dare behave like a Gentleman, let us go where I can furnish myself with one, and I will do by you as a Man of Honour ought.'

'Doth it become such a Villain as you are,' cries *Jones*, 'to contaminate the Name of Honour by assuming it? But I shall waste no Time in Discourse with you—Justice requires Satisfaction of you now, and shall have it.' Then turning to the Woman, he asked her, if she was near her Home, or if not, whether she was acquainted with any House in the Neighbourhood, where she might procure herself some decent Cloaths, in order to proceed to a Justice of the Peace.

She answered, She was an entire Stranger in that Part of the World. *Jones* then recollecting himself, said he had a Friend near, who would direct them; indeed he wondered at his not following; but, in Fact, the Good Man of the Hill, when our Hero departed, sat himself down on the Brow, where, tho' he had a Gun in his Hand, he with great Patience and Unconcern, had attended the Issue.

Jones then stepping without the Wood, perceived the old Man sitting as we have just described him; he presently exerted his utmost Agility, and with surprizing Expedition ascended the Hill.

The old Man advised him to carry the Woman to *Upton*,[1] which, he said, was the nearest Town, and there he would be sure of furnishing her with all manner of Conveniencies. *Jones* having received his Direction to the Place, took his Leave of the Man of the Hill, and desiring him to direct *Partridge* the same Way, returned hastily to the Wood.

Our Hero, at his Departure to make this Enquiry of his

[1] From the Worcestershire Beacon, the nearest settlement would have been Great Malvern; the nearest 'Town', however, was Upton-upon-Severn, some six miles to the south-east. And clearly for the purposes of his narrative, Fielding wished to bring Jones to Upton, where the threads of the plot could converge more naturally.

Friend, had considered, that as the Ruffian's Hands were tied behind him, he was incapable of executing any wicked Purposes on the poor Woman. Besides, he knew he should not be beyond the Reach of her Voice, and could return soon enough to prevent any Mischief. He had moreover declared to the Villain, that if he attempted the least Insult, he would be himself immediately the Executioner of Vengeance on him. But *Jones* unluckily forgot that tho' the Hands of *Northerton* were tied, his Legs were at Liberty; nor did he lay the least Injunction on the Prisoner, that he should not make what use of these he pleased. *Northerton* therefore having given no Parole of that Kind, thought he might, without any Breach of Honour, depart, not being obliged, as he imagined, by any Rules, to wait for a formal Discharge. He therefore took up his Legs, which were at Liberty, and walked off thro' the Wood, which favoured his Retreat; nor did the Woman, whose Eyes were perhaps rather turned towards her Deliverer, once think of his Escape, or give herself any Concern or Trouble to prevent it.

Jones therefore, at his Return, found the Woman alone. He would have spent some Time in searching for *Northerton*; but she would not permit him; earnestly entreating that he would accompany her to the Town whither they had been directed. 'As to the Fellow's Escape,' said she, 'it gives me no Uneasiness: For Philosophy and Christianity both preach up Forgiveness of Injuries. But for you, Sir, I am concerned at the Trouble I give you, nay indeed my Nakedness may well make me ashamed to look you in the Face; and if it was not for the Sake of your Protection, I should wish to go alone.'

Jones offered her his Coat; but, I know not for what Reason, she absolutely refused the most earnest Solicitations to accept it. He then begged her to forget both the Causes of her Confusion. 'With Regard to the former,' says he, 'I have done no more than my Duty in protecting you; and as for the latter, I will entirely remove it, by walking before you all the Way; for I would not have my Eyes offend you, and I could not answer for my Power of resisting the attractive Charms of so much Beauty.'

Thus our Heroe and the redeemed Lady walked in the same Manner as *Orpheus* and *Eurydice* marched heretofore:[1] But tho' I

---

[1] See Ovid, *Metamorphoses*, x. 1–63. To redeem his dead wife Eurydice, Orpheus descended to Hades and by his music so charmed Persephone that he was permitted to lead

cannot believe that *Jones* was designedly tempted by his Fair
One to look behind him, yet as she frequently wanted his
Assistance to help her over Stiles, and had besides many Trips
and other Accidents, he was often obliged to turn about. However, he had better Fortune than what attended poor *Orpheus*; for
he brought his Companion, or rather Follower, safe into the
famous Town of *Upton*.

CHAPTER III

The Arrival of Mr. Jones, *with his Lady, at the Inn, with a very full
Description of the Battle of* Upton.

THO' the Reader, we doubt not, is very eager to know who
this Lady was, and how she fell into the Hands of Mr.
Northerton; we must beg him to suspend his Curiosity for a short
Time, as we are obliged, for some very good Reasons, which
hereafter perhaps he may guess, to delay his Satisfaction a little
longer.

Mr. *Jones* and his fair Companion no sooner entered the Town,
than they went directly to that Inn[1] which, in their Eyes, presented
the fairest Appearance to the Street. Here *Jones*, having ordered
a Servant to shew a Room above Stairs, was ascending, when the
dishevelled Fair hastily following, was laid hold on by the
Master of the House, who cried, 'Hey day, where is that Beggar
Wench going? stay below Stairs, I desire you;' but *Jones* at that
Instant thundered from above, 'Let the Lady come up,' in so
authoritative a Voice, that the good Man instantly withdrew his
Hands, and the Lady made the best of her Way to the Chamber.

Eurydice from the underworld upon condition that he not look back. He forgot his promise and Eurydice was lost to him for ever.

[1] Situated on the river and along the main road, Upton was an important communications point between Gloucester and Worcester and a prosperous trading town in its own
right. It abounded with inns and ale-houses, but according to a tradition well established
by the mid-nineteenth century (see Lascelles's *Directory and Gazetteer of the City of Worcester
and Neighbourhood* [1851], p. 118), the particular hostel in which the central books of *Tom
Jones* are set is to be identified with the White Lion, a comfortable inn that still stands. (See
Mildred Berkeley, 'Some Old Worcestershire Inns', *Transactions of the Worcestershire
Archæological Society, 1924–5* [Worcester, 1925], ii. 108.) Advertisements in *The Weekly
Worcester Journal* reveal that the innkeeper was one John Hurst (see the numbers for 4–11
April 1746, 20–7 March 1747, 30 March 1749).

Here *Jones* wished her Joy of her safe Arrival, and then departed, in order, as he promised, to send the Landlady up with some Cloaths. The poor Woman thanked him heartily for all his Kindness, and said, She hoped she should see him again soon, to thank him a thousand Times more. During this short Conversation, she covered her white Bosom as well as she could possibly with her Arms: For *Jones* could not avoid stealing a sly Peep or two, tho' he took all imaginable Care to avoid giving any Offence.

Our Travellers had happened to take up their Residence at a House of exceeding good Repute, whither *Irish* Ladies of strict Virtue, and many Northern Lasses of the same Predicament, were accustomed to resort in their Way to *Bath*. The Landlady therefore would by no Means have admitted any Conversation of a disreputable Kind to pass under her Roof. Indeed so foul and contagious are all such Proceedings, that they contaminate the very innocent Scenes where they are committed, and give the Name of a bad House, or of a House of ill Repute, to all those where they are suffered to be carried on.

Not that I would intimate, that such strict Chastity as was preserved in the Temple of *Vesta* can possibly be maintained at a public Inn. My good Landlady did not hope for such a Blessing, nor would any of the Ladies I have spoken of, or indeed any others of the most rigid Note, have expected or insisted on any such Thing. But to exclude all vulgar Concubinage, and to drive all Whores in Rags from within the Walls, is within the Power of every one. This my Landlady very stiffly adhered to, and this her virtuous Guests, who did not travel in Rags, would very reasonably have expected of her.

Now it required no very blameable Degree of Suspicion, to imagine that Mr. *Jones* and his ragged Companion had certain Purposes in their Intention, which, tho' tolerated in some Christian Countries, connived at in others, and practised in all; are however as expressly forbidden as Murder, or any other horrid Vice, by that Religion which is universally believed in those Countries. The Landlady therefore had no sooner received an Intimation of the Entrance of the abovesaid Persons, than she began to meditate the most expeditious Means for their Expulsion. In order to this, she had provided herself with a long and deadly Instrument, with which, in Times of Peace, the Chambermaid was wont to demolish the Labours of the industrious

Spider. In vulgar Phrase, she had taken up the Broomstick, and was just about to sally from the Kitchen, when *Jones* accosted her with a Demand of a Gown, and other Vestments, to cover the half-naked Woman above Stairs.

Nothing can be more provoking to the human Temper, nor more dangerous to that cardinal Virtue, Patience, than Solicitations of extraordinary Offices of Kindness, on Behalf of those very Persons with whom we are highly incensed. For this Reason *Shakespear* hath artfully introduced[1] his *Desdemona* soliciting Favours for *Cassio* of her Husband, as the Means of enflaming not only his Jealousy, but his Rage, to the highest Pitch of Madness; and we find the unfortunate Moor less able to command his Passion on this Occasion, than even when he beheld his valued Present to his Wife in the Hands of his supposed Rival. In Fact, we regard these Efforts as Insults on our Understanding, and to such the Pride of Man is very difficultly brought to submit.

My Landlady, though a very good-tempered Woman, had, I suppose, some of this Pride in her Composition; for *Jones* had scarce ended his Request, when she fell upon him with a certain Weapon, which, tho' it be neither long, nor sharp, nor hard, nor indeed threatens from its Appearance with either Death or Wound, hath been however held in great Dread and Abhorrence by many wise Men; nay, by many brave ones; insomuch that some who have dared to look into the Mouth of a loaded Cannon, have not dared to look into a Mouth where this Weapon was brandished; and rather than run the Hazard of its Execution, have contented themselves with making a most pitiful and sneaking Figure in the Eyes of all their Acquaintance.

To confess the Truth, I am afraid Mr. *Jones* was one of these; for tho' he was attacked and violently belaboured with the aforesaid Weapon, he could not be provoked to make any Resistance; but in a most cowardly Manner applied, with many Entreaties, to his Antagonist to desist from pursuing her Blows; in plain *English*, he only begged her with the utmost Earnestness to hear him; but before he could obtain his Request, my Landlord himself entered into the Fray, and embraced that Side of the Cause which seemed to stand very little in need of Assistance.

There are a Sort of Heroes who are supposed to be determined

[1] Cf. *Othello*, III. iii–IV. i.

in their chusing or avoiding a Conflict by the Character and Behaviour of the Person whom they are to engage. These are said to know their Man, and *Jones*, I believe, knew his Woman; for tho' he had been so submissive to her, he was no sooner attacked by her Husband, than he demonstrated an immediate Spirit of Resentment, and enjoined him Silence under a very severe Penalty; no less than that, I think, of being converted into Fuel for his own Fire.

The Husband, with great Indignation, but with a Mixture of Pity, answered, 'You must pray first to be made able; I believe I am a better Man than yourself; ay, every Way, that I am;' and presently proceeded to discharge half a dozen Whores at the Lady above Stairs, the last of which had scarce issued from his Lips, when a swinging Blow from the Cudgel that *Jones* carried in his Hand assaulted him over the Shoulders.

It is a Question whether the Landlord or the Landlady was the most expeditious in returning this Blow. My Landlord, whose Hands were empty, fell to with his Fist, and the good Wife, up-lifting her Broom, and aiming at the Head of *Jones*, had probably put an immediate End to the Fray, and to *Jones* likewise, had not the Descent of this Broom been prevented,—not by the miracu-lous Intervention of any Heathen Deity, but by a very natural, tho' fortunate Accident; *viz.* by the Arrival of *Partridge*; who entered the House at that Instant (for Fear had caused him to run every Step from the Hill) and who, seeing the Danger which threatned his Master, or Companion, (which you chuse to call him) prevented so sad a Catastrophe, by catching hold of the Landlady's Arm, as it was brandished aloft in the Air.

The Landlady soon perceived the Impediment which pre-vented her Blow; and being unable to rescue her Arm from the Hands of *Partridge*, she let fall the Broom, and then leaving *Jones* to the Discipline of her Husband, she fell with the utmost Fury on that poor Fellow, who had already given some Inti-mation of himself, by crying, 'Zounds! do you intend to kill my Friend?'

Partridge, though not much addicted to Battle, would not however stand still when his Friend was attacked; nor was he much displeased with that Part of the Combat which fell to his Share: He therefore returned my Landlady's Blows as soon as he received them; and now the Fight was obstinately maintained on all Parts, and it seemed doubtful to which Side Fortune would incline, when the naked Lady, who had listened at the Top of the Stairs to the Dialogue which preceded the Engagement, descended suddenly from above, and without weighing the unfair Inequality of two to one, fell upon the poor Woman who was boxing with *Partridge*; nor did that great Champion desist, but rather redoubled his Fury, when he found fresh Succours were arrived to his Assistance.

Victory must now have fallen to the Side of the Travellers (for the bravest Troops must yield to Numbers) had not *Susan* the Chambermaid come luckily to support her Mistress. This *Susan* was as two-handed a Wench (according to the Phrase) as any in the Country, and would, I believe, have beat the famed *Thalestris* herself,[1] or any of her subject *Amazons*; for her Form was robust and manlike, and every way made for such Encounters. As her Hands and Arms were formed to give Blows with great Mischief to an Enemy, so was her Face as well contrived to receive Blows without any great Injury to herself: Her Nose being already flat to her Face; her Lips were so large, that no Swelling could be perceived in them, and moreover they were so hard, that a Fist could hardly make any Impression on them. Lastly, her Cheek-Bones stood out, as if Nature had intended them for two Bastions to defend her Eyes in those Encounters for which she seemed so well calculated, and to which she was most wonderfully well inclined.

This fair Creature entering the Field of Battle, immediately filed to that Wing where her Mistress maintained so unequal a Fight with one of either Sex. Here she presently challenged *Partridge* to single Combat. He accepted the Challenge, and a most desperate Fight began between them.

Now the Dogs of War being let loose,[2] began to lick their bloody Lips; now Victory with Golden Wings hung hovering in the Air. Now Fortune taking her Scales from her Shelf, began to weigh the Fates of *Tom Jones*, his Female Companion, and *Partridge*, against the Landlord, his Wife, and Maid; all which hung in exact Ballance before her; when a good-natured Accident

---

[1] Queen of the Amazons, who travelled to meet Alexander hoping to raise a race of heroes. (See Strabo, *Geography*, XI. v. 4.) In *Jonathan Wild* (1743), II. iii, she is said to be a popular character in the drolls at Bartholomew Fair. See also below, p. 846.

[2] Cf. *Julius Caesar*, III. i.

put suddenly an End to the bloody Fray, with which half of the Combatants had already sufficiently feasted. This Accident was the Arrival of a Coach and four; upon which my Landlord and Landlady immediately desisted from fighting, and at their Entreaty obtained the same Favour of their Antagonists; but *Susan* was not so kind to *Partridge*, for that *Amazonian* Fair having overthrown and bestrid her Enemy, was now cuffing him lustily with both her Hands, without any Regard to his Request of a Cessation of Arms, or to those loud Exclamations of Murder which he roared forth.

No sooner, however, had *Jones* quitted the Landlord, than he flew to the Rescue of his defeated Companion, from whom he with much Difficulty drew off the enraged Chambermaid; but *Partridge* was not immediately sensible of his Deliverance; for he still lay flat on the Floor, guarding his Face with his Hands, nor did he cease roaring till *Jones* had forced him to look up, and to perceive that the Battle was at an End.

The Landlord who had no visible Hurt, and the Landlady hiding her well scratched Face with her Handkerchief, ran both hastily to the Door to attend the Coach, from which a young Lady and her Maid now alighted. These the Landlady presently ushered into that Room where Mr. *Jones* had at first deposited his fair Prize, as it was the best Apartment in the House. Hither they were obliged to pass through the Field of Battle, which they did with the utmost Haste, covering their Faces with their Handkerchiefs, as desirous to avoid the Notice of any one. Indeed their Caution was quite unnecessary: For the poor unfortunate *Helen*, the fatal Cause of all the Bloodshed, was entirely taken up in endeavouring to conceal her own Face, and *Jones* was no less occupied in rescuing *Partridge* from the Fury of *Susan*; which being happily effected, the poor Fellow immediately departed to the Pump to wash his Face, and to stop that bloody Torrent which *Susan* had plentifully set a flowing from his Nostrils.

CHAPTER IV

In which the Arrival of a Man of War puts a final End to Hostilities, and causes the Conclusion of a firm and lasting Peace between all Parties.

A SERJEANT and a File of Musqueteers, with a Deserter in their Custody, arrived about this Time. The Serjeant presently enquired for the principal Magistrate of the Town, and was informed by my Landlord, that he himself was vested in that Office. He then demanded his Billets, together with a Mug of Beer, and complaining it was cold, spread himself before the Kitchen Fire.

Mr. *Jones* was at this Time comforting the poor distressed Lady, who sat down at a Table in the Kitchen, and leaning her Head upon her Arm, was bemoaning her Misfortunes; but lest my fair Readers should be in Pain concerning a particular Circumstance, I think proper here to acquaint them, that before she had quitted the Room above Stairs, she had so well covered herself with a Pillowbere which she there found, that her Regard to Decency was not in the least violated by the Presence of so many Men as were now in the Room.

One of the Soldiers now went up to the Serjeant, and whispered something in his Ear; upon which he stedfastly fixed his Eyes on the Lady, and having looked at her for near a Minute, he came up to her, saying, 'I ask Pardon, Madam, but I am certain I am not deceived, you can be no other Person than Captain *Waters's* Lady.'

The poor Woman, who in her present Distress had very little regarded the Face of any Person present, no sooner looked at the Serjeant, than she presently recollected him, and calling him by his Name, answered, 'That she was indeed the unhappy Person he imagined her to be;' but added, 'I wonder any one should know me in this Disguise.' To which the Serjeant replied, 'he was very much surprized to see her Ladyship in such a Dress, and was afraid some Accident had happened to her.' 'An Accident hath happened to me, indeed,' says she, 'and I am highly obliged to this Gentleman (pointing to *Jones*) that it was not a fatal one, or that I am now living to mention it.' 'Whatever the Gentleman hath done,' cries the Serjeant, 'I am sure the Captain will make him

Amends for it; and if I can be of any Service, your Ladyship may command me, and I shall think myself very happy to have it in my Power to serve your Ladyship; and so indeed may any one, for I know the Captain will well reward them for it.'

The Landlady who heard from the Stairs all that past between the Serjeant and Mrs. *Waters*, came hastily down, and running directly up to her, began to ask Pardon for the Offences she had committed, begging that all might be imputed to Ignorance of her Quality: For, 'Lud! Madam,' says she, 'how should I have imagined that a Lady of your Fashion would appear in such a Dress? I am sure, Madam, if I had once suspected that your Ladyship was your Ladyship, I would sooner have burnt my Tongue out, than have said what I have said: And I hope your Ladyship will accept of a Gown, till you can get your own Cloaths.'

'Prithee Woman,' says Mrs. *Waters*, 'cease your Impertinence: How can you imagine I should concern myself about any thing which comes from the Lips of such low Creatures as yourself. But I am surprized at your Assurance in thinking, after what is past, that I will condescend to put on any of your dirty Things. I would have you know, Creature, I have a Spirit above that.'

Here *Jones* interfered, and begg'd Mrs. *Waters* to forgive the Landlady, and to accept her Gown: 'For I must confess,' cries he, 'our Appearance was a little suspicious when first we came in; and I am well assured, all this good Woman did, was, as she professed, out of Regard to the Reputation of her House.'

'Yes, upon my truly was it,' says she; 'the Gentleman speaks very much like a Gentleman, and I see very plainly is so; and to be certain the House is well known to be a House of as good Reputation as any on the Road, and tho' I say it, is frequented by Gentry of the best Quality, both *Irish* and *English*. I defy any Body to say black is my Eye,[1] for that Matter. And, as I was saying, if I had known your Ladyship to be your Ladyship, I would as soon have burnt my Fingers as have affronted your Ladyship; but truly where Gentry come and spend their Money, I am not willing that they should be scandalized by a Set of poor shabby Vermin, that wherever they go, leave more Lice than Money behind them; such Folks never raise my Compassion: For to be certain, it is foolish to have any for them, and if our

---

[1] See above, p. 317, n. 2.

Justices did as they ought, they would be all whipt out of the Kingdom; for to be certain it is what is most fitting for them. But as for your Ladyship, I am heartily sorry your Ladyship hath had a Misfortune, and if your Ladyship will do me the Honour to wear my Cloaths till you can get some of your Ladyship's own, to be certain the best I have is at your Ladyship's Service.'

Whether Cold, Shame, or the Persuasions of Mr. *Jones* prevailed most on Mrs. *Waters*, I will not determine; but she suffered herself to be pacified by this Speech of my Landlady, and retired with that good Woman, in order to apparel herself in a decent Manner.

My Landlord was likewise beginning his Oration to *Jones*, but was presently interrupted by that generous Youth, who shook him heartily by the Hand; and assured him of entire Forgiveness, saying, 'If you are satisfied, my worthy Friend, I promise you I am;' and indeed in one Sense the Landlord had the better Reason to be satisfied; for he had received a Bellyfull of Drubbing, whereas *Jones* had scarce felt a single Blow.

Partridge, who had been all this Time washing his bloody Nose at the Pump, returned into the Kitchen at the Instant when his Master and the Landlord were shaking Hands with each other. As he was of a peaceable Disposition, he was pleased with those Symptoms of Reconciliation; and tho' his Face bore some Marks of *Susan's* Fist, and many more of her Nails, he rather chose to be contented with his Fortune in the last Battle, than to endeavour at bettering it in another.

The heroic *Susan* was likewise well contented with her Victory, tho' it had cost her a Black-Eye, which *Partridge* had given her at the first Onset. Between these two, therefore, a League was struck, and those Hands which had been the Instruments of War, became now the Mediators of Peace.

Matters were thus restored to a perfect Calm, at which the Serjeant, tho' it may seem so contrary to the Principles of his Profession, testified his Approbation. 'Why now, that's friendly,' said he; 'D—n me, I hate to see two People bear Ill-will to one another, after they have had a Tussel. The only Way when Friends quarrel, is to see it out fairly in a friendly Manner, as a Man may call it, either with a Fist, or Sword, or Pistol, according as they like, and then let it be all over: For my own Part, d—n me if ever I love my Friend better than when I am fighting with him. To bear Malice is more like a *Frenchman* than an *Englishman.*'

He then proposed a Libation[1] as a necessary Part of the Ceremony at all Treaties of this Kind. Perhaps the Reader may here conclude that he was well versed in antient History; but this, tho' highly probable, as he cited no Authority to support the Custom, I will not affirm with any Confidence. Most likely indeed it is, that he founded his Opinion on very good Authority, since he confirmed it with many violent Oaths.

Jones no sooner heard the Proposal, than immediately agreeing with the learned Serjeant, he ordered a Bowl, or rather a large Mug, filled with the Liquor used on these Occasions to be brought in, and then began the Ceremony himself. He placed his Right Hand in that of the Landlord, and seizing the Bowl with his Left, uttered the usual Words, and then made his Libation. After which the same was observed by all present. Indeed there is very little Need of being particular in describing the whole Form, as it differed so little from those Libations of which so much is recorded in ancient Authors, and their modern Transcribers. The principal Difference lay in two Instances: For first, the present Company poured the Liquor only down their Throats; and, secondly, The Serjeant, who officiated as Priest, drank the last; but he preserved, I believe, the antient Form in swallowing much the largest Draught of the whole Company, and in being the only Person present who contributed nothing towards the Libation, besides his good Offices in assisting at the Performance.

The good People now ranged themselves round the Kitchin Fire, where good Humour seemed to maintain an absolute Dominion, and *Partridge* not only forgot his shameful Defeat, but converted Hunger into Thirst, and soon became extremely facetious. We must, however, quit this agreeable Assembly for a while, and attend Mr. *Jones* to Mrs. *Waters's* Apartment, where the Dinner which he had now bespoke was on the Table. Indeed it took no long Time in preparing, having been all drest three Days before, and required nothing more from the Cook than to warm it over again.

---

[1] The Greek word for treaty or truce is σπονδαί, literally 'libations'. In the following passage Fielding parodies this ceremony as described, for instance, in the *Iliad*, xvi. 268 ff., where Achilles makes a libation to Zeus, pouring wine from the δέπας or 'Bowl' on to the ground. See also below, p. 546.25.

CHAPTER V

An Apology for all Heroes who have good Stomachs, with a Description of a Battle of the amorous Kind.

HEROES, notwithstanding the high Ideas, which by the Means of Flatterers they may entertain of themselves, or the World may conceive of them, have certainly more of mortal than divine about them. However elevated their Minds may be, their Bodies at least (which is much the major Part of most) are liable to the worst Infirmities and subject to the vilest Offices of human Nature. Among these latter the Act of Eating, which hath by several wise Men been considered as extremely mean and derogatory from the Philosophic Dignity, must be in some Measure performed by the greatest Prince, Heroe, or Philosopher upon Earth; nay, sometimes Nature hath been so frolicksome as to exact of these dignified Characters, a much more exorbitant Share of this Office, than she hath obliged those of the lowest Order to perform.

To say the Truth, as no known Inhabitant of this Globe is really more than Man, so none need be ashamed of submitting to what the Necessities of Man demand; but when those great Personages I have just mentioned, condescend to aim at confining such low Offices to themselves; as when by hoarding or destroying, they seem desirous to prevent any others from eating, they then surely become very low and despicable.

Now after this short Preface, we think it no Disparagement to our Heroe to mention the immoderate Ardour with which he laid about him at this Season. Indeed it may be doubted, whether *Ulysses*, who by the Way seems to have had the best Stomach of all the Heroes in that eating Poem of the Odyssey, ever made a better Meal. Three Pounds at least of that Flesh which formerly had contributed to the Composition of an Ox, was now honoured with becoming Part of the individual Mr. *Jones*.

This Particular we thought ourselves obliged to mention, as it may account for our Heroe's temporary Neglect of his fair Companion; who eat but very little, and was indeed employed in Considerations of a very different Nature, which passed unobserved by *Jones*, till he had entirely satisfied that Appetite which a Fast of twenty-four Hours had procured him; but his

Dinner was no sooner ended, than his Attention to other Matters revived; with these Matters therefore we shall now proceed to acquaint the Reader.

Mr. *Jones*, of whose personal Accomplishments we have hitherto said very little, was in reality, one of the handsomest young Fellows in the World. His Face, besides being the Picture of Health, had in it the most apparent Marks of Sweetness and Good-Nature. These Qualities were indeed so characteristical in his Countenance, that while the Spirit and Sensibility in his Eyes, tho' they must have been perceived by an accurate Observer, might have escaped the Notice of the less discerning, so strongly was this Good-nature painted in his Look, that it was remarked by almost every one who saw him.

It was, perhaps, as much owing to this, as to a very fine Complection, that his Face had a Delicacy in it almost inexpressible, and which might have given him an Air rather too effeminate, had it not been joined to a most masculine Person and Mein; which latter had as much in them of the *Hercules*, as the former had of the *Adonis*. He was besides active, genteel, gay and good-humoured, and had a Flow of Animal Spirits, which enlivened every Conversation where he was present.

When the Reader hath duly reflected on these many Charms which all centered in our Heroe, and considers at the same Time the fresh Obligations which Mrs. *Waters* had to him, it will be a Mark more of Prudery than Candour to entertain a bad Opinion of her, because she conceived a very good Opinion of him.

But whatever Censures may be passed upon her, it is my Business to relate Matters of Fact with Veracity. Mrs. *Waters* had, in Truth, not only a good Opinion of our Heroe, but a very great Affection for him. To speak out boldly at once, she was in Love, according to the present universally received Sense of that Phrase, by which Love is applied indiscriminately to the desirable Objects of all our Passions, Appetites, and Senses, and is understood to be that Preference which we give to one Kind of Food rather than to another.

But tho' the Love to these several Objects may possibly be one and the same in all Cases, its Operations however must be allowed to be different; for how much soever we may be in Love with an excellent Surloin of Beef, or Bottle of *Burgundy*; with a

Damask Rose, or *Cremona* Fiddle;[1] yet do we never smile, nor
ogle, nor dress, nor flatter, nor endeavour by any other Arts or
Tricks to gain the Affection of the said Beef, &c. Sigh indeed we
sometimes may; but it is generally in the Absence, not in the
Presence of the beloved Object. For otherwise we might possibly
complain of their Ingratitude and Deafness, with the same
Reason as *Pasiphae* doth of her Bull,[2] whom she endeavoured to
engage by all the Coquetry practised with good Success in the
Drawing Room, on the much more sensible, as well as tender,
Hearts of the fine Gentlemen there.

The contrary happens, in that Love which operates between
Persons of the same Species, but of different Sexes. Here we are
no sooner in Love, than it becomes our principal Care to engage
the Affection of the Object beloved. For what other Purpose
indeed are our Youth instructed in all the Arts of rendering
themselves agreeable? If it was not with a View to this Love, I
question whether any of those Trades which deal in setting off and
adorning the Human Person would procure a Livelihood. Nay,
those great Polishers of our Manners, who are by some thought
to teach what principally distinguishes us from the Brute Creation,
even Dancing-Masters themselves, might possibly find no Place
in Society. In short, all the Graces which young Ladies and young
Gentlemen too learn from others; and the many Improvements
which, by the Help of a Looking-glass, they add of their own, are
in Reality those very *Spicula et Faces Amoris*, so often mentioned
by *Ovid*;[3] or, as they are sometimes called in our own Language,
The whole Artillery of Love.

Now Mrs. *Waters* and our Heroe had no sooner sat down
together, than the former began to play this Artillery upon the
latter. But here, as we are about to attempt a Description hitherto
unessayed either in Prose or Verse,[4] we think proper to invoke
the Assistance of certain Aerial Beings, who will, we doubt not,
come kindly to our Aid on this Occasion.

---

[1] The town in Lombardy where the violins of Amati, Stradivari and Guarneri were made.

[2] Cf. Ovid, *Metamorphoses*, viii. 131–7, 152–6, ix. 735–43. In order to satisfy her unnatural passion for a bull, Pasiphaë had Daedalus fashion her a wooden cow, in which she
disguised herself.

[3] 'The stings and flames of love'—not a direct quotation, but these are among the
effects of love mentioned in Ovid's amatory verse (e.g. *Ars Amatoria*, ii. 520, 708; *Remedia
Amoris*, 140).

[4] Cf. *Paradise Lost*, i. 16: 'Things unattempted yet in prose or rhyme.'

'Say then, ye Graces, you that inhabit the heavenly Mansions of *Seraphina's* Countenance; for you are truly Divine, are always in her Presence, and well know all the Arts of charming, Say, what were the Weapons now used to captivate the Heart of Mr. *Jones.*'

'First, from two lovely blue Eyes, whose bright Orbs flashed Lightning at their Discharge, flew forth two pointed Ogles. But happily for our Heroe, hit only a vast Piece of Beef which he was then conveying into his Plate, and harmless spent their Force. The fair Warrior perceived their Miscarriage, and immediately from her fair Bosom drew forth a deadly Sigh. A Sigh, which none could have heard unmoved, and which was sufficient at once to have swept off a dozen Beaus; so soft, so sweet, so tender, that the insinuating Air must have found its subtle Way to the Heart of our Heroe, had it not luckily been driven from his Ears by the coarse Bubbling of some bottled Ale, which at that Time he was pouring forth. Many other Weapons did she assay; but the God of Eating (if there be any such Deity; for I do not confidently assert it) preserved his Votary; or perhaps it may not be *Dignus vindice nodus,*[1] and the present Security of *Jones* may be accounted for by natural Means: For as Love frequently preserves from the Attacks of Hunger, so may Hunger possibly, in some Cases, defend us against Love.

'The Fair One, enraged at her frequent Disappointments, determined on a short Cessation of Arms. Which Interval she employed in making ready every Engine of Amorous Warfare for the renewing of the Attack, when Dinner should be over.

'No sooner then was the Cloth removed, than she again began her Operations. First, having planted her Right Eye side-ways against Mr. *Jones,* she shot from its Corner a most penetrating Glance; which, tho' great Part of its Force was spent before it reached our Heroe, did not vent itself absolutely without Effect. This the Fair One perceiving, hastily withdrew her Eyes, and leveled them downwards as if she was concerned for what she had done: Tho' by this Means she designed only to draw him from his Guard, and indeed to open his Eyes, through which she intended to surprize his Heart. And now, gently lifting up those two bright Orbs which had already begun to make an Impression on poor *Jones,* she discharged a Volley of small Charms at

[1] See above, p. 397, n. 5.

once from her whole Countenance in a Smile. Not a Smile of
Mirth, nor of Joy; but a Smile of Affection, which most Ladies
have always ready at their Command, and which serves them to
show at once their Good-Humour, their pretty Dimples, and
their white Teeth.

'This Smile our Heroe received full in his Eyes, and was
immediately staggered with its Force. He then began to see the
Designs of the Enemy, and indeed to feel their Success. A
Parley now was set on Foot between the Parties; during which
the artful Fair so slily and imperceptibly carried on her Attack,
that she had almost subdued the Heart of our Heroe, before she
again repaired to Acts of Hostility. To confess the Truth, I am
afraid Mr. *Jones* maintained a Kind of *Dutch* Defence, and
treacherously delivered up the Garrison[1] without duly weighing
his Allegiance to the fair *Sophia*. In short, no sooner had the
amorous Parley ended, and the Lady had unmasked the Royal
Battery, by carelessly letting her Handkerchief drop from her
Neck, than the Heart of Mr. *Jones* was entirely taken, and the
fair Conqueror enjoyed the usual Fruits of her Victory.'

Here the Graces think proper to end their Description, and
here we think proper to end the Chapter.

CHAPTER VI

A friendly Conversation in the Kitchen, which had a very common,
tho' not very friendly Conclusion.

WHILE our Lovers were entertaining themselves in the
Manner which is partly described in the foregoing Chapter; they were likewise furnishing out an Entertainment for their
good Friends in the Kitchen. And this in a double Sense, by
affording them Matter for their Conversation, and, at the same
Time, Drink to enliven their Spirits.

---

[1] Throughout the war the English had complained of 'Towns given up and lost by
Dutch Governors' (*Considerations on the Conduct of the Dutch* [1745], p. 47). In 1747 this
became a constant theme in the newspapers, which accused the Dutch commanders of
taking bribes to surrender their fortresses to the enemy. In this way, it was alleged, General
La Roque had delivered up Hulst to the French, and Sluys, Axel, and Bergen-op-Zoom
had fallen. (See, for example, *The General Advertiser*, 9, 13, 28 May, 17 August,
12 September 1747.) See also above, p. 240, n. 3.

There were now assembled round the Kitchen Fire, besides my Landlord and Landlady, who occasionally went backward and forward, Mr. *Partridge*, the Serjeant, and the Coachman who drove the young Lady and her Maid.

Partridge having acquainted the Company with what he had learnt from the Man of the Hill, concerning the Situation in which Mrs. *Waters* had been found by *Jones*, the Serjeant proceeded to that Part of her History which was known to him. He said, she was the Wife of Mr. *Waters*, who was a Captain in their Regiment, and had often been with him at Quarters. 'Some Folks,' says he, 'used indeed to doubt whether they were lawfully married in a Church or no. But, for my Part, that's no Business of mine; I must own, if I was put to my Corporal Oath, I believe she is little better than one of us, and I fancy the Captain may go to Heaven when the Sun shines upon a rainy Day. But if he does, that is neither here nor there, for he won't want Company. And the Lady, to give the Devil his Due, is a very good Sort of Lady, and loves the Cloth, and is always desirous to do strict Justice to it; for she hath begged off many a poor Soldier, and, by her Good-will, would never have any of them punished. But yet, to be sure, Ensign *Northerton* and she were very well acquainted together, at our last Quarters, that is the very Right and Truth of the Matter. But the Captain he knows nothing about it; and as long as there is enough for him too, what does it signify! He loves her not a bit the worse, and I am certain would run any Man through the Body that was to abuse her, therefore I won't abuse her, for my Part. I only repeat what other Folks say; and to be certain, what every body says, there must be some Truth in.' 'Ay, ay, a great deal of Truth, I warrant you,' cries *Partridge*, '*Veritas odium parit*.'[1] 'All a Parcel of scandalous Stuff,' answered the Mistress of the House. 'I am sure now she is drest, she looks like a very good Sort of Lady, and she behaves herself like one; for she gave me a Guinea for the Use of my Cloaths.' 'A very good Lady indeed,' cries my Landlord, 'and if you had not been a little too hasty, you would not have quarrelled with her as you did at first.' 'You need mention that with my truly,' answered she, 'if it had not been for your Nonsense, nothing had happened. You must be meddling with

[1] Terence, *Andria*, I. i: 'Truth begets hatred.' Cf. Ausonius, *Ludus Septem Sapientum*, viii.

what did not belong to you, and throw in your Fool's Discourse.' 'Well, well,' answered he, 'what's past cannot be mended, so there's an End of the Matter.' 'Yes,' cries she, 'for this once, but will it be mended ever the more hereafter? This is not the first Time I have suffered for your Numscull's Pate. I wish you would always hold your Tongue in the House, and meddle only in Matters without Doors which concern you. Don't you remember what happened about seven Years ago?'—'Nay, my Dear,' returned he, 'don't rip up old Stories. Come, come, all's well, and I am sorry for what I have done.' The Landlady was going to reply, but was prevented by the Peace-making Serjeant, sorely to the Displeasure of *Partridge*, who was a great Lover of what is called Fun, and a great Promoter of those harmless Quarrels which tend rather to the Production of comical than tragical Incidents.

The Serjeant asked *Partridge* whither he and his Master were travelling. 'None of your Magisters,' answered *Partridge*, 'I am no Man's Servant, I assure you; for tho' I have had Misfortunes in the World, I write Gentleman after my Name; and as poor and simple as I may appear now, I have taught Grammar School in my Time. *Sed hei mihi non sum quod fui.*[1] 'No Offence, I hope, Sir,' said the Serjeant, 'where then, if I may venture to be so bold, may you and your Friend be travelling?'—'You have now denominated us right,' says *Partridge*. '*Amici Sumus.*[2] And I promise you my Friend is one of the greatest Gentlemen in the Kingdom,' (at which Words both Landlord and Landlady pricked up their Ears). 'He is the Heir of Squire *Allworthy*.' 'What, the Squire who doth so much Good all over the Country?' cries my Landlady. 'Even he,' answered *Partridge*. 'Then I warrant,' says she, 'he'll have a swinging great Estate hereafter.' 'Most certainly,' answered *Partridge*. 'Well,' replied the Landlady, 'I thought the first Moment I saw him he looked like a good Sort of Gentleman; but my Husband here, to be sure, is wiser than any body.' 'I own, my Dear,' cries he, 'it was a Mistake.' 'A Mistake indeed!' answered she; 'but when did you ever know me to make such Mistakes?'—'But how comes it, Sir,' cries the Landlord, 'that such a great Gentleman walks about the Country afoot?' 'I don't know,' returned *Partridge*, 'great Gentlemen have Humours sometimes. He hath now a dozen Horses and Servants

---

[1] 'But woe to me! I am not what I was.'   [2] 'We are friends.'

at *Gloucester*, and nothing would serve him, but last Night, it being very hot Weather, he must cool himself with a Walk to yon high Hill, whither I likewise walked with him to bear him Company; but if ever you catch me there again: For I was never so frightened in all my Life. We met with the strangest Man there.' 'I'll be hanged,' cries the Landlord, 'if it was not the Man of the Hill, as they call him; if indeed he be a Man; but I know several People who believe it is the Devil that lives there.' 'Nay, nay, like enough,' says *Partridge*, 'and now you put me in the Head of it, I verily and sincerely believe it was the Devil; tho' I could not perceive his cloven Foot; but perhaps he might have the Power given him to hide that, since evil Spirits can appear in what Shapes they please.' 'And pray, Sir,' says the Serjeant, 'no Offence I hope; but pray what Sort of a Gentleman is the Devil? For I have heard some of our Officers say, There is no such Person, and that it is only a Trick of the Parsons, to prevent their being broke; for if it was publickly known that there was no Devil, the Parsons would be of no more Use than we are in Time of Peace.' 'Those Officers,' says *Partridge*, 'are very great Scholars, I suppose.' 'Not much of Schollards neither,' answered the Serjeant, 'they have not half your Learning, Sir, I believe; and to be sure, I thought there must be a Devil, notwithstanding what they said, tho' one of them was a Captain; for methought, thinks I to myself, if there be no Devil, how can wicked People be sent to him, and I have read all that upon a Book.' 'Some of your Officers,' quoth the Landlord, 'will find there is a Devil, to their Shame, I believe. I don't question but he'll pay off some old Scores, upon my Account. Here was one quartered upon me half a Year, who had the Conscience to take up one of my best Beds, tho' he hardly spent a Shilling a Day in the House, and suffered his Men to roast Cabbages at the Kitchen Fire, because I would not give them a Dinner on a *Sunday*. Every good Christian must desire there should be a Devil for the Punishment of such Wretches.' 'Harkee, Landlord,' said the Serjeant, 'don't abuse the Cloth, for I won't take it.' 'D——n the Cloth,' answered the Landlord, 'I have suffered enough by them.' 'Bear Witness, Gentlemen,' says the Serjeant, 'he curses the King, and that's High Treason.' 'I curse the King! you Villain,' said the Landlord. 'Yes you did,' cries the Serjeant, 'you cursed the Cloth, and that's cursing the King. It's all one and the same; for every Man who curses the Cloth, would curse the King if he durst; so for Matter o' that, it's all one and the same Thing.' 'Excuse me there, Mr. Serjeant,' quoth *Partridge*, 'that's a *Non Sequitur*.' 'None of your outlandish Linguo,' answered the Serjeant, leaping from his Seat, 'I will not sit still and hear the Cloth abused.'— 'You mistake me, Friend,' cries *Partridge*, 'I did not mean to abuse the Cloth; I only said your Conclusion was a *Non Sequitur*.'* 'You are another,' cries the Serjeant, 'an you come to that. No more a *Sequitur* than yourself. You are a Pack of Rascals, and I'll prove it; for I will fight the best Man of you all for twenty Pound.' This Challenge effectually silenced *Partridge*, whose Stomach for drubbing did not so soon return, after the hearty Meal which he had lately been treated with; but the Coachman, whose Bones were less sore, and whose Appetite for Fighting was somewhat sharper, did not so easily brook the Affront, of which he conceived some Part at least fell to his Share. He started therefore from his Seat, and advancing to the Serjeant, swore he looked on himself to be as good a Man as any in the Army, and offered to box for a Guinea. The military Man accepted the Combat, but refused the Wager; upon which both immediately stript and engaged, till the Driver of Horses was so well mauled by the Leader of Men, that he was obliged to exhaust his small Remainder of Breath in begging for Quarter.

The young Lady was now desirous to depart, and had given Orders for her Coach to be prepared; but all in vain; for the Coachman was disabled from performing his Office for that Evening. An antient Heathen would perhaps have imputed this Disability to the God of Drink, no less than to the God of War; for, in Reality, both the Combatants had sacrificed as well to the former Deity as to the latter. To speak plainly, they were both dead drunk, nor was *Partridge* in a much better Situation. As for my Landlord, drinking was his Trade, and the Liquor had no more Effect on him, than it had on any other Vessel in his House.

The Mistress of the Inn being summoned to attend Mr. *Jones* and his Companion, at their Tea, gave a full Relation of the latter Part of the foregoing Scene; and at the same Time expressed great Concern for the young Lady, 'who,' she said, 'was under the utmost Uneasiness at being prevented from pursuing her

---

* This Word, which the Serjeant unhappily mistook for an Affront, is a Term in Logic, and means that the Conclusion doth not follow from the Premises.

Journey. She is a sweet pretty Creature,' added she, 'and I am certain I have seen her Face before. I fancy she is in Love, and running away from her Friends. Who knows but some young Gentleman or other may be expecting her, with a Heart as heavy as her own.'

Jones fetched a hearty Sigh at those Words; of which, tho' Mrs. *Waters* observed it, she took no Notice while the Landlady continued in the Room; but after the Departure of that good Woman, she could not forbear giving our Heroe certain Hints of her suspecting some very dangerous Rival in his Affections. The aukward Behaviour of Mr. *Jones* on this Occasion convinced her of the Truth, without his giving her a direct Answer to any of her Questions; but she was not nice enough in her Amours to be greatly concerned at the Discovery. The Beauty of *Jones* highly charmed her Eye; but, as she could not see his Heart, she gave herself no concern about it. She could feast heartily at the Table of Love, without reflecting that some other already had been, or hereafter might be, feasted with the same Repast. A Sentiment which, if it deals but little in Refinement, deals however much in Substance; and is less capricious, and perhaps less ill-natured and selfish than the Desires of those Females who can be contented enough to abstain from the Possession of their Lovers, provided they are sufficiently satisfied that no one else possesses them.

CHAPTER VII

Containing a fuller Account of Mrs. Waters, *and by what Means she came into that distressful Situation from which she was rescued by* Jones.

THOUGH Nature hath by no Means mixed up an equal Share either of Curiosity or Vanity in every human Composition, there is perhaps no Individual to whom she hath not allotted such a Proportion of both, as requires much Art, and Pains too, to subdue and keep under. A Conquest, however, absolutely necessary to every one who would in any Degree deserve the Characters of Wisdom or Good-Breeding.

As *Jones* therefore might very justly be called a well-bred Man, he had stifled all that Curiosity which the extraordinary Manner in which he had found Mrs. *Waters*, must be supposed to have occasioned. He had indeed at first thrown out some few Hints to the Lady; but when he perceived her industriously avoiding any Explanation, he was contented to remain in Ignorance, the rather as he was not without Suspicion, that there were some Circumstances which must have raised her Blushes, had she related the whole Truth.

Now, since it is possible that some of our Readers may not so easily acquiesce under the same Ignorance, and as we are very desirous to satisfy them all, we have taken uncommon Pains to inform ourselves of the real Fact, with the Relation of which we shall conclude this Book.

This Lady then had lived some Years with one Captain *Waters*, who was a Captain in the same Regiment to which Mr. *Norther-ton* belonged. She past for that Gentleman's Wife, and went by his Name; and yet, as the Serjeant said, there were some Doubts concerning the Reality of their Marriage, which we shall not at present take upon us to resolve.

Mrs. *Waters*, I am sorry to say it, had for some Time contracted an Intimacy with the above mentioned Ensign, which did no great Credit to her Reputation. That she had a remarkable Fondness for that young Fellow is most certain; but whether she indulged this to any very criminal Lengths, is not so extremely clear, unless we will suppose that Women never grant every Favour to a Man but one, without granting him that one also.

The Division of the Regiment to which Captain *Waters* belonged, had two Days preceded the March of that Company to which Mr. *Northerton* was the Ensign; so that the former had reached *Worcester*, the very Day after the unfortunate Rencounter between *Jones* and *Northerton*, which we have before recorded.

Now it had been agreed between Mrs. *Waters* and the Captain, that she should accompany him in his March as far as *Worcester*, where they were to take their Leave of each other, and she was thence to return to *Bath*, where she was to stay till the End of the Winter's Campaign against the Rebels.

With this Agreement Mr. *Northerton* was made acquainted. To say the Truth, the Lady had made him an Assignation at this very Place, and promised to stay at *Worcester* till his Division came thither; with what View, and for what Purpose must be left to the Reader's Divination: For though we are obliged to relate Facts, we are not obliged to do a Violence to our Nature by any Comments to the Disadvantage of the loveliest Part of the Creation.

Northerton no sooner obtained a Release from his Captivity, as we have seen, than he hasted away to overtake Mrs. *Waters*; which, as he was a very active nimble Fellow, he did at the last mentioned City, some few Hours after Captain *Waters* had left her: At his first Arrival he made no Scruple of acquainting her with the unfortunate Accident, which he made appear very unfortunate indeed: For he totally extracted every Particle of what could be called Fault, at least in a Court of Honour, though he left some Circumstances which might be questionable in a Court of Law.

Women, to their Glory be it spoken, are more generally capable of that violent and apparently disinterested Passion of Love, which seeks only the Good of its Object, than Men. Mrs. *Waters*, therefore, was no sooner apprized of the Danger to which her Lover was exposed, than she lost every Consideration besides that of his Safety; and this being a Matter equally agreeable to the Gentleman, it became the immediate Subject of Debate between them.

After much Consultation on this Matter, it was at length agreed, that the Ensign should go a-cross the Country to *Hereford*, whence he might find some Conveyance to one of the Sea-Ports in *Wales*, and thence might make his Escape abroad. In all which Expedition Mrs. *Waters* declared she would bear him Company; and for which she was able to furnish him with Money, a very material Article to Mr. *Northerton*, she having then in her Pocket three Bank Notes to the Amount of 90 *l.* besides some Cash, and a Diamond Ring of pretty considerable Value on her Finger. All which she, with the utmost Confidence, revealed to this wicked Man, little suspecting she should by these Means inspire him with a Design of robbing her. Now as they must, by taking Horses from *Worcester*, have furnished any Pursuers with the Means of hereafter discovering their Rout, the Ensign proposed, and the Lady presently agreed to make their first Stage on Foot; for which Purpose the Hardness of the Frost was very seasonable.

The main Part of the Lady's Baggage was already at *Bath*, and she had nothing with her at present besides a very small Quantity of Linnen, which the Gallant undertook to carry in his own Pockets. All Things, therefore, being settled in the Evening, they arose early the next Morning, and at Five o'Clock departed from *Worcester*, it being then above two Hours before Day. But the Moon which was then at the full, gave them all the Light she was capable of affording.[1]

Mrs. *Waters* was not of that delicate Race of Women who are obliged to the Invention of Vehicles for the Capacity of removing themselves from one Place to another, and with whom consequently a Coach is reckoned among the Necessaries of Life. Her Limbs were indeed full of Strength and Agility, and as her Mind was no less animated with Spirit, she was perfectly able to keep Pace with her nimble Lover.

Having travelled on for some Miles in a High Road, which *Northerton* said he was informed led to *Hereford*, they came at the Break of Day to the Side of a large Wood, where he suddenly stopped, and affecting to meditate a Moment with himself, expressed some Apprehensions from travelling any longer in so public a Way. Upon which he easily persuaded his fair Companion to strike with him into a Path which seemed to lead directly through the Wood, and which at length brought them both to the Bottom of *Mazard-Hill*.

Whether the execrable Scheme which he now attempted to execute, was the Effect of previous Deliberation, or whether it now first came into his Head, I cannot determine. But being arrived in this lonely Place, where it was very improbable he should meet with any Interruption; he suddenly slipped his Garter from his Leg, and laying violent Hands on the poor Woman, endeavoured to perpetrate that dreadful and detestable Fact, which we have before commemorated, and which the providential Appearance of *Jones* did so fortunately prevent.

Happy was it for Mrs. *Waters*, that she was not of the weakest Order of Females; for no sooner did she perceive by his tying a Knot in his Garter, and by his Declarations, what his Hellish

---

[1] If, as seems unlikely, Fielding had earlier troubled to consult an almanac when plotting the time-scheme of his narative (see above, p. 435, n. 1), at this point he was no longer doing so. The moon which had risen over Gloucester at 5.00 p.m., presumably on 29 November 1745, set the following morning at 3.05 (Greenwich time), some five hours before daybreak. (See Nathanael Culpepper, *The Family Almanack, for 1745.*)

Intentions were, than she stood stoutly to her Defence, and so strongly struggled with her Enemy, screaming all the while for Assistance, that she delayed the Execution of the Villain's Purpose several Minutes, by which Means Mr. *Jones* came to her Relief, at that very Instant when her Strength failed, and she was totally overpowered, and delivered her from the Ruffian's Hands, with no other Loss than that of her Cloaths, which were torn from her Back, and of the Diamond Ring, which during the Contention either dropped from her Finger, or was wrenched from it by *Northerton*.

Thus, Reader, we have given thee the Fruits of a very painful Enquiry, which for thy Satisfaction we have made into this Matter. And here we have opened to thee a Scene of Folly, as well as Villainy, which we could scarce have believed a human Creature capable of being guilty of; had we not remembered that this Fellow was at that Time firmly persuaded, that he had already committed a Murther, and had forfeited his Life to the Law. As he concluded therefore that his only Safety lay in Flight, he thought the possessing himself of this poor Woman's Money and Ring, would make him Amends for the additional Burthen he was to lay on his Conscience.

And here, Reader, we must strictly caution thee, that thou dost not take any Occasion from the Misbehaviour of such a Wretch as this, to reflect on so worthy and honourable a Body of Men, as are the Officers of our Army in general. Thou wilt be pleased to consider, that this Fellow, as we have already informed thee, had neither the Birth nor Education of a Gentleman, nor was a proper Person to be enrolled among the Number of such. If therefore his Baseness can justly reflect on any besides himself, it must be only on those who gave him his Commission.

The End of the Third Volume.

BOOK X

In which the History goes forward about Twelve Hours.

CHAPTER I

Containing Instructions very necessary to be perused by modern Critics.

READER, it is impossible we should know what Sort of Person thou wilt be: For, perhaps, thou may'st be as learned in Human Nature as *Shakespear* himself was, and, perhaps, thou may'st be no wiser than some of his Editors.[1] Now lest this latter should be the Case, we think proper, before we go any farther together, to give thee a few wholesome Admonitions; that thou may'st not as grosly misunderstand and misrepresent us, as some of the said Editors have misunderstood and misrepresented their Author.

---

[1] The incompetencies of Shakespeare's editors were a recurrent theme of Fielding's satire, his favourite target being Lewis Theobald. (See *Plutus* [1742], *Journey from This World to the Next* [1743; I. viii], *The True Patriot* [11–18 February 1746], and *The Covent-Garden Journal* [18 April 1752].) But the sarcasm of the present passage has a special point. In May 1747 William Warburton (see below, p. 687, n. 3) had published his pretentious edition of Shakespeare, based on Pope's (1725). The title-page declared that here the 'Genuine Text' was 'settled: Being restored from the *Blunders* of the first Editors, and the *Interpolations* of the two Last'. In the preface Warburton haughtily disparaged the editorial practices of Rowe (1709) and of Theobald (1734) and Sir Thomas Hanmer (1743–4), in particular. His own blunders and interpolations, however, together with his contemptuous manner of discrediting his predecessors, elicited a number of replies from the critics—some angry, some ironic, but nearly all hostile. Of these the most effective was Thomas Edwards (see below, p. 790, n. 1), whose *Canons of Criticism* (April 1748) went through three editions in two years.

Warburton was a close friend of Fielding's patron Ralph Allen—indeed, his edition of Shakespeare was dedicated to Allen's wife—and allusions to the learned divine, most of them complimentary, are frequent in Fielding's writings (see, for example, XIII. i; also *The Champion* [31 May 1740], *A Journey from This World to the Next* [I. viii], and 'Juvenal's Sixth Satire Modernized in Burlesque Verse' [*Miscellanies*, 1743]). Understandably, therefore, the satire here is carefully vague, being directed at 'some' of Shakespeare's editors; but Fielding's first readers would certainly have applied the passage to Warburton. Perhaps the motive for this disingenuous stroke at Warburton's expense may be found in the preface to his edition (p. xiii): among those who smarted under Warburton's universal condemnation of previous commentators was John Upton (see pp. 452, n. 1, and 524, n. 1), Fielding's good friend and author of *Critical Observations on Shakespeare* (1746).

First, then, we warn thee not too hastily to condemn any of the
Incidents in this our History, as impertinent and foreign to our
main Design, because thou dost not immediately conceive in what
Manner such Incident may conduce to that Design.[1] This Work

[1] Throughout this paragraph Fielding declares the 'Design' of his 'great Creation' in
a manner generally recalling Pope in the *Essay on Man* (1733–4), epistle i, and countless
other authors, both deists and divines, who argued that despite apparent imperfections in
the parts, God's world as a whole was orderly and regular. The idea is succinctly presented
in Pope's famous couplet, 'All Nature is but Art, unknown to thee;/ All Chance, Direction,
which thou canst not see' (i. 289–90). Fielding simply inverts the usual analogy comparing
the design of the creation to that of a well-made play or romance. In *The True Intellectual
System of the Universe* (1678), for example, Ralph Cudworth develops the comparison:

'But they, who, because judgment is not presently executed upon the ungodly, blame
the management of things as faulty, and Providence as defective, are like such spectators
of a dramatick poem, as when wicked and injurious persons are brought upon the stage,
for a while swaggering and triumphing, impatiently cry out against the dramatist, and
presently condemn the plot; whereas, if they would but expect the winding up of things,
and stay till the last close, they should then see them come off with shame and sufficient
punishment. The evolution of the world, as *Plotinus* calls it, is . . . a *truer poem*; and we
men histrionical actors upon the stage . . . but God Almighty is that skilful dramatist, who
always connecteth [our actions and His designs] . . . into good coherent sense, and will at
last make it appear, that a thread of exact justice did run through all, and that rewards
and punishments are measured out in geometrical proportion' (2nd ed., 1743; ii. 879–80).

Another version of this commonplace occurs in *The Sacred Theory of the Earth* (2nd ed.,
1691), where Thomas Burnet assures his readers that the history of the world, if truly
written, would reveal a 'harmony and correspondency' of parts far surpassing that of 'any
Poem or Romance': in such a history there must be, 'as I may so say, a *Plot* or *Mystery*
pursued through the whole Work, and certain Grand Issues or Events upon which the
rest depend, or to which they are subordinate; but these things we do not make or contrive
our selves, but find and discover them, being made already by the Great Author and
Governour of the Universe' (Carbondale, Ill., 1965; p. 17).

Considering the present context, moreover, Fielding's rather extraordinary metaphor may
be partly intended as a compliment to John Upton (see above, p. 452, n. 1), who in the
second edition of *Critical Observations on Shakespeare* (advertised in *The Jacobite's Journal*,
11 June 1748) had advised carping critics to keep their eye steadily on the whole work, not
allowing themselves to be distracted by apparent incidental flaws. Echoing his friend's
apology for the brashness of the comparison, Fielding merely applies to his own book the
analogy with the divine creation that Upton had reserved for the works of Shakespeare:

' 'Tis the artist of a lower class who finishes all alike. If you examine the designs of a
masterly hand, you'll perceive how rough these colours are laid on, how slightly that is
touched, in order to carry on your view to what is principal, and deserves the chief
attention: for by this correspondence and relation, and by thus making each part
subservient to the other, a *whole* is formed.

'And were it not a degree of prophanation, I might here mention the great Designer,
who has flung some things into such strong shades, that 'tis no wonder so much gloominess and melancholy is raised in rude and undisciplined minds, the sublime Maker, who
has set this universe before us as a book; yet what superficial readers are we in this
volume of nature? Here I am certain we must become good men, before we become
good critics, and the first step to wisdom is humility' (pp. 134–5).

may, indeed, be considered as a great Creation of our own; and for a little Reptile of a Critic to presume to find Fault with any of its Parts, without knowing the Manner in which the Whole is connected, and before he comes to the final Catastrophe, is a most presumptuous Absurdity. The Allusion and Metaphor we have here made use of, we must acknowledge to be infinitely too great for our Occasion, but there is, indeed, no other, which is at all adequate to express the Difference between an Author of the first Rate, and a Critic of the lowest.

Another Caution we would give thee, my good Reptile, is, that thou dost not find out too near a Resemblance between certain Characters here introduced; as for Instance, between the Landlady who appears in the Seventh Book, and her in the Ninth. Thou art to know, Friend, that there are certain Characteristics, in which most Individuals of every Profession and Occupation agree. To be able to preserve these Characteristics, and at the same Time to diversify their Operations, is one Talent of a good Writer. Again, to mark the nice Distinction between two Persons actuated by the same Vice or Folly is another; and as this last Talent is found in very few Writers, so is the true Discernment of it found in as few Readers; though, I believe, the Observation of this forms a very principal Pleasure in those who are capable of the Discovery: Every Person, for Instance, can distinguish between Sir *Epicure Mammon*, and Sir *Fopling Flutter*; but to note the Difference between Sir *Fopling Flutter* and Sir *Courtly Nice*,[1] requires a more exquisite Judgment: For want of which, vulgar Spectators of Plays very often do great Injustice in the Theatre; where I have sometimes known a Poet in Danger of being convicted as a Thief, upon much worse Evidence than the Resemblance of Hands hath been held to be in the Law.[2] In reality, I apprehend every amorous Widow on the Stage would run the Hazard of being condemned as a servile

---

[1] Characters who appear, respectively, in Jonson's *Alchemist* (1610), Etherege's *Man of Mode* (1676), and Crowne's *Sir Courtly Nice* (1685).

[2] Because of the possibility of forgery or of a coincidental resemblance between the handwritings of different persons, many judges rejected the 'similitude of hands' as evidence in cases involving disputed or incriminating documents. When in 1744 a new law made it treasonable to correspond with the sons of the Pretender, this legal question gained a special relevance. For a full account, see *A Dissertation Shewing the Invalidity of all Proof by Similitude of Hands, in Criminal Cases* (1744), translated from a French tract of 1704 and dedicated to the Earl of Chesterfield.

Imitation of *Dido*, but that happily very few of our Play-house Critics understand enough of *Latin* to read *Virgil*.

In the next Place, we must admonish thee, my worthy Friend, (for, perhaps, thy Heart may be better than thy Head) not to condemn a Character as a bad one, because it is not perfectly a good one.¹ If thou dost delight in these Models of Perfection, there are Books enow written to gratify thy Taste; but as we have not, in the Course of our Conversation, ever happened to meet with any such Person, we have not chosen to introduce any such here. To say the Truth, I a little question whether mere Man ever arrived at this consummate Degree of Excellence, as well as whether there hath ever existed a Monster bad enough to verify that

> ———*nulla virtute redemptum*
> *A vitiis*———*

in *Juvenal*:² Nor do I, indeed, conceive the good Purposes served by inserting Characters of such angelic Perfection, or such

* Whose Vices are not allayed with a single Virtue.

---

¹ In concluding this chapter, Fielding restates a standard doctrine of neoclassical critical theory: the notion that in order to achieve a greater degree of verisimilitude in characterization and to heighten the moral efficacy of the work, the protagonist of a play or epic poem should be a character neither perfectly good nor eminently vicious. Based on the *Poetics*, xiii. 5, the principle was reiterated by Le Bossu, Dryden, Addison, Dennis, Gildon, Broome, and many others. (See C. C. Green, *The Neo-classic Theory of Tragedy during the Eighteenth Century* [Cambridge, Mass., 1934], ch. vii, and H. T. Swedenberg, op. cit., ch. xii.) Blackmore's reasoning in the Preface to *A Paraphrase on the Book of Job* (1700) is typical: 'Whatever others assert, in my *Judgment* the *Hero* of the *Poem* ought not to be drawn without some defects; for as the representing of a perfect *Idea* of *Vertue*, which is never to be *found* in any *meer Man*, offends against the Establish'd Rule in *Epick Writings*, which excludes all things improbable, so instead of promoting, it rather obstructs the End of that *Poetry*: For a perfect *Idea* of *Vertue* and *Excellency* may amaze and dazle us; but when propounded for our *Imitation*, it will rather discourage, than excite us: But when the Examples of *Vertue* that are set before us, are discern'd to have a mixture of *Imperfection*, we are provok'd and embolden'd to *form* our selves according to such a Pattern, where there appears no *Impossibility*, as there does in the other, of becoming like it' (Sig. d1). In their different ways both Isaac Barrow and Shaftesbury similarly argued that the depiction of perfect characters defeated the moral ends of poetry (see Barrow's sermon, 'Of Being Imitators of Christ', in Alexander Napier [ed.], *Theological Works* [Cambridge, 1859], ii. 522, and Shaftesbury's 'Miscellaneous Reflections', *Characteristicks*, 5th ed. [1732], iii. 260–2 n.). For Fielding's earlier opinion against the use of paragon characters in fiction, see *Jonathan Wild* (1743; I. i, IV. iv).

² Juvenal, *Satires*, iv. 2–3.

diabolical Depravity, in any Work of Invention: Since from contemplating either, the Mind of Man is more likely to be overwhelmed with Sorrow and Shame, than to draw any good Uses from such Patterns; for in the former Instance he may be both concerned and ashamed to see a Pattern of Excellence, in his Nature, which he may reasonably despair of ever arriving at; and in contemplating the latter, he may be no less affected with those uneasy Sensations, at seeing the Nature, of which he is a Partaker, degraded into so odious and detestable a Creature.

In Fact, if there be enough of Goodness in a Character to engage the Admiration and Affection of a well-disposed Mind, though there should appear some of those little Blemishes, *quas humana parum cavit natura*,[1] they will raise our Compassion rather than our Abhorrence. Indeed, nothing can be of more moral Use than the Imperfections which are seen in Examples of this Kind; since such form a Kind of Surprize, more apt to affect and dwell upon our Minds, than the Faults of very vicious and wicked Persons. The Foibles and Vices of Men in whom there is great Mixture of Good, become more glaring Objects, from the Virtues which contrast them, and shew their Deformity; and when we find such Vices attended with their evil Consequence to our favourite Characters, we are not only taught to shun them for our own Sake, but to hate them for the Mischiefs they have already brought on those we love.

And now, my Friend, having given you these few Admonitions, we will, if you please, once more set forward with our History.

CHAPTER II

Containing the Arrival of an Irish *Gentleman, with very extraordinary Adventures which ensued at the Inn.*

NOW the little trembling Hare, which the Dread of all her numerous Enemies, and chiefly of that cunning, cruel, carnivorous Animal Man, had confined all the Day to her Lurking-place, sports wantonly o'er the Lawns: Now on some hollow

---

[1] Horace, *Ars Poetica*, 352–3: 'which . . . human frailty has failed to avert' (trans. H. R. Fairclough, Loeb Classical Library, 1929). See below, p. 570, where Fielding quotes the passage in full.

Tree the Owl, shrill Chorister of the Night, hoots forth Notes which might charm the Ears of some modern Conoisseurs in Music: Now in the Imagination of the half-drunk Clown, as he staggers through the Church-yard, or rather Charnel-yard, to his Home, Fear paints the bloody Hobgoblin: Now Thieves and Ruffians are awake, and honest Watchmen fast asleep: In plain *English*, it was now Midnight; and the Company at the Inn, as well those who have been already mentioned in this History, as some others who arrived in the Evening, were all in Bed. Only *Susan* Chambermaid, was now stirring, she being obliged to wash the Kitchin, before she retired to the Arms of the fond, expecting Ostler.

In this Posture were Affairs at the Inn, when a Gentleman arrived there Post. He immediately alighted from his Horse, and coming up to *Susan*, enquired of her, in a very abrupt and confused Manner, being almost out of Breath with Eagerness, whether there was any Lady in the House. The Hour of Night, and the Behaviour of the Man, who stared very wildly all the Time, a little surprized *Susan*, so that she hesitated before she made any Answer: Upon which the Gentleman, with redoubled Eagerness, begg'd her to give him a true Information, saying, he had lost his Wife, and was come in Pursuit of her. 'Upon my Shoul,' cries he, 'I have been near catching her already in two or three Places, if I had not found her gone just as I came up with her.

'If she be in the House, do carry me up in the Dark and shew her to me; and if she be gone away before me, do tell me which Way I shall go after her to meet her, and upon my Shoul, I will make you the richest poor Woman in the Nation.' He then pulled out a Handful of Guineas, a Sight which would have bribed Persons of much greater Consequence than this poor Wench, to much worse Purposes.

Susan, from the Account she had received of Mrs. *Waters*, made not the least Doubt but that she was the very identical Stray whom the right Owner pursued. As she concluded, therefore, with great Appearance of Reason, that she never could get Money in an honester Way than by restoring a Wife to her Husband, she made no Scruple of assuring the Gentleman, that the Lady he wanted was then in the House, and was presently afterward prevailed upon (by very liberal Promises, and some

Earnest paid into her Hands) to conduct him to the Bed-chamber of Mrs. *Waters*.

It hath been a Custom long established in the polite World, and that upon very solid and substantial Reasons, that a Husband shall never enter his Wife's Apartment without first knocking at the Door. The many excellent Uses of this Custom need scarce be hinted to a Reader who hath any Knowledge of the World: For by this Means the Lady hath Time to adjust herself, or to remove any disagreeable Object out of the Way; for there are some Situations, in which nice and delicate Women would not be discovered by their Husbands.

To say the Truth, there are several Ceremonies instituted among the polished Part of Mankind, which, tho' they may, to coarser Judgments, appear as Matters of mere Form, are found to have much of Substance in them, by the more discerning; and lucky would it have been, had the Custom abovementioned been observed by our Gentleman in the present Instance. Knock, indeed, he did at the Door, but not with one of those gentle Raps which is usual on such Occasions. On the contrary, when he found the Door locked, he flew at it with such Violence, that the Lock immediately gave Way, the Door burst open, and he fell headlong into the Room.

He had no sooner recovered his Legs, than forth from the Bed, upon his Legs likewise appeared—with Shame and Sorrow are we obliged to proceed—our Heroe himself, who, with a menacing Voice, demanded of the Gentleman who he was, and what he meant by daring to burst open his Chamber in that outrageous Manner.

The Gentleman at first thought he had committed a Mistake, and was going to ask Pardon and retreat, when, on a sudden, as the Moon shone very bright, he cast his Eyes on Stays, Gowns, Petticoats, Caps, Ribbons, Stockings, Garters, Shoes, Clogs, &c. all which lay in a disordered Manner on the Floor. All these operating on the natural Jealousy of his Temper, so enraged him, that he lost all Power of Speech; and without returning any Answer to *Jones*, he endeavoured to approach the Bed.

Jones immediately interposing, a fierce Contention arose, which soon proceeded to Blows on both Sides. And now Mrs. *Waters* (for we must confess she was in the same Bed) being, I suppose, awakened from her Sleep, and seeing two Men fighting in her Bed-chamber, began to scream in the most violent Manner, crying out Murder! Robbery! and more frequently Rape! which last, some, perhaps, may wonder she should mention, who do not consider that these Words of Exclamation are used by Ladies in a Fright, as Fa, la, la, ra, da, &c. are in Music, only as the Vehicles of Sound, and without any fixed Ideas.

Next to the Lady's Chamber was deposited the Body of an *Irish* Gentleman, who arrived too late at the Inn to have been mentioned before. This Gentleman was one of those whom the *Irish* call a Calabalaro, or Cavalier. He was a younger Brother of a good Family, and having no Fortune at Home, was obliged to look abroad in order to get one: For which Purpose he was proceeding to the *Bath* to try his Luck with Cards and the Women.

This young Fellow lay in Bed reading one of Mrs. *Behn's* Novels;[1] for he had been instructed by a Friend, that he would find no more effectual Method of recommending himself to the Ladies than the improving his Understanding, and filling his Mind with good Literature. He no sooner, therefore, heard the violent Uproar in the next Room, than he leapt from his Bolster, and taking his Sword in one Hand, and the Candle which burnt by him in the other, he went directly to Mrs. *Waters's* Chamber.

If the Sight of another Man in his Shirt at first added some Shock to the Decency of the Lady, it made her presently Amends by considerably abating her Fears; for no sooner had the Calabalaro enter'd the Room, than he cry'd out: 'Mr. *Fitzpatrick*, what the Devil is the *Maning* of this?' Upon which the other immediately answered, 'O, Mr. *Maclachlan*, I am rejoiced you are here,—This Villain hath debauched my Wife, and is got into Bed with her.'—'What Wife?' cries *Maclachlan*, 'do not I know Mrs. *Fitzpatrick* very well, and don't I see that the Lady, whom the Gentleman who stands here in his Shirt is lying in Bed with, is none of her?'

Fitzpatrick now perceiving, as well by the Glimpse he had of the Lady, as by her Voice, which might have been distinguished at a greater Distance than he now stood from her, that he had made a very unfortunate Mistake, began to ask many Pardons of the Lady; and then turning to *Jones* he said, 'I would have you take Notice I do not ask your Pardon, for you have *bate* me; for which I am resolved to have your Blood in the Morning.'

---

[1] Aphra Behn (1640–89), prolific and disreputable hackney authoress.

Jones treated this Menace with much Contempt; and Mr. *Maclachlan* answered, 'Indeed, Mr. *Fitzpatrick*, you may be ashamed of your ownself, to disturb People at this Time of Night: If all the People in the Inn were not asleep, you would have awakened them as you have me. The Gentleman has served you very rightly. Upon my Conscience, tho' I have no Wife, if you had treated her so, I would have cut your Throat.'

Jones was so confounded with his Fears for his Lady's Reputation, that he knew neither what to say or do; but the Invention of Women is, as hath been observed, much readier than that of Men. She recollected that there was a Communication between her Chamber and that of Mr. *Jones*; relying, therefore, on his Honour and her own Assurance, she answered, 'I know not what you mean, Villains! I am Wife to none of you. Help! Rape! Murder! Rape!'—And now the Landlady coming into the Room, Mrs. *Waters* fell upon her with the utmost Virulence, saying, 'She thought herself in a sober Inn, and not in a Bawdy-House; but that a Set of Villains had broke into her Room, with an Intent upon her Honour, if not upon her Life; and both, she said, were equally dear to her.'

The Landlady now began to roar as loudly as the poor Woman in Bed had done before. She cry'd, 'She was undone, and that the Reputation of her House, which was never blown upon before, was utterly destroyed.' Then turning to the Men, she cry'd, 'What, in the Devil's Name, is the Reason of all this Disturbance in the Lady's Room?' *Fitzpatrick*, hanging down his Head, repeated, 'that he had committed a Mistake, for which he heartily asked Pardon,' and then retired with his Countryman. *Jones*, who was too ingenious to have missed the Hint given him by his Fair One, boldly asserted, 'That he had run to her Assistance upon hearing the Door broke open; with what Design he could not conceive, unless of robbing the Lady; which if they intended,' he said, 'he had the good Fortune to prevent.' 'I never had a Robbery committed in my House since I have kept it,' cries the Landlady: 'I wou'd have you to know, Sir, I harbour no Highwaymen here; I scorn the Word, thof I say it. None but honest, good Gentlefolks, are welcome to my House; and, I thank good Luck, I have always had enow of such Customers; indeed as many as I could entertain. Here hath been my Lord——' and then she repeated over a Catalogue of Names and Titles, many of which we might, perhaps, be guilty of a Breach of Privilege by inserting.

Jones, after much Patience, at length interrupted her, by making an Apology to Mrs. *Waters*, for having appeared before her in his Shirt, assuring her, 'That nothing but a Concern for her Safety could have prevailed on him to do it.' The Reader may inform himself of her Answer, and, indeed, of her whole Behaviour to the End of the Scene, by considering the Situation which she affected, it being that of a modest Lady, who was awakened out of her Sleep by three strange Men in her Chamber. This was the Part which she undertook to perform; and, indeed, she executed it so well, that none of our Theatrical Actresses could exceed her, in any of their Performances, either on or off the Stage.

And hence, I think, we may very fairly draw an Argument, to prove how extremely natural Virtue is to the Fair Sex: For tho' there is not, perhaps, one in ten thousand who is capable of making a good Actress; and even among these we rarely see two who are equally able to personate the same Character; yet this of Virtue they can all admirably well put on; and as well those Individuals who have it not, as those who possess it, can all act it to the utmost Degree of Perfection.

When the Men were all departed, Mrs. *Waters* recovering from her Fear, recovered likewise from her Anger, and spoke in much gentler Accents to the Landlady, who did not so readily quit her Concern for the Reputation of the House, in Favour of which she began again to number the many great Persons who had slept under her Roof; but the Lady stopt her short, and having absolutely acquitted her of having had any Share in the past Disturbance, begged to be left to her Repose, which, she said, she hoped to enjoy unmolested during the Remainder of the Night. Upon which the Landlady, after much Civility, and many Curt'sies, took her Leave.

CHAPTER III

A Dialogue between the Landlady, and Susan *the Chambermaid, proper to be read by all Innkeepers, and their Servants; with the Arrival, and affable Behaviour of a beautiful young Lady; which may teach Persons of Condition how they may acquire the Love of the whole World.*

THE Landlady remembering that *Susan* had been the only Person out of Bed when the Door was burst open, resorted presently to her, to enquire into the first Occasion of the Disturbance, as well as who the strange Gentleman was, and when and how he arrived.

Susan related the whole Story which the Reader knows already, varying the Truth only in some Circumstances, as she saw convenient, and totally concealing the Money which she had received. But whereas her Mistress had in the Preface to her Enquiry spoken much in Compassion for the Fright which the Lady had been in concerning any intended Depredations on her Virtue, *Susan* could not help endeavouring to quiet the Concern which her Mistress seemed to be under on that Account, by swearing heartily she saw *Jones* leap out from her Bed.

The Landlady fell into a violent Rage at these Words. 'A likely Story truly,' cried she, 'that a Woman should cry out, and endeavour to expose herself, if that was the Case! I desire to know what better Proof any Lady can give of her Virtue than her crying out, which, I believe, twenty People can witness for her she did? I beg, Madam, you would spread no such Scandal of any of my Guests: For it will not only reflect on them, but upon the House; and I am sure no Vagabonds, nor wicked beggarly People come here.'

'Well,' says *Susan*, 'then I must not believe my own Eyes.' 'No, indeed must you not always,' answered her Mistress, 'I would not have believed my own Eyes against such good Gentlefolks. I have not had a better Supper ordered this half Year than they ordered last Night, and so easy and good-humoured were they, that they found no Fault with my *Worcestershire* Perry, which I sold them for *Champagne*;[1] and to be sure it is as well

---

[1] In *The Covent-Garden Journal* (3 March 1752) the practice of unscrupulous innkeepers in passing off perry for champagne served Fielding as the basis for an elaborate metaphor contrasting false wit and true.

tasted, and as wholesome as the best *Champagne* in the Kingdom, otherwise I would scorn to give it 'em, and they drank me two Bottles. No, no, I will never believe any Harm of such sober good Sort of People.'

Susan being thus silenced, her Mistress proceeded to other Matters. 'And so you tell me,' continued she, 'That the strange Gentleman came Post, and there is a Footman without with the Horses; why then, he is certainly some of your great Gentlefolks too. Why did not you ask him whether he'd have any Supper? I think he is in the other Gentleman's Room, go up and ask whether he called. Perhaps he'll order something when he finds any Body stirring in the House to dress it. Now don't commit any of your usual Blunders, by telling him the Fire's out, and the Fowls alive. And if he should order Mutton, don't blab out, that we have none. The Butcher, I know, killed a Sheep just before I went to Bed, and he never refuses to cut it up warm when I desire it. Go, remember there's all Sorts of Mutton and Fowls; go, open the Door, with, *Gentlemen d'ye call*, and if they say nothing, ask what his Honour will be pleased to have for Supper. Don't forget his Honour. Go; if you don't mind all these Matters better, you'll never come to any Thing.'

Susan departed, and soon returned with an Account, that the two Gentlemen were got both into the same Bed. 'Two Gentlemen,' says the Landlady, 'in the same Bed! that's impossible, they are two errant Scrubs, I warrant them, and, I believe, young Squire *Allworthy* guessed right, that the Fellow intended to rob her Ladyship: For if he had broke open the Lady's Door with any of the wicked Designs of a Gentleman, he would never have sneaked away to another Room to save the Expence of a Supper and a Bed to himself. They are certainly Thieves, and their searching after a Wife is nothing but a Pretence.'

In these Censures, my Landlady did Mr. *Fitzpatrick* great Injustice; for he was really born a Gentleman, though not worth a Groat; and tho', perhaps, he had some few Blemishes in his Heart as well as in his Head, yet being a sneaking, or a niggardly Fellow, was not one of them. In reality, he was so generous a Man, that whereas he had received a very handsome Fortune with his Wife, he had now spent every Penny of it, except some little Pittance which was settled upon her; and in order to possess himself of this, he had used her with such Cruelty, that together with his Jealousy, which was of the bitterest Kind, it had forced the poor Woman to run away from him.

This Gentleman then being well tired with his long Journey from *Chester* in one Day, with which, and some good dry Blows he had received in the Scuffle, his Bones were so sore, that added to the Soreness of his Mind, it had quite deprived him of any Appetite for eating. And being now so violently disappointed in the Woman, whom at the Maid's Instance, he had mistaken for his Wife, it never once entered into his Head, that she might nevertheless be in the House, though he had erred in the first Person he had attacked. He therefore yielded to the Dissuasions of his Friend from searching any farther after her that Night, and accepted the kind Offer of Part of his Bed.

The Footman and Post-boy were in a different Disposition. They were more ready to order than the Landlady was to provide; however, after being pretty well satisfied by them of the real Truth of the Case, and that Mr. *Fitzpatrick* was no Thief, she was at length prevailed on to set some cold Meat before them, which they were devouring with great Greediness, when *Partridge* came into the Kitchin. He had been first awaked by the Hurry which we have before seen, and while he was endeavouring to compose himself again on his Pillow, a Screech-Owl had given him such a Serenade at his Window, that he leapt in a most horrible Affright from his Bed, and huddling on his Cloaths with great Expedition, ran down to the Protection of the Company, whom he heard talking below in the Kitchin.

His Arrival detained my Landlady from returning to her Rest: For she was just about to leave the other two Guests to the Care of *Susan*; but the Friend of young Squire *Allworthy* was not to be so neglected, especially as he called for a Pint of Wine to be mulled. She immediately obeyed, by putting the same Quantity of Perry to the Fire: For this readily answered to the Name of every Kind of Wine.

The *Irish* Footman was retired to Bed, and the Post-boy was going to follow; but *Partridge* invited him to stay, and partake of his Wine, which the Lad very thankfully accepted. The Schoolmaster was indeed afraid to return to Bed by himself; and as he did not know how soon he might lose the Company of my Landlady, he was resolved to secure that of the Boy, in whose Presence he apprehended no Danger from the Devil, or any of his Adherents.

And now arrived another Post-Boy at the Gate; upon which *Susan* being ordered out, returned, introducing two young Women in Riding-habits, one of which was so very richly laced, that *Partridge* and the Post-boy instantly started from their Chairs, and my Landlady fell to her Curt'sies, and her Lady-ships, with great Eagerness.

The Lady in the rich Habit said, with a Smile of great Condescension, 'If you will give me Leave, Madam, I will warm my self a few Minutes at your Kitchin Fire, for it is really very cold; but I must insist on disturbing no one from his Seat.' This was spoken on account of *Partridge*, who had retreated to the other End of the Room, struck with the utmost Awe and Astonishment at the Splendor of the Lady's Dress. Indeed she had a much better Title to Respect than this: For she was one of the most beautiful Creatures in the World.

The Lady earnestly desired *Partridge* to return to his Seat, but could not prevail. She then pulled off her Gloves, and displayed to the Fire two Hands, which had every Property of Snow in them, except that of melting. Her Companion, who was indeed her Maid, likewise pulled off her Gloves, and discovered what bore an exact Resemblance, in Cold and Colour, to a Piece of frozen Beef.

. 'I wish, Madam,' quoth the latter, 'your Ladyship would not think of going any farther to Night. I am terribly afraid your Ladyship will not be able to bear the Fatigue.'

'Why sure,' cries the Landlady, 'her Ladyship's Honour can never intend it. O bless me, farther to Night indeed! Let me beseech your Ladyship not to think on't.—But to be sure, your Ladyship can't. What will your Honour be pleased to have for Supper? I have Mutton of all Kinds, and some nice Chicken.'——

'I think, Madam,' said the Lady, 'it would be rather Breakfast than Supper; but I can't eat any Thing, and if I stay, shall only lie down for an Hour or two. However, if you please, Madam, you may get me a little Sack-whey[1] made very small and thin.'

'Yes, Madam,' cries the Mistress of the House, 'I have some excellent White-wine.' 'You have no Sack then,' says the Lady. 'Yes, an't please your Honour, I have; I may challenge the Country for that.—But let me beg your Ladyship to eat something.'

'Upon my Word, I can't eat a Morsel,' answered the Lady;

1 See above, p. 382, n. 1.

'and I shall be much obliged to you, if you will please to get my Apartment ready as soon as possible: For I am resolved to be on Horseback again in three Hours.'

'Why *Susan*,' cries the Landlady, 'is there a Fire lit yet in the *Wild-goose*?—I am sorry, Madam, all my best Rooms are full. Several People of the first Quality are now in Bed. Here's a great young Squire, and a many other great Gentlefolks of Quality.'

Susan answered, 'That the *Irish* Gentlemen were got into the *Wild-goose*.'

'Was ever any Thing like it!' says the Mistress, 'why the Devil would you not keep some of the best Rooms for the Quality, when you know scarce a Day passes without some calling here?— If they be Gentlemen, I am certain, when they know it is for her Ladyship, they will get up again.'

'Not upon my Account,' says the Lady. 'I will have no Person disturbed for me. If you have a Room that is commonly decent, it will serve me very well, though it be never so plain. I beg, Madam, you will not give yourself so much Trouble on my Account.' 'O, Madam,' cries the other, 'I have several very good Rooms for that Matter, but none good enough for your Honour's Ladyship. However, as you are so condescending to take up with the best I have, do, *Susan*, get a Fire in the *Rose* this Minute. Will your Ladyship be pleased to go up now, or stay till the Fire is lighted?' 'I think, I have sufficiently warmed myself,' answered the Lady, 'so if you please I will go now; I am afraid I have kept People, and particularly that Gentleman (meaning *Partridge*) too long in the Cold already. Indeed I cannot bear to think of keeping any Person from the Fire this dreadful Weather.' She then departed with her Maid, the Landlady marching with two lighted Candles before her.

When that good Woman returned, the Conversation in the Kitchin was all upon the Charms of the young Lady. There is indeed in perfect Beauty a Power which none almost can withstand:[1] For my Landlady, though she was not pleased at the Negative given to the Supper, declared she had never seen so

---

[1] For the Platonic notion of the perfect and irresistible beauty of virtue, see the Dedication to Lyttelton, p. 7, n. 1. For the relation of this motif to Fielding's heroine, as in the present passage, see Battestin, 'Fielding's Definition of Wisdom: Some Functions of Ambiguity and Emblem in *Tom Jones*', *ELH*, xxxv (1968), 188–217.

lovely a Creature. *Partridge* ran out into the most extravagant Encomiums on her Face, though he could not refrain from paying some Compliments to the Gold Lace on her Habit; the Post-boy sung forth the Praises of her Goodness, which were likewise ecchoed by the other Post-boy, who was now come in. 'She's a true good Lady, I warrant her,' says he: 'For she hath Mercy upon dumb Creatures; for she asked me every now and tan upon the Journey, if I did not think she should hurt the Horses by riding too fast; and when she came in, she charged me to give them as much Corn as ever they would eat.'

Such Charms are there in Affability, and so sure is it to attract the Praises of all Kinds of People. It may indeed be compared to the celebrated Mrs. *Hussy*.* It is equally sure to set off every Female Perfection to the highest Advantage, and to palliate and conceal every Defect. A short Reflection which we could not forbear making in this Place, where my Reader hath seen the Loveliness of an affable Deportment; and Truth will now oblige us to contrast it, by shewing the Reverse.

---

* A celebrated Mantua-maker in the *Strand*, famous for setting off the Shapes of Women.[1]

---

[1] Probably Mrs. 'Amey Hussey, of St. Martin in the Fields, Mantua-Maker', listed in *The General Advertiser* (29 April 1748) among those persons of business with whom children of poor clergymen had been placed to learn a trade. Mrs. Hussey's friendship with Fielding and the pleasant story of her last-minute inclusion in *Tom Jones* are recalled by her grand-nephew, J. T. Smith, in *Nollekens and His Times* (1828):

'My aunt, who lived to the age of 105, had been blessed with four husbands, and her name had twice been changed to that of Hussey: she was of a most delightful disposition, of a retentive memory, highly entertaining, and liberally communicative; and to her, I have frequently been obliged for an interesting anecdote. She was after the death of her second husband, Mr. Hussey, a fashionable sacque and mantua-maker, and lived in the Strand, a few doors west of the residence of the celebrated Le Beck, a famous cook, who had a large portrait of himself for the sign of his house, at the north-west corner of Half-moon-street, since called Little Bedford-street. One day, Mr. Fielding observed to Mrs. Hussey, that he was then engaged in writing a novel, which he thought would be his best production; and that he intended to introduce in it the characters of all his friends. Mrs. Hussey, with a smile, ventured to remark, that he must have many niches, and that surely they must already be filled. "I assure you, my dear Madam," replied he, "there shall be a bracket for a bust of you." Sometime after this, he informed Mrs. Hussey, that the work was in the press; but, immediately recollecting that he had forgotten his promise to her, went to the printer, and was time enough to insert it . . .' (1949 ed., pp. 61–2).

CHAPTER IV

Containing infallible Nostrums for procuring universal Disesteem and Hatred.

THE Lady had no sooner laid herself on her Pillow, than the Waiting-woman returned to the Kitchin to regale with some of those Dainties which her Mistress had refused.

The Company at her Entrance, shewed her the same Respect which they had before paid to her Mistress, by rising; but she forgot to imitate her, by desiring them to sit down again. Indeed it was scarce possible they should have done so: For she placed her Chair in such a Posture, as to occupy almost the whole Fire. She then ordered a Chicken to be broiled that Instant, declaring if it was not ready in a Quarter of an Hour, she would not stay for it. Now tho' the said Chicken was then at Roost in the Stable, and required the several Ceremonies of catching, killing, and picking, before it was brought to the Grid-iron, my Landlady would nevertheless have undertaken to do all within the Time; but the Guest being unfortunately admitted behind the Scenes, must have been Witness to the *Fourberie*, the poor Woman was therefore obliged to confess that she had none in the House; 'but, Madam,' said she, 'I can get any kind of Mutton in an Instant from the Butcher's.'

'Do you think then,' answered the Waiting-Gentlewoman, 'that I have the Stomach of a Horse to eat Mutton at this Time of Night? Sure you People that keep Inns imagine your Betters are like yourselves. Indeed I expected to get nothing at this wretched Place. I wonder my Lady would stop at it. I suppose none but Tradesmen and Grasiers ever call here.' The Landlady fired at this Indignity offered to her House; however she suppressed her Temper, and contented herself with saying, 'Very good Quality frequented it, she thanked Heaven!' 'Don't tell me,' cries the other, 'of Quality! I believe I know more of People of Quality than such as you.—But, prithee, without troubling me with any of your Impertinence, do tell me what I can have for Supper; for tho' I cannot eat Horse-flesh, I am really hungry.' 'Why truly, Madam,' answered the Landlady, 'you could not take me again at such a Disadvantage: For I must confess, I have nothing in the House, unless a cold Piece of Beef, which indeed a Gentleman's Footman, and the Post-boy, have almost cleared to the Bone.' 'Woman,' said Mrs. *Abigail* (so for Shortness we will call her) 'I intreat you not to make me sick. If I had fasted a Month, I could not eat what had been touched by the Fingers of such Fellows. Is there nothing neat or decent to be had in this horrid Place?' 'What think you of some Eggs and Bacon, Madam,' said the Landlady. 'Are your Eggs new laid? Are you certain they were laid To-day? And let me have the Bacon cut very nice and thin; for I can't endure any Thing that's gross. —Prithee try if you can do a little tolerably for once, and don't think you have a Farmer's Wife, or some of those Creatures in the House.'—The Landlady began then to handle her Knife; but the other stopt her, saying, 'Good Woman, I must insist upon your first washing your Hands; for I am extremely nice, and have been always used from my Cradle to have every thing in the most elegant Manner.'

The Landlady, who governed herself with much Difficulty, began now the necessary Preparations; for as to *Susan*, she was utterly rejected, and with such Disdain, that the poor Wench was hard put to it, to restrain her Hands from Violence, as her Mistress had been to hold her Tongue. This indeed *Susan* did not entirely: For tho' she literally kept it within her Teeth, yet there it muttered many 'marry-come-ups, as good Flesh and Blood as yourself,' with other such indignant Phrases.

While the Supper was preparing, Mrs. *Abigail* began to lament she had not ordered a Fire in the Parlour; but she said, that was now too late. 'However,' said she, 'I have Novelty to recommend a Kitchin, for I do not believe I ever eat in one before.' Then turning to the Post-boys, she asked them, 'Why they were not in the Stable with their Horses? If I must eat my hard Fare here, Madam,' cries she to the Landlady, 'I beg the Kitchin may be kept clear, that I may not be surrounded with all the Black-guards in Town; as for you, Sir,' says she to *Partridge*, 'you look somewhat like a Gentleman, and may sit still if you please, I don't desire to disturb any body but Mob.'

'Yes, yes, Madam,' cries *Partridge*, 'I am a Gentleman, I do assure you, and I am not so easily to be disturbed. *Non semper vox causalis est verbo nominativus.*'[1] This *Latin* she took to be some

---

[1] Under 'Syntaxis', a rule in Lily's grammar: 'A casual [i.e., causal] word is not always the nominative case to the verb' (*Lily's Rules Construed* [1720], p. 38).

Affront, and answered, 'You may be a Gentleman, Sir, but you don't shew yourself as one, to talk *Latin* to a Woman.' *Partridge* made a gentle Reply, and concluded with more *Latin*; upon which she tossed up her Nose, and contented herself by abusing him with the Name of a great Scholar.

The Supper being now on the Table, Mrs. *Abigail* eat very heartily, for so delicate a Person; and while a second Course of the same was by her Order preparing, she said, 'And so, Madam, you tell me your House is frequented by People of great Quality?'

The Landlady answered in the Affirmative, saying, 'There were a great many very good Quality and Gentlefolks in it now. There's young Squire *Allworthy*, as that Gentleman there knows.'

'And pray who is this young Gentleman of Quality, this young Squire *Allworthy*?' said *Abigail*.

'Who should he be,' answered *Partridge*, 'but the Son and Heir of the great Squire *Allworthy* of *Somersetshire*.'

'Upon my Word,' said she, 'you tell me strange News: For I know Mr. *Allworthy* of *Somersetshire* very well, and I know he hath no Son alive.'

The Landlady pricked up her Ears at this, and *Partridge* looked a little confounded. However, after a short Hesitation, he answered, 'Indeed, Madam, it is true, every body doth not know him to be Squire *Allworthy*'s Son; for he was never married to his Mother; but his Son he certainly is, and will be his Heir too as certainly as his Name is *Jones*.' At that Word, *Abigail* let drop the Bacon, which she was conveying to her Mouth, and cried out, 'You surprize me, Sir. Is it possible Mr. *Jones* should be now in the House?' '*Quare non?*'[1] answered *Partridge*, 'it is possible, and it is certain.'

Abigail now made Haste to finish the Remainder of her Meal, and then repaired back to her Mistress, when the Conversation passed, which may be read in the next Chapter.

---

[1] 'Why not?'

CHAPTER V

Shewing who the amiable Lady, and her unamiable Maid, were.

AS in the Month of *June*, the Damask Rose, which Chance hath planted among the Lillies with their candid Hue mixes his Vermilion: Or, as some playsome Heifer in the pleasant Month of *May* diffuses her odoriferous Breath over the flowery Meadows: Or as, in the blooming Month of *April*, the gentle, constant Dove, perched on some fair Bough, sits meditating on her Mate; so looking a hundred Charms, and breathing as many Sweets, her Thoughts being fixed on her *Tommy*, with a Heart as good and innocent, as her Face was beautiful: *Sophia* (for it was she herself) lay reclining her lovely Head on her Hand, when her Maid entered the Room, and running directly to the Bed, cried, 'Madam—Madam—who doth your Ladyship think is in the House?' *Sophia* starting up, cried, 'I hope my Father hath not overtaken us.' 'No, Madam, it is one worth a hundred Fathers; Mr. *Jones* himself is here at this very Instant.' 'Mr. *Jones*!' says *Sophia*, 'it is impossible, I cannot be so fortunate.' Her Maid averred the Fact, and was presently detached by her Mistress to order him to be called; for she said she was resolved to see him immediately.

Mrs. *Honour* had no sooner left the Kitchin in the Manner we have before seen, than the Landlady fell severely upon her. The poor Woman had indeed been loading her Heart with foul Language for some Time, and now it scoured out of her Mouth, as Filth doth from a Mud-Cart, when the Board which confines it is removed. *Partridge* likewise shovelled in his Share of Calumny; and (what may surprize the Reader) not only bespattered the Maid, but attempted to sully the Lilly-white Character of *Sophia* herself. 'Never a Barrel the better Herring,'[1] cries he. '*Noscitur a socio*,[2] is a true Saying. It must be confessed indeed that the Lady in the fine Garments is the civiller of the two; but I warrant neither of them are a Bit better than they should be. A Couple of *Bath* Trulls, I'll answer for them; your Quality don't ride

---

[1] Nothing to choose between them. (W. G. Smith and P. Harvey, *Oxford Dictionary of English Proverbs*, 2nd ed. [Oxford, 1948], p. 24.)

[2] See above, p. 98, n. 1.

about at this Time o' Night without Servants.' 'Sbodlikins, and that's truc,' cries the Landlady, 'you have certainly hit upon the very Matter; for Quality don't come into a House without bespeaking a Supper, whether they eat or no.'

While they were thus discoursing, Mrs. *Honour* returned, and discharged her Commission, by bidding the Landlady immediately wake Mr. *Jones*, and tell him a Lady wanted to speak with him. The Landlady referred her to *Partridge*, saying, 'he was the Squire's Friend; but, for her Part, she never called Men Folks, especially Gentlemen,' and then walked sullenly out of the Kitchin. *Honour* applied herself to *Partridge*; but he refused; 'For my Friend,' cries he, 'went to Bed very late, and he would be very angry to be disturbed so soon.' Mrs. *Honour* insisted still to have him called, saying, 'She was sure, instead of being angry, that he would be to the highest Degree delighted when he knew the Occasion.' 'Another Time, perhaps, he might,' cries *Partridge*; 'but *non omnia possumus omnes*.[1] One Woman is enough at once for a reasonable Man.' 'What do you mean by one Woman, Fellow?' cries *Honour*. 'None of your Fellow,' answered *Partridge*. He then proceeded to inform her plainly, that *Jones* was in Bed with a Wench, and made use of an Expression too indelicate to be here inserted; which so enraged Mrs. *Honour*, that she called him saucy Jackanapes, and returned in a violent Hurry to her Mistress, whom she acquainted with the Success of her Errand, and with the Account she had received; which, if possible, she exaggerated, being as angry with *Jones*, as if he had pronounced all the Words that came from the Mouth of *Partridge*. She discharged a Torrent of Abuse on the Master, and advised her Mistress to quit all Thoughts of a Man who had never shewn himself deserving of her. She then ripped up the Story of *Molly Seagrim*, and gave the most malicious Turn to his formerly quitting *Sophia* herself; which, I must confess, the present Incident not a little countenanced.

The Spirits of *Sophia* were too much dissipated by Concern to enable her to stop the Torrent of her Maid. At last, however, she interrupted her, saying, 'I never can believe this; some Villain hath belied him. You say you had it from his Friend; but surely it is not the Office of a Friend to betray such Secrets.' 'I suppose,' cries *Honour*, 'the Fellow is his Pimp, for I never saw so ill-looked

[1] See above, p. 178, n. 3.

a Villain. Besides, such profligate Rakes as Mr. *Jones* are never ashamed of these Matters.'

To say the Truth, this Behaviour of *Partridge* was a little in-excusable; but he had not slept off the Effect of the Dose which he swallowed the Evening before; which had, in the Morning, received the Addition of above a Pint of Wine, or indeed rather of Malt Spirits; for the Perry was by no Means pure. Now that Part of his Head which Nature designed for the Reservoir of Drink, being very shallow, a small Quantity of Liquor over-flowed it, and opened the Sluices of his Heart; so that all the Secrets there deposited run out. These Sluices were indeed naturally very ill secured. To give the best-natured Turn we can to his Disposition, he was a very honest Man; for as he was the most inquisitive of Mortals, and eternally prying into the Secrets of others, so he very faithfully paid them by communicating, in Return, every thing within his Knowledge.

While *Sophia* tormented with Anxiety, knew not what to believe, nor what Resolution to take, *Susan* arrived with the Sack-Whey. Mrs. *Honour* immediately advised her Mistress, in a Whisper, to pump this Wench, who probably could inform her of the Truth. *Sophia* approved it, and began as follows: 'Come hither, Child, now answer me truly what I am going to ask you, and I promise you I will very well reward you. Is there a young Gentleman in this House, a handsome young Gentleman that —— ' Here *Sophia* blushed and was confounded.— 'A young Gentleman,' cries *Honour*, 'that came hither in Company with that saucy Rascal who is now in the Kitchin?' *Susan* answered, 'There was.'—'Do you know any Thing of any Lady,' continues *Sophia*, 'any Lady? I don't ask you whether she is handsome or no; perhaps she is not, that's nothing to the Purpose, but do you know of any Lady?' 'La, Madam,' cries *Honour*, 'you will make a very bad Examiner. Harkee, Child,' says she, 'Is not that very young Gentleman now in Bed with some nasty Trull or other?' Here *Susan* smiled, and was silent. 'Answer the Question, Child,' says *Sophia*, 'and here's a Guinea for you.' 'A Guinea! Madam,' cries *Susan*; 'La, what's a Guinea? If my Mistress should know it, I shall certainly lose my Place that very Instant.' 'Here's another for you,' says *Sophia*, 'and I promise you faith-fully your Mistress shall never know it.' *Susan*, after a very short Hesitation, took the Money, and told the whole Story, concluding with saying, 'If you have any great Curiosity, Madam, I can steal softly into his Room, and see whether he be in his own Bed or no.' She accordingly did this by *Sophia's* Desire, and returned with an Answer in the Negative.

Sophia now trembled and turned pale. Mrs. *Honour* begged her to be comforted, and not to think any more of so worthless a Fellow. 'Why there,' says *Susan*, 'I hope, Madam, your Ladyship won't be offended; but pray, Madam, is not your Ladyship's Name Madam *Sophia Western*?' 'How is it possible you should know me?' answered *Sophia*. 'Why that Man that the Gentlewoman spoke of, who is in the Kitchin, told about you last Night. But I hope your Ladyship is not angry with me.' 'Indeed, Child,' said she, 'I am not; pray tell me all, and I promise you I'll reward you.' 'Why, Madam,' continued *Susan*, 'that Man told us all in the Kitchin, that Madam *Sophia Western*—— Indeed I don't know how to bring it out.'—Here she stopt, till having received Encouragement from *Sophia*, and being vehemently pressed by Mrs. *Honour*, she proceeded thus:—'He told us, Madam, tho' to be sure it is all a Lie, that your Ladyship was dying for Love of the young Squire, and that he was going to the Wars to get rid of you. I thought to myself then he was a false-hearted Wretch; but now to see such a fine, rich, beautiful Lady as you be forsaken for such an ordinary Woman; for to be sure so she is, and another Man's Wife into the Bargain. It is such a strange unnatural thing, in a Manner.'

Sophia gave her a third Guinea, and telling her she would certainly be her Friend, if she mentioned nothing of what had passed, nor informed any one who she was, dismissed the Girl with Orders to the Post-Boy to get the Horses ready immediately.

Being now left alone with her Maid, she told her trusty Waiting-woman, 'That she never was more easy than at present. I am now convinced,' said she, 'he is not only a Villain, but a low despicable Wretch. I can forgive all rather than his exposing my Name in so barbarous a Manner. That renders him the Object of my Contempt. Yes, *Honour*, I am now easy. I am indeed. I am very easy,' and then she burst into a violent Flood of Tears.

After a short Interval, spent by *Sophia*, chiefly in crying and assuring her Maid that she was perfectly easy, *Susan* arrived with an Account that the Horses were ready, when a very extraordinary Thought suggested itself to our young Heroine, by which Mr.

Jones would be acquainted with her having been at the Inn, in a Way, which, if any Sparks of Affection for her remained in him, would be at least some Punishment for his Faults.

The Reader will be pleased to remember a little Muff, which hath had the Honour of being more than once remembered already in this History. This Muff, ever since the Departure of Mr. *Jones*, had been the constant Companion of *Sophia* by Day, and her Bedfellow by Night, and this Muff she had at this very Instant upon her Arm; whence she took it off with great Indignation, and having writ her Name with her Pencil upon a Piece of Paper which she pinned to it, she bribed the Maid to convey it into the empty Bed of Mr. *Jones*, in which, if he did not find it, she charged her to take some Method of conveying it before his Eyes in the Morning.

Then having paid for what Mrs. *Honour* had eaten, in which Bill was included an Account for what she herself might have eaten, she mounted her Horse, and once more assuring her Companion that she was perfectly easy, continued her Journey.

CHAPTER VI

Containing, among other Things, the Ingenuity of Partridge, *the Madness of* Jones, *and the Folly of* Fitzpatrick.

IT was now past Five in the Morning, and other Company began to rise and come to the Kitchin, among whom were the Serjeant and the Coachman, who being thoroughly reconciled, made a Libation, or, in the *English* Phrase, drank a hearty Cup together.

In this Drinking nothing more remarkable happened, than the Behaviour of *Partridge*, who, when the Serjeant drank a Health to King *George*, repeated only the Word King: Nor could he be brought to utter more: For tho' he was going to fight against his own Cause, yet he could not be prevailed upon to drink against it.

Mr. *Jones* being now returned to his own Bed (but from whence he returned we must beg to be excused from relating) summoned *Partridge* from this agreeable Company, who, after a ceremonious Preface, having obtained leave to offer his Advice, delivered himself as follows:

'It is, Sir, an old Saying, and a true one, that a wise Man may sometimes learn Counsel from a Fool;[1] I wish therefore I might be so bold as to offer you my Advice, which is to return home again, and leave these *Horrida Bella*,[2] these bloody Wars, to Fellows who are contented to swallow Gunpowder, because they have nothing else to eat. Now every body knows your Honour wants for nothing at home; when that's the Case, why should any Man travel abroad?'

'*Partridge*,' cries *Jones*, 'thou art certainly a Coward, I wish therefore thou would'st return home thyself, and trouble me no more.'

'I ask your Honour's Pardon,' cries *Partridge*, 'I spoke on your Account more than my own; for as to me, Heaven knows my Circumstances are bad enough, and I am so far from being afraid, that I value a Pistol, or a Blunderbuss, or any such Thing, no more than a Pop gun. Every Man must die once, and what signifies the Manner how; besides, perhaps, I may come off with the Loss only of an Arm or a Leg. I assure you, Sir, I was never less afraid in my Life; and so if your Honour is resolved to go on, I am resolved to follow you. But, in that Case, I wish I might give my Opinion. To be sure it is a scandalous Way of travelling, for a great Gentleman like you to walk afoot. Now here are two or three good Horses in the Stable, which the Landlord will certainly make no Scruple of trusting you with; but if he should, I can easily contrive to take them, and let the worst come to the worst, the King would certainly pardon you, as you are going to fight in his Cause.'

Now as the Honesty of *Partridge* was equal to his Understanding, and both dealt only in small Matters, he would never have attempted a Roguery of this Kind, had he not imagined it altogether safe; for he was one of those who have more Consideration of the Gallows than of the Fitness of Things; but, in Reality, he thought he might have committed this Felony without any Danger: For, besides that he doubted not but the Name of Mr. *Allworthy* would sufficiently quiet the Landlord, he conceived they should be altogether safe, whatever Turn Affairs might take;

---

[1] Cf. W. G. Smith and P. Harvey, *Oxford Dictionary of English Proverbs*, 2nd ed. (Oxford, 1948), p. 214.

[2] Virgil, *Aeneid*, vi. 466—used as a motto for *Spectator*, No. 239 (4 December 1711).

as *Jones*, he imagined, would have Friends enough on one Side, and as his Friends would as well secure him on the other.

When Mr. *Jones* found that *Partridge* was in earnest in this Proposal, he very severely rebuked him, and that in such bitter Terms, that the other attempted to laugh it off, and presently turned the Discourse to other Matters, saying, he believed they were then in a Bawdy-house, and that he had with much ado prevented two Wenches from disturbing his Honour in the Middle of the Night. 'Heyday!' says he, 'I believe they got into your Chamber whether I would or no, for here lies the Muff of one of them on the Ground.' Indeed, as *Jones* returned to his Bed in the Dark, he had never perceived the Muff on the Quilt, and in leaping into his Bed he had tumbled it on the Floor. This *Partridge* now took up, and was going to put into his Pocket, when *Jones* desired to see it. The Muff was so very remarkable, that our Heroe might possibly have recollected it without the Information annexed. But his Memory was not put to that hard Office, for at the same Instant he saw and read the Words *Sophia Western* upon the Paper which was pinned to it. His Looks now grew frantic in a Moment, and he eagerly cried out, 'Oh Heavens, how came this Muff here!' 'I know no more than your Honour,' cried *Partridge*; 'but I saw it upon the Arm of one of the Women who would have disturbed you, if I would have suffered them.' 'Where are they?' cries *Jones*, jumping out of Bed, and laying hold of his Clothes. 'Many Miles off, I believe, by this Time,' said *Partridge*. And now *Jones*, upon further Enquiry, was sufficiently assured that the Bearer of this Muff was no other than the lovely *Sophia* herself.

The Behaviour of *Jones* on this Occasion, his Thoughts, his Looks, his Words, his Actions, were such as *Beggar all Description*.[1] After many bitter Execrations on *Partridge*, and not fewer on himself, he ordered the poor Fellow, who was frightened out of his Wits, to run down and hire him Horses at any rate; and a very few Minutes afterwards, having shuffled on his Clothes, he hastened down Stairs to execute the Orders himself, which he had just before given.

But before we proceed to what passed on his Arrival in the Kitchin, it will be necessary to recur to what had there happened since *Partridge* had first left it on his Master's Summons.

[1] Cf. *Antony and Cleopatra*, ii. ii—Enobarbus describing the beauty of Cleopatra.

The Serjeant was just marched off with his Party, when the two *Irish* Gentlemen arose, and came down Stairs; both complaining, that they had been so often waked by the Noises in the Inn, that they had never once been able to close their Eyes all Night.

The Coach, which had brought the young Lady and her Maid, and which, perhaps, the Reader may have hitherto concluded was her own, was indeed a returned Coach belonging to Mr. *King* of *Bath*,[1] one of the worthiest and honestest Men that ever dealt in Horse-flesh, and whose Coaches we heartily recommend to all our Readers who travel that Road. By which Means they may, perhaps, have the Pleasure of riding in the very Coach, and being driven by the very Coachman, that is recorded in this History.

The Coachman having but two Passengers, and hearing Mr. *Maclachlan* was bound to *Bath*, offered to carry him thither at a very moderate Price. He was induced to this by the Report of the Ostler, who said, that the Horse which Mr. *Maclachlan* had hired from *Worcester*, would be much more pleased with returning to his Friends there, than to prosecute a long Journey; for that the said Horse was rather a two-legged than a four-legged Animal.

Mr. *Maclachlan* immediately closed with the Proposal of the Coachman, and, at the same Time, persuaded his Friend *Fitzpatrick* to accept of the fourth Place in the Coach. This Conveyance the Soreness of his Bones made more agreeable to him than a Horse, and being well assured of meeting with his Wife at *Bath*, he thought a little Delay would be of no Consequence.

Maclachlan, who was much the sharper Man of the two, no sooner heard that this Lady came from *Chester*, with the other Circumstances which he learned from the Ostler, than it came into his Head that she might possibly be his Friend's Wife; and presently acquainted him with this Suspicion, which had never once occurred to *Fitzpatrick* himself. To say the Truth, he was one of those Compositions which Nature makes up in too great a Hurry, and forgets to put any Brains into their Head.

---

[1] Perhaps Thomas King, who ran a coaching service between London, Bath, Bristol, and Chester. In London his coaches stopped at the White Bear Inn, Piccadilly. (See the notices in *The Daily Advertiser*, 3 November, 3–4 December 1747.) *The Bath and Bristol Guide* (1753) lists one Daniel King as a carrier between Bristol and towns to the north, 'Hampton, Nailsworth, Stroudwater, Kingstanley, &c.' (p. 37); his route, however, appears not to have included Bath.

Now it happens to this Sort of Men, as to bad Hounds, who never hit off a Fault[1] themselves; but no sooner doth a Dog of Sagacity open his Mouth, than they immediately do the same, and without the Guidance of any Scent, run directly forwards as fast as they are able. In the same Manner, the very Moment Mr. *Maclachlan* had mentioned his Apprehension, Mr. *Fitzpatrick* instantly concurred, and flew directly up Stairs to surprize his Wife before he knew where she was; and unluckily (as Fortune loves to play Tricks with those Gentlemen who put themselves entirely under her Conduct) ran his Head against several Doors and Posts to no Purpose. Much kinder was she to me, when she suggested that Simile of the Hounds, just before inserted, since the poor Wife may, on these Occasions, be so justly compared to a hunted Hare. Like that little wretched Animal she pricks up her Ears to listen after the Voice of her Pursuer; like her, flies away trembling when she hears it; and like her, is generally overtaken and destroyed in the End.

This was not however the Case at present; for after a long fruitless Search, Mr. *Fitzpatrick* returned to the Kitchin, where, as if this had been a real Chace, entered a Gentleman hallowing as Hunters do when the Hounds are at a Fault. He was just alighted from his Horse, and had many Attendants at his Heels.

Here, Reader, it may be necessary to acquaint thee with some Matters, which, if thou dost know already, thou art wiser than I take thee to be. And this Information thou shalt receive in the next Chapter.

CHAPTER VII

In which are concluded the Adventures that happened at the Inn at
Upton.

IN the first Place then, this Gentleman just arrived was no other Person than Squire *Western* himself, who was come hither in Pursuit of his Daughter; and had he fortunately been two Hours earlier, he had not only found her, but his Niece into the Bargain; for such was the Wife of Mr. *Fitzpatrick*, who had run away with her five Years before, out of the Custody of that sage Lady Madam *Western*.

---

[1] Recover a lost scent.

Now this Lady had departed from the Inn much about at the same Time with *Sophia*: For having been waked by the Voice of her Husband, she had sent up for the Landlady, and being by her apprized of the Matter, had bribed the good Woman, at an extravagant Price, to furnish her with Horses for her Escape. Such Prevalence had Money in this Family; and tho' the Mistress would have turned away her Maid for a corrupt Hussy, if she had known as much as the Reader, yet she was no more Proof against Corruption herself than poor *Susan* had been.

Mr. *Western* and his Nephew were not known to one another; nor indeed would the former have taken any Notice of the latter, if he had known him; for this being a stolen Match, and consequently an unnatural one in the Opinion of the good Squire, he had, from the Time of her committing it, abandoned the poor young Creature, who was then no more than Eighteen, as a Monster, and had never since suffered her to be named in his Presence.

The Kitchin was now a Scene of universal Confusion, *Western* enquiring after his Daughter, and *Fitzpatrick* as eagerly after his Wife, when *Jones* entered the Room, unfortunately having *Sophia's* Muff in his Hand.

As soon as *Western* saw *Jones*, he set up the same Holla as is used by Sportsmen when their Game is in View. He then immediately run up and laid hold of *Jones*, crying, 'We have got the Dog Fox, I warrant the Bitch is not far off.' The Jargon which followed for some Minutes, where many spoke different Things at the same Time, as it would be very difficult to describe, so would it be no less unpleasant to read.

Jones having, at length, shaken Mr. *Western* off, and some of the Company having interfered between them, our Heroe protested his Innocence as to knowing any thing of the Lady; when Parson *Supple* stepped up, and said, 'It is Folly to deny it; for why, the Marks of Guilt are in thy Hands. I will myself asseverate and bind it by an Oath, that the Muff thou bearest in thy Hand belongeth unto Madam *Sophia*; for I have frequently observed her, of later Days, to bear it about her.' 'My Daughter's Muff!' cries the Squire, in a Rage. 'Hath he got my Daughter's Muff! Bear Witness, the Goods are found upon him. I'll have him before a Justice of Peace this Instant. Where is my Daughter, Villain?' 'Sir,' said *Jones*, 'I beg you would be pacified. The Muff,

I acknowledge, is the young Lady's; but, upon my Honour, I have never seen her.' At these Words *Western* lost all Patience, and grew inarticulate with Rage.

Some of the Servants had acquainted *Fitzpatrick* who Mr. *Western* was. The good *Irishman* therefore thinking he had now an Opportunity to do an Act of Service to his Uncle, and by that Means might possibly obtain his Favour, stept up to *Jones*, and cried out, 'Upon my Conscience, Sir, you may be ashamed of denying your having seen the Gentleman's Daughter before my Face, when you know I found you there upon the Bed together.' Then turning to *Western*, he offered to conduct him immediately to the Room where his Daughter was; which Offer being accepted, he, the Squire, the Parson, and some others, ascended directly to Mrs. *Waters's* Chamber, which they entered with no less Violence than Mr. *Fitzpatrick* had done before.

The poor Lady started from her Sleep with as much Amazement as Terror, and beheld at her Bed-side a Figure which might very well be supposed to have escaped out of *Bedlam*. Such Wildness and Confusion were in the Looks of Mr. *Western*: who no sooner saw the Lady, than he started back, showing sufficiently by his Manner, before he spoke, that this was not the Person sought after.

So much more tenderly do Women value their Reputation than their Persons, that tho' the latter seemed now in more Danger than before, yet as the former was secure, the Lady screamed not with such Violence as she had done on the other Occasion. However, she no sooner found herself alone, than she abandoned all Thoughts of further Repose, and as she had sufficient Reason to be dissatisfied with her present Lodging, she dressed herself with all possible Expedition.

Mr. *Western* now proceeded to search the whole House, but to as little Purpose as he had disturbed poor Mrs. *Waters*. He then returned disconsolate into the Kitchin, where he found *Jones* in the Custody of his Servants.

This violent Uproar had raised all the People in the House; tho' it was yet scarcely Day-light. Among these was a grave Gentleman, who had the Honour to be in the Commission of the Peace for the County of *Worcester*. Of which Mr. *Western* was no sooner informed, than he offered to lay his Complaint before him. The Justice declined executing his Office, as he said he had no

Clerk present, nor no Book about Justice Business. And that he could not carry all the Law in his Head about stealing away Daughters, and such Sort of Things.

Here Mr. *Fitzpatrick* offered to lend him his Assistance; informing the Company that he had been himself bred to the Law. (And indeed he had served three Years as Clerk to an Attorney in the North of *Ireland*, when chusing a genteeler Walk in Life, he quitted his Master, came over to *England*, and set up that Business, which requires no Apprenticeship, namely, that of a Gentleman, in which he had succeeded as hath been already partly mentioned.)

Mr. *Fitzpatrick* declared that the Law concerning Daughters was out of the present Case; that stealing a Muff was undoubtedly Felony, and the Goods being found upon the Person, were sufficient Evidence of the Fact.

The Magistrate, upon the Encouragement of so learned a Coadjutor, and upon the violent Intercession of the Squire, was at length prevailed upon to seat himself in the Chair of Justice, where being placed, upon viewing the Muff which *Jones* still held in his Hand, and upon the Parson's swearing it to be the Property of Mr. *Western*, he desired Mr. *Fitzpatrick* to draw up a Commitment, which he said he would sign.

Jones now desired to be heard, which was at last, with Difficulty, granted him. He then produced the Evidence of Mr. *Partridge*, as to the finding it; but what was still more, *Susan* deposed that *Sophia* herself had delivered the Muff to her, and had ordered her to convey it into the Chamber where Mr. *Jones* had found it.

Whether a natural Love of Justice, or the extraordinary Comeliness of *Jones*, had wrought on *Susan* to make the Discovery, I will not determine; but such were the Effects of her Evidence, that the Magistrate, throwing himself back in his Chair, declared that the Matter was now altogether as clear on the Side of the Prisoner, as it had before been against him; with which the Parson concurred, saying, The Lord forbid he should be instrumental in committing an innocent Person to Durance. The Justice then arose, acquitted the Prisoner, and broke up the Court.

Mr. *Western* now gave every one present a hearty Curse, and immediately ordering his Horses, departed in Pursuit of his Daughter, without taking the least Notice of his Nephew *Fitzpatrick*, or returning any Answer to his Claim of Kindred, notwithstanding all the Obligations he had just received from that Gentleman. In the Violence, moreover, of his Hurry, and of his Passion, he luckily forgot to demand the Muff of *Jones*: I say luckily; for he would have died on the Spot rather than have parted with it.

Jones likewise, with his Friend *Partridge*, set forward the Moment he had paid his Reckoning, in Quest of his lovely *Sophia*, whom he now resolved never more to abandon the Pursuit of. Nor could he bring himself even to take Leave of Mrs. *Waters*; of whom he detested the very Thoughts, as she had been, tho' not designedly, the Occasion of his missing the happiest Interview with *Sophia*, to whom he now vowed eternal Constancy.

As for Mrs. *Waters*, she took the Opportunity of the Coach which was going to *Bath*; for which Place she set out in Company with the two *Irish* Gentlemen, the Landlady kindly lending her her Clothes; in Return for which she was contented only to receive about double their Value, as a Recompence for the Loan. Upon the Road she was perfectly reconciled to Mr. *Fitzpatrick*, who was a very handsome Fellow, and indeed did all she could to console him in the Absence of his Wife.

Thus ended the many odd Adventures which Mr. *Jones* encountered at his Inn at *Upton*, where they talk, to this Day, of the Beauty and lovely Behaviour of the charming *Sophia*, by the Name of the *Somersetshire* Angel.

CHAPTER VIII

In which the History goes backward.

BEFORE we proceed any farther in our History, it may be proper to look a little back, in order to account for the extraordinary Appearance of *Sophia* and her Father at the Inn at *Upton*.

The Reader may be pleased to remember, that in the Ninth Chapter of the Seventh Book of our History, we left *Sophia*, after a long Debate between Love and Duty, deciding the Cause, as it usually, I believe, happens, in Favour of the Former.

This Debate had arisen, as we have there shewn, from a Visit which her Father had just before made her, in order to force her

Consent to a Marriage with *Blifil*; and which he had understood
to be fully implied in her Acknowledgment, *that she neither must,
nor could refuse any absolute Command of his.*

Now from this Visit the Squire retired to his Evening Potation,
overjoyed at the Success he had gained with his Daughter; and
as he was of a social Disposition, and willing to have Partakers in
his Happiness, the Beer was ordered to flow very liberally into
the Kitchin; so that before Eleven in the Evening, there was not
a single Person sober in the House, except only Mrs. *Western*
herself, and the charming *Sophia.*

Early in the Morning a Messenger was dispatched to summon
Mr. *Blifil*: For tho' the Squire imagined that young Gentleman
had been much less acquainted than he really was, with the former
Aversion of his Daughter; as he had not, however, yet received
her Consent, he longed impatiently to communicate it to him, not
doubting but that the intended Bride herself would confirm it
with her Lips. As to the Wedding, it had the Evening before
been fixed, by the Male Parties, to be celebrated on the next
Morning save one.

Breakfast was now set forth in the Parlour, where Mr. *Blifil*
attended, and where the Squire and his Sister likewise were
assembled; and now *Sophia* was ordered to be called.

O, *Shakespear*, had I thy Pen! O, *Hogarth*,[1] had I thy Pencil!
then would I draw the Picture of the poor Serving-Man, who,
with pale Countenance, staring Eyes, chattering Teeth, faultering
Tongue, and trembling Limbs,[2]

(E'en such a Man, so faint, so spiritless,
So dull, so dead in Look, so woe-be-gone,
Drew *Priam's* Curtains in the dead of Night,
And would have told him, half his *Troy* was burn'd)

entered the Room, and declared,—*That Madam* Sophia *was not to
be found.*

'Not to be found!' cries the Squire, starting from his Chair;
'Zounds and D—nation! Blood and Fury! Where, when, how,
what,—— Not to be found! where?'

---

[1] See above, p. 66, n. 1.

[2] *2 Henry IV*, I. i. The servant reporting Sophia's flight to Western recalls Morton
bringing news to Northumberland of Hotspur's death. Northumberland describes the
messenger's behaviour—'Thou tremblest, and the whiteness in thy cheek/ Is apter than
thy tongue to tell thy errand'—and proceeds to speak the lines Fielding quotes.

'La! Brother,' said Mrs. *Western*, with true political Coldness, 'you are always throwing yourself into such violent Passions for nothing. My Niece, I suppose, is only walked out into the Garden. I protest you are grown so unreasonable, that it is impossible to live in the House with you.'

'Nay, nay,' answered the Squire, returning as suddenly to himself, as he had gone from himself; 'if that be all the Matter, it signifies not much; but, upon my Soul, my Mind misgave me, when the Fellow said she was not to be found.' He then gave Orders for the Bell to be rung in the Garden, and sat himself contentedly down.

No two Things could be more the Reverse of each other than were the Brother and Sister, in most Instances; particularly in this, That as the Brother never foresaw any Thing at a Distance, but was most sagacious in immediately seeing every Thing the Moment it had happened; so the Sister eternally foresaw at a Distance, but was not so quick-sighted to Objects before her Eyes. Of both these the Reader may have observed Examples: And, indeed, both their several Talents were excessive: For as the Sister often foresaw what never came to pass, so the Brother often saw much more than was actually the Truth.

This was not however the Case at present. The same Report was brought from the Garden, as before had been brought from the Chamber, that Madam *Sophia* was not to be found.

The Squire himself now sallied forth, and began to roar forth the Name of *Sophia* as loudly, and in as hoarse a Voice, as whileom did *Hercules* that of *Hylas*: And as the Poet tells us,[1] that the whole Shore ecchoed back the Name of that beautiful Youth; so did the House, the Garden, and all the neighbouring Fields, resound nothing but the Name of *Sophia*, in the hoarse Voices of the Men, and in the shrill Pipes of the Women; while Echo seemed so pleased to repeat the beloved Sound, that if there is really such a Person, I believe *Ovid* hath belied her Sex.[2]

Nothing reigned for a long Time but Confusion; till at last the Squire having sufficiently spent his Breath, returned to the

[1] Hylas was drowned while on a hunt. Hercules, believing that his friend had lost his way, ranged the hills and shores calling his name (cf. Theocritus xiii; Apollonius Rhodius, *Argonautica*, i. 1207 ff.; Valerius Flaccus, *Argonautica*, iii. 593–7). In *Hudibras*, i. iii. 183 ff., Butler anticipates Fielding's burlesque use of this episode.

[2] *Metamorphoses*, iii. 356–510.

Parlour, where he found Mrs. *Western* and Mr. *Blifil*, and threw himself, with the utmost Dejection in his Countenance, into a great Chair.

Here Mrs. *Western* began to apply the following Consolation:

'Brother, I am sorry for what hath happened; and that my Niece should have behaved herself in a Manner so unbecoming her Family; but it is all your own Doings, and you have no Body to thank but yourself. You know she hath been educated always in a Manner directly contrary to my Advice, and now you see the Consequence. Have I not a thousand Times argued with you about giving my Niece her own Will? But you know I never could prevail upon you: And when I had taken so much Pains to eradicate her headstrong Opinions, and to rectify your Errors in Policy, you know she was taken out of my Hands; so that I have nothing to answer for. Had I been trusted entirely with the Care of her Education, no such Accident as this had ever befallen you: So that you must comfort yourself by thinking it was all your own Doing; and, indeed, what else could be expected from such Indulgence?'——

'Zounds! Sister,' answered he, 'you are enough to make one mad. Have I indulged her? Have I given her her Will?—It was no longer ago than last Night that I threatened, if she disobeyed me, to confine her to her Chamber upon Bread and Water, as long as she lived.—You would provoke the Patience of *Job*.'

'Did ever Mortal hear the like?' replied she. 'Brother, if I had not the Patience of fifty *Jobs*, you would make me forget all Decency and Decorum. Why would you interfere? Did I not beg you, did I not entreat you to leave the whole Conduct to me? You have defeated all the Operations of the Campaign by one false Step. Would any Man in his Senses have provoked a Daughter by such Threats as these? How often have I told you, that *English* Women are not to be treated like *Ciracessian** Slaves. We have the Protection of the World: We are to be won by gentle Means only, and not to be hectored, and bullied, and beat into Compliance. I thank Heaven, no *Salique* Law[1] governs here. Brother, you have a Roughness in your Manner which no Woman but

* Possibly *Circassian*.

---

[1] By this law of the French monarchy, the female line and their descendants were excluded from the throne.

myself would bear. I do not wonder my Niece was frightned and terrified into taking this Measure; and to speak honestly, I think my Niece will be justified to the World for what she hath done. I repeat it to you again, Brother, you must comfort yourself by remembering that it is all your own Fault. How often have I advised——' Here *Western* rose hastily from his Chair, and, venting two or three horrid Imprecations, ran out of the Room.

When he was departed, his Sister expressed more Bitterness (if possible) against him, than she had done while he was present; for the Truth of which she appealed to Mr. *Blifil*, who, with great Complacence, acquiesced entirely in all she said; but excused all the Faults of Mr. *Western*, 'as they must be considered,' he said, 'to have proceeded from the too inordinate Fondness of a Father, which must be allowed the Name of an amiable Weakness.' 'So much the more inexcusable,' answer'd the Lady; 'for whom doth he ruin by his Fondness, but his own Child?' To which *Blifil* immediately agreed.

Mrs. *Western* then began to express great Confusion on the Account of Mr. *Blifil*, and of the Usage which he had received from a Family to which he intended so much Honour. On this Subject she treated the Folly of her Niece with great Severity; but concluded with throwing the whole on her Brother, who, she said, was inexcusable to have proceeded so far without better Assurances of his Daughter's Consent: 'But he was (says she) always of a violent, headstrong Temper; and I can scarce forgive myself for all the Advice I have thrown away upon him.'

After much of this Kind of Conversation, which, perhaps, would not greatly entertain the Reader, was it here particularly related, Mr. *Blifil* took his Leave, and returned home, not highly pleased with his Disappointment; which, however, the Philosophy which he had acquired from *Square*, and the Religion infused into him by *Thwackum*, together with somewhat else, taught him to bear rather better than more passionate Lovers bear these Kinds of Evils.

CHAPTER IX

The Escape of Sophia.

IT is now Time to look after *Sophia*; whom the Reader, if he loves her half so well as I do, will rejoice to find escaped from the Clutches of her passionate Father, and from those of her dispassionate Lover.

Twelve Times did the iron Register of Time beat on the sonorous Bell-metal, summoning the Ghosts to rise, and walk their nightly Round.—In plainer Language, it was Twelve o'Clock, and all the Family, as we have said, lay buried in Drink and Sleep, except only Mrs. *Western*, who was deeply engaged in reading a political Pamphlet, and except our Heroine, who now softly stole down Stairs, and having unbarred and unlocked one of the House Doors, sallied forth, and hastened to the Place of Appointment.

Notwithstanding the many pretty Arts, which Ladies sometimes practise, to display their Fears on every little Occasion, (almost as many as the other Sex uses to conceal theirs) certainly there is a Degree of Courage, which not only becomes a Woman, but is often necessary to enable her to discharge her Duty. It is, indeed, the Idea of Fierceness, and not of Bravery, which destroys the Female Character: For who can read the Story of the justly celebrated *Arria*,[1] without conceiving as high an Opinion of her Gentleness and Tenderness, as of her Fortitude? At the same Time, perhaps, many a Woman who shrieks at a Mouse, or a Rat, may be capable of poisoning a Husband; or, what is worse, of driving him to poison himself.

Sophia, with all the Gentleness which a Woman can have, had all the Spirit which she ought to have. When, therefore, she came to the Place of Appointment, and, instead of meeting her Maid, as was agreed, saw a Man ride directly up to her, she neither screamed out, nor fainted away: Not that her Pulse then beat with its usual Regularity; for she was, at first, under some Surprize and Apprehension: But these were relieved almost as soon as raised, when the Man, pulling off his Hat, asked her, in a very submissive Manner, 'If her Ladyship did not expect to meet

---

[1] When her husband, Caecina Paetus, was condemned to die by suicide (A.D. 42), Arria set him an example of courage by stabbing herself and then presenting him with the dagger, saying: 'It does not hurt, my Paetus'. (Pliny, *Letters*, III. xvi; trans. W. Melmoth, Loeb Classical Library, 1915.)

another Lady?' And then proceeded to inform her, 'that he was sent to conduct her to that Lady.'

Sophia could have no possible Suspicion of any Falshood in this Account: She therefore mounted resolutely behind the Fellow, who conveyed her safe to a Town about Five Miles distant,[1] where she had the Satisfaction of finding the good Mrs. *Honour*: For as the Soul of the Waiting-Woman was wrapt up in those very Habiliments which used to enwrap her Body, she could by no Means bring herself to trust them out of her Sight. Upon these, therefore, she kept Guard in Person, while she detached the aforesaid Fellow after her Mistress, having given him all proper Instructions.

They now debated what Course to take, in order to avoid the Pursuit of Mr. *Western*, who, they knew, would send after them in a few Hours. The *London* Road had such Charms for *Honour*, that she was desirous of going on directly; alledging, that as *Sophia* could not be missed till Eight or Nine the next Morning, her Pursuers would not be able to overtake her, even though they knew which Way she had gone. But *Sophia* had too much at Stake to venture any Thing to Chance; nor did she dare trust too much to her tender Limbs, in a Contest which was to be decided only by Swiftness. She resolved, therefore, to travel across the Country, for at least Twenty or Thirty Miles, and then to take the direct Road to *London*. So, having hired Horses to go Twenty Miles one Way, when she intended to go Twenty Miles the other, she set forward with the same Guide, behind whom she had ridden from her Father's House; the Guide having now taken up behind him, in the Room of *Sophia*, a much heavier, as well as much less lovely Burthen; being, indeed, a huge Portmanteau, well stuffed with those outside Ornaments, by Means of which the fair *Honour* hoped to gain many Conquests, and, finally, to make her Fortune in *London* City.

When they had gone about Two Hundred Paces from the Inn, on the *London* Road, *Sophia* rode up to the Guide, and, with a Voice much fuller of Honey than was ever that of *Plato*, though his Mouth is supposed to have been a Bee-hive,[2] begged him to take the first Turning which led towards *Bristol*.

---

[1] Probably Wells. See above, p. 315, n. 1.

[2] Cf. Cicero, *De Divinatione*, I. xxxvi. 78: 'Again, while Plato was an infant, asleep in his cradle, bees settled on his lips and this was interpreted to mean that he would have a

Reader, I am not superstitious, nor any great Believer of modern Miracles. I do not, therefore, deliver the following as a certain Truth; for, indeed, I can scarce credit it myself: But the Fidelity of an Historian obliges me to relate what hath been confidently asserted. The Horse, then, on which the Guide rode, is reported to have been so charmed by *Sophia's* Voice, that he made a full Stop, and exprest an Unwillingness to proceed any farther.

Perhaps, however, the Fact may be true, and less miraculous than it hath been represented; since the natural Cause seems adequate to the Effect: For as the Guide at that Moment desisted from a constant Application of his armed right Heel, (for, like *Hudibras*, he wore but one Spur)[1] it is more than possible, that this Omission alone might occasion the Beast to stop, especially as this was very frequent with him at other Times.

But if the Voice of *Sophia* had really an Effect on the Horse, it had very little on the Rider. He answered somewhat surlily, 'That Measter had ordered him to go a different Way, and that he should lose his Place, if he went any other than that he was ordered.'

Sophia finding all her Persuasions had no Effect, began now to add irresistible Charms to her Voice; Charms, which according to the Proverb,[2] makes the old Mare trot, instead of standing still; Charms! to which modern Ages have attributed all that irresistible Force, which the Ancients imputed to perfect Oratory. In a Word, she promised she would reward him to his utmost Expectation.

The Lad was not totally deaf to these Promises; but he disliked their being indefinite: For tho' perhaps he had never heard that Word, yet that in Fact was his Objection. He said, 'Gentlevolks did not consider the Case of poor Volks; that he had like to have been turned away the other Day, for riding about the Country with a Gentleman from Squire *Allworthy's*, who did not reward him as he should have done.'

'With whom?' says *Sophia* eagerly.—'With a Gentleman from Squire *Allworthy's*,' repeated the Lad, 'the Squire's Son, I think,

rare sweetness of speech' (trans. W. A. Falconer, Loeb Classical Library, 1927). Originally (editions 1–3) Fielding had applied this remark to Anacreon, the Greek lyric poet of the sixth century B.C.

  [1] Butler's *Hudibras*, I. i. 447.

  [2] 'Money makes the old mare trot' (W. G. Smith and P. Harvey, *Oxford Dictionary of English Proverbs*, 2nd ed. [Oxford, 1948], p. 430).

they call 'un.'—'Whither? which Way did he go?' says *Sophia.*
'Why a little o' one Side o' *Bristol*, about twenty Miles off,'
answered the Lad.—'Guide me,' says *Sophia*, 'to the same Place,
and I'll give thee a Guinea, or two, if one is not sufficient.' 'To be
certain,' said the Boy, 'it is honestly worth two, when your Ladyship considers what a Risk I run; but, however, if your Ladyship
will promise me the two Guineas, I'll e'en venture: To be certain
it is a sinful Thing to ride about my Master's Horses; but one
Comfort is, I can only be turned away, and two Guineas will
partly make me Amends.'

The Bargain being thus struck, the Lad turned aside into the
Bristol Road, and *Sophia* set forward in Pursuit of *Jones*, highly
contrary to the Remonstrances of Mrs. *Honour*, who had much
more Desire to see *London*, than to see Mr. *Jones*: For indeed she
was not his Friend with her Mistress, as he had been guilty of
some Neglect in certain pecuniary Civilities, which are by
Custom due to the Waiting-gentlewoman in all Love Affairs, and
more especially in those of a clandestine Kind. This we impute
rather to the Carelessness of his Temper, than to any Want of
Generosity; but perhaps she derived it from the latter Motive.
Certain it is that she hated him very bitterly on that Account, and
resolved to take every Opportunity of injuring him with her
Mistress. It was therefore highly unlucky for her, that she had
gone to the very same Town and Inn whence *Jones* had started,
and still more unlucky was she, in having stumbled on the same
Guide, and on this accidental Discovery which *Sophia* had made.

Our Travellers arrived at *Hambrook** at the Break of Day,
where *Honour* was against her Will charged to enquire the Rout
which Mr. *Jones* had taken. Of this, indeed, the Guide himself
could have informed them; but *Sophia*, I know not for what
Reason, never asked him the Question.

When Mrs. *Honour* had made her Report from the Landlord,
Sophia, with much Difficulty, procured some indifferent Horses,
which brought her to the Inn, where *Jones* had been confined
rather by the Misfortune of meeting with a Surgeon, than by
having met with a broken Head.

Here *Honour* being again charged with a Commission of

---

* This was the Village where *Jones* met the Quaker.[1]

[1] See VII. x.

Enquiry, had no sooner applied herself to the Landlady, and had described the Person of Mr. *Jones*, than that sagacious Woman began, in the vulgar Phrase, to smell a Rat. When *Sophia* therefore entered the Room, instead of answering the Maid, the Landlady addressing herself to the Mistress, began the following Speech. 'Good-lack-a-day! why there now, who would have thought it! I protest the loveliest Couple that ever Eye beheld. I-fackins, Madam, it is no Wonder the Squire run on so about your Ladyship. He told me indeed you was the finest Lady in the World, and to be sure so you be. Mercy on him, poor Heart, I bepitied him, so I did, when he used to hug his Pillow, and call it his dear Madam *Sophia*.—I did all I could to dissuade him from going to the Wars; I told him there were Men enow that were good for nothing else but to be killed, that had not the Love of such fine Ladies.' 'Sure,' says *Sophia*, 'the good Woman is distracted.' 'No, no,' cries the Landlady, 'I am not distracted. What doth your Ladyship think I don't know then? I assure you he told me all.' 'What saucy Fellow,' cries *Honour*, 'told you any Thing of my Lady?' 'No saucy Fellow,' answered the Landlady, 'but the young Gentleman you enquired after, and a very pretty young Gentleman he is and he loves Madam *Sophia Western* to the Bottom of his Soul.' 'He love my Lady! I'd have you to know, Woman, she is Meat for his Master.'—'Nay, *Honour*,' said *Sophia*, interrupting her, 'don't be angry with the good Woman, she intends no Harm.' 'No, marry don't I,' answered the Landlady, emboldened by the soft Accents of *Sophia*, and then launched into a long Narrative too tedious to be here set down, in which some Passages dropt, that gave a little Offence to *Sophia*, and much more to her Waiting-woman, who hence took Occasion to abuse poor *Jones* to her Mistress the Moment they were alone together, saying, 'that he must be a very pitiful Fellow, and could have no Love for a Lady, whose Name he would thus prostitute in an Alehouse.'

Sophia did not see his Behaviour in so very disadvantageous a Light, and was perhaps more pleased with the violent Raptures of his Love (which the Landlady exaggerated as much as she had done every other Circumstance) than she was offended with the rest; and indeed she imputed the whole to the Extravagance, or rather Ebullience of his Passion, and to the Openness of his Heart.

This Incident, however, being afterwards revived in her Mind, and placed in the most odious Colours by *Honour*, served to heighten and give Credit to those unlucky Occurrences at *Upton*, and assisted the Waiting-woman in her Endeavours to make her Mistress depart from that Inn without seeing *Jones*.

The Landlady finding *Sophia* intended to stay no longer than till her Horses were ready, and that without either eating or drinking, soon withdrew; when *Honour* began to take her Mistress to Task (for indeed she used great Freedom) and after a long Harangue, in which she reminded her of her Intention to go to *London*, and gave frequent Hints of the Impropriety of pursuing a young Fellow, she at last concluded with this serious Exhortation: 'For Heaven's Sake, Madam, consider what you are about, and whither you are going.'

This Advice to a Lady who had already rode near forty Miles, and in no very agreeable Season, may seem foolish enough. It may be supposed she had well considered and resolved this already; nay, Mrs. *Honour*, by the Hints she threw out, seemed to think so; and this I doubt not is the Opinion of many Readers, who have, I make no Doubt, been long since well convinced of the Purpose of our Heroine, and have heartily condemned her for it as a wanton Baggage.

But in reality this was not the Case. *Sophia* had been lately so distracted between Hope and Fear, her Duty and Love to her Father, her Hatred to *Blifil*, her Compassion, and (why should we not confess the Truth) her Love for *Jones*; which last the Behaviour of her Father, of her Aunt, of every one else, and more particularly of *Jones* himself, had blown into a Flame, that her Mind was in that confused State, which may be truly said to make us ignorant of what we do, or whither we go, or rather indeed indifferent as to the Consequence of either.

The prudent and sage Advice of her Maid, produced, however, some cool Reflection; and she at length determined to go to *Gloucester*, and thence to proceed directly to *London*.

But unluckily a few Miles before she entered that Town, she met the Hack-Attorney, who, as is beforementioned,[1] had dined there with Mr. *Jones*. This Fellow being well known to Mrs. *Honour*, stopt and spoke to her; of which *Sophia* at that Time took little Notice, more than to enquire who he was.

[1] See VIII. viii.

But having had a more particular Account from *Honour* of this Man afterwards at *Gloucester*, and hearing of the great Expedition he usually made in travelling, for which (as hath been before observed) he was particularly famous; recollecting likewise, that she had overheard Mrs. *Honour* inform him, that they were going to *Gloucester*, she began to fear lest her Father might, by this Fellow's Means, be able to trace her to that City; wherefore if she should there strike into the *London* Road, she apprehended he would certainly be able to overtake her. She therefore altered her Resolution; and having hired Horses to go a Week's Journey, a Way which she did not intend to travel, she again set forward after a light Refreshment, contrary to the Desire and earnest Entreaties of her Maid, and to the no less vehement Remonstrances of Mrs. *Whitefield*, who from good Breeding, or perhaps from good Nature (for the poor young Lady appeared much fatigued) press'd her very heartily to stay that Evening at *Gloucester*.

Having refreshed herself only with some Tea, and with lying about two Hours on the Bed, while her Horses were getting ready, she resolutely left Mrs. *Whitefield's* about eleven at Night, and striking directly into the *Worcester* Road, within less than four Hours arrived at that very Inn where we last saw her.

Having thus traced our Heroine very particularly back from her Departure, till her Arrival at *Upton*, we shall in a very few Words, bring her Father to the same Place; who having received the first Scent from the Post-boy, who conducted his Daughter to *Hambrook*, very easily traced her afterwards to *Gloucester*; whence he pursued her to *Upton*, as he had learned Mr. *Jones* had taken that Rout (for *Partridge*, to use the Squire's Expression, left every where a strong Scent behind him) and he doubted not in the least but *Sophia* travelled, or, as he phrased it, ran the same Way. He used indeed a very coarse Expression, which need not be here inserted; as Fox-hunters, who alone would understand it, will easily suggest it to themselves.

BOOK XI

Containing about three Days.

CHAPTER I

A Crust for the Critics.

IN our last initial Chapter, we may be supposed to have treated that formidable Set of Men, who are called Critics, with more Freedom than becomes us; since they exact, and indeed generally receive, great Condescension from Authors. We shall in this, therefore, give the Reasons of our Conduct to this august Body; and here we shall perhaps place them in a Light, in which they have not hitherto been seen.[1]

This Word Critic is of *Greek* Derivation, and signifies Judgement. Hence I presume some Persons who have not understood the Original, and have seen the *English* Translation of the Primitive, have concluded that it meant Judgment in the legal Sense, in which it is frequently used as equivalent to Condemnation.[2]

I am the rather inclined to be of that Opinion, as the greatest Number of Critics hath of late Years been found amongst the

---

[1] The basic rhetorical strategy of this chapter is clear enough: in order to censure contemporary critics, many of whom were lawyers at the Inns of Court (see the third paragraph), Fielding develops a double analogy comparing them to incompetent judges on the one hand and to slanderers on the other, those who rashly condemn and spitefully defame an author's 'good name'. Less obvious is the fact that in applying this strategy, Fielding wryly parodies a homiletic tradition best exemplified in Isaac Barrow's celebrated series of sermons '*tending*', as Tillotson expressed it, '*to reform the several Vices of the Tongue*' ('The Publisher to the Reader', Barrow's *Works*, 5th ed. [1741], i. a1ᵛ). Of Barrow's ten sermons on this subject, four in particular contain ideas and phrasing which Fielding may have recalled in composing his own, more facetious argument against censorious critics: these are sermons xvii–xviii, 'The Folly of Slander'; sermon xix, 'Against Detraction'; and sermon xx, 'Against rash censuring and judging'.

[2] With this paragraph, compare Barrow on the scriptural injunction to '*Judge not*': 'As to the word [judge] we may observe, that it being in it self according to its primitive sense of a middle and indifferent signification, is yet frequently in scripture used in the worst sense . . . for condemnation, and for infliction of punishment: And this sense here surely the word doth principally respect. . . . We are so prohibited the condemning and punishing our neighbour in his good name . . .' (sermon xx, op. cit., i. 196). In an earlier essay on the character and qualifications of critics (*The Champion*, 27 November 1739), Fielding had applied the derivation of the word to a different purpose. Cf. also Swift's *Tale of a Tub* (1704), sec. iii, 'A Digression concerning Critics'.

Lawyers. Many of these Gentlemen, from Despair, perhaps, of ever rising to the Bench in *Westminster-hall*, have placed themselves on the Benches at the Playhouse, where they have exerted their judicial Capacity, and have given Judgment, *i.e.* condemned without Mercy.

The Gentlemen would perhaps be well enough pleased, if we were to leave them thus compared to one of the most important and honourable Offices in the Commonwealth, and if we intended to apply to their Favour we would do so; but as we design to deal very sincerely and plainly too with them, we must remind them of another Officer of Justice of a much lower Rank; to whom, as they not only pronounce, but execute their own Judgment, they bear likewise some remote Resemblance.

But in reality there is another Light in which these modern Critics may with great Justice and Propriety be seen; and this is that of a common Slanderer. If a Person who prys into the Characters of others, with no other Design but to discover their Faults, and to publish them to the World, deserves the Title of a Slanderer of the Reputations of Men;[1] why should not a Critic, who reads with the same malevolent View, be as properly stiled the Slanderer of the Reputation of Books?

Vice hath not, I believe, a more abject Slave; Society produces not a more odious Vermin; nor can the Devil receive a Guest more worthy of him, nor possibly more welcome to him, than a Slanderer. The World, I am afraid, regards not this Monster with half the Abhorrence which he deserves, and I am more afraid to assign the Reason of this criminal Lenity shewn towards him; yet it is certain that the Thief looks innocent in the Comparison; nay, the Murderer himself can seldom stand in Competition with his Guilt: For Slander is a more cruel Weapon than a Sword, as the Wounds which the former gives are always incurable.[2] One Method, indeed, there is of killing, and that the

[1] Cf. Barrow, sermon xix: '. . . 'tis the property of a detractor, when he seeth a worthy person . . . to survey him thoroughly, and to sift all his actions, with intent to descry some failing, or any semblance of a fault, by which he may disparage him: when he vieweth any good action, he peereth into it, labouring to espy some pretence to derogate from the commendation apparently belonging to it. This in general is the nature of this fault' (op. cit., i. 189).

[2] Cf. Barrow, quoting Ecclesiasticus 28: 18–21: '*Many* (saith another wise man, the imitator of *Solomon*) *have fallen by the edge of the sword; but not so many as have fallen by the tongue.* . . . Incurable are the wounds which the slanderer inflicteth . . .' (sermon xviii, ibid., i. 183).

basest and most execrable of all, which bears an exact Analogy to the Vice here disclaimed against, and that is Poison. A Means of Revenge so base, and yet so horrible, that it was once wisely distinguished by our Laws from all other Murders, in the peculiar Severity of the Punishment.[1]

Besides the dreadful Mischiefs done by Slander, and the Baseness of the Means by which they are effected, there are other Circumstances that highly aggravate its atrocious Quality: For it often proceeds from no Provocation, and seldom promises itself any Reward, unless some black and infernal Mind may propose a Reward in the Thoughts of having procured the Ruin and Misery of another.

Shakespear hath nobly touched this Vice, when he says,[2]

> *Who steals my Purse steals Trash, 'tis something, nothing;*
> *'Twas mine, 'tis his, and hath been Slave to Thousands:*
> *But he that filches from me my good Name,*
> *Robs me of that* WHICH NOT ENRICHES HIM,
> BUT MAKES ME POOR INDEED.

With all this my good Reader will doubtless agree; but much of it will probably seem too severe, when applied to the Slanderer of Books. But let it here be considered, that both proceed from the same wicked Disposition of Mind, and are alike void of the Excuse of Temptation. Nor shall we conclude the Injury done this Way to be very slight, when we consider a Book as the Author's Offspring, and indeed as the Child of his Brain.

The Reader who hath suffered his Muse to continue hitherto in a Virgin State, can have but a very inadequate Idea of this Kind of paternal Fondness. To such we may parody the tender Exclamation of *Macduff*.[3] *Alas! Thou hast written no Book.* But the Author whose Muse hath brought forth, will feel the pathetic Strain, perhaps will accompany me with Tears (especially if his Darling be already no more) while I mention the Uneasiness with which the big Muse bears about her Burden, the painful Labour with which she produces it, and lastly, the Care, the Fondness,

---

[1] By 22 Henry VIII, cap. 9, those who committed murder by poisoning were punishable by boiling to death (Jacob, *New Law-Dictionary*, 4th ed. [1739], s.v. 'Poison').

[2] Iago in *Othello*, III. iii. In a similar context, Fielding had quoted this speech in *The Champion* (6 March 1739/40).

[3] *Macbeth*, IV. iii. When Malcolm urges him to control his grief for his murdered family, Macduff rejoins: 'He has no children.'

with which the tender Father nourishes his Favourite, till it be brought to Maturity, and produced into the World.

Nor is there any paternal Fondness which seems less to savour of absolute Instinct, and which may so well be reconciled to worldly Wisdom as this. These Children may most truly be called the Riches of their Father;[1] and many of them have with true filial Piety fed their Parent in his old Age; so that not only the Affection, but the Interest of the Author may be highly injured by these Slanderers, whose poisonous Breath brings his Book to an untimely End.

Lastly, The Slander of a Book is, in Truth, the Slander of the Author: For as no one can call another Bastard, without calling the Mother a Whore, so neither can any one give the Names of sad Stuff, horrid Nonsense, *&c.* to a Book, without calling the Author a Blockhead; which tho' in a moral Sense it is a preferable Appellation to that of Villain, is perhaps rather more injurious to his worldly Interest.

Now however ludicrous all this may appear to some, others, I doubt not, will feel and acknowledge the Truth of it; nay, may, perhaps, think I have not treated the Subject with decent Solemnity; but surely a Man may speak Truth with a smiling Countenance.[2] In reality, to depreciate a Book maliciously, or even wantonly, is at least a very ill-natured Office; and a morose snarling Critic, may, I believe, be suspected to be a bad Man.

I will therefore endeavour in the remaining Part of this Chapter, to explain the Marks of this Character, and to shew what Criticism I here intend to obviate: For I can never be understood, unless by the very Persons here meant, to insinuate, that there are no proper Judges of Writing, or to endeavour to exclude from the Commonwealth of Literature any of those noble Critics, to whose Labours the learned World are so greatly indebted. Such were *Aristotle, Horace,* and *Longinus* among the Ancients, *Dacier* and *Bossu*[3] among the *French,* and some perhaps

---

[1] A proverbial expression. (See W. G. Smith and P. Harvey, *Oxford Dictionary of English Proverbs,* 2nd ed. [Oxford, 1948], p. 92; and B. Stevenson, *English Proverbs, Maxims, and Familiar Phrases* [1949], p. 341.)

[2] Cf. Horace, *Satires,* I. i. 24–5: 'quamquam ridentem dicere verum/ quid vetat?'—translated in *The Covent-Garden Journal* (4 February 1752).

[3] On Dacier, see above, p. 396, n. 1. Fielding quotes him in *The Champion* (27 November 1739) and *The Covent-Garden Journal* (21 October 1752). Like Pope, Fielding had the highest regard for René Le Bossu (1631–80), author of *Traité du poëme épique*

among us; who have certainly been duly authorized to execute at least a judicial Authority in *Foro Literario*.[1]

But without ascertaining all the proper Qualifications of a Critic, which I have touched on elsewhere, I think I may very boldly object to the Censures of any one past upon Works which he hath not himself read.[2] Such Censurers as these, whether they speak from their own Guess or Suspicion, or from the Report and Opinion of others, may properly be said to slander the Reputation of the Book they condemn.

Such may likewise be suspected of deserving this Character, who without assigning any particular Faults, condemn the whole in general defamatory Terms; such as vile, dull, da—d Stuff, &c. and particularly by the Use of the Monosyllable Low; a Word which becomes the Mouth of no Critic who is not RIGHT HONOURABLE.

Again, tho' there may be some Faults justly assigned in the Work, yet if those are not in the most essential Parts, or if they are compensated by greater Beauties, it will savour rather of the Malice of a Slanderer, than of the Judgment of a true Critic, to pass a severe Sentence upon the whole, merely on account of some vicious Part. This is directly contrary to the Sentiments of *Horace*.[3]

> *Verum ubi plura nitent in carmine non ego paucis*
> *Offendor maculis, quas aut incuria fudit,*
> *Aut humana parum cavit natura——*

> But where the Beauties, more in Number, shine,
> I am not angry, when a casual Line
> (That with some trivial Faults unequal flows)
> A careless Hand, or human Frailty shows.
>
> Mr. FRANCIS.[4]

For as *Martial* says,[5] *Aliter, non fit, Avite, Liber. No Book can be otherwise composed.* All Beauty of Character, as well as of

---

(1675). The present passage may be compared to *Covent-Garden Journal* (4 January 1752), where Fielding again ranks Bossu, alone among the Moderns, in the company of Aristotle, Horace, and Longinus, and regrets that 'the Kingdom of Criticism', which had flourished under their 'Constitutions', has now been usurped by an anarchic mob of incompetent pretenders.   [1] In the literary court.

[2] Cf. the first qualification of the critic given in *The Champion* (27 November 1739).

[3] *Ars Poetica*, 351–3. (See above, p. 527, n. 1.)

[4] *Works of Horace*, 2nd ed. (1747), iv. 252–3. On Francis, see above, p. 472, n. 2.

[5] *Epigrams*, I. xvi.

Countenance, and indeed of every Thing human, is to be tried in this Manner. Cruel indeed would it be if such a Work as this History, which hath employed some Thousands of Hours in the composing, should be liable to be condemned, because some particular Chapter, or perhaps Chapters, may be obnoxious to very just and sensible Objections. And yet nothing is more common than the most rigorous Sentence upon Books supported by such Objections, which if they were rightly taken (and that they are not always) do by no Means go to the Merit of the whole. In the Theatre especially, a single Expression which doth not coincide with the Taste of the Audience, or with any individual Critic of that Audience, is sure to be hissed; and one Scene which should be disapproved, would hazard the whole Piece. To write within such severe Rules as these, is as impossible, as to live up to some splenetic Opinions; and if we judge according to the Sentiments of some Critics, and of some Christians, no Author will be saved in this World, and no Man in the next.

CHAPTER II

The Adventures which Sophia *met with, after her leaving* Upton.

OUR History, just before it was obliged to turn about, and travel backwards, had mentioned the Departure of *Sophia* and her Maid from the Inn; we shall now therefore pursue the Steps of that lovely Creature, and leave her unworthy Lover a little longer to bemoan his Ill-Luck, or rather his ill Conduct.

Sophia having directed her Guide to travel through Bye-Roads across the Country, they now passed the *Severn*, and had scarce got a Mile from the Inn, when the young Lady, looking behind her, saw several Horses coming after on full Speed. This greatly alarmed her Fears, and she called to the Guide to put on as fast as possible.

He immediately obeyed her, and away they rode a full Gallop. But the faster they went, the faster were they followed; and as the Horses behind were somewhat swifter than those before, so the former were at length overtaken. A happy Circumstance for poor *Sophia*; whose Fears, joined to her Fatigue, had almost overpowered her Spirits; but she was now instantly relieved by a female Voice, that greeted her in the softest Manner, and with the utmost Civility. This Greeting, *Sophia*, as soon as she could recover her Breath, with like Civility, and with the highest Satisfaction to herself, returned.

The Travellers who joined *Sophia*, and who had given her such Terror, consisted, like her own Company, of two Females and a Guide. The two Parties proceeded three full Miles together before any one offered again to open their Mouths; when our Heroine having pretty well got the better of her Fear; but yet being somewhat surprized that the other still continued to attend her, as she pursued no great Road, and had already passed through several Turnings, accosted the strange Lady in a most obliging Tone; and said, 'She was very happy to find they were both travelling the same Way.' The other, who, like a Ghost, only wanted to be spoke to,[1] readily answered, 'That the Happiness was entirely hers; that she was a perfect Stranger in that Country, and was so overjoyed at meeting a Companion of her own Sex, that she had perhaps been guilty of an Impertinence which required great Apology, in keeping Pace with her.' More Civilities passed between these two Ladies; for Mrs. *Honour* had now given Place to the fine Habit of the Stranger, and had fallen into the Rear. But tho' *Sophia* had great Curiosity to know why the other Lady continued to travel on through the same Bye-Roads with herself, nay, tho' this gave her some Uneasiness; yet Fear, or Modesty, or some other Consideration, restrained her from asking the Question.

The strange Lady now laboured under a Difficulty which appears almost below the Dignity of History to mention. Her Bonnet had been blown from her Head not less than five Times within the last Mile; nor could she come at any Ribbon or Handkerchief to tye it under her Chin. When *Sophia* was informed of this, she immediately supplied her with a Handkerchief for this Purpose; which while she was pulling from her Pocket, she perhaps too much neglected the Management of her Horse, for the Beast now unluckily making a false Step, fell upon his Fore-Legs, and threw his Fair Rider from his Back.

Tho' *Sophia* came Head foremost to the Ground, she happily received not the least Damage; and the same Circumstances

---

[1] For the belief that a ghost cannot speak until spoken to, see *Hamlet*, I. i. Fielding again alludes to the superstition in *The Covent-Garden Journal* (7 October 1752).

which had perhaps contributed to her Fall, now preserved her
from Confusion; for the Lane which thcy were then passing was
narrow and very much over-grown with Trees, so that the Moon
could here afford very little Light, and was moreover, at present,
so obscured in a Cloud, that it was almost perfectly dark. By
these Means the young Lady's Modesty, which was extremely
delicate, escaped as free from Injury as her Limbs, and she was
once more reinstated in her Saddle, having received no other
Harm than a little Fright by her Fall.

Day-light at length appeared in its full Lustre; and now the
two Ladies, who were riding over a Common[1] Side by Side, looking stedfastly at each other, at the same Moment both their
Eyes became fixed; both their Horses stopt, and both speaking
together, with equal Joy pronounced, the one the Name of
Sophia, the other that of *Harriet*.

This unexpected Encounter surprized the Ladies much more
than I believe it will the sagacious Reader, who must have
imagined that the strange Lady could be no other than Mrs.
Fitzpatrick, the Cousin of Miss *Western*, whom we before-
mentioned to have sallied from the Inn a few Minutes after her.

So great was the Surprize and Joy which these two Cousins
conceived at this Meeting (for they had formerly been most
intimate Acquaintance and Friends, and had long lived together
with their Aunt *Western*) that it is impossible to recount half the
Congratulations which passed between them, before either asked
a very natural Question of the other, namely, whither she was
going.

This at last, however, came first from Mrs. *Fitzpatrick*; but
easy and natural as the Question may seem, *Sophia* found it
difficult to give it a very ready and certain Answer. She begged
her Cousin therefore to suspend all Curiosity till they arrived at
some Inn, 'which I suppose,' says she, 'can hardly be far distant;
and believe me, *Harriet*, I suspend as much Curiosity on my
Side; for indeed I believe our Astonishment is pretty equal.'

The Conversation which passed between these Ladies on the

1 Possibly Defford Common. F. S. Dickson traced Sophia's flight from Upton in a
north-easterly direction leading eventually to the inn at Meriden—a distance of nearly
forty-five miles. Her route across country would take her through or near the villages of
Defford, Pershore, Bishampton, Alcester, Wootten Wawen, Nuthurst, and Solihull.
'*N & Q*, 11th Ser., ix [30 May 1914], 425–6.)

Road, was, I apprehend, little worth relating; and less certainly was that between the two Waiting-women: For they likewise began to pay their Compliments to each other. As for the Guides, they were debarred from the Pleasure of Discourse, the one being placed in the Van, and the other obliged to bring up the Rear.

In this Posture they travelled many Hours, till they came into a wide and well-beaten Road, which, as they turned to the Right, soon brought them to a very fair promising Inn;[1] where they all alighted: But so fatigued was *Sophia*, that as she had sat her Horse during the last five or six Miles with great Difficulty, so was she now incapable of dismounting from him without Assistance. This the Landlord, who had hold of her Horse, presently perceiving, offered to lift her in his Arms from her Saddle; and she too readily accepted the Tender of his Service. Indeed Fortune seems to have resolved to put *Sophia* to the Blush that Day, and the second malicious Attempt succeeded better than the first; for my Landlord had no sooner received the young Lady in his Arms, than his Feet, which the Gout had lately very severely handled, gave way, and down he tumbled; but at the same Time, with no less Dexterity than Gallantry, contrived to throw himself under his charming Burthen, so that he alone received any Bruise from the Fall; for the greatest Injury which happened to *Sophia*, was a violent Shock given to her Modesty, by an immoderate Grin which, at her rising from the Ground, she observed in the Countenances of most of the Bye-Standers. This made her suspect what had really happened, and what we shall not here relate, for the Indulgence of those Readers who are capable of laughing at the Offence given to a young Lady's Delicacy. Accidents of this Kind we have never regarded in a comical Light; nor will we scruple to say, that he must have a very inadequate Idea of the Modesty of a beautiful young Woman, who would wish to sacrifice it to so paultry a Satisfaction as can arise from Laughter.

1 Probably 'The Bull's Head', situated at Meriden on the main road between Birmingham and Coventry. According to one contemporary account, 'The Bull's Head' was locally reputed to be *'The handsomest Inn* in England: It is indeed a well-built genteelish House, has a neat Garden, good Fish-ponds, and a tolerable Prospect round it' (R. Patching, *Four Topographical Letters, written in July, 1755* [Newcastle upon Tyne, 1757]; letter iv, p. 64). This 'magnificent inn', observed George Alexander Cooke, was 'noted from time immemorial for its excellent malt liquor; various embellishments, such as ponds, statues, etc. enliven the spot greatly' (*Topographical and Statistical Description of the County of Warwick* [n.d.], pp. 94-5).

This Fright and Shock, joined to the violent Fatigue which both her Mind and Body had undergone, almost overcame the excellent Constitution of *Sophia*, and she had scarce Strength sufficient to totter into the Inn, leaning on the Arm of her Maid. Here she was no sooner seated than she called for a Glass of Water; but Mrs. *Honour*, very judiciously, in my Opinion, changed it into a Glass of Wine.

Mrs. *Fitzpatrick* hearing from Mrs. *Honour*, that *Sophia* had not been in Bed during the two last Nights, and observing her to look very pale and wan with her Fatigue, earnestly entreated her to refresh herself with some Sleep. She was yet a Stranger to her History, or her Apprehensions; but had she known both, she would have given the same Advice; for Rest was visibly necessary for her; and their long Journey through Bye-Roads so entirely removed all Danger of Pursuit, that she was herself perfectly easy on that Account.

Sophia was easily prevailed on to follow the Counsel of her Friend, which was heartily seconded by her Maid. Mrs. *Fitzpatrick* likewise offered to bear her Cousin Company, which *Sophia*, with much Complaisance, accepted.

The Mistress was no sooner in Bed, than the Maid prepared to follow her Example. She began to make many Apologies to her Sister *Abigail* for leaving her alone in so horrid a Place as an Inn; but the other stopped her short, being as well inclined to a Nap as herself, and desired the Honour of being her Bedfellow. *Sophia's* Maid agreed to give her a Share of her Bed, but put in her Claim to all the Honour. So after many Curt'sies and Compliments, to Bed together went the Waiting-women, as their Mistresses had done before them.

It was usual with my Landlord (as indeed it is with the whole Fraternity) to enquire particularly of all Coachmen, Footmen, Post-boys, and others, into the Names of all his Guests; what their Estate was, and where it lay. It cannot therefore be wondered at, that the many particular Circumstances which attended our Travellers, and especially their retiring all to Sleep at so extraordinary and unusual an Hour as ten in the Morning, should excite his Curiosity. As soon therefore as the Guides entered the Kitchin, he began to examine who the Ladies were, and whence they came; but the Guides, tho' they faithfully related all they knew, gave him very little Satisfaction. On the contrary, they rather enflamed his Curiosity than extinguished it.

This Landlord had the Character, among all his Neighbours, of being a very sagacious Fellow. He was thought to see farther and deeper into Things than any Man in the Parish, the Parson himself not excepted. Perhaps his Look had contributed not a little to procure him this Reputation; for there was in this something wonderfully wise and significant, especially when he had a Pipe in his Mouth; which, indeed, he seldom was without. His Behaviour, likewise, greatly assisted in promoting the Opinion of his Wisdom. In his Deportment he was solemn, if not sullen; and when he spoke, which was seldom, he always delivered himself in a slow Voice; and though his Sentences were short, they were still interrupted with many Hums and Ha's, Ay, Ays, and other Expletives: So that though he accompanied his Words with certain explanatory Gestures, such as shaking, or nodding the Head, or pointing with his Forefinger, he generally left his Hearers to understand more than he expressed; nay, he commonly gave them a Hint, that he knew much more than he thought proper to disclose. This last Circumstance alone, may, indeed, very well account for his Character of Wisdom, since Men are strangely inclined to worship what they do not understand. A grand Secret, upon which several Imposers on Mankind have totally relied for the Success of their Frauds.

This politic Person now taking his Wife aside, asked her, 'What she thought of the Ladies lately arrived?' 'Think of them!' said the Wife, 'why what should I think of them?' 'I know,' answered he, 'what I think. The Guides tell strange Stories. One pretends to be come from *Gloucester*, and the other from *Upton*; and neither of them, for what I can find, can tell whither they are going. But what People ever travel across the Country from *Upton* hither, especially to *London*? And one of the Maid-Servants, before she alighted from her Horse, asked, if this was not the *London* Road? Now I have put all these Circumstances together, and whom do you think I have found them out to be?' 'Nay,' answered she, 'you know I never pretend to guess at your Discoveries.'—'It is a good Girl,' replied he, chucking her under the Chin; 'I must own you have always submitted to my Knowledge of these Matters. Why then, depend upon it; mind what I say,—depend upon it, they are certainly some of the Rebel

Ladies,[1] who, they say, travel with the young Chevalier; and have taken a round-about Way to escape the Duke's Army.'

'Husband,' quoth the Wife, 'you have certainly hit it; for one of them is drest as fine as any Princess; and, to be sure, she looks for all the World like one.—But yet, when I consider one Thing——' 'When you consider,' cries the Landlord contemptuously—'Come, pray let's hear what you consider.'—'Why it is,' answered the Wife, 'that she is too humble to be any very great Lady; for while our *Betty* was warming the Bed, she called her nothing but Child, and my Dear, and Sweetheart; and when *Betty* offered to pull off her Shoes and Stockings, she would not suffer her, saying, she would not give her the Trouble.'

'Pugh!' answered the Husband, 'That is nothing. Dost think, because you have seen some great Ladies rude and uncivil to Persons below them, that none of them know how to behave themselves when they come before their Inferiors? I think I know People of Fashion when I see them. I think I do. Did not she call for a Glass of Water when she came in? Another Sort of Women would have called for a Dram; you know they would. If she be not a Woman of very great Quality, sell me for a Fool; and, I believe, those who buy me will have a bad Bargain. Now, would a Woman of her Quality travel without a Footman, unless upon some such extraordinary Occasion?' 'Nay, to be sure, Husband,' cries she, 'you know these Matters better than I, or most Folk.' 'I think I do know something,' said he. 'To be sure,' answered the Wife, 'the poor little Heart looked so piteous, when she sat down in the Chair, I protest I could not help having a Compassion for her, almost as much as if she had been a poor Body. But what's to be done, Husband? If an she be a Rebel, I suppose you intend to betray her up to the Court. Well, she's a sweet-tempered, good-humoured Lady, be she what she will, and I shall hardly refrain from crying when I hear she is hanged or beheaded.' 'Pooh!' answered the Husband.—'But as to what's to be done it is not so easy a Matter to determine. I hope, before she goes away, we shall have the News of a Battle: for if the Chevalier should get the better, she may gain us Interest at Court, and make our Fortunes, without betraying her.' 'Why that's true,' replied the Wife; 'and

[1] For an account of the 'Ladies' who accompanied the Young Pretender on his expedition into England, see Archibald Arbuthnot's colourful, if unreliable, biography, *Memoirs of the Remarkable Life and Surprizing Adventures of Miss Jenny Cameron* (1746), pp. 276–7.

I heartily hope she will have it in her Power. Certainly she's a sweet good Lady; it would go horribly against me to have her come to any Harm.' 'Pooh,' cries the Landlord, 'Women are always so tender-hearted. Why you would not harbour Rebels, would you?' 'No, certainly,' answered the Wife; 'and as for betraying her, come what will on't, Nobody can blame us. It is what any body would do in our Case.'

While our politic Landlord, who had not, we see, undeservedly the Reputation of great Wisdom among his Neighbours, was engaged in debating this Matter with himself, (for he paid little Attention to the Opinion of his Wife) News arrived that the Rebels had given the Duke the Slip, and had got a Day's March towards *London*;[1] and soon after arrived a famous *Jacobite* Squire, who, with great Joy in his Countenance, shook the Landlord by the Hand, saying, 'All's our own, Boy, ten thousand honest *Frenchmen* are landed in *Suffolk*. Old *England* for ever! Ten thousand *French*, my brave Lad! I am going to tap away directly.'

This News determined the Opinion of the wise Man, and he resolved to make his Court to the young Lady, when she arose; for he had now (he said) discovered that she was no other than Madam *Jenny Cameron* herself.[2]

[1] The rumours to which Fielding refers were reported in *The True Patriot* (10 December 1745). Expecting that the rebels intended to march toward Wales, Cumberland waited to intercept them at Stone, near Stafford. Under cover of darkness Charles moved instead toward Derby, where he arrived on 4 December 'after one of the longest Marches which hath perhaps been heard of'. On the 5th news from Admiral Vernon reached London that the French were embarking an army at Dunkirk with a design against the Coast of Suffolk. On the 6th, Fielding observed, 'the Alarm of the Rebels having given the Duke the Slip, and being in full March for this Town, together with the Express abovementioned from Admiral Vernon', caused a panic in the capital. These fears, however, were not substantiated. By the 6th, Cumberland's forces were deployed on Meriden Common, preventing any further advance of the rebels, and Charles began his long disastrous retreat toward Scotland.

[2] Jeanie or 'Jenny' Cameron (1699 ?–1767), the spirited, witty daughter of a Highland laird, was popularly supposed to be the Young Pretender's mistress and to have attended him in battle, leading the clan against the British at Prestonpans. (See, for example, Archibald Arbuthnot's *Memoirs*, cited above, p. 577, n. 1, and Fielding's references to her in *The Jacobite's Journal*, 12 December 1747, 27 February 1748.) Most of the stories about her were, however, fabrications. At the time of the rebellion she was a faded beauty in her mid-forties.

CHAPTER III

A very short Chapter, in which however is a Sun, a Moon, a Star, and an Angel.

THE Sun (for he keeps very good Hours at this Time of the Year) had been some Time retired to Rest, when *Sophia* arose greatly refreshed by her Sleep; which, short as it was, nothing but her extreme Fatigue could have occasioned; for tho' she had told her Maid, and perhaps herself too, that she was perfectly easy, when she left *Upton*, yet it is certain her Mind was a little affected with that Malady which is attended with all the restless Symptoms of a Fever, and is perhaps the very Distemper which Physicians mean (if they mean any thing) by the Fever on the Spirits.[1]

Mrs. *Fitzpatrick* likewise left her Bed at the same Time; and having summoned her Maid, immediately dressed herself. She was really a very pretty Woman, and had she been in any other Company but that of *Sophia*, might have been thought beautiful; but when Mrs. *Honour* of her own Accord attended (for her Mistress would not suffer her to be waked) and had equipped our Heroine, the Charms of Mrs. *Fitzpatrick* who had performed the Office of the Morning Star, and had preceded greater Glories, shared the Fate of that Star, and were totally eclipsed the Moment those Glories shone forth.

Perhaps *Sophia* never looked more beautiful than she did at this Instant. We ought not therefore to condemn the Maid of the Inn for her Hyperbole; who when she descended, after having lighted the Fire, declared, and ratified it with an Oath, that if ever there was an Angel upon Earth, she was now above Stairs.

Sophia had acquainted her Cousin with her Design to go to *London*; and Mrs. *Fitzpatrick* had agreed to accompany her; for the Arrival of her Husband at *Upton* had put an End to her Design of going to *Bath*, or to her Aunt *Western*. They had therefore no sooner finished their Tea, than *Sophia* proposed to set out, the Moon then shining extremely bright, and as for the Frost she defied it; nor had she any of those Apprehensions which many young Ladies would have felt at travelling by Night; for she had, as we have before observed, some little Degree of natural Courage;

[1] See above, p. 112, n. 1.

and this her present Sensations, which bordered somewhat on Despair, greatly encreased. Besides, as she had already travelled twice with Safety, by the Light of the Moon, she was the better emboldened to trust to it a third Time.

The Disposition of Mrs. *Fitzpatrick* was more timorous; for tho' the greater Terrors had conquered the less, and the Presence of her Husband had driven her away at so unseasonable an Hour from *Upton*, yet being now arrived at a Place where she thought herself safe from his Pursuit, these lesser Terrors of I know not what, operated so strongly, that she earnestly entreated her Cousin to stay till the next Morning, and not expose herself to the Dangers of travelling by Night.

Sophia, who was yielding to an Excess, when she could neither laugh nor reason her Cousin out of these Apprehensions, at last gave Way to them. Perhaps indeed, had she known of her Father's Arrival at *Upton*, it might have been more difficult to have persuaded her; for as to *Jones*, she had, I am afraid, no great Horror at the Thoughts of being overtaken by him; nay, to confess the Truth, I believe she rather wished than feared it; though I might honestly enough have concealed this Wish from the Reader, as it was one of those secret spontaneous Emotions of the Soul, to which the Reason is often a Stranger.[1]

When our young Ladies had determined to remain all that Evening in their Inn, they were attended by the Landlady, who desired to know what their Ladyships would be pleased to eat. Such Charms were there in the Voice, in the Manner, and in the affable Deportment of *Sophia*, that she ravished the Landlady to the highest Degree; and that good Woman, concluding that she had attended *Jenny Cameron*, became in a Moment a staunch *Jacobite*, and wished heartily well to the young Pretender's Cause, from the great Sweetness and Affability with which she had been treated by his supposed Mistress.

The two Cousins began now to impart to each other their reciprocal Curiosity, to know what extraordinary Accidents on both Sides occasioned this so strange and unexpected Meeting.

---

[1] Cf. 'An Essay on the Knowledge of the Characters of Men' (1743) where, in a quite different context, Fielding similarly explains the natural impulse to laugh at another's discomfiture: 'but as this is one of those first, and as it were, spontaneous Motions of the Soul, which few . . . attend to, and none can prevent; so it doth not properly constitute the Character.'

At last Mrs. *Fitzpatrick*, having obtained of *Sophia* a Promise of communicating likewise in her Turn, began to relate what the Reader, if he is desirous to know her History, may read in the ensuing Chapter.

CHAPTER IV

The History of Mrs. Fitzpatrick.

MRS. *Fitzpatrick*, after a Silence of a few Moments, fetching a deep Sigh, thus began:

'It is natural to the Unhappy to feel a secret Concern in re-collecting those Periods of their Lives which have been most delightful to them. The Remembrance of past Pleasures affects us with a kind of tender Grief, like what we suffer for departed Friends; and the Ideas of both may be said to haunt our Imaginations.

'For this Reason, I never reflect without Sorrow on those Days (the happiest far of my Life) which we spent together, when both were under the Care of my Aunt *Western*. Alas! why are Miss *Graveairs*, and Miss *Giddy* no more. You remember, I am sure, when we knew each other by no other Names. Indeed you gave me the latter Appellation with too just Cause. I have since experienced how much I deserved it. You, my *Sophia*, was always my Superior in every thing, and I heartily hope you will be so in your Fortune. I shall never forget the wise and matronly Advice you once gave me, when I lamented being disappointed of a Ball, though you could not be then fourteen Years old.—O my *Sophy*, how blest must have been my Situation, when I could think such a Dis-appointment a Misfortune; and when indeed it was the greatest I had ever known.'

'And yet, my dear *Harriet*,' answered *Sophia*, 'it was then a serious Matter with you. Comfort yourself therefore with think-ing, that whatever you now lament may hereafter appear as trifling and contemptible as a Ball would at this Time.'

'Alas, my *Sophia*,' replied the other Lady, 'you yourself will think otherwise of my present Situation; for greatly must that tender Heart be altered, if my Misfortunes do not draw many a Sigh, nay many a Tear, from you. The Knowledge of this should perhaps deter me from relating what I am convinced will so much affect you.'—Here Mrs. *Fitzpatrick* stopt, till at the repeated Entreaties of *Sophia*, she thus proceeded.

'Though you must have heard much of my Marriage, yet as Matters may probably have been misrepresented, I will set out from the very Commencement of my unfortunate Acquaintance with my present Husband; which was at *Bath*, soon after you left my Aunt, and returned home to your Father.

'Among the gay young Fellows, who were at this Season at *Bath*, Mr. *Fitzpatrick* was one. He was handsome, degagé, extremely gallant, and in his Dress exceeded most others. In short, my Dear, if you was unluckily to see him now, I could describe him no better than by telling you he was the very Reverse of every Thing which he is: For he hath rusticated himself so long, that he is become an absolute wild *Irishman*. But to proceed in my Story; the Qualifications which he then possessed so well recommended him, that though the People of Quality at that Time lived separate from the rest of the Company, and excluded them from all their Parties, Mr. *Fitzpatrick* found Means to gain Admittance. It was perhaps no easy Matter to avoid him; for he required very little or no Invitation; and as being handsome and genteel, he found it no very difficult Matter to ingratiate himself with the Ladies, so, he having frequently drawn his Sword, the Men did not care publickly to affront him. Had it not been for some such Reason, I believe he would have been soon expelled by his own Sex; for surely he had no strict Title to be preferred to the *English* Gentry; nor did they seem inclined to shew him any extraordinary Favour. They all abused him behind his Back, which might probably proceed from Envy; for by the Women he was well received, and very particularly distinguished by them.

'My Aunt, tho' no Person of Quality herself, as she had always lived about the Court, was enrolled in that Party: For by whatever Means you get into the Polite Circle, when you are once there, it is sufficient Merit for you that you are there. This Observation, young as you was, you could scarce avoid making from my Aunt, who was free, or reserved, with all People, just as they had more or less of this Merit.

'And this Merit, I believe, it was, which principally recommended Mr. *Fitzpatrick* to her Favour. In which he so well

succeeded, that he was always one of her private Parties. Nor was
he backward in returning such Distinction; for he soon grew so
very particular in his Behaviour to her, that the Scandal Club
first began to take Notice of it, and the better disposed Persons
made a Match between them. For my own Part, I confess, I
made no Doubt but that his Designs were strictly honourable, as
the Phrase is; that is, to rob a Lady of her Fortune by Way of
Marriage. My Aunt was, I conceived, neither young enough nor
handsome enough, to attract much wicked Inclination; but she
had matrimonial Charms in great Abundance.

'I was the more confirmed in this Opinion from the extraordinary Respect which he shewed to myself, from the first
Moment of our Acquaintance. This I understood as an Attempt
to lessen, if possible, that Disinclination which my Interest might
be supposed to give me towards the Match; and I know not but
in some Measure it had that Effect: for as I was well contented
with my own Fortune, and of all People the least a Slave to
interested Views, so I could not be violently the Enemy of a Man
with whose Behaviour to me I was greatly pleased; and the more
so, as I was the only Object of such Respect; for he behaved at
the same Time to many Women of Quality without any Respect
at all.

'Agreeable as this was to me, he soon changed it into another
Kind of Behaviour, which was perhaps more so. He now put on
much Softness and Tenderness, and languished and sighed
abundantly. At Times indeed, whether from Art or Nature I will
not determine, he gave his usual Loose to Gayety and Mirth;
but this was always in general Company, and with other Women;
for even in a Country Dance, when he was not my Partner, he
became grave and put on the softest Look imaginable, the
Moment he approached me. Indeed he was in all Things so very
particular towards me, that I must have been blind not to have
discovered it. And, and, and——' 'And you was more pleased
still, my dear *Harriet*,' cries *Sophia*; 'you need not be ashamed,'
added she sighing, 'for sure there are irresistible Charms in
Tenderness, which too many Men are able to affect.' 'True,'
answered her Cousin, 'Men, who in all other Instances want
common Sense, are very *Machiavels* in the Art of Loving. I wish
I did not know an Instance.—Well, Scandal now began to be as
busy with me as it had before been with my Aunt, and some good

Ladies did not scruple to affirm that Mr. *Fitzpatrick* had an Intrigue with us both.

'But what may seem astonishing; my Aunt never saw, nor in the least seemed to suspect that which was visible enough, I believe, from both our Behaviours. One would indeed think, that Love quite puts out the Eyes of an old Woman. In Fact, they so greedily swallow the Addresses which are made to them, that like an outragious Glutton, they are not at Leisure to observe what passes amongst others at the same Table. This I have observed in more Cases than my own; and this was so strongly verified by my Aunt, that tho' she often found us together at her Return from the Pump,[1] the least canting Word of his, pretending Impatience at her Absence, effectually smothered all Suspicion. One Artifice succeeded with her to Admiration. This was his treating me like a little Child, and never calling me by any other Name in her Presence, but that of pretty Miss. This indeed did him some Disservice with your humble Servant; but I soon saw through it, especially as in her Absence he behaved to me, as I have said, in a different Manner. However, if I was not greatly disobliged by a Conduct of which I had discovered the Design, I smarted very severely for it: For my Aunt really conceived me to be what her Lover (as she thought him) called me, and treated me, in all Rèspects, as a perfect Infant. To say the Truth, I wonder she had not insisted on my again wearing Leading-strings.

'At last, my Lover (for so he was) thought proper, in a most solemn Manner, to disclose a Secret which I had known long before. He now placed all the Love which he had pretended to my Aunt to my Account. He lamented, in very pathetic Terms, the Encouragement she had given him, and made a high Merit of the tedious Hours, in which he had undergone her Conversation. —What shall I tell you, my dear *Sophia?*—Then I will confess the Truth. I was pleased with my Man. I was pleased with my Conquest. To rival my Aunt delighted me; to rival so many other Women charmed me. In short, I am afraid, I did not behave as I should do, even upon the very first Declaration.—I wish I did not almost give him positive Encouragement before we parted.

'The *Bath* now talked loudly, I might almost say, roared against me. Several young Women affected to shun my Acquain-

---

[1] The Pump Room, where medicinal waters were dispensed. The original room was erected at the King's Bath in 1706 and later elaborated.

tance, not so much, perhaps, from any real Suspicion, as from a Desire of banishing me from a Company, in which I too much engrossed their favourite Man. And here I cannot omit expressing my Gratitude to the Kindness intended me by Mr. *Nash*;[1] who took me one Day aside, and gave me Advice, which if I had followed, I had been a happy Woman. "Child," says he, "I am sorry to see the Familiarity which subsists between you and a Fellow who is altogether unworthy of you, and I am afraid will prove your Ruin. As for your old stinking Aunt, if it was to be no Injury to you, and my pretty *Sophy Western* (I assure you I repeat his Words) I should be heartily glad, that the Fellow was in Possession of all that belongs to her. I never advise old Women: For if they take it into their Heads to go to the Devil, it is no more possible, than worth while, to keep them from him. Innocence and Youth and Beauty are worthy a better Fate, and I would save them from his Clutches. Let me advise you therefore, dear Child; never suffer this Fellow to be particular with you again." —Many more Things he said to me, which I have now forgotten, and indeed I attended very little to them at that Time: For Inclination contradicted all he said, and besides I could not be persuaded, that Women of Quality would condescend to Familiarity with such a Person as he described.

'But I am afraid, my Dear, I shall tire you with a Detail of so many minute Circumstances. To be concise therefore, imagine me married; imagine me, with my Husband, at the Feet of my Aunt, and then imagine the maddest Woman in *Bedlam* in a raving Fit, and your Imagination will suggest to you no more than what really happened.

'The very next Day, my Aunt left the Place, partly to avoid

---

[1] In the first decade of the century, Richard Nash (1674–1761), good-natured gambler and beau, established himself at Bath as Master of Ceremonies in the Guildhall ballroom and the Pump Room. Under his influence Bath became a splendid resort of the fashionable world. As self-appointed guardian of 'the Young, the Gay, the Heedless Fair', Nash made it his constant practice to interfere in their rash amours, admonishing them against the designs of philanderers and fortune-hunters. (See William Oliver, *A Faint Sketch of the Life, Character, and Manners, of the Late Mr. Nash* [Bath, 1761], pp. 4–5, and Oliver Goldsmith, *The Life of Richard Nash, of Bath, Esq.* [1762], pp. 77 ff.) Considering Nash's reputation as general counsellor to 'the Female Race', it is needless to assume, with his most recent biographer, that in this passage Fielding was remembering the tragic case of Fanny Braddock, who ruined herself by disregarding Nash's advice (Willard Connely, *Beau Nash* [1955], pp. 84–93, 142). For another reference to Nash, see the Dedication to *Shamela* (1741).

seeing Mr. *Fitzpatrick* or my self, and as much perhaps to avoid seeing any one else; for, tho' I am told she hath since denied every thing stoutly, I believe she was then a little confounded at her Disappointment. Since that Time, I have written to her many Letters; but never could obtain an Answer, which I must own sits somewhat the heavier, as she herself was, tho' undesignedly, the Occasion of all my Sufferings: For had it not been under the Colour of paying his Addresses to her, Mr. *Fitzpatrick* would never have found sufficient Opportunities to have engaged my Heart, which, in other Circumstances, I still flatter myself would not have been an easy Conquest to such a Person. Indeed, I believe, I should not have erred so grosly in my Choice, if I had relied on my own Judgment; but I trusted totally to the Opinion of others, and very foolishly took the Merit of a Man for granted, whom I saw so universally well received by the Women. What is the Reason, my Dear, that we who have Understandings equal to the wisest and greatest of the other Sex so often make Choice of the silliest Fellows for Companions and Favourites? It raises my Indignation to the highest Pitch, to reflect on the Numbers of Women of Sense who have been undone by Fools.' Here she paused a Moment; but *Sophia* making no Answer, she proceeded as in the next Chapter.

CHAPTER V

In which the History of Mrs. Fitzpatrick *is continued.*

'WE remained at *Bath* no longer than a Fortnight after our Wedding: For as to any Reconciliation with my Aunt, there were no Hopes; and of my Fortune, not one Farthing could be touched till I was at Age, of which I now wanted more than two Years. My Husband therefore was resolved to set out for *Ireland*; against which I remonstrated very earnestly, and insisted on a Promise which he had made me before our Marriage, that I should never take this Journey against my Consent; and indeed I never intended to consent to it; nor will any Body, I believe, blame me for that Resolution; but this, however, I never mentioned to my Husband, and petitioned only for the Reprieve of a Month; but he had fixed the Day, and to that Day he obstinately adhered.

'The Evening before our Departure, as we were disputing this Point with great Eagerness on both Sides, he started suddenly from his Chair, and left me abruptly, saying, he was going to the Rooms.[1] He was hardly out of the House, when I saw a Paper lying on the Floor, which, I suppose, he had carelesly pulled from his Pocket, together with his Handkerchief. This Paper I took up, and finding it to be a Letter, I made no Scruple to open and read it, and indeed I read it so often, that I can repeat it to you almost Word for Word. This then was the Letter.

"To Mr. Brian Fitzpatrick.

Sir,
    Yours received, and am surprized you should use me in this Manner, as have never seen any of your Cash, unless for one Linsey Woolsey Coat, and your Bill now is upwards of 150 *l.* Consider, Sir, how often you have fobbed me off with your being shortly to be married to this Lady, and t'other Lady; but I can neither live on Hopes or Promises, nor will my Woollen-draper take any such in Payment. You tell me you are secure of having either the Aunt or the Niece, and that you might have married the Aunt before this, whose Jointure you say is immense, but that you prefer the Niece on account of her ready Money. Pray, Sir, take a Fool's Advice for once, and marry the first you can get. You will pardon my offering my Advice, as you know I sincerely wish you well. Shall draw on you *per* next Post, in favour of Messieurs *John Drugget* and Company, at fourteen Days, which doubt not your honouring, and am,

Sir,
Your humble Servant,
SAM. COSGRAVE."

'This was the Letter Word for Word. Guess, my dear Girl, guess how this Letter affected me. *You prefer the Niece on account of her Ready Money!* If every one of these Words had been a Dagger, I could with Pleasure have stabbed them into his

---

[1] The Assembly Rooms, where the principal entertainments were dancing and card-playing. The original rooms were erected in 1708 and later enlarged. A second set of rooms, the Wiltshire Assembly Rooms, was built by John Wood the elder in 1728.

Heart; but I will not recount my frantic Behaviour on the
Occasion. I had pretty well spent my Tears before his Return
home; but sufficient Remains of them appeared in my swollen
Eyes. He threw himself sullenly into his Chair, and for a long
Time we were both silent. At length in a haughty Tone, he said,
"I hope, Madam, your Servants have packed up all your Things;
for the Coach will be ready by Six in the Morning." My Patience
was totally subdued by this Provocation, and I answered, No, Sir,
there is a Letter still remains unpacked, and then throwing it on
the Table, I fell to upbraiding him with the most bitter Language
I could invent.

'Whether Guilt, or Shame, or Prudence, restrained him, I
cannot say; but tho' he is the most passionate of Men, he exerted
no Rage on this Occasion. He endeavoured on the contrary to
pacify me by the most gentle Means. He swore the Phrase in the
Letter to which I principally objected was not his, nor had he ever
written any such. He owned indeed the having mentioned his
Marriage and that Preference which he had given to myself, but
denied with many Oaths the having assigned any such Reason.
And he excused the having mentioned any such Matter at all, on
account of the Straits he was in for Money, arising, he said, from
his having too long neglected his Estate in *Ireland*. And this, he
said, which he could not bear to discover to me, was the only
Reason of his having so strenuously insisted on our Journey. He
then used several very endearing Expressions, and concluded by
a very fond Caress, and many violent Protestations of Love.

'There was one Circumstance, which, tho' he did not appeal to
it, had much Weight with me in his Favour, and that was the
Word Jointure in the Taylor's Letter, whereas my Aunt never
had been married, and this Mr. *Fitzpatrick* well knew.—As I
imagined therefore that the Fellow must have inserted this of his
own Head, or from Hearsay, I persuaded myself he might have
ventured likewise on that odious Line on no better Authority.
What Reasoning was this, my Dear? Was I not an Advocate
rather than a Judge?—But why do I mention such a Circumstance as this, or appeal to it for the Justification of my Forgiveness!—In short, had he been guilty of twenty Times as much,
half the Tenderness and Fondness which he used, would have
prevailed on me to have forgiven him. I now made no farther
Objections to our setting out, which we did the next Morning,

and in a little more than a Week arrived at the Seat of Mr. *Fitzpatrick*.

'Your Curiosity will excuse me from relating any Occurrences which past during our Journey: For it would indeed be highly disagreeable to travel it over again, and no less so to you to travel it over with me.

'This Seat then, is an ancient Mansion-House; if I was in one of those merry Humours, in which you have so often seen me, I could describe it to you ridiculously enough. It looked as if it had been formerly inhabited by a Gentleman. Here was Room enough, and not the less Room on account of the Furniture: For indeed there was very little in it. An old Woman who seemed coeval with the Building, and greatly resembled her whom *Chamont* mentions in the *Orphan*,[1] received us at the Gate, and in a Howl scarce human, and to me unintelligible, welcomed her Master home. In short, the whole Scene was so gloomy and melancholy, that it threw my Spirits into the lowest Dejection; which my Husband discerning, instead of relieving, encreased, by two or three malicious Observations. "There are good Houses, Madam," says he, "as you find, in other Places besides *England*; but perhaps you had rather be in a dirty Lodgings at *Bath*."

'Happy, my Dear, is the Woman, who in any State of Life, hath a cheerful good-natured Companion to support and comfort her; but why do I reflect on happy Situations only to aggravate my own Misery! My Companion, far from clearing up the Gloom of Solitude, soon convinced me, that I must have been wretched with him in any Place, and in any Condition. In a Word, he was a surly Fellow, a Character you have perhaps never seen: For indeed no Woman ever sees it exemplified, but in a Father, a Brother, or a Husband; and tho' you have a Father, he is not of that Character. This surly Fellow had formerly appeared to me the very Reverse, and so he did still to every other Person. Good Heaven! how is it possible for a Man to maintain a constant Lie in his Appearance abroad and in Company, and to content himself with shewing disagreeable Truth only at home? Here, my Dear, they make themselves Amends for the uneasy Restraint which they put on their Tempers in the World; for I have observed the more merry and gay, and good-humoured my Husband hath at any Time been in Company, the more sullen and morose

[1] See above, p. 445, n. 1.

he was sure to become at our next private Meeting. How shall I describe his Barbarity? To my Fondness he was cold and insensible. My little comical Ways, which you, my *Sophy*, and which others have called so agreeable, he treated with Contempt. In my most serious Moments he sung and whistled; and whenever I was thoroughly dejected and miserable, he was angry, and abused me: for though he was never pleased with my good Humour, nor ascribed it to my Satisfaction in him; yet my low Spirits always offended him, and those he imputed to my Repentance of having (as he said) married an *Irishman*.

'You will easily conceive, my dear *Graveairs*; (I ask your Pardon, I really forgot myself) that when a Woman makes an imprudent Match in the Sense of the World; that is, when she is not an arrant Prostitute to pecuniary Interest, she must necessarily have some Inclination and Affection for her Man. You will as easily believe that this Affection may possibly be lessened; nay, I do assure you, Contempt will wholly eradicate it. This Contempt I now began to entertain for my Husband, whom I now discovered to be—I must use the Expression—an arrant Blockhead. Perhaps you will wonder I did not make this Discovery long before; but Women will suggest a thousand Excuses to themselves for the Folly of those they like: Besides, give me Leave to tell you it requires a most penetrating Eye to discern a Fool through the Disguises of Gayety and Good-breeding.

'It will be easily imagined, that when I once despised my Husband, as I confess to you I soon did, I must consequently dislike his Company; and indeed I had the Happiness of being very little troubled with it; for our House was now most elegantly furnished, our Cellars well stocked, and Dogs and Horses provided in great Abundance. As my Gentleman therefore entertained his Neighbours with great Hospitality, so his Neighbours resorted to him with great Alacrity; and Sports and Drinking consumed so much of his Time, that a small Part of his Conversation, that is to say, of his Ill-humours, fell to my Share.

'Happy would it have been for me, if I could as easily have avoided all other disagreeable Company; but alas! I was confined to some which constantly tormented me; and the more, as I saw no Prospect of being relieved from them. These Companions were my own racking Thoughts, which plagued, and in a Manner haunted me Night and Day. In this Situation I past through a Scene, the Horrors of which can neither be painted nor imagined. Think, my Dear, figure, if you can, to yourself what I must have undergone. I became a Mother by the Man I scorned, hated, and detested. I went through all the Agonies and Miseries of a Lying-in, (ten Times more painful in such a Circumstance, than the worst Labour can be, when one endures it for a Man one loves) in a Desart, or rather indeed a Scene of Riot and Revel, without a Friend, without a Companion, or without any of those agreeable Circumstances which often alleviate, and perhaps sometimes more than compensate the Sufferings of our Sex at that Season.'

CHAPTER VI

In which the Mistake of the Landlord throws Sophia *into a dreadful Consternation.*

MRS. *Fitzpatrick* was proceeding in her Narrative, when she was interrupted by the Entrance of Dinner, greatly to the Concern of *Sophia*: For the Misfortunes of her Friend had raised her Anxiety, and left her no Appetite, but what Mrs. *Fitzpatrick* was to satisfy by her Relation.

The Landlord now attended with a Plate under his Arm, and with the same Respect in his Countenance and Address, which he would have put on, had the Ladies arrived in a Coach and Six.

The married Lady seemed less affected with her own Misfortunes than was her Cousin: For the former eat very heartily, whereas the latter could hardly swallow a Morsel. *Sophia* likewise shewed more Concern and Sorrow in her Countenance than appeared in the other Lady; who having observed these Symptoms in her Friend, begged her to be comforted, saying, 'Perhaps all may yet end better than either you or I expect.'

Our Landlord thought he had now an Opportunity to open his Mouth, and was resolved not to omit it. 'I am sorry, Madam,' cries he, 'that your Ladyship can't eat; for to be sure you must be hungry after so long fasting. I hope your Ladyship is not uneasy at any Thing: For as Madam there says, all may end better than any body expects. A Gentleman who was here just now, brought excellent News, and perhaps some Folks who have given other Folks the Slip may get to *London* before they are overtaken, and if they do, I make no Doubt, but they will find People who will be very ready to receive them.'

All Persons under the Apprehension of Danger, convert whatever they see and hear into the Objects of that Apprehension. *Sophia* therefore immediately concluded from the foregoing Speech, that she was known and pursued by her Father. She was now struck with the utmost Consternation, and for a few Minutes deprived of the Power of Speech; which she no sooner recovered, than she desired the Landlord to send his Servants out of the Room, and then addressing herself to him, said; 'I perceive, Sir, you know who we are; but I beseech you;—nay, I am convinced, if you have any Compassion or Goodness, you will not betray us.'

'I betray your Ladyship!' quoth the Landlord; 'No; (and then he swore several very hearty Oaths) I would sooner be cut into ten thousand Pieces. I hate all Treachery. I! I never betrayed any one in my Life yet, and I am sure I shall not begin with so sweet a Lady as your Ladyship. All the World would very much blame me if I should, since it will be in your Ladyship's Power so shortly to reward me. My Wife can witness for me, I knew your Ladyship the Moment you came into the House: I said it was your Honour, before I lifted you from your Horse, and I shall carry the Bruises I got in your Ladyship's Service to the Grave; but what signified that, as long as I saved your Ladyship. To be sure some People this Morning would have thought of getting a Reward; but no such Thought ever entered into my Head. I would sooner starve than take any Reward for betraying your Ladyship.'

'I promise you, Sir,' says *Sophia*, 'if it be ever in my Power to reward you, you shall not lose by your Generosity.'

'Alack-a-day, Madam!' answered the Landlord, 'in your Ladyship's Power! Heaven put it as much into your Will. I am only afraid your Honour will forget such a poor Man as an Innkeeper; but if your Ladyship should not; I hope you will remember what Reward I refused—refused! that is I would have refused, and to be sure it may be called refusing; for I might have had it certainly, and to be sure you might have been in some Houses;—but for my Part, I would not methinks for the World have your Ladyship wrong me so much, as to imagine I ever thought of betraying you, even before I heard the good News.'

'What News pray?' says *Sophia*, somewhat eagerly.

'Hath not your Ladyship heard it then?' cries the Landlord, 'nay, like enough: For I heard it only a few Minutes ago; and if I had never heard it, may the Devil fly away with me this Instant, if I would have betrayed your Honour; no, if I would, may I——' Here he subjoined several dreadful Imprecations, which *Sophia* at last interrupted, and begged to know what he meant by the News.—He was going to answer, when Mrs. *Honour* came running into the Room, all pale and breathless, and cried out, 'Madam, we are all undone, all ruined, they are come, they are come!' These Words almost froze up the Blood of *Sophia*; but Mrs. *Fitzpatrick* asked *Honour*, who were come?—'Who?' answered she, 'why the *French*; several hundred thousands of them are landed, and we shall be all murdered and ravished.'

As a Miser, who hath in some well-built City a Cottage value Twenty Shillings, when at a Distance he is alarmed with the News of a Fire, turns pale and trembles at his Loss; but when he finds the beautiful Palaces only are burnt, and his own Cottage remains safe, he comes instantly to himself and smiles at his good Fortune: Or as (for we dislike something in the former Simile) the tender Mother, when terrified with the Apprehension that her darling Boy is drowned, is struck senseless and almost dead with Consternation; but when she is told that little Master is safe, and the *Victory* only with Twelve hundred brave Men gone to the Bottom,[1] Life and Sense again return, maternal Fondness enjoys the sudden Relief from all its Fears, and the general Benevolence which at another Time would have deeply felt the dreadful Catastrophe, lies fast asleep in her Mind.

So *Sophia*, than whom none was more capable of tenderly feeling the general Calamity of her Country, found such immediate Satisfaction from the Relief of those Terrors she had of being overtaken by her Father, that the Arrival of the *French* scarce made any Impression on her. She gently chid her Maid for the Fright into which she had thrown her; and said, 'she was glad it was no worse; for that she had feared somebody else was come.'

'Ay, ay,' quoth the Landlord smiling, 'her Ladyship knows

---

[1] Flagship of Admiral Sir John Balchen and considered the finest ship in the world, the *Victory* sank in a violent storm near Alderney on 4 October 1744. Her entire crew, more than one thousand men, was lost. (See William Laird Clowes, *The Royal Navy* [1898], iii. 108.)

better things; she knows the *French* are our very best Friends, and come over hither only for our good. They are the People who are to make old *England* flourish again. I warrant her Honour thought the Duke was coming; and that was enough to put her into a Fright. I was going to tell your Ladyship the News.—His Honour's Majesty, Heaven bless him, hath given the Duke the Slip; and is marching as fast as he can to *London*, and ten thousand *French* are landed to join him on the Road.'

Sophia was not greatly pleased with this News, nor with the Gentleman who related it; but as she still imagined he knew her (for she could not possibly have any Suspicion of the real Truth) she durst not shew any Dislike. And now the Landlord, having removed the Cloth from the Table, withdrew; but at his Departure frequently repeated his Hopes of being remembered hereafter.

The Mind of *Sophia* was not at all easy under the Supposition of being known at this House; for she still applied to herself many Things which the Landlord had addressed to *Jenny Cameron*; she therefore ordered her Maid to pump out of him by what Means he had become acquainted with her Person, and who had offered him the Reward for betraying her; she likewise ordered the Horses to be in Readiness by four in the Morning, at which Hour Mrs. *Fitzpatrick* promised to bear her Company, and then composing herself as well as she could, she desired that Lady to continue her Story.

CHAPTER VII

In which Mrs. Fitzpatrick *concludes her History.*

WHILE Mrs. *Honour*, in Pursuance of the Commands of her Mistress, ordered a Bowl of Punch, and invited my Landlord and Landlady to partake of it, Mrs. *Fitzpatrick* thus went on with her Relation.

'Most of the Officers who were quartered at a Town in our Neighbourhood were of my Husband's Acquaintance. Among these was a Lieutenant, a very pretty Sort of Man, and who was married to a Woman so agreeable both in her Temper and Conversation, that from our first knowing each other, which was soon after my Lying-in, we were almost inseparable Companions; for I had the good Fortune to make myself equally agreeable to her.

'The Lieutenant, who was neither a Sot nor a Sportsman, was frequently of our Parties; indeed he was very little with my Husband, and no more than good Breeding constrained him to be, as he lived almost constantly at our House. My Husband often expressed much Dissatisfaction at the Lieutenant's preferring my Company to his; he was very angry with me on that Account, and gave me many a hearty Curse for drawing away his Companions; saying, "I ought to be d—ned for having spoiled one of the prettiest Fellows in the World, by making a Milk-sop of him."

'You will be mistaken, my dear *Sophia*, if you imagine that the Anger of my Husband arose from my depriving him of a Companion; for the Lieutenant was not a Person with whose Society a Fool could be pleased; and if I should admit the Possibility of this, so little Right had my Husband to place the Loss of his Companion to me, that I am convinced it was my Conversation alone which induced him ever to come to the House. No, Child, it was Envy, the worst and most rancorous Kind of Envy, the Envy of Superiority of Understanding. The Wretch could not bear to see my Conversation preferred to his, by a Man of whom he could not entertain the least Jealousy. O my dear *Sophy*, you are a Woman of Sense; if you marry a Man, as is most probable you will, of less Capacity than yourself, make frequent Trials of his Temper before Marriage, and see whether he can bear to submit to such a Superiority.—Promise me, *Sophy*, you will take this Advice; for you will hereafter find its Importance.' 'It is very likely I shall never marry at all,' answered *Sophia*; 'I think, at least, I shall never marry a Man in whose Understanding I see any Defects before Marriage; and I promise you I would rather give up my own, than see any such afterwards.'—'Give up your Understanding!' replied Mrs. *Fitzpatrick*, 'Oh fie, Child, I will not believe so meanly of you. Every thing else I might myself be brought to give up; but never this. Nature would not have allotted this Superiority to the Wife in so many Instances, if she had intended we should all of us have surrendered it to the Husband. This indeed Men of Sense never expect of us; of which the Lieutenant I have just mentioned was one notable Example; for tho' he had a very good Understanding, he always acknowledged (as was really true) that his Wife had a better. And this, perhaps, was one Reason of the Hatred my Tyrant bore her.

' "Before he would be so governed by a Wife," he said, "especially such an ugly B—— (for indeed she was not a regular Beauty, but very agreeable, and extremely genteel) he would see all the Women upon Earth at the Devil," which was a very usual Phrase with him. He said, "he wondered what I could see in her to be so charmed with her Company; since this Woman," says he, "hath come among us, there is an End of your beloved Reading, which you pretended to like so much, that you could not afford Time to return the Visits of the Ladies, in this Country;" and I must confess I had been guilty of a little Rudeness this Way; for the Ladies there are at least no better than the mere Country Ladies here, and I think, I need make no other Excuse to you for declining any Intimacy with them.

'This Correspondence however continued a whole Year, even all the while the Lieutenant was quartered in that Town; for which I was contented to pay the Tax of being constantly abused in the Manner above-mentioned by my Husband; I mean when he was at home; for he was frequently absent a Month at a Time at *Dublin*, and once made a Journey of two Months to *London*; in all which Journeys I thought it a very singular Happiness that he never once desired my Company; nay, by his frequent Censures on Men who could not travel, as he phrased it, without a Wife tied up to their Tail, he sufficiently intimated that had I been never so desirous of accompanying him, my Wishes would have been in vain; but, Heaven knows, such Wishes were very far from my Thoughts.

'At length my Friend was removed from me, and I was again left to my Solitude, to the tormenting Conversation with my own Reflections, and to apply to Books for my only Comfort. I now read almost all Day long.—How many Books do you think I read in three Months?' 'I can't guess, indeed, Cousin,' answered *Sophia*.—'Perhaps half a Score!' 'Half a Score! half a thousand, Child,' answered the other. 'I read a good deal in *Daniel's English* History of *France*;[1] a great deal in *Plutarch's* Lives; the *Atalantis*,[2]

---

[1] *The History of France, from the Time the French Monarchy was Establish'd in Gaul, to the Death of Lewis the Fourteenth*, 5 vols. (1726), by the Jesuit, Gabriel Daniel (1649–1728).

[2] The scandalous *roman à clef, Secret Memoirs and Manners of Several Persons of Quality, of Both Sexes. From the New Atalantis* (1709), by Mrs. Mary de la Rivière Manley

Pope's Homer, Dryden's Plays, *Chillingworth,*[1] the Countess *D'Anois,*[2] and *Lock's* Human Understanding.

'During this Interval I wrote three very supplicating, and, I thought, moving Letters to my Aunt; but as I received no Answer to any of them, my Disdain would not suffer me to continue my Application.'—Here she stopt, and looking earnestly at *Sophia,* said, 'Methinks, my Dear, I read something in your Eyes which reproaches me of a Neglect in another Place, where I should have met with a kinder Return.' 'Indeed, dear *Harriet,*' answered *Sophia,* 'your Story is an Apology for any Neglect; but indeed I feel that I have been guilty of a Remissness, without so good an Excuse.—Yet pray proceed; for I long, tho' I tremble, to hear the End.'

Thus then Mrs. *Fitzpatrick* resumed her Narrative. 'My Husband now took a second Journey to *England,* where he continued upwards of three Months. During the greater Part of this Time, I led a Life which nothing but having led a worse, could make me think tolerable; for perfect Solitude can never be reconciled to a social Mind, like mine, but when it relieves you from the Company of those you hate. What added to my Wretchedness, was the Loss of my little Infant: Not that I pretend to have had for it that extravagant Tenderness of which I believe I might have been capable under other Circumstances; but I resolved, in every Instance, to discharge the Duty of the tenderest Mother, and this Care prevented me from feeling the Weight of that, heaviest of all Things, when it can be at all said to lie heavy on our Hands.

'I had spent full ten Weeks almost entirely by myself, having

(1663–1724). This popular novel found a place in the libraries of such frivolous young women as Leonora in *The Spectator,* No. 37 (12 April 1711), and Fielding's Miss Trifle (*The Champion,* 26 April 1740) and Shamela (letter xii). In *Joseph Andrews* (III. i) Fielding contrasts the true fictional 'Histories' of Cervantes, Scarron, Marivaux, and Le Sage to the unnatural productions of 'the modern Novel and *Atalantis* Writers'.

[1] William Chillingworth (1602–44), whose most famous work, *The Religion of Protestants, A Safe Way to Salvation* (1638), denied the infallibility of the Church of Rome, asserting that the Bible, as interpreted by the individual reason, was the only guide to salvation. His views profoundly influenced the development of latitudinarian theology, especially in Gilbert Burnet and Tillotson. A copy of Chillingworth's *Works,* 10th ed. (1742), was in Fielding's library.

[2] Marie Catherine de la Mothe, Comtesse d'Aulnoy (d. 1705), the popular author of novels and fairy tales. *The Diverting Works of the Countess D'Anois,* 4 vols., appeared in English in 1707; there were many other editions. For an earlier reference, see *The Champion* (20 March 1739/40).

seen no body all that Time, except my Servants, and a very few Visitors, when a young Lady, a Relation of my Husband, came from a distant Part of *Ireland* to visit me. She had staid once before a Week at my House, and I then gave her a pressing Invitation to return; for she was a very agreeable Woman, and had improved good natural Parts by a proper Education. Indeed she was to me a most welcome Guest.

'A few Days after her Arrival, perceiving me in very low Spirits, without enquiring the Cause, which indeed she very well knew, the young Lady fell to compassionating my Case. She said, "Tho' Politeness had prevented me from complaining to my Husband's Relations of his Behaviour, yet they all were very sensible of it, and felt great Concern upon that Account; but none more than herself:" and after some more general Discourse on this Head, which I own I could not forbear countenancing; at last, after much previous Precaution, and enjoined Concealment, she communicated to me, as a profound Secret—that my Husband kept a Mistress.

'You will certainly imagine, I heard this News with the utmost Insensibility.—Upon my Word, if you do, your Imagination will mislead you. Contempt had not so kept down my Anger to my Husband; but that Hatred rose again on this occasion. What can be the Reason of this? Are we so abominably selfish, that we can be concerned at others having the Possession even of what we despise? Or are we not rather abominably vain, and is not this the greatest Injury done to our Vanity? What think you, *Sophia*?'

'I don't know, indeed,' answered *Sophia*, 'I have never troubled myself with any of these deep Contemplations; but I think the Lady did very ill in communicating to you such a Secret.'

'And yet, my Dear, this Conduct is natural,' replied Mrs. *Fitzpatrick*; 'and when you have seen and read as much as myself, you will acknowledge it to be so.'

'I am sorry to hear it is natural,' returned *Sophia*; 'for I want neither Reading nor Experience, to convince me, that it is very dishonourable and very ill-natured: Nay, it is surely as ill-bred to tell a Husband or Wife of the Faults of each other, as to tell them of their own.'

'Well,' continued Mrs. *Fitzpatrick*, 'my Husband at last returned; and if I am thoroughly acquainted with my own

Thoughts, I hated him now more than ever; but I despised him rather less: For certainly nothing so much weakens our Contempt, as an Injury done to our Pride or our Vanity.

'He now assumed a Carriage to me, so very different from what he had lately worn, and so nearly resembling his Behaviour the first Week of our Marriage, that had I now had any Spark of Love remaining, he might, possibly, have rekindled my Fondness for him. But though Hatred may succeed to Contempt, and may, perhaps, get the better of it, Love, I believe, cannot. The Truth is, the Passion of Love is too restless to remain contented, without the Gratification which it receives from its Object; and one can no more be inclined to love without loving, than we can have Eyes without seeing. When a Husband, therefore, ceases to be the Object of this Passion, it is most probable some other Man— I say, my dear, if your Husband grows indifferent to you—if you once come to despise him—I say,—that is,—if you have the Passion of Love in you—Lud! I have bewildered myself so,— but one is apt, in these abstracted Considerations, to lose the Concatenation of Ideas, as Mr. *Locke* says.[1]—In short, the Truth is—— In short, I scarce know what it is; but, as I was saying, my Husband returned, and his Behaviour, at first, greatly surprized me; but he soon acquainted me with the Motive, and taught me to account for it. In a Word, then, he had spent and lost all the ready Money of my Fortune; and as he could mortgage his own Estate no deeper, he was now desirous to supply himself with Cash for his Extravagance, by selling a little Estate of mine, which he could not do without my Assistance; and to obtain this Favour, was the whole and sole Motive of all the Fondness which he now put on.

'With this I peremptorily refused to comply. I told him, and I told him truly, that had I been possessed of the *Indies* at our first Marriage, he might have commanded it all: For it had been a constant Maxim with me, that where a Woman disposes of her Heart, she should always deposite her Fortune; but as he had

---

[1] Cf. *Essay concerning Human Understanding*, IV. xvii. 15. Locke states that in rational demonstrations, 'each Agreement or Disagreement of the *Ideas* must be observed and seen in each Step of the whole Train, and retained in the Memory, just as it is, and the Mind must be sure, that no part of what is necessary to make up the Demonstration, is omitted or over-looked. This makes some Demonstrations long and perplexed, and too hard for those who have not Strength of Parts distinctly to perceive, and exactly to carry so many Particulars orderly in their Heads' (12th ed., 1741; ii. 304).

been so kind, long ago, to restore the former into my Possession, I was resolved, likewise, to retain what little remained of the latter.

'I will not describe to you the Passion into which these Words, and the resolute Air in which they were spoken, threw him: Nor will I trouble you with the whole Scene which succeeded between us. Out came, you may be well assured, the Story of the Mistress; and out it did come, with all the Embellishments which Anger and Disdain could bestow upon it.

'Mr. *Fitzpatrick* seemed a little Thunder-struck with this, and more confused than I had seen him; tho' his Ideas are always confused enough, Heaven knows. He did not, however, endeavour to exculpate himself; but took a Method which almost equally confounded me. What was this but Recrimination! He affected to be jealous;—he may, for ought I know, be inclined enough to Jealousy in his natural Temper: Nay, he must have had it from Nature, or the Devil must have put it into his Head: For I defy all the World to cast a just Aspersion on my Character: Nay, the most scandalous Tongues have never dared censure my Reputation. My Fame, I thank Heaven, hath been always as spotless as my Life; and let Falshood itself accuse that, if it dare. No, my dear *Graveairs*, however provoked, however ill treated, however injured in my Love, I have firmly resolved never to give the least Room for Censure on this Account.—And yet, my dear, there are some People so malicious, some Tongues so venomous, that no Innocence can escape them. The most undesigned Word, the most accidental Look, the least Familiarity, or most innocent Freedom, will be misconstrued, and magnified into I know not what, by some People. But I despise, my dear *Graveairs*, I despise all such Slander. No such Malice, I assure you, ever gave me an uneasy Moment. No, no, I promise you, I am above all that.— But where was I? O let me see, I told you, my Husband was jealous.—And of whom, pray?—Why of whom but the Lieutenant I mentioned to you before. He was obliged to resort above a Year and more back, to find any Object for this unaccountable Passion, if, indeed, he really felt any such, and was not an arrant Counterfeit, in order to abuse me.

'But I have tired you already with too many Particulars. I will now bring my Story to a very speedy Conclusion. In short, then, after many Scenes very unworthy to be repeated, in which my

Cousin engaged so heartily on my Side, that Mr. *Fitzpatrick* at last turned her out of Doors: when he found I was neither to be soothed nor bullied into Compliance, he took a very violent Method indeed. Perhaps you will conclude he beat me; but this, tho' he hath approached very near to it, he never actually did. He confined me to my Room, without suffering me to have either Pen, Ink, Paper, or Book; and a Servant every Day made my Bed, and brought me my Food.

'When I had remained a Week under this Imprisonment, he made me a Visit, and, with the Voice of a Schoolmaster, or, what is often much the same, of a Tyrant, asked me, "If I would yet comply?" I answered very stoutly, "That I would die first." "Then so you shall, and be d—n'd," cries he; "for you shall never go alive out of this Room."

'Here I remained a Fortnight longer; and, to say the Truth, my Constancy was almost subdued, and I began to think of Submission; when one Day, in the Absence of my Husband, who was gone abroad for some short Time, by the greatest good Fortune in the World, an Accident happened.—I—at a Time when I began to give Way to the utmost Despair—every Thing would be excusable at such a Time—at that very Time I received —— But it would take up an Hour to tell you all Particulars.—In one Word, then, (for I will not tire you with Circumstances) Gold, the common Key to all Padlocks, opened my Door, and set me at Liberty.

'I now made Haste to *Dublin*, where I immediately procured a Passage to *England*; and was proceeding to *Bath*, in Order to throw myself into the Protection of my Aunt, or of your Father, or of any Relation who would afford it me. My Husband overtook me last Night, at the Inn where I lay, and which you left a few Minutes before me; but I had the good Luck to escape him, and to follow you.

'And thus, my Dear, ends my History: A tragical one, I am sure, it is to myself; but, perhaps, I ought rather to apologize to you for its Dulness.'

Sophia heaved a deep Sigh, and answered, 'Indeed, *Harriet*, I pity you from my Soul;—But what could you expect? Why, why, would you marry an *Irishman*?'[1]

---

[1] Besides their reputation for impudence and a violent temper (see above, p. 396, n. 2), the Irish were particularly notorious for being fortune-hunters: see *A Modest Argument*

'Upon my Word,' replied her Cousin, your Censure is unjust. There are, among the *Irish*, Men of as much Worth and Honour, as any among the *English*: Nay, to speak the Truth, Generosity of Spirit is rather more common among them. I have known some Examples there too of good Husbands; and, I believe, these are not very plenty in *England*. Ask me, rather, what I could expect when I married a Fool; and I will tell you a solemn Truth; I did not know him to be so.'—'Can no Man,' said *Sophia*, in a very low and alter'd Voice, 'do you think, make a bad Husband, who is not a Fool?' 'That,' answered the other, 'is too general a Negative; but none, I believe, is so likely as a Fool to prove so. Among my Acquaintance, the silliest Fellows are the worst Husbands; and I will venture to assert, as a Fact, that a Man of Sense rarely behaves very ill to a Wife, who deserves very well.'

CHAPTER VIII

A dreadful Alarm in the Inn, with the Arrival of an unexpected Friend of Mrs. Fitzpatrick.

SOPHIA now, at the Desire of her Cousin, related—not what follows, but what hath gone before in this History: For which Reason the Reader will, I suppose, excuse me, for not repeating it over again.

One Remark, however, I cannot forbear making on her Narrative, namely, that she made no more mention of *Jones*, from the Beginning to the End, than if there had been no such Person alive. This I will neither endeavour to account for, nor to excuse. Indeed, if this may be called a Kind of Dishonesty, it seems the more inexcusable, from the apparent Openness and explicit Sincerity of the other Lady.—But so it was.

Just as *Sophia* arrived at the Conclusion of her Story, there arrived in the Room where the two Ladies were sitting, a Noise, not unlike, in Loudness, to that of a Pack of Hounds just let out from their Kennel; nor, in Shrillness, to Cats when caterwauling;

(1731), pp. 19 ff., and the article 'On the *Hibernian* Society of Fortune-Hunters', in *A Trip from St. James's to the Royal Exchange* (1744). See also below, p. 828. 21–2. Against these uncomplimentary allusions in *Tom Jones* one should balance Fielding's remarks in *The Champion* (29 March 1740) criticizing those who cast general aspersions upon the character of the Irish.

or, to Screech-Owls; or, indeed, more like (for what Animal can resemble a human Voice) to those Sounds, which, in the pleasant Mansions of that Gate,[1] which seems to derive its Name from a Duplicity of Tongues, issue from the Mouths, and sometimes from the Nostrils of those fair River Nymphs, ycleped of old the *Naïades*; in the vulgar Tongue translated Oyster-Wenches: For when, instead of the antient Libations of Milk and Honey and Oil, the rich Distillation from the Juniper-Berry, or, perhaps, from Malt, hath, by the early Devotion of their Votaries, been poured forth in great Abundance, should any daring Tongue, with unhallowed License prophane; i.e. depreciate the delicate fat *Milton* Oyster,[2] the Plaice sound and firm, the Flounder as much alive as when in the Water, the Shrimp as big as a Prawn, the fine Cod alive but a few Hours ago, or any other of the various Treasures, which those Water-Deities, who fish the Sea and Rivers, have committed to the Care of the Nymphs, the angry *Naïades* lift up their immortal Voices, and the prophane Wretch is struck deaf for his Impiety.

Such was the Noise, which now burst from one of the Rooms below; and soon the Thunder, which long had rattled at a Distance, began to approach nearer and nearer, till, having ascended by Degrees up Stairs, it at last entered the Apartment where the Ladies were. In short, to drop all Metaphor and Figure, Mrs. *Honour* having scolded violently below Stairs, and continued the same all the Way up, came in to her Mistress in a most outrageous Passion, crying out, 'What doth your Ladyship think? Would you imagine, that this impudent Villain, the Master of this House, hath had the Impudence to tell me, nay, to stand it out to my Face, that your Ladyship is that nasty, stinking Wh—re, (*Jenny Cameron* they call her) that runs about the Country with the Pretender? Nay, the lying, saucy Villain, had the Assurance to tell me, that your Ladyship had owned yourself to be so: But I have clawed the Rascal; I have left the Marks of my Nails in his impudent Face. My Lady!' says I, 'you saucy Scoundrel: My Lady is Meat for no Pretenders. She is a young Lady of as good Fashion, and Family, and Fortune, as any in

---

[1] i.e. Billingsgate, one of the gates of the City of London and the site of the fish market—famous for the foul, abusive language of the porters and fishmongers. Fielding's facetious derivation of the name from *bi-lingua* appears to be his own.

[2] Milton, near Sittingbourne, Kent, was famous for its oysters.

Somersetshire. Did you never hear of the great Squire *Western*, Sirrah? She is his only Daughter; she is,—and Heiress to all his great Estate. My Lady to be called a nasty *Scotch* Wh—re by such a Varlet.—To be sure, I wish I had knocked his Brains out with the Punch-bowl.'

The principal Uneasiness with which *Sophia* was affected on this Occasion, *Honour* had herself caused, by having in her Passion discovered who she was. However, as this Mistake of the Landlord sufficiently accounted for those Passages which *Sophia* had before mistaken, she acquired some Ease on that Account; nor could she, upon the whole, forbear smiling. This enraged *Honour*, and she cried, 'Indeed, Madam, I did not think your Ladyship would have made a laughing Matter of it. To be called Whore by such an impudent low Rascal. Your Ladyship may be angry with me, for ought I know, for taking your Part, since proffered Service, they say, stinks;[1] but to be sure I could never bear to hear a Lady of mine called Whore.—Nor will I bear it. I am sure your Ladyship is as virtuous a Lady as ever sat Foot on *English* Ground, and I will claw any Villain's Eyes out who dares for to offer to presume for to say the least Word to the contrary. No body ever could say the least ill of the Character of any Lady that ever I waited upon.'

Hinc illæ Lachrymæ;[2] in plain Truth, *Honour* had as much Love for her Mistress as most Servants have, that is to say—— But besides this, her Pride obliged her to support the Character of the Lady she waited on; for she thought her own was in a very close Manner connected with it. In Proportion as the Character of her Mistress was raised, hers likewise, as she conceived, was raised with it; and, on the contrary, she thought the one could not be lowered without the other.

On this Subject, Reader, I must stop a Moment to tell thee a Story. 'The famous *Nell Gwynn*,[3] stepping one Day from a House where she had made a short Visit into her Coach, saw a

---

[1] See W. G. Smith and P. Harvey, *Oxford Dictionary of English Proverbs*, 2nd ed. (Oxford, 1948), p. 519.

[2] See above, p. 415, n. 3.

[3] Eleanor 'Nell' Gwynn (1650–87), actress and mistress to Charles II. Fielding's appears to be the earliest published version of this anecdote. The anonymous author of *Memoirs of the Life of Eleanor Gwinn* (1752) gives substantially the same story, omitting, however, Fielding's final turn with its insight into the motivation of the footman (pp. 48–9).

great Mob assembled, and her Footman all bloody and dirty; the Fellow being asked, by his Mistress, the Reason of his being in that Condition, answered, "I have been fighting, Madam, with an impudent Rascal who called your Ladyship a Wh——re." "You Blockhead," replied Mrs. *Gwynn*, "at this Rate you must fight every Day of your Life; why, you Fool, all the World knows it." "Do they?" cries the Fellow, in a muttering Voice, after he had shut the Coach Door, "they shan't call me a Whore's Footman for all that." '

Thus the Passion of Mrs. *Honour* appears natural enough, even if it were to be no otherwise accounted for; but, in reality, there was another Cause of her Anger; for which we must beg Leave to remind our Reader of a Circumstance mentioned in the above Simile. There are indeed certain Liquors, which being applied to our Passions, or to Fire, produce Effects the very Reverse of those produced by Water, as they serve to kindle and inflame, rather than to extinguish. Among these, the generous Liquor called Punch is one. It was not therefore without Reason, that the learned Dr. *Cheney*[1] used to call drinking Punch pouring liquid Fire down your Throat.

Now Mrs. *Honour* had unluckily poured so much of this liquid Fire down her Throat, that the Smoke of it began to ascend into her Pericranium, and blinded the Eyes of Reason which is there supposed to keep her Residence, while the Fire itself from the Stomach easily reached the Heart, and there inflamed the noble

---

[1] George Cheyne (1671–1743), pious physician of Bath, was the author of several ungrammatical treatises on regimen advocating an abstemious vegetarian diet. In his *Essay of Health and Long Life* (1724) Cheyne, who feared that sottishness was fast becoming the universal vice, was particularly severe on punch—a '*Heathenish* Liquor' which makes its 'Votaries the soonest, and all of a sudden the deepest *drunk*; holds them longest in the Fit; and deprives them the most intirely of the Use of their *Intellectual Faculties*, and *Bodily Organs*, of any Liquor whatsoever' (10th ed., 1745; p. 59). He explained the inflammatory properties of punch with a special zest: 'The principal *Ingredient* is *Rum*, *Arrack*, *Brandy*, or *Malt Spirits*, as they are called, all of them raised by the *Fire*, from the *fermented Juices* of Plants brought from *Southern* Countries, or which have longest borne the *Heat* of the *Sun* in our own *Climate*: And 'tis observable, that every Thing that has passed the *Fire*, so that it has had due Time to divide and penetrate its Parts, as far as it possibly can, retains a *caustic, corrosive* and burning *Quality* ever afterwards. . . . And, in the continued *Distillation* of Spirits, this Action of the *Fire* is so strong, as to reduce them to liquid *Flames* at last . . .' (ibid., pp. 55–6). Earlier in *The Champion* Fielding had satirized Cheyne more than once, particularly for his unintelligible style (see the numbers for 15 November 1739, 17 May and 12 June 1740). For a later reference to Cheyne as a writer on regimen, see *The Journal of a Voyage to Lisbon* (1755), 'Sunday, July [14]'.

Passion of Pride. So that upon the whole, we shall cease to wonder at the violent Rage of the Waiting-woman; tho' at first Sight we must confess the Cause seems inadequate to the Effect.

Sophia, and her Cousin both, did all in their Power to extinguish these Flames which had roared so loudly all over the House. They at length prevailed; or, to carry the Metaphor one Step farther, the Fire having consumed all the Fuel which the Language affords, to wit, every reproachful Term in it, at last went out of its own Accord.

But tho' Tranquility was restored above Stairs, it was not so below; where my Landlady highly resenting the Injury done to the Beauty of her Husband, by the Flesh-Spades of Mrs. *Honour*, called aloud for Revenge and Justice. As to the poor Man who had principally suffered in the Engagement, he was perfectly quiet. Perhaps the Blood which he lost might have cooled his Anger: For the Enemy had not only applied her Nails to his Cheeks, but likewise her Fist to his Nostrils, which lamented the Blow with Tears of Blood in great Abundance. To this we may add Reflections on his Mistake; but indeed nothing so effectually silenced his Resentment, as the Manner in which he now discovered his Error; for as to the Behaviour of Mrs. *Honour*, it had the more confirmed him in his Opinion: but he was now assured by a Person of great Figure, and who was attended by a great Equipage, that one of the Ladies was a Woman of Fashion, and his intimate Acquaintance.

By the Orders of this Person, the Landlord now ascended, and acquainted our fair Travellers, that a great Gentleman below desired to do them the Honour of waiting on them. *Sophia* turned pale, and trembled at this Message, tho' the Reader will conclude it was too civil, notwithstanding the Landlord's Blunder, to have come from her Father; but Fear hath the common Fault of a Justice of Peace, and is apt to conclude hastily from every slight Circumstance, without examining the Evidence on both Sides.

To ease the Reader's Curiosity, therefore, rather than his Apprehensions, we proceed to inform him, that an *Irish* Peer had arrived very late that Evening at the Inn in his Way to *London*. This Nobleman having sallied from his Supper at the Hurricane before commemorated, had seen the Attendant of Mrs. *Fitzpatrick*, and upon a short Enquiry was informed, that her Lady, with whom he was very particularly acquainted, was above. This Information he had no sooner received, than he addressed himself to the Landlord, pacified him, and sent him up Stairs with Compliments rather civiler than those which were delivered.

It may perhaps be wondered at, that the Waiting-woman herself was not the Messenger employed on this Occasion; but we are sorry to say, she was not at present qualified for that, or indeed for any other Office. The Rum (for so the Landlord chose to call the Distillation from Malt) had basely taken the Advantage of the Fatigue which the poor Woman had undergone, and had made terrible Depredations on her noble Faculties, at a Time when they were very unable to resist the Attack.

We shall not describe this tragical Scene too fully; but we thought ourselves obliged by that historic Integrity which we profess, shortly to hint a Matter which we would otherwise have been glad to have spared. Many Historians indeed, for Want of this Integrity, or of Diligence, to say no worse, often leave the Reader to find out these little Circumstances in the Dark, and sometimes to his great Confusion and Perplexity.

Sophia was very soon eased of her causeless Fright by the Entry of the noble Peer, who was not only an intimate Acquaintance of Mrs. *Fitzpatrick*; but in reality a very particular Friend of that Lady. To say Truth, it was by his Assistance, that she had been enabled to escape from her Husband; for this Nobleman had the same gallant Disposition with those renowned Knights, of whom we read in heroic Story, and had delivered many an imprisoned Nymph from Durance. He was indeed as bitter an Enemy to the savage Authority too often exercised by Husbands and Fathers, over the young and lovely of the other Sex, as ever Knight Errant was to the barbarous Power of Enchanters: nay, to say Truth, I have often suspected that those very Enchanters with which Romance every where abounds, were in reality no other than the Husbands of those Days; and Matrimony itself was perhaps the enchanted Castle in which the Nymphs were said to be confined.

This Nobleman had an Estate in the Neighbourhood of *Fitzpatrick*, and had been for some Time acquainted with the Lady. No sooner therefore did he hear of her Confinement, than he earnestly applied himself to procure her Liberty; which he presently effected, not by storming the Castle, according to the

Example of ancient Heroes; but by corrupting the Governor, in Conformity with the modern Art of War;[1] in which Craft is held to be preferable to Valour, and Gold is found to be more irresistable than either Lead or Steel.

This Circumstance, however, as the Lady did not think it material enough to relate to her Friend, we would not at that Time impart it to the Reader. We rather chose to leave him a while under a Supposition, that she had found, or coined, or by some very extraordinary, perhaps supernatural Means, had possessed herself of the Money with which she had bribed her Keeper, than to interrupt her Narrative by giving a Hint of what seemed to her of too little Importance to be mentioned.

The Peer after a short Conversation, could not forbear expressing some Surprize at meeting the Lady in that Place, nor could he refrain from telling her, he imagined she had been gone to *Bath*. Mrs. *Fitzpatrick* very freely answered, 'That she had been prevented in her Purpose by the Arrival of a Person she need not mention. In short,' says she, 'I was overtaken by my Husband (for I need not affect to conceal what the World knows too well already). I had the good Fortune to escape in a most surprizing Manner, and am now going to *London* with this young Lady, who is a near Relation of mine, and who hath escaped from as great a Tyrant as my own.'

His Lordship concluding that this Tyrant was likewise a Husband, made a Speech full of Compliments to both the Ladies, and as full of Invectives against his own Sex; nor indeed did he avoid some oblique Glances at the matrimonial Institution itself, and at the unjust Powers given by it to Man over the more sensible, and more meritorious Part of the Species. He ended his Oration with an Offer of his Protection, and of his Coach and Six, which was instantly accepted by Mrs. *Fitzpatrick*, and at last, upon her Persuasions, by *Sophia*.

Matters being thus adjusted, his Lordship took his Leave, and the Ladies retired to Rest, where Mrs. *Fitzpatrick* entertained her Cousin with many high Encomiums on the Character of the noble Peer, and enlarged very particularly on his great Fondness for his Wife; saying, she believed he was almost the only Person of high Rank, who was entirely constant to the Marriage Bed. 'Indeed,' added she, 'my dear *Sophy*, that is a very rare Virtue amongst

[1] See above, pp. 240, n. 3, and 513, n. 1.

Men of Condition. Never expect it when you marry; for, believe
me, if you do, you will certainly be deceived.'

A gentle Sigh stole from *Sophia* at these Words, which perhaps
contributed to form a Dream of no very pleasant Kind; but as she
never revealed this Dream to any one, so the Reader cannot
expect to see it related here.

CHAPTER IX

The Morning introduced in some pretty Writing. A Stage Coach. The
Civility of Chambermaids. The heroic Temper of Sophia. *Her*
Generosity. The Return to it. The Departure of the Company, and
their Arrival at London; *with some Remarks for the Use of*
Travellers.

THOSE Members of the Society, who are born to furnish
the Blessings of Life, now began to light their Candles, in
order to pursue their daily Labours, for the Use of those who are
born to enjoy these Blessings. The sturdy Hind now attends the
Levee of his Fellow Labourer the Ox; the cunning Artificer, the
diligent Mechanic spring from their hard Mattress; and now
the bonny House-maid begins to repair the disordered Drum-
Room,[1] while the riotous Authors of that Disorder, in broken
interrupted Slumbers, tumble and toss, as if the Hardness of Down
disquieted their Repose.

In simple Phrase, the Clock had no sooner struck Seven, than
the Ladies were ready for their Journey, and at their Desire, his
Lordship and his Equipage were prepared to attend them.

And now a Matter of some Difficulty arose; and this was how
his Lordship himself should be conveyed: For tho' in Stage-
Coaches, where Passengers are properly considered as so much
Luggage, the ingenious Coachman stows half a Dozen with
perfect Ease into the Place of four: for well he contrives that the
fat Hostess, or well-fed Alderman, may take up no more Room
than the slim Miss, or taper Master; it being the Nature of Guts,
when well squeezed, to give Way, and to lie in a narrow Compass; yet in these Vehicles which are called, for Distinction-sake,
Gentlemen's Coaches, tho' they are often larger than the others,
this Method of packing is never attempted.

---

[1] Fielding defines a drum in XVII. vi.

His Lordship would have put a short End to the Difficulty, by very gallantly desiring to mount his Horse; but Mrs. *Fitzpatrick* would by no Means consent to it. It was therefore concluded that the *Abigails* should by Turns relieve each other on one of his Lordship's Horses, which was presently equipped with a Side-Saddle for that Purpose.

Every thing being settled at the Inn, the Ladies discharged their former Guides, and *Sophia* made a present to the Landlord, partly to repair the Bruise which he had received under herself, and partly on Account of what he had suffered under the Hands of her enraged Waiting-woman. And now *Sophia* first discovered a Loss which gave her some Uneasiness; and this was of the hundred Pound Bank Bill which her Father had given her at their last Meeting; and which, within a very inconsiderable Trifle, was all the Treasure she was at present worth. She searched every where, and shook and tumbled all her Things to no Purpose, the Bill was not to be found: And she was at last fully persuaded that she had lost it from her Pocket when she had the Misfortune of tumbling from her Horse in the dark Lane, as before recorded. A Fact that seemed the more probable, as she now recollected some Discomposure in her Pockets which had happened at that Time, and the great Difficulty with which she had drawn forth her Handkerchief the very Instant before her Fall, in order to relieve the Distress of Mrs. *Fitzpatrick*.

Misfortunes of this Kind, whatever Inconveniencies they may be attended with, are incapable of subduing a Mind in which there is any Strength, without the Assistance of Avarice. *Sophia* therefore, tho' nothing could be worse timed than this Accident, at such a Season, immediately got the better of her Concern, and with her wonted Serenity and Cheerfulness of Countenance, returned to her Company. His Lordship conducted the Ladies into the Vehicle, as he did likewise Mrs. *Honour*, who, after many Civilities, and more Dear Madams, at last yielded to the well-bred Importunities of her Sister *Abigail*, and submitted to be complimented with the first Ride in the Coach; in which indeed she would afterwards have been contented to have pursued her whole Journey, had not her Mistress, after several fruitless Intimations, at length forced her to take her Turn on Horse-back.

The Coach now having received its Company, began to move

forwards, attended by many Servants, and by two led Captains, who had before rode with his Lordship, and who would have been dismissed from the Vehicle upon a much less worthy Occasion, than was this of accommodating two Ladies. In this they acted only as Gentlemen; but they were ready at any Time to have performed the Office of a Footman, or indeed would have condescended lower, for the Honour of his Lordship's Company, and for the Convenience of his Table.

My Landlord was so pleased with the Present he had received from *Sophia*, that he rather rejoiced in than regretted his Bruise, or his Scratches. The Reader will perhaps be curious to know the *Quantum* of this Present, but we cannot satisfy his Curiosity. Whatever it was, it satisfied the Landlord for his bodily Hurt; but he lamented he had not known before how little the Lady valued her Money; 'For to be sure,' says he, 'one might have charged every Article double, and she would have made no Cavil at the Reckoning.'

His Wife however was far from drawing this Conclusion; whether she really felt any Injury done to her Husband more than he did himself, I will not say; certain it is, she was much less satisfied with the Generosity of *Sophia*. 'Indeed,' cries she, 'my Dear, the Lady knows better how to dispose of her Money than you imagine. She might very well think we should not put up such a Business without some Satisfaction, and the Law would have cost her an infinite deal more than this poor little Matter, which I wonder you would take.' 'You are always so bloodily wise,' quoth the Husband, 'It would have cost her more, would it? Dost fancy I don't know that as well as thee? But would any of that more, or so much, have come into our Pockets? Indeed, if Son *Tom* the Lawyer had been alive, I could have been glad to have put such a pretty Business into his Hands. He would have got a good Picking out of it; but I have no Relation now who is a Lawyer, and why should I go to Law for the Benefit of Strangers?' 'Nay, to be sure,' answered she, 'you must know best.' 'I believe I do,' replied he. 'I fancy when Money is to be got, I can smell it out as well as another. Every body, let me tell you, would not have talked People out of this. Mind that, I say, every body would not have cajoled this out of her, mind that.' The Wife then joined in the Applause of her Husband's Sagacity; and thus ended the short Dialogue between them on this Occasion.

We will therefore take our Leave of these good People, and attend his Lordship and his fair Companions, who made such good Expedition, that they performed a Journey of ninety Miles in two Days, and on the second Evening arrived in *London*, without having encountered any one Adventure on the Road worthy the Dignity of this History to relate. Our Pen, therefore, shall imitate the Expedition which it describes, and our History shall keep Pace with the Travellers who are its Subject. Good Writers will indeed do well to imitate the ingenious Traveller in this Instance, who always proportions his Stay at any Place, to the Beauties, Elegancies, and Curiosities, which it affords. At *Eshur*,[1] at *Stowe*,[2] at *Wilton*,[3] at *Eastbury*,[4] and at *Prior's*

---

[1] Esher Place, Surrey, was acquired in 1729 by Henry Pelham (1695 ?–1754), brother of the Duke of Newcastle (see above, p. 33, n. 2) and, as First Lord of the Treasury, prime minister of the 'Broad-Bottom' Administration. In the 1730s Pelham engaged William Kent to rebuild the house in the Gothic manner and to improve the park and gardens. In *Epilogue to the Satires: Dialogue II* (1738), 66–7, Pope was charmed by '*Esher*'s peaceful Grove/ (Where *Kent* and Nature vye for PELHAM's Love)'; and in *Summer* (*Seasons*, 1744 ed., 1421 ff.) Thomson was equally warm in praising the estate. To Fielding, Pelham was 'one of the best and worthiest Men in this Nation' (*Jacobite's Journal*, 24 September 1748); and throughout 1747–8 he continually defended the minister's policies against detractors. (See, for example, *A Dialogue between a Gentleman of London, etc.* [1747], *A Proper Answer to a late Scurrilous Libel* [1747], and *The Jacobite's Journal*, 2 July, 3 September, 8 October 1748.)

[2] Stowe, Buckinghamshire, the estate of Sir Richard Temple, Viscount Cobham (1675–1749), who was related by blood or marriage to several of Fielding's friends and patrons—Pitt (see below, p. 740, n. 2), Lyttelton (see above, p. 3, n. 1), and Dodington (see below, n. 4). Earlier in the century Cobham employed such able architects as Gibbs, Bridgeman, and Kent to lay out elaborate gardens and erect numerous ornamental buildings, in general developing Stowe into the most famous of all the great country estates. The process of naturalizing the formal gardens in conformity with the new English taste was seriously begun by 'Capability' Brown in the mid-1740s. In *Autumn* (*Seasons*, 1744 ed., 1053 ff.) Thomson celebrated the 'fair Majestic Paradise of STOWE', where 'All beauteous Nature fears to be outdone' by 'cool judicious Art'. Testifying to the keen contemporary interest in the estate, a guidebook to Stowe was published in 1744, and in 1748 appeared *A Dialogue upon the Gardens . . . at Stowe*, which reached a third edition in 1751.

[3] The seat, near Salisbury, of Henry Herbert (1693–1751), ninth Earl of Pembroke and one of the great 'building earls' of the century (see James Lees-Milne, *Earls of Creation* [1962], ch. ii). Roger Morris helped Pembroke design the splendid Palladian bridge there (1737) and Kent naturalized the formal gardens. The association of Wilton with 'Art' is clear from the first of James Harris's *Three Treatises* (1744), a dialogue on that subject prompted by a visit to Pembroke's estate, where 'The Beauties of Gardening, Architecture, Painting, and Sculpture . . . were the Subject of great Entertainment' (p. 4).

[4] The seat in Dorset of George Bubb Dodington (1691–1762), later Baron Melcombe. Dodington was Treasurer of the Navy in the 'Broad-Bottom' Administration and a patron of Thomson, Young, and Fielding among others. The house, rather more ornate than the best Palladian style of the period, was begun by Vanbrugh in 1718 and completed

Park,[1] Days are too short for the ravished Imagination; while we admire the wondrous Power of Art in improving Nature. In some of these, Art chiefly engages our Admiration; in others, Nature and Art contend for our Applause; but in the last, the former seems to triumph. Here Nature appears in her richest Attire, and Art dressed with the modestest Simplicity, attends her benignant Mistress. Here Nature indeed pours forth the choicest Treasures which she hath lavished on this World; and here Human Nature presents you with an Object which can be exceeded only in the other.

The same Taste, the same Imagination, which luxuriously riots in these elegant Scenes, can be amused with Objects of far inferior Note. The Woods, the Rivers, the Lawns of *Devon* and of *Dorset*, attract the Eye of the ingenious Traveller, and retard his Pace, which Delay he afterwards compensates by swiftly scouring over the gloomy Heath of *Bagshot*, or that pleasant Plain which extends itself Westward from *Stockbridge*,[2] where no other Object than one single Tree only in sixteen Miles presents itself to the View, unless the Clouds, in Compassion to our tired Spirits, kindly open their variegated Mansions to our Prospect.

Not so travels the Money-meditating Tradesman, the sagacious Justice, the dignified Doctor, the warm-clad Grazier, with all the numerous Offspring of Wealth and Dulness. On they jogg, with equal Pace, through the verdant Meadows, or over the barren Heath, their Horses measuring four Miles and a half *per* Hour with the utmost Exactness; the Eyes of the Beast and of his Master being alike directed forwards, and employed in

by Roger Morris, who also improved the gardens. In *Autumn* (*Seasons*, 1744 ed., 660 ff.) Thomson praised Eastbury, 'Where simple Nature reigns'. Compliments to Dodington are frequent in Fielding's works, though none equal in extravagance to that in *Amelia* (XI. ii), where he is represented as 'one of the greatest Men this Country ever produced'. Earlier Fielding had dedicated the poem *Of True Greatness* (1741) to Dodington, and in *The Champion* (29 January 1739/40) and 'An Essay on Conversation' (1743), he is distinguished for his politeness. For evidence of their continuing friendship, see Lewis M. Knapp, 'Fielding's Dinners with Dodington', *N & Q*, cxcvii (20 December 1952), 565–6.

[1] Ralph Allen's estate at Widcombe, near Bath. (See above, pp. 4, n. 1; 42, n. 1; and 403–4.) Designed by John Wood the elder, Allen's magnificent Palladian mansion was erected 1735–42. For a full description, see Boyce, *The Benevolent Man* (1967), ch. vi.

[2] Bagshot Heath and Salisbury Plain, through which—though in reverse order—the traveller from Devon or Dorset would pass along the Exeter Road to London. Cf. *Jonathan Wild* (III. vii), where marriage is described as an unchanging 'State of tranquil Felicity, so little concerned with Variety, that, like *Salisbury* Plain, it affords only one Prospect. ' very pleasant one it must be confest, but the same'.

contemplating the same Objects in the same manner. With equal Rapture the good Rider surveys the proudest Boasts of the Architect, and those fair Buildings, with which some unknown Name hath adorned the rich Cloathing-Town; where heaps of Bricks are piled up as a Kind of Monument, to shew that Heaps of Money have been piled there before.

And now, Reader, as we are in Haste to attend our Heroine, we will leave to thy Sagacity to apply all this to the *Bœotian* Writers,[1] and to those Authors who are their Opposites. This thou wilt be abundantly able to perform without our Aid. Bestir thyself therefore on this Occasion; for tho' we will always lend thee proper Assistance in difficult Places, as we do not, like some others, expect thee to use the Arts of Divination to discover our Meaning; yet we shall not indulge thy Laziness where nothing but thy own Attention is required, for thou art highly mistaken if thou dost imagine that we intended, when we began this great Work, to leave thy Sagacity nothing to do, or that without sometimes exercising this Talent, thou wilt be able to travel through our Pages with any Pleasure or Profit to thyself.

CHAPTER X

Containing a Hint or two concerning Virtue, and a few more concerning Suspicion.

OUR Company being arrived at *London*, were set down at his Lordship's House, where while they refreshed themselves after the Fatigue of their Journey, Servants were dispatched to provide a Lodging for the two Ladies; for as her Ladyship was not then in Town, Mrs. *Fitzpatrick* would by no Means consent to accept a Bed in the Mansion of the Peer.

Some Readers will perhaps condemn this extraordinary Delicacy, as I may call it, of Virtue, as too nice and scrupulous; but we must make Allowances for her Situation, which must be owned to have been very ticklish; and when we consider the Malice of censorious Tongues, we must allow, if it was a Fault, the Fault was an Excess on the right Side, and which every

---

[1] Though the birthplace of Pindar and Plutarch, Bœotia became proverbial for the stupidity of its inhabitants.

Woman who is in the self-same Situation will do well to imitate. The most formal Appearance of Virtue, when it is only an Appearance, may perhaps, in very abstracted Considerations, seem to be rather less commendable than Virtue itself without this Formality; but it will however be always more commended; and this, I believe, will be granted by all, that it is necessary, unless in some very particular Cases, for every Woman to support either the one or the other.

A Lodging being prepared, *Sophia* accompanied her Cousin for that Evening; but resolved early in the Morning to enquire after the Lady, into whose Protection, as we have formerly mentioned, she had determined to throw herself, when she quitted her Father's House. And this she was the more eager in doing, from some Observations she had made during her Journey in the Coach.

Now as we would by no Means fix the odious Character of Suspicion on *Sophia*, we are almost afraid to open to our Reader the Conceits which filled her Mind concerning Mrs. *Fitzpatrick*; of whom she certainly entertained at present some Doubts; which, as they are very apt to enter into the Bosoms of the worst of People, we think proper not to mention more plainly, till we have first suggested a Word or two to our Reader touching Suspicion in general.

Of this there have always appeared to me to be two Degrees. The first of these I chuse to derive from the Heart, as the extreme Velocity of its Discernment seems to denote some previous inward Impulse, and the rather, as this superlative Degree often forms its own Objects; sees what is not, and always more than really exists. This is that quick-sighted Penetration, whose Hawk's Eyes no Symptom of Evil can escape; which observes not only upon the Actions, but upon the Words and Looks of Men; and as it proceeds from the Heart of the Observer, so it dives into the Heart of the Observed, and there espies Evil, as it were, in the first Embryo; nay sometimes before it can be said to be conceived. An admirable Faculty, if it were infallible; but as this Degree of Perfection is not even claimed by more than one mortal Being, so from the Fallibility of such acute Discernment have arisen many sad Mischiefs and most grievous Heart-akes to Innocence and Virtue. I cannot help therefore regarding this vast Quicksightedness into Evil, as a vicious Excess, and as a

very pernicious Evil in itself. And I am the more inclined to this
Opinion, as I am afraid it always proceeds from a bad Heart, for
the Reasons I have above-mentioned, and for one more, namely,
because I never knew it the Property of a good one. Now from
this Degree of Suspicion I entirely and absolutely acquit *Sophia*.

A second Degree of this Quality seems to arise from the Head.
This is indeed no other than the Faculty of seeing what is before
your Eyes, and of drawing Conclusions from what you see. The
former of these is unavoidable by those who have any Eyes, and
the latter is perhaps no less certain and necessary a Consequence
of our having any Brains. This is altogether as bitter an Enemy to
Guilt, as the former is to Innocence, nor can I see it in an unamiable Light, even though, through human Fallibility, it should
be sometimes mistaken. For Instance, if a Husband should
accidentally surprize his Wife in the Lap or in the Embraces of
some of those pretty young Gentlemen who profess the Art of
Cuckoldmaking, I should not highly, I think, blame him for
concluding something more than what he saw, from the Fami-
liarities which he really had seen, and which we are at least
favourable enough to, when we call them innocent Freedoms.
The Reader will easily suggest great Plenty of Instances to himself; I shall add but one more, which however unchristian it may
be thought by some, I cannot help esteeming to be strictly
justifiable; and this is a Suspicion that a Man is capable of doing
what he hath done already, and that it is possible for one who hath
been a Villain once, to act the same Part again.[1] And to confess
the Truth, of this Degree of Suspicion I believe *Sophia* was
guilty. From this Degree of Suspicion she had, in Fact, conceived
an Opinion, that her Cousin was really not better than she should
be.

The Case, it seems, was this: Mrs. *Fitzpatrick* wisely considered, that the Virtue of a young Lady is, in the World, in the
same Situation with a poor Hare, which is certain, whenever it
ventures abroad, to meet its Enemies: For it can hardly meet any
other. No sooner therefore was she determined to take the first
Opportunity of quitting the Protection of her Husband, than

[1] Cf. Fielding's observation in 'An Essay on the Knowledge of the Characters of Men'
(1743): '. . . as the Actions of Men are the best Index to their Thoughts, as they do, if
well attended to and understood, with the utmost Certainty demonstrate the Character . . . I
think we may with Justice suspect, at least so far as to deny him our Confidence, that a
Man whom we once knew to be a Villain, remains a Villain still.'

she resolved to cast herself under the Protection of some other Man; and whom could she so properly chuse to be her Guardian as a Person of Quality, of Fortune, of Honour; and who, besides a gallant Disposition which inclines Men to Knight-Errantry; that is, to be the Champions of Ladies in Distress; had often declared a violent Attachment to herself, and had already given her all the Instances of it in his Power?

But as the Law hath foolishly omitted this Office of Vice-Husband, or Guardian to an eloped Lady; and as Malice is apt to denominate him by a more disagreeable Appellation; it was concluded that his Lordship should perform all such kind Offices to the Lady in secret, and without publicly assuming the Character of her Protector. Nay, to prevent any other Person from seeing him in this Light, it was agreed that the Lady should proceed directly to *Bath*, and that his Lordship should first go to *London*, and thence should go down to that Place by the Advice of his Physicians.

Now all this *Sophia* very plainly understood, not from the Lips or Behaviour of Mrs. *Fitzpatrick*; but from the Peer, who was infinitely less expert at retaining a Secret, than was the good Lady; and perhaps the exact Secrecy which Mrs. *Fitzpatrick* had observed on this Head in her Narrative, served not a little to heighten those Suspicions which were now risen in the Mind of her Cousin.

Sophia very easily found out the Lady she sought, for indeed there was not a Chairman in Town to whom her House was not perfectly well known; and as she received, in Return of her first Message, a most pressing Invitation, she immediately accepted it. Mrs. *Fitzpatrick* indeed did not desire her Cousin to stay with her with more Earnestness than Civility required. Whether she had discerned and resented the Suspicion above-mentioned, or from what other Motive it arose, I cannot say; but certain it is, she was full as desirous of parting with *Sophia*, as *Sophia* herself could be of going.

The young Lady, when she came to take Leave of her Cousin, could not avoid giving her a short Hint of Advice. She begged her, for Heaven's Sake, to take Care of herself, and to consider in how dangerous a Situation she stood; adding, she hoped some Method would be found of reconciling her to her Husband. 'You must remember, my Dear,' says she, 'the Maxim which my

Aunt *Western* hath so often repeated to us both; *That whenever the matrimonial Alliance is broke, and War declared between Husband and Wife, she can hardly make a disadvantageous Peace for herself on any Conditions.* These are my Aunt's very Words, and she hath had a great deal of Experience in the World.' Mrs. *Fitzpatrick* answered, with a contemptuous Smile, 'Never fear me, Child, take Care of yourself; for you are younger than I. I will come and visit you in a few Days; but, dear *Sophy*, let me give you one Piece of Advice: Leave the Character of *Graveairs* in the Country; for, believe me, it will sit very aukwardly upon you in this Town.'

Thus the two Cousins parted, and *Sophia* repaired directly to Lady *Bellaston*, where she found a most hearty, as well as a most polite Welcome. The Lady had taken a great Fancy to her when she had seen her formerly with her Aunt *Western*. She was indeed extremely glad to see her, and was no sooner acquainted with the Reasons which induced her to leave the Squire and fly to *London*, than she highly applauded her Sense and Resolution; and after expressing the highest Satisfaction in the Opinion which *Sophia* had declared she entertained of her Ladyship, by chusing her House for an Asylum, she promised her all the Protection which it was in her Power to give.

As we have now brought *Sophia* into safe Hands, the Reader will, I apprehend, be contented to deposite her there a while, and to look a little after other Personages, and particularly poor *Jones*, whom we have left long enough to do Pennance for his past Offences, which, as is the Nature of Vice, brought sufficient Punishment upon him themselves.

BOOK XII

Containing the same individual Time with the former.

CHAPTER I

Shewing what is to be deemed Plagiarism in a modern Author, and what is to be considered as lawful Prize.

THE learned Reader must have observed, that in the Course of this mighty Work, I have often translated Passages out of the best antient Authors, without quoting the Original, or without taking the least Notice of the Book from whence they were borrowed.

This Conduct in Writing is placed in a very proper Light by the ingenious Abbé *Bannier*,[1] in his Preface to his Mythology, a Work of great Erudition, and of equal Judgment. 'It will be easy,' says he, 'for the Reader to observe, that I have frequently had greater Regard to him, than to my own Reputation: For an Author certainly pays him a considerable Compliment, when, for his Sake, he suppresses learned Quotations that come in his Way, and which would have cost him but the bare Trouble of transcribing.'

To fill up a Work with these Scraps may indeed be considered as a downright Cheat on the learned World, who are by such Means imposed upon to buy a second Time in Fragments and by Retail what they have already in Gross, if not in their Memories, upon their Shelves; and it is still more cruel upon the Illiterate,[2] who are drawn in to pay for what is of no manner of Use to them.

---

[1] Abbé Antoine Banier (1673–1741), whose *Mythologie et les fables expliquées par l'histoire* (Paris, 1738–40) was translated into English in 1739–41, 4 vols.; Andrew Millar, Fielding's bookseller, was the publisher. The quotation is from 'The Author's Preface' (i. viii). (In the fourth ed. of *Tom Jones* the substitution of 'transcribing', the correct word, for 'translating' suggests that, in revising, Fielding compared his copy with the original.) When Millar reissued this work in January 1748, Fielding took a special interest in 'puffing' it in *The Jacobite's Journal* (9, 30 January, 20, 27 February 1748): the 'English *Translation*', he noted, '*is a most excellent one*' (9 January), and from his Bench in the Court of Criticism he ordered 'That the said Mythology be strongly recommended to the Public, as the most useful, instructive, and entertaining Book extant'.

[2] i.e. those who do not read Latin and Greek. For this usage, see also *Amelia*, xi. ii.

A Writer who intermixes great Quantity of *Greek* and *Latin* with his Works, deals by the Ladies and fine Gentlemen in the same paultry Manner with which they are treated by the Auctioneers, who often endeavour so to confound and mix up their Lots, that, in order to purchase the Commodity you want, you are obliged at the same Time to purchase that which will do you no Service.

And yet as there is no Conduct so fair and disinterested, but that it may be misunderstood by Ignorance, and misrepresented by Malice, I have been sometimes tempted to preserve my own Reputation, at the Expence of my Reader, and to transcribe the Original, or at least to quote Chapter and Verse, whenever I have made Use either of the Thought or Expression of another. I am indeed in some Doubt that I have often suffered by the contrary Method; and that by suppressing the original Author's Name, I have been rather suspected of Plagiarism, than reputed to act from the amiable Motive above-assigned by that justly celebrated *Frenchman*.

Now to obviate all such Imputations for the future, I do here confess and justify the Fact. The Antients may be considered as a rich Common,[1] where every Person who hath the smallest Tenement in *Parnassus* hath a free Right to fatten his Muse. Or, to place it in a clearer Light, we Moderns are to the Antients what the Poor are to the Rich. By the Poor here I mean, that large and venerable Body which, in *English*, we call The Mob. Now, whoever hath had the Honour to be admitted to any Degree of Intimacy with this Mob, must well know that it is one of their established Maxims, to plunder and pillage their rich Neighbours without any Reluctance; and that this is held to be neither Sin nor Shame among them. And so constantly do they abide and act by this Maxim, that in every Parish almost in the Kingdom, there is a Kind of Confederacy ever carrying on against a certain Person of Opulence called the Squire, whose Property is considered as Free-Booty by all his poor Neighbours; who, as they conclude that there is no Manner of Guilt in such Depredations, look upon it as a Point of Honour and moral Obligation to conceal, and to preserve each other from Punishment on all such Occasions.

In like Manner are the Ancients, such as *Homer*, *Virgil*, *Horace*, *Cicero*, and the rest, to be esteemed among us Writers,

[1] Cf. *Ars Poetica,* 131, where Horace refers to Homer and the epic authors as 'publica materies'.

as so many wealthy Squires, from whom we, the Poor of *Parnassus*, claim an immemorial Custom of taking whatever we can come at. This Liberty I demand, and this I am as ready to allow again to my poor Neighbours in their Turn. All I profess, and all I require from my Brethren, is to maintain the same strict Honesty among ourselves, which the Mob shew to one another. To steal from one another, is indeed highly criminal and indecent; for this may be strictly stiled defrauding the Poor (sometimes perhaps those who are poorer than ourselves) or, to see it under the most opprobrious Colours, robbing the Spittal.

Since therefore upon the strictest Examination, my own Conscience cannot lay any such pitiful Theft to my Charge, I am contented to plead guilty to the former Accusation; nor shall I ever scruple to take to my self any Passage which I shall find in an ancient Author to my Purpose, without setting down the Name of the Author from whence it was taken. Nay, I absolutely claim a Property in all such Sentiments the Moment they are transcribed into my Writings, and I expect all Readers henceforwards to regard them as purely and entirely my own. This Claim however I desire to be allowed me only on Condition, that I preserve strict Honesty towards my poor Brethren, from whom if ever I borrow any of that little of which they are possessed, I shall never fail to put their Mark upon it, that it may be at all Times ready to be restored to the right Owner.

The Omission of this was highly blameable in one Mr. *Moore*,[1] who having formerly borrowed some Lines of *Pope* and Company, took the Liberty to transcribe six of them into his Play of the *Rival Modes*. Mr. *Pope* however very luckily found them in the said Play, and laying violent Hands on his own Property, transferred it back again into his own Works; and for a further Punishment, imprisoned the said *Moore* in the loathsome Dungeon of the *Dunciad*, where his unhappy Memory now remains, and eternally will remain, as a proper Punishment for such his unjust Dealings in the poetical Trade.

[1] James Moore Smythe (1702–34), whom Pope pilloried as a plagiarist in *The Dunciad Variorum* (1729), ii. 46, explaining his reasons in the prefatory 'Testimonies of Authors'. Pope had given Moore permission to incorporate some of his verses (*Moral Essays*, ii. 243–8) in Moore's comedy, *The Rival Modes* (1727). When Pope withdrew his permission, Moore refused to delete the lines. For a full account of the situation, see Pope's *Epistles to Several Persons (Moral Essays)*, ed. F. W. Bateson, Twickenham Edition, III. ii (1951), p. 67 n.

CHAPTER II

*In which, tho' the Squire doth not find his Daughter, something is
found which puts an End to his Pursuit.*

THE History now returns to the Inn at *Upton*, whence we
shall first trace the Footsteps of Squire *Western*; for as he
will soon arrive at an End of his Journey, we shall have then full
Leisure to attend our Heroe.

The Reader may be pleased to remember, that the said Squire
departed from the Inn in great Fury, and in that Fury he
pursued his Daughter. The Hostler having informed him that
she had crossed the *Severn*, he likewise past that River with his
Equipage, and rode full Speed, vowing the utmost Vengeance
against poor *Sophia*, if he should but overtake her.

He had not gone far, before he arrived at a Cross-way. Here he
called a short Council of War, in which, after hearing different
Opinions, he at last gave the Direction of his Pursuit to Fortune,
and struck directly into the *Worcester* Road.

In this Road he proceeded about two Miles, when he began to
bemoan himself most bitterly, frequently crying out, 'What
Pity is it! Sure never was so unlucky a Dog as myself!' and then
burst forth a Volley of Oaths and Execrations.

The Parson attempted to administer Comfort to him on this
Occasion. 'Sorrow not, Sir,' says he, 'like those without Hope.[1]
Howbeit we have not yet been able to overtake young Madam,
we may account it some good Fortune, that we have hitherto
traced her Course aright. Peradventure she will soon be fati-
gated with her Journey, and will tarry in some Inn, in order to
renovate her corporeal Functions; and in that Case, in all moral
Certainty, you will very briefly be *compos voti*.'[2]

'Pogh! D——n the Slut,' answered the Squire, 'I am lamenting
the Loss of so fine a Morning for Hunting. It is confounded hard
to lose one of the best Scenting Days, in all Appearance, which
hath been this Season, and especially after so long a Frost.'

Whether Fortune, who now and then shews some Compassion in her wantonest Tricks, might not take Pity of the

---

[1] Cf. 1 Thessalonians 4: 13.
[2] 'Granted your wish'—cf. Horace, *Ars Poetica*, 76.

Squire; and as she had determined not to let him overtake his Daughter, might not resolve to make him Amends some other Way, I will not assert; but he had hardly uttered the Words just before commemorated, and two or three Oaths at their Heels, when a Pack of Hounds began to open their melodious Throats at a small Distance from them, which the Squire's Horse and his Rider both perceiving, both immediately pricked up their Ears, and the Squire crying, 'She's gone, she's gone! Damn me if she is not gone!' instantly clapped Spurs to the Beast, who little needed it, having indeed the same Inclination with his Master; and now the whole Company crossing into a Corn-field, rode directly towards the Hounds, with much Hollowing and Hooping, while the poor Parson, blessing himself, brought up the Rear.

Thus Fable reports, that the fair *Grimalkin*, whom *Venus*, at the Desire of a passionate Lover, converted from a Cat into a fine Woman, no sooner perceived a Mouse, than mindful of her former Sport, and still retaining her pristine Nature, she leapt from the Bed of her Husband to pursue the little Animal.

What are we to understand by this? Not that the Bride was displeased with the Embraces of her amorous Bridegroom: For tho' some have remarked that Cats are subject to Ingratitude, yet Women and Cats too will be pleased and purr on certain Occasions. The Truth is, as the sagacious Sir *Roger L'Estrange* observes, in his deep Reflections,[1] that 'if we shut Nature out at the Door, she will come in at the Window; and that Puss, tho' a Madam, will be a Mouser still.' In the same Manner we are not to arraign the Squire of any Want of Love for his Daughter: For in reality he had a great deal; we are only to consider that he was a Squire and a Sportsman, and then we may apply the Fable to him, and the judicious Reflections likewise.

The Hounds ran very hard, as it is called, and the Squire pursued over Hedge and Ditch, with all his usual Vociferation and Alacrity, and with all his usual Pleasure; nor did the Thoughts

---

[1] Sir Roger L'Estrange (1616–1704), journalist, translator, and Tory pamphleteer. In his *Fables of Æsop and Other Eminent Mythologists: With Morals and Reflexions* (1692), L'Estrange comments as follows on Fable 61, 'A Cat and Venus': 'The *Woman*'s Leaping at the *Mouse*, tells us also how Impossible it is to make Nature Change her Bias, and that *if we shut her out at the Door, She'll come in at the Window*. . . . We are further given to Understand that No Counterfeit is so Steady, and so Equally Drawn, but Nature by Starts will shew her self thorough it; for *Puss*, even when she's a *Madam*, will be a *Mouser* still' (5th ed. [1708], p. 76).

of *Sophia* ever once intrude themselves to allay the Satisfaction he enjoyed in the Chace, which, he said, was one of the finest he ever saw, and which he swore was very well worth going fifty Miles for. As the Squire forgot his Daughter, the Servants, we may easily believe, forgot their Mistress; and the Parson, after having express'd much Astonishment in *Latin* to himself, at length likewise abandoned all farther Thoughts of the young Lady, and jogging on at a Distance behind, began to meditate a Portion of Doctrine for the ensuing *Sunday*.

The Squire who owned the Hounds was highly pleased with the Arrival of his Brother Squire and Sportsman: For all Men approve Merit in their own Way, and no Man was more expert in the Field than Mr. *Western*, nor did any other better know how to encourage the Dogs with his Voice, and to animate the Hunt with his Holla.

Sportsmen, in the Warmth of a Chace, are too much engaged to attend to any Manner of Ceremony; nay, even to the Offices of Humanity: For if any of them meet with an Accident by tumbling into a Ditch, or into a River, the rest pass on regardless, and generally leave him to his Fate; during this Time, therefore, the two Squires, tho' often close to each other, interchanged not a single Word. The Master of the Hunt, however, often saw and approved the great Judgment of the Stranger in drawing the Dogs when they were at a Fault, and hence conceived a very high Opinion of his Understanding, as the Number of his Attendants inspired no small Reverence to his Quality. As soon therefore as the Sport was ended by the Death of the little Animal which had occasioned it, the two Squires met, and in all Squire-like Greeting, saluted each other.

The Conversation was entertaining enough, and what we may perhaps relate in an Appendix, or on some other Occasion; but as it nowise concerns this History, we cannot prevail on ourselves to give it a Place here. It concluded with a second Chace, and that with an Invitation to Dinner. This being accepted, was followed by a hearty Bout of Drinking, which ended in as hearty a Nap on the Part of Squire *Western*.

Our Squire was by no Means a Match either for his Host, or for Parson *Supple*, at his Cups that Evening; for which the violent Fatigue of Mind as well as Body that he had undergone, may very well account, without the least Derogation from his Honour. He was indeed, according to the vulgar Phrase, whistle-drunk;[1] for before he had swallowed the third Bottle, he became so entirely overpowered, that tho' he was not carried off to Bed till long after, the Parson considered him as absent, and having acquainted the other Squire with all relating to *Sophia*, he obtained his Promise of seconding those Arguments which he intended to urge the next Morning for Mr. *Western's* Return.

No sooner therefore had the good Squire shaken off his Evening, and began to call for his Morning Draught, and to summon his Horses in order to renew his Pursuit, than Mr. *Supple* began his Dissuasives, which the Host so strongly seconded, that they at length prevailed, and Mr. *Western* agreed to return home; being principally moved by one Argument, *viz.* That he knew not which Way to go, and might probably be riding farther from his Daughter instead of towards her. He then took Leave of his Brother Sportsman, and expressing great Joy that the Frost was broken (which might perhaps be no small Motive to his hastening home) set forwards, or rather backwards, for *Somersetshire*; but not before he had first dispatched Part of his Retinue in quest of his Daughter, after whom he likewise sent a Volley of the most bitter Execrations which he could invent.

CHAPTER III

The Departure of Jones *from* Upton, *with what past between him and* Partridge *on the Road.*

AT length we are once more come to our Heroe; and to say Truth, we have been obliged to part with him so long, that considering the Condition in which we left him, I apprehend many of our Readers have concluded we intended to abandon him for ever; he being at present in that Situation in which prudent People usually desist from enquiring any farther after their Friends, lest they should be shocked by hearing such Friends had hanged themselves.

But, in reality, if we have not all the Virtues, I will boldly say,

---

[1] Exceedingly drunk. Though Fielding implies that the phrase was commonplace, this is the only instance noted in Partridge, *Dictionary of Slang and Unconventional English* (1961).

neither have we all the Vices of a prudent Character; and tho' it is not easy to conceive Circumstances much more miserable than those of poor *Jones* at present, we shall return to him, and attend upon him with the same Diligence as if he was wantoning in the brightest Beams of Fortune.[1]

Mr. *Jones* then, and his Companion *Partridge*, left the Inn a few Minutes after the Departure of Squire *Western*, and pursued the same Road on Foot; for the Ostler told them, that no Horses were by any Means to be at that Time procured at *Upton*. On they marched with heavy Hearts; for tho' their Disquiet proceeded from very different Reasons, yet displeased they were both; and if *Jones* sighed bitterly, *Partridge* grunted altogether as sadly at every Step.

When they came to the Cross-roads where the Squire had stopt to take Council, *Jones* stopt likewise, and turning to *Partridge*, asked his Opinion which Track they should pursue. 'Ah, Sir!' answered *Partridge*, 'I wish your Honour would follow my Advice.' 'Why should I not?' replied *Jones*; 'for it is now indifferent to me whither I go, or what becomes of me?' 'My Advice then,' said *Partridge*, 'is that you immediately face about and return home: For who that had such a Home to return to, as your Honour, would travel thus about the Country like a Vagabond? I ask Pardon, *sed vox ea sola reperta est.*'[2]

'Alas!' cries *Jones*, 'I have no Home to return to;—but if my Friend, my Father would receive me, could I bear the Country from which *Sophia* is flown?—Cruel *Sophia*! Cruel! No. Let me blame myself.—No, let me blame thee. D—nation seize thee, Fool, Blockhead! thou hast undone me, and I will tear thy Soul from thy Body.'—At which Words he laid violent Hands on the Collar of poor *Partridge*, and shook him more heartily than an Ague Fit, or his own Fears had ever done before.

Partridge fell trembling on his Knees, and begged for Mercy, vowing he had meant no Harm—when *Jones*, after staring wildly on him for a Moment, quitted his Hold; and discharged a Rage on himself, that had it fallen on the other, would certainly have

---

[1] Cf. 'Of True Greatness' (1741), ll. 31–2: 'As the Sun Insects, Pow'r Court-Friends begets,/ Which wanton in its Beams, and vanish as it sets.'

[2] 'But that case alone is found'—so translated in the Eton Latin grammar, where the phrase occurs in the explanation of those heteroclite nouns which have but one case (*Introduction to the Latin Tongue* [Eton, 1758; reprinted 1794], p. 129).

put an End to his Being, which indeed the very Apprehension of it had almost effected.

We would bestow some Pains here in minutely describing all the mad Pranks which *Jones* played on this Occasion, could we be well assured that the Reader would take the same Pains in perusing them; but as we are apprehensive that after all the Labour which we should employ in painting this Scene, the said Reader would be very apt to skip it entirely over, we have saved ourself that Trouble. To say the Truth, we have, from this Reason alone, often done great Violence to the Luxuriance of our Genius, and have left many excellent Descriptions out of our Work, which would otherwise have been in it. And this Suspicion, to be honest, arises, as is generally the Case, from our own wicked Heart; for we have, ourselves, been very often most horridly given to jumping, as we have run through the Pages of voluminous Historians.

Suffice it then simply to say, that *Jones*, after having played the Part of a Madman for many Minutes, came, by Degrees, to himself; which no sooner happened, than turning to *Partridge*, he very earnestly begged his Pardon for the Attack he had made on him in the Violence of his Passion; but concluded, by desiring him never to mention his Return again; for he was resolved never to see that Country any more.

Partridge easily forgave, and faithfully promised to obey the Injunction now laid upon him. And then *Jones* very briskly cried out: 'Since it is absolutely impossible for me to pursue any farther the Steps of my Angel—I will pursue those of Glory. Come on, my brave Lad, now for the Army:—It is a glorious Cause, and I would willingly sacrifice my Life in it, even tho' it was worth my preserving.' And so saying, he immediately struck into the different Road from that which the Squire had taken, and, by mere Chance, pursued the very same thro' which *Sophia* had before passed.

Our Travellers now marched a full Mile, without speaking a Syllable to each other, tho' *Jones*, indeed, muttered many Things to himself; as to *Partridge*, he was profoundly silent: For he was not, perhaps, perfectly recovered from his former Fright; besides, he had Apprehensions of provoking his Friend to a second Fit of Wrath; especially as he now began to entertain a Conceit, which may not, perhaps, create any great Wonder in the Reader. In short, he began now to suspect that *Jones* was absolutely out of his Senses.

At length, *Jones* being weary of Soliloquy, addressed himself to his Companion, and blamed him for his Taciturnity: For which the poor Man very honestly accounted, from his Fear of giving Offence. And now this Fear being pretty well removed, by the most absolute Promises of Indemnity, *Partridge* again took the Bridle from his Tongue; which, perhaps, rejoiced no less at regaining its Liberty, than a young Colt, when the Bridle is slipt from his Neck, and he is turned loose into the Pastures.

As *Partridge* was inhibited from that Topic which would have first suggested itself, he fell upon that which was next uppermost in his Mind, namely, the Man of the Hill. 'Certainly, Sir,' says he, 'that could never be a Man, who dresses himself, and lives after such a strange Manner, and so unlike other Folks. Besides his Diet, as the old Woman told me, is chiefly upon Herbs, which is a fitter Food for a Horse than a Christian: Nay, Landlord at *Upton* says, that the Neighbours thereabouts have very fearful Notions about him. It runs strangely in my Head, that it must have been some Spirit, who, perhaps, might be sent to forewarn us: And who knows, but all that Matter which he told us, of his going to Fight, and of his being taken Prisoner, and of the great Danger he was in of being hanged, might be intended as a Warning to us, considering what we are going about: Besides, I dreamt of nothing all last Night, but of Fighting; and me-thought the Blood ran out of my Nose, as Liquor out of a Tap.[1] Indeed, Sir, *infandum, Regina, jubes renovare dolorem.*'[2]

'Thy Story, *Partridge*,' answered *Jones*, 'is almost as ill applied as thy *Latin*. Nothing can be more likely to happen than Death, to Men who go into Battle.[3] Perhaps we shall both fall in it,— and what then?' 'What then!' replied *Partridge*; 'Why then there is an End of us, is there not? When I am gone, all is over with me. What matters the Cause to me, or who gets the Victory, if I am

[1] According to the fortune-telling manuals, to dream of bleeding at the nose is an omen that whatever business or travel one is engaged in will prove unfortunate. (See above, p. 425, n. 1.)

[2] See above, p. 424, n. 1.

[3] The ensuing exchange between Tom and Partridge—the one bravely defying death for honour and his country's cause, the other preferring long life to both—recalls that between Prince Hal and Falstaff in 1 *Henry IV*, v. i, at a time when England was threatened by another rebellion from the north.

killed? I shall never enjoy any Advantage from it. What are all the ringing of Bells, and Bonfires, to one that is six Foot under Ground? There will be an End of poor *Partridge*.' 'And an End of poor *Partridge*,' cries *Jones*, 'there must be one Time or other. If you love *Latin*, I will repeat you some fine Lines out of *Horace*,[1] which would inspire Courage into a Coward.

> *Dulce et decorum est pro Patria mori,*
> *Mors et fugacem persequitur virum*
> *Nec parcit imbellis juventæ*
> *Poplitibus, timidoque tergo.'*

'I wish you would construe them,' cries *Partridge*, 'for *Horace* is a hard Author; and I cannot understand as you repeat them.'

'I will repeat you a bad Imitation, or rather Paraphrase of my own,' said *Jones*; 'for I am but an indifferent Poet.'

> 'Who would not die in his dear Country's Cause?
> Since if base Fear his dastard Step withdraws,
> From Death he cannot fly:—One common Grave
> Receives, at last, the Coward and the Brave.'

'That's very certain,' cries *Partridge*. 'Ay, sure, *Mors omnibus communis*:[2] But there is a great Difference between dying in one's Bed a great many Years hence, like a good Christian, with all our Friends crying about us; and being shot To-Day or Tomorrow, like a Mad-Dog; or, perhaps, hacked in twenty Pieces with a Sword, and that too, before we have repented of all our Sins. O Lord have Mercy upon us! To be sure, the Soldiers are a wicked Kind of People. I never loved to have any Thing to do with them. I could hardly bring myself ever to look upon them as Christians. There is nothing but Cursing and Swearing among them. I wish

---

[1] *Odes*, III. ii. 13–16. A correspondent in *The True Patriot* (15–22 April 1746) similarly invoked these lines, contrasting the spirit of Roman and old English patriotism to the cowardice and luxury of present-day Englishmen, too many of whom, in a time of national crisis, sought only their own ease and safety: '[They] think it much more *dulce & decorum* to have no Concern for their Country, and to keep out of Harm's Way; and whatever happens, to take Care to gratify their own Inclinations; and *mori pro patria* has too harsh a Sound in their fine Ears, who much more admire the charming, soft, engaging Notes of a foreign W[ho]re, or an *Italian* Eunuch, than the Grand, the Noble Majesty of Martial Music.'

[2] 'Death is common to all'—a proverbial expression used as an example in the grammar books, where it is attributed to Cicero. (See *Introduction to the Latin Tongue* [Eton, 1758; reprinted 1794], p. 86, and *A Short Introduction to Grammar* [1720], p. 143.) Cf. Cicero, *In Catilinam*, IV. X. 20.

your Honour would repent: I heartily wish you would repent, before it is too late; and not think of going among them.—Evil Communication corrupts good Manners.[1] That is my principal Reason. For as for that Matter, I am no more afraid than another Man, not I; as to Matter of that. I know all human Flesh must die; but yet a Man may live many Years for all that. Why I am a middle-aged Man now, and yet I may live a great Number of Years. I have read of several who have lived to be above a hundred, and some a great deal above a hundred. Not that I hope, I mean that I promise myself, to live to any such Age as that neither.— But if it be only to eighty or ninety: Heaven be praised, that is a great Ways off yet; and I am not afraid of dying then, no more than another Man: But, surely, to tempt Death before a Man's Time is come, seems to me downright Wickedness and Presumption.[2] Besides, if it was to do any Good indeed; but let the Cause be what it will, what mighty Matter of Good can two People do? And, for my Part, I understand nothing of it. I never fired off a Gun above ten Times in my Life; and then it was not charged with Bullets. And for the Sword, I never learned to fence, and know nothing of the Matter. And then there are those Cannons, which certainly it must be thought the highest Presumption to go in the Way of; and no Body but a Madman—I ask Pardon; upon my Soul, I meant no Harm: I beg I may not throw your Honour into another Passion.'

'Be under no Apprehension, *Partridge*,' cries *Jones*, 'I am now so well convinced of thy Cowardice, that thou couldst not provoke me on any Account.' 'Your Honour,' answered he, 'may call me Coward or any thing else you please. If loving to sleep in a whole Skin makes a Man a Coward, *non immunes ab illis malis sumus*.[3] I never read in my Grammar, that a Man can't be a good Man without fighting. *Vir bonus est quis? Qui consulta Patrum, qui*

[1] See above, p. 218, n. 1. With Partridge's advice that Tom should avoid bad company, compare Falstaff, who, playing the part of the King, admonishes Hal: 'Harry, I do not only marvel where thou spendest thy time, but also how thou art accompanied. . . . There is a thing, Harry, which thou hast often heard of, and it is known to many in our land by the name of pitch. This pitch, as ancient writers do report, doth defile; so doth the company thou keepest' (1 *Henry IV*, II. iv).

[2] Cf. Falstaff, reflecting on the prospect of his death: ''Tis not due yet. I would be loath to pay him before his day. What need I be so forward with him that calls not on me?' (1 *Henry IV*, v. i).

[3] 'We are not free from these evils'—an example in the grammar books (*A Short Introduction to Grammar* [1720], p. 143).

leges juraque servat.[1] Not a Word of Fighting; and I am sure the Scripture is so much against it, that a Man shall never persuade me he is a good Christian while he sheds Christian-blood.'

CHAPTER IV

The Adventure of a Beggar-Man.

JUST as *Partridge* had uttered that good and pious Doctrine, with which the last Chapter concluded, they arrived at another Cross-way, when a lame Fellow in Rags, asked them for Alms; upon which *Partridge* gave him a severe Rebuke, saying, 'Every Parish ought to keep their own Poor.' *Jones* then fell a laughing, and asked *Partridge*, if he was not ashamed with so much Charity in his Mouth to have no Charity in his Heart. 'Your Religion,' says he, 'serves you only for an Excuse for your Faults, but is no Incentive to your Virtue. Can any Man who is really a Christian abstain from relieving one of his Brethren in such a miserable Condition?' and at the same time putting his Hand in his Pocket, he gave the poor Object a Shilling.

'Master,' cries the Fellow, after thanking him, 'I have a curious Thing here in my Pocket, which I found about two Miles off, if your Worship will please to buy it. I should not venture to pull it out to every one; but as you are so good a Gentleman, and so kind to the Poor, you won't suspect a Man of being a Thief only because he is poor.' He then pulled out a little gilt Pocket-Book, and delivered it into the Hands of *Jones*.

Jones presently opened it, and (guess, Reader, what he felt) saw in the first Page the Words *Sophia Western*, written by her own fair Hand. He no sooner read the Name, than he prest it close to his Lips; nor could he avoid falling into some very frantic Raptures, notwithstanding his Company; but, perhaps, these very Raptures made him forget he was not alone.

While *Jones* was kissing and mumbling the Book, as if he had an excellent brown butter'd Crust in his Mouth, or as if he had

---

[1] Horace, *Epistles*, I. xvi. 40–1: 'Who is the good man? He who observes the Senate's decrees, the statutes and laws' (trans. H. R. Fairclough, Loeb Classical Library, 1929). The verses appear in the grammar books as an example illustrating the agreement of the relative pronoun and its antecedent (*A Short Introduction to Grammar* [1720], p. 138).

really been a Bookworm, or an Author, who hath nothing to eat but his own Works, a Piece of Paper fell from its Leaves to the Ground, which *Partridge* took up, and delivered to *Jones*, who presently perceived it to be a Bank-bill. It was, indeed, the very Bill which *Western* had given his Daughter, the Night before her Departure; and a *Jew* would have jumped to purchase it at five Shillings less than 100 *l.*

The Eyes of *Partridge* sparkled at this News, which *Jones* now proclaimed aloud; and so did (tho' with somewhat a different Aspect) those of the poor Fellow who had found the Book; and who (I hope from a Principle of Honesty) had never opened it: But we should not deal honestly by the Reader, if we omitted to inform him of a Circumstance, which may be here a little material, *viz.* That the Fellow could not read.

Jones, who had felt nothing but pure Joy and Transport from the finding the Book, was affected with a Mixture of Concern at this new Discovery: For his Imagination instantly suggested to him, that the Owner of the Bill might possibly want it, before he should be able to convey it to her. He then acquainted the Finder, that he knew the Lady to whom the Book belonged, and would endeavour to find her out as soon as possible, and return it her.

The Pocket-Book was a late Present from Mrs. *Western* to her Niece: It had cost five and twenty Shillings, having been bought of a celebrated Toyman,[1] but the real Value of the Silver, which it contained in its Clasp, was about 18*d.* and that Price the said Toyman, as it was altogether as good as when it first issued from his Shop, would now have given for it. A prudent Person would, however, have taken proper Advantage of the Ignorance of this Fellow, and would not have offer'd more than a Shilling, or perhaps Sixpence for it; nay, some perhaps would have given nothing, and left the Fellow to his Action of Trover,[2] which some

---

[1] Probably William Deard or Deards (d. 17 June 1761), a fashionable London jeweller and pawnbroker whose shop was located in the Strand. A tradesman, Fielding remarked in a note to *The Vernoniad* (1741), of the sort who, 'as we read in Scripture were driven out of the Temple', Deard was a frequent target of Fielding's satire: see *The Temple Beau* (1730), IV. vi; *The Miser* (1733), II. i; *Joseph Andrews,* III. vi; *Jonathan Wild,* II. iii; *A Journey from This World to the Next,* I. i; *Ovid's Art of Love Paraphrased* (1747); and *The Covent-Garden Journal,* 4 January 1752.

[2] To be valid, an 'action of trover' (from the French, *trouver*) would have to establish three things: (1) that the goods which had been lost or temporarily delivered into the possession of another were in fact the property of the plaintiff; (2) that the defendant had these goods in his possession; and (3)—the particular point of the action—that the

learned Serjeants may doubt whether he could, under these Circumstances, have maintained.

Jones, on the contrary, whose Character was on the Outside of Generosity, and may perhaps not very unjustly have been suspected of Extravagance, without any Hesitation, gave a Guinea in Exchange for the Book. The poor Man, who had not for a long Time before, been possessed of so much Treasure, gave Mr. *Jones* a thousand Thanks, and discovered little less of Transport in his Muscles, than *Jones* had before shewn, when he had first read the Name of *Sophia Western.*

The Fellow very readily agreed to attend our Travellers to the Place where he had found the Pocket-Book. Together, therefore, they proceeded directly thither; but not so fast as Mr. *Jones* desired; for his Guide unfortunately happened to be lame, and could not possibly travel faster than a Mile an Hour. As this Place, therefore, was at above three Miles Distance, though the Fellow had said otherwise, the Reader need not be acquainted how long they were in walking it.

Jones opened the Book a hundred Times during their Walk, kissed it as often, talked much to himself, and very little to his Companions. At all which the Guide exprest some Signs of Astonishment to *Partridge*; who more than once shook his Head, and cry'd, poor Gentleman! *orandum est ut sit mens sana in corpore sano.*[1]

At length, they arrived at the very Spot, where *Sophia* unhappily dropt the Pocket-Book, and where the Fellow had as happily found it. Here *Jones* offered to take Leave of his Guide, and to improve his Pace; but the Fellow, in whom that violent Surprize and Joy which the first Receipt of the Guinea had occasioned, was now considerably abated, and who had now had sufficient Time to recollect himself, put on a discontented Look, and, scratching his Head, said, 'He hoped his Worship would give him something more. Your Worship,' said he, 'will, I hope, take it into your Consideration, that if I had not been honest I might have kept the Whole.' And, indeed, this the Reader must

---

defendant *converted* these goods to his own use. (See Jacob, *New Law-Dictionary*, 4th ed. [1739], s.v. 'Trover'; and Wood, *Institutes*, 7th ed. [1745], pp. 562–3.) See also below, p. 947.

[1] Juvenal, *Satires*, x. 356: 'we must pray that he may have a sound mind in a sound body'—an example in the grammar books (*A Short Introduction to Grammar* [1720], p. 157).

confess to have been true. 'If the Paper there,' said he, 'be worth 100 *l*. I am sure the finding it deserves more than a Guinea. Besides, suppose your Worship should never see the Lady, nor give it her—and though your Worship looks and talks very much like a Gentleman, yet I have only your Worship's bare Word: And, certainly, if the right Owner ben't to be found, it all belongs to the first Finder. I hope your Worship will consider all these Matters. I am but a poor Man, and therefore don't desire to have all; but it is but reasonable I should have my Share.

'Your Worship looks like a good Man, and, I hope, will consider my Honesty: For I might have kept every Farthing, and no Body ever the wiser.' 'I promise thee, upon my Honour,' cries *Jones*, 'that I know the right Owner, and will restore it her.' 'Nay, your Worship,' answered the Fellow, 'may do as you please as to that, if you will but give me my Share, that is one half of the Money, your Honour may keep the rest yourself if you please;' and concluded with swearing by a very vehement Oath, 'that he would never mention a Syllable of it to any Man living.'

'Lookee, Friend,' cries *Jones*, 'the right Owner shall certainly have again all that she lost; and as for any further Gratuity, I really cannot give it you at present; but let me know your Name, and where you live, and it is more than possible, you may here-after have further Reason to rejoice at this Morning's Adventure.'

'I don't know what you mean by Venture,' cries the Fellow; 'it seems, I must venture whether you will return the Lady her Money or no: But I hope your Worship will consider——' 'Come, come,' said *Partridge*, 'tell his Honour your Name, and where you may be found; I warrant you will never repent having put the Money into his Hands.' The Fellow seeing no Hopes of recovering the Possession of the Pocket-Book, at last complied in giving in his Name and Place of Abode, which *Jones* writ upon a Piece of Paper with the Pencil of *Sophia*; and then placing the Paper in the same Page where she had writ her Name, he cry'd out: 'There, Friend, you are the happiest Man alive, I have joined your Name to that of an Angel.' 'I don't know any Thing about Angels,' answered the Fellow; 'but I wish you would give me a little more Money, or else return me the Pocket-Book.' *Partridge* now waxed wroth; he called the poor Cripple by several vile and opprobrious Names, and was absolutely pro-ceeding to beat him, but *Jones* would not suffer any such Thing:

And now telling the Fellow he would certainly find some Opportunity of serving him, Mr. *Jones* departed as fast as his Heels
would carry him; and *Partridge*, into whom the Thoughts of the
hundred Pound had infused new Spirits, followed his Leader;
while the Man who was obliged to stay behind, fell to cursing
them both, as well as his Parents; 'For had they,' says he, 'sent me
to Charity-School[1] to learn to write and read and cast Accounts,
I should have known the Value of these Matters as well as other
People.'

CHAPTER V

Containing more Adventures which Mr. Jones *and his Companion
met on the Road.*

OUR Travellers now walked so fast, that they had very little
Time or Breath for Conversation; *Jones* meditating all the
Way on *Sophia*, and *Partridge* on the Bank-Bill, which, though it
gave him some Pleasure, caused him at the same Time to repine
at Fortune, which, in all his Walks, had never given him such an
Opportunity of shewing his Honesty. They had proceeded above
three Miles, when *Partridge* being unable any longer to keep up
with *Jones*, called to him, and begged him a little to slacken his
Pace; with this he was the more ready to comply, as he had for
some Time lost the Footsteps of the Horses, which the Thaw had
enabled him to trace for several Miles, and he was now upon a
wide Common where were several Roads.

He here therefore stopt to consider which of these Roads he
should pursue, when on a sudden they heard the Noise of a Drum
that seemed at no great Distance. This Sound presently alarmed
the Fears of *Partridge*, and he cried out, 'Lord have Mercy upon
us all; they are certainly a coming!' 'Who is coming?' cries *Jones*,
for Fear had long since given Place to softer Ideas in his Mind,
and since his Adventure with the lame Man, he had been totally
intent on pursuing *Sophia*, without entertaining one Thought of
an Enemy. 'Who?' cries *Partridge*, 'why the Rebels; but why

---

[1] Established by the Society for the Promotion of Christian Knowledge in 1699, charity
schools offered vocational training and moral instruction for the children of the poor.

should I call them Rebels, they may be very honest Gentlemen, for any thing I know to the contrary. The Devil take him that affronts them, I say. I am sure, if they have nothing to say to me, I will have nothing to say to them but in a civil Way. For Heaven's Sake, Sir, don't affront them if they should come, and perhaps they may do us no Harm; but would it not be the wiser Way to creep into some of yonder Bushes till they are gone by? What can two unarmed Men do perhaps against fifty thousand? Certainly nobody but a Madman; I hope your Honour is not offended; but certainly no Man who hath *Mens sana in Corpore sano*[1]——'
Here *Jones* interrupted this Torrent of Eloquence, which Fear had inspired, saying, 'That by the Drum he perceived they were near some Town.' He then made directly towards the Place whence the Noise proceeded, bidding *Partridge* 'take Courage, for that he would lead him into no Danger; and adding, it was impossible the Rebels should be so near.'

Partridge was a little comforted with this last Assurance; and tho' he would more gladly have gone the contrary Way, he followed his Leader, his Heart beating Time, but not after the Manner of Heroes, to the Music of the Drum, which ceased not till they had traversed the Common, and were come into a narrow Lane.

And now *Partridge*, who kept even Pace with *Jones*, discovered something painted flying in the Air, a very few Yards before him, which fancying to be the Colours of the Enemy, he fell a bellowing, 'O Lord, Sir, here they are, there is the Crown and Coffin.[2] Oh Lord! I never saw any thing so terrible; and we are within Gun-shot of them already.'

Jones no sooner looked up than he plainly perceived what it was which *Partridge* had thus mistaken. '*Partridge*,' says he, 'I fancy

---

[1] See above, p. 633, n. 1.

[2] Before embarking for Scotland in 1745, Charles Edward supposedly assured his father that when he saw him next, either he would present him with the three crowns of Great Britain, or he would be dead in his coffin. None of Charles's flags actually bore this device, but from a distance one of them—a white flag bearing a representation in red of the Scottish Royal Crest (a lion sejant affrontee holding the sword and sceptre and sitting upon a crown)—resembled a coffin and a crown, and was consequently jeered at by the English soldiers. One satiric print entitled, 'The Rebellion Displayed' (1 November 1745), depicts 'an ass feeding on thistles, and bearing the Pretender's banner—three crowns above a coffin'. (See No. 2662, *Catalogue of Prints and Drawings in the British Museum*, Division I, Political and Personal Satires, iii [1734–*c*.1750], edd. F. G. Stephens and E. Hawkins. 1877.)

you will be able to engage this whole Army yourself; for by the Colours I guess what the Drum was which we heard before, and which beats up for Recruits to a Puppet-show.'

'A Puppet-show!' answered *Partridge*, with most eager Transport. 'And is it really no more than that? I love a Puppet-show of all the Pastimes upon Earth. Do, good Sir, let us tarry and see it. Besides I am quite famished to Death; for it is now almost dark, and I have not eat a Morsel since three o'Clock in the Morning.'

They now arrived at an Inn, or indeed an Alehouse, where *Jones* was prevailed upon to stop, the rather as he had no longer any Assurance of being in the Road he desired. They walked both directly into the Kitchin, where *Jones* began to enquire if no Ladies had passed that Way in the Morning, and *Partridge* as eagerly examined into the State of their Provisions; and indeed his Enquiry met with the better Success; for *Jones* could not hear News of *Sophia*; but *Partridge*, to his great Satisfaction, found good Reason to expect very shortly the agreeable Sight of an excellent smoking Dish of Eggs and Bacon.

In strong and healthy Constitutions Love hath a very different Effect from what it causes in the puny Part of the Species. In the latter it generally destroys all that Appetite which tends towards the Conservation of the Individual; but in the former, tho' it often induces Forgetfulness, and a Neglect of Food, as well as of every thing else, yet place a good Piece of well-powdered Buttock before a hungry Lover, and he seldom fails very handsomely to play his Part. Thus it happened in the present Case; for tho' *Jones* perhaps wanted a Prompter, and might have travelled much farther, had he been alone, with an empty Stomach, yet no sooner did he sit down to the Bacon and Eggs, than he fell to as heartily and voraciously as *Partridge* himself.

Before our Travellers had finished their Dinner, Night came on, and as the Moon was now past the full, it was extremely dark. *Partridge* therefore prevailed on *Jones* to stay and see the Puppet-show, which was just going to begin, and to which they were very eagerly invited by the Master of the said Show, who declared that his Figures were the finest which the World had ever produced, and that they had given great Satisfaction to all the Quality in every Town in *England*.

The Puppet-show was performed with great Regularity and

Decency.[1] It was called the fine and serious Part of the *Provok'd Husband*; and it was indeed a very grave and solemn Entertainment, without any low Wit or Humour, or Jests; or, to do it no more than Justice, without any thing which could provoke a Laugh. The Audience were all highly pleased. A grave Matron told the Master she would bring her two Daughters the next Night, as he did not shew any Stuff; and an Attorney's Clerk, and an Exciseman, both declared, that the Characters of Lord and Lady *Townly* were well preserved, and highly in Nature. *Partridge* likewise concurred with this Opinion.

[1] In their snobbish disdain for 'low' humour on the stage, the puppet-master and his audience typify those new standards of taste to which Fielding and Garrick objected. Cibber's *Provok'd Husband* (1728) provides the perfect focus for the opposing views. Produced at Drury Lane on 10 January 1728, Cibber's play was a genteeler version of *A Journey to London*, the unfinished comedy by Sir John Vanbrugh (1664–1726). Centring attention on the antics of Sir Francis Headpiece, an ale-drinking, fox-hunting country squire, Vanbrugh had relied precisely on those 'low' comic effects so despised by the puppet-master and his audience. Cibber, on the other hand, deliberately refined and moralized his original in the attempt, as he explained to the Queen, 'to Establish such [public diversions], as are fit to Entertain the Minds of a sensible Nation; and to wipe off that Aspersion of Barbarity, which the *Virtuosi* among our Neighbours, have sometimes thrown upon our Taste' (1728 ed., Sig. A2ᵛ). Despite his revisions, however, on opening night the audience, like Fielding's exciseman, objected to 'a Scene or two of the Lower Humour' which Cibber subsequently omitted—specifically, those scenes displaying the country manners and uncouth speech of the squire and his servant Moody. Fielding, whose own works were disparaged for being 'low', doubtless sided with Lady Grace in the play, who declares: 'I am in love with Nature, let her Dress be never so homely!' (p. 14). Cibber, however, chose to stress the loose, if genteel, behaviour of Lady Townly, and when 'the Town' approved, he took their response as 'Proof, that their Taste is not wholly vitiated, by the barbarous Entertainments that have been so expensively set off to corrupt it . . .' (Sig. A5).

In his Preface to *Plutus, the God of Riches* (1742), Fielding contrasted the comic genius of an Aristophanes or a Wycherley to the dullness of the modern stage, citing *The Provok'd Husband* as the principal case in point: '*This sort of Stuff, which is, I think, called genteel Comedy, and in which our Laureate succeeded so excellently well both as Author and Actor, had some Years ago taken almost sole Possession of our Stage, and banished* Shakespear, Fletcher, Johnson, &c. *from it*. . . .' Ten years later the prospects for English comedy were no less dim: 'The Theatres themselves', Fielding remarked in *The Covent-Garden Journal* (14 October 1752), 'are reduced to the strictest Rules of Modesty. Neither Pit nor Gallery will bear an indecent Idea, if they smell it out; and an obscene Jest would throw them into such a violent Fit of Groaning, that a Foreigner might suspect they were all bewitched.' Elsewhere the demands of the critics for decency and politeness on the stage are reflected in the castigation of Garrick for allowing 'Ribaldry . . . Farce and Buffoonry' at Drury Lane (see *Mr. Garrick's Conduct, As Manager of the Theatre-Royal in Drury-Lane, considered*, 2nd ed. [1747], p. 19), and in Samuel Foote's preference for *The Suspicious Husband* (1746) over Congreve and Vanbrugh on the grounds that Hoadly's comedy delights without 'recourse to the low usual Arts of Bawdy and Buffoonry' (*The Roman and English Comedy Consider'd and Compar'd* [1747], pp. 24–5, 27).

The Master was so highly elated with these Encomiums, that he could not refrain from adding some more of his own. He said, 'The present Age was not improved in any Thing so much as in their Puppet-shows; which, by throwing out *Punch* and his Wife *Joan*, and such idle Trumpery, were at last brought to be a rational Entertainment. I remember,' said he, 'when I first took to the Business, there was a great deal of low Stuff that did very well to make Folks laugh; but was never calculated to improve the Morals of young People, which certainly ought to be principally aimed at in every Puppet-show: For why may not good and instructive Lessons be conveyed this Way, as well as any other? My Figures are as big as the Life,[1] and they represent the Life in every Particular; and I question not but People rise from my little *Drama* as much improved as they do from the great.' 'I would by no Means degrade the Ingenuity of your Profession,' answered *Jones*; 'but I should have been glad to have seen my old Acquaintance Master *Punch*[2] for all that; and so far from improving, I think, by leaving out him and his merry Wife *Joan*, you have spoiled your Puppet-show.'

The Dancer of Wires conceived an immediate and high Contempt for *Jones*, from these Words. And with much Disdain in his Countenance, he replied, 'Very probably, Sir, that may be your Opinion; but I have the Satisfaction to know the best Judges differ from you, and it is impossible to please every Taste. I confess, indeed, some of the Quality at *Bath*, two or three Years ago, wanted mightily to bring *Punch* again upon the Stage. I believe I lost some Money for not agreeing to it; but let others do as they will, a little Matter shall never bribe me to degrade my own Profession, nor will I ever willingly consent to the spoiling the Decency and Regularity of my Stage, by introducing any such low Stuff upon it.'

'Right, Friend,' cries the Clerk, 'you are very right. Always avoid what is low. There are several of my Acquaintance in

---

[1] In 1734 the Abbé Prevost reported that 'marionettes of human size had been seen for several years past . . . with dress, gestures, walk, and moving lips and eyes, in every way resembling human beings' (quoted by George Speaight, *The History of the English Puppet Theatre* [1955], p. 163). One puppet-master, Isaac Fawkes, Jr. (*fl.* 1725–55), toured Bath and the West Country with waxwork figures five feet high.

[2] Fielding shared Jones's fondness for Punch and Joan, and for a brief season in the spring of 1748, as manager of 'Madame de la Nash's' puppet theatre in Panton Street, he brought them again on to the stage. (See the General Introduction, pp. xxxi–xxxii.)

London, who are resolved to drive every thing which is low from the Stage.' 'Nothing can be more proper,' cries the Exciseman, pulling his Pipe from his Mouth. 'I remember,' added he, '(for I then lived with my Lord) I was in the Footman's Gallery, the Night when this Play of the Provok'd Husband was acted first. There was a great deal of low Stuff in it about a Country Gentleman come up to Town to stand for Parliament Man; and there they brought a Parcel of his Servants upon the Stage, his Coachman I remember particularly; but the Gentlemen in our Gallery could not bear any thing so low, and they damned it. I observe, Friend, you have left all that Matter out, and you are to be commended for it.'

'Nay, Gentlemen,' cries *Jones*, 'I can never maintain my Opinion against so many; indeed if the Generality of his Audience dislike him, the learned Gentleman who conducts the Show may have done very right in dismissing *Punch* from his Service.'

The Master of the Show then began a second Harangue, and said much of the great Force of Example, and how much the inferior Part of Mankind would be deterred from Vice, by observing how odious it was in their Superiors; when he was unluckily interrupted by an Incident, which, though perhaps we might have omitted it at another Time, we cannot help relating at present, but not in this Chapter.

CHAPTER VI

From which it may be inferred, that the best Things are liable to be misunderstood and misinterpreted.

A VIOLENT Uproar now arose in the Entry, where my Landlady was well cuffing her Maid both with her Fist and Tongue. She had indeed missed the Wench from her Employment, and, after a little Search, had found her on the Puppetshow Stage in Company with the Merry Andrew, and in a Situation not very proper to be described.

Tho' *Grace* (for that was her Name)[1] had forfeited all Title to Modesty, yet had she not Impudence enough to deny a Fact in

---

[1] It is perhaps not entirely coincidental that Grace is also the name of Lord Townly's sister in *The Provok'd Husband*, who is described as a woman 'of Exemplary Virtue'.

which she was actually surprized; she therefore took another Turn, and attempted to mitigate the Offence. 'Why do you beat me in this Manner, Mistress?' cries the Wench. 'If you don't like my Doings, you may turn me away. If I am a Wh——e (for the other had liberally bestowed that Appellation on her) my Betters are so as well as I. What was the fine Lady[1] in the Puppet-show just now? I suppose she did not lie all Night out from her Husband for nothing.'

The Landlady now burst into the Kitchin, and fell foul on both her Husband and the poor Puppet-mover. 'Here, Husband,' says she, 'you see the Consequence of harbouring these People in your House. If one doth draw a little Drink the more for them, one is hardly made Amends for the Litter they make; and then to have one's House made a Bawdyhouse of by such lousy Vermin. In short, I desire you would be gone to-morrow Morning; for I will tolerate no more such Doings. It is only the Way to teach our Servants Idleness and Nonsense; for to be sure nothing better can be learned by such idle Shows as these. I remember when Puppet-shows were made of good Scripture Stories, as *Jephtha's Rash Vow,*[2] and such good Things, and when wicked People were carried away by the Devil.[3] There was some Sense in those Matters; but as the Parson told us last *Sunday,* nobody believes in the Devil now-a-days; and here you bring about a Parcel of Puppets drest up like Lords and Ladies, only to turn the Heads of poor Country Wenches, and when their Heads are once turned topsy turvy, no wonder every thing else is so.'

Virgil, I think, tells us,[4] that when the Mob are assembled in a riotous and tumultuous Manner, and all Sorts of missile Weapons fly about, if a Man of Gravity and Authority appears amongst them, the Tumult is presently appeased, and the Mob, which when collected into one Body, may be well compared to an Ass, erect their long Ears at the grave Man's Discourse.

[1] Lady Townly.

[2] *Jephthah's Rash Vow* (from Judges 11–12) was among the most popular of the puppet plays based on biblical themes; others were *The Creation of the World* and *Solomon and the Queen of Sheba.* (See G. Speaight, op. cit., p. 165.)

[3] A conventional ending of the old puppet-show: like the Vice in the morality plays, Punch was at last carried off to hell by the Devil; other wicked characters who suffered the same fate were Faustus, Mother Shipton, and Friar Bacon's servant. (See Speaight, op. cit., p. 171.) This was the sad demise of Punch in the play Fielding describes in *The True Patriot* (11–18 February 1746).

[4] *Aeneid,* i. 148–53.

On the contrary, when a Set of grave Men and Philosophers are disputing; when Wisdom herself may in a Manner be considered as present, and administring Arguments to the Disputants, should a Tumult arise among the Mob, or should one Scold, who is herself equal in Noise to a mighty Mob, appear among the said Philosophers; their Disputes cease in a Moment, Wisdom no longer performs her ministerial Office, and the Attention of every one is immediately attracted by the Scold alone.

Thus the Uproar aforesaid, and the Arrival of the Landlady, silenced the Master of the Puppet-show, and put a speedy and final End to that grave and solemn Harangue, of which we have given the Reader a sufficient Taste already. Nothing indeed could have happened so very inopportune as this Accident; the most wanton Malice of Fortune could not have contrived such another Stratagem to confound the poor Fellow, while he was so triumphantly descanting on the good Morals inculcated by his Exhibitions. His Mouth was now as effectually stopt, as that of a Quack must be, if in the Midst of a Declamation on the great Virtues of his Pills and Powders, the Corpse of one of his Martyrs should be brought forth, and deposited before the Stage, as a Testimony of his Skill.

Instead, therefore, of answering my Landlady, the Puppet-show Man ran out to punish his Merry Andrew; and now the Moon beginning to put forth her Silver Light, as the Poets call it, (tho' she looked at that Time more like a Piece of Copper) *Jones* called for his Reckoning, and ordered *Partridge*, whom my Landlady had just awaked from a profound Nap, to prepare for his Journey; but *Partridge* having lately carried two Points, as my Reader hath seen before, was emboldened to attempt a third, which was to prevail with *Jones* to take up a Lodging that Evening in the House where he then was. He introduced this with an affected Surprize at the Intention which Mr. *Jones* declared of removing; and after urging many excellent Arguments against it, he at last insisted strongly, that it could be to no manner of Purpose whatever: For that unless *Jones* knew which Way the Lady was gone, every Step he took might very possibly lead him the farther from her; 'for you find, Sir,' said he, 'by all the People in the House, that she is not gone this Way. How much better, therefore, would it be to stay till the Morning, when we may expect to meet with Some-body to enquire of?'

This last Argument had indeed some Effect on *Jones*, and while he was weighing it, the Landlord threw all the Rhetoric of which he was Master into the same Scale. 'Sure, Sir,' said he, 'your Servant gives you most excellent Advice: For who would travel by Night at this Time of the Year?' He then began in the usual Stile to trumpet forth the excellent Accommodation which his House afforded; and my Landlady likewise opened on the Occasion.—But not to detain the Reader with what is common to every Host and Hostess, it is sufficient to tell him, *Jones* was at last prevailed on to stay and refresh himself with a few Hours Rest, which indeed he very much wanted; for he had hardly shut his Eyes since he had left the Inn where the Accident of the broken Head had happened.

As soon as *Jones* had taken a Resolution to proceed no farther that Night, he presently retired to Rest, with his two Bed-fellows the Pocket-Book, and the Muff; but *Partridge*, who at several Times had refreshed himself with several Naps, was more inclined to Eating than to Sleeping, and more to Drinking than to either.

And now the Storm which *Grace* had raised being at an End, and my Landlady being again reconciled to the Puppet-man, who on his Side forgave the indecent Reflections which the good Woman in her Passion had cast on his Performances, a Face of perfect Peace and Tranquillity reigned in the Kitchin; where sat assembled round the Fire, the Landlord and Landlady of the House, the Master of the Puppet-show, the Attorney's Clerk, the Exciseman, and the ingenious Mr. *Partridge*; in which Company past the agreeable Conversation which will be found in the next Chapter.

CHAPTER VII

Containing a Remark or two of our own, and many more of the good Company assembled in the Kitchin.

THOUGH the Pride of *Partridge* did not submit to acknow-ledge himself a Servant, yet he condescended in most Particulars to imitate the Manners of that Rank. One Instance of this was his greatly magnifying the Fortune of his Companion, as he called *Jones*: such is a general Custom with all Servants among Strangers, as none of them would willingly be thought the Attendant on a Beggar: For the higher the Situation of the Master is, the higher consequently is that of the Man in his own Opinion; the Truth of which Observation appears from the Behaviour of all the Footmen of the Nobility.

But tho' Title and Fortune communicate a Splendor all around them, and the Footmen of Men of Quality and of Estate think themselves entitled to a Part of that Respect which is paid to the Quality and Estates of their Masters; it is clearly otherwise with Regard to Virtue and Understanding. These Advantages are strictly personal, and swallow themselves all the Respect which is paid to them. To say the Truth, this is so very little, that they cannot well afford to let any others partake with them. As these therefore reflect no Honour on the Domestic, so neither is he at all dishonoured by the most deplorable Want of both in his Master. Indeed it is otherwise in the Want of what is called Virtue in a Mistress, the Consequence of which we have before seen: For in this Dishonour there is a Kind of Contagion, which, like that of Poverty, communicates itself to all who approach it.

Now for these Reasons we are not to wonder that Servants (I mean among the Men only) should have so great Regard for the Reputation of the Wealth of their Masters, and little or none at all for their Character in other Points, and that tho' they would be ashamed to be the Footman of a Beggar, they are not so to attend upon a Rogue, or a Blockhead; and do consequently make no Scruple to spread the Fame of the Iniquities and Follies of their said Masters as far as possible, and this often with great Humour and Merriment. In reality, a Footman is often a Wit, as well as a Beau, at the Expence of the Gentleman whose Livery he wears.

After *Partridge*, therefore, had enlarged greatly on the vast Fortune to which Mr. *Jones* was Heir, he very freely communicated an Apprehension which he had begun to conceive the Day before, and for which, as we hinted at that very Time, the Behaviour of *Jones* seemed to have furnished a sufficient Foundation. In short, he was now pretty well confirmed in an Opinion, that his Master was out of his Wits, with which Opinion he very bluntly acquainted the good Company round the Fire.

With this Sentiment the Puppet-show Man immediately coincided. 'I own,' said he, 'the Gentleman surprized me very much, when he talked so absurdly about Puppet-shows. It is

indeed hardly to be conceived that any Man in his Senses should
be so much mistaken; what you say now, accounts very well for
all his monstrous Notions. Poor Gentleman, I am heartily
concerned for him; indeed he hath a strange Wildness about his
Eyes, which I took Notice of before, tho' I did not mention it.'

The Landlord agreed with this last Assertion, and likewise
claimed the Sagacity of having observed it. 'And certainly,'
added he, 'it must be so: for no one but a Madman would have
thought of leaving so good a House, to ramble about the Country
at that Time of Night.'

The Exciseman pulling his Pipe from his Mouth, said, 'He
thought the Gentleman looked and talked a little wildly,' and
then turning to *Partridge*, 'If he be a Madman,' says he, 'he should
not be suffered to travel thus about the Country, for possibly he
may do some Mischief. It is Pity he was not secured and sent
home to his Relations.'

Now some Conceits of this Kind were likewise lurking in the
Mind of *Partridge*: For as he was now persuaded that *Jones* had
run away from Mr. *Allworthy*, he promised himself the highest
Rewards, if he could by any Means convey him back. But Fear
of *Jones*, of whose Fierceness and Strength he had seen, and
indeed felt some Instances, had however represented any such
Scheme as impossible to be executed, and had discouraged him
from applying himself to form any regular Plan for the Purpose.
But no sooner did he hear the Sentiments of the Exciseman, than
he embraced that Opportunity of declaring his own, and expressed a hearty Wish that such a Matter could be brought about.

'Could be brought about?' says the Exciseman; 'why there is
nothing easier.'

'Ah! Sir,' answered *Partridge*; 'you don't know what a Devil
of a Fellow he is. He can take me up with one Hand, and throw
me out at Window, and he would too, if he did but imagine——'

'Pogh!' says the Exciseman. 'I believe I am as good a Man as
he. Besides here are five of us.'

'I don't know what five,' cries the Landlady, 'my Husband
shall have nothing to do in it. Nor shall any violent Hands be
laid upon any Body in my House. The young Gentleman is as
pretty a young Gentleman as ever I saw in my Life, and I believe
he is no more mad than any of us. What do you tell of his having
a wild Look with his Eyes? They are the prettiest Eyes I ever

saw, and he hath the prettiest Look with them; and a very modest civil young Man he is. I am sure I have bepitied him heartily ever since the Gentleman there in the Corner told us he was crost in Love. Certainly that is enough to make any Man, especially such a sweet young Gentleman as he is, to look a little otherwise than he did before. Lady, indeed! What the Devil would the Lady have better than such a handsome Man with a great Estate? I suppose she is one of your Quality-folks, one of your *Townly* Ladies that we saw last Night in the Puppet-show, who don't know what they would be at.'

The Attorney's Clerk likewise declared he would have no Concern in the Business, without the Advice of Council. 'Suppose,' says he, 'an Action of false Imprisonment should be brought against us, what Defence could we make? Who knows what may be sufficient Evidence of Madness to a Jury? But I only speak upon my own Account; for it don't look well for a Lawyer to be concerned in these Matters, unless it be as a Lawyer. Juries are always less favourable to us than to other People. I don't therefore dissuade you, Mr. *Thompson,* (to the Exciseman) nor the Gentleman, nor any Body else.'

The Exciseman shook his Head at this Speech, and the Puppet-show-Man said, 'Madness was sometimes a difficult Matter for a Jury to decide: For I remember,' says he, 'I was once present at a Trial of Madness, where twenty Witnesses swore that the Person was as mad as a *March* Hare; and twenty others, that he was as much in his Senses as any Man in *England.*—And indeed it was the Opinion of most People, that it was only a Trick of his Relations to rob the poor Man of his Right.'

'Very likely!' cries the Landlady, 'I myself knew a poor Gentleman who was kept in a Mad-house all his Life by his Family, and they enjoyed his Estate, but it did them no Good: For tho' the Law gave it them, it was the Right of another.'

'Pogh!' cries the Clerk, with great Contempt, 'Who hath any Right but what the Law gives them? If the Law gave me the best Estate in the Country, I should never trouble myself much who had the Right.'

'If it be so,' says *Partridge,* '*Fœlix quem faciunt aliena pericula cautum.*'[1]

---

[1] 'Happy is he who learns caution from the dangers of others'—cf. Tibullus, III. vi. 43–4.

My Landlord, who had been called out by the Arrival of a Horseman at the Gate, now returned into the Kitchin, and with an affrighted Countenance cried out, 'What do you think, Gentlemen? the Rebels have given the Duke the Slip, and are got almost to *London*.[1]—It is certainly true, for a Man on Horseback just now told me so.'

'I am glad of it with all my Heart,' cries *Partridge*, 'then there will be no fighting in these Parts.'

'I am glad,' cries the Clerk, 'for a better Reason; for I would always have Right take Place.'

'Ay but,' answered the Landlord, 'I have heard some People say this Man hath no Right.'

'I will prove the contrary in a Moment,' cries the Clerk; 'if my Father dies seized of a Right; do you mind me, seized of a Right, I say; Doth not that Right descend to his Son? And doth not one Right descend as well as another?'

'But how can he have any Right to make us Papishes?' says the Landlord.

'Never fear that,' cries *Partridge*. 'As to the Matter of Right, the Gentleman there hath proved it as clear as the Sun; and as to the Matter of Religion, it is quite out of the Case. The Papists themselves don't expect any such Thing.[2] A Popish Priest, whom I know very well, and who is a very honest Man, told me upon his Word and Honour they had no such Design.'

'And another Priest of my Acquaintance,' said the Landlady, 'hath told me the same Thing.—But my Husband is always so afraid of Papishes. I know a great many Papishes that are very honest Sort of People, and spend their Money very freely; and it is always a Maxim with me, that one Man's Money is as good as another's.'

'Very true, Mistress,' said the Puppet-show-Man, 'I don't care what Religion comes, provided the Presbyterians are not uppermost, for they are Enemies to Puppet-shows.'[3]

'And so you would sacrifice your Religion to your Interest?' cries the Exciseman; 'and are desirous to see Popery brought in, are you?'

'Not I truly,' answered the other, 'I hate Popery as much as any

---

[1] See above, p. 578, n. 1. [2] See above, p. 439, n. 1.

[3] The hostility of the Puritans toward puppet-shows, which they regarded as a profane diversion, provides an amusing scene in Ben Jonson's *Bartholomew Fayre* (1614), v. v.

Man; but yet it is a Comfort to one, that one should be able to live under it, which I could not do among Presbyterians. To be sure every Man values his Livelihood first, that must be granted; and I warrant if you would confess the Truth, you are more afraid of losing your Place than any Thing else; but never fear, Friend, there will be an Excise under another Government as well as under this.'

'Why certainly,' replied the Exciseman, 'I should be a very ill Man if I did not honour the King, whose Bread I eat. That is no more than natural, as a Man may say: For what signifies it to me that there would be an Excise-office under another Government, since my Friends would be out, and I could expect no better than to follow them. No, no, Friend, I shall never be bubbled out of my Religion in Hopes only of keeping my Place under another Government; for I should certainly be no better, and very probably might be worse.'

'Why, that is what I say,' cries the Landlord, 'whenever Folks say who knows what may happen? Odsooks! should not I be a Blockhead to lend my Money to I know not who, because mayhap he may return it again? I am sure it is safe in my own Bureau, and there I will keep it.'

The Attorney's Clerk had taken a great Fancy to the Sagacity of *Partridge*. Whether this proceeded from the great Discernment which the former had into Men, as well as Things, or whether it arose from the Sympathy between their Minds; for they were both truly *Jacobites* in Principle; they now shook Hands heartily, and drank Bumpers of Strong Beer to Healths which we think proper to bury in Oblivion.

These Healths were afterwards pledged by all present, and even by my Landlord himself, tho' reluctantly; but he could not withstand the Menaces of the Clerk, who swore he would never set his Foot within his House again, if he refused. The Bumpers which were swallowed on this Occasion soon put an End to the Conversation. Here, therefore, we will put an End to the Chapter.

CHAPTER VIII

In which Fortune seems to have been in a better Humour with Jones
than we have hitherto seen her.

AS there is no wholesomer, so perhaps there are few stronger
Sleeping Potions than Fatigue. Of this *Jones* might be said
to have taken a very large Dose, and it operated very forcibly
upon him. He had already slept nine Hours, and might perhaps
have slept longer, had he not been awakened by a most violent
Noise at his Chamber Door, where the Sound of many heavy
Blows was accompanied with as many Exclamations of Murder.
Jones presently leapt from his Bed, where he found the Master of
the Puppet-show belabouring the Back and Ribs of his poor
Merry Andrew, without either Mercy or Moderation.

Jones instantly interposed on Behalf of the Suffering Party,
and pinned the insulting Conqueror up to the Wall: For the
Puppet-show-Man was no more able to contend with *Jones*, than
the poor party-coloured Jester had been to contend with this
Puppet-man.

But tho' the Merry Andrew was a little Fellow, and not very
strong, he had nevertheless some Choler about him. He therefore
no sooner found himself delivered from the Enemy, than he
began to attack him with the only Weapon at which he was his
Equal. From this he first discharged a Volley of general abusive
Words, and thence proceeded to some particular Accusations.—
'D—n your Bl—d, you Rascal,' says he, 'I have not only supported you, (for to me you owe all the Money you get) but I have
saved you from the Gallows. Did you not want to rob the Lady of
her fine Riding-Habit, no longer ago than Yesterday, in the
Back-lane here? Can you deny that you wished to have her alone
in a Wood to strip her, to strip one of the prettiest Ladies that ever
was seen in the World? and here you have fallen upon me, and
have almost murdered me for doing no Harm to a Girl as willing
as myself, only because she likes me better than you.'

Jones no sooner heard this, than he quitted the Master, laying
on him at the same time the most violent Injunctions of For-
bearance from any further Insult on the Merry Andrew, and then
taking the poor Wretch with him into his own Apartment, he
soon learnt Tidings of his *Sophia*, whom the Fellow, as he was

attending his Master with his Drum the Day before, had seen pass by. He easily prevailed with the Lad to shew him the exact Place, and then having summoned *Partridge*, he departed with the utmost Expedition.

It was almost eight of the Clock before all Matters could be got ready for his Departure: For *Partridge* was not in any Haste; nor could the Reckoning be presently adjusted; and when both these were settled and over, *Jones* would not quit the Place before he had perfectly reconciled all Differences between the Master and the Man.

When this was happily accomplished, he set forwards, and was by the trusty Merry Andrew conducted to the Spot by which *Sophia* had past; and then having handsomely rewarded his Conductor, he again pushed on with the utmost Eagerness, being highly delighted with the extraordinary Manner in which he received his Intelligence. Of this *Partridge* was no sooner acquainted, than he, with great Earnestness, began to prophesy, and assured *Jones*, that he would certainly have good Success in the End: For, he said, 'two such Accidents could never have happened to direct him after his Mistress, if Providence had not designed to bring them together at last.' And this was the first Time that *Jones* lent any Attention to the superstitious Doctrines of his Companion.

They had not gone above two Miles, when a violent Storm of Rain overtook them, and as they happened to be at the same Time in Sight of an Alehouse, *Partridge*, with much earnest Entreaty, prevailed with *Jones* to enter, and weather the Storm.

Hunger is an Enemy (if indeed it may be called one) which partakes more of the *English* than of the *French* Disposition; for tho' you subdue this never so often, it will always rally again in Time; and so it did with *Partridge*, who was no sooner arrived within the Kitchin, than he began to ask the same Questions which he had asked the Night before. The Consequence of this was an excellent cold Chine being produced upon the Table, upon which not only *Partridge*, but *Jones* himself, made a very hearty Breakfast, tho' the latter began to grow again uneasy, as the People of the House could give him no fresh Information concerning *Sophia*.

Their Meal being over, *Jones* was again preparing to sally, notwithstanding the Violence of the Storm still continued; but

Partridge begged heartily for another Mugg, and at length casting his Eyes on a Lad at the Fire, who had entered into the Kitchin, and who at that Instant was looking as earnestly at him, he turned suddenly to *Jones*, and cried, 'Master, give me your Hand, a single Mugg shan't serve the Turn this Bout. Why here's more News of Madam *Sophia* come to Town. The Boy there standing by the Fire is the very Lad that rode before her. I can swear to my own Plaister on his Face.' 'Heavens bless you, Sir,' cries the Boy, 'it is your own Plaister sure enough; I shall have always Reason to remember your Goodness; for it hath almost cured me.'

At these Words *Jones* started from his Chair, and bidding the Boy follow him immediately, departed from the Kitchin into a private Apartment; for so delicate was he with regard to *Sophia*, that he never willingly mentioned her Name in the Presence of many People; and tho' he had, as it were, from the Overflowings of his Heart, given *Sophia* as a Toast among the Officers, where he thought it was impossible she should be known; yet even there the Reader may remember how difficultly he was prevailed upon to mention her Sir-name.

Hard therefore was it, and perhaps in the Opinion of many sagacious Readers, very absurd and monstrous, that he should principally owe his present Misfortune to the supposed Want of that Delicacy with which he so abounded; for in reality *Sophia* was much more offended at the Freedoms which she thought, and not without good Reason, he had taken with her Name and Character, than at any Freedoms, in which, under his present Circumstances, he had indulged himself with the Person of another Woman; and to say Truth, I believe *Honour* could never have prevailed on her to leave *Upton* without seeing her *Jones*, had it not been for those two strong Instances of a Levity in his Behaviour, so void of Respect, and indeed so highly inconsistent with any Degree of Love and Tenderness in great and delicate Minds.

But so Matters fell out, and so I must relate them; and if any Reader is shocked at their appearing unnatural, I cannot help it. I must remind such Persons, that I am not writing a System, but a History, and I am not obliged to reconcile every Matter to the received Notions concerning Truth and Nature. But if this was never so easy to do, perhaps it might be more prudent in me to avoid it. For Instance, as the Fact at present before us now stands, without any Comment of mine upon it, tho' it may at first Sight offend some Readers, yet upon more mature Consideration, it must please all; for wise and good Men may consider what happened to *Jones* at *Upton* as a just Punishment for his Wickedness, with Regard to Women, of which it was indeed the immediate Consequence; and silly and bad persons may comfort themselves in their Vices, by flattering their own Hearts that the Characters of Men are rather owing to Accident than to Virtue. Now perhaps the Reflections which we should be here inclined to draw, would alike contradict both these Conclusions, and would shew that these Incidents contribute only to confirm the great, useful and uncommon Doctrine, which it is the Purpose of this whole Work to inculcate, and which we must not fill up our Pages by frequently repeating, as an ordinary Parson fills his Sermon by repeating his Text at the End of every Paragraph.

We are contented that it must appear, however unhappily *Sophia* had erred in her Opinion of *Jones*, she had sufficient Reason for her Opinion; since, I believe, every other young Lady would, in her Situation, have erred in the same Manner. Nay, had she followed her Lover at this very Time, and had entered this very Alehouse the Moment he was departed from it, she would have found the Landlord as well acquainted with her Name and Person as the Wench at *Upton* had appeared to be. For while *Jones* was examining his Boy in Whispers in an inner Room, *Partridge*, who had no such Delicacy in his Disposition, was in the Kitchin very openly catechising the other Guide who had attended Mrs. *Fitzpatrick*; by which Means the Landlord, whose Ears were open enough on all such Occasions, became perfectly well acquainted with the Tumble of *Sophia* from her Horse, &c. with the Mistake concerning *Jenny Cameron*, with the many Consequences of the Punch, and, in short, with almost every thing which had happened at the Inn, whence we dispatched our Ladies in a Coach and Six, when we last took our Leaves of them.

CHAPTER IX

Containing little more than a few odd Observations.

JONES had been absent a full half Hour, when he returned into the Kitchin in a Hurry, desiring the Landlord to let him know that Instant what was to pay. And now the Concern which *Partridge* felt at being obliged to quit a warm Chimney-corner, and a Cup of excellent Liquor, was somewhat compensated by hearing that he was to proceed no farther on Foot; for *Jones*, by Golden Arguments, had prevailed with the Boy to attend him back to the Inn whither he had before conducted *Sophia*; but to this however the Lad consented, upon Condition that the other Guide would wait for him at the Alehouse; because, as the Landlord at *Upton* was an intimate Acquaintance of the Landlord at *Gloucester*, it might some Time or other come to the Ears of the latter, that his Horses had been let to more than one Person, and so the Boy might be brought to Account for Money which he wisely intended to put in his own Pocket.

We were obliged to mention this Circumstance, trifling as it may seem, since it retarded Mr. *Jones* a considerable Time in his setting out; for the Honesty of this latter Boy was somewhat high—that is, somewhat high-priced, and would indeed have cost *Jones* very dear, had not *Partridge*, who, as we have said, was a very cunning Fellow, artfully thrown in half a Crown to be spent at that very Alehouse, while the Boy was waiting for his Companion. This Half Crown the Landlord no sooner got Scent of, than he opened after it with such vehement and persuasive Outcry, that the Boy was soon overcome, and consented to take half a Crown more for his Stay. Here we cannot help observing, that as there is so much of Policy in the lowest Life, great Men often overvalue themselves on those Refinements in Imposture, in which they are frequently excelled by some of the lowest of the Human Species.

The Horses being now produced, *Jones* directly leapt into the Side-Saddle, on which his dear *Sophia* had rid. The Lad indeed very civilly offered him the Use of his; but he chose the Side-Saddle, probably because it was softer. *Partridge*, however, tho' full as effeminate as *Jones*, could not bear the Thoughts of degrading his Manhood, he therefore accepted the Boy's offer;

and now *Jones*, being mounted on the Side-Saddle of his *Sophia*, the Boy on that of Mrs. *Honour*, and *Partridge* bestriding the third Horse, they set forwards on their Journey, and within four Hours arrived at the Inn[1] where the Reader hath already spent so much Time. *Partridge* was in very high Spirits during the whole Way, and often mentioned to *Jones* the many good Omens of his future Success, which had lately befriended him; and which the Reader, without being the least superstitious, must allow to have been peculiarly fortunate. *Partridge* was moreover better pleased with the present Pursuit of his Companion, than he had been with his Pursuit of Glory; and from these very Omens, which assured the Pedagogue of Success, he likewise first acquired a clear Idea of the Amour between *Jones* and *Sophia*; to which he had before given very little Attention, as he had originally taken a wrong Scent concerning the Reasons of *Jones's* Departure; and as to what happened at *Upton*, he was too much frightened just before and after his leaving that Place, to draw any other Conclusions from thence, than that poor *Jones* was a downright Madman: A Conceit which was not at all disagreeable to the Opinion he before had of his extraordinary Wildness, of which, he thought, his Behaviour on their quitting *Gloucester*, so well justified all the Accounts he had formerly received. He was now however pretty well satisfied with his present Expedition, and henceforth began to conceive much worthier Sentiments of his Friend's Understanding.

The Clock had just struck Three when they arrived, and *Jones* immediately bespoke Post Horses; but unluckily there was not a Horse to be procured in the whole Place; which the Reader will not wonder at, when he considers the Hurry in which the whole Nation, and especially this Part of it,[2] was at this time engaged, when Expresses were passing and repassing every Hour of the Day and Night.

Jones endeavoured all he could to prevail with his former Guide to escorte him to *Coventry*; but he was inexorable. While he was arguing with the Boy in the Inn-yard, a Person came up to him, and saluting him by his Name, enquired how all the good Family did in *Somersetshire*; and now *Jones* casting his Eyes upon this Person, presently discovered him to be Mr. *Dowling* the Lawyer, with whom he had dined at *Gloucester*, and with much Courtesy returned his Salutation.

[1] See above, p. 574, n. 1.   [2] See above, p. 578, n. 1.

Dowling very earnestly pressed Mr. *Jones* to go no further that Night; and backed his Solicitations with many unanswerable Arguments, such as, that it was almost dark, that the Roads were very dirty, and that he would be able to travel much better by Day-light, with many others equally good, some of which *Jones* had probably suggested to himself before; but as they were then ineffectual, so they were still, and he continued resolute in his Design, even tho' he should be obliged to set out on Foot.

When the good Attorney found he could not prevail on *Jones* to stay, he as strenuously applied himself to persuade the Guide to accompany him. He urged many Motives to induce him to undertake this short Journey, and at last concluded with saying, 'Do you think the Gentleman won't very well reward you for your Trouble?'

Two to one are odds at every other thing, as well as at Football.[1] But the Advantage which this united Force hath in Persuasion or Entreaty, must have been visible to a curious Observer; for he must have often seen, that when a Father, a Master, a Wife, or any other Person in Authority, have stoutly adhered to a Denial against all the Reasons which a single Man could produce, they have afterwards yielded to the Repetition of the same Sentiments by a second or third Person, who hath undertaken the Cause without attempting to advance any thing new in its Behalf. And hence perhaps proceeds the Phrase of seconding an Argument or a Motion, and the great Consequence of which this is in all Assemblies of public Debate. Hence likewise probably it is, that in our Courts of Law we often hear a learned Gentleman (generally a Serjeant) repeating for an Hour together what another learned Gentleman who spoke just before him, had been saying.

Instead of accounting for this, we shall proceed in our usual Manner to exemplify it in the Conduct of the Lad abovementioned, who submitted to the Persuasions of Mr. *Dowling*, and promised once more to admit *Jones* into his Side-Saddle; but insisted on first giving the poor Creatures a good Bait, saying, they had travelled a great Way, and been rid very hard. Indeed this Caution of the Boy was needless; for *Jones*, notwithstanding his Hurry and Impatience, would have ordered this of himself;

---

[1] For another instance of this expression in Fielding, see *The True Patriot* (18–25 February 1746), under 'Apocrypha'.

for he by no Means agreed with the Opinion of those who consider Animals as mere Machines, and when they bury their
Spurs in the Belly of their Horse, imagine the Spur and the Horse
to have an equal Capacity of feeling Pain.

While the Beasts were eating their Corn, or rather were supposed to eat it; (for as the Boy was taking Care of himself in the
Kitchin, the Ostler took great Care that his Corn should not be
consumed in the Stable) Mr. *Jones*, at the earnest Desire of Mr.
Dowling, accompanied that Gentleman into his Room, where they
sat down together over a Bottle of Wine.

CHAPTER X

In which Mr. Jones *and Mr.* Dowling *drink a Bottle together.*

MR. *Dowling*, pouring out a Glass of Wine, named the Health
of the good Squire *Allworthy*; adding, 'If you please, Sir,
we will likewise remember his Nephew and Heir, the young
Squire: Come, Sir, here's Mr. *Blifil* to you, a very pretty young
Gentleman; and who, I dare swear, will hereafter make a very
considerable Figure in his Country. I have a Borough for him
myself in my Eye.'

'Sir,' answered *Jones*, 'I am convinced you don't intend to
affront me, so I shall not resent it; but, I promise you, you have
joined two Persons very improperly together; for one is the Glory
of the Human Species, and the other is a Rascal who dishonours
the Name of Man.'

Dowling stared at this. He said, 'He thought both the Gentlemen had a very unexceptionable Character. As for Squire
Allworthy himself,' says he, 'I never had the Happiness to see
him; but all the World talks of his Goodness. And, indeed, as to
the young Gentleman, I never saw him but once, when I carried
him the News of the Loss of his Mother; and then I was so
hurried, and drove, and tore with the Multiplicity of Business,
that I had hardly Time to converse with him; but he looked so
like a very honest Gentleman, and behaved himself so prettily,
that I protest I never was more delighted with any Gentleman
since I was born.'

'I don't wonder,' answered *Jones*, 'that he should impose upon you in so short an Acquaintance; for he hath the Cunning of the Devil himself, and you may live with him many Years without discovering him. I was bred up with him from my Infancy, and we were hardly ever asunder; but it is very lately only, that I have discovered half the Villainy which is in him. I own I never greatly liked him. I thought he wanted that Generosity of Spirit, which is the sure Foundation of all that is great and noble in Human Nature. I saw a Selfishness in him long ago which I despised; but it is lately, very lately, that I have found him capable of the basest and blackest Designs; for, indeed, I have at last found out, that he hath taken an Advantage of the Openness of my own Temper, and hath concerted the deepest Project, by a long Train of wicked Artifice, to work my Ruin, which at last he hath effected.'

'Ay! ay!' cries *Dowling*, 'I protest then, it is a Pity such a Person should inherit the great Estate of your Uncle *Allworthy*.'

'Alas, Sir,' cries *Jones*, 'you do me an Honour to which I have no Title. It is true, indeed, his Goodness once allowed me the Liberty of calling him by a much nearer Name; but as this was only a voluntary Act of Goodness, I can complain of no Injustice when he thinks proper to deprive me of this Honour; since the Loss cannot be more unmerited than the Gift originally was. I assure you, Sir, I am no Relation of Mr. *Allworthy*; and if the World, who are incapable of setting a true Value on his Virtue, should think, in his Behaviour by me, he hath dealt hardly by a Relation, they do an Injustice to the best of Men: For I—but I ask your Pardon, I shall trouble you with no Particulars relating to myself; only as you seemed to think me a Relation of Mr. *Allworthy*, I thought proper to set you right in a Matter that might draw some Censures upon him, which I promise you I would rather lose my Life, than give Occasion to.'

'I protest, Sir,' cried *Dowling*, 'you talk very much like a Man of Honour; but instead of giving me any Trouble, I protest it would give me great Pleasure to know how you came to be thought a Relation of Mr. *Allworthy's*, if you are not. Your Horses won't be ready this half Hour, and as you have sufficient Opportunity, I wish you would tell me how all that happened; for I protest it seems very surprizing that you should pass for a Relation of a Gentleman, without being so.'

Jones, who in the Compliance of his Disposition (tho' not in his Prudence) a little resembled his lovely *Sophia*, was easily prevailed on to satisfy Mr. *Dowling's* Curiosity, by relating the History of his Birth and Education, which he did, like *Othello*,[1]

——even from his boyish Years,
To th' very Moment he was bad to tell;

the which to hear, *Dowling*, like *Desdemona*, did *seriously incline*;

He swore 'twas strange, 'twas passing strange;
'Twas pitiful, 'twas wondrous pitiful.

Mr. *Dowling* was indeed very greatly affected with this Relation; for he had not divested himself of Humanity by being an Attorney. Indeed nothing is more unjust than to carry our Prejudices against a Profession into private Life, and to borrow our Idea of a Man from our Opinion of his Calling. Habit, it is true, lessens the Horror of those Actions which the Profession makes necessary, and consequently habitual; but in all other Instances, Nature works in Men of all Professions alike; nay, perhaps, even more strongly with those who give her, as it were, a Holiday, when they are following their ordinary Business. A Butcher, I make no doubt, would feel Compunction at the Slaughter of a fine Horse; and though a Surgeon can conceive no Pain in cutting off a Limb, I have known him compassionate a Man in a Fit of the Gout. The common Hangman, who hath stretched the Necks of Hundreds, is known to have trembled at his first Operation on a Head: And the very Professors of Human Blood-shedding, who in their Trade of War butcher Thousands, not only of their Fellow Professors, but often of Women and Children, without Remorse; even these, I say, in Times of Peace, when Drums and Trumpets are laid aside, often lay aside all their Ferocity, and become very gentle Members of civil Society. In the same Manner an Attorney may feel all the Miseries and Distresses of his Fellow Creatures, provided he happens not to be concerned against them.

Jones, as the Reader knows, was yet unacquainted with the very black Colours in which he had been represented to Mr. *Allworthy*; and as to other Matters he did not shew them in the most disadvantageous Light: For though he was unwilling to

---

[1] *Othello*, I. iii—slightly misquoted.

cast any Blame on his former Friend and Patron, yet he was not very desirous of heaping too much upon himself. *Dowling* therefore observed, and not without Reason, that very ill Offices must have been done him by some Body: 'For certainly,' cries he, 'the Squire would never have disinherited you only for a few Faults, which any young Gentleman might have committed. Indeed, I cannot properly say disinherited; for to be sure by Law you cannot claim as Heir. That's certain; that no Body need go to Counsel for. Yet when a Gentleman had in a Manner adopted you thus as his own Son, you might reasonably have expected some very considerable Part, if not the Whole; nay, if you had expected the Whole, I should not have blamed you: For certainly all Men are for getting as much as they can, and they are not to be blamed on that Account.'

'Indeed you wrong me,' said *Jones*; 'I should have been contented with very little: I never had any View upon Mr. *Allworthy's* Fortune; nay, I believe, I may truly say, I never once considered what he could or might give me. This I solemnly declare, if he had done a Prejudice to his Nephew in my Favour, I would have undone it again. I had rather enjoy my own Mind than the Fortune of another Man. What is the poor Pride arising from a magnificent House, a numerous Equipage, a splendid Table, and from all the other Advantages or Appearances of Fortune, compared to the warm, solid Content, the swelling Satisfaction, the thrilling Transports, and the exulting Triumphs, which a good Mind enjoys, in the Contemplation of a generous, virtuous, noble, benevolent Action? I envy not *Blifil* in the Prospect of his Wealth; nor shall I envy him in the Possession of it. I would not think myself a Rascal half an Hour, to exchange Situations. I believe, indeed, Mr. *Blifil* suspected me of the Views you mention; and I suppose these Suspicions, as they arose from the Baseness of his own Heart, so they occasioned his Baseness to me. But, I thank Heaven, I know, I feel,—I feel my Innocence, my Friend; and I would not part with that Feeling for the World.—For as long as I know I have never done, nor even designed an Injury to any Being whatever,

> *Pone me pigris ubi nulla campis*
> *Arbor æstiva recreatur aura*
> *Quod latus mundi nebulæ, malusque Jupiter urget.*

Pone, sub curru nimium propinqui
Solis, in Terra domibus negata;
Dulce ridentem Lalagen amabo Dulce loquentem.'[1]

He then filled a Bumper of Wine, and drank it off to the Health of his dear *Lalage*; and filling *Dowling's* Glass likewise up to the Brim, insisted on his pledging him. 'Why then here's Miss *Lalage's* Health, with all my Heart,' cries *Dowling*. 'I have heard her toasted often, I protest, though I never saw her; but they say she's extremely handsome.'

Though the *Latin* was not the only Part of this Speech which *Dowling* did not perfectly understand, yet there was somewhat in it, that made a very strong Impression upon him. And though he endeavoured, by winking, nodding, sneering, and grinning, to hide the Impression from *Jones*, (for we are as often ashamed of thinking right as of thinking wrong) it is certain he secretly approved as much of his Sentiments as he understood, and really felt a very strong Impulse of Compassion for him. But we may possibly take some other Opportunity of commenting upon this, especially if we should happen to meet Mr. *Dowling* any more in the Course of our History. At present we are obliged to take our Leave of that Gentleman a little abruptly, in Imitation of Mr. *Jones*; who was no sooner informed, by *Partridge*, that his Horses were ready, than he deposited his Reckoning, wished his Companion a good Night, mounted, and set forward towards *Coventry*, though the Night was dark, and it just then began to rain very hard.

> * Place me where never Summer Breeze
> Unbinds the Glebe, or warms the Trees;
> Where ever lowering Clouds appear,
> And angry *Jove* deforms th'inclement Year.
>
> Place me beneath the burning Ray,
> Where rolls the rapid Carr of Day;
> Love and the Nymph shall charm my Toils,
> The Nymph who sweetly speaks, and sweetly smiles.
>
> Mr. *Francis*.[2]

---

[1] Horace, *Odes*, I. xxii. 17–24.
[2] *Works of Horace*, 2nd ed. (1747), i. 90–1. On Francis, see above, p. 472, n. 2.

CHAPTER XI

The Disasters which befel Jones *on his Departure for* Coventry; *with the sage Remarks of* Partridge.

NO Road can be plainer than that from the Place where they now were to *Coventry*; and though neither *Jones* nor *Partridge*, nor the Guide, had ever travelled it before, it would have been almost impossible to have missed their Way, had it not been for the two Reasons mentioned in the Conclusion of the last Chapter.

These two Circumstances, however, happening both unfortunately to intervene, our Travellers deviated into a much less frequented Track; and after riding full Six Miles, instead of arriving at the stately Spires of *Coventry*, they found themselves still in a very dirty Lane, where they saw no Symptoms of approaching the Suburbs of a large City.

Jones now declared that they must certainly have lost their Way; but this the Guide insisted upon was impossible; a Word which, in common Conversation, is often used to signify not only improbable, but often what is really very likely, and, sometimes, what hath certainly happened: An hyperbolical Violence like that which is so frequently offered to the Words Infinite and Eternal; by the former of which it is usual to express a Distance of half a Yard; and by the latter, a Duration of five Minutes. And thus it is as usual to assert the Impossibility of losing what is already actually lost. This was, in fact, the Case at present: For notwithstanding all the confident Assertions of the Lad to the contrary, it is certain they were no more in the right Road to *Coventry*, than the fraudulent, griping, cruel, canting Miser is in the right Road to Heaven.

It is not, perhaps, easy for a Reader who hath never been in those Circumstances, to imagine the Horror with which Darkness, Rain, and Wind fill Persons who have lost their Way in the Night; and who, consequently, have not the pleasant Prospect of warm Fires, dry Cloaths, and other Refreshments, to support their Minds in struggling with the Inclemencies of the Weather. A very imperfect Idea of this Horror will, however, serve sufficiently to account for the Conceits which now filled the Head of *Partridge*, and which we shall presently be obliged to open.

Jones grew more and more positive that they were out of their Road; and the Boy himself, at last, acknowledged he believed they were not in the right Road to *Coventry*; tho' he affirmed, at the same Time, it was impossible they should have mist the Way. But *Partridge* was of a different Opinion. He said, 'When they first set out he imagined some Mischief or other would happen.— Did not you observe, Sir,' said he to *Jones*, 'that old Woman who stood at the Door just as you was taking Horse? I wish you had given her a small Matter, with all my Heart; for she said then you might repent it, and at that very Instant it began to rain, and the Wind hath continued rising ever since. Whatever some People may think, I am very certain it is in the Power of Witches to raise the Wind whenever they please.[1] I have seen it happen very often in my Time: And if ever I saw a Witch in all my Life, that old Woman was certainly one. I thought so to myself at that very Time; and if I had any Halfpence in my Pocket, I would have given her some: For to be sure it is always good to be charitable to those Sort of People, for Fear what may happen; and many a Person hath lost his Cattle by saving a Halfpenny.'

Jones, tho' he was horridly vexed at the Delay which this Mistake was likely to occasion in his Journey, could not help smiling at the Superstition of his Friend, whom an Accident now greatly confirmed in his Opinion. This was a Tumble from his Horse; by which, however, he received no other Injury than what the Dirt conferred on his Cloaths.

Partridge had no sooner recovered his Legs, than he appealed to his Fall, as conclusive Evidence of all he had asserted: But *Jones*, finding he was unhurt, answered with a Smile: 'This Witch of yours, *Partridge*, is a most ungrateful Jade, and doth not, I find, distinguish her Friends from others in her Resentment. If the old Lady had been angry with me for neglecting her, I don't see why she should tumble you from your Horse, after all the Respect you have expressed for her.'

'It is ill jesting,' cries *Partridge*, 'with People who have Power to do these Things; for they are often very malicious. I remember a Farrier, who provoked one of them, by asking her when the

---

1 On Fielding's attitude toward witchcraft and his association of the belief in witches with Jacobite superstitiousness, see above, p. 445, n. 2. The power of witches to raise the wind and to hurt cattle is mentioned in James I's *Demonology* (1597), II. v and III, and in the law against witches passed early in James's reign (1604) and subsequently repealed (1736).

Time she had bargained with the Devil for would be out; and within three Months from that very Day one of his best Cows was drowned. Nor was she satisfied with that; for a little Time afterwards he lost a Barrel of Best-Drink: For the old Witch pulled out the Spicket, and let it run all over the Cellar, the very first Evening he had tapped it, to make merry with some of his Neighbours. In short, nothing ever thrived with him afterwards; for she worried the poor Man so, that he took to Drinking; and in a Year or two his Stock was seized, and he and his Family are now come to the Parish.'

The Guide, and perhaps his Horse too, were both so attentive to this Discourse, that, either thro' Want of Care, or by the Malice of the Witch, they were now both sprawling in the Dirt.

Partridge entirely imputed this Fall, as he had done his own, to the same Cause. He told Mr. *Jones*, 'it would certainly be his Turn next,' and earnestly intreated him 'to return back, and find out the old Woman, and pacify her. We shall very soon,' added he, 'reach the Inn: For tho' we have seemed to go forward, I am very certain we are in the identical Place in which we were an Hour ago; and I dare swear if it was Day-light, we might now see the Inn we set out from.'

Instead of returning any Answer to this sage Advice, *Jones* was entirely attentive to what had happened to the Boy, who received no other Hurt than what had before befallen *Partridge*, and which his Cloaths very easily bore, as they had been for many Years inured to the like. He soon regained his Side-Saddle, and, by the hearty Curses and Blows which he bestowed on his Horse, quickly satisfied Mr. *Jones* that no Harm was done.

CHAPTER XII

Relates that Mr. Jones *continued his Journey contrary to the Advice of* Partridge, *with what happened on that Occasion.*

THEY now discovered a Light at some Distance, to the great Pleasure of *Jones*, and to the no small Terror of *Partridge*, who firmly believed himself to be bewitched, and that this Light was a *Jack* with a Lanthorn, or somewhat more mischievous.

But how were these Fears increased, when, as they approached nearer to this Light, (or Lights as they now appeared) they heard a confused Sound of Human Voices; of singing, laughing, and hallowing, together with a strange Noise that seemed to proceed from some Instruments;[1] but could hardly be allowed the Name of Music. Indeed, to favour a little the Opinion of *Partridge*, it might very well be called Music bewitched.

It is impossible to conceive a much greater Degree of Horror than what now seized on *Partridge*; the Contagion of which had reached the Post-boy; who had been very attentive to many Things that the other had uttered. He now therefore joined in petitioning *Jones* to return; saying he firmly believed what *Partridge* had just before said, that tho' the Horses seemed to go on, they had not moved a Step forwards during at least the last half Hour.

Jones could not help smiling in the midst of his Vexation, at the Fears of these poor Fellows. 'Either we advance,' says he, 'towards the Lights, or the Lights have advanced towards us; for we are now at a very little Distance from them; but how can either of you be afraid of a Set of People who appear only to be merry-making?'

'Merry-making, Sir!' cries *Partridge*, 'who could be merry-making at this Time of Night, and in such a Place, and such Weather? They can be nothing but Ghosts or Witches, or some Evil Spirits or other, that's certain.'

'Let them be what they will,' cries *Jones*, 'I am resolved to go up to them, and enquire the Way to *Coventry*. All Witches, *Partridge*, are not such ill-natured Hags, as that we had the Misfortune to meet with last.'

'Oh Lord, Sir!' cries *Partridge*, 'there is no knowing what Humour they will be in; to be sure it is always best to be civil to them; but what if we should meet with something worse than

---

[1] As will appear, the sounds issue from 'a Company of *Egyptians*, or as they are vulgarly called *Gypsies* . . . now celebrating the Wedding of one of their Society'. Since, throughout this chapter, Fielding develops an implicit parallel between these Egyptians and the Jacobites (see below, p. 666, n. 2, and following), the principal instrument producing this barbaric cacophony is doubtless the bagpipe. Thus Charles Perry describes the 'preposterous' marriage customs of the Egyptians: the brides are 'followed by a Symphony of Music, consisting of Drums, some kettle, some common, besides some other squeaking Instruments, which may be said to be a very scurvy Resemblance of Bag-pipes . . .' (*A View of the Levant* [1743], p. 249).

Witches, with Evil Spirits themselves?—Pray, Sir, be advised; pray, Sir, do. If you had read so many terrible Accounts as I have of these Matters, you would not be so Fool-hardy.—The Lord knows whither we have got already, or whither we are going: For sure such Darkness was never seen upon Earth, and I question whether it can be darker in the other World.'

Jones put forwards as fast as he could, notwithstanding all these Hints and Cautions, and poor *Partridge* was obliged to follow: For tho' he hardly dared to advance, he dared still less to stay behind by himself.

At length they arrived at the Place whence the Lights and different Noises had issued. This *Jones* perceived to be no other than a Barn where a great Number of Men and Women were assembled, and diverting themselves with much apparent Jollity.

Jones no sooner appeared before the great Doors of the Barn, which were open, than a masculine and very rough Voice from within demanded who was there?—To which *Jones* gently answered, A Friend; and immediately asked the Road to *Coventry*.

'If you are a Friend,' cries another of the Men in the Barn, 'you had better alight till the Storm is over,' (for indeed it was now more violent than ever) 'you are very welcome to put up your Horse, for there is sufficient Room for him at one End of the Barn.'

'You are very obliging,' returned *Jones*; 'and I will accept your Offer for a few Minutes, whilst the Rain continues; and here are two more who will be glad of the same Favour.' This was accorded with more Good-will than it was accepted: For *Partridge* would rather have submitted to the utmost Inclemency of the Weather, than have trusted to the Clemency of those whom he took for Hobgoblins; and the poor Post-boy was now infected with the same Apprehensions; but they were both obliged to follow the Example of *Jones*; the one because he durst not leave his Horse, and the other because he feared nothing so much as being left by himself.

Had this History been writ in the Days of Superstition, I should have had too much Compassion for the Reader to have left him so long in Suspense, whether *Beelzebub* or *Satan* was about actually to appear in Person, with all his Hellish Retinue; but as these Doctrines are at present very unfortunate, and have but few if any Believers, I have not been much aware of conveying any such Terrors. To say Truth, the whole Furniture of the infernal Regions hath long been appropriated by the Managers of Playhouses,[1] who seem lately to have lain them by as Rubbish, capable only of affecting the Upper Gallery; a Place in which few of our Readers ever sit.

However, tho' we do not suspect raising any great Terror on this Occasion, we have Reason to fear some other Apprehensions may here arise in our Reader, into which we would not willingly betray him, I mean that we are going to take a Voyage into Fairy Land, and to introduce a Set of Beings into our History, which scarce any one was ever childish enough to believe, tho' many have been foolish enough to spend their Time in writing and reading their Adventures.

To prevent therefore any such Suspicions, so prejudicial to the Credit of an Historian, who professes to draw his Materials from Nature only, we shall now proceed to acquaint the Reader who these People were, whose sudden Appearance had struck such Terrors into *Partridge*, had more than half frightened the Post-Boy, and had a little surprized even Mr. *Jones* himself.

The People then assembled in this Barn were no other than a Company of *Egyptians*, or as they are vulgarly called *Gypsies*,[2] and they were now celebrating the Wedding of one of their Society.

---

[1] A glance in particular at John Rich (see above, p. 213, n. 2), who, as theatrical manager first at Lincoln's Inn Fields and (after 1732) at Covent-Garden, produced such spectacular entertainments as Lewis Theobald's *Harlequin a Sorcerer* (1725) and *Orpheus and Eurydice* (1740), wherein audiences were diverted with extravagant scenes of devils and hell-fire. Pope satirized these productions in *The Dunciad Variorum* (1729; iii. 229–36, 305–14) and Fielding ridiculed them in *The Champion* (24 May 1740). In that journal for 3 May 1740, Fielding remarked that Rich's foolish spectacles appealed only to the occupants of 'the Gallery Superior, where the Apprentice, the Clerk, with all the viler Riff-Raff, the Tag-Rag, and Bob-Tail of the World, are mounted . . . above their Superiors . . .'.

[2] In describing the customs and polity of this gipsy band, Fielding develops an ironic parable of government designed to expose the Jacobite ideal of civil happiness under an absolute monarchy as nothing more than an alluring, if dangerous, fantasy. According to popular belief, the gipsies were in fact displaced Egyptians who had migrated to England from France. Fielding, therefore, facetiously attributes to the gipsies the manners and the form of government of their alleged ancestors, the ancient pharaohs, whom historians had represented as the exemplars *par excellence* of an enlightened despotism. (See, for instance, Diodorus Siculus and Herodotus, whose histories afforded the basis for such modern accounts as Charles Rollin's *Ancient History of the Egyptians . . . and Grecians* [Paris, 1730–8] and Charles Perry's *View of the Levant* [1743], esp. pp. 395–9.) Since the Revolution Settlement, the comparison between Jacobite and Egyptian principles of absolutism was often drawn—as in Perry, for example, or in Benjamin Hoadly's (see above, p. 105,

It is impossible to conceive a happier Set of People than appeared here to be met together. The utmost Mirth indeed shewed itself in every Countenance; nor was their Ball totally void of all Order and Decorum. Perhaps it had more than a Country Assembly is sometimes conducted with: For these People are subject to a formal Government and Laws of their own, and all pay Obedience to one great Magistrate whom they call their King.

Greater Plenty likewise was no where to be seen, than what flourished in this Barn. Here was indeed no Nicety nor Elegance, nor did the keen Appetite of the Guests require any. Here was good Store of Bacon, Fowls, and Mutton, to which every one present provided better Sauce himself, than the best and dearest *French* Cook can prepare.[1]

Æneas is not described under more Consternation in the Temple of *Juno,*

Dum stupet obtutuque hæret defixus in uno.[2]

than was our Heroe at what he saw in this Barn. While he was looking every where round him with Astonishment, a venerable Person approached him with many friendly Salutations, rather of too hearty a Kind to be called courtly. This was no other than the King of the *Gypsies* himself. He was very little distinguished in Dress from his Subjects, nor had he any *Regalia* of Majesty to support his Dignity; and yet there seemed (as Mr. *Jones* said) to be somewhat in his Air which denoted Authority, and inspired the Beholders with an Idea of Awe and Respect; tho' all this was perhaps imaginary in *Jones*, and the Truth may be, that such Ideas are incident to Power, and almost inseparable from it.

There was somewhat in the open Countenance and courteous

n. 1) frequently reprinted sermon in defence of the Hanoverian succession, *The Happiness of the present Establishment, and the Unhappiness of Absolute Monarchy* (1708). Indeed, in February or March 1748 there appeared an anonymous political satire, *De Toryismo Liber: or, A Treatise on Toryism*, which wryly anticipated Fielding's association of Jacobites and gipsies (pp. 11–15). For a discussion of this background and an interpretation of the political significance of the present chapter, see Battestin, 'Tom Jones and "His Egyptian Majesty": Fielding's Parable of Government', *PMLA*, lxxxii (1967), 68–77.

[1] On the simple diet of the Egyptian kings, cf. Diodorus, I. xlv. 2, and Rollin: 'His table was covered with nothing but the most common meats because eating in Egypt was designed, not to tickle the palate, but to satisfy the cravings of nature' (op. cit., 2nd ed. [1738–40], i. 31).

[2] *Aeneid*, i. 495: 'while in amazement he hangs rapt in one fixed gaze' (trans. H. R. Fairclough, Loeb Classical Library, 1916).

Behaviour of *Jones*, which being accompanied with much Comeliness of Person, greatly recommended him at first Sight to every Beholder. These were perhaps a little heightened in the present Instance, by that profound Respect which he paid to the King of the *Gypsies*, the Moment he was acquainted with his Dignity, and which was the sweeter to his *Gypseian* Majesty, as he was not used to receive such Homage from any but his own Subjects.

The King ordered a Table to be spread with the choicest of their Provisions for his Accommodation, and having placed himself at his Right Hand, his Majesty began to discourse our Heroe in the following Manner:

'Me doubt not, Sir, but you have often seen some of my People, who are what you call de Parties detache: For dey go about every where; but me fancy you imagine not we be so considrable Body as we be, and may be you will surprise more, when you hear de *Gypsy* be as orderly and well govern People as any upon Face of de Earth.

'Me have Honour, as me say, to be deir King, and no Monarch can do boast of more dutiful Subject, ne no more affectionate. How far me deserve deir Goodwill, me no say, but dis me can say, dat me never design any Ting but to do dem Good. Me sall no do boast of dat neider: For what can me do oderwise dan consider of de Good of dose poor People who go about all Day to give me always de best of what dey get. Dey love and honour me darefore, because me do love and take Care of dem; dat is all, me know no oder Reason.[1]

'About a tousand or two tousand Year ago, me cannot tell to a Year or two, as can neider write nor read, dere was a great what you call,—a Volution among de *Gypsy*;[2] for dere was de Lord

---

[1] On the affection between the pharaohs and their subjects, cf. Diodorus, i. lxxi. 4, and Rollin: 'The virtue in the highest esteem among the Egyptians, was gratitude. . . . Benefits are the band of concord, both publick and private. He who acknowledges favours, loves to do good to others; and in banishing ingratitude, the pleasure of doing good remains so pure and engaging, that 'tis impossible for a man to be insensible of it: But no kind of gratitude gave the Egyptians a more pleasing satisfaction, than that which was paid to their kings' (op. cit., 2nd ed. [1738–40], i. 35).

[2] According to the historians, Menes or Mizraim, grandson of Noah and the first king of Egypt, bequeathed his kingdom equally to his four sons. 'But,' as Perry observed, 'these Four Brothers quarrelling amongst themselves, after the Death of their Father, (so early a Footing had Faction and Discord in the World) each pretending to the sovereign Authority, and disdaining to suffer an Equal, they unanimously resolv'd to terminate their

Gypsy in dose Days; and dese Lord did quarrel vid one anoder about de Place; but de King of de *Gypsy* did demolish dem all, and made all his Subject equal vid each oder; and since dat time dey have agree very well: for dey no tink of being King, and may be it be better for dem as dey be: For me assure you it be ver troublesome ting to be King, and always to do Justice; me have often wish to be de private *Gypsy* when me have been forced to punish my dear Friend and Relation; for dough we never put to Death, our Punishments be ver severe. Dey make de *Gypsy* ashamed of demselves, and dat be ver terrible Punishment;[1] me ave scarce ever known de *Gypsy* so punish do Harm any more.'

The King then proceeded to express some Wonder that there was no such Punishment as Shame in other Governments. Upon which *Jones* assured him to the contrary: For that there were many Crimes for which Shame was inflicted by the *English* Laws, and that it was indeed one Consequence of all Punishment. 'Dat be ver strange,' said the King: 'For me know and hears good deal of your People, dough me no live among dem, and me ave often hear dat Sham is de Consequence and de Cause too of many your Rewards. Are your Rewards and Punishments den de same Ting?'

While his Majesty was thus discoursing with *Jones*, a sudden Uproar arose in the Barn, and as it seems, upon this Occasion: The Courtesy of these People had by Degrees removed all the Apprehensions of *Partridge*, and he was prevailed upon not only to stuff himself with their Food, but to taste some of their Liquors, which by Degrees entirely expelled all Fear from his Composition, and in its Stead introduced much more agreeable Sensations.

Differences by a Battle, and that the supreme Authority should be the Portion of him who got the Victory' (op. cit., p. 238). Copt, the youngest, defeated his brothers and began the long succession of despots who reigned thereafter.

    1 Rollin observes that the Egyptians valued personal honour above all other things, as 'the only human blessing of which death cannot deprive us' (op. cit., 2nd ed. [1738–40], i. 46). Diodorus, for instance, describes the Egyptian method of dealing with cowards on the battlefield: their punishment was 'not death, but the uttermost disgrace; but if later on such men wiped out their disgrace by a display of manly courage, they were restored to their former freedom of speech. Thus the lawgiver at the same time made disgrace a more terrible punishment than death, in order to accustom all the people to consider dishonour the greatest of evils, and he also believed that, while dead men would never be of value to society, men who had been disgraced would do many a good deed through their desire to regain freedom of speech' (i. lxxviii. 1–2; trans. C. H. Oldfather, Loeb Classical Library, 1933).

A young Female *Gypsy*, more remarkable for her Wit than her Beauty, had decoyed the honest Fellow aside, pretending to tell his Fortune. Now when they were alone together in a remote Part of the Barn, whether it proceeded from the strong Liquor, which is never so apt to inflame inordinate Desire as after moderate Fatigue, or whether the fair *Gypsy* herself threw aside the Delicacy and Decency of her Sex, and tempted the Youth *Partridge* with express Solicitations; but they were discovered in a very improper Manner by the Husband of the *Gypsy*, who from Jealousy, it seems, had kept a watchful Eye over his Wife, and had dogged her to the Place, where he found her in the Arms of her Gallant.

To the great Confusion of *Jones*, *Partridge* was now hurried before the King; who heard the Accusation, and likewise the Culprit's Defence, which was indeed very trifling: For the poor Fellow was confounded by the plain Evidence which appeared against him, and had very little to say for himself. His Majesty then turning towards *Jones*, said, 'Sir, you have hear what dey say, what Punishment do you tink your Man deserve?'

Jones answered, 'He was sorry for what had happened, and that *Partridge* should make the Husband all the Amends in his Power:' He said, he had very little Money about him at that Time, and putting his Hand into his Pocket, offered the Fellow a Guinea. To which he immediately answered, 'He hoped his Honour would not think of giving him less than five.'

This Sum after some Altercation was reduced to two, and *Jones* having stipulated for the full Forgiveness of both *Partridge* and the Wife, was going to pay the Money; when his Majesty restraining his Hand, turned to the Witness, and asked him, 'At what Time he had first discovered the Criminals?' To which he answered, 'That he had been desired by the Husband to watch the Motions of his Wife from her first speaking to the Stranger, and that he had never lost Sight of her afterwards till the Crime had been committed.' The King then asked, 'If the Husband was with him all that Time in his lurking Place?' To which he answered in the Affirmative. His *Egyptian* Majesty then addressed himself to the Husband as follows, 'Me be sorry to see any *Gypsy* dat have no more Honour dan to sell de Honour of his Wife for Money.[1]

---

[1] This was a fashionable vice of the age which Fielding regarded with a mixture of anger and loathing. Not only the gipsy husband, but Mr. Modern of *The Modern Husband*

If you had de Love for your Wife, you would have prevented dis Matter, and not endeavour to make her de Whore dat you might discover her. Me do order dat you have no Money given you, for you deserve Punishment not Reward; me do order derefore, dat you be de infamous *Gypsy*, and do wear Pair of Horns upon your Forehead for one Month, and dat your Wife be called de Whore, and pointed at all dat Time: For you be de infamous *Gypsy*, but she be no less de infamous Whore.'

The *Gypsies* immediately proceeded to execute the Sentence, and left *Jones* and *Partridge* alone with his Majesty.

Jones greatly applauded the Justice of the Sentence; upon which the King turning to him said, 'Me believe you be surprize: For me suppose you have ver bad Opinion of my People; me suppose you tink us all de Tieves.'

'I must confess, Sir,' said *Jones*, 'I have not heard so favourable an Account of them as they seem to deserve.'

'Me vil tell you,' said the King, 'how the Difference is between you and us. My People rob your People, and your People rob one anoder.'

Jones afterwards proceeded very gravely to sing forth the Happiness of those Subjects who live under such a Magistrate.

Indeed their Happiness appears to have been so compleat, that we are aware lest some Advocate for arbitrary Power should hereafter quote the Case of those People, as an Instance of the great Advantages which attend that Government above all others.[1]

And here we will make a Concession, which would not perhaps have been expected from us, That no limited Form of Government is capable of rising to the same Degree of Perfection, or of producing the same Benefits to Society with this. Mankind have never been so happy, as when the greatest Part of the then known World was under the Dominion of a single Master; and this State of their Felicity continued during the Reigns of five

(1732) and Col. Trent of *Amelia* (1751) are guilty of prostituting their wives for money. As Fielding observed in a note to *The Vernoniad* (1741), there was no surer sign of the moral depravity of the nation than that those who engaged in 'this infamous Trade' were neither ashamed of it themselves nor despised for it by others.

[1] In the monitory paragraphs that serve as an epilogue to the gipsy episode, Fielding's argument against political absolutism is based on Hoadly's well-known sermon, *The Happiness of the Present Establishment, and the Unhappiness of Absolute Monarchy*, originally published in 1708 and reprinted many times thereafter. For a discussion of the relationship between Hoadly's sermon and Fielding's remarks, see Battestin, *PMLA*, lxxxii (1967), 74–6. Cf. also Addison in *Spectator*, No. 287 (29 January 1712).

successive Princes.* This was the true Æra of the Golden Age, and the only Golden Age which ever had any Existence, unless in the warm Imaginations of the Poets, from the Expulsion from *Eden* down to this Day.

In reality, I know but of one solid Objection to absolute Monarchy. The only Defect in which excellent Constitution seems to be the Difficulty of finding any Man adequate to the Office of an absolute Monarch: For this indispensably requires three Qualities very difficult, as it appears from History, to be found in princely Natures: First, a sufficient Quantity of Moderation in the Prince, to be contented with all the Power which is possible for him to have. 2dly, Enough of Wisdom to know his own Happiness. And, 3dly, Goodness sufficient to support the Happiness of others, when not only compatible with, but instrumental to his own.

Now if an absolute Monarch with all these great and rare Qualifications should be allowed capable of conferring the greatest Good on Society, it must be surely granted, on the contrary, that absolute Power vested in the Hands of one who is deficient in them all, is likely to be attended with no less a Degree of Evil.

In short our own Religion furnishes us with adequate Ideas of the Blessing, as well as Curse which may attend absolute Power. The Pictures of Heaven and of Hell will place a very lively Image of both before our Eyes: For though the Prince of the latter can have no Power, but what he originally derives from the omnipotent Sovereign in the former; yet it plainly appears from Scripture, that absolute Power in his infernal Dominions is granted to their Diabolical Ruler. This is indeed the only absolute Power which can by Scripture be derived from Heaven. If therefore the several Tyrannies upon Earth can prove any Title to a divine Authority, it must be derived from this original Grant to the Prince of Darkness, and these subordinate Deputations must consequently come immediately from him whose Stamp they so expresly bear.

To conclude, as the Examples of all Ages shew us that Mankind in general desire Power only to do Harm, and when they obtain it, use it for no other Purpose; it is not consonant with even the

* *Nerva, Trajan, Adrian,* and the two *Antonini.*[1]

[1] The reigns of these enlightened emperors extended from A.D. 96 to 180.

least Degree of Prudence to hazard an Alteration, where our Hopes are poorly kept in Countenance by only two or three Exceptions out of a thousand Instances to alarm our Fears. In this Case it will be much wiser to submit to a few Inconveniencies arising from the dispassionate Deafness of Laws, than to remedy them by applying to the passionate open Ears of a Tyrant.

Nor can the Example of the *Gypsies,* tho' possibly they may have long been happy under this Form of Government, be here urged; since we must remember the very material Respect in which they differ from all other People, and to which perhaps this their Happiness is entirely owing, namely, that they have no false Honours among them; and that they look on Shame as the most grievous Punishment in the World.

CHAPTER XIII

A Dialogue between Jones *and* Partridge.

THE honest Lovers of Liberty will we doubt not pardon that long Digression into which we were led at the Close of the last Chapter, to prevent our History from being applied to the Use of the most pernicious Doctrine, which Priestcraft had ever the Wickedness or the Impudence to preach.

We will now proceed with Mr. *Jones,* who when the Storm was over, took Leave of his *Egyptian* Majesty, after many Thanks for his courteous Behaviour and kind Entertainment, and set out for *Coventry*; to which Place (for it was still dark) a *Gypsy* was ordered to conduct him.

Jones having, by Reason of his Deviation, travelled eleven Miles instead of six, and most of those through very execrable Roads, where no Expedition could have been made, in Quest of a Midwife, did not arrive at *Coventry* till near Twelve. Nor could he possibly get again into the Saddle till past Two; for Post-Horses were now not easy to get; nor were the Hostler or Post-Boy, in half so great a Hurry as himself, but chose rather to imitate the tranquil Disposition of *Partridge*; who being denied the Nourishment of Sleep, took all Opportunities to supply its Place with every other Kind of Nourishment, and was never better pleased than when he arrived at an Inn, nor ever more dissatisfied than when he was again forced to leave it.

Jones now travelled Post; we will follow him therefore, according to our Custom, and to the Rules of *Longinus*,[1] in the same Manner. From *Coventry* he arrived at *Daventry*, from *Daventry* at *Stratford*,[2] and from *Stratford* at *Dunstable*, whither he came the next Day a little after Noon, and within a few Hours after *Sophia* had left it; and though he was obliged to stay here longer than he wished, while a Smith, with great Deliberation, shoed the Post-Horse he was to ride, he doubted not but to overtake his *Sophia* before she should set out from *St. Albans*; at which Place he concluded, and very reasonably, that his Lordship would stop and dine.

And had he been right in this Conjecture, he most probably would have overtaken his Angel at the aforesaid Place; but unluckily my Lord had appointed a Dinner to be prepared for him at his own House in *London*, and in order to enable him to reach that Place in proper Time, he had ordered a Relay of Horses to meet him at *St. Albans*. When *Jones* therefore arrived there, he was informed that the Coach and Six had set out two Hours before.

If fresh Post-Horses had been now ready, as they were not, it seemed so apparently impossible to overtake the Coach before it reached *London*, that *Partridge* thought he had now a proper Opportunity to remind his Friend of a Matter which he seemed entirely to have forgotten; what this was the Reader will guess, when we inform him that *Jones* had eat nothing more than one poached Egg since he had left the Alehouse where he had first met the Guide returning from *Sophia*; for with the *Gypsies*, he had feasted only his Understanding.

---

[1] In setting forth the narrative principles of his 'new Province of Writing' (II. i), Fielding had distinguished his work from the productions of circumstantial historians and newspaper writers, whom he called the amanuenses of Time. Unlike these authors, who dutifully and dully record the most inconsequential events, he would 'fly' past those periods of his hero's life, whether days or months or years, in which nothing extraordinary happened. The reference to Longinus recalls several passages in the treatise *On the Sublime*, in which authors are advised to avoid the trivial and tedious, striving instead for aesthetic intensity: among 'the merits of great genius', for example, Longinus lists a 'sublime intensity' and 'speed—where speed is in season' (xxxiv. 4; trans. W. H. Fyfe, Loeb Classical Library, 1927).

[2] Stony Stratford. These are post-towns situated at intervals of about twenty miles along the Great Northwest Road from Coventry to London.

The Landlord so entirely agreed with the Opinion of Mr. *Partridge*, that he no sooner heard the latter desire his Friend to stay and dine, than he very readily put in his Word, and retracting his Promise before given of furnishing the Horses immediately, he assured Mr. *Jones* he would lose no Time in bespeaking a Dinner, which, he said, could be got ready sooner than it was possible to get the Horses up from Grass, and to prepare them for their Journey by a Feed of Corn.

Jones was at length prevailed on, chiefly by the latter Argument of the Landlord; and now a Joint of Mutton was put down to the Fire. While this was preparing, *Partridge* being admitted into the same Apartment with his Friend or Master, began to harangue in the following Manner.

'Certainly, Sir, if ever Man deserved a young Lady, you deserve young Madam *Western*; for what a vast Quantity of Love must a Man have, to be able to live upon it without any other Food, as you do. I am positive I have eat thirty times as much within these last twenty-four Hours as your Honour, and yet I am almost famished; for nothing makes a Man so hungry as travelling, especially in this cold raw Weather. And yet I can't tell how it is, but your Honour is seemingly in perfect good Health, and you never looked better nor fresher in your Life. It must be certainly Love that you live upon.'

'And a very rich Diet too, *Partridge*,' answered *Jones*. 'But did not Fortune send me an excellent Dainty Yesterday? Dost thou imagine I cannot live more than twenty-four Hours on this dear Pocket-Book?'

'Undoubtedly,' cries *Partridge*, 'there is enough in that Pocketbook to purchase many a good Meal. Fortune sent it to your Honour very opportunely for present Use, as your Honour's Money must be almost out by this Time.'

'What do you mean?' answered *Jones*; 'I hope you don't imagine I should be dishonest enough, even if it belonged to any other Person, besides Miss *Western*——'

'Dishonest!' replied *Partridge*; 'Heaven forbid I should wrong your Honour so much; but where's the Dishonesty in borrowing a little for present spending, since you will be so well able to pay the Lady hereafter. No indeed, I would have your Honour pay it again, as soon as it is convenient, by all Means; but where can be the Harm in making use of it now you want it. Indeed if it belonged to a poor Body, it would be another thing; but so great a Lady to be sure can never want it, especially now as she is along with a Lord, who it can't be doubted will let her have whatever she hath Need of. Besides, if she should want a little, she can't want the whole, therefore I would give her a little; but I would be hanged before I mentioned the having found it at first, and before I got some Money of my own; for *London*, I have heard, is the very worst of Places to be in without Money. Indeed, if I had not known to whom it belonged, I might have thought it was the Devil's Money, and have been afraid to use it; but as you know otherwise, and came honestly by it, it would be an Affront to Fortune to part with it all again, at the very Time when you want it most; you can hardly expect she should ever do you such another good Turn; for *Fortuna nunquam perpetuo est bona*.[1] You will do as you please, notwithstanding all I say; but for my Part, I would be hanged before I mentioned a Word of the Matter.'

'By what I can see, *Partridge*,' cries *Jones*, 'hanging is a Matter *non longe alienum a Scævolæ studiis*.'[2] 'You should say *alienus*,' says *Partridge*.—'I remember the Passage; it is an Example under *Communis, Alienus, immunis, variis casibus serviunt*.'[3] 'If you do remember it,' cries *Jones*, 'I find you don't understand it; but I tell thee, Friend, in plain *English*, that he who finds another's Property, and wilfully detains it from the known Owner, deserves *in Foro Conscientiæ*,[4] to be hanged no less than if he had stolen it. And as for this very identical Bill, which is the Property of my Angel, and was once in her dear Possession, I will not deliver it into any Hands but her own, upon any Consideration whatever; No, tho' I was as hungry as thou art, and had no other Means to satisfy my craving Appetite; this I hope to do before I sleep; but if it should happen otherwise, I charge thee, if thou wouldst not incur my Displeasure for ever, not to shock me any more by the bare Mention of such detestable Baseness.'

---

[1] Terence, *Hecyra*, 406: 'O Fortune, never constant in your kindness.' An example in *A Short Introduction to Grammar* (1720), p. 137.

[2] The quotation, with *alienus*, is from Cicero, *Letters to Atticus*, IV. xvi: 'not foreign to the interests of Scaevola.' Quintus Mucius Scaevola, 'the augur' (d. 88–2 B.C.), was a distinguished jurist and the teacher and friend of Cicero.

[3] '*Communis* [common], *alienus* [strange], *immunis* [free], serve divers cases'—from *A Short Introduction to Grammar* [1720], p. 143. Tom's quotation from Cicero is an example under this heading.

[4] See above, p. 192, n. 3.

'I should not have mentioned it now,' cries *Partridge*, 'if it had appeared so to me; for I'm sure I scorn any Wickedness as much as another; but perhaps you know better; and yet I might have imagined that I should not have lived so many Years, and have taught School so long, without being able to distinguish between *Fas et Nefas*;[1] but it seems we are to live and learn. I remember my old Schoolmaster, who was a prodigious great Scholar, used often to say, *Polly Matete cry Town is my Daskalon*.[2] The *English* of which, he told us, was, That a Child may sometimes teach his Grandmother to suck Eggs. I have lived to a fine Purpose truly, if I am to be taught my Grammar at this Time of Day. Perhaps, young Gentleman, you may change your Opinion if you live to my Years: For I remember I thought myself as wise when I was a Stripling of one or two and twenty as I am now. I am sure I always taught *alienus*, and my Master read it so before me.'

There were not many Instances in which *Partridge* could provoke *Jones*, nor were there many in which *Partridge* himself could have been hurried out of his Respect. Unluckily however they had both hit on one of these. We have already seen *Partridge* could not bear to have his Learning attacked, nor could *Jones* bear some Passage or other in the foregoing Speech. And now looking upon his Companion with a contemptuous and disdainful Air (a thing not usual with him) he cried, '*Partridge*, I see thou art a conceited old Fool, and I wish thou art not likewise an old Rogue. Indeed if I was as well convinced of the latter as I am of the former, thou shouldst travel no farther in my Company.'

The sage Pedagogue was contented with the Vent which he had already given to his Indignation; and, as the vulgar Phrase is, immediately drew in his Horns. He said, He was sorry he had uttered any thing which might give Offence, for that he had never intended it; but *Nemo omnibus horis sapit*.[3]

As *Jones* had the Vices of a warm Disposition, he was entirely free from those of a cold one; and if his Friends must have confest

---

[1] 'Right and wrong'.

[2] The source of Partridge's garbled Greek is an anonymous proverb in Stephanus's *Thesaurus* (s.v. μαθητής): πολλοὶ μαθηταὶ κρείττονες διδασκάλων ('many pupils are better than their teachers'). Fielding owned a copy of this work, the 1572 Paris edition.

[3] Pliny, *Natural History*, VII. xl. 131: 'No one is wise all the time.' Used as an example in *A Short Introduction to Grammar* [1720], p. 158. (See also above, p. 130.5. and below, p. 856.)

his Temper to have been a little too easily ruffled, his Enemies must at the same Time have confest, that it as soon subsided; nor did it at all resemble the Sea, whose Swelling is more violent and dangerous after a Storm is over, than while the Storm itself subsists. He instantly accepted the Submission of *Partridge*, shook him by the Hand, and with the most benign Aspect imaginable, said twenty kind Things, and at the same Time very severely condemned himself, tho' not half so severely as he will most probably be condemned by many of our good Readers.

Partridge was now highly comforted, as his Fears of having offended were at once abolished, and his Pride completely satisfied by *Jones* having owned himself in the wrong, which Submission he instantly applied to what had principally nettled him, and repeated, in a muttering Voice, 'To be sure, Sir, your Knowledge may be superior to mine in some Things; but as to the Grammar, I think I may challenge any Man living. I think, at least, I have that at my Finger's End.'

If any thing could add to the Satisfaction which the poor Man now enjoyed, he received this Addition by the Arrival of an excellent Shoulder of Mutton, that at this Instant came smoking to the Table. On which, having both plentifully feasted, they again mounted their Horses, and set forward for *London*.

CHAPTER XIV

What happened to Mr. Jones *in his* Journey from St. Albans.

THEY were got about two Miles beyond *Barnet*, and it was now the Dusk of the Evening, when a genteel looking Man, but upon a very shabby Horse, rode up to *Jones*, and asked him whether he was going to *London*, to which *Jones* answered in the affirmative. The Gentleman replied, 'I should be obliged to you, Sir, if you will accept of my Company; for it is very late, and I am a Stranger to the Road.' *Jones* readily complied with the Request; and on they travelled together, holding that Sort of Discourse which is usual on such Occasions.

Of this, indeed, Robbery was the principal Topic; upon which Subject the Stranger expressed great Apprehensions; but *Jones* declared he had very little to lose, and consequently as little to fear. Here *Partridge* could not forbear putting in his Word. 'Your Honour,' said he, 'may think it a little, but I am sure, if I had a hundred Pound Bank Note in my Pocket, as you have, I should be very sorry to lose it; but, for my Part, I never was less afraid in my Life; for we are four of us, and if we all stand by one another, the best Man in *England* can't rob us. Suppose he should have a Pistol, he can kill but one of us, and a Man can die but once, that's my Comfort, a Man can die but once.'

Besides the Reliance on superior Numbers, a kind of Valour which hath raised a certain Nation among the Moderns to a high Pitch of Glory,[1] there was another Reason for the extraordinary Courage which *Partridge* now discovered; for he had at present as much of that Quality as was in the Power of Liquor to bestow.

Our Company were now arrived within a Mile of *Highgate*, when the Stranger turned short upon *Jones*, and pulling out a Pistol, demanded that little Bank Note which *Partridge* had mentioned.

Jones was at first somewhat shocked at this unexpected Demand; however, he presently recollected himself, and told the Highwayman, all the Money he had in his Pocket was entirely at his Service; and so saying, he pulled out upwards of three Guineas, and offered to deliver it; but the other answered with an Oath, That would not do. *Jones* answered coolly, He was very sorry for it, and returned the Money into his Pocket.

The Highwayman then threatned, if he did not deliver the Bank Note that Moment, he must shoot him; holding his Pistol at the same Time very near to his Breast. *Jones* instantly caught hold of the Fellow's Hand, which trembled so that he could scarce hold the Pistol in it, and turned the Muzzle from him. A Struggle then ensued, in which the former wrested the Pistol from the Hand of his Antagonist, and both came from their Horses on the Ground together, the Highwayman upon his Back, and the victorious *Jones* upon him.

The poor Fellow now began to implore Mercy of the Conqueror; for, to say the Truth, he was in Strength by no Means a Match for *Jones*. 'Indeed, Sir,' says he, 'I could have had no Intention to shoot you, for you will find the Pistol was not loaded. This is the first Robbery I ever attempted, and I have been driven by Distress to this.'

[1] See above, p. 262, n. 1.

At this Instant, at about an hundred and fifty Yards Distance, lay another Person on the Ground, roaring for Mercy in a much louder Voice than the Highwayman. This was no other than *Partridge* himself, who endeavouring to make his Escape from the Engagement, had been thrown from his Horse, and lay flat on his Face, not daring to look up, and expecting every Minute to be shot.

In this Posture he lay, till the Guide, who was no otherwise concerned than for his Horses, having secured the stumbling Beast, came up to him and told him, his Master had got the better of the Highwayman.

Partridge leapt up at this News, and ran back to the Place, where *Jones* stood with his Sword drawn in his Hand to guard the poor Fellow; which *Partridge* no sooner saw, than he cried out, 'Kill the Villain, Sir, run him through the Body, kill him this Instant.'

Luckily however for the poor Wretch he had fallen into more merciful Hands; for *Jones* having examined the Pistol, and found it to be really unloaded, began to believe all the Man had told him before *Partridge* came up; namely, that he was a Novice in the Trade, and that he had been driven to it by the Distress he mentioned, the greatest indeed imaginable, that of five hungry Children, and a Wife lying in of a sixth, in the utmost Want and Misery. The Truth of all which the Highwayman most vehemently asserted, and offered to convince Mr. *Jones* of it, if he would take the Trouble to go to his House, which was not above two Miles off; saying, 'That he desired no Favour, but upon Condition of proving all he had alledged.'

Jones at first pretended that he would take the Fellow at his Word, and go with him, declaring that his Fate should depend entirely on the Truth of his Story. Upon this the poor Fellow immediately expressed so much Alacrity, that *Jones* was perfectly satisfied with his Veracity, and began now to entertain Sentiments of Compassion for him. He returned the Fellow his empty Pistol, advised him to think of honester Means of relieving his Distress, and gave him a couple of Guineas for the immediate Support of his Wife and his Family; adding, 'he wished he had more for his Sake, for the hundred Pound that had been mentioned, was not his own.'

Our Readers will probably be divided in their Opinions concerning this Action; some may applaud it perhaps as an Act of extraordinary Humanity, while those of a more saturnine Temper will consider it as a Want of Regard to that Justice which every Man owes his Country. *Partridge* certainly saw it in that Light; for he testified much Dissatisfaction on the Occasion, quoted an old Proverb, and said, 'He should not wonder if the Rogue attacked them again before they reached *London*.'

The Highwayman was full of Expressions of Thankfulness and Gratitude. He actually dropt Tears, or pretended so to do. He vowed he would immediately return home, and would never afterwards commit such a Transgression; whether he kept his Word or no, perhaps may appear hereafter.

Our Travellers having remounted their Horses, arrived in Town without encountering any new Mishap. On the Road much pleasant Discourse passed between *Jones* and *Partridge*, on the Subject of their last Adventure. In which *Jones* exprest a great Compassion for those Highwaymen who are, by unavoidable Distress, driven, as it were, to such illegal Courses, as generally bring them to a shameful Death. 'I mean,' said he, 'those only whose highest Guilt extends no farther than to Robbery, and who are never guilty of Cruelty nor Insult to any Person, which is a Circumstance that, I must say, to the Honour of our Country, distinguishes the Robbers of *England* from those of all other Nations; for Murder is, amongst those, almost inseparably incident to Robbery.'

'No doubt,' answered *Partridge*, 'it is better to take away one's Money than one's Life, and yet it is very hard upon honest Men, that they can't travel about their Business without being in Danger of these Villains. And to be sure it would be better that all Rogues were hanged out of the Way, than that one honest Man should suffer. For my own Part, indeed, I should not care to have the Blood of any of them on my own Hands; but it is very proper for the Law to hang them all. What Right hath any Man to take Sixpence from me, unless I give it him? Is there any Honesty in such a Man?'

'No surely,' cries *Jones*, 'no more than there is in him who takes the Horses out of another Man's Stable, or who applies to his own Use the Money which he finds, when he knows the right Owner.'

These Hints stopt the Mouth of *Partridge*, nor did he open it again till *Jones* having thrown some sarcastical Jokes on his

Cowardice, he offered to excuse himself on the Inequality of Fire Arms, saying, 'A thousand naked Men are nothing to one Pistol; for though, it is true, it will kill but one at a single Discharge, yet who can tell but that one may be himself.'

The End of the Fourth Volume.

BOOK XIII

Containing the Space of Twelve Days.

CHAPTER I

An Invocation.

COME, bright Love of Fame, inspire my glowing Breast: Not thee I call, who over swelling Tides of Blood and Tears, dost bear the Heroe on to Glory, while Sighs of Millions waft his spreading Sails; but thee, fair, gentle Maid,[1] whom *Mnesis*, happy Nymph, first on the Banks of *Hebrus* did produce. Thee, whom *Mæonia*[2] educated, whom *Mantua*[3] charm'd, and who, on that fair Hill[4] which overlooks the proud Metropolis of *Britain*, satst, with thy *Milton*, sweetly tuning the Heroic Lyre; fill my ravished Fancy with the Hopes of charming Ages yet to come. Foretel me that some tender Maid, whose Grandmother is yet unborn, hereafter, when, under the fictitious Name of *Sophia*, she reads the real Worth which once existed in my *Charlotte*,[5] shall, from her sympathetic Breast, send forth the heaving Sigh. Do thou teach me not only to foresee, but to enjoy, nay, even to feed on future Praise. Comfort me by a solemn Assurance, that when the little Parlour in which I sit at this Instant,[6] shall be reduced to a worse furnished Box, I shall be read, with Honour, by those who never knew nor saw me, and whom I shall neither know nor see.

And thou, much plumper Dame,[7] whom no airy Forms nor

---

[1] Calliope, the Muse of epic poetry and the mother of Orpheus. Mnesis—or, more usually, Mnemosyne, the Memory—was the mother of the Muses. Hebrus, the classical name for the modern Maritza, the principal river of Thrace, was associated with Dionysus and Orpheus; the latter was torn to pieces by the Thracian women and cast into its waters.

[2] The ancient name of Lydia and supposedly the birthplace of Homer.

[3] The town in Cisalpine Gaul famous as the birthplace of Virgil.

[4] Probably Ludgate Hill. Shortly after 1660, Milton was living in Jewin Street, St. Giles, where he completed the manuscript of *Paradise Lost*.

[5] See above, p. 156, n. 3.

[6] On Fielding's residences in 1748, when he was doubtless composing the prefatory chapters to the several books of *Tom Jones*, see the General Introduction, p. xxxiii.

[7] Having considered the 'bright Love of Fame' as a motive for writing his book, Fielding next addresses a more substantial Muse, who in some of her aspects resembles

Phantoms of Imagination cloathe: Whom the well-seasoned Beef, and Pudding richly stained with Plumbs delight. Thee, I call; of whom in a *Treckschuyte*[1] in some *Dutch* Canal the fat Ufrow Gelt,[2] impregnated by a jolly Merchant of *Amsterdam*, was delivered: In *Grubstreet*-School didst thou suck in the Elements of thy Erudition. Here hast thou, in thy maturer Age, taught Poetry to tickle not the Fancy, but the Pride of the Patron.[3] Comedy from thee learns a grave and solemn Air;[4] while Tragedy storms loud, and rends th' affrighted Theatres with its Thunder.[5] To sooth thy wearied Limbs in Slumber, Alderman History tells his tedious Tale;[6] and again to awaken thee, Monsieur Romance performs his surprizing Tricks of Dexterity. Nor less thy well-fed Bookseller obeys thy Influence. By thy Advice the heavy, unread, Folio Lump, which long had dozed on the dusty Shelf, piece-mealed into Numbers,[7] runs nimbly through the Nation. Instructed by thee some Books, like Quacks, impose on the World by promising Wonders; while others turn Beaus, and

Pope's Dulness. Like the Dunces, he thus weighs 'solid pudding against empty praise' (*Dunciad*, *A*, i. 52). Fielding's 'plumper' goddess is the daughter not of Chaos and Night (*A*, i. 10), but of Gain and Trade; and her own favourite seat is Grub-Street, close enough to Dulness's 'Cave of Poverty and Poetry' (*A*, i. 32).

With the opening lines of this paragraph, compare *Dunciad*, *A*, ii. 31–8, in which Dulness fashions a phantom prize to be competed for by the assembled scribblers and booksellers:

> A Poet's form she plac'd before their eyes,
> And bad the nimblest racer seize the prize;
> No meagre, muse-rid mope, adust and thin,
> In a dun night-gown of his own loose skin,
> But such a bulk as no twelve bards could raise,
> Twelve starveling bards of these degen'rate days.
> All as a partridge plump, full-fed, and fair,
> She form'd this image of well-bodied air. . . .

[1] *Trekschuit*—a canal boat. As 'Orbilius' sneeringly pointed out in his *Examen* (December 1749), p. 86, the original editions of *Tom Jones* mis-spelled this word.

[2] *Juffrouw geld*—'Madam Money'.

[3] Cf. Pope's Dulness, who, as the tickling contest begins, exhorts her votaries: 'He wins this Patron who can tickle best' (*Dunciad*, *A*, ii. 188).

[4] See above, p. 638, n. 1.

[5] Cf. Belinda's reaction to the loss of her lock: 'Then flash'd the living Lightning from her Eyes,/And Screams of Horror rend th'affrighted Skies' (*The Rape of the Lock*, iii. 155–6).

[6] See above, p. 150, n. 3.

[7] For a full discussion of the practice of publishing by numbers, see R. M. Wiles, *Serial Publication in England before 1750* (Cambridge, 1957). Fielding more than once criticized this mercenary device of the booksellers which he considered an imposition on the public: see especially the revised version of *The Author's Farce* (II. iv) and *Joseph Andrews* (II. i), where he satirizes the issuing of dictionaries in this manner.

trust all their Merits to a gilded Outside. Come, thou jolly Substance, with thy shining Face, keep back thy Inspiration, but hold forth thy tempting Rewards; thy shining, chinking Heap; thy quickly-convertible Bank-bill, big with unseen Riches; thy often-varying Stock; the warm, the comfortable House; and, lastly, a fair Portion of that bounteous Mother, whose flowing Breasts yield redundant Sustenance for all her numerous Offspring, did not some too greedily and wantonly drive their Brethren from the Teat.[1] Come thou, and if I am too tasteless of thy valuable Treasures, warm my Heart with the transporting Thought of conveying them to others. Tell me, that through thy Bounty, the prattling Babes,[2] whose innocent Play hath often been interrupted by my Labours, may one Time be amply rewarded for them.

And now this ill-yoked Pair, this lean Shadow and this fat Substance,[3] have prompted me to write, whose Assistance shall I invoke to direct my Pen?

First, Genius; thou Gift of Heaven; without whose Aid, in vain we struggle against the Stream of Nature. Thou, who dost sow the generous Seeds which Art nourishes, and brings to Perfection. Do thou kindly take me by the Hand, and lead me through all the Mazes, the winding Labyrinths of Nature. Initiate me into all those Mysteries which profane Eyes never beheld. Teach me, which to thee is no difficult Task, to know Mankind better than they know themselves. Remove that Mist which dims the Intellects of Mortals, and causes them to adore Men for their Art, or to detest them for their Cunning in deceiving others, when they are, in reality, the Objects only of Ridicule, for deceiving themselves. Strip off the thin Disguise

---

[1] Cf. 'Of Good-Nature' (1743), ll. 65 ff.:

> So full the Stream of Nature's Bounty flows,
> Man feels no Ill, but what to Man he owes.
> The Earth abundant furnishes a Store,
> To sate the Rich, and satisfy the Poor.
> These wou'd not want, if those did never hoard . . .

[2] Certainly Fielding's two surviving children by his first wife were alive when he wrote this chapter: Harriet (1737–66) and Henry (1742–50). (On the latter, about whom we have only recently learned, see T. C. Duncan Eaves and B. D. Kimpel, *N & Q*, N.S. xv [June 1968], 212.) The chorus of prattlers probably also included William (baptized 25 February 1748–1820), his first son by his second wife, and possibly even his short-lived daughter, Mary Amelia (baptized 6 January 1749—buried 17 December 1749).

[3] Cf. *The Dunciad, A*, i. 52, where the Dunces weigh 'solid pudding against empty praise'.

of Wisdom from Self-Conceit, of Plenty from Avarice, and of Glory from Ambition. Come thou, that hast inspired thy *Aristophanes*, thy *Lucian*, thy *Cervantes*, thy *Rabelais*, thy *Moliere*, thy *Shakespear*, thy *Swift*, thy *Marivaux*,[1] fill my Pages with Humour; till Mankind learn the Good-Nature to laugh only at the Follies of others, and the Humility to grieve at their own.

And thou, almost the constant Attendant on true Genius,

---

[1] Pierre Carlet de Chamblain de Marivaux (1688–1763), French comic dramatist and author of two novels, *La Vie de Marianne* (1731–41) and *Le Paysan parvenu* (1735–6), which Fielding praised in *Joseph Andrews* (III. i). When Warburton, whom Fielding compliments later in this chapter (see below, p. 687, n. 3), brought out his edition of Pope in 1751, he linked Marivaux and Fielding as the two modern writers who, by 'enriching' the new genre of prose fiction 'with the best part of the *Comic* art, may be said to have brought it to its perfection' (Pope's *Works* [1753], iv. 169).

The other names in Fielding's pantheon of wit are too well known to need identifying and his admiration for them is well attested. In the Preface to his own and William Young's translation of *Plutus* (1742), Fielding praised Aristophanes for 'good sense, manly wit, just satire, and true humour'. Later, however, his moralistic bias caused him to regret that Aristophanes, as well as Rabelais, had used his talents irresponsibly, indeed with a design 'to ridicule all Sobriety, Modesty, Decency, Virtue and Religion, out of the World' (*The Covent-Garden Journal*, 4 February 1752; see also 30 June 1752). Fielding's esteem for Molière is best known through his successful adaptations (1732–3) of *Le Médecin malgré lui* and *L'Avare* for the English stage. In *The Covent-Garden Journal* (4 January 1752) he ranked Molière with Le Bossu as pre-eminent among modern French authors, and a month later (4 February 1752) he repeated the compliment of the present passage by including Molière and Shakespeare in the company of 'that great Triumvirate, Lucian, Cervantes, and Swift'—masters all of 'Wit and Humour', who endeavoured 'to expose and extirpate those Follies and Vices which chiefly prevailed in their several Countries'.

Of this 'great Triumvirate' Fielding chiefly admired Lucian, 'the Father of true Humour', as he called him, and the author upon whom he had 'formed' his own style. Late in his career, Fielding and William Young projected a new English translation of Lucian (*The Covent-Garden Journal*, 30 June 1752); unfortunately, despite a rather obvious 'puff' from Booth in *Amelia* (VIII. v), the public appears to have received the proposal coolly and the work was abandoned. To Fielding the 'immortal' Swift was the greatest of Lucian's imitators, and, though on occasion he could therefore rank him 'Second to his Original' (*The Covent-Garden Journal*, 30 June 1752), he was usually disposed to praise him without even such modest qualification. From *The Masquerade* (1728) to *The Covent-Garden Journal* (1752) Fielding's published works pay tribute to the author who was, as Booth declares (*Amelia*, VIII. v), 'the greatest Master of Humour that ever wrote'. In the obituary for Swift appearing in *The True Patriot* (5 November 1745), Fielding lauded him as 'A Genius who deserves to be ranked among the first whom the World ever saw. He possessed the Talents of a *Lucian*, a *Rabelais*, and a *Cervantes*, and in his Works exceeded them all.' As for Cervantes, the third member of the triumvirate, Fielding paid him the compliment of imitation both in *Don Quixote in England* (1734) and especially in his first novel, *Joseph Andrews* (1742). If his admiration for *Don Quixote* (1605–15) was not quite uncritical (see the review of Charlotte Lennox in *The Covent-Garden Journal* [24 March 1752]), yet Fielding clearly regarded the book as a masterpiece—nothing less, indeed, than 'the History of the World in general' and the great model of that 'new species of writing' he had himself introduced into England.

Humanity, bring all thy tender Sensations. If thou hast already disposed of them all between thy *Allen* and thy *Lyttleton*,[1] steal them a little while from their Bosoms. Not without these the tender Scene is painted. From these alone proceed the noble, disinterested Friendship, the melting Love, the generous Sentiment, the ardent Gratitude, the soft Compassion, the candid Opinion; and all those strong Energies of a good Mind, which fill the moistened Eyes with Tears, the glowing Cheeks with Blood, and swell the Heart with Tides of Grief, Joy and Benevolence.

And thou, O Learning, (for without thy Assistance nothing pure, nothing correct, can Genius produce) do thou guide my Pen. Thee, in thy favourite Fields, where the limpid, gently rolling *Thames* washes thy *Etonian* Banks,[2] in early Youth I have worshipped. To thee, at thy birchen Altar, with true *Spartan* Devotion, I have sacrificed my Blood. Come, then, and from thy vast, luxuriant Stores, in long Antiquity piled up, pour forth the rich Profusion. Open thy *Mæonian* and thy *Mantuan* Coffers, with whatever else includes thy Philosophic, thy Poetic, and thy Historical Treasures, whether with *Greek* or *Roman* Characters thou hast chosen to inscribe the ponderous Chests: Give me a-while that Key to all thy Treasures, which to thy *Warburton*[3] thou hast entrusted.

Lastly, come Experience long conversant with the Wise, the Good, the Learned, and the Polite. Nor with them only, but with every Kind of Character, from the Minister at his Levee, to the Bailiff in his Spunging-House; from the Dutchess at her Drum,[4] to the Landlady behind her Bar. From thee only can the Manners of Mankind be known; to which the recluse Pedant, however great his Parts, or extensive his Learning may be, hath ever been a Stranger.

---

[1] See above, pp. 3, n. 1; 4, n. 1.

[2] Fielding attended Eton from 1719 to 1724.

[3] William Warburton (1698–1779), later Bishop of Gloucester and the intimate acquaintance of Pope, whose works he edited in 1751, and of Ralph Allen (see the preceding paragraph), whose niece he married in 1745. Though arrogant and disputatious, Warburton was indeed a learned man and an able polemicist. His best-known works were *The Alliance between Church and State* (1736; 3rd ed., 1748) and *The Divine Legation of Moses demonstrated* (1738–41). Though Fielding does indeed seem to have admired Warburton's erudition, the present compliment appears somewhat disingenuous when placed against Fielding's earlier ridicule of Shakespeare's editors, the most recent of whom was Warburton himself. (See above, p. 523, n. 1.)   [4] See below, pp. 897–8.

Come all these, and more, if possible; for arduous is the Task I have undertaken: And without all your Assistance, will, I find, be too heavy for me to support. But if you all smile on my Labours, I hope still to bring them to a happy Conclusion.

CHAPTER II

What befel Mr. Jones *on his Arrival in* London.

THE learned Dr. *Misaubin*[1] used to say, that the proper Direction to him was, *To Dr.* Misaubin, *in the World*; intimating, that there were few People in it to whom his great Reputation was not known. And, perhaps, upon a very nice Examination into the Matter, we shall find that this Circumstance bears no inconsiderable Part among the many Blessings of Grandeur.

The great Happiness of being known to Posterity, with the Hopes of which we so delighted ourselves in the preceding Chapter, is the Portion of few. To have the several Elements which compose our Names, as *Sydenham* expresses it,[2] repeated a thousand Years hence, is a Gift beyond the Power of Title and Wealth; and is scarce to be purchased, unless by the Sword and the Pen. But to avoid the scandalous Imputation, while we yet live, of being *one whom No-body knows*, (a Scandal, by the by, as old as the Days of *Homer*)* will always be the envied

* See the 2d Odyssey, ver. 175.[3]

---

[1] See above, p. 240, n. 4.

[2] Dr. Thomas Sydenham (1624–89), 'the English Hippocrates', whose best-known work was 'A Treatise of the Gout and Dropsy' (originally published in Latin, 1683). In *The Champion* (3 May 1740), an essay on the vanity of fame, Fielding had quoted the entire passage to which he here alludes, using the English translation of Dr. John Pechey. Philosophically remarking on the transiency of worldly reputation, Sydenham asks: 'For what Advantage will it be to me, after I am dead, that eight Alphabetical Elements, reduc'd into that Order that will compose my Name, shall be pronounc'd by those, who can no more frame an Idea of me in their Minds, than I can now conceive what those are to be, who will not know such as were dead in the foregoing Age . . .' (Dedication to 'A Treatise of the Gout and Dropsy', in Sydenham's *Whole Works*, trans. J. Pechey, 9th ed. [1729], p. 340). Fielding's admiration for 'the great *Sydenham*' is clear from *The True Patriot* (5 November 1745), where his name is linked with those of Shakespeare, Handel, and Coke.

[3] Alluding to Halitherses' prediction that, after an absence of twenty years, Odysseus would return home 'unknown to all'.

Portion of those, who have a legal Title either to Honour or Estate.

From that Figure, therefore, which the *Irish* Peer, who brought *Sophia* to Town, hath already made in this History, the Reader will conclude, doubtless, it must have been an easy Matter to have discovered his House in *London*, without knowing the particular Street or Square which he inhabited, since he must have been one *whom every Body knows*. To say the Truth, so it would have been to any of those Tradesmen who are accustomed to attend the Regions of the Great: For the Doors of the Great are generally no less easy to find, than it is difficult to get Entrance into them. But *Jones*, as well as *Partridge*, was an entire Stranger in *London*; and as he happened to arrive first in a Quarter of the Town, the Inhabitants of which have very little Intercourse with the Housholders of *Hanover* or *Grosvenor* Square, (for he entered through *Grays-Inn* Lane) so he rambled about some Time, before he could even find his Way to those happy Mansions, where Fortune segregates from the Vulgar, those magnanimous Heroes, the Descendants of antient *Britons*, *Saxons*, or *Danes*, whose Ancestors being born in better Days, by sundry Kinds of Merit, have entailed Riches and Honour on their Posterity.

Jones being at length arrived at those terrestrial *Elysian* Fields, would now soon have discovered his Lordship's Mansion; but the Peer unluckily quitted his former House when he went for *Ireland*; and as he was just entered into a new one, the Fame of his Equipage had not yet sufficiently blazed in the Neighbourhood: So that after a successless Enquiry till the Clock had struck Eleven, *Jones*, at last, yielded to the Advice of *Partridge*, and retreated to the *Bull* and *Gate* in *Holborn*,[1] that being the Inn where he had first alighted, and where he retired to enjoy that Kind of Repose, which usually attends Persons in his Circumstances.

Early in the Morning he again set forth in Pursuit of *Sophia*; and many a weary Step he took to no better Purpose than before. At last, whether it was that Fortune relented, or whether it was no longer in her Power to disappoint him, he came into the

---

[1] Situated in Holborn, the main road from London to the north-west, the Bull and Gate was a coaching house 'of very great business' (*The General Advertiser*, 23 March 1744). A print of the inn is reproduced in H. Phillips, *Mid-Georgian London* (1964), p. 201.

very Street which was honoured by his Lordship's Residence; and being directed to the House, he gave one gentle Rap at the Door.

The Porter, who, from the Modesty of the Knock, had conceived no high Idea of the Person approaching,[1] conceived but little better from the Appearance of Mr. *Jones*, who was drest in a Suit of Fustian, and had by his Side the Weapon formerly purchased of the Serjeant; of which, tho' the Blade might be composed of well-tempered Steel, the Handle was composed only of Brass, and that none of the brightest. When *Jones*, therefore, enquired after the young Lady, who had come to Town with his Lordship, this Fellow answered surlily, 'That there were no Ladies there.' *Jones* then desired to see the Master of the House; but was informed that his Lordship would see no Body that Morning. And upon growing more pressing, the Porter said, 'He had positive Orders to let no Person in; but if you think proper,' said he, 'to leave your Name, I will acquaint his Lordship; and if you call another Time, you shall know when he will see you.'

Jones now declared, 'that he had very particular Business with the young Lady, and could not depart without seeing her.' Upon which the Porter, with no very agreeable Voice or Aspect, affirmed, 'That there was no young Lady in that House, and,' consequently, 'none could he see;' adding, 'Sure you are the strangest Man I ever met with; for you will not take an Answer.'

I have often thought, that by the particular Description of *Cerberus* the Porter of Hell, in the 6th *Æneid*,[2] *Virgil* might possibly intend to satyrize the Porters of the great Men in his Time; the Picture, at least, resembles those who have the Honour to attend at the Doors of our great Men. The Porter in his Lodge, answers exactly to *Cerberus* in his Den, and, like him, must be appeased by a Sop, before Access can be gained to his Master. Perhaps *Jones* might have seen him in that Light, and have recollected the Passage, where the Sybil, in order to procure an Entrance for *Æneas*, presents the Keeper of the *Stygian* Avenue with such a Sop. *Jones*, in like Manner, now began to offer a Bribe to the human *Cerberus*, which a Footman overhearing, instantly advanced, and declared, 'if Mr. *Jones* would give him the Sum proposed, he would conduct him

---

[1] See below, p. 697, n. 1.　　　　[2] *Aeneid*, vi. 417–23.

to the Lady.' *Jones* instantly agreed, and was forthwith conducted to the Lodging of Mrs. *Fitzpatrick*, by the very Fellow
who had attended the Ladies thither the Day before.

Nothing more aggravates ill Success than the near Approach
to Good. The Gamester, who loses his Party at Piquet by a
single Point, laments his bad Luck ten Times as much as he who
never came within a Prospect of the Game. So in a Lottery, the
Proprietors of the next Numbers to that which wins the great
Prize, are apt to account themselves much more unfortunate
than their Fellow-Sufferers. In short, these kind of hair-breadth
Missings of Happiness, look like the Insults of Fortune, who
may be considered as thus playing Tricks with us, and wantonly
diverting herself at our Expence.

Jones, who more than once already had experienced this
frolicksome Disposition of the Heathen Goddess, was now again
doomed to be tantalized in the like Manner: For he arrived at the
Door of Mrs. *Fitzpatrick*, about ten Minutes after the Departure
of *Sophia*. He now addressed himself to the Waiting-woman
belonging to Mrs. *Fitzpatrick*; who told him the disagreeable
News, that the Lady was gone, but could not tell him whither;
and the same Answer he afterwards received from Mrs. *Fitzpatrick* herself. For as that Lady made no doubt but that Mr.
Jones was a Person detached from her Uncle *Western*, in Pursuit
of his Daughter, so she was too generous to betray her.

Though *Jones* had never seen Mrs. *Fitzpatrick*, yet he had
heard that a Cousin of *Sophia* was married to a Gentleman of that
Name. This, however, in the present Tumult of his Mind, never
once recurred to his Memory: But when the Footman, who had
conducted him from his Lordship's, acquainted him with the
great Intimacy between the Ladies, and with their calling each
other Cousin, he then recollected the Story of the Marriage which
he had formerly heard; and as he was presently convinced that
this was the same Woman, he became more surprized at the
Answer which he had received, and very earnestly desired Leave
to wait on the Lady herself; but she as positively refused him
that Honour.

Jones, who, though he had never seen a Court, was better
bred than most who frequent it, was incapable of any rude or
abrupt Behaviour to a Lady. When he had received, therefore,
a peremptory Denial, he retired for the present, saying to the

Waiting-woman, 'That if this was an improper Hour to wait
on her Lady, he would return in the Afternoon; and that he
then hoped to have the Honour of seeing her.' The Civility with
which he uttered this, added to the great Comeliness of his Person, made an Impression on the Waiting-woman, and she could
not help answering; 'Perhaps, Sir, you may:' And, indeed, she
afterwards said every Thing to her Mistress, which she thought
most likely to prevail on her to admit a Visit from the handsome
young Gentleman; for so she called him.

Jones very shrewdly suspected, that *Sophia* herself was now
with her Cousin, and was denied to him; which he imputed to
her Resentment of what had happened at *Upton*. Having, therefore, dispatched *Partridge* to procure him Lodgings, he remained
all Day in the Street, watching the Door where he thought his
Angel lay concealed; but no Person did he see issue forth, except
a Servant of the House. And in the Evening he returned to pay
his Visit to Mrs. *Fitzpatrick*, which that good Lady at last condescended to admit.

There is a certain Air of natural Gentility, which it is neither
in the Power of Dress to give, nor to conceal. Mr. *Jones*, as hath
been before hinted, was possessed of this in a very eminent
Degree. He met, therefore, with a Reception from the Lady,
somewhat different from what his Apparel seemed to demand;
and after he had paid her his proper Respects, was desired to
sit down.

The Reader will not, I believe, be desirous of knowing all the
Particulars of this Conversation, which ended very little to the
Satisfaction of poor *Jones*. For though Mrs. *Fitzpatrick* soon discovered the Lover, (as all Women have the Eyes of Hawks in
those Matters) yet she still thought it was such a Lover, as a
generous Friend of the Lady should not betray her to. In short,
she suspected this was the very Mr. *Blifil*, from whom *Sophia*
had flown, and all the Answers which she artfully drew from
Jones, concerning Mr. *Allworthy's* Family, confirmed her in this
Opinion. She therefore strictly denied any Knowledge concerning the Place whither *Sophia* was gone; nor could *Jones* obtain
more than a Permission to wait on her again the next Evening.

When *Jones* was departed, Mrs. *Fitzpatrick* communicated her
Suspicion concerning Mr. *Blifil*, to her Maid; who answered,
'Sure, Madam, he is too pretty a Man, in my Opinion, for any

Woman in the World to run away from. I had rather fancy it is
Mr. *Jones.*'—'Mr. *Jones,*' said the Lady, 'what *Jones?*' For *Sophia*
had not given the least Hint of any such Person in all their Conversation: But Mrs. *Honour* had been much more communicative, and had acquainted her Sister *Abigail* with the whole History
of *Jones,* which this now again related to her Mistress.

Mrs. *Fitzpatrick* no sooner received this Information, than she
immediately agreed with the Opinion of her Maid; and, what is
very unaccountable, saw Charms in the gallant, happy Lover,
which she had overlooked in the slighted Squire. '*Betty,*' says
she, 'you are certainly in the right: He is a very pretty Fellow,
and I don't wonder that my Cousin's Maid should tell you so
many Women are fond of him. I am sorry now I did not inform
him where my Cousin was: And yet if he be so terrible a Rake
as you tell me, it is a Pity she should ever see him any more;
for what but her Ruin can happen from marrying a Rake and a
Beggar against her Father's Consent. I protest, if he be such a
Man as the Wench described him to you, it is but an Office of
Charity to keep her from him; and, I am sure, it would be unpardonable in me to do otherwise, who have tasted so bitterly of
the Misfortunes attending such Marriages.'

Here she was interrupted by the Arrival of a Visitor, which was
no other than his Lordship; and as nothing passed at this Visit
either new or extraordinary, or any Ways material to this History,
we shall here put an End to this Chapter.

CHAPTER III

A Project of Mrs. Fitzpatrick, *and her Visit to Lady* Bellaston.

WHEN Mrs. *Fitzpatrick* retired to Rest, her Thoughts were
entirely taken up by her Cousin *Sophia* and Mr. *Jones.*
She was, indeed, a little offended with the former, for the Dis-
ingenuity which she now discovered. In which Meditation she
had not long exercised her Imagination, before the following
Conceit suggested itself: That could she possibly become the
Means of preserving *Sophia* from this Man, and of restoring
her to her Father, she should, in all human Probability, by so

great a Service to the Family, reconcile to herself both her Uncle and her Aunt *Western*.

As this was one of her most favourite Wishes, so the Hope of Success seemed so reasonable, that nothing remained but to consider of proper Methods to accomplish her Scheme. To attempt to reason the Case with *Sophia*, did not appear to her one of those Methods: For as *Betty* had reported from Mrs. *Honour*, that *Sophia* had a violent Inclination to *Jones*, she conceived, that to dissuade her from the Match, was an Endeavour of the same Kind as it would be, very heartily and earnestly to entreat a Moth not to fly into a Candle.

If the Reader will please to remember, that the Acquaintance which *Sophia* had with Lady *Bellaston*, was contracted at the House of Mrs. *Western*, and must have grown at the very Time when Mrs. *Fitzpatrick* lived with this latter Lady, he will want no Information, that Mrs. *Fitzpatrick* must have been acquainted with her likewise. They were, besides, both equally her distant Relations.

After much Consideration, therefore, she resolved to go early in the Morning to that Lady, and endeavour to see her, unknown to *Sophia*, and to acquaint her with the whole Affair. For she did not in the least doubt, but that the prudent Lady, who had often ridiculed romantic Love, and indiscreet Marriages, in her Conversation, would very readily concur in her Sentiments concerning this Match, and would lend her utmost Assistance to prevent it.

This Resolution she accordingly executed; and the next Morning before the Sun, she huddled on her Cloaths, and at a very unfashionable, unseasonable, unvisitable Hour went to Lady *Bellaston*, to whom she got Access, without the least Knowledge or Suspicion of *Sophia*, who though not asleep, lay at that Time awake in her Bed, with *Honour* snoring by her Side.

Mrs. *Fitzpatrick* made many Apologies for this early, abrupt Visit, at an Hour 'when,' she said, 'she should not have thought of disturbing her Ladyship, but upon Business of the utmost Consequence.' She then opened the whole Affair, told all she had heard from *Betty*; and did not forget the Visit which *Jones* had paid to herself the preceding Evening.

Lady *Bellaston* answered with a Smile, 'Then you have seen this terrible Man, Madam; pray is he so very fine a Figure as he is represented? For *Etoff* entertained me last Night almost two Hours with him. The Wench I believe is in Love with him by Reputation.' Here the Reader will be apt to wonder, but the Truth is that Mrs. *Etoff* who had the Honour to pin and unpin the Lady *Bellaston*, had received complete Information concerning the said Mr. *Jones*, and had faithfully conveyed the same to her Lady last Night (or rather that Morning) while she was undressing; on which Accounts she had been detained in her Office above the Space of an Hour and a half.

The Lady indeed, though generally well enough pleased with the Narratives of Mrs. *Etoff* at those Seasons, gave an extraordinary Attention to her Account of *Jones*, for *Honour* had described him as a very handsome Fellow, and Mrs. *Etoff* in her Hurry added so much to the Beauty of his Person to her Report, that Lady *Bellaston* began to conceive him to be a kind of Miracle in Nature.

The Curiosity which her Woman had inspired, was now greatly increased by Mrs. *Fitzpatrick*, who spoke as much in Favour of the Person of *Jones*, as she had before spoken in Dispraise of his Birth, Character and Fortune.

When Lady *Bellaston* had heard the whole, she answered gravely, 'Indeed Madam, this is a Matter of great Consequence. Nothing can certainly be more commendable than the Part you act, and I shall be very glad to have my Share in the Preservation of a young Lady of so much Merit, and for whom I have so much Esteem.'

'Doth not your Ladyship think,' says Mrs. *Fitzpatrick* eagerly, 'that it would be the best Way to write immediately to my Uncle, and acquaint him where my Cousin is?'

The Lady pondered a little upon this, and thus answered—'Why, no, Madam, I think not. *Di Western* hath described her Brother to me to be such a Brute, that I cannot consent to put any Woman under his Power who hath escaped from it. I have heard he behaved like a Monster to his own Wife; for he is one of those Wretches who think they have a Right to tyrannize over us, and from such I shall ever esteem it the Cause of my Sex to rescue any Woman who is so unfortunate to be under their Power.—The Business, dear Cousin, will be only to keep Miss *Western* from seeing this young Fellow, till the good Company, which she will have an Opportunity of meeting here, give her a properer Turn.'

'If he should find her out, Madam,' answered the other, 'your Ladyship may be assured he will leave nothing unattempted to come at her.'

'But Madam,' replied the Lady, 'it is impossible he should come here,—tho' indeed it is possible he may get some Intelligence where she is, and then may lurk about the House.—I wish therefore I knew his Person.

'Is there no Way, Madam, by which I could have a Sight of him? For otherwise you know, Cousin, she may contrive to see him here without my Knowledge.' Mrs. *Fitzpatrick* answer'd, 'that he had threatened her with another Visit that Afternoon, and that if her Ladyship pleased to do her the Honour of calling upon her then, she would hardly fail of seeing him between six and seven, and if he came earlier she would, by some Means or other, detain him till her Ladyship's Arrival.'—Lady *Bellaston* replied, 'she would come the Moment she could get from Dinner, which she supposed would be by seven at farthest, for that it was absolutely necessary she should be acquainted with his Person. Upon my Word, Madam,' says she, 'it was very good to take this Care of Miss *Western*, but common Humanity as well as Regard to our Family requires it of us both, for it would be a dreadful Match indeed.'

Mrs. *Fitzpatrick* failed not to make a proper Return to the Compliment which Lady *Bellaston* had bestow'd on her Cousin, and after some little immaterial Conversation withdrew, and getting as fast as she could into her Chair unseen by *Sophia* or *Honour*, returned home.

CHAPTER IV

Which consists of Visiting.

MR. *Jones* had walked within Sight of a certain Door during the whole Day, which, though one of the shortest,[1] appeared to him to be one of the longest in the whole Year. At length the Clock having struck five he returned to Mrs. *Fitz-*

---

[1] The assumption of most critics that Fielding organized the time-scheme of his novel in strict conformity to almanac and calendar seems doubtful. (See above, p. 435, n. 1.) According to this scheme, however, the date at this point in the narrative would be 5 December 1745, a Thursday.

patrick, who, though it was a full Hour earlier than the decent Time of visiting, receiv'd him very civilly; but still persisted in her Ignorance concerning *Sophia*.

Jones in asking for his Angel, had drop'd the Word Cousin; upon which Mrs. *Fitzpatrick* said, 'Then, Sir, you know we are related, and as we are, you will permit me the Right of enquiring into the Particulars of your Business with my Cousin.' Here *Jones* hesitated a good while, and at last answered, He had a considerable Sum of Money of hers in his Hands, which he desired to deliver to her. He then produced the Pocket-book, and acquainted Mrs. *Fitzpatrick* with the Contents, and with the Method in which they came into his Hands. He had scarce finished his Story when a most violent Noise shook the whole House. To attempt to describe this Noise to those who have heard it would be in vain, and to aim at giving any Idea of it to those who have never heard the like, would be still more vain: For it may be truly said,

———*Non acuta*
Sic geminant Corybantes Æra.[1]

The Priests of Cybele *do not so rattle their sounding Brass.*

In short a Footman knocked, or rather thundered at the Door. *Jones* was a little surprised at the Sound, having never heard it before; but Mrs. *Fitzpatrick* very calmly said, that as some Company were coming, she could not make him any Answer now; but if he pleased to stay till they were gone, she intimated she had something to say to him.

The Door of the Room now flew open, and, after pushing in her Hoop sideways before her,[2] entered Lady *Bellaston*, who

[1] Horace, *Odes*, I. xvi. 7–8. Cf. *Joseph Andrews* (IV. ix): when Beau Didapper mimics with his cane the ear-shattering rap of a London footman, Adams and his guests are thrown into confusion.

[2] Though the hoop-petticoat had been popular since the beginning of the century, in the early 1740s the introduction of 'the great hoop', which projected seven feet and more in either direction, was greeted by the men with a mixture of amusement and dismay, and it provoked a flurry of satires. In one of these—*The Enormous Abomination of the Hoop-Petticoat, as the Fashion Now is, And has been for about these Two Years Fully Display'd* (1745)—a certain 'A. W.' complained that 'this *prodigious Garment*' had become 'a perfect *publick Nuisance*' (p. 7). From the writer's description of 'the Fine Lady *coming into a Room*', one may imagine the spectacle Lady Bellaston presented: 'First *enters* wriggling, and sideling, and edging in by degrees, Two Yards and a half of *Hoop*; for as yet you see nothing else. Some time after appears the *Inhabitant* of the Garment herself; not with a

having first made a very low Curtesy to Mrs. *Fitzpatrick*, and as low a one to Mr. *Jones*, was ushered to the upper End of the Room.

We mention these minute Matters for the Sake of some Country Ladies of our Acquaintance, who think it contrary to the Rules of Modesty to bend their Knees to a Man.

The Company were hardly well settled, before the Arrival of the Peer lately mentioned caused a fresh Disturbance and a Repetition of Ceremonials.

These being over, the Conversation began to be (as the Phrase is) extremely brilliant. However, as nothing past in it which can be thought material to this History, or, indeed, very material in itself, I shall omit the Relation; the rather as I have known some very fine polite Conversation grow extreamly dull, when transcribed into Books,[1] or repeated on the Stage. Indeed this mental Repast is a Dainty, of which those who are excluded from polite Assemblies, must be contented to remain as ignorant as they must of the several Dainties of *French* Cookery, which are served only at the Tables of the Great. To say the Truth, as neither of these are adapted to every Taste, they might both be often thrown away on the Vulgar.

Poor *Jones* was rather a Spectator of this elegant Scene, than an Actor in it; for though in the short Interval before the Peer's Arrival, Lady *Bellaston* first, and afterwards Mrs. *Fitzpatrick*, had addressed some of their Discourse to him; yet no sooner was the noble Lord entered, than he engrossed the whole Attention of the two Ladies to himself; and as he took no more Notice of *Jones* than if no such Person had been present, unless by now and then staring at him, the Ladies followed his Example.

The Company had now staid so long, that Mrs. *Fitzpatrick* plainly perceived they all designed to stay out each other. She

full Face, but in Profile; the Face being turn'd to, or from the Company, according as they happen to be situated. Next, in due time again, follows Two Yards and a half of *Hoop* more. And now her whole Person, with all its Appurtenances, is *actually* arriv'd, fully and completely in the Room . . .' (pp. 10–11). The testy protestations of this unfashionable gentleman were answered by the gallant 'Jack Lovelass' in *The Hoop-Petticoat Vindicated* (1745). But the issue was not soon forgotten. In 1748 an anonymous Oxonian published a 'heroi-comical' poem called *The Hoop-Petticoat*, and hoops were among the 'Comical Humours of the Town' satirized in Fielding's puppet theatre (see Battestin, *PQ*, xlv [1966], 201).

1 e.g. Swift's—or rather 'Simon Wagstaff's'—*Complete Collection of Genteel and Ingenious Conversation* (1738).

therefore resolved to rid herself of *Jones*, he being the Visitant, to whom she thought the least Ceremony was due. Taking therefore an Opportunity of a Cessation of Chat, she addressed herself gravely to him, and said, 'Sir, I shall not possibly be able to give you an Answer To-night, as to that Business; but if you please to leave Word where I may send to you To-morrow——'

Jones had natural, but not artificial good Breeding. Instead therefore of communicating the Secret of his Lodgings to a Servant, he acquainted the Lady herself with it particularly, and soon after very ceremoniously withdrew.

He was no sooner gone, than the great Personages who had taken no Notice of him present, began to take much Notice of him in his Absence; but if the Reader hath already excused us from relating the more brilliant Part of this Conversation, he will surely be very ready to excuse the Repetition of what may be called vulgar Abuse: Though, perhaps, it may be material to our History to mention an Observation of Lady *Bellaston*, who took her Leave in a few Minutes after him, and then said to Mrs. *Fitzpatrick*, at her Departure. 'I am satisfied on the Account of my Cousin, she can be in no Danger from this Fellow.'

Our History shall follow the Example of Lady *Bellaston*, and take Leave of the present Company, which was now reduced to two Persons; between whom, as nothing passed, which in the least concerns us or our Reader, we shall not suffer ourselves to be diverted by it from Matters which must seem of more Consequence to all those who are at all interested in the Affairs of our Heroe.

CHAPTER V

An Adventure which happened to Mr. Jones, *at his Lodgings, with some Account of a young Gentleman who lodged there, and of the Mistress of the House, and her two Daughters.*

THE next Morning as early as it was decent, *Jones* attended at Mrs. *Fitzpatrick's* Door, where he was answered that the Lady was not at Home; an Answer which surprised him the more, as he had walked backwards and forwards in the Street from Break of Day; and if she had gone out, he must have seen her. This Answer, however, he was obliged to receive, and not only now, but to five several Visits which he made her that Day. To be plain with the Reader, the noble Peer had from some Reason or other, perhaps from a Regard for the Lady's Honour, insisted that she should not see Mr. *Jones*, whom he looked on as a Scrub, any more; and the Lady had complied in making that Promise to which we now see her so strictly adhere.

But as our gentle Reader may possibly have a better Opinion of the young Gentleman than her Ladyship, and may even have some Concern, should it be apprehended, that during this unhappy Separation from *Sophia*, he took up his Residence either at an Inn, or in the Street; we shall now give an Account of his Lodging, which was indeed in a very reputable House, and in a very good Part of the Town.

Mr. *Jones* then had often heard Mr. *Allworthy* mention the Gentlewoman at whose House he used to lodge when he was in Town. This Person, who as *Jones* likewise knew, lived in *Bond-Street*, was the Widow of a Clergyman, and was left by him at his Decease, in Possession of two Daughters, and of a compleat Set of Manuscript Sermons.[1]

Of these two Daughters, *Nancy*, the elder, was now arrived at the Age of seventeen, and *Betty*, the younger, at that of ten.

Hither *Jones* had dispatched *Partridge*, and in this House he was provided with a Room for himself in the second Floor, and with one for *Partridge* in the fourth.

The first Floor was inhabited by one of those young Gentlemen, who, in the last Age were called Men of Wit and Pleasure about Town, and properly enough: For as Men are usually denominated from their Business or Profession, so Pleasure may be said to have been the only Business or Profession of those Gentlemen to whom Fortune had made all useful Occupations unnecessary. Play-Houses, Coffee-Houses and Taverns were the Scenes of their Rendezvous. Wit and Humour were the Entertainment of their looser Hours, and Love was the Business of their more serious Moments. Wine and the Muses conspired to kindle the brightest Flames in their Breasts; nor did they only admire, but some were able to celebrate the Beauty they admired, and all to judge of the Merit of such Compositions.

Such therefore were properly called the Men of Wit and

---

[1] See above, p. 205, n. 1.

Pleasure; but I question whether the same Appellation may, with the same Propriety, be given to those young Gentlemen of our Times, who have the same Ambition to be distinguished for Parts. Wit certainly they have nothing to do with. To give them their due, they soar a Step higher than their Predecessors, and may be called Men of Wisdom and *Vertù*[1] (take heed you do not read Virtue). Thus at an Age when the Gentlemen abovementioned employed their Time in toasting the Charms of a Woman, or in making Sonnets in her Praise; in giving their Opinion of a Play at the Theatre, or of a Poem at *Will's* or *Button's*;[2] these Gentlemen are considering of Methods to bribe a Corporation, or meditating Speeches for the House of Commons, or rather for the Magazines.[3] But the Science of Gaming is that which above all others employs their Thoughts. These are the Studies of their graver Hours, while for their Amusements they have the vast Circle of Connoisseurship, Painting, Music, Statuary, and natural Philosophy, or rather *unnatural*, which deals in the Wonderful, and knows nothing of Nature, except her Monsters and Imperfections.[4]

[1] Love of the fine arts. Cf. Joseph Spence in *Polymetis* (1747), speaking of Italy past and present: 'As this people was of so military a turn, they generally gave Fortitude the name of Virtus, or the Virtue, by way of excellence: just as the same nation, now they are so debased and effeminated, call the love of the softer arts, Vertù' (p. 139).

[2] In the early part of the century these famous coffee-houses, situated in Russell Street, Covent Garden, were the favourite haunts of a brilliant circle of writers and wits. Will's, where Dryden had presided, maintained its reputation as 'the Wits' Coffee House' for some years, and from it Steele in *The Tatler* (1709–10) dated his literary articles. Soon after 1712–13, however, that enviable title passed to Button's, where Addison met with his 'Little Senate'.

[3] Since it was illegal to publish verbatim reports of the debates in Parliament, the editors of such periodicals as *The Gentleman's Magazine* (est. 1731) and *The London Magazine* (est. 1732) employed hackney authors to produce summaries of the proceedings from notes; owing less to fact than to the writer's imagination, these reports were quite untrustworthy. The best-known example is Samuel Johnson's series, 'Debates in the Senate of Lilliput', which ran in *The Gentleman's Magazine* (1741–3).

[4] Like Pope, Fielding believed that the philosopher, as well as the poet, must first follow Nature—by which he understood not the Baconian realm of shifting particularities, but rather the Christian humanist conception of *la belle Nature*, Nature as ideal form and universal type. Thus he repeatedly criticized modern novel- and romance-writers for preferring 'the Marvellous' to 'the Probable' (VIII. i), filling their works 'with Monsters, the Productions, not of Nature, but of distempered Brains' (IV. i). In similar terms he scorned the scientists of the Royal Society who, by occupying themselves with freaks and oddities, had lost sight of Nature and of Nature's God. These 'Virtuoso's', he declared, were 'The first great Corrupters' of the public taste, their 'Dexterities' seducing men from their proper study of morality and art (letter xl of Sarah Fielding's *Familiar Letters* [1747]). They were

When *Jones* had spent the whole Day in vain Enquiries after Mrs. *Fitzpatrick*, he returned at last disconsolate to his Apartment. Here while he was venting his Grief in private, he heard a violent Uproar below Stairs; and soon after a female Voice begged him for Heaven's Sake to come and prevent Murder. *Jones*, who was never backward on any Occasion, to help the Distressed, immediately ran down Stairs; when stepping into the Dining-room, whence all the Noise issued, he beheld the young Gentleman of Wisdom and *Vertù* just before mentioned, pinned close to the Wall by his Footman, and a young Woman standing by, wringing her Hands, and crying out, 'He will be murdered, he will be murdered;' and indeed the poor Gentleman seemed in some Danger of being choaked, when *Jones* flew hastily to his Assistance, and rescued him just as he was breathing his last, from the unmerciful Clutches of the Enemy.

Though the Fellow had received several Kicks and Cuffs from the little Gentleman, who had more Spirit than Strength, he had made it a kind of Scruple of Conscience to strike his Master, and would have contented himself with only choaking him; but towards *Jones* he bore no such Respect: He no sooner therefore found himself a little roughly handled by his new Antagonist, than he gave him one of those Punches in the Guts, which, tho' the Spectators at *Broughton's* Amphitheatre[1] have such exquisite Delight in Seeing them, convey but very little Pleasure in the Feeling.

The lusty Youth had no sooner received this Blow, than he meditated a most grateful Return; and now ensued a Combat between *Jones* and the Footman, which was very fierce, but short;

'*Triflers*' who busied themselves 'in hunting after Monsters of every Kind, as if they were at Enmity with Nature, and desirous of exposing all her Errors' (*The Covent-Garden Journal*, 24 March 1752). Later in *Tom Jones* (XVI. iii) Sophia's discovery of a letter concealed in a pullet leads to a further digression on the perverse interests of the virtuosi (see below, p. 842, n. 2). For a comprehensive analysis of Fielding's satires on the Royal Society, see H. K. Miller, *Fielding's 'Miscellanies'* (Princeton, N.J., 1961), pp. 315–31.

[1] John Broughton (1705–89), the most celebrated prize-fighter of his time, was champion from 1730 to 1750. From 1743 until it was closed by the legislature in 1750, Broughton's Amphitheatre in Oxford Road was the scene of bloody combats of all sorts—boxing matches, cudgel-playing, battles at broadsword. After one such exhibition resulted in a fighter's death, Fielding regretted '*the Encouragement of these Diversions*' in a Christian country (*The Jacobite's Journal*, 13 February 1748). See also the essay 'On Misery, and its Effects on MAN' in *The British Magazine*, iii (October 1748), 419–25, in which the writer similarly deplored the spectators' delight in cruelty (pp. 422–3). For other allusions to Broughton, see below, pp. 703, n. 1; 741, n. 2; and *Amelia* (XII. vi).

for this Fellow was no more able to contend with *Jones*, than his Master had before been to contend with him.

And now Fortune, according to her usual Custom, reversed the Face of Affairs, the former Victor lay breathless on the Ground, and the vanquished Gentleman had recovered Breath enough to thank Mr. *Jones* for his seasonable Assistance: He received likewise the hearty Thanks of the young Woman present, who was indeed no other than Miss *Nancy*, the eldest Daughter of the House.

The Footman having now recovered his Legs, shook his Head at *Jones*, and with a sagacious Look, cry'd,—O d—n me, I'll have nothing more to do with you, you have been upon the Stage, or I am d—nably mistaken: And indeed we may forgive this his Suspicion; for such was the Agility and Strength of our Heroe, that he was perhaps a Match for one of the first Rate Boxers, and could, with great Ease, have beaten all the muffled* Graduates of Mr. *Broughton's* School.

The Master foaming with Wrath, ordered his Man immediately to strip, to which the latter very readily agreed, on Condition of receiving his Wages. This Condition was presently complied with, and the Fellow was discharged.

And now the young Gentleman, whose Name was *Nightingale*, very strenuously insisted, that his Deliverer should take Part of a Bottle of Wine with him; to which *Jones*, after much

---

* Lest Posterity should be puzzled by this Epithet, I think proper to explain it by an Advertisement which was published *Feb*. 1. 1747.[1]

N. B. Mr. *Broughton* proposes, with proper Assistance, to open an Academy at his House in the *Hay-Market*, for the Instruction of those who are willing to be initiated in the Mystery of Boxing; where the whole Theory and Practice of that truly *British* Art, with all the various Stops, Blows, Cross-Buttocks, &c. incident to Combatants, will be fully taught and explain'd; and that Persons of Quality and Distinction may not be deterred from entering into *a Course of these Lectures*, they will be given with the utmost Tenderness and Regard to the Delicacy of the Frame and Constitution of the Pupil, for which Reason Mufflers are provided, that will effectually secure them from the Inconveniency of black Eyes, broken Jaws, and bloody Noses.

---

1 Fielding's dating is old-style: the advertisement appeared in *The Daily Advertiser* on 1, 2, 4, and 10 February 1748. 'Mufflers' were boxing gloves. Commencing with the performance of 18 April 1748, 'Muffle-Boxing' was another of the 'Comical Humours of the Town' ridiculed in Fielding's puppet theatre (see Battestin, *PQ*, xlv [1966], 201). With Fielding's views on the comfortable heroism of those who attended Broughton's 'Academy', compare William Kenrick in *The Town* (1748): 'Mufflers for those the naked Fist may fright,/ For here young Lords and Puppies learn to fight' (p. 24).

Entreaty, consented; tho' more out of Complaisance than Inclination; for the Uneasiness of his Mind fitted him very little for Conversation at this Time. Miss *Nancy* likewise, who was the only Female then in the House, her Mamma and Sister being both gone to the Play, condescended to favour them with her Company.

When the Bottle and Glasses were on the Table, the Gentleman began to relate the Occasion of the preceding Disturbance.

'I hope, Sir,' said he to *Jones*, 'you will not, from this Accident, conclude, that I make a Custom of striking my Servants; for I assure you this is the first Time I have been guilty of it in my Remembrance, and I have passed by many provoking Faults in this very Fellow, before he could provoke me to it; but when you hear what hath happened this Evening, you will, I believe, think me excuseable. I happened to come home several Hours before my usual Time, when I found four Gentlemen of the Cloth at Whisk by my Fire;—and my *Hoyle*, Sir,—my best *Hoyle*,[1] which cost me a Guinea, lying open on the Table, with a Quantity of Porter spilt on one of the most material Leaves of the whole Book. This, you will allow, was provoking; but I said nothing till the rest of the honest Company were gone, and then gave the Fellow a gentle Rebuke, who, instead of expressing any Concern, made me a pert Answer, "That Servants must have their Diversions as well as other People; that he was sorry for the Accident which had happened to the Book; but that several of his Acquaintance had bought the same for a Shilling; and that I might stop as much in his Wages if I pleased:" I now gave him a severer Reprimand than before, when the Rascal had the Insolence to—— In short he imputed my early coming Home to—— In short, he cast a Reflection,—— He mentioned the Name of a young Lady, in a Manner—— In such a Manner that incensed me beyond all Patience, and, in my Passion, I struck him.'

---

[1] Edmond Hoyle (1672–1769), author of *A Short Treatise on the Game of Whist, containing the Laws of the Game*, of which the first edition (1742) sold for a guinea a copy. This popular work, which had run through nine editions by 1748, made Hoyle the chief authority on the game until the mid nineteenth century. The rage for whist amused Fielding, as it did Hogarth (see Plate II of *Marriage à la Mode* [1745]). 'Whisk-Learning' is one of the 'Comical Humours of the Town' satirized in Fielding's puppet-theatre in 1748 (see Battestin, *PQ*, xlv [1966], 201); and in *The Covent-Garden Journal* (25 July 1752) 'the Whist Master' is said, 'of Modern Times', to be necessary to forming the character of a town lady.

Jones answered, 'That he believed no Person living would blame him; for my Part,' said he, 'I confess I should, on the last mentioned Provocation, have done the same Thing.'

Our Company had not sat long before they were joined by the Mother and Daughter, at their Return from the Play. And now they all spent a very chearful Evening together, for all but *Jones* were heartily merry, and even he put on as much constrained Mirth as possible. Indeed half his natural Flow of animal Spirits, joined to the Sweetness of his Temper, was sufficient to make a most amiable Companion; and notwithstanding the Heaviness of his Heart, so agreeable did he make himself on the present Occasion, that, at their breaking up, the young Gentleman earnestly desired his further Acquaintance. Miss *Nancy* was well pleased with him; and the Widow, quite charm'd with her new Lodger, invited him with the other, next Morning to Breakfast.

Jones, on his Part, was no less satisfied. As for Miss *Nancy*, tho' a very little Creature, she was extremely pretty, and the Widow had all the Charms which can adorn a Woman near fifty. As she was one of the most innocent Creatures in the World, so she was one of the most chearful. She never thought, nor spoke, nor wished any ill, and had constantly that Desire of pleasing, which may be called the happiest of all Desires in this, that it scarce ever fails of attaining its Ends, when not disgraced by Affectation. In short, though her Power was very small, she was in her Heart one of the warmest Friends. She had been a most affectionate Wife, and was a most fond and tender Mother.

As our History doth not, like a News-Paper, give great Characters to People who never were heard of before, nor will ever be heard of again;[1] the Reader may hence conclude, that this excellent Woman will hereafter appear to be of some Importance in our History.

---

[1] In his own periodicals, Fielding was fond of ridiculing the 'puffs' of newspaper writers, to whom every bride was a young lady 'of great Beauty, Merit, and Fortune' and every deceased shopkeeper a person '*of great Eminence*' (*The Jacobite's Journal*, 13 February 1748). Cf. the parody of Bridget Allworthy's wedding-notice, p. 78. 11–12. With the phrasing of the present passage compare *The Champion* (28 February 1739/40), which reports such puffs on behalf of 'Several Persons dead, who were never heard of while they liv'd. And some preferr'd, who will never be heard of any more till they die.' For other examples from Fielding's journals, see Glenn W. Hatfield, *Henry Fielding and the Language of Irony* (Chicago, Ill., 1968), pp. 86–8.

Nor was *Jones* a little pleased with the young Gentleman himself, whose Wine he had been drinking. He thought he discerned in him much good Sense, though a little too much tainted with Town Foppery; but what recommended him most to *Jones* were some Sentiments of great Generosity and Humanity, which occasionally dropt from him; and particularly many Expressions of the highest Disinterestedness in the Affair of Love. On which Subject the young Gentleman delivered himself in a Language which might have very well become an *Arcadian* Shepherd of Old, and which appeared very extraordinary when proceeding from the Lips of a modern fine Gentleman, but he was only one by Imitation, and meant by Nature for a much better Character.

CHAPTER VI

What arrived while the Company were at Breakfast, with some Hints concerning the Government of Daughters.

OUR Company brought together in the Morning the same good Inclinations towards each other, with which they had separated the Evening before; but poor *Jones* was extreme disconsolate; for he had just received Information from *Partridge*, that Mrs. *Fitzpatrick* had left her Lodging, and that he could not learn whither she was gone. This News highly afflicted him, and his Countenance, as well as his Behaviour, in Defiance of all his Endeavours to the contrary, betrayed manifest Indications of a disordered Mind.

The Discourse turned at present, as before, on Love; and Mr. *Nightingale* again expressed many of those warm, generous, and disinterested Sentiments upon this Subject, which wise and sober Men call romantic, but which wise and sober Women generally regard in a better Light. Mrs. *Miller*, (for so the Mistress of the House was called) greatly approved these Sentiments; but when the young Gentleman appealed to Miss *Nancy*, she answered only, 'That she believed the Gentleman who had spoke the least, was capable of feeling the most.'

This Compliment was so apparently directed to *Jones*, that we should have been sorry had he passed it by unregarded. He made her indeed a very polite Answer, and concluded with an oblique Hint, that her own Silence subjected her to a Suspicion of the same Kind: For indeed she had scarce opened her Lips either now, or the last Evening.

'I am glad, *Nancy*,' says Mrs. *Miller*, 'the Gentleman hath made the Observation; I protest I am almost of his Opinion. What can be the Matter with you, Child? I never saw such an Alteration. What is become of all your Gayety? Would you think, Sir, I used to call her my little Prattler. She hath not spoke twenty Words this Week.'

Here their Conversation was interrupted by the Entrance of a Maid-Servant, who brought a Bundle in her Hands, which, she said, 'was delivered by a Porter for Mr. *Jones*.' She added, 'that the Man immediately went away, saying, it required no Answer.'

Jones expressed some Surprize on this Occasion, and declared it must be some Mistake: But the Maid persisting that she was certain of the Name, all the Women were desirous of having the Bundle immediately opened; which Operation was at length performed by little *Betsy*, with the Consent of Mr. *Jones*; and the Contents were found to be a Domino, a Mask, and a Masquerade Ticket.

Jones was now more positive than ever, in asserting, that these Things must have been delivered by Mistake; and Mrs. *Miller* herself expressed some Doubt, and said, 'she knew not what to think.' But when Mr. *Nightingale* was asked, he delivered a very different Opinion. 'All I can conclude from it, Sir,' said he, 'is, that you are a very happy Man: For I make no doubt but these were sent you by some Lady whom you will have the Happiness of meeting at the Masquerade.'

Jones had not a sufficient Degree of Vanity to entertain any such flattering Imagination; nor did Mrs. *Miller* herself give much Assent to what Mr. *Nightingale* had said, till Miss *Nancy* having lifted up the Domino, a Card dropt from the Sleeve, in which was written as follows:

To Mr. Jones.
The Queen of the Fairies sends you this,
Use her Favours not amiss.

Mrs. *Miller* and Miss *Nancy* now both agreed with Mr. *Nightingale*; nay, *Jones* himself was almost persuaded to be of the same Opinion. And as no other Lady but Mrs. *Fitzpatrick*, he thought, knew his Lodging, he began to flatter himself with some

Hopes, that it came from her, and that he might possibly see his *Sophia*. These Hopes had surely very little Foundation; but as the Conduct of Mrs. *Fitzpatrick*, in not seeing him according to her Promise, and in quitting her Lodgings, had been very odd and unaccountable, he conceived some faint Hopes, that she (of whom he had formerly heard a very whimsical Character) might possibly intend to do him that Service, in a strange Manner, which she declined doing by more ordinary Methods. To say the Truth, as nothing certain could be concluded from so odd and uncommon an Incident, he had the greater Latitude to draw what imaginary Conclusions from it he pleased. As his Temper therefore was naturally sanguine, he indulged it on this Occasion, and his Imagination worked up a thousand Conceits, to favour and support his Expectations of meeting his dear *Sophia* in the Evening.

Reader, if thou hast any good Wishes towards me, I will fully repay them, by wishing thee to be possessed of this sanguine Disposition of Mind: Since, after having read much, and considered long on that Subject of Happiness which hath employed so many great Pens, I am almost inclined to fix it in the Possession of this Temper; which puts us, in a Manner, out of the Reach of Fortune, and makes us happy without her Assistance. Indeed the Sensations of Pleasure it gives are much more ·constant, as well as much keener than those which that blind Lady bestows; Nature having wisely contrived, that some Satiety and Languor should be annexed to all our real Enjoyments, lest we should be so taken up by them, as to be stopt from further Pursuits. I make no Manner of doubt but that, in this Light, we may see the imaginary future Chancellor just called to the Bar, the Archbishop in Crape, and the Prime-Minister at the Tail of an Opposition, more truly happy than those who are invested with all the Power and Profit of these respective Offices.

Mr. *Jones* having now determined to go to the Masquerade that Evening, Mr. *Nightingale* offered to conduct him thither. The young Gentleman, at the same Time, offered Tickets to Miss *Nancy* and her Mother; but the good Woman would not accept them. She said, 'She did not conceive the Harm which some People imagined in a Masquerade;[1] but that such

---

[1] This fashionable diversion—'that nocturnal Sacrifice to *Bacchus* and *Venus*' presided over by the notorious 'Count' Heidegger (see below, p. 712, n. 2)—had for some years

extravagant Diversions were proper only for Persons of Quality and Fortune, and not for young Women who were to get their Living, and could, at best, hope to be married to a good Tradesman.'—'A Tradesman!' cries *Nightingale*, 'you shan't undervalue my *Nancy*. There is not a Nobleman upon Earth above her Merit.' 'O fie! Mr. *Nightingale*,' answered Mrs. *Miller*, 'you must not fill the Girl's Head with such Fancies: But if it was her good Luck (says the Mother with a Simper) to find a Gentleman of your generous Way of thinking, I hope she would make a better Return to his Generosity, than to give her Mind up to extravagant Pleasures. Indeed where young Ladies bring great Fortunes themselves, they have some Right to insist on spending what is their own; and on that Account, I have heard the Gentlemen say, a Man has sometimes a better Bargain with a poor Wife, than with a rich one.—But let my Daughters marry whom they will, I shall endeavour to make them Blessings to their Husbands:—I beg, therefore, I may hear of no more Masquerades. *Nancy* is, I am certain, too good a Girl to desire to go; for she must remember when you carried her thither last Year, it almost turned her Head; and she did not return to herself, or to her Needle, in a Month afterwards.'

drawn the fire of critics, Fielding among them, who felt that few institutions quite so effectually served to corrupt the public morality. By 1726 masquerades had become so scandalous that a royal proclamation was issued against them, and in 1729 a Middlesex grand jury presented Heidegger as 'the principal promoter of vice and immorality'. Yet these entertainments continued to flourish. Even while the rebellion swept the north in 1745–6, the time of Fielding's narrative, lovers of pleasure crowded these 'lewd and dissolute Assemblies', much to the dismay of patriotic moralists: see, for instance, 'VERSES on the Affront offered to the Nation by a late PUBLIC MASQUERADE', *The Gentleman's Magazine*, xv (October 1745), 551; and 'Seasonable Reflections upon the late Frequency of Masquerades, and other publick Diversions', *The British Magazine*, i (March 1746), 13–15. That Mrs. Miller might well have 'conceived the Harm' to her daughter from these assemblies is clear from an article 'On Masquerades' in *The Craftsman* (10 January 1747), in which the writer asks: 'Would any parent wish his child to frequent an entertainment which consists of a large number of persons of both sexes in masks and antick dresses, where the principal conversation consists in abusive raillery and obscene discourse convey'd in whispers, with a continuance of musick and dancing to assist the designs of young fellows in their amours there, and where they have a variety of viands to heat them? All which are favourable instruments of debauchery' (quoted in *The Gentleman's Magazine*, xvii [January 1747], 35).

Fielding's first published work was the verse satire *The Masquerade* (1728), ironically dedicated to 'C——t H—D—G—R', and he continued his attacks throughout his career: see, for example, *The Champion* (19 February 1739/40), *Miss Lucy in Town* (1742), *A Charge delivered to the Grand Jury* (1749), *An Enquiry into the Causes of the late Increase of Robbers* (1751), section i; and *Amelia* (1751; x. ii–iv).

Though a gentle Sigh which stole from the Bosom of *Nancy*, seemed to argue some secret Disapprobation of these Sentiments, she did not dare openly to oppose them. For as this good Woman had all the Tenderness, so she had preserved all the Authority of a Parent; and as her Indulgence to the Desires of her Children, was restrained only by her Fears for their Safety and future Welfare, so she never suffered those Commands, which proceeded from such Fears, to be either disobeyed or disputed. And this the young Gentleman who had lodged two Years in the House, knew so well, that he presently acquiesced in the Refusal.

Mr. *Nightingale*, who grew every Minute fonder of *Jones*, was very desirous of his Company that Day to Dinner at the Tavern, where he offered to introduce him to some of his Acquaintance; but *Jones* begged to be excused, 'as his Cloaths,' he said, 'were not yet come to Town.'

To confess the Truth, Mr. *Jones* was now in a Situation, which sometimes happens to be the Case of young Gentlemen of much better Figure than himself. In short, he had not one Penny in his Pocket; a Situation in much greater Credit among the ancient Philosophers, than among the modern wise Men who live in *Lombard* Street,[1] or those who frequent *White's* Chocolate-House.[2] And, perhaps, the great Honours which those Philosophers have ascribed to an empty Pocket, may be one of the Reasons of that high Contempt in which they are held in the aforesaid Street and Chocolate-House.

Now if the antient Opinion, that Men might live very comfortably on Virtue only, be, as the modern wise Men just above-mentioned pretend to have discovered, a notorious Error; no less false is, I apprehend, that Position of some Writers of Romance, that a Man can live altogether on Love: For however delicious Repasts this may afford to some of our Senses or Appetites, it is most certain it can afford none to others. Those, therefore, who have placed too great a Confidence in such Writers, have experienced their Error when it was too late; and have found that Love was no more capable of allaying Hunger, than a Rose is capable of delighting the Ear, or a Violin of gratifying the Smell.

---

[1] This street in the City of London was inhabited chiefly by bankers, goldsmiths, and merchants.

[2] White's in St. James's Street was a private club, the resort especially of fashionable gamblers.

Notwithstanding, therefore, all the Delicacies which Love had set before him, namely, the Hopes of seeing *Sophia* at the Masquerade; on which, however ill-founded his Imagination might be, he had voluptuously feasted during the whole Day, the Evening no sooner came, than Mr. *Jones* began to languish for some Food of a grosser Kind. *Partridge* discovered this by Intuition, and took the Occasion to give some oblique Hints concerning the Bank-bill, and when those were rejected with Disdain, he collected Courage enough once more to mention a Return to Mr. *Allworthy*.

'*Partridge*,' cries *Jones*, 'you cannot see my Fortune in a more desperate Light than I see it myself; and I begin heartily to repent, that I suffered you to leave a Place, where you was settled, and to follow me. However, I insist now on your returning Home; and for the Expence and Trouble which you have so kindly put yourself to on my Account, all the Cloaths I left behind in your Care, I desire you would take as your own. I am sorry I can make you no other Acknowledgment.'

He spoke these Words with so pathetic an Accent, that *Partridge*, among whose Vices Ill-Nature or Hardness of Heart were not numbered, burst into Tears; and after swearing he would not quit him in his Distress, he began with the most earnest Intreaties to urge his return Home. 'For Heaven's Sake, Sir,' says he, 'do but consider: What can your Honour do? How is it possible you can live in this Town without Money? Do what you will, Sir, or go wherever you please, I am resolved not to desert you.—But pray, Sir, consider,—Do pray, Sir, for your own Sake, take it into your Consideration; and I'm sure,' says he, 'that your own Good-Sense will bid you return Home.'

'How often shall I tell thee,' answered *Jones*, 'that I have no Home to return to. Had I any Hopes that Mr. *Allworthy's* Doors would be open to receive me, I want no Distress to urge me:—Nay, there is no other Cause upon Earth, which could detain me a Moment from flying to his Presence, but, alas! that I am for ever banished from it. His last Words were,—O *Partridge*, they still ring in my Ears.—His last Words were, when he gave me a Sum of Money, what it was I know not, but considerable I'm sure it was.—His last Words were—"I am resolved from this Day forward, on no Account, to converse with you any more." '

Here Passion stopt the Mouth of *Jones*; as Surprize, for a Moment, did that of *Partridge*: But he soon recovered the Use of Speech, and after a short Preface, in which he declared he had no Inquisitiveness in his Temper, enquired, what *Jones* meant by a considerable Sum; he knew not how much; and what was become of the Money?

In both these Points he now received full Satisfaction; on which he was proceeding to comment, when he was interrupted by a Message from Mr. *Nightingale*, who desired his Master's Company in his Apartment.

When the two Gentlemen were both attired for the Masquerade, and Mr. *Nightingale* had given Orders for Chairs to be sent for, a Circumstance of Distress occurred to *Jones*, which will appear very ridiculous to many of my Readers. This was how to procure a Shilling;[1] but if such Readers will reflect a little on what they have themselves felt from the Want of a thousand Pound, or, perhaps, of ten or twenty, to execute a favourite Scheme, they will have a perfect Idea of what Mr. *Jones* felt on this Occasion. For this Sum, therefore, he applied to *Partridge*, which was the first he had permitted him to advance, and was the last he intended that poor Fellow should advance in his Service. To say the Truth, *Partridge* had lately made no Offer of this Kind; whether it was that he desired to see the Bank-bill broke in upon, or that Distress should prevail on *Jones* to return Home, or from what other Motive it proceeded, I will not determine.

CHAPTER VII

Containing the whole Humours of a Masquerade.

OUR Cavaliers now arrived at that Temple, where *Hey-degger*,[2] the great *Arbiter Deliciarum*, the great High-Priest of Pleasure presides; and, like other Heathen Priests, imposes on his Votaries by the pretended Presence of the Deity, when in reality no such Deity is there.

[1] In 1745, this was the rate for '*Hackney-Chairs*, for Distances not exceeding one Mile' (Parker's *Ephemeris for the Year of Our Lord 1745*, Sig. B7r).

[2] John James, known as 'Count', Heidegger (1659 ?–1749) was a Swiss immigrant who, though said to be the ugliest man in England, so ingratiated himself with London society

Mr. *Nightingale* having taken a Turn or two with his Companion, soon left him, and walked off with a Female, saying, 'Now you are here, Sir, you must beat about for your own Game.'

Jones began to entertain strong Hopes that his *Sophia* was present; and these Hopes gave him more Spirits than the Lights, the Music, and the Company; though these are pretty strong Antidotes against the Spleen. He now accosted every Woman he saw, whose Stature, Shape, or Air, bore any Resemblance to his Angel. To all of whom he endeavoured to say something smart, in order to engage an Answer, by which he might discover that Voice which he thought it impossible he should mistake. Some of these answered by a Question, in a squeaking Voice, *Do you know me?* Much the greater Numbers said, *I don't know you, Sir*; and nothing more. Some called him an impertinent Fellow; some made him no Answer at all; some said, *Indeed I don't know your Voice, and I shall have nothing to say to you*; and many gave him as kind Answers as he could wish, but not in the Voice he desired to hear.

Whilst he was talking with one of these last, (who was in the Habit of a Shepherdess) a Lady in a Domino came up to him, and slapping him on the Shoulder, whispered him, at the same Time, in the Ear, 'If you talk any longer with that Trollop, I will acquaint Miss *Western*.'

Jones no sooner heard that Name, than, immediately quitting his former Companion, he applied to the Domino, begging and entreating her to shew him the Lady she had mentioned, if she was then in the Room.

The Mask walked hastily to the upper End of the innermost Apartment before she spoke, and then, instead of answering him, sat down, and declared she was tired. *Jones* sat down by her, and still persisted in his Entreaties; at last the Lady coldly answered, 'I imagined Mr. *Jones* had been a more discerning

by promoting masquerades and other fashionable entertainments that he became manager of the Opera House in the Haymarket (which Fielding calls his 'Temple') and was appointed Master of the Revels to George II. (On the masquerades over which Heidegger presided, see above, p. 708, n. 1.) In a note to *The Dunciad, A*, i. 244, Pope had compared him with Nero's favourite voluptuary, '*Petronius, Arbiter Elegantiarum*'. Fielding's *The Masquerade* (1728) was ironically dedicated to Heidegger, and in the puppet show in *The Author's Farce* (revised version, 1734) he appears as 'Count Ugly', paying court to the goddess of Nonsense and representing himself as '*Surintendant des plaisirs d'Angleterre*'. See also *The Champion*, 19 February 1739/40.

Lover, than to suffer any Disguise to conceal his Mistress from
him.' 'Is she here then, Madam?' replied *Jones*, with much
Vehemence. Upon which the Lady cry'd,—'Hush, Sir, you will
be observed.—I promise you, upon my Honour, Miss *Western*
is not here.'

Jones now taking the Mask by the Hand, fell to entreating
her in the most earnest Manner, to acquaint him where he might
find *Sophia*: And when he could obtain no direct Answer, he
began to upbraid her gently for having disappointed him the
Day before; and concluded, saying, 'Indeed, my good Fairy
Queen, I know your Majesty very well, notwithstanding the
affected Disguise of your Voice. Indeed, Mrs. *Fitzpatrick*, it is a
little cruel to divert yourself at the Expence of my Torments.'

The Mask answered, 'Though you have so ingeniously discovered me, I must still speak in the same Voice, lest I should
be known by others. And do you think, good Sir, that I have no
greater Regard for my Cousin, than to assist in carrying on an
Affair between you two, which must end in her Ruin, as well as
your own? Besides, I promise you, my Cousin is not mad enough
to consent to her own Destruction, if you are so much her
Enemy as to tempt her to it.'

'Alas, Madam,' said *Jones*, 'you little know my Heart, when
you call me an Enemy of *Sophia*.'

'And yet to ruin any one,' cries the other, 'you will allow, is the
Act of an Enemy; and when by the same Act you must knowingly and certainly bring Ruin on yourself, is it not Folly or
Madness, as well as Guilt? Now, Sir, my Cousin hath very little
more than her Father will please to give her; very little for one of
her Fashion,—you know him, and you know your own Situation.'

Jones vowed he had no such Design on *Sophia*, 'That he would
rather suffer the most violent of Deaths than sacrifice her Interest to his Desires.' He said, 'he knew how unworthy he was
of her every Way; that he had long ago resolved to quit all such
aspiring Thoughts, but that some strange Accidents had made
him desirous to see her once more, when he promised he would
take Leave of her for ever. No, Madam,' concluded he, 'my Love
is not of that base Kind which seeks its own Satisfaction, at the
Expence of what is most dear to its Object. I would sacrifice
every Thing to the Possession of my *Sophia*, but *Sophia* herself.'

Though the Reader may have already conceived no very sublime Idea of the Virtue of the Lady in the Mask; and tho' possibly she may hereafter appear not to deserve one of the first Characters of her Sex; yet, it is certain, these generous Sentiments made a strong Impression upon her, and greatly added to the Affection she had before conceived for our young Heroe.

The Lady now, after a Silence of a few Moments, said, 'She did not see his Pretensions to *Sophia* so much in the Light of Presumption, as of Imprudence. Young Fellows,' says she, 'can never have too aspiring Thoughts. I love Ambition in a young Man, and I would have you cultivate it as much as possible. Perhaps you may succeed with those who are infinitely superior in Fortune, nay, I am convinced there are Women,—but don't you think me a strange Creature, Mr. *Jones*, to be thus giving Advice to a Man, with whom I am so little acquainted, and one with whose Behaviour to me I have so little Reason to be pleased?'

Here *Jones* began to apologize, and to hope he had not offended in any thing he had said of her Cousin.—To which the Mask answered, 'And are you so little versed in the Sex, to imagine you can well affront a Lady more, than by entertaining her with your Passion for another Woman? If the Fairy Queen had conceived no better Opinion of your Gallantry, she would scarce have appointed you to meet her at a Masquerade.'

Jones had never less Inclination to an Amour than at present; but Gallantry to the Ladies was among his Principles of Honour; and he held it as much incumbent on him to accept a Challenge to Love, as if it had been a Challenge to Fight. Nay, his very Love to *Sophia* made it necessary for him to keep well with the Lady, as he made no doubt but she was capable of bringing him into the Presence of the other.

He began therefore to make a very warm Answer to her last Speech, when a Mask, in the Character of an old Woman, joined them. This Mask was one of those Ladies who go to a Masquerade only to vent Ill-nature, by telling People rude Truths, and by endeavouring, as the Phrase is, to spoil as much Sport as they are able. This good Lady therefore, having observed *Jones*, and his Friend, whom she well knew, in close Consultation together in a Corner of the Room, concluded she could no where satisfy her Spleen better than by interrupting them. She attacked them therefore, and soon drove them from their Retirement; nor was she contented with this, but pursued them to every Place which they shifted to avoid her; till Mr. *Nightingale* seeing the Distress of his Friend, at last relieved him, and engaged the old Woman in another Pursuit.

While *Jones* and his Mask were walking together about the Room, to rid themselves of the Teazer, he observed his Lady speak to several Masks, with the same Freedom of Acquaintance as if they had been bare-faced. He could not help expressing his Surprise at this, saying, 'Sure, Madam, you must have infinite Discernment to know People in all Disguises.' To which the Lady answered, 'You cannot conceive any Thing more insipid and childish than a Masquerade to the People of Fashion, who in general know one another as well here, as when they meet in an Assembly or a Drawing-room; nor will any Woman of Condition converse with a Person with whom she is not acquainted. In short, the Generality of Persons whom you see here, may more properly be said to kill Time in this Place, than in any other; and generally retire from hence more tired than from the longest Sermon. To say the Truth, I begin to be in that Situation myself, and if I have any Faculty at guessing, you are not much better pleased. I protest it would be almost Charity in me to go Home for your Sake.' 'I know but one Charity equal to it,' cries *Jones*, 'and that is to suffer me to wait on you Home.' 'Sure,' answered the Lady, 'you have a strange Opinion of me, to imagine, that upon such an Acquaintance, I would let you into my Doors at this Time o' Night. I fancy you impute the Friendship I have shewn my Cousin, to some other Motive. Confess honestly; don't you consider this contrived Interview as little better than a downright Assignation? Are you used, Mr. *Jones*, to make these sudden Conquests?' 'I am not used, Madam,' said *Jones*, 'to submit to such sudden Conquests; but as you have taken my Heart by Surprize, the rest of my Body hath a Right to follow; so you must pardon me if I resolve to attend you wherever you go.' He accompanied these Words with some proper Actions; upon which the Lady, after a gentle Rebuke, and saying their Familiarity would be observed, told him 'She was going to sup with an Acquaintance, whither she hoped he would not follow her; for if you should,' said she, 'I shall be thought an unaccountable Creature, though my Friend indeed is not censorious, yet I hope you won't follow me: I protest I shall not know what to say, if you do.'

The Lady presently after quitted the Masquerade, and *Jones*, notwithstanding the severe Prohibition he had received, presumed to attend her. He was now reduced to the same Dilemma we have mentioned before, namely, the Want of a Shilling, and could not relieve it by borrowing as before. He therefore walked boldly on after the Chair in which his Lady rode, pursued by a grand Huzza from all the Chairmen present, who wisely take the best Care they can to discountenance all walking afoot by their Betters. Luckily however the Gentry who attend at the Opera-House were too busy to quit their Stations, and as the Lateness of the Hour prevented him from meeting many of their Brethren in the Street, he proceeded without Molestation, in a Dress, which, at another Season, would have certainly raised a Mob at his Heels.

The Lady was set down in a Street, not far from *Hanover-Square*, where the Door being presently opened, she was carried in, and the Gentleman, without any Ceremony, walked in after her.

Jones and his Companion were now together in a very well-furnished and well-warm'd Room, when the Female still speaking in her Masquerade Voice, said, she was surprized at her Friend, who must absolutely have forgot her Appointment; at which after venting much Resentment, she suddenly exprest some Apprehension from *Jones*, and asked him what the World would think of their having been alone together in a House at that Time of Night? But instead of a direct Answer to so important a Question, *Jones* began to be very importunate with the Lady to unmask, and at length having prevailed, there appeared not Mrs. *Fitzpatrick*, but the Lady *Bellaston* herself.

It would be tedious to give the particular Conversation which consisted of very common and ordinary Occurrences, and which lasted from two till six o'Clock in the Morning. It is sufficient to mention all of it that is any wise material to this History. And this was a Promise that the Lady would endeavour to find out *Sophia*, and in a few Days bring him to an Interview with her, on Condition that he would then take his Leave of her. When this was thoroughly settled, and a second Meeting in the Evening appointed at the same Place, they separated; the Lady returned to her House, and *Jones* to his Lodgings.

CHAPTER VIII

*Containing a Scene of Distress, which will appear very extraordinary
to most of our Readers.*

JONES having refreshed himself with a few Hours Sleep,
summoned *Partridge* to his Presence; and delivering him a
Bank Note of fifty Pounds, ordered him to go and change it.
Partridge received this with sparkling Eyes, though when he
came to reflect farther, it raised in him some Suspicions not very
advantagious to the Honour of his Master; to these the dreadful
Idea he had of the Masquerade, the Disguise in which his Master
had gone out and returned, and his having been abroad all
Night, contributed. In plain Language, the only Way he could
possibly find to account for the Possession of this Note, was by
Robbery; and, to confess the Truth, the Reader, unless he should
suspect it was owing to the Generosity of Lady *Bellaston*, can
hardly imagine any other.

To clear therefore the Honour of Mr. *Jones*, and to do Justice
to the Liberality of the Lady, he had really received this Present
from her, who, though she did not give much in to the Hackney
Charities of the Age, such as building Hospitals[1] &c., was not,
however, entirely void of that Christian Virtue; and conceived
(very rightly I think) that a young Fellow of Merit, without a
Shilling in the World, was no improper Object of this Virtue.

Mr. *Jones* and Mr. *Nightingale* had been invited to dine this
Day with Mrs. *Miller*. At the appointed Hour therefore the two
young Gentlemen, with the two Girls, attended in the Parlour,
where they waited from three till almost five before the good
Woman appeared. She had been out of Town to visit a Relation,
of whom, at her Return, she gave the following Account.

'I hope, Gentlemen, you will pardon my making you wait;
I am sure if you knew the Occasion.—I have been to see a Cousin
of mine, about six Miles off, who now lies in.—It should be a
Warning to all Persons (says she, looking at her Daughters)

---

[1] Cf. *The Champion* (21 February 1739/40), where Fielding praises his countrymen for
the charitable founding of hospitals. He mentions three in particular: St. George's Hospital
(established 1733); the General Hospital at Bath, which Ralph Allen helped to build (see
above, p. 38, n. 1); and the Foundling Hospital (established 1739; see below, p. 761, n. 3).
Subsequently others had been instituted, such as the London Infirmary (1740) and the
Middlesex Hospital (1745).

how they marry indiscreetly. There is no Happiness in this
World, without a Competency. O *Nancy*! how shall I describe
the wretched Condition in which I found your poor Cousin; she
hath scarce lain in a Week, and there was she, this dreadful
Weather, in a cold Room, without any Curtains to her Bed,
and not a Bushel of Coals in her House to supply her with Fire:
Her second Son, that sweet little Fellow, lies ill of a Quinzy
in the same Bed with his Mother, for there is no other Bed in the
House. Poor little *Tommy*! I believe, *Nancy*, you will never see
your Favourite any more, for he is really very ill. The rest of the
Children are in pretty good Health; but *Molly*, I am afraid, will
do herself an Injury; she is but thirteen Years old, Mr. *Nightingale*, and yet, in my Life, I never saw a better Nurse: She tends
both her Mother and her Brother; and what is wonderful in a
Creature so young, she shows all the Chearfulness in the World
to her Mother; and yet I saw her—I saw the poor Child, Mr.
Nightingale, turn about, and privately wipe the Tears from her
Eyes.' Here Mrs. *Miller*, was prevented, by her own Tears,
from going on, and there was not, I believe, a Person present,
who did not accompany her in them; at length she a little
recovered herself, and proceeded thus, 'In all this Distress the
Mother supports her Spirits in a surprising Manner. The
Danger of her Son sits heaviest upon her, and yet she endeavours
as much as possible to conceal even this Concern, on her Husband's Account. Her Grief, however, sometimes gets the better
of all her Endeavours; for she was always extravagantly fond of
this Boy, and a most sensible, sweet-tempered Creature it is.
I protest I was never more affected in my Life, than when I
heard the little Wretch, who is hardly yet seven Years old, while
his Mother was wetting him with her Tears, beg her to be comforted.—Indeed, Mamma, cry'd the Child, I shan't die, God
Almighty, I'm sure, wont take *Tommy* away; let Heaven be
ever so fine a Place, I had rather stay here and starve with you
and my Papa, than go to it.—Pardon me, Gentlemen, I can't
help it, (says she, wiping her Eyes) such Sensibility and Affection
in a Child.—And yet, perhaps, he is least the Object of Pity,
for a Day or two will, most probably, place him beyond the Reach
of all human Evils. The Father is indeed most worthy of Compassion. Poor Man, his Countenance is the very Picture of Horror,
and he looks rather like one dead than alive. Oh Heavens!

what a Scene did I behold at my first coming into the Room! The good Creature was lying behind the Bolster, supporting at once both his Child and his Wife. He had nothing on but a thin Waistcoat, for his Coat was spread over the Bed, to supply the Want of Blankets.——When he rose up, at my Entrance, I scarce knew him. As comely a Man, Mr. *Jones*, within this Fortnight, as you ever beheld; Mr. *Nightingale* hath seen him. His Eyes sunk, his Face pale, with a long Beard. His Body shivering with Cold, and worn with Hunger too; for my Cousin says, she can hardly prevail upon him to eat.——He told me himself in a Whisper——he told me——I can't repeat it——he said he could not bear to eat the Bread his Children wanted. And yet, can you believe it, Gentlemen? In all this Misery, his Wife has as good Cawdle[1] as if she lay in, in the midst of the greatest Affluence; I tasted it, and I scarce ever tasted better.——The Means of procuring her this, he said, he believed was sent him by an Angel from Heaven; I know not what he meant, for I had not Spirits enough to ask a single Question.

'This was a Love-Match, as they call it, on both Sides; that is, a Match between two Beggars. I must indeed say I never saw a fonder Couple; but what is their Fondness good for, but to torment each other?' 'Indeed, Mamma,' cries *Nancy*, 'I have always looked on my Cousin *Enderson* (for that was her Name) as one of the happiest of Women.' 'I am sure,' says Mrs. *Miller*, 'the Case at present is much otherwise; for any one might have discerned that the tender Consideration of each other's Sufferings, makes the most intolerable Part of their Calamity, both to the Husband and the Wife. Compared to which, Hunger and Cold, as they affect their own Persons only, are scarce Evils. Nay, the very Children, the youngest, which is not two Years old, excepted, feel in the same Manner; for they are a most loving Family; and if they had but a bare Competency, would be the happiest People in the World.' 'I never saw the least Sign of Misery at her House,' replied *Nancy*; 'I am sure my Heart bleeds for what you now tell me.'——'O Child,' answered the Mother, 'she hath always endeavoured to make the best of every Thing. They have always been in great Distress; but, indeed, this absolute Ruin hath been brought upon them by others.

---

[1] A warm drink consisting of thin gruel, spiced and mixed with wine or ale—usually given to sick people, especially women in childbed.

The poor Man was Bail for the Villain his Brother; and about a Week ago, the very Day before her Lying-in, their Goods were all carried away, and sold by an Execution. He sent a Letter to me of it by one of the Bailiffs, which the Villain never delivered.— What must he think of my suffering a Week to pass before he heard of me?'

It was not with dry Eyes that *Jones* heard this Narrative; when it was ended, he took Mrs. *Miller* apart with him into another Room, and delivering her his Purse, in which was the Sum of 50*l.* desired her to send as much of it as she thought proper to these poor People. The Look which Mrs. *Miller* gave *Jones*, on this Occasion, is not easy to be described. She burst into a Kind of Agony of Transport, and cry'd out,—'Good Heavens! Is there such a Man in the World?'—But recollecting herself, she said, 'Indeed I know one such; but can there be another?' 'I hope, Madam,' cries *Jones*, 'there are many who have common Humanity: For to relieve such Distresses in our Fellow-Creatures, can hardly be called more.' Mrs. *Miller* then took ten Guineas, which were the utmost he could prevail with her to accept, and said, 'she would find some Means of conveying them early the next Morning;' adding, 'that she had herself done some little Matter for the poor People, and had not left them in quite so much Misery as she found them.'

They then returned to the Parlour, where *Nightingale* express'd much Concern at the dreadful Situation of these Wretches, whom, indeed, he knew; for he had seen them more than once at Mrs. *Miller's.* He inveighed against the Folly of making one's self liable for the Debts of others;[1] vented many bitter Execrations against the Brother; and concluded with wishing something could be done for the unfortunate Family. 'Suppose, Madam,' said he, 'you should recommend them to Mr. *Allworthy?* Or what think you of a Collection? I will give them a Guinea with all my Heart.'

Mrs. *Miller* made no Answer; and *Nancy*, to whom her Mother had whispered the Generosity of *Jones*, turned pale upon the Occasion; though if either of them was angry with *Nightingale*,

---

[1] Nightingale's remark is particularly relevant to Fielding's own experience: like Enderson, in 1745 Fielding and James Harris had agreed to stand surety for a debt contracted by their mutual friend Arthur Collier—a debt which, a year later, they were obliged to pay. (See the General Introduction, pp. xxiv, xxvi.)

it was surely without Reason. For the Liberality of *Jones*, if he had known it, was not an Example which he had any Obligation to follow; and there are Thousands who would not have contributed a single Halfpenny, as indeed he did not in Effect, for he made no Tender of any thing; and therefore as the others thought proper to make no Demand, he kept his Money in his Pocket.

I have in Truth observed, and shall never have a better Opportunity than at present to communicate my Observation, that the World are in general divided into two Opinions concerning Charity, which are the very reverse of each other. One Party seems to hold, that all Acts of this Kind are to be esteemed as voluntary Gifts, and however little you give (if indeed no more than your good Wishes) you acquire a great Degree of Merit in so doing.—Others, on the contrary, appear to be as firmly persuaded, that Beneficence is a positive Duty, and that whenever the Rich fall greatly short of their Ability in relieving the Distresses of the Poor, their pitiful Largesses are so far from being meritorious, that they have only performed their Duty by Halves, and are in some Sense more contemptible than those who have entirely neglected it.

To reconcile these different Opinions is not in my Power. I shall only add, that the Givers are generally of the former Sentiment, and the Receivers are almost universally inclined to the latter.

CHAPTER IX

Which treats of Matters of a very different Kind from those in the preceding Chapter.

IN the Evening *Jones* met his Lady again, and a long Conversation again ensued between them; but as it consisted only of the same ordinary Occurrences as before, we shall avoid mentioning Particulars, which we despair of rendring agreeable to the Reader; unless he is one whose Devotion to the Fair Sex, like that of the Papists to their Saints, wants to be raised by the Help of Pictures.[1] But I am so far from desiring to exhibit

---

[1] The irreverent comparison between erotic pictures and the religious icons of the Roman Catholics is not new with Fielding. Cf. *The Whore's Rhetorick* (1683), referring to lascivious pictures as 'bawdy incentives' to love-making: 'In this particular all Men are of

such Pictures to the Public, that I would wish to draw a Curtain over those that have been lately set forth in certain *French* Novels; very bungling Copies of which have been presented us here, under the Name of Translations.[1]

Jones grew still more and more impatient to see *Sophia*; and finding, after repeated Interviews with Lady *Bellaston*, no Likelihood of obtaining this by her Means; for, on the contrary, the Lady began to treat even the Mention of the Name of *Sophia* with Resentment; he resolved to try some other Method. He made no Doubt but that Lady *Bellaston* knew where his Angel was, so he thought it most likely, that some of her Servants should be acquainted with the same Secret. *Partridge* therefore was employed to get acquainted with those Servants, in order to fish this Secret out of them.

Few Situations can be imagined more uneasy than that to which his poor Master was at present reduced; for besides the Difficulties he met with in discovering *Sophia*, besides the Fears he had of having disobliged her, and the Assurances he had received from Lady *Bellaston* of the Resolution which *Sophia* had taken against him, and of her having purposely concealed herself from him, which he had sufficient Reason to believe might be true; he had still a Difficulty to combat, which it was not in the Power of his Mistress to remove, however kind her Inclination might have been. This was the exposing of her to be disinherited of all her Father's Estate, the almost inevitable Consequence of their coming together without a Consent, which he had no Hopes of ever obtaining.

a Romish perswasion; in as much as their devotion at the Shrine of *Venus* is extreamly enlivened by the prospect of a naked Saint' (1960 reprint, p. 128). It appears that such pictures, concealed behind curtains, often adorned the walls of prostitutes' rooms (ibid., pp. 125 ff.).

[1] By 1745 translations of French pornography had become so numerous that the authorities took steps to suppress them. (See David Foxon, *Libertine Literature in England, 1660–1745* [1964], pp. 15–18.) The particular works in question included versions of *L'École des filles*, Jean Nicolas's *L'Académie des dames*, J. C. Gervaise de Latouche's *Histoire de Dom B * * **, *portier des Chartreux*, and Jean Barrin's *Vénus dans le cloître, ou la religieuse en chemise*—all of which were illustrated with cuts. Shamela (see letter xii) owns a copy of *Venus in the Cloister*, for selling which the 'unspeakable' Edmund Curll had been prosecuted. That some of these translations were 'very bungling Copies', as Fielding calls them, was also the complaint of John Stevens, publisher of *The School of Venus* (a version of *L'École des filles*), who assured readers that his was 'a true English Translation, without those innumerable Blunders which are to be found in every Page' of a competing edition (*The Daily Advertiser*, 25 August 1744; quoted in Foxon, op. cit., p. 3).

Add to all these the many Obligations which Lady *Bellaston*, whose violent Fondness we can no longer conceal, had heaped upon him; so that by her Means he was now become one of the best dress'd Men about Town; and was not only relieved from those ridiculous Distresses we have before mentioned, but was actually raised to a State of Affluence, beyond what he had ever known.

Now though there are many Gentlemen who very well reconcile it to their Consciences to possess themselves of the whole Fortune of a Woman, without making her any Kind of Return; yet to a Mind the Proprietor of which doth not deserve to be hang'd, nothing is, I believe, more irksome than to support Love with Gratitude only; especially where Inclination pulls the Heart a contrary Way. Such was the unhappy Case of *Jones*; for tho' the virtuous Love which he bore to *Sophia*, and which left very little Affection for any other Woman, had been entirely out of the Question, he could never have been able to have made an adequate Return to the generous Passion of this Lady, who had indeed been once an Object of Desire; but was now entered at least into the Autumn of Life; though she wore all the Gayety of Youth both in her Dress and Manner; nay, she contrived still to maintain the Roses in her Cheeks; but these, like Flowers forced out of Season by Art, had none of that lively blooming Freshness with which Nature, at the proper Time, bedecks her own Productions. She had, besides, a certain Imperfection, which renders some Flowers, tho' very beautiful to the Eye, very improper to be placed in a Wilderness of Sweets, and what above all others is most disagreeable to the Breath of Love.

Though *Jones* saw all these Discouragements on the one Side, he felt his Obligations full as strongly on the other; nor did he less plainly discern the ardent Passion whence those Obligations proceeded, the extreme Violence of which if he failed to equal, he well knew the Lady would think him ungrateful; and, what is worse, he would have thought himself so. He knew the tacit Consideration upon which all her Favours were conferred; and as his Necessity obliged him to accept them, so his Honour, he concluded, forced him to pay the Price. This therefore he resolved to do, whatever Misery it cost him, and to devote himself to her, from that great Principle of Justice, by which the Laws of some Countries oblige a Debtor who is no otherwise capable of discharging his Debt, to become the Slave of his Creditor.[1]

While he was meditating on these Matters, he received the following Note from the Lady.

'A very foolish, but a very perverse Accident hath happened since our last Meeting, which makes it improper I should see you any more at the usual Place. I will, if possible, contrive some other Place by To-morrow. In the mean Time, Adieu.'

This Disappointment, perhaps, the Reader may conclude was not very great; but if it was, he was quickly relieved; for in less than an Hour afterwards another Note was brought him from the same Hand, which contained as follows.

'I have altered my Mind since I wrote, a Change, which if you are no Stranger to the tenderest of all Passions, you will not wonder at. I am now resolved to see you this Evening, at my own House, whatever may be the Consequence. Come to me exactly at seven; I dine abroad, but will be at Home by that Time. A Day, I find, to those that sincerely love seems longer than I imagined.

'If you should accidentally be a few Moments before me, bid them shew you into the Drawing-Room.'

To confess the Truth, *Jones* was less pleased with this last Epistle, than he had been with the former, as he was prevented by it from complying with the earnest Entreaties of Mr. *Nightingale*, with whom he had now contracted much Intimacy and Friendship. These Entreaties were to go with that young Gentleman and his Company to a new Play,[2] which was to be acted that Evening, and which a very large Party had agreed to damn, from some Dislike they had taken to the Author, who was a Friend to one of Mr. *Nightingale's* Acquaintance. And this Sort of Funn,

---

[1] The treatment of debtors under English law struck Fielding as barbarous. (See the Wesleyan Edition of *Joseph Andrews*, p. 219, n. 1.) With the metaphor of the present passage, compare Job Vinegar's account of the customs of 'the PTFGHSIUMGSKI or the Inconstants' in *The Champion* (19 August 1740): 'The Virtue of Gratitude is so universal among these People, that when one Friend borrows Money of another, he always binds himself in an *Obligation* for it: So that, for the smallest Sum, he doth not only surrender his own Body to him, but those of his Heirs and Executors; and so excessive is their Gratitude, that I have known a Man who had borrowed 10s. of another, on a bare sending him a small Scrip to put him in mind of it, not being able to pay, shut himself up in a Prison, where he hath heavily prayed many Months for his Benefactor; and these Prayers their Law accounts a Satisfaction to the Lender.'

[2] See below, p. 729, n. 1.

our Heroe, we are ashamed to confess, would willingly have preferred to the above kind Appointment; but his Honour got the better of his Inclination.

Before we attend him to this intended Interview with the Lady, we think proper to account for both the preceding Notes, as the Reader may possibly be not a little surprized at the Imprudence of Lady *Bellaston* in bringing her Lover to the very House where her Rival was lodged.

First then the Mistress of the House where these Lovers had hitherto met, and who had been for some Years a Pensioner to that Lady, was now become a Methodist,[1] and had that very Morning waited upon her Ladyship, and after rebuking her very severely for her past Life, had positively declared, that she would, on no Account, be instrumental in carrying on any of her Affairs for the future.

The Hurry of Spirits into which this Accident threw the Lady, made her despair of possibly finding any other Convenience to meet *Jones* that Evening; but as she began a little to recover from her Uneasiness at the Disappointment, she set her Thoughts to work, when luckily it came into her Head to propose to *Sophia* to go to the Play, which was immediately consented to, and a proper Lady provided for her Companion. Mrs. *Honour* was likewise dispatched with Mrs. *Etoff* on the same Errand of Pleasure; and thus her own House was left free for the safe Reception of Mr. *Jones*, with whom she promised herself two or three Hours of uninterrupted Conversation, after her Return from the Place where she dined, which was at a Friend's House in a pretty distant Part of the Town, near her old Place of Assignation, where she had engaged herself before she was well apprized of the Revolution that had happened in the Mind and Morals of her late Confidante.

CHAPTER X

A Chapter which, though short, may draw Tears from some Eyes.

MR. *Jones* was just dress'd to wait on Lady *Bellaston*, when Mrs. *Miller* rapp'd at his Door; and being admitted, very earnestly desired his Company below Stairs to drink Tea in the Parlour.

---

[1] See above, p. 63, n. 1.

Upon his Entrance into the Room, she presently introduced a Person to him, saying, 'This, Sir, is my Cousin, who hath been so greatly beholden to your Goodness, for which he begs to return you his sincerest Thanks.'

The Man had scarce entered upon that Speech, which Mrs. *Miller* had so kindly prefaced, when both *Jones* and he looking stedfastly at each other, showed at once the utmost Tokens of Surprize. The Voice of the latter began instantly to faulter; and, instead of finishing his Speech, he sunk down into a Chair, crying, 'It is so, I am convinced it is so!'

'Bless me, what's the Meaning of this,' cries Mrs. *Miller*, 'you are not ill, I hope, Cousin? Some Water, a Dram this Instant.'

'Be not frighted, Madam,' cries *Jones*, 'I have almost as much Need of a Dram as your Cousin. We are equally surprized at this unexpected Meeting. Your Cousin is an Acquaintance of mine, Mrs. *Miller*.'

'An Acquaintance!' cries the Man,—'Oh Heaven!'

'Ay, an Acquaintance,' repeated *Jones*, 'and an honoured Acquaintance too. When I do not love and honour the Man who dares venture every thing to preserve his Wife and Children from instant Destruction, may I have a Friend capable of disowning me in Adversity.'

'O you are an excellent young Man,' cries Mrs. *Miller*,—'yes, indeed, poor Creature! he hath ventured every thing.—If he had not had one of the best of Constitutions it must have killed him.'

'Cousin,' cries the Man, who had now pretty well recovered himself; 'this is the Angel from Heaven whom I meant. This is he to whom before I saw you, I owed the Preservation of my *Peggy*. He it was to whose Generosity every Comfort, every Support which I have procured for her was owing. He is indeed the worthiest, bravest, noblest of all human Beings. O, Cousin, I have Obligations to this Gentleman of such a Nature!'

'Mention nothing of Obligations,' cries *Jones* eagerly, 'not a Word, I insist upon it, not a Word.' (Meaning, I suppose, that he would not have him betray the Affair of the Robbery to any Person.)—'If by the Trifle you have received from me, I have preserved a whole Family, sure Pleasure was never bought so cheap.'

'O, Sir,' cries the Man, 'I wish you could this Instant see my House. If any Person had ever a Right to the Pleasure you mention, I am convinced it is yourself. My Cousin tells me, she acquainted you with the Distress in which she found us. That, Sir, is all greatly removed, and chiefly by your Goodness.—My Children have now a Bed to lie on,—and they have—they have—eternal Blessings reward you for it,—they have Bread to eat. My little Boy is recovered; my Wife is out of Danger, and I am happy. All, all owing to you, Sir, and to my Cousin here, one of the best of Women. Indeed, Sir, I must see you at my House.—Indeed my Wife must see you, and thank you.—My Children too must express their Gratitude.—Indeed, Sir, they are not without a Sense of their Obligation; but what is my Feeling when I reflect to whom I owe, that they are now capable of expressing their Gratitude.—Oh, Sir! the little Hearts which you have warmed had now been cold as Ice without your Assistance.'——

Here *Jones* attempted to prevent the poor Man from proceeding; but indeed the Overflowing of his own Heart would of itself have stopped his Words. And now Mrs. *Miller* likewise began to pour forth Thanksgivings, as well in her own Name, as in that of her Cousin, and concluded with saying, she doubted not but such Goodness would meet a glorious Reward.

Jones answered, 'He had been sufficiently rewarded already. Your Cousin's Account, Madam,' said he, 'hath given me a Sensation more pleasing than I have ever known. He must be a Wretch who is unmoved at hearing such a Story; how transporting then must be the Thought of having happily acted a Part in this Scene. If there are Men who cannot feel the Delight of giving Happiness to others, I sincerely pity them, as they are incapable of tasting what is, in my Opinion, a greater Honour, a higher Interest, and a sweeter Pleasure, than the ambitious, the avaritious, or the voluptuous Man can ever obtain.'

The Hour of Appointment being now come, *Jones* was forced to take a hasty Leave, but not before he had heartily shaken his Friend by the Hand, and desired to see him again as soon as possible; promising, that he would himself take the first Opportunity of visiting him at his own House. He then stept into his Chair, and proceeded to Lady *Bellaston's*, greatly exulting in the Happiness which he had procured to this poor Family; nor could he forbear reflecting without Horror on the dreadful

Consequences which must have attended them, had he listened rather to the Voice of strict Justice, than to that of Mercy when he was attacked on the high Road.

Mrs. *Miller* sung forth the Praises of *Jones* during the whole Evening, in which Mr. *Enderson*, while he stayed, so passionately accompanied her, that he was often on the very Point of mentioning the Circumstances of the Robbery. However, he luckily recollected himself, and avoided an Indiscretion which would have been so much the greater, as he knew Mrs. *Miller* to be extremely strict and nice in her Principles. He was likewise well apprized of the Loquacity of this Lady; and yet such was his Gratitude, that it had almost got the better both of Discretion and Shame, and made him publish that which would have defamed his own Character, rather than omit any Circumstances which might do the fullest Honour to his Benefactor.

CHAPTER XI

In which the Reader will be surprized.

MR. *Jones* was rather earlier than the Time appointed, and earlier than the Lady, whose Arrival was hindered not only by the Distance of the Place where she dined, but by some other cross Accidents, very vexatious to one in her Situation of Mind. He was accordingly shewn into the Drawing-Room, where he had not been many Minutes before the Door opened, and in came—no other than *Sophia* herself, who had left the Play before the End of the first Act; for this, as we have already said, being a new Play,[1] at which two large Parties met, the one to damn,

---

[1] Though an anachronism in the time-scheme of his narrative, Fielding probably alludes to the tumultuous reception of *The Foundling*, a new comedy written by his friend Edward Moore (1712–57) and produced by Garrick at Drury Lane, 13 February 1748. Parties had been formed—one, led by Lord Hobart, to damn the play; the other, composed principally of Templars, to applaud it. (See G. W. Stone, Jr., *The London Stage, 1660–1800*, Pt. iv: *1747–76* [Carbondale, Ill., 1962], pp. 31–2.) Various motives were attributed to Moore's opponents, but, as Fielding learned, 'the true Reason' for the uproar was Faddle's declaration that he would '*as soon make love to a Milliner's* Doll' (II. v)—an allusion, supposedly, to the perverse sexual behaviour of a young nobleman, the putative hero of a salacious poem called *Adollizing: or, A Lively Picture of Adoll-worship* (published February 1748). (See *The Jacobite's Journal*, 12 March 1748.)

Whatever the cause, the clamour on the first night was violent indeed, 'to the great Terror of the Actresses, and of several Ladies of the first Quality among the Audience'

and the other to applaud, a violent Uproar, and an Engagement between the two Parties had so terrified our Heroine, that she was glad to put herself under the Protection of a young Gentleman, who safely conveyed her to her Chair.

As Lady *Bellaston* had acquainted her that she should not be at Home till late, *Sophia* expecting to find no one in the Room, came hastily in, and went directly to a Glass which almost fronted her, without once looking towards the upper End of the Room, where the Statue of *Jones* now stood motionless.—In this Glass it was, after contemplating her own lovely Face, that she first discovered the said Statue; when instantly turning about, she perceived the Reality of the Vision: Upon which she gave a violent Scream, and scarce preserved herself from fainting, till *Jones* was able to move to her, and support her in his Arms.

To paint the Looks or Thoughts of either of these Lovers is beyond my Power. As their Sensations, from their mutual Silence,

(*The Jacobite's Journal*, 20 February 1748). The following eyewitness account of the disturbance appeared in Sir John Hill's *British Magazine*, iii (February 1748), 70–5. By four o'clock, two hours before the curtain, the theatre was full:

'. . . the audience, who are ever merry in hopes of a damnation, entertained both themselves and me in a very humorous manner, till the curtain drew up: I cannot say indeed but we were noisy and mutinous enough. The musick must play nothing but ballad tunes and country dances, and the audience caper'd to the first, and sung in chorus to the latter. I cannot but say that I cou'd well have excus'd the dancing *butter'd peas* over my head, as I was in some fear that the gallery would have come down upon me; but I love King *George* well enough to own that I had afterwards ample amends in hearing the whole pit join with the next piece in singing, *God save our noble King*.

'After this, the long expected scene began, and the ador'd Mrs. *Pritchard* enter'd to claim the favour of the town in a new way, by a prayer from the petty-coat. We had, before this, had very strong proofs that there were cat-calls in the house ready upon occasion, and they were now soon us'd. I thank Heaven that I never have heard, nor I hope ver [*sic*] shall hear, quite so bad a prologue again, and we had not got ten lines forward in it, when an unlucky critick gave from his vocal lip the fatal signal of damnation. . . . Here had like to have sunk at once the whole fabrick; for, when the herd of the house are once let into the secret that they have a bad play coming, they never trouble themselves about enquiring into the merit of any thing afterwards, but ever damn all at a venture; at the signal however there up-rear'd in the midst a broad-shoulder'd and broad fac'd hero, to whom I can assure the author he owes all his third nights; this tremendous umpire between the poet and the audience, us'd no long arguments, but proceeded directly to the old *English* club-law, and Knock him down was thrice resounded thro' his raven-croaking throat. The friends of the play took spirit at this heroism; and finding they were more numerous than their antagonists, carried it afterwards with a high hand the whole night, and cram'd the worst parts of the performance down the peaceable critick's throats in glorious triumph.'

Despite sporadic outbursts from the gallery, *The Foundling* survived this ordeal and had a good run. For Fielding's criticism of the play, see *The Jacobite's Journal* (19 March 1748).

may be judged to have been too big for their own Utterance, it cannot be supposed, that I should be able to express them: And the Misfortune is, that few of my Readers have been enough in Love, to feel by their own Hearts what past at this Time in theirs.

After a short Pause, *Jones*, with faultering Accents, said,— 'I see, Madam, you are surprized.'— 'Surprized!' answered she; 'Oh Heavens! Indeed, I am surprized. I almost doubt whether you are the Person you seem.' 'Indeed,' cries he, 'my *Sophia*, pardon me, Madam, for this once calling you so, I am that very wretched *Jones*, whom Fortune, after so many Disappointments, hath, at last, kindly conducted to you. Oh! my *Sophia*, did you know the thousand Torments I have suffered in this long, fruitless Pursuit.'—'Pursuit of whom?' said *Sophia*, a little recollecting herself, and assuming a reserved Air.—'Can you be so cruel to ask that Question?' cries *Jones*. 'Need I say of you?' 'Of me?' answered *Sophia*: 'Hath Mr. *Jones* then any such important Business with me?' 'To some, Madam,' cries *Jones*, 'this might seem an important Business,' (giving her the Pocket-Book). 'I hope, Madam, you will find it of the same Value, as when it was lost.' *Sophia* took the Pocket-Book, and was going to speak, when he interrupted her, thus;—'Let us not, I beseech you, lose one of these precious Moments which Fortune hath so kindly sent us.—O my *Sophia*, I have Business of a much superior Kind.—Thus, on my Knees, let me ask your Pardon.'— 'My Pardon?' cries she;—'Sure, Sir, after what is past you cannot expect, after what I have heard——' 'I scarce know what I say,' answered *Jones*. 'By Heavens! I scarce wish you should pardon me. O my *Sophia*, henceforth never cast away a Thought on such a Wretch as I am. If any Remembrance of me should ever intrude to give a Moment's Uneasiness to that tender Bosom, think of my Unworthiness; and let the Remembrance of what past at *Upton* blot me for ever from your Mind.'——

Sophia stood trembling all this while. Her Face was whiter than Snow, and her Heart was throbbing through her Stays. But at the mention of *Upton*, a Blush arose in her Cheeks, and her Eyes, which before she had scarce lifted up, were turned upon *Jones* with a Glance of Disdain. He understood this silent Reproach, and replied to it thus: 'O my *Sophia*, my only Love, you cannot hate or despise me more for what happened there, than I do myself: But yet do me the Justice to think, that my *Heart* was never unfaithful to you. *That* had no Share in the Folly I was guilty of; it was even then unalterably yours. Though I despaired of possessing you, nay, almost of ever seeing you more, I doated still on your charming Idea, and could *seriously* love no other Woman. But if my Heart had not been engaged, she, into whose Company I accidentally fell at that cursed Place, was not an Object of serious Love. Believe me, my Angel, I never have seen her from that Day to this; and never intend, or desire, to see her again.' *Sophia*, in her Heart, was very glad to hear this; but forcing into her Face an Air of more Coldness than she had yet assumed; 'Why,' said she, 'Mr. *Jones*, do you take the Trouble to make a Defence, where you are not accused? If I thought it worth while to accuse you, I have a Charge of unpardonable Nature indeed.' 'What is it, for Heaven's Sake?' answered *Jones*, trembling and pale, expecting to hear of his Amour with Lady *Bellaston*. 'Oh,' said she, 'how is it possible! Can every Thing noble, and every Thing base, be lodged together in the same Bosom?' Lady *Bellaston*, and the ignominious Circumstance of having been *kept*, rose again in his Mind, and stopt his Mouth from any Reply. 'Could I have expected,' proceeded *Sophia*, 'such Treatment from you? Nay, from any Gentleman, from any Man of Honour? To have my Name traduced in Public; in Inns, among the meanest Vulgar! To have any little Favours, that my unguarded Heart may have too lightly betray'd me to grant, boasted of there! Nay, even to hear that you had been forced to fly from my Love!' Nothing could equal *Jones's* Surprize at these Words of *Sophia*; but yet, not being guilty, he was much less embarrassed how to defend himself, than if she had touched that tender String, at which his Conscience had been alarmed. By some Examination he presently found, that her supposing him guilty of so shocking an Outrage against his Love, and her Reputation, was entirely owing to *Partridge's* Talk at the Inns, before Landlords and Servants; for Sophia confessed to him, it was from them that she received her Intelligence. He had no very great Difficulty to make her believe that he was entirely innocent of an Offence so foreign to his Character; but she had a great deal to hinder him from going instantly Home, and putting *Partridge* to Death, which he more than once swore he would do. This Point being cleared up, they soon found themselves so well pleased with each other, that *Jones* quite forgot he had begun the Conversation with conjuring her to give up all Thoughts of him; and she was in a Temper to have given Ear to a Petition of a very different Nature: For before they were aware, they had both gone so far, that he let fall some Words that sounded like a Proposal of Marriage. To which she replied, 'That, did not her Duty to her Father forbid her to follow her own Inclinations, Ruin with him would be more welcome to her, than the most affluent Fortune with another Man.' At the mention of the Word Ruin he started, let drop her Hand, which he had held for some Time, and striking his Breast with his own, cried out, 'Oh, *Sophia*, can I then ruin thee? No; by Heavens, no! I never will act so base a Part. Dearest *Sophia*, whatever it costs me, I will renounce you; I will give you up: I will tear all such Hopes from my Heart, as are inconsistent with your real Good. My Love I will ever retain, but it shall be in Silence; it shall be at a Distance from you; it shall be in some foreign Land; from whence no Voice, no Sigh of my Despair, shall ever reach and disturb your Ears. And when I am dead——' He would have gone on, but was stopt by a Flood of Tears which *Sophia* let fall in his Bosom, upon which she leaned, without being able to speak one Word. He kissed them off, which, for some Moments, she allowed him to do without any Resistance; but then recollecting herself, gently withdrew out of his Arms; and, to turn the Discourse from a Subject too tender, and which she found she could not support, bethought herself to ask him a Question she never had Time to put to him before, 'How he came into that Room?' He began to stammer, and would, in all Probability, have raised her Suspicions by the Answer he was going to give, when, at once, the Door opened, and in came Lady *Bellaston*.

Having advanced a few Steps, and seeing *Jones* and *Sophia* together, she suddenly stopt; when after a Pause of a few Moments, recollecting herself with admirable Presence of Mind, she said,—tho' with sufficient Indications of Surprize both in Voice and Countenance—'I thought, Miss *Western*, you had been at the Play?'

Though *Sophia* had no Opportunity of learning of *Jones*, by what Means he had discovered her, yet as she had not the least Suspicion of the real Truth, or that *Jones* and Lady *Bellaston* were acquainted; so she was very little confounded: And the less, as the Lady had, in all their Conversations on the Subject, entirely taken her Side against her Father. With very little Hesitation, therefore, she went through the whole Story of what had happened at the Playhouse, and the Cause of her hasty Return.

The Length of this Narrative gave Lady *Bellaston* an Opportunity of rallying her Spirits, and of considering in what Manner to act. And as the Behaviour of *Sophia* gave her Hopes that *Jones* had not betray'd her, she put on an Air of Good-Humour, and said, 'I should not have broke in so abruptly upon you, Miss *Western*, if I had known you had Company.'

Lady *Bellaston* fixed her Eyes on *Sophia* whilst she spoke these Words. To which that poor young Lady, having her Face overspread with Blushes and Confusion, answered, in a stammering Voice, 'I am sure, Madam, I shall always think the Honour of your Ladyship's Company——' 'I hope, at least,' cries Lady *Bellaston*, 'I interrupt no Business.'—'No, Madam,' answered *Sophia*, 'our Business was at an End. Your Ladyship may be pleased to remember, I have often mentioned the Loss of my Pocket-Book, which this Gentleman having very luckily found, was so kind to return to me with the Bill in it.'

Jones, ever since the Arrival of Lady *Bellaston*, had been ready to sink with Fear. He sat kicking his Heels, playing with his Fingers, and looking more like a Fool, if it be possible, than a young booby Squire, when he is first introduced into a polite Assembly. He began, however, now to recover himself; and taking a Hint from the Behaviour of Lady *Bellaston*, who, he saw, did not intend to claim any Acquaintance with him, he resolved as entirely to affect the Stranger on his Part. He said, 'Ever since he had the Pocket-Book in his Possession, he had used great Diligence in enquiring out the Lady whose Name was writ in it; but never till that Day could be so fortunate to discover her.'

Sophia had, indeed, mentioned the Loss of her Pocket-Book to Lady *Bellaston*; but as *Jones*, for some Reason or other, had never once hinted to her that it was in his Possession, she believed not one Syllable of what *Sophia* now said, and wonderfully admired the extreme Quickness of the young Lady, in inventing such an Excuse. The Reason of *Sophia's* leaving the Play-house met with no better Credit; and though she could not account for the Meeting between these two Lovers, she was firmly perswaded it was not accidental.

With an affected Smile, therefore, she said—'Indeed, Miss *Western*, you have had very good Luck in recovering your Money. Not only as it fell into the Hands of a Gentleman of Honour, but as he happened to discover to whom it belonged. I think you would not consent to have it advertised.—It was great good Fortune, Sir, that you found out to whom the Note belonged.'

'O Madam,' cries *Jones*, 'it was inclosed in a Pocket-Book, in which the young Lady's Name was written.'

'That was very fortunate indeed,' cries the Lady;—'And it was no less so, that you heard Miss *Western* was at my House; for she is very little known.'

Jones had at length perfectly recovered his Spirits; and as he conceived he had now an Opportunity of satisfying *Sophia*, as to the Question she had asked him just before Lady *Bellaston* came in, he proceeded thus: 'Why, Madam,' answered he, 'it was by the luckiest Chance imaginable I made this Discovery. I was mentioning what I had found, and the Name of the Owner, the other Night, to a Lady at the Masquerade, who told me, she believed she knew where I might see Miss *Western*; and if I would come to her House the next Morning, she would inform me. I went according to her Appointment, but she was not at Home; nor could I ever meet with her till this Morning, when she directed me to your Ladyship's House. I came accordingly, and did myself the Honour to ask for your Ladyship; and upon my saying that I had very particular Business, a Servant shewed me into this Room; where I had not been long before the young Lady returned from the Play.'

Upon his mentioning the Masquerade, he look'd very slyly at Lady *Bellaston*, without any Fear of being remarked by *Sophia*; for she was visibly too much confounded to make any Observations. This Hint a little alarmed the Lady, and she was silent; when *Jones*, who saw the Agitations of *Sophia's* Mind, resolved to take the only Method of relieving her, which was by retiring: But before he did this, he said, 'I believe, Madam, it is customary to give some Reward on these Occasions;—I must insist on a very high one for my Honesty;—It is, Madam, no less than the Honour of being permitted to pay another Visit here.'

'Sir,' replied the Lady, 'I make no Doubt that you are a Gentleman, and my Doors are never shut to People of Fashion.'

Jones then, after proper Ceremonials, departed, highly to his own Satisfaction, and no less to that of *Sophia*; who was terribly alarmed lest Lady *Bellaston* should discover what she knew already but too well.

Upon the Stairs *Jones* met his old Acquaintance Mrs. *Honour*, who, notwithstanding all she had said against him, was now so well-bred to behave with great Civility. This Meeting proved indeed a lucky Circumstance, as he communicated to her the House where he lodged, with which *Sophia* was unacquainted.

CHAPTER XII

In which the Thirteenth Book is concluded.

THE elegant Lord *Shaftsbury* somewhere objects to telling too much Truth:[1] By which it may be fairly inferred, that, in some Cases, to lie, is not only excusable but commendable.

And surely there are no Persons who may so properly challenge a Right to this commendable Deviation from Truth, as young Women in the Affair of Love; for which they may plead Precept, Education, and above all, the Sanction, nay, I may say, the Necessity of Custom, by which they are restrained, not from submitting to the honest Impulses of Nature (for that would be a foolish Prohibition) but from owning them.

We are not, therefore, ashamed to say, that our Heroine now pursued the Dictates of the abovementioned Right Honourable Philosopher. As she was perfectly satisfied then, that Lady *Bellaston* was ignorant of the Person of *Jones*, so she determined to keep her in that Ignorance, though at the Expence of a little Fibbing.

Jones had not been long gone, before Lady *Bellaston* cry'd,

---

[1] In 'Sensus Communis: An Essay on the Freedom of Wit and Humour' (Pt. i, sec. ii) Shaftesbury observes: 'THERE is indeed a kind of *defensive Raillery* (if I may so call it) which I am willing enough to allow in Affairs of whatever kind; when the Spirit of Curiosity wou'd force a Discovery of more Truth than can conveniently be told. For we can never do more Injury to Truth, than by discovering too much of it, on some occasions' (*Characteristicks*, 5th ed. [1732], i. 62). For other references to Shaftesbury in *Tom Jones*, see above, pp. 217, n. 2; 398, n. 4; also p. 123, n. 1.

'Upon my Word, a good pretty young Fellow; I wonder who he is: For I don't remember ever to have seen his Face before.'

'Nor I neither, Madam,' cries *Sophia*. 'I must say he behaved very handsomely in relation to my Note.'

'Yes; and he is a very handsome Fellow,' said the Lady; 'don't you think so?'

'I did not take much Notice of him,' answered *Sophia*; 'but I thought he seemed rather awkward and ungenteel than otherwise.'

'You are extremely right,' cries Lady *Bellaston*: 'You may see, by his Manner, that he hath not kept good Company. Nay, notwithstanding his returning your Note, and refusing the Reward, I almost question whether he is a Gentleman.—I have always observed there is a Something in Persons well-born, which others can never acquire.—I think I will give Orders not to be at Home to him.'

'Nay sure, Madam,' answered *Sophia*, 'one can't suspect after what he hath done:—Besides, if your Ladyship observed him, there was an Elegance in his Discourse, a Delicacy, a Prettiness of Expression that, that——.'

'I confess,' said Lady *Bellaston*, 'the Fellow hath Words.— And indeed, *Sophia*, you must forgive me, indeed you must.'

'I forgive your Ladyship!' said *Sophia*.

'Yes indeed you must,' answered she laughing; 'for I had a horrible Suspicion when I first came into the Room—I vow you must forgive it; but I suspected it was Mr. *Jones* himself.'

'Did your Ladyship indeed?' cries *Sophia*, blushing, and affecting a Laugh.

'Yes, I vow I did,' answered she, 'I can't imagine what put it into my Head: For, give the Fellow his due, he was genteelly drest; which, I think, dear *Sophy*, is not commonly the Case with your Friend.'

'This Raillery,' cries *Sophia*, 'is a little cruel, Lady *Bellaston*, after my Promise to your Ladyship.'

'Not at all, Child,' said the Lady;—'It would have been cruel before; but after you have promised me never to marry without your Father's Consent, in which you know is implied your giving up *Jones*, sure you can bear a little Raillery on a Passion which was pardonable enough in a young Girl in the Country, and of which you tell me you have so entirely got the better. What must

I think, my dear *Sophy*, if you cannot bear a little Ridicule even
on his Dress? I shall begin to fear you are very far gone indeed;
and almost question whether you have dealt ingenuously with
me.'

'Indeed, Madam,' cries *Sophia*, 'your Ladyship mistakes me,
if you imagine I had any Concern on his Account.'

'On his Account?' answered the Lady: 'You must have mistaken me; I went no farther than his Dress;—for I would not
injure your Taste by any other Comparison.—I don't imagine,
my dear *Sophy*, if your Mr. *Jones* had been such a Fellow as
this——'

'I thought,' says *Sophia*, 'your Ladyship had allowed him to be
handsome.'——

'Whom, pray?' cried the Lady, hastily.

'Mr. *Jones*,' answered *Sophia*;—and immediately recollecting
herself, 'Mr. *Jones*!—no, no; I ask your Pardon;—I mean the
Gentleman who was just now here.'

'O *Sophy*! *Sophy*!' cries the Lady; 'this Mr. *Jones*, I am afraid,
still runs in your Head.'

'Then upon my Honour, Madam,' said *Sophia*, 'Mr. *Jones*
is as entirely indifferent to me, as the Gentleman who just now
left us.'

'Upon my Honour,' said Lady *Bellaston*, 'I believe it. Forgive
me, therefore, a little innocent Raillery; but I promise you I will
never mention his Name any more.'

And now the two Ladies separated, infinitely more to the
Delight of *Sophia*, than of Lady *Bellaston*, who would willingly
have tormented her Rival a little longer, had not Business of more
Importance called her away. As for *Sophia*, her Mind was not
perfectly easy under this first Practice of Deceit; upon which,
when she retired to her Chamber, she reflected with the highest
Uneasiness and conscious Shame. Nor could the peculiar Hard-
ship of her Situation, and the Necessity of the Case, at all reconcile her Mind to her Conduct; for the Frame of her Mind was too
delicate to bear the Thought of having been guilty of a Falshood,
however qualified by Circumstances. Nor did this Thought once
suffer her to close her Eyes during the whole succeeding Night.

BOOK XIV

Containing two Days.

CHAPTER I

An Essay to prove that an Author will write the better, for having some Knowledge of the Subject on which he writes.

AS several Gentlemen in these Times, by the wonderful Force of Genius only, without the least Assistance of Learning,[1] perhaps, without being well able to read, have made a considerable Figure in the Republic of Letters; the modern Critics, I am told, have lately begun to assert, that all kind of Learning is entirely useless to a Writer; and, indeed, no other than a kind of Fetters on the natural Spriteliness and Activity of the Imagination, which is thus weighed down, and prevented from soaring to those high Flights which otherwise it would be able to reach.

This Doctrine, I am afraid, is, at present, carried much too far: For why should Writing differ so much from all other Arts? The Nimbleness of a Dancing-Master is not at all prejudiced by

[1] Fielding seems to echo, and facetiously to extend, Addison's praise of such 'great Genius's' as Homer and Pindar, 'who by the mere Strength of natural Parts, and without any Assistance of Art or Learning, have produced Works that were the Delight of their own Times and the Wonder of Posterity' (*The Spectator*, No. 160 [3 September 1711]). By extending the unnecessary qualifications of authorship to include the ability to read, Fielding turns Addison's commendation into irony, resuming the fun he had had some years earlier at Cibber's expense. In *The Champion* (29 April 1740) he had delighted in Cibber's statement in the *Apology* that '*we have frequently Great Writers that cannot read*'— an opinion of the laureate's which was especially apt in view of the leader of 25 December 1739, where Fielding had observed: 'Those genteel Accomplishments which have been foolishly thought to ask the Assistance of Learning, have lately been discovered to require none at all. Poetry, for Instance, stands so little in need of it, that the Poet of our Age, most cherished at Court, never pretended to more than to read.' (On Cibber, see above, p. 75, n. 1.) Though the likes of Cibber might be preferred to the laureateship, and though Addison's more thoughtless followers might scour farms and dairies in search of untutored geniuses—a Stephen Duck or an Ann Yearsley—Fielding kept a sense of proportion; with the precepts of Horace in mind, Learning was among the tutelar deities he invoked to direct his own pen (IX. i, XIII. i). The new directions in criticism were, however, against him. The clearest expression of the cult of genius would of course be made by Richardson's friend, Edward Young, in his *Conjectures on Original Composition* (1759), but Young's views were by no means as novel as he liked to represent them (see the *Conjectures*, ed. Edith J. Morley [Manchester, 1918], pp. xiii–xv).

being taught to move;[1] nor doth any Mechanic, I believe, exercise his Tools the worse by having learnt to use them. For my own Part, I cannot conceive that *Homer* or *Virgil* would have writ with more Fire, if, instead of being Masters of all the Learning of their Times, they had been as ignorant as most of the Authors of the present Age. Nor do I believe that all the Imagination, Fire, and Judgment of *Pitt*[2] could have produced those Orations that have made the Senate of *England* in these our Times a Rival in Eloquence to *Greece* and *Rome*, if he had not been so well read in the Writings of *Demosthenes* and *Cicero*, as to have transferred their whole Spirit into his Speeches, and with their Spirit, their Knowledge too.

I would not here be understood to insist on the same Fund of Learning in any of my Brethren, as *Cicero* perswades us is necessary to the Composition of an Orator.[3] On the contrary, very little Reading is, I conceive, necessary to the Poet, less to the Critic, and the least of all to the Politician. For the first, perhaps, *Byshe's* Art of Poetry,[4] and a few of our modern Poets, may suffice; for the second, a moderate Heap of Plays; and for the last, an indifferent Collection of political Journals.

To say the Truth, I require no more than that a Man should have some little Knowledge of the Subject on which he treats, according to the old Maxim of Law, *Quam quisque norit artem in ea se exerceat*.[5] With this alone a Writer may sometimes do

---

[1] Cf. Pope, *Essay on Criticism* (1711), 362–3: 'True Ease in Writing comes from Art, not Chance,/ As those move easiest who have learn'd to dance.'

[2] William Pitt (1708–78), later first Earl of Chatham, was an eloquent speaker in the House of Commons whose abilities earned him the nickname of 'the Orator'. With his close friend Lyttelton (see above, p. 3, n. 1) he first came into prominence as a member of the Opposition, but, after Walpole's fall and the formation of the Broad-Bottom Administration, he was appointed Paymaster-General of the Forces (1746). Like Lyttelton, Pitt probably knew Fielding as a schoolboy at Eton, and their mutual friends and political interests served to keep them on friendly terms. According to tradition, Pitt was among the circle at Radway Grange to whom Fielding read from the manuscript of *Tom Jones*, and with Lyttelton he actively 'puffed' the novel before publication (see the General Introduction, pp. xxxii–xxxiii and n .1). For another compliment to him, see *The True Patriot* (7 January 1746).

[3] Cf. *De Oratore*, i. xxxiv. 155–9. Fielding also alludes to this passage in *The Champion* (25 December 1739) and *Joseph Andrews* (iii. ii).

[4] *The Art of English Poetry* (1702) by Edward Bysshe (*fl.* 1712) was a popular manual containing rules for versification, a rhyming dictionary, and a collection of poetical commonplaces. A copy of the book lies open before Hogarth's 'Distressed Poet'.

[5] From Cicero, *Tusculan Disputations*, i. xviii. 41: 'Let every man cultivate the talent he knows is in him.'

tolerably well; and indeed without this, all the other Learning in the World will stand him in little stead.

For Instance, let us suppose that *Homer* and *Virgil*, *Aristotle* and *Cicero*, *Thucydides* and *Livy* could have met all together, and have clubbed their several Talents to have composed a Treatise on the Art of Dancing; I believe it will be readily agreed they could not have equalled the excellent Treatise which Mr. *Essex*[1] hath given us on that Subject, entitled, *The Rudiments of genteel Education*. And, indeed, should the excellent Mr. *Broughton*[2] be prevailed on to set *Fist* to Paper, and to complete the abovesaid Rudiments, by delivering down the true Principles of Athletics, I question whether the World will have any Cause to lament, that none of the great Writers, either ancient or modern, have ever treated about that noble and useful Art.

To avoid a Multiplicity of Examples in so plain a Case, and to come at once to my Point, I am apt to conceive, that one Reason why many *English* Writers have totally failed in describing the Manners of upper Life, may possibly be, that in Reality they know nothing of it.

This is a Knowledge unhappily not in the Power of many Authors to arrive at. Books will give us a very imperfect Idea of it; nor will the Stage a much better: The fine Gentleman formed

---

[1] John Essex, the well-known dancing-master. Besides publishing a number of treatises on that art (see above, p. 211, n. 1), he was author of *The Young Ladies Conduct: or, Rules for Education* (1722), wherein he remarks of dancing: 'altho' other Arts and Sciences have their peculiar Use in Life, and are valuable in Education; yet few, if any, are so Necessary and Advantageous as this, especially under a good Master . . .' (p. 82). Fielding refers to this work again in *Amelia* (v. ii); and in *A Journey from This World to the Next* (I. xxv), he probably had Essex in mind when Julian, in his incarnation as an illiterate dancing-master, composes 'a Treatise on Education; the first Rudiments of which . . . were to instruct a Child in the Science of coming handsomely into a Room'. See, too, the series relating Job Vinegar's voyages in *The Champion*, which includes a satirical description of the role dancing-masters played in the education of females (4 September 1740). Essex is represented in Plate I of Hogarth's *Analysis of Beauty* (1753).

[2] Of the champion boxer John Broughton (see above, pp. 702, n. 1; 703, n. 1) one knowledgeable admirer asked: 'What can be stronger than to say, that for seventeen or eighteen Years, he has fought every able *Boxer* that appeared against him, and has never yet been beat ? . . . What is it that he wants ? Has he not all that others want, and all that the best can have ? Strength equal to what is human, Skill and Judgement equal to what can be acquired, undebauched Wind, and a bottom Spirit, never to pronounce the Word ENOUGH' (Capt. John Godfrey, *A Treatise upon the Useful Science of Defence* [1747], pp. 55–6). In 1748 Broughton opened an 'Academy' to initiate pupils into 'the Mystery of Boxing . . . that truly *British* Art' (see above, p. 703, n.).

upon reading the former will almost always turn out a Pedant, and he who forms himself upon the latter, a Coxcomb.

Nor are the Characters drawn from these Models better supported. *Vanbrugh* and *Congreve* copied Nature; but they who copy them draw as unlike the present Age, as *Hogarth*[1] would do if he was to paint a Rout or a Drum in the Dresses of *Titian* and of *Vandyke*.[2] In short, Imitation here will not do the Business. The Picture must be after Nature herself.[3] A true Knowledge of the World is gained only by Conversation, and the Manners of every Rank must be seen in order to be known.

Now it happens that this higher Order of Mortals is not to be seen, like all the rest of the Human Species, for nothing, in the Streets, Shops, and Coffee-houses: Nor are they shewn, like the upper Rank of Animals, for so much a Piece. In short, this is a Sight to which no Persons are admitted, without one or other of these Qualifications, *viz.* either Birth or Fortune; or what is equivalent to both, the honourable Profession of a Gamester. And very unluckily for the World, Persons so qualified, very seldom care to take upon themselves the bad Trade of Writing; which is generally entered upon by the lower and poorer Sort, as it is a Trade which many think requires no Kind of Stock to set up with.

Hence those strange Monsters in Lace and Embroidery, in Silks and Brocades, with vast Wigs and Hoops; which, under the Name of Lords and Ladies, strut the Stage, to the great Delight of Attornies and their Clerks in the Pit, and of the Citizens and their Apprentices in the Galleries; and which are no more to be found in real Life, than the Centaur, the Chimera, or any other Creature of mere Fiction.[4] But to let my Reader into a Secret, this Knowledge of upper Life, though very

[1] See above, p. 66, n. 1.

[2] Tiziano Vecellio (*c.* 1477–1576), the celebrated painter of the Venetian school; and Sir Anthony Vandyke (1599–1641), Flemish portrait painter to the court of Charles I.

[3] Cf. Dryden's observation in the Dedication to his translation of the *Æneis* (1697): ''Tis one thing to Copy, and another thing to imitate from Nature. The Copyer is that servile Imitator, to whom *Horace* gives no better a Name than that of Animal: He will not so much as allow him to be a Man. *Raphael* imitated Nature: They who Copy one of *Raphael*'s Pieces, imitate but him, for his Work is their Original' (sig. (d)1ʳ).

[4] Cf. letter cxxxi of Montesquieu's *Persian Letters* (Ozell trans., 1722), on romance-writers 'who spend their lives in seeking after Nature and never find her, and who create Heroes as unaccountably monstrous as winged Dragons and *Hippocentaurs*' (ii. 230).

necessary for preventing Mistakes, is no very great Resource to a Writer whose Province is Comedy, or that Kind of Novels, which, like this I am writing, is of the comic Class.

What Mr. *Pope* says of Women[1] is very applicable to most in this Station, who are indeed so entirely made up of Form and Affectation, that they have no Character at all, at least, none which appears. I will venture to say the highest Life is much the dullest, and affords very little Humour or Entertainment. The various Callings in lower Spheres produce the great Variety of humorous Characters; whereas here, except among the few who are engaged in the Pursuit of Ambition, and the fewer still who have a Relish for Pleasure, all is Vanity and servile Imitation. Dressing and Cards, eating and drinking, bowing and curtesying, make up the Business of their Lives.

Some there are however of this Rank, upon whom Passion exercises its Tyranny, and hurries them far beyond the Bounds which Decorum prescribes; of these, the Ladies are as much distinguished by their noble Intrepidity, and a certain superior Contempt of Reputation, from the frail ones of meaner Degree, as a virtuous Woman of Quality is by the Elegance and Delicacy of her Sentiments from the honest Wife of a Yeoman or Shopkeeper. Lady *Bellaston* was of this intrepid Character; but let not my Country Readers conclude from her, that this is the general Conduct of Women of Fashion, or that we mean to represent them as such. They might as well suppose, that every Clergyman was represented by *Thwackum*, or every Soldier by Ensign *Northerton*.

There is not indeed a greater Error than that which universally prevails among the Vulgar, who borrowing their Opinion from some ignorant Satyrists, have affixed the Character of Lewdness to these Times. On the contrary, I am convinced there never was less of Love Intrigue carried on among Persons of Condition, than now. Our present Women have been taught by their Mothers to fix their Thoughts only on Ambition and Vanity, and to despise the Pleasures of Love as unworthy their Regard; and being afterwards, by the Care of such Mothers, married without having Husbands, they seem pretty well confirmed in the Justness of those Sentiments; whence they content themselves,

---

[1] *Moral Essays*, II, 'To a Lady. Of the Characters of Women' (1735), 1–2: 'Nothing so true as what you once let fall,/ Most Women have no Characters at all.'

for the dull Remainder of Life, with the Pursuit of more innocent, but I am afraid more childish Amusements, the bare Mention of which would ill suit with the Dignity of this History. In
my humble Opinion, the true Characteristick of the present
Beau Monde, is rather Folly than Vice, and the only Epithet
which it deserves is that of *Frivolous*.

CHAPTER II

Containing Letters and other Matters which attend Amours.

JONES had not long been at Home, before he received the
following Letter.

'I was never more surprized than when I found you was gone.
When you left the Room, I little imagined you intended to have
left the House without seeing me again. Your Behaviour is all of a
Piece, and convinces me how much I ought to despise a Heart
which can doat upon an Idiot; though I know not whether I
should not admire her Cunning more than her Simplicity:
Wonderful both! For though she understood not a Word of
what passed between us, she yet had the Skill, the Assurance,
the—what shall I call it? to deny to my Face, that she knows
you, or ever saw you before.—Was this a Scheme laid between
you, and have you been base enough to betray me?—O how
I despise her, you, and all the World, but chiefly myself, for—
I dare not write what I should afterwards run mad to read; but
remember, I can detest as violently as I have loved.'

Jones had but little Time given him to reflect on this Letter,
before a second was brought him from the same Hand; and this,
likewise, we shall set down in the precise Words.

'When you consider the Hurry of Spirits in which I must have
writ, you cannot be surprised at any Expressions in my former
Note.—Yet, perhaps, on Reflection, they were rather too warm.
At least I would, if possible, think all owing to the odious Play-
house, and to the Impertinence of a Fool, which detained me
beyond my Appointment.—How easy is it to think well of those

we love?—Perhaps you desire I should think so. I have resolved to see you To-Night, so come to me immediately.

P.S. I have ordered to be at Home to none but yourself.

P.S. Mr. *Jones* will imagine I shall assist him in his Defence; for I believe he cannot desire to impose on me more than I desire to impose on myself.

P.S. Come immediately.'

To the Men of Intrigue I refer the Determination, whether the angry or the tender Letter gave the greatest Uneasiness to *Jones*. Certain it is, he had no violent Inclination to pay any more Visits that Evening, unless to one single Person. However he thought his Honour engaged, and had not this been Motive sufficient, he would not have ventured to blow the Temper of Lady *Bellaston* into that Flame of which he had Reason to think it susceptible, and of which he feared the Consequence might be a Discovery to *Sophia*, which he dreaded. After some discontented Walks therefore about the Room, he was preparing to depart, when the Lady kindly prevented him, not by another Letter, but by her own Presence. She entered the Room very disordered in her Dress, and very discomposed in her Looks, and threw herself into a Chair, where having recovered her Breath, she said,—'You see, Sir, when Women have gone one Length too far, they will stop at none. If any Person would have sworn this to me a Week ago, I would not have believed it of myself.' 'I hope, Madam,' said *Jones*, 'my charming Lady *Bellaston* will be as difficult to believe any thing against one who is so sensible of the many Obligations she hath conferred upon him.' —'Indeed!' says she, 'sensible of Obligations! Did I expect to hear such cold Language from Mr. *Jones*?' 'Pardon me, my dear Angel,' said he, 'if after the Letters I have received, the Terrors of your Anger, though I know not how I have deserved it——' 'And have I then,' says she with a Smile, 'so angry a Countenance?—Have I really brought a chiding Face with me?'— 'If there be Honour in Man,' said he, 'I have done nothing to merit your Anger.—You remember the Appointment you sent me—I went in Pursuance——' 'I beseech you,' cry'd she, 'do not run through the odious Recital.—Answer me but one Question, and I shall be easy.—Have you not betrayed my Honour to her?'—*Jones* fell upon his Knees, and began to utter the most violent Protestations, when *Partridge* came dancing and capering into the Room, like one drunk with Joy, crying out, 'She's found! she's found!—Here, Sir, here, she's here,—Mrs. *Honour* is upon the Stairs.' 'Stop her a Moment,' cries *Jones*,—'Here, Madam, step behind the Bed, I have no other Room nor Closet, nor Place on Earth to hide you in; sure never was so damn'd an Accident.'—'D—n'd indeed!' said the Lady as she went to her Place of Concealment; and presently afterwards in came Mrs. *Honour*. 'Hey day!' says she, 'Mr. *Jones*, what's the Matter?— That impudent Rascal, your Servant, would scarce let me come up Stairs. I hope he hath not the same Reason to keep me from you as he had at *Upton*.—I suppose you hardly expected to see me; but you have certainly bewitched my Lady. Poor dear young Lady! To be sure, I loves her as tenderly as if she was my own Sister. Lord have Mercy upon you, if you don't make her a good Husband; and to be sure, if you do not, nothing can be bad enough for you.' *Jones* begged her only to whisper, for that there was a Lady dying in the next Room. 'A Lady!' cries she; 'ay, I suppose one of your Ladies.—O Mr. *Jones*, there are too many of them in the World; I believe we are got into the House of one, for my Lady *Bellaston* I darst to say is no better than she should be.'—'Hush! hush!' cries *Jones*, 'every Word is overheard in the next Room.' 'I don't care a Farthing,' cries *Honour*, 'I speaks no Scandal of any one; but to be sure the Servants makes no Scruple of saying as how her Ladyship meets Men at another Place— where the House goes under the Name of a poor Gentlewoman, but her Ladyship pays the Rent, and many's the good Thing besides, they say, she hath of her.'—Here *Jones*, after expressing the utmost Uneasiness, offered to stop her Mouth.—'Hey day! why sure Mr. *Jones* you will let me speak, I speaks no Scandal, for I only says what I heard from others,—and thinks I to myself much good may it do the Gentlewoman with her Riches, if she comes by it in such a wicked Manner. To be sure it is better to be poor and honest.' 'The Servants are Villains,' cries *Jones*, 'and abuse their Lady unjustly.'—'Ay to be sure Servants are always Villains, and so my Lady says, and won't hear a Word of it.'— 'No, I am convinced,' says *Jones*, 'my *Sophia* is above listening to such base Scandal.' 'Nay, I believe it is no Scandal neither,' cries *Honour*, 'for why should she meet Men at another House?— It can never be for any Good: for if she had a lawful Design of being courted, as to be sure any Lady may lawfully give her Company to Men upon that Account; why where can be the Sense——' 'I protest,' cries *Jones*, 'I can't hear all this of a Lady of such Honour, and a Relation of *Sophia*; besides you will distract the poor Lady in the next Room.—Let me intreat you to walk with me down Stairs.'—'Nay, Sir, if you won't let me speak, I have done.—Here, Sir, is a Letter from my young Lady,—what would some Men give to have this? But, Mr. *Jones*, I think you are not over and above generous, and yet I have heard some Servants say; but I am sure you will do me the Justice to own I never saw the Colour of your Money.' Here *Jones* hastily took the Letter, and presently after slip'd five Pieces into her Hand. He then returned a thousand Thanks to his dear *Sophia* in a Whisper, and begged her to leave him to read her Letter; she presently departed, not without expressing much grateful Sense of his Generosity.

Lady *Bellaston* now came from behind the Curtain. How shall I describe her Rage? Her Tongue was at first incapable of Utterance; but Streams of Fire darted from her Eyes, and well indeed they might, for her Heart was all in a Flame. And now as soon as her Voice found Way, instead of expressing any Indignation against *Honour*, or her own Servants, she began to attack poor *Jones*. 'You see,' said she, 'what I have sacrificed to you, my Reputation, my Honour,—gone for ever! And what Return have I found? Neglected, slighted for a Country Girl, for an Idiot.'—'What Neglect, Madam, or what Slight,' cries *Jones*, 'have I been guilty of?'—'Mr. *Jones*,' said she, 'it is in vain to dissemble, if you will make me easy, you must entirely give her up; and as a Proof of your Intention, shew me the Letter.'—'What Letter, Madam?' said *Jones*. 'Nay, surely,' said she, 'you cannot have the Confidence to deny your having received a Letter by the Hands of that Trollop.' 'And can your Ladyship,' cries he, 'ask of me what I must part with my Honour before I grant? Have I acted in such a Manner by your Ladyship? Could I be guilty of betraying this poor innocent Girl to you, what Security could you have, that I should not act the same Part by yourself? A Moment's Reflection will, I am sure, convince you, that a Man with whom the Secrets of a Lady are not safe, must be the most contemptible of Wretches.' 'Very well,' said she—'I need not insist on your becoming this contemptible Wretch in your own Opinion; for the Inside of the Letter could inform me of nothing more than I know already. I see the Footing you are upon.'—Here ensued a long Conversation, which the Reader, who is not too curious, will thank me for not inserting at length. It shall suffice therefore to inform him, that Lady *Bellaston* grew more and more pacified, and at length believed, or affected to believe, his Protestations, that his meeting with *Sophia* that Evening was merely accidental, and every other Matter which the Reader already knows, and which as *Jones* set before her in the strongest Light, it is plain that she had in Reality no Reason to be angry with him.

She was not however in her Heart perfectly satisfied with his Refusal to shew her the Letter, so deaf are we to the clearest Reason, when it argues against our prevailing Passions. She was indeed well convinced that *Sophia* possessed the first Place in *Jones's* Affections; and yet, haughty and amorous as this Lady was, she submitted at last to bear the second Place; or to express it more properly in a legal Phrase, was contented with the Possession of that of which another Woman had the Reversion.[1]

It was at length agreed, that *Jones* should for the future visit at the House: for that *Sophia* her Maid, and all the Servants would place these Visits to the Account of *Sophia*; and that she herself would be considered as the Person imposed upon.

This Scheme was contrived by the Lady, and highly relished by *Jones*, who was indeed glad to have a Prospect of seeing his *Sophia* at any Rate; and the Lady herself was not a little pleased with the Imposition on *Sophia*, which *Jones*, she thought, could not possibly discover to her for his own Sake.

The next Day was appointed for the first Visit, and then, after proper Ceremonials, the Lady *Bellaston* returned Home.

CHAPTER III

Containing various Matters.

JONES was no sooner alone, than he eagerly broke open his Letter, and read as follows.

'Sir, it is impossible to express what I have suffered since

---

[1] In the laws of property, a reversion is the returning of an estate to the rightful owner after it had been temporarily granted to the use and possession of another (see Jacob, *New Law-Dictionary*, 4th ed. [1739], s.v. 'Reversion'). See also above, pp. 109. 10, 287. 6.

you left this House; and as I have Reason to think you intend coming here again, I have sent *Honour*, though so late at Night, as she tells me she knows your Lodgings, to prevent you. I charge you, by all the Regard you have for me, not to think of visiting here; for it will certainly be discovered; nay, I almost doubt from some Things which have dropt from her Ladyship, that she is not already without some Suspicion. Something favourable perhaps may happen; we must wait with Patience; but I once more entreat you, if you have any Concern for my Ease, do not think of returning hither.'

This Letter administred the same Kind of Consolation to poor *Jones*, which *Job* formerly received from his Friends. Besides disappointing all the Hopes which he promised to himself from seeing *Sophia*, he was reduced to an unhappy Dilemma, with Regard to Lady *Bellaston*; for there are some certain Engagements, which, as he well knew, do very difficultly admit of any Excuse for the Failure; and to go, after the strict Prohibition from *Sophia*, he was not to be forced by any human Power. At length, after much Deliberation, which during that Night supply'd the Place of Sleep, he determined to feign himself sick: For this suggested itself as the only means of failing the appointed Visit, without incensing Lady *Bellaston*, which he had more than one Reason of desiring to avoid.

The first Thing however which he did in the Morning was to write an Answer to *Sophia*, which he enclosed in one to *Honour*. He then dispatched another to Lady *Bellaston*, containing the abovementioned Excuse; and to this he soon received the following Answer.

'I am vexed that I cannot see you here this Afternoon, but more concerned for the Occasion; take great Care of yourself, and have the best Advice, and I hope there will be no Danger.—I am so tormented all this Morning with Fools, that I have scarce a Moment's Time to write to you. Adieu.

P.S. I will endeavour to call on you this Evening at nine.— Be sure to be alone.'

Mr. *Jones* now received a Visit from Mrs. *Miller*, who, after some formal Introduction, began the following Speech. 'I am very sorry, Sir, to wait upon you on such an Occasion; but I hope you will consider the ill Consequence which it must be to the

Reputation of my poor Girls, if my House should once be talked of as a House of ill Fame. I hope you won't think me therefore guilty of Impertinence, if I beg you not to bring any more Ladies in at that Time of Night. The Clock had struck two before one of them went away.' 'I do assure you, Madam,' said *Jones*, 'the Lady who was here last Night, and who staid the latest (for the other only brought me a Letter) is a Woman of very great Fashion, and my near Relation.' 'I don't know what Fashion she is of,' answered Mrs. *Miller*, 'but I am sure no Woman of Virtue, unless a very near Relation indeed, would visit a young Gentleman at ten at Night, and stay four Hours in his Room with him alone; besides, Sir, the Behaviour of her Chairmen shews what she was; for they did nothing but make Jests all the Evening in the Entry, and asked Mr. *Partridge* in the hearing of my own Maid, if Madam intended to stay with his Master all Night; with a great deal of Stuff not proper to be repeated. I have really a great Respect for you, Mr. *Jones*, upon your own Account, nay I have a very high Obligation to you for your Generosity to my Cousin. Indeed I did not know how very good you had been till lately. Little did I imagine to what dreadful Courses the poor Man's Distress had driven him. Little did I think when you gave me the ten Guineas, that you had given them to a Highwayman! O Heavens! What Goodness have you shewn? How have you preserved this Family.—The Character which Mr. *Allworthy* hath formerly given me of you, was, I find, strictly true.—And indeed if I had no Obligation to you, my Obligations to him are such, that, on his Account, I should shew you the utmost Respect in my Power.—Nay, believe me, dear Mr. *Jones*, if my Daughters and my own Reputation were out of the Case, I should, for your own Sake, be sorry that so pretty a young Gentleman should converse with these Women; but if you are resolved to do it, I must beg you to take another Lodging; for I do not myself like to have such Things carried on under my Roof; but more especially upon the Account of my Girls, who have little, Heaven knows, besides their Characters to recommend them.' *Jones* started and changed Colour at the Name of *Allworthy*. 'Indeed, Mrs. *Miller*,' answered he a little warmly, 'I do not take this at all kind. I will never bring any Slander on your House; but I must insist on seeing what Company I please in my own Room; and if that gives you any Offence, I shall, as soon as I am able, look for another

Lodging.' 'I am sorry we must part then, Sir,' said she, 'but I am convinced Mr. *Allworthy* himself would never come within my Doors, if he had the least Suspicion of my keeping an ill House.' —'Very well, Madam,' said *Jones.*—'I hope, Sir,' said she, 'you are not angry; for I would not for the World offend any of Mr. *Allworthy's* Family. I have not slept a wink all Night about this Matter.'—'I am sorry, I have disturbed your Rest, Madam,' said *Jones*, 'but I beg you will send *Partridge* up to me immediately;' which she promised to do, and then with a very low Courtesy retired.

As soon as *Partridge* arrived, *Jones* fell upon him in the most outrageous manner.—'How often,' said he, 'am I to suffer for your Folly, or rather for my own in keeping you? Is that Tongue of yours resolved upon my Destruction?'—'What have I done, Sir?' answered affrighted *Partridge*. 'Who was it gave you Authority to mention the Story of the Robbery, or that the Man you saw here was the Person?'—'I, Sir?' cries *Partridge*. 'Now don't be guilty of a Falshood in denying it,' said *Jones.*—'If I did mention such a Matter,' answers *Partridge*, 'I am sure, I thought no Harm: For I should not have opened my Lips, if it had not been to his own Friends and Relations, who, I imagined, would have let it go no farther.' 'But I have a much heavier Charge against you,' cries *Jones*, 'than this. How durst you, after all the Precautions I gave you, mention the Name of Mr. *Allworthy* in this House?' *Partridge* denied that he ever had, with many Oaths. 'How else,' said *Jones*, 'should Mrs. *Miller* be acquainted that there was any Connection between him and me? And it is but this Moment she told me, she respected me on his Account.'—'O Lord, Sir,' said *Partridge*, 'I desire only to be heard out; and to be sure, never was any thing so unfortunate; hear me but out, and you will own how wrongfully you have accused me. When Mrs. *Honour* came down Stairs last Night, she met me in the Entry, and asked me when my Master had heard from Mr. *Allworthy*; and to be sure Mrs. *Miller* heard the very Words; and the Moment Madam *Honour* was gone, she called me into the Parlour to her. "Mr. *Partridge*," says she, "What Mr. *Allworthy* is that the Gentlewoman mentioned? Is it the great Mr. *Allworthy* of *Somersetshire*?" "Upon my Word, Madam," says I, "I know nothing of the Matter."—"Sure," says she, "your Master is not the Mr. *Jones* I have heard Mr. *Allworthy* talk of?"

"Upon my Word, Madam," says I, "I know nothing of the Matter."—"Then," says she, turning to her Daughter *Nancy*, says she, "as sure as ten Pence this is the very young Gentleman, and he agrees exactly with the Squire's Description." The Lord above knows who it was told her, for I am the arrantest Villain that ever walked upon two Legs if ever it came out of my Mouth. —I promise you, Sir, I can keep a Secret when I am desired.— Nay, Sir, so far was I from telling her any thing about Mr. *Allworthy*, that I told her the very direct contrary: For though I did not contradict it at that Moment, yet as second Thoughts, they say, are best; so when I came to consider that some body must have informed her, thinks I to myself, I will put an End to the Story, and so I went back again into the Parlour some time afterwards, and says I, Upon my word, says I, whoever, says I, told you that this Gentleman was Mr. *Jones*, that is, says I, that this Mr. *Jones* was that Mr. *Jones*, told you a confounded Lie; and I beg, says I, you will never mention any such Matter, says I: for my Master, says I, will think I must have told you so, and I defy any body in the House, ever to say, I mentioned any such Word. To be certain, Sir, it is a wonderful Thing, and I have been thinking with myself ever since, how it was she came to know it; not but I saw an old Woman here t'other Day a begging at the Door, who looked as like her we saw in *Warwickshire*, that caused all that Mischief to us. To be sure it is never good to pass by an old Woman without giving her something, especially if she looks at you; for all the World shall never persuade me but that they have a great Power to do Mischief, and to be sure I shall never see an old Woman again, but I shall think to myself, *Infandum, Regina, jubes renovare Dolorem*.'[1]

The Simplicity of *Partridge* set *Jones* a laughing, and put a final end to his Anger, which had indeed seldom any long Duration in his Mind; and instead of commenting on his Defence, he told him he intended presently to leave those Lodgings, and ordered him to go and endeavour to get him others.

---

[1] See above, p. 424, n. 1.

CHAPTER IV

Which we hope will be very attentively perused by young People of both Sexes.

PARTRIDGE had no sooner left Mr. *Jones*, than Mr. *Nightingale*, with whom he had now contracted a great Intimacy, came to him, and after a short Salutation, said, 'So, *Tom*, I hear you had Company very late last Night. Upon my Soul, you are a happy Fellow, who have not been in Town above a Fortnight, and can keep Chairs waiting at your Door till two in the Morning.' He then ran on with much common-place Raillery of the same Kind, till *Jones* at last interrupted him, saying, 'I suppose you have received all this Information from Mrs. *Miller*, who hath been up here a little while ago to give me Warning. The good Woman is afraid, it seems, of the Reputation of her Daughters.' 'O she is wonderfully nice,' says *Nightingale*, 'upon that Account; if you remember, she would not let *Nancy* go with us to the Masquerade.' 'Nay, upon my Honour, I think she's in the Right of it,' says *Jones*; 'however I have taken her at her Word, and have sent *Partridge* to look for another Lodging.' 'If you will,' says *Nightingale*, 'we may, I believe, be again together; for to tell you a Secret, which I desire you won't mention in the Family, I intend to quit the House to-day.'— 'What, hath Mrs. *Miller* given you Warning too, my Friend?' cries *Jones*. 'No,' answered the other; 'but the Rooms are not convenient enough.—Besides, I am grown weary of this part of the Town. I want to be nearer the Places of Diversion; so I am going to *Pall-mall*.'—'And do you intend to make a Secret of your going away?' said *Jones*. 'I promise you,' answered *Nightingale*, 'I don't intend to bilk my Lodgings; but I have a private Reason for not taking a formal Leave.' 'Not so private,' answered *Jones*; 'I promise you, I have seen it ever since the second Day of my coming to the House.—Here will be some wet Eyes on your Departure.—Poor *Nancy*, I pity her, faith!—Indeed, *Jack*, you have play'd the Fool with that Girl.—You have given her a Longing, which I am afraid nothing will ever cure her of.'— *Nightingale* answered, 'What the Devil would you have me do? Would you have me marry her to cure her?'—'No,' answered *Jones*, 'I would not have had you make Love to her, as you have often done in my Presence. I have been astonished at the Blindness of her Mother in never seeing it.' 'Pugh, see it!' cries *Nightingale*, 'What the Devil should she see?' 'Why see,' said *Jones*, 'that you have made her Daughter distractedly in Love with you. The poor Girl cannot conceal it a Moment, her Eyes are never off from you, and she always colours every time you come into the Room. Indeed, I pity her heartily; for she seems to be one of the best natured, and honestest of human-Creatures.' 'And so,' answered *Nightingale*, 'according to your Doctrine, one must not amuse one's self by any common Gallantries with Women, for fear they should fall in love with us.' 'Indeed, *Jack*,' said *Jones*, 'you wilfully misunderstand me; I do not fancy Women are so apt to fall in love; but you have gone far beyond common Gallantries.'—'What do you suppose,' says *Nightingale*, 'that we have been a-bed together?' 'No, upon my Honour,' answered *Jones*, very seriously, 'I do not suppose so ill of you; nay, I will go farther, I do not imagine you have laid a regular premeditated Scheme for the Destruction of the Quiet of a poor little Creature, or have even foreseen the Consequence; for I am sure thou art a very good-natured Fellow, and such a one can never be guilty of a Cruelty of that Kind; but at the same time, you have pleased your own Vanity, without considering that this poor Girl was made a Sacrifice to it; and while you have had no Design but of amusing an idle Hour, you have actually given her Reason to flatter herself, that you had the most serious Designs in her Favour. Prithee, *Jack*, answer me honestly: To what have tended all those elegant and luscious Descriptions of Happiness arising from violent and mutual Fondness, all those warm Professions of Tenderness, and generous, disinterested Love? did you imagine she would not apply them? or speak ingenuously, did not you intend she should?' 'Upon my Soul, *Tom*,' cries *Nightingale*, 'I did not think this was in thee. Thou wilt make an admirable Parson.—So, I suppose, you would not go to Bed to *Nancy* now, if she would let you?'—'No,' cries *Jones*, 'may I be d—n'd if I would.' '*Tom, Tom*,' answered *Nightingale*, 'last Night, remember last Night.

　　——When every Eye was clos'd, and the pale Moon,
　　And silent Stars shone conscious of the Theft.'[1]

¹ Rowe's *The Fair Penitent* (1703), I. i. Lothario recounts his seduction of Calista:

'Lookee, Mr. *Nightingale*,' said *Jones*, 'I am no canting Hypocrite, nor do I pretend to the Gift of Chastity, more than my Neighbours. I have been guilty with Women, I own it; but am not conscious that I have ever injured any—nor would I to procure Pleasure to myself, be knowingly the Cause of Misery to any human Being.'[1]

'Well, well,' said *Nightingale*, 'I believe you, and I am convinced you acquit me of any such Thing.'

'I do, from my Heart,' answered *Jones*, 'of having debauched the Girl, but not from having gained her Affections.'

'If I have,' said *Nightingale*, 'I am sorry for it; but Time and Absence will soon wear off such Impressions. It is a Receipt I must take myself: For to confess the Truth to you—I never liked any Girl half so much in my whole Life; but I must let you into the whole Secret, *Tom*. My Father hath provided a Match for me, with a Woman I never saw, and she is now coming to Town, in order for me to make my Addresses to her.'

At these Words *Jones* burst into a loud Fit of Laughter; when *Nightingale* cried,—'Nay, prithee don't turn me into Ridicule. The Devil take me if I am not half mad about this Matter! My poor *Nancy*! Oh *Jones*, *Jones*, I wish I had a Fortune in my own Possession.'

'I heartily wish you had,' cries *Jones*; 'for if this be the Case, I sincerely pity you both: But surely you don't intend to go away without taking your Leave of her.'

> Once in a lone and secret Hour of Night,
> When ev'ry Eye was clos'd, and the pale Moon
> And Stars alone, shone conscious of the Theft,
> Hot with the *Tuscan* Grape, and high in Blood,
> Hap'ly I stole unheeded to her Chamber.

[1] At a time when the double standard was widely accepted, Fielding strove to define the morality of sexual relationships for men as well as women. With the present passage, compare *The Wedding Day* (1743), v. iii. Heartfort having declared that adultery is both vicious and dishonourable, Millamour exclaims: 'Heyday! thou art not turning Hypocrite, I hope. Thou dost not pretend to lead a Life equal to this Doctrine.' To which Heartfort replies: 'My Practice perhaps is not equal to my Theory; but I pretend to sin with as little Mischief as I can to others: and this I can lay my Hand on my Heart and affirm, that I never seduced a young Woman to her own Ruin, nor a married one to the Misery of her Husband.' Cf. also the narrator's plea before Minos in *A Journey from This world to the Next* (1743), I. vii: 'I confess'd I had indulged myself very freely with Wine and Women in my Youth, but had never done an Injury to any Man living, nor avoided an Opportunity of doing good; that I pretended to very little Virtue more than general Philanthropy, and private Friendship.'

'I would not,' answered *Nightingale*, 'undergo the Pain of taking Leave for ten thousand Pound; besides, I am convinced, instead of answering any good Purpose, it would only serve to inflame my poor *Nancy* the more. I beg therefore, you would not mention a Word of it to-day, and in the Evening or to-morrow morning I intend to depart.'

Jones promised he would not, and said, upon Reflection he thought, as he had determined and was obliged to leave her, he took the most prudent Method. He then told *Nightingale*, he should be very glad to lodge in the same House with him; and it was accordingly agreed between them, that *Nightingale* should procure him either the Ground Floor, or the two Pair of Stairs; for the young Gentleman himself was to occupy that which was between them.

This *Nightingale*, of whom we shall be presently obliged to say a little more, was in the ordinary Transactions of Life a Man of strict Honour, and what is more rare among young Gentlemen of the Town, one of strict Honesty too; yet in Affairs of Love he was somewhat loose in his Morals; not that he was even here as void of Principle as Gentlemen sometimes are, and oftner affect to be; but it is certain he had been guilty of some indefensible Treachery to Women, and had in a certain Mystery called making Love, practiced many Deceits, which if he had used in Trade he would have been counted the greatest Villain upon Earth.

But as the World, I know not well for what Reason, agree to see this Treachery in a better Light, he was so far from being ashamed of his Iniquities of this Kind, that he gloried in them, and would often boast of his Skill in gaining of Women, and his Triumphs over their Hearts, for which he had before this time received some Rebukes from *Jones*, who always exprest great Bitterness against any Misbehaviour to the fair Part of the Species, who, if considered, he said, as they ought to be, in the Light of the dearest Friends, were to be cultivated, honoured, and caressed with the utmost Love and Tenderness; but if regarded as Enemies, were a Conquest of which a Man ought rather to be ashamed than to value himself upon it.

CHAPTER V

A short Account of the History of Mrs. Miller.

JONES this Day eat a pretty good Dinner for a sick Man, that is to say, the larger Half of a Shoulder of Mutton. In the Afternoon he received an Invitation from Mrs. *Miller* to drink Tea: For that good Woman having learnt, either by Means of *Partridge*, or by some other Means natural or super-natural, that he had a Connection with Mr. *Allworthy*, could not endure the Thoughts of parting with him in an angry Manner.

Jones accepted the Invitation; and no sooner was the Tea-kettle removed, and the Girls sent out of the Room, than the Widow, without much Preface, began as follows: 'Well, there are very surprizing Things happen in this World; but certainly it is a wonderful Business, that I should have a Relation of Mr. *Allworthy* in my House, and never know any Thing of the Matter. Alas! Sir, you little imagine what a Friend that best of Gentle-men hath been to me and mine. Yes, Sir, I am not ashamed to own it; it is owing to his Goodness, that I did not long since perish for Want, and leave my poor little Wretches, two desti-tute, hclplcss, friendless Orphans, to the Care, or rather to the Cruelty of the World.

'You must know, Sir, though I am now reduced to get my Living by letting Lodgings, I was born and bred a Gentle-woman. My Father was an Officer of the Army, and died in a considerable Rank: But he lived up to his Pay; and as that expired with him, his Family, at his Death, became Beggars. We were three Sisters. One of us had the good Luck to die soon afterwards of the Small-pox: A Lady was so kind to take the second out of Charity, as she said, to wait upon her. The Mother of this Lady had been a Servant to my Grandmother; and having inherited a vast Fortune from her Father, which he had got by Pawnbroking, was married to a Gentleman of great Estate and Fashion. She used my Sister so barbarously, often upbraiding her with her Birth and Poverty, calling her in Derision a Gentle-woman, that I believe she at length broke the Heart of the poor Girl. In short, she likewise died within a Twelvemonth after my Father. Fortune thought proper to provide better for me, and within a Month from his Decease I was married to a Clergyman,

who had been my Lover a long Time before, and who had
been very ill-used by my Father on that Account; for though my
poor Father could not give any of us a Shilling, yet he bred us up
as delicately, considered us, and would have had us consider
ourselves as highly, as if we had been the richest Heiresses. But
my dear Husband forgot all this Usage, and the Moment we
were become fatherless, he immediately renewed his Addresses to
me so warmly, that I, who always liked, and now more than ever
esteemed him, soon comply'd. Five Years[1] did I live in a State
of perfect Happiness with that best of Men, till at last—— Oh!
cruel, cruel Fortune that ever separated us, that deprived me of
the kindest of Husbands, and my poor Girls of the tenderest
Parent.——O my poor Girls! you never knew the Blessing which
ye lost.——I am ashamed, Mr. *Jones*, of this womanish Weakness;
but I shall never mention him without Tears.'——'I ought rather,
Madam,' said *Jones*, 'to be ashamed that I do not accompany
you.'——'Well, Sir,' continued she, 'I was now left a second Time
in a much worse Condition than before; besides the terrible
Affliction I was to encounter, I had now two Children to provide
for; and was, if possible, more pennyless than ever, when that
great, that good, that glorious Man, Mr. *Allworthy*, who had
some little Acquaintance with my Husband, accidentally heard
of my Distress, and immediately writ this Letter to me. Here,
Sir;—here it is; I put it into my Pocket to shew it you. This is
the Letter, Sir; I must and will read it to you. "Madam, I
heartily condole with you on your late grievous Loss, which
your own good Sense, and the excellent Lessons you must have
learnt from the worthiest of Men, will better enable you to bear,
than any Advice which I am capable of giving. Nor have I any
Doubt that you, whom I have heard to be the tenderest of
Mothers, will suffer any immoderate Indulgence of Grief to
prevent you from discharging your Duty to those poor Infants,
who now alone stand in Need of your Tenderness.

"However, as you must be supposed at present to be incapable
of much worldly Consideration, you will pardon my having
ordered a Person to wait on you, and to pay you Twenty Guineas,
which I beg you will accept till I have the Pleasure of seeing you,
and believe me to be, Madam, *&c.*"

[1] In XIII. v, however, Mrs. Miller's daughter Nancy is said to be seven years older than
her sister.

'This Letter, Sir, I received within a Fortnight after the irreparable Loss I have mentioned, and within a Fortnight afterwards, Mr. *Allworthy*,—the blessed Mr. *Allworthy*, came to pay me a Visit, when he placed me in the House where you now see me, gave me a large Sum of Money to furnish it, and settled an Annuity of 50 *l.* a Year upon me, which I have constantly received ever since. Judge then, Mr. *Jones*, in what Regard I must hold a Benefactor, to whom I owe the Preservation of my Life, and of those dear Children, for whose Sake alone my Life is valuable.—Do not, therefore, think me impertinent, Mr. *Jones*, (since I must esteem one for whom I know Mr. *Allworthy* hath so much Value) if I beg you not to converse with these wicked Women. You are a young Gentleman, and do not know half their artful Wiles. Do not be angry with me, Sir, for what I said upon account of my House; you must be sensible it would be the Ruin of my poor, dear Girls. Besides, Sir, you cannot but be acquainted, that Mr. *Allworthy* himself would never forgive my conniving at such Matters, and particularly with you.'

'Upon my Word, Madam,' said *Jones*, 'you need make no farther Apology; nor do I in the least take any Thing ill you have said; but give me Leave, as no one can have more Value than myself for Mr. *Allworthy*, to deliver you from one Mistake, which, perhaps, would not be altogether for his Honour: I do assure you, I am no Relation of his.'

'Alas! Sir,' answered she, 'I know you are not. I know very well who you are; for Mr. *Allworthy* hath told me all: But I do assure you, had you been twenty Times his Son, he could not have expressed more Regard for you, than he hath often expressed in my Presence. You need not be ashamed, Sir, of what you are; I promise you no good Person will esteem you the less on that Account. No, Mr. *Jones*; the Words dishonourable Birth are Nonsense, as my dear, dear Husband used to say, unless the Word dishonourable be applied to the Parents; for the Children can derive no real Dishonour from an Act of which they are entirely innocent.'

Here *Jones* heaved a deep Sigh, and then said, 'Since I perceive, Madam, you really do know me, and Mr. *Allworthy* hath thought proper to mention my Name to you; and since you have been so explicit with me as to your own Affairs, I will acquaint you with some more Circumstances concerning myself.' And these Mrs. *Miller* having expressed great Desire and Curiosity to hear, he began and related to her his whole History, without once mentioning the Name of *Sophia*.

There is a Kind of Sympathy in honest Minds, by Means of which they give an easy Credit to each other. Mrs. *Miller* believed all which *Jones* told her to be true, and exprest much Pity and Concern for him. She was beginning to comment on the Story, but *Jones* interrupted her: For as the Hour of Assignation now drew nigh, he began to stipulate for a second Interview with the Lady that Evening, which he promised should be the last at her House; swearing, at the same Time, that she was one of great Distinction, and that nothing but what was entirely innocent was to pass between them; and I do firmly believe he intended to keep his Word.

Mrs. *Miller* was at length prevailed on, and *Jones* departed to his Chamber, where he sat alone till Twelve o'Clock, but no Lady *Bellaston* appeared.

As we have said that this Lady had a great Affection for *Jones*, and as it must have appeared that she really had so, the Reader may perhaps wonder at the first Failure of her Appointment, as she apprehended him to be confined by Sickness, a Season when Friendship seems most to require such Visits. This Behaviour, therefore, in the Lady, may, by some, be condemned as unnatural; but that is not our Fault; for our Business is only to record Truth.

CHAPTER VI

Containing a Scene which we doubt not will affect all our Readers.

MR. *Jones* closed not his Eyes during all the former Part of the Night; not owing it to any Uneasiness which he conceived at being disappointed by Lady *Bellaston*; nor was *Sophia* herself, though most of his waking Hours were justly to be charged to her Account, the present Cause of dispelling his Slumbers. In Fact, poor *Jones* was one of the best-natured Fellows alive, and had all that Weakness which is called Compassion, and which distinguishes this imperfect Character from that noble Firmness of Mind, which rolls a Man, as it were, within himself, and, like a polished Bowl, enables him to run through the World without being once stopped by the Calamities which happen to others.[1] He could not help, therefore, compassionating the Situation of poor *Nancy*, whose Love for Mr. *Nightingale* seemed to him so apparent, that he was astonished at the Blindness of her Mother, who had more than once, the preceding Evening, remarked to him the great Change in the Temper of her Daughter, 'who from being,' she said, 'one of the liveliest, merriest Girls in the World, was, on a sudden, become all Gloom and Melancholy.'

Sleep, however, at length got the better of all Resistance; and now, as if he had really been a Deity,[2] as the Ancients imagined, and an offended one too, he seemed to enjoy his dear-bought Conquest.—To speak simply, and without any Metaphor, Mr. *Jones* slept till Eleven the next Morning, and would, perhaps, have continued in the same quiet Situation much longer, had not a violent Uproar awakened him.

Partridge was now summoned, who, being asked what was the Matter, answered, 'That there was a dreadful Hurricane below Stairs; that Miss *Nancy* was in Fits; and that the other Sister and the Mother were both crying and lamenting over her.' *Jones* expressed much Concern at this News, which *Partridge* endeavoured to relieve, by saying, with a Smile, 'He fancied the young Lady was in no Danger of Death; for that *Susan* (which was the Name of the Maid) had given him to understand, it was nothing more than a common Affair. In short,' said he, 'Miss *Nancy* hath had a Mind to be as wise as her Mother, that's all. She was a little hungry, it seems, and so sat down to Dinner before Grace was said, and so there is a Child coming for the Foundling Hospital.'[3]—'Prithee leave thy stupid jesting,' cries *Jones*; 'is the Misery of these poor Wretches a Subject of Mirth? Go immediately to Mrs. *Miller*, and tell her, I beg Leave,— Stay, you will make some Blunder, I will go myself; for she

---

[1] Cf. Horace, *Satires*, II. vi. 86–8—quoted above, p. 472, n. 1.

[2] In Greek mythology, Hypnos; in Roman, Somnus.

[3] One of the notable charities of the age for which Fielding commended his countrymen (see above, p. 718, n. 1), the Foundling Hospital, 'for the Maintenance and Education of Exposed and Deserted Young Children', was established through the tireless efforts of Capt. Thomas Coram (1668 ?–1751), who in 1739 presented the Royal Charter to the Duke of Bedford. After 1745 it was situated in Bloomsbury Fields. Handel and Hogarth were among its many eminent benefactors.

desired me to breakfast with her.' He then rose and dressed himself as fast as he could; and while he was dressing, *Partridge*, notwithstanding many severe Rebukes, could not avoid throwing forth certain Pieces of Brutality, commonly called Jests, on this Occasion. *Jones* was no sooner dressed than he walked down Stairs, and knocking at the Door was presently admitted, by the Maid, into the outward Parlour, which was as empty of Company as it was of any Apparatus for eating. Mrs. *Miller* was in the inner Room with her Daughter, whence the Maid presently brought a Message to Mr. *Jones*, 'that her Mistress hoped he would excuse the Disappointment, but an Accident had happened, which made it impossible for her to have the Pleasure of his Company at Breakfast that Day, and begged his Pardon for not sending him up Notice sooner.' *Jones* 'desired she would give herself no Trouble about any Thing so trifling as his Disappointment; that he was heartily sorry for the Occasion; and that if he could be of any Service to her, she might command him.' He had scarce spoke these Words, when Mrs. *Miller*, who heard them all, suddenly threw open the Door, and coming out to him, in a Flood of Tears, said, 'O Mr. *Jones*, you are certainly one of the best young Men alive. I give you a thousand Thanks for your kind Offer of your Service; but, alas! Sir, it is out of your Power to preserve my poor Girl.—O my Child, my Child! She is undone, she is ruined for ever!' 'I hope, Madam,' said *Jones*, 'no Villain———' 'O Mr. *Jones*,' said she, 'that Villain who Yesterday left my Lodgings, hath betrayed my poor Girl; hath destroyed her,—I know you are a Man of Honour. You have a good—a noble Heart, Mr. *Jones*. The Actions to which I have been myself a Witness, could proceed from no other. I will tell you all: Nay, indeed, it is impossible, after what hath happened, to keep it a Secret. That *Nightingale*, that barbarous Villain hath undone my Daughter. She is—she is—oh! Mr. *Jones*, my Girl is with Child by him; and in that Condition he hath deserted her. Here! here, Sir, is his cruel Letter; read it, Mr. *Jones*, and tell me if such another Monster lives.' The Letter was as follows:

'Dear *Nancy*,

As I found it impossible to mention to you what I am afraid will be no less shocking to you, than it is to me, I have taken this

Method to inform you, that my Father insists upon my immediately paying my Addresses to a young Lady of Fortune, whom he hath provided for my—I need not write the detested Word. Your own good Understanding will make you sensible, how entirely I am obliged to an Obedience, by which I shall be for ever excluded from your dear Arms. The Fondness of your Mother may encourage you to trust her with the unhappy Consequence of our Love, which may be easily kept a Secret from the World, and for which I will take Care to provide, as I will for you. I wish you may feel less on this Account than I have suffered: But summon all your Fortitude to your Assistance, and forgive and forget the Man, whom nothing but the Prospect of certain Ruin, could have forced to write this Letter. I bid you forget me, I mean only as a Lover; but the best of Friends you shall ever find in

Your faithful, tho' unhappy

J. N.'

When *Jones* had read this Letter, they both stood silent during a Minute, looking at each other; at last he began thus: 'I cannot express, Madam, how much I am shocked at what I have read; yet let me beg you, in one Particular, to take the Writer's Advice. Consider the Reputation of your Daughter——' 'It is gone, it is lost, Mr. *Jones*,' cry'd she, 'as well as her Innocence. She received the Letter in a Room-full of Company, and immediately swooning away upon opening it, the Contents were known to every one present. But the Loss of her Reputation, bad as it is, is not the worst; I shall lose my Child; she hath attempted twice to destroy herself already: And though she hath been hitherto prevented, vows she will not out-live it; nor could I myself out-live any Accident of that Nature.—What then will become of my little *Betsy*, a helpless, infant Orphan? And the poor, little Wretch will, I believe, break her Heart at the Miseries with which she sees her Sister and myself distracted, while she is ignorant of the Cause.—O 'tis the most sensible, and the best-natured little Thing. The barbarous cruel—hath destroyed us all. O my poor Children! Is this the Reward of all my Cares? Is this the Fruit of all my Prospects? Have I so cheerfully undergone all the Labours and Duties of a Mother? Have I been so tender of their Infancy, so careful of their Education? Have I been toiling so many Years, denying myself even the Conveniencies of Life to provide some little Sustenance for them, to lose one or both in such a Manner?' 'Indeed, Madam,' said *Jones*, with Tears in his Eyes, 'I pity you from my Soul.'—'O Mr. *Jones*,' answered she, 'even you, though I know the Goodness of your Heart, can have no Idea of what I feel. The best, the kindest, the most dutiful of Children. O my poor *Nancy*, the Darling of my Soul; the Delight of my Eyes; the Pride of my Heart: Too much, indeed, my Pride; for to those foolish, ambitious Hopes, arising from her Beauty, I owe her Ruin. Alas! I saw with Pleasure the Liking which this young Man had for her. I thought it an honourable Affection; and flattered my foolish Vanity with the Thoughts of seeing her married to one so much her superior. And a thousand Times in my Presence, nay, often in yours, he hath endeavoured to sooth and encourage these Hopes by the most generous Expressions of disinterested Love, which he hath always directed to my poor Girl, and which I, as well as she, believed to be real. Could I have believed that these were only Snares laid to betray the Innocence of my Child, and for the Ruin of us all?'—At these Words little *Betsy* came running into the Room, crying, 'Dear Mamma, for Heaven's Sake come to my Sister, for she is in another Fit, and my Cousin can't hold her.' Mrs. *Miller* immediately obeyed the Summons; but first ordered *Betsy* to stay with Mr. *Jones*, and begged him to entertain her a few Minutes, saying, in the most pathetic Voice, 'Good Heaven! let me preserve one of my Children at least.'

Jones, in Compliance with this Request, did all he could to comfort the little Girl, though he was, in Reality, himself very highly affected with Mrs. *Miller's* Story. He told her, 'her Sister would be soon very well again: That by taking on in that Manner, she would not only make her Sister worse, but make her Mother ill too.' 'Indeed, Sir,' says she, 'I would not do any Thing to hurt them for the World. I would burst my Heart, rather than they should see me cry.—But my poor Sister can't see me cry.—I am afraid she will never be able to see me cry any more. Indeed, I can't part with her; indeed I can't.—And then poor Mamma too, what will become of her?—She says she will die too, and leave me; but I am resolved I won't be left behind.' 'And are you not afraid to die, my little *Betsy*?' said *Jones*. 'Yes,' answered she, 'I was always afraid to die; because I must have left my Mamma, and my Sister; but I am not afraid of going any where with those I love.'

Jones was so pleased with this Answer, that he eagerly kissed the Child; and soon after Mrs. *Miller* returned, saying, 'She thanked Heaven *Nancy* was now come to herself. And now, *Betsy*,' says she, 'you may go in, for your Sister is better, and longs to see you.' She then turned to *Jones*, and began to renew her Apologies for having disappointed him of his Breakfast.

'I hope, Madam,' said *Jones*, 'I shall have a more exquisite Repast than any you could have provided for me. This, I assure you, will be the Case, if I can do any Service to this little Family of Love.[1] But whatever Success may attend my Endeavours, I am resolved to attempt it. I am very much deceived in Mr. *Nightingale*, if, notwithstanding what hath happened, he hath not much Goodness of Heart at the Bottom, as well as a very violent Affection for your Daughter. If this be the Case, I think the Picture which I shall lay before him, will affect him. Endeavour, Madam, to comfort yourself and Miss *Nancy*, as well as you can. I will go instantly in quest of Mr. *Nightingale*; and I hope to bring you good News.'

Mrs. *Miller* fell upon her Knees, and invoked all the Blessings of Heaven upon Mr. *Jones*; to which she afterwards added the most passionate Expressions of Gratitude. He then departed to find Mr. *Nightingale*, and the good Woman returned to comfort her Daughter, who was somewhat cheered at what her Mother told her; and both joined in resounding the Praises of Mr. *Jones*.

CHAPTER VII

The Interview between Mr. Jones *and Mr.* Nightingale.

THE Good or Evil we confer on others, very often, I believe, recoils on ourselves. For as Men of a benign Disposition enjoy their own Acts of Beneficence, equally with those to whom they are done, so there are scarce any Natures so entirely diabolical, as to be capable of doing Injuries, without paying

---

[1] Cf. Mrs. Moneywood, the landlady in *The Author's Farce* (1730), who tells Luckless that before he came, 'We were the Family of Love' (I. vi). In *Jonathan Wild* (IV. xvi) Fielding describes the Heartfrees this way. Originally, the phrase was another name for the Familists, a religious sect founded in the sixteenth century by Henrick Niclaes.

themselves some Pangs, for the Ruin which they bring on their Fellow-Creatures.

Mr. *Nightingale*, at least, was not such a Person. On the contrary, *Jones* found him in his new Lodgings, sitting melancholy by the Fire, and silently lamenting the unhappy Situation in which he had placed poor *Nancy*. He no sooner saw his Friend appear, than he rose hastily to meet him; and after much Congratulation said, 'Nothing could have been more opportune than this kind Visit; for I was never more in the Spleen in my Life.'

'I am sorry,' answered *Jones*, 'that I bring News very unlikely to relieve you; nay, what I am convinced must, of all other, shock you the most. However, it is necessary you should know it. Without further Preface then, I come to you, Mr. *Nightingale*, from a worthy Family, which you have involved in Misery and Ruin.' Mr. *Nightingale* changed Colour at these Words; but *Jones*, without regarding it, proceeded, in the liveliest Manner, to paint the tragical Story, with which the Reader was acquainted in the last Chapter.

Nightingale never once interrupted the Narration, though he discovered violent Emotions at many Parts of it. But when it was concluded, after fetching a deep Sigh, he said, 'What you tell me, my Friend, affects me in the tenderest Manner. Sure there never was so cursed an Accident as the poor Girl's betraying my Letter. Her Reputation might otherwise have been safe, and the Affair might have remained a profound Secret; and then the Girl might have gone off never the worse; for many such Things happen in this Town; and if the Husband should suspect a little, when it is too late, it will be his wiser Conduct to conceal his Suspicion both from his Wife and the World.'

'Indeed, my Friend,' answered *Jones*, 'this could not have been the Case with your poor *Nancy*. You have so entirely gained her Affections, that it is the Loss of you, and not of her Reputation, which afflicts her, and will end in the Destruction of her and her Family.' 'Nay, for that Matter, I promise you,' cries *Nightingale*, 'she hath my Affections so absolutely, that my Wife, whoever she is to be, will have very little Share in them.' 'And is it possible then,' said *Jones*, 'you can think of deserting her?' 'Why what can I do?' answered the other. 'Ask Miss *Nancy*;' replied *Jones* warmly. 'In the Condition to which you have reduced her, I sincerely think she ought to determine what Reparation you shall make her. Her Interest alone, and not yours, ought to be your sole Consideration. But if you ask me what you shall do; what can you do less,' cries *Jones*, 'than fulfil the Expectations of her Family, and her own. Nay, I sincerely tell you, they were mine too, ever since I first saw you together. You will pardon me, if I presume on the Friendship you have favoured me with, moved as I am with Compassion for those poor Creatures. But your own Heart will best suggest to you, whether you have never intended, by your Conduct, to persuade the Mother, as well as the Daughter, into an Opinion, that you designed honourably: And if so, though there may have been no direct Promise of Marriage in the Case, I will leave to your own good Understanding, how far you are bound to proceed.'

'Nay, I must not only confess what you have hinted,' said *Nightingale*; 'but I am afraid even that very Promise you mention I have given.' 'And can you, after owning that,' said *Jones*, 'hesitate a Moment?' 'Consider, my Friend,' answered the other; 'I know you are a Man of Honour, and would advise no one to act contrary to its Rules; if there were no other Objection, can I, after this Publication of her Disgrace, think of such an Alliance with Honour?' 'Undoubtedly,' replied *Jones*; 'and the very best and truest Honour, which is Goodness, requires it of you. As you mention a Scruple of this Kind, you will give me Leave to examine it. Can you, with Honour, be guilty of having, under false Pretences, deceived a young Woman and her Family, and of having, by these Means, treacherously robbed her of her Innocence? Can you with Honour, be the knowing, the wilful Occasion, nay, the artful Contriver of the Ruin of a Human Being? Can you, with Honour, destroy the Fame, the Peace, nay, probably, both the Life and Soul too of this Creature? Can Honour bear the Thought, that this Creature is a tender, helpless, defenceless young Woman? A young Woman who loves, who doats on you, who dies for you; who hath placed the utmost Confidence in your Promises; and to that Confidence hath sacrificed every Thing which is dear to her? Can Honour support such Contemplations as these a Moment?'

'Common Sense, indeed,' said *Nightingale*, 'warrants all you say; but yet you well know the Opinion of the World is so contrary to it, that was I to marry a Whore, tho' my own, I should be ashamed of ever showing my Face again.'

'Fie upon it, Mr. *Nightingale*,' said *Jones*, 'do not call her by so ungenerous a Name: When you promised to marry her, she became your Wife,[1] and she hath sinned more against Prudence than Virtue. And what is this World, which you would be ashamed to face, but the Vile, the Foolish, and the Profligate? Forgive me, if I say such a Shame must proceed from false Modesty, which always attends false Honour as its Shadow.—But I am well assured there is not a Man of real Sense and Goodness in the World, who would not honour and applaud the Action. But admit no other would, would not your own Heart, my Friend, applaud it? And do not the warm, rapturous Sensations, which we feel from the Consciousness of an honest, noble, generous, benevolent Action, convey more Delight to the Mind, than the undeserved Praise of Millions? Set the Alternative fairly before your Eyes. On the one Side, see this poor, unhappy, tender, believing Girl, in the Arms of her wretched Mother, breathing her last. Hear her breaking Heart in Agonies sighing out your Name; and lamenting, rather than accusing, the Cruelty which weighs her down to Destruction. Paint to your Imagination the Circumstances of her fond, despairing Parent, driven to Madness, or, perhaps, to Death, by the Loss of her lovely Daughter. View the poor, helpless, Orphan-Infant: And when your Mind hath dwelt a Moment only on such Ideas, consider yourself as the Cause of all; the Ruin of this poor, little, worthy, defenceless Family. On the other Side, consider yourself as relieving them from their temporary Sufferings. Think with what Joy, with what Transports, that lovely Creature will fly to your Arms. See her Blood returning to her pale Cheeks, her Fire to her languid Eyes, and Raptures to her tortured Breast. Consider the Exultations of her Mother, the Happiness of all. Think of this little Family made, by one Act of yours, completely happy. Think of this Alternative, and sure I am mistaken in my Friend, if it requires any long Deliberation, whether he will sink these Wretches down for ever, or, by one generous, noble Resolution, raise them all from the Brink of Misery and Despair, to the highest Pitch of human Happiness. Add to this but one Consideration more; the Consideration that it is your Duty so to

---

[1] Cf. Jacob, *New Law-Dictionary*, 4th ed. (1739), s.v. 'Marriage': 'And it has been adjudged on a Promise of future *Marriage*, if the Parties afterwards lie together, the Contract passes thereby into a real *Marriage* in Construction of Law.'

do.—That the Misery from which you will relieve these poor
People, is the Misery which you yourself have wilfully brought
upon them.'

'O my dear Friend,' cries *Nightingale*, 'I wanted not your
Eloquence to rouse me. I pity poor *Nancy* from my Soul, and
would willingly give any Thing in my Power, that no Familiari-
ties had ever passed between us. Nay, believe me, I had many
Struggles with my Passion, before I could prevail with myself to
write that cruel Letter, which hath caused all the Misery in that
unhappy Family. If I had no Inclinations to consult but my
own, I would marry her Tomorrow Morning; I would, by
Heaven; but you will easily imagine how impossible it would
be to prevail on my Father to consent to such a Match; besides,
he hath provided another for me; and Tomorrow, by his express
Command, I am to wait on the Lady.'

'I have not the Honour to know your Father,' said *Jones*;
'but suppose he could be persuaded, would you yourself consent
to the only Means of preserving these poor People?' 'As eagerly
as I would pursue my Happiness,' answered *Nightingale*; 'for
I never shall find it in any other Woman.—O my dear Friend,
could you imagine what I have felt within these twelve Hours
for my poor Girl, I am convinced she would not engross all your
Pity. Passion leads me only to her; and if I had any foolish
Scruples of Honour, you have fully satisfied them: Could my
Father be induced to comply with my Desires, nothing would
be wanting to compleat my own Happiness, or that of my *Nancy*.'

'Then I am resolved to undertake it,' said *Jones*. 'You must
not be angry with me, in whatever Light it may be necessary to
set this Affair, which, you may depend on it, could not otherwise be long hid from him; for Things of this Nature make a
quick Progress, when once they get abroad, as this unhappily
hath already. Besides, should any fatal Accident follow, as upon
my Soul I am afraid will, unless immediately prevented, the
Public would ring of your Name, in a Manner which, if your
Father hath common Humanity, must offend him. If you will
therefore tell me where I may find the old Gentleman, I will
not lose a Moment in the Business; which while I pursue, you
cannot do a more generous Action, than by paying a Visit to the
poor Girl. You will find I have not exaggerated in the Account
I have given of the Wretchedness of the Family.'

Nightingale immediately consented to the Proposal; and now having acquainted *Jones* with his Father's Lodging, and the Coffee-house where he would most probably find him, he hesitated a Moment, and then said, 'My dear *Tom*, you are going to undertake an Impossibility. If you knew my Father, you would never think of obtaining his Consent.—Stay, there is one Way.—Suppose you told him I was already married, it might be easier to reconcile him to the Fact after it was done; and, upon my Honour, I am so affected with what you have said, and I love my *Nancy* so passionately, I almost wish it was done, whatever might be the Consequence.'

Jones greatly approved the Hint, and promised to pursue it. They then separated, *Nightingale* to visit his *Nancy*, and *Jones* in quest of the old Gentleman.

CHAPTER VIII

What passed between Jones *and old Mr.* Nightingale, *with the Arrival of a Person not yet mentioned in this History.*

NOTWITHSTANDING the Sentiment of the *Roman* Satyrist,[1] which denies the Divinity of Fortune; and the Opinion of *Seneca*[2] to the same Purpose; *Cicero*,[3] who was, I

---

[1] Juvenal, *Satires*, x. 365–6.

[2] Cf., for example, *Epistulae Morales*, lxxx. 5: 'Fortune has not the long reach with which we credit her; she can seize none except him that clings to her' (trans. R. M. Gummere, Loeb Classical Library, 1920).

[3] Cf. *Tusculan Disputations*, v. 9, where Cicero approves the maxim, 'Fortune, not wisdom, rules the life of men'. In an essay on Fortune in *The Champion* (6 December 1739) Fielding appears to concur in this opinion: disagreeing with Tacitus and Cardinal Richelieu, who attribute a man's success or failure to his conduct, whether wise or foolish, Fielding there imagines 'Wisdom to be of very little Consequence in the Affairs of this World: Human Life appears to me to resemble the game of *Hazard*, much more than that of *Chess*.' This essay, however, was in part motivated by the desire to embarrass Walpole, one of those great men whom Fortune '*picks . . . in Jest, out of the lowest of the People*' and whose greatness has been acquired by conduct 'visibly leading to Disgrace and Ruin'.

Fielding's usual view of the relation between Fortune and wisdom is expressed by Tom Jones in prison (XVIII. ii): 'Sure . . . Fortune will never have done with me, till she hath driven me to Distraction. But why do I blame Fortune ? I am myself the Cause of all my Misery. All the dreadful Mischiefs which have befallen me, are the Consequences only of my own Folly and Vice.' Jones's confession of moral responsibility is crucial to the theme of prudence in the novel (see p. 36, n. 1)—a theme to which Fielding would return in *Amelia* (I. i), where, contradicting the analogy he had used in *The Champion*, he propounded at length the lesson Jones learned: 'I question much, whether we may not by natural means

believe, a wiser Man than either of them, expresly holds the contrary; and certain it is there are some Incidents in Life so very strange and unaccountable, that it seems to require more than human Skill and Foresight in producing them.

Of this Kind was what now happened to *Jones*, who found Mr. *Nightingale* the elder in so critical a Minute, that Fortune, if she was really worthy all the Worship she received at *Rome*,[1] could not have contrived such another. In short the old Gentleman and the Father of the young Lady whom he intended for his Son, had been hard at it for many Hours; and the latter was just now gone, and had left the former delighted with the Thoughts that he had succeeded in a long Contention which had been between the two Fathers of the future Bride and Bridegroom; in which both endeavoured to over-reach the other, and, as it not rarely happens in such Cases, both had retreated fully satisfied of having obtained the Victory.

This Gentleman whom Mr. *Jones* now visited, was what they call a Man of the World, that is to say, a Man who directs his Conduct in this World, as one who being fully persuaded there is no other, is resolved to make the most of this. In his early Years he had been bred to Trade, but having acquired a very good Fortune, he had lately declined his Business; or to speak more properly, had changed it from dealing in Goods to dealing only in Money, of which he had always a plentiful Fund at Command, and of which he knew very well how to make a very plentiful Advantage; sometimes of the Necessities of private Men, and sometimes of those of the Public. He had indeed conversed so entirely with Money, that it may be almost doubted, whether he

account for the Success of Knaves, the Calamities of Fools, with all the Miseries in which Men of Sense sometimes involve themselves by quitting the Directions of Prudence, and following the blind Guidance of a predominant Passion; in short, for all the ordinary Phenomena which are imputed to Fortune; whom, perhaps, Men accuse with no less Absurdity in Life, than a bad Player complains of ill Luck at the Game of Chess.' What Fielding understood by 'Fortune' or 'Chance' is in fact subsumed within the concept of Christian Providence: see D. S. Thomas, 'Fortune and the Passions in Fielding's *Amelia*', *MLR*, lx (1965), 176–87; and Battestin, '*Tom Jones*: the Argument of Design', in H. K. Miller, E. Rothstein, and G. S. Rousseau (edd.), *The Augustan Milieu: Essays Presented to Louis A. Landa* (Oxford, 1970), pp. 289–319, esp. pp. 304–15.

[1] Cf. the article on 'Fortune' in *The Student's Companion* (1748): 'Among the Ancients, none, so much as the *Romans*, paid Honour to *Fortune*: They look'd on her as the Nurse, the Patroness, and the sole Defender of the City of *Rome*: They erected several Temples to her, under different Names, and worshipp'd her as a Goddess more powerful than *Virtue*' (p. 72).

imagined there was any other thing really existing in the World; this at least may be certainly averred, that he firmly believed nothing else to have any real Value.

The Reader will, I fancy, allow, that Fortune could not have culled out a more improper Person for Mr. *Jones* to attack with any Probability of Success, nor could the whimsical Lady have directed this Attack at a more unseasonable Time.

As Money then was always uppermost in this Gentleman's Thoughts, so the Moment he saw a Stranger within his Doors, it immediately occurred to his Imagination, that such Stranger was either come to bring him Money, or to fetch it from him. And according as one or other of these Thoughts prevailed, he conceived a favourable or unfavourable Idea of the Person who approached him.

Unluckily for *Jones*, the latter of these was the Ascendant at present; for as a young Gentleman had visited him the Day before, with a Bill from his Son for a Play Debt, he apprehended at the first Sight of *Jones*, that he was come on such another Errand. *Jones* therefore had no sooner told him that he was come on his Son's Account, than the old Gentleman, being confirmed in his Suspicion, burst forth into an Exclamation, 'That he would lose his Labour.' 'Is it then possible, Sir,' answered *Jones*, 'that you can guess my Business?' 'If I do guess it,' replied the other, 'I repeat again to you, you will lose your Labour. What, I suppose you are one of those Sparks who lead my Son into all those Scenes of Riot and Debauchery, which will be his Destruction; but I shall pay no more of his Bills I promise you. I expect he will quit all such Company for the future. If I had imagined otherwise I should not have provided a Wife for him; for I would be instrumental in the Ruin of no Body.' 'How, Sir,' said *Jones*, 'and was this Lady of your providing?' 'Pray, Sir,' answered the old Gentleman, 'how comes it to be any Concern of yours?' —'Nay, dear Sir,' replied *Jones*, 'be not offended that I interest myself in what regards your Son's Happiness, for whom I have so great an Honour and Value. It was upon that very Account I came to wait upon you. I can't express the Satisfaction you have given me by what you say; for I do assure you your Son is a Person for whom I have the highest Honour.—Nay, Sir, it is not easy to express the Esteem I have for you, who could be so generous, so good, so kind, so indulgent to provide such a Match for your Son; a Woman who, I dare swear, will make him one of the happiest Men upon Earth.'

There is scarce any thing which so happily introduces Men to our good Liking, as having conceived some Alarm at their first Appearance; when once those Apprehensions begin to vanish, we soon forget the Fears which they occasioned, and look on ourselves as indebted for our present Ease, to those very Persons who at first rais'd our Fears.

Thus it happened to *Nightingale*, who no sooner found that *Jones* had no Demand on him, as he suspected, then he began to be pleased with his Presence. 'Pray, good Sir,' said he, 'be pleased to sit down. I do not remember to have ever had the Pleasure of seeing you before; but if you are a Friend of my Son, and have any thing to say concerning this young Lady, I shall be glad to hear you. As to her making him happy, it will be his own Fault if she doth not. I have discharged my Duty, in taking Care of the main Article. She will bring him a Fortune capable of making any reasonable, prudent, sober Man happy.' 'Undoubtedly,' cries *Jones*, 'for she is in herself a Fortune; so beautiful, so genteel, so sweet-tempered, and so well educated; she is indeed a most accomplished young Lady; sings admirably well, and hath a most delicate Hand at the Harpsichord.' 'I did not know any of these Matters,' answered the old Gentleman, 'for I never saw the Lady; but I do not like her the worse for what you tell me; and I am the better pleased with her Father for not laying any Stress on these Qualifications in our Bargain. I shall always think it a Proof of his Understanding. A silly Fellow would have brought in these Articles as an Addition to her Fortune; but to give him his due, he never mentioned any such Matter; though to be sure they are no Disparagements to a Woman.' 'I do assure you, Sir,' cries *Jones*, 'she hath them all in the most eminent Degree: For my Part I own I was afraid you might have been a little backward, a little less inclined to the Match: For your Son told me you had never seen the Lady, therefore I came, Sir, in that Case, to entreat you, to conjure you, as you value the Happiness of your Son, not to be averse to his Match with a Woman who hath not only all the good Qualities I have mentioned, but many more.'—'If that was your Business, Sir,' said the old Gentleman, 'we are both obliged to you; and you may be perfectly easy, for I give you my Word I was very well satisfied with her Fortune.' 'Sir,' answered *Jones,* 'I honour you every Moment more and more. To be so easily satisfied, so very moderate on that Account, is a Proof of the Soundness of your Understanding, as well as the Nobleness of your Mind.'— 'Not so very moderate, young Gentleman, not so very moderate,' answered the Father.—'Still more and more noble,' replied *Jones,* 'and give me Leave to add sensible: For sure it is little less than Madness to consider Money as the sole Foundation of Happiness. Such a Woman as this with her little, her nothing of a Fortune.'—'I find,' cries the old Gentleman, 'you have a pretty just Opinion of Money, my Friend, or else you are better acquainted with the Person of the Lady than with her Circumstances. Why pray, what Fortune do you imagine this Lady to have?'—'What Fortune?' cries *Jones,* 'why too contemptible a one to be named for your Son.' 'Well, well, well,' said the other, 'perhaps he might have done better.'—'That I deny,' said *Jones,* 'for she is one of the best of Women.' 'Ay, ay, but in Point of Fortune I mean—' answered the other.—'And yet as to that now, how much do you imagine your Friend is to have?'— 'How much,' cries *Jones,* 'how much!—Why at the utmost, perhaps, 200 *l.*' 'Do you mean to banter me, young Gentleman?' said the Father a little angry.—'No, upon my Soul,' answered *Jones,* 'I am in Earnest, nay I believe I have gone to the utmost Farthing. If I do the Lady an Injury, I ask her Pardon.' 'Indeed you do,' cries the Father. 'I am certain she hath fifty Times that Sum, and she shall produce fifty to that before I consent that she shall marry my Son.' 'Nay,' said *Jones,* 'it is too late to talk of Consent now.—If she had not fifty Farthings your Son is married.'—'My Son married!' answered the old Gentleman with Surprise. 'Nay,' said *Jones,* 'I thought you was unacquainted with it.'—'My Son married to Miss *Harris!*' answered he again.—'To Miss *Harris!*' said *Jones,* 'no Sir, to Miss *Nancy Miller,* the Daughter of Mrs. *Miller,* at whose House he lodged; a young Lady, who, though her Mother is reduced to let Lodgings——' 'Are you bantering, or are you in Earnest?' cries the Father with a most solemn Voice. 'Indeed, Sir,' answered *Jones,* 'I scorn the Character of a Banterer. I came to you in most serious Earnest, imagining, as I find true, that your Son had never dared acquaint you with a Match so much inferior to him in Point of Fortune, tho' the Reputation of the Lady will suffer it no longer to remain a Secret.'

While the Father stood like one struck suddenly dumb at this News, a Gentleman came into the Room, and saluted him by the Name of Brother.

But though these two were in Consanguinity so nearly related, they were in their Dispositions almost the opposites to each other. The Brother who now arrived had likewise been bred to Trade, in which he no sooner saw himself worth 6000 *l.* than he purchased a small Estate with the greatest Part of it, and retired into the Country; where he married the Daughter of an unbeneficed Clergyman; a young Lady who, though she had neither Beauty nor Fortune, had recommended herself to his Choice, entirely by her good Humour, of which she possessed a very large Share.

With this Woman he had, during twenty-five Years, lived a Life more resembling the Model which certain Poets ascribe to the Golden Age, than any of those Patterns which are furnished by the present Times. By her he had four Children, but none of them arrived at Maturity except only one Daughter, whom in vulgar Language he and his Wife had spoiled; that is, had educated with the utmost Tenderness and Fondness; which she returned to such a Degree, that she had actually refused a very extraordinary Match with a Gentleman a little turned of forty, because she could not bring herself to part with her Parents.

The young Lady whom Mr. *Nightingale* had intended for his Son was a near Neighbour of his Brother, and an Acquaintance of his Niece; and in reality it was upon the Account of this projected Match, that he was now come to Town; not indeed to forward, but to dissuade his Brother from a Purpose which he conceived would inevitably ruin his Nephew; for he foresaw no other Event, from a Union with Miss *Harris*, notwithstanding the Largeness of her Fortune, as neither her Person nor Mind seemed to him to promise any Kind of matrimonial Felicity; for she was very tall, very thin, very ugly, very affected, very silly, and very ill-natured.

His Brother therefore no sooner mentioned the Marriage of his Nephew with Miss *Miller*, than he exprest the utmost Satisfaction; and when the Father had very bitterly reviled his Son, and pronounced Sentence of Beggary upon him, the Uncle began in the following Manner.

'If you was a little cooler, Brother, I would ask you whether you love your Son for his Sake, or for your own. You would answer, I suppose, and so I suppose you think, for his Sake; and doubtless it is his Happiness which you intended in the Marriage you proposed for him.

'Now, Brother, to prescribe Rules of Happiness to others, hath always appeared to me very absurd, and to insist on doing this very tyrannical. It is a vulgar Error I know; but it is nevertheless an Error. And if this be absurd in other Things, it is mostly so in the Affair of Marriage, the Happiness of which depends entirely on the Affection which subsists between the Parties.

'I have therefore always thought it unreasonable in Parents to desire to chuse for their Children on this Occasion, since to force Affection is an impossible Attempt; nay, so much doth Love abhor Force, that I know not whether through an unfortunate but uncurable Perverseness in our Natures, it may not be even impatient of Persuasion.

'It is, however, true, that though a Parent will not, I think, wisely prescribe, he ought to be consulted on this Occasion, and in Strictness perhaps should at least have a negative Voice. My Nephew therefore, I own, in marrying without asking your Advice, hath been guilty of a Fault. But honestly speaking, Brother, have you not a little promoted this Fault? Have not your frequent Declarations on this Subject, given him a moral Certainty of your Refusal, where there was any Deficiency in Point of Fortune? nay, doth not your present Anger arise solely from that Deficiency? And if he hath failed in his Duty here, did you not as much exceed that Authority, when you absolutely bargained with him for a Woman without his Knowledge, whom you yourself never saw, and whom if you had seen and known as well as I, it must have been Madness in you, to have ever thought of bringing her into your Family.

'Still I own my Nephew in a Fault; but surely it is not an unpardonable Fault. He hath acted indeed without your Consent, in a Matter in which he ought to have asked it; but it is in a Matter in which his Interest is principally concerned; you yourself must and will acknowledge, that you consulted his Interest only, and if he unfortunately differed from you, and hath been mistaken in his Notion of Happiness, will you, Brother, if you love your Son, carry him still wider from the Point? Will you encrease the ill Consequences of his simple Choice? Will you endeavour to make an Event certain Misery to him, which may accidentally prove so? In a Word, Brother, because he hath put it out of your Power to make his Circumstances as affluent as you would, will you distress them as much as you can?'

By the Force of the true Catholic Faith, St. *Anthony* won upon the Fishes.[1] *Orpheus* and *Amphion* went a little farther, and by the Charms of Music enchanted Things merely inanimate.[2] Wonderful both! But neither History nor Fable have ever yet ventured to record an Instance of any one, who by Force of Argument and Reason hath triumphed over habitual Avarice.

Mr. *Nightingale*, the Father, instead of attempting to answer his Brother, contented himself with only observing, that they had always differed in their Sentiments concerning the Education of their Children. 'I wish,' said he, 'Brother, you would have confined your Care to your own Daughter, and never have troubled yourself with my Son, who hath, I believe, as little profited by your Precepts, as by your Example:' For young *Nightingale* was his Uncle's Godson, and had lived more with him than with his Father. So that the Uncle had often declared, he loved his Nephew almost equally with his own Child.

Jones fell into Raptures with this good Gentleman; and when after much Perswasion, they found the Father grew still more and more irritated, instead of appeased, *Jones* conducted the Uncle to his Nephew at the House of Mrs. *Miller*.

CHAPTER IX

Containing strange Matters.

AT his Return to his Lodgings, *Jones* found the Situation of Affairs greatly altered from what they had been in at his Departure. The Mother, the two Daughters and young Mr. *Nightingale* were now sat down to Supper together, when the Uncle was, at his own Desire, introduced without any Ceremony into the Company, to all of whom he was well known; for he had several Times visited his Nephew at that House.

[1] St. Anthony of Padua (1195-1231), whose eloquence caused fish to leap out of the water to hear him.

[2] By the power of their music Orpheus enchanted the trees and rocks on Olympus, and Amphion built the walls of Thebes, charming the stones to dance into place.

The old Gentleman immediately walked up to Miss *Nancy*, saluted and wished her Joy, as he did afterwards the Mother and the other Sister; and lastly, he paid the proper Compliments to his Nephew, with the same good Humour and Courtesy, as if his Nephew had married his equal or superior in Fortune, with all the previous Requisites first performed.

Miss *Nancy* and her supposed Husband both turned pale, and looked rather foolish than otherwise upon the Occasion; but Mrs. *Miller* took the first Opportunity of withdrawing; and having sent for *Jones* into the Dining Room, she threw herself at his Feet, and in a most passionate Flood of Tears, called him her good Angel, the Preserver of her poor little Family, with many other respectful and endearing Appellations, and made him every Acknowledgment which the highest Benefit can extract from the most grateful Heart.

After the first Gust of her Passion was a little over, which she declared, if she had not vented, would have burst her, she proceeded to inform Mr. *Jones*, that all Matters were settled between Mr. *Nightingale* and her Daughter, and that they were to be married the next Morning: At which Mr. *Jones* having exprest much Pleasure, the poor Woman fell again into a Fit of Joy and Thanksgiving, which he at length with Difficulty silenced, and prevailed on her to return with him back to the Company, whom they found in the same good Humour in which they had left them.

This little Society now past two or three very agreeable Hours together, in which the Uncle, who was a very great Lover of his Bottle, had so well ply'd his Nephew, that this latter, though not drunk, began to be somewhat flustered; and now Mr. *Nightingale* taking the old Gentleman with him up Stairs into the Apartment he had lately occupied, unbosomed himself as follows.

'As you have been always the best and kindest of Uncles to me, and as you have shewn such unparalelled Goodness in forgiving this Match, which to be sure may be thought a little improvident; I should never forgive myself if I attempted to deceive you in any thing.' He then confessed the Truth, and opened the whole Affair.

'How, *Jack*!' said the old Gentleman, 'and are you really then not married to this young Woman?' 'No, upon my Honour,' answered *Nightingale*, 'I have told you the simple Truth.' 'My

dear Boy,' cries the Uncle, kissing him, 'I am heartily glad to
hear it. I never was better pleased in my Life. If you had been
married, I should have assisted you as much as was in my Power,
to have made the best of a bad Matter; but there is a great Difference between considering a Thing which is already done and
irrecoverable, and that which is yet to do. Let your Reason have
fair Play, *Jack*, and you will see this Match in so foolish and
preposterous a Light, that there will be no Need of any dis-
suasive Arguments.' 'How, Sir!' replies young *Nightingale*, 'is
there this Difference between having already done an Act, and
being in Honour engaged to do it?' 'Pugh,' said the Uncle,
'Honour is a Creature of the World's making, and the World hath
the Power of a Creator over it, and may govern and direct it as
they please. Now you well know how trivial these Breaches of
Contract are thought; even the grossest make but the Wonder
and Conversation of a Day. Is there a Man who afterwards
will be more backward in giving you his Sister or Daughter?
Or is there any Sister or Daughter who would be more backward
to receive you? Honour is not concerned in these Engagements.'
'Pardon me, dear Sir,' cries *Nightingale*, 'I can never think so;
and not only Honour, but Conscience and Humanity are concerned. I am well satisfied, that was I now to disappoint the
young Creature, her Death would be the Consequence, and I
should look upon myself as her Murderer; nay, as her Murderer
by the cruellest of all Methods, by breaking her Heart.' 'Break
her Heart, indeed! no, no, *Jack*,' cries the Uncle, 'the Hearts
of Women are not so soon broke; they are tough, Boy, they are
tough.' 'But, Sir,' answered *Nightingale*, 'my own Affections are
engaged, and I never could be happy with any other Woman.
How often have I heard you say, that Children should be always
suffered to chuse for themselves, and that you would let my
Cousin *Harriet* do so!' 'Why ay,' replied the old Gentleman, 'so
I would have them; but then I would have them chuse wisely.—
Indeed, *Jack*, you must and shall leave this Girl.'—'Indeed,
Uncle,' cries the other, 'I must and will have her.' 'You will,
young Gentleman?' said the Uncle; 'I did not expect such a
Word from you. I should not wonder if you had used such Lan-
guage to your Father, who hath always treated you like a Dog, and
kept you at the Distance which a Tyrant preserves over his Subjects; but I who have lived with you upon an equal Footing,

might surely expect better Usage: But I know how to account for it all; it is all owing to your preposterous Education, in which I have had too little Share. There is my Daughter now, whom I have brought up as my Friend, never doth any thing without my Advice, nor ever refuses to take it when I give it her.' 'You have never yet given her Advice in an Affair of this Kind,' said *Nightingale*, 'for I am greatly mistaken in my Cousin, if she would be very ready to obey even your most positive Commands in abandoning her Inclinations.' 'Don't abuse my Girl,' answered the old Gentleman with some Emotion; 'don't abuse my *Harriet*. I have brought her up to have no Inclinations contrary to my own. By suffering her to do whatever she pleases, I have enured her to a Habit of being pleased to do whatever I like.' 'Pardon me, Sir,' said *Nightingale*, 'I have not the least Design to reflect on my Cousin, for whom I have the greatest Esteem; and indeed I am convinced you will never put her to so severe a Trial, or lay such hard Commands on her as you would do on me.——But, dear Sir, let us return to the Company; for they will begin to be uneasy at our long Absence. I must beg one Favour of my dear Uncle, which is that he would not say any thing to shock the poor Girl or her Mother.' 'O you need not fear me,' answered he, 'I understand myself too well to affront Women; so I will readily grant you that Favour; and in Return I must expect another of you.' 'There are but few of your Commands, Sir,' said *Nightingale*, 'which I shall not very chearfully obey.' 'Nay, Sir, I ask nothing,' said the Uncle, 'but the Honour of your Company home to my Lodging, that I may reason the Case a little more fully with you: For I would if possible have the Satisfaction of preserving my Family, notwithstanding the headstrong Folly of my Brother, who, in his own Opinion, is the wisest Man in the World.'

Nightingale, who well knew his Uncle to be as headstrong as his Father, submitted to attend him Home, and then they both returned back into the Room, where the old Gentleman promised to carry himself with the same Decorum which he had before maintained.

CHAPTER X

A short Chapter which concludes the Book.

THE long Absence of the Uncle and Nephew had occasioned some Disquiet in the Minds of all whom they had left behind them; and the more, as during the preceding Dialogue, the Uncle had more than once elevated his Voice, so as to be heard down Stairs; which, though they could not distinguish what he said, had caused some evil foreboding in *Nancy* and her Mother, and indeed even in *Jones* himself.

When the good Company therefore again assembled, there was a visible Alteration in all their Faces; and the good Humour which, at their last Meeting, universally shone forth in every Countenance, was now changed into a much less agreeable Aspect. It was a Change indeed common enough to the Weather in this Climate, from Sunshine to Clouds, from *June* to *December*.

This Alteration was not however greatly remarked by any present; for as they were all now endeavouring to conceal their own Thoughts, and to act a Part, they became all too busily engaged in the Scene to be Spectators of it. Thus neither the Uncle nor Nephew saw any Symptoms of Suspicion in the Mother or Daughter; nor did the Mother or Daughter remark the overacted Complaisance of the old Man, nor the counterfeit Satisfaction which grinned in the Features of the young one.

Something like this, I believe, frequently happens, where the whole Attention of two Friends being engaged in the Part which each is to act, in order to impose on the other, neither sees nor suspects the Art practised against himself; and thus the Thrust of both (to borrow no improper Metaphor on the Occasion) alike takes Place.

From the same Reason it is no unusual Thing for both Parties to be over-reached in a Bargain, though the one must be always the greater Loser; as was he who sold a blind Horse, and received a bad Note in Payment.

Our Company in about half an Hour broke up, and the Uncle carried off his Nephew; but not before the latter had assured Miss *Nancy*, in a Whisper, that he would attend her early in the Morning, and fulfil all his Engagements.

Jones, who was the least concerned in this Scene, saw the most.

He did indeed suspect the very Fact; for besides observing the great Alteration in the Behaviour of the Uncle, the Distance he assumed, and his overstrained Civility to Miss *Nancy*; the carrying off a Bridegroom from his Bride at that Time of Night, was so extraordinary a Proceeding, that it could be accounted for only by imagining that young *Nightingale* had revealed the whole Truth, which the apparent Openness of his Temper, and his being flustered with Liquor, made too probable.

While he was reasoning with himself, whether he should acquaint these poor People with his Suspicion, the Maid of the House informed him, that a Gentlewoman desired to speak with him.—He went immediately out, and taking the Candle from the Maid, ushered his Visitant up Stairs, who in the Person of Mrs. *Honour* acquainted him with such dreadful News concerning his *Sophia*, that he immediately lost all Consideration for every other Person; and his whole Stock of Compassion was entirely swallowed up in Reflections on his own Misery, and on that of his unfortunate Angel.

What this dreadful Matter was, the Reader will be informed, after we have first related the many preceding Steps which produced it, and those will be the Subject of the following Book.

BOOK XV

In which the History advances about two Days.

CHAPTER I

Too short to need a Preface.

THERE are a Set of Religious, or rather Moral Writers, who teach that Virtue is the certain Road to Happiness, and Vice to Misery in this World. A very wholsome and comfortable Doctrine, and to which we have but one Objection, namely, That it is not true.

Indeed if by Virtue these Writers mean, the Exercise of those Cardinal Virtues, which like good House-wives stay at home, and mind only the Business of their own Family, I shall very readily concede the Point: For so surely do all these contribute and lead to Happiness, that I could almost wish, in Violation of all the antient and modern Sages, to call them rather by the Name of Wisdom, than by that of Virtue: For with regard to this Life, no System, I conceive, was ever wiser than that of the antient *Epicureans*,[1] who held this Wisdom to constitute the chief Good; nor foolisher than that of their Opposites, those modern *Epicures*, who place all Felicity in the abundant Gratification of every sensual Appetite.

But if by Virtue is meant (as I almost think it ought) a certain relative Quality, which is always busying itself without Doors, and seems as much interested in pursuing the Good of others as its own; I cannot so easily agree that this is the surest way to human

---

[1] According to Epicurus (342–270 B.C.) the *summum bonum* was pleasure, by which he meant not voluptuousness—he lived abstemiously on a diet of water and barley bread—but rather serenity and tranquillity of mind. Like the Stoics, he taught the severest rational control of the passions and disinterested detachment from worldly concerns. As his English translator, John Digby, remarked, Epicurus' wise man looks on the misfortunes of life 'as it were from a Fortress' (*Epicurus's Morals* [1712], p. 9), and he is too prudent to marry or to yield to 'the Charms of Love' (maxims ix, xii). The reward for such rigorous self-discipline was, he taught, the 'Happiness' of 'a Serene and undisturb'd Mind' (p. 167). In 'An Essay in Vindication of Epicurus, and his Doctrine' included in Digby's translation, Saint-Évremond properly dissociated the true disciples of Epicurus from those debauched hedonists who are called by that name.

Happiness; because I am afraid we must then include Poverty and Contempt, with all the Mischiefs which Backbiting, Envy, and Ingratitude can bring on Mankind in our Idea of Happiness; nay, sometimes perhaps we shall be obliged to wait upon the said Happiness to a Goal, since many by the above Virtue have brought themselves thither.

I have not now Leisure to enter upon so large a Field of Speculation, as here seems opening upon me; my Design was to wipe off a Doctrine that lay in my Way; since while Mr. *Jones* was acting the most virtuous Part imaginable in labouring to preserve his fellow Creatures from Destruction, the Devil, or some other evil Spirit, one perhaps cloathed in human Flesh, was hard at Work to make him completely miserable in the Ruin of his *Sophia.*

This therefore would seem an Exception to the above Rule, if indeed it was a Rule; but as we have in our Voyage through Life seen so many other Exceptions to it, we chuse to dispute the Doctrine on which it is founded, which we don't apprehend to be Christian, which we are convinced is not true, and which is indeed destructive of one of the noblest Arguments that Reason alone can furnish for the Belief of Immortality.[1]

But as the Reader's Curiosity (if he hath any) must be now awake, and hungry, we shall provide to feed it as fast as we can.

CHAPTER II

In which is opened a very black Design against Sophia.

I REMEMBER a wise old Gentleman, who used to say, when Children are doing nothing, they are doing Mischief. I will not enlarge this quaint Saying to the most beautiful Part of the Creation in general; but so far I may be allowed, that when the

---

[1] Fielding had similarly concluded an essay in *The Champion* (4 March 1739/40), reflecting on the fact that virtue is not always honoured in this life: 'a glorious Consideration to the virtuous Man, is that he may rejoyce even in the never attaining that which he so well deserves, since it furnishes him with a noble Argument for the Certainty of a future State. As it is inconsistent with the Justice of a supremely wise and good Being, to suffer his honest and worthy Endeavours to go unrewarded, can the Heart of Man be warmed with a more ecstatic Imagination, than that the most excellent Attribute of the great Creator of the Universe is concerned in rewarding him?'

Effects of female Jealousy do not appear openly in their proper Colours of Rage and Fury, we may suspect that mischievous Passion to be at work privately, and attempting to undermine, what it doth not attack above-ground.

This was exemplified in the Conduct of the Lady *Bellaston*, who under all the Smiles which she wore in her Countenance, concealed much Indignation against *Sophia*; and as she plainly saw that this young Lady stood between her and the full Indulgence of her Desires, she resolved to get rid of her by some Means or other; nor was it long before a very favourable Opportunity of accomplishing this, presented itself to her.

The Reader may be pleased to remember, that when *Sophia* was thrown into that Consternation at the Play-house, by the Wit and Humour of a Set of young Gentlemen, who call themselves the Town, we informed him, that she had put herself under the Protection of a young Nobleman, who had very safely conducted her to her Chair.

This Nobleman, who frequently visited Lady *Bellaston*, had more than once seen *Sophia* there, since her Arrival in Town, and had conceived a very great liking to her; which Liking, as Beauty never looks more amiable than in Distress, *Sophia* had in this Fright so encreased, that he might now without any great Impropriety be said to be actually in love with her.

It may easily be believed that he would not suffer so handsome an Occasion of improving his Acquaintance with the beloved Object as now offered itself to elapse, when even Good-breeding alone might have prompted him to pay her a Visit.

The next Morning therefore, after this Accident he waited on *Sophia*, with the usual Compliments and Hopes that she had received no Harm from her last Night's Adventure.

As Love, like Fire, when once thoroughly kindled, is soon blown into a Flame; *Sophia* in a very short time completed her Conquest. Time now flew away unperceived, and the Noble Lord had been two Hours in Company with the Lady, before it entered into his Head that he had made too long a Visit. Tho' this Circumstance alone would have alarmed *Sophia*, who was somewhat more a Mistress of Computation at present; she had indeed much more pregnant Evidence from the Eyes of her Lover of what past within his Bosom; nay, though he did not make any open Declaration of his Passion, yet many of his

Expressions were rather too warm, and too tender to have been imputed to Complaisance, even in the Age when such Complaisance was in Fashion; the very Reverse of which is well known to be the reigning Mode at present.

Lady *Bellaston* had been apprised of his Lordship's Visit at his first Arrival; and the Length of it very well satisfied her that Things went as she wished, and as indeed she had suspected the second time she saw this young Couple together. This Business she rightly, I think, concluded, that she should by no means forward by mixing in the Company while they were together; she therefore ordered her Servants, that when my Lord was going, they should tell him, she desired to speak with him, and employed the intermediate Time in meditating how best to accomplish a Scheme which she made no doubt but his Lordship would very readily embrace the Execution of.

Lord *Fellamar* (for that was the Title of this young Nobleman) was no sooner introduced to her Ladyship, than she attacked him in the following Strain: 'Bless me, my Lord, are you here yet? I thought my Servants had made a Mistake and let you go away; and I wanted to see you about an Affair of some Importance.'—'Indeed, Lady *Bellaston*,' said he, 'I don't wonder you are astonished at the Length of my Visit: For I have staid above two Hours, and I did not think I had staid above half a one.'—'What am I to conclude from thence, my Lord?' said she. 'The Company must be very agreeable which can make Time slide away so very deceitfully.'—'Upon my Honour,' said he, 'the most agreeable I ever saw. Pray tell me, Lady *Bellaston*, who is this blazing Star which you have produced among us all of a sudden?'—'What blazing Star, my Lord?' said she, affecting a Surprize.—'I mean,' said he, 'the Lady I saw here the other Day, whom I had last Night in my Arms at the Play-House, and to whom I have been making that unreasonable Visit.'—'O my Cousin *Western*,' said she, 'why that blazing Star, my Lord, is the Daughter of a Country Booby Squire, and hath been in Town about a fortnight, for the first Time.'—'Upon my Soul,' said he, 'I should swear she had been bred in a Court; for besides her Beauty, I never saw any thing so genteel, so sensible, so polite.' —'O brave!' cries the Lady, 'My Cousin hath you, I find.'— 'Upon my Honour,' answered he, 'I wish she had: for I am in Love with her to Distraction.'—'Nay, my Lord,' said she, 'it is

not wishing yourself very ill neither, for she is a very great Fortune, I assure you she is an only Child, and her Father's Estate is a
good 3000 *l.* a Year.' 'Then I can assure you, Madam,' answered
the Lord, 'I think her the best Match in *England.*' 'Indeed, my
Lord,' replied she, 'if you like her, I heartily wish you had her.'
'If you think so kindly of me, Madam,' said he, 'as she is a Relation of yours, will you do me the Honour to propose it to her
Father?' 'And are you really then in earnest?' cries the Lady,
with an affected Gravity. 'I hope, Madam,' answered he, 'you
have a better Opinion of me, than to imagine I would jest with
your Ladyship in an Affair of this Kind.' 'Indeed then,' said the
Lady, 'I will most readily propose your Lordship to her Father,
and I can, I believe, assure you of his joyful Acceptance of the
Proposal; but there is a Bar, which I am almost ashamed to mention, and yet it is one you will never be able to conquer. You have
a Rival, my Lord, and a Rival who, though I blush to name him,
neither you, nor all the World will ever be able to conquer.'
'Upon my Word, Lady *Bellaston*,' cries he, 'you have struck a
damp to my Heart which hath almost deprived me of Being.'
'Fie! my Lord,' said she, 'I should rather hope I had struck
Fire into you. A Lover, and talk of Damps in your Heart!
I rather imagined you would have asked your Rival's Name,
that you might have immediately entered the Lists with him.'
'I promise you, Madam,' answered he, 'there are very few Things
I would not undertake for your charming Cousin; but pray who
is this happy Man?'—'Why he is,' said she, 'what I am sorry to
say most happy Men with us are, one of the lowest Fellows in the
World. He is a Beggar, a Bastard, a Foundling, a Fellow in
meaner Circumstances than one of your Lordship's Footmen.'
'And is it possible,' cried he, 'that a young Creature with such
Perfections, should think of bestowing herself so unworthily?'
'Alas! my Lord,' answered she, 'consider the Country—the
Bane of all young Women is the Country. There they learn a
Set of romantic Notions of Love and I know not what Folly,
which this Town and good Company can scarce eradicate in a
whole Winter.' 'Indeed, Madam,' replied my Lord, 'your Cousin
is of too immense a Value to be thrown away: Such Ruin as this
must be prevented.' 'Alas!' cries she, 'my Lord, how can it be
prevented? The Family have already done all in their Power; but
the Girl is, I think, intoxicated, and nothing less than Ruin will

content her. And to deal more openly with you, I expect every Day to hear she is run away with him.' 'What you tell me, Lady *Bellaston*,' answered his Lordship, 'affects me most tenderly, and only raises my Compassion instead of lessening my Adoration of your Cousin. Some Means must be found to preserve so inestimable a Jewel. Hath your Ladyship endeavoured to reason with her?' Here the Lady affected a Laugh, and cried, 'My dear Lord, sure you know us better than to talk of reasoning a young Woman out of her Inclinations. These inestimable Jewels are as deaf as the Jewels they wear; Time, my Lord, Time is the only Medicine to cure their Folly; but this is a Medicine, which I am certain she will not take; nay, I live in hourly Horrors on her Account. In short nothing but violent Methods will do.' 'What is to be done?' cries my Lord, 'what Methods are to be taken?—Is there any Method upon Earth?—Oh! Lady *Bellaston*! there is nothing which I would not undertake for such a Reward.'—'I really know not,' answered the Lady, after a Pause, and then pausing again, she cried out,—'Upon my Soul, I am at my Wit's End on this Girl's Account.—If she can be preserved, something must be done immediately, and as I say, nothing but violent Methods will do.—If your Lordship hath really this Attachment to my Cousin, (and to do her Justice, except in this silly Inclination, of which she will soon see her Folly, she is every way deserving) I think there may be one Way, indeed it is a very disagreeable one, and what I am almost afraid to think of.—It requires a great Spirit, I promise you.' 'I am not conscious, Madam,' said he, 'of any Defect there, nor am I, I hope, suspected of any such. It must be an egregious Defect indeed, which could make me backward on this Occasion.' 'Nay, my Lord,' answered she, 'I am far from doubting you. I am much more inclined to doubt my own Courage: for I must run a monstrous Risque. In short, I must place such a Confidence in your Honour as a wise Woman will scarce ever place in a Man on any Consideration.' In this Point likewise my Lord very well satisfied her; for his Reputation was extremely clear, and common Fame did him no more than Justice, in speaking well of him. 'Well then,' said she, 'my Lord,—I—I vow, I can't bear the Apprehension of it.— No, it must not be.—At least every other Method shall be tried. Can you get rid of your Engagements and dine here to-day? Your Lordship will have an Opportunity of seeing a little more of Miss

Western.—I promise you we have no time to lose. Here will be no body but Lady *Betty*, and Miss *Eagle*, and Colonel *Hampsted*, and *Tom Edwards*, they will all go soon—and I shall be at home to no body. Then your Lordship may be a little more explicit. Nay, I will contrive some Method to convince you of her Attachment to this Fellow.' My Lord made proper Compliments, accepted the Invitation, and then they parted to dress, it being now past three in the Morning, or to reckon by the old Style, in the Afternoon.

CHAPTER III

A further Explanation of the foregoing Design.

THO' the Reader may have long since concluded Lady *Bellaston* to be a Member (and no inconsiderable one) of the Great World, she was in reality a very considerable Member of *the Little World*; by which Appellation was distinguished a very worthy and honourable Society which not long since flourished in this Kingdom.

Among other good Principles upon which this Society was founded, there was one very remarkable; for as it was a Rule of an honourable Club of Heroes, who assembled at the close of the late War,[1] that all the Members should every Day fight once at least; so 'twas in this, that every Member should, within the twenty-four Hours, tell at least one merry Fib, which was to be propagated by all the Brethren and Sisterhood.[2]

---

[1] The Treaty of Aix-la-Chapelle, ending the War of the Austrian Succession, was signed in October 1748. The 'Heroes' to whom Fielding alludes, however, may have been the so-called 'Derby Captains'—McManus, McNeal, Hardiman, Scroggs, and Marriot—a coterie of officers who, after the Peace of Utrecht (1713), went about seeking occasions to fight duels. According to an article in *Old England* (12 May 1750), these men 'were the Pests of human Society in those Days, and obtruded themselves into Company merely to quarrel; insomuch, that their Brother-Officers were made very uneasy by them, and took all Opportunities of shunning those fierce Beasts of the Forest, by retiring into distant Parts of the Town, and sometimes into the Country'.

[2] According to one contemporary writer who wished to erect an 'Academy for Lying', this was 'at present not only the most useful, but the most Gentleman-like Qualification in Fashion', necessary to the making of 'a compleat Man of the *Beau Monde*' (*The Museum*, ii [20 December 1746], 216). The 'honourable Society' to which Fielding refers, however, probably had its origin in Dr. Arbuthnot's prospectus for a treatise to be called 'The Art of Political Lying' (1727). After acknowledging the Devil to be the father of lies,

Many idle Stories were told about this Society, which from a certain Quality may be perhaps not unjustly supposed to have come from the Society themselves. As, that the Devil was the President, and that he sat in Person in an elbow Chair at the upper End of the Table; but upon very strict Enquiry, I find there is not the least Truth in any of those Tales, and that the Assembly consisted in reality of a Set of very good sort of People, and the Fibs which they propagated were of a harmless Kind, and tended only to produce Mirth and good Humour.

Edwards[1] was likewise a Member of this comical Society. To him therefore Lady *Bellaston* applied as a proper Instrument for her Purpose, and furnished him with a Fib, which he was to vent whenever the Lady gave him her Cue; and this was not to be till the Evening when all the Company but Lord *Fellamar* and himself were gone, and while they were engaged in a Rubbers at Whist.

To this Time then, which was between seven and eight in the

Arbuthnot proposes as the subject for ch. viii 'a Project for uniting the several smaller Corporations of Lyars into one Society'. In this society, he continues,

'there ought to be men of all Professions, that . . . *Decency* and *Probability*, may be observed as much as possible: That besides the persons above-mention'd [i.e., the heads of political parties], this Society ought to consist of the hopeful Genius's about the Town (of which there are great plenty to be pick'd up in the several Coffee-houses) Travellers, Virtuoso's, Fox-hunters, Jockies, Attornies, old Seamen and Soldiers out of the Hospitals of *Greenwich* and *Chelsea*: To this Society so constituted, ought to be committed the sole management of *Lying*: . . . That the rule of the Society be to invent a Lye, and sometimes two, for every day; in the choice of which great regard ought to be had to the weather, and the season of the year: Your . . . *Terrifying Lyes*, do mighty well in *November* and *December*, but not so well in *May* and *June*, unless the easterly winds reign: That it ought to be Penal, for any body to talk of any thing but the Lye of the day . . . That if any one of the Society were observ'd to blush, or look out of countenance, or want a necessary circumstance in telling the Lye, he ought to be expell'd, and declar'd incapable . . .' (*Miscellanies. By Dr. Swift, Dr. Arbuthnot, Mr. Pope, and Mr. Gay*, 4th ed. [1751], iii. 167–9).

For an account of an earlier 'Lying Club', of which it was said '*the Devil himself*' was alone fit to be the chairman, see Ned Ward's *Compleat and Humorous Account of all the Remarkable Clubs and Societies in the Cities of London and Westminster* (1745), pp. 203–27.

[1] Fielding could scarcely have been surprised if his first readers had seen in this accomplished prevaricator an allusion to the real-life Thomas Edwards (1699–1757) of Lincoln's Inn. An amateur scholar who had recently made sport of Warburton's edition of Shakespeare (see above, p. 523, n. 1), Edwards was also a close friend of Richardson's who seldom missed an opportunity to disparage Fielding's character and reputation. On the Warburton–Edwards controversy, see V. M. Gilbert, *N & Q*, cxcix (June–July 1954), 257–9, 291–3. For Edwards's slurs against Fielding, see his letters to Philip Yorke, 19 January 1749, 8 January 1752; to the Revd. Mr. Crusius, 3 May 1749; to Daniel Wray, 6 January 1752; and to the Revd. Mr. Lawry, 12 February 1752 (Bodl. MS. 1011).

Evening, we will convey our Reader; when Lady *Bellaston*, Lord *Fellamar*, Miss *Western*, and *Tom* being engaged at Whist, and in the last Game of their Rubbers, *Tom* received his Cue from Lady *Bellaston*, which was, 'I protest *Tom*, you are grown intolerable lately; you used to tell us all the News of the Town, and now you know no more of the World than if you lived out of it.'

Mr. *Edwards* then began as follows: 'The Fault is not mine, Madam; It lies in the Dulness of the Age that doth nothing worth talking of.—O la! tho' now I think on't, there hath a terrible Accident befallen poor Col. *Wilcox*.—Poor *Ned*—— You know him, my Lord, every body knows him; faith! I am very much concerned for him.'

'What is it, pray?' says Lady *Bellaston*.

'Why, he hath killed a Man this Morning in a Duel, that's all.'

His Lordship, who was not in the Secret, asked gravely, whom he had killed; to which *Edwards* answered, 'A young Fellow we none of us know; a *Somersetshire* Lad just come to town, one *Jones* his Name is; a near Relation of one Mr. *Allworthy*, of whom your Lordship I believe hath heard. I saw the Lad lie dead in a Coffee-house.—Upon my Soul he is one of the finest Corpses I ever saw in my Life.'

Sophia, who just began to deal as *Tom* had mentioned that a Man was killed, stopt her Hand, and listened with Attention, (for all Stories of that Kind affected her) but no sooner had he arrived at the latter part of the Story, than she began to deal again; and having dealt three Cards to one, and seven to another, and ten to a third, at last dropt the rest from her Hand, and fell back in her Chair.

The Company behaved as usually on these Occasions. The usual Disturbance ensued, the usual Assistance was summoned, and *Sophia* at last, as it is usual, returned again to Life, and was soon after, at her earnest Desire, led to her own Apartment; where, at my Lord's Request, Lady *Bellaston* acquainted her with the Truth, attempted to carry it off as a Jest of her own, and comforted her with repeated Assurances, that neither his Lordship, nor *Tom*, though she had taught him the Story, were in the true Secret of the Affair.

There was no farther Evidence necessary to convince Lord *Fellamar* how justly the Case had been represented to him by

Lady *Bellaston*; and now at her Return into the Room, a Scheme
was laid between those two noble Persons, which, though it
appeared in no very heinous Light to his Lordship, (as he faithfully promised, and faithfully resolved too, to make the Lady
all the subsequent amends in his Power by Marriage) yet many
of our Readers, we doubt not, will see with just Detestation.

The next Evening at seven was appointed for the fatal Purpose, when Lady *Bellaston* undertook that *Sophia* should be alone,
and his Lordship should be introduced to her. The whole Family
were to be regulated for the Purpose, most of the Servants dispatched out of the House, and for Mrs. *Honour* who, to prevent
any Suspicion, was to be left with her Mistress till his Lordship's
Arrival, Lady *Bellaston* herself was to engage her in an Apartment as distant as possible from the Scene of the intended Mischief, and out of the Hearing of *Sophia*.

Matters being thus agreed on, his Lordship took his Leave,
and her Ladyship retired to Rest, highly pleased with a Project
of which she had no reason to doubt the Success, and which
promised so effectually to remove *Sophia* from being any future
Obstruction to her Amour with *Jones*, by a Means of which she
should never appear to be guilty, even if the Fact appeared to the
World; but this she made no doubt of preventing by huddling up
a Marriage, to which she thought the ravished *Sophia* would
easily be brought to consent, and at which all the rest of her
Family would rejoice.

But Affairs were not in so quiet a Situation in the Bosom of
the other Conspirator. His Mind was tost in all the distracting
Anxiety so nobly described by *Shakespear*.[1]

> Between the Acting of a dreadful Thing,
> And the first Motion, all the Interim is
> Like a Phantasma, or a hideous Dream:
> The Genius and the mortal Instruments
> Are then in Council; and the State of Man,
> Like to a little Kingdom, suffers then
> The Nature of an Insurrection.——

Though the Violence of his Passion had made him eagerly
embrace the first Hint of this Design, especially as it came from
a Relation of the Lady, yet when that Friend to Reflection, a

[1] Brutus in *Julius Caesar*, II. i.

Pillow, had placed the Action itself in all its natural black Colours before his Eyes, with all the Consequences which must, and those which might probably attend it; his Resolution began to abate, or rather indeed to go over to the other Side; and after a long Conflict which lasted a whole Night between Honour and Appetite, the former at length prevailed, and he determined to wait on Lady *Bellaston* and to relinquish the Design.

Lady *Bellaston* was in Bed, though very late in the Morning, and *Sophia* sitting by her Bedside, when the Servant acquainted her that Lord *Fellamar* was below in the Parlour, upon which her Ladyship desired him to stay, and that she would see him presently; but the Servant was no sooner departed than poor *Sophia* began to intreat her Cousin not to encourage the Visits of that odious Lord (so she called him though a little unjustly) upon her Account. 'I see his Design,' said she, 'for he made downright Love to me Yesterday Morning; but as I am resolved never to admit it, I beg your Ladyship not to leave us alone together any more, and to order the Servants that if he enquires for me I may be always denied to him.'

'La! Child,' says Lady *Bellaston*, 'you Country Girls have nothing but Sweet-Hearts in your Head; you fancy every Man who is civil to you is making Love. He is one of the most gallant young Fellows about Town, and I am convinced means no more than a little Gallantry. Make Love to you indeed! I wish with all my Heart he would, and you must be an arrant mad Woman to refuse him.'

'But as I shall certainly be that mad Woman,' cries *Sophia*, 'I hope his Visits shall not be intruded upon me.'

'O Child,' said Lady *Bellaston*, 'you need not be so fearful, if you resolve to run away with that *Jones*, I know no Person who can hinder you.'

'Upon my Honour, Madam,' cries *Sophia*, 'your Ladyship injures me. I will never run away with any Man;[1] nor will I ever marry contrary to my Father's Inclinations.'

[1] Richardson's *Clarissa* was published in instalments during 1747–8 (vols. i–ii, 1 December 1747; vols. iii–iv, 28 April 1748; vols. v–vii, 6 December 1748). Fielding praised the novel both publicly and in a warm personal letter to the author (see above, p. 487, n. 1); yet, fully conscious of the rivalry between Richardson and himself, he seems to have designed certain passages in *Tom Jones* to invite comparison between his own heroine and Richardson's, who are caught in similar circumstances but comport themselves according to quite different standards of conduct. With Sophia's declaration that she 'will never run

'Well, Miss *Western*,' said the Lady, 'if you are not in a Humour to see Company this Morning, you may retire to your own Apartment; for I am not frightned at his Lordship, and must send for him up into my Dressing-Room.'

Sophia thanked her Ladyship and withdrew; and presently afterwards *Fellamar* was admitted up Stairs.

CHAPTER IV

By which it will appear how dangerous an Advocate a Lady is, when she applies her Eloquence to an ill Purpose.

WHEN Lady *Bellaston* heard the young Lord's Scruples, she treated them with the same Disdain with which one of those Sages of the Law, called *Newgate* Solicitors,[1] treats the Qualms of Conscience in a young Witness. 'My dear Lord,' said she, 'you certainly want a Cordial. I must send to Lady *Edgely* for one of her best Drams. Fie upon it! have more Resolution. Are you frightned by the Word Rape? Or are you apprehensive ——? Well, if the Story of *Helen* was modern, I should think it unnatural. I mean the Behaviour of *Paris*, not the Fondness of the Lady; for all Women love a Man of Spirit. There is another Story of the *Sabine* Ladies,—and that too, I thank Heaven, is very ancient. Your Lordship, perhaps, will admire my Reading; but I think Mr. *Hook* tells us[2] they made tolerable good Wives

away with any Man', compare Clarissa's letter to Anna Howe, confessing that she has eloped with Lovelace: 'You will soon hear (if already you have not heard from the mouth of common fame), that your Clarissa Harlowe is gone off with a man!—' (ii. 306). See also below, pp. 850, n. 1; 955, n. 1.

[1] Dishonest lawyers who, like Jonathan Wild's uncle, specialize 'in soliciting the Causes of the distressed Captives in *Newgate*' (I. ii). See also *Jonathan Wild* (II. v) and the Post-script to *A Clear State of the Case of Elizabeth Canning* (1753).

[2] *The Roman History, From the Building of Rome to the Ruin of the Commonwealth* by Pope's friend Nathaniel Hooke (d. 1763); it was published in 4 vols.—i (1738), ii (1745), and the two last posthumously. The story of the rape of the Sabine women is found in vol. i, where Hooke relates that because of 'the merit and fondness of their husbands', the women came to 'forget their native country and their fathers' houses' (p. 32) and 'became engaged by the strictest ties of affection, to those whom [they] formerly hated' (p. 38). Owing to their intercession, a treaty was effected between the Sabines and Romans. In *A Journey from This World to the Next* (I. ix) Fielding has Livy praise Hooke's *Roman History*, 'which he said was infinitely preferable to all others', most especially to Echard's (see above, pp. 273, n. 2; 421, n. 6).

Fielding and Hooke were certainly acquainted. Hooke had been employed by the

afterwards. I fancy few of my married Acquaintance were ravished by their Husbands.' 'Nay, dear Lady *Bellaston*,' cried he, 'don't ridicule me in this Manner.' 'Why, my good Lord,' answered she, 'do you think any Woman in *England* would not laugh at you in her Heart, whatever Prudery she might wear in her Countenance?—You force me to use a strange Kind of Language, and to betray my Sex most abominably: But I am contented with knowing my Intentions are good, and that I am endeavouring to serve my Cousin; for I think you will make her a Husband notwithstanding this; or, upon my Soul, I would not even persuade her to fling herself away upon an empty Title. She should not upbraid me hereafter with having lost a Man of Spirit; for that his Enemies allow this poor young Fellow to be.'

Let those who have had the Satisfaction of hearing Reflections of this Kind from a Wife or a Mistress, declare whether they are at all sweetened by coming from a Female Tongue. Certain it is they sunk deeper into his Lordship, than any Thing which *Demosthenes* or *Cicero* could have said on the Occasion.

Lady *Bellaston* perceiving she had fired the young Lord's Pride, began now, like a true Orator, to rouse other Passions to its Assistance. 'My Lord,' says she, in a graver Voice, 'you will be pleased to remember you mentioned this Matter to me first; for I would not appear to you in the Light of one who is endeavouring to put off my Cousin upon you. Fourscore thousand Pounds do not stand in Need of an Advocate to recommend them.' 'Nor doth Miss *Western*,' said he, 'require any Recommendation from her Fortune; for in my Opinion, no Woman ever had half her Charms.' 'Yes, yes, my Lord;' replied the Lady, looking in the Glass, 'there have been Women with more than half her Charms, I assure you; not that I need lessen her on that Account. She is a most delicious Girl, that's certain; and within these few Hours she will be in the Arms of one, who surely doth not deserve her, tho' I will give him his due, I believe he is truly a Man of Spirit.'

'I hope so, Madam,' said my Lord; 'though I must own he doth not deserve her; for unless Heaven, or your Ladyship disappoint me, she shall within that Time be in mine.'

Duchess of Marlborough to write her memoirs (published March 1742). When this work and its subject were attacked, Fielding rushed into print with his *Full Vindication* of the duchess (April 1742), to whom his mother's family was related by marriage.

'Well spoken, my Lord,' answered the Lady. 'I promise you no Disappointment shall happen from my Side; and within this Week I am convinced I shall call your Lordship my Cousin in Public.'

The Remainder of this Scene consisted entirely of Raptures, Excuses, and Compliments, very pleasant to have heard from the Parties; but rather dull when related at second Hand. Here, therefore, we shall put an End to this Dialogue, and hasten to the fatal Hour, when every Thing was prepared for the Destruction of poor *Sophia*.

But this being the most tragical Matter in our whole History, we shall treat it in a Chapter by itself.

CHAPTER V

Containing some Matters which may affect, and others which may surprize the Reader.

THE Clock had now struck Seven, and poor *Sophia*, alone and melancholy, sat reading a Tragedy. It was the *Fatal Marriage*,[1] and she was now come to that Part where the poor, distrest *Isabella* disposes of her Wedding-Ring.

Here the Book dropt from her Hand, and a Shower of Tears ran down into her Bosom. In this Situation she had continued a Minute, when the Door opened, and in came Lord *Fellamar*. *Sophia* started from her Chair at his Entrance; and his Lordship advancing forwards, and making a low Bow said, 'I am afraid, Miss *Western*, I break in upon you abruptly.' 'Indeed, my Lord,' says she, 'I must own myself a little surprized at this unexpected Visit.' 'If this Visit be unexpected, Madam,' answered Lord

---

[1] *The Fatal Marriage: or, The Innocent Adultery* (1694) by Thomas Southerne (1659–1746). The scene which moves Sophia (II. ii) is not far removed from her own distressed situation. Having been rejected by her father-in-law for marrying his son against his wishes, Isabella is in despair. Hounded by creditors and believing her husband to be dead, she reluctantly decides to sell her last thing of value, her wedding ring, to keep herself and her infant son from starving. After the tragic denouement, the father-in-law, Count Baldwin, speaks the moral:

> To erring Youth there's some Compassion due;
> But while with Rigour you their Crimes pursue,
> What's their Misfortune, is a Crime in you.
> Hence learn offending Children to forgive:
> Leave Punishment to Heav'n, 'tis Heav'n's Prerogative.

Fellamar, 'my Eyes must have been very faithless Interpreters of
my Heart, when last I had the Honour of seeing you: For surely
you could not otherwise have hoped to detain my Heart in your
Possession, without receiving a Visit from its Owner.' *Sophia*,
confus'd as she was, answered this Bombast (and very properly,
I think,) with a Look of inconceivable Disdain. My Lord then
made another and a longer Speech of the same Sort. Upon which
Sophia, trembling, said, 'Am I really to conceive your Lordship
to be out of your Senses? Sure, my Lord, there is no other Excuse
for such Behaviour.'—'I am, indeed, Madam, in the Situation you
suppose,' cries his Lordship; 'and sure you will pardon the
Effects of a Frenzy which you yourself have occasioned: For
Love hath so totally deprived me of Reason, that I am scarce
accountable for any of my Actions.' 'Upon my Word, my Lord,'
said *Sophia*, 'I neither understand your Words nor your Behaviour.'—'Suffer me then, Madam,' cries he, 'at your Feet to
explain both, by laying open my Soul to you, and declaring that
I doat on you to the highest Degree of Distraction. O most
adorable, most divine Creature! what Language can express the
Sentiments of my Heart?' 'I do assure you, my Lord,' said
Sophia, 'I shall not stay to hear any more of this.' 'Do not,'
cries he, 'think of leaving me thus cruelly: Could you know half
the Torments which I feel, that tender Bosom must pity what
those Eyes have caused.' Then fetching a deep Sigh, and laying
Hold of her Hand, he ran on for some Minutes in a Strain which
would be little more pleasing to the Reader, than it was to the
Lady; and at last concluded with a Declaration, 'That if he was
Master of the World, he would lay it at her Feet.' *Sophia* then
forcibly pulling away her Hand from his, answered, with much
Spirit, 'I promise you, Sir, your World and its Master, I should
spurn from me with equal Contempt.' She then offered to go,
and Lord *Fellamar* again laying Hold of her Hand, said, 'Pardon
me, my beloved Angel, Freedoms which nothing but Despair
could have tempted me to take.—Believe me, could I have had
any Hope that my Title and Fortune, neither of them inconsiderable, unless when compared with your Worth, would have been
accepted, I had, in the humblest Manner, presented them to your
Acceptance.—But I cannot lose you.—By Heaven, I will sooner
part with my Soul.—You are, you must, you shall be only mine.'
'My Lord,' said she, 'I intreat you to desist from a vain Pursuit;

for, upon my Honour, I will never hear you on this Subject. Let go my Hand, my Lord, for I am resolved to go from you this Moment, nor will I ever see you more.' 'Then, Madam,' cries his Lordship, 'I must make the best Use of this Moment; for I cannot, nor will I live without you.'—'What do you mean, my Lord?' said *Sophia*; 'I will raise the Family.' 'I have no Fear, Madam,' answered he, 'but of losing you, and that I am resolved to prevent, the only Way which Despair points to me.'—He then caught her in his Arms; upon which she screamed so loud, that she must have alarmed some one to her Assistance, had not Lady *Bellaston* taken Care to remove all Ears. But a more lucky Circumstance happened for poor *Sophia*; another Noise now broke forth, which almost drowned her Cries: For now the whole House rung with 'Where is she? D——n me, I'll unkennel her this Instant. Shew me her Chamber, I say. Where is my Daughter, I know she's in the House, and I'll see her if she's above Ground. Shew me where she is.'—At which last Words the Door flew open, and in came Squire *Western*, with his Parson, and a Set of Myrmidons at his Heels.

How miserable must have been the Condition of poor *Sophia*, when the enraged Voice of her Father was welcome to her Ears? Welcome indeed it was, and luckily did he come; for it was the only Accident upon Earth, which could have preserved the Peace of her Mind from being for ever destroyed.

Sophia, notwithstanding her Fright, presently knew her Father's Voice; and his Lordship, notwithstanding his Passion, knew the Voice of Reason, which peremptorily assured him, it was not now a Time for the Perpetration of his Villainy. Hearing, therefore, the Voice approach, and hearing likewise whose it was (for as the Squire more than once roared forth the Word Daughter, so *Sophia*, in the Midst of her Struggling, cried out upon her Father); he thought proper to relinquish his Prey, having only disordered her Handkerchief, and with his rude Lips committed Violence on her lovely Neck.

If the Reader's Imagination doth not assist me, I shall never be able to describe the Situation of these two Persons when *Western* came into the Room. *Sophia* tottered into a Chair, where she sat disordered, pale, breathless, bursting with Indignation at Lord *Fellamar*; affrighted, and yet more rejoiced at the Arrival of her Father.

His Lordship sat down near her, with the Bag of his Wig hanging over one of his Shoulders, the rest of his Dress being somewhat disordered, and rather a greater Proportion of Linnen than is usual appearing at his Bosom. As to the rest, he was amazed, affrighted, vexed, and ashamed.

As to Squire *Western*, he happened, at this Time, to be overtaken by an Enemy, which very frequently pursues, and seldom fails to overtake most of the Country Gentlemen in this Kingdom. He was literally speaking drunk; which Circumstance, together with his natural Impetuosity, could produce no other Effect, than his running immediately up to his Daughter, upon whom he fell foul with his Tongue in the most inveterate Manner; nay, he had probably committed Violence with his Hands, had not the Parson interposed, saying, 'For Heaven's Sake, Sir, animadvert that you are in the House of a great Lady. Let me beg you to mitigate your Wrath; it should minister a Fullness of Satisfaction that you have found your Daughter; for as to Revenge, it belongeth not unto us. I discern great Contrition in the Countenance of the young Lady. I stand assured, if you will forgive her, she will repent her of all past Offences, and return unto her Duty.'

The Strength of the Parson's Arms had at first been of more Service than the Strength of his Rhetoric. However, his last Words wrought some Effect, and the Squire answered, 'I'll forgee her if she wull ha un. If wot ha un, *Sophy*, I'll forgee thee all. Why dost unt speak? Shat ha un? D—n me, shat ha un? Why dost unt answer? Was ever such a stubborn Tuoad?'

'Let me intreat you, Sir, to be a little more moderate,' said the Parson; 'you frighten the young Lady so, that you deprive her of all Power of Utterance.'

'Power of mine A—,' answered the Squire. 'You take her Part then, you do? A pretty Parson, truly, to side with an undutiful Child. Yes, yes, I will gee you a Living with a Pox. I'll gee un to the Devil sooner.'

'I humbly crave your Pardon,' said the Parson, 'I assure your Worship, I meant no such Matter.'

My Lady *Bellaston* now entered the Room, and came up to the Squire, who no sooner saw her, than resolving to follow the Instructions of his Sister, he made her a very civil Bow, in the rural Manner, and paid her some of his best Compliments.

He then immediately proceeded to his Complaints, and said, 'There, my Lady Cousin, there stands the most undutiful Child in the World; she hankers after a beggarly Rascal, and won't marry one of the greatest Matches in all *England*, that we have provided for her.'

'Indeed, Cousin *Western*,' answered the Lady, 'I am persuaded you wrong my Cousin. I am sure she hath a better Understanding. I am convinced she will not refuse what she must be sensible is so much to her Advantage.'

This was a wilful Mistake in Lady *Bellaston*; for she well knew whom Mr. *Western* meant; tho' perhaps she thought he would easily be reconciled to his Lordship's Proposals.

'Do you hear there,' quoth the Squire, 'what her Ladyship says? All your Family are for the Match. Come, *Sophy*, be a good Girl, and be dutiful, and make your Father happy.'

'If my Death will make you happy, Sir,' answered *Sophia*, 'you will shortly be so.'

'It's a Lie, *Sophy*, it's a d—nd Lie, and you know it,' said the Squire.

'Indeed, Miss *Western*,' said Lady *Bellaston*, 'you injure your Father; he hath nothing in View but your Interest in this Match; and I and all your Friends must acknowledge the highest Honour done to your Family in the Proposal.'

'Ay, all of us,' quoth the Squire; 'nay, it was no Proposal of mine. She knows it was her Aunt proposed it to me first.—Come, *Sophy*, once more let me beg you to be a good Girl, and gee me your Consent before your Cousin.'

'Let me give him your Hand, Cousin,' said the Lady. 'It is the Fashion now-a-days to dispense with Time and long Courtships.'

'Pugh,' said the Squire, 'what signifies Time; won't they have Time enough to court afterwards? People may court very well after they have been a-bed together.'

As Lord *Fellamar* was very well assured, that he was meant by Lady *Bellaston*, so never having heard nor suspected a Word of *Blifil*, he made no doubt of his being meant by the Father. Coming up therefore to the Squire, he said, 'Though I have not the Honour, Sir, of being personally known to you; yet as I find, I have the Happiness to have my Proposals accepted, let me intercede, Sir, in Behalf of the young Lady, that she may not be more solicited at this Time.'

'You intercede, Sir!' said the Squire, 'why, who the Devil are you?'

'Sir, I am Lord *Fellamar*,' answered he, 'and am the happy Man, whom I hope you have done the Honour of accepting for a Son-in-law.'

'You are a Son of a B——,' replied the Squire, 'for all your laced Coat. You my Son-in-Law, and be d——nd to you!'

'I shall take more from you, Sir, than from any Man,' answered the Lord; 'but I must inform you, that I am not used to hear such Language without Resentment.'

'Resent my A——,' quoth the Squire. 'Don't think I am afraid of such a Fellow as thee art? Because hast a got a Spit there dangling at thy Side. Lay by your Spit and I'll give thee enough of meddling with what doth not belong to thee.—I'll teach you to Father-in-law me. I'll lick thy Jacket.'

'It's very well, Sir,' said my Lord, 'I shall make no Disturbance before the Ladies. I am very well satisfied. Your humble Servant, Sir; Lady *Bellaston*, your most obedient.'

His Lordship was no sooner gone, than Lady *Bellaston* coming up to Mr. *Western*, said, 'Bless me, Sir, what have you done? You know not whom you have affronted; he is a Nobleman of the first Rank and Fortune, and Yesterday made Proposals to your Daughter; and such as I am sure you must accept with the highest Pleasure.'

'Answer for yourself, Lady Cousin,' said the Squire, 'I will have nothing to do with any of your Lords. My Daughter shall have an honest Country Gentleman; I have pitched upon one for her,—and she shall ha' un.—I am sorry for the Trouble she hath given your Ladyship with all my Heart.' Lady *Bellaston* made a civil Speech upon the Word Trouble, to which the Squire answered, 'Why that's kind,—and I would do as much for your Ladyship. To be sure Relations should do for one another. So I wish your Ladyship a good Night.—Come, Madam, you must go along with me by fair Means, or I'll have you carried down to the Coach.'

Sophia said she would attend him without Force; but begged to go in a Chair, for she said she should not be able to ride any other Way.

'Prithee,' cries the Squire, 'wout unt persuade me canst not ride in a Coach, wouldst? That's a pretty Thing surely. No, no,

I'll never let thee out of my Sight any more till art married, that I promise thee.' *Sophia* told him 'she saw he was resolved to break her Heart.' 'O break thy Heart and be d—nd,' quoth he, 'if a good Husband will break it. I don't value a Brass Varden, not a Hapenny of any undutiful B—— upon Earth.' He then took violently hold of her Hand; upon which the Parson once more interfered, begging him to use gentle Methods. At that the Squire thundered out a Curse, and bid the Parson hold his Tongue, saying, 'At'n't in Pulpit now? when art a got up there I never mind what dost say; but I won't be Priest-ridden, nor taught how to behave myself by thee. I wish your Ladyship a good Night. Come along, *Sophy*, be a good Girl, and all shall be well. Shat ha un, d—n me, shat ha un.'

Mrs. *Honour* appeared below Stairs, and with a low Curtesy to the Squire, offered to attend her Mistress; but he pushed her away, saying, 'Hold, Madam, hold, you come no more near my House.' 'And will you take my Maid away from me?' said *Sophia*. 'Yes indeed, Madam, will I,' cries the Squire; 'you need not fear being without a Servant, I will get you another Maid, and a better Maid than this, who, I'd lay five Pound to a Crown, is no more a Maid than my Grannum. No, no, *Sophy*, she shall contrive no more Escapes I promise you.' He then packed up his Daughter and the Parson into the Hackney Coach, after which he mounted himself, and ordered it to drive to his Lodgings. In the Way thither he suffered *Sophia* to be quiet, and entertained himself with reading a Lecture to the Parson on good Manners, and a proper Behaviour to his Betters.

It is possible he might not so easily have carried off his Daughter from Lady *Bellaston*, had that good Lady desired to have detained her; but in reality she was not a little pleased with the Confinement into which *Sophia* was going; and as her Project with Lord *Fellamar* had failed of Success, she was well contented that other violent Methods were now going to be used in Favour of another Man.

CHAPTER VI

By what Means the Squire came to discover his Daughter.

THOUGH the Reader in many Histories is obliged to digest much more unaccountable Appearances than this of Mr. *Western*, without any Satisfaction at all; yet as we dearly love to oblige him whenever it is in our Power, we shall now proceed to shew by what Method the Squire discovered where his Daughter was.

In the third Chapter then of the preceding Book,[1] we gave a Hint (for it is not our Custom to unfold at any Time more than is necessary for the Occasion) that Mrs. *Fitzpatrick*, who was very desirous of reconciling herself to her Uncle and Aunt *Western*, thought she had a probable Opportunity by the Service of preserving *Sophia* from committing the same Crime which had drawn on herself the Anger of her Family. After much Deliberation therefore she resolved to inform her Aunt *Western* where her Cousin was, and accordingly she writ the following Letter, which we shall give the Reader at length for more Reasons than one.

'Honoured Madam,

    The Occasion of my writing this will perhaps make a Letter of mine agreeable to my dear Aunt, for the Sake of one of her Nieces, though I have little Reason to hope it will be so on the account of another.

    'Without more Apology, as I was coming to throw my unhappy Self at your Feet, I met, by the strangest Accident in the World, my Cousin *Sophy*, whose History you are better acquainted with than myself, though, alas! I know infinitely too much; enough indeed to satisfy me, that unless she is immediately prevented, she is in Danger of running into the same fatal Mischief, which, by foolishly and ignorantly refusing your most wise and prudent Advice, I have unfortunately brought on myself.

    'In short, I have seen the Man, nay I was most part of Yesterday in his Company, and a charming young Fellow I promise you he is. By what Accident he came acquainted with me is too tedious to tell you now; but I have this Morning changed my Lodging to avoid him, lest he should by my Means discover my

---

[1] Actually, of Book XIII.

Cousin; for he doth not yet know where she is, and it is adviseable he should not till my Uncle hath secured her.—No Time therefore is to be lost, and I need only inform you, that she is now with Lady *Bellaston*, whom I have seen, and who hath, I find, a Design of concealing her from her Family. You know, Madam, she is a strange Woman; but nothing could misbecome me more, than to presume to give any Hint to one of your great Understanding and great Knowledge of the World, besides barely informing you of the Matter of Fact.

'I hope, Madam, the Care which I have shewn on this Occasion for the Good of my Family, will recommend me again to the Favour of a Lady who hath always exerted so much Zeal for the Honour and true Interest of us all; and that it may be a Means of restoring me to your Friendship, which hath made so great a Part of my former, and is so necessary to my future Happiness. I am,

With the utmost Respect,
Honoured Madam,
Your most dutiful obliged Niece,
And most Obedient
Humble Servant,
Harriet Fitzpatrick.'

Mrs. *Western* was now at her Brother's House, where she had resided ever since the Flight of *Sophia*, in order to administer Comfort to the poor Squire in his Affliction. Of this Comfort which she doled out to him in daily Portions, we have formerly given a Specimen.

She was now standing with her Back to the Fire, and with a Pinch of Snuff in her Hand was dealing forth this daily Allowance of Comfort to the Squire while he smoaked his Afternoon Pipe, when she received the above Letter; which she had no sooner read than she delivered it to him, saying, 'There, Sir, there is an Account of your lost Sheep. Fortune hath again restored her to you, and if you will be governed by my Advice, it is possible you may yet preserve her.'

The Squire had no sooner read the Letter than he leap'd from his Chair, threw his Pipe into the Fire, and gave a loud Huzza for Joy. He then summoned his Servants, called for his Boots, and ordered the *Chevalier* and several other Horses to be saddled, and that Parson *Supple* should be immediately sent for. Having done this, he turned to his Sister, caught her in his Arms, and gave her a close Embrace, saying, 'Zounds! you don't seem pleased, one would imagine you was sorry I have found the Girl.'

'Brother,' answered she, 'the deepest Politicians who see to the Bottom discover often a very different Aspect of Affairs, from what swims on the Surface. It is true indeed, Things do look rather less desperate than they did formerly in *Holland*, when *Lewis* the fourteenth was at the Gates of *Amsterdam*;[1] but there is a Delicacy required in this Matter, which you will pardon me, Brother, if I suspect you want. There is a Decorum to be used with a Woman of Figure, such as Lady *Bellaston*, Brother, which requires a Knowledge of the World superior, I am afraid, to yours.'

'Sister,' cries the Squire, 'I know you have no Opinion of my Parts; but I'll shew you on this Occasion who is a Fool. Knowledge quotha! I have not been in the Country so long without having some Knowledge of Warrants and the Law of the Land. I know I may take my own wherever I can find it. Shew me my own Daughter, and if I don't know how to come at her, I'll suffer you to call me Fool as long as I live. There be Justices of Peace in *London*, as well as in other Places.'

'I protest,' cries she, 'you make me tremble for the Event of this Matter, which if you will proceed by my Advice, you may bring to so good an Issue. Do you really imagine, Brother, that the House of a Woman of Figure is to be attacked by Warrants and brutal Justices of the Peace? I will inform you how to proceed. As soon as you arrive in Town, and have got yourself into a decent Dress (for indeed, Brother, you have none at present fit to appear in) you must send your Compliments to Lady *Bellaston*, and desire Leave to wait on her. When you are admitted to her Presence, as you certainly will be, and have told her your Story, and have made proper Use of my Name, (for I think you just know one another only by Sight, though you are Relations) I am confident she will withdraw her Protection from my Niece, who hath certainly imposed upon her. This is the only Method.—Justices of Peace indeed! do you imagine any such Event can arrive to a Woman of Figure in a civilized Nation?'

'D—n their Figures,' cries the Squire; 'a pretty civilized

[1] In 1672.

Nation truly, where Women are above the Law. And what must
I stand sending a Parcel of Compliments to a confounded Whore,
that keeps away a Daughter from her own natural Father? I tell
you, Sister, I am not so ignorant as you think me.—I know you
would have Women above the Law, but it is all a Lie; I heard his
Lordship say at 'Size, that no one is above the Law. But this of
yours is *Hannover* Law, I suppose.'

'Mr. *Western*,' said she, 'I think you daily improve in Ignorance.—I protest you are grown an arrant Bear.'

'No more a Bear than yourself, Sister *Western*,' said the Squire.
—'Pox! you may talk of your Civility an you will, I am sure you
never shew any to me. I am no Bear, no, nor no Dog neither,
though I know Somebody, that is something that begins with a
B——, but Pox! I will shew you I have a got more good Manners
than some Folks.'

'Mr. *Western*,' answered the Lady, 'you may say what you
please, *Je vous mesprise de tout mon Cœur.*[1] I shall not therefore
be angry.—Besides, as my Cousin with that odious *Irish* Name
justly says, I have that Regard for the Honour and true Interest
of my Family, and that Concern for my Niece, who is a Part of
it, that I have resolved to go to Town myself upon this Occasion;
for indeed, indeed, Brother, you are not a fit Minister to be employed at a polite Court.—*Greenland*—*Greenland* should always
be the Scene of the Tramontane Negotiation.'[2]

'I thank Heaven,' cries the Squire, 'I don't understand you,
now. You are got to your *Hannoverian* Linguo. However, I'll
shew you I scorn to be behind-hand in Civility with you; and as
you are not angry for what I have said, so I am not angry for
what you have said. Indeed I have always thought it a Folly for
Relations to quarrel; and if they do now and then give a hasty
Word, why People should give and take; for my Part I never
bear Malice; and I take it very kind of you to go up to *London*,
for I never was there but twice in my Life, and then I did not
stay above a Fortnight at a Time; and to be sure I can't be expected to know much of the Streets and the Folks in that Time.
I never denied that you know'd all these Matters better than I.

---

[1] 'I despise you with all my heart.'

[2] On 'tramontane', see above, p. 438, n. 1. Cf. Steele, *The Tatler*, No. 222 (9 September
1710): 'as for our Tramontane Lovers. . . . A Man might as well serenade in *Greenland*
as in our Region.' Hans Egede's *Description of Greenland* (trans. 1745) confirmed the
reputation of that country as barbarous and uncivilized (see esp. ch. x).

For me to dispute that would be all as one, as for you to dispute the Management of a Pack of Dogs, or the finding a Hare sitting, with me.'—'Which I promise you,' says she, 'I never will.'— 'Well, and I promise you,' returned he, 'that I never will dispute the t'other.'

Here then a League was struck (to borrow a Phrase from the Lady) between the contending Parties; and now the Parson arriving, and the Horses being ready, the Squire departed, having promised his Sister to follow her Advice, and she prepared to follow him the next Day.

But having communicated these Matters to the Parson on the Road, they both agreed that the prescribed Formalities might very well be dispensed with; and the Squire having changed his Mind, proceeded in the Manner we have already seen.

CHAPTER VII

In which various Misfortunes befal poor Jones.

AFFAIRS were in the aforesaid Situation, when Mrs. *Honour* arrived at Mrs. *Miller's*, and called *Jones* out from the Company, as we have before seen, with whom, when she found herself alone, she began as follows.

'O my dear Sir, how shall I get Spirits to tell you; you are undone, Sir, and my poor Lady's undone, and I am undone.' 'Hath any thing happened to *Sophia?*' cries *Jones*, staring like a Madman. 'All that is bad,' cries *Honour*, 'O I shall never get such another Lady! O that I should ever live to see this Day!' At these Words *Jones* turned pale as Ashes, trembled and stammered; but *Honour* went on. 'O, Mr. *Jones*, I have lost my Lady for ever.' 'How! What! for Heaven's Sake tell me.—O my dear *Sophia!*'—'You may well call her so,' said *Honour*, 'she was the dearest Lady to me.—I shall never have such another Place.'— 'D—n your Place,' cries *Jones*, 'where is? what! what is become of my *Sophia?*' 'Ay, to be sure,' cries she, 'Servants may be d—n'd. It signifies nothing what becomes of them, tho' they are turned away, and ruined ever so much. To be sure they are not Flesh and Blood like other People. No to be sure, it signifies nothing what becomes of them.'—'If you have any Pity, any Compassion,' cries *Jones*, 'I beg you will instantly tell me what hath happened to *Sophia*?' 'To be sure I have more Pity for you than you have for me,' answered *Honour*; 'I don't d—n you because you have lost the sweetest Lady in the World. To be sure you are worthy to be pitied, and I am worthy to be pitied too: For to be sure if ever there was a good Mistress——' 'What hath happened,' cries *Jones*, in almost a raving Fit.—'What?'—'What?' said *Honour*; 'why the worst that could have happened both for you and for me.—Her Father is come to Town, and hath carried her away from us both.' Here *Jones* fell on his Knees in Thanksgiving that it was no worse.—'No worse!' repeated *Honour*, 'what could be worse for either of us? He carried her off, swearing she should marry Mr. *Blifil*; that's for your Comfort; and for poor me, I am turned out of Doors.' 'Indeed Mrs. *Honour*,' answered *Jones*, 'you frightned me out of my Wits. I imagined some most dreadful sudden Accident had happened to *Sophia*; something, compared to which, even the seeing her married to *Blifil* would be a Trifle; but while there is Life, there are Hopes, my dear *Honour*. Women in this Land of Liberty cannot be married by actual brutal Force.' 'To be sure, Sir,' said she, 'that's true. There may be some Hopes for you; but alack-a-day! what Hopes are there for poor me? And to be sure, Sir, you must be sensible I suffer all this upon your Account. All the Quarrel the Squire hath to me is for taking your Part, as I have done, against Mr. *Blifil*.' 'Indeed Mrs. *Honour*,' answered he, 'I am sensible of my Obligations to you, and will leave nothing in my Power undone to make you amends.' 'Alas, Sir,' said she, 'what can make a Servant amends for the Loss of one Place, but the getting another altogether as good!'—'Do not despair, Mrs. *Honour*,' said *Jones*, 'I hope to reinstate you again in the same.' 'Alack-a-day, Sir,' said she, 'how can I flatter myself with such Hopes, when I know it is a Thing impossible; for the Squire is so set against me: and yet if you should ever have my Lady, as to be sure I now hopes heartily you will; for you are a generous good-natured Gentleman, and I am sure you loves her, and to be sure she loves you as dearly as her own Soul; it is a Matter in vain to deny it; because as why, every Body that is in the least acquainted with my Lady, must see it; for, poor dear Lady, she can't dissemble; and if two People who loves one another a'n't happy, why who should be so? Happiness don't always depend upon ·

what People has; besides, my Lady has enough for both. To be sure therefore as one may say, it would be all the Pity in the World to keep two such Loviers asunder; nay, I am convinced for my Part, you will meet together at last; for if it is to be, there is no preventing it. If a Marriage is made in Heaven, all the Justices of Peace upon Earth can't break it off. To be sure I wishes that Parson *Supple* had but a little more Spirit to tell the Squire of his Wickedness in endeavouring to force his Daughter contrary to her Liking; but then his whole Dependance is on the Squire, and so the poor Gentleman, though he is a very religious good sort of Man and talks of the Badness of such Doings behind the Squire's Back, yet he dares not say his Soul is his own to his Face. To be sure I never saw him make so bold as just now, I was afeard the Squire would have struck him.—I would not have your Honour be melancholy, Sir, nor despair; Things may go better, as long as you are sure of my Lady, and that I am certain you may be, for she never will be brought to consent to marry any other Man. Indeed, I am terribly afeard the Squire will do her a Mischief in his Passion: For he is a prodigious passionate Gentleman, and I am afeard too the poor Lady will be brought to break her Heart, for she is as tender-hearted as a Chicken; it is pity methinks, she had not a little of my Courage. If I was in Love with a young Man, and my Father offered to lock me up, I'd tear his Eyes out, but I'd come at him; but then there's a great Fortune in the Case, which it is in her Father's Power either to give her or not; that, to be sure, may make some Difference.'

Whether *Jones* gave strict Attention to all the foregoing Harangue, or whether it was for want of any Vacancy in the Discourse, I cannot determine; but he never once attempted to answer, nor did she once stop, till *Partridge* came running into the Room, and informed him that the great Lady was upon the Stairs.

Nothing could equal the Dilemma to which *Jones* was now reduced. *Honour* knew nothing of any Acquaintance that subsisted between him and Lady *Bellaston*, and she was almost the last Person in the World to whom he would have communicated it. In this Hurry and Distress, he took (as is common enough) the worst Course, and instead of exposing her to the Lady, which would have been of little Consequence, he chose to expose the

Lady to her; he therefore resolved to hide *Honour*, whom he had but just time to convey behind the Bed, and to draw the Curtains.

The Hurry in which *Jones* had been all Day engaged on Account of his poor Landlady and her Family, the Terrors occasioned by Mrs. *Honour*, and the Confusion into which he was thrown by the sudden Arrival of Lady *Bellaston*, had altogether driven former Thoughts out of his Head; so that it never once occur'd to his Memory to act the Part of a sick Man; which indeed, neither the Gayety of his Dress, nor the Freshness of his Countenance would have at all supported.

He received her Ladyship therefore rather agreeably to her Desires than to her Expectations, with all the good Humour he could muster in his Countenance, and without any real or affected Appearance of the least Disorder.

Lady *Bellaston* no sooner entered the Room, than she squatted herself down on the Bed: 'So, my dear *Jones*,' said she, 'you find nothing can detain me long from you. Perhaps I ought to be angry with you, that I have neither seen nor heard from you all Day; for I perceive your Distemper would have suffered you to come abroad; Nay, I suppose you have not sat in your Chamber all Day drest up like a fine Lady to see Company after a Lying-in; but however, don't think I intend to scold you: For I never will give you an Excuse for the cold Behaviour of a Husband, by putting on the ill Humour of a Wife.'

'Nay, Lady *Bellaston*,' said *Jones*, 'I am sure your Ladyship will not upbraid me with neglect of Duty, when I only waited for Orders. Who, my dear Creature, hath Reason to complain? Who missed an Appointment last Night, and left an unhappy Man to expect, and wish, and sigh, and languish?'

'Do not mention it, my dear Mr. *Jones*,' cried she. 'If you knew the Occasion, you would pity me. In short, it is impossible to conceive what Women of Condition are obliged to suffer from the Impertinence of Fools, in order to keep up the Farce of the World. I am glad however, all your languishing and wishing have done you no harm: for you never looked better in your Life. Upon my Faith! *Jones*, you might at this Instant sit for the Picture of *Adonis*.'

There are certain Words of Provocation which Men of Honour hold can properly be answered only by a Blow. Among Lovers possibly there may be some Expressions which can be answered only by a Kiss. Now the Compliment which Lady *Bellaston* made *Jones* seems to be of this Kind, especially as it was attended with a Look in which the Lady conveyed more soft Ideas than it was possible to express with her Tongue.

Jones was certainly at this Instant in one of the most disagreeable and distrest situations imaginable; for to carry on the Comparison we made use of before, tho' the Provocation was given by the Lady, *Jones* could not receive Satisfaction, nor so much as offer to ask it, in the Presence of a third Person; Seconds in this kind of Duels not being according to the Law of Arms. As this Objection did not occur to Lady *Bellaston*, who was ignorant of any other Woman being there but herself, she waited some time in great Astonishment for an Answer from *Jones*, who conscious of the ridiculous Figure he made, stood at a Distance, and not daring to give the proper Answer, gave none at all. Nothing can be imagined more comic, nor yet more tragical than this Scene would have been, if it had lasted much longer. The Lady had already changed Colour two or three times; had got up from the Bed and sat down again, while *Jones* was wishing the Ground to sink under him, or the House to fall on his Head, when an odd Accident freed him from an Embarassment out of which neither the Eloquence of a *Cicero*, nor the Politicks of a *Machiavel* could have delivered him, without utter Disgrace.

This was no other than the Arrival of young *Nightingale* dead drunk; or rather in that State of Drunkenness which deprives Men of the Use of their Reason, without depriving them of the Use of their Limbs.

Mrs. *Miller* and her Daughters were in Bed, and *Partridge* was smoking his Pipe by the Kitchen Fire; so that he arrived at Mr. *Jones's* Chamber Door without any Interruption. This he burst open, and was entering without any Ceremony, when *Jones* started from his Seat, and ran to oppose him; which he did so effectually, that *Nightingale* never came far enough within the Door to see who was sitting on the Bed.

Nightingale had in Reality mistaken *Jones's* Apartment for that in which himself had lodged; he therefore strongly insisted on coming in, often swearing that he would not be kept from his own Bed. *Jones*, however, prevailed over him, and delivered him into the Hands of *Partridge*, whom the Noise on the Stairs soon summoned to his Master's Assistance.

And now *Jones* was unwillingly obliged to return to his own Apartment, where at the very Instant of his Entrance he heard Lady *Bellaston* venting an Exclamation, though not a very loud one; and at the same time, saw her flinging herself into a Chair in a vast Agitation, which in a Lady of a tender Constitution would have been an Hysteric Fit.

In reality the Lady, frightened with the Struggle between the two Men, of which she did not know what would be the Issue, as she heard *Nightingale* swear many Oaths he would come to his own Bed, attempted to retire to her known Place of Hiding, which to her great Confusion she found already occupied by another.

'Is this Usage to be borne, Mr. *Jones*?' cries the Lady,— 'basest of Men!—What Wretch is this to whom you have exposed me?' 'Wretch!' cries *Honour*, bursting in a violent Rage from her Place of Concealment—'marry come up!—Wretch forsooth!—As poor a Wretch as I am, I am honest, that is more than some Folks who are richer can say.'

Jones, instead of applying himself directly to take off the Edge of Mrs. *Honour's* Resentment, as a more experienced Gallant would have done, fell to cursing his Stars, and lamenting himself as the most unfortunate Man in the World; and presently after, addressing himself to Lady *Bellaston*, he fell to some very absurd Protestations of Innocence. By this time the Lady having recovered the Use of her Reason, which she had as ready as any Woman in the World, especially on such Occasions, calmly replied; 'Sir, you need make no Apologies, I see now who the Person is; I did not at first know Mrs. *Honour*; but now I do, I can suspect nothing wrong between her and you; and I am sure she is a Woman of too good Sense to put any wrong Constructions upon my Visit to you; I have been always her Friend, and it may be in my Power to be much more hereafter.'

Mrs. *Honour* was altogether as placable, as she was passionate. Hearing therefore Lady *Bellaston* assume the soft Tone, she likewise softened her's.—'I'm sure, Madam,' says she, 'I have been always ready to acknowledge your Ladyship's Friendships to me; sure I never had so good a Friend as your Ladyship—and to be sure now I see it is your Ladyship that I spoke to, I could almost bite my Tongue off for very mad.—I Constructions upon your Ladyship?—To be sure it doth not become a Servant as I am to think about such a great Lady—I mean I was a Servant: for indeed I am no Body's Servant now, the more miserable Wretch is me.—I have lost the best Mistress.'—Here *Honour* thought fit to produce a Shower of Tears.—'Don't cry, Child,' says the good Lady, 'Ways perhaps may be found to make you amends. Come to me to-morrow Morning.' She then took up her Fan which lay on the Ground, and without even looking at *Jones*, walked very majestically out of the Room; there being a kind of Dignity in the Impudence of Women of Quality, which their Inferiors vainly aspire to attain to in Circumstances of this Nature.

Jones followed her down Stairs, often offering her his Hand, which she absolutely refused him, and got into her Chair without taking any Notice of him as he stood bowing before her.

At his Return up Stairs, a long Dialogue past between him and Mrs. *Honour*, while she was adjusting herself after the Discomposure she had undergone. The Subject of this was his Infidelity to her young Lady; on which she enlarged with great Bitterness; but *Jones* at last found means to reconcile her, and not only so, but to obtain a Promise of most inviolable Secrecy, and that she would the next Morning endeavour to find out *Sophia*, and bring him a further Account of the Proceedings of the Squire.

Thus ended this unfortunate Adventure to the Satisfaction only of Mrs. *Honour*; for a Secret (as some of my Readers will perhaps acknowledge from Experience) is often a very valuable Possession; and that not only to those who faithfully keep it, but sometimes to such as whisper it about till it come to the Ears of every one, except the ignorant Person, who pays for the supposed concealing of what is publicly known.

CHAPTER VIII

Short and sweet.

NOTWITHSTANDING all the Obligations she had received from *Jones*, Mrs. *Miller* could not forbear in the Morning some gentle Remonstrances for the Hurricane which had happened the preceding Night in his Chamber. These were however so gentle and so friendly; professing, and indeed truly, to aim at nothing more than the real good of Mr. *Jones* himself, that he, far from being offended, thankfully received the Admonition of the good Woman, expressed much Concern for what had past, excused it as well as he could, and promised never more to bring the same Disturbances into the House.

But though Mrs. *Miller* did not refrain from a short Expostulation in private at their first meeting, yet the Occasion of his being summoned down Stairs that Morning was of a much more agreeable Kind; being indeed to perform the Office of a Father to Miss *Nancy*, and to give her in Wedlock to Mr. *Nightingale*, who was now ready drest, and full as sober as many of my Readers will think a Man ought to be who receives a Wife in so imprudent a Manner.

And here perhaps it may be proper to account for the Escape which this young Gentleman had made from his Uncle, and for his Appearance in the Condition in which we have seen him the Night before.

Now when the Uncle had arrived at his Lodgings with his Nephew, partly to indulge his own Inclinations (for he dearly loved his Bottle) and partly to disqualify his Nephew from the immediate Execution of his Purpose, he ordered Wine to be set on the Table; with which he so briskly ply'd the young Gentleman, that this latter, who, though not much used to Drinking, did not detest it so as to be guilty of Disobedience or of want of Complaisance by refusing, was soon completely finished.

Just as the Uncle had obtained this Victory, and was preparing a Bed for his Nephew, a Messenger arrived with a Piece of News, which so entirely disconcerted and shocked him, that he in a Moment lost all Consideration for his Nephew, and his whole Mind became entirely taken up with his own Concerns.

This sudden and afflicting News was no less than that his Daughter had taken the Opportunity of almost the first Moment of his Absence, and had gone off with a Neighbouring young Clergyman; against whom tho' her Father could have had but one Objection, namely, that he was worth nothing, yet she had never thought proper to communicate her Amour even to that Father; and so artfully had she managed, that it had never been once suspected by any, till now that it was consummated.

Old Mr. *Nightingale* no sooner received this Account, than in the utmost Confusion he ordered a Post-Chaise to be instantly got ready, and having recommended his Nephew to the Care of a Servant, he directly left the House, scarce knowing what he did, nor whither he went.

The Uncle being thus departed, when the Servant came to attend the Nephew to Bed, had waked him for that Purpose, and had at last made him sensible that his Uncle was gone, he, instead of accepting the kind Offices tendered him, insisted on a Chair being called; with this the Servant, who had received no strict Orders to the contrary, readily complied; and thus being conducted back to the House of Mrs. *Miller*, he had staggered up to Mr. *Jones's* Chamber, as hath been before recounted.

This Bar of the Uncle being now removed (though young *Nightingale* knew not as yet in what Manner) and all Parties being quickly ready, the Mother, Mr. *Jones*, Mr. *Nightingale*, and his Love stept into a Hackney-Coach, which conveyed him to Doctors Commons;[1] where Miss *Nancy* was, in vulgar Language, soon made an honest Woman, and the poor Mother became in the purest Sense of the Word, one of the happiest of all human Beings.

And now Mr. *Jones* having seen his good Offices to that poor Woman and her Family brought to a happy Conclusion, began to apply himself to his own Concerns; but here lest many of my Readers should censure his Folly for thus troubling himself with the Affairs of others, and lest some few should think he acted more disinterestedly than indeed he did, we think proper to assure our Reader, that he was so far from being unconcerned in this Matter, that he had indeed a very considerable Interest in bringing it to that final Consummation.

To explain this seeming Paradox at once, he was one who could truly say with him in *Terence, Homo sum: Humani nihil a me alienum puto*.[2] He was never an indifferent Spectator of the Misery

---

[1] Situated near St. Paul's in what is now Queen Victoria Street, Doctors' Commons was an ecclesiastical court where marriage licences could be obtained. Later, Jones and Sophia are also married in the chapel there (see below, p. 978).

[2] Spoken by Chremes in *Heauton Timorumenos* ('The Self-Tormentor'), 77: translated by Fielding in *The Covent-Garden Journal* (25 February 1752), 'I am a Man myself; and have an Interest in the Concerns of all other Men.' Like *Tom Jones*, Terence's play is about children whose wish to marry for love is opposed by their worldly parents. See also *Amelia* (1751), x. ix.

or Happiness of any one; and he felt either the one or the other in greater Proportion as he himself contributed to either. He could not therefore be the Instrument of raising a whole Family from the lowest State of Wretchedness to the highest Pitch of Joy without conveying great Felicity to himself; more perhaps than worldly Men often purchase to themselves by undergoing the most severe Labour, and often by wading through the deepest Iniquity.

Those Readers who are of the same Complexion with him will perhaps think this short Chapter contains abundance of Matter; while others may probably wish, short as it is, that it had been totally spared as impertinent to the main Design, which I suppose they conclude is to bring Mr. *Jones* to the Gallows, or if possible, to a more deplorable Catastrophe.

CHAPTER IX

Containing Love-Letters of several Sorts.

MR. *Jones* at his Return Home, found the following Letters lying on his Table, which he luckily opened in the Order they were sent.

LETTER I.

'Surely I am under some strange Infatuation; I cannot keep my Resolutions a Moment, however strongly made or justly founded. Last Night I resolved never to see you more; this Morning I am willing to hear if you can, as you say, clear up this Affair. And yet I know that to be impossible. I have said every Thing to myself which you can invent.—Perhaps not. Perhaps your Invention is stronger. Come to me therefore the Moment you receive this. If you can forge an Excuse, I almost promise you to believe it. Betrayed to—I will think no more.—Come to me directly.—This is the third Letter I have writ, the two former are burnt—I am almost inclined to burn this too—I wish I may preserve my Senses.—Come to me presently.'

LETTER II.

'If you ever expect to be forgiven, or even suffered within my Doors, come to me this Instant.'

LETTER III.

'I now find you was not at Home when my Notes came to your Lodgings. The Moment you receive this let me see you; —I shall not stir out; nor shall any Body be let in but yourself. Sure nothing can detain you long.'

Jones had just read over these three Billets, when Mr. *Nightingale* came into the Room. 'Well, *Tom*,' said he, 'any News from Lady *Bellaston*, after last Night's Adventure?' (for it was now no Secret to any one in that House who the Lady was.) 'The Lady *Bellaston*?' answered *Jones* very gravely.—'Nay, dear *Tom*,' cries *Nightingale*, 'don't be so reserved to your Friends. Though I was too drunk to see her last Night, I saw her at the Masquerade. Do you think I am ignorant who the Queen of the Fairies is?' 'And did you really then know the Lady at the Masquerade?' said *Jones*. 'Yes, upon my Soul, did I,' said *Nightingale*, 'and have given you twenty Hints of it since, though you seemed always so tender on that Point, that I wou'd not speak plainly. I fancy, my Friend, by your extreme Nicety in this Matter, you are not so well acquainted with the Character of the Lady, as with her Person. Don't be angry, *Tom*, but, upon my Honour, you are not the first young Fellow she hath debauched. Her Reputation is in no Danger, believe me.'

Though *Jones* had no Reason to imagine the Lady to have been of the vestal Kind when his Amour began, yet as he was thoroughly ignorant of the Town, and had very little Acquaintance in it, he had no Knowledge of that Character which is vulgarly called a Demirep; that is to say, a Woman who intrigues with every Man she likes, under the Name and Appearance of Virtue; and who, though some over-nice Ladies will not be seen with her, is visited, (as they term it) by the whole Town; in short, whom every Body knows to be what no Body calls her.

When he found, therefore, that *Nightingale* was perfectly acquainted with his Intrigue, and began to suspect, that so scrupulous a Delicacy as he had hitherto observed, was not quite necessary on the Occasion, he gave a Latitude to his Friend's Tongue, and desired him to speak plainly what he knew, or had ever heard of the Lady.

Nightingale, who in many other Instances, was rather too effeminate in his Disposition, had a pretty strong Inclination to

Tittle-Tattle. He had no sooner, therefore, received a full Liberty of speaking from *Jones*, than he entered upon a long Narrative concerning the Lady; which, as it contained many Particulars highly to her Dishonour, we have too great a Tenderness for all Women of Condition to repeat; we would cautiously avoid giving an Opportunity to the future Commentators on our Works, of making any malicious Application; and of forcing us to be, against our Will, the Author of Scandal, which never entered into our Head.

Jones having very attentively heard all that *Nightingale* had to say, fetched a deep Sigh, which the other observing, cried, 'Heyday! Why thou art not in Love I hope! Had I imagined my Stories would have affected you, I promise you should never have heard them.' 'O my dear Friend,' cries *Jones*, 'I am so entangled with this Woman, that I know not how to extricate myself. In Love indeed? No, my Friend, but I am under Obligations to her, and very great ones. Since you know so much, I will be very explicit with you. It is owing perhaps solely to her, that I have not, before this, wanted a Bit of Bread. How can I possibly desert such a Woman? And yet I must desert her, or be guilty of the blackest Treachery to one, who deserves infinitely better of me than she can: A Woman, my *Nightingale*, for whom I have a Passion which few can have an Idea of. I am half distracted with Doubts how to act.' 'And is this other, pray, an honourable Mistress?' cries *Nightingale*. 'Honourable?' answered *Jones*; 'No Breath ever yet durst sully her Reputation. The sweetest Air is not purer, the limpid Stream not clearer than her Honour. She is all over, both in Mind and Body, consummate Perfection. She is the most beautiful Creature in the Universe; and yet she is Mistress of such noble, elevated Qualities, that though she is never from my Thoughts, I scarce ever think of her Beauty, but when I see it.' 'And can you, my good Friend,' cries *Nightingale*, 'with such an Engagement as this upon your Hands, hesitate a Moment about quitting such a——' 'Hold,' said *Jones*, 'no more Abuse of her; I detest the Thought of Ingratitude.' 'Pooh!' answered the other, 'you are not the first upon whom she hath conferred Obligations of this Kind. She is remarkably liberal where she likes; though, let me tell you, her Favours are so prudently bestowed, that they should rather raise a Man's Vanity, than his Gratitude.' In short, *Nightingale* proceeded so far on this Head, and told his Friend so many Stories of the Lady, which he swore to the Truth of, that he entirely removed all Esteem for her from the Breast of *Jones*; and his Gratitude was lessened in Proportion. Indeed he began to look on all the Favours he had received, rather as Wages than Benefits, which depreciated not only her, but himself too in his own Conceit, and put him quite out of Humour with both. From this Disgust, his Mind, by a natural Transition, turned towards *Sophia*: Her Virtue, her Purity, her Love to him, her Sufferings on his Account, filled all his Thoughts, and made his Commerce with Lady *Bellaston* appear still more odious. The Result of all was, that though his turning himself out of her *Service*, in which Light he now saw his Affair with her, would be the Loss of his Bread, yet he determined to quit her, if he could but find a handsome Pretence; which being communicated to his Friend, *Nightingale* considered a little, and then said, 'I have it, my Boy; I have found out a sure Method: Propose Marriage to her, and I would venture Hanging upon the Success.' 'Marriage!' cries *Jones*. 'Ay, propose Marriage,' answered *Nightingale*, 'and she will declare off in a Moment. I knew a young Fellow whom she kept formerly, who made the Offer to her in earnest, and was presently turned off for his Pains.'

Jones declared he could not venture the Experiment. 'Perhaps,' said he, 'she may be less shocked at this Proposal from one Man than from another. And if she should take me at my Word, where am I then? Caught in my own Trap, and undone for ever.' 'No;' answered *Nightingale*, 'not if I can give you an Expedient, by which you may, at any Time, get out of the Trap.'—'What Expedient can that be?' reply'd *Jones*. 'This,' answered *Nightingale*. 'The young Fellow I mentioned, who is one of the most intimate Acquaintances I have in the World, is so angry with her for some ill Offices she hath since done him, that I am sure he would, without any Difficulty, give you a Sight of her Letters; upon which you may decently break with her, and declare off before the Knot is ty'd, if she should really be willing to tie it, which I am convinced she will not.'

After some Hesitation, *Jones*, upon the Strength of this Assurance, consented; but as he swore he wanted the Confidence to propose the Matter to her Face, he wrote the following Letter, which *Nightingale* dictated.

'*Madam*,

I am extremely concerned, that, by an unfortunate Engagement abroad, I should have missed receiving the Honour of your Ladyship's Commands the Moment they came; and the Delay which I must now suffer of vindicating myself to your Ladyship, greatly adds to this Misfortune. O Lady *Bellaston*, what a Terror have I been in for Fear your Reputation should be exposed by these perverse Accidents. There is one only Way to secure it. I need not name what that is. Only permit me to say, that as your Honour is as dear to me as my own, so my sole Ambition is to have the Glory of laying my Liberty at your Feet; and believe me when I assure you, I can never be made completely happy, without you generously bestow on me a legal Right of calling you mine for ever. I am,

Madam,
With most profound Respect,
Your Ladyship's most Obliged,
Obedient Humble Servant,

Thomas Jones.'

To this she presently returned the following Answer.

'*Sir*,

When I read over your serious Epistle, I could, from its Coldness and Formality, have sworn that you already had the legal Right you mention; nay, that we had, for many Years, composed that monstrous Animal a Husband and Wife. Do you really then imagine me a Fool? Or do you fancy yourself capable of so entirely persuading me out of my Senses, that I should deliver my whole Fortune into your Power, in order to enable you to support your Pleasures at my Expence. Are these the Proofs of Love which I expected? Is this the Return for—but I scorn to upbraid you, and am in great Admiration of your profound Respect.

'*P.S.* I am prevented from revising:—Perhaps I have said more than I meant.—Come to me at Eight this Evening.'

Jones, by the Advice of his Privy-Council, reply'd:

'*Madam*,

It is impossible to express how much I am shocked at the Suspicion you entertain of me. Can Lady *Bellaston* have conferred Favours on a Man whom she could believe capable of so base a Design? Or can she treat the most solemn Tie of Love with Contempt? Can you imagine, Madam, that if the Violence of my Passion, in an unguarded Moment, overcame the Tenderness which I have for your Honour, I would think of indulging myself in the Continuance of an Intercourse, which could not possibly escape long the Notice of the World; and which, when discovered, must prove so fatal to your Reputation? If such be your Opinion of me, I must pray for a sudden Opportunity of returning those pecuniary Obligations, which I have been so unfortunate to receive at your Hands; and for those of a more tender Kind, I shall ever remain, *&c.*' And so concluded in the very Words with which he had concluded the former Letter.

The Lady answered as follows.

'I see you are a Villain; and I despise you from my Soul. If you come here, I shall not be at Home.'

Though *Jones* was well satisfied with his Deliverance from a Thraldom which those who have ever experienced it will, I apprehend, allow to be none of the lightest, he was not, however, perfectly easy in his Mind. There was, in this Scheme, too much of Fallacy to satisfy one who utterly detested every Species of Falshood or Dishonesty: Nor would he, indeed, have submitted to put it in Practice, had he not been involved in a distressful Situation, where he was obliged to be guilty of some Dishonour, either to the one Lady or the other; and surely the Reader will allow, that every good Principle, as well as Love, pleaded strongly in Favour of *Sophia*.

Nightingale, highly exulted in the Success of his Stratagem, upon which he received many Thanks, and much Applause from his Friend. He answered, 'Dear *Tom*, we have conferred very different Obligations on each other. To me you owe the regaining your Liberty; to you I owe the Loss of mine. But if you are as happy in the one Instance, as I am in the other, I promise you we are the two happiest Fellows in *England*.'

The two Gentlemen were now summoned down to Dinner, where Mrs. *Miller*, who performed herself the Office of Cook, had exerted her best Talents, to celebrate the Wedding of her Daughter. This joyful Circumstance, she ascribed principally to the friendly Behaviour of *Jones*, her whole Soul was fired with

Gratitude towards him, and all her Looks, Words, and Actions were so busied in expressing it, that her Daughter, and even her new Son-in-Law, were very little the Objects of her Consideration.

Dinner was just ended when Mrs. *Miller* received a Letter; but as we have had Letters enough in this Chapter, we shall communicate the Contents in our next.

CHAPTER X

Consisting partly of Facts, and partly of Observations upon them.

THE Letter then which arrived at the End of the preceding Chapter was from Mr. *Allworthy*, and the Purport of it was his Intention to come immediately to Town, with his Nephew *Blifil*, and a Desire to be accommodated with his usual Lodgings, which were the first Floor for himself, and the second for his Nephew.

The Chearfulness which had before display'd itself in the Countenance of the poor Woman, was a little clouded on this Occasion. This News did indeed a good deal disconcert her. To requite so disinterested a Match with her Daughter, by presently turning her new Son-in-Law out of Doors, appeared to her very unjustifiable on the one Hand; and on the other, she could scarce bear the Thoughts of making any Excuse to Mr. *Allworthy*, after all the Obligations received from him, for depriving him of Lodgings which were indeed strictly his Due: For that Gentleman, in conferring all his numberless Benefits on others, acted by a Rule diametrically opposite to what is practised by most generous People. He contrived, on all Occasions, to hide his Beneficence not only from the World, but even from the Object of it. He constantly used the Words Lend and Pay, instead of Give; and by every other Method he could invent, always lessened with his Tongue the Favours he conferred, while he was heaping them with both his Hands. When he settled the Annuity of 50 *l.* a Year, therefore, on Mrs. *Miller*, he told her, 'It was in Consideration of always having her First-Floor when he was in Town,' (which he scarce ever intended to be) 'but that she might let it at any other Time, for that he would always send her a Month's Warning.' He was now, however, hurried to

Town so suddenly, that he had no Opportunity of giving such Notice; and this Hurry probably prevented him, when he wrote for his Lodgings, adding, *if they were then empty*: For he would most certainly have been well satisfied to have relinquished them on a less sufficient Excuse, than what Mrs. *Miller* could now have made.

But there are a Sort of Persons, who, as *Prior* excellently well remarks,[1] direct their Conduct by something

> Beyond the fix'd and settled Rules
> Of Vice and Virtue in the Schools:
> Beyond the Letter of the Law.

To these it is so far from being sufficient that their Defence would acquit them at the *Old-Bailey*, that they are not even contented, though Conscience, the severest of all Judges, should discharge them. Nothing short of the Fair and Honourable will satisfy the Delicacy of their Minds; and if any of their Actions fall short of this Mark, they mope and pine, are as uneasy and restless as a Murderer, who is afraid of a Ghost, or of the Hangman.

Mrs. *Miller* was one of these. She could not conceal her Uneasiness at this Letter; with the Contents of which she had no sooner acquainted the Company, and given some Hints of her Distress, than *Jones*, her good Angel, presently relieved her Anxiety. 'As for myself, Madam,' said he, 'my Lodging is at your Service at a Moment's Warning; and Mr. *Nightingale*, I am sure, as he cannot yet prepare a House fit to receive his Lady, will consent to return to his new Lodging, whither Mrs. *Nightingale* will certainly consent to go.' With which Proposal both Husband and Wife instantly agreed.

The Reader will easily believe, that the Cheeks of Mrs. *Miller* began again to glow with additional Gratitude to *Jones*; but, perhaps, it may be more difficult to persuade him that Mr. *Jones* having, in his last Speech, called her Daughter Mrs. *Nightingale*, (it being the first Time that agreeable Sound had ever reached her Ears) gave the fond Mother more Satisfaction, and warmed her Heart more towards *Jones*, than his having dissipated her present Anxiety.

The next Day was then appointed for the Removal of the

---

[1] Matthew Prior (1664–1721) in 'Paulo Purganti and His Wife: An Honest, but a Simple Pair' (1708), 1–3. The poem is referred to again in *Amelia* (xii. ii).

new-married Couple, and of Mr. *Jones*, who was likewise to be provided for in the same House with his Friend. And now the Serenity of the Company was again restored, and they past the Day in the utmost Chearfulness, all except *Jones*, who, though he outwardly accompanied the rest in their Mirth, felt many a bitter Pang on the Account of his *Sophia*; which were not a little heightened by the News of Mr. *Blifil's* coming to Town, (for he clearly saw the Intention of his Journey): And what greatly aggravated his Concern was, that Mrs. *Honour*, who had promised to enquire after *Sophia*, and to make her Report to him early the next Evening, had disappointed him.

In the Situation that he and his Mistress were in at this Time, there were scarce any Grounds for him to hope that he should hear any good News; yet he was as impatient to see Mrs. *Honour*, as if he had expected she would bring him a Letter with an Assignation in it from *Sophia*, and bore the Disappointment as ill. Whether this Impatience arose from that natural Weakness of the Human Mind, which makes it desirous to know the worst, and renders Uncertainty the most intolerable of Pains; or whether he still flattered himself with some secret Hopes, we will not determine. But that it might be the last, whoever has loved cannot but know. For of all the Powers exercised by this Passion over our Minds, one of the most wonderful is that of supporting Hope in the midst of Despair. Difficulties, Improbabilities, nay Impossibilities are quite overlook'd by it; so that to any Man extremely in Love, may be applied what *Addison* says of *Cæsar*,[1]

The Alps, *and* Pyrenæans *sink before him!*

Yet it is equally true, that the same Passion will sometimes make Mountains of Molehills, and produce Despair in the midst of Hope; but these cold Fits last not long in good Constitutions. Which Temper *Jones* was now in, we leave the Reader to guess, having no exact Information about it; but this is certain, that he had spent two Hours in Expectation, when being unable any longer to conceal his Uneasiness, he retired to his Room; where his Anxiety had almost made him frantick, when the following Letter was brought him from Mrs. *Honour*, with which we shall present the Reader *verbatim et literatim*.[2]

[1] Addison's *Cato* (1713), I. iii—spoken by Sempronius.
[2] 'Word for word and letter for letter.'

'SIR,

I shud sartenly haf kaled hon u a cordin too mi Prommiss haddunt itt bin that hur Lashipp prevent mee; for too bee sur, Sir, you nose veri wel that evere Persun must luk furst at ome, and sartenly such anuther offar mite not ave ever hapend, so as I shud ave bin justly to blam, had I not excepted of it when hur Laship wass so veri kind as to offar to mak mee hur one Uman without mi ever askin any such thing to bee sur shee is won of thee best Ladis in thee Wurld, and Pepil who sase to thee Kontrari must bee veri wiket Pepil in thare Harts. To be sur if ever I ave sad any thing of that Kine it as bin thru Ignorens and I am hartili sorri for it. I nose your Onur to be a Genteelman of more Onur and Onesty, if I ever said ani such thing to repete it to hurt a pore Servant that as alwais ad thee gratest Respect in thee World for ure Onur. To bee sur won shud kepe wons Tung within one's Teeth, for no Boddi nose what may hapen; and too bee sur if ani Boddi ad tolde mee Yesterday, that I shud haf bin in so gud a Plase to Day, I shud not haf beleeved it; for too bee sur I never was a dremd of any such Thing, nor shud I ever ha soft after ani other Boddi's Plase; but as her Laship wass so kine of her one a cord too give it mee without askin, to be sure Mrs. *Etoff* herself, nor no other Boddi can blam mee for exceptin such a Thing when it fals in mi Waye. I beg ure Onur not too menshon ani thing of what I haf sad, for I wish ure Onur all thee gud Luk in thee Wurld; and I don't cuestion butt thatt u wil haf Madam *Sofia* in the End; butt ass to miself ure Onur nose I kant bee of ani farder Sarvis to u in that Matar, nou bein under thee Cumand off anuthar Parson, and nott mi one Mistres. I begg ure Onur to say nothing of what past, and belive me to be, Sir,

Ure Onur's umble Sarvant
To Cumand till Deth,
Honour Blackmore.'

Various were the Conjectures which *Jones* entertained on this Step of Lady *Bellaston*; who in Reality had little further Design than to secure within her own House the Repository of a Secret, which she chose should make no farther Progress than it had made already; but mostly she desired to keep it from the Ears of *Sophia*; for tho' that young Lady was almost the only one who would never have repeated it again, her Ladyship could not persuade herself of this; since as she now hated poor *Sophia* with most implacable Hatred, she conceived a reciprocal Hatred to herself to be lodged in the tender Breast of our Heroine, where no such Passion had ever yet found an Entrance.

While *Jones* was terrifying himself with the Apprehension of a thousand dreadful Machinations, and deep political Designs, which he imagined to be at the Bottom of the Promotion of *Honour*, Fortune, who hitherto seems to have been an utter Enemy to his Match with *Sophia*, try'd a new Method to put a final End to it, by throwing a Temptation in his Way, which in his present desperate Situation it seemed unlikely he should be able to resist.

CHAPTER XI

Containing curious, but not unprecedented Matter.

THERE was a Lady, one Mrs. *Hunt*, who had often seen *Jones* at the House where he lodged, being intimately acquainted with the Women there, and indeed a very great Friend to Mrs. *Miller*. Her Age was about thirty, for she owned six and twenty; her Face and Person very good, only inclining a little too much to be fat. She had been married young by her Relations to an old *Turkey* Merchant, who having got a great Fortune, had left off Trade. With him she lived without Reproach, but not without Pain, in a State of great Self denial, for about twelve Years; and her Virtue was rewarded by his dying, and leaving her very rich. The first Year of her Widowhood was just at an End, and she had past it in a good deal of Retirement, seeing only a few particular Friends, and dividing her Time between her Devotions and Novels, of which she was always extremely fond. Very good Health, a very warm Constitution, and a good deal of Religion made it absolutely necessary for her to marry again; and she resolved to please herself in her second Husband, as she had done her Friends in the first. From her the following Billet was brought to *Jones*.

'Sir,

From the first Day I saw you I doubt my Eyes have told you too plainly, that you were not indifferent to me; but neither my

Tongue nor my Hand should have ever avowed it, had not the
Ladies of the Family where you are lodged given me such a
Character of you, and told me such Proofs of your Virtue and
Goodness, as convince me you are not only the most agreeable,
but the most worthy of Men. I have also the Satisfaction to hear
from them, that neither my Person, Understanding or Character
are disagreeable to you. I have a Fortune sufficient to make us
both happy, but which cannot make me so without you. In thus
disposing of myself I know I shall incur the Censure of the World,
but if I did not love you more than I fear the World I should not
be worthy of you. One only Difficulty stops me: I am informed
you are engaged in a Commerce of Gallantry with a Woman of
Fashion. If you think it worth while to sacrifice that to the Possession of me, I am yours; if not forget my Weakness, and let
this remain an eternal Secret between you and

Arabella Hunt.'

At the reading of this *Jones* was put into a violent Flutter. His
Fortune was then at a very low Ebb, the Source being stopt from
which hitherto he had been supplied. Of all he had received from
Lady *Bellaston* not above five Guineas remained, and that very
Morning he had been dunned by a Tradesman for twice that
Sum. His honourable Mistress was in the Hands of her Father,
and he had scarce any Hopes ever to get her out of them again.
To be subsisted at her Expence from that little Fortune she had
independent of her Father, went much against the Delicacy both
of his Pride and his Love. This Lady's Fortune would have been
exceeding convenient to him, and he could have no Objection
to her in any Respect. On the contrary, he liked her as well as he
did any Woman except *Sophia*. But to abandon *Sophia*, and marry
another, that was impossible; he could not think of it upon any
Account. Yet why should he not, since it was plain she could not
be his? Would it not be kinder to her, than to continue her
longer engaged in a hopeless Passion for him? Ought he not to do
so in Friendship to her? This Notion prevailed some Moments,
and he had almost determined to be false to her from a high
Point of Honour; but that Refinement was not able to stand
very long against the Voice of Nature, which cried in his Heart,
that such Friendship was Treason to Love. At last he called for
Pen, Ink and Paper, and writ as follows to Mrs. *Hunt*.

'Madam,

It would be but a poor Return to the Favour you have done me, to sacrifice any Gallantry to the Possession of you, and I would certainly do it, tho' I were not disengaged, as at present I am, from any Affair of that Kind. But I should not be the honest Man you think me, if I did not tell you, that my Affections are engaged to another, who is a Woman of Virtue, and one that I never can leave, though it is probable I shall never possess her. God forbid that in Return of your Kindness to me, I should do you such an Injury, as to give you my Hand, when I cannot give my Heart. No, I had much rather starve than be guilty of that. Even though my Mistress were married to another, I would not marry you unless my Heart had entirely effaced all Impressions of her. Be assured that your Secret was not more safe in your own Breast, than in that of

Your most obliged, and
Grateful Humble Servant,
T. Jones.'

When our Heroe had finished and sent this Letter, he went to his Scrutore, took out Miss *Western's* Muff, kiss'd it several Times, and then strutted some Turns about his Room with more Satisfaction of Mind than ever any *Irishman* felt in carrying off a Fortune of fifty Thousand Pounds.[1]

CHAPTER XII

A Discovery made by Partridge.

WHILE *Jones* was exulting in the Consciousness of his Integrity, *Partridge* came capering into the Room, as was his Custom when he brought, or fancied he brought, any good Tidings. He had been dispatched that Morning, by his Master, with Orders to endeavour, by the Servants of Lady *Bellaston*, or by any other Means, to discover whither *Sophia* had been conveyed; and he now returned, and with a joyful Countenance told our Heroe, that he had found the lost Bird. 'I have seen, Sir,' says he, '*Black George*, the Game-keeper, who is one of the

---

[1] See above, p. 601, n. 1.

Servants whom the Squire hath brought with him to Town. I
knew him presently, though I have not seen him these several
Years; but you know, Sir, he is a very remarkable Man, or to use
a purer Phrase, he hath a most remarkable Beard, the largest
and blackest I ever saw. It was some Time however before *Black
George* could recollect me.'—'Well, but what is your good News?'
cries *Jones*, 'what do you know of my *Sophia*?'—'You shall
know presently, Sir,' answered *Partridge*, 'I am coming to it as
fast as I can.—You are so impatient, Sir, you would come at the
Infinitive Mood, before you can get to the Imperative. As I was
saying, Sir, it was some Time before he recollected my Face.'—
'Confound your Face,' cries *Jones*, 'what of my *Sophia*?'—'Nay,
Sir,' answered *Partridge*, 'I know nothing more of Madam
Sophia, than what I am going to tell you; and I should have told
you all before this if you had not interrupted me; but if you look
so angry at me, you will frighten all of it out of my Head, or to
use a purer Phrase, out of my Memory. I never saw you look so
angry since the Day we left *Upton*, which I shall remember if I
was to live a thousand Years.'—'Well, pray go on in your own
Way,' said *Jones*, 'you are resolved to make me mad I find.' 'Not
for the World,' answered *Partridge*, 'I have suffered enough for
that already; which, as I said, I shall bear in my Remembrance
the longest Day I have to live.'—'Well, but *Black George*?' cries
Jones.—'Well, Sir, as I was saying, it was a long Time before he
could recollect me, for indeed I am very much altered since I saw
him. *Non sum qualis eram.*[1] I have had Troubles in the World, and
nothing alters a Man so much as Grief. I have heard it will
change the Colour of a Man's Hair in a Night. However, at last,
know me he did, that's sure enough; for we are both of an Age,
and were at the same Charity School.[2] *George* was a great Dunce,
but no Matter for that; all Men do not thrive in the World according to their Learning. I am sure I have Reason to say so; but it
will be all one a Thousand Years hence. Well, Sir,—where was I?
—O—well, we no sooner knew each other, than after many hearty
Shakes by the Hand, we agreed to go to an Alehouse and take a
Pot, and by good Luck the Beer was some of the best I have met
with since I have been in Town.—Now, Sir, I am coming to the
Point; for no sooner did I name you, and told him, that you and

---

[1] Horace, *Odes*, IV. i. 3: 'I am not what I was.'
[2] See above, p. 635, n. 1.

I came to Town together, and had lived together ever since, than he called for another Pot, and swore he would drink to your Health; and indeed he drank your Health so heartily, that I was overjoyed to see there was so much Gratitude left in the World; and after we had emptied that Pot, I said I would be my Pot too, and so we drank another to your Health; and then I made haste Home to tell you the News.'

'What News?' cries *Jones*, 'you have not mentioned a Word of my *Sophia*!'—'Bless me! I had like to have forgot that. Indeed we mentioned a great deal about young Madam *Western*, and *George* told me all; that Mr. *Blifil* is coming to Town in order to be married to her. He had best make haste then, says I, or some Body will have her before he comes, and indeed, says I, Mr. *Seagrim*, it is a Thousand Pities some Body should not have her; for he certainly loves her above all the Women in the World. I would have both you and she know, that it is not for her Fortune he follows her; for I can assure you as to Matter of that, there is another Lady, one of much greater Quality and Fortune than she can pretend to, who is so fond of Somebody, that she comes after him Day and Night.' Here *Jones* fell into a Passion with *Partridge*, for having, as he said, betrayed him; but the poor Fellow answered, he had mentioned no Name; 'Besides, Sir,' said he, 'I can assure you, *George* is sincerely your Friend, and wished Mr. *Blifil* at the Devil more than once; nay, he said he would do any thing in his Power upon Earth to serve you; and so I am convinced he will.—Betray you indeed! why I question whether you have a better Friend than *George* upon Earth, except myself, or one that would go farther to serve you.'

'Well,' says *Jones*, a little pacified, 'you say this Fellow, who I believe indeed is enough inclined to be my Friend, lives in the same House with *Sophia*?'

'In the same House!' answered *Partridge*, 'why, Sir, he is one of the Servants of the Family, and very well drest I promise you he is; if it was not for his black Beard you would hardly know him.'

'One Service then at least he may do me,' says *Jones*; 'sure he can certainly convey a Letter to my *Sophia*.'

'You have hit the Nail *ad unguem*,'[1] cries *Partridge*; 'how came

---

[1] Literally, 'to a fingernail'—i.e., done to a nicety. The phrase occurs in William Lily's charge to his scholars (*Short Introduction to Grammar* [1720], p. 61).

I not to think of it? I will engage he shall do it upon the very first mentioning.'

'Well then,' said *Jones*, 'do you leave me at present, and I will write a Letter which you shall deliver to him To-morrow Morning; for I suppose you know where to find him.'

'O yes, Sir,' answered *Partridge*, 'I shall certainly find him again, there is no Fear of that. The Liquor is too good for him to stay away long. I make no doubt but he will be there every Day he stays in Town.'

'So you don't know the Street then where my *Sophia* is lodged?' cries *Jones*.

'Indeed, Sir, I do,' says *Partridge*.

'What is the Name of the Street?' cries *Jones*.

'The Name, Sir, why here, Sir, just by,' answered *Partridge*, 'not above a Street or two off. I don't indeed know the very Name; for as he never told me, if I had asked, you know it might have put some Suspicion into his Head. No, no, Sir, let me alone for that. I am too cunning for that, I promise you.'

'Thou art most wonderfully cunning indeed,' replied *Jones*; 'however I will write to my Charmer, since I believe you will be cunning enough to find him To-morrow at the Alehouse.'

And now having dismissed the sagacious *Partridge*, Mr. *Jones* sat himself down to write, in which Employment we shall leave him for a Time. And here we put an End to the fifteenth Book.

The End of the Fifth Volume.

BOOK XVI

Containing the Space of Five Days.

CHAPTER I

Of Prologues.

I HAVE heard of a Dramatic Writer[1] who used to say, he would rather write a Play than a Prologue; in like manner, I think, I can with less Pains write one of the Books of this History, than the Prefatory Chapter to each of them.

To say the Truth, I believe many a hearty Curse hath been devoted on the Head of that Author,[2] who first instituted the Method of prefixing to his Play that Portion of Matter which is called the Prologue; and which at first was Part of the Piece itself, but of latter Years hath had usually so little Connexion with the Drama before which it stands, that the Prologue to one Play might as well serve for any other. Those indeed of more modern Date, seem all to be written on the same three Topics, *viz.* an Abuse of the Taste of the Town, a Condemnation of all Cotemporary Authors, and an Elogium on the Performance just about to be represented. The Sentiments in all these are very little varied, nor is it possible they should; and indeed I have often wondered at the great Invention of Authors, who have been capable of finding such various Phrases to express the same thing.

In like manner I apprehend, some future Historian (if any one shall do me the Honour of imitating my Manner) will, after much scratching his Pate, bestow some good Wishes on my Memory, for having first established these several initial Chapters; most of which, like Modern Prologues, may as properly be prefixed to any other Book in this History as to that which they introduce, or indeed to any other History as to this.

[1] Perhaps Terence in the Prologue to *Andria*: 'When the playwright first steered his thoughts towards authorship, he supposed his sole business was to see that his plays pleased the people. He now finds that it turns out much otherwise, for he spends his time in writing prologues . . .' (trans. John Sargeaunt, Loeb Classical Library, 1918).

[2] Euripides (485 ?–406 ? B.C.) is credited with having originated the convention of the prologue, which served as a comment on the action of the play.

But however Authors may suffer by either of these Inventions, the Reader will find sufficient Emolument in the one, as the Spectator hath long found in the other.

First, it is well known, that the Prologue serves the Critic for an Opportunity to try his Faculty of Hissing, and to tune his Cat-call to the best Advantage; by which means, I have known those Musical Instruments so well prepared, that they have been able to play in full Concert at the first rising of the Curtain.[1]

The same Advantages may be drawn from these Chapters, in which the Critic will be always sure of meeting with something that may serve as a Whetstone to his noble Spirit; so that he may fall with a more hungry Appetite for Censure on the History itself. And here his Sagacity must make it needless to observe how artfully these Chapters are calculated for that excellent Purpose; for in these we have always taken Care to intersperse somewhat of the sour or acid Kind, in order to sharpen and stimulate the said Spirit of Criticism.

Again, the indolent Reader, as well as Spectator, finds great Advantage from both these; for as they are not obliged either to see the one or read the others, and both the Play and the Book are thus protracted, by the former they have a Quarter of an Hour longer allowed them to sit at Dinner, and by the Latter they have the Advantage of beginning to read at the fourth or fifth Page instead of the first; a Matter by no means of trivial Consequence to Persons who read Books with no other View than to say they have read them, a more general Motive to reading than is commonly imagined; and from which not only Law Books, and Good Books, but the Pages of *Homer* and *Virgil*, of *Swift* and *Cervantes* have been often turned over.

Many other are the Emoluments which arise from both these, but they are for the most part so obvious that we shall not at present stay to enumerate them; especially since it occurs to us that the principal Merit of both the Prologue and the Preface is that they be short.

---

[1] The prologue to Moore's *The Foundling* (1748) had served the critics in just this way (see above, p. 729, n. 1).

CHAPTER II

A whimsical Adventure which befel the Squire, with the distressed Situation of Sophia.

WE must now convey the Reader to Mr. *Western's* Lodgings which were in *Piccadilly*, where he was placed by the Recommendation of the Landlord at the *Hercules Pillars* at *Hide-Park-Corner*;[1] for at that Inn, which was the first he saw on his Arrival in Town, he placed his Horses, and in those Lodgings, which were the first he heard of, he deposited himself.

Here when *Sophia* alighted from the Hackney-Coach, which brought her from the House of Lady *Bellaston*, she desired to retire to the Apartment provided for her, to which her Father very readily agreed, and whither he attended her himself. A short Dialogue, neither very material nor pleasant to relate minutely, then passed between them, in which he pressed her vehemently to give her Consent to the Marriage with *Blifil*, who, as he acquainted her, was to be in Town in a few Days; but instead of complying, she gave a more peremptory and resolute Refusal than she had ever done before. This so incensed her Father, that after many bitter Vows that he would force her to have him whether she would or no, he departed from her with many hard Words and Curses, locked the Door and put the Key into his Pocket.

While *Sophia* was left with no other Company than what attend the closest State Prisoner, namely, Fire and Candle, the Squire sat down to regale himself over a Bottle of Wine, with his Parson and the Landlord of the *Hercules Pillars*, who, as the Squire said, would make an excellent third Man, and could inform them of the News of the Town, and how Affairs went; for to be sure, says he, he knows a great deal since the Horses of a many of the Quality stand at his House.

In this agreeable Society, Mr. *Western* past that Evening and great part of the succeeding Day, during which Period nothing happened of sufficient Consequence to find a Place in this

---

[1] At mid century this famous inn was the first the traveller would have encountered as he entered London along the Knightsbridge Turnpike. For a contemporary print of the building, see H. Phillips, *Mid-Georgian London* (1964), p. 75. In 1748 the landlord of the Hercules Pillars was one John Douglas (see *Licensed Victuallers Register* [Westminster] 1748. Ref. MCRO L.V. (W) 68/333. At the Middlesex Records Office).

History. All this time *Sophia* past by herself; for her Father swore she should never come out of her Chamber alive, unless she first consented to marry *Blifil*; nor did he ever suffer the Door to be unlocked unless to convey her Food, on which Occasions he always attended himself.

The second Morning after his Arrival, while he and the Parson were at Breakfast together on a Toast and Tankard, he was informed that a Gentleman was below to wait on him.

'A Gentleman!' quoth the Squire, 'who the Devil can he be? Do, Doctor, go down and see who 'tis. Mr. *Blifil* can hardly be come to Town yet.—Go down, do, and know what his Business is.'

The Doctor returned with an Account that it was a very well drest Man, and by the Ribbon in his Hat, he took him for an Officer of the Army; that he said he had some particular Business, which he could deliver to none but Mr. *Western* himself.

'An Officer!' cries the Squire, 'what can any such Fellow have to do with me? If he wants an Order for Baggage-Waggons,[1] I am no Justice of Peace here, nor can I grant a Warrant.—Let un come up then, if he must speak to me.'

A very genteel Man now entered the Room; who, having made his Compliments to the Squire, and desired the Favour of being alone with him, delivered himself as follows.

'Sir, I come to wait upon you by the Command of my Lord *Fellamar*, but with a very different Message from what I suppose you expect, after what past the other Night.'

'My Lord who?' cries the Squire, 'I never heard the Name o' un.'

'His Lordship,' said the Gentleman, 'is willing to impute every thing to the Effect of Liquor, and the most trifling Acknowledgment of that Kind will set every thing right; for as he hath the most violent Attachment to your Daughter, you, Sir, are the last Person upon Earth, from whom he would resent an Affront; and happy is it for you both that he hath given such public Demonstrations of his Courage, as to be able to put up an Affair of this Kind, without Danger of any Imputation on his Honour. All he desires therefore, is, that you will before me, make some Acknowledgment, the slightest in the World will be sufficient,

---

[1] The annual 'Mutiny Act' (e.g. 19 George II, cap. 11) required justices of the peace to issue warrants to constables to provide baggage-wagons when troops were on the march.

and he intends this Afternoon to pay his Respects to you, in order to obtain your Leave of visiting the young Lady on the Footing of a Lover.'

'I don't understand much of what you say, Sir,' said the Squire; 'but I suppose, by what you talk about my Daughter, that this is the Lord which my Lady Cousin *Bellaston* mentioned to me, and said something about his courting my Daughter. If so be, that how, that be the Case—you may give my Service to his Lordship, and tell un the Girl is disposed of already.'

'Perhaps, Sir,' said the Gentleman, 'you are not sufficiently apprized of the Greatness of this Offer. I believe such a Person, Title, and Fortune, would be no where refused.'

'Lookee, Sir,' answered the Squire, 'to be very plain, my Daughter is bespoke already; but if she was not, I would not marry her to a Lord upon any Account; I hate all Lords; they are a Parcel of Courtiers and *Hannoverians*, and I will have nothing to do with them.'——

'Well, Sir,' said the Gentleman, 'if that is your Resolution, the Message I am to deliver to you, is, that my Lord desires the Favour of your Company this Morning in *Hide-Park*.'[1]

'You may tell my Lord,' answered the Squire, 'that I am busy and cannot come. I have enough to look after at home, and can't stir abroad on any Account.'

'I am sure, Sir,' quoth the other, 'you are too much a Gentleman to send such a Message; you will not, I am convinced, have it said of you, that after having affronted a noble Peer, you refuse him Satisfaction. His Lordship would have been willing, from his great Regard to the young Lady, to have made up matters in another way; but unless he is to look on you as a Father, his Honour will not suffer his putting up such an Indignity as you must be sensible you offered him.'

'I offered him!' cries the Squire; 'it is a d—n'd Lie, I never offered him any Thing.'

Upon these Words the Gentleman returned a very short verbal Rebuke, and this he accompanied at the same time with some manual Remonstrances, which no sooner reached the Ears of Mr. *Western*, than that worthy Squire began to caper very

---

[1] In London duels commonly took place in Hyde Park in the spot 'which may be properly called the Field of Blood, being that Part a little to the Left of the Ring, which Heroes have chosen for the Scene of their Exit out of this World' (*Amelia*, v. v).

briskly about the Room, bellowing at the same time with all his Might, as if desirous to summon a greater Number of Spectators to behold his Agility.

The Parson, who had left great part of the Tankard unfinished, was not retired far; he immediately attended therefore on the Squire's Vociferation, crying, 'Bless me! Sir, what's the Matter?' —'Matter!' quoth the Squire, 'here's a Highway-Man, I believe, who wants to rob and murder me—for he hath fallen upon me with that Stick there in his Hand, when I wish I may be d—n'd if I gid un the least Provocation.'

'How, Sir,' said the Captain, 'did you not tell me, I ly'd.'

'No, as I hope to be saved,' answered the Squire.—'I believe I might say, " 'Twas a Lie that I had offered any Affront to my Lord,"—but I never said the Word *you lie.*—I understand myself better, and you might have understood yourself better than to fall upon a naked Man. If I had had a Stick in my Hand, you would not have dared strike me. I'd have knocked thy Lanthorn Jaws about thy Ears. Come down into Yard this Minute, and I'll take a Bout with thee at single Stick for a broken Head, that I will; or I will go into naked Room and box thee for a Belly full. At unt half a Man, at unt I'm sure.'

The Captain, with some Indignation, replied, 'I see, Sir, you are below my Notice, and I shall inform his Lordship you are below his.—I am sorry I have dirtied my Fingers with you.'— At which Words he withdrew, the Parson interposing to prevent the Squire from stopping him, in which he easily prevailed, as the other, though he made some Efforts for the Purpose, did not seem very violently bent on Success. However, when the Captain was departed, the Squire sent many Curses and some Menaces after him; but as these did not set out from his Lips till the Officer was at the Bottom of the Stairs, and grew louder and louder as he was more and more remote, they did not reach his Ears, or at least did not retard his Departure.

Poor *Sophia* however, who, in her Prison, heard all her Father's Outcries from first to last, began now first to thunder with her Foot, and afterwards to scream as loudly as the old Gentleman himself had done before, though in a much sweeter Voice. These Screams soon silenced the Squire, and turned all his Consideration towards his Daughter, whom he loved so tenderly, that the least Apprehension of any Harm happening to her, threw him presently into Agonies: For except in that single Instance in which the whole future Happiness of her Life was concerned, she was sovereign Mistress of his Inclinations.

Having ended his Rage against the Captain, with swearing he would take the Law of him, the Squire now mounted up Stairs to *Sophia*, whom, as soon as he had unlocked and opened the Door, he found all pale and breathless. The Moment however that she saw her Father, she collected all her Spirits, and catching him hold by the Hand, she cry'd passionately, 'O my dear Sir, I am almost frightned to Death; I hope to Heaven no Harm hath happened to you.'—'No, no,' cries the Squire, 'no great Harm. The Rascal hath not hurt me much, but rat me if I don't ha the Laa o'un.' 'Pray, dear Sir,' says she, 'tell me what's the Matter, who is it that hath insulted you?' 'I don't know the Name o'un,' answer'd *Western*, 'some Officer Fellow I suppose that we are to pay for beating us, but I'll make him pay this Bout, if the Rascal hath got any thing, which I suppose he hath not. For thof he was drest out so vine, I question whether he hath got a Voot of Land in the World.' 'But, dear Sir,' cries she, 'what was the Occasion of your Quarrel?' 'What should it be, *Sophy*?' answered the Squire, 'but about you, *Sophy*? All my Misfortunes are about you; you will be the Death of your poor Father at last. Here's a Varlet of a Lord, the Lord knows who forsooth! who hath a taan a Liking to you, and because I would not gi un my Consent, he sent me a Kallenge. Come, do be a good Girl, *Sophy*, and put an End to all your Father's Troubles; come do, consent to ha un; he will be in Town within this Day or two; do but promise me to marry un as soon as he comes, and you will make me the happiest Man in the World, and I will make you the happiest Woman; you shall have the finest Cloaths in *London*, and the finest Jewels, and a Coach and Six at your Command. I promised *Allworthy* already to give up half my Estate,—Odrabbet it! I should hardly stick at giving up the whole.' 'Will my Papa be so kind,' says she, 'as to hear me speak?'—'Why wout ask, *Sophy*?' cries he, 'when dost know I had rather hear thy Voice, than the Music of the best Pack of Dogs in *England*.—Hear thee, my dear little Girl! I hope I shall hear thee as long as I live; for if I was ever to lose that Pleasure, I would not gee a Brass Varden to live a Moment longer. Indeed, *Sophy*, you do not know how I love you, indeed you don't, or you never could have run away, and left your poor Father, who hath

no other Joy, no other Comfort upon Earth but his little *Sophy*.'
At these Words the Tears stood in his Eyes; and *Sophia*, (with
the Tears streaming from hers) answered, 'Indeed, my dear
Papa, I know you have loved me tenderly, and Heaven is my
Witness how sincerely I have returned your Affection; nor could
any thing but an Apprehension of being forced into the Arms of
this Man, have driven me to run from a Father whom I love so
passionately, that I would, with Pleasure, sacrifice my Life to his
Happiness; nay, I have endeavoured to reason myself into doing
more, and had almost worked up a Resolution, to endure the
most miserable of all Lives, to comply with your Inclination. It
was that Resolution alone to which I could not force my Mind;
nor can I ever.' Here the Squire began to look wild, and the
Foam appeared at his Lips, which *Sophia* observing, begged to be
heard out, and then proceeded, 'If my Father's Life, his Health,
or any real Happiness of his was at Stake, here stands your
resolved Daughter, may Heaven blast me, if there is a Misery I
would not suffer to preserve you.—No, that most detested, most
loathsome of all Lots would I embrace. I would give my Hand to
Blifil for your Sake.'—'I tell thee, it will preserve me,' answers
the Father; 'it will gee me Health, Happiness, Life, every
thing.—Upon my Soul I shall die if dost refuse me; I shall break
my Heart, I shall upon my Soul.'—'Is it possible,' says she, 'you
can have such a Desire to make me miserable?' 'I tell thee noa,'
answered he loudly, 'my whole Desire is to make thee happy;
me! d—n me if there is a Thing upon Earth I would not do to see
thee happy.'—'And will not my dear Papa allow me to have the
least Knowledge of what will make me so? If it be true that
Happiness consists in Opinion; what must be my Condition,
when I shall think myself the most miserable of all the Wretches
upon Earth.' 'Better think yourself so,' said he, 'than know it by
being married to a poor bastardly Vagabond.' 'If it will content
you, Sir,' said *Sophia*, 'I will give you the most solemn Promise
never to marry him nor any other while my Papa lives, without
his Consent. Let me dedicate my whole Life to your Service; let
me be again your poor *Sophy*, and my whole Business and Pleasure
be, as it hath been, to please and divert you.' 'Lookey, *Sophy*,'
answered the Squire, 'I am not to be choused[1] in this Manner.
Your Aunt *Western* would then have Reason to think me the

---

[1] Tricked.

Fool she doth. No, no, *Sophy*, I'd have you to know I have a got more Wisdom, and know more of the World than to take the Word of a Woman in a Matter where a Man is concerned.' 'How, Sir, have I deserved this Want of Confidence?' said she, 'have I ever broke a single Promise to you? Or have I ever been found guilty of a Falshood from my Cradle?' 'Lookee, *Sophy*,' cries he, 'that's neither here nor there. I am determin'd upon this Match, and have him you shall, d—n me if shat unt. D—n me if shat unt, though dost hang thyself the next Morning.' At repeating which Words he clinched his Fist, knit his Brows, bit his Lips, and thundered so loud, that the poor afflicted, terrified *Sophia* sunk trembling into her Chair, and had not a Flood of Tears come immediately to her Relief, perhaps worse had followed.

Western beheld the deplorable Condition of his Daughter with no more Contrition or Remorse, than the Turnkey of *Newgate* feels at viewing the Agonies of a tender Wife, when taking her last Farewel of her condemned Husband; or rather he looked down on her with the same Emotions which arise in an honest fair Tradesman, who sees his Debtor dragged to Prison for 10 *l.* which, though a just Debt, the Wretch is wickedly unable to pay. Or, to hit the Case still more nearly, he felt the same Compunction with a Bawd when some poor Innocent whom she hath ensnared into her Hands, falls into Fits at the first Proposal of what is called seeing Company. Indeed this Resemblance would be exact, was it not that the Bawd hath an Interest in what she doth, and the Father, though perhaps he may blindly think otherwise, can in Reality have none in urging his Daughter to almost an equal Prostitution.

In this Condition he left his poor *Sophia*, and departing with a very vulgar Observation on the Effect of Tears, he locked the Room, and returned to the Parson, who said every Thing he durst in Behalf of the young Lady, which though perhaps it was not quite so much as his Duty required, yet was it sufficient to throw the Squire into a violent Rage, and into many indecent Reflections on the whole Body of the Clergy, which we have too great an Honour for that sacred Function to commit to Paper.

CHAPTER III

What happened to Sophia *during her Confinement.*

THE Landlady of the House where the Squire lodged had begun very early to entertain a strange Opinion of her Guests. However as she was informed that the Squire was a Man of a vast Fortune, and as she had taken Care to exact a very extraordinary Price for her Rooms, she did not think proper to give any Offence; for though she was not without some Concern for the Confinement of poor *Sophia*, of whose great Sweetness of Temper and Affability, the Maid of the House had made so favourable a Report, which was confirmed by all the Squire's Servants, yet she had much more Concern for her own Interest, than to provoke one, whom, as she said, she perceived to be a very hastish Kind of a Gentleman.

Though *Sophia* eat but little, yet she was regularly served with her Meals; indeed I believe if she had liked any one Rarity, that the Squire, however angry, would have spared neither Pains nor Cost to have procured it for her; since however strange it may appear to some of my Readers, he really doated on his Daughter, and to give her any Kind of Pleasure was the highest Satisfaction of his Life.

The Dinner Hour being arrived, *Black George* carried her up a Pullet, the Squire himself (for he had sworn not to part with the Key) attending the Door. As *George* deposited the Dish, some Compliments passed between him and *Sophia* (for he had not seen her since she left the Country, and she treated every Servant with more Respect than some Persons shew to those who are in a very slight Degree their Inferiors.) *Sophia* would have had him take the Pullet back, saying, she could not eat; but *George* begged her to try, and particularly recommended to her the Eggs, of which he said it was full.

All this Time the Squire was waiting at the Door; but *George* was a great Favourite with his Master, as his Employment was in Concerns of the highest Nature, namely, about the Game, and was accustomed to take many Liberties. He had officiously carried up the Dinner, being, as he said, very desirous to see his young Lady; he made therefore no Scruple of keeping his Master standing above ten Minutes, while Civilities were passing between him and *Sophia*, for which he received only a good-humoured Rebuke at the Door when he returned.

The Eggs of Pullets, Partridges, Pheasants, *&c.* were, as *George* well knew, the most favourite Dainties of *Sophia*. It was therefore no Wonder, that he who was a very good-natured Fellow, should take Care to supply her with this Kind of Delicacy, at a Time when all the Servants in the House were afraid she would be starved; for she had scarce swallowed a single Morsel in the last forty Hours.

Though Vexation hath not the same Effect on all Persons, as it usually hath on a Widow, whose Appetite it often renders sharper than it can be rendered by the Air on *Bansted* Downs, or *Salisbury* Plain,[1] yet the sublimest Grief, notwithstanding what some People may say to the contrary, will eat at last. And *Sophia* herself, after some little Consideration, began to dissect the Fowl, which she found to be as full of Eggs as *George* had reported it.

But if she was pleased with these, it contained something which would have delighted the Royal Society[2] much more; for if a Fowl with three Legs be so invaluable a Curiosity, when perhaps Time hath produced a Thousand such, at what Price shall we esteem a Bird which so totally contradicts all the Laws of Animal Œconomy, as to contain a Letter in its Belly?[3] *Ovid* tells

---

[1] The chalk downs on which stands the village of Banstead, Surrey, were famous for fresh, wholesome air and hence were prescribed by physicians as a resort for the infirm. On Salisbury Plain, see above, p. 613, n. 2.

[2] On Fielding's attitude toward the '*unnatural*' philosophers of the Royal Society, see above, p. 701, n. 4. The perverse interests of the 'virtuosi' may be illustrated by an article appearing in the *Philosophical Transactions*, No. 456 (January–June 1740), pp. 294–307. In '*Some Reflections on* Generation, *and on* Monsters, *with a Description of some particular* Monsters', Daniel de Superville, a German physician, proudly displayed his personal collection of freaks, among them 'a Pig, that has eight Feet . . . four Ears, three Eyes, and the Snout seems double. I have also the Head of a Foal, which is double, and has three Eyes. I have a *Turkish* Duck, which is double, the two Bodies are joined by the Breast; each Body has two Wings, and two Legs; but they have only one Neck with one Head. I keep a Chicken, which has a second Rump fixed to its Breast, with the two Legs, and two Paws. I even have a Frog, which besides its four Paws, has a Fifth as well formed as the others, which comes out at the Right Shoulder' (vol. xli, pt. 1, pp. 301–2). Fielding's parodies of the *Philosophical Transactions* include *The Champion* (16 August 1740), *Some Papers Proper to be Read before the R[oyal] Society* (1743), and *An Attempt towards a Natural History of the Hanover Rat* (1744).

[3] Sophia's guardians were less vigilant than Atterbury's at the time of his incarceration in the Tower. In a letter of 11 September 1722 included in his published correspondence, Pope wrote to Gay: 'Pray tell Dr. *Arbuthnot* that even Pigeon-pyes and Hogs-puddings

us[1] of a Flower into which *Hyacinthus* was metamorphosed, that
bears Letters on its Leaves, which *Virgil* recommended[2] as a
Miracle to the Royal Society of his Day; but no Age nor Nation
hath ever recorded a Bird with a Letter in its Maw.

But though a Miracle of this Kind might have engaged all
the *Academies des Sciences* in *Europe*, and perhaps in a fruitless
Enquiry, yet the Reader by barely recollecting the last Dialogue
which passed between Messieurs *Jones* and *Partridge*, will be
very easily satisfied from whence this Letter came, and how it
found its Passage into the Fowl.

Sophia, notwithstanding her long Fast, and notwithstanding
her favourite Dish was there before her, no sooner saw the Letter
than she immediately snatched it up, tore it open, and read as
follows.

'Madam,

'Was I not sensible to whom I have the Honour of writing,
I should endeavour, however difficult, to paint the Horrors of my
Mind, at the Account brought me by Mrs. *Honour*: but as
Tenderness alone can have any true Idea of the Pangs which
Tenderness is capable of feeling; so can this most amiable
Quality which my *Sophia* possesses in the most eminent Degree,
sufficiently inform her what her *Jones* must have suffered on this
melancholy Occasion. Is there a Circumstance in the World
which can heighten my Agonies, when I hear of any Misfortune
which hath befallen you? Surely there is one only, and with that
I am accursed. It is, my *Sophia*, the dreadful Consideration that
I am myself the wretched Cause. Perhaps I here do myself too
much Honour, but none will envy me an Honour which costs me
so extremely dear. Pardon me this Presumption, and pardon me
a greater still, if I ask you whether my Advice, my Assistance, my
Presence, my Absence, my Death or my Tortures can bring you
any Relief? Can the most perfect Admiration, the most watchful

are thought dangerous by our Governors; for those that have been sent to the Bishop of
Rochester, are open'd and prophanely pry'd into at the *Tower*: 'Tis the first time dead
Pigeons have been suspected of carrying Intelligence' (George Sherburn, ed. *The Corre-
spondence of Alexander Pope* [Oxford, 1956], ii. 133–4).

[1] *Metamorphoses*, x. 215 ff. The letters are 'Ai, Ai', signifying Apollo's grief for the
dead Hyacinthus.

[2] *Eclogues*, iv. 106–7. In *Some Papers Proper to be Read before the R[oyal] Society* (1743),
a parody of the *Philosophical Transactions*, Fielding had quoted Virgil's lines with a
similarly facetious intent.

Observance, the most ardent Love, the most melting Tenderness, the most resigned Submission to your Will, make you Amends for what you are to sacrifice to my Happiness? If they can, fly, my lovely Angel, to those Arms which are ever open to receive and protect you; and to which, whether you bring yourself alone, or the Riches of the World with you, is, in my Opinion, an Alternative not worth regarding. If, on the contrary, Wisdom shall predominate, and, on the most mature Reflection, inform you, that the Sacrifice is too great; and if there be no Way left to reconcile your Father, and restore the Peace of your dear Mind, but by abandoning me, I conjure you drive me for ever from your Thoughts, exert your Resolution, and let no Compassion for my Sufferings bear the least Weight in that tender Bosom. Believe me, Madam, I so sincerely love you better than myself, that my great and principal End is your Happiness. My first Wish (why would not Fortune indulge me in it?) was, and pardon me if I say, still is to see you every Moment the happiest of Women; my second Wish is to hear you are so; but no Misery on Earth can equal mine, while I think you owe an uneasy Moment to him who is,

Madam,

In every Sense, and to every Purpose,

Your devoted

Thomas Jones.'

What *Sophia* said, or did, or thought upon this Letter, how often she read it, or whether more than once, shall all be left to our Reader's Imagination. The Answer to it he may perhaps see hereafter, but not at present; for this Reason, among others, that she did not now write any, and that for several good Causes, one of which was this, she had no Paper, Pen, nor Ink.

In the Evening while *Sophia* was meditating on the Letter she had received, or on something else, a violent Noise from below disturbed her Meditations. This Noise was no other than a round Bout at Altercation between two Persons. One of the Combatants, by his Voice, she immediately distinguished to be her Father; but she did not so soon discover the shriller Pipes to belong to the Organ of her Aunt *Western*, who was just arrived in Town, where having by means of one of her Servants, who stopt at the *Hercules Pillars*, learnt where her Brother lodged, she drove directly to his Lodgings.

We shall therefore take our Leave at present of *Sophia*, and with our usual Good-Breeding, attend her Ladyship.

CHAPTER IV

In which Sophia *is delivered from her Confinement.*

THE Squire and the Parson (for the Landlord was now otherwise engaged) were smoaking their Pipes together, when the Arrival of the Lady was first signified. The Squire no sooner heard her Name, than he immediately ran down to usher her up Stairs; for he was a great Observer of such Ceremonials, especially to his Sister, of whom he stood more in Awe than of any other human Creature, though he never would own this, nor did he perhaps know it himself.

Mrs. *Western*, on her Arrival in the Dining-Room, having flung herself into a Chair, began thus to harangue. 'Well, surely no one ever had such an intolerable Journey. I think the Roads, since so many Turnpike Acts,[1] are grown worse than ever. La, Brother, how could you get into this odious Place? No Person of Condition, I dare swear, ever set Foot here before.' 'I don't know,' cries the Squire, 'I think they do well enough; it was Landlord recommended them. I thought as he knew most of the Quality, he could best shew me where to get among um.' 'Well, and where's my Niece?' says the Lady, 'have you been to wait upon Lady *Bellaston* yet?' 'Ay, ay,' cries the Squire, 'your Niece is safe enough; she is up Stairs in Chamber.' 'How,' answered the Lady, 'is my Niece in this House, and doth she not know of my being here?' 'No, no Body can well get to her,' says the Squire, 'for she is under Lock and Key. I have her safe; I vetched her from my Lady Cousin the first Night I came to Town, and I have taken Care o' her ever since; she is as secure as a Fox in a Bag, I promise you.' 'Good Heaven!' returned Mrs. *Western*, 'what do I hear! I thought what a fine Piece of Work would be the Consequence of my Consent to your coming to Town yourself; nay, it was indeed your own headstrong Will, nor can I charge

[1] Throughout the 1740s and after, many bills were passed for the improvement of roads and the financing of such repairs by the erection of turnpikes, where tolls were collected. Public resentment against this form of taxation ran so high that riots erupted in several places (see, for example, *The Gentleman's Magazine*, xix [August 1749], 376-7).

/myself with having ever consented to it. Did not you promise me, Brother, that you would take none of these headstrong Measures. Was it not by those headstrong Measures that you forced my Niece to run away from you in the Country? Have you a Mind to oblige her to take such another Step?' 'Z—ds and the Devil,' cries the Squire, dashing his Pipe on the Ground, 'did ever Mortal hear the like? when I expected you would have commended me for all I have done, to be fallen upon in this Manner!' 'How! Brother,' said the Lady, 'have I ever given you the least Reason to imagine I should commend you for locking up your Daughter? Have I not often told you, that Women in a free Country are not to be treated with such arbitrary Power? We are as free as the Men, and I heartily wish I could not say we deserve that Freedom better. If you expect I should stay a Moment longer in this wretched House, or that I should ever own you again as my Relation, or that I should ever trouble myself again with the Affairs of your Family, I insist upon it that my Niece be set at Liberty this Instant.' This she spoke with so commanding an Air, standing with her Back to the Fire, with one Hand behind her, and a Pinch of Snuff in the other, that I question whether *Thalestris*[1] at the Head of her Amazons, ever made a more tremendous Figure. It is no Wonder therefore that the poor Squire was not Proof against the Awe which she inspired. 'There,' he cried, throwing down the Key, 'There it is, do whatever you please. I intended only to have kept her up till *Blifil* came to Town, which can't be long; and now if any Harm happens in the mean Time, remember who is to be blamed for it.'

'I will answer it with my Life,' cry'd Mrs. *Western*, 'but I shall not intermeddle at all, unless upon one Condition, and that is, that you will commit the whole entirely to my Care, without taking any one Measure yourself, unless I shall eventually appoint you to act. If you ratify these Preliminaries, Brother, I yet will endeavour to preserve the Honour of your Family; if not, I shall continue in a neutral State.'

'I pray you, good Sir,' said the Parson, 'permit yourself this once to be admonished by her Ladyship; peradventure by communing with young Madam *Sophia*, she will effect more than you have been able to perpetrate by more rigorous Measures.'

---

[1] See above, p. 503, n. 1.

'What dost thee open upon me?' cries the Squire. 'If thee dost begin to babble, I shall whip thee in presently.'

'Fie, Brother,' answered the Lady, 'is this Language to a Clergyman? Mr. *Supple* is a Man of Sense, and gives you the best Advice, and the whole World, I believe, will concur in his Opinion; but I must tell you I expect an immediate Answer to my categorical Proposals. Either cede your Daughter to my Disposal, or take her wholly to your own surprizing Discretion, and then I here, before Mr. *Supple*, evacuate the Garrison, and renounce you and your Family for ever.'

'I pray you let me be a Mediator,' cries the Parson; 'let me supplicate you.'

'Why there lies the Key on the Table,' cries the Squire. 'She may take un up, if she pleases; who hinders her?'

'No, Brother,' answered the Lady, 'I insist on the Formality of its being delivered me, with a full Ratification of all the Concessions stipulated.'

'Why then I will deliver it to you.—There 'tis,' cries the Squire. 'I am sure, Sister, you can't accuse me of ever denying to trust my Daughter to you. She hath a lived wi' you a whole Year and muore to a Time, without my ever zeeing her.'

'And it would have been happy for her,' answered the Lady, 'if she had always lived with me. Nothing of this Kind would have happened under my Eye.'

'Ay, certainly,' cries he, 'I only am to blame.'

'Why, you are to blame, Brother,' answered she, 'I have been often obliged to tell you so, and shall always be obliged to tell you so. However, I hope you will now amend, and gather so much Experience from past Errors, as not to defeat my wisest Machinations by your Blunders. Indeed, Brother, you are not qualified for these Negotiations. All your whole Scheme of Politics is wrong. I once more, therefore, insist, that you do not intermeddle. Remember only what is past.'——

'Z—ds and Bl—d, Sister,' cries the Squire, 'What would you have me say? You are enough to provoke the Devil.'

'There now,' said she, 'just according to the old Custom. I see, Brother, there is no talking to you. I will appeal to Mr. *Supple*, who is a Man of Sense, if I said any Thing which could put any Human Creature into a Passion; but you are so wrong-headed every Way.'

'Let me beg you, Madam,' said the Parson, 'not to irritate his Worship.'

'Irritate him?' said the Lady;—'Sure you are as great a Fool as himself. Well, Brother, since you have promised not to interfere, I will once more undertake the Management of my Niece. Lord have Mercy upon all Affairs which are under the Directions of Men. The Head of one Woman is worth a thousand of yours.' And now having summoned a Servant to shew her to *Sophia*, she departed, bearing the Key with her. She was no sooner gone, than the Squire (having first shut the Door) ejaculated twenty Bitches, and as many hearty Curses against her, not sparing himself for having ever thought of her Estate; but added, 'Now one hath been a Slave so long, it would be Pity to lose it at last, for want of holding out a little longer. The Bitch can't live for ever, and I know I am down for it upon the Will.'

The Parson greatly commended this Resolution; and now the Squire having ordered in another Bottle, which was his usual Method when any Thing either pleased or vexed him, did, by drinking plentifully of this medicinal Julap, so totally wash away his Choler, that his Temper was become perfectly placid and serene, when Mrs. *Western* returned with *Sophia* into the Room. The young Lady had on her Hat and Capuchin, and the Aunt acquainted Mr. *Western*, 'that she intended to take her Niece with her to her own Lodgings; for, indeed, Brother,' says she, 'these Rooms are not fit to receive a Christian Soul in.'

'Very well, Madam,' quoth *Western*, 'whatever you please. The Girl can never be in better Hands than yours; and the Parson here can do me the Justice to say, that I have said fifty Times behind your Back, that you was one of the most sensible Women in the World.'

'To this,' cries the Parson, 'I am ready to bear Testimony.'

'Nay, Brother,' says Mrs. *Western*, 'I have always, I'm sure, given you as favourable a Character. You must own you have a little too much Hastiness in your Temper; but when you will allow yourself Time to reflect, I never knew a Man more reasonable.'

'Why then, Sister, if you think so,' said the Squire, 'here's your good Health with all my Heart. I am a little passionate sometimes, but I scorn to bear any Malice. *Sophy*, do you be a good Girl, and do every Thing your Aunt orders you.'

'I have not the least Doubt of her,' answered Mrs. *Western*. 'She hath had already an Example before her Eyes, in the Behaviour of that Wretch her Cousin *Harriet*, who ruined herself by neglecting my Advice.—O Brother, what think you? You was hardly gone out of Hearing, when you set out for *London*, when who should arrive but that impudent Fellow with the odious *Irish* Name—that *Fitzpatrick*. He broke in abruptly upon me without Notice, or I would not have seen him. He ran on a long, unintelligible Story about his Wife, to which he forced me to give him a Hearing; but I made him very little Answer, and delivered him the Letter from his Wife, which I bid him answer himself. I suppose the Wretch will endeavour to find us out; but I beg you will not see her, for I am determined I will not.'

'I zee her?' answered the Squire; 'you need not fear me. I'll ge no Encouragement to such undutiful Wenches. It is well for the Fellow her Husband, I was not at Huome. Od rabbit it, he should have taken a Dance thru the Horse-pond, I promise un. You zee, *Sophy*, what Undutifulness brings Volks to. You have an Example in your own Family.' 'Brother,' cries the Aunt, 'you need not shock my Niece by such odious Repetitions. Why will you not leave every Thing entirely to me?' 'Well, well; I wull, I wull;' said the Squire. And now Mrs. *Western*, luckily for *Sophia*, put an End to the Conversation, by ordering Chairs to be called. I say luckily; for had it continued much longer, fresh Matter of Dissention would, most probably, have arisen between the Brother and Sister; between whom Education and Sex made the only Difference; for both were equally violent and equally positive, they had both a vast Affection for *Sophia*, and both a sovereign Contempt for each other.

CHAPTER V

In which Jones *receives a Letter from* Sophia, *and goes to a Play with* Mrs. Miller *and* Partridge.

THE Arrival of *Black George* in Town, and the good Offices which that grateful Fellow had promised to do for his old Benefactor, greatly comforted *Jones* in the Midst of all the Anxiety and Uneasiness which he had suffered on the Account of

Sophia; from whom, by the Means of the said *George*, he received the following Answer to his Letter, which *Sophia*, to whom the Use of Pen, Ink, and Paper was restored with her Liberty, wrote the very Evening when she departed from her Confinement.

'*Sir*,

As I do not doubt your Sincerity in what you write, you will be pleased to hear that some of my Afflictions are at an End, by the Arrival of my Aunt *Western*, with whom I am at present, and with whom I enjoy all the Liberty I can desire. One Promise my Aunt hath insisted on my making, which is, that I will not see or converse with any Person without her Knowledge and Consent. This Promise I have most solemnly given, and shall most inviolably keep: And tho' she hath not expresly forbidden me writing, yet that must be an Omission from Forgetfulness; or this, perhaps, is included in the Word conversing. However, as I cannot but consider this as a Breach of her generous Confidence in my Honour, you cannot expect that I shall, after this, continue to write myself, or to receive Letters without her Knowledge. A Promise is with me a very sacred Thing, and to be extended to every Thing understood from it, as well as to what is expressed by it;[1] and this Consideration may perhaps, on Reflection, afford you some Comfort. But why should I mention a Comfort to you of this Kind? For though there is one Thing in which I can never comply with the best of Fathers, yet am I firmly resolved never to act in Defiance of him, or to take any Step of Consequence without his Consent. A firm Perswasion of this, must teach you

---

[1] Fielding again shapes this episode so as to invite comparison with *Clarissa* (see pp. 487, n. 1; 793, n. 1; 955, n. 1). Though Richardson's heroine, despite her close confinement, is never at a loss for writing materials, Sophia in similar circumstances 'had no Paper, Pen, nor Ink' (XVI. iii). Now, even though these things have been 'restored with her Liberty', she is too honourable to violate not merely the letter, but the spirit, of her promise to her aunt. Clarissa, on the other hand, carries on a voluminous 'clandestine' correspondence with Anna Howe and Lovelace, wilfully disobeying her family's strict orders to the contrary: she declares to Anna, 'as to [the prohibition] of not corresponding with you, nothing but the menace, that our letters shall be intercepted, can engage my observation of it' (i. 51). 'How', she continues, 'do needless watchfulness and undue restraint produce artifice and contrivance! I should abhor these clandestine correspondencies, were they not forced upon me. They have so mean, so low an appearance . . .' (i. 53). The technical exigencies of his novel—a novel in letters, after all—may have forced Richardson into such improbabilies, but Fielding may be pardoned his implicit criticism of a somewhat surreptitious and insubordinate young woman whom the author's Preface proposes as a model of '*Delicacy*' and of '*the strictest Notions of filial Duty*' (I. ix).

to divert your Thoughts from what Fortune hath (perhaps) made impossible. This your own Interest persuades you. This may reconcile, I hope, Mr. *Allworthy* to you; and if it will, you have my Injunctions to pursue it. Accidents have laid some Obligations on me, and your good Intentions probably more. Fortune may, perhaps, be sometimes kinder to us both than at present. Believe this, that I shall always think of you as I think you deserve, and am,

Sir,
Your Obliged Humble Servant,
Sophia Western.'

'I charge you write to me no more—at present at least; and accept this, which is now of no Service to me, which I know you must want, and think you owe the Trifle only to that Fortune by which you found it.'*

A Child who hath just learnt his Letters, would have spelt this Letter out in less Time than *Jones* took in reading it. The Sensations it occasioned were a Mixture of Joy and Grief; somewhat like what divide the Mind of a good Man, when he peruses the Will of his deceased Friend, in which a large Legacy, which his Distresses make the more welcome, is bequeathed to him. Upon the whole, however, he was more pleased than displeased; and indeed the Reader may probably wonder that he was displeased at all; but the Reader is not quite so much in Love as was poor *Jones*: And Love is a Disease, which, tho' it may in some Instances resemble a Consumption, (which it sometimes causes) in others proceeds in direct Opposition to it, and particularly in this, that it never flatters itself, or sees any one Symptom in a favourable Light.

One Thing gave him complete Satisfaction, which was, that his Mistress had regained her Liberty, and was now with a Lady where she might at least assure herself of a decent Treatment. Another comfortable Circumstance, was the Reference which she made to her Promise of never marrying any other Man: For however disinterested he might imagine his Passion, and notwithstanding all the generous Overtures made in his Letter, I very much question whether he could have heard a more afflicting Piece of News, than that *Sophia* was married to another tho' the Match had been never so great, and never so likely to end in

---

* Meaning, perhaps, the Bank-bill for 100 *l.*

making her completely happy. That refined Degree of *Platonic* Affection which is absolutely detached from the Flesh, and is indeed entirely and purely spiritual, is a Gift confined to the female Part of the Creation; many of whom I have heard declare, (and doubtless with great Truth) that they would, with the utmost Readiness, resign a Lover to a Rival, when such Resignation was proved to be necessary for the temporal Interest of such Lover. Hence, therefore, I conclude, that this Affection is in Nature, though I cannot pretend to say, I have ever seen an Instance of it.

Mr. *Jones* having spent three Hours in reading and kissing the aforesaid Letter, and being, at last, in a State of good Spirits, from the last-mentioned Considerations, he agreed to carry an Appointment which he had before made into Execution. This was to attend Mrs. *Miller* and her younger Daughter into the Gallery at the Playhouse, and to admit Mr. *Partridge* as one of the Company. For as *Jones* had really that Taste for Humour which many affect, he expected to enjoy much Entertainment in the Criticisms of *Partridge*; from whom he expected the simple Dictates of Nature, unimproved indeed, but likewise unadulterated by Art.[1]

In the first Row then of the first Gallery[2] did Mr. *Jones*, Mrs. *Miller*, her youngest Daughter, and *Partridge* take their Places. *Partridge* immediately declared, it was the finest Place he had ever been in. When the first Musick was played, he said, 'It was a Wonder how so many Fidlers could play at one Time, without putting one another out.' While the Fellow was lighting the upper Candles, he cry'd out to Mrs. *Miller*, 'Look, look, Madam, the very Picture of the Man in the End of the Common-Prayer Book, before the Gunpowder-Treason Service:'[3] Nor could he help observing, with a Sigh, when all the Candles were lighted, 'That here were Candles enough burnt in one Night, to keep an honest poor Family for a whole Twelvemonth.'

---

[1] The following scene was doubtless inspired by *Spectator*, No. 335 (25 March 1712), in which Sir Roger de Coverley attends a performance of Philips's *The Distrest Mother*, Mr. Spectator valuing his friend's ingenuous remarks 'as a Piece of Natural Criticism'.

[2] See above, p. 326, n. 1.

[3] The nation's deliverance from the Roman Catholic plot to blow up Parliament (1605) was commemorated annually in the service for 5 November, Guy Fawkes' Day. The picture to which Partridge refers depicts a man with a lantern approaching the doors of Parliament (*The Book of Common Prayer* [1745], Plate 50, entitled 'Gunpowder Treason').

As soon as the Play, which was *Hamlet* Prince of *Denmark*,[1] began, *Partridge* was all Attention, nor did he break Silence till the Entrance of the Ghost; upon which he asked *Jones*, 'what Man that was in the strange Dress; something,' said he, 'like what I have seen in a Picture. Sure it is not Armour, is it?' *Jones* answered, 'That is the Ghost.' To which *Partridge* replied with a Smile, 'Perswade me to that, Sir, if you can. Though I can't say I ever actually saw a Ghost in my Life, yet I am certain I should know one, if I saw him, better than that comes to. No, no, Sir, Ghosts don't appear in such Dresses as that, neither.' In this Mistake, which caused much Laughter in the Neighbourhood of *Partridge*, he was suffered to continue, till the Scene between the *Ghost* and *Hamlet*, when *Partridge* gave that Credit to Mr. *Garrick*,[2] which he had denied to *Jones*, and fell into so violent a Trembling, that his Knees knocked against each other. *Jones* asked him what was the Matter, and whether he was afraid of the Warrior upon the Stage? 'O la! Sir,' said he, 'I perceive now it is what you told me. I am not afraid of any Thing; for I know it is

---

[1] The present episode provides further evidence that Fielding made no consistent attempt to square the events of his narrative with those that historically occurred in 1745. (See above, pp. 435, n. 1; 729, n. 1.) In that year Garrick spent the season in Dublin. Furthermore, the only production of *Hamlet* to take place in December was on the 28th, at Goodman's Fields with Furnival in the lead, whereas, if Fielding had been following a calendar, Jones and Partridge attend the theatre on the 19th.

[2] On Garrick, see above, pp. 327, n. 2; 493, n. 1. In 1748 Garrick played Hamlet at Drury Lane on 14 October and 17 December. By stressing Garrick's ability to project the passions, especially of terror and grief, Fielding throughout this episode becomes his friend's advocate in a recent critical controversy. In *A Treatise on the Passions, So far as they regard the Stage* (1747), Samuel Foote had remarked on Garrick's ineffectiveness in conveying 'the Passions of Love, Grief, and Horror' (p. 15). He was promptly answered by one who shared Fielding's opinion that Garrick was 'the greatest Actor that ever trod the *English* Stage, the little Miracle who has all the Passions at Command, the real *Proteus*, who can instantly transform himself into what Shape he pleases . . .' ('J. T.', *A Letter of Compliment to the ingenious Author of a Treatise on the Passions* [1747], p. 20). Garrick's expression of grief in Lear, writes this author, 'communicates itself to the whole Audience; and fills even the most obdurate Heart with Distress and Pity unfelt before'. And 'When *Macbeth* sees the *horrid Shadow* of his murder'd Friend, seated at his Banquet; when Guilt and Fear, with all their hideous Train of Images, at once assail him, and goad and sting his iron Heart; nothing cou'd paint the dreadful Scene, but the Words of the immortal *Shakespear*, delivered by Mr. *G.* I have observ'd the Refuse of the Theatre, *Macbeth*'s Company, Creatures who seldom betray any Idea of Nature or Feeling, behave in the justest Manner in this Scene, merely from the Infection they have caught from the Countenance of their *Roscius*' (p. 16). Some years later, Fielding similarly remarked that when Garrick plays Macbeth, 'it is scarce an Hyperbole to say, I have seen the Hair of the Audience stand on End' (*An Enquiry into the Causes of the late Increase of Robbers* [1751], section xi).

but a Play: And if it was really a Ghost, it could do one no Harm
at such a Distance, and in so much Company; and yet if I was
frightened, I am not the only Person.' 'Why, who,' cries *Jones*,
'dost thou take to be such a Coward here besides thyself?' 'Nay,
you may call me Coward if you will; but if that little Man¹ there
upon the Stage is not frightned, I never saw any Man frightned
in my Life. Ay, ay; *go along with you!* Ay, to be sure! Who's Fool
then? Will you? Lud have Mercy upon such Fool-Hardiness!—
Whatever happens, it is good enough for you.—*Follow you?* I'd
follow the Devil as soon. Nay, perhaps, it is the Devil—for they
say he can put on what Likeness he pleases.—Oh! here he is
again.—*No farther!* No, you have gone far enough already;
farther than I'd have gone for all the King's Dominions.' *Jones*
offered to speak, but *Partridge* cried, 'Hush, hush, dear Sir, don't
you hear him!' And during the whole Speech of the Ghost, he sat
with his Eyes fixed partly on the Ghost, and partly on *Hamlet*, and
with his Mouth open; the same Passions which succeeded each
other in *Hamlet*, succeeding likewise in him.

When the Scene was over, *Jones* said, 'Why, *Partridge*, you
exceed my Expectations. You enjoy the Play more than I conceived possible.' 'Nay, Sir,' answered *Partridge*, 'if you are not
afraid of the Devil, I can't help it; but to be sure it is natural to be
surprized at such Things, though I know there is nothing in
them: Not that it was the Ghost that surprized me neither; for I
should have known that to have been only a Man in a strange
Dress: But when I saw the little Man so frightned himself, it was
that which took Hold of me.' 'And dost thou imagine then,
Partridge,' cries *Jones*, 'that he was really frightned?' 'Nay, Sir,'

---

¹ Foote had complained that Garrick's smallness of stature detracted from his effective-
ness in heroic roles:

'And as the Eye is the Scence [*sic*] first gratified, or disgusted, it may not be improper
to enquire what kind of Prepossession arises in the Mind, from the Appearance of Mr.
G's Figure, and here I am afraid frail Nature has been a little unkind, and tho' I must
own I have very distinct Ideas of big and great, yet such is the Folly of the Million,
that they expect a more than ordinary Appearance from a Man, who is to perform
extraordinary Actions; it is in vain, to tell them, that *Charles* of *Sweden*, was but five-
feet five, or *Alexander* the Great, a very little Man, the false Association is so deeply
rooted into their Minds, that you may as well attempt to persuade them that Night and
Apparitions have no connection: they are dissatisfied, when they see a Bulls-Pizzle, a
dried Elves-Skin, in *Falstaff*'s Language, bullying a Congregation of Heroes . . .'
(*A Treatise on the Passions* [1747], p. 14).
'J. T.' tersely dismissed this criticism by reminding Foote 'of this common Observation;
when Mr. G. is on the Stage, no Body else is seen' (*A Letter of Compliment* [1747], p. 15).

said *Partridge*, 'did not you yourself observe afterwards, when he found it was his own Father's Spirit, and how he was murdered in the Garden, how his Fear forsook him by Degrees, and he was struck dumb with Sorrow, as it were, just as I should have been, had it been my own Case.—But hush! O la! What Noise is that? There he is again.—Well, to be certain, though I know there is nothing at all in it, I am glad I am not down yonder, where those Men are.' Then turning his Eyes again upon *Hamlet*, 'Ay, you may draw your Sword; what signifies a Sword against the Power of the Devil?'

During the second Act, *Partridge* made very few Remarks. He greatly admired the Fineness of the Dresses; nor could he help observing upon the King's Countenance. 'Well,' said he, 'how People may be deceived by Faces? *Nulla fides fronti*[1] is, I find, a true Saying. Who would think, by looking in the King's Face,[2] that he had ever committed a Murder?' He then enquired after the Ghost; but *Jones*, who intended he should be surprized, gave him no other Satisfaction, than 'that he might possibly see him again soon, and in a Flash of Fire.'

Partridge sat in fearful Expectation of this; and now when the Ghost made his next Appearance, *Partridge* cried out, 'There, Sir, now; what say you now? Is he frightned now or no? As much frightned as you think me, and, to be sure, no Body can help some Fears, I would not be in so bad a Condition as what's his Name, Squire *Hamlet*, is there, for all the World. Bless me! What's become of the Spirit? As I am a living Soul, I thought I saw him sink into the Earth.' 'Indeed, you saw right,' answered *Jones*. 'Well, well,' cries *Partridge*, 'I know it is only a Play; and besides, if there was any Thing in all this, Madam *Miller* would not laugh so: For as to you, Sir, you would not be afraid, I believe, if the Devil was here in Person.—There, there—— Ay, no Wonder you are in such a Passion; shake the vile wicked Wretch to Pieces. If she was my own Mother I should serve her so. To be sure, all Duty to a Mother is forfeited by such wicked Doings.—Ay, go about your Business; I hate the Sight of you.'

---

[1] Slightly altered from Juvenal, *Satires*, ii. 8: 'Men's faces are not to be trusted.'

[2] Partridge is probably seeing '*Honest Billy Mills*' (see above, p. 329, n. 1) in the role of Claudius—a part Mills often played, even though his 'honest Face', as Fielding remarked (VII. i), made him an unlikely villain. (See O. W. Ferguson, *PQ*, xliii [1964], 73–8.) See also below, p. 856, n. 2.

Our Critic was now pretty silent till the Play, which *Hamlet* introduces before the King. This he did not at first understand, till *Jones* explained it to him; but he no sooner entered into the Spirit of it, than he began to bless himself that he had never committed Murder. Then turning to Mrs. *Miller*, he asked her, 'If she did not imagine the King looked as if he was touched; though he is,' said he, 'a good Actor, and doth all he can to hide it. Well, I would not have so much to answer for, as that wicked Man there hath, to sit upon a much higher Chair than he sits upon.—No wonder he run away; for your Sake I'll never trust an innocent Face again.'

The Grave-digging Scene next engaged the Attention of *Partridge*, who expressed much Surprize at the Number of Skulls thrown upon the Stage. To which *Jones* answered, 'That it was one of the most famous Burial-Places about Town.' 'No wonder then,' cries *Partridge*, 'that the Place is haunted. But I never saw in my Life a worse Grave-digger. I had a Sexton, when I was Clerk, that should have dug three Graves while he is digging one. The Fellow handles a Spade as if it was the first Time he had ever had one in his Hand. Ay, ay, you may sing. You had rather sing than work, I believe.'—Upon *Hamlet's* taking up the Skull, he cry'd out, 'Well, it is strange to see how fearless some Men are: I never could bring myself to touch any Thing belonging to a dead Man on any Account.—He seemed frightned enough too at the Ghost I thought. *Nemo omnibus horis sapit.*'[1]

Little more worth remembering occurred during the Play; at the End of which *Jones* asked him, 'which of the Players he had liked best?' To this he answered, with some Appearance of Indignation at the Question, 'The King without Doubt.'[2] 'Indeed, Mr. *Partridge*,' says Mrs. *Miller*, 'you are not of the same Opinion with the Town; for they are all agreed, that *Hamlet* is acted by the best Player who ever was on the Stage.' 'He the best Player!' cries *Partridge* with a contemptuous Sneer,

---

[1] See above, pp. 130.5, 677, n. 3.

[2] If, as is likely, Fielding was imagining 'Billy' Mills as Claudius (see above, p. 855, n. 2), it is instructive to note the comparison he had made between the abilities of Mills and Garrick in *The Jacobite's Journal* (23 April 1748): '[Mills] was at all times a very safe Actor; and as he never shock'd you with any Absurdity, so he never raised Horror, Terror, Admiration, or any of those turbulent Sensations, to that dangerous Height to which Mr. *Garrick* (however good a Man he may otherwise be) hath been guilty of carrying them.'

'why I could act as well as he myself. I am sure if I had seen a Ghost, I should have looked in the very same Manner, and done just as he did. And then, to be sure, in that Scene, as you called it, between him and his Mother, where you told me he acted so fine, why, Lord help me, any Man, that is, any good Man, that had such a Mother, would have done exactly the same. I know you are only joking with me; but, indeed, Madam, though I was never at a Play in *London*, yet I have seen acting before in the Country; and the King for my Money; he speaks all his Words distinctly, half as loud again as the other.—Any Body may see he is an Actor.'

While Mrs. *Miller* was thus engaged in Conversation with *Partridge*, a Lady came up to Mr. *Jones*, whom he immediately knew to be Mrs. *Fitzpatrick*. She said, she had seen him from the other Part of the Gallery, and had taken that Opportunity of speaking to him, as she had something to say, which might be of great Service to himself. She then acquainted him with her Lodgings, and made him an Appointment the next Day in the Morning; which, upon Recollection, she presently changed to the Afternoon; at which Time *Jones* promised to attend her.

Thus ended the Adventure at the Playhouse; where *Partridge* had afforded great Mirth, not only to *Jones* and Mrs. *Miller*, but to all who sat within hearing, who were more attentive to what he said, than to any Thing that passed on the Stage.

He durst not go to Bed all that Night, for Fear of the Ghost, and for many Nights after, sweated two or three Hours before he went to sleep, with the same Apprehensions, and waked several Times in great Horrors, crying out, 'Lord have Mercy upon us! there it is.'

CHAPTER VI

In which the History is obliged to look back.

IT is almost impossible for the best Parent to observe an exact Impartiality to his Children, even though no superior Merit should biass his Affection; but sure a Parent can hardly be blamed, when that Superiority determines his Preference.

As I regard all the Personages of this History in the Light of my Children, so I must confess the same Inclination of Partiality to *Sophia*; and for that I hope the Reader will allow me the same Excuse, from the Superiority of her Character.

This extraordinary Tenderness, which I have for my Heroine, never suffers me to quit her any long Time without the utmost Reluctance. I could now, therefore, return impatiently to enquire what hath happened to this lovely Creature since her Departure from her Father's, but that I am obliged first to pay a short Visit to Mr. *Blifil*.

Mr. *Western*, in the first Confusion into which his Mind was cast, upon the sudden News he received of his Daughter, and in his first Hurry to go after her, had not once thought of sending any Account of the Discovery to *Blifil*. He had not gone far, however, before he recollected himself, and accordingly stopt at the very first Inn he came to, and dispatched away a Messenger to acquaint *Blifil* with his having found *Sophia*, and with his firm Resolution to marry her to him immediately, if he would come up after him to Town.

As the Love which *Blifil* had for *Sophia* was of that violent Kind, which nothing but the Loss of her Fortune, or some such Accident, could lessen, his Inclination to the Match was not at all altered by her having run away, though he was obliged to lay this to his own Account. He very readily, therefore, embraced this Offer. Indeed, he now proposed the Gratification of a very strong Passion besides Avarice, by marrying this young Lady, and this was Hatred: For he concluded that Matrimony afforded an equal Opportunity of satisfying either Hatred or Love; and this Opinion is very probably verified by much Experience. To say the Truth, if we are to judge by the ordinary Behaviour of married Persons to each other, we shall, perhaps, be apt to conclude, that the Generality seek the Indulgence of the former Passion only in their Union of every Thing but of Hearts.

There was one Difficulty, however, in his Way, and this arose from Mr. *Allworthy*. That good Man, when he found by the Departure of *Sophia*, (for neither that, nor the Cause of it, could be concealed from him) the great Aversion which she had for his Nephew, began to be seriously concerned that he had been deceived into carrying Matters so far. He by no Means concurred with the Opinions of those Parents, who think it as immaterial to consult the Inclinations of their Children in the Affair of Marriage, as to solicit the good Pleasure of their Servants when they intend to take a Journey; and who are, by Law or Decency at least, withheld often from using absolute Force. On the contrary, as he esteemed the Institution to be of the most sacred Kind, he thought every preparatory Caution necessary to preserve it holy and inviolate; and very wisely concluded, that the surest Way to effect this, was by laying the Foundation in previous Affection.

Blifil indeed soon cured his Uncle of all Anger on the Score of Deceit, by many Vows and Protestations that he had been deceived himself, with which the many Declarations of *Western* very well tallied; but now to persuade *Allworthy* to consent to the renewing his Addresses, was a Matter of such apparent Difficulty, that the very Appearance was sufficient to have deterred a less enterprizing Genius; but this young Gentleman so well knew his own Talents, that nothing within the Province of Cunning, seemed to him hard to be atchieved.

Here then he represented the Violence of his own Affection, and the Hopes of subduing Aversion in the Lady by Perseverance. He begged that in an Affair on which depended all his future Repose, he might at least be at Liberty to try all fair Means for Success. Heaven forbid, he said, that he should ever think of prevailing by any other than the most gentle Methods. 'Besides, Sir,' said he, 'if they fail, you may then (which will be surely time enough) deny your Consent.' He urged the great and eager Desire which Mr. *Western* had for the Match, and lastly, he made great Use of the Name of *Jones*, to whom he imputed all that had happened, and from whom, he said, to preserve so valuable a young Lady was even an Act of Charity.

All these Arguments were well seconded by *Thwackum*, who dwelt a little stronger on the Authority of Parents than Mr. *Blifil* himself had done. He ascribed the Measures which Mr. *Blifil* was desirous to take to Christian Motives; 'and though,' says he, 'the good young Gentleman hath mentioned Charity last, I am almost convinced it is his first and principal Consideration.'

Square, possibly, had he been present, would have sung to the same Tune, though in a different Key, and would have discovered much Moral Fitness in the Proceeding; but he was now gone to *Bath* for the Recovery of his Health.

Allworthy, though not without Reluctance, at last yielded to the Desires of his Nephew. He said, he would accompany him to

London, where he might be at Liberty to use every honest Endeavour to gain the Lady: 'But I declare,' said he, 'I will never give my Consent to any absolute Force being put on her Inclinations, nor shall you ever have her, unless she can be brought freely to Compliance.'

Thus did the Affection of *Allworthy* for his Nephew, betray the superiour Understanding to be triumphed over by the inferiour; and thus is the Prudence of the best of Heads often defeated by the Tenderness of the best of Hearts.

Blifil having obtained this unhoped for Acquiescence in his Uncle, rested not till he carried his Purpose into Execution. And as no immediate Business required Mr. *Allworthy's* Presence in the Country, and little Preparation is necessary to Men for a Journey, they set out the very next Day, and arrived in Town that Evening when Mr. *Jones*, as we have seen, was diverting himself with *Partridge* at the Play.

The Morning after his Arrival, Mr. *Blifil* waited on Mr. *Western*, by whom he was most kindly and graciously received, and from whom he had every possible Assurance (perhaps more than was possible) that he should very shortly be as happy as *Sophia* could make him; nor would the Squire suffer the young Gentleman to return to his Uncle, till he had, almost against his Will, carried him to his Sister.

CHAPTER VII

In which Mr. Western *pays a Visit to his Sister, in company with Mr.* Blifil.

MRS. *Western* was reading a Lecture on Prudence, and Matrimonial Politics to her Niece, when her Brother and *Blifil* broke in with less Ceremony than the Laws of Visiting require. *Sophia* no sooner saw *Blifil*, than she turned pale, and almost lost the Use of all her Faculties; but her Aunt on the contrary waxed red, and having all her Faculties at Command, began to exert her Tongue on the Squire.

'Brother,' said she, 'I am astonished at your Behaviour, will you never learn any Regard to Decorum? Will you still look upon every Apartment as your own, or as belonging to one of your

Country Tenants? Do you think yourself at Liberty to invade the Privacies of Women of Condition, without the least Decency or Notice?'—'Why, what, a Pox! is the Matter now,' quoth the Squire, 'one would think, I had caught you at——' 'None of your Brutality, Sir, I beseech you,' answered she.—'You have surprized my poor Niece so, that she can hardly, I see, support herself.—Go, my dear, retire, and endeavour to recruit your Spirits; for I see you have Occasion.' At which Words, *Sophia*, who never received a more welcome Command, hastily withdrew.

'To be sure, Sister,' cries the Squire, 'you are mad, when I have brought Mr. *Blifil* here to court her, to force her away.'

'Sure, Brother,' says she, 'you are worse than mad, when you know in what Situation Affairs are, to—I am sure, I ask Mr. *Blifil* pardon, but he knows very well to whom to impute so disagreeable a Reception. For my own part, I am sure, I shall always be very glad to see Mr. *Blifil*; but his own good Sense would not have suffered him to proceed so abruptly, had you not compelled him to it.'

Blifil bowed and stammered and looked like a Fool; but *Western* without giving him time to form a Speech for the Purpose, answered, 'Well, well, I am to blame if you will, I always am, certainly; but come, let the Girl be fetched back again, or let Mr. *Blifil* go to her.—He's come up on Purpose, and there is no time to be lost.'

'Brother,' cries Mrs. *Western*, 'Mr. *Blifil*, I am confident, understands himself better than to think of seeing my Niece any more this Morning after what hath happened. Women are of a nice Contexture, and our Spirits when disordered are not to be recomposed in a Moment. Had you suffered Mr. *Blifil* to have sent his Compliments to my Niece, and to have desired the Favour of waiting on her in the Afternoon, I should possibly have prevailed on her to have seen him; but now I despair of bringing about any such Matter.'

'I am very sorry, Madam,' cried *Blifil*, 'that Mr. *Western's* extraordinary Kindness to me, which I can never enough acknowledge, should have occasioned——' 'Indeed, Sir,' said she interrupting him, 'you need make no Apologies, we all know my Brother so well.'

'I don't care what any Body knows of me,' answered the

Squire,—'but when must he come to see her; for consider, I tell you, he is a come up on purpose, and so is *Allworthy*.' 'Brother,' said she, 'whatever Message Mr. *Blifil* thinks proper to send to my Niece, shall be delivered to her, and I suppose she will want no Instructions to make a proper Answer. I am convinced she will not refuse to see Mr. *Blifil* at a proper Time.'—'The Devil she won't,' answered the Squire.—'Odsbud!—Don't we know— I say nothing, but some Volk are wiser than all the World.—If I might have had my will, she had not run away before: And now I expect to hear every Moment she is guone again. For as great a Fool as some Volk think me, I know very well she hates——' 'No Matter, Brother,' replied Mrs. *Western*, 'I will not hear my Niece abused. It is a Reflection on my Family. She is an Honour to it, and she will be an Honour to it, I promise you. I will pawn my whole Reputation in the World on her Conduct.—I shall be glad to see you, Brother, in the Afternoon; for I have somewhat of Importance to mention to you.—At present Mr. *Blifil*, as well as you, must excuse me, for I am in haste to dress.'—'Well but,' said the Squire, 'do, appoint a Time.'—'Indeed,' said she, 'I can appoint no Time.—I tell you, I will see you in the Afternoon.'— 'What the Devil would you have me do,' cries the Squire, turning to *Blifil*, 'I can no muore turn her, than a Beagle can turn an old Hare. Perhaps, she will be in a better Humour in the Afternoon.' —'I am condemned, I see, Sir, to Misfortune,' answered *Blifil*, 'but I shall always own my Obligations to you.'—He then took a ceremonious Leave of Mrs. *Western*, who was altogether as ceremonious on her Part, and then they departed, the Squire muttering to himself with an Oath, that *Blifil* should see his Daughter in the Afternoon.

If Mr. *Western* was little pleased with this Interview, *Blifil* was less. As to the former, he imputed the whole Behaviour of his Sister to her Humour only, and to her Dissatisfaction at the omission of Ceremony in the Visit; but *Blifil* saw a little deeper into Things. He suspected somewhat of more Consequence, from two or three Words which dropt from the Lady; and, to say the Truth, he suspected right, as will appear when I have unfolded the several Matters which will be contained in the following Chapter.

CHAPTER VIII

Schemes of Lady Bellaston *for the Ruin of* Jones.

LOVE had taken too deep a Root in the Mind of Lord *Fellamar* to be plucked up by the rude Hands of Mr. *Western*. In the Heat of Resentment he had indeed given a Commission to Captain *Egglane*, which the Captain had far exceeded in the Execution; nor had it been executed at all, had his Lordship been able to find the Captain after he had seen Lady *Bellaston*, which was in the Afternoon of the Day after he had received the Affront; but so industrious was the Captain in the Discharge of his Duty, that having after long Enquiry found out the Squire's Lodgings very late in the Evening, he sat up all Night at a Tavern, that he might not miss the Squire in the Morning, and by that Means missed the Revocation which my Lord had sent to his Lodgings.

In the Afternoon then next after the intended Rape of *Sophia*, his Lordship, as we have said, made a Visit to Lady *Bellaston*, who laid open so much of the Character of the Squire, that his Lordship plainly saw the Absurdity he had been guilty of in taking any Offence at his Words, especially as he had those honourable Designs on his Daughter. He then unbosomed the violence of his Passion to Lady *Bellaston*, who readily undertook the Cause, and encouraged him with certain Assurance of a most favourable Reception, from all the Elders of the Family, and from the Father himself when he should be sober, and should be made acquainted with the Nature of the Offer made to his Daughter. The only Danger, she said, lay in the Fellow she had formerly mentioned, who, though a Beggar and a Vagabond, had by some Means or other, she knew not what, procured himself tolerable Cloaths, and past for a Gentleman. 'Now,' says she, 'as I have, for the sake of my Cousin, made it my Business to enquire after this Fellow, I have luckily found out his Lodging;' with which she then acquainted his Lordship. 'I am thinking, my Lord,' added she, '(for this Fellow is too mean for your personal Resentment) whether it would not be possible for your Lordship to contrive some Method of having him pressed and sent on board a Ship.[1]

[1] Though the impressment of recruits for the Navy had been practised in England since the thirteenth century, in 1744 a new law went into effect (17 George II, cap. 15) explicitly

Neither Law nor Conscience forbid this Project: for the Fellow, I promise you, however well drest, is but a Vagabond, and as proper as any Fellow in the Streets to be pressed into the Service; and as for the conscientious Part, surely the Preservation of a young Lady from such Ruin is a most meritorious Act; nay, with regard to the Fellow himself, unless he could succeed (which Heaven forbid) with my Cousin, it may probably be the means of preserving him from the Gallows, and perhaps may make his Fortune in an honest Way.'

Lord *Fellamar* very heartily thanked her Ladyship, for the Part which she was pleased to take in the Affair, upon the Success of which his whole future Happiness entirely depended. He said, he saw at present no Objection to the pressing Scheme, and would consider of putting it in Execution. He then most earnestly recommended to her Ladyship, to do him the Honour of immediately mentioning his Proposals to the Family; to whom he said, he offered a *Carte Blanche*, and would settle his Fortune in almost any manner they should require. And after uttering many Extasies and Raptures concerning *Sophia*, he took his leave and departed, but not before he had received the strongest Charge to beware of *Jones*, and to lose no time in securing his Person where he should no longer be in a Capacity of making any Attempts to the Ruin of the young Lady.

The Moment Mrs. *Western* was arrived at her Lodgings, a Card was dispatched with her Compliments to Lady *Bellaston*; who no sooner received it, than with the Impatience of a Lover, she flew to her Cousin, rejoiced at this fair Opportunity, which beyond her Hopes offered itself: for she was much better pleased with the Prospect of making the Proposals to a Woman of Sense, and who knew the World, than to a Gentleman whom she honoured with the Appellation of *Hottentot*; though indeed from him she apprehended no Danger of a Refusal.

The two Ladies being met, after very short previous Ceremonials, fell to Business, which was indeed almost as soon concluded as begun; for Mrs. *Western* no sooner heard the Name of Lord *Fellamar* than her Cheeks glowed with Pleasure, but when she was acquainted with the Eagerness of his Passion, the Earnestness

empowering local authorities to conscript as soldiers or marines all 'such able-bodied Men as do not follow or exercise any lawful Calling or Employment, or have not some other lawful and sufficient Support and Maintenance'.

of his Proposals, and the Generosity of his Offer, she declared her full Satisfaction in the most explicit Terms.

In the Progress of their Conversation their Discourse turned to *Jones*, and both Cousins very pathetically lamented the unfortunate Attachment, which both agreed, *Sophia* had to that young Fellow; and Mrs. *Western* entirely attributed it to the Folly of her Brother's Management. She concluded however at last, with declaring her Confidence in the good Understanding of her Niece, who though she would not give up her Affection in Favour of *Blifil*, will, I doubt not, says she, soon be prevailed upon to sacrifice a simple Inclination to the Addresses of a fine Gentleman, who brings her both a Title and a large Estate: 'For indeed,' added she, 'I must do *Sophy* the Justice to confess, this *Blifil* is but a hideous kind of Fellow, as you know, *Bellaston*, all Country Gentlemen are, and hath nothing but his Fortune to recommend him.'

'Nay,' said Lady *Bellaston*, 'I don't then so much wonder at my Cousin; for I promise you, this *Jones* is a very agreeable Fellow, and hath one Virtue which the Men say is a great Recommendation to us. What do you think, *Bell*[1]—I shall certainly make you laugh; nay, I can hardly tell you myself for laughing.—Will you believe that the Fellow hath had the Assurance to make Love to me? But if you should be inclined to disbelieve it, here is Evidence enough, his own Hand-writing, I assure you.' She then delivered her Cousin the Letter with the Proposals of Marriage, which if the Reader hath a Desire to see, he will find already on Record in the XVth Book of this History.

'Upon my Word, I am astonished,' said Mrs. *Western*, 'this is indeed a Masterpiece of Assurance. With your leave, I may possibly make some use of this Letter.' 'You have my full Liberty,' cries Lady *Bellaston*, 'to apply it to what Purpose you please. However, I would not have it shewn to any but Miss *Western*, nor to her unless you find Occasion.' 'Well, and how did you use the Fellow?' returned Mrs. *Western*. 'Not as a Husband,' said the Lady, 'I am not married, I promise you, my Dear. You know, *Bell*, I have try'd the Comforts once already, and once I think is enough for any reasonable Woman.'

This Letter Lady *Bellaston* thought would certainly turn the Balance against *Jones* in the Mind of *Sophia*, and she was

---

[1] Earlier Lady Bellaston had called her cousin 'Di' Western (XIII. iii).

emboldened to give it up, partly by her Hopes of having him instantly dispatched out of the way, and partly by having secured the Evidence of *Honour*, who, upon sounding her, she saw sufficient Reason to imagine, was prepared to testify whatever she pleased.

But perhaps the Reader may wonder why Lady *Bellaston*, who in her Heart hated *Sophia*, should be so desirous of promoting a Match, which was so much to the Interest of the young Lady. Now I would desire such Readers to look carefully into human Nature, Page almost the last, and there he will find, in scarce legible Characters, that Women, notwithstanding the preposterous Behaviour of Mothers, Aunts, &c. in matrimonial Matters, do in Reality think it so great a Misfortune to have their Inclinations in Love thwarted, that they imagine they ought never to carry Enmity higher than upon these Disappointments; again he will find it written much about the same Place, that a Woman who hath once been pleased with the Possession of a Man, will go above half way to the Devil, to prevent any other Woman from enjoying the same.

If he will not be contented with these Reasons, I freely confess I see no other Motive to the Actions of that Lady, unless we will conceive she was bribed by Lord *Fellamar*, which for my own Part I see no Cause to suspect.

Now this was the Affair which Mrs. *Western* was preparing to introduce to *Sophia*, by some prefatory Discourse on the Folly of Love, and on the Wisdom of legal Prostitution for Hire,[1] when her Brother and *Blifil* broke abruptly in upon her; and hence arose all that Coldness in her Behaviour to *Blifil*, which tho' the Squire, as was usual with him, imputed to a wrong Cause, infused into *Blifil* himself, (he being a much more cunning Man) a Suspicion of the real Truth.

CHAPTER IX

In which Jones *pays a Visit to Mrs.* Fitzpatrick.

THE Reader may now perhaps be pleased to return with us to Mr. *Jones*, who at the appointed Hour attended on Mrs. *Fitzpatrick*; but before we relate the Conversation which now past,

---

[1] On the currency of this phrase in the period, see C. J. Rawson, *N & Q*, N.S. xi (August 1964), 298.

it may be proper, according to our Method, to return a little back, and to account for so great an Alteration of Behaviour in this Lady, that from changing her Lodging principally to avoid Mr. *Jones*, she had now industriously, as hath been seen, sought this Interview.

And here we shall need only to resort to what happened the preceding Day, when hearing from Lady *Bellaston*, that Mr. *Western* was arrived in Town, she went to pay her Duty to him, at his Lodgings at *Piccadilly*, where she was received with many scurvy Compellations too coarse to be repeated, and was even threatned to be kicked out of Doors. From hence an old Servant of her Aunt *Western*, with whom she was well acquainted, conducted her to the Lodgings of that Lady, who treated her, not more kindly, but more politely; or, to say the Truth, with Rudeness in another Way. In short, she returned from both, plainly convinced not only that her Scheme of Reconciliation had proved abortive, but that she must for ever give over all Thoughts of bringing it about by any Means whatever. From this Moment Desire of Revenge only filled her Mind; and in this Temper meeting *Jones* at the Play, an Opportunity seemed to her to occur of effecting this Purpose.

The Reader must remember, that he was acquainted by Mrs. *Fitzpatrick*, in the Account she gave of her own Story, with the Fondness Mrs. *Western* had formerly shewn for Mr. *Fitzpatrick* at *Bath*, from the Disappointment of which, Mrs. *Fitzpatrick* derived the great Bitterness her Aunt had expressed toward her. She had therefore no Doubt but that the good Lady would as easily listen to the Addresses of Mr. *Jones*, as she had before done to the other, for the Superiority of Charms was clearly on the side of Mr. *Jones*, and the Advance which her Aunt had since made in Age, she concluded (how justly I will not say) was an Argument rather in Favour of her Project than against it.

Therefore, when *Jones* attended after a previous Declaration of her Desire of serving him, arising, as she said, from a firm Assurance how much she should by so doing oblige *Sophia*; and after some Excuses for her former Disappointment, and after acquainting Mr. *Jones* in whose Custody his Mistress was, of which she thought him ignorant; she very explicitly mentioned her Scheme to him, and advised him to make sham Addresses to the older Lady, in order to procure an easy Access to the Younger, informing him at the same time of the Success which Mr. *Fitzpatrick* had formerly owed to the very same Stratagem.

Mr. *Jones* exprest great Gratitude to the Lady for the kind Intentions towards him which she had expressed, and indeed testified, by this Proposal; but besides intimating some Diffidence of Success from the Lady's Knowledge of his Love to her Niece, which had not been her Case in regard to Mr. *Fitzpatrick*, he said, he was afraid Miss *Western* would never agree to an Imposition of this Kind, as well from her utter Detestation of all Fallacy, as from her avowed Duty to her Aunt.

Mrs. *Fitzpatrick* was a little nettled at this; and indeed if it may not be called a Lapse of the Tongue, it was a small Deviation from Politeness in *Jones*, and into which he scarce would have fallen, had not the Delight he felt in praising *Sophia*, hurried him out of all Reflection; for this Commendation of one Cousin was more than a tacit Rebuke on the other.

'Indeed, Sir,' answered the Lady, with some Warmth, 'I cannot think there is any thing easier than to cheat an old Woman with a Profession of Love, when her Complexion is amorous; and, tho' she is my Aunt, I must say, there never was a more liquorish one than her Ladyship. Can't you pretend that the Despair of possessing her Niece, from her being promised to *Blifil*, had made you turn your Thoughts towards her? As to my Cousin *Sophia*, I can't imagine her to be such a Simpleton as to have the least Scruple on such an Account, or to conceive any Harm in punishing one of these Haggs for the many Mischiefs they bring upon Families, by their Tragi-comic Passions; for which I think it is pity they are not punishable by Law. I had no such Scruple myself, and yet I hope my Cousin *Sophia* will not think it an Affront when I say she cannot detest every real Species of Falshood more than her Cousin *Fitzpatrick*. To my Aunt indeed I pretend no Duty, nor doth she deserve any. However, Sir, I have given you my Advice, and if you decline pursuing it, I shall have the less Opinion of your Understanding, that's all.'

Jones now clearly saw the Error he had committed, and exerted his utmost Power to rectify it; but he only faultered and stuttered into Nonsense and Contradiction. To say the Truth, it is often safer to abide by the Consequences of the first Blunder, than to endeavour to rectify it; for by such Endeavours, we generally plunge deeper instead of extricating ourselves; and few Persons will on such Occasions, have the good Nature, which Mrs. *Fitzpatrick* display'd to *Jones*; by saying, with a Smile, 'You need attempt no more Excuses; for I can easily forgive a real Lover, whatever is the Effect of Fondness for his Mistress.'

She then renewed her Proposal, and very fervently recommended it, omitting no Argument which her Invention could suggest on the Subject; for she was so violently incensed against her Aunt, that scarce any Thing was capable of affording her equal Pleasure with exposing her, and, like a true Woman, she would see no Difficulties in the Execution of a favourite Scheme.

Jones however persisted in declining the Undertaking, which had not indeed the least Probability of Success. He easily perceived the Motives which induced Mrs. *Fitzpatrick* to be so eager in pressing her Advice. He said he would not deny the tender and passionate Regard he had for *Sophia*; but was so conscious of the Inequality of their Situations, that he could never flatter himself so far as to hope that so divine a young Lady would condescend to think on so unworthy a Man; nay he protested he could scarce bring himself to wish she should. He concluded with a Profession of generous Sentiments, which we have not at present Leisure to insert.

There are some fine Women (for I dare not here speak in too general Terms) with whom Self is so predominant, that they never detach it from any Subject; and as Vanity is with them a ruling Principle, they are apt to lay hold of whatever Praise they meet with; and, though the Property of others, convey it to their own Use. In the Company of these Ladies it is impossible to say any thing handsome of another Woman, which they will not apply to themselves; nay they often improve the Praise they seize; as for Instance, if her Beauty, her Wit, her Gentility, her good Humour deserve so much Commendation, what do I deserve who possess those Qualities in so much more eminent a Degree?

To these Ladies a Man often recommends himself while he is commending another Woman; and while he is expressing Ardour and generous Sentiments for his Mistress, they are considering what a charming Lover this Man would make to them, who can feel all this Tenderness for an inferiour Degree of Merit. Of this, strange as it may seem, I have seen many Instances besides Mrs.

Fitzpatrick, to whom all this really happened, and who now began to feel a Somewhat for Mr. *Jones*, the Symptoms of which she much sooner understood than poor *Sophia* had formerly done.

To say the Truth, perfect Beauty in both Sexes is a more irresistible Object than it is generally thought; for notwithstanding some of us are contented with more homely Lots, and learn by Rote (as Children are to repeat what gives them no Idea) to despise Outside, and to value more solid Charms; yet I have always observed at the Approach of consummate Beauty, that these more solid Charms only shine with that Kind of Lustre which the Stars have after the rising of the Sun.

When *Jones* had finished his Exclamations, many of which would have become the Mouth of *Oroondates* himself,[1] Mrs. *Fitzpatrick* heaved a deep Sigh, and taking her Eyes off from *Jones*, on whom they had been some time fixed, and dropping them on the Ground, she cry'd, 'Indeed Mr. *Jones*, I pity you; but it is the Curse of such Tenderness to be thrown away on those who are insensible of it. I know my Cousin better than you, Mr. *Jones*, and I must say, any Woman who makes no Return to such a Passion and such a Person, is unworthy of both.'

'Sure, Madam,' said *Jones*, 'you can't mean——' 'Mean?' cries Mrs. *Fitzpatrick*, 'I know not what I mean; there is something, I think, in true Tenderness bewitching; few Women ever meet with it in Men, and fewer still know how to value it when they do. I never heard such truly noble Sentiments, and I can't tell how it is, but you force one to believe you. Sure she must be the most contemptible of Women who can overlook such Merit.'

The Manner and Look with which all this was spoke infused a Suspicion into *Jones*, which we don't care to convey in direct Words to the Reader. Instead of making any Answer, he said, 'I am afraid, Madam, I have made too tiresome a Visit,' and offered to take his Leave.

'Not at all, Sir,' answered Mrs. *Fitzpatrick*.—'Indeed I pity you, Mr. *Jones*, indeed I do; but if you are going, consider of the

---

[1] The hero of La Calprenède's voluminous romance, *Cassandre* (1644–50), Oroöndates became the very type of the noble lover. Speaking of Colonel James's addresses to Amelia, Mrs. Atkinson asks: 'Did he not make use of an Expression which might have become the Mouth of *Oroondates* himself?—If I remember, the Words were these, "That had he been *Alexander the Great*, he should have thought it more Glory to have wiped off a Tear from the bright Eyes of *Statira*, than to have conquered Fifty Worlds"' (VIII. vii). See also, *Spectator*, No. 377 (13 May 1712).

Scheme I have mentioned, I am convinced you will approve it, and let me see you again as soon as you can.—To-morrow Morning if you will, or at least some time to-morrow. I shall be at Home all Day.'

Jones then, after many Expressions of Thanks, very respect- fully retired; nor could Mrs. *Fitzpatrick* forbear making him a Present of a Look at parting, by which if he had understood nothing, he must have had no Understanding in the Language of the Eyes. In Reality it confirmed his Resolution of returning to her no more; for faulty as he hath hitherto appeared in this History, his whole Thoughts were now so confined to his *Sophia*, that I believe no Woman upon Earth could have now drawn him into an Act of Inconstancy.

Fortune however, who was not his Friend, resolved, as he in- tended to give her no second Opportunity, to make the best of this; and accordingly produced the tragical Incident which we are now in sorrowful Notes to record.

CHAPTER X

The Consequence of the preceding Visit.

MR. *Fitzpatrick* having received the Letter before-mentioned, from Mrs. *Western*, and being by that Means acquainted with the Place to which his Wife was retired, returned directly to *Bath*, and thence the Day after set forward to *London*.

The Reader hath been already often informed of the jealous Temper of this Gentleman. He may likewise be pleased to remember the Suspicion which he had conceived of *Jones* at *Upton*, upon his finding him in the Room with Mrs. *Waters*; and though sufficient Reasons had afterwards appeared entirely to clear up that Suspicion, yet now the reading so handsome a Character of Mr. *Jones* from his Wife caused him to reflect that she likewise was in the Inn at the same Time, and jumbled to- gether such a Confusion of Circumstances in a Head which was naturally none of the clearest, that the whole produced that green- ey'd Monster mentioned by *Shakespear* in his Tragedy of *Othello*.[1]

And now as he was enquiring in the Street after his Wife, and

[1] *Othello,* III. iii.

had just received Directions to the Door, unfortunately Mr. *Jones* was issuing from it.

Fitzpatrick did not yet recollect the Face of *Jones*; however seeing a young well-dressed Fellow coming from his Wife, he made directly up to him, and asked him what he had been doing in that House: 'For I am sure,' said he, 'you must have been in it, as I saw you come out of it.'

Jones answered very modestly, 'That he had been visiting a Lady there.' To which *Fitzpatrick* replied, 'What Business have you with the Lady?' Upon which *Jones*, who now perfectly re-membred the Voice, Features, and indeed Coat, of the Gentle-man, cried out,—'Ha, my good Friend! give me your Hand; I hope there is no ill Blood remaining between us upon a small Mistake which happened so long ago.'

'Upon my Soul, Sir,' said *Fitzpatrick*, 'I don't know your Name, nor your Face.' 'Indeed, Sir,' said *Jones*, 'neither have I the Pleasure of knowing your Name, but your Face I very well remember to have seen before, at *Upton*, where a foolish Quarrel happened between us, which, if it is not made up yet, we will now make up over a Bottle.'

'At *Upton*!' cried the other.—'Ha! upon my Soul, I believe your Name is *Jones*.' 'Indeed,' answered he, 'it is.'—'O, upon my Soul,' cries *Fitzpatrick*, 'you are the very Man I wanted to meet.—Upon my Soul I will drink a Bottle with you presently; but first I will give you a great Knock over the Pate. There is for you, you Rascal. Upon my Soul, if you do not give me Satis-faction for that Blow, I will give you another.' And then drawing his Sword, put himself in a Posture of Defence, which was the only Science he understood.

Jones was a little staggered by the Blow which came somewhat unexpectedly; but presently recovering himself he also drew, and tho' he understood nothing of Fencing, prest on so boldly upon *Fitzpatrick* that he beat down his Guard, and sheathed one half of his Sword in the Body of the said Gentleman who had no sooner received it than he stept backwards, dropt the Point of his Sword, and leaning upon it, cried, 'I have Satisfaction enough; I am a dead Man.'

'I hope not,' cries *Jones*, 'but whatever be the Consequence you must be sensible you have drawn it upon yourself.' At this Instant a Number of Fellows rushed in and seized *Jones*, who told them he should make no Resistance, and begged some of them at least would take Care of the wounded Gentleman.

'Ay,' cries one of the Fellows, 'the wounded Gentleman will be taken Care enough of; for I suppose he hath not many Hours to live. As for you, Sir, you have a Month at least good yet.' 'D—n me, *Jack*,' said another, 'he hath prevented his Voyage; he's bound to another Port now;' and many other such Jests was our poor *Jones* made the Subject of, by these Fellows, who were indeed the Gang employed by Lord *Fellamar*, and had dogged him into the House of Mrs. *Fitzpatrick*, waiting for him at the Corner of the Street when this unfortunate Accident happened.

The Officer who commanded this Gang very wisely concluded, that his Business was now to deliver his Prisoner into the Hands of the Civil Magistrate. He ordered him therefore to be carried to a publick House, where having sent for a Constable, he delivered him to his Custody.

The Constable seeing Mr. *Jones* very well drest, and hearing that the Accident had happened in a Duel, treated his Prisoner with great Civility, and, at his Request, dispatched a Messenger to enquire after the wounded Gentleman, who was now at a Tavern under the Surgeon's Hands. The Report brought back was that the Wound was certainly mortal, and there were no Hopes of Life. Upon which the Constable informed *Jones*, that he must go before a Justice. He answered, 'Wherever you please; I am indifferent as to what happens to me, for tho' I am convinced I am not guilty of Murder in the Eye of the Law, yet the Weight of Blood I find intolerable upon my Mind.'

Jones was now conducted before the Justice, where the Surgeon who drest Mr. *Fitzpatrick* appeared, and deposed that he believed the Wound to be mortal; upon which the Prisoner was committed to the *Gatehouse*.[1] It was very late at Night, so that *Jones* would not send for *Partridge* till the next Morning; and as he never shut his Eyes till seven, so it was near twelve before the poor Fellow, who was greatly frightned at not hearing from his Master so long, received a Message which almost deprived him of his Being, when he heard it.

He went to the *Gatehouse* with trembling Knees and a beating Heart, and was no sooner arrived in the Presence of *Jones*,

---

[1] The chief prison for the district of Westminster (pulled down in 1776). It was situated at the east end of Tothill Street facing Westminster Abbey.

than he lamented the Misfortune that had befallen him with many Tears, looking all the while frequently about him in great Terror; for as the News now arrived that Mr. *Fitzpatrick* was dead, the poor Fellow apprehended every Minute that his Ghost would enter the Room. At last he delivered him a Letter, which he had like to have forgot, and which came from *Sophia* by the Hands of *Black George*.

Jones presently dispatched every one out of the Room, and having eagerly broke open the Letter, read as follows.

'You owe the hearing from me again to an Accident which I own surprizes me. My Aunt hath just now shewn me a Letter from you to Lady *Bellaston*, which contains a Proposal of Marriage. I am convinced it is your own Hand; and what more surprizes me is, that it is dated at the very Time when you would have me imagine you was under such Concern on my Account.— I leave you to comment on this Fact. All I desire is, that your Name may never more be mentioned to

S. W.'

Of the present Situation of Mr. *Jones's* Mind, and of the Pangs with which he was now tormented, we cannot give the Reader a better Idea, than by saying his Misery was such, that even *Thwackum* would almost have pitied him. But bad as it is, we shall at present leave him in it, as his good Genius (if he really had any) seems to have done. And here we put an End to the sixteenth Book of our History.

BOOK XVII

Containing three Days.

CHAPTER I

Containing a Portion of introductory Writing.

WHEN a Comic Writer hath made his principal Characters as happy as he can; or when a Tragic Writer hath brought them to the highest Pitch of human Misery, they both conclude their Business to be done, and that their Work is come to a Period.

Had we been of the Tragic Complexion, the Reader must now allow we were very nearly arrived at this Period, since it would be difficult for the Devil, or any of his Representatives on Earth, to have contrived much greater Torments for poor *Jones*, than those in which we left him in the last Chapter; and as for *Sophia*, a good-natured Woman would hardly wish more Uneasiness to a Rival, than what she must at present be supposed to feel. What then remains to complete the Tragedy but a Murder or two, and a few moral Sentences.

But to bring our Favourites out of their present Anguish and Distress, and to land them at last on the Shore of Happiness, seems a much harder Task; a Task indeed so hard that we do not undertake to execute it. In Regard to *Sophia* it is more than probable, that we shall somewhere or other provide a good Husband for her in the End, either *Blifil*, or my Lord, or Somebody else; but as to poor *Jones*, such are the Calamities in which he is at present involved, owing to his Imprudence, by which if a Man doth not become a Felon to the World, he is at least a *Felo de se*;[1] so destitute is he now of Friends, and so persecuted by Enemies, that we almost despair of bringing him to any good; and if our Reader delights in seeing Executions, I think he ought not to lose any Time in taking a first Row at *Tyburn*.[2]

This I faithfully promise, that notwithstanding any Affection which we may be supposed to have for this Rogue, whom we have unfortunately made our Heroe, we will lend him none of that

---

[1] See above, p. 477, n. 1.　　　　　　[2] See above, p. 406, n. 1.

supernatural Assistance with which we are entrusted, upon Condition that we use it only on very important Occasions.[1] If he doth not therefore find some natural Means of fairly extricating himself from all his Distresses, we will do no Violence to the Truth and Dignity of History for his Sake; for we had rather relate that he was hanged at *Tyburn* (which may very probably be the Case) than forfeit our Integrity, or shock the Faith of our Reader.

In this the Antients had a great Advantage over the Moderns. Their Mythology, which was at that Time more firmly believed by the Vulgar than any Religion is at present, gave them always an Opportunity of delivering a favourite Heroe. Their Deities were always ready at the Writer's Elbow, to execute any of his Purposes; and the more extraordinary the Intervention was, the greater was the Surprize and Delight of the credulous Reader. Those Writers could with greater Ease have conveyed a Friend from one Country to another, nay from one World to another, and have brought him back again, than a poor circumscribed Modern can deliver him from a Goal.

The *Arabians* and *Persians* had an equal Advantage in Writing their Tales from the *Genii*[2] and *Fairies*, which they believe in as an Article of their Faith, upon the Authority of the *Koran* itself. But we have none of these Helps. To natural Means alone are we confined; let us try therefore what by these Means may be done for poor *Jones*; though to confess the Truth, something whispers me in the Ear, that he doth not yet know the worst of his Fortune; and that a more shocking Piece of News than any he hath yet heard remains for him in the unopened Leaves of Fate.

---

[1] An allusion to Horace: see above, pp. 397, n. 5; 512. When the condemned Heartfree is luckily reprieved at the eleventh hour in *Jonathan Wild* (IV. vi), Fielding similarly protests that the happy event is 'at least as natural as delightful; for, we assure [the reader], we would rather have suffered half Mankind to be hang'd, than have saved one contrary to the strictest Rules of Writing and Probability'.

[2] 'This word signifies properly the *genus* of rational, *invisible* beings, whether angels, devils, or that intermediate species called *genii*'—so defined in George Sale, trans. *The Koran* (1734), p. 109, n.h. On the genii, see ch. lxxii.

CHAPTER II

The generous and grateful Behaviour of Mrs. Miller.

MR. *Allworthy* and Mrs. *Miller* were just sat down to Breakfast, when *Blifil*, who had gone out very early that Morning,
returned to make one of the Company.

He had not been long seated before he began as follows, 'Good
Lord! my dear Uncle, what do you think hath happened? I
vow I am afraid of telling it you, for fear of shocking you with the
Remembrance of ever having shewn any Kindness to such a Villain.'
'What is the Matter, Child,' said the Uncle, 'I fear I have shewn
Kindness in my Life to the Unworthy more than once. But
Charity doth not adopt the Vices of its Objects.' 'O, Sir,' returned
Blifil, 'it is not without the secret Direction of Providence that
you mention the Word Adoption. Your adopted Son, Sir, that
Jones, that Wretch whom you nourished in your Bosom, hath
proved one of the greatest Villains upon Earth.' 'By all that's
sacred 'tis false,' cries Mrs. *Miller*. 'Mr. *Jones* is no Villain. He
is one of the worthiest Creatures breathing; and if any other
Person had called him Villain, I would have thrown all this
boiling Water in his Face.' Mr. *Allworthy* looked very much
amazed at this Behaviour. But she did not give him Leave to
speak, before turning to him, she cry'd, 'I hope you will not be
angry with me; I would not offend you, Sir, for the World; but
indeed I could not bear to hear him called so.' 'I must own,
Madam,' said *Allworthy* very gravely, 'I am a little surprized to
hear you so warmly defend a Fellow you do not know.' 'O I do
know him, Mr. *Allworthy*,' said she, 'indeed I do; I should be the
most ungrateful of all Wretches if I denied it. O he hath preserved me and my little Family; we have all Reason to bless him
while we live.—And I pray Heaven to bless him, and turn the
Hearts of his malicious Enemies. I know, I find, I see he hath
such.' 'You surprize me, Madam, still more,' said *Allworthy*,
'sure you must mean some other. It is impossible you should have
any such Obligations to the Man my Nephew mentions.' 'Too
surely,' answered she, 'I have Obligations to him of the greatest
and tenderest Kind. He hath been the Preserver of me and mine.
—Believe me, Sir, he hath been abused, grosly abused to you,
I know he hath, or you, whom I know to be all Goodness and

Honour, would not, after the many kind and tender Things I have heard you say of this poor helpless Child, have so disdainfully called him Fellow. Indeed, my best of Friends, he deserves a kinder Appellation from you, had you heard the good, the kind, the grateful Things which I have heard him utter of you; he never mentions your Name but with a Sort of Adoration. In this very Room I have seen him on his Knees, imploring all the Blessings of Heaven upon your Head. I do not love that Child there better than he loves you.'

'I see, Sir, now,' said *Blifil*, with one of those grinning Sneers with which the Devil marks his best Beloved, 'Mrs. *Miller* really doth know him. I suppose you will find she is not the only one of your Acquaintance to whom he hath exposed you. As for my Character, I perceive by some Hints she hath thrown out, he hath been very free with it, but I forgive him.' 'And the Lord forgive you, Sir,' says Mrs. *Miller*, 'we have all Sins enough to stand in Need of his Forgiveness.'

'Upon my Word, Mrs. *Miller*,' said *Allworthy*, 'I do not take this Behaviour of yours to my Nephew, kindly; and I do assure you as any Reflections which you cast upon him must come only from that wickedest of Men, they would only serve, if that were possible, to heighten my Resentment against him: For I must tell you, Mrs. *Miller*, the young Man who now stands before you, hath ever been the warmest Advocate for the ungrateful Wretch whose Cause you espouse. This, I think, when you hear it from my own Mouth, will make you wonder at so much Baseness and Ingratitude.'

'You are deceived, Sir,' answered Mrs. *Miller*, 'if they were the last Words which were to issue from my Lips, I would say you are deceived; and I once more repeat it, the Lord forgive those who have deceived you. I do not pretend to say the young Man is without Faults; but they are all the Faults of Wildness and of Youth; Faults which he may, nay which I am certain he will relinquish, and if he should not, they are vastly over-ballanced by one of the most humane tender honest Hearts that ever Man was blessed with.'

'Indeed, Mrs. *Miller*,' said *Allworthy*, 'had this been related of you, I should not have believed it.' 'Indeed, Sir,' answered she, 'you will believe every Thing I have said, I am sure you will; and when you have heard the Story which I shall tell you, (for

I will tell you all) you will be so far from being offended, that you will own (I know your Justice so well) that I must have been the most despicable and most ungrateful of Wretches, if I had acted any other Part than I have.'

'Well, Madam,' said *Allworthy*, 'I shall be very glad to hear any good Excuse for a Behaviour which I must confess, I think wants an Excuse. And now, Madam, will you be pleased to let my Nephew proceed in his Story without Interruption. He would not have introduced a Matter of slight Consequence with such a Preface. Perhaps even this Story will cure you of your Mistake.'

Mrs. *Miller* gave Tokens of Submission, and then Mr. *Blifil* began thus. 'I am sure, Sir, if you don't think proper to resent the ill Usage of Mrs. *Miller*, I shall easily forgive what affects me only. I think your Goodness hath not deserved this Indignity at her Hands.' 'Well, Child,' said *Allworthy*, 'but what is this new Instance? What hath he done of late?' 'What?' cries *Blifil*, 'notwithstanding all Mrs. *Miller* hath said, I am very sorry to relate, and what you should never have heard from me, had it not been a Matter impossible to conceal from the whole World. In short he hath killed a Man; I will not say murdered,—for perhaps it may not be so construed in Law, and I hope the best for his Sake.'

Allworthy looked shocked, and blessed himself; and then turning to Mrs. *Miller*, he cried, 'Well, Madam, what say you now?'

'Why, I say, Sir,' answered she, 'that I never was more concerned at any Thing in my Life; but, if the Fact be true, I am convinced the Man, who ever he is, was in Fault. Heaven knows there are many Villains in this Town, who make it their Business to provoke young Gentlemen. Nothing but the greatest Provocation could have tempted him; for of all the Gentlemen I ever had in my House, I never saw one so gentle, or so sweet-tempered. He was beloved by every one in the House, and every one who came near it.'

While she was thus running on, a violent Knocking at the Door interrupted their Conversation, and prevented her from proceeding further, or from receiving any Answer; for as she concluded this was a Visiter to Mr. *Allworthy*, she hastily retired, taking with her her little Girl, whose Eyes were all over blubbered at the melancholy News she heard of *Jones*, who used to call her his little Wife, and not only gave her many Playthings, but spent whole Hours in playing with her himself.

Some Readers may perhaps be pleased with these minute Circumstances, in relating of which we follow the Example of *Plutarch*,[1] one of the best of our Brother Historians; and others to whom they may appear trivial, will, we hope, at least pardon them, as we are never prolix on such Occasions.

CHAPTER III

The Arrival of Mr. Western, *with some Matters concerning the Paternal Authority.*

MRS. *Miller* had not long left the Room, when Mr. *Western* entered; but not before a small wrangling Bout had pass'd between him and his Chairmen; for the Fellows who had taken up their Burden at the *Hercules Pillars*, had conceived no Hopes of having any future good Customer in the Squire; and they were moreover farther encouraged by his Generosity, (for he had given them of his own Accord Sixpence more than their Fare) they therefore very boldly demanded another Shilling, which so provoked the Squire, that he not only bestowed many hearty Curses on them at the Door, but retained his Anger after he came into the Room; swearing, that all the *Londoners* were like the Court, and thought of nothing but plundering Country Gentlemen. 'D—n me,' says he, 'if I won't walk in the Rain rather than get into one of their Handbarrows again. They have jolted me more in a Mile than Brown Bess would in a long Fox Chace.'

When his Wrath on this Occasion was a little appeased, he resumed the same passionate Tone on another. 'There,' says he, 'there is fine Business forwards now. The Hounds have changed at last, and when we imagined we had a Fox to deal with, Od-rat-it, it turns out to be a Badger at last.'

'Pray, my good Neighbour,' said *Allworthy*, 'drop your Metaphors, and speak a little plainer.' 'Why then,' says the Squire, 'to tell you plainly, we have been all this Time afraid of a Son of a

---

[1] Beginning his life of Alexander, Plutarch asserts: 'For it is not Histories I am writing but Lives, and in the most illustrious deeds there is not always a manifestation of virtue or vice, nay, a slight thing like a phrase or jest often makes a greater revelation of character than battles ...' (trans. B. Perrin, Loeb Classical Library, 1919). Boswell followed Plutarch's advice in his *Life of Johnson* (1791), where he quotes this passage (G. B. Hill and L. F. Powell, edd. [Oxford, 1934], i. 31–2).

Whore of a Bastard of Somebody's, I don't know who's not I——
And now here is a confounded Son of a Whore of a Lord, who
may be a Bastard too for what I know or care, for he shall never
have a Daughter of mine by my Consent. They have beggared
the Nation, but they shall never beggar me. My Land shall
never be sent over to *Hannover*.'[1]

'You surprize me much, my good Friend,' said *Allworthy*.
'Why, zounds! I am surprized myself,' answered the Squire.
'I went to zee Sister *Western* last Night, according to her own
Appointment, and there I was a had into a whole Room-full of
Women.—There was my Lady Cousin *Bellaston*, and my Lady
Betty, and my Lady *Catharine*, and my Lady I don't know who;
d—n me if ever you catch me among such a Kennel of Hoop-
petticoat B—s. D—n me, I'd rather be run by my own Dogs, as
one *Acton*[2] was, that the Story Book says was turned into a Hare;
and his own Dogs kill'd un, and eat un. Od-rabbet-it, no Mortal
was ever run in such a Manner; if I dodged one Way, one had
me, if I offered to clap back, another snap'd me. O! certainly one
of the greatest Matches in *England*, says one Cousin (here he
attempted to mimic them); A very advantageous Offer indeed,
cries another Cousin (for you must know they be all my Cousins,
thof I never zeed half oum before.) "Surely," says that fat a—se
B——, my Lady *Bellaston*, "Cousin, you must be out of your
Wits to think of refusing such an Offer." '

'Now I begin to understand,' says *Allworthy*, 'some Person
hath made Proposals to Miss *Western*, which the Ladies of
the Family approve, but is not to your Liking.'

'My Liking!' said *Western*, 'how the Devil should it? I tell
you it is a Lord, and those are always Volks whom you know I
always resolved to have nothing to do with. Did unt I refuse a
matter of vorty Years Purchase now for a Bit of Land, which
one oum had a Mind to put into a Park, only because I would
have no Dealings with Lords, and dost think I would marry my
Daughter zu? Besides, ben't I engaged to you, and did I ever
go off any Bargain when I had promised?'

'As to that Point, Neighbour,' said *Allworthy*, 'I entirely release
you from any Engagement. No Contract can be binding between

[1] See above, p. 321, n. 2.

[2] i.e., Actæon. To punish him for spying on her while she bathed, Diana transformed
Actæon into a stag and he was killed by his own hounds (Ovid, *Metamorphoses*, iii. 138 ff.).

Parties who have not a full Power to make it at the Time, nor ever afterwards acquire the Power of fulfilling it.'

'Slud! then,' answered *Western*, 'I tell you I have Power, and I will fulfil it. Come along with me directly to *Doctors Commons*,[1] I will get a Licence; and I will go to Sister and take away the Wench by Force, and she shall ha un, or I will lock her up and keep her upon Bread and Water as long as she lives.'

'Mr. *Western*,' said *Allworthy*, 'shall I beg you will hear my full Sentiments on this Matter?' 'Hear thee! ay to be sure, I will,' answered he. 'Why then, Sir,' cries *Allworthy*, 'I can truly say, without a Compliment either to you or the young Lady, that when this Match was proposed, I embraced it very readily and heartily, from my Regard to you both. An Alliance between two Families so nearly Neighbours, and between whom there had always existed so mutual an Intercourse and good Harmony, I thought a most desirable Event; and with Regard to the young Lady, not only the concurrent Opinion of all who knew her, but my own Observation assured me that she would be an inestimable Treasure to a good Husband. I shall say nothing of her personal Qualifications, which certainly are admirable; her Goodnature, her charitable Disposition, her Modesty are too well known to need any Panegyric: but she hath one Quality which existed in a high Degree in that best of Women, who is now one of the first of Angels, which as it is not of a glaring Kind, more commonly escapes Observation; so little indeed is it remarked, that I want a Word to express it. I must use Negatives on this Occasion. I never heard any thing of Pertness, or what is called Repartee out of her Mouth; no Pretence to Wit, much less to that Kind of Wisdom, which is the Result only of great Learning and Experience; the Affectation of which, in a young Woman, is as absurd as any of the Affectations of an Ape.[2] No dictatorial Sentiments, no judicial Opinions, no profound Criticisms. Whenever I have seen her in the Company of Men, she hath been all Attention, with the Modesty of a Learner, not the Forwardness of a Teacher. You'll pardon me for it, but I once, to try her

---

[1] See above, p. 815, n. 6.

[2] These views of Allworthy are shared by Dr. Harrison in *Amelia* (x. i, iv), who declares to Mrs. Atkinson, the bluestocking, that learning is a masculine virtue, neither useful nor becoming in a woman. Earlier in *Tom Jones* (i. vi), Fielding had remarked on the 'Folly' of Partridge, who gave Jenny Jones a scholarly education and thereby spoiled her for her station in society.

only, desired her Opinion on a Point which was controverted between Mr. *Thwackum* and Mr. *Square*, To which she answered with much Sweetness, "You will pardon me, good Mr. *Allworthy*, I am sure you cannot in Earnest think me capable of deciding any Point in which two such Gentlemen disagree." *Thwackum* and *Square*, who both alike thought themselves sure of a favourable Decision, seconded my Request. She answered with the same good Humour, "I must absolutely be excused; for I will affront neither so much, as to give my Judgment on his Side." Indeed, she always shewed the highest Deference to the Understandings of Men; a Quality, absolutely essential to the making a good Wife. I shall only add, that as she is most apparently void of all Affectation, this Deference must be certainly real.'

Here *Blifil* sighed bitterly; upon which *Western*, whose Eyes were full of Tears at the Praise of *Sophia*, blubbered out, 'Don't be Chicken-hearted, for shat ha her, d——n me, shat ha her, if she was twenty Times as good.'

'Remember your Promise, Sir,' cried *Allworthy*, 'I was not to be interrupted.' 'Well, shat unt,' answered the Squire, 'I won't speak another Word.'

'Now, my good Friend,' continued *Allworthy*, 'I have dwelt so long on the Merit of this young Lady, partly as I really am in Love with her Character, and partly that Fortune (for the Match in that Light is really advantageous on my Nephew's Side) might not be imagined to be my principal View in having so eagerly embraced the Proposal. Indeed I heartily wished to receive so great a Jewel into my Family; but tho' I may wish for many good Things, I would not therefore steal them, or be guilty of any Violence or Injustice to possess myself of them. Now to force a Woman into a Marriage contrary to her Consent or Approbation, is an Act of such Injustice and Oppression, that I wish the Laws of our Country could restrain it; but a good Conscience is never lawless in the worst regulated State, and will provide those Laws for itself, which the Neglect of Legislators hath forgotten to supply. This is surely a Case of that Kind; for is it not cruel, nay impious, to force a Woman into that State against her Will; for her Behaviour in which she is to be accountable to the highest and most dreadful Court of Judicature, and to answer at the Peril of her Soul. To discharge the Matrimonial Duties in an adequate Manner is no easy Task, and shall we lay this Burthen upon a

Woman while we at the same Time deprive her of all that Assistance which may enable her to undergo it? Shall we tear her very Heart from her, while we enjoin her Duties to which a whole Heart is scarce equal. I must speak very plainly here, I think Parents who act in this Manner are Accessaries to all the Guilt which their Children afterwards incur, and of Course must, before a just Judge, expect to partake of their Punishment; but if they could avoid this, good Heaven! is there a Soul who can bear the Thought of having contributed to the Damnation of his Child?

'For these Reasons, my best Neighbour, as I see the Inclinations of this young Lady are most unhappily averse to my Nephew, I must decline any further Thoughts of the Honour you intended him, tho' I assure you I shall always retain the most grateful Sense of it.'

'Well, Sir,' said *Western*, (the Froth bursting forth from his Lips the Moment they were uncorked) 'you cannot say but I have heard you out, and now I expect you'll hear me; and if I don't answer every Word o't, why then I'll consent to gee the Matter up. First then I desire you to answer me one Question, Did not I beget her? Did not I beget her? answer me that. They say indeed it is a wise Father that knows his own Child; but I am sure I have the best Title to her, for I bred her up. But I believe you will allow me to be her Father, and if I be, am I not to govern my own Child? I ask you that, am I not to govern my own Child? And if I am to govern her in other Matters, surely I am to govern her in this which concerns her most. And what am I desiring all this while? Am I desiring her to do any Thing for me? To give me any thing?—Zu much on t'other Side, that I am only desiring her to take away half my Estate now, and t'other half when I die. Well, and what is it all vor? Why is unt it to make her happy? It's enough to make one mad to hear Volks talk; if I was going to marry myself, then she would ha Reason to cry and to blubber; but, on the contrary, han't I offered to bind down my Land in zuch a Manner, that I could not marry if I woud, seeing as narro' Woman upon Earth would ha me. What the Devil in Hell can I do more? I contribute to her Damnation!—Zounds! I'd zee all the World d—d bevore her little Vinger should be hurt. Indeed, Mr. *Allworthy*, you must excuse me, but I am surprized to hear you talk in zuch a Manner, and I must say, take it how you will, that I thought you had more Sense.'

Allworthy resented this Reflection only with a Smile; nor could he, if he would have endeavoured it, have conveyed into that Smile any Mixture of Malice or Contempt. His Smiles at Folly were indeed such as we may suppose the Angels bestow on the Absurdities of Mankind.

Blifil now desired to be permitted to speak a few Words. 'As to using any Violence on the young Lady, I am sure I shall never consent to it. My Conscience will not permit me to use Violence on any one, much less on a Lady for whom, however cruel she is to me, I shall always preserve the purest and sincerest Affection; but yet I have read, that Women are seldom Proof against Perseverance. Why may I not hope then by such Perseverance at last to gain those Inclinations, in which for the future I shall, perhaps, have no Rival; for as for this Lord, Mr. *Western* is so kind to prefer me to him; and sure, Sir, you will not deny but that a Parent hath at least a negative Voice in these Matters; nay I have heard this very young Lady herself say so more than once, and declare, that she thought Children inexcuseable who married in direct Opposition to the Will of their Parents. Besides, though the other Ladies of the Family seem to favour the Pretensions of my Lord, I do not find the Lady herself is inclined to give him any Countenance; alas, I am too well assured she is not; I am too sensible that wickedest of Men remains uppermost in her Heart.'

'Ay, ay, so he does,' cries *Western*.

'But surely,' says *Blifil*, 'when she hears of this Murder which he hath committed, if the Law should spare his Life——'

'What's that,' cries *Western*, 'Murder, hath he committed a Murder, and is there any Hopes of seeing him hanged?—Tol de rol, tol lol de rol.' Here he fell a singing and capering about the Room.

'Child,' says *Allworthy*, 'this unhappy Passion of yours distresses me beyond Measure. I heartily pity you, and would do every fair Thing to promote your Success.'

'I desire no more,' cries *Blifil*. 'I am convinced my dear Uncle hath a better Opinion of me than to think that I myself wou'd accept of more.'

'Lookee,' says *Allworthy*, 'you have my Leave to write, to

visit, if she will permit it,—but I insist on no Thoughts of Violence. I will have no Confinement, nothing of that Kind attempted.'

'Well, well,' cries the Squire, 'nothing of that Kind shall be attempted; we will try a little longer what fair Means will effect; and if this Fellow be but hanged out of the Way—Tol lol de rol. I never heard better News in my Life; I warrant every Thing goes to my Mind.—Do, prithee, dear *Allworthy*, come and dine with me at the *Hercules Pillars*: I have bespoke a Shoulder of Mutton roasted, and a Spare-rib of Pork, and a Fowl and Egg-Sauce. There will be Nobody but ourselves, unless we have a Mind to have the Landlord; for I have sent Parson *Supple* down to *Basingstoke* after my Tobacco Box, which I left at an Inn there, and I would not lose it for the World; for it's an old Acquaintance of above Twenty Years standing. I can tell you Landlord is a vast comical Bitch, you will like un hugely.'

Mr. *Allworthy* at last agreed to this Invitation, and soon after the Squire went off, singing and capering at the Hopes of seeing the speedy tragical End of poor *Jones*.

When he was gone, Mr. *Allworthy* resumed the aforesaid Subject with much Gravity. He told his Nephew, 'he wished with all his Heart he would endeavour to conquer a Passion, in which I cannot,' says he, 'flatter you with any Hopes of succeeding. It is certainly a vulgar Error, that Aversion in a Woman may be conquered by Perseverance. Indifference may, perhaps, sometimes yield to it; but the usual Triumphs gained by Perseverance in a Lover, are over Caprice, Prudence, Affectation, and often an exorbitant Degree of Levity, which excites Women not over-warm in their Constitutions, to indulge their Vanity by prolonging the Time of Courtship, even when they are well-enough pleased with the Object, and resolve (if they ever resolve at all) to make him a very pitiful Amends in the End. But a fixed Dislike, as I am afraid this is, will rather gather Strength, than be conquered by Time. Besides, my dear, I have another Apprehension which you must excuse. I am afraid this Passion which you have for this fine young Creature, hath her beautiful Person too much for its Object, and is unworthy of the Name of that Love, which is the only Foundation of matrimonial Felicity. To admire, to like, and to long for the Possession of a beautiful Woman, without any Regard to her Sentiments towards us, is, I am afraid, too natural: But Love, I believe, is the Child of Love only; at least, I am pretty confident, that to love the Creature who we are assured hates us, is not in Human Nature. Examine your Heart, therefore, thoroughly, my good Boy, and if, upon Examination, you have but the least Suspicion of this Kind, I am sure your own Virtue and Religion will impel you to drive so vicious a Passion from your Heart, and your good Sense will soon enable you to do it without Pain.'

The Reader may pretty well guess *Blifil's* Answer; but if he should be at a Loss, we are not, at present, at Leisure to satisfy him, as our History now hastens on to Matters of higher Importance, and we can no longer bear to be absent from *Sophia*.

CHAPTER IV

An extraordinary Scene between Sophia *and her Aunt.*

THE lowing Heifer, and the bleating Ewe in Herds and Flocks, may ramble safe and unregarded through the Pastures. These are, indeed, hereafter doomed to be the Prey of Man; yet many Years are they suffered to enjoy their Liberty undisturbed. But if a plump Doe be discovered to have escaped from the Forest, and to repose herself in some Field or Grove, the whole Parish is presently alarmed, every Man is ready to set his Dogs after her; and if she is preserved from the rest by the good Squire, it is only that he may secure her for his own eating.

I have often considered a very fine young Woman of Fortune and Fashion, when first found strayed from the Pale of her Nursery, to be in pretty much the same Situation with this Doe. The Town is immediately in an Uproar, she is hunted from Park to Play, from Court to Assembly, from Assembly to her own Chamber, and rarely escapes a single Season from the Jaws of some Devourer or other: For if her Friends protect her from some, it is only to deliver her over to one of their own chusing, often more disagreeable to her than any of the rest: While whole Herds or Flocks of other Women securely, and scarce regarded, traverse the Park, the Play, the Opera, and the Assembly; and though, for the most Part at least, they are at last devoured, yet for a long Time do they wanton in Liberty, without Disturbance or Controul.

Of all these Paragons, none ever tasted more of this Persecution than poor *Sophia*. Her ill Stars were not contented with all that she had suffered on Account of *Blifil*, they now raised her another Pursuer, who seemed likely to torment her no less than the other had done. For though her Aunt was less violent, she was no less assiduous in teazing her, than her Father had been before.

The Servants were no sooner departed after Dinner, than Mrs. *Western*, who had opened the Matter to *Sophia*, informed her, 'That she expected his Lordship that very Afternoon, and intended to take the first Opportunity of leaving her alone with him.' 'If you do, Madam,' answered *Sophia*, with some Spirit, 'I shall take the first Opportunity of leaving him by himself.' 'How! Madam!' cries the Aunt; 'is this the Return you make me for my Kindness, in relieving you from your Confinement at your Father's?' 'You know, Madam,' said *Sophia*, 'the Cause of that Confinement was a Refusal to comply with my Father, in accepting a Man I detested; and will my dear Aunt, who hath relieved me from that Distress, involve me in another equally bad?' 'And do you think then, Madam,' answered Mrs. *Western*, 'that there is no Difference between my Lord *Fellamar* and Mr. *Blifil*?' 'Very little, in my Opinion,' cries *Sophia*; 'and if I must be condemned to one, I would certainly have the Merit of sacrificing myself to my Father's Pleasure.' 'Then my Pleasure I find,' said the Aunt, 'hath very little Weight with you; but that Consideration shall not move me. I act from nobler Motives. The View of aggrandizing my Family, of ennobling yourself is what I proceed upon. Have you no Sense of Ambition? Are there no Charms in the Thoughts of having a Coronet on your Coach?' 'None, upon my Honour,' said *Sophia*. 'A Pincushion upon my Coach would please me just as well.' 'Never mention Honour,' cries the Aunt. 'It becomes not the Mouth of such a Wretch. I am sorry, Niece, you force me to use these Words; but I cannot bear your groveling Temper; you have none of the Blood of the *Westerns* in you. But however mean and base your own Ideas are, you shall bring no Imputation on mine. I will never suffer the World to say of me, that I encouraged you in refusing one of the best Matches in *England*; a Match which,

besides its Advantage in Fortune, would do Honour to almost
any Family, and hath indeed, in Title, the Advantage of ours.'
'Surely,' says *Sophia*, 'I am born deficient, and have not the Senses
with which other People are blessed: There must be certainly
some Sense which can relish the Delights of Sound and Show,
which I have not: For surely Mankind would not labour so much,
nor sacrifice so much for the obtaining; nor would they be so
elate and proud with possessing what appeared to them, as it
doth to me, the most insignificant of all Trifles.'

'No, no, Miss,' cries the Aunt; 'you are born with as many
Senses as other People; but I assure you, you are not born with a
sufficient Understanding to make a Fool of me, or to expose my
Conduct to the World. So I declare this to you upon my Word,
and you know, I believe, how fixed my Resolutions are, unless you
agree to see his Lordship this Afternoon, I will, with my own
Hands, deliver you Tomorrow Morning to my Brother, and will
never henceforth interfere with you, nor see your Face again.'
Sophia stood a few Moments silent after this Speech, which was
uttered in a most angry and peremptory Tone; and then bursting
into Tears, she cry'd, 'Do with me, Madam, whatever you please;
I am the most miserable, undone Wretch upon Earth; if my
dear Aunt forsakes me, where shall I look for a Protector?'—
'My dear Niece,' cries she, 'you will have a very good Protector
in his Lordship; a Protector, whom nothing but a Hankering
after that vile Fellow *Jones* can make you decline.' 'Indeed,
Madam,' said *Sophia*, 'you wrong me. How can you imagine,
after what you have shewn me, if I had ever any such Thoughts,
that I should not banish them for ever. If it will satisfy you, I
will receive the Sacrament upon it, never to see his Face again.'—
'But Child, dear Child,' said the Aunt, 'be reasonable: Can you
invent a single Objection?'—'I have already, I think, told you a
sufficient Objection,' answered *Sophia*.—'What?' cries the Aunt;
'I remember none.' 'Sure, Madam,' said *Sophia*, 'I told you he
had used me in the rudest and vilest Manner.' 'Indeed, Child,'
answered she, 'I never heard you, or did not understand you:—
But what do you mean by this rude and vile Manner?' 'Indeed,
Madam,' says *Sophia*, 'I am almost ashamed to tell you. He
caught me in his Arms, pulled me down upon the Settee, and
thrust his Hand into my Bosom, and kissed it with such Violence, that I have the Mark upon my left Breast at this Moment.'

—'Indeed!' said Mrs. *Western*. 'Yes indeed, Madam,' answered *Sophia*; 'my Father luckily came in at that Instant, or Heaven knows what Rudeness he intended to have proceeded to.' 'I am astonished and confounded,' cries the Aunt. 'No Woman of the Name of *Western* hath been ever treated so, since we were a Family. I would have torn the Eyes of a Prince out, if he had attempted such Freedoms with me. It is impossible: Sure, *Sophia*, you must invent this to raise my Indignation against him.' 'I hope, Madam,' said *Sophia*, 'you have too good an Opinion of me, to imagine me capable of telling an Untruth. Upon my Soul it is true.' 'I should have stabbed him to the Heart had I been present,' returned the Aunt. 'Yet surely he could have no dishonourable Design: It is impossible; he durst not: Besides, his Proposals shew he had not; for they are not only honourable but generous. I don't know; the Age allows too great Freedoms. A distant Salute is all I would have allowed before the Ceremony. I have had Lovers formerly, not so long ago neither; several Lovers, tho' I never would consent to Marriage, and I never encouraged the least Freedom. It is a foolish Custom, and what I never would agree to. No Man kissed more of me than my Cheek. It is as much as one can bring oneself to give Lips up to a Husband; and, indeed, could I ever have been persuaded to marry, I believe I should not have soon been brought to endure so much.' 'You will pardon me, dear Madam,' said *Sophia*, 'if I make one Observation: You own you have had many Lovers, and the World knows it, even if you should deny it. You refused them all, and I am convinced one Coronet at least among them.' 'You say true, dear *Sophy*,' answered she; 'I had once the Offer of a Title.' 'Why then,' said *Sophia*, 'will you not suffer me to refuse this once?' 'It is true, Child,' said she, 'I have refused the Offer of a Title; but it was not so good an Offer; that is, not so very, very good an Offer.'—'Yes, Madam,' said *Sophia*; 'but you have had very great Proposals from Men of vast Fortunes. It was not the first, nor the second, nor the third advantageous Match that offered itself.' 'I own it was not,' said she. 'Well, Madam,' continued *Sophia*, 'and why may not I expect to have a second perhaps better than this? You are now but a young Woman, and I am convinced would not promise to yield to the first Lover of Fortune, nay, or of Title too. I am a very young Woman, and sure I need not despair.' 'Well, my dear,

dear *Sophy*,' cries the Aunt, 'what would you have me say?'
'Why I only beg that I may not be left alone, at least this Evening:
Grant me that, and I will submit, if you think, after what is past,
I ought to see him in your Company.' 'Well, I will grant it,'
cries the Aunt. '*Sophy*, you know I love you, and can deny you
nothing. You know the Easiness of my Nature; I have not always
been so easy. I have been formerly thought cruel; by the Men I
mean. I was called the cruel *Parthenissa*.¹ I have broke many a
Window that has had Verses to the cruel *Parthenissa* in it. *Sophy*,
I was never so handsome as you, and yet I had something of you
formerly. I am a little altered. Kingdoms and States, as *Tully
Cicero* says in his Epistles,² undergo Alterations, and so must the
human Form.' Thus run she on for near half an Hour upon
herself, and her Conquests and her Cruelty, till the Arrival of
my Lord, who, after a most tedious Visit, during which Mrs.
Western never once offered to leave the Room, retired, not much
more satisfied with the Aunt than with the Niece. For *Sophia*
had brought her Aunt into so excellent a Temper, that she consented to almost every Thing her Niece said; and agreed, that a
little distant Behaviour might not be improper to so forward a
Lover.

Thus *Sophia* by a little well directed Flattery, for which
surely none will blame her, obtained a little Ease for herself, and,
at least, put off the evil Day. And now we have seen our Heroine
in a better Situation than she hath been for a long Time before,
we will look a little after Mr. *Jones*, whom we left in the most
deplorable Situation that can well be imagined.

¹ The eminently chaste and beautiful heroine of a romance (1654–69) by Roger Boyle,
the first Earl of Orrery (1621–79). Because of its romantic associations, Bridget in Steele's
Tender Husband (1705), II. i, prefers the name 'Parthenissa' to her own.

² If Mrs. Western can be thought to have in fact read Cicero's *Epistulae ad Familiares*,
wherein reflections on political change abound, she may recall v. xvii. 3: 'remember, that,
though a mortal, you are yet a man; in other words, to bear philosophically our common
lot of fickle change and chance, which no single one of us can either avoid or vouch for,
to defy sorrow and misfortune with a stout heart; and to reflect that in our state, as in all
others that have risen to empire, the like calamities have befallen the bravest and best of
men . . .' (trans. W. G. Williams, Loeb Classical Library, 1958). Cf. also I. ix. 21, V. xvi. 2–3
and *passim*.

CHAPTER V

Mrs. Miller *and Mr.* Nightingale *visit* Jones *in the Prison.*

WHEN Mr. *Allworthy* and his Nephew went to meet Mr. *Western*, Mrs. *Miller* set forwards to her Son-in-Law's Lodgings, in order to acquaint him with the Accident which had befallen his Friend *Jones*; but he had known it long before from *Partridge*, (for *Jones*, when he left Mrs. *Miller*, had been furnished with a Room in the same House with Mr. *Nightingale*.) The good Woman found her Daughter under great Affliction on Account of Mr. *Jones*, whom having comforted as well as she could, she set forwards to the *Gatehouse*, where she heard he was, and where Mr. *Nightingale* was arrived before her.

The Firmness and Constancy of a true Friend is a Circumstance so extremely delightful to Persons in any Kind of Distress, that the Distress itself, if it be only temporary and admits of Relief, is more than compensated by bringing this Comfort with it. Nor are Instances of this Kind so rare, as some superficial and inaccurate Observers have reported. To say the Truth, Want of Compassion is not to be numbered among our general Faults. The black Ingredient which fouls our Disposition is Envy. Hence our Eye is seldom, I am afraid, turned upward to those who are manifestly greater, better, wiser, or happier than ourselves, without some Degree of Malignity; while we commonly look downwards on the Mean and Miserable, with sufficient Benevolence and Pity. In Fact, I have remarked, that most of the Defects which have discovered themselves in the Friendships within my Observation have arisen from Envy only; a hellish Vice; and yet one from which I have known very few absolutely exempt. But enough of a Subject which, if pursued, would lead me too far.

Whether it was that Fortune was apprehensive lest *Jones* should sink under the Weight of his Adversity, and that she might thus lose any future Opportunity of tormenting him; or whether she really abated somewhat of her Severity towards him, she seemed a little to relax her Persecution, by sending him the Company of two such faithful Friends, and what is perhaps more rare, a faithful Servant. For *Partridge*, tho' he had many Imperfections, wanted not Fidelity; and tho' Fear would not suffer him to be hanged for his Master, yet the World, I believe, could not have bribed him to desert his Cause.

While *Jones* was expressing great Satisfaction in the Presence of his Friends, *Partridge* brought an Account that Mr. *Fitzpatrick* was still alive, tho' the Surgeon declared that he had very little Hopes. Upon which *Jones* fetching a deep Sigh, *Nightingale* said to him; 'My dear *Tom*, why should you afflict yourself so upon an Accident, which, whatever be the Consequence, can be attended with no Danger to you, and in which your Conscience cannot accuse you of having been in the least to blame. If the Fellow should die, what have you done more than taken away the Life of a Ruffian in your own Defence? So will the Coroner's Inquest certainly find it; and then you will be easily admitted to Bail: And though you must undergo the Form of a Trial, yet it is a Trial which many Men would stand for you for a Shilling.' 'Come, come, Mr. *Jones*,' says Mrs. *Miller*, 'cheer yourself up. I knew you could not be the Aggressor, and so I told Mr. *Allworthy*, and so he shall acknowledge too before I have done with him.'

Jones gravely answered, 'That whatever might be his Fate, he should always lament the having shed the Blood of one of his Fellow-Creatures, as one of the highest Misfortunes which could have befallen him. But I have another Misfortune of the tenderest Kind.—O! Mrs. *Miller*, I have lost what I held most dear upon Earth.' 'That must be a Mistress,' said Mrs. *Miller*. 'But come, come; I know more than you imagine;' (for indeed *Partridge* had blabbed all) 'and I have heard more than you know. Matters go better, I promise you, than you think; and I would not give *Blifil* Sixpence for all the Chance which he hath of the Lady.'

'Indeed, my dear Friend, indeed,' answered *Jones*, 'you are an entire Stranger to the Cause of my Grief. If you was acquainted with the Story, you wou'd allow my Case admitted of no Comfort. I apprehend no Danger from *Blifil*. I have undone myself.' 'Don't despair,' replied Mrs. *Miller*; 'you know not what a Woman can do, and if any Thing be in my Power, I promise you I will do it to serve you. It is my Duty. My Son, my dear Mr. *Nightingale*, who is so kind to tell me he hath Obligations to you on the same Account, knows it is my Duty. Shall I go to the Lady myself? I will say any Thing to her you would have me say.'

'Thou best of Women,' cries *Jones*, taking her by the Hand, 'talk not of Obligations to me;—but as you have been so kind to mention it, there is a Favour which, perhaps, may be in your Power. I see you are acquainted with the Lady (how you came by your Information I know not) who sits indeed very near my Heart. If you could contrive to deliver this, (giving her a Paper from his Pocket) I shall for ever acknowledge your Goodness.'

'Give it me,' said Mrs. *Miller*. 'If I see it not in her own Possession before I sleep, may my next Sleep be my last. Comfort yourself, my good young Man; be wise enough to take Warning from past Follies, and I warrant all shall be well, and I shall yet see you happy with the most charming young Lady in the World; for so I hear from every one she is.'

'Believe me, Madam,' said he, 'I do not speak the common Cant of one in my unhappy Situation. Before this dreadful Accident happened, I had resolved to quit a Life of which I was become sensible of the Wickedness as well as Folly. I do assure you, notwithstanding the Disturbances I have unfortunately occasioned in your House, for which I heartily ask your Pardon, I am not an abandoned Profligate. Though I have been hurried into Vices, I do not approve a vicious Character; nor will I ever, from this Moment, deserve it.'

Mrs. *Miller* expressed great Satisfaction in these Declarations, in the Sincerity of which she averred she had an entire Faith; and now, the Remainder of the Conversation past in the joint Attempts of that good Woman and Mr. *Nightingale*, to cheer the dejected Spirits of Mr. *Jones*, in which they so far succeeded, as to leave him much better comforted and satisfied than they found him; to which happy Alteration nothing so much contributed as the kind Undertaking of Mrs. *Miller*, to deliver his Letter to *Sophia*, which he despaired of finding any Means to accomplish: For when *Black George* produced the last from *Sophia*, he informed *Partridge*, that she had strictly charged him, on pain of having it communicated to her Father, not to bring her any Answer. He was moreover not a little pleased, to find he had so warm an Advocate to Mr. *Allworthy* himself in this good Woman, who was in Reality one of the worthiest Creatures in the World.

After about an Hour's Visit from the Lady, (for *Nightingale* had been with him much longer) they both took their leave promising to return to him soon; during which Mrs. *Miller* said, she hoped to bring him some good News from his Mistress, and Mr. *Nightingale* promised to enquire into the State of Mr. *Fitzpatrick's* Wound, and likewise to find out some of the Persons who were present at the Rencounter.

The former of these went directly in quest of *Sophia*, whither we likewise shall now attend her.

CHAPTER VI

In which Mrs. Miller *pays a Visit to* Sophia.

ACCESS to the young Lady was by no means difficult; for as she lived now on a perfect friendly Footing with her Aunt, she was at full Liberty to receive what Visitants she pleased.

Sophia was dressing, when she was acquainted that there was a Gentlewoman below to wait on her. As she was neither afraid, nor ashamed, to see any of her own Sex, Mrs. *Miller* was immediately admitted.

Curt'sies, and the usual Ceremonials between Women who are Strangers to each other being past, *Sophia* said, 'I have not the Pleasure to know you, Madam.' 'No Madam,' answered Mrs. *Miller*, 'and I must beg Pardon for intruding upon you. But when you know what has induced me to give you this Trouble, I hope ——' 'Pray, what is your Business, Madam?' said *Sophia*, with a little Emotion. 'Madam, we are not alone,' replied Mrs. *Miller*, in a low Voice. 'Go out, *Betty*,' said *Sophia*.

When *Betty* was departed, Mrs. *Miller* said, 'I was desired, Madam, by a very unhappy young Gentleman to deliver you this Letter.' *Sophia* changed Colour when she saw the Direction, well knowing the Hand, and after some Hesitation, said—'I could not conceive, Madam, from your Appearance, that your Business had been of such a Nature.—Whomever you brought this Letter from I shall not open it. I should be sorry to entertain an unjust Suspicion of any one; but you are an utter Stranger to me.'

'If you will have Patience, Madam,' answered Mrs. *Miller*, 'I will acquaint you who I am, and how I came by that Letter.' 'I have no Curiosity, Madam, to know any thing,' cries *Sophia*, 'but I must insist on your delivering that Letter back to the Person who gave it you.'

Mrs. *Miller* then fell upon her Knees, and in the most passionate Terms, implored her Compassion; to which *Sophia* answered: 'Sure, Madam, it is surprizing you should be so very strongly interested in the Behalf of this Person. I would not think, Madam——' 'No, Madam,' says Mrs. *Miller*, 'you shall not think any thing but the Truth. I will tell you all, and you will not wonder that I am interested. He is the best natured Creature that ever was born.'—She then began and related the Story of Mr. *Enderson*.—After this she cried, 'This, Madam, this is his Goodness; but I have much more tender Obligations to him. He hath preserved my Child.'—Here after shedding some Tears, she related every thing concerning that Fact, suppressing only those Circumstances which would have most reflected on her Daughter, and concluded with saying, 'Now, Madam, you shall judge whether I can ever do enough for so kind, so good, so generous a young Man, and sure he is the best and worthiest of all Human Beings.'

The Alterations in the Countenance of *Sophia*, had hitherto been chiefly to her Disadvantage, and had inclined her Complexion to too great Paleness; but she now waxed redder if possible, than Vermilion, and cry'd, 'I know not what to say, certainly what arises from Gratitude cannot be blamed.—But what Service can my reading this Letter do your Friend, since I am resolved never——' Mrs. *Miller* fell again to her Entreaties, and begged to be forgiven, but she could not, she said, carry it back. 'Well, Madam,' says *Sophia*, 'I cannot help it, if you will force it upon me.—Certainly you may leave it whether I will or no.' What *Sophia* meant, or whether she meant any thing, I will not presume to determine; but Mrs. *Miller* actually understood this as a Hint, and presently laying the Letter down on the Table took her Leave, having first begged Permission to wait again on *Sophia*, which Request had neither Assent nor Denial.

The Letter lay upon the Table no longer than till Mrs. *Miller* was out of Sight; for then *Sophia* opened and read it.

This Letter did very little Service to his Cause; for it consisted of little more than Confessions of his own Unworthiness, and bitter Lamentations of Despair, together with the most solemn Protestations of his unalterable Fidelity to *Sophia*, of which he said, he hoped to convince her if he had ever more the Honour of being admitted to her Presence; and that he could account for the Letter to Lady *Bellaston*, in such a Manner, that though it would not intitle him to her Forgiveness, he hoped at least to obtain it from her Mercy. And concluded with vowing that nothing was ever less in his Thoughts than to marry Lady *Bellaston*.

Though *Sophia* read the Letter twice over with great Attention, his Meaning still remained a Riddle to her, nor could her Invention suggest to her any Means to excuse *Jones*. She certainly remained very angry with him, though indeed Lady *Bellaston* took up so much of her Resentment that her gentle Mind had but little left to bestow on any other Person.

That Lady was most unluckily to dine this very Day with her Aunt *Western*, and in the Afternoon, they were all three by Appointment to go together to the Opera, and thence to Lady *Thomas Hatchet's* Drum. *Sophia* would have gladly been excused from all, but she would not disoblige her Aunt; and as to the Arts of counterfeiting Illness, she was so entirely a Stranger to them, that it never once entered into her Head. When she was drest, therefore, down she went, resolved to encounter all the Horrours of the Day, and a most disagreeable one it proved; for Lady *Bellaston* took every Opportunity very civilly and slily to insult her; to all which her Dejection of Spirits disabled her from making any Return; and indeed, to confess the Truth, she was at the very best but an indifferent Mistress of Repartee.

Another Misfortune which befel poor *Sophia*, was the Company of Lord *Fellamar*, whom she met at the Opera, and who attended her to the Drum. And though both Places were too publick to admit of any Particularities, and she was farther relieved by the Musick at the one Place, and by the Cards at the other, she could not however enjoy herself in his Company: for there is something of Delicacy in Women, which will not suffer them to be ever easy in the Presence of a Man whom they know to have Pretensions to them, which they are disinclined to favour.

Having in this Chapter twice mentioned a Drum, a Word which our Posterity, it is hoped, will not understand in the Sense it is here applied, we shall, notwithstanding our present Haste, stop a Moment to describe the Entertainment here meant, and the rather as we can in a Moment describe it.

A Drum then is an Assembly of well dressed Persons of both Sexes, most of whom play at Cards, and the rest do nothing at all; while the Mistress of the House performs the Part of the Landlady at an Inn, and like the Landlady of an Inn prides herself in the Number of her Guests, though she doth not always, like her, get any Thing by it.

No wonder then as so much Spirits must be required to support any Vivacity in these Scenes of Dulness, that we hear Persons of Fashion eternally complaining of the Want of them; a Complaint confined entirely to upper Life. How insupportable must we imagine this Round of Impertinence to have been to *Sophia*, at this time; how difficult must she have found it to force the Appearance of Gaiety into her Looks, when her Mind dictated nothing but the tenderest Sorrow, and when every Thought was charged with tormenting Ideas.

Night, however at last, restored her to her Pillow, where we will leave her to soothe her Melancholy at least, though incapable we fear of Rest, and shall pursue our History, which something whispers us is now arrived at the Eve of some great Event.

CHAPTER VII

A pathetic Scene between Mr. Allworthy *and Mrs.* Miller.

MRS. *Miller* had a long Discourse with Mr. *Allworthy* at his Return from Dinner, in which she acquainted him with *Jones's* having unfortunately lost all which he was pleased to bestow on him at their Separation; and with the Distresses to which that Loss had subjected him; of all which she had received a full Account from the faithful Retailer *Partridge*. She then explained the Obligations she had to *Jones*; not that she was entirely explicit with regard to her Daughter; for though she had the utmost Confidence in Mr. *Allworthy*, and though there could be no Hopes of keeping an Affair secret, which was unhappily known to more than half a Dozen; yet she could not prevail with herself to mention those Circumstances which reflected most on the Chastity of poor *Nancy*; but smothered that Part of her Evidence as cautiously as if she had been before a

Judge, and the Girl was now on her Trial for the Murder of a Bastard.

Allworthy said, there were few Characters so absolutely vicious as not to have the least Mixture of Good in them. 'However,' says he, 'I cannot deny but that you had some Obligations to the Fellow, bad as he is, and I shall therefore excuse what hath past already, but must insist you never mention his Name to me more; for I promise you, it was upon the fullest and plainest Evidence that I resolved to take the Measures I have taken.' 'Well, Sir,' says she, 'I make not the least doubt, but Time will shew all Matters in their true and natural Colours, and that you will be convinced this poor young Man deserves better of you than some other Folks that shall be nameless.'

'Madam,' cries *Allworthy*, a little ruffled, 'I will not hear any Reflections on my Nephew, and if you ever say a Word more of that Kind, I will depart from your House that Instant. He is the worthiest and best of Men; and I once more repeat it to you, he hath carried his Friendship to this Man to a blameable Length, by too long concealing Facts of the blackest Die. The Ingratitude of the Wretch to this good young Man is what I most resent; for, Madam, I have the greatest Reason to imagine he had laid a Plot to supplant my Nephew in my Favour, and to have disinherited him.'

'I am sure, Sir,' answered Mrs. *Miller*, a little frightened (for though Mr. *Allworthy* had the utmost Sweetness and Benevolence in his Smiles, he had great Terrour in his Frowns) 'I shall never speak against any Gentleman you are pleased to think well of. I am sure, Sir, such Behaviour would very little become me, especially when the Gentleman is your nearest Relation; but, Sir, you must not be angry with me, you must not indeed, for my good Wishes to this poor Wretch. Sure, I may call him so now, though once you would have been angry with me, if I had spoke of him with the least Disrespect. How often have I heard you call him your Son? How often have you prattled to me of him with all the Fondness of a Parent? Nay, Sir, I cannot forget the many tender Expressions, the many good Things you have told me of his Beauty, and his Parts, and his Virtues; of his Good-nature and Generosity.—I am sure, Sir, I cannot forget them: For I find them all true. I have experienced them in my own Cause. They have preserved my Family. You must pardon my

Tears, Sir, indeed you must, when I consider the cruel Reverse of Fortune which this poor Youth, to whom I am so much obliged, hath suffered; when I consider the Loss of your Favour, which I know he valued more than his Life, I must, I must lament him. If you had a Dagger in your Hand, ready to plunge into my Heart, I must lament the Misery of one whom you have loved, and I shall ever love.'

Allworthy was pretty much moved with this Speech, but it seemed not to be with Anger: For after a short Silence, taking Mrs. *Miller* by the Hand, he said very affectionately to her; 'Come, Madam, let us consider a little about your Daughter. I cannot blame you, for rejoicing in a Match which promises to be advantageous to her; but you know this Advantage, in a great Measure, depends on the Father's Reconciliation. I know Mr. *Nightingale* very well, and have formerly had Concerns with him; I will make him a Visit, and endeavour to serve you in this Matter. I believe he is a worldly Man; but as this is an only Son, and the Thing is now irretrievable, perhaps he may in Time be brought to Reason. I promise you I will do all I can for you.'

Many were the Acknowledgments which the poor Woman made to *Allworthy*, for this kind and generous Offer, nor could she refrain from taking this Occasion again to express her Gratitude towards *Jones*, to whom, said she, I owe the Opportunity of giving you, Sir, this present Trouble. *Allworthy* gently stopped her; but he was too good a Man to be really offended with the Effects of so noble a Principle as now actuated Mrs. *Miller*; and indeed had not this new Affair inflamed his former Anger against *Jones*, it is possible he might have been a little softened towards him by the Report of an Action which Malice itself could not have derived from an evil Motive.

Mr. *Allworthy* and Mrs. *Miller* had been above an Hour together, when their Conversation was put an End to by the Arrival of *Blifil*, and another Person, which other Person was no less than Mr. *Dowling*, the Attorney, who was now become a great Favourite with Mr. *Blifil*, and whom Mr. *Allworthy*, at the Desire of his Nephew, had made his Steward, and had likewise recommended him to Mr. *Western*, from whom the Attorney received a Promise of being promoted to the same Office upon the first Vacancy; and in the mean Time was employed in transacting some Affairs which the Squire then had in *London*, in Relation to a Mortgage.

This was the principal Affair which then brought Mr. *Dowling* to Town, therefore he took the same Opportunity to charge himself with some Money for Mr. *Allworthy*, and to make a Report to him of some other Business; in all which as it was of much too dull a Nature to find any Place in this History, we will leave the Uncle, Nephew, and their Lawyer concerned, and resort to other Matters.

CHAPTER VIII

Containing various Matters.

BEFORE we return to Mr. *Jones*, we will take one more View of *Sophia*.

Though that young Lady had brought her Aunt into great good Humour by those soothing Methods, which we have before related, she had not brought her in the least to abate of her Zeal for the Match with Lord *Fellamar*; this Zeal was now inflamed by Lady *Bellaston*, who had told her the preceding Evening, that she was well satisfied from the Conduct of *Sophia*, and from her Carriage to his Lordship, that all Delays would be dangerous, and that the only Way to succeed, was to press the Match forward with such Rapidity, that the young Lady should have no Time to reflect, and be obliged to consent, while she scarce knew what she did. In which Manner, she said, one half of the Marriages among People of Condition were brought about. A Fact very probably true, and to which I suppose is owing the mutual Tenderness which afterwards exists among so many happy Couples.

A Hint of the same Kind was given by the same Lady to Lord *Fellamar*; and both these so readily embraced the Advice that the very next Day was, at his Lordship's Request, appointed by Mrs. *Western* for a private Interview between the young Parties. This was communicated to *Sophia* by her Aunt, and insisted upon in such high Terms, that, after having urged every Thing she possibly could invent against it, without the least Effect, she at last agreed to give the highest Instance of Complaisance which any young Lady can give, and consented to see his Lordship.

As Conversations of this Kind afford no great Entertainment, we shall be excused from reciting the whole that past at this Interview; in which, after his Lordship had made many Declarations of the most pure and ardent Passion, to the silent, blushing *Sophia*; she at last collected all the Spirits she could raise, and with a trembling low Voice, said, 'My Lord, you must be yourself conscious whether your former Behaviour to me hath been consistent with the Professions you now make.' 'Is there,' answered he, 'no Way by which I can attone for Madness? What I did, I am afraid must have too plainly convinced you, that the Violence of Love had deprived me of my Senses.' 'Indeed, my Lord,' said she, 'it is in your Power to give me a Proof of an Affection which I much rather wish to encourage, and to which I should think myself more beholden.' 'Name it, Madam,' said my Lord, very warmly.—'My Lord,' says she, looking down upon her Fan, 'I know you must be sensible how uneasy this pretended Passion of yours hath made me.'—'Can you be so cruel to call it pretended?' says he. 'Yes, my Lord,' answered *Sophia*, 'all Professions of Love to those whom we persecute, are most insulting Pretences. This Pursuit of yours is to me a most cruel Persecution; nay, it is taking a most ungenerous Advantage of my unhappy Situation.' 'Most lovely, most adorable Charmer, do not accuse me,' cries he, 'of taking an ungenerous Advantage, while I have no Thoughts but what are directed to your Honour and Interest, and while I have no View, no Hope, no Ambition but to throw myself, Honour, Fortune, every Thing at your Feet.' 'My Lord,' says she, 'it is that Fortune and those Honours which give you the Advantage of which I complain. These are the Charms which have seduced my Relations, but to me they are Things indifferent. If your Lordship will merit my Gratitude, there is but one Way.'—'Pardon me, divine Creature,' said he, 'there can be none. All I can do for you is so much your due, and will give me so much Pleasure, that there is no room for your Gratitude.'—'Indeed, my Lord,' answered she, 'you may obtain my Gratitude, my good Opinion, every kind Thought and Wish which it is in my Power to bestow, nay you may obtain them with Ease; for sure to a generous Mind it must be easy to grant my Request. Let me beseech you then, to cease a Pursuit, in which you can never have any Success. For your own Sake as well as mine, I entreat this Favour; for sure you are too noble to have any Pleasure in tormenting an unhappy Creature. What can your Lordship propose but Uneasiness to yourself, by a Perseverance, which, upon my Honour, upon my Soul, cannot, shall not prevail with me, whatever Distresses you may drive me to.' Here my Lord fetched a deep Sigh, and then said,— 'Is it then, Madam, that I am so unhappy to be the Object of your Dislike and Scorn; or will you pardon me if I suspect there is some other?'—Here he hesitated, and *Sophia* answered with some Spirit, 'My Lord, I shall not be accountable to you for the Reasons of my Conduct. I am obliged to your Lordship for the generous Offer you have made; I own it is beyond either my Deserts or Expectations; yet I hope, my Lord, you will not insist on my Reasons, when I declare I cannot accept it.' Lord *Fellamar* returned much to this, which we do not perfectly understand, and perhaps it could not all be strictly reconciled either to Sense or Grammar; but he concluded his ranting Speech with saying, 'That if she had pre-engaged herself to any Gentleman, however unhappy it would make him, he should think himself bound in Honour to desist.' Perhaps my Lord laid too much Emphasis on the Word Gentleman; for we cannot else well account for the Indignation with which he inspired *Sophia*, who, in her Answer, seemed greatly to resent some Affront he had given her.

While she was speaking, with her Voice more raised than usual, Mrs. *Western* came into the Room, the Fire glaring in her Cheeks, and the Flames bursting from her Eyes. 'I am ashamed,' says she, 'my Lord, of the Reception which you have met with. I assure your Lordship we are all sensible of the Honour done us; and I must tell you, Miss *Western*, the Family expect a different Behaviour from you.' Here my Lord interfered on Behalf of the young Lady, but to no Purpose; the Aunt proceeded till *Sophia* pulled out her Handkerchief, threw herself into a Chair, and burst into a violent Fit of Tears.

The Remainder of the Conversation between Mrs. *Western* and his Lordship, till the latter withdrew, consisted of bitter Lamentations on his Side, and on hers of the strongest Assurances that her Niece should and would consent to all he wished. 'Indeed, my Lord,' says she, 'the Girl hath had a foolish Education, neither adapted to her Fortune nor her Family. Her Father, I am sorry to say it, is to blame for every Thing. The Girl hath silly Country

Notions of Bashfulness. Nothing else, my Lord, upon my Honour; I am convinced she hath a good Understanding at the Bottom, and will be brought to Reason.'

This last Speech was made in the Absence of *Sophia*, for she had sometime before left the Room with more Appearance of Passion than she had ever shewn on any Occasion; and now his Lordship, after many Expressions of Thanks to Mrs. *Western*, many ardent Professions of Passion which nothing could conquer, and many Assurances of Perseverance which Mrs. *Western* highly encouraged, took his Leave for this Time.

Before we relate what now passed between Mrs. *Western* and *Sophia*, it may be proper to mention an unfortunate Accident which had happened, and which had occasioned the Return of Mrs. *Western* with so much Fury as we have seen.

The Reader then must know, that the Maid who at present attended on *Sophia*, was recommended by Lady *Bellaston*, with whom she had lived for some Time in the Capacity of a Combbrush; she was a very sensible Girl, and had received the strictest Instructions to watch her young Lady very carefully. These Instructions, we are sorry to say, were communicated to her by Mrs. *Honour*, into whose Favour Lady *Bellaston* had now so ingratiated herself, that the violent Affection which the good Waiting-Woman had formerly borne to *Sophia*, was entirely obliterated by that great Attachment which she had to her new Mistress.

Now when Mrs. *Miller* was departed, *Betty* (for that was the Name of the Girl) returning to her young Lady, found her very attentively engaged in reading a long Letter, and the visible Emotions which she betrayed on that Occasion, might have well accounted for some Suspicions which the Girl entertained; but indeed they had yet a stronger Foundation, for she had overheard the whole Scene which passed between *Sophia* and Mrs. *Miller*.

Mrs. *Western* was acquainted with all this Matter by *Betty*, who, after receiving many Commendations, and some Rewards for her Fidelity, was ordered, that if the Woman who brought the Letter, came again, she should introduce her to Mrs. *Western* herself.

Unluckily Mrs. *Miller* returned at the very time when *Sophia* was engaged with his Lordship. *Betty*, according to Order, sent her directly to the Aunt; who being Mistress of so many Circumstances relating to what had past the Day before, easily imposed upon the poor Woman to believe that *Sophia* had communicated the whole Affair; and so pumped every thing out of her which she knew, relating to the Letter, and relating to *Jones*.

This poor Creature might indeed be called Simplicity itself. She was one of that Order of Mortals, who are apt to believe every thing which is said to them; to whom Nature hath neither indulged the offensive nor defensive Weapons of Deceit, and who are consequently liable to be imposed upon by any one, who will only be at the Expence of a little Falshood for that Purpose. Mrs. *Western* having drained Mrs. *Miller* of all she knew, which indeed was but little, but which was sufficient to make the Aunt suspect a great deal, dismissed her, with Assurances that *Sophia* would not see her, that she would send no Answer to the Letter, nor ever receive another; nor did she suffer her to depart, without a handsome Lecture on the Merits of an Office, to which she could afford no better Name than that of Procuress.—

This discovery had greatly discomposed her Temper, when coming into the Apartment next to that in which the Lovers were, she overheard *Sophia* very warmly protesting against his Lordship's Addresses. At which the Rage already kindled, burst forth, and she rushed in upon her Niece in a furious Manner, as we have already described together with what past at that time till his Lordship's Departure.

No sooner was Lord *Fellamar* gone, than Mrs. *Western* returned to *Sophia*, whom she upbraided in the most bitter Terms, for the ill Use she had made of the Confidence reposed in her; and for her Treachery in conversing with a Man, with whom she had offered but the Day before to bind herself in the most solemn Oath, never more to have any Conversation. *Sophia* protested she had maintained no such Conversation. 'How! Miss *Western*,' said the Aunt, 'will you deny your receiving a Letter from him yesterday?' 'A Letter, Madam,' answered *Sophia*, somewhat surprized. 'It is not very well bred, Miss,' replies the Aunt, 'to repeat my Words. I say a Letter, and I insist upon your shewing it me immediately.' 'I scorn a Lie, Madam,' said *Sophia*, 'I did receive a Letter, but it was without my Desire, and indeed I may say against my Consent.' 'Indeed, indeed, Miss,' cries the Aunt, 'you ought to be ashamed of owning you had received it at all; but where is the Letter? for I will see it.'

To this peremptory Demand *Sophia* paused some Time before she returned an Answer; and at last only excused herself by declaring she had not the Letter in her Pocket, which was indeed true; upon which her Aunt losing all manner of Patience, asked her Niece this short Question, whether she would resolve to marry Lord *Fellamar* or no? to which she received the strongest Negative. Mrs. *Western* then replied with an Oath, or something very like one, that she would early the next Morning deliver her back into her Father's Hands.

Sophia then began to reason with her Aunt in the following manner; 'Why, Madam, must I of Necessity be forced to marry at all? consider how cruel you would have thought it in your own Case, and how much kinder your Parents were in leaving you to your Liberty. What have I done to forfeit this Liberty? I will never marry contrary to my Father's Consent, nor without asking yours.—And when I ask the Consent of either improperly it will be then time enough to force some other Marriage upon me.' 'Can I bear to hear this,' cries Mrs. *Western*, 'from a Girl, who hath now a Letter from a Murderer in her Pocket?' 'I have no such Letter, I promise you,' answered *Sophia*; 'and if he be a *Murderer*, he will soon be in no Condition to give you any further Disturbance.' 'How, Miss *Western*,' said the Aunt, 'have you the Assurance to speak of him in this Manner, to own your Affection for such a Villain to my Face!' 'Sure, Madam,' said *Sophia*, 'you put a very strange Construction on my Words.' 'Indeed, Miss *Western*,' cries the Lady, 'I shall not bear this Usage; you have learnt of your Father this manner of treating me; he hath taught you to give me the Lie. He hath totally ruined you by his false System of Education; and please Heaven he shall have the Comfort of its Fruits: For once more I declare to you, that to-morrow Morning I will carry you back. I will withdraw all my Forces from the Field, and remain henceforth, like the wise King of *Prussia*,[1] in a State of perfect Neutrality. You are both too wise to

---

[1] Frederick the Great (1712–84). In order to pursue the war against France more effectually, the Pelham administration was eager to end the hostilities between England's Austrian allies and Prussia. This goal was accomplished when the Treaty of Dresden was signed in December 1745. To 'this truly great and political Negotiation', Fielding declared, is 'justly to be ascribed the Preservation of *Europe*, and the whole Turn of Affairs abroad' (*The True Patriot*, 22–9 April 1746).

be regulated by my Measures; so prepare yourself, for to-morrow Morning you shall evacuate this House.'

Sophia remonstrated all she could; but her Aunt was deaf to all she said. In this Resolution therefore we must at present leave her, as there seems to be no Hopes of bringing her to change it.

CHAPTER IX

What happened to Mr. Jones *in the Prison.*

MR. *Jones* past above twenty-four melancholy Hours by himself, unless when relieved by the Company of *Partridge*, before Mr. *Nightingale* returned; not that this worthy young Man had deserted or forgot his Friend; for indeed, he had been much the greatest part of the time employed in his Service.

He had heard upon Enquiry that the only Persons who had seen the Beginning of the unfortunate Rencounter, were a Crew belonging to a Man of War, which then lay at *Deptford*. To *Deptford* therefore he went, in search of this Crew, where he was informed that the Men he sought after were all gone ashore. He then traced them from Place to Place, till at last he found two of them drinking together, with a third Person, at a Hedge-Tavern,¹ near *Aldersgate*.

Nightingale desired to speak with *Jones* by himself (for *Partridge* was in the Room when he came in.) As soon as they were alone, *Nightingale* taking *Jones* by the Hand, cried, 'Come, my brave Friend, be not too much dejected at what I am going to tell you, I am sorry I am the Messenger of bad News; but I think it my Duty to tell you.' 'I guess already what that News is,' cries *Jones*. 'The poor Gentleman then is dead.'—'I hope not,' answered *Nightingale*. 'He was alive this Morning; though I will not flatter you; I fear from the Accounts I could get, that his Wound is mortal. But if the Affair be exactly as you told it, your own Remorse would be all you would have reason to apprehend, let what would happen; but forgive me, my dear *Tom*, if I entreat you to make the worst of your Story to your Friends. If you disguise any thing to us, you will only be an Enemy to yourself.'

'What Reason, my dear *Jack*, have I ever given you,' said

---

¹ A tavern frequented by 'low' and disreputable persons.

Jones, 'to stab me with so cruel a Suspicion?' 'Have Patience,' cries *Nightingale*, 'and I will tell you all. After the most diligent Enquiry I could make, I at last met with two of the Fellows who were present at this unhappy Accident, and I am sorry to say, they do not relate the Story so much in your Favour, as you your-self have told it.' 'Why, what do they say?' cries *Jones*. 'Indeed, what I am sorry to repeat, as I am afraid of the Consequence of it to you. They say that they were at too great a Distance to over-hear any Words that passed between you; but they both agree that the first Blow was given by you.' 'Then upon my Soul,' answered *Jones*, 'they injure me. He not only struck me first, but struck me without the least Provocation. What should induce those Villains to accuse me falsely?' 'Nay, that I cannot guess,' said *Nightingale*, 'and if you yourself, and I who am so heartily your Friend, can-not conceive a Reason why they should belie you, what Reason will an indifferent Court of Justice be able to assign why they should not believe them? I repeated the Question to them several times, and so did another Gentleman who was present, who, I believe, is a sea-faring Man, and who really acted a very friendly part by you; for he begged them often to consider, that there was the Life of a Man in the Case; and asked them over and over if they were certain; to which they both answered, that they were, and would abide by their Evidence upon Oath. For Heaven's Sake, my dear Friend, recollect yourself; for if this should appear to be the Fact, it will be your Business to think in time of making the best of your Interest. I would not shock you; but you know, I believe, the Severity of the Law, whatever verbal Provocations may have been given you.' 'Alas! my Friend,' cries *Jones*, 'what Interest hath such a Wretch as I? Besides, do you think I would even wish to live with the Reputation of a Murderer? If I had any Friends, (as alas! I have none) could I have the Confidence to solicit them to speak in the Behalf of a Man condemned for the blackest Crime in Human Nature? Believe me I have no such Hope; but I have some Reliance on a Throne still greatly superior; which will, I am certain, afford me all the Protection I merit.' He then concluded with many solemn and vehement Protestations of the Truth of what he had at first asserted.

The Faith of *Nightingale* was now again staggered, and began to incline to credit his Friend, when Mrs. *Miller* appeared, and made a sorrowful Report of the Success of her Embassy; which when *Jones* had heard, he cried out most heroically, Well, my Friend, I am now indifferent as to what shall happen, at least with Regard to my Life; and if it be the Will of Heaven that I shall make an Atonement with that for the Blood I have spilt, I hope the Divine Goodness will one Day suffer my Honour to be cleared, and that the Words of a dying Man, at least, will be believed, so far as to justify his Character.'

A very mournful Scene now past between the Prisoner and his Friends, at which, as few Readers would have been pleased to be present, so few, I believe, will desire to hear it particularly related. We will, therefore, pass on to the Entrance of the Turnkey, who acquainted *Jones*, that there was a Lady without who desired to speak with him, when he was at Leisure.

Jones declared his Surprize at this Message. He said, 'he knew no Lady in the World whom he could possibly expect to see there.' However, as he saw no Reason to decline seeing any Person, Mrs. *Miller* and Mr. *Nightingale* presently took their Leave, and he gave Orders to have the Lady admitted.

If *Jones* was surprized at the News of a Visit from a Lady, how greatly was he astonished when he discovered this Lady to be no other than Mrs. *Waters*. In this Astonishment then we shall leave him awhile, in order to cure the Surprize of the Reader, who will likewise, probably, not a little wonder at the Arrival of this Lady.

Who this Mrs. *Waters* was, the Reader pretty well knows; what she was he must be perfectly satisfied. He will therefore be pleased to remember, that this Lady departed from *Upton* in the same Coach with Mr. *Fitzpatrick* and the other *Irish* Gentleman, and in their Company travelled to the *Bath*.

Now there was a certain Office in the Gift of Mr. *Fitzpatrick* at that Time vacant, namely, that of a Wife; for the Lady who had lately filled that Office had resigned, or at least deserted her Duty. Mr. *Fitzpatrick* therefore having thoroughly examined Mrs. *Waters* on the Road, found her extremely fit for the Place, which, on their Arrival at *Bath*, he presently conferred upon her, and she, without any Scruple, accepted. As Husband and Wife this Gentleman and Lady continued together all the Time they stayed at *Bath*, and as Husband and Wife they arrived together in Town.

Whether Mr. *Fitzpatrick* was so wise a Man as not to part with one good Thing till he had secured another, which he had at present only a Prospect of regaining; or whether Mrs. *Waters* had so well discharged her Office, that he intended still to retain her as Principal, and to make his Wife (as is often the Case) only her Deputy, I will not say; but certain it is he never mentioned his Wife to her, never communicated to her the Letter given him by Mrs. *Western*, nor ever once hinted his Purpose of re-possessing his Wife; much less did he ever mention the Name of *Jones*. For though he intended to fight with him wherever he met him, he did not imitate those prudent Persons who think a Wife, a Mother, a Sister, or sometimes a whole Family, the safest Seconds on these Occasions. The first Account therefore which she had of all this, was delivered to her from his Lips, after he was brought home from the Tavern where his Wound had been drest.

As Mr. *Fitzpatrick* however had not the clearest Way of telling a Story at any Time, and was now, perhaps, a little more confused than usual, it was some Time before she discovered, that the Gentleman who had given him this Wound was the very same Person from whom her Heart had received a Wound, which, though not of a mortal Kind, was yet so deep that it had left a considerable Scar behind it. But no sooner was she acquainted that Mr. *Jones* himself was the Man who had been committed to the *Gatehouse* for this supposed Murder, than she took the first Opportunity of committing Mr. *Fitzpatrick* to the Care of his Nurse, and hastened away to visit the Conqueror.

She now entered the Room with an Air of Gayety, which received an immediate Check from the melancholy Aspect of poor *Jones*, who started and blessed himself when he saw her. Upon which she said, 'Nay, I do not wonder at your Surprize; I believe you did not expect to see me; for few Gentlemen are troubled here with Visits from any Lady, unless a Wife. You see the Power you have over me, Mr. *Jones*. Indeed I little thought when we parted at *Upton*, that our next Meeting would have been in such a Place.' 'Indeed, Madam,' says *Jones*, 'I must look upon this Visit as kind; few will follow the Miserable, especially to such dismal Habitations.' 'I protest, Mr. *Jones*,' says she, 'I can hardly persuade myself you are the same agreeable Fellow I saw at *Upton*. Why, your Face is more miserable than any Dungeon in the Universe. What can be the Matter with you?' 'I thought,

Madam,' said *Jones*, 'as you knew of my being here, you knew
the unhappy Reason.' 'Pugh,' says she, 'you have pinked a Man
in a Duel, that's all.' *Jones* exprest some Indignation at this
Levity, and spoke with the utmost Contrition for what had happened. To which she answered, 'Well then, Sir, if you take it so
much to Heart, I will relieve you; the Gentleman is not dead;
and, I am pretty confident, is in no Danger of dying. The
Surgeon indeed who first dressed him was a young Fellow, and
seemed desirous of representing his Case to be as bad as possible,
that he might have the more Honour from curing him; but the
King's Surgeon[1] hath seen him since, and says, unless from a
Fever, of which there are at present no Symptoms, he apprehends
not the least Danger of Life.' *Jones* shewed great Satisfaction in
his Countenance at this Report; upon which she affirmed the
Truth of it, adding, 'By the most extraordinary Accident in the
World I lodge at the same House, and have seen the Gentleman;
and I promise you he doth you Justice, and says, Whatever be the
Consequence, that he was entirely the Aggressor, and that you
was not in the least to blame.'

Jones expressed the utmost Satisfaction at the Account which
Mrs. *Waters* brought him. He then informed her of many
Things which she well knew before, as who Mr. *Fitzpatrick* was,
the Occasion of his Resentment, &c. He likewise told her several
Facts of which she was ignorant, as the Adventure of the Muff,
and other Particulars, concealing only the Name of *Sophia*. He
then lamented the Follies and Vices of which he had been guilty;
every one of which, he said, had been attended with such ill
Consequences, that he should be unpardonable if he did not take
Warning, and quit those vicious Courses for the future. He
lastly concluded with assuring her of his Resolution to sin no
more, lest a worse Thing should happen to him.

Mrs. *Waters* with great Pleasantry ridiculed all this, as the
Effects of low Spirits and Confinement. She repeated some
Witticisms about *the Devil when he was sick*,[2] and told him,
'She doubted not but shortly to see him at Liberty, and as lively
a Fellow as ever; and then,' says she, 'I don't question but your

---

[1] Doubtless another compliment to John Ranby (see above, p. 468, n. 1).

[2] 'The Devil was sick, The devil a monk would be; the devil was well, the devil a monk
was he' (W. G. Smith and P. Harvey, *Oxford Dictionary of English Proverbs*, 2nd ed.
[1948], p. 142).

Conscience will be safely delivered of all these Qualms that it is now so sick in breeding.'

Many more Things of this Kind she uttered, some of which it would do her no great Honour, in the Opinion of some Readers, to remember; nor are we quite certain but that the Answers made by *Jones* would be treated with Ridicule by others. We shall therefore suppress the rest of this Conversation, and only observe, that it ended at last with perfect Innocence, and much more to the Satisfaction of *Jones* than of the Lady: For the former was greatly transported with the News she had brought him; but the latter was not altogether so pleased with the penitential Behaviour of a Man whom she had at her first Interview conceived a very different Opinion of from what she now entertained of him.

Thus the Melancholy occasioned by the Report of Mr. *Nightingale* was pretty well effaced; but the Dejection into which Mrs. *Miller* had thrown him still continued. The Account she gave, so well tallied with the Words of *Sophia* herself in her Letter, that he made not the least Doubt but that she had disclosed his Letter to her Aunt, and had taken a fixed Resolution to abandon him. The Torments this Thought gave him were to be equalled only by a Piece of News which Fortune yet had in Store for him, and which we shall communicate in the second Chapter of the ensuing Book.

BOOK XVIII

Containing about Six Days.

CHAPTER I

A Farewel to the Reader.

WE are now, Reader, arrived at the last Stage of our long Journey. As we have therefore travelled together through so many Pages, let us behave to one another like Fellow-Travellers in a Stage-Coach, who have passed several Days in the Company of each other; and who, notwithstanding any Bickerings or little Animosities which may have occurred on the Road, generally make all up at last, and mount, for the last Time, into their Vehicle with Chearfulness and Good-Humour; since, after this one Stage, it may possibly happen to us, as it commonly happens to them, never to meet more.

As I have here taken up this Simile, give me Leave to carry it a little farther. I intend then in this last Book to imitate the good Company I have mentioned in their last Journey. Now it is well known, that all Jokes and Raillery are at this Time laid aside; whatever Characters any of the Passengers have for the Jest-sake personated on the Road, are now thrown off, and the Conversation is usually plain and serious.

In the same Manner, if I have now and then, in the Course of this Work, indulged any Pleasantry for thy Entertainment, I shall here lay it down. The Variety of Matter, indeed, which I shall be obliged to cram into this Book, will afford no Room for any of those ludicrous Observations which I have elsewhere made, and which may sometimes, perhaps, have prevented thee from taking a Nap when it was beginning to steal upon thee. In this last Book thou wilt find nothing (or at most very little) of that Nature. All will be plain Narrative only; and, indeed, when thou hast perused the many great Events which this Book will produce, thou wilt think the Number of Pages contained in it, scarce sufficient to tell the Story.

And now, my Friend, I take this Opportunity (as I shall have no other) of heartily wishing thee well. If I have been an entertaining Companion to thee, I promise thee it is what I have desired. If in any Thing I have offended, it was really without any Intention. Some Things perhaps here said, may have hit thee or thy Friends; but I do most solemnly declare they were not pointed at thee or them. I question not but thou hast been told, among other Stories of me, that thou wast to travel with a very scurrilous Fellow: But whoever told thee so, did me an Injury. No Man detests and despises Scurrility more than myself; nor hath any Man more Reason; for none hath ever been treated with more: And what is a very severe Fate, I have had some of the abusive Writings of those very Men fathered upon me, who in other of their Works have abused me themselves with the utmost Virulence.[1]

All these Works, however, I am well convinced, will be dead long before this Page shall offer itself to thy Perusal: For however short the Period may be of my own Performances, they will most probably outlive their own infirm Author, and the weakly Productions of his abusive Cotemporaries.

[1] From the Preface to the *Miscellanies* (1743) to the 'Advertisement' prefixed to the revised edition of *Jonathan Wild* (1754), Fielding publicly complained against his detractors—and against those in particular who fathered upon him the scurrilous productions of his anonymous contemporaries. In the Preface to the second edition of his sister's novel, *David Simple* (1744), of which it was rumoured he was the author, Fielding protested that he had been 'reputed and reported the Author of half the Scurrility, Bawdy, Treason and Blasphemy, which these few last Years have produced'. Of all these 'Scurrilities' he was especially incensed at the attribution to him of *The Causidicade* (1743), 'that infamous, paultry Libel' against certain prominent members of the legal profession. The real author of this satire (possibly Macnamara Morgan [d. 1762]) signed himself 'Porcupinus Pelagius'. Some years later, when Fielding took up *The Jacobite's Journal* in behalf of the Pelham ministry, this same hack—or so Fielding believed (see *The Jacobite's Journal*, 12 March 1748)—was maligning him in the pages of *Old England*, one of the 'weakly Productions' of the Opposition press. Stung by this abuse, Fielding responded in *The Jacobite's Journal* for 16 April 1748:

'. . . before my Paper hath reached the 20th Number, a heavier Load of Scandal hath been cast upon me, than I believe ever fell to the Share of a single Man. The Author of the Journal was soon guess'd at. . . . Of this [his name] several Writers were no sooner possessed, than they attempted to blacken it with every kind of Reproach; pursued me into private Life, *even to my boyish Years*; where they have given me almost every Vice in Human Nature. Again, they have followed me, with uncommon Inveteracy, into a Profession, in which they have very roundly asserted, that I have neither Business nor Knowledge: And lastly, as an Author, they have affected to treat me with more Contempt, than Mr. *Pope*, who had great Merit and no less Pride in the Character of a Writer, hath thought proper to bestow on the lowest Scribbler of his Time. All this, moreover, they have poured forth in a Vein of Scurrility, which hath disgraced the Press with every abusive Term in our Language.'

CHAPTER II

Containing a very tragical Incident.

WHILE *Jones* was employed in those unpleasant Meditations, with which we left him tormenting himself, *Partridge* came stumbling into the Room with his Face paler than Ashes, his Eyes fixed in his Head, his Hair standing an End, and every Limb trembling. In short, he looked as he would have done had he seen a Spectre, or had he indeed been a Spectre himself.

Jones, who was little subject to Fear, could not avoid being somewhat shocked at this sudden Appearance. He did indeed himself change Colour, and his Voice a little faultered, while he asked him what was the Matter.

'I hope, Sir,' said *Partridge*, 'you will not be angry with me. Indeed I did not listen, but I was obliged to stay in the outward Room. I am sure I wish I had been a hundred Miles off, rather than have heard what I have heard.' 'Why what is the Matter?' said *Jones*. 'The Matter, Sir? O good Heaven!' answered *Partridge*, 'was that Woman who is just gone out, the Woman who was with you at *Upton*?' 'She was, *Partridge*,' cries *Jones*. 'And did you really, Sir, go to Bed with that Woman?' said he trembling.—'I am afraid what past between us is no Secret,' said *Jones*.—'Nay, but pray, Sir, for Heaven's Sake, Sir, answer me,' cries *Partridge*. 'You know I did,' cries *Jones*.—'Why then the Lord have Mercy upon your Soul, and forgive you,' cries *Partridge*; 'but as sure as I stand here alive, you have been a-Bed with your own Mother.'

Upon these Words, *Jones* became in a Moment a greater Picture of Horror than *Partridge* himself. He was indeed, for some Time, struck dumb with Amazement, and both stood staring wildly at each other. At last his Words found Way, and in an interrupted Voice he said—'How! how! What's this you tell me?' 'Nay, Sir,' cries *Partridge*, 'I have not Breath enough left to tell you now—but what I have said is most certainly true.— That Woman who now went out is your own Mother. How unlucky was it for you, Sir, that I did not happen to see her at that Time, to have prevented it? Sure the Devil himself must have contrived to bring about this Wickedness.'

'Sure,' cries *Jones*, 'Fortune will never have done with me, till she hath driven me to Distraction. But why do I blame Fortune? I am myself the Cause of all my Misery. All the dreadful Mischiefs which have befallen me, are the Consequences only of my own Folly and Vice. What thou hast told me, *Partridge*, hath almost deprived me of my Senses. And was Mrs. *Waters* then ―――― But why do I ask? for thou must certainly know her.――If thou hast any Affection for me; nay, if thou hast any Pity, let me beseech thee to fetch this miserable Woman back again to me. O good Heavens! Incest―with a Mother! To what am I reserved?' He then fell into the most violent and frantic Agonies of Grief and Despair, in which *Partridge* declared he would not leave him: But at last having vented the first Torrent of Passion, he came a little to himself; and then having acquainted *Partridge* that he would find this wretched Woman in the same House where the wounded Gentleman was lodged, he dispatched him in quest of her.

If the Reader will please to refresh his Memory, by turning to the Scene at *Upton* in the Ninth Book, he will be apt to admire the many strange Accidents which unfortunately prevented any Interview between *Partridge* and Mrs. *Waters*, when she spent a whole Day there with Mr. *Jones*. Instances of this Kind we may frequently observe in Life, where the greatest Events are produced by a nice Train of little Circumstances; and more than one Example of this may be discovered by the accurate Eye, in this our History.

After a fruitless Search of two or three Hours, *Partridge* returned back to his Master, without having seen Mrs. *Waters*. *Jones*, who was in a State of Desperation at his Delay, was almost raving mad when he brought him this Account. He was not long however in this Condition before he received the following Letter.

'*Sir*,

Since I left you, I have seen a Gentleman, from whom I have learnt something concerning you which greatly surprizes and affects me; but as I have not at present Leisure to communicate a Matter of such high Importance, you must suspend your Curiosity till our next Meeting, which shall be the first Moment I am able to see you. O Mr. *Jones*, little did I think, when I past that happy Day at *Upton*, the Reflection upon which is like to embitter all my future Life, who it was to whom I owed such perfect Happiness. Believe me to be ever sincerely your unfortunate

J. Waters.

P.S. I would have you comfort yourself as much as possible, for Mr. *Fitzpatrick* is in no Manner of Danger; so that whatever other grievous Crimes you may have to repent of, the Guilt of Blood is not among the Number.'

Jones having received the Letter, let it drop (for he was unable to hold it, and indeed had scarce the Use of any one of his Faculties.) *Partridge* took it up, and having received Consent by Silence, read it likewise; nor had it upon him a less sensible Effect. The Pencil, and not the Pen, should describe the Horrors which appeared in both their Countenances. While they both remained speechless, the Turnkey entered the Room, and without taking any Notice of what sufficiently discovered itself in the Faces of them both, acquainted *Jones* that a Man without desired to speak with him. This Person was presently introduced, and was no other than *Black George*.

As Sights of Horror were not so usual to *George* as they were to the Turnkey, he instantly saw the great Disorder which appeared in the Face of *Jones*. This he imputed to the Accident that had happened, which was reported in the very worst Light in Mr. *Western's* Family; he concluded therefore that the Gentleman was dead, and that Mr. *Jones* was in a fair Way of coming to a shameful End. A Thought which gave him much Uneasiness; for *George* was of a compassionate Disposition, and notwithstanding a small Breach of Friendship which he had been over-tempted to commit, was, in the main, not insensible of the Obligations he had formerly received from Mr. *Jones*.

The poor Fellow therefore scarce refrained from a Tear at the present Sight. He told *Jones* he was heartily sorry for his Misfortunes, and begged him to consider if he could be of any Manner of Service. 'Perhaps, Sir,' said he, 'you may want a little Matter of Money upon this Occasion; if you do, Sir, what little I have is heartily at your Service.'

Jones shook him very heartily by the Hand, and gave him many Thanks for the kind Offer he had made; but answered, 'He had not the least Want of that Kind.' Upon which *George* began to press his Services more eagerly than before. *Jones* again thanked him, with Assurances that he wanted nothing which was in the Power of any Man living to give. 'Come, come, my good Master,' answered *George*, 'do not take the Matter so much to Heart. Things may end better than you imagine; to be sure you ant the first Gentleman who hath killed a Man, and yet come off.' 'You are wide of the Matter, *George*,' said *Partridge*, 'the Gentleman is not dead, nor like to die. Don't disturb my Master, at present, for he is troubled about a Matter in which it is not in your Power to do him any good.' 'You don't know what I may be able to do, Mr. *Partridge*,' answered *George*; 'if his Concern is about my young Lady, I have some News to tell my Master.'—'What do you say, Mr. *George?*' cry'd *Jones*, 'Hath any thing lately happened in which my *Sophia* is concerned? My *Sophia*! How dares such a Wretch as I mention her so prophanely.'—'I hope she will be yours yet,' answered *George*.—'Why, yes, Sir, I have something to tell you about her. Madam *Western* hath just brought Madam *Sophia* home, and there hath been a terrible to do. I could not possibly learn the very Right of it; but my Master he hath been in a vast big Passion, and so was Madam *Western*, and I heard her say as she went out of Doors into her Chair, that she would never set her Foot in Master's House again. I don't know what's the Matter, not I, but every thing was very quiet when I came out; but *Robin*, who waited at Supper, said he had never seen the Squire for a long while in such good Humour with young Madam; that he kiss'd her several Times, and swore she should be her own Mistress, and he never would think of confining her any more. I thought this News would please you, and so I slipp'd out, though it was so late, to inform you of it.' Mr. *Jones* assured *George* that it did greatly please him; for though he should never more presume to lift his Eyes towards that incomparable Creature, nothing could so much relieve his Misery as the Satisfaction he should always have in hearing of her Welfare.

The rest of the Conversation which passed at the Visit is not important enough to be here related. The Reader will therefore forgive us this abrupt breaking off, and be pleased to hear how this great good Will of the Squire towards his Daughter was brought about.

Mrs. *Western*, on her first Arrival at her Brother's Lodging, began to set forth the great Honours and Advantages which would accrue to the Family by the Match with Lord *Fellamar*, which her Niece had absolutely refused; in which Refusal, when the Squire took the Part of his Daughter, she fell immediately into the most violent Passion, and so irritated and provoked the Squire, that neither his Patience nor his Prudence could bear it any longer; upon which there ensued between them both so warm a Bout at Altercation, that perhaps the Regions of *Billingsgate*[1] never equalled it. In the Heat of this Scolding Mrs. *Western* departed, and had consequently no Leisure to acquaint the Brother with the Letter which *Sophia* received, which might have possibly produced ill Effects; but to say Truth I believe it never once occurred to her Memory at this Time.

When Mrs. *Western* was gone, *Sophia*, who had been hitherto silent, as well indeed from Necessity as Inclination, began to return the Compliment which her Father had made her, in taking her Part against her Aunt, by taking his likewise against the Lady. This was the first Time of her so doing, and it was in the highest Degree acceptable to the Squire. Again he remembred that Mr. *Allworthy* had insisted on an entire Relinquishment of all violent Means; and indeed as he made no doubt but that *Jones* would be hanged, he did not in the least question succeeding with his Daughter by fair Means; he now therefore once more gave a Loose to his natural Fondness for her, which had such an Effect on the dutiful, grateful, tender and affectionate Heart of *Sophia*, that had her Honour given to *Jones*, and something else perhaps in which he was concerned, been removed, I much doubt whether she would not have sacrificed herself to a Man she did not like, to have obliged her Father. She promised him she would make it the whole Business of her Life to oblige him, and would never marry any Man against his Consent; which brought the old Man so near to his highest Happiness, that he was resolved to take the other Step, and went to Bed completely drunk.

[3] See above, p. 603, n. 1.

CHAPTER III

Allworthy *visits old* Nightingale; *with a strange Discovery that he made on that Occasion.*

THE Morning after these Things had happened, Mr. *Allworthy* went according to his Promise to visit old *Nightingale*, with whom his Authority was so great, that after having sat with him three Hours, he at last prevailed with him to consent to see his Son.

Here an Accident happened of a very extraordinary Kind; one indeed of those strange Chances, whence very good and grave Men have concluded that Providence often interposes in the Discovery of the most secret Villany, in order to caution Men from quitting the Paths of Honesty, however warily they tread in those of Vice.

Mr. *Allworthy*, at his Entrance into Mr. *Nightingale's*, saw *Black George*; he took no Notice of him, nor did *Black George* imagine he had perceived him. However, when their Conversation on the principal Point was over, *Allworthy* asked *Nightingale* whether he knew one *George Seagrim*, and upon what Business he came to his House. 'Yes,' answered *Nightingale*, 'I know him very well, and a most extraordinary Fellow he is, who, in these Days, hath been able to hoard up 500 *l.* from renting a very small Estate of 30 *l.* a Year.' 'And is this the Story which he hath told you?' cries *Allworthy*. 'Nay, it is true, I promise you,' said *Nightingale*, 'for I have the Money now in my own Hands, in five Bank Bills, which I am to lay out either in a Mortgage, or in some Purchase in the North of *England.*' The Bank Bills were no sooner produced at *Allworthy's* Desire, than he blessed himself at the Strangeness of the Discovery. He presently told *Nightingale*, that these Bank Bills were formerly his, and then acquainted him with the whole Affair. As there are no Men who complain more of the Frauds of Business than Highwaymen, Gamesters, and other Thieves of that Kind; so there are none who so bitterly exclaim against the Frauds of Gamesters, &c. as Usurers, Brokers, and other Thieves of this Kind; whether it be that the one Way of cheating is a Discountenance or Reflection upon the other, or that Money, which is the common Mistress of all Cheats, makes them regard each other in the Light of Rivals; but *Nightingale* no sooner heard the Story, than he exclaimed against the Fellow in Terms much severer than the Justice and Honesty of *Allworthy* had bestowed on him.

Allworthy desired *Nightingale* to retain both the Money and the Secret till he should hear farther from him; and if he should in the mean Time see the Fellow, that he would not take the least Notice to him of the Discovery which he had made. He then returned to his Lodgings, where he found Mrs. *Miller* in a very dejected Condition, on Account of the Information she had received from her Son-in-law. Mr. *Allworthy*, with great Chearfulness, told her that he had much good News to communicate; and with little further Preface, acquainted her, that he had brought Mr. *Nightingale* to consent to see his Son, and did not in the least doubt to effect a perfect Reconciliation between them; though he found the Father more sowered by another Accident of the same Kind, which had happened in his Family. He then mentioned the running away of the Uncle's Daughter, which he had been told by the old Gentleman, and which Mrs. *Miller*, and her Son-in-law, did not yet know.

The Reader may suppose Mrs. *Miller* received this Account with great Thankfulness and no less Pleasure; but so uncommon was her Friendship to *Jones*, that I am not certain whether the Uneasiness she suffered for his Sake, did not over-ballance her Satisfaction at hearing a Piece of News tending so much to the Happiness of her own Family; nor whether even this very News, as it reminded her of the Obligations she had to *Jones*, did not hurt as well as please her; when her grateful Heart said to her, 'While my own Family is happy, how miserable is the poor Creature, to whose Generosity we owe the Beginning of all this Happiness.'

Allworthy having left her a little while to chew the Cud (if I may use that Expression) on these first Tidings, told her, he had still something more to impart, which he believed would give her Pleasure. 'I think,' said he, 'I have discovered a pretty considerable Treasure belonging to the young Gentleman, your Friend; but perhaps indeed, his present Situation may be such, that it will be of no Service to him.' The latter Part of the Speech gave Mrs. *Miller* to understand who was meant, and she answered with a Sigh, 'I hope not, Sir.' 'I hope so too,' cries *Allworthy*,

'with all my Heart, but my Nephew told me this Morning, he
had heard a very bad Account of the Affair.'—'Good Heaven!
Sir,' said she—'Well, I must not speak, and yet it is certainly
very hard to be obliged to hold one's Tongue when one hears——'
'Madam,' said *Allworthy*, 'you may say whatever you please, you
know me too well to think I have a Prejudice against any one;
and as for that young Man, I assure you I should be heartily
pleased to find he could acquit himself of every thing, and particularly of this sad Affair. You can testify the Affection I have
formerly borne him. The World, I know, censured me for loving
him so much. I did not withdraw that Affection from him without
thinking I had the justest Cause. Believe me, Mrs. *Miller*, I
should be glad to find I have been mistaken.' Mrs. *Miller* was
going eagerly to reply, when a Servant acquainted her, that a
Gentleman without desired to speak with her immediately.
Allworthy then enquired for his Nephew, and was told, that he
had been for some Time in his Room with the Gentleman who
used to come to him, and whom Mr. *Allworthy*, guessing rightly
to be Mr. *Dowling*, he desired presently to speak with him.

When *Dowling* attended, *Allworthy* put the Case of the Bank-
Notes to him, without mentioning any Name, and asked in what
manner such a Person might be punished. To which *Dowling*
answered, he thought he might be indicted on the Black Act;[1]
but said, as it was a Matter of some Nicety, it would be proper
to go to Counsel. He said he was to attend Counsel presently
upon an Affair of Mr. *Western's*, and if Mr. *Allworthy* pleased
he would lay the Case before them. This was agreed to; and then
Mrs. *Miller* opening the Door, cry'd, 'I ask pardon, I did not
know you had Company;' but *Allworthy* desired her to come in,
saying, he had finished his Business. Upon which Mr. *Dowling*
withdrew, and Mrs. *Miller* introduced Mr. *Nightingale* the
younger, to return thanks for the great Kindness done him by
Allworthy; but she had scarce Patience to let the young Gentleman finish his Speech before she interrupted him, saying, 'O
Sir, Mr. *Nightingale* brings great News about poor Mr. *Jones*,

---

[1] This statute of 1723 (9 George I, cap. 22) was directed chiefly against the so-called
'Blacks', a gang of deer-stalkers and extortionists who blackened their faces and assumed
other disguises to prevent detection. Besides poaching they sent threatening letters demanding money under fictitious names. For another reference, see *The Jacobite's Journal*
(9 January 1748).

he hath been to see the wounded Gentleman, who is out of all Danger of Death, and what is more, declares he fell upon poor Mr. *Jones* himself, and beat him. I am sure, Sir, you would not have Mr. *Jones* be a Coward. If I was a Man myself, I am sure if any Man was to strike me, I should draw my Sword. Do pray, my Dear, tell Mr. *Allworthy*, tell him all yourself.' *Nightingale* then confirmed what Mrs. *Miller* had said; and concluded with many handsome Things of *Jones*, who was, he said, one of the best-natured Fellows in the World, and not in the least inclined to be quarrelsome. Here *Nightingale* was going to cease, when Mrs. *Miller* again begged him to relate all the many dutiful Expressions he had heard him make use of towards Mr. *Allworthy*. 'To say the utmost Good of Mr. *Allworthy*,' cries *Nightingale*, 'is doing no more than strict Justice, and can have no Merit in it; but indeed I must say, no Man can be more sensible of the Obligations he hath to so good a Man, than is poor *Jones*. Indeed, Sir, I am convinced the Weight of your Displeasure is the heaviest Burthen he lies under. He hath often lamented it to me, and hath as often protested in the most solemn Manner he hath never been intentionally guilty of any Offence towards you; nay, he hath sworn he would rather die a Thousand Deaths than he would have his Conscience upbraid him with one disrespectful, ungrateful, or undutiful Thought towards you. But I ask pardon, Sir, I am afraid I presume to intermeddle too far in so tender a Point.' 'You have spoke no more than what a Christian ought,' cries Mrs. *Miller*. 'Indeed, Mr. *Nightingale*,' answered *Allworthy*, 'I applaud your generous Friendship, and I wish he may merit it of you. I confess I am glad to hear the Report you bring from this unfortunate Gentleman; and if that Matter should turn out to be as you represent it (and indeed I doubt nothing of what you say) I may perhaps, in Time, be brought to think better than lately I have of this young Man: For this good Gentlewoman here, nay all who know me, can witness that I loved him as dearly as if he had been my own Son. Indeed I have considered him as a Child sent by Fortune to my Care. I still remember the innocent, the helpless Situation in which I found him. I feel the tender Pressure of his little Hands at this Moment.— He was my Darling, indeed he was.' At which Words he ceased, and the Tears stood in his Eyes.

As the Answer which Mrs. *Miller* made may lead us into fresh

Matters, we will here stop to account for the visible Alteration in Mr. *Allworthy's* Mind, and the Abatement of his Anger to *Jones*. Revolutions of this Kind, it is true, do frequently occur in Histories and dramatic Writers, for no other Reason than because the History or Play draws to a Conclusion,[1] and are justified by Authority of Authors; yet though we insist upon as much Authority as any Author whatever, we shall use this Power very sparingly, and never but when we are driven to it by Necessity, which we do not at present foresee will happen in this Work.

This Alteration then in the Mind of Mr. *Allworthy*, was occasioned by a Letter he had just received from Mr. *Square*, and which we shall give the Reader in the Beginning of the next Chapter.

CHAPTER IV

Containing two Letters in very different Stiles.

'*My worthy Friend*,

I informed you in my last, that I was forbidden the Use of the Waters, as they were found by Experience rather to encrease than lessen the Symptoms of my Distemper.[2] I must now acquaint you with a Piece of News, which, I believe, will afflict my Friends more than it hath afflicted me. Dr. *Harrington*[3] and Dr. *Brewster*[4] have informed me, that there is no Hopes of my Recovery.

---

[1] Cf. above, p. 406.

[2] Perhaps a clue to the nature of Square's illness. According to Dr. Cheyne (see above, p. 605, n. 1), only three sorts of distempers could not be beneficially treated by bathing in the Bath waters, chief among these being 'Those Distempers which impair the *rational* Faculties, or affect the *Head* with Pain, or Giddiness. Because *Hot-bathing* might send Fumes, or Vapours upwards, and so increase these Distempers, such are *hysteric* Disorders, *Convulsions, Epilesies* [sic] &c.' (*An Account of the Nature and Quality of Bath-Waters, the Manner of using them, and the Diseases in which they are proper*, 8th ed. [1737], p. 59).

[3] Dr. Edward Harrington, or Harington (1696–1757), originally of Kelston, Somerset. He attended Wadham College, Oxford (B.A. 1715, M.A. 1718, B.M. 1722, D.M. 1726) and established his practice at Bath. (See Francis J. Poynton, *Memoranda, Historical and Genealogical, Relating to the Parish of Kelston, in the County of Somerset* [1885], pt. iv, pp. 51–8.) Harrington's name appears among the subscribers to Fielding's *Miscellanies* (1743).

[4] Dr. Thomas Brewster (b. 1705), originally of Eardestand, Hereford, was a Fellow of St. John's College, Oxford (B.A. 1728, M.A. 1732, B.M. and D.M. 1738) and practised medicine at Bath. In a modest way he was also a man of letters, being author of a verse translation of Persius' satires (ii, 1733; i, 1741; iii–vi, 1742). Fielding's complimentary reference to him as 'the late ingenious Translator of that obscure Author' ('An Essay on Conversation' [1743]) has been taken to mean that Brewster died shortly before the

'I have somewhere read, that the great Use of Philosophy is to learn to die.[1] I will not therefore so far disgrace mine, as to shew any Surprize at receiving a Lesson which I must be thought to have so long studied. Yet, to say the Truth, one Page of the Gospel teaches this Lesson better than all the Volumes of antient or modern Philosophers.[2] The Assurance it gives us of another

Miscellanies were published (see J. P. de Castro, *N & Q*, 12th Ser., ii [2 December 1916], 441–3), but this inference is improbable. From the phrasing of the advertisement to the second edition of *The Satires of Persius*, it seems clear that Brewster was still alive in 1751, and his name appears among the subscribers to Sarah Fielding's *Lives of Cleopatra and Octavia* (1757). Like Dr. Harrington, Brewster also subscribed to the *Miscellanies*, wherein he would have found, besides the compliment on his abilities as a translator, another on his skill in his profession: in the poem 'TO Miss H—AND at *Bath*. Written *Extempore* in the Pump-Room, 1742', Fielding lamented that the pains inflicted by the lady's eyes, 'Not *Brewster*, Glory of his Art, can cure'.

[1] Cf., among many other possible references, Cicero, *Tusculan Disputations*, I. xxx. 74, xxxi. 75, and Montaigne, *Essayes*, I. xix.

[2] Cf. above, p. 470, n. 1. As these paragraphs will make clear, Square's conversion to Christianity is owing to his new-found conviction that natural philosophy alone is inadequate to establish the doctrine of immortality. During 1745–7 this important issue became the focus of a controversy in which Fielding's friends Warburton (see above, p. 687, n. 3) and Lyttelton (see above, p. 3, n. 1) sought to confute Deism by proving the superiority of the Christian revelation. As early as *The Divine Legation of Moses demonstrated*, i (1738), Warburton had insisted '*that none of the ancient Philosophers believed the Doctrine of a future State of Reward sand Punishments*' (Bk. III, sections 2–3). In 1745 this view was expressly denied by one John Jackson in a tract entitled, *The Belief of a Future State Proved to be a Fundamental Article of the Religion of the Hebrews. And the Doctrine of the ancient Philosophers concerning a Future State, shewn to be consistent with Reason, and their Belief of it demonstrated*. In due course Jackson's thesis was assailed by an anonymous clergyman in *A Critical Inquiry into the Opinions and Practice of the Ancient Philosophers concerning the Nature of the Soul and a Future State* (1747), to which Warburton contributed a Preface. Jackson, in turn, replied to both his antagonists in *A Farther Defence of the Ancient Philosophers* (1747).

What must have especially interested Fielding is that, in the same year, his friend and patron entered the dispute on the side of Warburton. Lyttelton's *Observations on the Conversion and Apostleship of St. Paul* (1747) was designed to explode the position of the freethinkers by a thorough consideration of St. Paul's miraculous conversion to Christianity. Lyttelton remarked that the Apostle was opposed by the proud philosophers of his day, whose wisdom, like that of Square, 'chiefly consisted in vain metaphysical speculations, in logical subtleties, in endless disputes, in high-flown conceits of the perfection and self-sufficiency of human wisdom, in dogmatical positiveness about doubtful opinions, or sceptical doubts about the most clear and certain truths' (*Works*, ed. G. E. Ayscough [1774], p. 299). The absurdities of the philosophers and the views of the theists on 'the nature of God and the soul' are proof of the inadequacy of their beliefs; 'But', Lyttelton continues, 'I will not enlarge on a subject which the most learned Mr. Warburton has handled so well' in *The Divine Legation* and *A Critical Inquiry* (p. 300). In the light of Square's repudiation of his former beliefs and of his confession (in the succeeding paragraph) that he had been 'intoxicated' by the 'Pride of Philosophy', consider Lyttelton's argument:

'If it were necessary to enter particularly into this argument [i.e., Warburton's], I

Life is a much stronger Support to a good Mind, than all the Consolations that are drawn from the Necessity of Nature, the Emptiness or Satiety of our Enjoyments here, or any other Topic of those Declamations which are sometimes capable of arming our Minds with a stubborn Patience in bearing the Thoughts of Death; but never of raising them to a real Contempt of it, and much less of making us think it is a real Good. I would not here be understood to throw the horrid Censure of Atheism, or even the absolute Denial of Immortality, on all who are called Philosophers. Many of that Sect, as well antient as modern, have, from the Light of Reason, discovered some Hopes of a future State; but, in Reality, that Light was so faint and glimmering, and the Hopes were so uncertain and precarious, that it may be justly doubted on which Side their Belief turned. *Plato* himself concludes his *Phædon*, with declaring that his best Arguments amount only to raise a Probability,[1] and *Cicero* himself seems rather to profess an Inclination to believe,[2] than any actual Belief in the Doctrines of Immortality. As to myself, to be very sincere with you, I never was much in earnest in this Faith, till I was in earnest a Christian.

could easily prove, that there was not one of all the different philosophical sects then upon earth, not even the Platonicks themselves, who are thought to favour it most, that did not maintain some opinions fundamentally contrary to those of the gospel. And in this they all agreed, to explode as most unphilosophical, and contrary to every notion that any among them maintained, that great article of the Christian religion, upon which the foundations of it are laid, and without which St. Paul declares to his proselytes, *their faith would be vain* [1 Corinthians 15: 17, 20], the resurrection of the dead with their bodies, of which resurrection Christ was the *first-born* [Colossians 1: 18]. Besides the contrariety of their tenets to those of the gospel, the pride that was common to all the philosophers, was of itself an almost invincible obstacle against the admission of the evangelical doctrines calculated to humble that pride, and teach them, that *professing themselves to be wise they became fools* [Romans 1: 22].' (p. 300.)
(For an earlier allusion to Lyttelton's *Observations* in *Tom Jones*, see above, p. 405, n. 2.)

   1 Cf. *Phaedo*, 107b, 114d.
   2 Cf. *Tusculan Disputations*, 1. ix. 17. Commenting on this passage, Conyers Middleton remarked that though Cicero 'believed *a future state*, was fond of the opinion, and declares himself resolved *never to part with it*; yet he believed it as *probable* onely, not as *certain*' (*The History of the Life of Marcus Tullius Cicero* [1741], ii. 561). He continues, confirming the lesson Square has learned: 'FROM this general view of CICERO's *religion*, one cannot help observing, that the most exalted state of human reason is so far from superseding the use, that it demonstrates the benefit of a *more explicit revelation*: for though the *natural law*, in the perfection, to which it was carried by CICERO, might serve for a sufficient guide to the few, such as himself, of enlarged minds and happy dispositions, yet it . . . could not produce in them at last any thing more than a hope, never a full persuasion' (ii. 562, n. x).

'You will perhaps wonder at the latter Expression; but I assure you it hath not been till very lately, that I could, with Truth, call myself so. The Pride of Philosophy had intoxicated my Reason, and the sublimest of all Wisdom appeared to me, as it did to the *Greeks* of old, to be Foolishness.[1] God hath however been so gracious to shew me my Error in Time, and to bring me into the Way of Truth, before I sunk into utter Darkness for ever.

'I find myself beginning to grow weak, I shall therefore hasten to the main Purpose of this Letter.

'When I reflect on the Actions of my past Life, I know of nothing which sits heavier upon my Conscience, than the Injustice I have been guilty of to that poor Wretch, your adopted Son. I have indeed not only connived at the Villany of others, but been myself active in Injustice towards him. Believe me, my dear Friend, when I tell you on the Word of a dying Man, he hath been basely injured. As to the principal Fact, upon the Misrepresentation of which you discarded him, I solemnly assure you he is innocent. When you lay upon your supposed Death-bed, he was the only Person in the House who testified any real Concern; and what happened afterwards arose from the Wildness of his Joy on your Recovery; and, I am sorry to say it, from the Baseness of another Person (but it is my Desire to justify the Innocent, and to accuse none.) Believe me, my Friend, this young Man hath the noblest Generosity of Heart, the most perfect Capacity for Friendship, the highest Integrity, and indeed every Virtue which can enoble a Man. He hath some Faults, but among them is not to be numbred the least want of Duty or Gratitude towards you. On the contrary, I am satisfied when you dismissed him from your House, his Heart bled for you more than for himself.

'Worldly Motives were the wicked and base Reasons of my concealing this from you so long; to reveal it now I can have no Inducement but the Desire of serving the Cause of Truth, of doing Right to the Innocent, and of making all the Amends in my Power for a past Offence. I hope this Declaration therefore will have the Effect desired, and will restore this deserving young

---

[1] Cf. 1 Corinthians 1: 17–23, contrasting the wisdom of this world with the gospel of 'Christ crucified', which appeared 'unto the Greeks foolishness'. In *Jonathan Wild* (1743), IV. xiv, the Ordinary of Newgate preaches a sermon on this text.

Man to your Favour; the hearing of which, while I am yet alive, will afford the utmost Consolation to,

> *Sir,*
> *Your most obliged,*
> *Obedient humble Servant,*
> Thomas Square.'

The Reader will, after this, scarce wonder at the Revolution so visibly appearing in Mr. *Allworthy*, notwithstanding he received from *Thwackum*, by the same Post, another Letter of a very different Kind, which we shall here add, as it may possibly be the last Time we shall have Occasion to mention the Name of that Gentleman.

'*Sir*,

I am not at all surprized at hearing from your worthy Nephew a fresh Instance of the Villany of Mr. *Square* the Atheist's young Pupil. I shall not wonder at any Murders he may commit; and I heartily pray that your own Blood may not seal up his final Commitment to the Place of Wailing and gnashing of Teeth.

'Though you cannot want sufficient Calls to Repentance for the many unwarrantable Weaknesses exemplified in your Behaviour to this Wretch, so much to the Prejudice of your own lawful Family, and of your Character. I say, tho' these may sufficiently be supposed to prick and goad your Conscience at this Season; I should yet be wanting to my Duty, if I spared to give you some Admonition in order to bring you to a due Sense of your Errors. I therefore pray you seriously to consider the Judgment which is likely to overtake this wicked Villain; and let it serve at least as a Warning to you, that you may not for the future despise the Advice of one who is so indefatigable in his Prayers for your Welfare.

'Had not my Hand been withheld from due Correction, I had scourged much of this diabolical Spirit out of a Boy, of whom from his Infancy I discovered the Devil had taken such entire Possession; but Reflections of this Kind now come too late.

'I am sorry you have given away the Living of *Westerton* so hastily. I should have applied on that Occasion earlier, had I thought you would not have acquainted me previous to the Disposition.—Your Objection to Pluralities is being righteous over-much.[1] If there were any Crime in the Practice, so many godly Men would not agree to it. If the Vicar of *Aldergrove* should die (as we hear he is in a declining Way) I hope you will think of me, since I am certain you must be convinced of my most sincere Attachment to your highest Welfare. A Welfare to which all worthy Considerations are as trifling as the small Tithes mentioned in Scripture[2] are, when compared to the weighty Matters of the Law.

I am, Sir,

Your faithful humble Servant,

Roger Thwackum.'

This was the first Time *Thwackum* ever wrote in this authoritative Stile to *Allworthy*, and of this he had afterwards sufficient Reason to repent, as in the Case of those who mistake the highest Degree of Goodness for the lowest Degree of Weakness. *Allworthy* had indeed never liked this Man. He knew him to be proud and ill-natured; he also knew that his Divinity itself was tinctured with his Temper, and such as in many Respects he himself did by no means approve: But he was at the same Time an excellent Scholar, and most indefatigable in teaching the two Lads. Add to this the strict Severity of his Life and Manners, an unimpeached Honesty, and a most devout Attachment to Religion. So that upon the whole, though *Allworthy* did not esteem nor love the Man, yet he could never bring himself to

---

[1] Ecclesiastes 7: 16: 'Be not righteous over much; neither make thyself over wise: why shouldest thou destroy thyself?' Some years earlier, this text became the focus of an angry controversy between that complacent representative of the Established Church, Dr. Joseph Trapp, and the fiery Methodist, George Whitefield (see above, p. 430, n. 1; also pp. 63, n. 1; 79, n. 4; 93, n. 1; 96, n. 2), who had denounced the worldliness of the Anglican clergy. In 1739 Trapp reproved his antagonist in a series of four sermons entitled, *The Nature, Folly, Sin, and Danger of being Righteous over-much*; Whitefield at once replied in *An Explanatory Sermon on that Mistaken Text, Be not Righteous over-much*. Though Fielding was steadily opposed to Whitefield's theology, he—together with Parson Adams (*Joseph Andrews*, I. xvii)—was in perfect agreement with the Methodist's desire to reform 'the Luxury and Splendour of the Clergy'. In *Shamela* (1741), letter ix, he makes the debauched Arthur Williams preach a specious sermon on Trapp's text; and in *The Champion* (5 April 1740) he sides with Whitefield on this one point: 'without *being righteous over much*, we may, I think, conclude, that if the Clergy are not to abandon all they have to their Ministry, neither are they to get immense Estates by it; and I would recommend it to the Consideration of those who do, whether they do not make a Trade of Divinity?'

[2] Matthew 23: 23: 'Woe unto you, scribes and Pharisees, hypocrites! for ye pay tithe of mint and anise and cummin, and have omitted the weightier *matters* of the law, judgment, mercy, and faith: these ought ye to have done, and not to leave the other undone.'

part with a Tutor to the Boys, who was both by Learning and Industry, extremely well qualified for his Office; and he hoped, that as they were bred up in his own House, and under his own Eye, he should be able to correct whatever was wrong in *Thwackum's* Instructions.

CHAPTER V

In which the History is continued.

M R. *Allworthy*, in his last Speech, had recollected some tender Ideas concerning *Jones*, which had brought Tears into the good Man's Eyes. This Mrs. *Miller* observing, said, 'Yes, yes, Sir, your Goodness to this poor young Man is known, notwithstanding all your Care to conceal it; but there is not a single Syllable of Truth in what those Villains said. Mr. *Nightingale* hath now discovered the whole Matter. It seems these Fellows were employed by a Lord, who is a Rival of poor Mr. *Jones*, to have pressed him on board a Ship.—I assure them I don't know who they will press next. Mr. *Nightingale* here hath seen the Officer himself, who is a very pretty Gentleman, and hath told him all, and is very sorry for what he undertook, which he would never have done had he known Mr. *Jones* to have been a Gentleman; but he was told that he was a common strolling Vagabond.'

Allworthy stared at all this, and declared he was a Stranger to every Word she said. 'Yes, Sir,' answered she, 'I believe you are. —It is a very different Story, I believe, from what those Fellows told the Lawyer.'

'What Lawyer, Madam? what is it you mean?' said *Allworthy*. 'Nay, nay,' said she, 'this is so like you to deny your own Goodness; but Mr. *Nightingale* here saw him.' 'Saw whom, Madam?' answered he. 'Why your Lawyer, Sir,' said she, 'that you so kindly sent to enquire into the Affair.' 'I am still in the Dark, upon my Honour,' said *Allworthy*. 'Why then do you tell him, my dear Sir,' cries she. 'Indeed, Sir,' said *Nightingale*, 'I did see that very Lawyer who went from you when I came into the Room, at an Alehouse in *Aldersgate*, in Company with two of the Fellows who were employed by Lord *Fellamar* to press Mr. *Jones*, and who were by that Means present at the unhappy Rencounter between him and Mr. *Fitzpatrick*.' 'I own, Sir,' said Mrs. *Miller*, 'when I saw this Gentleman come into the Room to you, I told Mr. *Nightingale* that I apprehended you had sent him thither to enquire into the Affair.' *Allworthy* shewed Marks of Astonishment in his Countenance at this News, and was indeed for two or three Minutes struck dumb by it. At last, addressing himself to Mr. *Nightingale*, he said, 'I must confess myself, Sir, more surprized at what you tell me, than I have ever been before at any Thing in my whole Life. Are you certain this was the Gentleman?' 'I am most certain,' answered *Nightingale*. 'At *Aldersgate*?' cries *Allworthy*. 'And was you in Company with this Lawyer and the two Fellows?'—'I was, Sir,' said the other, 'very near half an Hour.'—'Well, Sir,' said *Allworthy*, 'and in what Manner did the Lawyer behave? Did you hear all that past between him and the Fellows?' 'No, Sir,' answered *Nightingale*, 'they had been together before I came.—In my Presence the Lawyer said little; but after I had several Times examined the Fellows, who persisted in a Story directly contrary to what I had heard from Mr. *Jones*, and which I find by Mr. *Fitzpatrick* was a rank Falshood, the Lawyer then desired the Fellows to say nothing but what was the Truth, and seemed to speak so much in Favour of Mr. *Jones*, that when I saw the same Person with you, I concluded your Goodness had prompted you to send him thither.'—'And did you not send him thither?' says Mrs. *Miller*.—'Indeed I did not,' answered *Allworthy*; 'nor did I know he had gone on such an Errand till this Moment.'—'I see it all!' said Mrs. *Miller*: 'Upon my Soul, I see it all! No Wonder they have been closetted so close lately. Son *Nightingale*, let me beg you run for these Fellows immediately—find them out if they are above Ground. I will go myself.'—'Dear Madam,' said *Allworthy*, 'be patient, and do me the Favour to send a Servant up Stairs to call Mr. *Dowling* hither, if he be in the House, or if not, Mr. *Blifil*.' Mrs. *Miller* went out muttering something to herself, and presently returned with an Answer, 'That Mr. *Dowling* was gone; but that the t'other (as she called him) was coming.'

Allworthy was of a cooler Disposition than the good Woman, whose Spirits were all up in Arms in the Cause of her Friend. He was not however without some Suspicions which were near a-kin to hers. When *Blifil* came into the Room, he asked him with a very serious Countenance, and with a less friendly Look than he had ever before given him, 'Whether he knew any Thing of Mr. *Dowling's* having seen any of the Persons who were present at the Duel between *Jones* and another Gentleman?'

There is nothing so dangerous as a Question which comes by Surprize on a Man, whose Business it is to conceal Truth, or to defend Falshood. For which Reason those worthy Personages, whose noble Office it is to save the Lives of their Fellow-Creatures at the *Old-Bailey*, take the utmost Care, by frequent previous Examination, to divine every Question which may be asked their Clients on the Day of Trial, that they may be supply'd with proper and ready Answers, which the most fertile Invention cannot supply in an Instant. Besides, the sudden and violent Impulse on the Blood, occasioned by these Surprizes, causes frequently such an Alteration in the Countenance, that the Man is obliged to give Evidence against himself. And such indeed were the Alterations which the Countenance of *Blifil* underwent from this sudden Question, that we can scarce blame the Eagerness of Mrs. *Miller*, who immediately cry'd out, 'Guilty, upon my Honour! Guilty, upon my Soul!'

Mr. *Allworthy* sharply rebuked her for this Impetuosity; and then turning to *Blifil*, who seemed sinking into the Earth, he said, 'Why do you hesitate, Sir, at giving me an Answer? You certainly must have employed him, for he would not, of his own Accord, I believe, have undertaken such an Errand, and especially without acquainting me.'

Blifil then answered, 'I own, Sir, I have been guilty of an Offence, yet may I hope your Pardon?'—'My Pardon?' said *Allworthy* very angrily.—'Nay, Sir,' answered *Blifil*, 'I knew you would be offended; yet surely my dear Uncle will forgive the Effects of the most amiable of Human Weaknesses. Compassion for those who do not deserve it, I own, is a Crime; and yet it is a Crime from which you yourself are not entirely free. I know I have been guilty of it in more than one Instance to this very Person; and I will own I did send Mr. *Dowling*, not on a vain and fruitless Enquiry, but to discover the Witnesses, and to endeavour to soften their Evidence. This, Sir, is the Truth; which though I intended to conceal from you, I will not deny.'

'I confess,' said *Nightingale*, 'this is the Light in which it appeared to me from the Gentleman's Behaviour.'

'Now, Madam,' said *Allworthy*, 'I believe you will once in your

Life own you have entertained a wrong Suspicion, and are not so angry with my Nephew as you was.'

Mrs. *Miller* was silent; for though she could not so hastily be pleased with *Blifil*, whom she looked upon to have been the Ruin of *Jones*, yet in this particular Instance he had imposed upon her as well as upon the rest; so entirely had the Devil stood his Friend. And, indeed, I look upon the vulgar Observation, *That the Devil often deserts his Friends, and leaves them in the Lurch*, to be a great Abuse on that Gentleman's Character. Perhaps he may sometimes desert those who are only his Cup Acquaintance; or who, at most, are but half his; but he generally stands by those who are thoroughly his Servants, and helps them off in all Extremities till their Bargain expires.

As a conquered Rebellion strengthens a Government,[1] or as Health is more perfectly established by Recovery from some Diseases; so Anger, when removed, often gives new Life to Affection. This was the Case of Mr. *Allworthy*; for *Blifil* having wiped off the greater Suspicion, the lesser, which had been raised by *Square's* Letter, sunk of Course, and was forgotten; and *Thwackum*, with whom he was greatly offended, bore alone all the Reflections which *Square* had cast on the Enemies of *Jones*.

As for that young Man, the Resentment of Mr. *Allworthy* began more and more to abate towards him. He told *Blifil*, 'he did not only forgive the extraordinary Efforts of his Good-Nature, but would give him the Pleasure of following his Example.' Then turning to Mrs. *Miller*, with a Smile which would have become an Angel, he cry'd, 'What say you, Madam; shall we take a Hackney-Coach, and all of us together pay a Visit to your Friend? I promise you it is not the first Visit I have made in a Prison.'

Every Reader, I believe, will be able to answer for the worthy Woman; but they must have a great deal of Good-Nature, and

---

[1] In *A Dialogue between a Gentleman of London . . . and an Honest Alderman of the Country Party* (1747) Fielding had made this same observation, referring to the Hanoverian Establishment and the Pelham ministry after the 'Forty-Five': 'What a Hurricane did we go through, when, besides two great foreign Wars, we had a Rebellion to contend with at Home! What an Advantage did that give to our Enemies! Yet, by the Blessing of God, by the Wisdom of his Majesty, the Valour and Conduct of his Son, and the Care of his Administration, that Danger hath been conquered, and his Throne and Kingdom, nay, I may say, the whole Constitution have gained an additional Strength from the Attempt so wickedly made to overturn them.'

be well acquainted with Friendship, who can feel what she felt on this Occasion. Few, I hope, are capable of feeling what now past in the Mind of *Blifil*; but those who are, will acknowledge, that it was impossible for him to raise any Objection to this Visit. Fortune, however, or the Gentleman lately mentioned above, stood his Friend, and prevented his undergoing so great a Shock: For at the very Instant when the Coach was sent for, *Partridge* arrived, and having called Mrs. *Miller* from the Company, acquainted her with the dreadful Accident lately come to Light; and hearing Mr. *Allworthy's* Intention, begged her to find some Means of stopping him; 'for,' says he, 'the Matter must at all Hazards be kept a Secret from him; and if he should now go, he will find Mr. *Jones* and his Mother, who arrived just as I left him, lamenting over one another the horrid Crime they have ignorantly committed.'

The poor Woman, who was almost deprived of her Senses at this dreadful News, was never less capable of Invention than at present. However, as Women are much readier at this than Men, she bethought herself of an Excuse, and returning to *Allworthy* said, 'I am sure, Sir, you will be surprized at hearing any Objection from me to the kind Proposal you just now made; and yet I am afraid of the Consequence of it, if carried immediately into Execution. You must imagine, Sir, that all the Calamities which have lately befallen this poor young Fellow, must have thrown him into the lowest Dejection of Spirits: And now, Sir, should we all on a sudden fling him into such a violent Fit of Joy, as I know your Presence will occasion, it may, I am afraid, produce some fatal Mischief, especially as his Servant, who is without, tells me he is very far from being well.'

'Is his Servant without?' cries *Allworthy*; 'pray call him hither. I will ask him some Questions concerning his Master.'

Partridge was at first afraid to appear before Mr. *Allworthy*; but was at length persuaded, after Mrs. *Miller*, who had often heard his whole Story from his own Mouth, had promised to introduce him.

Allworthy recollected *Partridge* the Moment he came into the Room, though many Years had passed since he had seen him. Mrs. *Miller* therefore might have spared here a formal Oration, in which indeed she was something prolix: For the Reader, I believe, may have observed already that the good Woman, among other Things, had a Tongue always ready for the Service of her Friends.

'And are you,' said *Allworthy* to *Partridge*, 'the Servant of Mr. *Jones*?' 'I can't say, Sir,' answered he, 'that I am regularly a Servant, but I live with him, an't please your Honour, at present. *Non sum qualis eram,*[1] as your Honour very well knows.'

Mr. *Allworthy* then asked him many Questions concerning *Jones*, as to his Health, and other Matters; to all which *Partridge* answered, without having the least Regard to what was, but considered only what he would have Things appear; for a strict Adherence to Truth was not among the Articles of this honest Fellow's Morality, or his Religion.

During this Dialogue Mr. *Nightingale* took his Leave, and presently after Mrs. *Miller* left the Room, when *Allworthy* likewise dispatched *Blifil*; for he imagined that *Partridge*, when alone with him, would be more explicit than before Company. They were no sooner left in private together, than *Allworthy* began as in the following Chapter.

CHAPTER VI

In which the History is farther continued.

'SURE, Friend,' said the good Man, 'you are the strangest of all Human Beings. Not only to have suffered as you have formerly, for obstinately persisting in a Falshood; but to persist in it thus to the last, and to pass thus upon the World for a Servant of your own Son? What Interest can you have in all this? What can be your Motive?'

'I see, Sir,' said *Partridge*, falling down upon his Knees, 'that your Honour is prepossessed against me, and resolved not to believe any Thing I say, and therefore what signifies my Protestations; but yet there is one above who knows that I am not the Father of this young Man.'

'How!' said *Allworthy*, 'Will you yet deny what you was formerly convicted of upon such unanswerable, such manifest Evidence? Nay, what a Confirmation is your being now found with this very Man, of all which twenty Years ago appeared against you. I thought you had left the Country; nay, I thought

---

[1] See above, p. 829, n. 1.

you had been long since dead.—In what Manner did you know any Thing of this young Man? Where did you meet with him, unless you had kept some Correspondence together. Do not deny this; for I promise you it will greatly raise your Son in my Opinion, to find that he hath such a Sense of filial Duty, as privately to support his Father for so many Years.'

'If your Honour will have Patience to hear me,' said *Partridge*, 'I will tell you all.'—Being bid go on, he proceeded thus: 'When your Honour conceived that Displeasure against me, it ended in my Ruin soon after; for I lost my little School; and the Minister, thinking I suppose it would be agreeable to your Honour, turned me out from the Office of Clerk; so that I had nothing to trust to but the Barber's Shop, which, in a Country Place like that, is a poor Livelihood; and when my Wife died, (for till that Time I received a Pension of 12 *l.* a Year from an unknown Hand, which indeed I believe was your Honour's own, for no Body that ever I heard of doth these Things besides) but as I was saying, when she died, this Pension forsook me; so that now as I owed two or three small Debts, which began to be troublesome to me, (particularly one* which an Attorney brought up by Law-charges from 15*s.* to near 30 *l.*) and as I found all my usual Means of living had forsook me, I packed up my little All as well as I could, and went off.

'The first Place I came to was *Salisbury*, where I got into the Service of a Gentleman belonging to the Law,[1] and one of the

---

* This is a Fact which I knew happen to a poor Clergyman in *Dorsetshire*,[2] by the Villainy of an Attorney, who not contented with the exorbitant Costs to which the poor Man was put by a single Action, brought afterwards another Action on the Judgment, as it is called. A Method frequently used to oppress the poor, and bring Money into the Pockets of Attornies, to the great Scandal of the Law, of the Nation, of Christianity, and even of Human Nature itself.

---

[1] If Fielding intends to compliment an actual acquaintance—and the language here suggests that he does—the most likely possibility is Robert Stillingfleet, the Salisbury attorney whom, in 1737, he twice employed to represent him—once in the conveyance of the estate at East Stour and a second time in defending him against an action (see Cross, i. 240, and J. P. de Castro, *N & Q*, 12th Ser., iii [November 1917], 467). Fielding's biographers have too easily credited a vague tradition that Stillingfleet was the original of Dowling and hence a scoundrel (see Cross, ii. 167–8, and Dudden, ii. 650); but, as de Castro has shown, the evidence, such as it is, all points to Fielding's having trusted this man and respected his abilities as a lawyer.

[2] Perhaps Fielding refers to his good friend and occasional collaborator, William Young (1702 ?–57), who from 1731 to 1740 served as curate of East Stour (a chapelry of Gillingham), the village in Dorset where Fielding grew up. The original of Parson Adams in

best Gentlemen that ever I knew; for he was not only good to me, but I know a thousand good and charitable Acts which he did while I staid with him; and I have known him often refuse Business because it was paultry and oppressive.'—'You need not be so particular,' said *Allworthy*; 'I know this Gentleman, and a very worthy Man he is, and an Honour to his Profession.'—'Well, Sir,' continued *Partridge*, 'from hence I removed to *Lymington*, where I was above three Years in the Service of another Lawyer,[1] who was likewise a very good Sort of a Man, and to be sure one of the merriest Gentlemen in *England*. Well, Sir, at the End of the three Years I set up a little School, and was likely to do well again, had it not been for a most unlucky Accident. Here I kept a Pig; and one Day, as ill Fortune would have it, this Pig broke out, and did a Trespass I think they call it, in a Garden belonging to one of my Neighbours, who was a proud, revengeful Man, and employed a Lawyer, one—one—I can't think of his Name; but he sent for a Writ against me, and had me to Size. When I came there, Lord have Mercy upon me—to hear what the Counsellors said. There was one that told my Lord a Parcel of the confoundedst Lies about me; he said, that I used to drive my Hogs into other Folks Gardens, and a great deal more; and at last he said, He hoped I had at last brought my Hogs to a fair Market. To be sure, one wou'd have thought, that instead of being Owner only of one poor, little Pig, I had been the greatest Hog-Merchant in *England*. Well——' 'Pray,' said *Allworthy*, 'do not be so particular. I have heard nothing of your Son yet.' 'O it was a great many Years,' answered *Partridge*, 'before I saw my Son, as you are pleased to call him.—I went over to *Ireland*

Joseph Andrews, Young was certainly poor enough to fit the description—he had to support a wife and six children on a stipend of £30 a year or less—and, according to one contemporary account, he was so improvident 'as to run into every tradesman's debt, and had went to gaol if [his friends] had not raised money to redeem him' (from a manuscript dated 18 December 1742 and quoted in the *Salisbury and Wiltshire Herald*, 25 February 1837; see the Wesleyan Edition of *Joseph Andrews*, ed. M. C. Battestin [1967], xxi–xxii, n. 2).

[1] As J. Paul de Castro believed (*N & Q*, 12th Ser., i [17 June 1916], 484–5), the allusion may be to Odber Knapton (1696–20 November 1746), attorney, mayor (1727–8), and Town Clerk (1744) of Lymington, Hampshire. Since Odber Knapton was dead when Fielding presumably wrote this passage, de Castro's hypothesis is questionable; but the compliment may be addressed to Knapton's family, particularly his first cousins, the booksellers John and Paul Knapton, to whom there are friendly allusions in *The Champion* (17 June 1740, under 'Index to the Times') and *The True Patriot* (25 March–1 April 1746).

after this, and taught School at *Cork* (for that one Suit ruined me again, and I lay seven Years in *Winchester* Goal.)'—'Well,' said *Allworthy*, 'pass that over till your Return to *England*.'— 'Then, Sir,' said he, 'it was about half a Year ago that I landed at *Bristol*, where I stayed some Time, and not finding it do there, and hearing of a Place between that and *Gloucester*, where the Barber was just dead, I went thither, and there I had been about two Months, when Mr. *Jones* came thither.' He then gave *Allworthy* a very particular Account of their first Meeting, and of every Thing as well as he could remember, which had happened from that Day to this, frequently interlarding his Story with Panegyrics on *Jones*, and not forgetting to insinuate the great Love and Respect which he had for *Allworthy*. He concluded with saying, 'Now, Sir, I have told your Honour the whole Truth:' And then repeated a most solemn Protestation, 'That he was no more the Father of *Jones* than of the Pope of *Rome*;' and imprecated the most bitter Curses on his Head if he did not speak Truth.

'What am I to think of this Matter?' cries *Allworthy*. 'For what Purpose should you so strongly deny a Fact, which I think it would be rather your Interest to own?'—'Nay, Sir,' answered *Partridge*, (for he could hold no longer) 'if your Honour will not believe me, you are like soon to have Satisfaction enough. I wish you had mistaken the Mother of this young Man, as well as you have his Father.'—And now being asked what he meant, with all the Symptoms of Horror both in his Voice and Countenance, he told *Allworthy* the whole Story, which he had a little before expressed such Desire to Mrs. *Miller* to conceal from him.

Allworthy was almost as much shocked at this Discovery as *Partridge* himself had been while he related it. 'Good Heavens!' says he, 'in what miserable Distresses do Vice and Imprudence involve Men! How much beyond our Designs are the Effects of Wickedness sometimes carried!' He had scarce uttered these Words, when Mrs. *Waters* came hastily and abruptly into the Room. *Partridge* no sooner saw her, than he cry'd, 'Here, Sir, here is the very Woman herself. This is the unfortunate Mother of Mr. *Jones*; I am sure she will acquit me before your Honour. —Pray, Madam——'

Mrs. *Waters*, without paying any Regard to what *Partridge* said, and almost without taking any Notice of him, advanced to

Mr. *Allworthy*. 'I believe, Sir, it is so long since I had the Honour
of seeing you, that you do not recollect me.'—'Indeed,' answered
Allworthy, 'you are so very much altered, on many Accounts,
that had not this Man already acquainted me who you are, I
should not have immediately called you to my Remembrance.
Have you, Madam, any particular Business which brings you to
me?'—*Allworthy* spoke this with great Reserve; for the Reader
may easily believe he was not well pleased with the Conduct of this
Lady; neither with what he had formerly heard, nor with what
Partridge had now delivered.

Mrs. *Waters* answered,—'Indeed, Sir, I have very particular
Business with you; and it is such as I can impart only to yourself.
—I must desire therefore the Favour of a Word with you alone;
for I assure you what I have to tell you is of the utmost Importance.'

Partridge was then ordered to withdraw, but before he went,
he begged the Lady to satisfy Mr. *Allworthy* that he was perfectly
innocent. To which she answered—'You need be under no
Apprehension, Sir, I shall satisfy Mr. *Allworthy* very perfectly of
that Matter.'

Then *Partridge* withdrew, and that past between Mr. *Allworthy* and Mrs. *Waters* which is written in the next Chapter.

CHAPTER VII

Continuation of the History.

MRS. *Waters* remaining a few Moments silent, Mr. *Allworthy* could not refrain from saying, 'I am sorry, Madam,
to perceive by what I have since heard, that you have made so
very ill a Use——' 'Mr. *Allworthy*,' says she, interrupting him,
'I know I have Faults, but Ingratitude to you is not one of them.
I never can nor shall forget your Goodness, which I own I have
very little deserved; but be pleased to wave all Upbraiding me at
present, as I have so important an Affair to communicate to you
concerning this young Man, to whom you have given my Maiden
Name of *Jones*.' 'Have I then,' said *Allworthy*, 'ignorantly
punished an innocent Man in the Person of him who hath just
left us? was he not the Father of the Child?'—'Indeed he was

not,' said Mrs. *Waters*. 'You may be pleased to remember, Sir, I formerly told you, you should one Day know; and I acknowledge myself to have been guilty of a cruel Neglect, in not having discovered it to you before.—Indeed I little knew how necessary it was.'—'Well, Madam,' said *Allworthy*, 'be pleased to proceed.' 'You must remember, Sir,' said she, 'a young Fellow, whose Name was *Summer*.' 'Very well,' cries *Allworthy*, 'he was the Son of a Clergyman of great Learning and Virtue, for whom I had the highest Friendship.' 'So it appeared, Sir,' answered she; 'for I believe you bred the young Man up, and maintained him at the University; where, I think, he had finished his Studies, when he came to reside at your House; a finer Man, I must say, the Sun never shone upon; for, besides the handsomest Person I ever saw, he was so genteel, and had so much Wit and good Breeding.' 'Poor Gentleman,' said *Allworthy*, 'he was indeed untimely snatch'd away; and little did I think he had any Sins of this kind to answer for; for I plainly perceive, you are going to tell me he was the Father of your Child.' 'Indeed, Sir,' answered she, 'he was not.' 'How?' said *Allworthy*, 'to what then tends all this Preface?' 'To a Story, Sir,' said she, 'which I am concerned falls to my Lot to unfold to you.—O, Sir, prepare to hear something which will surprize you, will grieve you.' 'Speak,' said *Allworthy*, 'I am conscious of no Crime, and cannot be afraid to hear.'— 'Sir,' said she, 'that Mr. *Summer*, the Son of your Friend, educated at your Expence, who, after living a Year in the House as if he had been your own Son, died there of the small Pox, was tenderly lamented by you, and buried as if he had been your own; that *Summer*, Sir, was the Father of this Child.'—'How!' said *Allworthy*, 'you contradict yourself.'—'That I do not,' answered she, 'he was indeed the Father of this Child, but not by me.' 'Take care, Madam,' said *Allworthy*, 'do not to shun the Imputation of any Crime be guilty of Falsehood. Remember there is one from whom you can conceal nothing, and before whose Tribunal Falsehood will only aggravate your Guilt.' 'Indeed, Sir,' says she, 'I am not his Mother; nor would I now think myself so for the World.' 'I know your Reason,' said *Allworthy*, 'and shall rejoice as much as you to find it otherwise; yet you must remember, you yourself confessed it before me.'—'So far what I confess,' said she, 'was true, that these Hands conveyed the Infant to your Bed, conveyed it thither at the Command of its

Mother; at her Commands I afterwards owned it, and thought myself by her Generosity nobly rewarded, both for my Secrecy and my Shame.' 'Who could this Woman be?' said *Allworthy.*—'Indeed I tremble to name her,' answered Mrs. *Waters.* 'By all this Preparation I am to guess that she was a Relation of mine,' cried he. 'Indeed she was a near one.' At which Words *Allworthy* started, and she continued.—'You had a Sister, Sir.'—'A Sister!' repeated he, looking aghast.—'As there is Truth in Heaven,' cries she, 'your Sister was the Mother of that Child you found between your Sheets.' 'Can it be possible,' cries he, 'good Heavens!' 'Have Patience, Sir,' said Mrs. *Waters*, 'and I will unfold to you the whole Story. Just after your Departure for *London,* Miss *Bridget* came one Day to the House of my Mother. She was pleased to say she had heard an extraordinary Character of me for my Learning and superior Understanding to all the young Women there, so she was pleased to say. She then bid me come to her to the great House; where when I attended, she employed me to read to her. She expressed great Satisfaction in my reading, shewed great Kindness to me, and made me many Presents. At last she began to catechise me on the Subject of Secrecy, to which I gave her such satisfactory Answers, that at last having locked the Door of her Room, she took me into her Closet, and then locking that Door likewise, she said, she should convince me of the vast Reliance she had on my Integrity, by communicating a Secret in which her Honour and consequently her Life was concerned. She then stopt, and after a Silence of a few Minutes, during which she often wiped her Eyes, she enquired of me, if I thought my Mother might safely be confided in. I answered, I would stake my Life on her Fidelity. She then Imparted to me the great Secret which laboured in her Breast, and which, I believe, was delivered with more Pains than she afterwards suffered in Child-birth. It was then contrived, that my Mother and myself only should attend at the Time, and that Mrs. *Wilkins* should be sent out of the way, as she accordingly was to the very furthest Part of *Dorsetshire* to enquire the Character of a Servant; for the Lady had turned away her own Maid near three Months before, during all which Time I officiated about her Person, upon Trial as she said, tho', as she afterwards declared, I was not sufficiently handy for the Place. This and many other such Things which she used to say of me, were all thrown out to prevent any Suspicion which *Wilkins* might hereafter have when I was to own the Child; for she thought it could never be believed she would venture to hurt a young Woman with whom she had intrusted such a Secret. You may be assured, Sir, I was well paid for all these Affronts, which, together with being informed of the Occasion of them, very well contented me. Indeed the Lady had a greater Suspicion of Mrs. *Wilkins* than of any other Person; not that she had the least Aversion to the Gentlewoman, but she thought her incapable of keeping a Secret, especially from you, Sir: For I have often heard Miss *Bridget* say, that if Mrs. *Wilkins* had committed a Murder, she believed she would acquaint you with it. At last the expected Day came, and Mrs. *Wilkins*, who had been kept a Week in Readiness, and put off from Time to Time, upon some Pretence or other, that she might not return too soon, was dispatched. Then the Child was born in the Presence only of myself and my Mother, and was by my Mother conveyed to her own House, where it was privately kept by her till the Evening of your Return, when I, by the Command of Miss *Bridget*, conveyed it into the Bed where you found it. And all Suspicions were afterwards laid asleep by the artful Conduct of your Sister, in pretending Ill-will to the Boy, and that any Regard she shew'd him was out of meer Complaisance to you.' Mrs. *Waters* then made many Protestations of the Truth of this Story, and concluded by saying, 'Thus, Sir, you have at last discovered your Nephew, for so I am sure you will hereafter think him, and I question not but he will be both an Honour and a Comfort to you under that Appellation.' 'I need not, Madam,' said *Allworthy*, 'express my Astonishment at what you have told me; and yet surely you would not, and could not, have put together so many Circumstances to evidence an Untruth. I confess, I recollect some Passages relating to that *Summer*, which formerly gave me a Conceit that my Sister had some Liking to him. I mentioned it to her: For I had such a Regard to the young Man, as well on his own account, as on his Father's, that I should willingly have consented to a Match between them; but she exprest the highest Disdain of my unkind Suspicion, as she called it, so that I never spoke more on the Subject. Good Heavens! well, the Lord disposeth all Things.— Yet sure it was a most unjustifiable Conduct in my Sister to carry this Secret with her out of the World.' 'I promise you, Sir,' said

Mrs. *Waters*, 'she always profest a contrary Intention, and frequently told me she intended one Day to communicate it to you. She said indeed, she was highly rejoiced that her Plot had succeeded so well, and that you had of your own accord taken such a Fancy to the Child, that it was yet unnecessary to make any express Declaration. Oh! Sir, had that Lady lived to have seen this poor young Man turned like a Vagabond from your House; nay, Sir, could she have lived to hear that you had yourself employed a Lawyer to prosecute him for a Murder of which he was not guilty—— Forgive me, Mr. *Allworthy*, I must say it was unkind.—Indeed you have been abused, he never deserved it of you.' 'Indeed, Madam,' said *Allworthy*, 'I have been abused by the Person whoever he was that told you so.' 'Nay, Sir,' said she, 'I would not be mistaken, I did not presume to say you were guilty of any wrong. The Gentleman who came to me, proposed no such Matter: He only said, taking me for Mr. *Fitzpatrick's* Wife, that if Mr. *Jones* had murdered my Husband, I should be assisted with any Money I wanted to carry on the Prosecution, by a very worthy Gentleman, who, he said, was well apprized what a Villain I had to deal with. It was by this Man I found out who Mr. *Jones* was; and this Man, whose Name is *Dowling*, Mr. *Jones* tells me, is your Steward. I discovered his Name by a very odd Accident, for he himself refused to tell it me; but *Partridge*, who met him at my Lodgings the second Time he came, knew him formerly at *Salisbury*.'

'And did this Mr. *Dowling*,' says *Allworthy*, with great Astonishment in his Countenance, 'tell you that I would assist in the Prosecution?'—'No, Sir,' answered she, 'I will not charge him wrongfully. He said, I should be assisted, but he mentioned no Name.—Yet you must pardon me, Sir, if from Circumstances I thought it could be no other.'—'Indeed, Madam,' says *Allworthy*, 'from Circumstances I am too well convinced it was another.—Good Heavens, by what wonderful Means is the blackest and deepest Villany sometimes discovered!—Shall I beg you, Madam, to stay till the Person you have mentioned comes, for I expect him every Minute; nay, he may be perhaps already in the House.' *Allworthy* then stept to the Door, in order to call a Servant, when in came, not Mr. *Dowling*, but the Gentleman who will be seen in the next Chapter.

CHAPTER VIII

Further Continuation.

THE Gentleman who now arrived was no other than Mr. *Western*. He no sooner saw *Allworthy*, than without considering in the least the Presence of Mrs. *Waters*, he began to vociferate in the following Manner. 'Fine Doings at my House! A rare Kettle of Fish I have discovered at last; who the Devil would be plagued with a Daughter?' 'What's the Matter, Neighbour,' said *Allworthy*. 'Matter enough,' answered *Western*, 'when I thought she was a just coming to, nay, when she had in a Manner promised me to do as I would ha her, and when I was a hoped to have had nothing more to do than to have a sent for the Lawyer and finished all. What do you think I have found out? that the little B—— hath bin playing Tricks with me all the while, and carrying on a Correspondence with that Bastard of yours. Sister *Western*, whom I have a quarrelled with upon her Account, sent me Word o't, and I ordered her Pockets to be searched when she was asleep, and here I have got un signed with the Son of a Whore's own Name. I have not had Patience to read half o't, for 'tis longer than one of Parson *Supple's* Sermons; but I find plainly it is all about Love, and indeed what should it be else? I have packed her up in Chamber again, and To-morrow Morning down she goes into the Country, unless she consents to be married directly, and there she shall live in a Garret upon Bread and Water all her Days; and the sooner such a B—— breaks her Heart the better, though d—n her, that I believe is too tough. She will live long enough to plague me.' 'Mr. *Western*,' answered *Allworthy*, 'you know I have always protested against Force, and you yourself consented that none should be used.' 'Ay,' cries he, 'that was only upon Condition that she would consent without. What the Devil and Doctor *Faustus*,[1] shan't I do what I will with my own Daughter, especially when I desire nothing but her own Good?' 'Well, Neighbour,' answered *Allworthy*, 'if you will give me Leave, I will undertake once to argue with the young Lady.' 'Will you,' said *Western*, 'why that

---

[1] For an explanation of the proverbial expression, 'as great as the Devil and Dr. Faustus [or Dr. Foster]', see Defoe's *Political History of the Devil*, 4th ed. [1739], pp. 325–6.

is kind now and neighbourly, and mayhap you will do more than I have been able to do with her; for I promise you she hath a very good Opinion of you.' 'Well, Sir,' said *Allworthy*, 'if you will go Home and release the young Lady from her Captivity, I will wait upon her within this half Hour.'—'But suppose,' said *Western*, 'she should run away with un in the mean Time? for Lawyer *Dowling* tells me there is no Hopes of hanging the Fellow at last, for that the Man is alive, and like to do well, and that he thinks *Jones* will be out of Prison again presently.'—'How,' said *Allworthy*, 'what, did you employ him then to enquire or to do any Thing in that Matter?' 'Not I,' answered *Western*, 'he mentioned it to me just now of his own Accord.'—'Just now!' cries *Allworthy*, 'why where did you see him then? I want much to see Mr. *Dowling*.'—'Why you may see un an you will presently at my Lodgings; for there is to be a Meeting of Lawyers there this Morning, about a Mortgage.—Icod! I shall lose two or dree Thousand Pounds, I believe, by that honest Gentleman, Mr. *Nightingale*.'—'Well, Sir,' said *Allworthy*, 'I will be with you within the half Hour.' 'And do for once,' cries the Squire, 'take a Fool's Advice; never think of dealing with her by gentle Methods, take my Word for it, those will never do. I have try'd um long enough. She must be frightned into it, there is no other Way. Tell her I'm her Father, and of the horrid Sin of Disobedience, and of the dreadful Punishment of it in t'other World, and then tell her about being lock'd up all her Life in a Garret in this, and be kept only upon Bread and Water.' 'I will do all I can,' said *Allworthy*, 'for I promise you there is nothing I wish more than an Alliance with this amiable Creature.' 'Nay, the Girl is well enough for Matter o' that,' cries the Squire, 'a Man may go farther and meet with worse Meat; that I may declare o' her, thof she be my own Daughter. And if she will but be obedient to me, there is n'arrow a Father within a hundred Miles o' the Place that loves a Daughter better than I do; but I see you are busy with the Lady here, so I will go Huome and expect you, and so your humble Servant.'

As soon as Mr. *Western* was gone, Mrs. *Waters* said, 'I see, Sir, the Squire hath not the least Remembrance of my Face. I believe, Mr. *Allworthy*, you would not have known me neither. I am very considerably altered since that Day when you so kindly gave me that Advice, which I had been happy had I followed.'—'Indeed, Madam,' cries *Allworthy*, 'it gave me great Concern when I first heard the contrary.' 'Indeed, Sir,' says she, 'I was ruined by a very deep Scheme of Villany, which if you knew, though I pretend not to think it would justify me in your Opinion, it would at least mitigate my Offence, and induce you to pity me; you are not now at Leisure to hear my whole Story; but this I assure you, I was betrayed by the most solemn Promises of Marriage; nay in the Eye of Heaven I was married to him; for after much reading on the Subject, I am convinced that particular Ceremonies are only requisite to give a legal Sanction to Marriage, and have only a worldly Use in giving a Woman the Privileges of a Wife;[1] but that she who lives constant to one Man, after a solemn private Affiance, whatever the World may call her, hath little to charge on her own Conscience.' 'I am sorry, Madam,' said *Allworthy*, 'you made so ill an Use of your Learning. Indeed it would have been well that you had been possessed of much more, or had remained in a State of Ignorance. And yet, Madam, I am afraid you have more than this Sin to answer for.' 'During his Life,' answered she, 'which was above a Dozen Years, I most solemnly assure you, I had not. And consider, Sir, on my Behalf, what is in the Power of a Woman stript of her Reputation, and left destitute, whether the good-natured World will suffer such a stray Sheep to return to the Road of Virtue, even if she was never so desirous. I protest then I would have chose it had it been in my Power; but Necessity drove me into the Arms of Capt. *Waters*, with whom, though still unmarried, I lived as a Wife for many Years, and went by his Name. I parted with this Gentleman at *Worcester*, on his March against the Rebels, and it was then I accidentally met with Mr. *Jones*, who rescued me from the Hands of a Villain. Indeed he is the worthiest of Men. No young Gentleman of his Age is, I believe, freer from Vice, and few have the twentieth Part of his Virtues; nay, whatever Vices he hath had, I am firmly persuaded he hath now taken a Resolution to abandon them.' 'I hope he hath,' cries *Allworthy*, 'and I hope he will preserve that Resolution. I must

---

1 Marriage being 'one of the Rights of human Nature', nothing more was required for 'a compleat *Marriage* by the Laws of *England*, than a full, free, and mutual Consent' between the parties. Formal solemnization of the marriage was necessary, however, if the husband and wife were to enjoy the 'legal Advantages' of their union, such as the rights of dower, inheritance, etc. (See Jacob, *New Law-Dictionary*, 4th ed. [1739], s.v. 'Marriage'; see also above, p. 768, n. 1.)

say I have still the same Hopes with Regard to yourself. The
World, I do agree, are apt to be too unmerciful on these Occa-
sions, yet Time and Perseverance will get the better of this their
Disinclination, as I may call it, to Pity, for though they are not,
like Heaven, ready to receive a penitent Sinner, yet a continued
Repentance will at length obtain Mercy even with the World.
This you may be assured of, Mrs. *Waters*, that whenever I find
you are sincere in such good Intentions, you shall want no
Assistance in my Power to make them effectual.'

Mrs. *Waters* fell now upon her Knees before him, and, in a
Flood of Tears, made him many most passionate Acknowledgments of his Goodness, which, as she truly said, savoured more of
the divine than human Nature.

Allworthy raised her up, and spoke in the most tender Manner,
making use of every Expression which his Invention could suggest to comfort her, when he was interrupted by the Arrival of
Mr. *Dowling*, who, upon his first Entrance, seeing Mrs. *Waters*,
started, and appeared in some Confusion; from which he soon
recovered himself as well as he could, and then said, he was in the
utmost Haste to attend Counsel at Mr. *Western*'s Lodgings;
but however thought it his Duty to call and acquaint him with
the Opinion of Counsel upon the Case which he had before told
him, which was that the Conversion of the Moneys in that Case
could not be questioned in a Criminal Cause, but that an Action
of Trover[1] might be brought, and if it appeared to the Jury to be
the Moneys of Plaintiff, that Plaintiff would recover a Verdict
for the Value.

Allworthy, without making any Answer to this, bolted the Door,
and then advancing with a stern Look to *Dowling*, he said,
'Whatever be your Haste, Sir, I must first receive an Answer to
some Questions. Do you know this Lady?'—'That Lady, Sir?'
answered *Dowling* with great Hesitation. *Allworthy* then, with
the most solemn Voice, said, 'Look you, Mr. *Dowling*, as you
value my Favour, or your Continuance a Moment longer in my
Service, do not hesitate nor prevaricate; but answer faithfully
and truly to every Question I ask.—Do you know this Lady?'—
'Yes, Sir,' said *Dowling*, 'I have seen the Lady.' 'Where, Sir?'
'At her own Lodgings.'—'Upon what Business did you go
thither, Sir, and who sent you?' 'I went, Sir, to enquire, Sir, about

[1] See above, p. 632, n. 2.

Mr. *Jones.*' 'And who sent you to enquire about him?' 'Who, Sir, why, Sir, Mr. *Blifil* sent me.' 'And what did you say to the Lady concerning that Matter?' 'Nay, Sir, it is impossible to recollect every Word.' 'Will you please, Madam, to assist the Gentleman's Memory?' 'He told me, Sir,' said Mrs. *Waters,* 'that if Mr. *Jones* had murdered my Husband, I should be assisted by any Money I wanted to carry on the Prosecution, by a very worthy Gentleman, who was well apprized what a Villain I had to deal with. These I can safely swear were the very Words he spoke.'— 'Were these the Words, Sir?' said *Allworthy.* 'I cannot charge my Memory exactly,' cries *Dowling,* 'but I believe I did speak to that Purpose.'—'And did Mr. *Blifil* order you to say so?' 'I am sure, Sir, I should not have gone on my own Accord, nor have willingly exceeded my Authority in Matters of this Kind. If I said so, I must have so understood Mr. *Blifil's* Instructions.' 'Look you, Mr. *Dowling,*' said *Allworthy,* 'I promise you before this Lady, that whatever you have done in this Affair by Mr. *Blifil's* Order, I will forgive, provided you now tell me strictly the Truth; for I believe what you say, that you would not have acted of your own Accord, and without Authority, in this Matter. —Mr. *Blifil* then likewise sent you to examine the two Fellows at *Aldersgate?*'—'He did, Sir.'—'Well, and what Instructions did he then give you? Recollect as well as you can, and tell me, as near as possible, the very Words he used.'—'Why, Sir, Mr. *Blifil* sent me to find out the Persons who were Eye-Witnesses of this Fight. He said, he feared they might be tampered with by Mr. *Jones,* or some of his Friends. He said, Blood required Blood; and that not only all who concealed a Murderer, but those who omitted any Thing in their Power to bring him to Justice, were Sharers in his Guilt. He said, he found you was very desirous of having the Villain brought to Justice, though it was not proper you should appear in it.'—'He did so?' says *Allworthy.*—'Yes, Sir,' cries *Dowling,* 'I should not, I am sure, have proceeded such Lengths for the Sake of any other Person living but your Worship.'—'What Lengths, Sir?' said *Allworthy.* —'Nay, Sir,' cries *Dowling,* 'I would not have your Worship think I would, on any Account, be guilty of Subordination of Perjury; but there are two Ways of delivering Evidence. I told them therefore that if any Offers should be made them on the other Side, they should refuse them, and that they might be assured they should lose nothing by being honest Men, and telling the Truth. I said, we were told, that Mr. *Jones* had assaulted the Gentleman first, and that if that was the Truth, they should declare it; and I did give them some Hints that they should be no Losers.'—'I think you went Lengths indeed,' cries *Allworthy*.—'Nay, Sir,' answered *Dowling*, 'I am sure I did not desire them to tell an Untruth,—nor should I have said what I did, unless it had been to oblige you.'—'You would not have thought, I believe,' says *Allworthy*, 'to have obliged me, had you known that this Mr. *Jones* was my own Nephew.'—'I am sure, Sir,' answered he, 'it did not become me to take any Notice of what I thought you desired to conceal.'—'How,' cries *Allworthy*, 'and did you know it then?'—'Nay, Sir,' answered *Dowling*, 'if your Worship bids me speak the Truth, I am sure I shall do it. —Indeed, Sir, I did know it; for they were almost the last Words which Madam *Blifil* ever spoke, which she mentioned to me as I stood alone by her Bedside, when she delivered me the Letter I brought your Worship from her.'—'What Letter?' cries *Allworthy*.—'The Letter, Sir,' answered *Dowling*, 'which I brought from *Salisbury*, and which I delivered into the Hands of Mr. *Blifil*.'—'O Heavens!' cries *Allworthy*, 'well, and what were the Words? What did my Sister say to you?'—'She took me by the Hand,' answered he, 'and as she delivered me the Letter, said, I scarce know what I have written. Tell my Brother, Mr. *Jones* is his Nephew.—He is my Son—Bless him, says she, and then fell backward, as if dying away. I presently called in the People, and she never spoke more to me, and dy'd within a few Minutes afterwards.'—*Allworthy* stood a Minute silent, lifting up his Eyes, and then turning to *Dowling*, said,—'How came you, Sir, not to deliver me this Message?' 'Your Worship,' answered he, 'must remember that you was at that Time ill in Bed; and being in a violent Hurry, as indeed I always am, I delivered the Letter and Message to Mr. *Blifil*, who told me he would carry them both to you, which he hath since told me he did, and that your Worship, partly out of Friendship to Mr. *Jones*, and partly out of Regard to your Sister, would never have it mentioned; and did intend to conceal it from the World; and therefore, Sir, if you had not mentioned it to me first, I am certain I should never have thought it belonged to me to say any Thing of the Matter, either to your Worship, or any other Person.'

We have remarked somewhere already, that it is possible for a Man to convey a Lie in the Words of Truth; this was the Case at present: For *Blifil* had in Fact told *Dowling* what he now related; but had not imposed upon him, nor indeed had imagined that he was able so to do. In Reality, the Promises which *Blifil* had made to *Dowling*, were the Motives which had induced him to Secrecy; and as he now very plainly saw *Blifil* would not be able to keep them, he thought proper to make this Confession, which the Promises of Forgiveness, joined to the Threats, the Voice, the Looks of *Allworthy*, and the Discoveries he had made before, extorted from him, who was besides taken unawares, and had no Time to consider of Evasions.

Allworthy appeared well satisfied with this Relation, and having enjoined on *Dowling* strict Silence as to what had past, conducted that Gentleman himself to the Door, lest he should see *Blifil*, who was returned to his Chamber, where he exulted in the Thoughts of his last Deceit on his Uncle, and little suspected what had since passed below Stairs.

As *Allworthy* was returning to his Room, he met Mrs. *Miller* in the Entry, who with a Face all pale and full of Terror, said to him, 'O! Sir, I find this wicked Woman hath been with you, and you know all; yet do not on this Account abandon the poor young Man. Consider, Sir, he was ignorant it was his own Mother, and the Discovery itself will most probably break his Heart, without your Unkindness.' 'Madam,' says *Allworthy*, 'I am under such an Astonishment at what I have heard, that I am really unable to satisfy you; but come with me into my Room. Indeed, Mrs. *Miller*, I have made surprising Discoveries, and you shall soon know them.'

The poor Woman followed him trembling; and now *Allworthy* going up to Mrs. *Waters*, took her by the Hand, and then turning to Mrs. *Miller* said, 'What Reward shall I bestow upon this Gentlewoman for the Services she hath done me?—O! Mrs. *Miller*, you have a Thousand Times heard me call the young Man to whom you are so faithful a Friend, my Son. Little did I then think he was indeed related to me at all.—Your Friend, Madam, is my Nephew, he is the Brother of that wicked Viper which I have so long nourished in my Bosom.—She will herself tell you the whole Story, and how the Youth came to pass for her Son. Indeed, Mrs. *Miller*, I am convinced that he hath been wronged, and that I have been abused, abused by one whom you too justly suspected of being a Villain. He is, in Truth, the worst of Villains.'

The Joy which Mrs. *Miller* now felt, bereft her of the Power of Speech, and might perhaps have deprived her of her Senses, if not of Life, had not a friendly Shower of Tears come seasonably to her Relief. At length recovering so far from her Transport as to be able to speak, she cry'd, 'And is my dear Mr. *Jones* then your Nephew, Sir? and not the Son of this Lady? and are your Eyes opened to him at last? and shall I live to see him as happy as he deserves?' 'He certainly is my Nephew,' says *Allworthy*, 'and I hope all the rest.'—'And is this the dear, good Woman, the Person,' cries she, 'to whom all this Discovery is owing!' '—She is indeed,' says *Allworthy*.—'Why then,' cry'd Mrs. *Miller*, upon her Knees, 'may Heaven shower down its choicest Blessings upon her Head, and for this one good Action, forgive her all her Sins be they never so many.'

Mrs. *Waters* then informed them, that she believed *Jones* would very shortly be released; for that the Surgeon was gone, in Company with a Nobleman, to the Justice who committed him, in order to certify that Mr. *Fitzpatrick* was out of all Manner of Danger, and to procure the Prisoner his Liberty.

Allworthy said, he should be glad to find his Nephew there at his Return home; but that he was then obliged to go on some Business of Consequence. He then called to a Servant to fetch him a Chair, and presently left the two Ladies together.

Mr. *Blifil* hearing the Chair ordered, came down Stairs to attend upon his Uncle, for he never was deficient in such Acts of Duty. He asked his Uncle if he was going out, which is a civil Way of asking a Man whither he is going; to which the other making no Answer, he again desired to know when he would be pleased to return.—*Allworthy* made no Answer to this neither, till he was just going into his Chair, and then turning about he said—'Harkee, Sir, do you find out, before my Return, the Letter which your Mother sent me on her Death-bed.' *Allworthy* then departed, and left *Blifil* in a Situation to be envied only by a Man who is just going to be hanged.

CHAPTER IX

A further Continuation.

ALLWORTHY took an Opportunity whilst he was in the Chair of reading the Letter from *Jones* to *Sophia*, which *Western* delivered him; and there were some Expressions in it concerning himself, which drew Tears from his Eyes. At length he arrived at Mr. *Western's*, and was introduced to *Sophia*.

When the first Ceremonies were past, and the Gentleman and Lady had taken their Chairs, a Silence of some Minutes ensued; during which, the latter, who had been prepared for the Visit by her Father, sat playing with her Fan, and had every Mark of Confusion both in her Countenance and Behaviour. At length *Allworthy*, who was himself a little disconcerted, began thus; 'I am afraid, Miss *Western*, my Family hath been the occasion of giving you some Uneasiness; to which, I fear, I have innocently become more instrumental than I intended. Be assured, Madam, had I at first known how disagreeable the Proposals had been, I should not have suffered you to have been so long persecuted. I hope therefore you will not think the Design of this Visit is to trouble you with any further Solicitations of that kind, but entirely to relieve you from them.'

'Sir,' said *Sophia*, with a little modest Hesitation, 'this Behaviour is most kind and generous, and such as I could expect only from Mr. *Allworthy*: But as you have been so kind to mention this Matter, you will pardon me for saying, it hath indeed given me great Uneasiness, and hath been the occasion of my suffering much cruel Treatment from a Father, who was, till that unhappy Affair, the tenderest and fondest of all Parents. I am convinced, Sir, you are too good and generous to resent my Refusal of your Nephew. Our Inclinations are not in our own Power; and whatever may be his Merit, I cannot force them in his Favour.' 'I assure you, most amiable young Lady,' said *Allworthy*, 'I am capable of no such Resentment, had the Person been my own Son, and had I entertain'd the highest Esteem for him. For you say truly, Madam, we cannot force our Inclinations, much less can they be directed by another.' 'Oh! Sir,' answered *Sophia*, 'every Word you speak proves you to deserve that good, that great, that benevolent Character the whole World allows you. I assure you, Sir, nothing less than the certain Prospect of future Misery could have made me resist the Commands of my Father.' 'I sincerely believe you, Madam,' replied *Allworthy*, 'and I heartily congratulate you on your prudent Foresight, since by so justifiable a Resistance you have avoided Misery indeed.' 'You speak now, Mr. *Allworthy*,' cries she, 'with a Delicacy which few Men are capable of feeling; but surely in my Opinion, to lead our Lives with one to whom we are indifferent, must be a State of Wretchedness.—Perhaps that Wretchedness would be even increased by a Sense of the Merits of an Object to whom we cannot give our Affections. If I had married Mr. *Blifil*——' 'Pardon my interrupting you, Madam,' answered *Allworthy*, 'but I cannot bear the Supposition.—Believe me, Miss *Western*, I rejoice from my Heart, I rejoice in your Escape.—I have discovered the Wretch, for whom you have suffered all this cruel Violence from your Father, to be a Villain.' 'How, Sir!' cries *Sophia*,—'you must believe this surprises me.'—'It hath surprised me, Madam,' answered *Allworthy*, 'and so it will the World.—But I have acquainted you with the real Truth.' 'Nothing but Truth,' says *Sophia*, 'can, I am convinced, come from the Lips of Mr. *Allworthy*.—Yet, Sir, such sudden, such unexpected News—— Discovered, you say—— may Villany be ever so.'—'You will soon enough hear the Story,' cries *Allworthy*,—'at present let us not mention so detested a Name.— I have another Matter of a very serious Nature to propose.— O! Miss *Western*, I know your vast Worth, nor can I so easily part with the Ambition of being allied to it.—I have a near Relation, Madam, a young Man whose Character is, I am convinced, the very opposite to that of this Wretch, and whose Fortune I will make equal to what his was to have been.—Could I, Madam, hope you would admit a Visit from him?' *Sophia*, after a Minute's Silence, answered, 'I will deal with the utmost Sincerity with Mr. *Allworthy*. His Character, and the Obligation I have just received from him demand it. I have determined at present to listen to no such Proposals from any Person. My only Desire is to be restor'd to the Affection of my Father, and to be again the Mistress of his Family. This, Sir, I hope to owe to your good Offices. Let me beseech you, let me conjure you by all the Goodness which I, and all who know you, have experienced; do not the very Moment when you have released me from one

Persecution, do not engage me in another, as miserable and as fruitless.' 'Indeed, Miss *Western*,' replied *Allworthy*, 'I am capable of no such Conduct; and if this be your Resolution, he must submit to the Disappointment, whatever Torments he may suffer under it.' 'I must smile now, Mr. *Allworthy*,' answered *Sophia*, 'when you mention the Torments of a Man whom I do not know, and who can consequently have so little Acquaintance with me.' 'Pardon me, dear young Lady,' cries *Allworthy*, 'I begin now to be afraid he hath had too much Acquaintance for the Repose of his future Days; since, if ever Man was capable of a sincere, violent and noble Passion, such, I am convinced, is my unhappy Nephew's for Miss *Western*.' 'A Nephew of yours! Mr. *Allworthy*,' answered *Sophia*. 'It is surely strange, I never heard of him before.' 'Indeed! Madam,' cries *Allworthy*, 'it is only the Circumstance of his being my Nephew to which you are a Stranger, and which, till this Day, was a Secret to me.—Mr. *Jones*, who has long loved you, he! he is my Nephew.'—'Mr. *Jones* your Nephew, Sir?' cries *Sophia*, 'Can it be possible?'— 'He is indeed, Madam,' answered *Allworthy*: 'He is my own Sister's Son—as such I shall always own him; nor am I ashamed of owning him. I am much more ashamed of my past Behaviour to him; but I was as ignorant of his Merit as of his Birth. Indeed, Miss *Western*, I have used him cruelly—— Indeed I have.'— Here the good Man wiped his Eyes, and after a short Pause proceeded—'I never shall be able to reward him for his Sufferings without your Assistance.—Believe me, most amiable young Lady, I must have a great Esteem of that Offering which I make to your Worth. I know he hath been guilty of Faults; but there is great Goodness of Heart at the Bottom. Believe me, Madam, there is.'—Here he stopped, seeming to expect an Answer, which he presently received from *Sophia*, after she had a little recovered herself from the Hurry of Spirits into which so strange and sudden Information had thrown her: 'I sincerely wish you Joy, Sir, of a Discovery in which you seem to have such Satisfaction. I doubt not but you will have all the Comfort you can promise yourself from it. The young Gentleman hath certainly a thousand good Qualities, which makes it impossible he should not behave well to such an Uncle.'—'I hope, Madam,' said *Allworthy*, 'he hath those good Qualities which must make him a good Husband.—He must, I am sure, be of all Men the most abandoned, if a Lady of your Merit should condescend——' 'You must pardon me, Mr. *Allworthy*,' answered *Sophia*, 'I cannot listen to a Proposal of this Kind. Mr. *Jones*, I am convinced, hath much Merit; but I shall never receive Mr. *Jones* as one who is to be my Husband.—Upon my Honour I never will.'—'Pardon me, Madam,' cries *Allworthy*, 'if I am a little surprized after what I have heard from Mr. *Western*.—I hope the unhappy young Man hath done nothing to forfeit your good Opinion, if he had ever the Honour to enjoy it.—Perhaps he may have been misrepresented to you, as he was to me. The same Villainy may have injured him every where.—He is no Murderer, I assure you, as he hath been called.'—'Mr. *Allworthy*,' answered *Sophia*, 'I have told you my Resolution. I wonder not at what my Father hath told you; but whatever his Apprehensions or Fears have been, if I know my Heart, I have given no Occasion for them; since it hath always been a fixed Principle with me, never to have marry'd without his Consent. This is, I think, the Duty of a Child to a Parent; and this, I hope, nothing could ever have prevailed with me to swerve from. I do not indeed conceive, that the Authority of any Parent can oblige us to marry, in direct Opposition to our Inclinations. To avoid a Force of this Kind, which I had Reason to suspect, I left my Father's House, and sought Protection elsewhere.[1] This is the Truth of my Story; and if the World, or my Father, carry my Intentions any farther, my own Conscience will acquit me.' 'I hear you, Miss *Western*,' cries *Allworthy*, 'with Admiration. I admire the Justness of your Sentiments; but

---

[1] Cf. the situation in *Clarissa*, where Richardson's heroine, threatened by her family with marriage to the detestable Solmes, is forced to elope with Lovelace. As Richardson stated in his Preface, one of 'the principal Views' of *Clarissa* was 'To caution Parents against the undue Exertion of their natural Authority over their Children, in the great Article of Marriage' (I. viii). This certainly was an interest shared by Fielding in presenting the story of his own heroine, whose views on the nature and extent of filial duty and parental authority in the arrangement of marriages may be compared to those expressed by Clarissa to Anna Howe: 'Let me but be permitted to avoid the man I hate; and I will give up, with all my heart, the man I could prefer. To renounce the one, were I really to value him . . . can give but a temporary concern, which time and discretion will make light: This is a sacrifice which a child owes to parents and friends, if they insist upon its being made. But the other, to marry a man one *cannot endure*, is not only a dishonest thing, as to the man; but it is enough to make a creature, who wishes to be a good wife, a bad or indifferent one . . . And then she can hardly be either a good mistress; a good friend; or any thing but a discredit to her family, and a bad example to all around her' (ii. 90–1). For other passages in which Fielding invites comparison between Sophia and Clarissa, see above, pp. 793, n. 1; 850, n. 1.

surely there is more in this. I am cautious of offending you, young Lady; but am I to look on all which I have hitherto heard or seen, as a Dream only? And have you suffered so much Cruelty from your Father on the Account of a Man to whom you have been always absolutely indifferent?' 'I beg, Mr. *Allworthy*,' answered *Sophia*, 'you will not insist on my Reasons;—Yes, I have suffered indeed: I will not, Mr. *Allworthy*, conceal—I will be very sincere with you—I own I had a great Opinion of Mr. *Jones*—I believe—I know I have suffered for my Opinion— I have been treated cruelly by my Aunt, as well as by my Father; but that is now past—I beg I may not be farther press'd; for whatever hath been, my Resolution is now fixed. Your Nephew, Sir, hath many Virtues—he hath great Virtues, Mr. *Allworthy*. I question not but he will do you Honour in the World, and make you happy.'—'I wish I could make him so, Madam,' replied *Allworthy*; 'but that I am convinced is only in your Power. It is that Conviction which hath made me so earnest a Solicitor in his Favour.' 'You are deceived; indeed, Sir, you are deceived,' said *Sophia*,—'I hope not by him.—It is sufficient to have deceived me. Mr. *Allworthy*, I must insist on being prest no farther on this Subject.—I should be sorry—— Nay, I will not injure him in your Favour. I wish Mr. *Jones* very well. I sincerely wish him well; and I repeat it again to you, whatever Demerit he may have to me, I am certain he hath many good Qualities. I do not disown my former Thoughts; but nothing can ever recall them. At present there is not a Man upon Earth whom I would more resolutely reject than Mr. *Jones*; nor would the Addresses of Mr. *Blifil* himself be less agreeable to me.'

Western had been long impatient for the Event of this Conference, and was just now arrived at the Door to listen; when having heard the last Sentiments of his Daughter's Heart, he lost all Temper, and bursting open the Door in a Rage, cried out, —'It is a Lie. It is a d—n'd Lie. It is all owing to that d—n'd Rascal *Juones*; and if she could get at un, she'd ha un any Hour of the Day.' Here *Allworthy* interposed, and addressing himself to the Squire with some Anger in his Look, he said, 'Mr. *Western*, you have not kept your Word with me. You promised to abstain from all Violence.'—'Why so I did,' cries *Western*, 'as long as it was possible; but to hear a Wench telling such confounded Lies.—Zounds! Doth she think if she can make Vools of other Volk, she can make one of me?—No, no, I know her better than thee dost.' 'I am sorry to tell you, Sir,' answered *Allworthy*, 'it doth not appear by your Behaviour to this young Lady, that you know her at all. I ask Pardon for what I say; but I think our Intimacy, your own Desires, and the Occasion justify me. She is your Daughter, Mr. *Western*, and I think she doth Honour to your Name. If I was capable of Envy, I should sooner envy you on this Account, than any other Man whatever.'—'Od-rabbit-it,' cries the Squire, 'I wish she was thine with all my Heart—wouldst soon be glad to be rid of the Trouble o' her.'—'Indeed, my good Friend,' answered *Allworthy*, 'you yourself are the Cause of all the Trouble you complain of. Place that Confidence in the young Lady which she so well deserves, and I am certain you will be the happiest Father on Earth.'— 'I Confidence in her!' cries the Squire.—'Sblood! what Confidence can I place in her, when she won't do as I wou'd ha her? Let her gi but her Consent to marry as I would ha her, and I'll place as much Confidence in her as wouldst ha me.'—'You have no Right, Neighbour,' answered *Allworthy*, 'to insist on any such Consent. A negative Voice your Daughter allows you, and God and Nature have thought proper to allow you no more.' 'A negative Voice?' cries the Squire,—'Ay! ay! I'll shew you what a negative Voice I ha.—Go along, go into your Chamber, go, you Stubborn——' 'Indeed, Mr. *Western*,' said *Allworthy*,—'Indeed, you use her cruelly—I cannot bear to see this.—You shall, you must behave to her in a kinder Manner. She deserves the best of Treatment.' 'Yes, yes,' said the Squire, 'I know what she deserves: Now she's gone, I'll shew you what she deserves.— See here, Sir, here is a Letter from my Cousin, my Lady *Bellaston*, in which she is so kind to gi me to understand, that the Fellow is got out of Prison again; and here she advises me to take all the Care I can o' the Wench. Odzookers! Neighbour *Allworthy*, you don't know what it is to govern a Daughter.'

The Squire ended his Speech with some Compliments to his own Sagacity; and then *Allworthy*, after a formal Preface, acquainted him with the whole Discovery which he had made concerning *Jones*, with his Anger to *Blifil*, and with every Particular which hath been disclosed to the Reader in the preceding Chapters.

Men over-violent in their Dispositions, are, for the most Part, as changeable in them. No sooner then was *Western* informed of Mr. *Allworthy's* Intention to make *Jones* his Heir, than he joined heartily with the Uncle in every Commendation of the Nephew, and became as eager for her Marriage with *Jones*, as he had before been to couple her to *Blifil.*

Here Mr. *Allworthy* was again forced to interpose, and to relate what had passed between him and *Sophia,* at which he testified great Surprize.

The Squire was silent a Moment, and looked wild with Astonishment at this Account.—At last he cried out, 'Why what can be the Meaning of this, Neighbour *Allworthy?* Vond o'un she was, that I'll be sworn to.—Odzookers! I have hit o't. As sure as a Gun I have hit o' the very right o't. It's all along o' *Zister.* The Girl hath got a Hankering after this Son of a Whore of a Lord. I vound 'em together at my Cousin, my Lady *Bellaston's.* He hath turned the Head o' her that's certain—but d—n me if he shall ha her—I'll ha no Lords nor Courtiers in my Vamily.'

Allworthy now made a long Speech, in which he repeated his Resolution to avoid all violent Measures, and very earnestly recommended gentle Methods to Mr. *Western,* as those by which he might be assured of succeeding best with his Daughter. He then took his Leave, and returned back to Mrs. *Miller,* but was forced to comply with the earnest Entreaties of the Squire, in promising to bring Mr. *Jones* to visit him that Afternoon, 'that he might,' as he said, 'make all Matters up with the young Gentleman.' At Mr. *Allworthy's* Departure, *Western* promised to follow his Advice in his Behaviour to *Sophia,* saying, 'I don't know how 'tis, but d—n me, *Allworthy,* if you don't make me always do just as you please, and yet I have as good an Esteate as you, and am in the Commission of the Peace as well as yourself.'

CHAPTER X

Wherein the History begins to draw towards a Conclusion.

WHEN *Allworthy* returned to his Lodgings, he heard Mr. *Jones* was just arrived before him. He hurried therefore instantly into an empty Chamber, whither he ordered Mr. *Jones* to be brought to him alone.

It is impossible to conceive a more tender or moving Scene, than the Meeting between the Uncle and Nephew (for Mrs. *Waters*, as the Reader may well suppose, had at her last Visit discovered to him the Secret of his Birth.) The first Agonies of Joy which were felt on both Sides, are indeed beyond my Power to describe: I shall not therefore attempt it. After *Allworthy* had raised *Jones* from his Feet, where he had prostrated himself, and received him into his Arms, 'O my Child,' he cried, 'how have I been to blame! How have I injured you! What Amends can I ever make you for those unkind, those unjust Suspicions which I have entertained; and for all the Sufferings they have occasioned to you?' 'Am I not now made Amends?' cries *Jones*, 'Would not my Sufferings, if they had been ten Times greater, have been now richly repaid? O my dear Uncle! this Goodness, this Tenderness overpowers, unmans, destroys me. I cannot bear the Transports which flow so fast upon me. To be again restored to your Presence, to your Favour; to be once more thus kindly received by my great, my noble, my generous Benefactor——' 'Indeed, Child,' cries *Allworthy*, 'I have used you cruelly.'—He then explained to him all the Treachery of *Blifil*, and again repeated Expressions of the utmost Concern, for having been induced by that Treachery to use him so ill. 'O talk not so,' answered *Jones*; 'Indeed, Sir, you have used me nobly. The wisest Man might be deceived as you were, and, under such a Deception, the best must have acted just as you did. Your Goodness displayed itself in the Midst of your Anger, just as it then seemed. I owe every thing to that Goodness of which I have been most unworthy. Do not put me on Self-accusation, by carrying your generous Sentiments too far. Alas, Sir, I have not been punished more than I have deserved; and it shall be the whole Business of my future Life to deserve that Happiness you now bestow on me; for believe me, my dear Uncle, my Punishment hath not been thrown away upon me: Though I have been a great, I am not a hardened Sinner; I thank Heaven I have had Time to reflect on my past Life, where, though I cannot charge myself with any gross Villainy, yet I can discern Follies and Vices more than enough to repent and to be ashamed of; Follies which have been attended with dreadful Consequences to myself, and have brought me to the Brink of Destruction.' 'I am rejoiced, my dear Child,' answered *Allworthy*, 'to hear you talk thus sensibly; for as I am convinced Hypocrisy (good Heaven how have I been imposed on by it in others!) was never among your Faults, so I can readily believe all you say. You now see, *Tom*, to what Dangers Imprudence alone may subject Virtue (for Virtue, I am now convinced, you love in a great Degree.) Prudence is indeed the Duty which we owe to ourselves; and if we will be so much our own Enemies as to neglect it, we are not to wonder if the World is deficient in discharging their Duty to us; for when a Man lays the Foundation of his own Ruin, others will, I am afraid, be too apt to build upon it. You say, however, you have seen your Errors; and will reform them. I firmly believe you, my dear Child; and therefore, from this Moment, you shall never be reminded of them by me. Remember them only yourself so far, as for the future to teach you the better to avoid them; but still remember, for your Comfort, that there is this great Difference between those Faults which Candour may construe into Imprudence, and those which can be deduced from Villainy only. The former, perhaps, are even more apt to subject a Man to Ruin; but if he reform, his Character will, at length, be totally retrieved; the World, though not immediately, will, in Time, be reconciled to him; and he may reflect, not without some Mixture of Pleasure, on the Dangers he hath escaped: But Villainy, my Boy, when once discovered, is irretrievable; the Stains which this leaves behind, no Time will wash away. The Censures of Mankind will pursue the Wretch, their Scorn will abash him in Public, and if Shame drives him into Retirement, he will go to it with all those Terrors with which a weary Child, who is afraid of Hobgoblins, retreats from Company to go to Bed alone. Here his murdered Conscience will haunt him. Repose, like a false Friend, will fly from him. Where-ever he turns his Eyes, Horror presents itself; if he looks backward, unavailable Repentance treads on his Heels; if forward, incurable Despair stares him in the Face; till, like a condemned Prisoner, confined in a Dungeon, he detests his present Condition, and yet dreads the Consequence of that Hour which is to relieve him from it. Comfort yourself, I say, my Child, that this is not your Case; and rejoice, with Thankfulness to him who hath suffered you to see your Errors, before they have brought on you that Destruction to which a Persistance in even those Errors must have led you. You have deserted them, and the Prospect now before you is such, that

Happiness seems in your own Power.'—At these Words *Jones* fetched a deep Sigh; upon which, when *Allworthy* remonstrated, he said, 'Sir, I will conceal nothing from you: I fear there is one Consequence of my Vices I shall never be able to retrieve. O my dear Uncle, I have lost a Treasure.'—'You need say no more,' answered *Allworthy*; 'I will be explicit with you; I know what you lament; I have seen the young Lady, and have discoursed with her concerning you. This I must insist on, as an Earnest of your Sincerity in all you have said, and of the Stedfastness of your Resolution, that you obey me in one Instance. To abide intirely by the Determination of the young Lady, whether it shall be in your Favour, or no. She hath already suffered enough from Sollicitations which I hate to think of; she shall owe no further Constraint to my Family: I know her Father will be as ready to torment her now on your Account, as he hath formerly been on another's; but I am determined she shall suffer no more Confinement, no more Violence, no more uneasy Hours.'—'O my dear Uncle,' answered *Jones*, 'lay, I beseech you, some Command on me, in which I shall have some Merit in Obedience. Believe me, Sir, the only Instance in which I could disobey you, would be to give an uneasy Moment to my *Sophia*. No, Sir, if I am so miserable to have incurred her Displeasure beyond all Hope of Forgiveness, that alone, with the dreadful Reflection of causing her Misery, will be sufficient to overpower me. To call *Sophia* mine is the greatest, and now the only additional Blessing which Heaven can bestow; but it is a Blessing which I must owe to her alone.' 'I will not flatter you, Child,' cries *Allworthy*; 'I fear your Case is desperate: I never saw stronger Marks of an unalterable Resolution in any Person, than appeared in her vehement Declarations against receiving your Addresses; for which, perhaps, you can account better than myself.'—'Oh, Sir! I can account too well,' answered *Jones*; 'I have sinned against her beyond all Hope of Pardon; and, guilty as I am, my Guilt unfortunately appears to her in ten Times blacker than the real Colours. O my dear Uncle, I find my Follies are irretrievable; and all your Goodness cannot save me from Perdition.'

A Servant now acquainted them, that Mr. *Western* was below Stairs; for his Eagerness to see *Jones* could not wait till the Afternoon. Upon which *Jones*, whose Eyes were full of Tears, begged his Uncle to entertain *Western* a few Minutes, till he a little recovered himself: To which the good Man consented, and having ordered Mr. *Western* to be shewn into a Parlour, went down to him.

Mrs. *Miller* no sooner heard, that *Jones* was alone, (for she had not yet seen him since his Release from Prison) than she came eagerly into the Room, and, advancing towards *Jones*, wished him heartily Joy of his new-found Uncle, and his happy Reconciliation; adding, I wish I could give you Joy on another Account, my dear Child; but any thing so inexorable I never saw. *Jones*, with some Appearance of Surprize, asked her, what she meant. 'Why then,' says she, 'I have been with your young Lady, and have explained all Matters to her, as they were told me by my Son *Nightingale*. She can have no longer any Doubt about the Letter, of that I am certain; for I told her my Son *Nightingale* was ready to take his Oath, if she pleased, that it was all his own Invention, and the Letter of his inditing. I told her the very Reason of sending the Letter ought to recommend you to her the more, as it was all upon her Account, and a plain Proof, that you was resolved to quit all your Profligacy for the future; that you had never been guilty of a single Instance of Infidelity to her since your seeing her in Town. I am afraid I went too far there; but Heaven forgive me: I hope your future Behaviour will be my Justification. I am sure I have said all I can; but all to no Purpose. She remains inflexible. She says, she had forgiven many Faults on account of Youth; but expressed such Detestation of the Character of a Libertine, that she absolutely silenced me. I often attempted to excuse you; but the Justness of her Accusation flew in my Face. Upon my Honour she is a lovely Woman, and one of the sweetest and most sensible Creatures I ever saw. I could have almost kissed her for one Expression she made use of. It was a Sentiment worthy of *Seneca*, or of a Bishop. "I once fancied, Madam," said she, "I had discovered great Goodness of Heart in Mr. *Jones*; and for that I own I had a sincere Esteem; but an entire Profligacy of Manners will corrupt the best Heart in the World; and all which a good-natured Libertine can expect is, that we should mix some Grains of Pity with our Contempt and Abhorrence." She is an angelic Creature, that is the Truth on't.'—'O Mrs. *Miller*,' answered *Jones*, 'can I bear to think I have lost such an Angel.'—'Lost! No,' cries Mrs. *Miller*; 'I hope you have not lost her yet. Resolve to leave such vicious Courses, and you may yet have Hopes: Nay, if she should remain inexorable, there is another young Lady, a sweet pretty young Lady, and a swinging Fortune, who is absolutely dying for Love of you. I heard of it this very Morning, and I told it to Miss *Western*; nay, I went a little beyond the Truth again; for I told her you had refused her; but indeed I knew you would refuse her.—And here I must give you a little Comfort: When I mentioned the young Lady's Name, who is no other than the pretty Widow *Hunt*, I thought she turned pale; but when I said you had refused her, I will be sworn her Face was all over Scarlet in an Instant; and these were her very Words, "I will not deny but that I believe he has some Affection for me." '

Here the Conversation was interrupted by the Arrival of *Western*, who could no longer be kept out of the Room even by the Authority of *Allworthy* himself; though this, as we have often seen, had a wonderful Power over him.

Western immediately went up to *Jones*, crying out, 'My old Friend *Tom*, I am glad to see thee with all my Heart. All past must be forgotten. I could not intend any Affront to thee, because, as *Allworthy* here knows, nay, dost know it thyself, I took thee for another Person; and where a Body means no Harm, what signifies a hasty Word or two; one Christian must forget and forgive another.' 'I hope, Sir,' said *Jones*, 'I shall never forget the many Obligations I have had to you; but as for any Offence towards me, I declare I am an utter Stranger.'—'A't,' says *Western*, 'then give me thy Fist, a't as hearty an honest Cock as any in the Kingdom. Come along with me; I'll carry thee to thy Mistress this Moment.' Here *Allworthy* interposed; and the Squire being unable to prevail either with the Uncle or Nephew, was, after some Litigation, obliged to consent to delay introducing *Jones* to *Sophia* till the Afternoon; at which Time *Allworthy*, as well in Compassion to *Jones*, as in Compliance with the eager Desires of *Western*, was prevailed upon to promise to attend at the Teatable.

The Conversation which now ensued was pleasant enough; and with which, had it happened earlier in our History, we would have entertained our Reader; but as we have now Leisure only to attend to what is very material, it shall suffice to say, that Matters being intirely adjusted as to the Afternoon-visit, Mr. *Western* again returned home.

CHAPTER XI

The History draws nearer to a Conclusion.

WHEN Mr. *Western* was departed, *Jones* began to inform Mr. *Allworthy* and Mrs. *Miller*, that his Liberty had been procured by two noble Lords, who, together with two Surgeons, and a Friend of Mr. *Nightingale's*, had attended the Magistrate by whom he had been committed, and by whom, on the Surgeons Oaths that the wounded Person was out of all Manner of Danger from this Wound, he was discharged.

One only of these Lords, he said, he had ever seen before, and that no more than once; but the other had greatly surprized him, by asking his Pardon for an Offence he had been guilty of towards him, occasioned, he said, entirely by his Ignorance who he was.

Now the Reality of the Case with which *Jones* was not acquainted till afterwards, was this. The Lieutenant whom Lord *Fellamar* had employed, according to the Advice of Lady *Bellaston*, to press *Jones*, as a Vagabond, into the Sea Service, when he came to report to his Lordship the Event which we have before seen, spoke very favourably of the Behaviour of Mr. *Jones* on all Accounts, and strongly assured that Lord, that he must have mistaken the Person, for that *Jones* was certainly a Gentleman, insomuch that his Lordship, who was strictly a Man of Honour, and would by no Means have been guilty of an Action which the World in general would have condemned, began to be much concerned for the Advice which he had taken.

Within a Day or two after this, Lord *Fellamar* happened to dine with the *Irish* Peer, who, in a Conversation upon the Duel, acquainted his Company with the Character of *Fitzpatrick*; to which indeed he did not do strict Justice, especially in what related to his Lady. He said, she was the most innocent, and most injured Woman alive, and that from Compassion alone he had undertaken her Cause. He then declared an Intention of going the next Morning to *Fitzpatrick's* Lodgings, in order to prevail with him, if possibly, to consent to a Separation from his Wife, who, the Peer said, was in Apprehensions for her Life, if she should ever return to be under the Power of her Husband. Lord *Fellamar* agreed to go with him, that he might satisfy him-

self more concerning *Jones*, and the Circumstances of the Duel;
for he was by no Means easy concerning the Part he had acted.
The Moment his Lordship gave a Hint of his Readiness to assist
in the Delivery of the Lady, it was eagerly embraced by the other
Nobleman, who depended much on the Authority of Lord
Fellamar, as he thought it would greatly contribute to awe
Fitzpatrick into a Compliance; and perhaps he was in the right;
for the poor *Irishman* no sooner saw these noble Peers had under-
taken the Cause of his Wife, than he submitted, and Articles of
Separation were soon drawn up and signed between the Parties.

Fitzpatrick had been so well satisfied by Mrs. *Waters* concerning the Innocence of his Wife with *Jones* at *Upton*, or perhaps from some other Reasons was now become so indifferent
to that Matter, that he spoke highly in Favour of *Jones*, to Lord
Fellamar, took all the Blame upon himself, and said the other had
behaved very much like a Gentleman, and a Man of Honour;
and upon that Lord's further Enquiry concerning Mr. *Jones*,
Fitzpatrick told him he was Nephew to a Gentleman of very great
Fashion and Fortune, which was the Account he had just received
from Mrs. *Waters*, after her Interview with *Dowling*.

Lord *Fellamar* now thought it behoved him to do every Thing
in his Power to make Satisfaction to a Gentleman whom he had
so grosly injured, and without any Consideration of Rivalship,
(for he had now given over all Thoughts of *Sophia*) determined
to procure Mr. *Jones's* Liberty, being satisfied as well from
Fitzpatrick as his Surgeon, that the Wound was not mortal. He
therefore prevailed with the *Irish* Peer to accompany him to the
Place where *Jones* was confined, to whom he behaved as we have
already related.

When *Allworthy* returned to his Lodgings,[1] he immediately
carried *Jones* into his Room, and then acquainted him with the
whole Matter, as well what he had heard from Mrs. *Waters*,
as what he had discovered from Mr. *Dowling*.

Jones expressed great Astonishment, and no less Concern at
this Account; but without making any Comment or Observation upon it. And now a Message was brought from Mr. *Blifil*,

---

[1] Fielding apparently forgets that Allworthy had returned to his lodgings in the
previous Chapter, and that Jones was then acquainted with Blifil's designs against him.
Other errors in this chapter attest to the haste in which Fielding brought his novel to a
close (see below, p. 966, nn. 1–2).

desiring to know if his Uncle was at Leisure, and he might wait upon him. *Allworthy* started and turned pale, and then in a more passionate Tone than, I believe, he had ever used before, bid the Servant tell *Blifil*, he knew him not. 'Consider, dear Sir,'—cries *Jones* in a trembling Voice.—'I have considered,' answered *Allworthy*, 'and you yourself shall carry my Message to the Villain. —No one can carry him the Sentence of his own Ruin so properly as the Man whose Ruin he hath so villainously contrived.'—'Pardon me, dear Sir,' said *Jones*; 'a Moment's Reflection will, I am sure, convince you of the contrary. What might be perhaps but Justice from another Tongue, would from mine be Insult; and to whom?—My own Brother, and your Nephew.—Nor did he use me so barbarously.—Indeed that would have been more inexcuseable than any Thing he hath done. Fortune may tempt Men of no very bad Dispositions to Injustice; but Insults proceed only from black and rancorous Minds, and have no Temptations to excuse them.—Let me beseech you, Sir, to do nothing by him in the present Height of your Anger. Consider, my dear Uncle, I was not myself condemned unheard.' *Allworthy* stood silent a Moment, and then embracing *Jones*, he said, with Tears gushing from his Eyes, 'O my Child! to what Goodness have I been so long blind!'

Mrs. *Miller* entring the Room at that Moment, after a gentle Rap, which was not perceived, and seeing *Jones* in the Arms of his Uncle, the poor Woman, in an Agony of Joy, fell upon her Knees, and burst forth into the most extatic Thanksgivings to Heaven, for what had happened.[1]—Then running to *Jones*, she embraced him eagerly, crying, 'My dearest Friend, I wish you Joy a Thousand and a Thousand Times of this blest Day;' and next Mr. *Allworthy* himself received the same Congratulations. To which he answered, 'Indeed, indeed, Mrs. *Miller*, I am beyond Expression happy.' Some few more Raptures having passed on all Sides, Mrs. *Miller* desired them both to walk down to Dinner in the Parlour, where she said there were a very happy Set of People assembled; being indeed no other than Mr. *Nightingale* and his Bride, and his Cousin *Harriet*[2] with her Bridegroom.

---

[1] At the beginning of the chapter Mrs. Miller is said to be already in the room with Allworthy and Jones, whom she had earlier congratulated on his good fortune (XVIII. x).

[2] For "Harris". Harriet is the name of Nightingale's cousin (XIV. ix); Harris, of the disagreeable young woman to whom his father had intended to marry him (XIV. viii).

Allworthy excused himself from dining with the Company, saying he had ordered some little Thing for him and his Nephew
in his own Apartment; for that they had much private Business to
discourse of, but would not resist promising the good Woman,
that both he and *Jones* would make Part of her Society at Supper.

Mrs. *Miller* then asked what was to be done with *Blifil*; 'for
indeed,' says she, 'I cannot be easy while such a Villain is in my
House.'—*Allworthy* answered, 'He was as uneasy as herself on
the same Account.' 'O,' cries she, 'if that be the Case, leave the
Matter to me; I'll soon shew him the Outside of my Doors, I
warrant you. Here are two or three lusty Fellows below Stairs.'
'There will be no need of any Violence,' cries *Allworthy*, 'if you
will carry him a Message from me, he will, I am convinced, depart
of his own Accord.' 'Will I?' said Mrs. *Miller*, 'I never did any
Thing in my Life with a better Will.' Here *Jones* interfered, and
said, 'He had considered the Matter better, and would, if Mr.
Allworthy pleased, be himself the Messenger. I know,' says he,
'already enough of your Pleasure, Sir, and I beg Leave to
acquaint him with it by my own Words. Let me beseech you,
Sir,' added he, 'to reflect on the dreadful Consequences of driving
him to violent and sudden Despair. How unfit, alas! is this poor
Man to die in his present Situation.' This Suggestion had not the
least Effect on Mrs. *Miller*. She left the Room crying, 'You are
too good, Mr. *Jones*, infinitely too good to live in this World.'
But it made a deeper Impression on *Allworthy*. 'My good Child,'
said he, 'I am equally astonished at the Goodness of your Heart,
and the Quickness of your Understanding. Heaven indeed forbid
that this Wretch should be deprived of any Means or Time for
Repentance. That would be a shocking Consideration indeed.
Go to him therefore, and use your own Discretion; yet do not
flatter him with any Hopes of my Forgiveness; for I shall never
forgive Villainy farther than my Religion obliges me,[1] and that
extends not either to our Bounty or our Conversation.'

Jones went up to *Blifil's* Room, whom he found in a Situation
which moved his Pity, though it would have raised a less amiable
Passion in many Beholders. He had cast himself on his Bed, where
he lay abandoning himself to Despair, and drowned in Tears;
not in such Tears as flow from Contrition, and wash away Guilt

---

[1] Fielding regarded the Christian injunction to forgive the acts of one's enemies as 'the
highest Maxim of Morality' (see above, p. 52, n. 1).

from Minds which have been seduced or surprised into it unawares, against the Bent of their natural Dispositions, as will
sometimes happen from human Frailty, even to the Good: No,
these Tears were such as the frighted Thief sheds in his Cart,
and are indeed the Effects of that Concern which the most
savage Natures are seldom deficient in feeling for themselves.

It would be unpleasant and tedious to paint this Scene in full
Length. Let it suffice to say, that the Behaviour of *Jones* was
kind to Excess. He omitted nothing which his Invention could
supply, to raise and comfort the drooping Spirits of *Blifil*, before
he communicated to him the Resolution of his Uncle, that he
must quit the House that Evening. He offered to furnish him
with any Money he wanted, assured him of his hearty Forgiveness of all he had done against him, that he would endeavour to
live with him hereafter as a Brother, and would leave nothing
unattempted to effectuate a Reconciliation with his Uncle.

Blifil was at first sullen and silent, balancing in his Mind
whether he should yet deny all: But finding at last the Evidence
too strong against him, he betook himself at last to Confession.
He then asked Pardon of his Brother in the most vehement
Manner, prostrated himself on the Ground, and kissed his
Feet: In short, he was now as remarkably mean, as he had been
before remarkably wicked.

Jones could not so far check his Disdain, but that it a little
discovered itself in his Countenance at this extreme Servility.
He raised his Brother the Moment he could from the Ground,
and advised him to bear his Afflictions more like a Man; repeating, at the same Time, his Promises, that he would do all in his
Power to lessen them: For which *Blifil* making many Professions
of his Unworthiness, poured forth a Profusion of Thanks: And
then he having declared he would immediately depart to another
Lodging, *Jones* returned to his Uncle.

Among other Matters, *Allworthy* now acquainted *Jones* with
the Discovery which he made concerning the 500 *l.* Bank-Notes.
'I have,' said he, 'already consulted a Lawyer, who tells me, to
my great Astonishment, that there is no Punishment for a Fraud
of this Kind.[1] Indeed, when I consider the black Ingratitude of

---

[1] Swift in *Gulliver's Travels* (I. vi) devotes a paragraph to this fact, remarking on the
difference between the laws of England and Lilliput, whose people 'look upon Fraud as a
greater Crime than Theft'.

this Fellow toward you, I think a Highwayman, compared to him, is an innocent Person.'

'Good Heaven!' says *Jones*, 'is it possible?—I am shocked beyond Measure at this News. I thought there was not an honester Fellow in the World.—The Temptation of such a Sum was too great for him to withstand; for smaller Matters have come safe to me through his Hand. Indeed, my dear Uncle, you must suffer me to call it Weakness rather than Ingratitude; for I am convinced the poor Fellow loves me, and hath done me some Kindnesses, which I can never forget; nay, I believe he hath repented of this very Act: For it is not above a Day or two ago, when my Affairs seemed in the most desperate Situation, that he visited me in my Confinement, and offered me any Money I wanted. Consider, Sir, what a Temptation to a Man who hath tasted such bitter Distress, it must be to have a Sum in his Possession, which must put him and his Family beyond any future Possibility of suffering the like.'

'Child,' cries *Allworthy*, 'you carry this forgiving Temper too far. Such mistaken Mercy is not only Weakness, but borders on Injustice, and is very pernicious to Society, as it encourages Vice.[1] The Dishonesty of this Fellow I might perhaps have pardoned, but never his Ingratitude. And give me Leave to say, when we suffer any Temptation to attone for Dishonesty itself, we are as candid and merciful as we ought to be; and so far I confess I have gone: for I have often pitied the Fate of a Highwayman, when I have been on the Grand Jury; and have more than once applied to the Judge on the Behalf of such as have had any mitigating Circumstances in their Case; but when Dishonesty is attended with any blacker Crime, such as Cruelty, Murder, Ingratitude, or the like, Compassion and Forgiveness then become Faults. I am convinced the Fellow is a Villain, and he shall be punished; at least as far as I can punish him.'

This was spoke with so stern a Voice, that *Jones* did not think proper to make any Reply: Besides, the Hour appointed by Mr. *Western* now drew so near, that he had barely Time left to dress himself. Here therefore ended the present Dialogue, and *Jones* retired to another Room, where *Partridge* attended, according to Order, with his Cloaths.

Partridge had scarce seen his Master since the happy Discovery.

---

[1] Fielding shared this view (see above, p. 102, n. 2).

The poor Fellow was unable either to contain or express his Transports. He behaved like one frantic, and made almost as many Mistakes while he was dressing *Jones*, as I have seen made by Harlequin[1] in dressing himself on the Stage.

His Memory, however, was not in the least deficient. He recollected now many Omens and Presages of this happy Event, some of which he had remarked at the Time, but many more he now remembered; nor did he omit the Dreams he had dreamt the Evening before his meeting with *Jones*; and concluded with saying, 'I always told your Honour something boded in my Mind, that you would one Time or other have it in your Power to make my Fortune.' *Jones* assured him, that this Boding should as certainly be verified with regard to him, as all the other Omens had been to himself; which did not a little add to all the Raptures which the poor Fellow had already conceived on account of his Master.

CHAPTER XII

Approaching still nearer to the End.

*J*ONES being now completely dressed, attended his Uncle to Mr. *Western's*. He was indeed one of the finest Figures ever beheld, and his Person alone would have charmed the greater Part of Womankind; but we hope it hath already appeared in this History, that Nature, when she formed him, did not totally rely, as she sometimes doth, on this Merit only, to recommend her Work.

Sophia, who, angry as she was, was likewise set forth to the best Advantage, for which I leave my female Readers to account, appeared so extremely beautiful, that even *Allworthy*, when he saw her, could not forbear whispering *Western*, that he believed she was the finest Creature in the World. To which *Western* answered, in a Whisper overheard by all present, 'So much the better for *Tom*;—for d—n me if he shan't ha the tousling her.' *Sophia* was all over Scarlet at these Words, while *Tom's* Countenance was altogether as pale, and he was almost ready to sink from his Chair.

[1] The role made popular by John Rich, 'the Inventor of . . . the *English* Pantomime' (see above, p. 214, n. 1).

The Tea-table was scarce removed, before *Western* lugged *Allworthy* out of the Room, telling him, 'He had Business of Consequence to impart, and must speak to him that Instant in private before he forgot it.'

The Lovers were now alone, and it will, I question not, appear strange to many Readers, that those who had so much to say to one another when Danger and Difficulty attended their Conversation, and who seemed so eager to rush into each others Arms when so many Bars lay in their Way, now that with Safety they were at Liberty to say or do whatever they pleased, should both remain for some Time silent and motionless; insomuch, that a Stranger of moderate Sagacity might have well concluded they were mutually indifferent: But so it was, however strange it may seem; both sat with their Eyes cast downwards on the Ground, and for some Minutes continued in perfect Silence.

Mr. *Jones*, during this Interval, attempted once or twice to speak, but was absolutely incapable, muttering only, or rather sighing out some broken Words; when *Sophia* at length, partly out of Pity to him, and partly to turn the Discourse from the Subject which she knew well enough he was endeavouring to open, said;—

'Sure, Sir, you are the most fortunate Man in the World in this Discovery.' 'And can you really, Madam, think me so fortunate,' said *Jones*, sighing, 'while I have incurred your Displeasure?'—'Nay, Sir,' says she, 'as to that, you best know whether you have deserved it.' 'Indeed, Madam,' answered he, 'you yourself are as well apprized of all my Demerits. Mrs. *Miller* has acquainted you with the whole Truth. O! my *Sophia*, am I never to hope for Forgiveness?'—'I think, Mr. *Jones*,' said she, 'I may almost depend on your own Justice, and leave it to yourself to pass Sentence on your own Conduct.'—'Alas! Madam,' answered he, 'it is Mercy, and not Justice, which I implore at your Hands. Justice I know must condemn me.—Yet not for the Letter I sent to Lady *Bellaston*. Of that I most solemnly declare, you have had a true Account.' He then insisted much on the Security given him by *Nightingale* of a fair Pretence for breaking off, if, contrary to their Expectations, her Ladyship should have accepted his Offer; but confest, that he had been guilty of a great Indiscretion to put such a Letter as that into her Power, 'which,' said he, 'I have dearly paid for, in the Effect it has upon you.' 'I do not, I cannot,' says she, 'believe otherwise of that Letter than you would have me. My Conduct, I think, shews you clearly I do not believe there is much in that. And yet, Mr. *Jones*, have I not enough to resent? After what past at *Upton*, so soon to engage in a new Amour with another Woman, while I fancied, and you pretended, your Heart was bleeding for me!—Indeed, you have acted strangely. Can I believe the Passion you have profest to me to be sincere? Or if I can, what Happiness can I assure myself of with a Man capable of so much Inconstancy?' 'O! my *Sophia*,' cries he, 'do not doubt the Sincerity of the purest Passion that ever inflamed a human Breast. Think, most adorable Creature, of my unhappy Situation, of my Despair.—Could I, my *Sophia*, have flatter'd myself with the most distant Hopes of being ever permitted to throw myself at your Feet, in the Manner I do now, it would not have been in the Power of any other Woman to have inspired a Thought which the severest Chastity could have condemned. Inconstancy to you! O *Sophia*! if you can have Goodness enough to pardon what is past, do not let any cruel future Apprehensions shut your Mercy against me.—No Repentance was ever more sincere. O! let it reconcile me to my Heaven in this dear Bosom.' 'Sincere Repentance, Mr. *Jones*,' answered she, 'will obtain the Pardon of a Sinner, but it is from one who is a perfect Judge of that Sincerity. A human Mind may be imposed on; nor is there any infallible Method to prevent it. You must expect however, that if I can be prevailed on by your Repentance to pardon you, I will at least insist on the strongest Proof of its Sincerity.'—'O! name any Proof in my Power,' answered *Jones* eagerly. 'Time,' replied she; 'Time alone, Mr. *Jones*, can convince me that you are a true Penitent, and have resolved to abandon these vicious Courses, which I should detest you for, if I imagined you capable of persevering in them.' 'Do not imagine it,' cries *Jones*. 'On my Knees I intreat, I implore your Confidence, a Confidence which it shall be the Business of my Life to deserve.' 'Let it then,' said she, 'be the Business of some Part of your Life to shew me you deserve it. I think I have been explicit enough in assuring you, that when I see you merit my Confidence, you will obtain it. After what is past, Sir, can you expect I should take you upon your Word?'

He replied, 'Don't believe me upon my Word; I have a better Security, a Pledge for my Constancy, which it is impossible to see and to doubt.' 'What is that?' said *Sophia*, a little surprised. 'I will show you, my charming Angel,' cried *Jones*, seizing her Hand, and carrying her to the Glass. 'There, behold it there, in that lovely Figure, in that Face, that Shape, those Eyes, that Mind which shines through those Eyes: Can the Man who shall be in Possession of these be inconstant? Impossible! my *Sophia*. They would fix a *Dorimant*,[1] a Lord *Rochester*. You could not doubt it, if you could see yourself with any Eyes but your own.' *Sophia* blushed, and half smiled; but forcing again her Brow into a Frown, 'If I am to judge,' said she, 'of the future by the past, my Image will no more remain in your Heart, when I am out of your Sight, than it will in this Glass when I am out of the Room.' 'By Heaven, by all that is sacred,' said *Jones*, 'it never was out of my Heart. The Delicacy of your Sex cannot conceive the Grossness of ours, nor how little one Sort of Amour has to do with the Heart.' 'I will never marry a Man,' replied *Sophia*, very gravely, 'who shall not learn Refinement enough to be as incapable as I am myself of making such a Distinction.' 'I will learn it,' said *Jones*. 'I have learnt it already. The first Moment of Hope that my *Sophia* might be my Wife taught it me at once; and all the rest of her Sex from that Moment became as little the Objects of Desire to my Sense, as of Passion to my Heart.' 'Well,' said *Sophia*, 'the Proof of this must be from Time. Your Situation, Mr. *Jones*, is now altered, and I assure you I have great Satisfaction in the Alteration. You will now want no Opportunity of being near me, and convincing me that your Mind is altered too.' 'O! my Angel,' cries *Jones*, 'how shall I thank thy Goodness? And are you so good to own, that you have a Satisfaction in my Prosperity?—Believe me, believe me, Madam, it is you alone have given a Relish to that Prosperity, since I owe to it the dear Hope—— O! my *Sophia*, let it not be a distant one.—— I will be all Obedience to your Commands. I will not dare to press any thing further than you permit me. Yet let me intreat you to appoint a short Trial. O! tell me, when I may expect you will be convinced of what is most solemnly true.' 'When I have gone voluntarily thus far, Mr. *Jones*,' said she, 'I expect not to be

---

[1] The dissolute hero of Etherege's *The Man of Mode* (1676)—a character supposedly modelled on Lord Rochester, himself a notorious libertine (see above, p. 155, n. 5).

pressed. Nay, I will not.'—'O don't look unkindly thus, my *Sophia*,' cries he. 'I do not, I dare not press you.—Yet permit me at least once more to beg you would fix the Period. O! consider the Impatience of Love.'—'A Twelvemonth perhaps,' said she.—'O! my *Sophia*,' cries he, 'you have named an Eternity.'—'Perhaps it may be something sooner,' says she, 'I will not be teazed. If your Passion for me be what I would have it, I think you may now be easy.'—'Easy, *Sophia*, call not such an exulting Happiness as mine by so cold a Name.—O! transporting Thought! am I not assured that the blessed Day will come, when I shall call you mine; when Fears shall be no more; when I shall have that dear, that vast, that exquisite, extatic Delight of making my *Sophia* happy?'—'Indeed, Sir,' said she, 'that Day is in your own Power.'—'O! my dear, my divine Angel,' cried he, 'these Words have made me mad with Joy.—But I must, I will thank those dear Lips which have so sweetly pronounced my Bliss.' He then caught her in his Arms, and kissed her with an Ardour he had never ventured before.

At this Instant, *Western*, who had stood some Time listening, burst into the Room, and with his hunting Voice and Phrase, cry'd out, 'To her Boy, to her, go to her.—That's it, little Honeys, O that's it. Well, what is it all over? Hath she appointed the Day, Boy? What, shall it be to-morrow or next Day? It shan't be put off a Minute longer than next Day, I am resolved.' 'Let me beseech you, Sir,' says *Jones*, 'don't let me be the Occasion——' 'Beseech mine A—,' cries *Western*, 'I thought thou had'st been a Lad of higher Mettle, than to give way to a Parcel of maidenish Tricks.—I tell thee 'tis all Flimflam. Zoodikers! she'd have the Wedding to-Night with all her Heart. Would'st not, *Sophy*? Come confess, and be an honest Girl for once. What, art dumb? Why do'st not speak?' 'Why should I confess, Sir,' says *Sophia*, 'since it seems you are so well acquainted with my Thoughts.'—'That's a good Girl,' cries he, 'and do'st consent then?' 'No indeed, Sir,' says *Sophia*, 'I have given no such Consent.'—'And wut nut ha un then to-Morrow, nor next Day?' says *Western*.—'Indeed, Sir,' says she, 'I have no such Intention.' 'But I can tell thee,' replied he, 'why hast nut, only because thou dost love to be disobedient, and to plague and vex thy Father.'—'Pray, Sir,' said *Jones*, interfering.—'I tell thee, thou art a Puppy,' cries he. 'When I forbid her, then it was all nothing but sighing and whining, and languishing and writing; now I am vor thee, she is against thee. All the Spirit of contrary, that's all. She is above being guided and governed by her Father, that is the whole Truth on't. It is only to disoblige and contradict me.' 'What would my Papa have me do?' cries *Sophia*. 'What would I ha thee do?' says he, 'why gi un thy Hand this Moment.'—'Well, Sir,' said *Sophia*, 'I will obey you.—There is my Hand, Mr. *Jones*.' 'Well, and will you consent to ha un to-morrow Morning?' says *Western*.—'I will be obedient to you, Sir,' cries she.—'Why then to-morrow Morning be the Day,' cries he.—'Why then to-morrow Morning shall be the Day, Papa, since you will have it so,' says *Sophia*. *Jones* then fell upon his Knees, and kissed her Hand in an Agony of Joy, while *Western* began to caper and dance about the Room, presently crying out,—'Where the Devil is *Allworthy*? He is without now a-talking with that d—d Lawyer *Dowling*, when he should be minding other Matters.' He then sallied out in quest of him, and very opportunely left the Lovers to enjoy a few tender Minutes alone.

But he soon returned with *Allworthy*, saying, 'If you won't believe me, you may ask her yourself. Hast nut gin thy Consent, *Sophy*, to be married to-morrow?' 'Such are your Commands, Sir,' cries *Sophia*, 'and I dare not be guilty of Disobedience.' 'I hope, Madam,' cries *Allworthy*, 'my Nephew will merit so much Goodness, and will be always as sensible as myself of the great Honour you have done my Family. An Alliance with so charming and so excellent a young Lady, would indeed be an Honour to the greatest in *England*.' 'Yes,' cries *Western*, 'but if I had suffered her to stand shill I shall I, dilly dally, you might not have had that Honour yet awhile; I was forced to use a little fatherly Authority to bring her to.' 'I hope not, Sir,' cries *Allworthy*. 'I hope there is not the least Constraint.' 'Why there,' cries *Western*, 'you may bid her unsay all again, if you will. Do'st repent heartily of thy Promise, do'st not, *Sophy*?' 'Indeed, Papa,' cries she, 'I do not repent, nor do I believe I ever shall, of any Promise in favour of Mr. *Jones*.' 'Then, Nephew,' cries *Allworthy*, 'I felicitate you most heartily; for I think you are the happiest of Men. And, Madam, you will give me leave to congratulate you on this joyful Occasion; indeed I am convinced you have bestowed yourself on one who will be sensible of your great Merit, and who will at least use his best Endeavours to deserve it.' 'His best Endeavours!' cries *Western*, 'that he will I warrant un.—Harkee, *Allworthy*, I'll bet thee five Pound to a Crown we have a Boy to-morrow nine Months; but prithee tell me what wut ha? wut ha Burgundy, Champaigne, or what? for please *Jupiter*, we'll make a Night on't.' 'Indeed, Sir,' said *Allworthy*, 'you must excuse me; both my Nephew and I were engaged before I suspected this near Approach of his Happiness.'—'Engaged!' quoth the Squire, 'never tell me.— I won't part with thee to-night upon any Occasion. Shalt sup here, please the Lord *Harry*.' 'You must pardon me, my dear Neighbour,' answered *Allworthy*; 'I have given a solemn Promise, and that you know I never break.' 'Why, prithee, who art engaged to?' cries the Squire.—*Allworthy* then informed him, as likewise of the Company.—'Odzookers!' answered the Squire, 'I will go with thee, and so shall *Sophy*; for I won't part with thee to-night; and it would be barbarous to part *Tom* and the Girl.' This Offer was presently embraced by *Allworthy*; and *Sophia* consented, having first obtained a private Promise from her Father, that he would not mention a Syllable concerning her Marriage.

CHAPTER *The last.*

In which the History is concluded.

YOUNG *Nightingale* had been that Afternoon by Appointment to wait on his Father who received him much more kindly than he expected. There likewise he met his Uncle, who was returned to Town in quest of his new-married Daughter.

This Marriage was the luckiest Incident which could have happened to the young Gentleman; for these Brothers lived in a constant State of Contention about the Government of their Children, both heartily despising the Method which each other took. Each of them therefore now endeavoured as much as he could to palliate the Offence which his own Child had committed, and to aggravate the Match of the other. This Desire of triumphing over his Brother, added to the many Arguments which

Allworthy had used, so strongly operated on the old Gentleman, that he met his Son with a smiling Countenance, and actually agreed to sup with him that Evening at Mrs. *Miller's*.

As for the other, who really loved his Daughter with the most immoderate Affection, there was little Difficulty in inclining him to a Reconciliation. He was no sooner informed by his Nephew where his Daughter and her Husband were, than he declared he would instantly go to her. And when he arrived there, he scarce suffered her to fall upon her Knees, before he took her up, and embraced her with a Tenderness which affected all who saw him; and in less than a Quarter of an Hour was as well reconciled to both her and her Husband, as if he had himself joined their Hands.

In this Situation were Affairs when Mr. *Allworthy* and his Company arrived to complete the Happiness of Mrs. *Miller*, who no sooner saw *Sophia*, than she guessed every Thing that had happened; and so great was her Friendship to *Jones*, that it added not a few Transports to those she felt on the Happiness of her own Daughter.

There have not, I believe, been many Instances of a Number of People met together, where every one was so perfectly happy, as in this Company. Amongst whom the Father of young *Nightingale* enjoyed the least perfect Content; for notwithstanding his Affection for his Son, notwithstanding the Authority and the Arguments of *Allworthy*, together with the other Motive mentioned before, he could not so entirely be satisfied with his Son's Choice; and perhaps the Presence of *Sophia* herself tended a little to aggravate and heighten his Concern, as a Thought now and then suggested itself, that his Son might have had that Lady, or some such other. Not that any of the Charms which adorned either the Person or Mind of *Sophia*, created the Uneasiness: It was the Contents of her Father's Coffers which set his Heart a longing. These were the Charms which he could not bear to think his Son had sacrificed to the Daughter of Mrs. *Miller*.

The Brides were both very pretty Women; but so totally were they eclipsed by the Beauty of *Sophia*, that had they not been two of the best-tempered Girls in the World, it would have raised some Envy in their Breasts; for neither of their Husbands could long keep his Eyes from *Sophia*, who sat at the Table like a

Queen receiving Homage, or rather like a superiour Being receiving Adoration from all around her. But it was an Adoration which they gave, not which she exacted: For she was as much distinguished by her Modesty and Affability, as by all her other Perfections.

The Evening was spent in much true Mirth. All were happy, but those the most, who had been most unhappy before. Their former Sufferings and Fears gave such a Relish to their Felicity, as even Love and Fortune in their fullest Flow could not have given without the Advantage of such a Comparison. Yet as great Joy, especially after a sudden Change and Revolution of Circumstances, is apt to be silent,[1] and dwells rather in the Heart than on the Tongue, *Jones* and *Sophia* appeared the least merry of the whole Company. Which *Western* observed with great Impatience, often crying out to them, 'Why do'st not talk Boy! Why do'st look so grave! Hast lost thy Tongue Girl! Drink another Glass of Wine, sha't drink another Glass?' And the more to enliven her, he would sometimes sing a merry Song, which bore some Relation to Matrimony, and the Loss of a Maidenhead. Nay, he would have proceeded so far on that Topic, as to have driven her out of the Room, if Mr. *Allworthy* had not checkt him sometimes by Looks, and once or twice by a *Fie! Mr. Western.* He began indeed once to debate the Matter, and assert his Right to talk to his own Daughter as he thought fit; but as no Body seconded him, he was soon reduced to Order.

Notwithstanding this little Restraint, he was so pleased with the Chearfulness and Good-Humour of the Company, that he insisted on their meeting the next Day at his Lodgings. They all did so; and the lovely *Sophia*, who was now in private become a Bride too, officiated as the Mistress of the Ceremonies, or, in the polite Phrase, did the Honours of the Table. She had that Morning given her Hand to *Jones*, in the Chapel at *Doctors Commons*,[2] where Mr. *Allworthy*, Mr. *Western*, and Mrs. *Miller* were the only Persons present.

Sophia had earnestly desired her Father, that no others of the Company, who were that Day to dine with him, should be acquainted with her Marriage. The same Secrecy was enjoined to Mrs. *Miller*, and *Jones* undertook for *Allworthy*. This somewhat reconciled the Delicacy of *Sophia* to the public Entertainment,

---

[1] See above, p. 44, n. 1.   [2] See above, p. 815, n. 1.

which, in Compliance with her Father's Will, she was obliged to go to, greatly against her own Inclinations. In Confidence of this Secrecy, she went through the Day pretty well, till the Squire, who was now advanced into the second Bottle, could contain his Joy no longer, but, filling out a Bumper, drank a Health to the Bride. The Health was immediately pledged by all present, to the great Confusion of our poor blushing *Sophia*, and the great Concern of *Jones* upon her Account. To say Truth, there was not a Person present made wiser by this Discovery; for Mrs. *Miller* had whispered it to her Daughter, her Daughter to her Husband, her Husband to his Sister, and she to all the rest.

Sophia now took the first Opportunity of withdrawing with the Ladies, and the Squire sat in to his Cups, in which he was, by Degrees, deserted by all the Company, except the Uncle of young *Nightingale*, who loved his Bottle as well as *Western* himself. These two therefore sat stoutly to it, during the whole Evening, and long after that happy Hour which had surrendered the charming *Sophia* to the eager Arms of her enraptured *Jones*.

Thus, Reader, we have at length brought our History to a Conclusion, in which, to our great Pleasure, tho' contrary perhaps to thy Expectation, Mr. *Jones* appears to be the happiest of all human Kind: For what Happiness this World affords equal to the Possession of such a Woman as *Sophia*, I sincerely own I have never yet discovered.

As to the other Persons who have made any considerable Figure in this History, as some may desire to know a little more concerning them, we will proceed in as few Words as possible, to satisfy their Curiosity.

Allworthy hath never yet been prevailed upon to see *Blifil*, but he hath yielded to the Importunity of *Jones*, backed by *Sophia*, to settle 200 *l.* a Year upon him; to which *Jones* hath privately added a third. Upon this Income he lives in one of the northern Counties, about 200 Miles distant from *London*, and lays up 200 *l.* a Year out of it, in order to purchase a Seat in the next Parliament from a neighbouring Borough, which he hath bargained for with an Attorney there.[1] He is also lately turned

---

[1] Throughout the century it was common practice to purchase seats in Parliament. The candidate contracted with an attorney, known as an election agent, who used his influence to secure the nomination. The market value of a nomination was generally £5,000–6,000 for the duration of a Parliament. (See Edward Porritt, *The Unreformed*

Methodist,[1] in hopes of marrying a very rich Widow of that Sect, whose Estate lies in that Part of the Kingdom.

Square died soon after he writ the before-mentioned Letter; and as to *Thwackum*, he continues at his Vicarage. He hath made many fruitless Attempts to regain the Confidence of *Allworthy*, or to ingratiate himself with *Jones*, both of whom he flatters to their Faces, and abuses behind their Backs. But in his stead, Mr. *Allworthy* hath lately taken Mr. *Abraham Adams*[2] into his House, of whom *Sophia* is grown immoderately fond, and declares he shall have the Tuition of her Children.

Mrs. *Fitzpatrick* is separated from her Husband, and retains the little Remains of her Fortune. She lives in Reputation at the polite End of the Town, and is so good an Œconomist, that she spends three Times the Income of her Fortune, without running in Debt. She maintains a perfect Intimacy with the Lady of the *Irish* Peer; and in Acts of Friendship to her repays all the Obligations she owes to her Husband.

Mrs. *Western* was soon reconciled to her Niece *Sophia*, and hath spent two Months together with her in the Country. Lady *Bellaston* made the latter a formal Visit at her Return to Town, where she behaved to *Jones*, as to a perfect Stranger, and with great Civility, wished him Joy on his Marriage.

Mr. *Nightingale* hath purchased an Estate for his Son in the Neighbourhood of *Jones*, where the young Gentleman, his Lady, Mrs. *Miller*, and her little Daughter reside, and the most agreeable Intercourse subsists between the two Families.

As to those of lower Account, Mrs. *Waters* returned into the Country, had a Pension of 60 *l.* a Year settled upon her by Mr. *Allworthy*, and is married to Parson *Supple*, on whom, at the Instance of *Sophia*, *Western* hath bestowed a considerable Living.

Black George hearing the Discovery that had been made, run away, and was never since heard of; and *Jones* bestowed the Money on his Family, but not in equal Proportions, for *Molly* had much the greatest Share.

As for *Partridge*, *Jones* hath settled 50 *l.* a Year on him; and he hath again set up a School, in which he meets with much

House of Commons: Parliamentary Representation before 1832 [Cambridge, 1903], i. 353–64.)

1 On Fielding's attitude towards Methodism, see above, p. 63, n. 1.

2 The learned and good-natured parson of Fielding's first novel, *Joseph Andrews* (1742).

better Encouragement than formerly; and there is now a Treaty of Marriage on Foot, between him and Miss *Molly Seagrim*, which through the Mediation of *Sophia*, is likely to take Effect.

We now return to take Leave of Mr. *Jones* and *Sophia*, who, within two Days after their Marriage, attended Mr. *Western* and Mr. *Allworthy* into the Country. *Western* hath resigned his Family Seat, and the greater Part of his Estate to his Son-in-law, and hath retired to a lesser House of his, in another Part of the Country, which is better for Hunting. Indeed he is often as a Visitant with Mr. *Jones*, who as well as his Daughter, hath an infinite Delight in doing every Thing in their Power to please him. And this Desire of theirs is attended with such Success, that the old Gentleman declares he was never happy in his Life till now. He hath here a Parlour and Anti-chamber to himself, where he gets drunk with whom he pleases, and his Daughter is still as ready as formerly to play to him whenever he desires it; for *Jones* hath assured her, that as next to pleasing her, one of his highest Satisfactions is to contribute to the Happiness of the old Man; so the great Duty which she expresses and performs to her Father renders her almost equally dear to him, with the Love which she bestows on himself.

Sophia hath already produced him two fine Children, a Boy and a Girl, of whom the old Gentleman is so fond, that he spends much of his Time in the Nursery, where he declares the tattling of his little Grand-Daughter, who is above a Year and half old, is sweeter Music than the finest Cry of Dogs in *England*.

Allworthy was likewise greatly liberal to *Jones* on the Marriage, and hath omitted no Instance of shewing his Affection to him and his Lady, who love him as a Father. Whatever in the Nature of *Jones* had a Tendency to Vice, hath been corrected by continual Conversation with this good Man, and by his Union with the lovely and virtuous *Sophia*. He hath also, by Reflexion on his past Follies, acquired a Discretion and Prudence very uncommon in one of his lively Parts.

To conclude, as there are not to be found a worthier Man and Woman, than this fond Couple, so neither can any be imagined more happy. They preserve the purest and tenderest Affection for each other, an Affection daily encreased and confirmed by mutual Endearments, and mutual Esteem. Nor is their Conduct towards their Relations and Friends less amiable, than towards one another. And such is their Condescension, their Indulgence, and their Beneficence to those below them, that there is not a Neighbour, a Tenant, or a Servant, who doth not most gratefully bless the Day when Mr. *Jones* was married to his *Sophia*.

FINIS.

APPENDICES

APPENDIX I

Chronology of Important Dates

	Fielding's Life	The Age
1707	April 22: Fielding born at Sharpham Park, near Glastonbury, Somerset.	
1711		May: Pope's *Essay on Criticism*.
1714		August: death of Queen Anne and accession of George I.
1715–16		September–February: Jacobite Rebellion.
1719–24	Education at Eton.	April, 1719: Defoe's *Robinson Crusoe*.
1721		Sir Robert Walpole begins his twenty-year tenure as Prime Minister.
1726		October: Swift's *Gulliver's Travels*.
1727		June: death of George I and accession of George II.
1728	January 29: his earliest extant work published—*The Masquerade*, a satiric poem. February 16: his first play produced—*Love in Several Masques*. March 16: registers as student of letters, University of Leyden.	January: Gay's *Beggar's Opera*. May: Pope's *Dunciad* in three books.
1729	August: discontinues studies at Leyden. Autumn: takes up residence in London.	
1730–37	His career as a dramatist. During this period his plays—all of them comedies—included *The Author's Farce* (1730), *Rape upon Rape* (1730), *Tom Thumb* (1730), *The Modern Husband* (1732), *The Miser* (1733), *Don Quixote in England* (1734), *Pasquin* (1736), *The Historical Register* (1737).	
1731		April: death of Defoe.
1732		December: death of Gay.
1733–34		February–January: Pope's *Essay on Man*.
1734	November 28: elopement and marriage with Charlotte Cradock.	
1737	November 1: begins study of law at the Middle Temple.	June: passage of the Theatrical Licensing Act.

	Fielding's Life	*The Age*
1739	November 15–June, 1741: edits *The Champion*.	October: war with Spain.
1740	June 20: called to the Bar.	November: Richardson's *Pamela*.
1741	April 4: *Shamela*.	
1742	February 22: *Joseph Andrews*.	February: Walpole resigns. March: Pope's *New Dunciad*.
1743	April 12: *Miscellanies*, including *Jonathan Wild* and *A Journey from This World to the Next*.	
1744	November: death of his wife.	March: war with France. May: death of Pope. December: formation of "Broad-Bottom" Administration.
1745	October: pamphlets supporting the Hanoverian government against the Jacobites—*A Serious Address to the People of Great Britain, The History of the Present Rebellion,* and *A Dialogue between the Devil, the Pope, and the Pretender.*	October: death of Swift.
1745–46	November 5–June 17, 1746: edits *The True Patriot*.	August–April 16: Jacobite Rebellion, under the Young Pretender, Charles Edward Stuart.
1747	November 27: marries Mary Daniel. December 5–November 5, 1748: edits *The Jacobite's Journal*.	December–December, 1748: Richardson's *Clarissa*.
1748	March 28–June 2: manages puppet theatre under name of "Mme. de la Nash." October 15: writes to Richardson praising *Clarissa*. October 25: final writ empowering him to act as magistrate for district of Westminster, London.	January: Smollett's *Roderick Random*. October: Treaty of Aix-la-Chapelle, ending war with France.
1749	January: commissioned magistrate for County of Middlesex. February 3–10: *Tom Jones*.	
1751	January: *Enquiry into the Causes of the Late Increase of Robbers*. December 19: *Amelia*.	February: Smollett's *Peregrine Pickle*.
1752	January 4–November 25: *The Covent-Garden Journal*.	
1753	January: *Proposal for Making an Effectual Provision for the Poor*. Autumn–winter: successfully executes plan for suppressing crime in London.	November–March, 1754: Richardson's *Sir Charles Grandison*.
1754	April: seriously ill, he resigns from the magistracy.	

1754   June 26–August 7: his voyage to
Lisbon, the *Journal* of which was
posthumously published in 1755.
October 8: his death in Junqueira
near Lisbon.

APPENDIX II
Select Bibliography

THE standard edition of *Tom Jones*, with text by Fredson Bowers and an historical introduction and explanatory annotations by M. C. Battestin, was published in two volumes in 1975 as part of the definitive Wesleyan Edition of Fielding's complete works, now in progress. The text of the present Wesleyan paperback edition has been printed by offset from this standard edition; but, as Professor Bowers explains in the Preface, care has been taken to correct several misprints and to revise certain passages in Book VIII, chapters xiii–xv. In this corrected and revised form the Wesleyan text of *Tom Jones* may be considered authoritative.

Despite its inaccuracies, the standard biography of Fielding is still Wilbur L. Cross's *The History of Henry Fielding* (New Haven: Yale University Press, 1918), 3 vols., which also contains a full, though not always trustworthy, bibliography of Fielding's works. F. Homes Dudden's *Henry Fielding: His Life, Works, and Times* (Oxford: The Clarendon Press, 1952), 2 vols., adds nothing to Cross's research on the life and canon and repeats all his errors; however, Dudden's discussions of the novels and of the political and social background often are informative.

For a more accurate account of the canon, as well as a list of critical studies of Fielding from 1744 to 1968, see George Watson, ed., *New Cambridge Bibliography of English Literature*, Vol. II (1971). Readers who wish to acquaint themselves with the principal features of this extensive body of criticism will find them summarized by M. C. Battestin in *The English Novel: Select Bibliographical Guides*, ed. A. E. Dyson (Oxford: Oxford University Press, 1973). Those who wish to have a first-hand impression of Fielding's developing reputation may consult Ronald Paulson and Thomas Lockwood's *Henry Fielding: The Critical Heritage* (London: Routledge & Kegan Paul, 1969), which reprints a generous sample of the early criticism, and Claude Rawson's *Henry Fielding: A Critical Anthology* in the Penguin Critical Anthologies series (Harmondsworth: Penguin, 1973), which supplies excerpts from the critics from 1730 to 1968. Paulson's *Fielding: A Collection of Critical Essays* (Englewood Cliffs, N. J.: Prentice-Hall, 1962) is an excellent selection of the best critical essays that had appeared by 1960, including essays on *Tom Jones* by Gide, Kettle, Middleton Murry, Watt, and Empson. Fielding's own critical writings have been collected by Ioan Williams in *The Criticism of Henry Fielding* (London: Routledge & Kegan Paul, 1970).

For students perhaps the best brief introduction to Fielding and his writing is John Butt's *Fielding*, Writers and Their Work, No. 57 (London: Long-mans, Green & Company, 1954; revised 1959). The best introduction to Fielding's art of fiction is probably still Robert Alter's lively and perceptive study, *Fielding and the Nature of the Novel* (Cambridge: Harvard University Press, 1968). On the nature and background of Fielding's ethical and religious views, see Battestin, *The Moral Basis of Fielding's Art* (Middle-town, Conn.: Wesleyan University Press, 1959; paperback, 1975), and Henry Knight Miller's *Essays on Fielding's "Miscellanies": A Commentary on Volume One* (Princeton: Princeton University Press, 1961). On Fielding's social thought, see Malvin R. Zirker, Jr., *Fielding's Social Pamphlets* (Berkeley and Los Angeles: University of California Press, 1966).

In recent years *Tom Jones* has been the subject of more stimulating critical discussion than any other novel of its time. It is of course impossible to do justice here to this impressive body of interpretation and commentary. Some of these studies, however, may be mentioned for their usefulness to the student. Irvin Ehrenpreis provides an excellent introduction to the book in *Fielding: Tom Jones*, Studies in English Literature, No. 23 (London: Edward Arnold, 1964). This helpful little book may be supplemented by two critical anthologies: Battestin's *Twentieth Century Interpretations of "Tom Jones"* (Englewood Cliffs, N. J.: Prentice-Hall, 1968), including discussions of the novel by Leavis, Watt, Empson, Wright, Crane, Booth, and Alter; and Neil Compton's *Henry Fielding: Tom Jones: A Casebook* (London: Macmillan, 1970), reprinting essays by Kettle, Van Ghent, Middleton Murry, Watt, Empson, Paulson, Preston, and others. Two recent monographs deserve special notice. Anyone wishing to improve his understanding of Fielding's view of human nature and the quality of his moral thought should read Bernard Harrison's *Henry Fielding's "Tom Jones": The Novelist as Moral Philosopher* (London: Sussex University Press, 1975). In another vein, but equally fresh and illuminating, is H. K. Miller's generic study, *Henry Fielding's "Tom Jones" and the Romance Tradition*, English Literary Studies, No. 6 (Victoria, B.C.: University of Victoria, 1976).

The following books and articles consider *Tom Jones* from a variety of viewpoints. For the most part, essays included in the anthologies mentioned above have been omitted from the list.

Battestin, Martin C. "Fielding: The Argument of Design" and "Fielding: The Definition of Wisdom," in *The Providence of Wit: Aspects of Form in Augustan Literature and the Arts*. Oxford: The Clarendon Press, 1974.

———. "Osborne's *Tom Jones*: Adapting a Classic," *Virginia Quarterly Review*, 42 (1966), 378–93.

Blanchard, Frederic T. *Fielding the Novelist: A Study in Historical Criticism*. New Haven: Yale University Press, 1926; reprinted 1966.

Coley, William B. "Gide and Fielding," *Comparative Literature*, 11 (1959), 1–15.

Golden, Morris. *Fielding's Moral Psychology*. Amherst: University of Massachusetts Press, 1966.

Hatfield, Glenn W. "The Serpent and the Dove: 'Prudence' in *Tom Jones*," in *Henry Fielding and the Language of Irony*. Chicago and London: University of Chicago Press, 1968.

Hilles, Frederick W. "Art and Artifice in *Tom Jones*," in *Imagined Worlds: Essays on Some English Novels and Novelists in Honour of John Butt*, ed. Maynard Mack and Ian Gregor. London: Methuen, 1968.

Hunter, J. Paul. Chapters 6–8, in *Occasional Form: Henry Fielding and the Chains of Circumstance*. Baltimore: Johns Hopkins University Press, 1975.

Hutchens, Eleanor N. *Irony in "Tom Jones."* University, Ala.: University of Alabama Press, 1965.

Irwin, Michael. *"Tom Jones,"* in *Henry Fielding: The Tentative Realist*. Oxford: The Clarendon Press, 1967.

Johnson, Maurice. Chapters 5–8, in *Fielding's Art of Fiction*. Philadelphia: University of Pennsylvania Press, 1961.

McKillop, Alan D. "Fielding," in *The Early Masters of English Fiction*. Lawrence: University of Kansas Press, 1956.

Miller, Henry Knight. "Some Functions of Rhetoric in *Tom Jones*," *Philological Quarterly*, 45 (1966), 209–35.

———. "The Voices of Henry Fielding: Style in *Tom Jones*," in *The Augustan Milieu: Essays Presented to Louis A. Landa*, ed. Henry Knight Miller, Eric Rothstein, and G. S. Rousseau. Oxford: The Clarendon Press, 1970.

Paulson, Ronald. "Fielding the Novelist," in *Satire and the Novel in Eighteenth-Century England*. New Haven: Yale University Press, 1967.

Preston, John. Chapters 5–6, in *The Created Self: The Reader's Role in Eighteenth-Century Fiction*. London: Heinemann, 1970.

Price, Martin. "Fielding: The Comedy of Forms," in *To the Palace of Wisdom: Studies in Order and Energy from Dryden to Blake*. New York: Doubleday, 1964.

Sacks, Sheldon. *Fiction and the Shape of Belief: A Study of Fielding with Glances at Swift, Johnson, and Richardson*. Berkeley and Los Angeles: University of California Press, 1964.

Williams, Aubrey. "Interpositions of Providence and the Design of Fielding's Novels," *South Atlantic Quarterly*, 70 (1971), 265–86.

APPENDIX III

Index to the Corrections

In preparing the text and notes of the present paperback edition of *Tom Jones*, the editors have corrected certain inaccuracies and entered some revisions in the original Wesleyan clothbound edition. The following Index will enable readers to locate the page and line of the clothbound edition where such corrections have been made. References in roman type are to the text; those in italics are to the notes.

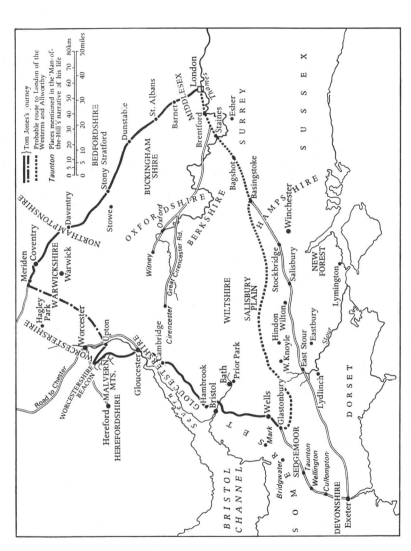

A GEOGRAPHY OF *TOM JONES*

(Based on Thomas Kitchin, 'An Accurate Map of England and Wales', 1760)

Tom Jones's journey
Probable route to London of the Westerns and Allworthy
Taunton Places mentioned in the 'Man-of-the-Hill's narrative' of his life